[英 汉 对 照]

西方学术经典文库

# 法律社会学基本原理

FUNDAMENTAL PRINCIPLES OF THE SOCIOLOGY OF LAW

[奥] 尤根·埃利希 著

叶名怡 袁震 译

(一)

九州出版社
JIUZHOUPRESS

**图书在版编目(CIP)数据**

法律社会学基本原理:英汉对照/(奥)埃利希著;叶名怡,袁震译. —北京:九州出版社,2007.4
(西方学术经典文库)
ISBN 978-7-80195-580-7

Ⅰ.法… Ⅱ.①埃…②叶…③袁… Ⅲ.社会法学—英、汉 Ⅳ.D90-052

中国版本图书馆 CIP 数据核字(2007)第 048730 号

**法律社会学基本原理**

| | |
|---|---|
| 作　　者 | [奥]尤根·埃利希 著　　叶名怡 袁 震 译 |
| 责任编辑 | 云岩涛　张皖莉 |
| 出版发行 | 九州出版社 |
| 地　　址 | 北京市西城区阜外大街甲 35 号(100037) |
| 发行电话 | (010)68992190/2/3/5/6 |
| 网　　址 | www.jiuzhoupress.com |
| 电子信箱 | jiuzhou@jiuzhoupress.com |
| 印　　刷 | 三河市东方印刷厂 |
| 开　　本 | 630×970mm　1/16 |
| 印　　张 | 70.75 |
| 字　　数 | 754 千字 |
| 版　　次 | 2007 年 4 月第 1 版 |
| 印　　次 | 2007 年 4 月第 1 次印刷 |
| 书　　号 | ISBN 978-7-80195-580-7/C·131 |
| 定　　价 | 140.00 元(全三册) |

# 出版说明

在西方学术思想的发展流变中，出现过很多影响深远的经典著作，这些著作穿越时空，为人们长久研读，有的甚至影响了整个人类文明的发展进程。这套《西方学术经典文库》（英汉对照本），精选了其中最有代表性的一些名著，计划达到一百部，将陆续分批出版直至全部完成。

《西方学术经典文库》由多位专家学者指导分类选目，内容涵盖哲学、文学、宗教学、政治学、经济学、社会学、人类学、心理学、法学、历史学等类，注重权威性、学术性和影响性，收录了不同国家、不同时代、不同流派的诸多名著。

《西方学术经典文库》中译本译自英文原著或其他文种的英文译本，以英汉对照的形式出版，读者可以参照原文对作品有更加客观的理解，更好地把握西方学术思想的精髓。

为加以区别，原文中的英文注释，注释号用①、②……形式表示；中文译者注释则以〔1〕、〔2〕……形式表示。至于英译本中出现的原文页码和特殊索引等问题，中文译者在“译者后记”中将予以解释、说明。另外，在英文原著中，有一些表示着重意义的斜体或大写等字体，考虑到读者可以在对照英文阅读中看到，因此在中译文中，没有照样标出，还望读者理解。

九州出版社

Fundamental Principles Of The Sociology Of Law

By *Eugen Ehrlich*

English Translation

By *Walter L. Moll*

本书根据 Harvard University Press 1936 年版本译出

# FOREWORD

It Is often said that a book must be written in a manner that permits of summing up its content in a single sentence. If the present volume were to be subjected to this test, the sentence might be the following: At the present as well as at any other time, the center of gravity of legal development lies not in legislation, nor in juristic science, nor in judicial decision, but in society itself. This sentence, perhaps, contains the substance of every attempt to state the fundamental principles of the sociology of law.

THE AUTHOR

Paris, on Christmas Day, 1912.

# 前　言

人们常说著书应采取这样的方式，即该书的内容可以用一个句子来概括。若将此检验标准适用于本书，则本书可用下面这句来概括：不论是现在还是其他任何时候，法律发展的重心不在立法、法学，也不在司法裁决，而在社会本身。或许，这句话涵括了对法律社会学基本原理作出阐释的每一次尝试的主旨。

作　者

1912 年圣诞节于巴黎

# CONTENTS

# 目　录

## （一）

(二)



(三)

# I

# The Practical Concept Of Law

There was a time, and indeed it does not lie very far behind us, when the university trained the physician for his future profession by requiring him to commit to memory the symptoms of the various diseases and the names of such remedies for them as were known at the time. This time is past. The modern physician is a natural scientist who has chosen the human body as his field of investigation. Similarly, not much more than a century ago, the mechanical engineer was little more than a mechanician to whom his master had imparted the manual skill required for the building of machines. Here too a change has taken place. The present-day mechanical engineer is a physicist who studies the nature of the materials which he is to use and the extent to which their reactions to various external influences take place in conformity with observed and observable laws. Neither the physician nor the mechanical engineer any longer, in a purely craftsmanlike manner, acquires merely the skill required for his profession, but chiefly an understanding of its scientific basis. The same development has taken place long ago in countless other fields.

In jurisprudence, however, the distinction between the theoretical science of law (*Rechtswissenschaft*) and the practical science of law (*Rechtslehre*), i. e. practical juristic science, is being made only

# 第一章　法律的实用观念

曾经有一个时代,这一时代离我们确实并不遥远。那时候,大学培养未来的执业医师时,会要求他们牢记当时已知的各种疾病的症状和相应的治疗方法名称。这一时代已经过去了。现代的医师是选择了人体作为其研究领域的自然科学家。同样地,不到一个世纪以前,机械工程师和从师傅那儿学习机械制造所必需的手工技艺的技工并无差别。这一点上也已经发生了变化。当代的机械工程师是一个物理学家,他要研究他所使用的材料的性质,并探究在何种程度上这些材料在各种外界影响下的反应会与已发现、可发现的规律相一致。医师和机械工程师都不再单纯以手艺人的方式仅仅掌握职业所必需的技巧,而主要是理解其技艺的科学基础。很久以前,在无数的其他领域中也发生了同样的变化。

但是,在法学[1]中,理论法学(*Rechtswissenschaft*)与实用法学(*Rechtslehre*)二者只是在最近才被区分开来。并且在这一领域从

---

〔1〕 德国著者通常将广义上的法学/法律科学(Science of law)分为狭义上的法学(Jurisprudence,对应的德语单词为 *Jurisprudenz*)和法哲学(Philosophy of law)。这是欧洲大陆,特别是法国的用法,在那里,Jurisprudence 实际上类似于“Practical science of law”或“caselaw”。不过,本书的英译者采用

just now, and, for the time being, the greater number of those that are working in this field are not aware that it is being made. This distinction, however, is the basis of an independent science of law, whose purpose is not to subserve practical ends but to serve pure knowledge, which is concerned not with words but with facts. This change, then, which has taken place long since in the natural sciences is taking place in jurisprudence also, in the science which Anton Menger has called the most backward of all sciences, "to be likened to an out-of-the-way town in the provinces, where the discarded fashions of the metropolis are being worn as novelties." And it will not be barren of good results. The new science of law will bring about much enlightenment as to the nature of law and of legal institutions that has hitherto been withheld from us, and doubtless it will also yield results that are of practical usefulness.

There is little that is more instructive to the jurist than the study of those spheres of juristic knowledge in which the change has already taken place, e. g. that of the general theory of the state or that of history of law. Let us glance at the latter for a moment. The idea that the law is to be interpreted in its historical relations was not unknown to the Romans. Both Gaius and the fragments of the Digest abound with historical references. Even the glossators and the postglossators have made abundant use of the data of legal history. Moreover the great French scholars and the fine Dutch scholars of the sixteenth, seventeenth, and eighteenth centuries can properly be referred to as historical and philological jurists. The German publicists of the seventeenth century have also worked along historical lines. The same is true of the English, possibly from the days of Fortescue. Blackstone is a

事研究的多数学者暂时还没有注意到这种区分。但是,这种区分是独立的法律科学的基础,这一法律科学的目的不是为了促进实用的目的而是为了服务于纯粹的知识。这种区分所关注的不是用语本身,而是事实。由此,这一早已在自然科学领域发生的转变也在法学领域发生了,安东·门格将法学这个所有学科中最为滞后的学科比作是“外省的一个偏远的城镇,人都市已经抛弃的服装式样在这里还正在被当作新潮流行着”。这一变化并非毫无善果。这种新的法律科学将促成那些迄今我们仍无从知晓的法律和法律制度之性质的启蒙。无疑,它也将会带来实用的结果。

对法学家而言,几乎没有什么比那些已经发生变化的法学领域的知识的研究有更多启发了。诸如国家的一般理论[1]或法律史。让我们稍稍浏览一下法律史。罗马人并非不知法律应当在历史的关联中得以阐释这一理念。盖尤斯和《学说汇纂》的诸段落中都充斥着历史概述。甚至连注释法学派与后注释法学派都运用了大量的法律史资料。此外伟大的法国学者和16、17、18世纪杰出的荷兰学者都可以完全称得上是历史的和语言学的法学家。德国17世纪的国际法学家也是沿着历史路径展开研究工作的。英国也是如此,并且很可能是从福蒂斯丘的时代就是如此。布莱克斯通是一位用历史方法解释现行法中看似无法解释的那些部分

---

美国的习惯用法,在表达广义的法学/法律科学时使用“Jurisprudence”或“Science of law”,在表达实用法学时用“Practical science of law”或“Juristic science”。由于此中译本从该英译本转译而来,因而对照阅读时宜分清。

〔1〕 *Allegmeine Staatslehre*,这是十九世纪末二十世纪初发展起来的科学,这一学科和政治学之间区分界线并未获得相当程度上的统一。

perfect master of the art of explaining historically such parts of the existing law as appear to be inexplicable. But it was the Historical School of jurisprudence that first made the history of law, which until then had been studied exclusively for the sake of a better understanding of the positive law, an independent science; made her the mistress of her own household. To the modern legal historian it is a matter of indifference whether the results of his investigations are of any practical usefulness or not. They are to him not a means, but an end. Nevertheless, ever since legal history ceased to be a handmaiden to dogmatic legal science, she has rendered the most invaluable services to the latter. Present-day dogmatics owes its greatest scientific achievements to fructification by legal history. The importance of legal history for legal science, however, rests not so much upon the fact that it is history as upon the fact that it is a pure science, perhaps the only science of law that is in existence today. And what an inexhaustible source of stimulation and instruction legal history has become for theoretical and practical economics, as well as for legislation! Would this have been possible if it had not given up its original limited aims and methods?

Human thinking is necessarily dominated by the concept of purpose, which determines its direction, the selection of its materials, and its methods. And with reference to these things the thinking of the jurist is conditioned by the practical purposes pursued by juristic science. When a structural-iron engineer is thinking of iron, he does not have the chemical element in mind, but the article of commerce with which the foundries are supplying him for his buildings. He will be interested only in those properties of iron that are of moment for iron construction, and when he studies these properties he will employ such methods as are suitable for the workshop of the builder who erects iron structures. He will not take thought to develop methods of scientific investigation, for the structural-iron engineer is not interested in scientific results; for practical purposes scientific exactness would be not only superfluous, but too expensive, time-consuming, and difficult. It is sufficient if the structural-iron engineer does those things which he can do best, and leaves to others the things which they can do better. This, of course, is not, in itself, a detriment.

的完美艺术大师。不过,第一次使法律史学成为一门独立学科的当属法学中的历史法学派,直到那时,法学研究的目的还是完全为了对实证法有更好的理解,历史法学派还使得法律史成为她自己家庭的女主人。现代的法律史学者对他们的研究结果是否具有任何实用处漠不关心。研究结果对于他们来说,不是一种手段而是一种目标。尽管如此,自从法律史学不再是法教义学的女仆之后,它还是为法教义学提供了最无价的服务。当今法教义学把它所取得的最辉煌科学成就归功于法律史学的成果。但是法律史学对于法律科学的重要性与其说在于它本身是历史学这一事实,倒不如说在于它是纯粹的科学,或许还是当今唯一存在的科学。法史学不仅对于立法,而且对于理论法学与实用法学,[1]已经成了怎样一种永不枯竭的激励和指导之源啊!倘若它当初没有放弃它有限的目标与方法的话,这一切会是可能的吗?

人类思维必然受到目的观念的支配。目的观念决定着思维方向、材料选择和思维方法。关于这些,法学家的思维受到法学所追求的实践目的的制约。当一个铁结构建筑工程师想到铁的时候,他不会去思考铁的化学成分,而是去思考铸造厂提供给他作为建筑材料的商品。他仅仅对铁的属性——这对于铁结构建筑物很重要——感兴趣,并且,当他研究这些属性的时候,他会采用那些适于搭建铁结构的建筑工人所在工场的研究方法。他不会寻思发展一种科学的研究方法,因为铁结构工程师对科学的结果不感兴趣。对于实用目的来说,科学的精确性不仅多余,而且昂贵、耗时和困难。铁结构建筑工程师把他们最擅长的事情做好就足够了,而把其余的事情留给那些可以做得更好的人。当然,

〔1〕 economics 疑为英译者笔误,中译者认为应为 science of law。

It is true that, because of this necessary limitation, the structural-iron engineer fails to observe many a thing that might be of importance not only for science but for the technic of iron construction. But as soon as men of science and specialists in other branches of iron work find something that is of value for iron construction, he will avail himself of it. Good work done by him within his narrow sphere and with the limited means at his disposal is of scientific as well as of practical value. The observations of the practical man have at all times been providing nourishment for science; a great deal of the scientific botany of our time has been derived from the old herbalism of the apothecaries.

The situation would be quite different if there were no science dealing with iron but structural-iron engineering; if there were no botany but the herbalism of the apothecaries: not only research but practical work as well would suffer tremendously. In addition to pharmacognosy and pharmacology, which have replaced the herbalism of the apothecaries, the nature of plants is being studied by the sciences of agriculture, forestry, horticulture, and many others. Scientific botany studies it quite independently, and the results of its investigations, of course, avail the practical sciences referred to; and at the same time the results of the labor of the practical men working in all of these fields offer to the botanist a multitude of suggestions.

It is the tragic fate of juristic science that, though at the present time it is an exclusively practical science of law, it is at the same time the only science of law in existence. The result of this situation is that its teaching on the subject of law and legal relations is, as to tendency, subject matter, and method, only that which the practical science of law can give. Indeed it is as if mineralogy and chemistry could teach us no more about iron than that which has been discovered for the purposes of structural-iron engineering; as if botany could teach us no more about plants than is contained in the text-books on pharmacognosy and pharmacology. This state of the science of law is an extremely sad one, particularly in view of the fact that the present-day practical science of law is far from covering the whole field of the practical activity of the jurist. Properly speaking there ought to be as many practical sciences of law as there are juristic activities.

这本身不是一种损害。的确,由于这种必要的限制,铁结构建筑工程师无法观察到许多对科学、铁结构建筑技术而言也许很重要的东西。但是,一旦科学家和炼铁厂其他部门的专家发现对铁建筑有价值的东西,铁结构建筑工程师就会加以利用。他可以在自己的狭窄的领域中以可支配的有限方法创造杰作,这些杰作都是具有科学与实践价值的。在任何时代,实践者的观察都会带来科学的繁荣;现代植物学的许多部分都来源自药剂师古老的本草学。

如果没有研究铁的科学,而只有铁结构工程学;如果没有植物学,而仅有配药师的本草学,那情况将会大为不同,因为不仅是研究,而且连实践工作也会遭受巨大损失。除了取代药剂师的本草学的生药学和药理学外,农学、林学、园艺学和其他学科也在研究植物的特性。植物学相当独立地研究植物,当然,植物学的研究成果会有益于相关的实践科学;与此同时,在所有这些领域工作的实践者的劳动成果也为植物学家提供了大量的建议。

尽管目前法学纯粹是实用法学,但同时它也是当前存在的唯一的法学,这就是它的悲剧性命运所在。这种状况带来的结果就是,涉及法律和法律关系问题的法学教学,在法学趋势、主题和方法方面,只能是实用法学能够给予的东西。实际上这就像矿物学和化学除了告诉我们铁确实可用于铁结构工程之外无法告诉我们更多相关知识一样;又好比植物学在介绍植物时只会讲授那些生药学教材和药理学教材中已有的知识。关于法学的这句话让人极为伤感,特别是考虑到当前实用法学的范围远不能涵盖法学家实践活动的全部领域这一事实,尤为如此。确切地讲,实用法律学科应当与法学实践活动一样多。古罗马人把法学家的活动

The Romans divided the activity of the jurist into *respondere*, *agere*, *cavere*; which, being expressed in modern terminology, is: the activity of the judge, of the draftsman of legal documents, and of the attorney; and it seems that in the days of the Republic at least, research, literature, and instruction were engaged in the service of each of these three activities. In England practical juristic science (*Rechtslehre*) is concerned with the activity of the judge and the attorney; whereas the art of drafting legal documents (conveyancing) exists as a distinct, highly developed branch of legal science. But the judge, the draftsman of legal documents, and the attorney are by no means the only representatives of professional juristic activity. In addition to the administration of the affairs of the state, the administration of private affairs is a fruitful sphere of juristic activity, e. g. agriculture, commerce, and industry. To these may be added participation in legislation, politics, journalism.

The practical juristic science of the Continent is considerably poorer than that of the Romans and of the English. Since the reception of Roman law, it has made its abode exclusively at the universities, which, for the most part, were founded, and are being maintained, by the state, and to which, after the rise of a learned judiciary, the task of training the future judge for his calling has chiefly been assigned. Had legal instruction been given in private schools, undoubtedly there would have been schools for attorneys and notaries in addition to schools for judges, and the various practical sciences of law would have enjoyed a corresponding development. As it was, a juristic science arose whose content can be defined exhaustively as practical instruction in the performance of the duties of a judge. Slowly and halt-

分为解答、[1]协助[2]和提供,[3]用现在的法律术语来讲,就是法官的活动、法律文件起草人的活动和律师的活动。[4]看上去至少在共和国时期,法律研究、法律文献和法律讲授都服务于这三方面的活动。在英国,实用法学(*Rechtslehre*)关注法官与律师的活动;另一方面,法律文件的起草活动(财产或其他权益让与之法律事务)是作为一项独特的、高度发展的法学存在的。但是法官、法律文件的起草人和律师绝不是法律职业活动的唯一代表。除了管理国家事务外,管理私人事务也是法学活动的一个有成果的领域,例如在农业、商业和工业等方面的管理。另外,法学活动的范围还涉及立法、政治和新闻业等方面的参与。

跟古罗马人和英国人的实用法学相比,欧陆实用法学更加薄弱。自从罗马法继受以来,法学就专门将大学作为自己的住所,大学多半由国家建立和维持,在出现学识渊博的法官以后,为这一行业培养未来法官的任务主要就落到了这些大学的头上。倘若私立大学可以讲授法学,则毫无疑问,除了培养法官的学校外,肯定还会有培养律师和公证人的学校,并且各类实用法律学科就会获得相应的发展。像现在这样出现的法学,其内容倒是可以彻底被界定为是对法官履行职责的实践指导。慢慢地并且有些犹

---

[1] (拉)*Respondere*(解答),指法学家针对向其提出的、涉及具体案件的法律问题所作出的答复。这种答复对于当事人或者审判员一般具有参考意义,但享有公开解答权的法学家的解答则被认为具有法律上的约束力。

[2] (拉)*agere*(协助),即为当事人进行诉讼、办案子。

[3] (拉)*cavere*(提供),即为当事人拟定书面契约、遗嘱等。

[4] 此处,英译本把 *agere* 与 *cavere* 所对应的现代法律活动前后顺序弄颠倒了,应予注意。

ingly there was added the preparation for the diplomatic and administrative services. Accordingly the practical and the theoretical science of law began to comprise also international law and public law. Paulsen therefore quite properly described the present-day juristic faculties as technical training schools for judges and administrative officials. Since the majority of students, however, were bent upon a career on the bench, the law that the judge requires remained in the center of legal teaching. This may perhaps account for the fact that the study of public law and international law became a scientific study long before private law, penal law, and procedure. Public law in the narrow sense (*allgemeines Staatsrecht*, later called *allgemeine Staatslehre*) was the first branch of juristic science, which, disregarding the practical utility of its results, pursued purely scientific aims. But the juristic faculties could and would not become anything but training schools for judges and government officials; and this aim became the determining factor not only in legal education but also in research and literature. For this reason it is not very likely that the draftsman of legal documents or the attorney-at-law will find a book from which he can learn how to perform the duties of his profession, difficult, important, and involving grave responsibilities though they be. Most of the information he needs he must obtain in a purely tradesmanlike fashion in the practice, and the most valuable knowledge gained by professional experience dies with him who has acquired it. But—and this is the important consideration here—these things are also being ignored by the science of law, which knows only the law required by the judge, although even a hasty glance at legal life shows that a great deal of the administration of justice and of the development of law takes place in the offices of attorneys and notaries, and that legal science can gather valuable material therefrom. Moreover the modern jurist can, if need be, get all the information he requires as to the importance of the legal document as a lever for the development of law from any handbook of legal

豫地,法学中增加了为外交和行政职业而作准备的内容。相应的,实用法学和理论法学也开始涵盖国际法和公法。因此,保尔森非常恰当地将如今的法学系描述为培训法官和行政官员的专门学校。不过,既然大部分学生都立志当法官,那么法官所需要的法律知识就仍是法学教育的核心。这或许可以解释这样的一个事实:与私法、刑法与诉讼法相比,公法和国际法很久之前就成为了一门科学研究。狭义上的公法(*allgemeines Staatsrecht*,后被称为 *allgemeine Staatslehre*)[1]是法律科学的第一个分支,它漠视其研究结果的实践应用,追求的是纯科学的目标。但是大学的法律院系只能且只会是培养法官和政府官员的学校;这一目标不仅在法学教育中,而且在法学的研究与文献中成为决定性因素。由于这一原因,尽管法律文件起草者或者律师的执业难度大、重要,并且涉及重大职责,但他们也不太可能找到一本可以学习如何执业的书籍。法律文件的起草者或者律师必须在实践中以一种纯粹工匠式的方式获得他所需要的知识,他通过职业经历所获得的最有价值的知识也随着他的逝世而消失。但是我们在此必须慎重考虑,这些知识同样被法学所忽略,后者仅仅知道法官所需要的法律,尽管哪怕是对法律生活的匆匆一瞥也能看到,大量的司法与法律发展发生在律师和公证人的办公室中,并且法学可以从那里收集到珍贵的素材。而且,如果需要的话,现代法学家可以获得他所需要的重要法律文件的所有信息,这与从任何法律史手

[1] *allgemeines Staatsrecht*,后被称为 *allgemeine Staatslehre*。*allgemeines Staatslehre* 翻译成狭义上的公法,区分于 *Staatsrecht* 和国际法。*Staatrecht* 分为 *Verfassungsrecht*(宪法)和 *Verwaltungsrecht*(行政法)。

history. The fact that practical juristic science limits itself in its own sphere in accordance with the same point of view is quite in keeping with this. It excludes important matters from discussion if the judge does not generally concern himself with them in his professional capacity. About a decade ago, Lotmar first discovered for juristic science the existence of law concerning contracts of labor—after the great industrial development in Germany had begun to make it a matter of ever-increasing concern to the administration of justice. The most significant juristic problems of our time, the problems of trade unions, of trusts, and of cartels, do not exist for practical juristic science; doubtless for the simple reason that, although they play an important part in legal life, their rôle is not nearly so important in the administration of justice.

The most disastrous consequence of this state of affairs has been its effect on the method of juristic science. The first and foremost function of all research is to find a method adapted to its subject matter. The life of many a great scholar has been spent in the endeavor to find a method. Once the method was found, the work could be carried on by inferior minds. Ultimately, even the analysis of the spectrum is nothing more than a method. With the sole exception of the general theory of the state (*Staatslehre*), which is already infused with a scientific spirit, the science of law knows no other method than that which has been developed by practical juristic science for the application of law by the judge. According to the prevailing conception of the judicial office, which arose in the sixteenth century, the judge must derive his decision of the individual case from the existing general propositions. Practical juristic science, which had been designed for the use of the judge, was to supply the judge with legal propositions, formulated in the most general terms possible, in order that the greatest possible number of decisions might be derived from them. It was to teach the judge how to apply the general propositions to the specific cases. Its method therefore had to be a method of abstraction and deduction. With the exception of public law in the narrow sense, however, juristic science as a whole proceeds by abstraction and deduction just as if the human mind were incapable of any higher attainment than the creation of bloodless shapes that lose contact with reality proportionately to the measure of abstractness that they attain. In this respect it is altogether different from true science, the prevailing

册中获知法律发展一样。基于同样的观点，实用法学将其自身限制在自己领域内，这一事实与此相一致。如果法官在他的职业角色上通常不关心一些重要的问题，那么这些重要问题就被排除在讨论范围之外。大约十年前，在德国工业大发展开始受到司法的日益关注后，洛特曼首次发现法学中有关劳动契约法的存在。当代最为重要的法学问题——工会问题、托拉斯问题和卡特尔问题对于实用法学而言并不存在；毫无疑问，原因显而易见，尽管它们在法律生活中发挥了重要的作用，但它们在司法中的角色还不是那么重要。

事情的这种状况最为不幸的后果是它对法学研究方法的影响。学术研究的首要功能是找到一个适合于自己研究课题的研究方法。许多著名学者花费毕生的精力来寻找一种方法。一旦有了研究的方法，研究工作就可以由那些能力稍弱的人来完成。最终，甚至光谱分析也仅仅成为一种方法了。除了早就灌输了科学精神的国家一般理论（*Staatslehre*）这一唯一的例外，法学仅仅了解实用法学为法官适用法律而发展起来的方法。按照16世纪发展起来的司法部门的主流观点，法官必须按照现有的一般命题来裁决个案。为法官的使用目的而存在的实用法学，是为了给法官提供法律命题，并采用可能的最一般的术语做出阐释，以便法官能尽可能多地依靠它做出裁决。这是为了教会法官如何将法律命题应用到具体案件中。因此，它的方法必然是抽象和演绎。但是，除了狭义上的公法外，整体上法学仍依照抽象与演绎的方式行事，正如人类的思维除了创造与他们所达到的抽象方法相称的脱离现实的苍白形式外不能达致任何更高的成就。在这方面，法学总的说来还不同于真正的科学，后者主流的方法是归纳性

method of which is inductive, and which seeks to increase the depth of our insight into the nature of things through observation and experience.

Accordingly juristic science has no scientific concept of law. Just as the technical expert in iron construction, when speaking of iron, is not thinking of the chemically pure substance which the chemist or the mineralogist refers to as iron, but rather of the chemically very impure compound that is used in iron construction, so the jurist does not mean by law that which lives and is operative in human society as law, but, apart from a few branches of public law, exclusively that which is of importance as law in the judicial administration of justice. an occasional flash of deeper insight ought not to mislead anyone. A technical expert in iron construction may perhaps, in making an attempt to be scientific, state the chemical formula of the compound which is being used in iron construction as iron, but in the course of his practical discussion he will deal only with this compound; for iron in the scientific sense is of no interest to him. The important thing is not the definitions that are found in the introductory chapters of handbooks or monographs, but the concept of law with which juristic science actually works; for concepts are not merely external ornamentation, but implements for the erection of a structure of scientific thought.

From the point of view of the judge, the law is a rule according to which the judge must decide the legal disputes that are brought before him. According to the definition which is current in juristic science, particularly in Germany, the law is a rule of human conduct. The rule of human conduct and the rule according to which the judges decide legal disputes may be two quite distinct things; for men do not always act according to the rules that will be applied in settling their disputes. No doubt the legal historian conceives of law as a rule of human conduct; he states the rules according to which, in antiquity or in the Middle Ages, marriages were entered into, husband and wife, parents and children lived together in the family; he tells whether property was held individually or in common, whether the soil was tilled by the owner or by a lessee paying rent or by a serf rendering services; how contracts were entered into, and how property descended. One would hear the same thing if one should ask a traveler returning from foreign lands to give an account of the law of the peoples he has become

的,它通过观察与经验来寻求增进我们对事物性质的深刻洞察。

因此,法学根本没有科学的法律概念。正如铁结构建筑方面的技术专家一样,当他说起铁的时候,他所想到的不是化学家或者矿物学者所说的纯粹的铁物质,而是指在化学上非常不纯的、用于铁结构建筑的混合物;法学家提到法律时,他也不是指人类社会中如法律那样存在并发挥效用的东西,而是——除了公法中的几个分支以外——专门指在司法审判中如法律一般重要的东西。偶然一闪而过的深刻洞察力不应当误导任何人。一个在铁结构建筑方面的技术专家,在努力显得专业一些时,或许可以说出用于铁结构建筑的铁作为混合物的化学公式,但是他在实际讨论中,可能仅仅关注铁本身,因为他对科学意义上的铁丝毫没有兴趣。重要的不是在手册或专著中的介绍章节中所看到的关于法的定义,而是法学实际运作中所使用的法律概念。因为概念绝不仅仅是外部的装饰品,而且还是架起科学思想大厦的工具。

自法官的角度言之,法律是其断案必须遵循的一个规则。依目前流行(特别是在德国)的法律定义,法律是行为规则。行为规则和法官据以断案的规则是两种截然不同的规则;因为人们并不是总是依照裁判中用来解决纠分的规则行事。毫无疑问,法律史学家认为法律是人类的行为规则。他讲述了在古代或中世纪婚姻据以缔结的规则以及夫妻、父母和子女在一个家庭内共同生活所遵循的规则。他告诉世人:当时财产是个人所有还是共同所有,土地是所有人耕种还是支付租金的承租人或提供服务的农奴耕种,契约是如何缔结的,财产是怎样继承的。倘若你让一个从外国归来的旅行者来描述一下他所熟悉的民族的法律,你就会听到与此相同的事

acquainted with. He will tell of marriage customs, of family life, of the manner of entering into contracts; but he will have little to say about the rules according to which law-suits are being decided.

This concept of law, which the jurist adopts quite instinctively when he is studying the law of a foreign nation or of remote times for a purely scientific purpose, he will give up at once when he turns to the positive law of his own country and of his own time. Without his becoming aware of it, secretly as it were, the rule according to which men act becomes the rule according to which their acts are being adjudged by courts and other tribunals. The latter, indeed, is also a rule of conduct, but it is such for but a small part of the people, i. e. for the authorities, entrusted with the application of the law; but not like the former, for the generality of the people. The scientific view has given way to the practical view, adapted to the requirements of the judicial official, who, to be sure, is interested in knowing the rule according to which he must proceed. It is true, jurists look upon these rules as rules of conduct as well, but they arrive at this view by a jump in their thinking. They mean to say that the rules according to which courts decide are the rules according to which men ought to regulate their conduct. To this is added a vague notion that in the course of time men will actually regulate their conduct in accordance with the rules according to which the courts render their decisions. Now it is true that a rule of conduct is not only a rule according to which men customarily regulate their conduct, but also a rule according to which they ought to do so, but it is an altogether inadmissible assumption that this "ought" is determined either exclusively or even preponderantly by the courts. Daily experience teaches the contrary. Surely no one denies that judicial decisions influence the conduct of men, but we must first of all inquire to what extent this is true and upon what circumstances it depends.

Every page of a law book, every lecture on a legal subject, bears out the statement just made. Each and every word shows that the jurist who is discussing a legal relation invariably has in mind the problem how the legal disputes arising from this relation are to be adjudged, and not the totally different question how men

情。他会告诉你婚姻习俗、家庭生活和合同的缔结方式;但是,关于依据什么规则来裁决诉讼,他会无可奉告。

当法学家为了纯粹的科学目的研究外国或者远古时代法律的时候,他不假思索所采用的法律概念,在他回到他所处国家和时代的实证法时,他会立刻放弃。在法学家未加注意的时候,如同暗中进行的一样,人类的行为规则转变成了法院或者其他审判机构的裁判规则。实际上后者也是一种行为规则,但它仅仅适用于一小部分人,亦即被赋予了法律执行权的权威机构;而不像前者,前者是一般大众的行为规则。科学性观点让位于实用观点。适应了司法官员的需要,后者当然有兴趣知道所要依循的规则。事实上,法学家也把这些规则看作是人们的行为规则,只不过这一观点是思维跳跃性的结果。他们想要表达的是,法院据以裁判的规则就是人们应当用以规范行为的规则。除此之外,还有一个含糊的观念:随着时间的推移,人们实际上将会根据法院的裁判规则来规范他们的行为。目前,行为规则的确不仅仅是人们习惯上规范他们行为的规则,也是人们应当如此的规则,但是,这个“应当”要么纯粹由法院决定,要么主要由法院决定——这是一个让人根本无法接受的假定。日常经验告诉我们的是相反的情形。当然没有人否认司法裁决影响人们的行为,但我们首先必须探究它的真实程度以及它所依赖的环境。

法律书籍中的每一页、法律主题的每一种讲稿都证实了我们刚得出的结论。每一个用词都说明正在讨论法律关系的法学家们总是在思考这一问题——从这一关系中出现的法律纠纷应当怎么样裁决,而不是在思考另外一个完全不同的问题——人们如

conduct themselves, and how they ought to conduct themselves in this relation. Even a man of the mental stature of a Maitland said that to write the history of the English actions is to write the history of English law. This juristic line of thought has been given a positively naïve expression in the doctrine of error in law. A juristic science which conceives of law as a rule of conduct could not consistently have laid down a principle that men are bound by the law even though they do not know it; for one cannot act according to a rule that one does not know. On the contrary, it ought to have discussed the question how much of a given legal material is known as a rule of conduct and is followed as such, and, at most, what can be done to make it known. In fact, Binding understood the whole problem in this way years ago, and posited the proposition that only the norms of penal law, not the penal law itself, are generally known, and in fact regulate human conduct. Only Max Ernst Mayer has followed him, without however adding anything to the requisite experiential material. But if we say, as is usually done, that the law binds him who does not know the law as well as him who does, we are evidently giving up the concept of law as a rule of human conduct altogether; we are laying down a rule for the courts and other tribunals, which the latter are to apply whether the person concerned knew it or not. We are not improving the situation by requiring everyone to know the law or by setting up the fiction that the law, if properly published, is known to everyone.

The prevailing notion as to the origin of law is a result of this very line of thought. Whence comes the rule of law, and who breathes life and efficacy into it? It is extremely interesting to note the answers that have been made in reply to these questions; for they clearly and unambiguously reflect the fact that even perfectly correct scientific knowledge is not sufficient to guide the human mind when the necessity of serving a practical need suggests another path. Today, a century after Savigny and Puchta, no scientifically trained jurist doubts that a considerable part of the law of the past was not created by the state, and

何规范自己的行为、在这一关系中他们应当如何行为。甚至连睿智如梅特兰的人也曾说过，写英国的诉讼史就是写英国的法律史。该法律思维路径已经在法律的错误学说中被赋予了一种绝对幼稚的表述。将法律设想为人们行为规则的法学不可能始终如一规定这一原则——人们受法律拘束，即便是他们不知道法律——因为一个人不可能按照他不知道的规则行事。相反，法学应当讨论这样的问题：有多少已知的法律材料是作为行为规则为人所知并被遵循，以及至多做了哪些使它们为人所知。事实上布林丁已经在几年前以此种方式理解了整个问题，他提出如下主张：人们普遍熟知的只是刑法的规范，而不是刑法本身，并且实际上规范人们行为的也是前者。仅有马克斯·厄恩斯特·迈耶追随他，但前者并没有增加任何必不可少的经验素材。但是，如果我们说（如通常所言）法律约束那些了解法律和不了解法律的人，那么我们显然完全放弃了法律是人类行为规则这一观念；我们为法院和其他裁决机构制定规则——不管相关人员是否知道它，它都要被适用。我们并不是通过要求人人都要知晓法律的方式，或者通过建立一种拟制——即适当公布之法律推定人人皆知——的方式来改善此种状况。

当前关于法律起源的主流观点正是这一思考路径的结果。法律规则从哪里来，谁赋予了他生命与效力？注意一下对这些问题的回答是极为有趣的；因为它们清楚且毫不含糊地反映出了这一事实——当满足实践需要的必要性使人想到另外一条路径时，即使是完全正确的科学的知识也不足以引导人们的思想。在萨维尼和普赫塔一个世纪以后的今天，受过科学训练的法学家均不再怀疑：过去法律相当多一部分并非由国家制定，即使在今天，

that even today it is derived to a great extent from other sources. That is the theory. Now comes the question: Where is this non-state law to be studied? Where is an exposition of it to be found? Where is it being taught? Perhaps we are not too daring if we make the assertion that today research, literature, and legal education on the Continent know of no other law than statute law.

To be sure one soothes one's conscience by saying that customary law—a collective term, an expression which for centuries has been used to lump together the whole heterogeneous mass of non-state law—is a "negligible quantity" at the present time. This statement is found in the writings of Savigny and Puchta themselves. Since that time it has been repeated time and again in various forms, and even writers who do not make the statement in so many words adhere to it. A jurist who holds this opinion has ceased to look upon law as a rule of general human conduct; he has clearly demonstrated that law is to him, preponderantly at least, a rule for the conduct of courts and other tribunals; for even the believers in the doctrine of the omnipotence of the state have not very often seriously thought that the state can make rules to regulate the whole field of human conduct. Perhaps the only exception within the whole range of European civilization was the Emperor Josef II, whose program split on the rock of this idea. For this reason the relation of juristic science to non-state law, quite independently of scientific conviction, has been undergoing changes in accordance with the changing attitude of the state toward the courts. And if juristic science today is devoted exclusively to state law, the reason for this must be sought in the fact that tile state, in the course of historical development, has come to believe that it is able to add to the monopoly of the administration of law, which it acquired long ago, a monopoly of the creation of law. And I do not doubt, therefore, that the modern free-finding-of-law movement marks not only an advance in

法律也在很大程度上得自于其他源头。那就是这一理论。接下来的问题是:非国家法[1]要在哪里研究呢?有关它的讲解要在哪里找到呢?哪里正在教授它呢?假使我们断言,当今欧洲大陆上的研究、文献以及法律教育除了知道制定法外就再也不知道有其他任何法律,或许我们还不算太鲁莽。

的确,有人以当今习惯法——一个集合名词,数世纪以来用于囊括整个非国家法中全部的异源法律——"数量微不足道"来平息内心的不安。这种表述可以在萨维尼和普赫塔的著作中找到。从那时起,它就以各种形式一次又一次地重复,甚至那些没有用如此多言语来作此表述的作者也支持它。持此看法的法学家不再把法律看作是人们一般性的行为规则;他清楚地证明,在他看来,法律至少主要是法院和其他裁决机构的行为规则;因为即使是国家万能学说的信奉者,也并非经常真的以为国家能够制定规范人类所有领域的行为规则。或许在整个欧洲文明史上唯一的例外就是约瑟夫二世皇帝,他的计划由于这一观念破碎了。因此法学与非国家法之间的关系,与科学信念完全无关,而是随着国家对法院态度的变化而变化。如果今天的法学完全专注于国家制定法,它的原因必然可以在下述事实中找到:在历史的发展进程中,国家相信它能够增加早已获得的对法律实施的垄断,增加对法律创制的垄断。因而,我并不怀疑现代的法律的自由发现运动不但标示着科学洞察力的提升,而且也标示着国家和社会之

---

〔1〕 埃里希提到"*ausserstaatliches Recht*"和"*staatliches Recht*"。前者译为"非国家法 ",后者译为"国家法",亦即分别是"非由国家创制的法律"和"由国家创制的法律"。

scientific insight, but also an actual shift in the relation of the state and society—a shift which has taken place long ago in other spheres.

Where the judge renders his decisions chiefly according to custom, as was done almost everywhere down to a very late stage of development, e. g. in Rome in the days of the Republic, or in Germany in the Middle Ages, the idea, self-evidently, does not enter the head of anyone to derive the law as such from the state. As late as the end of the Republic, the Romans considered their national customary law, the *ius civile*, at least as valuable as a source of law as the *leges*. And the law-books of the Middle Ages mention provisions of statutes or regulations only in exceptional instances. In the Middle Ages, the *corpus iuris civilis*, the *corpus iuris canonici*, even the Golden Bull, are merely very high authorities to which one turns for aid in the solution of difficult and important problems as one might turn to any other authorities, e. g. the Bible or the ancient writers—for in the Middle Ages scientific work was done chiefly on the basis of authority, in law no less than in theology, philosophy, or medicine. It is only after the state has grown extremely powerful, and has begun to tend toward an absolute form of government, that the thought begins to germinate, and the impulse awakens, to make the state the authoritative, and in the course of time the sole, source of law. This was done in Rome in the days of the Empire and in western Europe in the sixteenth century. Attempts were made to tie nonstate creation of law to authorization by the state, particularly in the very earliest days of the Empire, by means of

间关系的实际转变——这种转变在其他领域早已发生了。

在法官主要依据习惯作出裁判——直至非常晚近的发展阶段几乎到处(例如共和国时期的罗马或中世纪的德国)还都是这样做——的地方,不言而喻,任何人的头脑中都没有像现在这样的观点:法律本身来自于国家。直到共和国的晚期,罗马人认为他们民族的习惯法、法学家法,至少和作为法源的法律[1]一样有价值。在中世纪的法律典籍中,只有在例外情况下才提到制定法或法令中的条款。在中世纪,《民法大全》、《教会法大全》,甚至金玺诏书,[2]也仅仅是很高的权威——人们在解决疑难且重要的问题求助它,就好比人们也可能像其他任何权威(例如圣经或古代著作)求助一样,因为在中世纪,科学著作主要是以权威为基础的,此点在法学上和在神学、哲学和医学上并没有不同。直到国家变得极端强大并开始朝着专制政府的方向发展之后,这种思想才开始产生。推动力的觉醒使得在历史的进程中,国家成为权威的、唯一的法律来源。这一进程在古罗马帝国时期和 16 世纪的西欧得以完成,特别是在罗马帝国的最初时期,通过法律解答权——[3]罗马帝国皇帝授予法学家创制法律的权力——的方式,

〔1〕 (拉)*leges*(法律),后古典时期人们对君主谕令(*constitutiones principum*)的笼统称呼,与另一种规范渊源——法(*iura*)相对应。

〔2〕 金玺诏书(Golden Bull),盖有金印章或金玺的特许状的总称,但特别用于少数非常重要的政治性特许状。

〔3〕 (拉)*ius respondendi*(法律解答权),某些具有较高威望的法学家根据君主授权就公众提出的法律问题作出解答的权力,在此解答中发表的见解和意见被认为具有法律效力。此权力也被称为“经君主批准的解答权(*ius respondendi ex auctoritate principis*)”。

the *ius respondendi*, which was conferred by the Emperor upon jurists empowered to create law. The power to create law was limited to questions not yet regulated by law. Very strict precepts as to the validity of customary law were embodied in the statutes. Attempts were made to render it superfluous by means of codifications, which purported to comprise the whole law; occasionally, even to exclude it in express terms. Even the scientific legal work of the jurists was looked upon askance, and occasionally was expressly forbidden because the powers that were realized that it gave rise to a new sort of non-state law, i. e. to juristic law. The final word of this trend was spoken, perhaps, by Justinian: *Tam conditor quam inter pres legum solus imperator iuste existimabitur, nihil hac lege derogante veteris iuris conditoribus, quia et eis hoc maiestas imperialis permisit.*

Juristic science steadfastly follows in the path of this development of state law, paying very little attention to the progress of scientific knowledge. Having made a curt obeisance to the teachings of science, she returns at once to the task which she considers her true function, i. e. to furnish that which the administration of law requires. The decisive step had already been taken when the judge was no longer required to know both non-state and state law; when only a knowledge of state law was presupposed, while non-state law had to be proved by the parties. Henceforth only state law is "law" in the full sense of the term; every other kind of law is merely "fact". Juristic science arrived at this stage when the judge became a learned official of the state, i. e., in Germany, as early as the sixteenth century. The doctrine, which was becoming more and more firmly established, was that customary law, which today comprises all non-state law with the exception of juristic law, is law of an inferior kind, which, as to its origin and as to its validity, is conditioned upon authorization, recognition, or confirmation by the legislator, who could, if he chose, forbid its

非国家制定法被试图与国家权威联结起来。这种创制法律的权力仅限于针对法律尚未规范的问题。制定法中包含了对习惯法有效性问题的严格规定。国家试图通过号称包含所有法律的法典编纂,使习惯法变得多余;有时甚至用明确的措辞将其排除在外,甚至法学家的法学著作也不被信任,并且有时被明确禁止,因为这些主张获得实现的有影响力的人会引致一种新的国家法,即法学家法。或许是优士丁尼对这一倾向作了总结陈词:皇帝应该被正当地看做是唯一的立法者和法律的解释者。这一规定不损害古法的建构者,因为他们的特权本来就是由皇帝授予的。

法学坚定地沿着国家法的这种发展道路前进,它很少关注科学知识的进步。在向科学教义草草表示尊重以后,它马上回到了它认为是真正功能的任务上去,也就是,提供法律实施所需要的东西。一方面,当法官不再被要求同时熟知非国家法和国家法时,当仅有国家法的知识成为先决条件时,另一方面,非国家法不得不由当事人举证证明时,决定性的一步就已经迈出。自此以后,只有国家制定的法律才是该术语完整意义上的“法律”,而其他任何的法律仅仅是“事实”。德国早在 16 世纪时,法官成为渊博的政府官员,法律科学就达到了这个阶段。已经被越来越牢固地树立起来的学说就是,习惯法——如今包含了除法学家法之外所有的非国家法——是一种劣等的法律,它在起源和效力方面都取决于立法者的批准、认可或确认,后者如果愿意,他可以完全禁

use altogether, it was held in low esteem, even ridiculed occasionally, proof of it was made more difficult, and the conditions upon which it was recognized were insisted upon with increasing strictness. Studies investigating and presenting non-state law became fewer and fewer in number, until, finally, in the eighteenth century they ceased to appear altogether. In the teaching of law, customary law became a mere name. This was the state of affairs at the beginning of the nineteenth century. Juristic science thought that it was its function not to determine what is law, but to point out to the judge, who was appointed and commissioned by the state, what he should apply as law according to the will of his employer. There never was a time when the law promulgated by the state in statutory form was the only law, even for the courts and other tribunals, and there has always been an undercurrent, therefore, which strove to secure proper recognition for law that was not promulgated by the state. This undercurrent forced its way to the surface at two different periods: in the writings of the teachers of the law of nature school in the seventeenth and eighteenth centuries, and again in the writings of Savigny and Puchta, the founders of the Historical School. To what extent the teachers of the law of nature were the precursors of the historical conception of law, and to what extent the pioneers of the Historical School were carrying out the ideas of the Natural Law School, has, unfortunately, been realized only very rarely, and has never been properly investigated by anyone. These two schools have this in common: neither has blindly accepted as law what the state declared to be law; both have sought to ascertain the nature of law in a scientific manner. Both have found its origin outside of the state: one, in the nature of man; the other, in the legal consciousness of the people.

Neither of these schools has fully followed out its ideas. Doubtless they were hindered by the idea which has dominated all juristic thinking down to our day, i. e. the idea that only that is law which the judge applies in the administration of justice. In spite of their radicalism, the teachers of the law of nature, particularly those outside of France, where the situation was somewhat different from that in the other countries of Europe, never dared to assert, with any show of firmness at least, that a judge can ever

止它。习惯法很少被尊重,甚至偶尔还成为嘲讽对象,习惯法的证明被规定得更加困难,并且它获得认可的条件也越来越严格。调查和介绍非国家法的研究在数量上日益减少,最终,到了18世纪这种研究彻底消失了。在法律教学中,习惯法也仅仅是个名称而已。这是19世纪初的状况。法学认为,它的功能不是去决定什么是法律,而是向被国家任命并委以职权的法官指出他应当如何依据任命者的意志来运用法律。国家以制定法的形式颁布的法律是唯一法律的时代从来没有过。因此,即使对法院和其他裁决机构来说,始终存在一种潜流,即努力获得对非由国家颁布之法的确定的适当的了解。这种潜流在两个不同的时期浮出水面:先是在17世纪和18世纪自然法学派教授者的著作中,然后是在历史法学派的创始人萨维尼和普赫塔的著作中。不幸的是,在多大程度上自然法学启蒙学者是历史法观念的先驱和在多大程度上历史法学派遵循了自然法学派的思想很少被意识到,也从未被任何人适当地研究过。这两个学派具有以下共同点:他们都没有盲目地接受法律就是国家所颁布的法律的观念;他们都在努力以科学的方式探知法律的性质。他们都发现法律的根源在国家之外:一个认为法律的根源存在于人性之中;另一个认为它存在于民族的法律意识之中。

这两个学派都没有完全贯彻他们的观点。毫无疑问他们受到那种直到今天仍然主导所有法学思维的理念的阻碍,这个理念就是只有法官在司法中运用的东西才是法律。尽管他们中有激进主义者,但自然法的教授者,特别是法国(那儿的情形颇不同于欧洲其他国家)以外的自然法启蒙学者,他们从来都不敢断言——至少是不敢带有丝毫肯定地声称——法官可能永远有义

be under a duty to apply a rule of law that has not, tacitly at least, been approved by the state. Accordingly the law of nature is, in fact, suspended in mid-air. Only that is law which is binding on the judge; but the law of nature is not binding on the judge. At this point the doctrine of the school of the law of nature completely reverses itself. The protagonists of natural law as nonstate law based on the nature of man in the end demand legislation by the state in order that the law of nature may be realized.

Savigny and Puchta perhaps were the first to conceive, vaguely at least, the idea of a science of law the exclusive object of which is to promote knowledge. Their whole life-work bears witness to a disdain, unconscious perhaps, never expressly admitted certainly, clearly marked however, for a science of law which serves only practical purposes. Even in their studies in the common law, i. e. the positive law of their day, they sought to arrive at a scientific understanding of that element of the common law which constitutes the nature of all law; they sought to comprehend not a system of law, but law itself. Far in advance of their time, they turned away from the insignificant figure of the personal legislator and directed their attention to the great elemental forces that are at work in the creation of law. These natural forces prevail in customary law, which, it is true, was to them a symbol of all that is superhuman in law rather than a clearly discerned concept. Nevertheless the task of creating a science of law proved too great even for them. They made a beginning, but were unable to carry it out.

The founders of the Historical School never attempted actually to apply in their dogmatic works the methodological principles which they professed in theory. Their interest in non-state law led them to strive for a clear understanding of the concept of customary law; but they never took the trouble to investigate the customary law of Germany; they made no attempt to perfect the methods, highly imperfect then as well as now, for the ascertainment of customary law; they rejected Beseler's suggestions, which, inadequate to be sure, were nevertheless worthy of serious consideration; they did not discuss a single case taken from the

务去适用一个至少尚未被国家默认的法律规则。因此,事实上,自然法被悬空了。只有拘束法官的才是法律,但是自然法却不拘束法官。在这一点上,自然法学派的学说完全和自己的观点相悖。与非国家法一样基于人性之上的自然法学,其倡导者为了自然法能够实现,最终还是会要求由国家来立法。

萨维尼和普赫塔或许第一次——至少是非常模糊地——秉持这样的法学理念:法学的唯一目标是为了提升知识。他们毕生的事业证明存在一种对那种仅为实践目的服务的法学的蔑视,这种蔑视或许是无意识的,当然也从未明确被承认过,但却有清晰的标记。甚至在他们对共同法——即他们那个年代的实证法——的研究中,他们也寻求达到对构成所有法律性质的共同法要素的科学理解;他们不是试图理解一个法律制度,而是法律本身。他们厌恶立法者个人这一无关紧要的角色,并将他们的注意力转向了在创制法律运转中重要的自然力上,远远超越了他们那个时代。事实上,这些在习惯法中普遍存在的自然力量,对于他们来说,是法律中所有的超人类力量的象征,而不是清晰可辨的观念。尽管如此,即使对他们而言,创立法律科学的任务对他们来说也还是太难了。他们仅仅开了个头,却未能进行到底。

历史法学派的创立者从来没有试图在他们的教义学著作中应用他们在理论中所宣称的方法原则。他们在非国家法方面的兴趣引导他们去努力获得对习惯法概念的清楚理解;但是他们从没有不辞劳苦地去调查德国的习惯法;他们没有试图去完善他们的方法,在探查习惯法的方法方面,他们的方法如同现在一样极不完善;他们拒绝了贝塞勒的建议,这些建议虽然并不足以让人确信,但是还是值得认真考虑;他们从没有讨论过源自法律文献

living customary law that was not already known in legal literature. They do indeed insist that the law develops in the popular legal consciousness (*Rechtsbewusstsein des Volkes*), but barring the much decried method of legislation, they cannot tell us how new law is received into the body of already existing positive law; they never express an opinion as to the method by which legal science recognizes and receives new law, unless, indeed, it is supplied ready-made by legislation. The legal material that they deal with is comprised in its entirety in the common law juristic science of the eighteenth century. They arrange it much more carefully, observe much more closely, occasionally merely more subtly, the states of fact previously discussed by their predecessors; they test it by the content of the sources which they have re-examined historically and, occasionally, doctrinally; they often correct the traditional definitions with remarkable acumen; but they make no attempt to enrich it or to introduce new methods.

They have had few continuators and no followers. Beseler, it is true, in obedience to a splendid inspiration, made an attempt to begin afresh where the thread had been cut. But though he saw many things in their true relations, he thought few of them out to their logical conclusions; at any rate, he did not express his thoughts clearly, and therefore the general judgment as to the value of his work was easily misled by malevolent critics. Only a few Germanists and a few teachers of ecclesiastical law are actually working in the field of legal dogmatic in the spirit of the Historical School. The former confine themselves to searching out the vestiges of ancient German legal institutions that have been received into the codifications of German particular law, i. e. the so-called common German private law. The latter limit themselves to a very narrow field.

未知的、生活中现行有效的习惯法任何一种情形。他们确实坚持法律的发展在于民众的法律意识(*Rechtsbewusstsein des Volks*)中,但是除了这种受到谴责的立法方法外,他们不能告诉我们新的法律如何被现存的实证法接纳;他们从来没有明确表述一种有关法律科学以何种方法认可和接纳新法律的观点,除非,立法确实早已提供了现成的规定。他们所处理的法律素材包含了18世纪共同法法学中的全部内容。他们更为认真地安排、更为严密地观察,有时候仅仅是更为精巧地处理他们的前辈们已经讨论过的事实状况;他们通过在历史上——偶尔也在学说上——他们已经再次检验过的原始文献的内容来验证它;他们经常以非凡的敏锐来修正传统的定义;但是他们并未试图丰富它或者引入新的方法。

他们的继承者极少,追随者则是一个也没有。确实,贝塞勒在思路被切断的地方,受一种绝妙的灵感的牵引,开始了一种新的探索。不过尽管他看到了在他们真实关系中的许多东西,但是他几乎没有对它们作彻底的思考并得出它们的逻辑结论;至少,他没有清楚地表述他的思想;因此,对他作品价值的一般评判很容易被一些恶意的批评家所误导。只有少数的日耳曼法学家和教会法的教授者以历史法学派的精神在法律教义学领域中实际耕耘着。日耳曼法学家将自己的研究限于探寻已经被日耳曼特别法[1]的法律汇编纳入的古代日耳曼法律制度的残余,即所谓的德国私法之共同法中。教会法学的教授者将自己的研究限于一个非常狭窄的领域内。

---

〔1〕 *Partikulaes Recht*,即产生于德国各个州的特殊来源的法律。

Particularly as to the all-important matter of customary law, retrogression rather than progress is observable. The epigone of the Historical School who are working in the field of historical dogmatic pass by Savigny and Puchta's doctrine of customary law, which is one of the great achievements of the human mind, with little or no appreciation of its importance. Ignoring Savigny and Puchta, they start from the common law juristic science of the eighteenth century. To them customary law no longer is a power which governs the creation of law, the laws of which must be made the subject of scientific inquiry. The only question in their minds is: What are the conditions under which, according to the intention of the legislator, which is to be ascertained by interpretation of the *corpus iuris civilis* and *canonici* or of a modern statute, customary law is binding upon the judge? That is to say, it still is nothing more than a practical juristic science which is concerned only with the duties of the judge. At the same time, it manifests no interest in non-state law. The doctrine of customary law is disposed of in a few introductory paragraphs of the institutional books and of the handbooks; a few smaller works discuss the controversial questions that are sufficiently well known. There is no thought of systematic inquiry. They do not even know of a method for it. The small number of scholars who did examine individual cases of customary law (Bruns, Fitting) dealt only with written sources, especially with juristic literature, i. e. they proceeded very much as if they were dealing with a statute. Under the heading *The Interpretation of the Rules of Law*, they actually discuss only the interpretation of statutes. To introduce, as Windscheid and Baehr have done, the course of judicial decisions into the presentation of the positive law is considered a pioneering innovation.

Accordingly practical juristic science has, in spite of Savigny and Puchta, remained what it has been ever since the rise of the state-controlled judiciary, i. e. the science of the application of the law created by the state. Practically all modern juristic writing

特别是,从关于习惯法方面最为重要的事项可以看到,习惯法是在退化而不是在进步。历史法学派的模仿者——那些在历史教义学领域中从事研究的人——绕过了人类思想的最伟大成就之一的、萨维尼和普赫塔的习惯法学说,他们极少或者根本不能正确评价它的重要性。忽略了萨维尼和普赫塔,他们从 18 世纪共同法法学重新开始。对于他们来说,习惯法不再是一种支配法律创制的力量,习惯法必须作为科学探究的主题。他们大脑中的唯一的问题就是:在何种条件下,按照立法者的意图——该意图要透过对《民法大全》、《教会法大全》或现代制定法的解释来确定,习惯法对法官具有拘束力?换句话说,这仍然是一种只关注法官职责的实用法学。与此同时,该法学对非国家法没有表现出任何兴趣。习惯法的学说仅在有关基本原理的书籍与手册的一些介绍性片段中被少量提及;一些更不重要的作品则探讨了若干足够众所周知的争议性问题。那里没有系统探究的思想。他们甚至还不知道研究这一问题的方法。数量很少的、深入检视过习惯法个案的学者——如布伦斯、菲廷——仅仅涉及到一些书面的渊源、特别是法学文献,即,他们像研究一部制定法一样做了很多。在名为《法律规则的解释》这本书中,他们实际上仅仅论述了制定法的解释。像温德沙伊德和巴赫所做的那样,将司法裁决的过程引入到实证法的阐述当中去,这被认为是一种开拓性的创新。

因此,尽管有萨维尼和普赫塔的理论,但实用法学仍然保持了自从国家控制的司法系统出现后就存在的样子,即,实用法学是国家制定法的应用科学。实际上,所有现代的法学著述和教

and teaching, within the sphere of private law at least, pretends to be nothing but a setting forth, as clear, as faithful, as complete, as is possible, of the content of statute law in its finest ramifications and its remotest applications. Such a literature and such teaching cannot, however, be termed scientific; in fact, they are merely a more emphatic form of publication of statutes. The ultimate inference which is drawn by the exponents of this school is the doctrine of the perfection and completeness of the legal system. When the Historical School makes this assertion, it reverses itself just as the Law of Nature School did when it demanded legislation by the state. This conception of law, which was first stated in express terms by Brinz, but which had actually been applied at an earlier date by the exponents of the Historical School, so effectively brought down the fate of the Historical School upon its head on lines parallel to the fate of the Law of Nature School that one is tempted to see the sway of a higher justice therein. There is a veritable gulf fixed between the *Weltanschauung* (world-view, or philosophy) of the two great vanquishers of the Law of Nature School, who founded the Historical School, and the proposition that there is within the positive law an answer for every question that might arise, and that one need but find it. And this theorem—for it is nothing more than a practically meaningless theorem—makes it perfectly obvious that practical juristic science, in its entirety, does not purport to be anything but a system of norms according to which the judge must render his decisions; for surely no man has ever entertained the preposterous thought that the law in its entirety is a complete system of rules which regulate in advance all human conduct in all possible relations. Jellinek has made the remark that the dogma of the logical perfection of the legal system does not apply to public law "but only to those parts of the legal order in which the final decision of the individual case lies in the hands of the judge." By way of proof, Jellinek adduces a great number of problems of public law for which the existing public law offers no solution whatever. But the situation would be the same if the final decision did lie in the hands of a judge—and this is possible in each and every one of the cases adduced by Jellinek. Only, if that were the case, it would be incumbent upon

学，至少是在私法范围之内，都自称仅仅是对制定法的内容就其最纤细的分支和最间接的应用方面予以尽可能清晰、忠实、完整的阐释。但是，这样的著述和教学不可能被称为科学；事实上，它们仅仅是制定法颁布的一种更引人注目的形式。从该学派的倡导者那里所得到的最终推论是完善和完备法律制度的学说。当历史法学派作此论断的时候，它已经与自身相矛盾了，正如自然法学派在要求国家立法的时候所制造的悖论那样。布林茨首先用明确的法律术语对该法律观念作了说明，但是，实际上历史法学派的倡导者们早在很久以前就已运用了它；此种法律观念如此有效地令历史法学派招致厄运——与自然法学派的命运如出一辙——以至于人们十分想去那里看看更高正义的影响。在自然法学派的两个伟大的征服者——他们创立了历史法学派——的。*Weltanschauung*（世界观或哲学）方面以及在实证法中对每一个可能出现之问题（人们只需要找到它）的回答意见上，存在名副其实的鸿沟。并且由于这一定理不过是一个实际上毫无意义的定理，因而使得以下事实更为明了：实用法学整体上声称它只是法官必须据以断案的规则体系；因为确信无疑，没有人会接受这种荒谬想法：法律整体上是在所有可能的关系上预先规范人类行为的一个完整的规则体系。耶里内克对此作出评论，即法律制度的逻辑完备的教条并不适用于公法，“而仅仅适用于个案最终判决掌握在法官手中的那部分的法律秩序”。作为证明，耶里内克列举了现行公法根本无法解决的大量公法问题。但是，如果最终判决真的在法官的掌握中，情况还是一样——这在耶里内克所引证的任何一个案件中都是可能发生的。只是，若在那种情况下，法官有义

the judge to find a solution, but he would not find it on the basis of the logically perfect system; for it is not contained therein. What Jellinek considers a peculiarity of public law, therefore, holds true, in fact, for every department of law, and the principle of the logically perfect system of law does not state a scientifically established fact, but merely expresses the practical endeavor to supply the judge with a store of norms for decision sufficient for all cases that might arise and to make them binding upon him as effecttively as possible.

In the light of these considerations, it is possible to understand the view, which still prevails at the present time, that the law is a compulsory order, that it is an essential element of the law to recognize enforceable claims and to impose enforceable duties. First of all we must arrive at a clear understanding of what is meant by compulsion. It cannot mean psychological compulsion of any kind; for man always acts under some kind of psychological compulsion, even quite outside of the legal sphere. It can, therefore, mean only such compulsion as is considered characteristic of law; i. e. only such psychological compulsion as is exercised by threat of penalty or of compulsory execution. That these two kinds of compulsion have been considered essential characteristics of law can be explained only by the fact that law has always been believed to be the rule to be applied by the judge. With rare exceptions, cases are brought before the judge solely in order to have the judge impose a penalty or in order to secure compulsory enforcement of the claim after the judge has recognized its validity, and, with rare exceptions, a judgment of a court of law can actually be executed in our day. Law applied by the court and law that can be enforced by compulsion are practically synonymous today. To a person, however, whose conception of law is that of a rule of conduct, compulsion by threat of penalty as well as of compulsory execution becomes a secondary matter. To him the scene of all human life is not the court room. It is quite obvious that a man lives in innumerable legal relations, and that, with few exceptions, he quite voluntarily performs the duties incumbent upon him because of these relations. One performs one's duties as father or son, as husband or wife, does not

务去发现一个解决方案,但是他却不能以这一逻辑上完善的体系为基础找到答案;因为答案不在上述体系中。因此,耶里内克所考察的公法的特性事实上对于每一个法律部门来说都是正确的,并且,逻辑上完善的法律体系的原则并未说出一个在科学上已被确证的事实。这一原则仅仅表达了一种实践的努力——为法官提供大量的、足以解决所有可能发生之案件的裁判规则,并使这些规则尽可能有效地拘束法官。

鉴于这些考虑,才有可能理解当前仍占主流的观点:法律是一种强制的规则,承认可执行请求权与强加可执行义务是法律的基本元素。首先我们必须清楚地理解强制这一用语的含义。它不可能指任何种类心理上的强制,因为人们总是在某种心理强制下行动,甚至心理强制完全在法律的范围之外。所以,它仅指那些被认为是法律特征的强制,即诸如通过刑罚或强制执行威胁而实施的那种心理强制。这两种强制被认为是法律的本质特征,这只能通过如下事实来解释:法律总是被认为是法官适用的规则。除了极少的例外,案件提交到法官面前仅仅是为了让法官施以刑罚,或者仅仅是为了在法官承认请求权的效力后获得有关该权利的强制执行,并且在我们这个时代,除了极少的例外,法院作出的法律裁决实际上都获得了强制执行。现今法院所适用的法律与可以被强制执行的法律实际上是相同的。不过,对于秉持法律是行为规范这种法律观念的人来说,刑罚威胁与强制执行都是次要事项。对于他来说,一个人所有的生活场景都不在法院的房间里。很显然,一个人总是生活在数不清的法律关系中,并且由于这些(对他而言十分重要的)关系,他总是非常自愿地履行其所负有的义务,很少有例外。一个人履行作为父亲或儿子、作为丈夫或

interfere with one's neighbor's enjoyment of his property, pays one's debts, delivers that which one has sold, and renders to one's employer the performance to render which one has obligated oneself. The jurist, of course, is ready with the objection that all men perform their duties only because they know that the courts could eventually compel them to perform them. If he should take the pains, to which, indeed, he is not accustomed, to observe what men do and leave undone, he would soon be convinced of the fact that, as a rule, the thought of compulsion by the courts does not even enter the minds of men. In so far as they do not simply act instinctively, as indeed is usually the case, their conduct is determined by quite different motives: they might otherwise have quarrels with their relatives, lose their positions, lose custom, get the reputation of being quarrelsome, dishonest, iresponsible persons. The jurist ought to be the last person of all to overlook the fact that that which men do or leave undone as a legal duty in this sense often is something quite different from, occasionally is much more than, that which the authorities could ever compel them to do or leave undone. The rule of conduct, not infrequently, is quite different from the rule that is obeyed because of compulsion (*Zwangsnorm*).

It was observed long ago that in a considerable part of public law in the narrow sense (*Staatsrecht*) and administrative law there is no compulsion in this sense whatever. If, in reply to this argument, one would urge the compulsion that lies in the responsibility of cabinet ministers or in the parliamentary or the disciplinary responsibility of officials, one should show whether or not this compulsion can, at this stage, be said to be identical with the compulsion that lies in compulsory execution. These two things seem to lie pretty far apart from each other. At this point we may disregard altogether the psychological question whether or not a weapon so dull as the impeachment of a minister practically always turns out to be, or as the parliamentary and the disciplinary responsibility of an official turns out to be in many cases

妻子的责任,不干涉邻居对其财产的享有,偿还债务,交付售出的商品,并且履行对雇主应尽的义务。当然,法学家很可能会表示反对:所有的人履行他们的义务,仅仅因为他们知道法院将最终强迫他们履行。如果他耐心去观察——确实他不习惯于这样做——人们做了什么和没有做什么,他将会很快确信这一事实:法院灌输的强制思想通常并没有进入人们的大脑。在他们并非简单地依本能行事的范围内——事实上的确如此,他们的行为由迥然相异的动机决定:他们可能在其他方面和他们的亲戚争吵,丢掉他们的职位,失去主顾,并获得爱争吵、不诚实和不负责任的坏名声。法学家应该是所有人中最后忽略如下事实的人:在作为一种法律义务的意义上说,人们的作为或者不作为经常完全不同于当局始终强制他们的作为或不作为,就内容而言,有时候前者要比后者多得多。行为规则与因强制而被遵守的规则(*Zwangsnorm*)[1]十分不同,这种情形并非罕见。

很久以前,人们就发现在相当一部分的狭义公法(*Staatsrecht*)和行政法中不存在任何意义上的强制。如果某人在回复这一论点时极力主张,这种强制性存在于内阁部长或者议会议员的责任中,或者存在于官员的纪律性责任中,那么他应当说明,在目前这个阶段,一般是否认为这种强制与强制执行中的强制相同。这两种强制看上去相距极为遥远。在这一点上,我们可以完全忽略下述心理学问题:无论是诸如在实践中最终总是被证明很笨拙的对部长的弹劾、还是诸如很多情况下最后总是被证明效果很差的议会议员的责任与官员的纪律责任那样驽钝的武器是否可以被

〔1〕 (德)强制性规则。

can be said to amount to a means of compulsion. But even this resource will fail in the case of international law, ecclesiastical law, and public law in the narrow sense (*Staatsrecht*), as well as in a considerable part of the administrative law of an absolute or of a non-parliamentary constitutional state, and particularly in the case of almost all precepts regulating the competence and the order of business of parliamentary representative bodies. It has often been said that almost any breach of the constitution may be perpetrated without the perpetrators being held to account, provided the majority of the parliament or of any other representative body and the presiding officer are in agreement. It is true, in such case there remains the "restraint exercised by public opinion," "popular indignation or resentment," and, lastly, the possibility of revolution. But can a sanction of this kind, which is not prescribed by law and is not regulated by law, be considered an essential characteristic of law? There are no social norms, whether they be norms of morality, of ethical custom, of honor, of tact, of etiquette, or of fashion, but have recourse to a sanction of this kind whenever they are being transgressed. And in the case of a few of these non-legal norms, this sanction is often more effective than in the case of a legal norm; occasionally it is so powerful as to overcome even the compulsion exercised by legal execution. Many a man pays his gambling debts although he fails to pay his tailor, fights a duel with the person who challenges him, contemptuous of the criminal law, but blindly obedient to the social sanction.

All of this has been stated often enough, and it is perhaps superfluous to revert to it here. Therefore I will emphasize but one point—a point which has been neglected hitherto, i. e. the great number of situations in private law for which no effective legal sanction has been provided. This is true particularly in the case of all purely personal claims strictly limited to a certain time which arise from permanent legal relations. Many precepts that determine the mutual rights and duties of the members of a family or of a partnership, the duties of the organs of a corporation, of the board of directors, of the members, or of the meeting

说成是一种强制方式。但是,即便是这一对策,也会在涉及国际法、教会法和狭义上的公法(*Staatsrecht*),以及专制国家或非议会制国家中相当大部分的行政法等法域遭到挫败,特别是在几乎所有规范代议团体的资格和议事的规定方面,它会失灵。人们常说,倘若议会中的大多数人或者其他任何代议团体和主持官员同意,则几乎所有的违反先法的行为人都不用承担法律责任。[1] 诚然,在上述情况下存在着“公共舆论产生出的限制”、“大众的愤怒或者怨恨”,并且最后还存在着革命的可能性;但是,这样一种法律未为规定、也不受法律调整的制裁,它是否可以被认为是法律的本质特征呢?没有任何一种社会规范,不管是道德规范、伦理习俗规范、荣誉规范、言行得体规范、礼节规范还是时尚规范,每逢遭到违反之时,会求助于这种意义上的制裁。在一些违反非法律性规范的情况下,这种制裁经常比违反法律规范的制裁更为有效;有时候它甚至强大到足以超过法律执行所产生出的强制。许多人偿还赌债却并不偿还其对裁缝的债务,蔑视刑法而与向他挑战的人决斗,但是却盲目地服从于社会的制裁。

所有的这些都已经被足够多地一再陈述,在这里重提此事或许是多余的。因此,我仅强调一点——迄今一直被忽视的一点,即,法律并没有对私法中的大量情形规定有效的法律制裁。特别是在严格限于特定时期的、源于永久性法律关系的所有的纯粹人身权利方面,此点尤为真实。许多确定家庭成员或者合伙成员间的相互权利与义务的规定,确定公司机构、董事会、公司成员和社

[1] 这样的一个表述不适用于像美国这样的国家,美国不奉行“议会至上”主义,议会通过的法案也不得违宪。

of the members, fail to create an enforceable legal situation because, as the jurists say, they create no subjective law: there is no legal remedy to enforce them. And in many cases of this kind there is no possibility of availing oneself of an existing legal remedy. Would a member of an association sue the board of directors because the reading room has not been placed at his disposal? Would an employer sue a servant girl for not tidying the house? What would a suit of this kind avail him? The claim for damages would not afford relief, for no matter how much importance he may have attached to his right at the moment, in the end he will not be able to prove damage that is worth mentioning. It is only where the obligor has, by his conduct, made the relation unendurable, that the obligee is given an effectual legal remedy, i. e. the right to demand the dissolution of the relation and damages. But this does not involve a legal sanction which effectively compels the other party to perform his duties; for the latter very often embarks upon his illegal course of conduct in order to bring about the dissolution of the relation in exchange for the payment of damages. The order of human society is based upon the fact that, in general, legal duties are being performed, not upon the fact that failure to perform gives rise to a cause of action.

Three elements therefore must, under all circumstances, be excluded from the concept of law as a compulsory order maintained by the state—a concept to which the traditional juristic science has clung tenaciously in substance, though not always in form. It is not an essential element of the concept of law that it be created by the state, nor that it constitute the basis for the decisions of the courts or other tribunals, nor that it be the basis of a legal compulsion consequent upon such a decision. A fourth element remains, and that will have to be the point of departure, i. e. the law is an ordering. It is the deathless merit of Gierke that he discovered this characteristic of law in the bodies which he called associations (*Genossenschaften*), and among

员大会职责的规定都不能产生出一种可强制的法律情势，因为，如法学家们所说，它们没有创造出任何主观权利，相应地，那里不存在强制实现它们的任何法律救济手段。此类情形中许多情况下，都不存在当事人可以利用的救济手段。一个联合体成员是否会因为董事会没有按照他的意愿安排阅读室而起诉董事会？一个雇主是否会因为女仆没有收拾房间而起诉女仆？这样的诉讼对他会有任何益处吗？赔偿金的请求不能为其提供救济，因为无论他怎么强调在这一时刻他的权利是如何重要，最终他都不能证明损失是值得一提的。仅仅是在债务人的[1]行为使得这一法律关系无法再忍受时，债权人才被赋予了一项有效的法律救济权利，亦即要求解除这一关系和要求赔偿损失的权利。但是这并不涉及一项有效强迫另一方履行义务的法律制裁；因为后者经常采取非法的一连串行动致使法律关系解除，并籍此换得赔偿金的支付。人类社会的秩序基于通常法律义务会被履行这一事实，而不是基于不履行法律义务将会引发诉由这一事实。

因此，无论如何，这三种因素应当被排除在作为一种由国家维持的强制性秩序的法律概念之外，传统法学尽管形式上未必总是坚持该概念，但实质上却一直墨守它。法律必须由国家创制不是法律概念中的本质因素，它也构不成法院或其他裁决机构裁决的基础，它也不是裁决必然产生的法律强制的基础。第四种要素保留下来，并且它将必须成为一个分界点，即，法律是一种规整。基尔克在被他称做联合体(*Genossenschaften*)的团体——他把国家

〔1〕 德国法上的债务人(Obligor 或 debtor)比英美法的债务人含义更为宽泛。前者指称任何负有给付义务的人。

which he numbered the state, and that he gave an account of it in a detailed study. As a result of his labors, we may consider it established that, within the scope of the concept of the association, the law is an organization, that is to say, a rule which assigns to each and every member of the association his position in the community, whether it be of domination or of subjection (*Überordnung*, *Unterordnung*), and his duties; and that it is now quite impossible to assume that law exists within these associations chiefly for the purpose of deciding controversies that arise out of the communal relation. The legal norm according to which legal disputes are being decided, the norm for decision, is merely a species of legal norm with limited functions and purposes. ①

Gierke's doctrine is open to the objection that it is taking a partial view of things, but only inasmuch as it presents as applying only to the law of associations that which holds true for the whole legal sphere. His own book shows plainly that the law of associations does not organize human beings only, but things as well. It is a question

① It has been said, by way of reproach (Battaglioni, Le norme del diritto penale, Rome, undated), that the distinction between legal norms that are forms of organization and the norms for decision coincides with the distinction first made by Max Ernst Mayer between norms of law and norms of civilization (*Kultur*). I would say first of all that I first spoke of the distinction between forms of organization and norms for decision in my address, "Freie Rechtsfindung und freie Rechtswissenschaft," which I delivered on March 4, 1903, before the Vienna Juristic Society, and which was printed in the year 1903. The preface is dated June 1903. The discussion referred to appears on p. 9 of this edition. The book of Max Ernst Mayer was published in 1903, and the preface bears the date of August 8, 1903. One cannot, therefore, speak of a borrowing either by Max Ernst Mayer or by myself. Moreover an attentive reader ought not to have failed to observe that my doctrine, although it reaches the same results that were reached by Max Ernst Mayer, is based upon a conception quite different from that of Mayer and has a totally different aim. —*Author's note*.

也包括在内——中发现了这一法律特征,并且在一个详实的研究中对其给予了说明。这是他的不朽功绩。由于他的劳动,我们可以认为如下概念已被确证:在联合体之概念的范围内,法律是一种构造方式,换句话说,法律是一种为联合体每一个成员分配在团体中地位——不管这些成员在团体内是支配者还是被支配者(*Überordnung*, *Unterordnung*)——和职责的规则;现今完全不可能承认存在于这些联合体中的法律其主要目的是为了裁决因社区关系而产生的争端。据以裁判法律纠纷的法律规范即裁判规范仅仅是一种具有有限功能和目的的法律规范。①

基尔克的学说容易遭到这种反驳:该学说采取了一个特殊的事物观,但仅仅因为(如它所述)只适用于联合体的法律,即认为对所有法律领域有效。他自己的著作也清楚地表明,联合体的法律不仅组织人类,也组织事物。这不仅是联合体的成员做了

---

① 据说(作为一种指责),(*Battaglioni*, *Le norme del diritto penale*, *Rome*, *undated*)作为构造方法的法律规范和用以裁判的规范二者之间的区分与和马克斯·厄恩斯特·迈耶(Max Ernst Mayer)首先作出区分的法律规范与文明规范(*Kultur*)相一致。首先,我要说的是,在我的讲演中我第一次提到了构造方法的规范与裁判规范的区分,我在1903年3月4日发表了《法律的自由发现和自由法学》。这早于1903年出版的《维也纳法律社会》。该书的序言写于1903年的6月。这里所说的讨论出现在这一版的第9页。马克斯·厄恩斯特·迈耶的这本书出版于1903年。它的序言的日期是1903年8月8日。因此,任何人都不能说马克斯·厄恩斯特·迈耶和我借鉴了彼此的观点。此外,细心的读者还会注意到虽然我得出了与马克斯·厄恩斯特·迈耶相同的结论。但是,我是基于一个和马克斯·厄恩斯特·迈耶完全不同的观念而得出该结论的,并且怀有一个和他完全不同的目的。

not only of what the members of the association do or leave undone, but of the extent to which they should be permitted to avail themselves of the property of the association. It was observed long ago that Gierke has formulated his concept so broadly as to include practically the entire German law within its scope. And herein lies the germ of a true and great conception of the nature of law. Just as we find the ordered community wherever we follow its traces, far beyond the limits set by Gierke, so we also find law everywhere, ordering and upholding every human association.

The term social sciences, at the present time, comprises every manner of science of human society, theoretical as well as practical; and therefore it includes not only the theoretical science of economics but the practical science (*Nationalökonomie*, as it is called), statistics, and politics as well. At the beginning of the last century, the French philosopher Auguste Comte created the term sociology to designate the totality of the theoretical social sciences. Attempts are making to give to sociology a specific content, to make it an independent science, the function of which is to present a synthesis of the content of all theoretical social sciences, which might constitute a unitary "general part" of the social sciences. The existence of such a science may be justified, but it would not be advisable to call it sociology, for in that case it would be necessary to find a new term for the social sciences as a whole. The term *Jurisprudenz* hitherto has comprised both the theoretical and the practical science of law; and it is likely that this customary terminology will be retained, but it will be necessary to distinguish between the theory of law in the proper sense of the term, the science of law, on the one hand, and the practical juristic science (*Jurisprudenz*) and, where there is no danger of misunderstanding, juristic science (*Jurisprudenz*) simply, on the other. Since the taw is a social phenomenon, every kind of legal science (*Jurisprudenz*) is a social science; but legal science in the

什么或没有做什么的问题,而且还是在多大的程度上他们可以利用联合体的财产的问题。很久以前人们就发现,基尔克阐述的观念广阔到实际上将整个德国法都包括在其范围内的程度。这里包含着真正而伟大的自然法观念的萌芽。正如无论在哪里我们发现了有秩序的共同体,我们就会追寻它的足迹,远远超越基尔克所设定的边界,同样,我们也会在各处发现法律,规整和支撑着每一个人类联合体。

当前,社会科学这一术语包含了人类社会科学的任何一个方面——理论科学和实用科学。因此,它不仅包括了理论经济学,还包括应用经济学(如被称做 *Nationalökonomie*)、[1]统计学和政治学。在上个世纪初,法国哲学家奥古斯特·孔德创造了社会学这一术语用来指称理论社会科学的整体。人们试图赋予社会学以特有的内容,使它成为一门独立的学科。社会学的功能是对所有的理论社会科学的内容进行综合,这样就可以组成一个单一的社会科学的"总论部分"。那样一种科学的存在可能是合理的,但是将它叫做社会学并不可取,因为那样的话,我们就有必要寻找一个指称作为整体的社会科学的术语。迄今法学这一术语包含理论法学和实用法学,并且很可能这一习惯性术语还将被继续保留。但是,一方面,我们也有必要区分在这一术语恰当意义上的法律理论即法律科学和实用法学(*Jurisprudenz*)——另一方面,在没有被误解的危险之处,直接用法律科学(*Jurisprudenz*)。既然法律是一种社会现象,则每一种法律科学(*Jurisprudenz*)都是社会

---

〔1〕(德)国民经济学。

proper sense of the term is a part of the theoretical science of society, of sociology. The sociology of law is the theoretical science of law (*die wissenschaftliche Lehre vom Recht*).

科学;但是法律科学这一术语在恰切的意义上是理论性社会科学的一部分,即社会学的部分。法律社会学是理论性法律科学(*die wissenschaftliche Lehre vom Recht*)。

# II

# The Inner Order Of The Social Associations

It is axiomatic that all study in the field of social science is based on the concept of human society. Society is the sum total of the human associations that have mutual relations with one another. And these associations that constitute human society are very heterogeneous. The state, the nation, the community of states which are bound together by the ties of international law, i. e. the political, economic, intellectual, and social association of the civilized nations of the earth extending far beyond the bounds of the individual state and nation, the religious communions and the individual churches, the various sects and religious groups, the corporations, the classes, the professions, the political parties within the state, the families in the narrowest and in the widest sense, the social groups and cliques—this universe of interlacing rings and intersecting circles—constitute a society to the extent that acting and reacting upon one another is at all perceptible among them. There is then, first of all, a society consisting of the civilized nations of the earth; within this society are various narrower societies, e. g. a society of the Christian and of the Mohammedan nations, and lastly societies that comprise only the individual civilized nations. Nations that are altogether outside of this sphere of mutual action and reaction are beyond the pale of human society, e. g. the savage and the barbarous nations of the earth, and, until recent times, the Japanese and the Chinese, who, however, in their seclusion, constituted a society of their own.

From these various kinds of groups of human beings, we must select, first of all, a certain kind of organized association, which

# 第二章　社会联合体的内部秩序

社会科学领域的所有研究均基于人类社会之观念，此乃不证自明之理。人类社会是彼此具有相互关系的人类联合体的总和。这些构成人类社会的社会联合体性质迥异。国家、民族以及通过国际法纽带联系在一起的国家联合体，亦即，已远远超越了单个国家和民族疆界、宗教团体和各个教会、各种各样的教派和宗教组织、一个国家内部的法人社团、社会阶层、职业团体和政治党派，最狭义和最广义的家庭以及社会组织和派系的——地球上文明民族的政治联合体、经济联合体、智识联合体和社会联合体——这种交错的帮派和交叉的圈子形成的世界——在某种程度上构成了一个社会，其中，这些联合体彼此之间的作用与反作用完全清晰可见。首先，这是一个由世界上文明的民族所组成的社会；在这个社会中又有各种各样更小的社会团体——例如，基督教社团和伊斯兰教民族社团——以及最终只包括独立的文明民族的社会。所有处于相互作用和反作用之外的民族都超出了人类社会的界限，例如地球上原始和野蛮的民族，但是，直到最近这一时代，中国人和日本人，在隔离的状态下，仍然建立了他们自己的社会。

首先，我们必须从这些形式多样的人类组织中选择特定的有

we shall hereafter designate as the primitive (genetic) association. We meet with it in primitive times in various forms as clan (*Geschlecht*, *gens*, *Sippe*), family, house community. The clan and the family are its original forms. It cannot as yet be determined which of these two must be considered the true original form (*Urform*); whether the clan is nothing more than a full-grown, enlarged family, or whether the family developed at a much later time than, and within, the clan. It is self-evident that, from the moment in which men begin to form associations, increased capacity for association with others becomes a weapon in the struggle for existence. It effects the gradual exclusion and extinction of those in whom self-seeking and predatory instincts predominate, and the survival of those that have capacity for socialization, who henceforth are the stronger because they can avail themselves of the strength of the whole association. Accordingly natural selection and heredity produce a race of human beings which is increasingly capable of socialization. This feeling of solidarity which has its roots in the dim consciousness of mutual interdependence begets the clan, and, strengthened by the consciousness of common ancestry, the (cognatic, based on blood relationship) family. Among breeders of cattle and tillers of the soil, whose common toil leads them to dwell together, the family develops into the house community, which is usually also called family. Out of the union of genetic associations, clans, families, house communities, grows the tribe, and, in course of time, the nation.

In lower stages of development, the social order of mankind rests exclusively upon the genetic associations and their union into

组织的联合体,这些联合体就是我们随后所称的基本的(原生性的)联合体。在原始时代,我们看到的是以像氏族(*Geschlecht*,*Gens*,*Sippe*)、家族、家庭共同体等[1]各种形式出现的有组织的团体。氏族和家族是有组织联合体的最初形式。至今我们还不能确定这两者中的哪一个可以被看做真正的人类社会最初形态(*Urform*);氏族是否仅是一个完全发展了的扩大了的家族,或者家族是在氏族内部、远远晚于氏族发展起来的。不言而喻,自从人们开始组织联合体那一时刻起,人与人之间日益增强的交往能力就成为了人类生存斗争的武器。联合体渐渐排斥那些以追逐私利和掠夺为主导的人,并使他们逐渐消失,同时使得那些具有社会化能力的人存活下来,自此以后人们更加强大,因为他们可以利用整个联合体的力量。从而,自然选择和遗传产生出了一个种族,他们具有日益提高的、使联合体社会化的能力。源于模糊的相互依赖的意识中的这种团结一致的感觉使氏族得以产生,又由于共同的祖先和(有血缘关系、以血统关系为基础的)家族,这种意识得以强化。在牲畜饲养者和土地耕种者中间,共同的辛苦劳动使他们居住到了一起,家庭发展成了家庭共同体,这种住户共同体也经常被称之为家族。由于这些原生性联合体、氏族、家族、住户共同体,慢慢地形成部落,然后,随着时间的推移,民族也产生了。

在发展的低级阶段,人类社会的秩序完全取决于原生性联合

---

〔1〕 英译本中,family、house、household、house community 经常并列出现。依据英译者的表达,除另有说明外,family 应该指“家族”,而 house 指的是“住户”或“家庭”。

tribe and nation. These associations therefore fulfil a number of functions. The clan, the house community, the family, is an association economic, religious, military, and legal; it is a community of language, ethical custom, and social life. But in more advanced societies, these functions are gradually severing from the genetic associations; groups of a different kind arise, which add to their new functions by taking over the original functions of the genetic associations. These are: the commune, the state, the religious communion, the society, the political party, the social coterie, the social club, the economic association in agriculture, shop, and factory, the cooperative society, the association of the members of a calling, all the associations connected with the transportation of persons or goods. Among the peoples of the highest degree of civilization, a man becomes a member of an almost incalculable number of associations of the most diverse kinds; his life becomes richer, more varied, more complex. And in consequence, the once powerful genetic associations languish and, in part, fall into decay. Only the house community of the nearest blood relatives, who dwell under the same roof, the family in the narrowest sense of the word, has been able to maintain itself in full vigor down to our day; the wider family has largely faded out, and of the clan only a few scarcely perceptible traces remain, and these are to be found exclusively among the higher nobility and among the peasantry.

All later associations are in a relation of pronounced contrast to the genetic associations. With few exceptions every man belongs to a genetic association; there is no such necessity as to the other associations. One is born into the genetic associations; but membership in the other associations is a matter of voluntary joining and reception. The genetic association owes its existence to unconscious impulses; the later associations are the result of conscious human activity. And this contrast is heightened with every advance in civilization. One hundred years ago, a man's occupation or his profession, his religious fellowship, his political affiliations, and his social connections, were determined to a much greater extent than they are today, by his descent, i. e. by the genetic association to which he belonged. All

体以及他们联合而成的部落和民族。因此，这种联合体履行了大量的职能。氏族、住户共同体、家族是经济、宗教、军事和法律的联合体，也是语言、伦理习俗和社会生活的共同体。但是在一个更为发达的社会中，这些功能会逐渐从原生性联合体中分离出来。各种形式的组织发展起来，它们通过接收原生性联合体的原始职能，向其中加入了它们的新职能。这些组织是：公社、国家、宗教团体、社团、政党、社会行业团体、社交俱乐部、农业经济联合体、商店、工厂、合作型社团和职业会员联合体。所有这些团体都是通过成员和货物的输送而连接起来。在最高文明程度的民族中，每个人都成了几乎数不尽的类别迥异的联合体成员。他的人生变得更为丰富、多样和复杂。结果，曾经强大的原生性联合体开始衰退并且部分衰亡了。只有由居住在同一个屋檐下的至亲血缘所组成的住户共同体——最为狭义的家庭——还以顽强的生命力维持到今天。大家族已经在很大程度上衰退，并且宗族仅仅在少数几个可以观察到的种族中保存着，这些唯独还可以在豪门贵族阶层和农民阶层中看到。

所有的后面这些联合体处在一种和原生性联合体迥异的关系中。除了很少的例外情况外，每个人都属于一个原生性联合体；而其他的联合体都没有这样的必然性。一个人生来就属于特定的原生性联合体，但要成为其他联合体的成员还需要自愿地加入和批准。原生性联合体的存在乃是基于无意识的冲动，后面的这些联合体则是人们有意识行为的结果。这种差异随着文明的进步而加深。一百多年前，跟今天相比，一个人的职业或事业、宗教信仰、政治关系和他的社会联系在更大程度上由他的出身决定，也就是说，由他所属的原生性联合体决定，人们自由选择决定

these things were determined by free choice to a much lesser extent than they are today.

Though we know very little of the law of the early times of the peoples from whom the civilized nations of Europe have sprung, there can be no doubt that of what today is mostly, and sometimes even exclusively, called law, i. e. of the fixed rule of law, formulated in words, which issues from a power superior to the individual, and which is imposed upon the latter from without, only a few negligible traces can be found among them. Their law is chiefly the order of the clans, families, houses. It determines the prerequisites and the consequences of a valid marriage, the mutual relation of the spouses, of parents and children, and the mutual relations of the other members of the clan, family, and household. Each association creates this order for itself quite independently. It is not bound by the order which exists in other associations for the same relations. And if the orders in associations of the same kind differ very little from each other, this must be attributed to the similarity of the conditions of life; often to borrowing; but by no means to a uniform order in some manner prescribed for them from without. In the language of German scholarship, there may possibly be a general law (*allgemeines Recht*) in these associations, but not a common law (*gemeines Recht*).

As soon as ownership of land becomes established, law arises concerning it, but without any general rules of law. Each settle ment creates its own land law; each landlord imposes it independently upon his villeins; each royal grant, quite independently of all others, makes provision for the legal status of the estate it grants. There are concrete legal relations in the various communes, settlements, and manors, but no law of ownership in land such as is found in the *corpus iuris* or in modern statute-books.

The same holds true for the contract. The law of contracts is based solely upon the content of the contracts that are being entered into. There are no general legal propositions governing contracts. There is an utter absence of all those rules of compulsion, of eking out, and of interpretation with which the *corpus iuris* and

上述事情的可能性在很大程度上低于今天。

虽然我们对于欧洲文明民族演进之源头的早期民族的法律几乎一无所知,但是毫无疑问,今天大部分的、有时甚至是全部的被称做法律的事物——即由超越个人的强权发布的、从外界强加给个人的、以言辞清晰表达出来的确定的法律规则——在上述早期的民族中都能找得到。他们的法律主要是关于氏族、家族和家庭的秩序。这种秩序决定着有效婚姻的先决条件和后果,配偶之间的相互关系,父母和子女之间的相互关系,氏族、家族以及家庭的其他成员之间的相互关系。每个联合体都相当独立地创立自身的秩序,并且每个联合体均不受其他联合体中为了处理相同的关系而存在的规则的拘束。如果相同类型的联合体的规则彼此差异极小,这肯定是因为它们的生活条件具有相似性;这经常也是移植的结果,但这绝非是从外部以某种特定的方式给他们规定的统一秩序的结果。用德国的学术话语来说就是,这些联合体中很可能存在一般法(*allgemeines Recht*),而不是共同法(*gemeines Recht*)。

土地的所有权一建立,法律就开始关注它,但是并没有产生任何一般性的法律规则。每一个聚居区都创制它自己的土地法;每一个地主都独立地在其农奴中强制推行该土地法;每一个王室财产授予(状)——独立于所有其他财产授予——都为它所授予的土地规定法律地位。在各类各样的社区、聚居区和庄园中都存在具体的法律关系,但是却没有像可以在《国法大全》中或现代法令全书中找到的那种土地所有权法律。

对于契约法,也同样是如此。契约法完全以(当时流行的)契约内容为基础。规范契约的一般性法律命题是不存在的。《国法大全》和现代法令全书中所充斥的那些关于强制性的、补充性的

modern statute books abound. Where the contract is silent, there is no law; and the literal, narrow interpretation of contracts, which is so characteristic of the older law, is not based upon formalism, which is usually imputed to primitive times, but which in reality is quite foreign to them, but upon the fact that, outside of the language of the contract, there is nothing to stand on.

General rules of law are found first of all, perhaps, in the law of inheritance. In the most ancient times, only the members of the household of the deceased take by inheritance; and these general rules concern only the rights of distant relatives. Even the Twelve Tables say nothing of the *sui heredes*, but do speak of the agnates and the gentiles; and we encounter the same situation in the ancient Germanic folk laws and in the Slavic law books. This shows that these rules belong to a later stratum. The disposition by the members of a household of the goods of one of their own number who had died was determined independently, even in historical times, by each and every house and clan. It was only for the event that there were no members of the household in existence that general precepts arose at a comparatively early time.

The earliest state is based exclusively upon the agreement entered into by the noble clans that found it; and over and above this agreement there is nothing that might determine the position, rights, and duties of the individual organs of the state. After kingship for life, and, at a later time hereditary kingship, has begun to replace temporary leadership, everything is dependent upon the personality, the wealth, the influence of the king, and upon the number, the bravery, and the loyalty of his retainers. If the king can rely upon his retainers, his power may be very great; if not, he must, in matters of important governmental action, secure the consent of the influential men among the people, possibly of all the people. Accordingly the

和解释性的法律规则也完全不存在。合同保持沉默的地方，就不存在任何法律。对契约的字面的、狭义的解释（这是古法的典型特征之一）不是基于通常可归咎于原始时代但事实上却与原始时代完全没有关系的形式主义，而是基于这一事实：除了契约用语外，没有任何可以依赖的东西。

或许，一般性法律规则首先存在于继承法中。在极其远古的时代，只有亡者的家庭成员才能获得遗产；这些一般性的规则仅涉及到远亲的权利。《十二铜表法》甚至没有提及合法继承人，[1]但确实提到了父系亲属和氏族亲属。在古日耳曼的民间亲属法和斯拉夫人的法律书籍中我们会遇到相同的情形。这表明这些规则属于后来的阶层。由家庭成员对自己家庭中已故者财产的支配，即使在历史上，也是由每个家庭和氏族独立决定的。仅仅针对一个家族没有任何活着的成员这种情形，在一个相对较早的时期才产生了相应的一般性规则。

最早的国家纯粹基于显贵氏族之间的立国协议。除这个协议之外，没有任何的东西可以确定国家各独立机构的地位、权利和职责。在终身王位制和稍后的世袭王位制取代临时的领导权以后，所有的一切都依赖于国王的个性、财富、影响力以及他的扈从的数目、英勇度和忠诚度。如果国王能够信赖他的扈从，他的权力可能会非常强大；如果不能信赖他的扈从，他必须在涉及重要的政府行为方面，获得在人民中有影响力的人的同意，可能还

---

〔1〕 *Sui heredes* 疑为 *Sui haeredes*；*Sui haeredes*（拉），合法继承人，正统继承人。

council of the elders and the popular assembly are not constitutional institutions, but merely means employed by the king to enforce his will. The authority of the royal officials is based on the king's mandate and upon the royal power. Therefore there are no legal propositions concerning it.

The present-day private law of princes is a part of the most ancient legal order of the human race which has been preserved for our day like an antediluvian gnat encased in amber. Von Dungern has conclusively shown that the private law of princes has no material content of any kind. It merely provides that the families of the high nobility may determine their legal relations independently. What that determination shall be lies exclusively within their discretion. This present-day condition of the private law of princes was the condition of all law in time past. The self-determination of the families of the high nobility, however, extends solely to a few questions of the law of the family and of the law of inheritance; whereas in primitive times each and every association and, within the association, each and every legal relation, contract, or parcel of ground had its own law; and, apart from this law of the individual legal relation, there was no law in ancient human society.

This legal order is reflected in the Homeric poems, the Scandinavian sagas, and the *Germania* of Tacitus. The legal traditions of the Twelve Tables and of the most ancient Germanic legal records, indeed, to a certain extent, present a later development. The latter contain general legal propositions relating to the system of penalties, to penal procedure, and to a few matters of public and private law. These are in part, it is true, merely borrowings from Roman law; in part, they have originated under the influence of Roman law; but for the most part, they bear witness to a more advanced stage of legal development. The Slavic legal sources bear a similar relation to Byzantine law.

But even the highly developed Roman law of historical times contains untold survivals which point to an older condition such as has been described. The whole of human life and all relations

要获得所有人的同意。因此,长者议事会和民众大会不是宪法性机构,仅是国王用来实现他的意志的机构。王室官员的权威基于国王的委任授权和王权。因此,不存在关于皇家官员的权威的法律命题。

如今的王室私法是人类最古老法律秩序的一部分,这些像大洪水前装入琥珀的极其古老的小昆虫一样被保存到了今天。冯·敦根已经确凿无疑地证明,王室私法没有任何类型的实质内容,它仅仅规定显贵家庭可以独立地决定他们的法律关系。此类决定纯属他们的自由裁量权。今天王室私法的状况就是过去所有法律的状况。不过,显贵家族的自我决定权只能延伸到家庭法和继承法的若干问题上。但在远古时期,每一个联合体以及每一个联合体内的每一个法律关系、契约或者每一宗土地都有它自己的法律;而且除了这些有关个体法律关系的法律外,古代的人类社会没有任何别的法律。

这种法律秩序在荷马史诗、斯堪的纳维亚的传奇故事和塔西佗的《赫马尼亚》中都能反映出来。《十二铜表法》和最古老的日耳曼法律记载的传统确实在一定程度上展现了法律的新发展。最古老的日耳曼法律记载中包含了关于刑罚制度、刑事诉讼程序以及一些公法和私法事项的一般性法律命题。的确,这些法律部分地从罗马法移植而来,部分在罗马法的影响下产生;但是,极大程度上,它们构成了一个法律发展较高阶段的证据。斯拉夫人的法律渊源和拜占庭法有着相似的关系。

但是,即使历史上高度发达的罗马法中也包含着体现上述古老情形的无法列举的残余。在罗马人家庭和氏族中的人类生活

within the Roman house and clan are based on the autonomy of each house and clan. In the earlier stratum of Roman contracts, the words of the contracts determine all rights and duties arising therefrom. This is an inevitable consequence of the lack of general rules concerning the presuppositions and consequences of contractual duties. From the earliest times, the right and law of inheritance of the *sui heredes* was never governed by any regulations. This is shown by the sovereign power of disposition of the testament as well as by the lack of all regulations governing settlements made by the heirs of the body in the *actio familiae herciscundae*. According to clear evidence, the right of inheritance of the gentiles was regulated quite independently by each *gens*. And what in actual fact is Roman *Staatsrecht* (public law in the narrow sense)? Barring the content of the small number of *leges* that contain *Staatsrecht*, everything that Mommsen sets forth under this head is merely a presentation of the practice of the organs of the Roman state during the existence of the Empire. Mommsen does, indeed, arrive at general legal propositions at every point; but with very few exceptions these were the product of his own intellectual labor; they were abstracted by him from the facts; they never were the rules that regulated the facts. Indeed one may call this Roman public law in the narrow sense, but it certainly is not a constitution of the Roman state. Since Oriental aristocrats have begun to travel in Europe and have been receiving a European education, there is no lack of statutes in the Orient, occasionally even of written constitutions; but these are mere toys, not without significance for the far distant future perhaps, but utterly ineffectual at the present time. If one would become acquainted with the actual public law in the narrow sense of an Oriental state, one must try to understand the activity of the individual organs of the state from actual observation, which is more than a substitute for the *Corpus Inscriptionum Latinarum*. The methodological significance of Von Dun-

的整体和所有关系都是基于每一个家庭和氏族的自治。在罗马契约法早期发展阶段，契约中的措辞决定着该契约的所有权利和义务。这是缺少有关契约责任先决条件和后果的一般规则的必然结果。从最早期开始，合法继承人的继承权从未被任何法令规范过。这既被遗嘱处分的至高权所证明，也被遗产分割之诉[1]中规范继承人和解之法令的缺乏所证明。确凿的证据表明，氏族成员的继承权由各个氏族自己独立规范。实际情形上，罗马 *Staatsrecht*（狭义上的公法）是什么呢？除了包含 *Staatsrecht* 的少量法律外，蒙森在这一标题下阐述的所有内容，仅仅是对罗马帝国存在期间的罗马国家机构实践活动的表述。莫姆森确实在每一点上都得出了一般性法律命题，但是除了极少数的例外，这些都是他自己智力劳动的成果；这些都是他从事实当中提炼出来的；它们从来不是规范这些事实的规则。的确，人们可以将这称做狭义上的罗马公法，但它肯定不是罗马国家的宪法。自从东方的贵族们开始到欧洲来旅游并接受欧洲式的教育后，东方就不再缺少制定法，甚至偶尔也不缺少成文宪法；不过，这些仅仅是小饰物，它们或许对遥远的未来意义重大，但是当前它们是彻底无效的。如果某人熟悉东方国家的狭义上的公法，他肯定会设法通过实际观察去理解这个国家各个机构的活动，这不仅仅是《拉丁铭文大全》

---

〔1〕（拉）*actio familiae hercisundae*（遗产分割之诉），此诉讼是由《十二铜表法》创设的；某个或某几个共同继承人可以要求与其他共同继承人分割由他们共同继承的遗产的集合体。当共同继承人中的某个人得到先取遗赠时，他可以通过遗产分割之诉要求从共同继承的遗产中提取受赠物。

gem's work on the public law in the narrow sense of Egypt rests on his appreciation of this fact.

In the primitive stage, the whole legal order consists in the inner order of the human associations, of which, indeed, the state is one. Each association creates this order for itself, even though it is true that an association often copies an order existing in other associations, or in case of a splitting up of an association, takes over an order and continues it. Because of these facts, to which must be added the similarities caused by the similarity of the relations, common features will not be lacking. To an observer from the outside these common features might appear to constitute a common law of the nation. But this is only a generalization made by the observer himself on the basis of what he has seen and heard. Tacitus makes a number of statements about the legal relations of the ancient Germans, but a cursory glance at his account suffices to show that it contains no legal propositions, but only statements about what the Germans customarily did and left undone. Society, if one may use the term with reference to those times, maintained its balance not by means of rules of law, but by means of the inner order of its associations.

Passing over a great number of generations of men, we reach the feudal state. It has been extremely difficult for the modern man to understand the feudal state, for the reason that, for a long time, he had been trying to find a constitution of the feudal state; whereas the chief characteristic of the feudal state is the fact that it has no constitution, but only agreements. The relation between the king and the great lords to whom he has granted fiefs is a contractual one. Likewise the relation between the great lords and those whom they have enfeoffed; likewise the relation between the latter and those whom they, in turn, have enfeoffed. On the lowest rung of the ladder are the serfs. Of course, one or more rungs may be omitted, and the feudal lords may have serfs at any level in this scale. In order to write an exhaustive description of the feudal state, one must be able to state the content of

的替代办法。冯·敦根关于埃及狭义公法方面的著作在方法论上的重要意义在于,他尊重了这一事实。

在原始阶段,整个的法律秩序存在于人类联合体的内部秩序,事实上,国家也是这些联合体之一。每个联合体都为自己创制法律秩序,尽管事实上有些联合体经常模仿存在于其他联合体中的秩序,或者在一个联合体分裂的情形下,一个联合体接受了原来的秩序并继续适用。由于这些事实,在上述事实中必须增加因为关系的相似性所导致的类似性,共同的特征将不可缺少。对于一个外部的观察者来说,这些共同特征看上去像是构成了这个民族的共同法。但这仅仅是观察者自己以其所看和所听为基础所作的一种概括。塔西佗就古代德国的法律关系作了大量陈述,但是,对其说明的粗略一瞥就足以明了,其陈述中并不包含法律命题,而主要是关于德国人习惯上的作为和不作为。社会——如果那个时代人们会使用这个术语——不是凭借法律规则来维持它的平衡,而是依靠其联合体的内部秩序来维持它的平衡。

略过许多代人不提,我们探讨一下封建国家。让现代人理解封建国家是相当困难的,原因是,长期以来,现代人一直试图寻找一部封建国家的宪法;然而,封建国家的主要特征就是它根本没有宪法,只有协议。国王和由国王授予封地的大封建主之间的关系是一种契约关系。大封建主和由他们授予封地的封建主之间的关系也是如此;同样,后者与他授予封地的对象之间的关系还是如此。处于封建梯级最底层的是农奴。当然,一个或者更多的梯级可以省略,并且封建主可能在这一范围内有任何等级的农奴。为了完整地描述封建国家,人们必须能够说明封建主和臣民

all the agreements entered into between the lords and their liegemen and of the relation between the lords and the villeins, which often is merely contractual. The agreements and the relation between the lord and the villeins may be very much alike in a certain district and among a certain people. But this similarity also is based upon the similarity of the attendant circumstances, upon direct imitation or borrowing, not upon a general rule. What is called "feudal law" is primarily a scientific elaboration of the common element in the individual agreements, which at a later period is transformed into a general rule of law which ekes out the content of the agreements.

It is true, in the more developed feudal law, assemblies of the feudal tenants of the individual feudal lords are not unknown. Occasionally these are assemblies not only of the immediate tenants of the feudal lord, but also of the tenants of the intermediate feudatories. Sometimes there are assemblies of villeins. These assemblies adopt common resolutions. But before the idea of law had made its way, these resolutions did not contain legal propositions in the modern sense of the term. They are merely expressions of the common will, and their legal significance is based upon the fact that they are being accepted by the feudal lord, and thereby become collective agreements with the feudal lord. Collective agreements in this sense of the term were: the most ancient resolutions of the German Imperial Diet, the Magna Charta Libertatum, which to the present day has remained the foundation of the English constitution, and on the whole, the law of the German manorial rights and of the corresponding services.

But the feudal constitution was far from being the whole content of the social order of the feudal state. Within the feudal state, the clan, the family, the house continued; but the clan was weakened considerably. Side by side with it, new local associations arose, which took over a considerable number of social functions. Among the local associations, the city soon became very important, and achieved a considerable measure of independence, which in effect placed it outside of the feudal constitution. The feudal constitution, in fact, has always remained a constitution of the open country. Within the walls of the city, a vast number of social associations, which were unknown elsewhere,

之间缔结的所有契约的内容以及封建主和农奴之间的关系，这种关系经常只是契约性的。封建主和农奴之间的协议和关系在一个特定的地区和在特定的人群中是非常相似的。这种相似性也是以相似的伴随环境、直接的模仿或移植为基础的，而不是以一个一般规则为基础的。所谓的“封建法”主要是对单个协议中共同要素的科学而详尽的论述，在稍后的一段时期内，单个协议被改造为补充协议内容的一般性法律规则。

的确，在更为发达的封建法中，人们对单个封建主的封地佃户的集会并不陌生。有时候，这些集会不仅仅是封建主的直接佃户的集会，也是中间的封建封臣之佃户的集会。有时候，也存在农奴的集会。这些集会会正式通过共同的决议。但是在法律观念还没有形成以前，这些决议并不包含现代术语意义上的法律命题。它们仅仅是共同意愿的表达，它们的重要性基于封建主准备接受这些共同意愿的事实，因此，它们变成了和封建主缔结的集体协议。在这一术语意义上的集体协议有：“德意志神圣罗马帝国议会”中最古老的决议；直到今天还是英国宪法基础的《自由大宪章》；在整体上，德国的庄园权利和相应劳务的法律。

但是，封建宪法远不是封建国家社会秩序的全部内容。在封建国家内部，氏族、家族和家庭还继续存在；但是氏族已经相当地削弱了。与此同时，新的地区性联合体产生了，它们接管了相当多的社会职能。在这些地区性联合体中，城市很快变得极为重要，并且获得了相当大的独立性，即城市实质上已经脱离了封建宪法。事实上，封建宪法一直都是开放国家的宪法。在城市围墙内，大量在别处所不曾知悉的社会联合体和活跃的法律生活发展

and an active legal life developed. Here for the first time fully developed legal institutions were exapressed in a number of legal propositions: the law of real property, of pledge, of contract, of inheritance.

But these legal propositions constitute an infinitesimal part of the legal order. In the feudal state as well as elsewhere, the great bulk of the legal order is not based upon the legal propositions, but upon the inner order of the social associations, of the older ones (the clan, the family, the house community), as welt as of those of more recent origin—the feudal association, the manor, the mark community, the urban community, the guilds and trade unions, the corporations and foundations. If one would obtain a knowledge of the law of mediaeval society, one must not confine oneself to a study of the legal propositions, but must study it in the deeds of grant, the charters, the land registers, the records of the guilds, the city books, the regulations of the guilds. Even at this period, the center of gravity of the law lies in the inner order of the human associations.

If one compares the law of the present with that of past centuries, one cannot but be struck at the first glance by the great importance which in the course of centuries has attached to the legal proposition, authoritatively pronounced and formulated. With the sole exception of Great Britain, the *Staatsrecht* (public law in the narrow sense) of all European states has been put into this form, as well as the law of the state magistracies, administrative law, procedural law, and, apparently, the whole body of private law and of penal law. For this reason the idea that the law is nothing but a body of legal propositions dominates legal thinking today.

This idea, however, contains so many contradictory elements that it refutes itself. This inner inconsistency is least apparent in *Sta-*

起来了。在这里完整发展起来的法律制度第一次通过大量的法律命题表达出来了:不动产法、担保法、契约法和继承法。

不过这些法律命题只构成法律秩序中微小的一部分。在封建国家和其他地方,大量的法律秩序不是基于法律命题,而是基于社会联合体的内部秩序、基于旧有的联合体(氏族、家族和家庭共同体)的内部秩序和新近产生的联合体——封建联合体、庄园和马尔克公社、城市社区、同业协会和贸易协会、公司和基金会的内部秩序。如果任何人想获得关于中世纪社会的法律知识,那么他不应该把自己限制在研究法律命题上,他必须研究财产转让契据、商业租约、土地登记簿、行业协会的登记记录、城市名册、行业协会的规章。即使在这一时期,法律的重心也在于人类联合体的内部秩序。

如果有人将现在的法律和过去几个世纪的法律比较,那么他在看到第一眼时,就会情不自禁被在过去的几个世纪里经权威性宣告和阐述的法律命题的重要意义所震动。除了英国这唯一的例外,欧洲所有国家的 *Staatsrecht*(狭义的公法)都采用了法律命题的形式,当然还有国家的地方执法官法、行政法、诉讼法,很显然,还包括全部的私法和刑法。由于这一个原因,法律就是法律命题集合的观点,主导了今天的法律思维。

然而,这一观点中包含了太多的自我冲突的矛盾因素。这种内在的不协调性在 *Staatsrecht*(狭义上的公法)、行政法和诉讼法中最不明显。不过,对该事实的现代规范性意义的实际调查、对传

*atsrecht* (public law in the narrow sense), in administrative law, and in the law of procedure. But modern investigation of the normative significance of the factual, of the *Konventional*regel, and of the practice of administrative boards has shown that this branch of the law too does not consist exclusively of legal propositions. On the other hand, the legal rules barely touch the surface of the modern order of the family. The law of corporations and of foundations is based in the main upon the articles of association. In spite of the detailed provisions of the law of contracts, the content of the contract is of greater importance in the individual casc than the rules of law governing contracts. Testamentary declarations of will, nuptial agreements, contracts of inheritance, agreements among heirs, are of much greater importance in the law of inheritance than the rules of law concerning it. Every judge, every administrative official, knows that, comparatively speaking, he rarely renders a decision based solely on legal propositions. By far the greatest number of decisions are based upon documents, testimony of witnesses or experts, contracts, articles of association, last wills and testaments, and other declarations. In other words, in the language of jurists, in a much greater number of instances judgment is being rendered upon questions of fact than upon questions of law. And the fact is a matter of the inner order of the human associations, as to which the judge obtains information from the testimony of witnesses and experts, from contracts, agreements among heirs, declarations by last will and testament. Even today, just as in primitive times, the fate of man is determined to a much greater extent by the inner order of the associations than by legal propositions.

This truth is hidden from the eye of the jurist by the fact that to him an adjudication upon a question of fact merely amounts to a subsumption of the ascertained facts under a legal proposition. But this is due solely to a juristic habit of thought. The state existed before the constitution; the family is older than the order of the family;

统规则或法律[1]的现代调查以及对行政管理委员实际运作的现代调查显示，这些法律部门也并非纯粹由法律命题组成。另一方面，法律规范仅仅触及现代家庭秩序的表面。公司的法律和基金会的法律也主要是基于联合体章程。尽管有详备的契约法的法律命题，个案中的契约内容比规范契约的法律规则更为重要。遗嘱的宣告、婚姻契约、遗产契约、继承人之间的协议在继承法中要比法律在这方面的规定更为重要。每一位法官和每一位行政官员都知道，相比较而言，他不会单单依据法律的条文作出判决。到目前为止，数量最多的判决都是基于文件材料、证人或专家的证言、契约、联合体的章程、遗嘱和其他声明。换句话说，在法学家的语言中，在更多的情况下，法官都是基于事实问题作出判决，而不是基于法律问题。事实就是人类联合体的内部秩序，关于这一秩序，法官从证人和专家的证言、契约、继承人之间的协议、遗嘱的宣告中获得信息。即便是今天，也正如原始时代一样，个人的命运在很大程度上由联合体的内部秩序决定，而不是由法律命题来决定。

这一真理被法学家眼中的下述事实所掩盖：对他来说，对事实问题作出的裁决实际上不过是将待决事实涵摄到一个法律命题之下。但是，这完全是一种法学思维习惯的结果。国家在宪法出现前就已经存在，家庭也比家庭秩序更为久远；占有先于所有

---

〔1〕 *Konventionalregel*，即传统规则或法律，由当事人协议创立，只要选择了就要受其拘束。该协议可以基于言辞表达亦可基于当事人的行为而成立。

possession antedates ownership; there were contracts before there was a law of contracts; and even the testament, where it is of native origin, is much older than the law of last wills and testaments. If the jurists think that before a binding contract was entered into, before a valid testament was made, there must have been in existence a legal proposition according to which agreements or testaments are binding, they are placing the abstract before the concrete. Perhaps it seems more readily understandable to a jurist that a legal proposition concerning the law of contracts or the law of wills might be binding than that a contract or a will might be binding without a legal proposition. But the mental processes of nations and of men, excepting the jurists among them, do not function in this fashion. It can be shown that the idea that prevailed among men in the past was that their right had arisen from a contract or from a grant; the idea that it had arisen from a legal proposition was altogether foreign to them. And at the present time, unless legal theory exerts its influence, men generally assume that their rights arise not from legal propositions but from the relations of man to man, from marriage, contract, last will and testament. That anyone might owe his rights to a legal proposition, is a notion that even today is current only among jurists. Social phenomena, however, can be explained not by construing them juristically but by inferring from facts the modes of thought that underlie them.

Up to this point, I have been confining this presentation intentionally to the nations of Europe; but its application is not limited to these. Among primitive races, the law is generally identical with the inner order of their associations. At this stage of development there are no legal propositions at all. At a somewhat higher stage, they appear in the form of religious commands. And it seems that until man has reached a very high stage of development, he cannot fully conceive the idea that the abstract rules of law can force their will upon life. It is true, the German folk laws of the early Middle Ages contain very detailed legal propositions, but probably they were applied only in those parts of the country in which there was a Roman population sufficiently large to bring about the continuation of Roman modes of thought even

权;契约先于契约法;甚至自然产生出来的遗嘱也远比遗嘱法更为古老。如果法学家们认为在一个有拘束力的契约缔结以前、在一个有效的遗嘱作出以前,必定存在一个法律命题,依此命题协议或者遗嘱才具有拘束力,那么他们是把抽象置于具体之前。一项涉及契约法或遗嘱法的法律命题比没有法律命题基础的契约或遗嘱可能更具有拘束力,这对于法学家来说似乎更容易理解。但是,除了法学家外的整个民族和人们的思维过程都不是以这种方式运作的。事实能够表明,过去人们的主流观点是,他们的权利来自于契约或者特许;他们对权利产生于一个法律命题的观念是完全陌生的。目前,除非法律理论发挥它的影响,否则人们会通常认为他们的权利不是源于法律命题,而是源于人与人之间的关系、婚姻、契约和遗嘱。将自己权利归因于法律命题的观念,甚至在今天,也仅仅在法学家中流行。然而,社会现象不是通过法学上对它们进行推演而获得解释,而是通过对构成社会现象之基础的思维模式的事实进行推理而获得解释。

到目前为止,我一直都有意地将我的陈述限定在欧洲民族的范围之内;但是这一理论的应用并不仅限于这些国家。在原始种族中,法律通常情况下是和联合体的内部秩序相一致的。在这发展阶段,根本就没有法律命题。在稍微发达一点的阶段,法律以宗教命令的形式出现。并且看起来,在人类达到了一个很高的发展阶段之前,人类是不可能完全理解这种理念:法律的抽象规则可以把它们的意志强加给生活。诚然,中世纪早期的德意志民间法中包含非常详尽的法律命题,然而,这些命题可能仅仅适用于该国的如下这些地区——在这些地区罗马居民的数量足够大,以至于即使在日耳曼社会中,罗马人的思维方式仍然继续着。

in a Germanic society. How small the influence of legislation was, even in the Middle Ages, is sufficiently well known. Travelers in backward countries, in the Orient, in parts of eastern and southern Europe, are struck by the general disorder. This disorder is caused by the fact that general legal propositions, even if there are such, are not being followed. There is a strange contrast between this lack of order in public life and the strictness with which the traditional order of the small association, of the household, of the family, of the clan, is followed.

The great master of comparative legal science, Sir Henry Sumner Maine, has pointed this out in another connection. He was the first to state that at all times the oldest law has been the procedural law. Taken literally, this statement, of course, is absurd. A society, be it never so simple and primitive, whose whole order is based upon procedural law is unthinkable. Even legal disputes are nowhere decided solely on the basis of procedural norms. It is true, often a complaint is dismissed because of a mistake of form on the part of the plaintiff, or a complaint is permitted to succeed because of a mistake of form on the part of the defendant; but in every case where defects of form did not enter into consideration, the decision had to be rendered on the basis of the material law. This would have been impossible if there had been no material law. But although the procedural law was not, indeed, the oldest law, Maine's doctrine is correct in so far as the oldest legal propositions were those of procedural law; perhaps the propositions connected with provisions for penalties. Undoubtedly the material law was already in existence, even though it had not yet been formulated in legal propositions.

The inner order of the associations of human beings is not only the original, but also, down to the present time, the basic form of law. The legal proposition not only comes into being at a much

即便是在中世纪,人们也已经足够充分认识到立法影响力的微不足道!在落后国家、在东方、在东欧与南欧部分地区的旅行者都被普遍的无秩序状态所震动。这种无秩序状态的缘由是:尽管存在着那样的一般性法律命题,也没有人遵守。这种公共生活秩序的缺失与人们对小联合体、家庭、家族和氏族中传统秩序的严格遵循形成了奇妙的对比。

比较法的伟大学者,亨利·萨姆勒·梅因爵士在另外一个背景下指出了这一问题。他首次阐明,在任何时代最古老的法律是诉讼法。当然,照字面意思去理解,这一陈述是荒诞的。一个社会——不管它如何的简单和原始——的所有秩序都是以诉讼法为基础,这是无法想象的。甚至在任何地方,都不能完全以诉讼法为基础裁判法律纠纷。的确,一项诉讼请求经常因为原告方面起诉形式的错误而被驳回,或者一项诉讼请求因为被告方面答辩方式的错误而被认可;但是,在不考虑形式方面瑕疵的每一个案件中,判决都不得不以实体法[1]为基础作出。如果没有任何实体法,是不可能作出判决的。但是,尽管诉讼法确实不是最古老的法律,就最古老的法律命题是诉讼法法律命题而言,梅因的学说是正确的;或许这些命题和刑罚规定相联系。毫无疑问,即使迄今实体法尚未以法律命题的方式被系统阐述过,实体法也早已存在。

人类联合体的内部秩序不但在最初是法律的基本形式,而且到目前为止也是如此。法律命题不但是在稍后的时期才形成,而

---

〔1〕 实体法和形式法相区分,这种区分大体上对应于实体法和诉讼法的区分。

later time, but is largely derived from the inner order of the associations. In order to explain the beginnings, the development, and the nature of law, one must first of all inquire into the order of the associations. All attempts that have been made until now to comprehend the nature of law have failed because the investigation was not based on the order of the associations but on the legal propositions.

The inner order of the associations is determined by legal norms. Legal norms must not be confused with legal propositions. The legal proposition is the precise, universally binding formulation of the legal precept in a book of statutes or in a law book. The legal norm is the legal command, reduced to practice, as it obtains in a definite association, perhaps of very small size, even without any formulation in words. As soon as there are legal propositions within an association that have actually become effective, they give rise to legal norms. But in every society there is a much greater number of legal norms than of legal propositions; for there always is much more law that is applicable to individual cases than is applicable to all relations of a similar kind; much more law than the contemporary jurists who have attempted to formulate it in words have realized. Every modern legal historian knows how small a portion of the law that was valid at the time is contained in the Twelve Tables or in the *Lex* Salica. Modern codes are in the same case. In the past centuries, all legal norms that were determinative of the inner order of the associations were based upon custom, upon contracts, and upon articles of association of corporations. In the main, this is the situation today.

且也主要来源于联合体的内部秩序。为了解释法律的产生、发展及其性质,他必须首先考察联合体的内部秩序。迄今为止,所有理解法律之性质的尝试都归于失败,因为这些调查研究不是基于联合体的秩序,而是基于法律命题。

联合体的内部秩序由法律规范决定。不应该混淆法律规范和法律命题。法律命题是制定法卷册或者法律书籍中法律规定精确的、具有普遍约束力的系统表达。法律规范是一种落实到实践中的法律命令,如同在一个确定的(或许规模很小的)联合体内获得普遍遵守的法律命令——哪怕并没有对它进行任何言语上的清晰阐明。一个联合体中一旦存在生效的法律命题,则这些法律命题就可以产生出法律规范。但是,在每一个社会中,法律规范的数量都大大多于法律命题;因为在个案中适用的法律总是要比适用到同类所有法律关系的法律更多,也要比当代试图用语言系统表述法律的法学家所认识到的法律更多。每一个现代法律史学家都知道当时包含在《十二铜表法》或《萨利克法》[1]中的法律占当时全部有效法律的比例有多小。现代的法典也同样如此。在过去的几个世纪里,决定联合体内部秩序的所有法律规范都是以习惯、契约和公司的社团章程为基础的。大体上,这就是今天的情形。

[1] 现残存的最古老的日耳曼法典。

# III

# The Social Assoclations And The Social Norms

A scial association is a plurality of human beings who, in their relations with one another, recognize certain rules of conduct as binding, and, generally at least, actually regulate their conduct according to them. These rules are of various kinds, and have various names: rules of law, of morals, of religion, of ethical custom, of honor, of decorum, of tact, of etiquette, of fashion. To these may be added some of lesser importance, e. g. rules of games, the rule that one must wait one's turn, for instance at the ticket window or in the waiting room of a busy physician. These rules are social facts, the resultants of the forces that are operative in society, and can no more be considered separate and apart from society, in which they are operative, than the motion of the waves can be computed without considering the element in which they move. As to form and content, they are norms, abstract commands and prohibitions, concerning the social life within the association and directed to the members of the association. In addition to rules of conduct of this kind, there are rules that are not norms because they do not refer to the social life of human beings: e. g. the rules of language, of taste, or of hygiene.

The legal norm, therefore, is merely one of the rules of conduct, of the same nature as all other rules of conduct. For reasons readily understood, the prevailing school of juristic science does not stress this fact, but, for practical reasons, emphasizes the antithesis between law and the other norms, especially the ethical norms,

# 第三章 社会联合体和社会规范

一个社会联合体是这样一群人，他们在相互关系中，承认一些行为规则具有拘束力，并且至少在通常情况下，实际上按照这些规则来调节他们的行为。这些规则类型各式各样，名称也各不相同：法律规则、道德规则、宗教规则、伦理习俗规则、荣誉规则、礼仪规则、言行得体规则、礼节规则和时尚规则。除了这些，还有一些不太重要的规则，例如：游戏规则、排队规则，比如在购票窗口，或在繁忙医师的候诊室里。这些规则是社会事实、社会中起作用之力量的结果，不能被认为是独立、分离于它们正生效于其中的社会，正如，波浪的运动不可能被计算——倘若不考虑其中它们移动的因素。至于形式和内容，它们是关于联合体内部社会生活和指导联合体成员的规范、抽象的命令和禁令。除了这种行为规则外，社会中还存在着不是规范的行为规则，因为这些行为规则并不涉及人类的社会生活，例如语言规则、品味规则或者卫生规则。

因此，法律规范仅仅是行为规则的一种，具有和其他行为规则一样的性质。因为容易理解的原因，主流的法学学派没有强调这一事实，而是基于实践的原因，强调法律和其他规范的对立，

in order to urge upon the judge at every turn as impressively as possible that he must render his decisions solely according to law and never according to other rules. Where the state has not obtained a complete monopoly of lawmaking, this antithesis is not emphasized very much. In Rome, where the law has been defined as the *ars aequi et boni*, it was hardly ever heard of; and among the present-day English, it is not stressed nearly so forcibly. In those fields of law in which juristic science does not subserve the practical purposes of judicial decision, in international law, in *Staatsrecht* (public law in the narrow sense), in administrative law, law is by no means so carefully distinguished from morals, ethical custom, decorum, and tact, from the so-called *Konventionalregeln* (conventional rules), and even from considerations of expediency, as is the case, in theory at least, in private and penal law.

Every human relation within the association, whether transient or permanent, is sustained exclusively by the rules of conduct. If the rules cease to be operative, the community disintegrates; the weaker they become, the less firmly knit the organization becomes. The religious communion dissolves if the precepts of religion lose their validity. The family breaks up if the members of the family no longer consider themselves bound by the order of the family. Among the northern Slavs of Austria, the last vestiges of the greater family have completely disappeared in the last fifty years because the more distant members of the family no longer recognize the rules of the communal family life as binding.

Not all human associations are being regulated by legal norms, but manifestly only those associations are parts of the legal order whose order is based upon legal norms. The sociology of law deals exclusively with these; the others are the subject matter of other branches of sociology. Among the legal associations there are some that are readily recognizable by external criteria, i. e. those that jurists style juristic persons, corporations, institutions, foundations, and, first and foremost, the state. But even in

特别是法律和伦理规范的对立,以便尽可能令人难忘地处处督促法官,他只能依照法律而决不可依照其他规范作出裁判。在国家没有获得完全垄断性立法权的地方,这一对立没有被过多地强调。在罗马,在法律被定义为法律乃良善与公正之艺术的地方,几乎不曾听到这一论调;在今天的英国,也没有如此着力地强调这一点。在法学并非旨在促进司法裁判这一实践目的的那些法律领域中,在国际法中,在 *Staatsrecht*(狭义上的公法)中、在行政法中,法律绝不会如此谨慎地跟道德、伦理习俗、礼仪和言行得体性区分开来,也不会和所谓的 *Konventionalregeln*(习俗规则)区分开来,甚至不会与合目的性考量区分开来,不过事实通常就是这样,至少理论上在私法和刑法中对它们作了区分。

在联合体中的每一个人际关系,不管是短暂的还是长久的,全都完全依靠行为规则来维持。如果这些规则不再有效,这一团体就会分裂;这些规则的效力越弱,这一组织间的联系就越弱。如果宗教规则失去效力,宗教团体就会解体。如果家庭的成员认为他们不再受家庭秩序的约束,家庭就会破裂。在奥地利北部的斯拉夫人当中,大家庭的遗迹在过去的五十年中完全消失了,因为家庭中较远的成员不再认为公共家庭生活的规则具有约束力。

并非所有的人类联合体都受法律规范调整,但是很显然,只有那些联合体是基于法律规范之法律秩序的一部分。法律社会学专门处理这些法律规范,其余的规范是社会学其他分支所研究的主题。在法律联合体中,有一些很容易被外部的标准所认可,亦即那些法学家所称的法人、公司、公共机构、基金会以及最重要的国家。但是即便是在公法中,也有大量的不具有法律人格的

public law, there are numerous legal associations that have no legal personality; such as administrative boards, public institutions, the people, the army, the various classes, ranks, and professions. Much more of this is to be found in private law.

In all legal associations the legal norm constitutes the backbone of the inner order; it is the strongest support of their organization. By organization we mean that rule in the association which assigns to each member his relative position in the association (whether of domination or of subjection) and his function. This rule may deal not only with the relation of man to man, but also with the relation of man to things. Indirectly it deals with the relation of man to man even in the latter case. For the owner of articles of consumption determines what performance is to be rendered in return by those at whose disposal he places the goods; the owner of the factory determines the order in the factory and its management; the creditor determines the fate of the subjectmatter of the obligation, and often of the debtor; just as often, however, it is the debtor that determines the fate of the subject matter of the obligation and of the creditor, for, being the possessor of the thing, he has a great deal of legal power over it. But only those rules of law have a share in the creation of the legal order of the association that have actually become rules of conduct in the association, i. e. that are being recognized and followed by men, in a general way at least. Rules of law that have remained mere norms for decision, that become effective only in the very rare cases of legal controversy, do not take part in the ordering of the associations. This may be said, a *fortiori*, of those legal propositions, in reality quite numerous, that do not affect life at all. The same holds true for the norms of morality, ethical custom, and religion. It is always necessary therefore to ask not only how much of what has been promulgated by the lawgiver, proclaimed by the founder of a religion, or taught by the philosopher has been applied by the courts, preached from the pulpits, or taught in books or schools, but how much has actually been

法律联合体,例如管理委员会、公共机构、人民大众、军队、各种阶级、阶层以及职业团体。在私法中我们可以发现更多的这种联合体。

在所有的法律联合体中,法律规范构成了内部秩序的支柱;法律规范是它们构造方法的最强有力的支撑。关于构造方法,我们意指联合体中的那种规则——根据该规则,联合体中的每一个成员都被分配以相应的地位(不管是统治的还是从属的)和职责。这一规则不仅处理人和人之间的关系,而且也处理人与物之间的关系。即便是在后一种情况之下,它也间接地处理人与人之间的关系。因为消费品的所有权人决定提供何种履行义务,是以接受该商品之人的相应回报为条件的。工厂的所有者决定着工厂内的秩序和管理;债权人决定着与债务相关标的物的命运,也经常决定着债务人的命运;正如另一方面,经常也正是债务人决定着债务标的物及债权人的命运,因为,债务人作为物的占有者,债务人对物拥有大量的法律权利。但是,只有那些规则参与了联合体法律秩序的创建,这些规则实际上也变成了联合体内的行为规则,即,至少在一般情况下,它们被联合体成员所认可和遵守。仅仅作为裁判规范和仅在极少数法律争端中有效的法律规范,并不参与联合体的规整。此主张可能更有理由适用于那些现实中大量存在、但根本不影响生活的法律命题。对于道德规范、伦理习俗和宗教,这一说法同样正确。因此,如下做法总是必要的:不仅要去探求立法者颁布了多少法律,宗教的创立者宣布了多少教义,或者哲学家宣扬的理论有多少被法院适用,神职人员鼓吹了多少说教,或者书籍或学校教授了什么,而且也要去探问

practiced and lived. Only that which becomes part and parcel of life becomes a living norm; everything else is mere doctrine, norm for decision, dogma, or theory. Norms of ethical custom, of honor, of decorum, of tact, of etiquette, of fashion are only rules of human conduct; and though a new code of honor (rules for the duel) should appear at every moment, it would remain absolutely without any significance whatever if it did not actually become part and parcel of life.

The first and most important function of the sociological science of law, therefore, is to separate those portions of the law that regulate, order, and determine society from the mere norms for decision, and to demonstrate their organizing power. This was recognized first of all in *Staatsrecht* (public law in the narrow sense) and in administrative law. Indeed hardly anyone doubts today that *Staatsrecht* is an ordering of the state, whose purpose is not to decide legal disputes, but to determine the positions and the functions of the organs of the state, as well as the duties and functions of the authorities of the state. But the state is above all a social association; the forces that are operative in the state are social forces; everything that proceeds from the state, the activity of the authorities of the state and particularly legislation by the state, is something that is done by society through the association created for that purpose, i. e. the state. The same classes, orders, and interests that control society prevail in the state; and if the state makes war on any one of these, we know that the state has passed under the control of one of the others. *Staatsrecht* (public law in the narrow sense) therefore comprises both a state and a social ordering.

The rich life of a great scholar has been consumed to a great extent by the labor of demonstrating the organizing power of the law of corporations and the contributions which the corporations and their law have been making and are still making today to civilization, particularly to the civilization of Germany. Every page of history teaches the significance of the corporations as associations for the organization of political, intellectual, religious, economic, and social life; and any English or American

上述东西有多少被实际应用并具有生命力。只有成为生活必不可少之一部分的规范才是活的规范;其余的任何东西都仅仅是学说、裁判规范、教义或者理论。伦理习俗规则、荣誉规则、礼仪规则、言行得体规则、礼节规则和时尚规则仅仅是人类行为规则;虽然在任何时刻都可能产生一种新的荣誉规则(如决斗规则),但如果它不能实际成为生活的重要部分,那么不管是什么,它绝对是毫无意义的。

因此,法律社会学最主要的功能就是要把管控、规整和决定社会的那部分法律从纯粹的裁判规范中区分出来,并证明它们的组织力。此点首先在 *Staatsrecht*(狭义的公法)和行政法中被认可。确实,今天几乎没有任何人怀疑 *Staatsrecht*(狭义的公法)是对国家的一种规整,它的目的不是为了裁断法律纠纷,而是为了确定国家机构的地位和职能,也是为了确定权威机构的责任和职能。但是国家首先是一个社会联合体,在国家中起作用的力量是社会力量;来自于国家、国家权威机构活动的所有事务,特别来源于国家立法活动的事务,都是由社会通过为这一目的所创立的联合体——国家所完成的事务。控制社会的相同的阶级、阶层和势力在国家中占据主导地位;并且如果国家跟上述的任何一方展开斗争,我们知道,国家是在另外一方的控制下做出的。因此,*Staatsrecht*(狭义的公法)既包括国家规整,也包括社会规整。

在很大程度上,论证法人社团法的组织力量、法人社团及其法律已经并至今仍对人类文明、特别是对德国文明所作的贡献这样的工作,已经消耗掉一个伟大学者丰富的一生。历史的每一页都在告诉人们,法人社团作为政治、智识、宗教、经济和社会生活组织而存在的联合体的重要性。任何英国或者美国涉及法人社

work on corporations and trusts can complete this picture. It would be needless for the purposes of this book to add anything to these statements.

Gierke contrasts the law of the state and of the corporations of public and private law, which he styles social law, with the entire remaining private law, which he styles individual law. But this antithesis is unwarranted. There is no individual law. All law is social law. Life knows not man as an utterly detached, individual, and isolated being, nor does the law know such a being. The law always sees in man solely a member of one of the countless associations in which life has placed him. These associations, inasmuch as they bear a legal stamp, are being ordered and regulated by law and the other social norms; it is the norms that assign to each individual his position of domination or of subjection and his function. It is true, membership in the association occasionally, but by no means always, gives rise to individual rights and duties of the individual, but this is not its purpose, is not its essential content.

In the prevailing system of private law, however, the association is given very inadequate expression. Thanks to the analytical method of the juristic science of private law, the great majority of associations have been taken to pieces for the purpose of placing their component parts under the magnifying glass and studying them separately as subjects or objects of rights, as real or personal rights. This may be necessary for practical purposes, but it is unscientific at all events, just as the alphabetical order of the dictionary is unscientific though necessary for practical purposes. The sociological science of law, not being bound by any practical considerations, must reunite the severed parts into a whole. Even when viewed solely from without, the juristic persons of private law, the societies that are not juristic persons, the partnerships, and other communities, and the family self-evidently are clearly seen to be associations. But in actual fact the entire private law is a law of associations. For the private law is preponderantly, and, apart from family law, exclusively, the law of economic life, and economic life goes on exclusively in associations.

团和信托方面的论著都可以完成此类描述。考虑到本书宏旨,对这些论述再多费笔墨,都是不必要的。

基尔克将国家法与公法法人及私法法人(他所称的社会法),跟余下的整个的私法(他所指称的个人法)作了对比分析。但是这一对比没有正当理由。根本没有个人法存在。所有的法都是社会法。生活无法了解完全分离的、单独的、孤立的个人存在,法律也不能认识到这种存在。法律总是将人看作是生活于无数联合体之一里面的单独一员。因为这些联合体具有法律的特征,所以法律和其他的社会规范规整和管控这些联合体;正是这些规范,分配给每一个人或支配或服从的地位及职能。的确,联合体成员的身份,偶尔但绝非总是,赋予个人独立的权利和义务,但是,这并非其目的,也非其本质内容。

但是在私法的主要制度中,对联合体的表述十分不充分。由于私法的法学分析方法,联合体的绝大部分被分解成一块块细小的部分,以便能够把联合体的组成部分置于放大镜下,并分别作为权利的主体或者客体、不动产权利或者动产权利来研究它们,这可能对于实践的目的来说是必要的,但是这无论如何也是不科学的,就像辞典按字母顺序编纂一样,虽然按实践的目的,这是必要的,但并不科学。不受任何实践性考虑拘束的法律社会学,必须把这些分离的部分重新组合成一个整体。甚至仅仅从外部看,不言而喻,私法中的法人、非法人社团、合伙关系、其他共同体以及家庭显然都可以被看做是联合体。但是,事实上整个私法都是联合体的法律。因为私法主要——并且除了家庭法之外,私法完全——是经济生活法,经济生活完全在联合体内进行。

Economic life comprises production of goods, exchange of goods, and consumption of goods. Accordingly the economic associations subserve these three functions. Just at this point, however, there is an enormous contrast between the economic undertakings of today and those of a not far distant past. In antiquity and in the Middle Ages, the economically self-sufficing household of the free farmer and the *Oikenwirtschaft* (self-sufficing economic establishment) of the royal court and of the seigniorial manor were the prevailing forms. These manifestly were economic associations, and their legal order was apparent. Today economically self-sufficing households are to be found in Europe perhaps only in some secluded region. Until the present day, among the peasantry at least, and, where work is done at home, in rare cases also among handicraftsmen, the family has remained a laboring association which produces goods; but it is no longer self-sufficing, and even among the peasantry it performs its labors only in part for its own needs. And even among handicraftsmen and among the peasantry, these cases are merely instances of survival of forms of economic management which are disappearing. The family generally no longer is a place where goods are produced, but where they are being consumed; and only the very last part of the preparation of goods that are being consumed takes place in the family. Apart from this, the home and the workshop are definitely separated from each other. The workshop sends the goods that it has produced to the market, from which the home obtains the goods it requires. The manufactured products become merchandise. The course that merchandise must travel from the producing to the consuming economic unit is steadily lengthening, and every lengthening enlarges the sphere of trade, of commerce. It is generally true therefore at the present time that the production of goods takes place in the workshop; the exchange, in commerce; the consumption, in the home. And to this three-fold division the legal order of the economic associations of our day must conform.

In every economic association, three things must be distinguished: the working or consuming group of human beings; the material basis of economic life, i. e. the instruments of production and raw materials; and finally the juristic form in which this group of human beings receives the protection of the courts and of the other tribunals of the state for their entire associational life. This, we might say, is a statement of the basic features of the relation between the economic

经济生活由产品生产、产品交换和产品消费构成。因此,经济联合体也服务于这三种职能。不过,正是在这一点上,今天的经济企业和过去不远的企业有着巨大的差异。在古代和中世纪,经济上自给自足的自由民家庭、王室宫廷的*Oikenwirtschaft*(自足的经济机构)和领主的庄园是主要的组织形式。这些显然就是经济性联合体,它们的法律秩序也清楚可见。目前,经济上自足的家庭可能仅在欧洲的一些与世隔绝的地区还能见到。直至今天,至少在那些工作主要是在家庭中完成的农民中——在手工业者中也零星存在这种现象——家庭仍然是一个生产产品的劳动联合体;但是它已不再自给自足,甚至在农民中,他们的劳动也只是部分为了满足自己的需要。即使是在手工业者和农民中,这些情况也仅仅是正在渐渐消失的经济管理方式残存的实例。一般说来,家庭已经不再是生产产品的场所,而是消费产品的场所。仅仅是即将被消费之产品最后的准备这一阶段的工作还发生在家庭中。除此之外,家庭和工场彼此已经完全分离。工场将它所生产的产品送到市场上,家庭再从市场中获取它所需要的产品。制造的产品变成了商品。商品从生产的经济单位到消费的经济单位之间的过程不断地延长,并且每一次延长都会扩大贸易和商业的范围。因此,在通常情况下,如下情形属实:目前产品生产在工场中;产品交换在商业领域;产品消费在家庭中。所以,目前的经济联合体的法律秩序必须遵循这三个方面的职能划分。

在每一个经济联合体中,三种事物必须区分:人类的工作群组或消费群组;经济生活的物质基础,即产品的生产工具和原材料;以及最终这一人类群体为了整个联合体的生活,获得的国家法院和其他裁决机构保护的法律形式。我们可以说,这是对社会经

structure of society and its juristic forms.

On the farm, which the farmer manages with the assistance of his wife and children, his men-servants and women-servants, he raises grain and tubers, cattle and sheep. This is the economic content of this association. Its juristic form is ownership, the real right of usufruct or of usufructuary lease in the farm, the family law which unites the members of the family, the contract of Service which binds the men-servants and women-servants to the farm. In part, the great landed proprietor cultivates his lands himself; in part, he has put them out on lease to lessees or to usufructuaries. This economic organization of the great landed estate determines its juristic forms: ownership, lease, real rights of usufruct. The tradesman, together with his journeymen and apprentices, works in a rented workshop with his own materials and his own tools; the right of tenancy in the shop, the ownership of tools and materials, the contract for wages with the journeyman, and the contract of apprenticeship constitute both the juristic form and the economic content of the trade. The factories of a share company can throw goods on the market whose value amounts to millions of dollars. The share company with its board of directors and board of supervisors, its members and the meeting of the members, with an army of officers and employees, with its right of ownership, its relations of usufruct and ordinary lease in factories, machinery, sources of power, raw materials, and merchandise—all of these constitute the economic order of the manufacturing establishment, which is reflected in the contract of association, in a multitude of legal relations involving real rights, in countless contractual relations with employers and workmen, with ordinary and usufructuary lessors.

A discussion of the other economic associations, of the commercial establishment, of the bank, of the household as a community of consumers, leads to similar results. The association in the commercial establishment and in the bank, very much like that in the factory, consists of the owner and the employees and servants, who are in a contractual relation with each other. In addition to the contracts for wages, there are many contracts concerning the execution of commissions and the performance of duties of other kinds.

济结构和其法律形式之间关系基本特征的陈述。

在农场里,农民在他的妻儿、男仆和女仆的帮助下经营农场,种植着谷物和块茎农产品、饲养牛羊。这是这一联合体的经济内容。它的法律形式是所有权、农场不动产用益权或附用益权租约、使家庭成员结合的家庭法、将男仆和女仆约束在农场劳动的服务契约。大土地所有者自己耕种一部分土地;他把另一部分土地通过租约转给承租人或者用益权人耕种。这种大的拥有土地不动产的经济组织形式决定了它的法律形式:所有权、租赁权和不动产用益权。商人与其手下的临时工和学徒一起用他们自己的材料和工具在租来的工场里工作;商店的租赁权、对工具和材料的所有权、与临时工之间的工资契约、与学徒的身份契约共同构成了贸易的法律形式和经济内容。股份公司的工厂可以将价值百万美元的产品投入到市场中。股份公司与它的董事会和监事会、公司成员和成员大会、大批高级职员和雇员,加上它的所有权、在工厂中的附用益权租约与普通租约关系以及机器设备、电源、原材料和商品——所有的这些构成了生产性公司的经济秩序,这些秩序都反映在联合体的契约、大量的涉及不动产的法律关系、与公司雇员和工人之间以及与普通租约出租人和附用益权租约出租人间的数不清的契约关系之中。

对其他的经济性联合体、商业机构、银行、作为消费团体之家庭的讨论导向了相似的结果。商业机构和银行内的联合体非常类似于工厂内的联合体,它由互相处于契约关系的所有者、雇员和服务人员组成。除了工资契约外,还存在着大量的关于委任事务之履行以及其他类型义务之履行的契约。商业机构和银行的

The order of the commercial establishment and of the bank, to a much greater extent than that of the factory, is arranged with a view to dealings with the outside world. For this reason the contracts for services entered into with the individual employees are connected with various powers of agency such as do not exist in the case of the factory. The material basis here appears in the juristic form of ownership or of right of tenancy in the shop and the warehouses, the ownership of merchandise and of sums of money. In addition to the members, the family and the household, as associations for consumption, include the servants. The material basis is the right of tenancy in the dwelling, and the right of ownership in the articles of consumption that are to be found in kitchen, cellar, and storeroom.

The family law within the family, the contract of service, of wages, and of employment in the factory, in the workshop, in the commercial establishment and in the bank, accomplish the same results everywhere that are accomplished in the corporation by the articles of association; in the state, in the commune, in the church, by the public law relation of service; i. e. they bring about the inner order of the group of human beings that has its being within these economic associations. This applies, however, not only to the contract of service, of wages, and of employment, but also to all other kinds of agreements; especially to the contract of barter, to contracts for supplying things for use (contracts of lease, of usufruct, and of loan for use), and to the contract for the extension of credit (*Kreditvertrag*). The organizing power of all these contracts appears at once if one considers not merely, as is usually done for purely practical juristic purposes, the two parties that enter into the contract, but the whole group of persons who are brought into relation with one another by means of the regular exchange of goods arranged for by contract. All persons that are in this group constitute an economic association, which produces the goods and offers the services that are needed, and which thereby supplies its members with the goods and services they require. In this association the sum total of contracts entered into, or to be entered into, assigns to each individual his station, his position of domination or of subjection—the latter, it is true, only in a very rudimentary manner—and his functions. In com-

秩序,在很大程度上比工厂的规范更广,此种秩序的安排要着眼于与外部世界的许多交易。因为这一原因,和单个的雇员缔结的服务契约与各种各样的代理权联系在一起,后者在工厂的情形下是不存在的。在这里,物质基础存在于对商店、仓库的所有权或者租赁权的法律形式、对商品和一笔款项的所有权中。除了它们自身的成员外,作为消费联合体的家庭和住户还包括佣人,其物质基础是对住所的租赁权,是对可以在厨房、地下室和储存室中发现的消费品的所有权。

家庭内部的家庭法、服务契约、工资契约,以及工厂中、车间里、商业机构和银行中的雇佣契约,它们达到的结果与法人团体通过其社团章程所达到的结果完全相同。在国家、社区、教堂内,通过公法的服务关系也达到了同样的效果;也就是说,它们带来了存在于这些经济联合体之中的人类群体的内部秩序。但是,这不仅仅适用于服务契约、工资契约和雇佣契约中,而且还适用于其他各种契约中,特别是易货契约、提供使用物品的契约(租赁契约、用益契约和使用借贷契约)和信贷契约(*Kreditvertrag*)中。如果人们考虑的不仅仅是签订契约的双方——虽然事实上基于纯粹的使用法学目的通常是这么考虑的——而是考虑到通过基于契约安排经常性地交换货物而互相之间建立起关系的整群人的话,那么所有这些契约的组织力就会立刻显现出来。这一群体中的所有人就组成了一个经济联合体,这个经济联合体生产货物并提供社会所需的服务,从而,这个经济联合体提供给他们成员所需的商品和服务。在这一联合体中,已经订立和将要订立的契约之全部为每个人指定了各自的身份、他的支配地位或从属地位——后者的确仅仅是通过一种非常初步的方式而实现的——

mercial intercourse, contracts, at least those concerning performances that can be delegated to an assignee, are not being entered into as with definite persons, but as with the whole group of persons who are in a mutual relation of exchange of goods with each other. That is the significance of negotiability, of endorsement, of clearance of accounts, and, in part, of negotiable paper payable to bearer.

The social nature of the contract appears most clearly in credit transactions. Every credit transaction is conditioned upon the existence of stores of material goods in society. As long as mankind produces only so much as it needs for the moment, as long as it lives from hand to mouth, as it always does in primitive stages of development, there are no credit transactions. Even in the stage of economic development in which only natural produce is exchanged, the farmer cannot help his neighbor out with seed corn unless he has harvested more than he requires for his immediate needs; he must have a supply. In present-day society, supplies appear in the form of money. A person who produces more economic goods than he requires for his own needs disposes of them and receives money in exchange. If he spends the money, he buys other goods in order to use them; if he keeps the money, the value of the goods corresponding to the sum of money must exist unconsumed somewhere in the economic system. Extension of credit by the seller for the sale price implies that for the present he will not secure other goods in the place of those sold, that this value, for the time being, will remain unconsumed in society. Every instance of extension of credit for a sum of money therefore is the exercise of a right and power to determine what disposition is to be made of stores of material goods that are in existence in one economic unit in favor of another economic unit; and every credit transaction imports a decision of the question whether or not there is in existence in society a store of goods corresponding to the presumable intention of the person who asks for credit; the credit transaction, therefore, is always conditioned socially. In the most highly developed national economic systems, everyone carries the money that he does not use immediately to the bank. The greater part of the stores, therefore, which the several economic units are laying by for the purposes of the other

和他的职责。在商业交往中,契约——至少那些有关义务履行可以委派给受托人的契约——并非是与确定的人签订的协议,而是与彼此存在货物交换关系的一群人签订协议。这就是流通性、背书转让、账户清算以及部分程度上能向持票人付款的可转让性票据的重要性。

契约的社会属性在信用交易中表现得最为清楚。每一笔信用交易的条件就是社会中存在着大量的物质商品。只要人类只能生产当前所需要的商品,只要人类的生产仅能糊口——如同原始发展阶段总是存在的情形一样——那就不会存在信用交易。即便在只有自然产品用于交换的经济发展阶段,农民也不可能用谷种帮助他的邻居渡过难关,除非他收获了能大大满足自己当前需要的农产品;他必须有储备物资。在今天的社会中,供给以货币的形式出现。一个能生产出比自己的需要还多的经济产品的人,卖掉这些经济产品并换回货币。如果他花掉这些货币,他会买回他所需的产品。如果他留有这些货币,那么在经济体系中的什么地方肯定有等同于这笔货币价值的、未被消费的商品。卖方为该售价提供信用,意味着卖方暂时不会去购买其他商品以取代被售商品,还意味着这些货币的价值当前仍将以未消费的状态存在于社会中。因此,每一次提供金钱信贷的实例,都是一种权利和权力的行使,即决定将要采取何种措施处置存于一个经济单位中的库存商品,以支持另外一个经济体;并且每一笔信用交易都意味着对以下问题的一个决断:在社会中是否存在对应于申请信用者可推测之意图相一致的丰富商品。因此,信用交易必须与社会条件相适应。在高度发展的国民经济体系中,每个人都会将他并不马上要用的钱存入银行。因此,几个经济单位为了其他经济

economic units is accumulating in the banks in the form of money. And since the banks have the right and power to determine what disposition is to be made of these funds in favor of the individual economic units, they actually obtain control over the production, the exchange, and the consumption of goods in society. Their calculations more and more become the basis for the genesis, the development, and the continued existence of economic operations.

The contract, then, is the juristic form for the distribution and utilization of the goods and personal abilities (services) that are in existence in society. Not only the making of the contract, but also its content, is a result of social interrelations. In connection with any one of the ordinary contracts of daily life, it may suffice to raise the question which part of it is peculiar to this specific contract and which part is determined by the social order and by the organization of economic life and of commercial intercourse, in order to satisfy ourselves of the extent to which the latter elements preponderate. The fact that we are in a position today to satisfy our needs as to food, clothing, and housing by means of the everyday contracts of sale and lease and the contracts for work and labor, we owe to the other fact that in the community in which we live commerce and production of goods have been regulated sufficiently to make this manner of satisfying one's needs possible. Assuredly five hundred years ago this was not possible anywhere, and there is many a part of the world in which it is not possible today. One cannot rent a dwelling in a mountain village where there are none to let; one cannot provide oneself daily with food and clothing unless they are offered for sale in the vicinity; and one cannot hire a man to perform services which are not being rendered in exchange for wages in the form of money. This applies, self-evidently, not only to the subject matter of the contract but to every individual provision of the contract. If one examines a contract point by point, one can easily find the social reason why it is worded exactly as it is. It may be the fact that one of the parties occupies a position of social or economic advantage over the other, or the condition of the market, or the custom of the particular line of business. A person who has changed his residence will notice at once that he is making contracts of an entirely different nature from those that he made before.

单位的目的而作的更大部分的储藏,都被银行以货币的形式蓄积起来。既然银行有权利和权力,为了个别经济单位的利益去决定这些资金的用途,他们实际上就获得了对社会中产品的生产、交换和消费的控制权。银行的这种计算日益成为经济运行的起始、发展和持续存在的基础。

这样,契约就是人类社会中存在的货物和个人能力(服务)分配和利用的法律形式。契约的签订及内容都是社会相互关系的结果。就日常生活中任一普通契约而言,它足以提出这一问题:契约中的哪一部分是这一特定契约的特有部分,契约中的哪一部分由社会秩序以及经济生活和商业交往的组织形式所决定,如此我们可以弄清楚,后一部分究竟在多大程度上占据优势。我们能够通过每天的买卖和租赁契约以及劳动契约来满足我们对食物、衣服和住房的需要——我们可以将此种事实归功于以下事实:在我们所生活的社会内,货物的贸易和生产获得了充分的规制,使得满足我们需要的这种方式成为可能。可以确信,在五百年以前,这在任何一个地方都不可能,并且今天这在世界上的很多地方都无法实现。在一个不允许租赁的山区小村庄内,任何人不能为自己租得一个住处;任何人都不能每天为自己提供食物和衣物,除非食物和衣物在附近就有销售;如果不是通过支付货币形式的工资进行交换,任何人都不能雇佣其他人提供服务。不言而喻,这不仅适用于契约的标的,而且还适用于契约的每一单个条款。如果一个人逐条审视一个契约,他很容易就会发现事实上契约用词准确的原因。这可能是因为如下事实:一方当事人占据了比另一方当事人更为优越的社会和经济地位或市场条件,或者是特殊行业的商业惯例。一个更换居住地的当事人,将会马上注意

And though he be ever so firmly resolved not to change his mode of living in any way, the world round about him has changed, and he must conform to it even in his contractual intent. In England, as a rule, one does not rent an apartment but a whole house; one does not purchase one's daily supply of meat at the butcher's, but has it delivered weekly at one's residence. Accordingly rental contracts and contracts for the purchase of meat in England have a quite different content from those on the Continent. The writer has intentionally chosen contracts of the retail trade as illustrations, for in these the peculiar features of each individual case appear most clearly. It has often been shown to what extent the contracts of the wholesale trade and of industry are merely expressions of the general conditions of the market or of the special needs of the particular economic sphere. Most written contracts are drawn up according to printed forms, the content of which often is not made known to the parties, for it is determined by society quite independently of their individual wills. Nevertheless, it is true that the individualizing data that are written into the form are also a result of social interrelations.

The individual contract is so far from being the resultant of the individual wills of the parties that it was possible for the Austrian school of economists to undertake to compute the most important part of the leading contract involving exchange of goods, i. e. the purchase price, exclusively on the basis of its social and economic presuppositions; and an eminent economist, Walras, has made a successful attempt to reduce it to a mathematical formula. Perhaps the results of all these investigations are directly applicable to those contracts of exchange in which the counter-performance is to be rendered in money: contracts of labor (*Arbeitsverträge*) and of lease (*Mietverträge*), and contracts for work (*Werkverträge*); and though it will never be possible perhaps to reduce the remainder of the content of the contract to a mathematical formula, this must be attributed to the fact that the elements that enter into the computation cannot be evaluated readily rather than to the irresolvability of the problem in principle.

到他正在签订和他以前签订的契约性质完全不同的契约。虽然，他曾经坚决表示不以任何方式改变自己的生活方式，但是他周围的世界在变化，他必须遵循这一变化，甚至在他签订契约的意图方面也是如此。在英国，作为一项规则，任何人都不是去租赁一套单元住宅，而是整座房子；任何人都不从屠户那里购买他自己每天所需要的肉类，而是由人每周送到他的住处。因此，英国的租赁契约和肉类购买契约具有和欧洲大陆的同类契约不同的内容。作者在这里有意地选择了零售贸易契约作为范例，因为在零售贸易契约中每一个个别情形的特性都显示得清清楚楚。一些情形显示，批发贸易契约和工业契约在多大的程度上仅仅是市场的通常条件或特殊经济领域内的特别需求的表达。大部分的书面契约都是按照已印制好的形式起草，这些契约的内容也经常不为双方当事人所知晓，因为这些内容都是由社会、完全独立于他们的个别意志决定的。尽管，事实上写进契约中的个别化的数据是社会交往的结果。

个别的契约远不是双方当事人独立意愿的结果，以至于对于奥地利经济学派而言，完全以社会和经济预设为基础，计算涉及到货物交易的最主要类型契约的最为重要的部分——即买卖价格——是可能实现的。一位非常著名的经济学家沃尔拉斯先生非常成功地尝试了将这种计算简化为了一个数学公式。或许，所有这些研究的结果可以直接适用于那些通过金钱来进行对待履行的交易契约：劳动契约（*Arbertsverträge*）、租赁契约（*Mietverträge*）和承揽契约（*Werkverträge*）。尽管，或许从来都不可能将契约内容的剩余部分简化为一个数学公式，但这肯定是因为无法非常容易地评估纳入计算的要素，而非因为原则上问题的无法解决性。

But to speak of the social nature of the contract is merely another way of saying that it must serve the purposes of society. It exists in its innumerable forms for the purpose of regulating the production, the exchange, and the consumption of goods in human society, which is based on private ownership of the soil, of the means of production, and of the goods for consumption. On the material basis created by ownership, real rights, and, perhaps, agreements to supply things for use (lease, usufruct, loan), the contract creating a partnership or the contract which creates a mercantile association and which is closely related to the former unites several adventurers in a partnership or in a mercantile association; the contracts of labor and of service keep the army of officials and laborers of a manor and of workmen in a factory together; the various contracts of exchange, as instrumentalities of commerce, direct the products of agriculture and of the various handicrafts to the places where they are needed; the contract for the extension of credit makes it possible for the various economic units to obtain the capital that happens to be available for their purposes. In these vast economic machines, ranged one above the other, i. e. in individual, national, and world-wide economic undertakings, each human being that lives and moves creatively within them amounts to a small spring, a wheel, or a screw; and his position as well as his function within them is being assigned to him, in the main, by the sum total of contracts he enters into.

There is not another branch of the law whose organizing significance legal science has so thoroughly failed to recognize, which it has disfigured so mercilessly, and abused so pitilessly, as the modern Continental law of inheritance. If one reads a juristic exposition, searches a code, or studies a collection of decisions, one is occasionally tempted to believe that the law of inheritance is like a lottery; the part of the orphan boy is played by the sections of the code through whose tortuous sentences a mysterious goddess of fate distributes her gifts to the fortunate ones according to a decree that is past finding out. Indeed the mischief began everywhere at a very early date. The clear lines of the law of inheritance of the Twelve Tables and of the German law-books,

但是,谈及契约的社会属性,仅仅是以另一种方式来说明,契约必须服务于社会目的。此点存在于为了调整人类社会中商品生产、商品交换和商品消费的目的的数不清楚的形式中,而这些形式是基于对土地、生产工具和消费品的私人所有权。此点还存在于:在所有权、物权或许还有提供使用物的协议(租赁、用益权、借贷)所创造的物质基础上,创立合伙的契约或者创立与合伙有密切关系的商业联合体——将几个企业家联合到了合伙或者商业联合体中——的契约;劳动契约和服务契约将大批高级职员和庄园中的劳动者以及工厂中的工人团结在了一起;作为商业媒介手段的各种各样的交易契约指引着农业产品和不同种类的手工艺品到需要它们的地方;提供信用的契约使得各种经济体可以获取适合于他们意图的资金。在这一个接一个排列的巨大经济体系中,即在个体的经济企业、全国性经济企业和全球性的经济企业中,每个生活于其中并从事创造性活动的人都相当于它们中的一个小弹簧、一个轮子,或者一个螺丝钉;个人在这些经济体系中的地位和作用,大体上也是通过他所签订的全部契约被分配给他的。

不存在其他任何一个法律部门——其构建秩序的意义完全没有被法律科学所承认——能像现代欧洲大陆的继承法一样,被如此无情地扭曲,那样冷酷地滥用。如果某人阅读一篇法律讲解文字、查看一部法典,或者研究一本判例集,他偶尔会不由自主地相信继承法就像一种抽奖;法典的这一部分通过拐弯抹角的语句戏弄了一部分孤儿,一个神秘的命运女神按照过去发现的大意把她的礼物分给了幸运的孩子。的确,很早的时候此种误导就无处不在了。透过《十二铜表法》和德国法律书籍中关于继承法的清

from which one can, even today, gather, almost without any effort whatever, the social organization of the time, have lost all sense and meaning, since the societies in which they were valid have vanished. A new order has arisen meanwhile, but, strange to say, has been unable, either in Rome or elsewhere, to find clear-cut and universally valid propositions for a law of inheritance adapted to its needs. At the many points of invasion, it has indeed, on several occasions, wrought grave destruction, but has scarcely anywhere built up anything worth preserving. Accordingly almost everything is left to the foresight of the individual. Declaration by last will and testament, family ordinance, *pactum et providentia maiorum*, marriage contract, parental division of inheritance, transfer of goods during one's lifetime, agreement among the heirs out of court, must step into the breach. Such is the chaos of the presentday law of inheritance; a few decaying fragments remaining from times long since past, on which some incoherent patchwork has been placed quite thoughtlessly. The greater part of the burden must be borne by the art of drafting legal documents, a branch of legal science which has been taken notice of by but few, and appreciated by none, and which has undertaken the difficult but fruitful task of making a pathway through this confusion for the needs of life.

Our task here can only be to sketch with a few strokes of the pen the great ever-present organizing basic problem of the law of inheritance of every legal system. The head of the family, the soul of all its undertakings, who had been furnishing bread and, in part, a sphere of activity to the members of the family, has departed this life. How should his work be continued? What disposition is to be made of all those things to which his spirit gave life and which his strong arm maintained? Every economic undertaking, the farm, the factory, the mercantile house, and the mine, is an association within which not only the human beings

晰线索,即便是在今天,任何人都可以几乎毫不费劲地收集到当时的社会组织的任何信息,但自从那样的社会——其中那些线索仍然是有效的探求依据——消失后,这些线索就已经失去了它全部的意义和价值。与此同时,一种新的秩序正在生成,但是说来奇怪,不管是在罗马还是其他任何地方,都未能找到适合于其需要的、清晰且普遍有效的继承法命题。在遭受入侵的很多地方,若干场合下,该新生秩序确实造成了严重破坏,但是几乎在任何地方都没有建立任何值得保存的东西。因此几乎所有的东西都留给了个人对未来的谋划计算。遗嘱声明、家庭传统风俗习惯、先人的约定和安排、婚姻契约、父母遗产的分割、生前的财物转让、继承人庭外所达成的协议,这些必须要临时填补法律缺失留下来的空白。这就是如今继承法的混乱状况;这种混乱还表现在很久以前的几个时期保存下来的一些正在消散的碎片中,其中一些毫不连贯的拼凑物完全未经思考就被堆放在一起。法律文件的起草技艺必然承担了更为巨大的负担,但这样一个法学部门却只有极少的人注意到,更是未被任何人重视,它承担起了——为生活需要而开辟穿越此种混乱局面的道路——这一困难重重但却硕果累累的任务。

在这里,我们的任务仅仅是粗线条地勾绘出每一个法律制度中继承法里经常存在的、重大的、有关构造的基本问题。家庭中所有事业的核心、养家糊口并部分地为家庭成员提供活动领域的一家之主逝世了。他的事业应当如何继续?他的精神所赋予生命的、他强大的权威所维系的那些事业,应当如何处置?每一个经济企业、农场、工厂、商业机构、矿场都是一个联合体,在这一联

but also the material things are ordered and regulated. In it, all persons and all things are combined into a unified whole in the manner in which they can best serve the purposes of the economic undertaking. Rent asunder or divided into their "conceptual" parts, they at most retain the value of the material that the fragments consist of, and uncounted wealth is lost for all time not only to the surviving members of the family, but to the whole national economic system. Apart from the jurists, perhaps no one who has given thought to these things has failed to observe that this is a matter of solicitude to every strong and able man who, after a life of achievement, is thinking of death. What is to be done in order to prevent disintegration, to put the right man in the right place in every economic organization which the deceased has created, and to assign the right tasks to him? Unless one has had actual experience in such matters, one can form no conception of what goes on after the death of such a man when his affairs fall into the hands of the lawyers; of the way everything works at cross purposes with him, the whole juristic *πολυπραγματεία* of the codes, the attorneys, the notaries, and the courts; of the sedulous determination with which his intentions are being defeated and weapons are being supplied to folly and malice for a work of destruction. But all this is infinitesimal when compared with the infinitely more thorough work that must be done when there is no last will, or, indeed, when the custody of wards committed to the charge of the authorities gives the latter greater powers. Of course, where the past has exercised forethought, as shown in the law of inheritance of the ruling families, of the nobility, of the peasantry, it is true that occasionally, in spite of the violent resistance of the lawyers, in many an instance economic undertakings have been preserved from destruction, or, where destruction has already taken place, have been rebuilt. But these usually are like saplings that have no vitality whatsoever; much more frequently they are surviving frag ments that are past hope. Jurists have become conscious, only vaguely however, of the

合体内不仅仅人员，而且物质材料也被规整和调整。在联合体内，所有的人和物都被通过一种能最好地服务于经济企业的方式组合成为统一的整体。地产收益被分成数部分，或分成“观念上”的数部分，它们至多维持着各部分所组成的物质的价值，这，不但对于仍健在的家庭成员而且对于整个国民经济体系而言，数不清的财富都被永远浪费了。除了法学家外，曾经思考着这些事情的人没有谁不会注意到，对一个强壮和有能力的人，在他取得人生的成就后，却要考虑死亡，这是一件令人焦虑的事情。应采取什么样的措施来防止经济组织的解体，使恰当的人在每一个已故者所创办的经济组织中找到恰当的位置，并给他分配恰当的任务？除非一个人对这样的事情有实际经验，否则他无法了解，在那样一个人死后——那时他的事务落入律师之手——事情如何演变下去；他无法了解，法典、律师、公证人和法院的整个法律的(忙乱活动)与他意图相反的所有这一切运作的方式；他无法了解孜孜以求的决定，这决定令他的目标遭到挫败，同时他的手段为着一项毁灭工作供给愚行与恶念使用。但是，这些事情与那些在没有遗嘱或者当由官方管理的被监护人的监护被给予更大权力的情况下所需要做的、无穷多的、更周到的工作相比，都是微不足道的。当然，在过去已作过长远规划的情形下——比如统治家庭、贵族阶层、农民阶层的继承法所显示的那样——尽管律师们作出激烈的抵抗，但许多时候，经济企业确实偶尔还是能免于毁灭，或者在毁灭已经发生的情形下企业能够重建。不过，这些通常就像没有任何活力的小树苗一样；更多时候，它们经常是过去之希望的残留碎片。法学家已经开始意识到——但仅仅是模糊地意识到——一种责任，即创设一种考虑到现

duty to create a law of inheritance that takes into account the multiform and peculiar requirements of modern life. But at the present time the necessary foundation has not yet been laid by anyone. The beginning would have to be made by juristic science. First of all it would be necessary to investigate all the living law that is contained in testamentary provisions, in parental divisions of inheritance, in transfers of property during the lifetime of the donors, in settlements out of court by the heirs, and to discover its guiding principles. One is most likely to find something of this nature in the Swiss Civil Code.

Inasmuch as the law is an inner order of the social associations, its content is determined with absolute necessity by the structure of these associations and by their method of conducting their economic enterprises. Every social and economic change causes a change in the law, and it is impossible to change the legal bases of society and of economic life without bringing about a corresponding change in the law. If the changes in the law are arbitrary and of such a nature that the economic institutions cannot adapt themselves to them, the order of the latter is destroyed without compensation. The farmer is able to produce on his farm the goods that he requires in order to supply not only himself but also the other classes of society with raw materials only so long as the legal order guarantees to him, in a great measure at least, the returns of his labor. If therefore a class which is all-powerful in the state should force upon the farmer a legal order which compels him to give up all that he has harvested, the farm would be deserted, and the powerful in the state would soon be without the means of preserving the state and of maintaining their own economic position. Even foreign conquerors, therefore, have been content with reducing the free farmers to a state of serfdom or of making them their tenants, but have always left them so much of the returns of their labor as they absolutely needed for the maintenance of their economic activity.

The entire private law therefore, inasmuch as it has an organizing content, is social law in precisely the same sense as the law of the state and the law of corporations. It is always concerned with the human associations: it determines the position of the individual in the group of

代生活的多种形式和特殊需要的继承法。但是,目前任何人都没有为这种继承法建立必要的基础。法学将不得不创造一个开端。首先,有必要去研究所有的活法——存在于遗嘱条款、父母遗产分割、捐赠人生前的财产转让、继承人庭外和解中的所有活法,并发掘它们的指导性原则。在瑞士民法典中,人们很容易找到这种性质的东西。

因为法律是一个社会联合体的内部规则,它的内容取决于这些联合体结构的绝对必要性与经营经济企业的方式。社会和经济的每一次变化都会导致法律的变化,如果社会和经济的变化不导致相应的法律变化,它们就不可能改变社会的法律基础。如果法律的变化是恣意的,并且具有这种恣意的性质以至于经济制度无法适应它们,则经济制度之秩序就会遭到破坏,且没有任何弥补。农民能够在其农场上生产他所需的产品,以便为自己和社会的其他阶层提供原材料,只要法律秩序能够确保——至少在很大程度上确保——他的劳动会产生利润。因此,如果国家中的一个最强大阶层强加给农民一种法律秩序——强迫农民放弃所有的收成,那么农场将会荒芜,并且这个最强大阶层很快就会失去维持这个国家、维系他们自己经济地位的手段。因此,即便是外国的征服者,也仅会满足于将自由的农民降格为农奴状态或者是将自由农民降格为他们的佃户,但是他们还总是留给农民一定的收益,可以让农民维持他们的经济活动所绝对必需的物质条件。

因此,整个的私法因为具有构造联合体的内容,所以是社会法,正如国家法和法人社团法在完全同样的意义上也是社会法。私法总是关注人类联合体:它决定着个人在人类工作群体中的位

working human beings and the relation of the group to its tools. Like *Staatsrecht* (public law in the narrow sense) and the law of corporations, private law primarily creates associations, not individual rights and duties; and though individual spheres (*Individualbereiche*) arise for the individhal in the organized community, this is a reflex effect of organization, in public law no less than in private law. The fact that in this case the association is not based on a constitution or on articles of association, but on the law of things and of contract and on the order of the family, must not hide this great truth from us, for in this case the law of things and of contract and the order of the family serve the same purpose that is accomplished elsewhere by a constitution or by articles of association. A hermit may have a truly "individual sphere" not only in the juristic but also in the sociological and economic sense, but a man living among men cannot. One may have individual rights in economically insignificant articles of use and consumption, e. g. in clothing, in jewelry, in a portfolio, or in stationery, but even in the matter of the furnishings of a dwelling, except in the case of single men or women, there is the common use by the family. And even the true individual rights are social rights, to the same extent at least as is the legal claim of the member of the commune to participation in the use of the pasture belonging to the commune or of the member of a reading club to participation in the use of the books and periodicals. In conceding to the individual the possession of these things and permitting him to dispose of them according to his pleasure, society regulates their use and consumption; ownership of the goods which it concedes to the individual is merely a result of this social order. The individual enjoys this ownership as a member of an ordered community which respects private ownership and protects it without, in the case of certain things, concerning itself about the way in which they are being utilized. Society could regulate individual use and consumption in a manner quite different from, and much more detailed than, the manner in which it does this today, and we shall be convinced of this at a much earlier date perhaps than we should like as soon as the exhaustion of the resources of nature, which is

置以及人类群体和其使用的工具间的关系。与*Staatsrecht*(狭义上的公法)和法人社团法一样,私法主要也是创立联合体,而不是创设个人的权利和义务;虽然对于处于有机联系的共同体内的个人而言,私人领域(*Individualbereiche*)也随之出现,但这是组织体的一种反射效果,在公法中与在私法中情形都一样。这种情形下,联合体并没有以宪法或者联合体的章程为基础,而是以物权法、契约法和家庭秩序为基础——此等事实无法遮蔽我们身边的这一重大的真相,因为这种情况下,物权法和契约法以及家庭秩序都服务于由宪法或联合体章程在任何别处所实现的相同目的。一个隐士可能会有这种不仅在法学,而且也在社会学和经济学意义上的真正的"私人领域",但是,一个生活在群体中的人是不可能做到这样的。一个人可以对经济意义不大的使用权和消费品拥有个人权利,例如对衣物、珠宝、一个文件夹或者文具。但是即使就住处的家具而论,除了男人或女人单独居住的情况外,这些家具也通常由家庭共同使用。甚至真正的个人权利也是社会权利,至少在同样的程度上,个人权利如同对社区所有的牧场分享使用的社区成员的合法请求权,或是像对俱乐部所有的书籍和期刊分享阅读的俱乐部成员的合法请求权。在承认个人对这些物品的个人占有,并允许他依据自己的喜好自由处分的同时,社会也规范着这些物品的使用和消费;社会所认可的个人的物品所有权,也仅仅是社会秩序的结果。个人作为一个有序社会的成员,享有这种所有权,这一有序的社会尊重私人所有权并从外部保护它,在特定的物的情形下,社会还关注这些物的利用方式。社会可以采取一种不同于今天所采用的,但比今天所采用的方式更为明细的方式,来规范个人的使用和消费,并且,相比直到自然资源

even now threatening, shall have drawn much nearer. Whenever society actually accords to the individual an individual sphere, it refrains, on principle, from any and all interference. The inner life of the adult man, for instance, is his individual sphere; it lies within the domain of art, of religion, of philosophy, but not of law or of the extra-legal social norms.

The jural associations of human society therefore are, in the main, the following: the state with its courts and magistracies; the family, and the other bodies, associations, and communities with or without juristic personality; associations created by means of contract and inheritance, and, in particular, national and world-wide economic systems. Possession and ownership, which for the purposes of sociological discussions might be treated as, to a certain extent, convertible terms, real rights and claims based on obligation, create the inner order of these associations. This is the part that law plays in the ordering of the political, intellectual, economic, and social life of present-day society. This by no means exhausts the entire material of the law, but it is the part of the law which has power to regulate and order. Apart from this, there is another part of the law, which does not directly regulate and order the associations, but only protects them against attacks. It is connected with the social associations as a sort of secondary order; it maintains and strengthens them, but does not give them shape or form. This applies to the law of procedure before the courts and other tribunals; for it is merely a part of the order of the tribunals which have been created for the protection of social institutions; it is without direct influence upon society. It applies also to penal law, for the latter creates no social institutions; it merely protects goods that are already in existence in society and institutions that have already been established. And, lastly, it applies also to all those provisions of the material private law that concern only the protection afforded by law; like penal law, they create neither goods nor social institutions; they but regulate the already existing protection afforded by the courts and other tribunals. These norms did not come into being within the social associations themselves as the inner order of the latter, but arose in juristic law or in the

枯竭——现在这种危险正在逼近——我们才立刻醒悟，或许我们应该在一个早得多的日子就相信这一点。当社会实际上授予个人私人空间时，原则上，它要限制任何的和所有的干涉。例如，成人的内心生活是他的个人的空间，它存在于艺术、宗教、哲学领域之中，但并不存在于法律或者法律外的社会规范中。

因此，人类社会的法律上的联合体大体上如下：拥有法院和地方执法官员的国家；家庭、其他的实体、协会和具有或者不具有法律人格的团体；通过契约和继承方式建立的联合体，特别是全国性和全球性的经济体系。占有和所有权——为了社会学的讨论方便，在一定程度上把这两个看做可互换的术语——物权和债权创设了这些联合体的内部秩序。这就是法律在今天社会的政治、智识、经济和社会生活的规整中所起的作用。这绝不会枯竭全部的法律素材，但是它是有权去管控和规整之法律的一部分。除了这一部分法律外，还存在着另外一部分法律——这些法律不直接管控和规整联合体而仅仅保护它们免受侵害。这些法律作为一种次级秩序，与社会联合体相联系；它维持和强化着联合体，但不界定联合体的形态和形式。这涉及到法院和其他裁决机构所适用的程序法；因为这些法律仅仅是裁决机构秩序的一部分，这些裁决秩序的创设是为了保护社会制度；这些法律并不对社会产生直接影响。这也适用于刑事法律，因为刑事法律并不创立社会制度；它仅仅保护已经存在于社会中的货物和已经建立的社会制度。最后，这也同样适用于那些仅涉及提供法律保护的实体私法的所有条款；像刑事法律一样，它们既不创造货物也不创立社会制度；但是，它们管控法院和其他裁决机构已经提供的保护。这些规范不像社会联合体的内部秩序一样在社会联合体内自

law created by the state. All rights of monopoly, especially patent rights and copyrights, are created by the state. They consist in a command, addressed to all who are subjected to the will of the state, except the person who holds the right, to refrain from engaging in any activity in a certain sphere. Norms of similar nature have occasionally arisen in juristic law also.

And now we must point out the significance, but slightly considered hitherto, of the extra-legal norms for the inner ordering of the associations. The statement that legal institutions are based exclusively on legal norms is not true. Morality, religion, ethical custom, decorum, tact, even etiquette and fashion, do not order the extra-legal relations only; they also affect the legal sphere at every turn. Not a single one of the jural associations could maintain its existence solely by means of legal norms; all of them, at all times, require the aid of extra-legal norms which increase or eke out their force. Nothing short of the cooperation of the social norms of every description can offer a complete picture of the social mechanism.

A glance at what is going on round about us every day will serve to convince us of the truth of these statements. There is no state in which a government would be possible for any length of time which relies solely on the law. Even Macchiavelli urges his *Principe* to observe, outwardly at least, certain precepts of morality, religion, ethical custom and honor, decorum and tact. No administrative tribunal would be able to function if it were guided solely by rules of law; and for a government official it is positively a matter of official duty in his dealings with the public as well as with his colleagues to observe not only the precepts of law but also those of morality, ethical custom, honor, decorum, and tact. Certainly there is no institution of public life in which so many things are regulated by organizing legal norms as the army; and even this highly developed law does not suffice. It is well known how highly the army esteems the organizing value of morality, ethical custom, religion, honor, decorum, tact; nay,

发形成,而是产生于法学家法或者国家创制的法律。所有的垄断性权利,特别是专利权和著作权都是由国家创设的。它们存在于一项命令之中,该命令是要求所有那些服从国家意志的人——享有相关权利的人除外——在特定领域不得从事任何行为。同类性质的规范也偶尔产生自法学家法。

现在,我们必须指出那些迄今较少被考虑的非法律性规范对联合体内部规整形成的重要性。那种法律制度完全以法律规范为基础的陈述并不正确。道德、宗教、伦理习俗、礼仪、言行得体,甚至是礼节和时尚都不仅仅处理非法律关系;它们也常常影响法律领域。没有任何一个法律上的联合体能完全依靠法律规范的方式来维持它的存在;法律规范一直都需要能强化和弥补他们效力的非法律规范的协助。缺少上述所提及的每一种社会规范的合作,任何东西都不能提供社会机制运转的完整图景。

对我们周围每天所发生事情的粗略观察,会帮助我们相信这些陈述的真实性。没有一个国家、政府,在任何时候都可能完全依靠法律进行统治。甚至马基雅维利也督促他的君主至少在表面上遵守道德、宗教、伦理习俗、荣誉、礼仪和言行得体的特定规则。如果仅仅是依靠法律规则的指导,没有一个行政裁决机构能够正常运转;对于一位政府官员来说,在处理他和公众以及他与同僚的关系时,不仅遵守法律规则,而且也遵守那些道德、伦理习俗、荣誉、礼仪和言行得体行为规则——这肯定是一种公务上的职责。当然,不存在任何像军队一样的公共生活机构,如此多的事情被组织性的法律规范所调整;但是即使是如此高度发展的法律也不足备。众所周知,军队是多么重视道德、伦理习俗、宗教、荣誉、礼仪和言行得体的组织价值;不仅如此,军队也重视礼节

even of etiquette and of fashion. Indeed examples taken from the past show that an army which knows only legal norms can become a mob which is beyond the pale of society, and which is controlled solely by means of barbaric discipline. The term parliamentary courtesy, which undoubtedly is known to all civilized nations, sufficiently demonstrates the role which the extra-legal norms play in public representative bodies. And it is in this connection that they first became the object of scientific investigation as *Konventionalregeln* (rules arising from convention or agreement).

Is it otherwise in family and property law? A family the members of which reciprocally insist upon their legal rights has already disintegrated in most cases as a social and economic association. If they appeal to the judge, they have arrived at the point where they part company. The prohibition of the abusive exercise of legal rights (*Chicane*) shows that even real rights may not be exercised without giving heed to certain extra-legal norms; and where land or dwellings adjoin, there is the further requirement of customary observance of the dictates of morality, ethical custom, decorum, tact, and etiquette. Contracts must be interpreted and performed according to the requirements of good faith and commercial custom. That is to say that many other things must be considered besides the rule of law and the meaning and language of the contract. Nevertheless life demands a great deal more than even the most liberal-minded jurist would concede on the basis of good faith and business custom. There is perhaps no other contractual relation which is so thoroughly stripped of extra-legal content as is the contract of ordinary lease in a large city; nevertheless even in this relation the "good landlord" and "the desirable tenant" are valued highly. These two expressions are in common use in Vienna; the "thing itself," doubtless, is in existence everywhere. In the case of a usufructuary lease, however, the personal characteristics of the parties to the contract often are of even greater importance than the content of the agreement. No man of experience in business affairs will enter into a usufructuary lease without having made the most searching inquiry concerning the personal characteristics of the other party. He does this in order to make sure that he is justified in assuming that the other party will observe the non-legal norms that are customary in the relation of lessor and lessee. The organizing significance of the extra-legal norms appears with particular clear-

和时尚。来自过去的实例确实证明,仅仅知道法律规范的军队,会变成超越社会界限和完全依靠野蛮纪律控制的暴徒。议会的礼貌这一术语充分证明了非法律性规范在公共代表性机构中所起的作用,毫无疑问所有文明的国家都知道这个。正是在这一点上,它们首先变成了对作为 *Konventionalregeln*(源于习俗或协议的规则)进行科学研究的对象。

在家庭法和财产法领域内是否有所不同呢?在一个家庭中,若家庭中的成员相互主张他们的法律权利,则如大多数情况下的社会和经济联合体一样,这一家庭早已解体了。如果他们诉诸于法官,那么他们已经到了断绝关系的地步。法律权利(*Chicane*)滥用的禁止表明,即便是物权,若不注意特定的非法律性规范,它也不能得以行使;在土地和居所相邻的地方,就更有必要习惯性遵从道德命令、伦理习俗、礼仪、言行得体和礼节等戒律。契约必须依据诚实信用和商业习惯的要求来解释和履行。这就是说,除了法律的规则和契约的含义及用语外,还有很多的因素要考虑。尽管如此,生活常常要求得甚至比最具有自由主义意识的法学家基于诚实信用和商业习惯所承认的还要多。可能没有其他的契约关系像大城市中的普通租赁一样,如此彻底地剥离了非法律的内容。然而,即使在这样的一个关系中,"好房东"和"令人渴望的承租人"也价值重大。在维也纳,人们普遍使用这两种表达;无疑的,这种"事物本身"在任何地方都存在。然而,在附用益权租约的情况下,契约双方当事人的个人品行经常要比契约的内容更为重要。不对另一方当事人的个人品行作最大限度的调查取证,具有处理商业事务经验的人是不会订立用益性租约的。他做这些调查是为了能确信,他有正当理由认为另一方当事人能遵守出租人与承租人间的习惯性非法律规范。非法律性规范的组织重要

ness in the contract for services and wages. On the part of the entrepreneur or of his authorized representative, a certain firm insistence upon his legal right, together with an instinct for morality, ethical custom, decorum, and tact constitutes the principal part of the aptitude which is usually called a talent for organization; if this is lacking, a contract is without value not only for him but also for the workmen and employees. On the other hand an entrepreneur could not work with people who recognize only the legal point of view. Moreover such people could not get on with one another; the undertaking would be disorganized. The influence of extra-legal norms was recognized first and most clearly in the case of contracts for the extension of credit. They mark the dividing line between morally unexceptionable investment of capital and usury, which is always proscribed morally, and usually also legally. Although it is said that mercantile strictness should always obtain in mercantile intercourse, a merchant who is ever ready to insist on the letter of the law will quickly alienate his customers and those with whom he has business connections. Business custom, business honor, and business decorum constitute elements of commercial legal life. The content of these terms may be described as fair dealing (*Kulanz*). At a time in which the prevailing sexual morality is being violently attacked even by some choice spirits, it may not be altogether superfluous to call to mind that the existing order of the family is based upon it. If there is any ulterior motive behind these often well directed attacks, it can only be the thought that they are preparing the way for an entirely new order of the family. It would be absurd to believe that the family in its present form can be maintained if the present conception of sexual morality, without which it cannot exist, is given up.

We may say therefore that the law is the order of state or political, social, intellectual, and economic life, but it is not the only order. There are many others which are of equal value, and which, taken together, perhaps, are of much greater effectiveness. Indeed life would become a hell if it were regulated by law alone. It is true, the extra-legal norms are not being observed inviolably,

性在服务契约和工资契约中表现得至为清楚。就企业家或者他的全权代表而言，对其法定权利某种坚定的坚持，以及道德、伦理习俗、礼仪和言行得体的本能，共同构成了通常被称做组织才能的天资的首要部分；若缺少这些，则契约不但对于他自己，而且对于工人和雇员来说都是毫无价值的。另一方面，企业家不可能与那些仅仅认可法律观点的人一起共事。而且，这种人也无法和其他人融洽相处；企业可能会因此而解体。在信贷契约这种情况下，非法律性规范的影响首先并非常明确地被认可了。他们标注出道德上无懈可击的资本投资与高利贷之间的界线，这一界限总是道德上的，通常也是法律上的。虽然，据说在商业的交往中，商业的严格性总是获得公认，但是时刻准备坚守法律文本的商人，将会很快地疏远了他的客户以及与他有商业联系的商人。商业习惯、商业信誉和商业礼俗组成了商业法律生活的要素。这些术语的内容可以被描述为公平交易(*Kulanz*)。在一个主流的性道德正在受到激烈抨击、甚至受到精英人士抨击的时代，回想一下现存的家庭秩序正是基于其上，可能并不是完全多余的。如果这些有明确导向的抨击背后有任何别有用心的动机，那只可能是准备为全新的家庭秩序开辟道路的思想。认为如果放弃现在的性道德观念——没有这种观念，家庭不能维持——现在的家庭形式仍能够保持，这种想法是荒谬的。

因此，我们可以说，法律是国家秩序或者是政治生活、社会生活、智识生活和经济生活的秩序，但不是唯一的秩序。还有另外一些秩序具有与法律同等的价值，这些秩序可能在整体上要比法律具有更强的效力。的确，如果生活由法律独自规范，那么生活将会变成地狱。事实上，非法律性规范并未被始终不渝地遵从，但是

but this is equally true of the legal norms. The order of the social machine is continually being interfered with. And though it does its work with much creaking and groaning, the important thing is that it shall continue to functiom. To this extent, at least, its norms must be observed; and to this extent they are being observed in every country in which there is a tolerably well ordered life. And lastly, a breach of the existing order often is more than a merely local or temporary disorder; not infrequently it indicates the beginning of a new stage of development.

Let us for a moment compare our present-day society and its legal order with a socialistic society as various socialists have so often pictured it. Both, as it were, may be compared to enormous hoisting machines, by means of which humanity is to be supplied with the goods it requires in order to maintain its life and to develop its powers. In a socialistic society, as well as in our present-day society, there will be farms, mines, and factories, in which goods are being produced; there will be means of transportation like our railroads, steamboats, and vehicles, which deliver these goods at large magazines and storehouses where they will have to be stored, as is done in our warehouses and shops, until there is a demand for them; finally there will have to be smaller undertakings in which goods are being prepared for immediate consumption, as is being done today in the workshop of the mechanic and also in the kitchen and in housekeeping generally. In a socialistic society, as well as in our present-day society, untold millions of busy hands will be stirring on the farms, in the mines, the factories, the agencies of transportation, the warehouses and storehouses, in order to supply the goods which humanity requires, to transport them to the places where they are needed, and to distribute them. But above them all will hover an all-knowing and all-overseeing official body which makes an advance estimate of the total requirement, orders its production, directs the work man to the places where the work is to be done, and orders the products to be sent where they are needed. Our present-day society indeed has no official body of this kind. But the

法律性规范也是同样如此。社会机器的秩序总是不停地受到干扰。虽然它行进的过程中总是伴随着咯吱声和吱嘎声,但是重要的事情是,它将一直在发挥功效。至少在这一范围内,它的规范必须被遵守。在这一范围内,在任何一个具有良好有序的生活的国家,这些规范都正在被遵守。最后,对这种已存秩序的违反经常不仅仅意味着局部的或暂时的混乱,有时这种违反还预示着一个新的发展阶段的开始。

让我们利用片刻把我们现今的社会及其法律秩序与形形色色的社会主义者所经常描绘的社会主义社会作一下比较。可以说,这两个社会都可以被比做巨大的升降机器,依赖这种机器,这两个社会提供给人类所必需的物品,从而维持人类的生命和发展人类的能力。社会主义社会也像我们今天的社会一样,存在着生产物品的农场、矿场和工厂;那里也存在着像我们这里的铁路、汽船和车辆这样的运输货物的交通工具,这些交通工具把货物全部运送至各类仓库中被储存起来——这与我们的仓库和商店的功能一样——一直等到对这些储存产品有需求为止;最后,那里必然也有一些较小的企业,它们准备要立即消耗一些产品,如同今天我们通常在机械车间、也像在厨房和在家政公司里正在做的那样。在一个社会主义社会中,与在我们如今的社会中一样,为了提供人类所需要的货物并把它们运输到需要它们的地方以及分配它们,数不清的、数以百万计的劳动者要在农场、矿场、工厂、运输机构和储存仓库里辛勤工作。但是,在这所有的一切上面盘旋着一个全知的和鸟瞰一切的官方机构,这一机构能够提前对总需求做出预算,定购产品,指挥工人到需要人手的地方,命令将产品送到需要它们的地方。我们今天的社会中确实没有这样类型的官

task which, in a socialistic society, is to be performed by this omnipotent board of superhuman stature is performed in our present-day society by the law acting automatically and with such simple instrumentalities as the family order, possession, contract, and the law and right of inheritance. The owners, as entrepreneurs, provide the establishments at which goods are being produced, the means of transportation, the warehouses, and the salerooms; they assemble the workers by means of contracts of service and wages, and secure the necessary capital by means of contracts for the extension of credit. The merchants estimate in advance how much merchandise the human race will require, and, by means of agreements of exchange, direct it to the places where it is needed. And they accomplish all of this, it is true, not without a considerable amount of error, friction, and opposition, but certainly with much less friction and expenditure of energy than the most efficient purely bureaucratic board could accomplish it. Possession, ownership, real rights, contract, inheritance, and, for purpose of consumption, the family accomplish almost automatically in our society those things for which a socialistic society would require a complicated network of bureaucratic boards.

方机构。但是,在社会主义国家中由这一具有超人地位的全能的部门所履行的任务,在我们今天的社会中,依据法律而被自动履行或者由家庭秩序、占有、契约和继承权这些简单的手段完成了。作为企业家的所有人提供了一个生产商品的机构,提供了运输工具、仓库和拍卖行。他们通过服务和工资契约来召集工人,通过信贷契约获得必要的资本。商人们预先估计人类需要多少商品,并依靠交换契约将它们分配到需要它们的地方。的确,他们完成所有这些工作的过程中并没有相当数量上的错误、摩擦和阻挠,当然,这要比由最为有效的纯粹官僚机构可能来完成这些而所产生的摩擦和能源消耗要少得多。在我们的社会中,占有、所有权、物权、契约、继承权以及基于消费目的的家庭几乎自动地完成了那些在社会主义社会中需要由一个复杂的官僚机构网络来完成的事情。

# IV

# Social And State Sanction Of The Norms

A doctrine which has a great vogue at the present time, and which derives from various sources, seeks to explain the origin of the legal norms and, occasionally, also of the other social norms, especially those of morality, by the power of the dominant groups in society, which have established them, and are enforcing them in their own interest. But power over men can be maintained and exercised permanently only by uniting them in associations and prescribing rules of conduct for them within the association, i. e. by organizing them. In this sense the doctrine referred to would be in harmony with that taught here, according to which the social norms are but the order of the human associations. But the statement that the dominant groups of the associations set up the norms of conduct for the other members of their association solely in their own interest is meaningless or incorrect. Man always acts in his own interest, and he who is able to state exhaustively the interests which motivate human conduct is able to solve not only the question of the sanction of the norms but practically all questions of social science. On the other hand, it is quite incorrect to say that the interests of the dominant groups in the associations conflict with those of the whole association or with those of the other members. To a certain extent the interests of the dominant groups must coincide with the interests of the whole association, or at least with those of the majority of the members of the association; for if this were not so, the other members would not obey the norms established by the dominant group. It is unlikely that one could ever gain the support of a great

# 第四章　规范的社会制裁和国家制裁

当前有一种非常流行且发端于各种各样来源的学说，它总是试图通过社会中统治集团的权力来解释法律规范的起源，偶尔也用此解释其他社会规范特别是道德规范的起源，统治集团创制了这些规范并为了他们自己的利益而实施这些规范。但是，只有通过把人统一到联合体中并且为联合体中的人规定行为规则——即把人组织起来——权力统治才能永久地得以维持和实施。在这种意义上，该学说可能和我们此处所讲授的学说相一致，按照我们的学说，社会规范只是人类联合体的秩序。但是，联合体中的统治集团单单出于他们自己的利益而为联合体的其他成员设定行为规范——这一陈述是毫无意义或是不正确的。人总是为自己的利益行事，一个能够详尽说明激励人类行为之各种利益的人，不仅能解决规范的制裁问题，也能够解决实践中社会科学的所有问题。另一方面，如果说联合体中统治集团的利益与整个联合体的利益或者与联合体内其他成员的利益冲突的话，这是相当不正确的。在一定程度上，联合体内统治集团的利益肯定与整个联合体的利益相一致，或至少与联合体内大多数成员的利益相一致；因为如果情况不是如此，联合体内的其他成员不会遵守由统治集团所创立的规范。一个人的任何行动计划不大可能永远获

number of men for any project unless every individual had at least a vague idea that the project, if realized, would redound to the advantage of all. And this idea is never altogether without foundation. The order of an association, abstractly considered, may be a poor one, may perhaps afford undue advantages to its leaders, may impose heavy burdens upon the others, but it is always better than no order at all. And the fact that there is no better order in existence is always a cogent proof that the association, in its given spiritual and moral condition, and in view of the economic supplies it has had at its disposal, has been unable to create a better order.

The question then is by what means do the social associations induce their individual members to obey the norms of the association. There is, certainly, nothing more untenable psychologically than the idea, which has such a vogue, that men refrain from laying violent hands upon other men's property only because they fear the criminal law; that they pay their debts only because they fear that their goods will be levied on. Even at times when penal laws lose their force—as is often the case temporarily in time of war or of domestic disorder—it is always only a very small portion of the population that participates in murder, robbery, theft, and plundering; and in times of tranquillity most men perform the obligations they have assumed without thinking of levy of execution. From this it does not indeed follow that the great majority of men conform to the norms because they are prompted by an inner impulse; but it does follow that fear of punishment or of levy of execution is not the only consideration that prompts them to do so, quite apart from the fact that there is a sufficiently large number of social norms which threaten the transgressor neither with punishment nor with levy of execution, but which nevertheless are not ineffectual.

Sanction is not a peculiarity of the legal norms. The norms of ethical custom, morality, religion, tact, decorum, etiquette, and fashion would be quite meaningless if they did not exercise a certain amount of coercion. They too constitute the order of the human associ-

得大多数人的支持,除非每一个成员至少都模糊地认为,如果这一计划实现,它将对所有人有益。这一观点是完全有基础的。从抽象的意义上来考虑,一个联合体的秩序或许是一种很糟糕的秩序,它或许给其领导者提供了过度的有利条件,可能给其他人施加了过重的负担,但这总比根本没有秩序要好得多。现实中没有更好的秩序存在——这一事实总是有力地证明了如下命题:联合体在其既定的精神和道德条件下,考虑到其可以自由支配的经济供给,无法创造一个更好的秩序。

接下来的问题是,社会联合体借助什么样的手段来促使其单个成员服从联合体的规范。无疑,没有什么东西比如下那样一种流行理念在心理学上更站不住脚:人们之所以克制自己不向他人财产伸出暴力之手,其原因仅在于他们惧怕刑法;人们之所以清偿债务仅仅是因为他们担心他们的货物会遭到扣押。即使有时刑法失去其效力——如在战争时期和国内混乱时期经常出现的这种暂时情况,也总是仅有非常少的一部分人参与到谋杀、抢劫、偷窃和侵占中;在社会安定的时代,大部分人履行其承担的义务,却根本没有考虑到执行强制的问题。从这一点上看,此种情形,的确并不符合大部分人遵守规范是因为他们受到内在刺激的驱动这样的观点;但是它符合对刑法或强制执行的惧怕并非是促使他们这样做的唯一考虑因素这样的说法,此外,它还与如下事实相照应:存在足够多的社会规范,它们威胁犯规者的手段既不是惩罚也不是强制执行,但尽管如此,这些社会规范并非没有实效。

制裁并非法律规范的特性。如果不具有一定程度的强制,那么伦理习俗规范、道德规范、宗教规范、言行得体规范、礼仪规范、礼节规范和时尚规范这些就毫无意义。它们也构成了人类联合

ations, and it is their specific function to coerce the individual members of the association to submit to the order. All compulsion exercised by the norms is based upon the fact that the individual is never actually an isolated individual; he is enrolled, placed, embedded, wedged, into so many associations that existence outside of these would be unendurable, often even impossible, to him. We are speaking now of basic facts of the inner, the emotional, life of man. The psychic needs of ordinary commonplace creatures, who everywhere constitute the compact majority, must indeed be appraised none too highly; nevertheless there is no one to whom country, native land, religious communion, family, friends, social relations, political party, are mere words. Most people perhaps will set little store by one or the other of these, but doubtless there would be very few who do not cling with all their hearts and minds to one group at least. It is within his circle that each man seeks aid in distress, comfort in misfortune, moral support, social life, recognition, respect, honor. In the last analysis it is his group that supplies him with everything that he sets store by in life. But the importance of these associations is not limited to these moral, intangible considerations, for on them depends success in one's profession and business. On the other hand, one's profession and business draw one into a number of professional and business associations.

All of us then are living within numberless, more or less compactly, occasionally quite loosely, organized associations, and our fate in life will, in the main, be conditioned by the kind of position we are able to achieve within them. It is clear that in this matter there must be a reciprocity of services rendered. It is impossible for the associations to offer something to each one of its members unless each individual is at the same time a giver. And in fact all these associations—whether they are organized or unorganized, and whether they are called country, home, residence, religious communion, family, circle of friends, social life, political party, industrial association, or good will of a business—

体的秩序，特别是强迫联合体的个体成员去服从这种秩序是它们的特定功能。规范所产生的所有强制都是基于个人实际上从来都不是一个孤立的个体这一事实；他被招收、被安置、被包裹、被锲进到众多的联合体中，以至于脱离这些联合体而存在对他来说是无法忍受的、甚至经常是不可能的。现在我们说说人们内心和情感生活的一些基本事实。尽管普通人——他们在任何地方都构成紧密相连的大多数——的精神需求的确决不应获得过高的评析。但对于任何人，国家、国土、宗教团体、家庭、朋友、社会关系和政党都不仅仅是一个语汇。大部分人或许会不喜欢其中的一个或者另外一个群体，但是毫无疑问，很少有人不全身心地依赖至少一个群体。每个人，正是在这样一个群体圈子内，在危难时寻求帮助，在不幸时寻求安慰，寻求道德的支持、社会生活、认可、尊敬和荣誉。归根到底，正是他的群体为他提供了生活中所钟爱的一切东西。但是这些联合体的重要性并不仅仅局限于这些道德的、无形的考量，因为正是依靠这些联合体，一个人在职业和行业上才取得成功。另一方面，一个人的职业和行业又把这个人带入更多的职业和行业联合体中。

于是，我们所有的人都生活在无数的、紧凑程度不等的、偶尔也非常宽松的有组织的联合体中，我们一生的命运大体上将取决于我们在所属联合体中能取得的这种地位。非常清楚，在这个问题上，提供的服务必须具有相互性。除非联合体中的每个个体同时都是给予者，否则联合体不可能给每个成员提供东西。事实上，所有的这些联合体——不管他们是有组织的还是没有组织的，不管他们被称做国家、住户、居所、宗教团体、家庭、朋友圈子、社会生活、政党、工业协会或者企业营业权——都会提出一些需

make certain demands in exchange for that which they give; and the social norms which prevail in these communities are nothing more than the universally valid precipitate of the claims which the latter make upon the individual. He therefore who is in need of the support of the circle to which he belongs—as who is not? —does wisely if he conforms, at least in a general way, to its norms. He who refuses to conform to them must face the fact that his conduct will loosen the bonds of solidarity with his own circle. He who persistently refuses obedience has himself loosened the bonds which until now have united him with his associates. He will gradually be deserted, avoided, excluded. Here then, in the social association, is the source of the coercive power, the sanction, of all social norms, of law no more than of morality, ethical custom, religion, honor, decorum, etiquette, fashion, at least as far as the outward observance of the precepts is concerned. Especially as to etiquette and fashion, Jhering, many years ago, in two articles published in the Berlin *Gegenwart* and entitled, "Das soziale Motiv der Mode" (The Social Motive of Fashion) and "Das soziale Motiv der Tracht" (The Social Motive of Dress), showed that this is their very nature. These articles, with some omissions and changes, were subsequently incorporated in the author's *Zweck im Recht*. Etiquette and fashion are the norms of a privileged social circle; they are the external indicia of belonging. In order to be received and enjoy the advantages of being a member, one must know and observe them.

A man therefore conducts himself according to law, chiefly because this is made imperative by his social relations. In this respect the legal norm does not differ from the other norms. The state is not the only association that exercises coercion; there is an untold number of associations in society that exercise it much more forcibly than the state. One of the most vigorous of these associations is the family. Modern legislation more and more does away with the possibility of execution of a decree for the restitution of conjugal relations. But even if the family law were abolished in its entirety, families would not bear an

求,以此交换他们所给予的;而且,盛行于这些共同体中的社会规范不过是联合体对个人所提要求的普遍有效的沉淀物。因此,一个人若需要他所归属圈子给予支持——谁不需要呢?至少通常情况下,则他遵守该圈子的规范就是明智的。拒绝遵循联合体规范的人将必须面对他的行为使他及他自己的圈子的紧密结合趋于松散这一事实。一个坚持拒不服从联合体规范的人等于解开了迄今还连接着他与联合体的纽带。他将逐渐被遗弃,疏离和驱逐。这样看来,至少就涉及到的规范的外部遵守而言,在社会联合体中,存在着所有社会规范的强制力和制裁的根源,也存在道德、伦理习俗、宗教、荣誉、礼仪、礼节、时尚的强制力和制裁的根源。特别是对于礼节和时尚,在许多年以前耶林在柏林《风采》杂志中发表了题为《时尚的社会动机》和《着装的社会动机》这两篇文章,表明这是他们的本性。这些文章经过一些删略和改动后,最终被收录进作者的《法律的目的》一书。礼节和时尚是特权社会圈子的规范;它们是身份属性的外部标志。一个人为了被某个圈子接纳并享受到身为其成员才具有的诸多好处,他必须了解和遵守圈子的规范。

因此,一个人按照法律引导他自己的行为,主要是因为受到他的社会关系的强制。在这方面,法律规范与其他的规范并无不同。国家并非实施强制的唯一联合体;社会中存在着无数比国家更强有力的实施强制的联合体。这些联合体中最有力的一个就是家庭。为了恢复婚姻关系,现代立法越来越多地消除这方面法令执行的可能性。但是即使全面废除了家庭法,家庭所展示的面

aspect much different from that which they bear today; for fortunately the family law requires state sanction only in rare instances. If the workman, the employee, the office-holder, the military officer, do not perform their contractual and official duties from a sense of duty, they do so because they wish to keep their positions, perhaps because they wish to rise to better ones. The physician, the attorney, the mechanic, the merchant, are interested in exact performance of their contracts because they wish to satisfy their patients, clients, and customers and to increase the number of the latter; at any rate, because they wish to establish or strengthen their credit. Penalty and levy of execution is the last thing that enters their minds. There are large mercantile houses which, as a matter of principle, do not bring suit on a matter arising in their commercial relations, and as a rule do not permit themselves to be sued, but satisfy even an unfounded claim in full. They meet refusal of payment and frivolous demands by severing commercial relations. To this extent their own power is sufficient unto them; to this extent they can dispense with the aid of the courts and with legal protection. Likewise persons of superior social position avoid litigation of controversies, e. g. with servants, employees, workmen, mechanics. Their social and economic influence affords sufficient protection from imposition. For decades the English trade unions have declined all recognition by the state, thereby consciously and intentionally foregoing legal protection. Manifestly they did not fare badly by doing so. Modern trusts and cartels have at their disposal a complete system of means of coercion, by which they are enabled, without ever calling upon the power of the state or upon the courts, to enforce their just, as well as their often altogether unjustifiable, demands against everyone who happens to come within their sphere of power. In the course of the investigation of the iron cartel instituted by the Austrian government one of the chiefs of the cartel, Director Kestranek, made the statement that it was a matter of minor importance to him whether the iron cartel was legally efficacious or not, since the

貌也不会和今天的家庭有太大区别；因为幸运的是，家庭法在极少的情况下需要国家的强制。如果工人、雇员、政府官员、军官不是出于责任感来履行他们的契约和公务上的职责的话，那么他们之所以这么做，是因为他们想保住职位，或许他们希望能升迁到一个更好的位置上。医师、律师、机械师、商人对准确地履行他们的契约感兴趣，因为他们想使他们的病人、客户和顾客满意以便增加他们的病人、客户和顾客的数量；至少，因为他们希望建立或者加固他们的信用。刑罚和强制执行是他们最不会考虑的事情。有很多的商业机构，原则上，他们不会对由商业关系中所引起的事件提起诉讼，同样，他们通常也不会放任自己至被起诉的境地，但他们却甚至要满足一个完全没有理由的要求。他们通过断绝商业关系的方式来处理拒绝付款和无理的要求。在此程度上，他们自己的力量对他们来说是充分的；在此程度上，他们无需法院的帮助和司法的保护。同样的，社会地位很高的人避免通过诉讼来解决争端，例如与仆人、雇员、工人和机械师间的争端。他们的社会和经济影响力给他们提供免受外界强迫的充分保护。几十年来，英国工会一直拒绝国家的一切认可，因此，工会也自觉地、有意地拒绝了上述的法律保护。显然，他们这么做的效果并不差。现代托拉斯和卡特尔已经有一整套能够自由支配的强制方式体制，在不需要借助国家力量和法院权力的情况下，通过这套体制，现代托拉斯和卡特尔强制实现他们的公平，同时也强制实现了——针对偶然进入他们权力领域的每个人——经常是完全不合情理的要求。在对由奥地利政府所组建的钢铁卡特尔的调查过程中，卡特尔的其中一位董事克斯特拉内科作出如下陈述：钢铁卡特尔合法有效与否，对他来说是无足轻重的，因为这些协议，

agreements, whether legally valid or not, were being kept as if they were legally valid. He said: "The iron-masters are men who keep agreements, even if they have no legal validity." He might have added that the individual ironmaster can be coerced by means as efficacious as any that are at the disposal of the courts of the state. Likewise legally binding force of trade-union agreements would be without great significance to the workingmen since they are being kept for all that as if they were legally binding, chiefly for the same reasons for which the agreements of the iron magnates are being kept. Both friend and foe admire the compact structure which is seen everywhere in the Catholic Church, in its legal order no less than in other respects. Nevertheless the ecclesiastical law is enforced only to a very small extent by the state; and where separation of church and state is in effect, not at all. It rests, as a whole, chiefly on a social basis. In France, since the enactment of the law of separation, church taxes are being paid conscientiously even by non-believing Catholics. Nothnagel, of whose services science was deprived by his untimely death, devoted the highly interesting first-fruits of his juristic labor to the question of enforcement by social *Interessengruppen* (groups having common interests).

There is nothing that is better adapted to throw light upon what has just been said than a brief consideration of modern strikes. For years the factory worker has most conscientiously been performing all obligations arising from the contract for work and wages. What has impelled him to do this? If it is not his sense of duty, it is fear of dismissal and unemployment, the prospect of getting on better in the factory in which he is working, or of the respect of his associates and of his superiors. Compared with this, law-suit and compulsory execution are to him little more than mere words; for he has nothing that he can call his own but the strength of his hands. Now he joins the newly organized union, which passes a resolution that its members must not work with non-union workmen. It is true, the law which is being applied in the courts of the state and in the other tribunals

不管在法律上有效与否,都会被当做具有法律效力的协议来信守。他说:“制铁业者会遵守这些协议,即便这些协议不具有任何法律效力。”他或许还会加上:那些个体制铁业者会受到像国家法院采取的强制措施一样有效的方式的限制。同样,法律上具有拘束力的工会协议对于工人而言应该没有什么重大意义,因为他们一直就遵守该协议,如同该协议以前就具有法律拘束力一样,这种情形的发生主要原因与钢铁巨头的协议被遵守的原因完全相同。敌友均赞赏这种在天主教堂随处可见的紧密的结构,这在法律秩序中和在其他方面都一样。然而,国家仅在一个很小的范围内实施教会法;并且在那里,教会和国家的分离是根本做不到的。总的说来,教会法主要以社会为基础。在法国,自从教会与国家分离法颁布后,甚至那些不信奉天主教的人也真心实意地承担教会的税负。诺特纳戈的英年早逝剥夺了他为科学服务的机会,他把法学劳动中极为有趣的初次成果献给了由社会 *Interessengruppen*(利益共同体)来执行的问题。

没有任何东西比对现代罢工的简要描述更适合阐明刚才所说的了。多年来,工厂里的工人认真负责地履行着由劳动契约与工资契约所载明的全部义务。是什么驱使他们这么做呢?如果不是责任感,那么就是害怕被解雇和失业,期待在他工作的工厂中有更好发展的前景,或是对他的同事和上司的尊敬。和这相比,法律诉讼和强制实行对他来说只不过是语汇;因为除了两只手的力气外,他没有什么可以支配的了。现在他参加了一个新组织起来的工会,工会通过决议,它的成员不能和未参加工会的人一起工作。事实上,国家法院和其他裁决机构所适用的法律否认这

denies to this norm all legal efficacy; but the workman will accept it without objection, for it was created by an association with which he is most intimately connected. And when his associates lay down their tools in obedience to this resolution, he does not hesitate for one moment to join them, to break the contract which he has faithfully kept for years, and to expose himself and his family to the perils of unemployment. Adversity and destitution, which follow dismissal, have lost all their terrors for him; the force of the contractual norm, which is an enforceable legal norm, has been completely shattered by another norm. The strike has divided the entrepreneurs and the workmen in this branch of industry into two belligerent armies; and in each camp the commands of the leaders are being blindly obeyed although doubtless they are legally unenforceable. Ultimately peace is brought about, i. e. a wage agreement. Whether this can be sued upon is a question that has, as is well known, generally been answered in the negative, and it is unlikely that, according to existing law, a suit on it can be maintained in court. But that is not the important consideration. It will nevertheless be kept inviolate by both parties, even by entrepreneurs who are not parties to it as well as by workmen who may enter the employment long after the agreement has been made. For now the wage-scale agreement is the basis for the order of the work in this branch of business. And though the parties may not be satisfied with the agreement, they know that even a bad order is better than continued warfare.

There are two forms of sanction which are preponderantly, though not exclusively, peculiar to the legal norms; to wit penalty and compulsory execution. What is the significance of these two forms? Do they, as is usually assumed, impart to the legal norm such efficacy as it has? If the law were without sanction, or to put it accurately, without the coercion effected by penalty and compulsory execution, would it really be merely a fire that does not burn as Jhering thinks? (There are,

些规范的一切法律效力；但是工人却会毫无异议地接受它们，因为这些规范是由与他们最密切相连的联合体所创设的。当他的同事遵照这一个决议而放下手中的生产工具时，他会毫不犹豫地加入他们，违背他多年来一直切实遵守的契约，并把他自己和他的家人置于失业的危险当中。因被解雇而带来的不幸与穷困，不会给他带来恐惧；契约规范这种可强制执行的法律规范，它的效力已经完全让另外一种规范给破坏了。罢工已经把在同一工业部门内的企业家与工人分成了处于对立状态的两个阵营；在每一个阵营内，尽管领导者的命令无疑不具有法律上的强制执行性，但该命令还是被盲目地遵从。最终和平来临了，即一个工资协议最终会达成。对于能否对这一新的工资协议提起诉讼这一问题，众所周知，回答经常是否定的，并且根据现行法，法院是不可能支持这一起诉的。但这不是重要的考虑因素。然而，双方当事人都会完全遵守这一协议，即使那些不是当事人的企业家，以及那些在新的工资协议签订后很久才加入雇佣关系的劳动者也会遵守它们。因为现在工资标准协议是这一商业部门劳动秩序的基础。尽管双方当事人对这一协议都不满意，但是他们知道甚至一个不好的秩序也要胜过延续的冲突。

特别是对于法律规范来说，主要的——虽然不是全部的——制裁有两种形式，即刑罚和强制执行。这两种形式的重要性何在？难道它们真像通常所假设的那样，赋予了法律规范应当具有的法律效力吗？如果法律没有制裁，或者更精确地讲，如果法律没有由刑罚和强制执行产生出强制力，那么法律难道真的正如耶林所认为的那样仅仅是不燃烧的火吗？（顺便说一下，确实有很

incidentally, many kinds of fire that do not burn. ) To answer these questions exhaustively would probably require a detailed study of the coercive effect of penalty and of compulsory execution; but a fleeting glance at life will suffice to convince us that both are of importance in a very limited measure and in certain situations only. If we exclude the cases in which appeal is made to the courts because the question of fact or of law is in dispute, in which it is not a matter of enforcing law and right by coercion but of showing what is law and right in the given case, it will appear that the coercive force of penalty and of compulsory execution, as mass phenomena at least—and only these are of moment here—is effective only in a very limited measure and in so far as, for some reason or other, the other sanctions of the social organizations fail to function.

As to penalty, its true significance is shown by penal statistics. It is true, penal offenses occur in all social circles. But if we disregard persons of inferior social value who are not amenable to social restraints; if we leave out of consideration a few misdeeds as to which social influences are less effective because these misdeeds as such do not affect social position (insult, duel, political crime, and, among a large part of the German peasantry, bodily injury); if we consider not individual cases, but the great bulk of the daily work done by the criminal courts, we shall see that criminal law is directed almost exclusively against those whom descent, economic distress, neglected education or moral degradation has excluded from the human associations. It is only in the case of these outcasts that the widest association, which includes even them, i. e. the state, steps in with its power to punish. The state as an organ of society protects society against those that are outside the pale of society. The measure of its success is shown by its experience extending over thousands of years. The conviction is steadily gaining ground that the only serious weapon against crime is the possibility of regaining the criminal for human society and thus again subjecting him to social restraint.

Is the situation otherwise in case of compulsory execution? The writer has already pointed out that in the case of claims arising

多种不燃烧的火。)要全面地回答这些问题,很可能需要对刑罚和强制执行的强制效果作一个详尽的研究;但是对生活的粗略观察也将足以使我们相信,这两种制裁仅仅在有限的范围和特定的情况下才很重要。如果我们排除以下这种情形——此种情形下,之所以诉诸法院是因为事实问题或法律问题存在争议,所要解决的问题,并非是通过强制而实施权利的问题,而是揭示在给定案件中的权利是什么的问题,则看起来,刑法和强制执行的强制力,至少如同大多数现象一样——此时只有这些较重要——只在非常有限的程度上有效,并且在此程度上,由于某种原因,社会组织的其他制裁不能发挥效用。

至于刑法,它的真实意义被刑事统计数据所表明。的确,刑事违法出现在所有的社会圈子中。但是,如果我们忽略那些不服从社会约束的具有较低社会价值的人;如果我们不考虑社会影响力对其效力很小的少数违法行为,因为它们同样不会影响社会形势(侮辱、决斗、政治罪行,以及存在于大部分德国农民中的身体伤害行为);如果我们不考虑个别的情形,而仅考虑刑事法庭每天所做的日常事务的话,那么我们就会发现刑法几乎完全针对那些由于出身、经济压力、教育缺乏或道德堕落而被排除于人类联合体的人。仅仅是在面对这些被驱逐者的情况下,最广泛的联合体,甚至包括他们,即国家,才会插手用它的权力来惩罚这些人。国家作为社会的一个机构,它保护社会免受那些处于社会范围以外的人的侵犯。延续了千年的经验揭示了国家成功的措施。制止犯罪的唯一真正的武器是使罪犯重归社会,从而使他再次服从于社会约束的可能性,这一信念正在获得越来越多的认同。

在强制执行的情况下情形会不同吗?作者已经指出,在请求

from contracts of service, wages, and labor it plays a very insignificant part. It is of social significance only in the case of obligations to pay money, i. e. in but a small fraction of legal life. At this point it may suffice to raise the question whether the agreements from which obligations to pay money arise are being entered into with an eye to compulsory execution. For when the creditor extends credit he doubtless takes into consideration everything that might prompt the debtor to make repayment. A single glance, however, at the organization of credit shows of what small significance compulsory execution is in business which is done on credit. We are fully justified in saying that in a developed economic system a person may not safely be granted credit if the creditor has to take into consideration the possibility of the necessity of compulsory execution. Whether or not credit can safely be extended is determined in general by means of a thorough social and psychological investigation of the person who is asking for credit. In a case of ordinary extension of credit the actual basis for the investigation is furnished by experience in the affairs of everyday life; in case of mercantile credit, by a widely ramified organization. If this investigation shows that litigation or compulsory execution might result, the question whether credit can safely be extended is answered in the negative.

The security of credit depends upon the wealth, the social position, the personal relations, and the honesty of the person asking for credit. All of these things must warrant the assumption that he will always bear in mind and fulfil his obligations. The most imperfectly organized form of extension of credit, i. e. the usurious credit, which seeks to guard against loss by exacting excessive interest, is the very one that relies most strongly on the debtor's being prompted to pay by his sense of duty or by his position in life. All these things indicate the importance of the social associations which credit presupposes. And if, as may happen at any time, credit is extended to a stranger, this can be accounted for only by the fact that somehow the bearing of the borrower has created the impression that his position, his situation, his wealth,

权从服务合同、薪金合同和劳动合同中产生出来的情况下，强制执行无关紧要。只在支付金钱债务的情况下，强制执行才有社会意义，即，强制执行的意义仅存在于一小部分的法律生活中。在这一点上，足以提出这一问题：据以支付金钱债务的协议在订立时是否要考虑到强制执行。因为当债权人提供信用时，毫无疑问，他要考虑能促使债务人偿还的所有因素。但是，匆匆留意一下信用组织状态，就能明了强制执行在信用交易中的意义是多么微不足道。我们完全可以证明如下的陈述是正当的：在一个发达的经济体系中，如果债权人不得不考虑实施必要的强制执行的可能性，那么一个人是不会被放心地授予信用的。通常情况下，是否可以安全地授予信用，主要通过对要求商业信用的人进行全面的社会和心理调查的方式来决定。在普通信用授予中，日常生活事务的经验为调查提供了实际基础；在商业信用授予中，头绪繁多的组织为调查提供了实际基础。如果这一调查证明诉讼或强制执行可能产生，那么对是否可以安全授予信用这一问题的回答就是否定的。

信用的安全性取决于请求信用的人的财产、社会地位、私人关系和诚实度。所有这些必须确保这一假定：申请信用的人将一直牢记并履行义务。最不完善的授予信用的形式，即高利贷信用，它通过勒索过量利益来确保不受损失，它正是那种极度依赖债务人受自己责任感或者生活地位的敦促而偿付的形式。所有这些都说明了作为信用存在之前提条件的社会联合体的重要性。并且，如同任何时候都能发生的一样，如果信用提供给了一个陌生人，那么这只能用这一事实来解释：借款人的行为方式以某种方式制造了这样一个印象：他的地位、他的处境和他的财富足

warrant the assumption that he is solvent. In Rome, where every sale, because of the liabilities arising from the transaction, was in fact a credit transaction, one did not, as the sources show, readily buy from a person one did not know.

To say then that credit can safely be extended is not to make a prediction as to the result of compulsory execution. It is rather to make a statement as to the social relations upon which the creditor relies when he extends credit. One does not extend credit to a person whose position does not warrant the assumption that the obligation will be performed; one deals with him for cash or in reliance upon security given, e. g. a pledge. Transactions for cash or transactions secured by a pledge however are transfers of possession, and therefore not only do not presuppose compulsory execution but do not presuppose so much as a legal order. One would enter into a cash or a pledge transaction even with savages who have never before seen a white man, provided one were protected, by an escort for instance, against violence on the part of the savages. In civilized society, possession is rendered sufficiently secure by the inner order of the associations; and, ultimately, it is protected also by the state, the most inclusive association known to society, as an organ of society. Transactions for cash or secured by a pledge can be entered into with anyone because they are transactions that involve only a transfer of possession, and therefore do not presuppose compulsory execution, but are designed to render the latter superfluous. The right of pledge of the lessor therefore has the beneficial effect that anyone can lease a dwelling without reference to his credit rating. If the lessor does not get his rent, he can take possession of the chattels which the lessee has brought into the house, and is protected by the community in doing so. In England, where the right of pledge of the lessor does not exist, references are required in case of lease which show that credit can safely be extended to the lessee. Only the innkeeper, who has no option as to the customer with whom

以保证他是有清偿能力的这一假定。在罗马——由于在那里债务产生于交易，所以每一笔出售事实上都是信用交易——正如原始文献所表明的，人们并不乐意从他不认识的人那里购买东西。

因而，可以说，能够安全提供信用并不是要对强制执行的后果作出预测。它毋宁是有关社会关系的一个陈述：当债权人提供信用时他信赖该陈述。人们不会给那种所处地位不能保证债务履行这一假定的人提供商业信用；人们会和这样的人进行现金交易，或者通过特定的安全保障——例如担保——来和此类人交易。但是现金交易和由担保物保障的交易都是占有的转移，因此，这不仅没有预设强制执行，甚至也没有预设一个法律秩序。一个人甚至可以和以前从未见过白人的野蛮人进行现金交易或担保交易，只要这个人获得使其免受来自野蛮人方面暴力侵害的保护，例如得到一个护卫队的保护。在一个文明的社会，联合体的内部秩序就已经提供了对占有的充分保护；并且最终，国家——对社会来说这是最具有包容性的联合体——作为一个社会机构，也对占有提供了保护。任何人都可以进行现金交易和由担保物保障的交易，因为上述交易仅仅涉及占有的转移，因此，上述交易不以强制执行为先决条件，而且这些交易也使得强制执行成为多余。因此，出租人的担保权有一种有利的效果，任何人都可以租得住处，不论他的信用等级如何。如果出租人拿不到租金，他就会占有承租人带到他的房子里的动产，并且他这样做会受到他所在社区的保护。在英国——那里并不存在出租人的担保权，承租人租赁房屋时，通常需要提供一份信用证明以证明房东可以安全地向他提供信用。只有对交易客户没有选择权的旅

he will deal, has a legal right of pledge (lien) on all of the goods which the guest has brought into the inn. Here again security based on possession takes the place of the organization of credit in civilized society.

To consider the right of compulsory execution, as jurists often do, as the basis of the legal order involves a tremendous overestimation of its scope. Limited in its effectiveness to a small fraction of legal life, i. e. the obligation to pay money, it is secondary even within this sphere to the force of the social interrelations which urge us to perform our obligations. There can be no doubt that the creditor usually makes a correct calculation as to whether credit may safely be granted to the debtor, i. e. that the considerations which prompt him to extend credit coincide with those that prompt the debtor to meet his obligations. In fact, a person to whom his personal reputation, his social standing, his business relations, in short his credit, mean anything surely will never even think of hazarding a compulsory execution. All these things mean too much to him to endanger them for the sake of a momentary advantage. The gambler pays his unenforceable gambling debts under a merely social compulsion, and the average man is at least as sensitive to social sanction as the average gambler. Even unenforceable debts arising from stock-exchange differences are usually being paid, although in these cases the social and economic consequences of failure to do so are much less than in case of true business debts. The generally known ineffectiveness of the usury laws demonstrates that the persons from whom usury is being exacted can be compelled to pay even without compulsory execution. The reports of mercantile credit associations show that the well known purely economic means of coercion, to wit boycott and black list, are effective even where compulsory execution has remained altogether fruitless. Nothnagel, in the book referred to above, mentions older material, which however is still valuable. Compulsory execution, like penalty, we may therefore say, exists only for those that have come down in the world and for those whom society has cast out. It is

店主才拥有一项对客人带到旅店内所有物品的法律上担保权(留置权)。在这里,以占有为基础的安全保障又一次替代文明社会中的信用组织结构。

如同法学家经常做的那样,将强制执行权看做法律规范的基础,这必然是对强制执行范围的过分高估。强制执行的效果仅限于法律生活中的一小部分,即支付金钱的债务,即使在这一个范围内,强制执行对于敦促我们履行债务的社会相互关系力量而言,也是次要的。毫无疑问,债权人通常会做出关于是否可以安全授予债务人信用的正确盘算,即,促使债权人提供信用的考量与促使债务人履行义务的考量相一致。事实上,对于一个将个人声誉、社会地位、商业关系——简而言之也就是他的信用——视为一切的人来说,他的确不会想到遭受强制执行的危险。所有的这些对他来说意义重大,以至于他不会为了暂时的利益使它们受到危害。赌徒们在只有社会强制的情况下支付他的不能被强制执行的赌债,一般人至少会像一般的赌徒一样对社会制裁敏感。即使那些因为股票交易差额所产生的不能强制执行的债务,通常情况下也会被支付,尽管在这种情况下,不支付这种债务的社会和经济后果要比不支付真正的商业债务的社会和经济后果要小得多。通常所知的高利贷在法律上的无效性,证明了即便是在没有强制执行的情况下,被勒索的人也会被迫偿还债务。商业信用协会的报告表明,即便是在强制执行仍是完全无效的地方,众所周知的纯粹经济强制方式即联合抵制和黑名单,也是有效的。在上面所参引的书中,诺特纳戈提到了一些早期的但仍然非常有价值的材料。因此,我们可以说,强制执行像刑罚一样仅仅适用于那些非常落魄的人和为社会所驱逐的人。强制执行对于那些鲁

effective against the reckless borrower, the cheat, the bankrupt, and against him who has become insolvent through misfortune. However much of a burden these classes of borrowers may be on business life, they are too insignificant to warrant the statement that the value of the legal order depends upon the protection it affords against such elements.

On the whole the effect of the coercive order of the state is limited to protection of one's person, of one's possession, and of claims against those who are outside of the pale of society. Whatsoever else the state may do in order to maintain the law is of much less significance, and one might reasonably maintain that society would not go to pieces even if the state should exercise no coercion whatever. After all, commerce was able to eke out a precarious existence even in the ancient Polish republic; and it pursues its way even in the Orient today, although the corrupt and extermely incompetent administration of justice there scarcely deserves the name. Before the judicial reform of the thirties of the last century, the benefits of the expensive and cumbersome English civil procedure did not extend far beyond the well-to-do upper crust of English society. This however did not prevent the English from becoming a rich and highly civilized nation. Moreover legal protection in Germany and Austria under the older procedure was not much more effective. Under such circumstances one extends credit more sparingly, or protects oneself by carefully thought-out safeguards; the rest must be done by the social associations. Goethe, who did not fail to observe that the Imperial Supreme Court had extremely little influence upon the administration of justice, quite correctly pointed out the things that are really important. It is a more serious matter if the administration of criminal justice breaks down also. But Hungary, southern Italy, and Spain prove that a nation can survive centuries of brigandage.

Not only in primitive times, when society as a whole consisted chiefly of small associations, but much later, even at the present time, there is no lack of instances of societies maintained exclusively by the inner order of its associations. Wherever the power of the state is extremely feeble, there is no order but this. And indeed on this order, societies have been built up in Europe even in modern times, e. g. that of the former Polish Republic, of Hungary in the seventeenth and eighteenth centuries, of the kingdom

莽的借款人、骗子、破产者以及那些因为命运的不幸而无力偿债的人而言，是有效的。这些阶层的借款者无论对商业生活会产生怎样重的负担，他们都太无关紧要了，并不能由此证明，法律秩序的价值取决于法律对那些因素提供保护的陈述。

大体上，国家强制秩序的效力限于对人身的保护、对占有的保护和对针对那些处于社会范围外的人的请求权的保护。国家为了维护法律所做的任何其他事情意义极小，并且人们有理由认为：即使国家不实施任何强制，社会也不会分崩离析。毕竟，即使在古波兰共和国，贸易也能弥补这种不稳定的存在；即便是在今天的东方，贸易还是按自己的方式运行，尽管那里腐败、极端无能的司法绝大多数时候都已名不副实。在上世纪30年代司法改革之前，昂贵繁琐的英国民事诉讼的好处远没有普及到英国社会富裕的上层以外。但是，这并没有阻止英国变成一个富裕并高度文明的国家。而且，在旧的诉讼程序下，德国和奥地利的法律保护并不是很有效。在这种情况下，任何人都更加谨慎地提供信用，或采用深思熟虑的保证条款来保护自己；其余的都由社会联合体来完成。成功地洞察到帝国高等法院对司法的影响已经微乎其微的歌德，正确指出了一些确实非常重要的事情。若刑事司法也停顿的话，那么形势将更为严峻。但是，匈牙利、南意大利和西班牙证明了一个国家能平安度过强盗横行的几个世纪。

不仅在社会整体上主要由小的联合体所组成的原始时代，而且在后来的时期，甚至是在当代，也不缺乏社会完全是由联合体的内部秩序维持的实例。在国家权力极端脆弱的任何地方，只存在联合体的内部秩序。的确，在这种联合体的内部秩序之上，甚至在现代欧洲——例如，前波兰共和国、17和18世纪的匈牙利，

of Naples, of Sicily. This is true, in part, of the Orient also. In the Middle Ages, the weakness of the state brought about special associations for legal protection and caused men to resort to commendation. In modern times similar formations can be found, e. g. the confederations of the former Polish Republic, the Camorra and the Maffia in Naples and Sicily. In conclusion, the studies of Noeldeke on the Arabs of the sixth century may be referred to in order to prove that the existence of a great nation, nay, what is more, of a large and opulent commercial city, may be maintained solely by the inner strength of its associations. "Here it is important to note that among the Arabs there are no traces of the formation of states. The clan, the tribe, are moral units of great authority, but without any power of coercion. He who refuses to take part in an undertaking of the tribe or of the family may incur derision, even contempt, but there is no means of coercing him. Only the vengeance of blood guarantees a certain measure of security. If any other crime can be punished by any means other than private vengeance, I have no knowledge of that fact. To rob a member of one's tribe or a guest was disgraceful, but the robbed had no other means of redress than to try to get back that of which he had been robbed. This was the prevailing state of affairs not only among the Bedouins, but also in the cities; even in Mecca. It is almost incredible that a city whose inhabitants were engaged extensively in commerce, who were very much superior mentally to the Bedouins, and who soon after successfully undertook to conquer and rule one half of the world, had no actual government. But we must always emphasize the fact that the authority of the most prominent citizens offsets this defect fairly well. After the heads of the clan—who exercised only a moral authority over the latter—had agreed upon an

还有那不勒斯王国和西西里——社会也被建立了起来。事实上，东方社会部分地也是如此。在中世纪，国家的脆弱导致了维护法律保护的特殊联合体的出现，并促使人们采取领主附庸的形式。[1] 在现代，也可以发现同样的组织形式，例如，前波兰共和国联盟和那不勒斯和西西里的克莫拉[2]和黑手党。总之，为了证明一个强大国家、甚或一个庞大而富裕的商业城市的存在也可以完全由联合体的内部力量来维持，我们可以引用诺伊德克对6世纪阿拉伯人的研究。“在此，重要的是注意，在阿拉伯人当中，并没有国家形成的痕迹。氏族、部落，是有崇高权威的道德单位，但是它们没有任何强制权力。那些拒绝参加部落或者家庭事业的人会招致嘲笑，甚至侮辱，但决不会受到强制。只有血亲的复仇才会保障一定范围内的安全。如果其他任何犯罪可以被私人复仇以外的方式惩罚，那么我对此并不知晓。抢劫一个部落的成员或客人是不名誉的，但是被抢劫者除了尽力取回被抢物品之外，没有其他的救济措施。这种普遍的事态不仅存在于贝多因人[3]中，也存在于城市中，甚至在麦加城中。一个城市——其居民广泛从事着贸易，他们在智力上优越于贝多因人，不久之后他们又成功地征服和统治了半个世界——居然没有一个实际存在的政府，这几乎是难以置信的。但是我们必须始终强调这样的一个事实，最杰出公民的权威相当令人满意地弥补了这一不足。在氏族首领——只能对后者施加道德权威——已经同意某一项事业之

---

〔1〕 拥有自由土地的自由又将自己和土地置于某一领主的庇护之下，并使自己成为其封臣或附庸。

〔2〕 1820年前后在意大利那不勒斯组成的一个秘密团体，一度发展成颇有势力的政治组织，后因从事诈骗、抢劫等非法恐怖活动而被取缔。

〔3〕 一个居无定所的阿拉伯游牧民族。

undertaking, an individual or an individual family would not be likely to dare to refuse to cooperate; this has happened however." From the last remark of Noeldeke's, it follows that only the extraordinarily close cohesion of the Arabic clans, which continues down to the present time, and the support which each individual found among his own people have made the existence of such a society possible.

A study of the beginnings of human society discloses the fact that the force of the legal norm, which at the time is as yet undifferentiated from the norm of religion, of morals, and of ethical custom, is based exclusively or almost exclusively on the influence exerted upon every individual by the members of the narrower association of which he is a member. Generally everyone conforms without making objection to the order of the family or of the clan. True legal or peaal coercion is scarcely ever employed against a fellow-member of a narrower association. Obstinate resistance is met with exclusion from the association, which is considered the greatest misfortune that can befall a man. Note the Homeric words ἀφρήτωρ, ἀνέστιος, ἀθέμιστς. Enforcement of one's rights by violence as well as defense by violence are resorted to only against outsiders, as to whom the norms of the association are ineffectual. It is an error to believe that we have advanced far beyond such a state of affairs. Even today, just as in the beginnings of legal development, the force of law is based on the silent, uninterrupted sway of the associations which embrace the individual. From this point of view, the law appears even today to be related, in its essential nature, to the other social norms, i. e. to the norms of religion, morals, ethical custom, decorum, tact, etiquette, fashion. Even today exclusion from the community (the church, the association, society (*aus der Gesellschaft*) in the social as well as in the juristic sense), withdrawal of credit, loss

后，该个人或者家庭不大可能敢于拒绝合作；但是这种事情还是发生了。”从诺伊德克的最后评论中可以得出这样的结论：只有阿拉伯人氏族一直延续到如今的、超乎寻常的凝聚力，以及在该民族中的每个人都可以感受到的支持，才使得那样一个社会的存在成为可能。

对人类社会起源的研究揭示了这样一个事实：当时，还没有跟宗教规范、道德规范和伦理习俗规范区分开来的法律规范，后者的效力完全或者几乎完全基于它所属的狭小联合体对其每一个成员所施加的影响。一般说来，每个人都毫无异议地遵守家庭或氏族的规范。真正的法律或者 peaal〔1〕强制很少对狭小联合体的内部成员施用。顽固的抵抗会遭遇到联合体的驱逐，这种驱逐被认为是降临到一个人身上的最大不幸。注意荷马的话：没有手足之情，没有家园，没有法律。〔2〕通过暴力和防卫来强行实现权利，仅仅被用来对付外来者，因为联合体的规范对后者没有约束效力。认为我们已经远远地超越了这样一种状态是错误的。甚至在今天——正如在法律发展的开端时一样——法律的效力也是基于包含个人之联合体默默的、未曾中断的影响之上。由此看来，即使在今天，法律在本质属性上也似乎与其他社会规范相关联，即与宗教规范、道德规范、伦理习俗规范、礼仪规范、言行得体规范、礼节规范和时尚规范相关联。即使在今天（在社会意义和法律意义上），将不服从者从共同体（如教会、社团、社会）中驱逐出去（*aus der Gesellschaft*），以及信用的撤销、地位或客户的

〔1〕一古老的家族。

〔2〕根据英译者注译出。

of position or of custom, is the most efficacious means of coinbating insubordination. Even today punishment and compulsory execution, which the jurist is accustomed to look upon as the basis of all legal order, are merely the extreme means of combat against those that have been excluded from the associations, just as the feud was the extreme means of combat against a member of a strange community.

Nevertheless the fact that the force of the social norms is so universally traced to the coercive power of the state requires explanation. Every false doctrine must, in the nature of things, be based on a correct observation of some sort or other. All our perceptions and sensations are always true; only the conclusions we draw from them can be false. In the first place, the validity of only a part of the law is maintained by the coercive power of the state. This part is neither very great nor very important, but it is the part which is of greatest interest to the jurist; because the latter is not concerned until coercion becomes necessary. In the second place there are doubtless many norms which most people would not observe if there were no sanction in the form of penalty or compulsory execution. In this connection the norms of police law (Max Ernst Mayer), which incidentally are applied not only by the judges of the police courts and of the criminal courts, but also by the judges of the civil courts, are of minor importance. Being norms for decision and having been created by the sovereign power of the state, they are foreign to the life of society, and often do not become known except through the decisions rendered in accordance with them, and they become rules of conduct only through these decisions. These decisions then appear to be the real promulgation of the law, and the rule *ignorantia legis nocet* appears in its true significance. It is a fact of greater importance that the entire military system and the entire tax system of the modern state, that is to say, the very thing which customarily is considered the basis of the life of the state, could not exist for a single moment without coercion exercised by the state. All this however merely amounts to saying that the state and a considerable portion of society have consciously become antagonistic to each other. In consequence of this antagonism, the military and the tax system of the state have remained so unrelated to society that they have become state institutions exclusively. History will probably show that this is merely a

丧失，这些也是与不服从作斗争的最有效方式。即使在今天，被法学家习惯看做是法律秩序基础的惩罚和强制执行也仅仅是与被驱逐出联合体的成员作斗争的极端方式，正如世仇是与一个来自陌生共同体的成员作斗争的极端方式一样。

尽管如此，社会规范的效力普遍要追溯到国家强制力这一事实仍需要解释。理所当然地，每种错误的学说必定基于这种或者那种正确的观察。我们的感知和感觉总是正确的；只是我们从它们推出的结论可能是错误的。首先，只有一部分法律的有效性由国家强制力量来维持。这一部分既非数量巨大，也非十分重要，但它们是法学家最为感兴趣的部分；因为不等到强制成为必需时，法学家不会关注。其次，毫无疑问，确实存在许多规范——如果没有惩罚或强制执行这些形式的制裁，那么这些规范不会获得大多数人的遵守。关于这一点，警察法规范（Max Ernst Mayer）并不重要，尽管不但治安法院和刑事法院的法官偶尔适用这些法律规范，而且民事法院的法官也顺带地适用它们。作为裁判规范和由国家主权所创设的规范，警察法规范对社会生活是陌生的，除非依据它们作出裁决，否则它们常常不为人所知，只有通过这些裁决，它们才能变成行为规范。于是，这些裁决似乎是法律的真正颁布，并且不知法亦不免责规则似乎也落实了它真正的意义。以下这个事实更为重要：若没有国家产生的强制，现代国家的整个军事体制和税收体制，亦即，通常被视为国家生活基础的东西，就不能存在片刻。然而，所有的这些仅仅是等于说：国家和相当一部分的社会已经变得有意识地相互对立了。由于相互敌对的缘故，国家的军事与税收体制保持了与社会不相关的状态以至于它们成了国家所独有的制度。历史或许会表明这仅仅是一个

transition stage. It was not the case in antiquity. The whole military system and that part of the services required by the state which had to be rendered by the commonalty were socially organized. This is true even today in small states.

The conception of law as a coercive order therefore is based upon the fact that its exponents have one-sidedly taken into consideration only those portions of the law that derive their force solely from the state. But that is not the whole story. To a considerable extent, this conception has been derived from a consideration not merely of law, but of social life as a whole. It is being observed that there is an enormous contrast in society between the rich and the poor; that the entire burden of the work of society rests upon the poor; that in exchange they receive little more than the bare necessaries of life; that the legal order compels them to render valuable services to society in exchange for services of much less value. That this state of affairs is endured by those to whom it causes such losses can be understood only if one assumes that it is being forcibly maintained by the sovereign power of the state. This thought has been followed through to its logical conclusion in the socialist philosophy of history. The latter begins with a discussion of the older economic organization of mankind, of the ordering of the clan and of the family, of the household as a self-sufficing economic unit, of industry carried on by organized crafts, whereby an equal division of the fruits of labor among all who participated therein was secured (Engels, Rodbertus); and shows that this state of affairs, under the influence of capitalism, is continually shifting, to the disadvantage of an ever increasing majority of those who have not and to the advantage of an ever decreasing number of those who have (Marx). The older economic order, it is contended, was sustained by the great majority, who found it to be to their advantage to do so; the later capitalistic order is being maintained exclusively by the state, which is a powerful, elaborate organization of those who have for the protection of the legal order, which is based on property, contract, and the law of inheritance. The socialists therefore quite consistently urge those who have not to oppose to the organization of those who have the organization of the masses in order to bring about a legal

转变的阶段。在古代情形不是如此。整个的军事制度和国家需要的由大众提供的部分服务都是通过社会方式组织的。在一些小的国家中,即便是今天实情也是如此。

因此,法律作为强制性秩序的观念基于这样的事实:这一观念的阐述者片面地考虑了那些效力完全源自国家的那部分法律。但是这并不是事情的全部。在一个相当的程度上,这种观念不仅仅起源自对法律的考虑,而是对作为整体的社会生活的考虑。我们可以观察到社会上的富人和穷人之间存在着巨大的差异;整个社会劳动的重担落在了穷人肩上;在交换中,穷人仅仅得到最低的生活必需品。法律秩序强迫他们向社会提供颇有价值的服务而换回社会提供给他们的价值很少的服务。穷人们一直在忍受那种不断给他们带来损失的状况——若想理解此点,只有通过如下的看法才能办到:上述事态是由国家主权强制维持的。在社会主义者的哲学史上,这一思想被贯彻到底并得出逻辑结论。社会主义者首先讨论了人类的古老的经济组织、氏族和家庭的规整、作为自给自足的经济单位的住户、有组织的手工业者所从事的工业,凭借着这些,在所有参加到上述组织的人中,劳动成果的平等分配得以确保(恩格斯、洛贝图斯);(马克思)证明这一情势在资本主义制度的影响下,正在不断向着对人数占大多数且不断增加的无产者的不利方向和对人数不断减少的有产者的有利方向转变。大多数人发现维持旧的经济秩序对他们有利,因而维持着这种旧的经济秩序;后来的资本主义秩序完全由国家——有产者强大而精密的组织——来维持,其目的是为了保护基于财产权、契约和继承法的法律秩序。因此,社会主义者始终如一地敦促无产者反对有产者的组织——这些大众组织是为了给有产者带来

order which is more favorable to the latter.

If it were true that the legal order of the present day cannot be maintained without the help of the state and that the latter is nothing but an organization of the small and ever decreasing minority of those who have against the great mass of those who have not, the legal order and the state were condemned already. But the present inquiry has shown that the resources of the state for the protection of the legal order are, in actual fact, not being employed against the great masses of the people but only against the small minority of those who have been cast out, who are cut off from all social relations. There is no need for any exertion on the part of the state to subdue the great mass of the people; the latter submit to the legal order willingly because they realize that the legal order is their order, the order of the economic and social associations, of which each one of them is a member. It cannot be true therefore that a small minority makes use of these associations for the purpose of exploiting the great majority. To say that this can be done for a long period of time without eruptions of violence is to contradict all historical experience and all mass psychology. Every great strike which is accompanied by a breach of agreement demonstrates that the means at the disposal of the state are insufficient to enforce legal claims against hundreds or thousands of resisting human beings. If therefore the great majority of human beings—and this includes, as can readily be seen, the whole working class—render obedience to the legal order, they undoubtedly must be actuated by a very strong conviction, though not perhaps a clear understanding, that it is necessary to do this—necessary in order to secure their own interests. This same conviction is clearly manifested in every revolt the object of which is not political but economic revolution. By far the greater number will be found on the side of the sovereign power of the state, and a revolutionary movement of this sort has never been successful even to the extent of being able to maintain itself permanently in a state of any considerable magnitude.

In fact, since the present legal order is at the same time an organization of production and exchange of goods it is not possible

了更为有利的法律秩序。

倘若以下情形属实:没有国家的帮助,目前的法律秩序无法维持,并且国家仅仅是一个那些反对无产者大众的少数人(本来数量很少而且一直在减少)的组织,那么法律秩序和国家早就应当受到谴责。但是,目前的调查证明,事实上,国家保护法律秩序的各种对策并没有用来针对大多数人,而仅仅是用来针对那些被社会所抛弃的、已经断绝一切社会关系的人中的少数。在国家方面,国家没有必要采取任何措施使大多数人服从法律;大多数人自愿地遵守法律秩序,是因为他们意识到法律秩序是他们的秩序,是他们作为其中一员的经济和社会联合体的秩序。因此,少数人为了剥削大多数人的目的而利用联合体,这不可能是真实的。在没有暴乱的很长一段时间内,少数人能够实现利用联合体来剥削大多数人的目的,这种说法与历史经验和大众心理相悖。每一次大罢工——同时必然有违约情势发生——证明,国家可自由采取的手段不足以强制执行对数以百计、数以千计的罢工者的法律请求权。因此,如果大多数人——显而易见包括工人阶级——遵守法律秩序,则毫无疑问,他们受到了一个必须这样做的强有力的信念的驱使,尽管这种信念或许不是很清晰,该信念即,为了确保他们自己的利益,罢工是必要的。每一次以经济革命而不是以政治革命为目标的反抗也清楚地证明了同样的信念。显然,支持国家主权更多的信念还将会被发现,并且,这种形式的革命运动永远不会取得成功,哪怕仅仅是在能够使其自身永久维持在任何相当重要的程度上。

事实上,因为现行法律秩序同时也是货物生产和交换的组织状态,所以在不剥夺大多数人——同样也是少数人的——生存方

to abolish it without, at the same time, depriving the great majority as well as the small minorities of the means of subsistence. It is necessary, therefore, if civilization is to continue, that the existing legal order should not be abolished, unless it can at once be replaced by another, a socialistic order. That this can be accomplished at any time without further ado is no longer contended by anyone competent to judge, even a socialist. Intelligent socialists have long since been speaking only of a gradual development of the capitalistic economy into a socialistic one. Incidentally, I believe that I have shown elsewhere (Südd. Monatshefte, 3 Jahrg.) that even this cannot be accomplished within a calculable period of time. If therefore the present-day social order, in spite of the great sacrifices it exacts from the majority of the people, exhibits a tolerably firm structure, this is due to the fact that, for the moment, there is no other order available that could do more, or even as much, not only for those who have, but also for those who have not. The question of the ultimate goal (*Endziel*) may safely be passed over. As a practical matter, even the socialistic working class of Europe is concerned only about such an improvement of the present legal order as secures to it a modest, but attainable, social advancement.

In view of the coercion by means of which the social associations enforce observance of the norms, it may be said that the individual manifestly is at all times both active and passive; every member of the association takes part in bringing pressure to bear, and every individual, in turn, must submit to pressure. The coercive power of the norms—a fact of mass psychology—posits at the same time the observance of the latter—a fact of individual psychology. It would be a mistake, nevertheless, to lay too much stress upon this particular fact. With the great mass of men who throughout their whole lives permit themselves, without objection, to be fitted into the vast social mechanism, it is not a matter of conscious thinking, but of unconsciously habituating themselves to the emotions and thoughts of their surroundings, which are with them from the cradle to the grave. The most important norms function only through suggestion. They come to man in the form of commands or of prohibitions; they are addressed to him without a statement of the reason on

式的同时，废除现在的法律秩序是不可能的。因此，如果现存的文明继续，则现行法律秩序必然不应该被废除，除非它立即被另外的一种法律秩序——社会主义的法律秩序所代替。有判断力的任何人，即使是社会主义者，也不再主张，任何时候这种代替无需多费周折就能完成。聪明的社会主义者很早以前仅仅提及从逐步发展的资本主义经济过渡到社会主义经济。顺便说一下，我相信我在别处（Südd. Monatshefte，3 Jahrg.）已经证明，甚至在可预测的期间内该转变也不可能完成。因此，不管现行的社会秩序要求大多数人做出了多么巨大的牺牲，如果它展示了一种可以忍受的坚固结构，那是因为这样的一个事实：目前没有任何其他的可能秩序不仅能够为有产者而且也能为无产者做得更多或者做得一样好。终极目标（*Endziel*）这一问题确实可以被忽略。实际上，即使欧洲的社会主义工人阶级，也只关心诸如确保获得一个适度但可达到的社会进步这样的现行法律秩序的改善。

鉴于社会联合体据以使得规范获得遵守的强制，或许可以这么说，显然个人一直既是主动的又是被动的；每个联合体的成员都会带来要承担的压力，反过来，每个联合体的成员也要忍受压力。规范的强制力即这样一个大众心理事实，同时假定会有"对规范的遵守"这样一个个人心理事实。然而，对于这个特殊的事实过于强调将是一个错误。对于那些整个一生中都毫无异议地让自己适应到巨大社会机器中去的绝大多数人来说，这种对社会的适应不是出于一种有意识的思考，而是自发地让自身习惯于他们周遭的情感和思维的过程，并且这个过程伴随他们从摇篮走向坟墓。最为重要的规范仅仅通过建议起作用。这些规范通过命令或者禁止的形式走入人的意识中；它们针对个人提出，却没有

which they are based; and he obeys them without a moment's reflection. They have not subdued man but have educated him. They are being impressed upon his mind in his childhood; an "It is not done," "It is not proper," "Thus hath God commanded" follows him through his whole life. And he submits with a willingness which is the greater the more emphatically experience brings home to him the advantages of obedience and the disadvantages of disobedience. The advantages and disadvantages are not only social but also individual; for he who obeys a command is spared the arduous labor of doing his own thinking, and the still more arduous labor of making his own decision. Liberty and independence are ideals of the poet, the artist, and the thinker only. The average man is a Philistine, without much appreciation of these things. He loves that to which he has become habituated, the instinctive, and hates nothing more than intellectual exertion. That is the reason why women become enthusiastic over men of strong will. The latter make their decisions for them, and do not even give the thought of resistance opportunity to arise. For all the trouble and pains that they are thereby freed from they are sincerely grateful to their husbands.

In this way, obedience to norms ultimately impresses its stamp upon the whole man. It makes not only the individual act, but the man himself, just, moral, faithful, tenacious of ethical custom, dignified, tactful, honorable, well-mannered, modern. He submits to the norms from conviction, and this imparts stability to his conduct. After the social pressure which is brought to bear upon the individual in each case by the habit of obedience to the norms has fashioned the character of the individual, it can no longer be effectively counteracted by other influences. The social norms give shape and form to the individuality of man.

It might not be amiss for everyone who is investigating the origin and the effects of the legal norms to make an attempt to answer the much simpler question why he does not meet a man in the street wearing conventional civilian clothes without a cravat. It cannot be a matter of mere fastidiousness; for undoubtedly there is a great number of men who are quite indifferent to matters of dress, who nevertheless would

附有任何它们赖以存在之理由的陈述;个人未经片刻反思也就服从了它们。它们并没有压制个人而是教育了他。还在个人的孩童时代,这些规范就深深印在了他的大脑中。“这不妥当”,“这不合适”,“这是上帝的命令”,这些话跟随人的一生。个人自愿地服从,这种自愿更为重要,也更为有利,经验使他认识到,服从带来利益而不服从带来不利益。这种利益和不利益不但是社会的,而且也是个人的;因为服从命令的人可以省掉自己思考这一艰辛的劳动,也可以省掉自己做出决定这一更为艰辛的劳动。自由和独立仅仅是诗人、艺术家和思想家的理想。普通的人都是不怎么欣赏这些价值的庸人。普通的人热爱他已经习惯的事物,痛恨的却不过是智识的运用。这就是女人们为什么会对意志坚强的男人如此狂热的原因。意志坚强的男人为女人们作出决定,甚至不给她们产生抵制思想的机会。由于女人们摆脱了作决定过程中所有的麻烦与痛苦,所以她们真诚地感激她们的丈夫。

这样,遵守规范最终成了印在整个人类身上的标签。遵守规范不仅塑造着一个人的行为,而且塑造这个人本身,使这个人成为了一个正直、有道德、忠实、坚守伦理习俗、高贵、机智、值得尊敬、有礼貌和时髦的人。他基于信念而服从规范,这也赋予其行为以稳定性。由于遵守规范的习惯而带给个人的社会压力塑造了个人的性格之后,任何其他的社会影响都已经无法再有效地抵消它。社会规范塑造和培养了人们的个性。

对于正在调查法律规范的起源和效果的所有人而言,试图回答他为什么不会在街上遇到身着普通便装不带领带的人这样一个很简单的问题,可能不会有差错。这不可能仅仅是一种吹毛求疵;因为毫无疑问,很多人对于着装漠不关心,尽管如此,他们不

never appear in public without a cravat. In order to facilitate the inevitable historical investigation, I will say that this in itself rather superfluous article of dress, which, incidentally, is not of impeccable taste, is descended from the garb of the Croatian regiments in Paris in the days of Louis XIV, from whom, by the way, it got its Austrian and French name (cravat). And for the very reason that at the present time it is not readily seen that the social norm requiring every civilized European man who has any self-respect to wear a cravat fulfils any function in the creation or preservation of the social order, a detailed study of it would yield a great amount of information to the jurist.

Accordingly social norms, whether they are legal norms or norms of another kind, always have their origin in an association; they impose an obligation only on the members of this association; and this obligation is binding upon them only in their dealings with members of the association. They have no effect upon anyone outside of the association. If these propositions had been enunciated in classical antiquity they would not have required further proof, for they would have been accepted as self-evident truths. At that time, no one doubted that law, religion, morality, ethical custom, were in existence only for one's own people, and that one's own people occasionally did not even include all those that dwelt within the walls of the city; at any rate, that it never extended beyond the closest tribal or lingual relationship. Beyond this, there was no bond that was not established by treaty of guest-friendship, of friendship, or of commerce. This is the situation even today among all peoples that are outside the pale of European civilization. It is true, in most cases the person of the guest is sacred, but the moment the guest crosses the threshold he becomes a member of the household; and often enough the protection extended ceases the moment he leaves the house.

At the present time, it is true, this is no longer the case to the same extent. It is clear however that the norms of ethical custom, decorum, tact, etiquette, fashion, have no validity beyond a certain circle. But the legal norms, in part at least, impose an

会不带领带在公共场合露面。为了促进这一不可避免的历史调查，我会说：领带就其本身来说是一件相当多余的装饰，顺便提一下，这也不是一种无懈可击的品味，领带源自路易十四时代巴黎的克罗地亚军团的服装。顺便说到，在路易十四那里，领带有了它的奥地利和法国的名字（领带）。正因为这个原因，目前，不容易看到以下情形：社会规范要求每一个有自尊的文明欧洲人去佩戴领带，它履行社会秩序的创造或者保存上的任何功能，与此相关的一个详细研究会给法学家提供大量信息。

因此，社会规范——不管是法律规范还是其他类型的规范——总是起源于一个联合体；它们仅仅对这一联合体的成员施加一个义务；这一义务对联合体成员的拘束力也仅存在于联合体的成员的交往中。它们对联合体外的任何人都不产生效力。在古典时期曾被清晰阐明的这些命题是不需要任何进一步的证据的，因为它们已经作为不证自明的真理被接受了。那时候，没有人怀疑：法律、宗教、道德、伦理习俗仅仅为自己的民族而存在，并且自己的民族有时甚至不包括那些已经居住在城墙里面的人。无论如何，它都不会超越最近的部落或者语言关系。除此之外，任何的约束都是通过宾客友好条约、友好条约或者商业条约建立起来。甚至在今天这种情形也存在于欧洲文明范围以外的所有民族中。的确，在大多数情况下，客人是受尊敬的，但是，客人在越过家庭门槛的这一刻变成了家庭成员，并且常常从客人离开家庭这一刻起，对其提供的保护也随之终止。

日前，的确情形不再完全一样。然而，清楚的是，伦理习俗规范、礼仪规范、言行得体规范、礼节规范和时尚规范超出一个特定的范围就不再有效。但是，至少法律规范部分地强加给每一个人

obligation on everyone; and this obligation is binding upon everyone in his dealings with every other human being. Three or four world-religions proclaim their truths to all mankind. Modern morality likewise no longer recognizes the ancient limitation that its norms order the relations of those only that belong to the same people. The question is, what is the meaning of all this?

The religions, to begin with, both in their doctrines and in their ritual norms, appeal only to those that profess the faith. The fact that they proclaim themselves world-religions means simply that their doors are open to everyone that accepts their truths. In this respect they differ from the religions of antiquity, which were limited to their respective peoples, but this difference lies in a different sphere.

As to modern ethics, however, the situation is quite different, irrespective of whether its basis is religious or philosophical. Its object is to impose the moral commandment upon all men and to make it binding upon them in their dealings with every being that bears a human countenance. It must be emphatically denied, however, that this has ever amounted to more than a preachment or a teaching, that this morality has in fact become a rule of conduct for the great masses of mankind. Even today commandments of morality are actually being obeyed with any degree of exactness only in the intimate circle of the family, at most among friends. Outside this circle the effectiveness of the moral command decreases steadily; and as to the stranger, the average man recognizes no teaching of morality which obligates him to do anything more than to extend courtesies which require no effort; and hatred of the enemy of one's country is considered as praiseworthy today as it was in the most remote antiquity. A glance at the atrocities occasionally perpetrated in the colonies of this or that great power shows the depths to which the morality of modern man may sink where there are no associational bonds; and these atrocities are only a small fraction of the atrocities which the nationals of the most highly civilized nations of the earth believe they have a right to perpetrate upon defenseless natives.

It is true there is a series of legal norms that are valid in favor

一个义务;这一义务拘束他和任何其他人之间的交往。三个或者四个世界性宗教宣称他们的真理对全人类有效。现代人的道德也不再承认道德规范仅仅调整属于同一民族人的关系这一古代限制。问题是,所有这一切的意义是什么?

首先,宗教在宗教教义上和仪式规范上都仅仅对那些表示信仰的人有吸引力。它们宣称自己是世界性宗教的事实仅仅意味着它们的大门向所有接收它们的真理的人敞开着。在这一方面,它们不同于古代的宗教,古代的宗教仅限于它们各自的民族。但是这种差异仅存在于一个不同的范围。

但是,至于现代的道德规范,不管它的基础是宗教性的还是哲学性的,情形就完全不同了。现代的道德规范的目标是把道德戒律强加给所有的人,并拘束每一个拥有人类面庞的人之间的交往行为。但是,我们可以断然否认以下说法:道德戒律曾经不仅仅是一种说教或者教导,这种道德事实上已经变为了大多数人的行为准则。甚至今天,在任何非常精确的程度上,道德戒律实际上仅在家庭的亲密圈子内被遵守,至多在朋友中间被遵守。在这一范围外,道德戒律的效力稳步下降;至于陌生人,普通人除了承认要求陌生人给予不费任何力气就可以做到的礼貌外,不承认要求他去做任何事情的、任何其他的道德教导。如在远古时代一样,仇恨一个国家的敌人如今还被认为是值得称道的。回顾一下这个或者那个强权在殖民地不时犯下的暴行,就会明白,在没有联合体约束的地方,现代人的道德会下降到的程度;而且这些暴行仅仅是地球上最文明国家的国民相信他们有权对毫无防备的土著居民犯下的暴行的一小部分。

的确,存在一系列有效的法律规范,它们既对任何人有利,同

of everyone and bind everyone. But these are either a part of the law created by the state or they are but norms for decision, not rules of conduct. Even the so-called private international law and criminal law contain only norms for decision, are addressed to the authorities and not to the people. The living law, even where it is created by the state, is preponderantly, as to its content, limited to an association. The rights and duties arising from *Staatsrecht* (public law in the narrow sense) presuppose the right of citizenship in the state; the law of the family presupposes membership in the family; the law of corporations presupposes membership in the corporation; the law of contract presupposes a contract; the law of inheritance presupposes membership in the family or the acceptance of a testamentary gift (of which the mere non-repudiation, according to some laws, is an equivalent). Other rights and duties arise from the position of an official, of a servant of the state. It is only as to the claim to life, liberty, and property that a different rule obtains at the present time; for this claim is being recognized, at least within the territory in which European civilization holds undisputed sway, as a valid claim of everyone, irrespective of nationality. This is a relatively modern achievement. As late as the sixteenth century, the life and the property of the alien were by no means secure in Europe. Even today it is not an indispensable element of civilization, as is shown by the history of colonies everywhere and by the fate of the Negroes in America. The anti-slavery legislation of the nineteenth century shows how difficult it was to instil into the most highly civilized nations of the earth respect for the life and the liberty of the defenseless Negro. But with these temporal and local limitations, respect for the life, the liberty, and the property of every man is today not merely a norm for decision and a policy of the state, but has actually become a principle of the living law. To this modest extent, the whole human race has already become a vast legal association. This cannot be said, however, of other legal relations, especially of the law of contract. The uncertainty of credit relations in far distant countries—a standing phrase in trade reports—bears eloquent witness to this fact.

时也拘束着任何人。不过,这些法律规范或者是国家所创制之法律的一部分,或者仅仅是裁判规范,不是行为规范。即使所谓的国际私法和刑法也仅仅包含裁判规范,它们也仅仅向当局发布而不是向人民发布。甚至在国家创立法律的地方,活法就其内容而言,也主要限于一个联合体内。产生自 *Staatsrecht*(狭义上的公法)的权利和义务以国家中公民权的存在为前提;家庭法以家庭中成员身份为前提;公司法以公司中的成员身份为前提;契约法以契约为前提;继承法以家庭成员身份或者接受了遗嘱馈赠(按照某些法律,仅仅对遗嘱馈赠不加拒绝,也视为接受)为前提。其他的权利和义务产生自官员的职位、国家公务员的职位。目前,仅仅有关对生命、自由和财产的请求权,还在适用不同的规则。因为至少在欧洲文明无可置辩的影响范围内,这一请求权被认可为每个人的合法请求权,而不考虑他的国籍。这是一个相对现代的成就。迟至 16 世纪,外国侨民的生命和财产权在欧洲也绝没有获得保障。甚至在今天,这也不是文明不可或缺的一个因素,如同任何地方的殖民地历史和美洲黑人的命运所揭示的那样。19 世纪反对奴隶制的立法表明,向地球上最高文明程度的国家灌输尊敬毫无抵抗力的黑人的生命和财产权利这样的观念是多么的困难。但是,尽管有这些临时的和地域的局限,但是,如今,尊敬每个人的生命、自由和财产已经不仅仅是一项裁判规范和国家政策,而且实际上也已经成了活法的一项基本原则。在此适当的程度上,整个的人类群体早已变成了一个巨大的法律联合体。然而,这并不适用于其他法律关系,特别是契约法律关系。遥远的国家中信用关系的不确定性——国际贸易报告中一个固定不变的措辞——雄辩地证明了这一事实。

Nevertheless the fact remains that at the present time there is in existence a religious and philosophical system of ethics which does not limit its morality to an individual human association. This fact requires explanation. Its import is that, at least among the select spirits of the world, there exists a conception of a morality which embraces all men, a conception of law not confined within any boundaries. Although it is at the present time nothing more than a dream of the noblest and best which promises a better future, it has been realized in the living law to the extent of securing, in the seats of the highest civilization, life, liberty, and property to every man.

尽管如此,但目前如下事实仍然保持未变:存在一个宗教性和哲学性的伦理体系,它并未将其道德限于单个的人类联合体。此事实需要解释。它的意义在于,至少在世界的精英人群中,存在着一种包容所有人的道德观念,存在着一种不受任何边界限制的法律观念。虽然,它目前只不过是一个预示更好未来的、最崇高和最美好的梦想,但是,在人类最高文明之所在,它已经在——确保每个人的生命、自由和财产——这样范围内的活法中实现。

# V

# The Facts Of The Law

The modern jurist is accustomed to seeing a world ruled by law and legal coercion. To this world, which is his world, he owes his *Weltanschauung* (world-view, philosophy of life), which assumes that law and legal coercion have been in existence from the beginning of time. He cannot conceive of human communal life without them. A family that is not held together, or at least supervised, by the constituted authorities, property that is not protected by the courts, a contract that cannot be sued upon, or that may not, to say the least, be set up as a defense, an inheritance that cannot be obtained by legal means, are to him things that are altogether outside of the legal sphere, that are without legal significance. In this way, legal order, court, and legal sanction become a unit in his mode of thinking, and he will unhesitantingly speak of law or legal relation only where he finds a court and legal coercion, or perhaps an administrative tribunal and administrative coercion.

In this narrow world of ideas the purely juristic concept of the sources of law had its origin. Manifestly it could only be a matter of explaining the origin of the rules according to which legal coercion is being exercised by courts and administrative tribunals. Following this path, the prevailing juristic science arrived at the well known theory of the two sources—a theory which derives all law from statute or custom. It is manifestly based on the precepts of the *corpus iuris civilis* and of the *corpus iuris canonici*, which recognize only the *leges* and, in addition thereto, *consuetudo* as sources of law. Its epistemological basis might well be the logical theorem of the excluded middle. Since all law which is not statute law must needs be customary law, the

# 第五章　法律事实

现代法学家习惯透过法律和法律强制来理解世界。对于这个他自己的世界，他拥有自己的*Weltanschauung*（世界观、生活哲学），这种世界观认为法律和法律强制从一开始就存在。他无法设想没有法律和法律强制的人类共同生活。不是由合法当局主持下——或至少在其监督下——团结在一起的家庭、不受法院保护的财产、不能据以起诉——或至少说不可构成抗辩——的契约以及不能通过法律手段获得的遗产，这些对于法学家来说，完全超出了法律范围，它们也不具有任何法律意义。这样，法律秩序、法院和法律制裁变成了他的思维模式中的一个单元，只有当他发现了法院和法律强制，或者，或许当他发现一个行政裁决机构和行政强制时，他才会毫不迟疑地谈及法律或者法律关系。

在此狭隘的观念世界里，法源的纯粹法学观念从中产生。显然，它只可能是对法院或者行政裁决机构据以实施法律强制之规则效力来源的解释。循此路径，主流法学得出了众所周知的有关法源的二源论——所有的法律都来源于制定法或者习惯。显然，它基于《民法大全》和《教会法大全》，它们仅承认法律和除此之外的习惯法是法律的渊源。它的认识论基础很可能是排中律。既然所有非制定法的法律，必然应当是习惯法，则习惯法的观念问

question as to the concept of customary law resolves itself into the question: What must be the nature of law that is not statute law? We are not told why there can be no sources of law other than statute and customary law. No suggestion is being made that a scientific inquiry into the nature of law should be instituted. Whatsoever is said about customary law moves within a circle of commonplaces. In the last analysis the Romans proceeded in a much more scientific manner inasmuch as they were content with simply enumerating the six or eight methods according to which, in their system of law, legal rules that were binding on the judge arose. Nevertheless not one of the attempts to add as much as a third source to the two that have been recognized until now has met with success, i. e. the addition of science or judicial usage or the rule established by agreement or customary dealings between the parties (*Konventionalregel*) or, as has been attempted by writers on commercial law, commercial usage (*usance*).

The saddest part of the matter perhaps is the fact that those who are struggling with the concepts of statute and customary law are not looking for the difficulty in the quarter in which it may be found. In the matter of the sources of law, it is not a question of how the rules of law which the judge or the administrative official must apply assume the form in which they are binding on him. The law does not consist of legal propositions, but of legal institutions. In order to be able to state the sources of law one must be able to tell how the state, the church, the commune, the family, the contract, and inheritance came into being, how they change and develop. The function of a theory of the sources of law is to discover the vital forces that bring about the development of legal institutions. It is not sufficient to state the forms in which legal propositions, or, to be more exact, legal propositions of a certain kind, are to be found. Law and legal relation is a matter of intellectual concept which does not exist in the sphere of tangible reality, but in the minds of men. There would be no law if there were not men who bear the concept of law in their consciousness. But here, as everywhere else, our concepts are fashioned from the material which we take from tangible reality.

题本身也归结为如下问题:非制定法的法律其性质必定是什么?没有人告诉我们,为什么除了制定法和习惯法外就不存在任何其他法源?没有人提议应当着手对法律的性质进行科学的探究。任何关于习惯法的论述都没于超出老生常谈的范围。归根到底,罗马人以一种更为科学的方法展开了研究,因为他们满足于简单地列举他们法律制度中的六种或者八种在他们的法律制度中约束法官的法律规则产生的方法。然而,直到现在,没有一个企图向已获承认的两种法源中增加第三种法源的尝试取得成功;这些被尝试加入的第三种法源包括:科学或者司法惯例;当事人间通过协议或者通行的交易建立起来的规则(*Konventionalregel*);或者商法的著述者曾经尝试增加的商业惯例(*usance*)。

事情最令人痛心的一方面或许是这一事实:那些与制定法和习惯法观念作斗争的人并没有在本来可以发现困难的地方寻找困难。在法源这一问题上,它并不是法官或者行政官员必须适用的法律规则应采取何种形式来约束法官或者行政官员的问题。法律并不是由法律命题组成,而是由法律制度组成。为了能够说明法源,人们应当能说出国家、教堂、公社、家庭、契约和继承是怎么形成的,它们又是如何变化和发展的。法源理论的功能是揭示促使法律制度发展的核心性力量。仅仅说明法律命题——或者更确切地说,某种法律命题——的发现形式是不够的。法律和法律关系是一种并非存在于有形现实的领域内、而仅存在于人之思想中的智识。如果不存在意识中有法律观念的人,那么就不存在法律。但是此处,如同在任何别处一样,我们的观念形塑于我们取自有形现实的素材。它们总是以我们可以观察到的事实为

They are always based on facts which we have observed. These facts must have been in existence before the concept of law and legal relation began to dawn in the human brain. And at the present time certain facts at least must be in existence before we can speak of law and legal relation. It is here that we must look for the workshop of the law. The first question of juristic science, the question as to the origin of law, accordingly becomes the question: Which are the factual institutions that become legal relations in the course of legal development, and which are the social processes through which this comes about?

A group of human beings becomes an association through organization. Organization is the rule which assigns to each individual his position and his functions. We are chiefly concerned therefore with determining the facts with which the human mind associates such rules. These facts, though apparently very heterogeneous, may be traced back to a very small number. They are—if we may be permitted to state the results of our inquiry in advance—the following: usage, domination, possession, declaration of will.

Usage here does not mean "customary law." We are not speaking of the customary application of legal propositions. Usage here means: The custom of the past shall be the norm for the future. Usage determines the position of the head as well as of the members of the association, the relation of superiority and of inferiority, and the functions of each individual member. Usage creates the order of all genetic associations: of the clan, the family, the household. In the family and in the home this is true perhaps even up to the present time. In a primitive stage, usage is still essentially normative in all local associations and in the state. But even in a highly developed commonwealth, like the Roman republic or present-day Great Britain, the constitutional law position of the organs of the state rests on usage. As to Rome, one

基础。这些事实在人们的大脑开始形成法律和法律关系的观念以前就必定已经存在。而且目前,特定的法律事实肯定至少在我们谈论法律和法律关系以前就已经存在了。我们必须在此寻觅生产、加工法律的车间。法学的第一个问题——关于法源的问题,因而变成了另一个问题:在法律的发展过程中,哪些事实上的制度变成了法律关系,这一转变通过哪些社会步骤得以发生?

一个人类群体通过组织构造而变成了一个联合体。组织构造是为每个个人分配位置和职能的规则。因此,我们主要关注确定那些人类的心智将那些规则与其相连的事实。这些事实尽管明显种类各异,但我们还是可以追溯到数量很少的一部分事实。它们是——如果允许我们提前说明我们的调查结果——如下一些:习惯、支配、占有和意思表示。

习惯在这里的意思并不是指“习惯法”。我们并不是指法律命题的习惯性应用。此处的习惯意指:过去的惯例可以成为未来的规范。习惯决定着联合体首领和联合体成员间的地位、地位优越者和地位低微者的关系以及联合体中每一个成员的角色。习惯创造了每一个原生性联合体的秩序:氏族的秩序、家族的秩序和家庭的秩序。甚至或许直到今天,在家族和家庭中也是如此。在原始时期,习惯实质上仍然在所有的地方性联合体和在国家中具有规范性。但是,即便是在高度发达的共和国中,像罗马共和国或今天的大不列颠,国家机构的宪法地位仍基于习惯之上。关于罗马,为了确信这一陈述的真实性,一个人只需要通

need only page through Mommsen's "*Römisches Staatsrecht*" in order to convince oneself of the truth of this statement. The small number of Roman statutes that have a public law (*staatsrechtlich*) content refer exclusively to the *comitia*. Moreover down to the days of the Empire even Mommsen knows of no other means whereby to determine the rights and duties of a Roman magistrate than to state what his duties were according to traditional usage, and what he actually did do. And in order to make a presentation of British public law, one must proceed in the same way. The King, the Parliament, the ministers, the highest officials, all the organs of the state, regulate their course of conduct chiefly according to usage, or, in English terminology, according to precedents. The dominant associations of antiquity and of the Middle Ages likewise maintained their order through usage.

The majority of present-day associations have an order which is based on agreement, articles of association, legal proposition, and constitution. Nevertheless even in these, usage has by no means lost all significance. Wherever agreement, articles of association, legal proposition, or constitution has left a doubt or has failed to make provision as to the position and duties of an individual, usage governs. Even in a constitutional state, therefore, usage is of the utmost importance (*Konventionalregel*); and in labor unions (in the factory) it is the indispensable basis of associational life.

Usage, to use Jellinek's phrase, is effective through the "nor-

读蒙森[1]的《罗马国家法》[2]即可。包含有公法内容(*staatsrechtlich*)的少量的罗马制定法完全是指民众会议。[3] 而且下至罗马帝国时期,甚至连蒙森,除了说罗马地方官员的职责取决于传统习惯以及说明他实际是如何做的之外,对于确定罗马地方官权利和义务的其他方式也是一无所知。同样,为了叙述英格兰的公法,一个人必须采取同样的方式。国王、议会、大臣,高级官员和所有的国家机关主要是依据习惯来调控他们的一系列行为,或者用英格兰的术语来说,依据先例。在古代和中世纪居于支配地位的联合体同样通过习惯来维持它们的秩序。

今天,大多数联合体都有一种以协议、联合体章程、法律命题和宪法为基础的秩序。然而即便在这些联合体中,习惯也绝不会失去所有的意义。无论在什么情况下,只要协议、联合体章程、法律命题或者宪法留有疑问或者未能对个体的地位和职责作出规定,习惯就会起作用。因此,即便在一个宪政国家,习惯(*Konventionalregel*)也至关重要;并且,在(工厂里的)工会中,它还是联合体生活不可或缺的基础。

用耶里内克的话说,习惯通过"实际的规范性力量"起作用。

---

〔1〕 Mommsen(1817 ~ 1903),蒙森,德国历史学家、古典学家,曾获1902年诺贝尔文学奖。

〔2〕 罗马公法(狭义上的)。

〔3〕 (拉)*Comitia*(民众会议),全体罗马市民都有资格参加的议会。会议的主要内容是审议法律议案、选举执法官和履行某些审判职能。民众会议一般由一位有权代表民众行事的执法官主持。召集之前应当发布告示,公布准备审议的法律草案的内容、候选人名单或者作为审判对象的被指控者的姓名。会议必须选在吉日举行。

mative power of the factual." Its ordering and regulative power in the association is based on the fact that it reflects the equilibration of the forces existing within the association. The interest which all members have in the associational life, their interest in the proper utilization of every force which is operative in the association, in placing every one of its members where he can render most service, in assigning to him rights and duties according to the needs of the whole, are counterbalanced by the aspirations of the individual to live his own life, to assert his own personality, to pursue his own interests. Usage always reflects the final equilibration of the forces. In general, a usage which produces norms for the future arises when a person who has been placed in a certain position claims a certain right without encountering opposition; when a person to whom a task has been assigned undertakes its performance without a protest; or when a protest that has arisen is overcome. In genetic associations, the decisive factors are physical strength, mental power, experience, personal prestige, age. In other associations they are wealth, birth, personal relations. The rights and duties connected by usage with a certain position usually pass from the holder to his successor; but if the distribution of power is changed by the successsion, usage at once adapts itself to the changed situation.

The only association whose order, even today, depends chiefly upon usage is the house community of the family, not only as a moral and social, but also as an economic association. Among the peasantry it is an association for the purpose of production and consumption; among the urban middle classes, for consumption only; among a part of the working classes, almost exclusively for dwelling together. There is a great difference, economically, between the middle-class family and the working-class family, even where the latter is also an association for consumption; for the former is usually maintained exclusively by the earnings of the head of the family, while the latter is maintained by the earnings of all the able-bodied members of the family. A

习惯在联合体中的规整和调节力量是基于这一事实:习惯反映联合体中现有力量的平衡。联合体中所有成员在联合体生活中的利益、他们适当运用联合体内起作用的每一种力量的过程中的利益、他们在安置每一个联合体成员至其能提供最佳服务之位置过程中的利益,在按照整体需要分配给他权利和义务过程中的利益,这些利益与个人对自己生活的热情、对自己个性的坚持、对自己利益的追求构成了一种平衡。习惯总是反映了各种力量的最终平衡。一般而言,下列情况下为未来制定规范的习惯就产生了:当处于特定地位的人要求一种特定的权利而未遇到反对时;当被分配了一项任务的人毫无异议地开始履行义务时;或者当一项提出的反对被压服时。在原生性联合体中,决定性的因素是体力、精神力量、经验、个人的威望和年龄。在其他联合体中,决定性因素是财富、出身和个人关系。通过习惯与特定职位相关联的权利和义务,通常由现在的持有者传给他的继任者;但是,如果通过继任,权利的分配发生了改变,习惯马上会使自己适应改变后的情形。

其秩序甚至在今天仍然主要依靠习惯的唯一的联合体,是家庭的居住共同体,它不仅作为一个道德和社会的联合体,而且还作为一个经济联合体。在农民中间,这是一个为了生产和消费的目的而建立的联合体;在城市的中产阶级当中,这一团体的目的仅是消费;在部分的工人阶级中,这一团体几乎完全是为了居住在一起。经济上,在中产阶层的家庭和工人阶级的家庭之间存在着巨大的差异,甚至纯消费的工人阶级家庭中也是如此。中产阶级家庭通常完全由一家之主的收入来维持,而一般的工人阶级家庭由有劳动能力的所有成员的收入来维持。简单观察一下这三种

glance at these three kinds of families shows that each one of them has its own law not merely as to personal subordination but also as to property and earnings, and that the contents of the documents that are drawn up concerning family affairs (nuptial agreements, wills) differ to such an extent according to the station of the maker that it is possible without more ado to determine the station of the latter from the documents. The absolute supremacy of the peasant within his household becomes a mere general guidance among the middle classes, and among the working classes it is attenuated to what amounts, at most, to a moral influence. Among the peasantry, property and consumption is in common; among the middle classes there is individual ownership of property, but consumption is in common; among the working classes everything is separate; each member of the family owns his share and contributes his quota to defray the common expenses. Similarly in all other associations the content of usage and the order which is created thereby is determined by the economic bases of the associational life.

A careful distinction must be observed between the relation of superiority and inferiority, which exists in every organized association, and which is the expression of the inner order of the association, and the relation of domination and subjection. A command issued by a person occupying a position of superiority in an organized association is quite different from a command issued by a person who has the power of domination. The former is issued in behalf of the association, the latter in behalf of the person who issues it. A person who is in a position of superiority as well as a person who is in a position of inferiority acts in the consciousness of serving the association, but a person who is in a relation of subjection to another is conscious primarily of serving the person to whom he is subjected, and only occasionally of serving the association at the same time. The association remains unitary in spite of the relation of superiority and inferiority, which is necessarily produced by its organization; but relations of domination and subjection divide it into ruler and ruled. In an association thus organized, the rulers and often the ruled, too, from associations of their own, or associations within the association.

类型的家庭，就会发现每一个家庭都有自己的法律，这些不仅仅涉及个人的从属关系，而且也涉及财产和收入的法律；还会发现，起草的关于家庭事务（婚姻协议、遗嘱）文件的内容也因起草者的身份的不同而有很大的不同，以至于依据所起草内容无需多费周折就可能确定文件起草者的身份。农民在他的家庭中的绝对至高无上的地位在中产阶级中成了一种一般性的指引，这种地位在工人阶级中被削弱到至多是一种道德影响的程度。在农民中，财产和消费是共同的；在中产阶级中存在着个人财产的所有权，但消费是共同的；在工人阶级中，所有的一切都是分开的；家庭中的每一个成员都有自己的那一份财产，并且拿出一部分收入用于共同开支。同样，在所有其他联合体中，共同生活的经济基础决定着习惯的内容和由习惯所创造的秩序。

上下级关系中的一种精细的区分必定被遵循，这种区分存在于每一个有组织的联合体中，它是联合体内部秩序以及支配与服从关系的一种表述。在一有组织的联合体中，位居上级的人发布的命令与有支配权的人发布的命令大不相同。前一种命令的颁布代表了联合体的利益，后一种命令的颁布代表了颁布者的利益。位居上级的人和位居下级的人都有意识地为联合体服务，但是居于服从地位者主要是有意识地为他的支配者服务，并且仅仅偶尔同时也为联合体服务。尽管联合体中的组织结构中必然会产生上级和下级关系，但是联合体仍然是一个整体；然而，支配和被支配的关系将联合体分成了统治者和被统治者。在如此组织的联合体中，统治者——被统治者经常也——组成他们自己的联合体或者组成处于这一联合中的联合体。

We must distinguish two kinds of relations of domination and subjection, to wit those relations that flow from the family relationship—the subjection of children to the power of the father, of the wife to that of the husband—and relations of subjection of a purely social origin, slavery and serfdom. The idea presents itself most naturally to refer to legal precepts all the manifold and variously gradated relationships of domination and subjection, which are found in all stages of social development, down to the very latest, down to that which has been attained only by the most advanced nations of Europe and America. In fact the prevailing idea is that it is the legal proposition which subjects the wife to the husband, the children to the father, the ward to the guardian, the slave and the serf to the master. But the relations of domination and subjection were actually in existence everywhere before there was a legal proposition which regulated them as constituent parts of the legal order. Domination in every instance is merely the counterpart of the defenselessness and helplessness of the person subjected. The latter is subjected to domination because he enjoys no legal protection (*Rechtsschutz*); and he receives no protection because he is not a member of an association which might protect him, or because the association to which he belongs is too weak to protect him.

The situation of the slave and of the serf, and perhaps that of the guest and of the ward, it is true, is seemingly quite different from that of the women and the children. The former do not belong to the association of the rulers, but are strangers who have come within their sphere of power. Women and children however are members of the same association as the rulers. Recent study of the relation of the sexes and of the various groups of people of the same age in the most ancient society has shown that in primitive society the two sexes and the several groups of people of the same age everywhere form separate associations. To a certain extent this is true even at the present time. Even today we see women and men combining in groups for the protection of their separate interests, and even today there are traces of opposition between the groups of people of the same age. The latter is a common phenomenon in secondary schools, likewise between

我们必须区分两种类型的支配和服从关系,即,那些产生自家庭关系——孩子对父亲权力的服从、妻子对丈夫权力的服从——和那种纯粹具有社会根源的支配关系,如奴隶和农奴。这种观念的提出,最自然地涉及到那些千丝万缕、种类多样、逐渐显示出层次的支配与服从关系的法律规定,这些关系在社会发展的每一个阶段,下至最近的这一阶段,甚至直到最为发达的欧洲和美洲民族所达到的阶段都能发现。事实上,流行的观点是:法律命题使得妻子服从丈夫、孩子服从父亲、被监护人服从监护人、奴隶和农奴服从他的主人。但是,在法律命题把它们作为法律秩序的构成部分进行规范以前,这种支配和服从关系就已经存在了。支配在每一个场合中仅仅是被支配者的无保护状态和无助状态的对应物。后者服从于支配是因为他并不享有法律上的保护(*Rechtsschutz*);而且,他没有受到保护是因为他不是可以保护他的联合体中的一员,或者是因为他所归属的联合体太弱小而无法保护他。

事实上,奴隶和农奴的情形——或许还有客人和被监护者情形——看上去非常不同于妇女和孩子的情形。前者不属于支配者的联合体,而是进入支配者权力范围的陌生人。但是妇女和孩子与支配者一样是同一联合体的成员。对最远古社会中的两性关系和同一年龄人多个群体的最新研究证明,原始社会中在任何地方两性和同一年龄人群体都形成了各自独立的联合体。即使在当前,一定程度上,这也是真实的。甚至在今天,我们也可以看到男人们和女人们为了保护他们独立的利益在群体中联合起来;甚至在今天,同龄人的群体相互反对的痕迹依然存在。后者在中学里是常见现象,同样,这种现象也存在于商业中的熟练工人和

journeymen and apprentices in a trade. Both surely are survivals of stages of development which have long since had their day rather than the beginning of a new development.

In the most ancient societies an association is formed at the outset by the efficient (*vollwertig*) members, who in case of need would be able to repel an attack single-handed and who could extend to others the same measure of assistance that they ask of the latter. The woman, the child, the youth who as yet is unable to bear arms, cannot do this, for they, by themselves, cannot form an association capable of self-defense. The stranger living in isolation cannot do this, for he has no association to take his part; the member of a vanquished tribe or nation cannot do it, for the community of which he is a member has just been crushed; the poor oppressed man cannot do it in unsettled times, for the protection which the association to which he belongs might possibly extend to him is ineffectual against the arbitrary dealings of the powerful. All of these, the woman, the child, the stranger, the vanquished, therefore are subjected to the domination of the man who is inclined to protect them, i. e. the husband, the father, the guest-friend, the victor. Every other person who lacks confidence in his own strength voluntarily places himself under the protection of another. If the defenseless one fails to find a protector, he becomes the prey of anyone who seizes him and spares his life; he becomes a slave of the latter. The weak person who has a master is no longer defenseless, for every attack upon him is now an attack on the master. ①

But all of these protective relationships presuppose that the protected is in position to offer some advantage to the protector. The

---

① An Austrian naval officer who is familiar with conditions in Africa told me one day that he ascribed Stanley's successes mostly to the agreements which the latter made with his black carriers. Other African explorers were in the habit of hiring carriers for short stretches only, for the territory occupied by the tribe to which they belonged, of dismissing them when they came to the border, and of looking there for other carriers at the same terms. Stanley, however, hired them at the coast for the entire journey Now an African negro, when outside of the confines of the territory of his tribe, is usually in the position of an outlaw. As soon as Stanley, therefore, had entered foreign territory, the caravan was the only protection the carriers had. They were absolutely in his power and at his discretion. He was their protector, and therefore their absolute lord and master. —*Author's note*.

学徒中。但是,二者确实都是很久以前兴盛发展阶段的残余,而不是新发展的开端。

在最远古社会中,开始时联合体由最能干(*vollwertig*)的成员组织,这些成员能够在需要的时候单独徒手击退一次进攻,而且能够在其余成员要求帮助时为他们提供同样程度的帮助。妇女、孩子和那些到那时为止还不能携带武器的青年不能这样做,因为他们自己不能组成能够自卫的联合体。那些孤立生活的陌生人也不能这样做,因为他没有联合体可以加入;那些被征服的部落和民族的成员也不能这样做,因为他所属的社区已经被摧毁了;在动荡时期贫穷的被压迫者也不能这样做,因为他归属的联合体可以给他提供的保护对于强权者的独裁行为是无效的。因此,所有的这些人——妇女、孩子、陌生人、被征服者都服从倾向于保护他们的人,也就是丈夫、父亲、宾客之友和胜利者。其余对自己的力量缺乏自信的每个人都自愿地将自己置于他人保护之下。如果缺乏防卫力的人没能够找到一个保护者,他变成了任何一个可以捕获他并自由处置他生命的人的猎物;他变成了捕获者的 个奴隶。一个拥有主人的弱者不再是一个没有防卫力的人,因为现在每一个对他的攻击都是对他主人的攻击。①

但是,所有的这些保护关系都以被保护者能够为保护者提供

① 有一天,一个熟悉非洲情况的奥地利海军军官告诉我,史坦利的成功主要归功于他与黑奴贩运者之间的协议。其他的非洲探险家有仅仅为穿越贩运者所属部落占领的领土而短暂地雇佣贩运者的习惯。当他们通过边界后,他们就遣散这些贩运者并以同样的条件寻找新的贩运者。然而,史坦利在海岸边整个旅程都雇佣了他们。当一个非洲黑人处在他所属部落领土范围以外的时候,他通常处在完全不受法律保护的状态。因此,一旦史坦利进入外国的领土,旅行队是这些运输者唯一的保护。运输者完全处在史坦利的权力和判断的支配之下。因此,史坦利是他们的保护者,也是他们的绝对的主人。

relationship of ruler and ruled exists for the benefit of the ruler and not of the ruled. A man who with the utmost exertion can produce no more than he himself requires for a bare existence, as for instance a very poor hunter or shepherd, has no lord and master. The lord would derive no benefit from his lordship. A captured enemy therefore is not reduced to slavery, but is slaughtered, or in exceptional cases, received into the conquering tribe. Only the woman is of value even at this stage of development, for she is the object not only of economic, but also of sexual exploitation. For this reason her life is spared, and she is compelled to do work which the man disdains either because he deems it beneath his dignity, or because it requires too much exertion.

Defenselessness alone cannot serve as the basis of a legal relation. It abandons the defenseless person like an ownerless chattel or beast to him who reduces him to possession, but it does not give him an owner. It does not give anyone a right in him. Domination however is more than mere possession of a person and exploitation of his labor, for it is a legally regulated relation between the person who has the power and the person who is subjected to the latter. The fact of personal subjection is based on the economic productivity of his labor, but it becomes a part of the legal order only in a case where the labor of the subjugated person is of decisive significance for the economic order of society. The unfree person may be a laborer on a farm or a groom of the chamber at the court of a king; he may, together with thousands of fellow-sufferers, toil on plantations or in mines; he may together with his wife and children live in a cottage on the land of his lord as a tenant-farmer paying rent to the latter, or he may till the soil on his own account as a serf for a moderate return on the plot of ground allotted to him; he may become a teacher or a manager

一些利益为前提。支配和被支配关系是为了支配者的利益而不是为了被支配者的利益而存在。一个尽自己最大努力都仅能生产出只够维持自己生存所需物品的人——比如一个非常贫穷的猎人或者牧羊者——是没有支配者和主人的。领主不能从他的支配中获得利益。因此，一个被捕获的敌人没有被转化为奴隶，而是被屠杀，或者在极为特殊的情形下，被接受为征服者部落的一员。只有女人才有价值，甚至在发达阶段也一样，因为她不仅是经济剥削的对象，而且也是性盘剥的对象。因为这一原因，她的生命获得宽宥，而且她被迫去从事那些男人鄙视的工作——因为男人认为这些有辱尊严或者需要付出艰辛劳动。

毫无防御能力的状态不能单独被视为法律关系的基础。这种状态使一个毫无防备能力的人沉溺于一种——对于占有他的人来说——像无主动产或者动物一样的状态，但是这种状态并不能为他带来一个所有者。这种状态却是给了任何人一种针对他的权利。然而，支配绝不仅仅是对一个人的占有和对他的劳动的剥削，因为它是拥有权力者和服从权力者之间的一种法律上的规范关系。一个人受支配的事实是以他劳动的经济生产率为基础，但是只有在受支配者的劳动对社会的经济秩序具有决定性意义的情况下，这个受支配的事实才能变为法律秩序的一部分。这个不自由的人可能是农场里的一个劳动者或者国王宫廷内庭来的一个马夫；他可能和上千受苦的同伴一起在种植园或者矿场辛勤工作；他可能作为一个向他的领主支付地租的租种土地的农民和他的妻子儿女一起居住在属于他的领主土地上的一个小村庄里，或者他可能作为农奴在分配给他的小块土地上为了自己能获得一个适度的回报耕作着；或者在为他的领主服务中，他可能变成

in the service of his lord or he may render knight's service to the latter or he may engage independently in a trade or a business in the city. Whether he is one or the other of these is determined not by the arbitrary will of the master, but by the economic constitution of the country as a whole and by the qualities of the human beings that constitute the mass of the unfree population. Doubtless it was impossible in the days of the early Roman Empire to conduct an agricultural establishment on the basis of a system of villeinage; likewise it was impossible in mediaeval Germany to raise cane sugar and tobacco on plantations. The legal position of the unfree man depends upon his position in the economic system. The farm-hand, the slave on the plantation, the groom of the chamber, the tenant-farmer, the villein, the man rendering knight's service, the civil official, the tradesman, are in totally different situations as unfree persons, in fact as well as in law. In Roman slavery this fact did not meet the eye except to a very limited extent. This however is due to the fact that the Roman jurists, who concern themselves only with the law that is applied by law courts, tell us nothing of the inner order of the household. A presentation of the Roman law of slavery which is not limited to the legal sources but which takes into account inscriptions and documents would most emphatically set forth the differences in the legal relations, of which the legal sources merely give slight intimations. A legal system which is less enamored of abstractions than is the Roman will give outward form and expression to the differences in the legal situations of the unfree as determined by their economic functions. Accordingly from the very beginning of the Middle Ages the several types of serfdom of the Continental law have corresponded to differences in the economic constitution. The two later types, *Grundherrschaft* and *Gutsherrschaft*, correspond to differences in economic management

教师或者管理者,或者他为领主提供骑士[1]的服务,或者他可能在城市中独立地从事贸易或者买卖。上述工作他从事哪一项,不是由其主人的专断意愿所决定,而是由这个国家的整体经济制度和组成这个国家的大多数非自由人口的素质决定。毫无疑问,在罗马帝国早期的岁月中,以农奴制为基础管理农业机构是不可能的;同样地,在中世纪的德国,以农奴制为基础那样在大种植园里种植蔗糖和烟草也是不可能的。非自由人的法律地位依赖于他们在经济体制中的地位。农场工人、种植园中的奴隶、宫廷里的马夫、租种土地的农民、农奴、提供骑士服务的人、政府官员、商人作为非自由人在事实上和法律上都是完全不同的境况。在罗马奴隶制下,除了在一个非常有限的范围内,这一事实并没有呈现在眼前。但是,这是由于那些仅关心法院所适用法律的罗马法学家没有告诉我们家庭内部秩序的缘故。对奴隶制罗马法的介绍,若不局限于法律的原始文献,同时也考虑到各种批注和文件,则将会最为显著地表达出——法律渊源仅仅给予过最少暗示的——法律关系中的不同。一个不像罗马法那样倾心于抽象概念的法律制度,将会对非自由民的法律境况中的差异给出外在的形式和表达,而他们的法律境况是由他们的经济功能所决定的。因此,从中世纪开始的那一刻起,大陆法系的几种不同类型的农奴身份就适应了经济制度的不同。后来的两种类型封建领主所有制和地主所有制[2]对应于对非自由人经济管理和

---

〔1〕 *Ritterlicher Ministeriale*,最初是指不自由的随侍。

〔2〕 在 *Grundherrschaft*(封建领主所有制)中,非自由人被降格为隶农;在 *Gutsherrschaft*(地主所有制)中,非自由人以租赁的形式拥有他们自己的土地,并承担特定的劳役义务。

as well as in legal treatment of the unfree. In my book entitled *Rechtsfähigkeit* (in Franz Kobler's collection entitled "*Das Recht*"), I have shown in detail that the legal capacity of the individual and his position in the economic order are always interrelated.

Perhaps originally all domination, viewed as a legal institution, was a property interest in the person subjected to domination. Serfdom undoubtedly began with man-stealing; marriage, possibly, with woman-stealing; and the parental power is possibly based on the possession of the children as long as they are quite small. But domination can be permanently maintained as possession only in very rare instances, perhaps in the case of slaves on a plantation, who are kept under uninterrupted surveillance and are locked up at night. In general, domination presupposes something more, something different, a certain state of mind, a certain placing and fitting oneself into the relation of domination and subjection. Domination without this state of mind could be maintained only by uninterrupted surveillance and in most cases would be perfectly worthless to the lord and master.

For the process of economic utilization of a thing, the legal relations respecting the thing doubtless are immaterial. The field will bear cabbage even if the husbandman who has planted it has acquired the field by an invalid will; the loom weaves the thread into cloth without inquiring how the manufacturers acquired it; and a slice of bread appeases the hunger even if a person who has stolen it. The important thing in the process of economic utilization is possession. Goethe has expressed this thought very clearly in the famous passage in *Dichtung und Wahrheit*, in which he sums up his reflections on the Imperial Supreme Court sitting at Wetzlar. It is perhaps the best thing that has ever been written on the reason for protecting possession. We are not indeed concerned here with possession in the sense of any doctrinal formulation, but, to speak in the words of the famous master of the doctrine of possession, with possession "as the possibility of actual control over the thing; and the extent of this control is the extent to which our will to control is, as a matter of experience, habitually deferred to. Whether

法律待遇上的不同。在我的名为《权利能力》的书中（在弗朗茨·考布勒名为《法律》的选集中），我已经详细地证明了个人的权利能力和他在经济秩序中的地位总是相关的。

或许最初的时候，被视为法律制度的所有支配都是对服从支配的人的一种财产利益。毫无疑问，农奴制度产生于绑架；婚姻或许也产生于绑架；父母的权力可能基于子女很小的时候就对他们进行占有的事实。但是，支配作为占有关系仅在极少情形下能永久地维持，其中或许包括在种植园中的奴隶的例子，奴隶处在不间断的监视中并且晚上会被锁起来。一般情况下，支配需要预先假定更多且不同的东西、特定的思想状态以及对支配与服从关系的融入和配合。没有意识状态的支配只有通过不间断的监视才能维持，并且，在大部分情况下它对于主人而言完全没有价值。

对于物的经济利用过程来说，物的法律关系无疑是无关紧要的。即使种植某块地的农夫是通过一份无效遗嘱而获得该土地的，也不影响这块土地将会生产出卷心菜；织布机会把细线编制成布而不会过问厂商是如何获得细线的；即便是一个人所偷来的面包也可以为其充饥。在经济的利用过程中，重要的事情是占有。歌德在《诗歌与真实》的著名的一节中将这一思想表达得非常清楚，在这一段中他总结了他对位于韦茨拉的帝国最高法院的思考。歌德的表达可能是对保护占有之理由最好的论述。在这里我们确实不关心任何教义学表达意义上的占有，而是关注——用有关占有学说之名家的话说——“作为对物实际支配可能性的占有，这种支配的限度就是我们意志支配的范围，作为一种经验事实，占有被习惯性地遵从。是否有这样的一种情形是一个现实

this is the case, is a question of actual life, which must be answered according to the diversity of the relations, especially of those of the object, according to the means at the disposal of the subject for carrying out his will, according to the state of public safety, of public morals, and of economic development." (Randa.)

Whether possession is recognized or not, then, is a "question of actual life." The important thing is not the legal precept of positive law, but the rule of conduct which governs life. The possession of the lessee, the borrower, the depositary, "as a matter of experience, was habitually respected" in the Continental common law by the other party to the contract even after Savigny had shown that according to Roman law they were not entitled to this. Again the Continental common law doubtless did not "as a matter of experience habitually" respect the possession of the thief or of the robber in spite of what the Roman law said on this point. When a third person found property that had been taken by theft or robbery in the possession of a thief or robber, he did not hesitate, because of these precepts, to take it forcibly if possible, and to deliver it to the person injured or to the authorities. Was the law otherwise in Rome? One would have to imagine a strange case indeed in which a thief or a robber whose possession had been interfered with would have applied for the *interdictum unde vi or utrubi*, An actual case of this kind cannot, to my knowledge, be found in the sources.

Possession is a fact of the law in the sense that it is the possessor

生活的问题,回答这一问题则必须依据现实关系的多样性、特别是客体关系的多样性,还必须依据主体实现其意志时可以自由采取的方式、公共安全状态、公共道德状态以及经济发展的状态。”(兰达)

于是,占有是否被承认的问题是一个“现实生活问题”。重要的不是实证法的法律规定,而是支配生活的行为规则。在欧陆共同法中,承租人、借用人和保管人的占有,被契约的另一方当事人“依据经验而习惯性地尊重”,甚至在萨维尼证明,依据罗马法承租人、借用人和保管人无权那样做之后,情况还是如此。同样,欧陆共同法毫无疑问并没有“依据经验习惯性”地尊重小偷和强盗的占有,尽管罗马法在这一点上如是说。当第三人发现小偷或者强盗占有他们偷来或者抢来的财产的时候,由于这些规定,如果可能他会毫不犹豫地强行夺下财产并把它交给受到损害的人或者当局。罗马的法律会是另一种样子吗?人们得想一个真的比较奇怪的案例,其中,一个占有受到干涉的小偷或者强盗可能申请制止暴力剥夺令[1]或者动产占有保持禁令。[2] 就我所知,这种类型的实际案例在原始文献中无法找到。

占有是一种如下意义上的法律事实——依据物的经济效用

---

〔1〕 (拉)*interdictum unde vi*(制止暴力剥夺令),恢复占有令状的一种,针对以暴力(但未使用武器)剥夺他人对物的占有时采用。有关该令状的申请应当在占有被剥夺后的一年内提起,并且以占有的正当行为为前提条件。

〔2〕 (拉)*utrubi*(动产占有保持禁令),该禁令是为了保护对动产的占有。

who employs and utilizes the thing according to its economic purpose. Every system of law protects the possessor in the economic use of the thing. It is a matter of indifference whether the protection is secured by means of independent legal remedies, as in Roman law, by means of private delictual actions (trespass), as in English law, or chiefly by means of the criminal law, as in Scandinavian law. Even as it is, protection of possession is everywhere, to a great extent, a matter for the criminal courts and the police. In the case of movable things, the protection afforded by the criminal law is sufficient at the present time to protect against theft and embezzlement; the independent remedies are used very little. The French Civil Code therefore has abolished the independent protection of possession of movables. True, the action of ownership may be used, just as under the German Civil Code, by any possessor against anyone except the person who has just been deprived of the thing by theft or loss. Accordingly it serves the purpose of a possessory action as well. In the case of immovables specific protection of possession is indispensable in Roman law and in the Continental legal systems derived from the latter because the protection afforded by the criminal law as well as that of the law of delicts is altogether too ineffectual. Since in the *Code de Procédure Civile* the action for interference with possession, *la complainte*, presupposes uninterrupted proprietary possession for one year, and thus has become a petitory action, and since there is no true possessory action, the French administration of justice has invented a means of protecting possession which is purely a police remedy, *la réintegrande*, which requires neither proprietary nor uninterrupted possession: *attendu que les voies de fait ne peuvent pas étre tolerées dens une société civilisée et que si cette action n'existait pas il faudrait l'inventer.*

而使用、利用占有物的是占有人。每一种法律制度都保护占有者对物的经济利用。至于是否像在罗马法中,可以获得独立的法律救济方式的保护;是否像在英格兰法中那样,受到私人不法侵害诉讼(侵权诉讼)保护;或者是否像在斯堪的纳维亚法律中那样,主要受到刑事法律方式的保护,这些都不重要。甚至目前的情形,所有地方的占有保护很大程度上都是刑事法院和警察的事情。对于动产,目前刑法所提供的保护就足以使其免受偷窃和侵占的侵害;独立的救济方法很少适用。因此,《法国民法典》废除了对动产占有的独立保护。诚然,所有权之诉可以被采用——正如在《德国民法典》中规定的那样——任何占有人都可以对除了刚被小偷盗窃或者丢失物品的人以外的任何人提起所有权之诉。因此,它也解决占有之诉的问题。因为刑法和不法侵害法的保护太没有效力,所以在罗马法以及由其衍生出来的大陆法系制度中,在动产情形下,占有的特殊保护必不可少。由于在《法国民事诉讼法典》中,排除妨害所有权之诉以不间断地自主占有一年为前提条件,因而,排除妨害所有权之诉变成了确认所有权之诉,并且,由于法国并不存在真正的占有之诉,所以,法国司法创造了一种纯属治安救济的占有保护方式——恢复占有之诉,它既不要求所有权也不要求不间断的占有:由于在一个文明的社会,抢劫是无法容忍的,因此,如果没有这样一种诉讼救济制度,即恢复占有之诉的话,那么我们应该创设这样的制度。

Possession, as a purely economic relation to a thing, is distinguished from ownership and the other real rights. Economically the owner as such has no dealings with the thing; he remains the owner even though he does not concern himself about the thing for years, even though he knows nothing about it. This proves at all events that the concept of ownership was formulated, in part at least, by influences other than economic. To carry out the distinction between possession on the one hand and ownership as an independent concept on the other to its logical conclusion is to say that the law completely disregards the economic order, which takes form and shape in possession, and recognizes only the order based on ownership and real rights. The sharp distinction made in Roman law between ownership and possession might indeed lead to this view. This is the view of the juristic literature also inasmuch as it manifestly assumes that it is not the protection of ownership but that of possession that requires justification. The primary thing however is not ownership, but possession. A glance at mediaeval German law presents a legal order which is predominantly based on *Gewere* (i. e. the right of possession) and not on ownership. The vital energy of this thought has been demonstrated by its subsequent history; it has not only made its way against all opposition in the Continental common law, but has attained full development in England, and there meets the requirements of one of the greatest mercantile nations of the whole world; it prevails in the modern codes, the French Civil Code, the German Civil Code and the Swiss Civil Code. A comparison of the results of the entire legal development with Roman law shows that in all questions that are of significance for life, the latter strives for the same goal as German law, i. e. to make the order of ownership conform as closely as possible to the economic order, which is embodied in possession.

The person who makes use of a thing according to its economic purpose is entitled to *Gewere*. In the case of immovable things, at

占有作为一种对物的纯粹经济关系,不同于所有权和其他的物权。经济上,如此意义的所有权人本身并不对物为任何行为;即使所有权人已经数年没有关注所有物,即使所有权人对所有物一无所知,他仍是物的所有者。无论如何这证明了所有权观念的形成至少部分地受到经济以外其他因素的影响。贯彻一方面是占有与另一方面作为独立观念的所有权的区分的逻辑结果,就是法律完全忽视以占有为基础形成的经济秩序,并仅仅承认以所有权和物权为基础的秩序。罗马法对所有权和占有的明显区分可能的确导致了这一见解。这也是法学文献中的见解,因为它显然认为:这不是对所有权的保护,而是对需要正当理由之占有的保护。但是最主要的事情,不是所有权而是占有。对中世纪的德国法的粗略浏览,就会发现一种主要以总有(即占有权)〔1〕而不是以所有权为基础的法律秩序。这种思想的生命力已经被其随后的历史所证明。这种思想不仅仅在欧陆共同法中战胜了各种反对思想、一路向前;而且它在英格兰也获得充分的发展,在那里,这种思想符合了世界上最伟大的商业民族之一的需要;这种思想还广泛存在于现代的民法典中,如《法国民法典》、《德国民法典》和《瑞士民法典》。整个法律发展的结果与罗马法的比较表明:在对生活具有重大意义的所有问题上,罗马法都像德国法一样努力争取达到相同的目标,即让所有权的秩序尽可能地符合占有所体现的经济秩序。

那些依照经济效用来利用物的人被赋予了总有权。至少在

〔1〕 *Gewere* 是日耳曼法的概念,学界在 *Gewere* 仅指占有还是也包括占有权方面存在争论。

least, the latter conforms perfectly to the economic order; for everyone who has a share in the returns yielded by a thing, or derives any economic advantage from it has *Gewere* in it, and yields only to him who has shown a better right. Until this happens, his share in the economic yield is a matter of right, he has the power of disposition over the thing, and is entitled to the true *Gewere* as soon as the person who has a better right has lost it through failure to assert it. *Gewere* therefore actually presents a pretty complete picture of the economic constitution for the time being, to the extent that it has its roots in the law of things. If it were possible to describe the kind and extent of all the *Gewere* (rights of possession) that exist in all the things within a certain legal sphere, the result would be, barring the shifts conditioned upon purely obligatory rights, a fairly faithful picture of the economic situation in that sphere of law. English law has developed this basic idea of German law inasmuch as it actually grants to the possessor all the rights of an owner until he has been deprived of *Gewere* (possession) by a person who has a better right. He receives the fruits of the thing (he that sows shall reap), he controls the thing with full legal effect, but he is unable to give a better right to the transferee than he himself has. The transferee, like the transferor, yields to the person who has a better right, and must surrender all profits received (*mesne* profits) to the latter, but is preferred to every third party whose right is inferior to that of his transferor. Since English law does not recognize any absolute right of ownership, but invariably lets the decision hinge upon the question which of the two persons entitled has the better right, English jurists can say now and then that every possessor is an owner until he is deprived of the thing by litigation. And finally the right of the possessor becomes the best right as soon as the period of prescription has run against the claim of the person who had the better right. Where the law is couched in these terms there can, of course, be no usucapion. In Roman law, in conesquence of the concept of absolute ownership, the economic point of view apparently recedes into the background. In actual fact

不动产的情形下，总有权完全符合了经济秩序；因为从物之孳息拥有份额、或自物中获取任何利益的每个人，都对物拥有总有权，并且他也仅仅服从那些能够证明拥有更优权利的人。在后者发生之前，他对经济产出的份额是一种权利标的，他拥有了对物的处分权，一旦拥有更优权利的人因为没有主张权利而丧失权利，他就获得了真正的总有权。因此，在总有权扎根于物权法的这一范围内，总有权实际上呈现了经济秩序暂时的完整图景。如果有可能描述在一个特定法律范围内存在所有物上的总有权（占有权）的类型和范围，结果将是——除基于纯粹债权的变动外——对那一法律范围内经济情形的忠实体现。英格兰法发展出了这样的一种基本的日耳曼法观念，因为，英格兰法实际上授予了占有者全部的所有人权利，直到他被拥有更优权利的人剥夺总有权（占有权）。他收取了物的孳息（播种的人要收获），他支配着物，且具有完全法律效力，但是，他不能将比自己所拥有的权利更大的权利转让给受让人。受让人和出让人一样，服从拥有更优权利的人，并且必须把收到的所有利益（中间收益）交给后者，但是他的权利优于每一个权利劣于他的转让者的第三人。因为英格兰法不承认任何绝对的所有权，所以不可避免，裁决总是纠缠在——两个有权利的人哪一个人权利更优——这一问题上，英格兰法学家偶尔可以说：在诉讼剥夺其占有物以前，每一个占有者都是所有者。最后，更优权利人之请求权的诉讼时效一旦届满，占有者的权利就成为最优的权利。当然，在由这些术语组成的法律中，不可能存在取得时效。在罗马法中，由于绝对所有权的观念，经济的视角显然不再重要。但是，事实上罗马

however the Roman law merely denies to the possessor the use of a certain action, the *rei vindicatio*, and in its stead grants him the *actio Publiciana* and, to the fullest extent, the possessory actions. In Roman law also the possessor may keep the thing and utilize it economically until he is deprived of it by litigation; and in the litigation as to ownership he occupies a favored position. He acquires the fruits of the thing provisionally at least, and—here Roman law goes further than English law—after he has consumed them in good faith, definitely and without making compensation. If he has utilized, it in his trade or business in good faith, he acquires ownership. This is the meaning of the Roman provisions as to specification. Since the validity of an agreement entered into with reference to the thing does not depend on the ownership of the thing, and since the *actio Publiciana* which follows the terms of the agreement is regularly available to the goodfaith transferee, the possessor also has the power of disposition over the thing to this extent. Finally, according to Roman law, the economic relationship becomes ownership through usucapion; through the running of the period of prescription, it becomes the "best right." In all these things, the modern Continental law follows the Roman law. Only, in case of movables that were found or stolen, it has made provision to prevent the possessor

法仅仅不许占有者采取特定的诉讼——返还所有物之诉，[1]而且作为替代，赋予他善意占有之诉[2]和一个最完整范围内的占有之诉。在罗马法中，占有者也可以保有物并且可以为了经济目的利用它，直到他因诉讼而被剥夺对物的占有；并且在所有权诉讼中，他占据一个有利的地位。他至少暂时获得了孳息——此点上罗马法比英格兰法走得更远，并且，在他善意消费孳息后，被消费部分将是确定无需作任何补偿的。如果他在贸易或营业中善意地利用了物，他将获得所有权。这是有关加工他人动产所得新物之权利的罗马法规定的含义。由于涉及物的协议的有效性并不依赖于物的所有权，同时善意受让人一般可以利用符合协议条件的善意占有之诉，因而在这范围内，占有者也有权处分物。最后，按照罗马法，经济关系由于时效取得制度变成了所有权关系，由于诉讼时效制度，这种权利变成了"最优权利"。在所有的这些方面，现代大陆法系追随了罗马法。仅仅是在动产被发现或者被偷窃的情况下，法律规定了一些禁止占有者利用物的条款；这主要

---

〔1〕（拉）*rci vindicatio*（返还所有物之诉），典型的据以要求维护市民法所有权的诉讼，表现为物品的所有主针对非法占据其物品的人提出归还该物品的要求。在这种诉讼中首先需要认定的是物品的归属，它最初采取的是对物的誓金法律诉讼形式，即：双方当事人当着执法官的面相互提出所有权主张并进行赌誓，宣称有关物品归自己所有。

〔2〕（拉）*actio Publiciana*（善意占有之诉），也被译为"布布里其诉讼"，由共和国末期的裁判官布布里其（*Publicio*）创设，并以其名字命名。它曾经是一种拟制诉讼。当原告对某物的占有受到侵夺时，如果裁判官查明原告已根据正当原因取得该物并且因法定时间经过而实现了时效取得，就责成审判员对被告判罚。在这种返还所有物之诉中虚拟的因素就是时效取得所要求的时间已经届满；至于时效取得的其他要件，审判员则应当根据事实进行审查。

from utilizing the thing; and this chiefly in order to protect the owner against injury.

Roman law goes beyond German and English law; possibly, too, beyond practical necessity, inasmuch as it protects the possession of the thief and the robber, which has been acquired in an uneconomic manner, although doubtless in actual life such possession is not considered a legal relation. It does not go so far as the above-named legal systems inasmuch as it does not treat the economic relationship to the thing that is based solely upon relations of the law of obligation, e. g. relationship of lease, both ordinary and usufructuary, as possession. It does however, with a few insignificant exceptions, place the good-faith possessor in the position of an owner to the same extent at least as do German and English law, and since good-faith possession alone is of significance for the economic constitution, we can say that manifestly, even in Roman law, the economic point of view prevails over the legal concept of ownership. The modern Continental legal systems have, in general, adopted these basic ideas of the Roman law of possession, albeit with a few historically conditioned concessions to Germanic law.

It is only on one point that the right of the owner rather than that of the possessor has become the rule of conduct, i. e. inasmuch as only the owner can validly transfer ownership, or the "best right." This principle, which is binding in Roman and English law with reference to all things, is limited in the law of the Continent to immovables. Where this principle governs, the transferee must needs make inquiry as to the right of the transferor or protect himself against loss by means of a contractual warranty. The security of the buyer is based on the warranty of the seller, i. e., as in Roman law, on his credit; and every sate becomes a credit transaction. In England, in case of immovables, there is the liability of the attorney who draws up the contract and undertakes to investigate the title of the seller (investigation of title). In the case of movables, on the other hand, the possession of the seller is generally sufficient on the Continent to transfer title to a good-faith purchaser. It is extremely interesting to observe how the effect which has been given to possession has made its way in the course of the last century even where no effect had been given to it before that time; how, on the Continent,

是为了保护物的所有权人免受损害。

罗马法比德国法和英格兰法走得更远；可能，罗马法也超越了实践的需要，因为罗马法保护小偷和强盗通过非经济方式获得的占有，尽管毫无疑问，现实生活中那样的占有不被认为是一种法律关系。它又没有和上述法律制度走得一样远，因为它并没有将单纯基于债法关系——例如租赁关系，不管是普通租赁还是附用益权租赁——之上物的经济关系视为占有。不过，除了一些无关紧要的例外，至少罗马法如同德国法和英格兰法那样，在同样的程度上使善意占有人处在所有者的位置上，既然单单善意占有就对经济制度意义重大，我们可以说，显然即便在罗马法中，经济的观念也胜过法律所有权的观念。虽然现代大陆法律制度历史上曾对日耳曼法有条件地做出了让步，但是，在整体上它还是采纳了罗马法中关于占有的这些基本概念。

仅仅在这一点上，所有者的权利而不是占有者的权利成为了行为规则，即，因为只有所有者可以合法有效地转让所有权或者“最优权利”。这一在罗马法和英格兰法中对所有物均具有拘束力的原则在大陆法系仅限于不动产法。在受这一原则支配的地方，受让人需要调查转让者的权利或者依靠契约担保的方式使自己免受损失。买方的安全是以卖方的保证为基础的，即如同在罗马法中以卖方的信用为基础；并且每一笔买卖都变成了信用交易。在英格兰，在不动产情况下，律师对于起草契约和调查卖方权利（权利调查）负有责任。另一方面，在欧洲大陆，对于动产，卖方的占有通常情况下足以使善意买受人取得所有权。观察下列事情是极为有趣的：在上一个世纪里，甚至在先前未曾赋予过占有任何效力的地方，赋予占有的效力是如何一路向前发展的；在

it developed into the related principle of the "public assurance" of the land register, into "the reliance on collateral states of fact" (*Wellspacher*); how the French hypothec registers gradually became land registers; how the land registers are gaining in importance even in England; how in England the maxim "*Hand muss Hand wahren*," which until quite recently had been limited to purchases made in the open market (and in part also in a retailer's shop), is, thanks to modern legislation, steadily gaining ground.

The law of possession, therefore, is the true law of the economic order and is most closely related to the living law of economics. For this very reason it is one of the most fluid fields of the law. Every economic change at once results in a change in the law of possession. On questions of possession the statements of the Roman jurist very often are conflicting. This must be attributed, in part at least, to changes of opinion. On no other point has German law offered such unyielding resistance to Roman law, and still it has itself been changing continually. The English action of trespass, too, bears a different aspect in every century. The law of possession as found in the codes of the nineteenth century is out of date at the present time; both Austrian and French judicial decision must resort to legal material not contained in the codes.

In this sense the legal relations of possession were at all times nothing but the legal side of the economic system of landholding. What does one mean when one speaks of nations of hunters and of shepherds? Clearly, that in general these peoples do not know of

欧洲大陆,这一原则如何发展成了与之相关的土地登记的“公信原则”和“对担保情势的信赖原则”(*Wellspacher*);法国的抵押登记如何逐步演变为土地登记;甚至在英格兰,土地登记如何日益变得重要;在英格兰,直到最近,其适用范围还仅限于在公开市场(部分在零售商店)〔1〕发生之购买的“以手护手”原则〔2〕由于现代立法活动正如何稳步取得更多的阵地。

因此,占有法是经济秩序的真正法律,并且它和经济生活中的活法关系最为密切。正是因为这一原因,占有法是最富有变动性的法律领域之一。每一次经济领域的变革马上会导致占有法的变化。在占有问题上,罗马法学家的陈述经常互相矛盾。这至少部分地可归因于观念的变化。德国法在任何一点上都没有对罗马法进行了如此不屈不挠的抵制,德国法本身也处在不断的变动之中。英格兰法中的侵害之诉在每一个世纪中都呈现出不同的面貌。19世纪法典中的占有法今天早已过时;奥地利和法国的司法判决都必须求助于法典中没有包含的法律材料。

在这种意义上,占有法律关系一直都仅仅是土地占有经济制度的一个法律面向而已。当某人谈起狩猎民族或者牧羊民族的时候,他的意思是什么?显然,通常情况下,这些民族不知道土地

---

〔1〕 公开市场原则。

〔2〕 善意第三人可以从不是所有权人却因所有权人的同意而占有物的占有人那里获得所有权。按照“以手护手”原则,原来的所有权人只能向受托保管人,即未经授权而实施了对户转让的人进行追索。因此,善意第三人不可以从不是所有权人,却因所有权人的同意而占有物的占有人那里获得所有权。现代的善意取得制度与“以手护手”原则具有一定的关联性。

ownership in land, that they merely assert a claim to a tribal sovereignty over the territory they occupy—a sovereignty which grants to each member of the tribe the right of hunt and pasture. The earliest form of agriculture, however, the raising of field grass, implies possession of the cultivated land—a possession which is protected at least by legal self-help. Fixed relationships arise when the two and three-field system comes into vogue: unrestricted ownership of the *Hofstätte*, partition of the *Feldmark* among the individual families that had settled in the *Höfe*, ownership in the arable land in *Gemenglage* limited by *Flurzwang* and *Nachbarrechte*, common ownership of the *Allmende*, of woodland, and of meadowland. A more intensive system of agriculture, especially the *Fruchtwechsel*, leads to freeing the soil from feudal burdens, and, in part, to the arising—not until the most recent times, it is true—of individual rights in the common mark. And lastly, the financial and credit systems transform the parcel of ground into an object of commerce and create the modern land law.

It is true, because of the free ownership of Roman law and of the modern legal system, the immediate connection between the legal order of possession and the economic order, between land law and the possessory order, does not appear at once. Free ownership is apparently the same in every tract of land, whether there be on it a forest, a mine, arable land, or a house subject to ground rent. The explanation of this lies in the fact that the Roman as well as the modern immovable is a result of the process of freeing the soil from the burdens that had been resting upon it—a process which created the free Italic soil in Rome at a time prior to the beginning of historical tradition that cannot be definitely ascertained, and which began to operate in England in the seventeenth century, and on the Continent in the eighteenth

所有权,他们仅仅对他们占据的地区主张部落统治权——一种授予每一个部落成员狩猎和放牧的权利。然而,最早的农业形式(草地的出现)暗示了对可耕种土地的占有——一种至少受到法律自力救济保护的占有。当两田制或者三田制开始流行的时候,固定的关系随之产生,它包括以下形式:不受限制的农民建立的独立机构所有权;居住在一单块土地中各家庭对村庄周围空闲土地的分割;在混合地带[1]上受乡村公社规定的种植方式与相邻权限制的可耕地的所有权;对未分割公地、对林地和牧场的共同所有权。农业中一种更为精耕细作的体制,特别是轮流种植生产食用草和坚果的制度使得土地摆脱了封建负担,并且——的确,直到最近才——部分地导致了公共土地上个人权利的产生。最终,金融和信用制度将一块块土地转变为商业的客体,并建立起了现代土地法。

的确,因为罗马法和现代法律制度中的绝对所有权,占有法律秩序和经济秩序之间、土地法和占有秩序之间的直接联系无法马上显现。绝对所有权在每一块土地上都是相同的,不论是在森林、矿场、耕地还是附属于租来土地的住房上。对这一问题的解释存在于这样的一个事实里:罗马和现代的不动产制度都是使土地摆脱其负担这一进程的结果——这一进程在罗马,在无法明确查明的历史传统开始以前的一个时期,建立了意大利自由土地;这一进程在17世纪的英格兰和18世纪、19世纪的欧洲大陆开

〔1〕 混合地带。自由农民的份地遍布在马克公社的混合地带,即整个马克公社地域。

and nineteenth centuries. Before the soil has been freed from these burdens, landed property occupies a definite place in a clearly defined economic and social relationship: The *Hof* in the village settlement, the arable field in the *Gemenglage*, woodland and pasture in the *Allmende*—all these are an integral part of the social order of the region. Likewise the claims of the ultimate owner, as well as the burdens and duties of the usufructuary, are conditioned by their position in society, in the state, in the whole economic interrelationship. Thus the extent and the content of the right of ownership in each immovable is determined, either positively or negatively, by law, i. e. the nature of the right of ownership in a certain immovable cannot be derived from the concept of ownership. As to the arable field in the *Gewann*, as to woodland and pasture in the *Allmende*, as to the *Hof* of every husbandman in the village, and as to every knight's estate, (*Rittergut*), the extent and manner of usage, everything that a neighbor can demand or is under obligation to permit, everything that the ultimate owner has a right to demand and that the usufructuary owner must render, is fixed in each individual case. These restrictions and limitations, which at a very early period had existed in ancient Rome as well as, though perhaps not to the same extent as, in the Middle Ages, disappeared when the soil was freed from its burdens.

As soon as the soil is freed from its burdens, it is no longer necessary to say anything about the content of ownership; the owner no longer has to consider neighbor or inferior. He can do or leave undone what he pleases. This of course does not mean that the content of ownership is no longer conditioned by the whole economic order. It means primarily something negative; i. e. that one kind of constraint which has prevailed until now has been done away with by the change of the economic constitution. Ownership must now create its new legal order for itself in accordance with the economic order. It does this in the sphere of the law of the family and of the law of slavery as well as by means of free agreement with owners of adjacent land (*Nachbarrecht*, i. e. law and right of neighbors) and with hired workmen. The legal

始产生作用。在土地从这些负担中解放出来以前,地产在一个被清楚地界定的经济和社会关系中占据了一个明确的位置。在村落中的四方庭院、在混合地带中的可耕地和未分割公地上的林地和牧场——所有的这些都是地区社会秩序中一个组成部分。同样地,最终所有者的请求权连同用益权上的负担和义务都以它们在社会、国家以及整个经济相互关系中的地位为条件。每一个不动产所有权的范围和内容都由法律或积极或消极地确定,即,特定不动产所有权的性质不可能起源于所有权的概念。至于村庄四方形区域中的可耕地、未分割公地上的林地和牧场、村庄中每一个农民的四方庭院、每一块骑士封地、封地、习惯的范围和使用方式、邻居可以主张权利或有义务允许的所有情形,以及最终所有权人有权利要求和用益所有权人必须提供的所有事情,都在每一个个案中得以明确。当土地从其上各种负担中解脱出来的时候,在一个很早的时期就已经存在于古罗马和中世纪(尽管或许没有达到前者那样的程度)的这些约束和限制消失了。

一旦土地上没有了各种负担,就没有必要对所有权的内容再作任何说明;所有权人不必再考虑他的邻居和具有次优权利的人。他可以做或者不做他乐意的任何事情。当然,这不是说所有权的内容不再以整个的经济秩序为条件。这主要指消极的方面;即,社会经济结构的变化已经废除了在那之前一直盛行的某种类型的限制。现在所有权必须依据经济秩序为自己创造新的法律秩序。在家庭法和奴隶制法的范围内,通过和邻近土地所有人以及雇工之间的自由合意(*Nachbarrecht*,即相邻权),此种

order is busily at work fashioning, by means of a series of economic precepts, a law of ownership that is adapted to the thing itself as well as to its economic purpose. These precepts however are usually being treated as parts of administrative law and therefore, from the juristic point of view, ostensibly no longer affect the law of ownership. This results in the conceptually absolute, unconditioned "Roman" right of ownership, which permits not merely a certain, but any conceivable, use of the object of ownership. "Roman" ownership is ownership which, by means of juristic intellectual labor, has been wrested out of its social and economic connection.

But after all, this ownership is merely a kind of juristic fiction. The doctrine of the "absolute power of control over the thing" is usually presented today as if it constituted the entire content of the concept of ownership, as if there were no *Forstrecht* (law of forests), *Wasserrecht* (law of water), *Bergrecht* (mining law), no *Agrarrecht* (agrarian law), no *Bauordnungen* (building-regulations), and no *Gewerbeordnungen* (trade-regulations), as if there were no "conceptual" difference between ownership of a tract of woodland and ownership of a pocketbook. This was not correct even in the case of the *fundus* of the *solum Italicum*, which, to the fullest extent possible, was kept free from all burdens and restrictions, and which forms the only empirical basis for the modern concept of ownership; for Roman law, too, knew of *Forst-*, *Wasser-*, *Agrarrecht*, as well as of *Bauordnungen* and *Gewerbeordnungen*, even though the greater part of all this has not been handed down to us, and though, in part, it must be gleaned from inscriptions, scattered legal sources, and other records. Ownership (including the real right of usufruct, the right of a usufructuary lessee, at any rate of the ordinary lessee) of woodland, of water, of a mine, of arable land, of a building, are from inner necessity quite different things, both economically and legally. Likewise ownership of, and the real right of usufruct or of usufructuary lease in, the objects that constitute the aggregate of things employed in an industrial

新的法律秩序得以建立。法律秩序正在忙于通过一系列经济规则来塑造适于物自身与经济目的的所有权法。然而,这些规则通常被视做行政法的一部分,因而从法学家的视角来看,这些规则在表面上不再影响所有权法。这就导致了观念上绝对的、无条件的"罗马人的"所有权,这种所有权不仅允许所有权人对所有权的客体为特定的使用,而且允许所有权人通过任何可以想象到的方式使用所有物。"罗马人的"所有权是一种通过法学家的智力劳动,从其社会和经济方面费力取得的所有权。

但是,这种所有权毕竟仅仅是一种法学的虚构。"对物的绝对控制力"的学说如今常常被提及,仿佛这一学说构成了所有权观念的全部内容,仿佛 *Forstrecht*(森林法)、*Wasserrecht*(水法)、*Bergrecht*(矿业法)、*Agrarrecht*(农业法)、*Bauordnungen*(建筑法规)和 *Gewerbeordnungen*(贸易法规)统统根本不存在,仿佛一块林地的所有权与笔记本的所有权之间并不存在任何"概念上"的区别。即使是在涉及罗马法中意大利的土地——在可能的最大程度上,罗马法中意大利的土地上一直都免于任何负担和限制,而且,它也构成了现代所有权观念的唯一经验主义基础——的情况下,这也是不正确的;因为罗马法也知道上述森林法、水法、农业法、建筑法以及贸易法等法规,尽管这些规则的大部分都没有传下来,尽管这些知识必须部分地从各种批注、分散的原始文献和其他的各种记录中收集。森林、水、矿山、耕地和建筑物的所有权(包括用益物权、用益承租人的权利、任何形式的普通承租人的权利),这些所有权在经济上和法律上,就内部的必要性而言,都是完全不同的。同样地,构成一个工业企业中物之总和(即企业财团)的客体,其所有权、用益物权或附用益权租约,根

undertaking may have a totally dissimilar content according to the kind of undertaking. This is not referable to diversity in the precepts of the lawmaker. In this field, even more than elsewhere, the legal precepts are nothing more than a precipitate of that which has actually been practiced at all times. It is referable to the fact that it is impossible to exercise the rights of ownership in things of totally dissimilar natures according to identical principles. The economic nature of a thing determines the relation between the owner and a neighbor; it determines the inner organization of the undertaking which it subserves and the position of the latter in commerce. Inasmuch as the agreements through which ownership is utilized form part of the exercise of the right of ownership,① the content of these agreements determines the content of the right of ownership. Accordingly ownership of a factory is a different thing from ownership of a mine; for the contract of employment entered into with a miner is quite different from a contract with a factory worker; and ownership of a railroad, for the same reason, is different from ownership of a tract of woodland, for the railroad freight contract is different from a contract for removing stumps. For the precepts governing the agreements upon which the order of property rights in things that serve a particular economic purpose is based constitute the essential content of the particular law that exists for these things, e. g. the law of mines, of forests, of railroads.

Possession everywhere becomes a legal relation in virtue of its being fitted into the economic order. Man subjects the natural world surrounding him to his will by means of his economic activity. In this sense possession is merely the factual side of the economic order. The objects of possession increase in number as soon as their usefulness is understood.

Wild animal taming is contemporaneous with the beginnings of cattle-breeding; land-taking, with the beginnings of agriculture. But methodical management presupposes not only possession, but also protection of possession. For it is possible to provide for the future by gathering supplies and producing goods only in case

---

① The statutory limitation of the working day in factories is a most incisive limitation of the ownership of the factory owner; not, indeed, of the liberty of contract of the worker, as is often assumed. —*Author's note.*

据企业种类的不同，都可能有完全不同的内容。这不能归因于立法者颁布规定的多样性。在这一领域，甚至在其他任何地方，法律规定也都是一直实际应用之习惯的沉淀。其原因在于：依据同样的原则，对具有完全不同性质的物行使所有权是不可能的。物的经济性质决定了所有人与其邻居的关系；它也决定了企业的内部构造（后者有益于该企业的发展）和企业在商业中的地位。因为，所有权据以获得利用的协议构成了所有权行使的一部分，[①]所以这些协议的内容决定了所有权的内容。据此，工厂所有权不同于矿场所有权，因为与矿工缔结的雇佣契约不同于与工人缔结的雇佣契约；同理，铁路所有权也不同于对一片林地的所有权，因为铁路运输契约不同于移除树桩的契约。因为那些调整服务于特定经济目的的物之上的财产权秩序所赖以存在之协议的规定构成了为这些物服务而存在的特别法的本质内容，例如矿业法、森林法和铁路法。

由于占有契合于经济秩序，因而它在每个地方都成为了法律关系。人类依靠自身的经济活动，使周围的自然界服从于自己的意志。在此意义上，占有仅仅是经济秩序的一个事实面向。一旦人们了解了物的有用性，被占有之客体的数量就会增加。

野生动物的驯养与家畜饲养的开始属于同一时代的事；土地占有和农业的早期阶段亦属同一时代。但是有条不紊的管理不但要以占有为条件，而且要以对占有的保护为条件。因为只有在占有受到某种程度保护的情况下，才可能通过积聚供应品和生产货物的方式为未

---

① 工厂中工作日的法定限制是对工厂主所有权的最有力的限制，它的确不是人们通常认为的是对工人契约自由的限制。

possession is protected to some extent; not until possession is protected can a possessor count on actually retaining the proceeds of the labor he bestows upon preserving, augmenting, and utilizing his possession; and therefore in an established economic order, relations of possession must become legally protected relations of possession. In every instance therefore the order of possession is a reflection of the economic order. There can therefore be no doubt as to the reason for the protection of possession. It lies in the fact that agriculture, trade, industry, commerce, would be unthinkable without security. The difficulty which the concept of possession caused to the jurists who had been trained in Roman law lay in the fact that they were always striving to define possession without reference to the economic order—an impossible undertaking. It is much more difficult to explain the reason for the existence of ownership, except in so far as it closely follows the order which is based on possession. Here complicated social relations are contributing factors, and the whole question belongs to the subject matter of another field of inquiry.

From this discussion it follows that the sociology of law must, to a certain extent, treat possession and ownership as interchangeable terms. The necessity of doing this is accentuated by the fact that both statutes and juristic science as a rule do not differentiate between the two. Let anyone attempt to make a clear-cut distinction between these two concepts in the law of finance, mines, water, forest, or agriculture. Whatsoever is stated in these departments of law as to ownership, with rare exceptions, applies also to possession, and vice versa. This is the case also in everyday life, which at every moment finds it necessary to treat possession as ownership. Only in those parts of the law of possession that deal specifically with possession and ownership is a clear-cut distinction made between the two. In these exceptional cases the sociology of law will also observe the distinction. In such case, ownership, as distinguished from possession, implies the sum total of legal remedies that are available to a non-possessor in order to acquire proprietary possession of a thing.

We have now arrived at the point where we must enter upon the discussion of the legal declaration of will as a fact of the law.

来做准备;在占有受到保护前,占有人不可能指望实际保留他通过维护、加工、利用占有物而获得的劳动收益。因此,在每一个既有经济秩序中,占有关系必须成为受法律保护的占有关系。在所有情况下,占有秩序都是经济秩序的一种反映。关于对占有进行保护的原因没有任何疑问。这个原因就是:如果没有安全保障,那么农业、贸易、工业和商业这些都无法想像。占有的概念实际上给受过罗马法训练的法学家带来了困难,这是因为:他们总是努力在不考虑经济秩序的前提下界定占有这一概念——这是一项不可能完成的任务。除了所有权严密遵循了以占有为基础的秩序之外,解释所有权存在的原因会更加困难。在这里,复杂的社会关系是促成因素,并且整个问题属于另外一个研究领域的主题内容。

从这里的论述中可以得出结论:法律社会学必须在一定程度上将占有和所有权看做可以相互替换的术语。制定法和法学通常都不区分占有和所有权这一事实更强调了这样做的必要性。让任何人试图在财政法、矿业法、水法、森林法或者农业法中对这两个概念作一个清晰的区分吧。除了很少的例外,这些部门法中关于所有权任何陈述也适用于占有,反之亦然。这也正是日常生活中的情形,在生活中的每一刻都有必要将占有视做所有权。只有明确涉及占有和所有权的那部分占有法中,才会在占有和所有权之间作出了清晰的区分。在这些例外的情形中,法律社会学也将遵循这一区分。那种情况下,区别于占有的所有权暗示了——非占有人为了使其获得对物的自主占有而可以运用的一切法律救济的总和。

现在,我们来讨论作为法律事实的意思表示。在这一点上,研究所有法学分支中意思表示和法律处分的事实基础既无必要

It is neither necessary nor possible at this point to investigate the factual bases of the legal declaration of will and of the legal disposition in all its ramifications. There are only two classes that are of significance in the legal history of the world, to wit agreement (*Vertrag*) and disposition by last will and testament. The articles of association of the law of corporations were originally a statement of the existing usage or a form of agreement, and therefore are not of independent significance as a fact of the law.

At this point, our discussion will deal in the first place only with the agreement. Just as a distinction was made between possession on the one hand and ownership and real right on the other, so a distinction must be made between the mere fact of understanding and the *Vertrag* (agreement). Germanistic legal science, spinning out a thought first expressed by Brinz, has worked out the distinction between *Schuld* (debt, obligation) and *Haftung* (liability) with extraordinary precision, and by doing so has laid the foundation not only for the historical but also for the sociological discussion of the contract. *Schuld* is the *Sollen* of the debtor; it is that which according to the experience of life is considered the content of the obligation; liability (*Haftung*) is the right of the creditor to enforce his claim, a right which secures satisfaction even against the will of the debtor. And the understanding is converted from a bare fact into a fact of the law and thereby into a *Vertrag* (agreement), even though no liabilities (*Haftungen*) arise, but merely a debt, or obligation (*Schuld*). The Roman *contractus* gives rise to obligation (*Schuld*) and liability (*Haftung*); the

也不可能。在世界法律史上,只有两类意义重大,即契约(*Vertrag*)[1]和遗嘱处分。法人社团法中的联合体章程最初是现行习惯的陈述,或是一种协议形式,因此它们作为法律的事实并不具有独立意义。

在这一点上,我们将首先只对契约进行讨论。正如区分占有和所有权及物权一样,我们同样必须区分单纯默示协议的事实和 *Vertrag*(契约)。日耳曼法学中,由布林兹首先表达的一种思想对 *Schuld*(债务)和 *Haftung*(责任)作出了极为精细的区分,这样做不但为对契约进行历史讨论奠定了基础,而且也为对契约进行社会学讨论奠定了基础。债务是债务人的当为,是依据生活经验被认定为义务内容的东西;责任(*Haftung*)是债权人强制实现其请求权的权利,是一种即使违逆债务人的意志也能获得实现的权利。这种默示协议从一种单纯的事实转变为法律事实,从而变成了 *Vertrag*(契约),即使在这里也没有责任(*Haftungen*)产生,而仅仅是一种债务(*Schuld*)。罗马的契约[2]会产生

---

〔1〕 英译者在此将 *Vertrag* 翻译为协议(agreement),以便与他处的契约(contract)相区别;此种处理源于两大法系对契约的界定不同。由于中国法主要属于大陆法系,因此仍将 *Vertrag* 直接翻译为契约。与此相类似的还有 *Schuld*(债)这个词,由于两大法系术语的差异,英译者为求周全,选了两个词与其对应,即 debt、obligation;基于前述理由,中译者径自将 *Schuld* 译为"债"或"债务"。

〔2〕 (拉)*contractus*(契约),根据古典罗马法学家的观点,契约是指数个当事人之间创设债关系的法律行为;它由两个要素构成,第一个要件是作为债根据的客观事实或原因,第二个要素是当事人之间的协议。在罗马法中,并非当事人之间的所有协议都可被称做契约,实际上,只有那些产生债关系的协议才能算是契约;契约是最重要的法律渊源。

*pactum* (pact) brings about no liability (*Haftung*), but as a rule brings about an obligation (*Schuld*). The *pactum* (pact) therefore usually amounts to a *Vertrag*; the *contractus*, always. The traditional juristic science, which, following the Romans, devoted sufficient attention to the distinction between possession and real right, does not know how to deal with a parallel phenomenon in the sphere of the law of contracts, although the Romans have done some preparatory work also in this sphere, by means of their concept of *naturalis obligatio*, which Windscheid in his day estimated at its true value as merely an obligation according to the *Verkehrsauffassung* (the view of commercial custom).

One root of the law of contracts is the present exchange of goods, or barter. This did not arise from friendly intercourse between neighbors. Within the clan, in his own village, man in the lower stages of development was as little given to making contracts as he is given to doing so today in his own family group. Interchange of goods was brought about by means of taking booty or by means of gifts exchanged between a guest and his host. The oldest merchant is the pirate at a more advanced stage of development, who has become convinced that it is of greater advantage to himself to trade with a stranger than to rob him. And the oldest known forms of trading are closely related to robbery. Shortly before the harvest, the pygmies of Africa make raids into the fields of the negroes, carry off the bananas, peanuts, and maize which grow there, and by way of exchange leave behind dried meat, the chief product of their economic activity. The

债务(*Schuld*)和责任(*Haftung*),*pactum*(简约)[1]不会产生责任(*Haftung*),通常简约仅仅产生债务(*Schuld*)。因此,*pactum*(简约)通常等同于一项契约,*contractus*(契约)则总是等同于一项契约。追随罗马人的传统法学对占有和物权的区分给予了足够的重视,却不知道如何处理在契约法领域中的这一个类似现象,尽管罗马人依靠自然债务[2]的观念在这一领域也做了一些准备性工作,温德沙伊德在他那个时代,认为自然债务仅仅作为一种 *Verkehrsauffassung*(商业惯例上)的债务才有其真正的价值。

契约法的一个根源就是现在的货物交易或者易物交易。这并非源自邻居间的友好交往。在人类发展的低级阶段,在氏族中,在他自己的村庄里,一个人就像今天在自己的家庭群体里那样,很少有机会缔结契约。货物的交换借助于获得战利品或者客人和主人之间交换礼物的方式而达成。最古老的商人是一个较高发展阶段的海盗,他确信和陌生人做生意比抢劫陌生人对自己更有利。已知的最古老的贸易形式与抢掠密切相连。在丰收在即的时刻,非洲的俾格米人会突然袭击黑人的领地,夺走生长在那里的香蕉、花生和玉米,作为交换他们留下干肉——他们经济活动的主要成果。希罗多

[1] (拉)*Pactum*(简约)。指两个以上当事人采用法定契约形式以外的方式达成的协议,也被称为无形式简约。从法律上讲,简约不导致权利的转移,不产生严格意义上的债,也不产生诉权,除非它作为法律行为的附带约定或者具效力得到法律的承认。但在实践中,执法官往往对当事人之间的简约给与考虑和维护。

[2] (拉)*naturalis obligatio*(自然债务),不受法律保障、不可被强制执行的债务,但债务人自愿履行的,不得反悔。

silent trading that Herodotus and Pliny tell of belongs to a more advanced stage. "The oldest agreement is the agreement for the exchange of goods; it can be entered into without any personal, verbal relations; the chronicles tell of silent trading between Russians and strangers, neither party understanding the language of the other." This is Budanow-Wladimirski's introduction to the history of the contract in his history of Russian law.

The second root of the law of contracts is subjection to the domination of another. An instance of this is the sale of one's own person. The man who is in need of seed corn for his economic activity or who has lost more at gambling than he can pay surrenders himself as a slave to the wealthy lord, who takes the man into custody for the advance and lets the latter work for him. Another instance is the enfeoffment with a knight's fee, which obligated the feoffee to render military and knight's services; another, the enfeoffment for rent and services, which imposed on the feoffee the payment of rent and the performance of services; another, the agreement of commendation, whereby a freeman places his person and his property under the dominion of a more powerful man, who in exchange for services and rent promises protection against attack.

In the contract of barter as well as in the contract of submission, there is a granting of possession; in the former, possession of the thing; in the latter, of the person. But there are certain subsidiary agreements which are connected with the transfer of possession,

德[1]和普林尼所讲述的“无声交易”属于一种更为高级的阶段。“最古老的契约是货物交换契约；缔结这种契约不需要任何人身的和口头的关系，编年史讲述了俄国人和陌生人之间的无声交易，双方当事人都不理解对方的语言。”这是布达诺·乌拉迪密斯基为他的俄国法律史中的契约史部分写的导言。

契约法的另外一个根源是对另外一个人支配的服从。出卖个人的人身就是这样的一个例子。因为经济活动而急需谷物种子的人或者在赌博中输得一贫如洗无法偿还债务的人，会放弃自己的人身自由而成为富裕领主的奴隶，领主会为了这些预付款项而将放弃人身自由的人置于自己的监护下并让这个人为自己劳动。另外的一个例子，就是骑士封地的授予，受领封地的人有义务提供军事和骑士服务；另外就是为了获取租金和服务而授予封地，这种形式强加给了受领封地者支付租金和提供服务的义务。再有就是领主附庸契约，在这种协议中，自由民把自己人身和财产置于一个更强大的人的支配下，后者为了获取租金和服务而承诺对前者提供免受攻击的保护。

在易物契约和臣服契约中，都存在着占有转移。在前者中，转移的是对物的占有；在后者中，转移的是对人的占有。但是，也存在着特定的与占有转移相联系的附属协议，例如在易

〔1〕 Herodotus，希罗多德（约公元前485～约公元前425），希腊历史学家，他的作品主要涉及波斯战争，系人们所知的叙述体史书的最早样品。

e. g. in the case of a contract of barter, the warranty that the thing has not been stolen; in the case of a contract of submission, an understanding about mutual performances, the promise of the creditor to release the debtor as soon as the debt has been paid or worked out. In this case the obligation or debt incurred is greater than the liability (*Haftung*); for there is no liability in case of subsidiary agreements of this nature.

But a debt can be secured by means of the possession of a person other than that of the debtor, or of a thing other than that which was the subject of the contractual agreement. This happens when a debtor gives a third person to the creditor as a hostage, or delivers a pledge to him. Until now the liability (*Haftung*) consisted in the creditor's keeping the debtor or the thing that was owed in his own possession until he had been paid. At this stage however the contractual obligation is severed from the possession of the person or of the thing which constitutes the subject or object of the contract. The liability (*Haftung*) becomes selfexistent, and the extent, content, and duration of the liability (*Haftung*) is determined by the extent, content, and duration of the obligation; in the last analysis, by the contract. The creditor who refuses to release a hostage or to return a pledge although the debt has been extinguished is guilty of man-stealing or of theft, and this at quite an early time constituted the basis of a claim which could be prosecuted by appeal to the courts. In the early stages, perhaps, the penalty for such conduct was death. Limited to the duty to return the person or thing, the widely entertained view may be correct that contractual obligation became enforceable by legal action because of the fact that the person obligated who had not performed was treated as liable to punishment. Apart from that, the idea that a person who performs his obligations poorly or not at all is liable for the resulting damage arose at a very late time, much later than the immediate liability (*Haftung*) based on the contract.

All further development of contractual liability (*Vertragshaftung*) is a progressive severance of liability (*Haftung*) from possession of the object of the liability (*Haftung*) and a progressive reception of the content of the obligation, or debt (*Schuld*), into

物契约的情形下，对物不是偷盗来的保证；在臣服协议中，则是有关互相履行的默契，即债权人的允诺——一旦债务人还清债务或者完成工作，债权人就释放债务人。在这种情况下，产生的债务要远远大于责任（*Haftung*），因为在这种性质的附属性协议中不存在责任。

但是，债务可以通过对第三人的占有或对契约标的物以外的物的占有来保障实现。当债务人将第三人交给债权人作为人质时，或向债权人交付担保物时，即属这种情况。责任（*Haftung*）存在于债权人在其债权获偿之前所保管的债务人或担保物。但是，在这一阶段，契约债务与构成契约主体或客体的人或物的占有相分离。责任（*Haftung*）变成了独立存在的东西，责任（*Haftung*）的范围、内容和持续期间都由债务的范围、内容和持续期间来决定；归根到底，责任由契约决定。如果债务已经清偿，但债权人拒绝释放人质或者归还质物，他就会触犯绑架罪或者偷窃罪，这在很早的时候就构成了可诉诸法院的请求权的基础。在较早的阶段，对这种行为的刑罚或许是死刑。广泛流行的观点将债权人的责任限于返还质人或质物上，并认为，契约债务通过法律诉讼变得可以强制执行，因为没有履行义务的债务人被认为应受到惩罚，这种观点可能是正确的。除此之外，在非常晚的时期，还产生了这样的观念：不完全履行债务或者根本没有履行债务的人要对由此导致的损失承担责任，这种责任出现的时间要比基于契约的直接责任（*Haftung*）晚得多。

契约责任（*Vertragshaftung*）所有的进一步发展都是责任（*Haftung*）与对责任（*Haftung*）对象之占有的渐次分离，以及责任（*Haftung*）对债务（*Schuld*）内容的逐渐接纳。提供债务人人身和人质

the liability (*Haftung*). The immediate sale by the debtor of his person and the giving of hostages is superseded by a conditional sale and by the finding of a surety or sureties. The debtor sells his person to the creditor only in case he fails to make payment (the *Treugelöbnis* of the Germans, the *nexum* of the Romans, numerous examples in ancient Russian law), or he finds a surety against this event. The pledge becomes a wager, i. e. a thing of no value or of lesser value is given as a symbol. In this way the contracts of subjection and of pledge gradually become *real* contracts. At a later time the contract of barter ceases to be a contract of present exchange and becomes a *real* contract, i. e. the very fact that one party has accepted the performance of the other obligates the former to render a counter-performance. At a later period, the acceptance of part performance is sufficient, and finally even the acceptance of an apparent performance (*Arrha*, earnest-money). This brings about the liability (*Haftung*) for the promised performance not only of the giver but also of the taker. Whether, apart from this, the promise under oath, whereby the debtor had called down upon himself the vengeance of the gods if he should fail to keep his promise, was, at this early stage, of decisive importance for the development of law as a formal contract cannot be ascertained at the present state of our knowledge. Originally the formal promise served merely to confirm the compromise providing for payment of *wergild* or penalty.

This imports chiefly that the liability (*Haftung*) no longer results from possession but from the contract. The creditor obtains

的即刻买卖被有条件的买卖所取代,或者被保证所取代。债务人只有在未能清偿债务(德国人的信用担保,罗马人的债务口约,[1]古俄国法中的无数例子)的情况下,才会将其人身出质给债权人,债务人对这种事项作了保证。担保变成了一种保证,即没有任何价值或价值极小的物作为象征而被交付。这样,臣服契约和担保契约逐渐变成要物契约。后来,易物契约也不再是当面交易的契约,而是变成了一种要物契约,也就是说,一方当事人接受另一方当事人履行的事实使得前者有义务提供对待履行。再后来,对部分履行的接受也足以构成契约,到最后,即使是表面履行的接受(*Arrha*,定金),也足以构成契约。这就产生了允诺者和接受允诺者对允诺履行的责任(*Haftung*),我们当前的知识状态无法确定:除此之外,宣誓允诺——债务人诅咒自己如果他不能信守允诺他将被上帝惩罚——作为正式的契约是否对这一早期的契约发展具有决定性的意义。最初,正式的允诺仅仅是为了确认规定刑事赔偿金[2]或刑罚的和解契约。

这主要表明,责任(*Haftung*)不再产生于占有而是产生于契

---

〔1〕 (拉)*Nexum*(债务口约),一种古老的契约形式,类似于要式买卖。当事人在见证人和司秤面前缔结关于消费借贷方面的契约,所不同的是,缔约一方(债务人)采用出卖人身的方式为借贷担保,这意味着:如果债务人不能清偿债务或者未能实现债务口约的解除,将根据该契约成为债权人的债务奴隶,接受债权人的役使。

〔2〕 *Wergild*,赎罪赔偿金。中世纪的日耳曼法中规定的,由造成伤害的人向受害者本人,或者造成死亡时向死者的亲属支付的一定数额的金钱赔偿。最初,赎罪赔偿金的数额是不确定的,后来逐渐由法律和中世纪的一些法典固定下来。

a right of enforcement against the person or property of the debtor which is independent of possession, and whose nature and extent are determined by the content of the contractual debt, or obligation (*Vertragsschuld*). This whole development has been placed beyond all doubt as to Germanic law by modern research; and Roman law, although it has become known to us in a much later stage of development, has preserved numerous traces of it. I think that most probably the few words that Festus has handed down to us from the *foedus Latinum* under the key-word *nancitor* refer to the right of the creditor to take possession of the property of the debtor. The oldest Roman action, the *legis actio per manus iniectionem*, even in historical times, is a living vestige of the creditor's right against the person of the debtor. The creditor seizes the debtor wheresoever he finds him, and leads him away into custody. This is not man-stealing but legal self-help, and therefore does not give rise to a feud. Anyone who would defend the debtor must go to the praetor with the creditor. The prevailing view that the creditor did not perform the *manus iniectio* until he got into court is manifestly erroneous. We find the *legis*

约。债权人获得了一项独立于占有的、针对债务人的人身或者财产强制执行的权利,这种权利的属性和范围由契约之债务(*Vertragsschuld*)的内容决定。通过现代的研究,日耳曼法整个这方面的发展毫无疑问已被认定;尽管我们了解罗马法是在一个较晚的发展阶段,但罗马法中仍留下了大量的线索。我认为:费斯特斯从拉丁条约[1]传给我们的、在关键词获得的少许文字中,最为可能涉及的是债权人对债务人财产取得占有的权利。甚至在历史上,最古老的罗马诉讼拘禁之诉[2]就是债权人针对债务人人身的权利的一个现存的残余。无论在何处,只要债权人发现债务人就可以将其抓获,并将他置于自己的监禁之下。这不是绑架,而是一种法律上的自力救济,因此,这不会导致一种世仇。任何想要保护债务人的人必须和债权人一起到裁判官[3]那里。未进入法庭前债权人不能对债务人实行拘禁的流行观点明显是错误的。

---

〔1〕 (拉)*foedus Latinum*(拉丁条约),罗马和其他民族或国家签订的协定。

〔2〕 (拉)*the legis actio per manus iniectionem*(拘禁之诉),一种较为古老的、以强制执行为目的的法律诉讼,主要针对的是得到司法裁决确认的债务关系。债权人在作出司法裁决的30日后要求(可采取强制手段)未清偿的债务人在执法官前出庭应诉,并且要求对债务人实施人身拘禁;如果债务人不能向执法官提供推迟应诉保证人,执法官将允许债权人对债务人实行60日的人身监禁,为债务人套上枷锁,强迫他劳动或者将其在城市内市场出卖;如果在60日后债务仍未得到清偿,债权人甚至有权杀死被拘禁的债务人或者将其卖到城邦之外。

〔3〕 Praetor,裁判官。古罗马共和国一年选举一次的裁判官,位列执政官之下,但具有与执政官几乎相同的职权。

*actio per manus iniectionem* among the southern Slavs as late as the end of the Middle Ages under the name Udawa. It has been described very vividly by Novakovic, together with the mitigation which it underwent in the course of time, in a treatise published by the Serbian Academy of Sciences, chiefly on the basis of Ragusan sources.

It was not until liability (*Haftung*) was completely severed from possession and the extent of the liability (*Haftung*) coincided with the content of the obligation (*Schuld*), at least in principle, that the road was cleared for the credit contract (*Kreditvertrag*). The credit contract however brings about a complete change in the nature of the contract. The contracts of barter and of subjection thereby lose their original peculiar nature, so that it becomes possible to extend credit to the debtor, or obligor, for the counterperformance for which he is liable. The sale of his person by the debtor becomes a loan of money or of things, the enfeoffment for services and rent becomes a contract of ordinary and usufructuary lease, to which all personal subjection and the obligation to labor are foreign (although this was not fully carried out in Roman law); so that in more advanced stages of development only the contract for services and wages and the mandate (*Auftrag*) remind one of the fact that, at some time in the past, the contract could bring about personal subjection. The extension of credit converts the contract of barter into a consensual contract.

Tracing the development of the understanding into a fact of the law, one must distinguish the following stages: the *Barvertrag* (contract for present exchange), the *Schuldvertrag* (contract creating a debt or obligation), the *Haftungsvertrag* (contract creating a liability), and the *Kreditvertrag* (credit contract). The *Barvertrag* (contract for present exchange) merely effects the acquisition of possession of the subject matter of the contract. The fact of the law here is not the contract, but the possession; all the legal consequences that ensue are consequences of the transfer of possession, not of the contract. As soon as promises are connected with the transfer of possession, and obligation (*Schuld*) is attached to these, the contract, in addition to the exchange of possession, effectuates an obligation (*Schuld*), and thereby becomes a self-

我们发现在中世纪晚期,拘禁之诉以 Udawa 的名义存在于南部斯拉夫人中。在主要以拉谷桑的原始资料为基础的由塞尔维亚科学院发表的一篇论文中,诺瓦克维克对拘禁诉讼及其在时间推移中历经的缓和作了非常生动的描述。

直到责任(*Haftung*)与占有完全分离、责任(*Haftung*)内容与债务(*Schuld*)内容相一致,至少在原则上,通向信用契约(*Kreditvertrag*)的大道才开辟出来。然而,信用契约导致了契约性质的彻底转变。由此,易物契约和服从契约丧失了它们最初的独特性质,因而,向债务人提供信用以便换取后者的对待给付,成为了可能。债务人人身的出卖变成了货币借贷或者物品借贷,为获取服务和租金而进行的封地授予变成了普通的契约和附用益权租约,对于它们来说,所有的人身隶属和劳动义务都是不相关的(尽管这在罗马法中并没有完全贯彻);所以,在更为发达的发展阶段,只有服务和工资契约和委任契约(*Auftrag*)才会让人想起:在过去的某一个时期,契约可以导致人身的隶属。信用的提供将易物契约变成了诺成契约。

探索对法律事实理解的发展过程,任何人都必须区分下列阶段:*Barvertrag*(当场交易契约)、*Schuldvertrag*(债权契约)、*Haftungsvertrag*(产生责任的契约)和 *Kreditvertrag*(信用契约)。*The Barvertrag*(当场交易契约)仅仅实现对契约标的物占有的获得。在这里,法律事实不是契约而是占有;随后发生的所有的结果都是占有转移的后果,而不是契约引发的后果。一旦允诺与占有转移相联系,并且债务(*Schuld*)基于它们而发生,则该契约,除了占有的交换外,还使债务(*Schuld*)得以生效,从而,契约也变成是一种独立存在的法律事实。正是通过

existent fact of the law. It is through the *Haftungsvertrag* ( contract creating liability), which gives to the creditor the right to proceed against the person or property of the debtor which he has in his possession, that the contract, as a fact of the law which creates liability (*Haftung*), is gradually being emancipated from all connection with possession.

The principle of the Continental common law that informal contracts are actionable implies that every contract, on principle, brings about debt or obligation (*Schuld*) as well as liability (*Haftung*), and that the extent of the liability is determined by the extent of the debt, or obligation. This fact has made it difficult for the common-law jurist to perceive that today, as well as in the hoary past, in addition to *contractus* there are *pacta* (pacts) ; that in addition to contracts creating liability there are contracts creating merely an obligation.

We must therefore emphasize so much the more vigorously that the important thing for the economic life is not the liability (*Haftung*) but the debt, or obligation (*Schuld*); that in the great majority of cases it is immaterial whether a contract is actionable or not, provided only that according to the rule of conduct which governs life one can count upon its being performed. In view of the fact that contracts are actionable on principle, it seems very natural to suppose that in actual life contracts are being performed only because they are actionable ; not only legal history, however, but also a glance at modern life shows that, on the contrary, contracts have become actionable because, as a rule, they are being performed in life. Even today, the contract which cannot be sued upon, and which effects merely an obligation (*Schuld*), plays an important role in economic and social life. A very important part of industry is based on child labor, and most of the contracts for work and labor that were made with children undoubtedly were absolutely invalid down to the time of the legislation for the protection of working-men, and many are invalid today. But that has not prevented exploitation of children from being at all times a most profitable business. For a century at least, a large part of the business transacted at the Exchange has been beyond the bounds of the legally enforcible, and, in part, beyond the bounds of the legally permissible.

*Haftungsvertrag*（产生责任的契约）的方式——该契约赋予债务人起诉处于其占有下的债务人人身或其财产的权利——契约作为一种产生责任（*Haftung*）的法律事实逐渐从与占有的各种联系中解脱出来。

欧陆共同法的原则——非正式的契约也是可诉的——意味着：原则上，每一种契约都会导致债（*Schuld*）的产生，也会导致责任（*Haftung*）的产生，并且责任的范围由债的范围来决定。这一事实使得欧陆共同法法学家很难察觉在今天和在遥远的过去，除了契约外，还存在着 *pacta*（简约）；除了产生责任的契约外，还存在着仅仅产生债的契约。

因此，我们必须强调，使经济生活更具活力的重要事情不是责任（*Haftung*），而是债（*Schuld*）；在大多数的情形下，只要依据支配生活的行为规则人们能够对契约的履行寄予依赖，一个契约是否可诉就无关紧要。鉴于原则上契约都是可诉的这一事实，做以下推想似乎非常自然：现实生活中，契约之所以会被履行仅仅是因为契约是可诉的。然而，不仅法律史，而且对现代生活的粗略观察表明：恰恰相反，契约之所以可诉，通常是因为它们在现实生活中被人们履行。即使是今天，那些不可诉的契约和仅仅产生债务（*Schuld*）的契约，也在经济和社会生活中起到了重要的作用。工业很重要的一部分是以童工劳动为基础，毫无疑问，和童工签订的大部分工作和劳动契约直至劳工保护立法的时代都是绝对无效的，并且在今天，许多契约也是无效的。因为剥削童工一直都是一项有利可图的事业，所以这种无效认定并没有阻止对童工的剥削。至少一个世纪以来，证券市场进行的大量交易都已经超出了法律强制的范围，并且部分地超出了法律许可的范围。特别是社会斗争和经济

Particularly, the social struggles and the economic movements have brought about a whole series of contracts that are not enforcible; numerous cartel agreements of entrepreneurs, many wage agreements among working-men, and most agreements between representatives of labor and of employers (*Tarifverträge*) probably are not legally enforcible.

It is necessary therefore to bear in mind that, not only in history but also in the law that is valid today, in addition to understandings that are altogether outside of the legal sphere, there are agreements that import an obligation (*Schuld*) but no liability (*Haftung*); that import a rule according to which men regulate their conduct in life, but not a rule according to which the authorities proceed; and that these contracts are as significant for the economic life as legally enforceable contracts. Juristic science must not overlook this. And it must go further. It must bear in mind that the enforcible contract does not rule the world to the extent that it is being enforced by the authorities, but to the extent that it has become a rule of conduct.

Legal history shows us that whenever the contract becomes a fact of the law, this does not amount to a recognition of the sovereignty of the human will, but of the role actually played by the contract in social and in economic life. To the law the contract is nothing more than an instrument of the social and economic order. But the contract becomes a fact of the law, though only to the extent to which there is a social and economic need therefor; and it disappears from life as soon as the need which brought it about has disappeared. Entering into a relation of protection or into a contract of enfeoffment would be as impossible today as it would have been to secure a loan by a hypothec in the Germany of Tacitus. The law of contracts, too, is nothing more than the legal form of the social and economic order.

Up to this point it has been possible to base our discussion upon generally recognized results of comparative legal science and upon

运动导致了一系列不具有强制执行力的契约;企业主间大量的卡特尔协议、劳工间以及劳工代表和雇主间的大部分工资协议(*Tarifverträge*)很可能都是不具有法律强制执行力的。

因此,有必要记住,不仅在历史上而且在今天有效的法律中,除了那些完全超出法律范围的默示协议外,还存在着只引起债(*Schuld*)不引起责任(*Haftung*)的协议;这意味着生活中人们据以调节自己行为的规则不是当局依据来进行诉讼的规则;并且,对于经济生活来说,这些契约与法律上可强制执行的契约一样重要。法学不能忽视这些,而且法学必须走得更远。必须记住,可强制执行的契约并不在它被当局强制执行的范围内统治着世界,而是在它成为一种行为规则的范围内统治着世界。

法律史告诉我们:当契约变成一种法律事实的时候,这并不等同于对人类意思自治的认可,而是对契约在社会和经济生活中的实际作用的认可。对于法律来说,契约仅仅是一种实现社会和经济秩序的工具。但是契约还是变成了一种法律事实,尽管仅仅在经济和社会需要的范围内;一旦导致契约产生的经济和社会需要消失,契约也会从生活中消失。如今,缔结一种保护关系或者订立封地授予契约,就如同在塔西佗[1]时代的德国通过抵押权来担保一笔贷款一样不可能。契约法也仅仅是社会和经济生活秩序的法律形式。

到现在为止,我们还是可以将我们的讨论建立在比较法学和

---

〔1〕 Tacitus · Publius · Cornelius,塔西佗 · 普布留斯 · 科内利乌斯,古罗马官员和历史学家,他的两部最伟大的著作——《历史》(Histories)和《编年史》(Annals),记述了从奥古斯都之死(公元 14 年)到多米西安之死(公元 96 年)期间的史实。

the history of law. The same cannot be said of the law of inheritance. The prevailing doctrine derives the law of inheritance from the common ownership of the family; even where the latter no longer exists, it still produces after-effects according to the prevailing view inasmuch as it gives to certain kinsmen who in time past had been members of the family community an inchoate right of inheritance. If this were true, the law of inheritance would be a development from another legal relation and we should find it necessary to investigate, not the facts that have led to the law of inheritance, but those that have led to the inchoate rights of kinsmen.

Sir Henry Sumner Maine, however, in his day, expressed doubts as to the correctness of this doctrine. It has been refuted, it seems to me, by Ficker, at least as to the Germanic peoples, to whom it was originally attributed. Ficker has, as I believe, conclusively shown that the law of inheritance is older, even among the Germans, than the inchoate right of the members of the house community, that the owner may, at a time at which there exists a fully developed right of inheritance of the kinsmen, dispose of his property freely without concerning himself about the claims of his children, to say nothing of the claims of more distant kinsmen.

The early history of the law of inheritance must begin with the house community. The law of inheritance has its roots in the house. We are concerned here with two questions. First of all, to whom did the estate belong if the deceased lived in a house community; and, secondly, to whom did it belong if he lived alone, perhaps surrounded only by unfree persons or servants? The latter case manifestly occurs very rarely in primitive society, perhaps never; but it does occur with increasing frequency at a later period in a well ordered state, which makes it possible for a person to live alone. It is easily understood that the property of the deceased that was not put into the grave with him became the property of the members of his house community who had dwelt and worked together with him in the household. This indeed applies only to his movable possessions, for this order obtains even

法律史学公认的结果上。但此判断不能适用于继承法。主流学说从家庭的共同所有权中推导出继承法;甚至在共同所有权不再存在的地方,依据主流观点,它还可以产生后继效应,因为共同所有权赋予了曾是家族共同体成员的同族男性亲属一种尚未成熟的继承权。如果事实如此,那么继承法可能是从另外一种法律关系中发展而来的,我们认为有必要调查的是那些导致同族亲属尚未成熟之继承权的事实,而不是调查导致继承法产生的事实。

然而,亨利·萨姆纳·梅因爵士在他那个年代就表达了对这一学说正确性的怀疑。至少在关于日耳曼民族方面,我认为菲克尔早已将这一学说驳倒,不过该学说最初也归功于他。我相信,菲克尔确凿无疑地证明:即使在日耳曼民族中,继承法也比家族成员尚不成熟的继承权要早;在男性亲属继承权充分发展的时代,所有者也可以在不考虑其子女请求权的情况下自由处分自己的财产,更不用说考虑远亲的请求权了。

继承法早期的历史必定从家庭共同体开始。继承法最先根源于家庭。这里我们关注两个问题:首先,如果亡者先前居住在家族共同体中,遗产应当属于谁?其次,如果亡者是独自一人,或许有一些非自由人或者仆人跟随他,那么财产又归谁所有?非常明显,第二种情况在原始社会中极少发生,或许从来就没有发生过。但第二种情况在稍后的时期,在一个秩序良好的国家中发生的频率日益增加,秩序良好的国家使得一个人单独生活成为了可能。非常容易理解,那些没有成为殉葬品的财产成为了那些和他在家庭中一起居住和工作的其他成员的财产。这一规则的确仅仅适用于亡者的动产,因为这种秩序即

among hunters and cattle-breeders, and is therefore older than ownership of land. The members of the house community of the deceased need not take possession of the goods of the latter, for they are in possession at the moment of his death, and they are in position to resist interference by a third person with the same means as during the lifetime of the deceased. The members of the household remain in possession of the goods the latter left behind, and carry on as they always did; the situation has changed very little; the number of persons in the house has merely been decreased by one. The fact of the law, then, at this stage, is possession. But the primitive law of inheritance has not progressed much beyond this remaining in possession on the part of the members of the house community. Accordingly if the deceased has not lived in a house community, his estate becomes ownerless. Among the Romans and the Germanic peoples clear traces of this state of affairs remain even in historical times. The most important traces however are to be found among the Slavic people, whose oldest legal monuments present a most interesting, very early stage of development, which the other people of Europe had passed through long before their legal tradition was recorded in writing. To the Russians, the Poles, the Masovians, the Czechs, the Moravians, and perhaps the Serbs, of the eighteenth century, the right of inheritance of the collateral kindred is still an unknown thing; in the case of a death without an heir, the estate is "*leer*," and escheats to the ruler, or, in case of an unfree person, to the lord.

As to the limited recognition by the Slavic codes of the fourteenth century (the statute of Wislica, and the code of Tsar Duschan) of the right of inheritance of the collateral kindred, the very wording shows that it is an innovation. Among the Slavic peoples, the princes, whose power had developed very rapidly, manifestly acting in their own interest, retarded the right of inheritance

使在猎人和家畜的饲养者中也普遍存在。因此,这种秩序要比土地所有权更古老。亡者的家庭共同体成员不需要接管亡者的财产,因为在亡者去世的那一刻,亡者的家庭共同体的成员已占有了财产,他们有权利凭借亡者生前所采取的同样方式来抵制第三人干涉。家庭共同体的成员仍然保有着亡者遗留下来的财产,并可以一如既往继续保有下去;局面基本上没有什么变化,仅仅只是家庭成员减少了一个。因而,在这一阶段法律事实仍是占有。但是,原始继承法的发展并没有超越家庭共同体成员对亡者遗留财产的占有。因此,如果亡者不是居住在一个家庭共同体中,他的遗产就变成了无主财产。甚至历史上,在罗马人和日耳曼民族中,这种事态的清晰痕迹依然残存。然而,我们在斯拉夫人中发现这种事态的最重要的踪迹,斯拉夫人的最古老的法律著作展现了这一非常有趣的早期发展阶段,而欧洲的其他民族在他们的法律传统有记录时,就早已经历了这一阶段。18 世纪的俄国人、波兰人、马索维亚人、捷克人和摩拉维亚人仍然不知旁系亲属的继承权为何物,或许 18 世纪的塞尔维亚人也是如此。在亡者死后没有继承人的情况下,不动产成了“无主财产”,并被充作统治者的公产;若亡者是非自由人,则财产归领主所有。

关于 14 世纪斯拉夫法典(韦斯里卡的制定法和沙皇杜显的法典)对旁系亲属继承权的有限承认,恰当的措辞表明那是一种创新。在斯拉夫民族中,权力迅速膨胀的国王为了自己的利益行事,在很长的一段时间内延迟了旁系亲属继承权的发展,

of the collateral relatives for a long time because it curtailed the right of escheat. Among the Bohemians and the Poles, the right of escheat of the princes may be traceable to German influences; among the Russians and the Serbs, to Byzantine influences.

It has been shown that the declaration by last will and testament did not become an effective *post mortem* disposition until a very late date. Before that time all that could be done was to receive a stranger into the house, and this had the effect that the goods of the head of the house would pass to the person so received equally with the other member of the house community. A little later the gift *morris causa* with present delivery, but with legal effect postponed until the death of the donor, made its appearance; then the *Treuhand* transaction, whose importance for universal legal history was shown in the truly pioneering work of Robert Caillemer: In the Roman law of inheritance the *Treuhänder* appears twice: as *familiae emptor* and as a fiduciary. The English uses and trusts also have their roots in the *Treuhänder* transaction. Here too, therefore, the law of inheritance shows no independent characteristic features; it follows the order of possession and makes use of the contract. The effect of receiving a person into the house (*arrogatio*, *adoptio*, *adfatomie*) is that the

因为这种继承权剥夺了国王没收无继承人之财产的权利。在波希米亚人和波兰人中，国王的此项权利可以追溯到德国法的影响。在俄国和塞尔维亚人中，此项权利可以追溯到拜占廷帝国的影响。

这表明，直到后来很晚的某个时期，遗嘱声明才变成有效的死因处分。在这之前，要做的所有事情就是家庭接纳一个陌生人，这种接纳具有如下效力：家庭头领的财产将平等传继给包括新入者在内的家庭共同体的所有成员。稍后，当场交付标的物但直到赠予者逝世赠予才生效的死因赠予出现了；随后，信托交易出现了，这种交易对世界法律史的重要意义由罗勃特·凯勒默在他的真正的拓荒性作品中有所表达。在罗马法中，信托[1]继承出现了两次：作为家产买受人[2]和作为受托人。英国的用益和信托也源于受托人交易。因此，在这里，继承法也没有显示出任何独立的典型特征，而只是遵循占有秩序并使用契约的形式。家庭接纳一个成员（*arrogatio*、[3] *adoptio*、[4]

---

〔1〕 古日耳曼法中的Salmann。

〔2〕 （拉）*familiae emptor*（家产买受人），在家产要式买卖（*mancipatio familiae*）中购买全部家庭财产的人。此人只是为了安排遗产继承的目的而设置，具有虚拟意义，他将按照家产出卖人的指示在后者去世后对买得的家产进行分配。

〔3〕 对成年人的收养。

〔4〕 （拉）*adoptio*（收养），对其他家庭的子女取得父权（*patria potestas*）的方式。

person received has immediate possession of the goods of the deceased; the gift *mortis causa* and the *Treuhand* transaction are effective in conjunction with transfer of possession. The disposition did not become a self-existent fact of the law of inheritance until the testament came into use.

The economic significance of the law of inheritance does not appear so clearly as that of the other legal institutions, for in this department several currents frequently cross and interfere with each other. The chief concern is the continuation of the economic undertaking. This appears quite clearly in the case of the peasant family household. In this case the economic undertaking is continued without much ado by the survivors; but this is not, properly speaking, a law of inheritance, for the family household is immortal. If there are no survivors, the economic association collapses, for there is no one to continue the undertaking. This is simply another way of saying that the estate is ownerless, or that the ruler, supported by the military power of the state, takes possession of it. Before long however endeavor is being made to preserve the inheritance for the former members of the household or for the kinsmen. The purpose of the law of inheritance thereafter is to serve not an economic but a purely social association, the family. Undoubtedly there is the secondary thought that the kinsmen will continue the economic undertaking of the deceased, but a glance at the actual state of the law of inheritance shows to what extent in this very matter of the succession of the kindred the economic point of view has been thrust into the background by the social. It is self-evident that only where, as in English law, the right of inheritance of the firstborn prevails, has precaution been taken against the destruction of the economic undertaking through the collapse occasioned by the succession; but the motive in this case, too, was consideration for the family, and the whole institution was not thought out on economic lines. Hence the strong and significant endeavor to preserve the economic undertaking by means of adoption or of dispositions *mortis causa*. Where the law of inheritance is non-economic in an especially high

*adfatomie*)[1]的效果是,被接纳者马上就取得对亡者财产的占有。死因赠与和信托交易的效力都与占有的转移相联系。直到遗嘱这种形式开始被运用,遗嘱处分才变成一种独立存在的继承法事实。

继承法的经济意义看上去并不如其他法律制度那样明显,因为,这个法律部门中,几种潮流经常彼此交叉和冲突。首要的关切是经济事业的持续。这在农民家庭住户中表现得非常明显。在这种情况下,生者会毫不费力地将经济事业持续下去;但是,准确地说,这并不是继承法,因为家庭住户是永续存在的。如果没有生者,经济联合体就瓦解,因为没有人继续这一事业。以下只是这种情形的另外一种说法:遗产是无主财产,或者国家军事力量所支持的统治者取得了这些财产。然而,不久以后,人们就试图为先前的住户成员或男性亲属保留遗产。从那以后,继承法的目的就不是服务于经济联合体,而是服务于纯粹的社会联合体——家族。毫无疑问,次要的思考是男性亲属将继续亡者留下的事业,但是对继承法实际状态的粗略观察表明:在这件事情上,社会在怎样的程度上把经济视角的亲属继承置于了一个无关紧要的位置。不言而喻,仅仅在那些长子继承权盛行的地方(如英国),才会采取预防措施,以避免经济事业因继承失败而导致毁灭。但是,在这种情况下,其动机也是为了家族而着想,并且整个制度不是出于经济方面的考量。因此,依靠收养和死因处分的方式维系经济事业是一种有力且有意义的尝试。在那些继承法非出于经济考量的地方,特别是二者疏离程度很高的地方,

---

[1] *Adfatomie* 或者 *affatomie* 是古日耳曼法的两种收养方式之一。

degree like the later Roman or the modern Continental law, making a last will and testament is considered a duty; and dying intestate is a great misfortune. Even where there is a declaration of will by last will and testament, non-economic influences are brought into play; such as consideration for the family, which is often protected against loss of the inheritance by means of a testamentary disposition; consideration for the church; consideration for institutions for the public welfare; and finally reverence for the dead. These were purely social forces, but they gave effect to declarations by last will and testament long before the latter were recognized by the authorities.

Without doubt it would be a great mistake to consider the economic phenomena and fail to take the other social phenomena into consideration. The state, the church, education, art, science, social life, entertainment, play a role in the life of society no less than economic labor. We have therefore pointed out the significance of noneconomic influences, particularly in the discussion of the human associations and of the law of inheritance. It is self-evident that they assert themselves at every moment in the relations of domination and subjection and in the law of possession and of contract. We must not forget in this connection that the economic situation is the presupposition for every form of noneconomic activity. The state can be maintained, the church can be served, education can be provided, art and science can be fostered, time and means for social life and entertainment can exist, only to the extent that the national economy produces returns that are greater than the amount required to satisfy the needs of the workers. For this reason an understanding of the economic order is the basis for an understanding of the other parts of the social order, especially of the legal order of society.

If we fix our attention on the facts of the law in the very beginnings of social life, we shall see that all of them can be traced back to two, to wit the human association, which is kept together and regulated by usage, as the subject, and possession, the social relation which becomes a legal relation within the association, as the object. In the beginning all domination seems to have been based on possession of the subjected person in an association. The contract consists in unilateral or reciprocal transfer of possession or in self-surrender into the possession of another; the law of inheritance

如后来的罗马法或现代欧陆法中，立遗嘱被认为是一种责任；未留有遗嘱而死亡是一种最大的不幸。甚至在那些有遗嘱声明的地方，非经济的影响力也在起作用；这些非经济因素包括基于家庭方面的考虑，其目的通常是依靠遗嘱处分的方式来防止遗产的丧失；还包括教会方面的考虑；公共福利制度方面的考虑；以及对亡者的尊敬。这些都是纯粹的社会力量，但是，它们在遗嘱声明被当局认可的很久以前就已经影响着它了。

毋庸置疑，考虑经济现象的同时不考虑其他社会现象是一个巨大的错误。国家、教会、教育、艺术、科学、社会生活、娱乐在社会生活中起着不低于经济劳动的作用。因此，特别是在讨论人类联合体和继承法的时候，我们指出了非经济影响因素的重要意义。不证自明的是：在支配和服从关系中，在占有法和契约法中，这些影响因素在每一刻都在彰显着它们的力量。在这一点上，我们不能忘记，经济状况是每一种非经济活动形式的先决条件。只有在国民经济创造的利润大于满足工人所需之消耗的范围内，国家才能维持，教会才能运作，教育才得以提供，艺术和科学才得以培育，社会生活与娱乐的时间和手段才得以存在。因此，对经济秩序的理解是理解社会秩序具他部分的基础，特别是理解社会法律秩序的基础。

如果我们将注意力集中到社会生活开始时的法律事实上，我们就会发现所有的法律事实都可以追溯到两种基本的法律事实，即，作为主体而存在的、由习惯撮合并调整的人类联合体；作为客体而存在的、在联合体内变成法律关系的社会关系——占有。最初，所有的支配都是基于对联合体内被支配者的占有。契约存在于单方或者相互的占有转移中，或者存在于对他人占有的甘心屈

consists in this, that the kindred of a deceased keep for themselves that which hitherto they have possessed in common with the latter, and that they divide among themselves that which the latter possessed for himself in the common household. All law then arises from the fact that within the association there is added to respect for the person of the members respect for his possessions, and that this becomes the basis of the general order and the general rule of conduct. At a later stage, the possession of a human being becomes the right in the human being (relations of domination and family relations), and finally the right to demand a performance from a human being (personal liability); possession of a thing becomes a right in the thing or the right to various emoluments of the thing (ownership and real rights); and finally possession of the thing on the basis of a contract becomes a right in the thing based on a declaration of the previous possessor. From this time forth all development of law consists in the slow development of the norms which command respect for the person of the member of the association and for his possessions and in the development of the latter into norms for the peaceful exchange and transportation of goods, in the extension and the differentiation of the human associations into an increasingly comprehensive, intricate, and diversified organization of the human family.

We may perhaps be permitted to spin this thought out a little further. In the simple associations of the peoples on the lowest level of development known to us, there is neither possession of things nor contracts. The order of the association is based chiefly on usage, and perhaps on domination over women and minors. The fact of this domination is sufficiently explained by the fact that the peoples who are found on the lowest level of development known to us have, after all, reached a certain stage of development at which differences of sex and of age give rise to associations within the associations. In the oldest associations, which have long since disappeared, usage, most probably, was the sole ordering element. And also in the original association of our present-day society, in the community of the family household, possession and contract are very far from being looked upon as facts of the law. Here too the whole order is based on usage; the more so, the better and more intimately the family life is organized. Contracts that are made with reference to family relationships

从中;继承法存在于:亡者的亲属为自身保有到那时为止他们和亡者共同占有的财产,亡者的亲属将亡者在共同居住中为自己利益而占有的财产进行分割。于是,所有的法律都产生于如下事实:联合体内的成员因为其占有而受人尊重,而且这变成了一般秩序和一般行为规则的基础。后来,对人的占有变成了对人的权利(支配关系和家庭关系),最终变成了要求他人履行的权利(个人责任);对物的占有变成了对物的权利或获取物的各种收益的权利(所有权和物权)。而且,最后,以契约为基础的、对物的占有变成了基于前手占有人意思表示的物权。从这一时刻起,全部的法律发展存在于——那些命令尊重联合体成员和联合体成员财产的——规范的缓慢发展中,存在于这些规范的发展中——从起初仅要求尊重的规范转变为商品和平交易和运输的规范,存在于人类联合体不断的扩展和分化中——人类联合体从最初简单的形式演变为日益广泛、复杂、多样化的人类家庭组织。

或许我们可以将这一思想讲述得再深入一点。在我们所知发展程度最低的民族的简单联合体中,对物的占有和契约都是不存在的。联合体的秩序主要基于习惯,并且,或许是基于对妇女和未成年人的支配。此种支配的事实完全可以由下面的事实来解释:我们所知处在最低发展阶段的民族毕竟达到了特定的发展阶段,在此阶段,性别和年龄的差异已经促生了联合体内的联合体。在早已消失的最古老的联合体中,习惯,最有可能是唯一的规整元素。同样地,在我们今天社会里的原始联合体中,在家庭住户共同体中,占有和契约还远没有被看做法律事实。在这里,整个秩序的基础也是习惯;在组织得越好、越亲密的家庭生活中,就越是如此。涉及家庭关系的契约(特别是涉及与婚姻有关的财

(especially contracts concerning matrimonial property) are made solely for the purpose of regulating the situation in case of dissolution of the community of the household. So long as the family is not disrupted, and its members get along well with one another, usually no one gives thought to contracts, much less to possession. Among all the facts of the law, therefore, usage is the sole primitive one. Possession and contract become facts of the law only in the higher associations, which are composed of several simple associations, and they are not found at all where there are no composite associations of this kind. As to these two facts of the law, possession is evidently older and more primitive than the contract. Where possession does not govern the relations within the associations, the latter either have not yet been combined into an association of a higher order or they have already dissolved the latter; in either case they are at war with each other. Even today possession determines the reciprocal relations of people who, being associated in a but loosely knit association, wish to get along peaceably with one another. One may instance the occupying of seats and chairs in a railway coach and on a ship, and the monopolizing of newspapers in a cafe; the rules as to standing in line at a ticket-window or waiting one's turn in a waiting room are also related to the rules of possession. The contract presupposes a much closer relationship; the closer, the more completely it is severed from the bare transfer of possession. A contract that involves more than a present exchange, even an understanding that has absolutely no binding force, is usually made only with acquaintances, persons of the same social class, business friends, or business men, in foreign countries perhaps with fellow-countrymen.

The whole economic and social order of the human race is based upon the following small number of facts: usage, domination, possession, disposition (usually by contract or by testamentary disposition). These facts by their very existence determine the rules of conduct for the human associations that are comprised in human society. These rules, self-evidently, are not exclusively legal norms. They are the elements into which the infinite diversity of the phenomena of our legal world, and in part of the world of the other norms, resolves itself. Every small human society creates its own order self-actively and where the smaller associations combine, or are combined, into larger associations the combined association must indeed, in its relations with its com-

产方面的契约)都纯粹为了调整家庭共同体解体的情形。因此,只要家庭不瓦解,家庭中的成员彼此和睦相处,通常没有人会想到契约,更不用说占有。因此,在所有的法律事实中,习惯是唯一最原始的一个。仅仅在由几个简单联合体组成的更高级联合体中,占有和契约才变成了法律事实,而且,若是这种类型的复合联合体不存在,占有和契约根本不存在。至于这两种法律事实中,占有明显地要比契约更古老和原始。在占有不支配联合体内部关系的地方,这种内部关系要么还没有被整合成一种较高等级的联合体,要么这种内部关系已经使联合体解体。在任一情况下,它们都处于竞争状态。甚至今天,占有也决定着那些已组成了松散联合体、同时希望彼此和平相处的人的相互关系。一个人可以举出在铁路客车和轮船上占座位和椅子的例子,以及在一间咖啡馆中垄断报纸的例子;甚至在售票口排队或者在等候室等待的规则也和占有的规则有关。契约以一种更近的关系为前提;这种关系越亲近,契约和单纯的占有移转就分离得越完全。不仅仅涉及当场交易的契约,甚至绝对没有拘束力的默示协议,通常也仅与熟人、同一个社会阶层的人、商业朋友或者商人缔结,在外国或许会与本国同胞缔结。

人类整个经济和社会秩序建立在如下的少数几个事实之上:习惯、支配、占有、处分(通常通过契约或者遗嘱处分)。这些事实通过它们的存在决定着组成人类社会的人类联合体的行为规则。不言而喻,这些规则并不完全是法律规则。它们是我们的法律世界无穷多样的现象,或者部分是其他规范世界的现象。每一个小的人类联合体都会主动创造自己的秩序,在较小的联合体组合或者被组合成一个较大的联合体时,合成的联合体在处理它及其组成部分

ponent parts, create a new order, but must needs also, substantially, take over the order which has already been in existence in the original cells, and in general leave it in the form into which it had developed there. Indeed it is very simple, but extremely superficial, to believe that, at the present time, the state creates the order everywhere. In spite of the state law of the family, which allegedly is the same everywhere, there are no two families exactly alike; in spite of the state law of communes, there are no two communes exactly alike; in spite of the law of societies, there are no two societies exactly alike; in spite of identical laws of property, of contract, and of trades, there are no two agricultural establishments, workshops, factories, and, self-evidently, contracts, that are exactly alike. The differences appear much more distinctly if one considers not only the wording of the regulation and of the contract (a superficial proceeding), but also the way in which these are being applied and habitually entered into in the individual associations. The center of gravity everywhere lies in the order which the associations create for themselves, and life in the state and in society depends more upon the order of the associations than upon the order which proceeds from the state and from society.

But this great diversity must not cause us to overlook the uniformities. The latter are based on the fact that the conditions of the economic and of the social life of the various associations are to a great extent, both as to time and place, and in part too, independently of time and place, so uniform that a great number of identical rules necessarily result from this uniformity. In addition, there are direct borrowings. For as to content norms do not arise anew with every new association. In every society there is in existence a great store of legal and extra-legal norms which live in the consciousness of men. In the course of millennia it has been accumulating within the associations which came into being in the far distant past. And men who unite to form a new association bring this store of norms with them, having inherited it, or having acquired it by study. Each new generation has begun with that which the primitive ages, lying far behind us, have

的关系过程中，必定创造新的秩序，但是同时，它也非得实质上接管联合体中原先单元中已存的秩序不可，并且通常还要让后者保持旧有的形式。相信国家目前在任何地方都创造秩序，这种想法的确非常简单，但也极端浅薄。尽管有规范家庭的国家法——据称此类法律各处都一样——但没有两个家庭是完全相似的；尽管有规范公社的国家法，但是没有两个完全相似的公社；尽管有规范社团的国家法，却没有两个完全相似的社团；尽管有相同的财产法、契约法和贸易法，却没有两个完全相似的农业公司、车间和工厂，并且不言而喻，也没有完全相似的契约。如果一个人不仅考虑法令和契约（一种粗浅的纪录）的措辞，而且还考虑到这些法令和契约的实际应用和习惯性订立的方式，那么这些区别看上去将更加明显。在任何地方，重心都在于联合体为其自身所创造的秩序中，国家与社会中的生活依赖于联合体的秩序，而不是依赖于源自国家和社会的秩序。

但是，巨大的差异性不应当导致我们对一致性的忽略。该一致性基于如下事实：各种各样的联合体的经济和社会生活状况，就时间和地点方面而言——部分也与时间和地点无关——在很大程度上都是如此的一致，以至于大量的相同规范都必然因此而产生。除此之外，还有规则的直接移植。因为就内容而言，每一个新联合体并不重新产生新的规范。每一个社会中，都存在着大量的法律规范和非法律规范，它们都居于人类的意识当中。在千年的时光中，这些规范在远古时代即已形成的联合体内不断地累积。那些联合起来组成新的联合体的人们通过继承或者通过研究习得的方式把这些大量的规范带给了新的联合体。每个新的时代，都是以在离我们很久远的原始年代即已创设了至今仍是很

created in their as yet very simple associations. It has taken over the greater part of it unaltered; that which has become unsuitable it has discarded; other parts it has moulded over into special forms for special purposes; some parts, especially in case of organizations of a legal nature, it has posited expressly by means of statute or contract. Each new family, in essentials, reflects the existing family order; each new economic undertaking, in its characteristic features, follows the legal as well as the extra-legal constitution of undertakings of a similar nature; every newly made contract derives the greater part of its content from the traditional content of contracts of the same kind. And every new development which arises for new purposes, and which stands the test of time, is added to the treasure of social norms, and serves to guide later associations. There is an endless and uninterrupted process of adaptation to new needs and situations, in which is embodied, at the same time, the development of the human race and of its norms. It may suffice to instance the great number of new norms, not only of law, but also of morals, ethical custom, honor, good manners, tact, and perhaps, at least in a certain sense, etiquette and fashion, which have come into existence in the course of the last decades in consequence of the social movement in the various associations which it has occasioned or for which it has created a new order.

A fact which is an isolated occurrence in society is not a social fact; it cannot bring about social norms, and it will remain unnoticed by society. It cannot be considered a component part of the social order until it has become a common phenomenon. When a group of human beings of a certain kind, let us say a particular form of family life, a new church, a new political tendency, a relation of subjection, a form of possession, a content of a contract, becomes an important and permanent phenomenon because of common occurrence, then, and not until then, society must take

简单的联合体的时代为起点。新的联合体原封不动地接受了旧联合体的大部分规范;它抛弃了那些不适合自己的规范;其他一些部分,新的联合体则重新将它们塑造成特殊的形式,以适应特殊的目的;有些部分,特别是在具有法律性质的组织情形下,新的联合体通过制定法或者契约的形式对它们进行了专门的安排。每一个新的家庭在本质上都反映着既存的家庭秩序;每一个新的经济企业在典型特征上都遵循着具有类似属性的企业制度的法律和非法律规范;每一个新近订立之契约的绝大部分内容都来源于同种类契约的传统内容。出于新的意图、经受了时间考验的每一次新的发展都会使社会规范的宝库增加,并用以引导后来的联合体。适应新的需要和形式是一个永无止境的和从不间断的过程,同时这一过程也体现了人类和人类规范的发展。我们可以举出大量的新的规范,这些规范不但包括法律规范,而且还包括道德、伦理习俗、荣誉、良好举止、言行得体规范,或许至少还在一定程度上包括礼节和时尚规范。过去 10 年间,各种各样的联合体中的社会运动导致了这些规范的形成,这些社会运动既催生了联合体,也为这些联合体创造了新的秩序。

一个事实若仅仅是在社会中发生的孤立事件,则该事实并不是社会事实;这种事实不会导致社会规范的产生,也不会受到社会的关注。在这种事实成为一种常见现象之前,它不可能被认为是社会秩序的一个组成部分。当特定类型的一群人,让我们假定,特定类型的家庭生活、新的教会、一种新的政治趋势、一种服从关系、一种占有形式、一类契约的内容因为经常发生而变为一种重要、恒久的社会现象时,那时,直到那时,社会必须认可它。它要么必须拒绝它——必要时会坚决反对它,要么必须将其作为

cognizance of it. It must either reject it, if need be, combat it, or it must receive it into the general social and economic order as a suitable means for the satisfaction of social and economic needs. After this has been done, it becomes a new form for the organization of society, and thereby a social relation; under certain circumstances, a legal relation.

一种满足经济和社会需要的一种恰当方式,使其成为社会和经济秩序的一部分。在社会接受这一现象之后,这一现象就变成了社会组织的一种新的形式,从而变成了一种社会关系;在某种情况下,这种现象会成为一种法律关系。

# VI

# The Norms For Decision

Courts do not come into being as organs of the state, but of society. Their function originally was merely to determine, upon authority given by clans or families which had entered into a close relationship with one another, whether a quarrel between the members of different associations could be composed by payment of a penalty or whether it could be expiated only in blood, and eventually to determine the amount of the penalty. It is not until a much later date that courts are being erected by the state for matters that directly concern the state, e. g. attempts on the life of the king, trading with the enemy, violation of the military order. At a later time, the state gains control also over the courts of the former class; but the distinction between administration of justice by the state and by society continues today in the distinction between the jurisdiction of criminal and of civil causes, in spite of the extensive encroachments of the criminal courts upon the one-time purely social sphere. But the courts were never completely converted into state institutions. Society has always had, and has kept to the present day, courts of its own that are independent of the state; and courts of this kind come into existence from time to time even today. Though the prevailing juristic science applies the term courts only to the state organs for the administration of justice, with which it must concern itself professionally, the sociology of law, when it defines the term court, is concerned only with the question whether or not the institution involved performs the general functions of a court. Considered functionally, the court is a person or a group of persons who are not parties to the controversy and whose function is to establish peace by the opinion which they express about the subject matter of the controversy. This opinion has no binding

# 第六章　裁判规范

法院并不是作为国家的机构而产生，而是作为社会的机构而产生。法院的最初功能不过是依据彼此间建立起紧密联系的氏族或者家族授予的权威来裁决这样的问题：不同联合体之成员间的争端是否可以通过支付赔偿金的方式来调解，或是犯罪人必须通过流血的方式来赎罪，并最终决定赔偿金的幅度。直到后来很晚的时期，国家才设立法院，以便处理直接涉及国家的事务，例如对国王生活的攻击、通敌、军事命令的违反等。稍后，国家也获得对前种类型法院的控制权；尽管刑事法院广泛入侵了曾经是纯粹的社会事务的范围，但是国家的司法与社会的司法的区分一直延续到今天，它体现在刑事诉讼管辖权和民事诉讼管辖权的区分上。但是，法院从没有彻底转变为国家的机构。社会始终拥有——并且直到今天仍然保有——自己的独立于国家的法院；甚至在今天，这种类型的法院有时也会形成。虽然主流法学将法院这一术语仅仅运用于自己在专业上必须关注的、为司法目的而存在的国家机构之上，但是法律社会学在界定法院这一术语时，仅仅关注相关机构是否执行法院的一般职能这个问题。从功能上来考虑，法院就是非属争议当事人的一个人或者一群人，他们的职责是通过对争议事项给予裁断意见从而带来和平。甚至当这

force even when pronounced by a state court of primitive times; it is a mere opinion. He who refuses to submit may resort to self-help, to a feud, but he puts himself in the wrong, and loses the purely social advantage of having a just quarrel. At the beginning the court, even the state court, has no means whereby to coerce a contumacious person who refuses to appear though he has been summoned, or who flouts its decision, other than exclusion from the community (exile), whereby the person excluded becomes an outlaw, and must wander about, seeking rest and finding none, until he is either killed, or reduced to slavery, or received into another community. At this stage the death penalty, which is found at a very early time, is merely a sacrifice to the gods, among the classical peoples, to the gods of the nether world, the victim for which is the outlawed person.

If we consider only the functions of the court, we must include among the courts quite a number of variously named institutions for the social administration of justice, whose relation to the state is a more or less distant one: courts of honor, courts of discipline, courts of arbitration, courts of societies, courts of conciliation. For the social jurisdiction of English clubs a special body of law and a special technique have been developed. The decisions of these tribunals are subject to attack in the courts of the state and to review by the latter. Nothnagel discusses all these phenomena in the work already referred to, entitled *Exekution durch soziale, Interessengruppen*. The judgments of all of these courts, like

种裁断意见是由原始时期国家的法院宣布时，它也没有拘束效力，它仅仅是一个裁断意见。拒绝服从的人可以采取自己自助的方式，可以诉诸于复仇，但是，他这样就等于是有了过错，并会丧失进行公正辩论这种纯粹的社会利益。开始时，法院——即使是国家的法院——除了将他驱逐出社区外（放逐），也不能通过任何方式强制已经被传唤但拒绝出庭、或藐视法院裁决的违令者，被驱逐出社区的人就变成了一个不受法律保护的被放逐者，他必须四处游荡，寻求安身之所，但一无所获，直到他被杀死或被迫成为奴隶，或者被另一个社区收留。在这一阶段，我们在很早的时代中发现的死刑仅仅是一种对神灵的献祭，在古典的民族中，死刑是对阴间的神灵的献祭，受害者也都是不受法律保护的人。

如果我们只考虑法院的功能，我们讨论时必须包括法院中那些——和国家关系或远或近并执行社会司法职能的——相当多的名称各异的机构：荣誉法院、[1]纪律法院、仲裁法庭，社团法院，调解法庭。[2] 由于英格兰会所的社会性裁判权，一种特殊的法律体和特殊的技术发展起来了。这些特殊裁决机构的裁决在国家法院中受到攻击并受到国家法院审查。在前引名为《通过社会共同利益体来实施》中，诺特纳戈讨论了该书中已提到的所有的这些现象。如同原

〔1〕 在欧洲的某些国家，这一名称用以指有权调查军官提出的有碍其军官荣誉的指控，惩罚违反荣誉法典的失职行为和决定军官之间的决斗的原因、场合及方式的军事法庭。

〔2〕 （美）courts of conciliation（调解法院），对当事人在债务或者婚姻等方面的纠纷予以调解，避免争执。

those of the courts in primitive times, are limited to exclusion from the group. On the other hand administrative tribunals created by the state, especially the police and in part the presiding officers of bodies of representatives of the public, doubtless exercise a judicial function, Courts, of whatsoever description they may be, must not render their judgments arbitrarily or without giving reasons, but must base them on general principles. The norms for decision upon which the latter are based invariably appear as the result of an inspiration of higher power and wisdom; nay, indeed, at a lower stage, as the result of an illumination by the godhead. The norm for decision, like all social norms, is primarily a rule of conduct, but only for the courts. It is not, primarily at least, a rule for the men who are the doers in life, but for the men who sit in judgment upon the doers. In so far as the norm for decision is a legal norm, it appears to be a legal norm of a special kind, different from the legal norms that contain general rules of conduct.

Whence do the courts draw their norms for decision? To render a decision in case of a quarrel means to delimit the spheres that are in dispute, above all things to delimit them just as they had been delimited before the quarrel arose. This delimitation is indicated, in the first instance, by the inner order of the associations as it existed at the beginning of the quarrel. Every norm for decision therefore is based primarily upon this inner order, i. e. the facts of the law, which create the order, upon the usages, which assign to each individual his position and his function in the association, upon relations of domination and possession, contracts, articles of association, testamentary dispositions. In every quarrel the point involved is that a norm which is based on these facts has been violated, and in all litigation, in order to be able to render a decision, the judge must ascertain these facts either from his own knowledge or from the evidence. All these facts constitute the basis of the decision just as they have developed and taken shape in the concrete association before the quarrel arose.

In the past there has frequently been a toying, especially among exponents of the natural law theory, with the thought that the

始时期的法院裁决一样,所有这些法院的裁决也限于将成员开除出团体。另一方面,国家建立的行政裁决机构,尤其是警察和部分公共代表机构的首脑,毫无疑问地执行着一种司法功能。任何一种描述下的法院都不能恣意或者不给任何理由地作出裁决,他们必须将自己的裁决建立在一般原则之上。作为裁决基础的裁判规范看上去总是像一种来自更高的权力和智慧的启示的结果;不仅如此,在一个较低的阶段,裁判规范确实是作为一种神灵启迪的结果。裁判规范如同所有的社会规范一样,主要是一种行为规则,但仅仅是法院的行为规则。裁判规范至少主要不是生活中行为人的规则,而是对行为人的行为作出裁判的裁判者的规则。就裁判规范是法律规范而言,裁判规范看上去是一种特殊类型的行为规范,这种规范不同于包含一般行为规则的法律规范。

法院的裁判规范来自何处?在出现争端的情况下,作出一项裁决意味着要界定争端的范围,最重要的是,要按照争端发生以前的状态界定它们的范围。这种界定首先需要依据争端开始时即已经存在的联合体的内部秩序。因此,每一个裁判规范都主要是基于这种内部秩序,即这些法律事实,这些法律事实依靠习惯创造了秩序,依靠支配和占有关系、契约、社团章程、遗嘱处分为联合体中每一个人确定在联合体中的地位和职责。每一个争端中相关要点都是对基于这些法律事实的规范违反,在所有的诉讼中,法官为了作出一项裁决都必须通过自己的知识或者证据来查明这些事实。正如这些事实在争端产生以前就已经在具体的联合体内发展和成形一样,所有的这些法律事实也构成了裁判的基础。

在过去,尤其是在自然法理论的倡导者中间,时常有一些草

whole law must be susceptible of being summed up in a few clear propositions that are obvious to unaided human reason. They evidently had an idea, quite vague indeed, that the existing usages, relations of possession, contracts, articles of association, testamentary dispositions, were sufficient for the rendering of judicial decisions, and required only a few additional rules to complement them. But he who adopts this view fails to see that the norm for decision is always something more than and distinct from the inner order of the association. Even where the norm for decision is based directly upon an order of an association that is formulated in express words, even where it goes back to a bylaw of a society, to a contract, or to a last will and testament, it is always a thing quite distinct from the inner order of the association; for a relation as to which there is a dispute is something different from the same relation at peace. That which before had been adaptable and flexible has become rigid, immovable; vague outlines have become clear and sharply drawn, and often a meaning must be read into the words that the parties had never been clearly conscious of. But the judge in a law-suit has duties to perform with reference to the relation submitted to him for decision which involve more than this relation, which have remained altogether foreign to the experience of the associations so long as they were left to themselves; and as to these duties he can learn nothing from the inner order of the associations. For such cases, he must have at his disposal norms for decision which are independent of this latter order.

We must consider chiefly the requirements of the administration of justice as such. Every social association is, to be accurate, a special case that cannot be duplicated anywhere in the world. There are no two families in which the position of the father, the mother, the children, the servants, is exactly the same; no two parts of the world in which the identical relations as to landholding obtain; no two contracts, bylaws of corporations, testamentary declarations, that do not differ from each other; in addition to the differences in words and phrasing, there are differences in the relations of persons and things. It is self-evident

率的想法:整个法律必须很容易地被概括为——对于独立的人类理性来说容易理解的——几个清晰的命题。他们显然持有这样的一种实际上非常模糊的观点:既有的习惯、占有关系、契约、社团章程、遗嘱处分对于作出司法裁判而言已经足够,仅仅需要一些附加的规则去补足它们。但是采纳这一观点的人没有注意到,裁判规范始终不仅仅是联合体的内部秩序,而且和联合体的内部秩序并不相同。即使在裁判规范直接基于以明确的语言阐述联合体内部秩序的地方,即使在裁判规范可以追溯回社团章程细则、契约或遗嘱的地方,它也总是一种非常不同于联合体内部秩序的事物;因为处于纠纷中的关系总是和处于和平时期的同种关系有所不同。那些曾经是适应的和灵活的东西变得僵硬和呆板;模糊的轮廓变得清晰并被精确地刻画出来,并且一个意思经常被曲解为当事人从未意识到的文字。但是,在一起讼案中,只要当事人提交某种关系给法官要求裁判,法官就有义务根据那种关系来履行职责,尽管那种被提交的关系可能超越这种发生争议的关系,并且是与联合体的经验完全不同的关系;关于这些职责,法官不能从联合体的内部秩序中学到任何东西。对于那样的情形,法官必须自主获得独立于联合体内部秩序的裁判规范。

我们必须主要考虑司法本身的要求。精确地说,每一个社会联合体都是在世界上任何地方无法被复制的一个特别情形。没有两个父亲、母亲、孩子、仆人的地位完全相同的家庭;世界上不存在在土地所有关系方面流行同一种关系的两个地方;没有两份彼此没有差异的契约、公司章程细则和遗嘱声明;除了措辞方面的不同外,在对人和物的关系方面也存在不同。当一个人考虑的

that one sees these differences becoming greater and greater as one considers wider spheres; in different communes, provinces, nations, the associations present different pictures. The administration of justice cannot function where there is such a medley; for technical reasons, if for no others, it must reduce the same to simple formulae. This is done by means of universalization and reduction to unity. Social relations are judged according to the form of relations of this kind that prevails in a given locality, or the social relations of a whole country are judged indiscriminately by the form of these relations that prevails in a certain part of the country or in a certain social class. If it is customary in a given locality for the husband to have absolute power of disposition over the property of his wife, a disposition actually made by a husband is held binding on the wife with utter disregard of the question whether or not this was the custom in the given family. If it is a general custom of the country that everything that the lessee has inseparably attached to the soil becomes the property of the owner of the land, this custom is treated as the common law of the country, and an action by the lessee for such expenditures is dismissed everywhere even though this custom cannot be shown to exist in this or that part of the country. This is the process called universalization. But courts go further than this. An order which is in conflict with the general norm is held invalid even though its existence is clearly proved. By this means the law is made unitary. This results in general and unitary norms for decision, but not in a general and unitary living law; and individual as well as local differences may well continue to exist beneath the crust of external uniformity.

But the associations themselves require norms for decision for their own completion and perfection. In their normal state, they are supplied with norms for those situations only which the parties involved have anticipated; every new situation, which has not been anticipated, confronts them with the necessity of finding new rules of conduct. This indispensable task of completing the structure of the associations is usually performed from within. If a

范围越宽广时,他就会看到越来越多的差异,这是不言而喻的。在不同的乡镇、省、国家内,联合体都呈现出不同的图景。司法不能在如此混杂的地方发挥功能;如果不是因为其他原因,单单因为技术性的原因,法律也必须将相同的事物化约为简单的公式。通过一般化和化而为一的方式,此项工作得以完成。社会关系依据在一特定地域盛行的同种类型的关系形式来裁断,或者整个国家的社会关系依据在国家特定地域或者特定阶级中盛行的这些关系形式不加区别地来裁断。如果在一特定地域,丈夫对妻子的财产享有绝对的处分权,此种情形合乎习惯,由丈夫所作的处分实际上被认定对妻子具有拘束力,而完全不用理会这是否是一个特定家庭中习惯的问题,如果——承租人添附到土地上、且与土地无法分离的东西都变为了土地所有人的财产——这是一个国家通常的习惯,则这种习惯就被认为是该国的共同法,承租人为了这种支出提起的诉讼在这个国家的任何地方都会被驳回,即使这一习惯无法被证明在该国的此地或彼地存在。这一过程被称做一般化。但是法院走得比这还远。法院认为和一般规范相冲突的秩序是无效的,尽管这种秩序的存在可以被清楚地证明。通过这种方式法律取得了统一。这就促生了一般的和统一的裁判规范,但是却没有促生一般和统一的活法。个体的差异和地区的差异在外观统一的外壳下有充分的理由继续存在下去。

但是联合体为了自己的完整和完善也需要裁判规范。在正常状态下,联合体只为有关当事人已经预见的情形设定行为规范;没有预见到的每一种新的情形都让联合体有发现新的行为规则的必要。这种完善联合体结构的必不可少的任务通常由联合体

father contracts a second marriage, the relations of the members of the family to each other are dislocated at once; the family must try to create a new order for itself; a few norms that have prevailed hitherto are given up, and new ones are received. If leased property is employed in a new form of economic enterprise as to which nothing is said in the contract of lease, the parties must arrange their relations accordingly. In many cases an unconscious adaptation takes place; in others a new contract is entered into. But it is the difficulties created by such an unanticipated event that most frequently cause the parties to appeal to the judge. The judge cannot find the solution in the inner order of the association; for the latter has at this very juncture proved unable to create an order. He must have special norms for the decision of the case at hand.

In addition it must be remembered that in every case when a quarrel or controversy arises, the associations have usually got out of their established order into a state of disorder. It would be foolish thereafter to try to make the norms of the association the basis of a decision, for the latter have lost their ordering power in the association. Special norms are required, not for the peaceful relation but for the legal dispute. And these will often differ from the former even as to content.

The compilers of the Civil Code for the German Empire were ill-advised when they made the *Verwaltungsgemeinschaft* the normal statutory matrimonial regime. As long as the spouses get on well with each other, the marriage will automatically establish the *Verwaltungsgemeinschaft* of the Civil Code as its order; the wife will entrust her husband with the management of her property even though there be no

在内部完成。如果一个父亲订立了第二个婚约,家庭成员彼此间的关系就会马上陷入混乱;家庭必须设法为自己创造一种新的秩序;一些迄今为止盛行的新的规范被抛弃,新的规范被采纳。如果租赁来的财产被投入到租赁契约没有提及的一种新的经济企业形式中,则双方当事人必须重新安排他们之间的关系。在很多情况下,无意识的适应发生了;在另外的一些情形下,当事人订立了新的契约。但是,正是这种未预计到的事件所引发的困难,经常导致当事人诉诸于法官。法官不能从联合体的内部秩序中找到解决办法;因为在这一关键时刻,联合体的内部秩序被证明它无法创设出一种规则。法官必须为手头的案件寻找专门的裁判规范。

此外,必须记住,每一项争执或者争议产生时,联合体通常已经脱离了现有秩序而进入一种无秩序的状态。此后,还设法将联合体的规范作为裁判的基础是愚蠢的,因为联合体的规范已经丧失了在联合体中的规整力。联合体需要特别的规范,不是为了和平的关系,而是为了法律纠纷。而且这些规范即使在内容上,也与和平时期的联合体规范不同。

德意志帝国《民法典》的编纂者在将联合管理[1]变为正常的制定法的婚姻制度时,不够明智。只要婚姻双方相处得很好,婚姻会自动地建立作为《民法典》秩序的联合管理关系;即使没有制定法的规定,妻子也会把她自己的财产委托给她的丈夫管理,她也不会进

〔1〕 *Verwaltungsgemeinschaft*,管理共同体、联合管理,这一术语描述了德国制定法上的婚姻制度,在此种制度下,夫妻双方结婚后,各自所有的财产合并为夫妻财产,由丈夫管理,当夫妻关系终止时,妻子的原有财产由其本人收回或由其继承人继承。

statutory provision, will not exercise a special supervision or demand a detailed accounting. The spouses who get on well with each other have no need of a judge, and it was a superfluous thing to establish *Verwaltungsgemeinschaft* by statutory enactment where it was already in existence. But if the marriage relation has become inharmonious, the love and confidence which hitherto has induced the wife to live with her husband in *Verwaltungsgemeinschaft* has disappeared. The statute ought to have selected the regime of separation of goods; for this regime alone can protect the wife, in the case of an ill-starred marriage, against abuse of the husband's power. No one has failed to see this in the case of ordinary community of property. It is just barely conceivable that an able and honest business man might enter into a partnership with an utterly incapable and indiscreet man, and in such case it would be a good arrangement if the former should by contractual agreement take away from the latter the right to inspect books, letters, and accounts. But such a prohibition is effective only as long as the partnership relation is peaceful, as long as the other party submits to it, in order to maintain the partnership perhaps, but it is not effective as a norm for decision. If the partnership relation should give rise to litigation, the courts must not be bound by this prohibition.

The legal dispute also has its peculiar needs. Certain questions do not arise until the quarrel has begun. How they are to be solved cannot be determined by the inner order of the association; for the latter is not an order of war, but of peace. In the very earliest beginnings of administration of justice, in the most common case that came before him, the judge had to find norms for decision that went beyond the inner order of the associations themselves. If it was a question of homicide, it was incumbent upon him to decide not only whether the complainant was entitled, on the basis of the inner order of his clan, to demand a penalty, and whether the defendants, were liable according to the order of the clan, perhaps as members of the clan, but over and above that, what the amount of the penalty was to be. On these points, he cannot find anything in the inner order. This is true to

行特别监督或者要求一份详细的会计账目。那些相处融洽的配偶是不需要法官的，并且在那些联合管理已经存在的地方，通过制定法的规定设定联合管理也是多余的。但是如果婚姻关系变得不和谐了，则联合管理关系中迄今让妻子和丈夫一起生活的爱情与信任也会消失。制定法应当选择分别财产制；因为在一个不幸的婚姻里，这种制度单独就可以保护妻子免遭丈夫权利的滥用。在普通的夫妻共同财产制的情况下，没有人不会注意到这种情况。几乎不能想象一个有才干的、诚实的商人会和没有才干的、轻率的商人建立合伙关系，那种情况下，如果有才能的、诚实的商人通过契约的安排剥夺了没有才能的、轻率的商人检查簿册、函件和账目的权利，这将是一种绝佳的安排。但是这种禁止只有在合伙关系处于和平状态时才有效，只有在另一方当事人或许为了维持合伙关系而服从这种安排时才有效，但是这种禁止条款并不具有裁判规范的效力。如果合伙关系引发诉讼，法院不得受此禁止条款的约束。

法律纠纷也有其特殊的需要。特定的问题直到争执开始时才出现。这些纠纷如何解决不能依据联合体的内部秩序，因为后者不是斗争时的秩序，而是和平时的秩序。在司法的最早阶段，在提交到法官面前的大部分普通案件中，法官都不得不超越他们自己联合体的内部秩序来寻找裁判规范。如果那是一个有关杀人的纠纷，法官有责任不仅要依据原告氏族的内部秩序来裁定原告是否有权要求赔偿金以及被告（他或许是氏族成员）是否负有责任，而且除此之外，法官还要判定赔偿金的数额。在这些事情上，法官无法从内部秩序中发现任何裁判依据。在稍后时期更困难和更

a still greater degree in the more difficult and more complicated relations of later times. It will not suffice to award the parcel of land to its owner with all the powers and privileges which ownership gives in the experience of life. What is to be done about the crops which the previous owner has planted, about the work and labor he has done and the expenditures he has made? It will not suffice to enforce the contract as it was made; the judge must render judgment on things that the parties never thought of. What happens if the thing the debtor was obligated to deliver has perished before performance could be rendered? What if it is of a nature quite different from that which has been presupposed? The person who renders the decision can answer questions of this kind creatively only if he is guided by the form which the relations of life have assumed, not in peaceful development, but during the course of the litigation. To this group belongs the whole law of damages, of compensation for unjust enrichment, the right of avoidance (*actio Pauliana*), the provision of the material law concerning the protection of legal rights, the principles concerning the duty of allegation and proof, and the legal effect of a judgment. We are here presupposing throughout, not a living order, but litigation about an order that is dead.

The last group consists of those norms for decision that have arisen from the clash of the spheres of influence of several associations. In our present-day society, every human being primarily is a member of the state; the spheres of the various other associations to which he belongs are largely intertwined, and all are within

复杂的关系中，情形就更是如此。它仍然不足以把一宗土地连同生活经验中所有权展现出来的所有权利和特权赋予所有权人。如何处理先前所有人在土地上种植的庄稼？如何处理先前所有人在土地付出的劳动和支出的费用？它也不足以按照契约订立的内容强制履行契约；法官必须基于当事人从未考虑的事情来作出裁决。如果债务人有义务交付的物在契约可以履行以前已经毁坏，将会产生什么样的后果？如果契约的性质已经完全不同于原来预设的契约，那又将如何？作出裁决者只有受到并非在和平发展时期、而是在诉讼期间呈现出来的生活关系形式的指引，才能够创造性地回答这种类型的问题。全部损害赔偿法、不当得利补偿法、撤销权(*actio Pauliana*)、[1]关于合法权利保护的实体法规定、关于答辩义务和举证责任的原则以及裁决的法律效力都属于这一类。此处，我们自始至终预设的不是一种“活”的秩序，而是有关一种“死”的秩序的诉讼。

最后一个类群由那些因几个联合体影响范围相互冲突而产生的裁判规范组成。在我们如今的社会中，每一个人首先是国家的一个成员；一个人所属的各种其他联合体的范围广泛交织在一

---

〔1〕 (拉)*actio Pauliana*(保利安诉讼或撤销转让行为之诉)。如果资不抵债的债务人为对债权人实行欺诈而将自己的财产转让给第三人，从而使债权人得不到清偿，即可对该债务人提起此诉讼，要求执法官撤销债务人实施的转让行为。提起此诉讼所需具备的三项条件是：1. 债务人有意采取减少自己财产的手段致使债权人得不到清偿，即具有欺诈意图；2. 对债权人造成损害结果；3. 接受转让的第三人对上述欺诈知情。保利安诉讼是由优士丁尼法创设的，在此之前，它表现为两种不同的诉讼手段，一种叫做欺诈给付令状，它要求欺诈知情的第三人必须返还所获得的财物；另一种叫做恢复原状。

the sphere of power of the state. The forces inherent in the associations which cross and embrace one another are variously distributed, and the struggle among them is usually carried on within several spheres at the same time. This struggle, to a very great extent, is about the norms according to which the courts render their decisions. An extreme measure of parental or marital authority may be proportionate to the distribution of power within a certain family or within the family in a certain class or locality; but it is in conflict with the general order of the family in the state and in society, which have impressed their stamp upon the prevailing norms of law of morality, of ethical custom, of etiquette. The state and society therefore will not tolerate it, and will attempt to bring about an order which is more in harmony with the views that prevail generally, at least when appeal is made to its courts for the settling of disputes. Every wage contract, however disadvantageous to the working-man, will reflect quite accurately the relation of power that obtained between the employer and the employe at the time the contract was made. But if the working class obtains a greater measure of influence in society, it will attempt to shape the wage contract according to its ideas; a movement will arise within society which will stigmatize one or the other provision of the contracts of wages as contrary to morality and decency, and which, perhaps, will attain power enough to influence even the norms for decision applicable to wage contracts.

The courts decide on the basis of their norms for decision whether a social norm has been transgressed or not. The prevailing juristic science takes for granted that it must be a legal norm that has been transgressed, that the object for which courts have been erected is not the protection of non-legal norms. But it is evident that this can apply only to the organs of the state for the administration of justice. And even as to these it is true only if we call every norm according to which a court renders a decision a legal norm. But if we do that, the question becomes a mere question of terminology. If we consider the inner content of the norms according to which the courts must render their

起,这些联合体都处于国家权力的范围之内。相互交叉和包容的联合体内固有的各种力量在不同的时间里以不同的名称分布着,这些力量间的斗争通常也在几个范围内同时进行着。这一斗争在很大程度上是关于法院据以作出裁决的规范。父母亲或者婚姻权威的极限可能会与特定家庭内的权力分配或特定阶层与地区中的家庭内相称,或者与在特定阶层或者地域的家庭内的权力分配相称;但是,它可能会与在国家和社会中一般的家庭秩序相冲突,这种一般的家庭秩序已经在主流的法律规范以及道德、伦理习俗、礼节规范上刻下它们的印记。因此,国家和社会将不会容忍这种权威,并且会试图造就一种与普遍流行的见解更加和谐一致的秩序,至少在有人为了解决纠纷向法院起诉时是这样的。每一份工资契约无论怎样对工人不利,它会非常精确地反映出契约订立时雇主与雇员得到的权力关系。如果工人阶级在社会中获得更大程度的影响力,他们就会尝试按照自己的主张来塑造工资契约;社会上将会出现一次运动,它将会把与道德和行为准则相反的一些内容烙印在工资契约的一个或者另外一个条款上。或许它还会获得甚至足以影响适用到工资契约之上的裁判规范的力量。

法院依据他们的裁判规范来裁断一个社会规范是否被违反。主流的法学想当然地以为:被违反的规范必定是法律规范,法院建立的目标并不是对非法律规范提供保护。但是,很明显,这仅仅适用于国家的司法机构。并且,甚至在这一范围内,也仅仅当我们把法院据以作出裁判的所有规范都称做法律规范时,这种看法才是正确的。但是如果我们这样做,这一问题就变成一个仅仅是术语学的问题。如果我们考虑到法院据以作出裁判之规范的

decisions—and that is the only fair way to proceed—we shall be convinced that the non-legal norms play an important role even in the courts of the state.

In a primitive stage of development, there is so little differentiation between law on the one hand and morality, religion, ethical custom, decorum, on the other, that the administration of justice utilizes them all indiscriminately. The Roman *prudentes* and the German *Schöffen* appeal without hesitation to morality, ethical custom and decorum; the English judge, who at the present time is perhaps the only heir of the traditions of the ancient judicial office, does the same thing. But all of these are bound by the ever recurring limitation that non-legal norms may be used only to eke out the positive law, to act as stop-gaps; the judge therefore is not authorized to disregard the legal norms in favor of the nonlegal ones. The principle is extremely elastic, and occasionally the limitation which it imposes upon the discretion of the judges can scarcely be felt; nevertheless it is of very great importance. It imports that the bases of our social order that have been expressed in legal norms may not be disturbed by other social orderings and rules. It does not apply therefore when the state itself intervenes in the administration of justice. The Roman praetor, the king in the Frankish and in the German kingdom, the English chancellor, render decisions according to fairness or according to morals, i. e. according to non-legal norms, and occasionally even contrary to the established law. From these decisions, it is true, legal propositions subsequently evolve. Although the praetorian law and English equity grew chiefly out of norms of morality, ethical custom, and decorum, they became separate and distinct legal systems in the course of time. This however merely shows that the chief difference between law and non-legal norms of this kind is a matter of stability, certainty,

内在内容——这是唯一合宜的思考方式——我们将会确信非法律规范即使在国家的法院里也发挥着重大的作用。

在原始发展阶段,法律与道德、宗教、伦理习俗、礼仪规范之间几乎没有什么差别,司法机构不加区分地适用它们。罗马的法学家和德国的法官助理[1]会毫不犹豫地诉诸道德、伦理习俗和礼仪。当前或许是这一古代司法部门传统的唯一继承人——英格兰的法官,也在做着同样的事情。但是,所有的这些都受到始终反复出现的限制——即这些规范仅仅作为补缺者用于弥补制定法的不足——的约束。因此法官并没有被授权在支持非法律规范的时候漠视法律规范。该原则具有极端的弹性,有时候它给法官自由裁量权施加的限制几乎令人无法感觉;尽管如此,它还是非常重要的。这表明,以法律规范表达的我们社会的基础不可受到其他社会规整和规则干扰。所以当国家自己干预司法的时候,这一原则不适用。罗马人的裁判官、法兰克和日耳曼王国的国王、英格兰的御前大臣依据公平或者道德作出裁判,即他们依据非法律规范作出裁判,而且有些时候这些裁判甚至违反了已制定的法律。的确,法律命题随即从这些裁决中产生出来。虽然裁判官法和英格兰的衡平法主要在道德、伦理习俗和礼仪规范的基础上发展起来,但是,随着时间的推移,它们也变成了独立的和独特的法律体系。然而,这仅仅表明法律规范和这一类型的非法律规范之间的主要区别在于它们的稳定性、确定性和关于它们的社会

---

〔1〕 (德)*Schöffen*(法官助理),一个普通人,在法院中作为受过法律训练的法官的助手。

and the general conviction as to their social importance, not of content.

Even in the courts of the Continent, however, which had been completely transformed into state courts, which had become exclusively organs of the administration of justice, the principle that the courts must base their decisions exclusively upon the law was never more than a matter of seeming. The rule of law itself continually refers them to other social norms; it will tolerate no abuse of the law which violates morality, ethical custom, or decorum; it forbids immoral contracts; commands performance of contracts according to good faith and the custom of everyday life; provides penalties for insults, for violation of the proprieties and for gross mischief. It entrusts the decision to the free discretion of the judge; and that often means to a discretion based on other than purely legal considerations. But the administration of justice actually goes much further than the law. The fact that the judge was rigidly confined to the law in every respect has hitherto merely prevented the judges from openly making non-legal norms the bases of their decisions, but not from doing so in various, sometimes very transparent, disguises. The holding of the French courts that the owner of a building may not let a shop to a competitor of his tenant in the same building, on the ground that according to the statute he has impliedly given to the latter a warranty *de tout trouble*, amounts to a recognition of a principle of propriety which the wording of the statute does not express even approximately. Generally speaking, the non-legal norms of morality, ethical custom, and decorum become legal norms so readily that in most cases a differentiation is altogether impossible. In Lotmar's book *Der unmoralische Vertrag*, (The Immoral Contract), the basic features of this process are presented with reference to a single instance in an incontrovertible manner, although in other respects the ideas we have presented here are quite foreign to this book.

All of this, of course, does not mean that the courts should, without more ado, render their decisions according to non-legal norms. All legal propositions are not suitable for norms for decisions;

重要性的一般确信等方面，而并非在内容方面。

然而，即便是在欧洲大陆的法院——这些法院已经完全变为了国家的法院，也变成了司法的专门机构，法院作出的裁判必须全部以法律为基础——这样的原则也从来都只是一种表面现象。法律规则自身也不断参考其他的社会规范。任何违反道德、伦理习俗或礼仪规范的法律滥用都是令人无法容忍的。法律禁止不道德契约，它要求按照诚信和日常生活习俗来履行契约，它规定了对侮辱、侵犯财产和严重伤害的惩罚。法律将裁判委托给了法官的自由裁量；这意味着裁判经常基于不同于纯粹法律考虑的裁量权。但是，实际上司法走得比法律更远。法官在各方面都严格受到法律的限制——这一事实迄今为止仅仅防止了法官公开将非法律规范作为他们的裁判基础，但是，这一事实不能阻止法官在各种各样——有时候很明显——的伪装形式下这样做。法国法院的观点——建筑物所有人不可将同一建筑物内的商店租给其承租人的竞争者，其根据在于，依制定法，他含蓄地给予后者一个免受任何争扰的保证，此种观点等于承认，在制定法的文字中，甚至没有近似表述的一个财产原则。一般说来，道德、伦理习俗、礼仪等非法律规范如此容易地转变为法律规范，以至于大多数情况下，那样的区别完全是不可能的。在洛特马的《不道德的契约》一书中，作者通过一个例子以一种无可争议的方式对这一进程的基本特征进行了描述，尽管在其他方面，我们这里提出的理念与这本书完全无关。

当然，这一切并不是说法院应该直接干脆地依据非法律规范作出裁判。并非所有的法律命题都适合作裁判规范，更何况非法

*a fortiori* all non-legal norms, taken indiscriminately, are still less so. To make a proper selection is a task of enormous difficulty—a task which makes much higher demands upon the powers of the judge than the mere application of law. The strong tendency on the Continent to make the judge merely a ministerial servant of the statute who has no right to exercise any discretion whatever arises, I am convinced, from a suspicion that he is not equal to so difficult a task. The Roman *prudentes*, the English, and, in part, the French judges, have proved their ability in this matter; and the *Oberappellationsgericht* at Lübeck as well as the *Oberhandelsgericht* at Leipzig have demonstrated that the German judge, too, possesses the necessary ability. And, lastly, the work must be done at all events, and it is being done today. And if it must be admitted that, as a result of the imperfect regulation of the administration of justice, it is being done in a most exceptionable manner, we may nevertheless say that one cannot solve a difficulty of this nature by closing one's eyes to it.

As to courts other than those that are organs of the state for the administration of justice, the contention is no longer made that they arrive at their decisions on the basis of legal propositions. The administrative tribunals of the state, the police, the courts of discipline, the presiding officers of bodies of representatives of the people, must very often render judgments based on the norms of morality, ethical custom, honor, decorum, tact, etiquette. This applies [to an even higher degree] to the non-state courts, the various courts of arbitration, courts of societies, courts of honor, courts of cartels, courts of trusts, courts of tradeunions, courts of clubs. In ecclesiastical courts, religious norms also play an important role. The police imposing a penalty for a violation of decency; the presiding officer of the *Abgeordnetenhaus* reprimanding a member for violation of parliamentary custom; the court of honor compelling an officer to resign because of a breach of the code of honor; the disciplinary court condemning an official for injuring the reputation of the class (by failure to exercise sufficient tact); the court of a club excluding a member for non-payment of a

律规范,不偏袒地说,所有的非法律规范更是如此。作出一个恰当的选择是一项非常困难的任务,这项任务对法官的权力提出了比仅仅适用法律更高的要求。我确信,欧洲大陆上——令法官仅仅成为制定法的工具性仆人,无论发生什么他都不能行使裁量权——这种强烈的趋势来自对法官能否胜任这一困难任务的怀疑。罗马的法学家、英格兰的法官和法国的部分法官已经证明,他们的能力足以胜任此项工作。并且,在吕贝克的高等上诉法院和在莱比锡的高等商事上诉法院早已证明德国的法官也拥有必要的能力。最后,无论如何,审判工作必须要做,并且今天审判工作也正在做着。如果必须承认,由于司法条例的不完善,寻找恰当规范的工作正在以一种可能有极大争议的方式来做,则我们仍然可以说,任何人都不能以视而不见的方式解决这种性质的困难。

至于那些非属国家司法机构的法庭,人们不再主张,此类法庭必须以法律命题为基础来裁判案件。国家的行政法庭、警察机关、纪律法院、人民代表机构的首脑必须经常基于道德、伦理习俗、荣誉、礼仪、言行得体、礼节等规范作出裁判。这更加适用于非国家的法庭、各种各样的仲裁法庭、社会法院、荣誉法庭、卡特尔法庭、信托法院、工会法院和会所法院。在教会法庭里,宗教规范也发挥着重要的作用。警察会对行为不端者施以处罚;下议院的议长严厉训斥一个违反议会习惯的官员;荣誉法庭会勒令违反荣誉法规的官员辞职;纪律法院会因为一位官员损害所属阶层的名誉而谴责他(因为其言行不够得体);会所法院将没有支付赌债的一个成员除名;卡特尔法庭对于——

gaming debt; the court of a cartel ordering a boycott against an entrepreneur for furnishing goods to an entrepreneur against whom a boycott had been declared; the court of a union declaring that a member is not in good standing for having worked during a strike—all of these are courts which are erected and maintained by society itself, and which, on the basis of norms which are preponderantly extralegal, display a fruitful and ever increasing activity, and, in part, have means of compulsion at their disposal which are of greater effectiveness than those of the state tribunals. In the book of Nothnagel, to which I have referred repeatedly, much material has been gathered on this point, which, though somewhat out of date, is nevertheless useful at all times.

The norm for decision contains the general proposition on which the decision is based, and thereby sets up the pretension that it is a truth which is valid, not only for the specific case under discussion but for every like or similar case. A judgment decreeing that the *wergild* is to be paid to the brother of the slain man by the brother of the slayer establishes a rule that, in the clan of the slain man at least, a brother always has the right to assert the claim; that, in the clan of the slayer, a brother is always liable. A judgment allowing recovery against the defendant on the basis of a contract implies that under the circumstances of the case an enforceable claim arises from a contract of the kind in question. Even a decision of the question by casting lots, as is often done on a lower level of development, amounts to a general acknowledgment that in cases like the one in dispute the party in whose favor the lot is cast wins.

This is the law of the stability of legal norms, which is of such vast importance for the creation of law. It is based, in the first place, on social psychology. Rendering contrary decisions in like or in similar cases would not be law and right, but arbitrariness or caprice. It is based also on a certain sound economic quality of thinking. The expenditure of intellectual labor which undoubtedly is always involved in seeking norms for decision can often be avoided by rendering a decision according to a norm which has

向一个联合抵制令所针对的企业供应货物的——企业,发布一项联合抵制命令;工会法院宣布一个成员在罢工中没有遵守规则,以上所有的这些法庭都是由社会自己建立和维持的法院,它们的裁决主要以非法律规范为基础,它们开展了富有成效的、日益增加的活动,而且,在某种程度上,这些法庭有其自主决定的强制手段,这些强制手段比国家裁决机构的强制手段更有效。在我反复提到的诺特纳戈的书中,在这一点上已经收集到了大量的材料,虽然这些材料中的部分已经过时,然而它们无论什么时候都是有用的。

裁判规范中包含了裁决所基于的一般命题,也由此建立了这样的要求,该命题不仅对于具体案件有效,而且对于每一种类似或相同的案件都是有效的。一项有关凶手的兄弟向被害人的兄弟支付赔偿金的判决确立了一项规则:至少在被害人所在的氏族里,被害人的兄弟总是有权主张权利,在凶手所在的氏族里,凶手的兄弟总是对此负有责任。一项有关允许原告依据契约向被告索回财产的判决表明,在那种情况下,从涉讼那种契约中能够产生一种可强制执行的请求权。即使相关问题的裁决是通过抓阄的方式——如同在较低发展水平时经常做的那样,这也相当于一种普遍的共识:在类似这样一个纠纷中,有运气抓到阄的当事人就是胜诉方。

这就是对法律的创制来说至关重要的法律规范的稳定性规则。首先,这一规则以社会心理因素为基础。在相同或者类似的案件中作出相反的裁决是不合法、不正确的,那是一种恣意和任性。这一规则同样也建立在某种合理的经济性思考之上。根据已经存在的规范作出裁判经常可以避免智力劳动——其目的毫无

already been found. Moreover there is a great social need of stable norms for decision, which make it possible in a limited measure to foresee and predict the decisions and thereby to put a man in position to make his arrangements accordingly.

The law of the stability of the norms for decision functions chiefly in time. The court will not, without good cause, depart from a norm which it has applied in the decision of a case as long as the norm is remembered, and often special measures are being taken to prevent its being forgotten. But it functions in space also; for the norms for decision which have been found by one court will readily be applied by other courts which exist in the same sphere of influence, if for no other reason, in order to avoid the labor incident to finding norms. Since the courts, in a more advanced stage of development, at least inasmuch as they are the organs of the state for the administration of justice, are given a local competence, their norms for decision also become competent and fixed for this territory, and where several courts enter into reciprocal relations, for the territory of all of these courts.

The sovereignty of the state in the field of law, which is so significant for modern law, is based on the stability of the legal norms. The prevailing modern belief that *Rechtsgebiet* and *Staatsgebiet* are identical arises from the fact that the courts within the territory of a certain state consistently follow certain norms of decision. The stability of the norms for decision receives a special significance because of the fact that it extends not merely to like or similar cases but also to cases that are only approximately similar. This makes it possible to apply a norm to cases as to which it is not a decision at all, on the sole ground that the latter are similar to the decided cases. Every such decision, indeed, is based on a new norm for decision, but the content

疑问总是为了探寻裁判规范——的付出。而且,社会对稳定的裁判规范也有巨大需求,裁判规范的稳定性使得以有限的方法来预见裁决成为可能,由此,这种稳定性可以让人适得其所地安排自己的事务。

裁判规范的稳定性主要在时间向度内发挥作用。在没有很好理由的情形下,只要这一规范还能被记得,法院就不会偏离已经适用于某一案件中的裁判规范,而且为了防止这一裁判规范被遗忘,法院还经常采取一些特殊的措施。但是裁判规范的稳定性也主要在一定的空间中发挥作用;因为如果没有其他理由,为了避免寻找规范难免要付出的劳动,一个法院会欣然适用与该法院处于相同影响范围内的其他法院发现的裁判规范。在更高的发展阶段,至少由于法院变成了国家专门的司法机构,因而法院获得了对特定地域的权限,它们的裁判规范也变成了特定地域适当的和固定的裁判规范,而且在几个法院建立了相互关系的地方,它们的裁判规范变成了所有这些法院管辖地域的适当且固定的裁判规范。

对现代法律有重大意义的法律领域中的国家主权是以法律规范的稳定性为基础的。法律施行区域与国土二者完全重合——这一普遍的现代信念产生于如下事实:特定国土内的法院始终如一地适用特定的裁判规范。由于裁判规范的稳定性不仅仅为相同或者类似的案件提供了裁判基础,而且也为只是大致近似的案件提供裁判基础这一事实,因而,裁判规范的稳定性具有特别重要的意义。这使得将一个规范适用于根本不符合判例的案件成为可能,此种适用的唯一基础就在于后者类似于已有判例。的确,每个那样的裁决都是基于一个新的裁判规范,

of this new norm is merely this: that the existing norm is applicable to the case. The new norm has extended the sphere of application of the original norm and enriched its content; and every such extension and enrichment in turn functions according to the law of the stability of the norms for decision. Juristic lawmaking is based chiefly on this continued projection, as Wurzel has called it, of the norm to new cases. Thanks to this law of stability, the norms acquire an extremely tenacious life and an enormous extensibility. Every reception of foreign law is an instance of the operation of the law of the stability of the norms. Many a norm which, possibly, the Roman *pontifices* have thought out, continues to function today. One might raise the question here: If it is true that the norms grow out of the situations themselves for the decision concerning which they are to constitute the basis, how does it come about that a norm can still be applicable so long after it was created and under a totally different social and economic order; that the present-day German law contains norms which as to content are identical with those of the *corpus iuris*, nay, with those of the Twelve Tables and the Decalogue; that the French Civil Code can be valid for two so dissimilar societies as the French and the Roumanian?

The answer is this: The norms, especially those that have been derived from Roman law, have become so general and so abstract, by the uninterrupted process of extension and of enrichment of their content in the course of the millennia, that they are adaptable to the most diverse situations. This shows however that after all the law of the stability of the norms is based on a superficial view of things. In actual fact it is not the same norm at all; it has remained unchanged in appearance only; it has received an

但该新裁判规范的内容仅仅是:现有规范可适用于该案件。新的规范扩展了原有规范的适用范围,并丰富了原有规范的内容;每一次这样的扩展和丰富反过来也在按照裁判规范的稳定性法则发挥作用。如乌策尔所言,法学家立法主要是基于对适用于新型案件之规范的不断预估。得益于法律的这种稳定性,法律规范获得了极为顽强的生命力和巨大的延伸性。每一次外国法律的继受都是法律规范稳定性运作的例子。许多很可能是罗马祭司[1]设计出来的法律在今天仍在发挥作用。有人可能在这里提出这样的问题:如果规范的确产生于构成裁判基础的那些情势之中,那么一个规范被创造出来后的很长时间里在一个完全不同的社会、经济秩序中仍然能够适用,这是如何发生的?今天的德国法中包含着在内容上与《国法大全》一样的规范,不仅如此,而且也包含着那些在内容上与《十二铜表法》及《摩西十诫》一样的规范,这又是如何发生的?《法国民法典》可以在法国和罗马尼亚这样两个不同的社会有效,这又是如何发生的?

答案是这样的:在几千年的进程中,规范尤其是那些起源于罗马法的规范,通过内容上不间断的延伸和丰富的进程,它们已经变得如此的一般和抽象,以至于能够适用于最多样的情形。然而,这毕竟表明,规范稳定性的所有法则都是基于一种肤浅的事物观。事实上,后者根本就不是相同的规范,它仅仅在外表上没有改变而已,它已经接纳了全新的核心内容。

[1] (拉)*pontifices*(祭司),罗马社会的僧侣,他们曾经垄断着法律文献和有关的解释。

entirely new inner content.

The great contrasts between the law of the past and the law of the present, the differences between the laws of the various countries and nations, are based on the facts of the law, in every instance, rather than on the legal norms. The usages, relations of domination and subjection, relations of possession, contracts, testamentary dispositions, change to a much greater extent than the norms, and react upon the latter even though the wording of the latter has remained unchanged. In the *Eigentumsklage*, the principles of compensation for fruits or expenditures may be worded, in the main, just as they were among the Romans, but it is by no means immaterial whether they are applied to a Roman *fundus* or to a modern knight's estate or to securities amounting to millions. One need only bear in mind what is meant by the terms *fruits* and *expenditures* in each of these three cases to see at once what changes the norms have undergone meanwhile. The Roman law of obligations has, in a certain sense, manifested an astonishing power of resistance. But in Rome both the creditor and the debtor were *patres familiae*, heads of families the membership of each of which often comprised more than half of a hundred persons. Today the creditor and the debtor are, formally at least, individuals. In view of this vast difference, what is the significance of the fact that today the liability of the individual for fault and accident is similar to that of the liability of the *pater familias* in time past in Rome? If one strikes glass or iron with the same hammer, there will be a different sound in each case.

Nevertheless one must not assume that this pouring of a new content into the norms obviates all difficulties involved in the law of the stability of the norms. The bulk of the complaints about unsatisfactory laws amounts to this: that the norms, because of their stability, function in situations for which they were not created, and to which therefore they are not adapted. But the evil effects are limited considerably by the fact that these norms are not norms of conduct but of decision.

过去的和现在的法律间的巨大差异、不同国家和民族间法律的差异都是基于每一种情况下法律事实的不同，而不是法律规范的不同。习惯、支配与臣服关系、占有关系、契约以及遗嘱处分，所有这些的改变比规范的改变在程度上要大得多，并且对后者产生了影响，即使后者的措辞表达保持未变。在所有权确认之诉中，对孳息和支出之补偿原则的表述，大体上恰如罗马人对相应原则的表述。但是，它们是适用于罗马的土地还是适用于近代的骑士封地，或是适用于数百万计的证券，就绝对不是无关紧要的。任何人只需牢记在这三种情形下，孳息和支出这两个术语在不同情形中的含义，他就能立刻明白，法律规范与此同时经历了怎样的变迁。罗马债法在某种意义上显示了一种令人惊异的抵制力量。但是在古罗马，债权人和债务人都是家父，都是各自——成员经常超过半百的——家庭中的首脑。今天，至少在形式上，债权人和债务人都是个人。考虑到此种巨大差异，今天的个人过错责任和意外事故责任与古罗马时的家父责任相似，这一事实有何重要意义？如果一个人用同样的铁锤敲打玻璃或者铁，在每种情形下将会产生不同的声音。

尽管如此，人们不能以为，往规范中注入新内容就能排除规范稳定性法则中的一切困难。针对令人不满意之法律的大量抱怨实际上是这种情形：由于规范的稳定性，规范（经常不得不）在那种并非专门为其量身定做的境况下继续运行，并且因此而不能适应后者。不过，这种不幸的效果在相当程度上被这些不是行为规范而是裁判规范的事实限制了。倘若罗马法规范的稳定性实

If the stability of the Roman norms should actually compel us to live according to Roman law, e. g. in the enlarged family of the Romans with its *manus* marriage or its free marriage arbitrarily dissoluble, if it should actually compel us to adapt our system of landholding to the Roman *fundus*, the resulting situation would be unendurable. In actual fact, all that it comes to is that occasionally a law-suit is decided according to Roman law. The part of our daily life that appears in the courts is by far too insignificant to make it impossible for us to endure the most unjust decisions. Much though we may suffer under this state of affairs, we submit to the inevitable; for stability of the norms, as a basis for judicial decision and for juristic science, is inevitable.

The stability of the norms for decision causes them to lose their original form and to become legal propositions. One of the most important results achieved by Jung in his book, *The Problem of Natural Law*, is that "the power of the *Praejudiz* (which rests on the stability of the norms for decision) is part of the conceptual presuppositions for the formation of legal propositions." Before we can discuss the norm for decision in the form of the legal proposition, however, we must consider another form of law in general, the law created by the state.

际上迫使我们不得不依照罗马法生活,例如,在存在夫权婚姻或者可任意解除的自由婚姻的罗马人大家庭中生活;倘若它实际上迫使我们不得不把我们的土地所有制度变为罗马的土地制度,则产生的情形将是无法忍受的。事实上,提及的所有这些仅仅是:偶尔一个法律诉讼是依据罗马法作出裁判的。出现在法庭上的我们日常生活的那一部分对于我们来说,太过于无关紧要,以至于我们能够忍受与之相关的最不公正的判决。尽管此种情形下我们可能遭受许多损失,但是我们忍受这种不可避免的结果;因为规范的稳定性,作为司法裁判和法学的基础,是不可避免的。

规范的稳定性使得规范失去了它们最初的形式,变成了法律命题。耶林在其《自然法的问题》一书中所得出的最重要结论之一就是:"(基于裁判规范的稳定性之上的)先例的力量是法律命题形成之观念预设的一部分。"然而,在我们可以讨论以法律命题形式存在的裁判规范之前,我们必须对另外一种法律形式——国家创制之法——予以大致的考量。

# VII
# The State And The Law

A clear-cut distinction must be made between state law and statute. State law is created by the state, not indeed as to its form, but as to its content; it is law that came into being solely through the state, and that could not exist without the state. The form in which it arises is immaterial. Not every statutory precept contains state law. There are statutes whose sole function is to create the inner order for a legal relation, e. g. articles of association, regulations for the conduct of a commercial enterprise; moreover the state can enter into a contract by enacting a statute. Articles of association, regulation of commercial enterprises, contract do not become state law because they have been put into statutory form; they remain what they were, the inner order of a legal relation. In the same way, jurist-made law can be put into statutory form, i. e. the legislator may confine himself, in the manner of the jurist, to universalizing, reducing to unity, to finding norms according to what seems to him to be justice. The resolutions of many mediaeval corporate bodies of the state, especially of the German Diet and of the English Parliament, normally were *Weistumer*, i. e. they were juristic law not only in content but also in form. On the other hand state law can come into existence not only in the form of statutes, but also in the form of administrative or police regulation, of magisterial law, of judge-made law. The Roman praetor

# 第七章 国家和法

国家法和制定法必须明确区分。国家法是由国家创制的法律,当然并不是指在形式上由国家创制,而是在内容上由国家创制。国家法是仅仅经由国家而形成的法律,而且国家法离开了国家也无法存在下去。国家法通过何种形式产生是无关紧要的。并不是每一条制定法的规定都包含国家法。唯一功能是创造法律关系内在秩序的制定法也存在,例如联合体的章程、商业企业的管理条例等;而且国家可以通过颁布一项制定法建立一份契约。联合体的章程、商业企业的条例、契约并没有因为它们采取了制定法的形式而变为国家法;它们保持了它们本来的法律关系的内在秩序。同样地,法学家制定的法律也可以采取制定法的形式,即立法者可以采取法学家的方式,只限于使之一般化并将之化而为一,发现对他来说似乎是正义的规范。中世纪的许多国家的法人团体的决议,尤其是德国议会和英国议会的决议,通常是法律的宣布,即它们不仅在内容上而且在形式上也是法学家法。另一方面,国家法的形成不仅可以采取制定法的形式,也可以采取行政规章或治安条例、地方执法官法和法官法的形式。罗马的裁判

was essentially a *Gerichtsherr* ; his praetorian edict therefore contains mostly magisterial law (*Amtsrecht*), occasionally when his object was merely to resolve doubts and difficulties, judge-made law; but the *edictum de posito et suspenso or de calumniatoribus* is state law, police regulation, and criminal law. The English judges, acting as organs of the state, have created the most important parts of the English criminal law of the state in their legal decisions. English equity also contains much state law.

Most jurists would be slightly astonished if they were asked how it happens that the state, which they are accustomed to look upon as the source of all law, concerns itself about law at all. But the question is not altogether unjustified. In its origin the state is a military association, whose relation to the affairs of the legal order is very loose; and, with the exception of a few modern states, established in the former and the present English colonies in North America and in other parts of the world, it has remained an essentially military association to the present day. It is possible to place the origin of the state in the far distant past, but one must not look for it in the clan or in the community of the household. The earliest formation which is at all historically connected with the present state is the confederation of the warlike nobility of several tribes related by language, who, followed by the remaining freemen, choose a military leader, not only for the

官本质上是一个至高的司法权威,[1]因此,他的裁判官告示主要包括职务法(*Amtsrecht*),有时候,当裁判官的目的仅仅是解决一些疑惑和困难的时候,裁判官的告示也包括法官法;关于搁置物和悬挂物的告示或关于诬告的告示是国家法、治安条例和刑法。英国的法官作为发挥作用的国家机构,在他们的裁决中创制了英国国家刑法的最重要的部分。英国的衡平法也包含大量的国家法。

如果大部分法学家被问及——国家(他们习惯性地把国家看做所有法律的来源)在根本上关切法律——这是怎样发生的,那么他们可能会稍稍有些吃惊。但是这一问题并非完全没有道理的。在国家的起源方面,国家是一种与法律秩序事务联系非常松散的军事联合体。而且,除了一些现代国家外,先前建立的和现在在北美洲和世界其他地方的英国殖民地,直到今天在本质上仍然是军事联合体。国家的起源可以追溯到遥远的过去,但是,任何人不能在氏族或者家庭共同体中寻觅最初的国家。与现代国家有着根本性历史联系的最初形态,是因语言而相关的、几个部落好战贵族的同盟,贵族在余留的自由民的拥护下选择一位军事首领,这位军事首领不仅仅是为了特别的紧急情况而产生,

〔1〕 *Gerichtsherr*,至高的司法权威。法治国的基本原则要求,法官必须服从法律;在实现正义方面,法官的职责就是适用法律。但是在古罗马,情况并非如此。在法院里行使职权的裁判官并不受法律的束缚,他拥有广泛的自由裁量权,因此,他是至高的司法权威。

special emergency, but as a permanent leader. The state has never denied its military origin; at every stage of its development military interests were in the foreground; and with the exception of the English colonies referred to above and a few minor European states, this is true everywhere today.

To the purely military functions of the young state two others were added at an early date, which however are closely connected with the former. First of all, it is the function of the state to supply the king, the permanent military leader, and his followers with the necessary material means. This is done in the earliest times by means of urgent demands for gifts—a method which later, especially in the Orient, becomes out and out extortion. The Romans, in their provinces, appear to have been the first to develop an orderly system of taxation. In addition, the state at an early period developed a crude police activity, especially in cases of insurrection and rebellion. The great territorial states of the Orient did not develop beyond this stage until the middle of the nineteenth century. This stage is followed, after a long interval, in small territorial and in city states at first, later also in large territorial states, in the Roman Empire, in the Carolingian Empire, in England, by a well ordered system of administration of justice by the state; and much later, in the same states, by legislation. A true administration by the state, even approximately comparable in the diversity of its purposes with that of the present day, did not arise until the seventeenth century in France. Prior to this time, there is nothing like it except in city states. In the Orient scarcely anything like it is to be found down to the most recent period, or in the old Republic of Poland, or in England down to the nineteenth century. We might therefore speak with Adolf Wagner of a law of an ever increasing, and more than that, of an ever more rapidly increasing, activity of the state, if it were not for the fact that the culminating

而且也是一位常设的领导。国家从来没有否认它的军事起源;在国家发展的每一个阶段,军事利益都处于最显著的位置;而且,除了上面所提到的英国殖民地和欧洲的一些很小的国家外,这在今天每一个地方都是正确的。

在早期,单纯的执行军事职能的初期的国家又增加了另外两项职能,然而这两项职能还是和军事职能密切相关。首先,这项国家职能是为国王——国家永久的军事首领——和其追随者提供必要的物质财富。这一职能在最初的时候是通过对财物的紧急征收方式完成的,这种方法后来,尤其是在东方变成了一种彻底的掠夺。似乎罗马人在他们的行省里第一次发展了一种有序的税收制度。另外,早期的国家发展出了野蛮的警察活动,尤其是在出现起义和叛乱的情况下。地域极其辽阔的东方国家直到 19 世纪中期也没有超越这一发展阶段。在经历一段很长的间隔期后,首先在一些地域狭小的国家和城市国家,后来也在一些地域辽阔的国家,在罗马帝国、加洛林帝国、[1]英国,出现了依赖国家的秩序良好的司法制度。一种真正的依靠国家的行政,甚至在目的多样性上可以大致和今天的国家行政相比的国家行政,直到 17 世纪才在法国产生。在这以前,除了在城市国家外,没有这种依靠国家的行政。在东方,直到最近,也没有发现任何类似的这种行政,在古波兰共和国以及在 19 世纪以前的英国也是如此。因此,如果不是因为这一顶点已经过去或在不久的将来即将过去,我们可以和阿道夫·瓦格纳

〔1〕 Carolingian Empire,加洛林帝国:751 年矮子丕平创立了法兰克王朝,该王朝在法国一直延续到 987 年,在德国延续到 911 年。

point either has already been passed or will have been passed in the near future.

There are, manifestly, four things that cause the state to appear, in such an eminent degree, to be the source of law. These are the following. First its participation in lawmaking through legislation; secondly, its participation in the administration of law through the state courts and in part through other tribunals; thirdly, its power and control over the state tribunals, by which it is enabled to give effect to its statutes; lastly, the idea that the preservation of a factual situation corresponding to the law can be effected primarily, or at least ultimately, through the state's power of compulsion. This last point however is of no importance here since it is without influence upon the creation and development of state law.

The history of law has shown that originally both legislation and administration of law were beyond the sphere and province of the state. The administration of justice does not derive from the state; it has its roots in the time before the existence of the state. Its oldest form appears quite clearly in the judgment scene on the shield of Achilleus, for the only possible interpretation of which we are indebted to Hoffmeister. Two men are quarreling over the *wergild* for a man who was slain. One boasted that he would pay all; the other disputed this, saying he would not accept anything. In other words, the kinsman of the slain man insists on the vengeance of blood, and the wise judges are called upon to decide whether he shall prevail, or whether he is obligated to accept the penalty. The court has not been commissioned by the state, and the judgment is not made effective by compulsion exercised by the state. If the other party refuses to submit, he may have his vengeance in spite of the judgment. The only consequence of doing so is the loss of the purely social advantages of a just feud. Traces of this stage in the development of the administration of justice can readily be found in the criminal law of the sagas of Iceland, as it has recently been set forth with such vividness by Andreas Heusler, the younger. It is easily recognizable not only in the legal

一起商谈不断增加的法律,不仅如此,也可以一起商谈更快增加的国家活动。

显然,四个因素导致了国家在一个如此显著的程度上成为法律的来源。它们是:首先,国家通过立法活动参与法律的制定;其次,国家通过法院并且部分地通过其他裁决机构参与司法;再次,国家拥有对国家裁决机构的权威和支配权,据此国家可以使自己的制定法产生效力;最后,符合法律之事实情形的维持,主要或者至少最终要通过国家强制力产生作用的观念。然而,最后这一点在这里是不重要的,因为这一点对国家法的创制和发展不产生影响。

法律史证明:最初立法和司法都超出了国家的范围和领域。司法并不起源于国家,它在国家存在之前就已产生。它最古老的形式在阿基里斯之盾的裁决场面中呈现得十分清楚,对于相关的唯一可能的解释,我们要感激霍夫迈斯特。两个人对因凶杀案而支付赔偿金一事产生争执。其中一方夸口说他将支付所有的赔偿金;另一方对此表示反对,说他将不接受任何的赔偿金。换句话说,被害人的族人坚持要血亲复仇。英明的法官需要裁决,凶手是应胜诉还是有责任接受惩罚。法院并没有国家的授权,而且裁决也并不是因为国家实施的强制力而有效。如果另一方当事人拒绝服从,即使存在裁决,他也可以复仇。这样做的唯一结果是丧失一次公正斗争的纯粹社会利益。如同小安德里亚·霍伊斯勒最近如此生动地阐述的那样,司法在此阶段发展的线索可以很容易在冰岛传说中的刑法中找到。不仅仅在前加洛林王朝时期的法律诉讼程序中,而且也在罗马《十二铜表法》

procedure in the pre-Carolingian period but also in the much more highly developed procedure of the Roman Twelve Tables. At this stage, penalties in fixed amounts have already been prescribed, but the injured party is not yet obligated to accept them; the judgment delivers up the party who has done the injury to the injured party unless an agreement is reached (*ni cum eo pacit*). The procedure is rigid and formal, as indeed it must be between deadly enemies; the competence of the court is limited, in the main, to cases demanding the death penalty (homicide, man-stealing, bodily injury, theft).

Zallinger has pointed out that this procedure could not possibly have been the only procedure in the primitive period of the history of the Germanic peoples. Surely even in primitive times quarrels arose not only between deadly enemies but also between members of a close association; and some of these most likely because of minor wrong-doings. In actual fact it can easily be shown that provision had been made everywhere for the composition of quarrels of this nature, but the reports that we have concerning them are meagre since the jurists, for obvious reasons, are not interested in them. We find the jurisdiction of the head of the clan, of the head of the house, of the elder of the village. We find family courts and village courts. The procedure is quite informal. The legal principles according to which the decisions are arrived at are unsettled and uncertain; the judgment is a sort of amicable settlement unless it pronounces exclusion from the community. The head of the household in Rome did indeed have the *ius vitae ac necis*. But things of this kind are rare in antiquity as the Romans themselves point out and cannot readily be found in other courts of a close association. (Can it be shown to have existed among the ancient Russians?) It probably arose after politically organized states had come into existence.

The work of Pachman, *Russian Customary Private Law* (*Obytschnoje graschdanskoje prawo w Rosii*), contains a full discussion of this kind of administration of justice. In Russia communal courts, which perhaps are rooted in a very early period, and which

中更为发达的诉讼程序中,此点都可以非常容易地辨认出来。在这一阶段,固定数量的刑法已有规定,但是受害方当事人仍然没有义务接受它们;除非达成一项协议(*ni cum eo pacit*),否则法官要把致害方交给受害方。这种诉讼程序是刻板的和正式的,因为,这种诉讼程序的确是在势不两立的敌人间进行的。法院的权限大体上被限制在要求判处死刑的案件上(杀人、绑架、身体伤害、盗窃)。

察林格早已指出这种诉讼程序无论如何也不会是日耳曼民族在原始时期的唯一诉讼程序。当然,在原始时代争执不仅仅出现在势不两立的敌人中间,而且也出现在一个紧密联合体的成员之间。后者部分可能因为一些很小的不道德行为。事实上,很容易证明,任何地方都制定了调解这种性质争执的条款,但是,我们拥有的有关它们的报告却非常不详尽,因为,基于很明显的理由,法学家们对它们不感兴趣。我们发现了氏族首领的司法权、家族首领的司法权和村庄里年长者的司法权。我们发现了家庭法院和村庄法院,这些法院的诉讼程序非常不正式。据以作出裁决的法律原则是变动不居的。裁决是一种友善的解决方式,除非裁决宣告将某一成员驱逐出社区。罗马家庭中的家长确实有生杀予夺的权利。但正如罗马人他们自己所指出的那样,这种情况在古代是罕见的,而且在紧密型联合体的其他法庭上也不容易找到。(能够证明在古代俄罗斯人中也存在这种情况吗?)这种情况可能产生在政治上组织形成的国家形成以后。

帕赫曼的著作《俄国习惯私法》(*Obytschnoje graschdanskoje prawo w Rosii*),对这种类型的司法予以了透彻的讨论。在俄国,社区法院可能在一个非常早的时期就已经存在,并且社区法院

are devoted to the administration of the affairs of the peasantry, have maintained their existence down to the present day. Legislation has merely circumscribed their jurisdiction, but has left their freedom unrestricted down to the most recent times. In the sixties and seventies their activity was investigated by a government commission, which published a six-volume report of its findings. The work of Pachman is based on this report (with the exception of the article on *Artele*). The results are, as Nalyschew and Kowalewsky point out, extremely open to attack, for the courts at the present time are in a state of the utmost disintegration. Nevertheless the work of Pachman is not without value. The sole legal proposition which is met with in all parts of Russia in communal administration of justice is extremely significant. It is *Grech po polu* (the damage is equally divided between the parties). If the court cannot make up its mind what decision it is to render, it divides the damage equally between the parties.

But there is a third class of courts. These are exclusively of state origin; they arise from the military leader's power and control over his followers. The military leader self-evidently acts as soon as the commonwealth is endangered, especially in case of treason, or of trading with the enemy. But he does not confine himself to these cases. The military leader must maintain discipline among his troops and, particularly, prevent feuds: he cannot permit vengeance of blood to become prevalent while he is face to face with the enemy. For this reason a certain jurisdiction over private affairs is inevitable at an early time. At a more advanced stage, the king has it as a matter of course. The sovereign power which the king attains in time of peace enables him to administer justice in times of peace also. This however is done according to principles, and according to a procedure, quite different from those of other courts and, at all events, not according to the sole discretion of the king, but according to that of the counsel of his advisers.

The next step in the development is that, in consequence of the loosening of the bonds of the old associations, the composition of

专门处理农民的事务，这种社区法院直到今天仍然存在。立法仅仅限制了它们的司法权，但是直到最近，立法仍留给了它们不受限制的自由。在6世纪和7世纪，一个政府委员会调查了它们的活动并出版了一部六卷本的调查结果。帕赫曼的著作主要以这一份报告为基础（除了关于合作社的文章外）。正如纳吕舒和科瓦列夫斯卡雅所指出的，帕赫曼的结论极端容易受到攻击，因为当前的法院处于一种极度分裂状态。然而帕赫曼的著作并非毫无价值。俄国所有地方社区司法都能碰到的唯一法律命题具有极端重要的意义。这就是 *Grech po polu*（损失平等地在双方当事人间分配）。如果法院不能决定应当作出什么样的裁决，就会让损失在当事人之间平等分配。

但是还存在第三种法院。这些法院纯粹源自国家。它们因军事首领对其追随者的权威和支配权而产生。不言而喻，国家一遭受危险——尤其是出现叛国和通敌的情况下——军事首领就会采取行动，但是他不会将自己的权力限于这些情形。军事首领必须维持军队的纪律，特别是防止长期的争斗。当他和敌人进行正面冲突的时候，他不能允许血亲复仇大行其道。因为这一原因，对私人事务的特定司法权在早期是不可避免的。在更进步的阶段，国王照例拥有了这种对私人事务的司法权。国王在和平时期获得的至高无上的权力使他在和平时代也能管理司法事务。然而，国王管理司法事务要依据一些原则，依据一种和其他法院完全不同的诉讼程序，而且无论如何都不是依据国王的独断，而是依据他的顾问们商议之后的判断。

发展的下一步是这样的：由于旧联合体的联结松散，具有亲

quarrels among people in a close relationship loses most of its importance, and that, consequently, the disputes between persons within close relationships are also brought into the regularly established courts. Since the latter henceforth are no longer limited to sitting in judgment in cases involving the death penalty, it becomes their task not only to compose quarrels, but to render decisions. The second step is the organization of these courts by the state. This has been done in various ways. Either the power to institute proceedings is put into the hands of a state official, as was done in Rome, or the state supplies the courts with a presiding officer, as was done in the kingdom of the Franks by Charles the Great, and in England after the conquest. At the same time the royal administration of justice as a function of the state continues. This is followed by the third step, the development of the king's jurisdiction. The king's advisers become self-dependent judges and actually displace all the old established courts in virtue of their special privileges, or perhaps because of the superior quality of their administration of justice (as in England), or they are converted into courts of appeal (the Parliaments in France, the *Hofgericht* of the German kingdom). The personal jurisdiction of the king however is not yet abolished by any means. Finally the lay assessors (*Beisitzer*), who are chosen from among the populace, are eliminated from the regularly constituted courts, and the latter become purely state courts manned by state officials. Perhaps there is a later stage of development, at which popular elements are again employed in the administration of justice. This was done in England as early as the days of Henry II in the assizes, and at a somewhat later date in the trial by jury. On the Continent this tendency, which did not appear until after the French Revolution and which was at first limited to criminal causes, has been extended more and more to certain kinds of private-law causes.

This conversion of the administration of justice into a function of the state is limited to Europe however. The Orient, where it has

密关系的人之间的争议和解失去了其大部分的重要性，具有亲密关系的人之间争议也提交给了按照规则建立起来的法院。因此，自此以后，法院的权限不仅仅限于听审涉及死刑的案件，除了调解争执作出裁决也成为了法院的任务。第二步是国家对这些法院的构造。这是通过各种不同的方式完成的。或者像在罗马社会一样，创制诉讼程序形式的权力掌握在国家官员手中，或者像在伟大的查尔斯统治下的法兰克王国和被征服后的英国一样，国家任命主管法院的官员。同时，作为国家职能的皇家司法也继续存在。紧接下来的是发展的第三步，即国王司法权的发展。国王的顾问变成了独立法官，并且事实上借助着他们的特权取代了所有的已经建立起来的古老法院，或许是因为它们司法的卓越品质（如在英国），或者它们转变成为了上诉法院（法国的国会、德意志王国的国王法院）。[1] 不过无论如何，国王的人身管辖权至今仍未被废除。最后，从平民中选出的非职业陪审员（*Beisitzer*）被排除出常规设立的法院。后者变成了纯粹由国家官员组成的国家法院。或许还存在着发展得更晚的一个阶段，大众化的因素被重新应用到司法中了。在英国，这最早出现在亨利二世时期的咨审团中，在稍晚一段时期，这也应用在了陪审团参加的裁决中。在欧洲大陆，这一趋势直到法国大革命以后才出现，这种趋势首先限于刑事诉讼中，随后越来越扩展到特定类型私法诉讼中。

然而，司法向国家职能的转变仅限于欧洲。未受到欧洲影响

〔1〕 字面上的意思是统治者的法院，也就是国王的法院。

remained untouched by European influences, to the present day knows nothing of state administration of justice. The Kadi is appointed by a spiritual authority, and is independent of the state. Likewise, in Mohammedan countries justice is administered either by temporal or by spiritual local authorities which are neither appointed nor commissioned by the state. Turkey alone established state courts, when it began to adopt European ways after the Crimean war, but it has preserved the jurisdiction of spiritual courts for a great number of causes.

State law appears in history at a much later date than state administration of justice. The state, in the first place, creates its own order, *Staatsrecht*, and when it creates tribunals of any kind whatsoever, it prescribes their competence, their order of conducting business, and occasionally also their procedure. At an early date, statements of law are being drawn up by private individuals at the behest of the state, or are being recognized by the state, which are collections of the norms according to which the courts conduct their business or render their decisions. These collections, however, are not state law even though additions and modifications have been added to the traditional element. Such additions are found in collections of this kind that are of an altogether private nature, and this fact merely demonstrates that man has ever been unable and unwilling, both then and at a later period, to observe the distinction between stating law and positing law, just as the medicine man who was closely related to the jurist found it necessary not only to know but also to discover his remedies.

The presuppositions under which state law can arise are conditioned upon the nature of the latter as a command addressed to the courts and other tribunals and directing them how to proceed. It can proceed only from a person who has control over the courts and the other tribunals. Before the state can create law in this manner, the administration of the affairs of the state and the order of the administration of justice must be unitary, to a certain extent. The powers of the state must have reached a degree of development sufficient to compel the performance of the commands of the central power throughout the whole territory of the state. This includes a certain military development and a police department of some sort. Lastly, the law of the state is conditioned upon certain factors of popular psychology. The state must find material from which it can select pliant judges

的东方国家至今对国家的司法一无所知。下级法官由一个宗教权威任命，并且独立于国家。同样地，在伊斯兰国家，司法由世俗的或者宗教的地方当局来执掌，他们都不是由国家指定或者委任的。克里米亚战争之后，当土耳其开始接受欧洲的方式时，它独自建立了国家法院，但是土耳其因为许多原因也保留了宗教法院的司法权。

在历史上，国家法在远远晚于国家司法产生的时期才出现。国家首先创制了自己的秩序——狭义上的公法，而且当国家无论创制何种类型的裁决机构时，都会规定它们的权限、处理事务的秩序，有时候也规定了它们的诉讼程序。在早期，法律的表述由私人按照国家的要求起草，或者被国家所认可，它们是法院据以行事或作出裁决的规范集。然而，这些规范集不是国家法，即使在传统元素之上有所增加或者修改。这种增加可以在完全是私人性的规范集中找到，而且这一事实仅仅证明：在那时和在稍晚一个时期，人们曾经不能且不愿遵从表述法律和提出法律之间的这种区分，正如和法学家密切相关的教士医生发现不但要知道而且要找到他的治疗方法一样。

国家法得以产生的预设是：国家法的性质作为一种对法院与其他裁决机构发布的命令，指令后者如何行事。它只来自于掌控法院与其他裁决机构的人。在国家可以如此创制法律以前，国家的行政事务和司法秩序必须在一定程度上统一。国家的权力必须达到足以在整个国家的领土上强制执行中央权力机关的命令的发展程度。这包含了特定军事力量的发展和某种警察部门的发展。最后，国家法也以特定的大众心理因素为条件。国家必须找到适当的人选，国家可以从中选择出顺从的法官

and officials. In this matter, the ability to read and write is of great importance. It must be reserved for the as yet unwritten history of legislation by the state to show how legislation everywhere followed the development of the administration of the affairs of the state. We can imagine of what value a study of the laws of Hammurabi and of other Assyrian law would be as long as we know nothing of the nature of the Assyrian state. The mere thought that the state can create law which is as effective as the law that arises from long continued custom, i. e. in the words of the gloss to the *Sachsenspiegel* that " the will of the country is to be treated like law," presupposes an enormous power of abstraction which man possesses only in an advanced stage of development. Since the German lay judges (*Schöffen*) of the early Middle Ages were not endowed with the latter, there could be no true legis lation in the Empire. It is well known that the small number of German imperial statutes that had been enacted by the time of the thirteenth century, imitations of Roman models, have received scant attention. For this reason statutes are, in general, unknown in the Orient down to the present time. When Turkey began to promulgate statutes, it had to create entirely new courts. If the Sultan had sent a copy of the commercial code to a Kadi, the latter, most likely, would not have known what to do with it. Furthermore there can be no legislation by the state without an administration of law that is subservient to the state. This too was lacking in the Middle Ages. After the French Parliaments had, to a limited extent, emancipated themselves from state control, they offered resistance even to the statutes of an absolute king. The German territories undoubtedly would not have attained a system of state law as early as the sixteenth and seventeenth centuries if the universities had not supplied them with excellent material for judges and officials who were in a situation of complete dependence upon the state. Finally there must be effective means of publishing state regulations, and the populace must have some understanding and appreciation of the content and purpose of a statute. If, nevertheless, statutes are frequently met with in a country where all of these presuppositions are nonexistent, we are likely to find that they are utterly ineffectual imitations of foreign models. The Frankish kings imitated the

和官员。在这方面,阅读和写作能力至关重要。这种能力必定专门用于到那时为止不成文的国家立法律史,以便揭示各个地方立法都是如何追随国家行政事务而发展的。我们可以设想在我们对亚述国的性质一无所知的时候,研究《汉谟拉比法典》和其他亚述法会有什么价值。纯粹那种思想——国家能够创制与长期习惯而形成的法律一样有效的法律,亦即用《萨克森法典》注释中的话来说就是“国家的意志将被视为法律”,预设了一种人类只有在高级发展阶段才有的超乎寻常的抽象力。既然中世纪早期德国非职业法官(*Schöffen*)还不具有后来的这种抽象力,那么在帝国中就不存在真正的立法。众所周知,德意志帝国 13 世纪前模仿罗马人颁布的少量制定法没有引起什么注意。因为这一原因,制定法在东方直到现在普遍不为人所知。当土耳其开始颁布制定法时,它不得不创立全新的法院。如果苏丹给下级法院的法官送去一份商法典的副本,下级法院的法官最有可能不知道如何依据法典裁决。而且,在没有服务于国家之司法的情况下,也不会有任何的国家立法。服务于国家的司法在中世纪也是缺失的。在法国的议会有限地从国家的控制中解放出来后,他们甚至对独裁国王的制定法进行了抵制。如果德国大学不能够为他们提供完全充当依赖于国家的法官和政府官员的优秀候选人,毫无疑问,德国不可能早在 16 世纪和 17 世纪就建立起国家法的制度。最后,国家法令必须存在有效的出版方式,而且民众也必须能够对制定法的内容和目的有所理解并做出正确评价。然而,如果在这些先决条件都不存在的国家,那么我们可能会发现:制定法经常完全是对外国模式的无效的模仿。法兰克的国王仿效罗马的

Roman Caesars; Tsar Duschan of Serbia, the Byzantine emperors; and in modern times many an Oriental state strives to imitate the Europeans, e. g. Siam, which had a Frenchman draw up a civil code.

State law is found only where the administration of justice and of the affairs of the state is directed from a central point and is based on a strong military and police power. At first these conditions exist only in states of small territorial extent; in antiquity, in Egypt with its unusually powerful state, and especially in the city states, Athens and Rome; in the Middle Ages, in the city states of Italy and Germany. The Roman citizen and the Roman official did indeed carry the concept of state law into every part of the enormous Empire; but it did not begin to prevail until the later days of the Empire, after the *constitutio Antonina*. Modern investigation has shown that there was much of seeming and little of actuality in this. The Germanic states that arose on the wreckage of the Roman Empire did have state law, as the Capitulary legislation shows, but this can be explained by the fact that they had taken over a great deal of Roman civilization and of the Roman bureaucratic institutions, It is very difficult to determine whether and to what extent these statutes really were valid, whether they were actually applied. On this very point doubts have been raised in recent days, especially by Dopsch, whose work, I regret to state, I have not been in position to avail myself of. The greater the distance between the Germanic states and the Roman Empire, both in time and in space, the more their legislation fades out. Jenks, the English legal historian, has ap-

统治者;塞尔维亚的沙皇仿效拜占庭的皇帝;而且,现代许多东方国家努力仿效欧洲国家,例如暹罗[1]邀请法国人起草了一部民法典。

国家法只有在司法和国家行政事务受到中央的指导并且有强大的军事和警察力量为基础的地方才能建立起来。起先,这些条件仅仅存在于地域范围狭小的国家;在古代,异常强大的国家存在于埃及,更存在于一些城邦,如雅典和罗马;在中世纪,在意大利和德国的城邦。罗马市民和罗马官员确实把国家法的观念传播到了庞大帝国的每一部分。但是这种观念直到帝国的晚期,在安东尼敕令[2]颁布之后,才开始盛行。现代研究表明,其中国家法的观念大多是表面上的,真正实在的极少。如同教会的立法显示的那样,在罗马帝国的残骸上建立起来的日耳曼国家确实拥有国家法,但是这可以通过日耳曼国家继承了大量的罗马文明和接管了大量的罗马官僚机构这一事实来解释。确定这些制定法是否实际有效以及在多大程度上有效,确定这些制定法是否被实际应用过,都是非常困难的。正是在这一点上,最近人们已经提出许多怀疑,尤其是道普什,不过非常遗憾,我未能利用道普什的著作。日耳曼国家在时间和空间上距离罗马帝国愈远,它们的立法就愈弱。英格兰的法律史学家詹克斯在他的著作《中世纪的

---

〔1〕 泰国的旧称。

〔2〕 公元212年,罗马皇帝卡拉卡颁布的一项敕令。这一敕令扩大了罗马公民资格的范围。之前,罗马公民的范围仅限于意大利,之后的范围,一般认为是整个帝国。自此,公民资格已失去了其政治上的重要含义,而仅仅具有帝国整体象征的意义。

pended to his book, *Law and Politics in the Middle Ages*, a table of the sources of the mediaeval law in Italy, Germany, France, England, Scotland, Spain, and Scandinavia. It is very instructive. The columns devoted to Italy and to the kingdom of the Franks are filled for the period from the sixth to the ninth century; there is an occasional entry concerning Spain. True, these entries are chiefly declarations of the existing law, but these statements, as is well known, contain legislative innovations; moreover, they also contain true state law. In the column devoted to England a few statements of law appear and these as of the sixth century only. In the tenth and eleventh centuries, legislation in all these states is at a standstill. Statements of law are found in England and Scotland. In the eleventh century, the systems of law in the cities of Italy are beginning to attract attention. True statutes, Schupfer informs us, are found first in Milan (as of the dates 1026, 1061, 1065). As to this point nothing appears in Jenks' table. At a somewhat later date the *Landfrieden* appear in Germany, which however, it seems, first developed from ecclesiastical commands and voluntary agreements into statutes in the eleventh century. To these the laws of the cities are added in the twelfth century.

This discussion of externals does not teach us very much. There are two questions that are of much greater importance than the question whether the will of the state has been proclaimed as law anywhere—perhaps under foreign influence or by some accident. These questions are: first, when the idea that the state has a call, and is able, to create law independently was first seriously entertained, and

法律和政治》中附加了一份意大利、德国、法国、英格兰、苏格兰、西班牙和斯堪的纳维亚半岛的中世纪法律来源的表格。这份表格非常具有启发意义。用来说明意大利和法兰克王国的专栏被从6世纪到9世纪的内容填满了;在这些专栏中偶尔有一个条目是关于西班牙的。确实,这些条目主要是现存法律的公告,但是,众所周知,这些条目中包含有立法方面的创新。而且,它们同样也包含了真正的国家法。在用来说明英格兰法的专栏中,出现了大量的仅关于6世纪的英格兰法律的法律综述。在10世纪和11世纪的这些国家中,立法都处于一种停顿状态。在英格兰和苏格兰发现了法律综述。在11世纪里,意大利城邦的法律制度才开始引起注意。舒普费尔告诉我们真正的制定法首先出现在米兰(大约在1026年、1061年和1065年)。在这一点上,詹克斯的表格并没有提到任何东西。稍迟一些时候,国家安宁法[1]出现在德国,然而,它似乎首先在11世纪时从教会命令与自愿协议发展为制定法。12世纪时,城邦法又加入其中。

这种表面上的讨论无法告诉我们太多。相对于——(或许在外国的影响下,或许由于某些偶发事件)国家的意志是否在任何地方被宣布为法律——这个问题,如下两个问题更为重要。它们是:第一个问题,国家有职责并有能力独立创制法律——这样的观念首次被郑重接受是在什么时候,这种观念是如何生根的;第

〔1〕 国家安宁,社会安宁;类似于英格兰的国王安宁。在这里:规范 *Landfrieden* 的法律。

how it took root; and secondly, when the idea that only the state can create law begins to gain ground. Neither of these questions has been investigated. In Greece, outside of Athens, there are few traces of state law. In Sparta, the utter absence, in earlier times, of the concept of state law later developed into a prohibition forbidding any change in the old customary law, the so-called legislation of Lycurgus. The idea of a state monopoly of law remained foreign even to the Romans until the last days of the Empire. It is clearly expressed for the first time by Constantinus. Until that time only the *ius publicum* is considered a creation of the state. And, as I have shown in my *Beiträge zur Theorie der Rechtsquellen*, in addition to *Staatsrecht* (public law), the Romans consider the positive law, i. e. the *leges*, *senatus consulta*, *edicta magistratuum*, *constitutiones*, a part of the *ius publicum*; but not the law which has not been posited, the *ius quod sine scripto venit compositum a prudentibus*, the *ius civile* in the technical

二个问题,只有国家才可以创制法律——这样的观念是什么时候获得人们赞同的。这些问题都没有被研究过。在希腊,除雅典外很少有国家法的痕迹。在斯巴达,更早时,国家法观念的完全缺失,它后来发展为一种禁令,即禁止对古老习惯法——所谓的赖库尔戈斯立法——〔1〕作任何改动。甚至罗马人直到帝国后期仍然对国家垄断法律的观念感到陌生。君士坦丁第一次明确地阐述了国家垄断法律的观念。直到那时,只有公法才被认为是国家创制的法律。并且,如同我在我的《法源理论的贡献》一书中证明的那样,除了 *Staatsrecht*(公法)外,罗马人认为实证法,即法律、〔2〕元老院决议、〔3〕执法官告示、皇帝敕令——〔4〕都是公法的一部分,而不是未被分类的法律,通过法学家的活动而产生的

〔1〕 斯巴达国王赖库尔戈斯,传说中古代斯巴达的立法者。

〔2〕 (拉)*leges*(法律),在罗马法中,*lex* 一般是指共同体的权力机构根据执法官的提议并经过元老院认可的法律规范,从更广的意义上讲,它是指由某一权力机构(例如民众会议、元老院、执政官、皇帝等)依照法定程序制定和发布的规范,因此一些学者将法律区分为官定法律和民决法律。

〔3〕 (拉)*senatus consulta*(元老院决议),罗马法的重要渊源之一,表现为以书面形式向最高执法官提供的咨询意见。由于元老院成员所享有的威望和权力,这类咨询意见在事实上具有法律(*lex*)的效力。

〔4〕 (拉)*constitutiones*(法令),指帝国法令、由皇帝颁布的敕令。后则指法律汇编。法令有不同的形式,包括呈交元老院决议的提案(*orations*)、无需元老院同意而直接由皇帝公布的敕令(*edicta*)、向帝国官吏所作的敕训(*mandata*)、皇帝对法律案件所作的敕裁(*decreta*)和皇帝对提交的法律问题所作的敕答(*rescrepta*)等。

sense, which to-gether with the *ius gentium* and the *ius naturale* they subsume under the head of *ius privatum*. It is impossible to determine when the Romans began to create law by means of statutes. But even in historical times, they hesitated to modify the *ius civile*, the traditional customary law, by means of statutes. This is shown by the fact that their older *leges*, which are directed against abuses, do not abolish these abuses by directly doing away with the legal propositions upon which the abuse is based, but by giving the injured party a right to demand restitution. They are all *leges imperfectae* (*lex Plaetoria*, *lex Furia testamentaria*, *lex Marcia*, *lex Cincia*); and Gaius, in his day, still speaks of the matter as if the old *ius civile* were still in existence side by side with the *leges* which had abolished it. In the Middle Ages, from about the time of the collapse of the Carolingian Empire, the idea that the state can create law or modify it is altogether non-existent. At

不成文法，技术意义上的市民法和万民法以及自然法，它们都列在私法的门类之下。要确定罗马人什么时候开始通过制定法的方式来创制法律是非常困难的。但是，即使在历史上，罗马人也对通过制定法修改市民法、传统的习惯法犹豫不决。以下事实可以证明这一点：他们专门针对法律滥用的古老法律，达致目标的方式并非是直接废除那些滥用赖以存在的法律命题，而是给予受害方一个要求恢复原状的权利。它们都是不完善的法律〔1〕(《普莱多里法》,〔2〕《关于遗嘱的富里法》,〔3〕《马尔其法》,〔4〕《琴其亚法》);〔5〕并且盖尤斯在他生活的年代仍然提及了这一问题，仿佛旧的市民法和废止它的法律同时并存一样。在中世纪，大约从加洛林帝国崩溃时起，国家可以创制法律或者修改法律的观

---

〔1〕 (拉)*leges imperfectae*(不完善的法律)，罗马法学家对禁止性法律所划分的三个类别之一，指禁止某一行为、但并不认为违反有关禁令的行为是无效的且未规定罚则的法律规范。

〔2〕 (拉)*lex Plaetoria*(《普莱多里法》)，颁布于公元前191年，该法针对以欺骗手段与不满25岁未成年人(无论是自权人还是他权人)缔结契约的人规定了惩罚措施，允许上述未成年人为维护自己的权益而针对有关适法行为(*negozio giuridico*)的有效性提出抗辩(*exceptio*)。

〔3〕 (拉)*lex Furia testamentaria*(《关于遗嘱的富里法》)，一项颁布于公元前200年的法律，该法规定：遗嘱的数量不得超过1000阿斯(*as*)，对于超过此限额的部分，受遗赠人应支付四倍的罚金，或者予以充公。

〔4〕 (拉)*lex Marcia*(《马尔其法》)，颁布年代不详。该法规定，对于收取高利贷的人，可以通过拘禁之诉(*legis actio per manus iniectio*)要求获得返还。

〔5〕 (拉)*lex Cincia*(《琴其亚法》)，一项于公元前204年颁布的平民会决议，它对随意的私人赠与(*donatio*)行为加以限制，针对非以亲属为对象的赠与规定了最高限额。

the diet of Stela, in the reign of Otto I, in the year 942, the right of grandsons to inherit from their grandfather is not determined by a statute but is established by the *Gottesurteil* (judgment of God) of the legal combat. No trace of this idea is found in the *Sachsenspiegel*. And surely the two-sword theory does not refer to it. It expressly denies to the pope, the bearer of the spiritual sword, the right to modify the law of the land and of feudal tenancy. The gloss to the *Sachsenspiegel* concedes that Willkür is to be treated as law, but only within very narrow falimits. The *Weistum* of the Parliament of Merton (1235-1236) is famous: *Acrogaverunt omnes episcopi Magnates, ut consentirent, quod nati ante matrimonium essent legitimi, sicut illi qui nati sunt post matrimonium quantum ad successionem hereditariam, quia ecclesia tales habet pro legitimis, et omnes Comites et Barones una voce responderunt, quod nolunt leges Angliae mutate, quae usitatae sunt et approbatae.* This attitude of the *Comites* and *Barones* is by no means to be explained as caused by a disinclination to accept the principle of legitimation—for there were illegitimate children at that time in England as well as elsewhere—but by the absence of the idea that law can be created or modified by resolution of Parliament.

念还完全不存在。在 942 年奥托一世统治时期的斯泰拉三政会中，孙子对祖父的继承权并非由制定法确定，而是建立在对合法争斗的 *Gottesurteil*（上帝判决）之上。没有迹象表明在《萨克森法典》存在这一观点。的确，“双剑理论”并没有提到这一点。这一理论明确否认了教皇（灵魂之剑持有人）修改土地法和封地租赁制度的权利。对《萨克森法典》的注释勉强承认自由意志可以被视同为法律，但这也仅仅适用于一个非常狭小的范围内。默顿[1]（1235～1236）议会的法律颁布很著名：*Acrogaverunt omnes episcopi Magnates, ut consentirent, quod nati ante matrimonium essent legitimi, sicut illi qui nati sunt post matrimonium quantum ad successionem hereditariam, quia ecclesia*（古代雅典的人民会议）*tales habet pro legitimis, et omnes Comites et Barones una voce responderunt, quod nolunt leges Angliae mutate, quae usitatae sunt et approbatae.*[2]可科米蒂斯和巴罗尼斯的态度决不能被解释为是由于他们不愿意接受非婚生子女准正原则——[3]因为那时在英格兰和在其他地方一样都存在着非婚生子女——而是因为议会的决议可以创制或者修改法律这种观念当时并不存在。

---

〔1〕 英格兰东南部城市。

〔2〕 此段拉丁文大意是：允许那些在婚姻之前出生的非婚生子女与那些在婚姻之后出生的子女一样，享有对遗产的继承权。而在教会法上，通常采取的是有利于婚生子的原则。

〔3〕 非婚生子女准正是指给与非婚生子女以婚生子女的地位。准正在确定非婚生子女的继承权方面有重要意义。

And when a statute is enacted, it is by no means "the will of the State." Its oldest form seems to have been that of contract. This may have been the case among the Romans. The Roman *leges sacratae* may originally have been an agreement sworn to by all citizens whom they concerned. Similar situations are found in ancient Greece. There is no doubt that this applies to the oldest statutes of the German kingdom, the *Landfrieden*. They had to be sworn to and had validity only for those who had sworn to them. They derived their power not from the will of the state, but from the oath, although the individual often took the oath under compulsion. Even in England, a statute was agreed upon between King and Parliament like a contract. Another form is the "*Privileg.*" *Privilegia*, granted to cities by the lords of cities, are in the first place the city charters in Germany and Italy as well as the confirmation of city statutes. Very often the statute is disguised as a *Weistum* (declaration of law). Jenks says of the English Parliament that it is a law-declaring rather than a law-making body. It has been said of the Magna Charta, one of the most

当一部制定法颁布时,它绝对不是“国家的意志”。制定法最古老的形式似乎是契约。在罗马人中可能正是这种情形。罗马人的神圣约法[1]可能起源于所有相关市民共同宣誓的协议。在古希腊,也可以发现同样的情形。毫无疑问,这也适用于日耳曼王国古老的制定法《国家安宁法》。它们的创设必须经过宣誓,而且也只对那些宣过誓的人有效。虽然个人经常被迫宣誓,但是它们的权力并不是来源于国家的意志,而是来源于誓约。甚至在英格兰,一部制定法也像契约一样在国王和议会间达成。另外的一种形式是“法律的公布”。城市领主授予城市的 *Privilegia*,[2]首先是在德国和意大利城市的宪章,其次也是对城市制定法的确认。制定法时常伪装成 *Weistum*(法律的公布)。詹克斯说英格兰的议会是一种法律公布机构,而不是法律制定机构。《大宪章》[3]被说成是人类历史上最著

---

〔1〕(拉)*leges sacratae*(神圣约法),早期罗马社会的平民在圣山(*Monte Sacro*)上制定的法律,其主要内容是调整平民代表机构的活动和平民护民官的职责。

〔2〕*A Privilegia*,法律创设的一种形式,是国家主权对直接基于其上的主观性权利的一种公布。

〔3〕英格兰国王约翰(King John)在封建领主的强迫下于1215年6月15日在伦尼梅特(Runnynede)签署的保证公民自由和政治权利的宪法性文件,被公认为英格兰宪法自由权的基础。大宪章共63条,后世国王曾经多次协定确认。其主要内容是针对当时一些不公正的社会现象从法律上规定了补救措施,如司法职权的公正实施,世俗和教会裁判权的界定,公民人身自由和财产权的保障,征税限制和教会权利不受侵犯等。大宪章对后世的巨大影响不在于其具体条款而是其语言的内在重要含义。如大宪章保障自由民除经合法裁决外,不得被任意逮捕、监禁、没收财产和放逐出境。在司法公正方面规定,不得任意出卖权利和公正,也不得任意拒绝或拖延赋予任何人权利或公正。

famous sources of state law in the history of mankind, that"the form of this solemn instrument is that of a deed of grant" (Maitland). With such difficulty, and so gradually, the idea of state law, which indeed is anything but easily comprehensible, has made its way even among the most advanced nations of the human race. The fact that the concept of law as created by the state is found among the glossators and later also among the postglossators and the canonists in the early Middle Ages with reference to the church is not in conflict with this view. For the latter reflect not their own ideas, but the doctrines of the *corpus iuris* of the Byzantine age. We may disregard the question how much of this can be traced to political, especially Ghibelline, ambitions.

In the Orient, traces of state law are as few and far between as traces of state administration of justice. Whatsoever is called statute in extra-European states is either a declaration of law like the law of Moses or of Zarathustra or of Manu, or it is a regulation issued by the sovereign power of the state, without any general significance beyond the special case for which it was issued. We may disregard imitations of European models made without serious intent.

As to content, state law originally contained only norms for decision. It is merely a direction to the courts, which by this time have become state courts, directing them how to adjudge legal disputes. The government of the state, as developed first of all in France after the collapse of Rome, was concerned only with collecting taxes and with military affairs (the *intendants*). It knows of state law, therefore, only as to these things. The financial and military authorities receive special directions for individual cases; later, directions couched in quite general

名的国家法渊源之一，“此神圣的法律文件采取的是一种授权行为的形式”（梅特兰语）。尽管如此困难又如此缓慢，不过，的确绝非容易理解的国家法观念甚至在人类最发达的民族中也开辟了道路。国家创制法律的观念，出现在注释法学者中，后来也出现在后注释法学者和中世纪早期与教会有关的宗教法学者中——该事实与这一观念并不冲突。因为这一观念并不反映他们自己的观点，而是拜占庭时代的《国法大全》中的法律原则。我们可以忽略这个问题——它在多大程度上可以追溯到政治上的野心，尤其是皇帝党人的野心。[1]

在东方，国家法的线索和国家司法的线索一样稀少。在欧洲以外的国家被称为制定法的任何东西或者是一种法律的公布，如摩西的法律或者拜火教的创始人的法律或者摩奴的法律；或者是一种国家主权发布的条例，它们并不具有任何超越特殊情形的一般意义。我们可以忽略没有严肃意图的、对欧洲模式的模仿。

就内容而言，国家法最初仅仅包含了裁判规范。制定法仅仅是对法院（到此刻已经成为国家法院）的一种指令，制定法指令他们如何裁决法律纠纷。在罗马帝国崩溃后首先在法国发展起来的国家政府，仅仅关心税收和军事事务。因此，当时已知道的国家法，也仅限于这些事情。财政和军事机构接受对个别情形的特别指导；后来用相当一般性的术语表述的指令在某些明确界定的

〔1〕 中世纪拥护德国皇帝控制意大利的贵族政党成员，反对归尔甫派和教皇派。

terms to act in certain clearly defined cases; and finally detailed directions issued by the central power instructing them how to proceed. This constitutes the basis of a new kind of state law, the law governing state action, i. e. state administrative law. From France, this law spreads over the whole continent of Europe. Where there are no state administrative authorities, as in the ancient German kingdom, in England, in Poland, in Hungary, there is no effective administrative legislation. Occasionally the state resorts to charging the autonomous administrative bodies of the lesser associations, especially of the communes (*Gemeinde*), the districts (*Bezirk*), the counties (*Komitat*), with the execution of the statutes; in England it also commissions the justices of the peace. But these means are as a rule poorly adapted to this purpose. If the will of the state is to be carried out effectively, special agencies must be constituted for this purpose. When the English, therefore, enacted legislation for relief of the poor, they created a board for this purpose, and when they enacted legislation for the protection of factory workers, they created a board of factory inspectors. These institutions have frequently served as models for similar purposes elsewhere.

Now, what is the propulsive force in this whole development? What prompts the state to take over, to an ever increasing extent, the administration of justice and the creation of law, which originally belong to the lesser associations of which society is composed, and finally to assert, in theory at least, supreme power over all these things? If we consider the state by itself, quite apart from society, this conduct is incomprehensible; we cannot understand it as long as we think of the estate as an institution suspended in mid-air. We must think of it as an organ of society. The cause of it is the steadily progressing unification of society; the quickened consciousness that the lesser associations in society,

情形中得以适用;最后,中央权力机关发布了详细指令指导法院如何进行诉讼。这些构成一种新型国家法的基础——控制国家行为的法律,即国家行政法。从法国开始,这种法律蔓延到整个欧洲大陆。在没有国家行政机构的地方,如在古日耳曼王国、英格兰、波兰、匈牙利等地方,那里不会有有效的行政立法。偶尔,国家会让较小联合体的独立行政机关来实施制定法,尤其是社区(*Gemeinde*)、地区(*Bezirk*)、县(*Komitat*)的行政机关。在英格兰,国家也委任治安法官。[1] 但是通常这些方式都不太适合这一目的。若要有效贯彻国家意志,必须为此目的组建专门的机构。因此,当英国人制定了救济穷人的立法时,他们为此建立了一个委员会,当他们制定了保护工厂工人的立法时,他们建立了一个工厂巡视员委员会。这些机构经常作为其他地方为同样目的而效仿的典范。

那么,在这整个发展过程中,推进力是什么?是什么促使国家在越来越大的范围内接管最初属于组成人类社会之较小联合体的司法和法律创制,并且至少在理论上宣称对这些事务拥有至高的权力?如果我们完全脱离社会考察国家本身,这种行为是无法理解的。只要我们认为地产权是脱离现实的一种制度,我们就无法理解它;我们必须把地产权看做是社会的一个元件。地产权的起因是社会统一的稳步发展;另外一个缘由是如下意识的不

[1] 1327年,英格兰的一项制定法最早设置了治安法官一职。1344年,立法规定在每一郡都应以国王的委任状指定几人维持治安。起初,其职能仅为提起公诉及看管王室法院审理的被告人。但到14世纪时,他们即有权审理囚犯,随后又有制定法对治安法官的人数及其权限予以限制。

which in part include one another, in part intersect one another, in part are interlaced with one another, are merely the building-stones of a greater association, of which they become parts. The structure of every association is conditioned by the constitution of the individual associations of which it is composed. The interdependence of all social associations upon one another and the dependence of the whole upon its component parts constitute the *consensus universel* of Comte and the social consensus of Herbert Spencer, without which the concept of society is incomprehensible, and a science of society is unthinkable.

An association which is absolutely unconditioned by anything other than itself, e. g. a clan on a distant island or in the desert, could, of course, create an order for itself quite independently. What it considers marriage, is marriage; and what it considers ownership, is ownership. This applies also to the smaller associations that constitute society to the extent that they live independently of one another. But as the associations coalesce and become members of society, the situation changes accordingly. Each association in society, and society itself, becomes more and more sensitive to everything that goes on within the associations that compose the whole. And they thereby sense something that really exists, i. e. that their existence as a whole is conditioned by the state of the parts. Doubtless a society is possible in which marriage is replaced by a much looser union of the sexes; but it would be something quite different from our present-day society. Not only the marriage relation but numberless other things will also have to undergo a radical transformation if society is to regain its equilibrium on this changed basis. The production

断增长：那些彼此部分地相互包含、相互交叉、相互交错的社会较小联合体，仅仅是那些较大联合体的建构石材，从而成为后者的一个构成部分。每一个联合体的结构都取决于构成其部分的各个联合体的构造。所有社会联合体之间的相互依赖以及整体独立于其组成部分，构成了孔德[1]的普遍民意和赫伯特·斯宾塞[2]的社会民意，没有这样一种认识，社会观念是无法理解的，而且社会学也是不可想象的。

一个绝对不以自己之外的任何事物为存在条件的联合体，例如在偏远的岛上或者沙漠中的一个民族，当然可以完全独立地为自己创制一种秩序。这种联合体所认为的婚姻，就是婚姻；这种联合体所认为的所有权，就是所有权。这同样适用于组成社会的、在一定程度上相互独立存在的较小联合体。但是，当联合体结合成一个整体并成为社会成员的时候，形势也发生了相应的变化。社会中每一个联合体和社会本身也越来越对组成整体之联合体的内部运行的一切事物越来越敏感。在那里，它们感觉到一些真正存在的东西，即，整体上，它们的存在是以各个部分的状态为条件的。毫无疑问，可能存在这样一种社会，更加松散的两性结合取代了婚姻；但这一社会可能和我们今天的社会大不相同。如果社会在这一变化了的基础上重新获得平衡，那么不仅婚姻关系而且无数的其他关系也将会经历一种急剧的转变。产品的生

---

〔1〕 孔德(1798～1857)，法国哲学家，以实证主义创始人闻名。他还使社会学成为系统的科学。

〔2〕 赫伯特·斯宾塞(1820～1903)，英格兰哲学家，他试图在其系列论著合成哲学（1855～1893年)中将进化论运用于哲学及伦理学。

of goods, especially in agriculture, is based to a considerable extent, and the consumption of goods is based practically altogether, upon the marriage relation and on the family, the latter of which is also based on the marriage relation; for the greater part of mankind, as is well known, still dwells, and makes provision for its sustenance, in the home. The rearing of children, the educational system, morality—all of these things would have to be provided for according to quite new principles if the demands of the various innovators in the sphere of marriage were to be acceded to. The difficulties which would be created for society by these changes cannot be estimated today. The Cyclopean wall which has outlasted thousands of years is shaken if but one stone is moved out of its place. Society has rigid forms for matrimony and the family, as to which not even non-essentials may be changed lightly. At each and every innovation society trembles for the whole, and carefully eliminates everything that is found to be out of harmony with the existing situation.

This explains the endeavor of society to effect a unitary inner order of the associations according to its needs, and upon this endeavor the various kinds of general social norms are based. One may contend that each and every, even the smallest, social association, every family, every house, every village, every commune, every country, every nation, has its own law, its own religion, its morality, its ethical custom, its code of decorum, of tact, of fashion. Accordingly a person who has an accurate knowledge of the circumstances often is able to tell at the first glance where a certain individual belongs. Side by side with these, however, there is a law, a religion, a code of morality, of ethical custom, of tact, of decorum, of fashion, which have their origin in the larger association, and which the latter imposes upon the smaller ones that it is composed of; and in the end norms of this kind proceed from society as a whole. Accordingly each society has legal norms of general validity through which it acts upon the inner order of the associations of which it is composed. We find everywhere not only individuals who are placed under a disadvantage by society, but also associations which are being slighted, outlawed, persecuted,

产,尤其是农业品的生产,在相当大程度上是以婚姻关系和家庭为基础的,产品的消费实际上也完全基于婚姻和家庭关系之上,当然,家庭关系也是以婚姻关系为基础的。众所周知,因为大部分人都居住在家庭中并为生计作安排。如果在婚姻领域中形形色色改革者的要求被采纳,则子女抚养、教育制度、道德——所有的这些都不得不依据全新的原则来规定。今天,我们无法预估这些变革给社会带来的困难。只要一块石头被移出了它原来的位置,延续了几千年的“独眼巨人墙”都会摇晃。社会对于婚姻和家庭方面有严格的形式,在这方面,即使是非本质的因素也不可被轻易改变。在每一次革新中,社会都会为整体担忧,并且会小心地消除与现有形势不和谐的任何东西。

这解释了社会按照自己的需要、影响联合体统一的内在秩序的努力,这种努力也是各种不同类型的一般社会规范的基础。人们可能会声称每一联合体甚至是最小的联合体——每个家庭、每个家族、每个村庄、每个乡镇、每个国家、每个民族——都有自己的法律以及自己的宗教、道德、伦理习俗、礼仪、言行得体和时尚。因此,一个对各种情况有准确了解的人经常能够看第一眼,就能说出某个人来自哪里。然而,与这些准则并存的,还有另外一种法律以及宗教、道德法典、伦理习俗、言行得体、礼仪和时尚,后者产生于一个较大联合体,并且这个较大联合体把这些东西强加给组成它的较小联合体。最终,这种类型的规范总体上产生于社会。因此,每个社会都有普遍有效的法律规范,通过它们,社会对其组成部分之联合体的内在秩序产生影响。我们在各处不但发现那些被社会置于不利地位的个人,而且还发现了那些被蔑视、被剥夺法律保护、被迫害的联合体,例如婚姻关系、特定类

e. g. marital relations; certain kinds of families; peoples; religious communities; political parties, to whom society makes life a burden; contracts which are not considered binding even by society. These norms are made effective through the same kinds of social pressure that are employed by the smaller associations in enforcing their norms against the individual. These norms, however, and especially the legal norms, do not constitute the inner order of the associations, but the inner order of society, which imposes them upon the smaller associations as an external order. This order, to a much greater extent than the inner order of the associations, bears the stamp of an order of domination, of conflict. To a great extent, it is the expression of the relation of the associations that rule in society to those that are being ruled and of the struggle of the associations that constitute organized society with those that refuse to be fitted into the organization. And a whole series of social norms by no means serves the purpose of directly creating an order in the associations, but merely of carrying the order which is created by society into the associations. They are secondary norms therefore. As long as the administration of justice has not yet been taken over by the state, the administration of justice as a whole, the procedure of the courts, which as yet are purely social, is based on such purely social secondary norms. But we meet this phenomenon even today in so far as there are social courts which are independent of the state, to wit courts of honor, courts of societies, courts of clubs, courts of arbitration. Their jurisdiction and procedure are regulated solely by social norms of the second rank. The enormous importance of the state for the law is based upon the fact that society avails itself of the state as its organ in order to give effectual support to the law that arises in society. It is not impossible to conceive a state which is independent of society. This concept has long since been expressed theoretically in the doctrine of the "social kingdom." It would be a state which is composed exclusively of the sovereign, an army, and a class of civil officials—a state in which the sovereign is an absolute ruler, in which the army is blindly devoted to the latter, in which all of these are altogether out of touch with the remainder of the population, withdrawn from the influ-

型的家庭、民族、宗教团体、政党(社会使生存成为它们的一种负担)以及社会甚至认为不具有拘束力的契约。这些规范通过与较小联合体针对个人使用的社会压力同种类型的社会压力而发生效力。然而这些规范尤其是法律规范,并没有构成这些联合体的内在秩序,而是构成了作为一种外在秩序强加给较小联合体的社会内在秩序。与这些联合体内在秩序相比,此种社会内在秩序在更大程度上带有支配秩序和冲突秩序的标记。很大程度上,这种秩序是对居于社会统治地位的联合体与居于被统治地位的联合体之间关系的表达,也是对构成有组织之社会的联合体与那些拒绝适应社会的联合体之间斗争关系的表达。整个一系列的社会规范绝不是为了直接创立联合体的秩序的目的,而是仅仅将已经由社会创立的秩序贯彻到其内部的每一个联合体中。因此,它们是第二性的规范。只要司法还没有被国家接管,则总体上的司法、到目前为止仍是纯粹社会性的法院的诉讼程序以这些纯粹的社会次级规范为基础。不过,就独立于国家的社会法院——即荣誉法庭、社团法院、会所法院、仲裁法庭——而言,甚至今天我们也能碰到这种现象。它们的司法权和司法诉讼程序完全受次级社会规范调整。国家对于法律的巨大意义乃基于这样一个事实:为了给产生于社会的法律以有效的支持,社会利用了作为自己机构的国家。设想一个独立于社会的国家并非不可能。这一观念很久以前就在“社会王国”学说中得到了理论上的表达。可能会存在一个完全由主权者、军队和一个政府官员阶层组成的国家,在这样的一个国家中,最高统治者是绝对的统治者,军队盲目地效忠于统治者;在这样的一个国家中,所有的这些人都不和剩余的其他人往来、不受每一个社会倾向的影响。当然这是设想出

ence of each and every social tendency. This is conceivable, of course, only in the case of an army of mercenaries, commanded by foreign officers, and a class of officials which is self-perpetuating and the members of which will marry only within their class. The not infrequent marriage regulations for officials and for officers of the army or of the navy are evidently prompted by the desire to make the latter independent of society, at least of certain strata of society. It would be difficult to adduce historical examples of states altogether dissevered from society. An approximation perhaps is a state which consciously places itself into opposition to society even though it be only as to one point, e. g. the government of the Emperor Joseph II in Austria, Frederick the Great in Prussia, Peter the Great in Russia, Napoleon III in France, and perhaps the activity of Stein and Hardenberg in Prussia, of Struensee in Denmark. But even under the most favorable circumstances governmental systems of this kind have been unable to maintain themselves anywhere for any length of time; they collapsed, at the very latest, at the death of the ruler. If the ideas which they tried to realize were taken up again at a later time, this was brought about by the fact that meanwhile society had undergone such changes that at that time society itself demanded those things which formerly it would have been necessary to do against its will.

Apart from these exceptions, the state is, from almost every point of view, and particularly in matters of law, merely an organ of society. But even in an absolutist state, the sovereign, the army, the civil officials, are connected in so many ways with the influential classes and strata of society that they generally do only those things which the latter demand. If resistance to society or even an attempt to act in opposition to society should appear in the state at any point, society would find innumerable means to make its will effective. Social forces are elemental forces, against which the will of man cannot prevail, not for any length of time at least. The whole question of the constitution of

来的，这仅存在于外国军官指挥雇佣军队的情形以及一个等级的官员之中，他们能使自身长久存在，并且其成员只在该等级内部通婚之中。针对官员和陆军或者海军军官的、并非罕见的婚姻条例，明显是由想使他们独立于社会、至少独立于特定社会阶层的意愿促成的。举出完全与社会区分开的国家的历史实例是非常困难的。一个近似的例子可能就是一个故意使自己处于与社会对立位置的国家，即使对立处仅仅在一点上，例如奥地利皇帝约瑟二世的政府、普鲁士腓特烈二世、俄国彼得大帝、法国拿破仑三世，还有或许就是在普鲁士的施泰因和哈登堡的活动和丹麦的斯特鲁恩西的政府。但是，即使在最有利的环境下，此种政府制度也不可能在任何地方维持多久；最迟，当统治者死亡时，它们就会崩溃。如果它们设法实现的理念在后来某个时候又受到响应，那么这是由于：其间社会经历了如此的变迁，以至于当时社会自身需要那些先前曾不得不违背己意去做的事情。

除了这些例外，几乎从所有视角、尤其是从法律的角度来看，国家都仅仅是社会的一个机构。但是，即使在专制国家里，最高统治者、军队、公务员也在如此多的方面和有影响力的社会阶级和阶层相联系，以至于他们通常都在做有影响力的社会阶级和阶层要求他们去做的事情。如果国家在任何一点上出现对社会的抵制，或者甚至出现反对社会的企图，那么社会将会找到无数的方法使自己的意志生效。社会力量是基本的力量，反对社会力量的个人力量不会成功，至少不会永远成功。正如孟德斯

the state, as Montesquieu understood it in his day, and as it has been mooted again and again since then, concerns the technical task of fashioning the state so that it may carry out the will of society with as little resistance and friction as possible. In a free state, the head of the state and the judiciary are still, in theory, independent of society; in actual fact, however, they are so restricted by the constitution and the legislature, so exposed to the influences of power, that they cannot possibly resist the trends that prevail in society.

Society utilizes the state as its organ to impose its order upon the associations belonging to it. A considerable part of the law created by the state does indeed contain norms of the first rank, which are being posited by the state as an organ of society. Norms of this kind are: the constitution of the state, the purely state norms for decision, the precepts established by the state for various departments of social and economic life (e. g. education, trades, finance). But another very important part of state law is designed exclusively for the protection of social or state law by means of norms of the second rank; this is the law of crimes and the law of procedure, since these have become state law; furthermore the *Gefährdungsverbote*, police precepts. Law of crimes, law of procedure and police law, therefore, contain norms of the second rank exclusively; they do not order life directly, but are designed merely to maintain the order established by other means.

It is readily understood, therefore, that state law, in all essentials, merely follows the social development. If society wishes to get rid of, exploit, or suppress a certain association, e. g. a people,

鸠[1]在他生活的年代中所理解的，而且也正如此后反复争论的，国家宪法的整个问题涉及到塑造国家的技术方面的任务，所以国家可以在尽可能小的抵制和摩擦的情况下实现社会意志。在一个自由国家中，国家首脑和司法部门首脑仍然在理论上独立于社会。然而事实上，他们受到宪法和立法机关的限制，受到各种影响力的影响，所以他们可能无法抵制社会中流行的趋势。

社会利用国家作为自己的机构将其秩序强加给它所属的联合体。国家制定的相当多的一部分法律确实都包括一级规范，它们由作为社会机构的国家进行了设置。这类规范有：国家的宪法规范、纯粹的国家裁判规范、国家为各种社会和经济生活部门建立起来的规定（例如：教育、贸易和金融）。但是，另外非常重要的一部分国家法，其设计完全是为了通过次级规范来保护社会法或国家法；自从这些法律变成了国家法之后，它们就被称为刑法和诉讼法；此外，还有禁止危害生命、健康或者财产之行为的法令和治安条例。因此刑法、诉讼法和治安法所包含的纯粹是次级规范；它们不直接对生活发布命令，而是仅用于维护其他手段已建立起来的秩序。

因此不难理解，在一切本质上而言，国家法仅仅是在追随社会的发展。如果社会想要除去、剥削或者压迫一个特定的联合

〔1〕 孟德斯鸠：法国哲学家和法学家。他是早期法国启蒙运动的杰出人物。著有隐含攻击君主制和古代政体的有影响力的作品如《波斯人信札》（1721 年）和谴责政府的《论法的精神》（1748 年）。

a religious communion, a social rank, a class, a political party, the state with its agencies, its courts, in so far as they are dependent upon the state, and especially with its legal propositions of the second rank, the law of crimes, the law of procedure, the police law, espouses the cause of the persecutors. It dissolves societies, forbids assemblies, attacks religions, political parties, scientific doctrines, and provides a legal basis for these things through legislation. The rare exceptions, a few of which have just been mentioned, merely confirm the rule. But society will shift its position if it appears that the persons attacked cannot be overcome. It is then faced with the necessity of receiving the new cell into the old structure as well as possible. This involves an adaptation to society on the part of the association which hitherto has been the subject of attack by society; and at the same time, an adaptation on the part of society to the association. Society must recover its equilibrium. The greater part of the process therefore takes place within society itself. Another part of the task must be performed by juristic science. New legal propositions must be created for the new relation. Roman juristic science has often enough performed this duty in a splendid manner. The juristic science of the Continental common law as well as juristic science in England and France have likewise rendered outstanding services in this sphere. Lastly, the constitution of the state, the method of administrative procedure, and the state law in its entirety must be adapted to the new order. But if the distribution of power in society is changed to such an extent that they who hitherto have been the oppressed party obtain control of the state —a thing that does not happen, of course, where there is a mere military, or palace, revolution in which case the social structure remains untouched, but only where there is a social revolution—the law of the state and the agencies of the state espouse the cause of the victors; and often enough the persecutors have become the persecuted.

In reality, therefore, the historical fact that state law is manifestly gaining ground is merely the expression of the intensified solidarity of society. As the conviction grows stronger that everything that is in society concerns society, the idea appears that it would be a great advantage if the state should prescribe a unitary legal basis for each and every inde-

体,例如一个民族、宗教团体、社会阶层、阶级、政党,则拥有附属机构与法院,特别是拥有其次级法律命题——刑法、诉讼法、治安法——的国家会支持迫害者的事业。国家会解散社团,禁止集会,攻击宗教、政党及科学学说,并且会通过立法为这些事情提供一个法律根据。罕见例外——刚刚提到了一些——是仅仅确认规则。但是如果看上去被攻击者无法被战胜时,社会将会改变立场。于是,社会就有必要在旧结构中尽可能好地接纳新细胞。这必然涉及到迄今为止一直是社会攻击对象的联合体对社会的适应;与此同时,这也涉及到社会对联合体的适应。社会必须重新恢复它的平衡。因此,更大一部分进程发生在了社会自身内部。该任务的另外一部分必须由法学来完成,必须为新的关系创设新的法律命题。罗马法学经常以一种令人满意的方式充分完成此项任务。欧陆共同法学、英格兰法学和法国法学在这一领域同样有出色的表现。最后,国家的宪法、行政诉讼的方法和在整体意义上的国家法必须适应这一新秩序。但是如果社会的权力分配发生了那样一种程度的变化以至于迄今被压迫的一方获得了对国家的控制权——当然这种情形不会发生在那些仅仅是军队革命或者宫廷政变的背景中,那种背景下社会的结构并未被触及,这种情形只会发生在一种社会革命的背景下,则国家的法律、国家的机构将会支持胜利者的事业,并且足够多的情形是,压迫者变成了被压迫者。

因此,实际上,国家法明显获得支持的历史事实仅仅是增强后的社会团结的一种表述。随着社会中的所有事物都关系到社会这种确信不断加强,出现了如下理念:如果国家为社会中每一个独立的联合体规定一个统一的法律基础,那么它将具有巨大的

pendent association in society. I may be permitted to elucidate this idea by means of a few illustrations.

Let us consider the legal situation of the Roman household. Where, as here, about thirty or forty adult free persons were living together, subjected to the power of a superior, there could, selfevidently, be neither complete anarchy nor purely arbitrary rule by the head of the household. The Romans possessed too much administrative efficiency to permit either one or the other. Indeed what we do know about the Roman household shows that a firm legal order obtained therein. There were family laws which could be asserted even against the *pater familias*. We know, at any rate, that the marital rights of a married son of the house and of a married daughter of the house were always respected by the parents and that the *manus* belonged to the son of the house, not to the *pater familias*. The persons who were subjected to the *potestas* had their own property, which had been bestowed upon them by the holder of the *potestas* or which they had acquired by their own efforts, e. g. land, cattle, business undertakings; obligatory rights existed among them; and we are told of a family court. From the point of view of Roman society, these relations, in the beginning at any rate, were not legal relations; for society, on principle, did not concern itself about what went on within the household. Roman society knew only one kind of law—the law which regulated the relation of household to household, and which was administered by the magistrate and by the court.

优势。请允许我借助一些例子来阐明这一理念。

让我们考察一下罗马家庭的法律情形。那里和这里一样，大约三十或者四十个自由人生活在一起，服从于长者的权力，不言而喻，那里既不可能是完全的混乱状态也不可能是家庭首脑纯粹的恣意统治。罗马人拥有的管理效率不允许上述任一情形存在。的确，我们所知道的关于罗马家庭的情况也证明，那里有一种稳定的法律秩序运行着。那里存在据称甚至是反对家父[1]的家庭法。我们至少知道，已婚的儿子[2]或者已婚的女儿总是受到父母的尊重，至少夫权是属于男性家子而不属于家父的。那些服从支配权[3]的人有他们自己的财产，这些财产可能是支配权的享有人授予他们的，或者是服从支配权者通过自己的努力获得的，例如：土地、牲畜、商业企业；他们中间也存在债权；而且我们也听说存在一个家事法院。从罗马社会的角度来看，这些关系至少在最初时都不是法律关系。社会原则上并不关心家庭里发生了什么事情。罗马社会仅仅知道一种法律——那就是调整家庭和家庭之间关系的、由地方执法官和法院执行的法律。随着时间的推移，

---

〔1〕（拉）*pater familias*（家父），指罗马法家庭的家长。在这里“家父”不是亲属关系的术语，而是指家庭的主权者，他可以是丈夫、父亲、祖父或者曾祖父，总之，必须是在家庭中不从属他们的父权的自权人。在罗马法中，家父对于家子拥有生杀权、弃子权、出卖权、移交罪犯权。

〔2〕（拉）*Filius familias*（家子），在罗马的家庭中处于父权支配下的子女。家子属于他权人，他们因为家父死亡或者脱离父权而成为自权人。家子的地位可由于婚姻法中的生育、收养、归顺父权等原因而取得。

〔3〕（拉）*potestas*（支配权），一般是指某一个主体根据法律或者习俗对其他主体行使的权力。例如：家父对家子行使的父权。在公法领域它也指执法官享有的治权。

In the course of time this situation underwent a change; for the son of the house became a business man and the goods in the house that belonged to him, his *peculium*, became the foundation of his credit. In this way, the son of the house began to assume a position in the world that lay outside of the household, and his legal position within the household became a matter of importance for trade and commerce. To this extent the inner order of the household became a part of the social law: the praetor publishes regulations concerning it in his edict, and the jurists discuss it in their writings. Finally the legislation of Imperial times directly intervenes in the relation between the bearer of the *potestas* and those *in potestate*, protects the son of the house against abuse of the parental power; grants to him the right to own property, which the *pater familias* cannot take away from him. The Roman law of slavery developed in a manner somewhat different but very similar in principle.

In the mediaeval system of landholding, a similar process goes on, albeit on a much grander scale. The unfree tenants by custom of the Middle Ages surely had definite rules regulating their relations to each other and to the lord. These rules were recorded at an early day and in this way the Continental *Hof und Dienstrechte*, the byrlowes, by-laws, customs of the English manor arose. These regulations doubtless were law and they are treated as such by modern legal history. But they were law only within the association; for at the outset, seigniory in mediaeval times, like the

这种情形经历了一个变化；因为家子变成了一个商人，并且家庭中的货物是属于他的，他的特有产[1]变成了其信用的基础。这样，家子就在家庭外面的世界中取得了一个位置，并且因为贸易和商业，家子在家庭中的法律地位也变得重要了。在此范围内，家庭内在秩序变成了社会法的一部分，裁判官在其告示中发布了有关该问题的规定，法学家在他们的著作中也讨论了该问题。最后，帝国时代的立法直接干预支配权人和受支配人之间的关系，保护家子免受父母权力滥用的侵害；授予家子对其自身财产的权利，且家父不能剥夺它。罗马人之奴隶制法的发展方式与此稍微有些差别，但大体上非常相似。

在中世纪的土地所有制中，也存在一个相似的发展进程，虽然它的范围更广。中世纪土地非自由保有人按照习惯确实有一些调整他们之间相互关系以及与封建领主之间关系的明确规则。这些规则在早期就被记录下来，而且通过这种方式，欧洲大陆的庄园习惯和役务习惯、地方法、市政条例、英格兰庄园习惯产生了。这些规则无疑是法律，并且现代的法律史也如此看待它们。但他们仅仅是联合体内部的法律；因为在最初时候，中世纪的领

---

〔1〕（拉）*peculium*（特有产），主人允许奴隶或者家父允许家子保留的小笔财产，该财产的所有权在名义上归主人或者家父所有，但奴隶或者家子对其享有处分和经管权，他们可以使用特有产独立地对外进行交易，而主人或者家父只在此特有产的范围内为有关交易承担民事责任。特有产是可撤销的，在解放奴隶的情况下，它将被推定为是向奴隶的赠与。家子对于某些特有产享有不断扩大的权利，可以对之实行赠与、转让或者死因处置。

Roman house, constituted a world of its own, whose inner order was of no concern to the outside world; and as late as the seventeenth century, Coke, the English jurist, refers to the relation between the lord and the copyholder as "a little commonwealth," although in Coke's day only vestiges of this situation had remained. In the later Middle Ages, seigniory gradually merges into society generally, and, in consequence, that which originally has been law solely within the inner association of the manor, henceforth becomes a law recognized outside of the manor, and is recognized as such by mediaeval society as a whole. In this way, that which had belonged to the copyholder solely by the custom of the manor became property that was protected by the common law both in Germany and in England. A very famous passage by Littleton, who about the middle of the fifteenth century wrote a work on landholding (Upon Tenures) indicates the transition by the fact that his first sentence on tenants by custom flatly contradicts what he says in the second. The passage reads as follows: "It is said that if the lord do oust them, they have no other remedy but to sue to their lords by petition, for if they should have any other remedy they should

主权像罗马的家庭一样，构建了一个内在秩序与外部世界毫不相关的自己的世界；迟至17世纪，英国法学家柯克[1]指出，领主与依据公簿纪录保有土地者[2]之间的关系像一个"小的共和国"，尽管在他生活的年代这种情形仅仅剩下一些残留的痕迹。在中世纪后期，领主权逐渐广泛融入到社会中。结果，起初完全是庄园内部联合体的法律自此以后成为在庄园外也获得承认的法律，并且，它也同样被中世纪整个社会所承认。这样，仅仅依据庄园的习惯，属于公簿纪录土地保有人的财产受到了德国共同法和英格兰普通法的保护。利特尔顿大约在15世纪时，写下了一本关于土地保有制度的著作(《论保有》)，他在一个非常有名的章节中以如下事实指出了这种转变：他论及习惯上的土地保有人的第一个句子与他在第二个句子所说的产生了截然冲突。这一段文字如下："据说，如果他们的领主确实驱逐了他们，他们除了通过请愿书向他们的领主请愿外，没有任何其他救济方式。因为如果他们有其他救济方式的话，那么不应

---

〔1〕 柯克·爱德华(Coke Edward)(1552～1634)，英格兰法学家、高等民事法庭的首席法官(1606～1616年)，他认为即使在国王不同意的情况下仍裁定习惯法是最高法。

〔2〕 Copyhold，英格兰的土地保有形式之一，于1925年被取消。公簿保有源于庄园制。庄园本是分配给领主占有并作为一个经济组织的一片土地，当封建制土地保有方式于诺曼征服后被引进到英格兰时，原来持有庄园的领主被接纳为国王的直属封臣，原来从他那里以自由身份保有土地的人变成了他的自由封臣，而那些虽占有土地身份却不自由的人被称之为农奴，亦译做"维兰"(villain)。农奴以向领主提供农役为条件保有土地，但这种农役是不确定的，他服从领主的意志，这是他与自由保有的地产的最大区别。大约在15世纪，劳务地租转变为实物地租，农奴保有转变为公簿保有。公簿保有是根据庄园习惯法依领主的意志保有的一片庄园内领主自留地。

not be said to be tenants at the will of the lord, according to the custom of the manor. Tenant by the custom is as well inheritor to have his land according to the custom as he which hath a freehold at the common law. " The second sentence, moreover, is said to be not by Littleton, but to be a later interpolation. The further development is this: ultimately the relations governed by the custom of the manor are completely merged into the law of society, the association of the manor disintegrates, and the several tenants by the custom enter into a direct relation to society.

A third example is the development of the state itself. Every great territorial state, at the beginning, consists of commonwealths which have created their own order. Up to the time of the social war, Roman Italy was merely an international law alliance of Italic city states with the city state of Rome; the modern centralized states of Europe, at first, were associations of cities and provinces, which in turn were composed of communes; and each of these city states, each province, each commune, had its traditional or its posited order which, with the exception of possible *privilegia* and city charters, had arisen and developed quite independently of the state. In Roman Italy, the change was first brought about by the creation of the *municipia*. From that time on, the order of the city was based on a Roman statute. And since the rise of the modern centralized state, the provinces are being put on a legal basis by the state, or are being completely fused with the latter, as e. g. in France and Italy; and the law of the communes is being regulated by state ordinances for the government of cities and communes. It has often been said that this did not, as a matter of fact, necessarily bring about a thoroughgoing

当称他们为依据庄园习惯受到领主意志支配的土地保有人。习惯上的土地保有人也是依习惯拥有土地的继承人,因为他拥有普通法上的自由保有权。”而且,据说第二个句子不是利特尔顿写下的,而是后来增补上去的。进一步的发展是:最终,受到庄园习惯法支配的关系完全融入到社会法之中,庄园联合体解体了,若干习惯上的土地保有人直接和社会建立了关系。

第三个例子是国家自身的发展。每一个幅员辽阔的国家在开始时都是由自己创制自身秩序的共和国组成。直到社会战争开始的时候,罗马人的意大利在国际法上还仅仅是一个意大利城邦和罗马城邦之间的联盟。欧洲现代的中央集权国家最初是一些城市和行省的联合体,这些城市和行省反过来是由社区组成的。而且每一个这样的城邦、每一个行省、每一个社区都有自己传统的或设定好的秩序,除了可能的私法[1]和城市宪章外,这些秩序的产生和发展都完全独立于国家。在罗马帝国时的意大利,这种变化首先是因为自治城市[2]的创设所导致的。从那时起,城市的秩序都以罗马制定法为基础。而且自从现代中央集权国家产生以后,行省建立在国家确立的法律基础之上,或者完全和国家融合在一起,比如在法国和意大利;社区法律受到国家为管理城市和社区而制定的国家法令的调整。经常有人说,事实上这并不必然导致法律的彻底变革,

---

〔1〕（拉）*privilegia*（罗马法中的私法）。

〔2〕（拉）*municipia*（自治城市）,指独立享有某些民事权利的城市或居民共同体。不同于享有主权的国家,它在私法领域拥有一定的权利能力,可以在与居民的个人关系中成为原告或者被告,可以成为遗赠或遗产信托的受益人,甚至在后来还拥有接受遗产的权利。

change of law, for the Roman municipal constitution did not differ much from the constitution which had obtained until then in the Italic city states, and the modern ordinances for the government of provinces and communes, too, have often been following tradition. But it did bring about an enormous revolution in principle inasmuch as the original order of all these commonwealths, which had been independent of the state, was replaced by an order derived from the state. Every province, every city, every commune was thereby converted from an independent living organism into a mere administrative unit of the state. The federal states of the German Empire however, down to the present day, have constitutions which have not been derived from that of the German Empire.

Now these facts are the standard according to which the prevailing concept of the nature of law is to be judged. This concept is, in the main, that a norm is a legal norm only if it has been posited by the state as a legal norm. This view has, I think, been refuted by our present discussion, for we have seen that only a small part of the law, i. e. state law, is, in actual fact, created by the state. As a rule, however, when writers attribute the creation of all law to the state, they mean only that a norm, whatsoever may have been its origin, becomes a legal norm only when the state recognizes it as a legal norm, and surrounds it with norms of the second rank, penal provisions, procedure, administrative regulations. If this is really a constituent element of the concept "legal norm," the formations which we have discussed hitherto, i. e. the order of the Roman household, of the mediaeval manor, of the primitive community (unless one looks upon the latter as states) are not parts of the law. One might indeed contend that the Roman son of the house (*filius familias*), except in those cases in which he could, at a later time, assert his claims in court, had no *Recht* (law and right). It is well known that that was not the view of the Romans, for the sources clearly show that the *manus* is in the *filius familias* and not in the bearer of the *potestas*, that the *peculium* was the property of the *filius familias* (eventually

因为罗马的市政宪法与直到那时意大利城邦先前一直广泛适用的宪法并没有多大差别,现代为行省和社区颁布的条例也经常遵循传统。然而,这的确带来了原则上的巨大变革,因为所有这些独立于国家的秩序的共和国的最初秩序被起源于国家的秩序代替了。每一个省、每一个城市、每一个社区从而也从一个独立的、有生命的有机体转变为国家的一个纯粹行政单位。然而,德意志帝国的各联邦共和国直到今天还拥有并非起源于德意志帝国的宪法。[1]

如今这些事实成了据以判断法律性质之主流观念的标准。这种观念大体上是:一种规范只要被国家安排归类为法律规范,那它就是法律规范。我认为,这种观念已经被我们现在的讨论驳倒,因为我们已经看到,只有很少一部分的法律即国家法,实际上是由国家创制的。然而,当著作家把所有法律的创制都归因于国家时,通常他们仅仅意指,一个规范无论其起源为何,只有当国家认可它是一个法律规范时,它才成为一个法律规范,而且次级规范、刑事规定、诉讼程序规则和行政规章围绕着它。如果这真的是"法律规范"概念的构成要素,则迄今为止我们所讨论的形态,即罗马家庭秩序、中世纪庄园秩序、原始公社秩序(除非把原始公社看做国家)都不是法律的一部分。人们确实可以主张,除了后来家子(*filius familias*)可在法庭主张其请求权的那些情形外,罗马的家子没有任何 *Recht*(权利)。众所周知,那不是罗马人的见解。因为原始文献清楚地表明夫权由家子享有,而非属于拥有支配权的人,特有产是家子的财产

〔1〕 这已不再正确。1919 年,魏玛宪法的颁布改变了这种状况。

of the slaves), that *obligationes naturales* could subsist between the bearer of the *potestas* and the person subject to the *potestas*, even though all of these relations were not protected by the courts—the possible protection given by the censor, which was not a legal protection, cannot of course, be considered here—and though legal remedies against third persons were given only to the *pater familias*. As well deny the validity of the German *Hofrechte*, the English manorial customs, for the tenant could not appeal to them in any court of the state. But the most accurate students of the law of the Middle Ages have expressed a different opinion, to wit: "hen as to the case between lord and tenant, the tenant cannot sue the lord in the lord's court; the tenant in villeinage ejected by the lord has no remedy anywhere. But is this, we may ask, a denial of legal right? The king disseises the Earl of Gloucester; the earl has no remedy anywhere; yet we do not deny that the honor of Gloucester is the earl's by law or that in disseising him the king will break the law." (Maitland.) And another, whose knowledge certainly is not inferior to that of Maitland,

（最终也是奴隶的财产），自然之债[1]可存在于享有支配权的人与服从支配权的人之间，即使所有的这些关系都不受法院的保护——检察官[2]所可能提供的保护并不是一种法律保护，当然此处不能考虑它——尽管防御第三人的法律救济仅仅给予了家父。同样，那种观念势必也要否认德国的领主法和英格兰庄园习惯的合法性，因为土地保有人不能向任何国家法院起诉。但是，对中世纪法律有最精确研究的学者表达了不同的意见，即："至于领主和土地保有人之间的情形，土地保有人不能在领主的法院起诉领主；隶奴制下的土地保有人若被领主驱逐，则他在任何地方都没有救济途径。但是我们可以设问，这是对法律权利的否定吗？国王侵占了格洛斯特伯爵的土地，伯爵在任何地方都没有救济方式；但是我们不能否认，依据法律，格洛斯特的领主特权是属于伯爵的，或者说我们不能否认，国王强占他的不动产会违反法律。"（梅特兰语）另外一个知识无疑并不比梅特兰少的人说：

---

〔1〕（拉）*obligationes naturales*（自然之债），因缺乏法律规定的条件而不产生诉权的债的关系。虽然这种债务不能得到法律的承认和保护，但是在债务人自动清偿的情况下，债权人有权保留被给付物并且拒绝返还或者对抗错债索回之诉。罗马法中的自然之债有：由奴隶缔结的债，由家子缔结的债，受监护人在未获得监护人许可的情况下缔结的债等。

〔2〕（拉）*censor*（罗马的检察官），罗马的执法官之一，产生于公元前443年；最初为两人，从已卸任的执政官中选举产生，任职期限为18月。检察官最初的职责与人口登记有关，负责审核和增补市民登记并且按照等级和部落加以划分，因而他们的设立往往是不定期的，只是在要搞人口登记时才感到必要。检察官可以将不够条件的市民排除在骑士百人团甚至百人团之外，这使得此官职获得尊严和威信；后来他甚至可以监察记过，对市民的名誉进行评判。

says: "The concept that that which the lord is under obligation to give to the man is owed to the latter in the legal sense is immanent in all Germanic law of associations. Enforcible duties however arose from this situation only in case a higher power in the association was authorized to intervene for the protection of the rights of the members of the association. Nevertheless in all cases the conduct of the bearer of the power who refuses to grant to the person subjected to the power that which the latter is entitled to or demands something that he is not authorized to demand is considered a violation of law (Unrecht). (Gierke).

The view that law is created by the state therefore will not bear the test of historical analysis. And we may therefore say that it has been refuted; for if it be essential to the concept of law that it be created by the state, how could it have been in existence without the state throughout long epochs of history? The only remaining question is whether the concept which we associate with the term law is of such a nature that the view that the law is created by the state can be justified. It seems necessary therefore to form a clear idea of its significance in every detail.

In all spheres of life we find relations which in every respect are like those which the state recognizes, regulates, protects, and to which the state is by no means opposed, but for whose protection it has provided no legal remedy. Among these are numerous economic, social, and religious associations, political bodies, and many a contract. In addition there are similar phenomena in the law of things and in the law of inheritance. In a limited measure, this is true, in the German civil law, of an association that does not possess legal capacity. The so-called "freedom of coalition" of the working classes in the second half of the nineteenth century was based on the same idea. The state by no means disapproves, nay, perhaps it actually approves, of the idea that men as a matter of

"领主有义务给予该封臣的那些东西,在法律意义上属于后者——这种观念在日耳曼所有的联合体法律中是固有的内容。不过,可强制执行的义务仅产生于这种情形:为了保护联合体成员的权利,必须授权联合体内一个更高的权力对此进行干涉。然而在所有的情况下,某权力的拥有者下述这种行为都被视为违法:他拒绝给予该权力的服从者那些后者有权享有的东西,或者要求一些他无权要求的东西。"(基尔克)

因此,法律由国家创制的观念经受不住历史分析的检验。因而我们可以说这一观念已被驳倒。因为如果法律由国家创制——这是法律概念的本质因素,那么在历史上没有国家的漫长年代里,法律又如何能够存在?剩下的唯一问题是:与法律这一术语相连的观念是否具有那样一种性质,以至于法律由国家创制这种见解显得理由极其充分。因此,似乎有必要在每一个细节上形成该观念之意义的清晰的观点。

在生活的所有领域,我们发现了这样一些关系,它们在每个方面都与国家认可、调整、保护的那些关系相似,对于它们,国家绝对不会反对,不过对于它们的保护,国家也没有为它们提供任何法律上的救济。在这些当中有无数的经济、社会和宗教联合体,政治团体和许许多多的契约。此外,在物权法和继承法方面也有许多类似的现象。在有限的程度上,这也适用于德国民法上不具有权利能力的联合体。19 世纪后半叶所谓的工人阶级"自由联盟"[1] 就是基于这样的观念产生的。国家绝对不会不赞成——而且或许实际上会赞同——依照特定的秩序进行司法和

---

[1] 也就是,工人组成工会、同意罢工和宣布罢工的权利。

justice and law proceed according to a certain order, but its will is that they should do this voluntarily or solely under social pressure. Very often it is merely a matter of the technical difficulty of finding an adequate juristic rule and an adequate form for the legal protection; the relation is not "juristically" construable. This is frequently true in the case of rights, particularly of special rights of the members of juristic persons, of the rights of the beneficiaries of a given foundation or institution. The German jurists, for example, were unable to fit the duty to supply beets, which is incumbent upon the shareholders in a beetsugar factory, into their legal system; and the Austrian jurists are unable, even today, to fit the South Slavic Sadruga into their legal system. Similar technical difficulties are standing in the way of recognition of the *Tarifvertrag*. Moreover it happens occasionally that people intentionally decline the legal protection of institutions which they have created although they might enjoy it. This was done for a long time in the case of the English trade unions, and is being done in the case of the Roman Catholic church in France today. Writers who have expert knowledge of the situation in France say that this attitude strengthens the church considerably, e. g. Bureau, in his book *La séparation de l' Eglise et de l' État*. In the case of cartels and trusts it seems that both sides object to legal protection by the state. And contracts are occasionally entered into, and testamentary provisions made, in such a way that, according to the declared will of the person making the disposition, no legally enforceable claim can arise therefrom.

法律诉讼,但是,国家的意愿是:它们应当自愿这样做或者完全在社会的压力下这么做。寻找一个适当的法律规则和适当的法律保护形式,大多数时候仅仅是一个技术难题;这种关系并不是“法学上”可以解释的。此点在下列情形往往是对的:存在许多权利、特别是在法人成员的特殊权利的情况下;存在特定基金或者机构受益人的权利的情况下。例如,德国法学家不能够使提供甜菜的义务——那是甜菜工厂里股东的义务——适于他们的法律制度;甚至今天奥地利的法学家不能使南部斯拉夫的家长制家庭公社[1]适于他们的法律制度。同样地,技术困难也突出表现在集体劳动合同[2]的认可方面。而且,虽然人们可能珍爱他们创立的法律制度,但人们故意拒绝他们所创设的制度所提供之法律保护的事情也时有发生。就英格兰工会来说,这已经发生了很长的时间;而且,就今天法国罗马天主教会而言,这正在发生。对此种局面有内行知识的法国作者说,这种态度在相当大的程度上强化了教会组织,例如卜闳,在他的《教会与国家的分离》一书中。就卡特尔和托拉斯而言,似乎双方当事人都拒绝国家提供的法律保护。有时候契约订立和遗嘱条款的签署也采取这样一种方式,依照当事人表示意思作出处分,其中不会产生任何可强制

〔1〕 也被称做 *Zadruga*,音译为扎德鲁加,指古代南部斯拉夫人、克尔特人的家长制家庭公社,这种公社包括几个或十几个在血缘、经济、土地上有联系的家庭。

〔2〕 *Tarifvertrag*,即集体劳动合同,一个雇主或者许多雇主和一群有组织或者没有组织的工人之间确定在什么条件下进行劳动的契约,例如确定劳动报酬、工作时间、休息休假、劳动安全卫生条件等。

Still more important is the fact that the greater part of legal life goes on in a sphere far removed from the state, the state tribunals, and state law. What is the important consideration here? It is clear, to begin with, that the confused mass of statutes cannot possibly cover the variegated diversity of legal life. New communities, new relations of possession, new contracts, new regulations as to inheritance, all as yet unknown to the statutes, are continually coming into existence even today, just as they did in the hoary past. Must these relations wait until they receive mention in a statute before they can become legal relations, in spite of the fact that the basic institutions of our society furnished the order for the affairs of mankind for thousands of years without this aid? And what of the enforceability of these claims by courts or by other tribunals? In the long run it is only a very few of the incalculable number of the relations of human life that attract the attention of the courts and of other tribunals. There are millions of human beings who enter into untold legal relations, and who are fortunate enough never to find it necessary to appeal for aid to a tribunal of any sort. Since the relation which has never come into contact with legislation and judicial adjudication, after all, is the normal relation, it follows that in the very cases that constitute the rule, everything would be lacking that is necessary to determine whether we are dealing with a legal relation or not. Moreover the line of demarcation between that which the courts and the other tribunals are able to do and that which they think they must leave undone is continually shifting; and this shifting is brought about not only by legislation, but also by actual usage. Should every change of this nature, should every variation, imperceptible though it be, react upon all the relations which have never been and never should be brought to the attention of the courts?

After all, even today there are two legal systems which are absolutely independent of the state, or, to be more accurate, independent of state legislation, state adjudication, and state administration. These are ecclesiastical law and international law. A person to whom law always means state law could not regard

执行的请求权。

尽管如此,更为重要的是:更大一块的法律生活,在远离国家、国家裁决机构和国家法的领域内运行。在这里,重要的考量是什么?首先,非常清楚,混成一团的制定法不可能囊括法律生活的斑驳多样性。所有的这些制定法迄今并不熟悉的新的共同体、新占有关系、新契约和新继承规则甚至在今天也不断涌现,正如在遥远的过去发生的情形一样。难道这些关系必须等到国家制定法接受并提及它们时才能变为法律关系——尽管我们社会的基本制度几千年来在没有此种帮助下,已经为这些人类事务提供了秩序?这些请求权由法院或其他裁决机构的可强制执行性又是如何?最后,无法计算的人类关系中,只有一小部分吸引了法院和其他裁决机构的注意。数以百万计的人们建立不知名的法律关系,而且他们非常幸运,从来没有发现有必要向任何类型的裁决机构求助。既然这些从未与立法和司法裁判产生联系的关系是正常的关系,那么由此可以得出结论:在制定法律规则的那些情形下,确定我们是否正在涉及某种法律关系的一切必要东西都将缺乏。而且,在法院和其他裁决机构认为他们能够去做的事情和他们认为他们不得做的事情之间的划分界线也在不断地移动;这种移动不仅是因为立法的缘故,而且也会因现实惯例而产生。尽管这种变化无法觉察,但是,难道每一次这种性质的改变、每一次更新,都应当对法院从未也从不应注意的所有关系产生影响吗?

毕竟,甚至在今天也存在着两种完全独立于国家的法律制度,或者更准确地说独立于国家立法、国家裁决和国家行政的法律制度。它们是教会法和国际法。一个在观念中认为法律就是

ecclesiastical law as law unless it is state ecclesiastical law. But this is in conflict with the general view which, as we know, is the strongest support of the prevailing doctrine. Ecclesiastical law is law, irrespective of what the attitude of the state may be, for the reason that it is the legal order of the church. And ecclesiastical law has lost nothing of its legal quality through a complete separation of the church from the state, such as obtains in France. Likewise the opposition to the recognition of the legal nature of international law has been silenced altogether. It was based, from the very beginning, not upon a scientific investigation of the nature of law in general and of international law in particular but exclusively upon the fact that the latter did not fit into a ready-made pattern.

If the ideal of the most advanced state socialist should be realized; if all goods were produced by the state in state-owned workshops through its employes, and furthermore if these goods were distributed by the state through its employes among those entitled to consume them, then indeed we should have a system of law which is state law in the fullest sense of the term, not merely a few legal propositions which have been created by the state. In that case, state legal institutions will have taken the place of ownership and contract as well as of private production and private exchange of goods. A picture of a commonwealth whose law is exclusively state law is presented by Bellamy, the American writer, in his utopian *Looking Backward*. Whether we should be happier in such a state, we shall not discuss here. At any rate the present discussion has shown that as yet we are far from a state of that description.

The view, therefore, that all law is state law is scientifically untenable. It is based, in part, upon the fact that, by means of certain utterly impermissible artifices, its proponents refer every legal norm, whatsoever may be its nature, and from whatsoever

国家法的人，可能不会承认教会法是法律，除非教会法是国家教会法。但是这与——如我们所知、是通说最强的支持者的——一般观点冲突。因为教会法是教会的法律秩序，因而不管国家的态度如何，教会法都是法律。教会与国家的完全分离，丝毫不会让教会法丧失其法律的属性。譬如发生在法国的情形。同样地，反对承认国际法的法律性质的观点也已经完全沉寂了。从一开始，那种反对观点就不是基于对法律性质总体上的、特别是国际法性质的科学研究，而是完全基于国际法并不符合既定模式这一事实。

倘若最发达国家中的社会主义者的理想实现，倘若所有产品都由国家通过其雇员在国有工厂中生产，而且这些产品也由国家通过其雇员在有权消费它们的人中间分配，那么，我们的确会有一种法律制度，它是国家法这个术语最完整意义上的表达，而不仅仅有一些由国家创设的法律命题。假使那样的话，国家的法律制度将会取代所有权和契约，也会取代私人生产和私人间的货物交易。美国作家贝拉米[1]在他的乌托邦式小说《回顾》中呈现了一幅法律完全是国家法的共和国图景。我们在这里不讨论在这样的一个国家中我们是否幸福。无论如何，现在的讨论证明我们还离描述的那样一种状态很遥远。

因此，所有法律都是国家法的观点在科学上是站不住脚的。这种观点部分地基于这一事实：借助某些完全不被允许的技巧方式，这一观点的倡导者将每一个法律规范——无论其性质是什

〔1〕 贝拉米·爱德华(1850～1898)，美国作家和幻想社会主义者，通过其流行小说《回顾》(1888年)宣传其政治观点。

source it may be derived, and by whatsoever means it may preserve its existence, to the state, and upon the fact that, in part, they forcibly close their eyes to the great mass of law that has come into being independently of the state and exists independently of the state. But the highly one-sided concept of law which has come into existence thereby has exerted a fateful influence upon true scientific study as well as upon practical juristic science and upon the teaching of law, not only inasmuch as it is false in itself, but inasmuch as it has deprived the investigator of the law of a field of investigation which is highly stimulating and extremely fruitful. By confining the attention of the investigator to the state, to tribunals, to statutes, and to procedure, this concept of law has condemned the science of law to the poverty under which it has been suffering most terribly down to the present day. Its further development presupposes liberation from these shackles and a study of the legal norm not only in its connection with the state but also in its social connection.

Wherever the legal norm attracted the attention of the sociologist, irrespective of whether it was a matter of tracing its origin, of determining the concept, of examining its social function, it has always been found in the company of other social norms. Nevertheless there can be no doubt that there is an unmistakable difference between it and the non-legal norms. It is as impossible to deny the existence of this difference as it is difficult, in view of the present state of the science of law, to indicate precisely wherein it consists; and the object of the discussion that follows is rather to define the problem than to offer a solution. This problem is not peculiar to the law; for indeed one is also under the necessity of instituting inquiry as to how ethics differs from religion and ethical custom, how the latter differs from decorum and tact, how decorum and tact differ from honor or etiquette, how etiquette differs from fashion. On the other hand the lines of demarcation between the various kinds of norms are undoubtedly somewhat arbitrary. Here as everywhere else the concepts do not lie in the nature of things, and every sharp line of distinction is imported into things by man. Within the various species of

么,无论其源自何处,无论其采取什么手段维持其存在——归因于国家;它同时还部分地基于这一事实:这种观点的倡导者硬是对独立于国家而产生和存在的大量法律视而不见。但是已经藉此形成的、极为片面的法律观念,对真正的科学研究、实用法学和法律教学产生了致命的影响,不仅仅因为这一观念自身是错误的,也因为它排除了这一领域法律研究者一个极具刺激性和极富有成果的研究。由于把研究者的注意力限制在国家、裁决机构、制定法及诉讼程序方面,这一法律观念宣告了法学的贫乏,在这一观念下,直到今天它仍蒙受着巨大损失。法学的进一步发展的前提条件是法学必须从这些桎梏中解放出来,并且,不仅要研究与国家有关的法律规范,也要研究与社会相关的法律规范。

法律规范吸引社会学者注意的任何地方,不管它是否关涉到追溯法律起源、确定法律概念、审查法律的社会功能,该法律规范总是和其他社会规范相伴出现。然而毫无疑问,在法律规范和其他非法律规范之间存在着明显的区别。否认这种区分的存在是不可能的,同时鉴于现今法学的状况,精确指明该区分究竟何在,也是同样的困难。随后的讨论目标就是界定这一问题,而不是提供一个解答。这个问题并非是一个专门属于法律的问题;因为人们也有必要探究:伦理如何不同于宗教和伦理习俗,宗教和伦理习俗如何不同于礼仪和言行得体行为,礼仪和言行得体行为如何不同于荣誉或礼节,礼节如何不同于时尚等。另一方面,各种不同类型规范之间的界限划分,无疑也是稍微有些任意的。在这里也和其余的任何地方一样,概念并不存在于事物的本质之中,每一个明显的区分界限都是由人类强加给事物的。在各种不同种类的规范中,存在着构成事物从一组类型向另一组类型过渡的

norms there are sub-species which constitute the transition from one group to the other, and in the case of many a phenomenon it is scarcely possible to determine accurately to which group it belongs.

Difficult though it may be to draw the line with scientific exactitude between the legal norm and other kinds of norms, practically this difficulty exists but rarely. In general anyone will be in position to tell without hesitation whether a given norm is a legal norm or whether it belongs to the sphere of religion, ethical custom, morality, decorum, tact, fashion, or etiquette. This fact must be made the basis of the discussion. The question as to the difference between the legal and the non-legal norm is a question not of social Science but of social psychology. The various classes of norms release various overtones of feeling, and we react to the transgression of different norms with different feelings. Compare the feeling of revolt that follows a violation of law with the indignation at a violation of a law of morality, with the feeling of disgust occasioned by an indecency, with the disapproval of tactlessness, the ridiculousness of an offense against etiquette, and lastly with the critical feeling of superiority with which a votary of fashion looks down upon those who have not attained the heights which he has scaled. Peculiar to the legal norm is the reaction for which the jurists of the Continental common law have coined the term *opinio necessitatis*. This is the characteristic feature which enables one to identify the legal norm.

But the question arises at once what has caused the variety of overtones of feeling as reactions to violations of the various species of norms? We find that norms with apparently identical content, at different times, in different countries, in different classes and ranks of society, manifestly belong to different groups, and that they readily pass from one group to another. In the course of the millennia the prohibition of marriage outside of one's own rank has been a norm of law, of religion, of morality, of ethical custom, of decorum, and today, perhaps, it is merely a norm of tact, of etiquette, or even of fashion. At the present time, judging from the overtones of feeling that are released, it is based among the Polish nobility upon the code of morals

亚种规范,并且在很多现象的情形下,精确判定一个规范属于哪一组类型几乎是不可能的。

虽然在法律规范和其他类型规范之间划出合乎科学的精确性的界限是困难的,但实践中,这一困难极少存在。通常,任何人都会毫不犹豫地指出一个给定的规范是法律规范还是宗教、伦理习俗、道德、礼仪、言行得体、时尚或者礼节规范。这一事实必须作为讨论的基础。关于法律规范和非法律规范之间的区别问题不是一个社会科学问题,而是一个社会心理学问题。各种不同类型的规范释放出不同类型的感情暗示,而且我们对不同类型规范的违反也会做出不同的感情反应。比如对违反法律的反应是产生对抗情绪,对违反道德准则的反应是愤慨,对下流行为的反应是厌恶,对言行不得体的反应是不赞成,对冒犯礼节的反应是产生可笑之感,最后,时尚的追随者轻视那些未能和他保持同一高度的人,对他们会产生一种挑剔感。专门对应于法律规范的是这样一种反应——欧陆共同法学家为此创造了一个术语必然之念。这是人们能够识别法律规范的典型特征。

不过,马上就产生了如下问题:是什么导致了——作为对不同类型规范违反的反应——不同类型的情感暗示?我们发现,显然具有相同内容的规范在不同的时代、在不同的国家、在不同的社会阶级和阶层中却明明白白属于不同的类型,并且它们很容易从一种类型转变为另一种类型。几千年来,禁止与自身所属阶层外的人结婚曾经是一个法律规范以及宗教、道德、伦理习俗、礼仪规范,如今,或许它仅仅是一种行为得体规范、礼节规范,或者甚至是一种时尚规范。目前,根据释放出来的感情暗示来判断,在波兰贵族中它是以那里通行的道德准则为基础的;在奥地利贵族

prevailing there; among the Austrian nobility upon the conceptions of decorum; among the French nobility upon their ideas of etiquette. It prevails, perhaps, in the same locality at the same time with widely divergent effects. A marriage of the young farmer to his maidservant may be looked upon as an offense against morality; that of the merchant prince to his servant-girl, as a violation of the rules of etiquette. How can we account for these different reactions? In the first place by the different structure of the various social classes in question, and the different structure of the same social classes at different times and in different countries. But the assumption is obvious that where there is a difference in the structure of the community in which the norm is valid, the norm, though it retains its wording unchanged, nevertheless serves a different purpose and accordingly has a changed content.

On the other hand, it is easy to convince oneself that, though a norm of the same wording can indeed belong to two different groups, it has a different content in each case. The agreement in wording therefore is a purely external thing. The proposition, "Honor thy father and thy mother," can be considered a command of law, of morality, of religion, of ethical custom, of decorum, of tact, of etiquette, and of fashion. As a legal norm it commands a child to honor his parents by means of certain outward demonstrations; as a norm of morality, in general, by means of conduct evincing honor and respect. Religion, unless it simply repeats the command of morality, prescribes religious duties in addition, especially prayers for one's father and one's mother. Ethical custom demands that one show such respect for one's parents as is customary in good families. As a norm of decorum it forbids such omission of manifestations of respect as would be offensive to others; as a norm of tact it disapproves of much less serious offenses which might release a feeling of displeasure among those that happen to be present. Etiquette refers solely to deportment toward one's father and mother in society. If respectful demeanor toward one's parents were fashionable at a given time in fashionable circles, a person moving in these circles who should omit it

之中，它以一种礼仪观念为基础的；在法国贵族中，它是以他们的礼节观念为基础的。或许同一个规范通行于相同的地方、相同的时期，却有着迥异效果。一位年轻农民和他的女仆之间的婚姻可能被认为是对道德的违反；一位商业巨子和他的女仆的婚姻可能被认为是对礼节规则的违反。我们如何解释这些不同的反应？首先，我们要借助于多种相关社会阶层的不同结构，以及同一社会阶层在不同时期、不同国家的不同结构。但是，显然存在这种假定：在社区——其中存在某有效规范——结构存在差异的地方，该规范的字面表述虽然未变，但它服务于不同的目的，因而其内容实际上有所改变。

另一方面，人们很容易充分弄明白，虽然拥有同样措辞的规范可能确实属于两类不同的规范，每一种情形下，它有不同的内容。因此，措辞上的一致纯粹是外在的东西。“尊敬你的父亲和母亲”这一命题可以被认为是法律命令、道德命令、宗教命令、伦理习俗命令、礼仪命令、言行得体命令、礼节命令和时尚命令。作为一个法律规范，它命令一个孩子通过某种外在表示来尊敬他的父母；作为一个道德规范，通常它命令孩子通过行为来表示尊敬；宗教，除非它只是重复道德命令，否则还会要求附加的宗教义务，尤其是为他的父母亲祈祷的义务。伦理习俗要求一个人表现出对父母的那种尊重就像良好家庭的习惯一样。作为一项礼仪规范，它禁止那种可能冒犯他人的、对尊敬表露的省略。作为言行得体规范，它不赞同那种可能会使那些碰巧在场的人产生不快的更轻佻的冒犯。礼节仅仅涉及社会中对自己的父亲和母亲的行为举止。如果在特定时期，尊敬父母的言行在一个时尚圈子里很流行，则进入这些圈子的人要是忽略了那种尊敬的言行，就会因

would be guilty of an offense against fashion.

At any rate one must not state the difference between law and morals, as is frequently done today, as consisting in this, that law is heteronomous; morals, autonomous; that law is imposed from without; morals comes from within. All norms as rules of conduct—and they are to be considered here only as such—are autonomous and heteronomous at the same time. They are heteronomous, for they originate in the associations; they are autonomous, for their basis is the attitude of the individuals of whom the association is composed. The norms are autonomous also in the sense that obedience to the norms is considered of fult value only when its proceeds from a conviction which has been given shape by the norms. This is the true kernel of Bierling' s *Anerkennungslehre* (doctrine of recognition). A norm, whether it be a legal norm or a norm of some other kind, must be *recognized* in the sense that men actually regulate their conduct according to it. A system of law or of ethics that no one gives heed to is like a fashion that no one follows. Only we must bear in mind that what has been said about the rule of conduct must not be applied to the norm for decision; for courts may at any time draw forth a legal proposition which has been slumbering for centuries and make it the basis of their decisions. And we must not conceive of this doctrine as Bierling did, as implying that the norm must be recognized by each individual. The norms operate through the social force which recognition by a social association imparts to them, not through recognition by the individual members of the association. Even the moral anarchist, if he is well advised, will conform to the norms which prevail in the community; perhaps, as indeed happens occasionally, with gnashing of teeth and vociferous imprecations upon the hypocrisy of society, prompted, nevertheless, by consideration of his own interest; if for no other reason, because he does not wish to lose the advantages which he gains by doing so, because he wishes to avoid the disadvantages incident to rebellion.

The sociological science of law, therefore, will not be able to state the difference between law and morals in a brief simple formula in the manner of the juristic science that has hitherto been current. Only a thorough examination of the psychic and social

为违反这种时尚而感到愧疚。

无论如何,任何人都不能说法律和道德的区别就在于——如今人们经常有此误解——法律是他律的,道德是自律的;法律是从外部强加给人的,道德来自人的内心。所有的规范作为行为规范——在这里只把它们如此看待——同时是自律的也是他律的。它们是他律的,因为它们产生自联合体;它们是自律的,因为它们的基础是组成联合体的个人的态度。规范是自律的,这另外一层意义是:只有当服从规范是源于一种由该规范所形成的确信时,这种服从才被认为具有完整的价值。这就是比尔林的 *Anerkennungslehre*(认可原则)的真正精髓。一个规范不管是法律规范还是其他类型的规范,它必须在人们实际据以调控他们自身行为的意义上被认可。一个没有人注意的法律制度或者道德制度,正如无人追随的时尚一样。只是我们必须牢记,我们就行为规则所说的东西不得应用于裁判规则;因为法院在任何时候都可以拾起一项可能已经沉睡了几个世纪的法律命题并将其作为它们的裁决基础。我们也不能像比尔林理论构想那样,暗示所有规范必须被每一个个人认可。规范通过社会联合体给予他们认可的社会力量运作,而不是通过联合体的个别成员的认可运作。甚至连道德虚无主义者,如果他够明智,他也会遵循社区通行规范;或许这确实偶然会发生,他会咬牙切齿并且大声诅咒社会的虚伪,尽管如此,他还是会受到自己利益考量的驱动。如果不是因为其他原因,那是因为他不想失去这样做可能获得的利益,或者他希望避免不服从带来的不利益。

因此,法律社会学不能像迄今流行的法学那样以一个简单公式来表述法律和道德的区别。只有全面研究——那些目前甚至

facts, which at the present time have not even been gathered, can shed light upon this difficult question. Though we are well aware of the great degree of caution made imperative by the present state of juristic science, we may perhaps be permitted to assume, at this time, the following essential characteristics of law. The legal norm regulates a matter which, at least in the opinion of the group within which it has its origin, is of great importance, of basic significance. The individual act which is commanded by the legal proposition may not be of great weight, as for instance in the case of statutes regulating foods, or concerning prevention of fires or infectious diseases of cattle, but we must always consider the consequences if violations of these statutes should assume the dimension of a mass phenomenon. Only matters of lesser significance are left to other social norms. Therefore the proposition, "Thou shalt honor thy father and thy mother" is considered a legal proposition only where the organization of the state and of society is based chiefly on the order of the family. A community which conceives of God as being in an immediate relation to its affairs will be inclined to elevate religious norms to the rank of legal norms. On the other hand, the legal norm, as contrasted with the other norms, can always be stated in clear definite terms. It thereby gives a certain stability to the associations that are based on legal norms, whereas associations not based on legal norms, e. g. political parties, religious communions, groups of relatives, social relations, are characterized by a looseness, a lack of stability, until they assume a legal form. Norms of morality, too, of ethical custom, of decorum, often become legal norms as soon as they lose their universal character, and, couched in clear precise terms, assume basic significance for the legal order of society. In this way, the Roman *prudentes* and the praetor often succeeded in introducing them into the legal system; in this way, equity arose in England, which is today a system of law as fully developed as the common law. It may well be possible therefore that the normal precept of good faith in contractual relations may, in the course of time, be compressed into a series of definite and clear legal propositions.

尚未搜集到的——心理和社会事实，才能清楚地说明这一难题。虽然我们充分意识到了面对目前这种法学状况不得不抱有的极度谨慎，但我们现在或许还是可以认定，法律具有如下本质特征。法律规范所调整一个事项，它至少在其发源之群体的观念中具有极大的重要性，具有最根本的意义。受法律命题支配的个体行为不可能很重要，例如有关食品的制定法、或者涉及防火或防止家畜传染病的制定法之下的个体行为，但是，我们必须始终考虑到，如果对这些制定法的违反呈现出一种群体现象的规模则会导致何种结果。只有一些不是很重要的事项才由其他社会规范调整。因此，“你应当尊敬你的父亲和母亲”的命题，只有在国家和社会组织主要是建立在家庭秩序之上的地方才会被认为是一个法律命题。一个把上帝想象为一种直接涉及其事务之存在的社会，倾向于把宗教规范提升到法律规范的等级。另一方面，与其他的规范相比，法律规范总是用清晰而明确的术语表述。从而，法律给了那些以法律规范为基础的联合体以特定的稳定性，然而，不以法律规范为基础的联合体，例如政党、宗教团体、亲戚群体、社会关系，除非它们都采取了法律形式，否则它们都具有松散性和缺乏稳定性的特征。一旦道德规范、伦理习俗规范、礼仪规范丧失了它们的普遍特征，并且也用明确的术语表述，对社会法律秩序具有根本性意义，则它们也经常可以变为法律规范。通过这种方式，罗马的法学家和裁判官经常成功地把它们引入到法律制度中；通过这种方式，今天已是像普通法一样充分发展的法律制度——衡平法在英格兰产生了。因此，以下这一点极有可能：契约关系中正常的诚信原则，随着时间的推移，可能被压缩为一系列明确而清晰的法律命题。

Correct observation therefore underlies the habit of speaking of the heteronomy of law and of the autonomy of morals. This is not a matter of essential characteristics but of differences of degree. In the case of legal norms, society devotes much more thought to the matter of formulating than in the case of norms of morals and of the other non-legal norms; in view of the importance it attaches to law it is anxious to have not merely a general direction, but a detailed precept. Everyone ought to be able to know from the mere wording of the legal norm how he is to regulate his conduct in a given case; whereas the non-legal norms, couched as they are, in general terms, are little more than general guides; and on this basis, everyone must make his own rules of conduct in the individual case. It is true therefore that, in case of norms of morality, it is to a much greater extent a matter of the inner attitude of mind than in the case of law. A man without any inner sense of law knows how to perform his duties as a citizen of the state, knows that he must perform his contracts, respect the property right of others; but in order to be able to conduct himself correctly from the point of view of morals, religion, ethical custom, decorum, etiquette, and fashion, he requires a sense of morality, religion, ethical custom, decorum, tact, etiquette, and fashion. Without this sense, he cannot hit upon the correct thing. For this reason, when non-legal norms are involved, the center of gravity is inwardly within a man's self to a much greater extent than when legal norms are involved.

If we bear these characteristics in mind, it may be possible to give a more exact definition of the legal norm. Legal norms are those norms that flow from the facts of the law, to wit from usages, which assign to each member of the social association his position and function, from the relations of domination and subjection, from the relations arising from possession, from articles of association, from contracts, from testamentary and other dispositions; furthermore, those norms are legal norms that arise from the legal propositions of state and of juristic law. The *opinio necessitatis* is found only in connection with these, and therefore we may say there are no legal norms other than these. But this prop-

因此，确切的观察成了法律他律性和道德自律性这种习惯性说法的基础。但是这并不是一种本质特征，而是一定程度上的差别。在法律规范的情况下，社会要比在道德规范和其他非法律规范的情况下，更多地考虑法律的明确表达；鉴于社会强调的法律的重要性，社会不仅仅渴望有一般性的指导，而且还有详细的规定。每个人都应当能够仅仅通过法律规范的措辞就知道，在一给定情形下，他应当如何调整他的行为；然而，正如非法律规范以一般的术语表述一样，它们大体上也是一般性的指引；在此基础上，每个人都必须在单个情形下，找到自己的行为规则。因此，事实上，在道德规范的情形下，要比在法律规范的情形下，那个过程更大程度上是一个内在的心理态度问题。一个对法律毫无深层理解的人也知道如何履行他作为国家公民的义务，知道他必须履行契约、尊重其他人的财产权利；但是为了能使他自己正确地从道德、宗教、伦理习俗、礼仪、礼节和时尚等视角出发来调整自己的行为，他需要一种道德、宗教、伦理习俗、礼仪、言行得体、礼节和时尚等方面的感受力。没有这种感受力，他就不能想到正确的东西。因为这一原因，当涉及非法律规范时，相对于涉及法律规范时，重心更大程度上在于一个人的内心。

如果我们记住这些特征，就可能给法律规范下一个更准确的定义。法律规范是那些来自法律事实的规范，即来自为社会联合体中每个成员分配地位和职责的习惯、支配和服从关系、因占有而产生的关系、联合体的章程、契约、遗嘱和其他处分；此外，那些规范是源自国家和法学家法之法律命题的法律规范。必然之念只有与这些相关时，它才能被发觉。因此我们可以说，除了这些之外，不存在任何其他的法律规范。但是这一命题在逻辑

osition is not convertible. Not all norms that arise in this way are legal norms. In the first place legal propositions contain much that is not norm but "*unverbindlicher Gesetzesinhalt.*" Again there are norms that flow from legal propositions and from facts of the law, which however do not belong to the sphere of law, but of ethics, of ethical custom (regulations as to clothing), of honor (compulsory dueling among officers). Even religious dogmas have been posited by statute. These characteristics therefore do not furnish a positive delimitation of legal norms from other norms. Such delimitation would require first of all a thorough study of the nature of the non-legal norms.

Whether we can consider a norm which is socially valid but which violates a prohibition issued by the state a legal norm in the sociological sense, is a question of social power. The decisive question in this connection is whether or not it releases the overtones of feeling which are peculiar to the legal norm, the *opinio necessitatis* of the common law jurists. It is precisely in this matter that the juristic science of the Continental common law, in a manner deserving our deepest gratitude, has prepared the ground for the work of the sociology of law through its doctrine of the so-called abrogative power of customary law; it has assumed and demonstrated that legal propositions that are in conflict with the legal consciousness may languish and die. Let me cite as illustrations the fate of many a penal provision of the *Carolina*, the Prussian order in cabinet cited by Adickes, which provided the death penalty for handing a petition to the king in person; the order of the Austrian council of ministers, which declared that the possession and the acquisition of money tokens of the revolutionary propaganda, e. g. of Mazzini ducats, Kossuth dollar notes,

上不能自由换位。并非所有以这种方式产生的规范都是法律规范。首先，一些法律命题并不包含规范，而是包含“非强行性法律内容”。其次，一些规范产生自法律命题和法律事实，然而它们却不属于法律的范围，而是属于道德规范、伦理习俗（关于着装的规则）、荣誉规范（军官之间的强制性决斗）。甚至宗教教义也由制定法设定。因此，这些特征并没有提供一个法律规范和其他规范之间的绝对定界。这种定界首先需要对所有非法律规范的性质作彻底研究。

我们是否可以认为，一个在社会上有效却违反了国家发布之禁令的规范，在社会学意义上，是一个社会力量的问题。这方面的决定性问题是：它是否会释放出专属于法律规范的那种情感暗示——普通法法学家的必然之念。正好是在这一方面，欧陆共同法法学，以一种值得我们最深感激的方式，通过所谓的习惯法之废除力的学说为法律社会学的工作准备好了基础。该学说假定并证明了，与法律意识冲突的法律命题，将会枯萎和死亡。我们可以列举卡罗莱纳的许多刑事条款为例，类似的还有阿迪克斯所引的普鲁士内阁之命令：如果一个人私自向国王呈交一份请愿书就会被处以死刑；奥地利内政会议的命令：宣布占有和获得革命宣传的货币纪念品——诸如马志尼[1]硬币、

〔1〕 马志尼·朱森珀（1805～1872），意大利爱国者，以其政治性文章和秘密策划推行独立、统一的意大利的运动，大部分是在伦敦流亡期间实施的。

which one can now purchase as curiosities in the shops of Vienna, was high treason. In general, a legal relation entered into in spite of a legal prohibition, a forbidden society, a forbidden contract, a forbidden marriage, a forbidden testamentary gift, a forbidden club, will not be considered legal institutions. Compulsory dueling also is not considered such even among officers of the army or navy. It is otherwise when a transaction which the state has not prohibited but merely treats as ineffective becomes common in society generally, e. g. marriage entered into by church ceremony only, the unrecorded transfer of land, the *Treuhandgeschäft*, as a form of testamentary disposition. These, as experience has shown, can readily compel recognition by society as legal institutions; and, in the course of time, by the courts and the state.

科苏特[1]纸币等,如今人们出于好奇也能在维也纳的商店里买到这些东西——是最严重的叛国罪。通常,尽管存在法律禁令,某种法律关系——被禁止的社团、被禁止的契约、被禁止的婚姻、被禁止的遗嘱赠与、被禁止的俱乐部——仍然会建立,但它们都不会被认为是合法的制度。强制性决斗,甚至在陆军和海军军官之间,也不被认为是合法的。当国家对一种交易并不禁止但仅仅将其视为没有效力时,该种交易就会以某种不同的方式在社会中变得普遍起来,例如仅通过宗教仪式建立的婚姻、未经登记的土地转让、作为一种遗嘱处分形式的信托。经验表明,这些很容易会迫使社会承认它们是法律制度,并且,总有一天也会迫使法院和国家承认它们。

---

〔1〕 科苏特·拉约斯(1802～1894),匈牙利革命领导人,他为匈牙利脱离奥地利获得独立不懈努力,宣称哈布斯堡王朝灭亡,他曾作过很短一段时间的临时政府首脑(1849 年),直到俄国代表奥地利进行干预(德)(土地的)从物。

[英 汉 对 照]

西方学术经典文库

# 法律社会学基本原理

FUNDAMENTAL PRINCIPLES OF THE SOCIOLOGY OF LAW

[奥] 尤根·埃利希 著

叶名怡 袁震 译

(二)

九 州 出 版 社
JIUZHOUPRESS

# VIII

# The Creation Of The Legal Proposition

The most diversified content may be clothed in the form of a legal proposition, in particular, in the form of a statute. There are therefore legal propositions without any normative content whatsoever, with a non-obligatory legal content, statutes in a purely formal sense. And there are legal propositions from which no legal norms can be derived, but only social norms of some other kind. We shall not discuss either of these species, but only legal propositions which contain legal norms. Their purpose is to serve as the basis for judicial decisions or for direct administrative action.

Every legal proposition which is to serve as the basis for judicial decisions is itself a norm for decision, formulated in words, and published in an authoritative manner, asserting claim to universal validity, but without reference to the case that may have occasioned it. The prevailing school of juristic science treats the judicial decision as a logical syllogism in which a legal proposition is the major premise; the matter litigated, the minor; and the judgment of the court, the conclusion. This idea presupposes that every judgment is preceded in time by a legal proposition. Historically this is quite incorrect. The judge who, in the beginnings of the administration of justice, awards a penalty to the plaintiff has found the existence of a concrete relation of domination and subjection, a relation of possession, a usage, or a contract, and a violation thereof, and thereupon has independently found the norm fixing the penalty. Perhaps in each of these decisions the thought is germinating that in a similar situation, a like or a similar decision ought to be arrived at; but this germ at this time is

# 第八章 法律命题的创设

法律命题的形式之下,特别是制定法的形式之下可能包含最多样的内容。因为,也存在一些没有任何规范性内容的法律命题,存在包含非强行性的法律内容,存在纯粹形式意义上的制定法。而且存在一些法律命题,从它们无法导出任何法律规范,而只能得出一些其他种类的社会规范。我们此处不讨论这些类型的法律命题,而仅讨论含有法律规范的法律命题。它们的目的是为了作为司法裁判或直接的行政行为的基础。

每一个作为司法裁判基础的法律命题,自己也是一个裁判规范,每一个法律命题都用语言清楚地表达出来,通过权威的方式发布,宣称具有普遍的效力,而不论何种情形会导致该命题的适用。主流法学学派把司法裁决看作是一个逻辑上的三段论,在这个逻辑三段论里,法律命题是大前提,诉讼事实是小前提;法院的判决是结论。这一个观点预设法律命题在时间上早于判决。在历史上,这是完全不正确的。在司法的早期,判决给原告赔偿金的法官发现了具体的支配与服从关系、占有关系、习惯或者契约以及对它们之违反等诸多情势的存在,因此法官要独立地发现确定赔偿金的规范。或许,在每一个这样的判决中,思想的萌芽是这样的:在一个相似的情形中,应当得出一个相同或者类似的判

buried deep in the subliminal consciousness of the judge. If we assume that the judge in primitive times protected possession or contract only because he had assumed the existence of a legal proposition according to which possession or contract ought to be protected by law, we are attributing our own conception to him. He thinks only of the concrete, not of the abstract. The legal historian, who is trying to gather the law of the past from such judgments, may at most read out of them that which was universal, the universal usage, but not that which was universally valid. Nevertheless, in spite of the lack of legal propositions, the norm for decision was not a matter of pure caprice. The judge always drew it from the facts of the law, which had been established either on the basis of his own knowledge or of evidence, i. e. from usages, from relations of domination and of possession, from declarations of wilt, and, chiefly, from contracts. Given these facts, the norm was given; it was impossible to separate the question of fact from the question of law.

Today we have the identical situation when there is no legal proposition in existence for the case that is to be decided. The judge can only ascertain the existence of the usages, of the relations of domination, of the legal relations, of the contract, of the articles of association, of the testamentary disposition involved in the litigation, and on this basis find a legal norm independently. Neither the ascertainment of the facts nor the free finding of the norm for decision appears as a subsumption of the case in litigation under a proposition relating to possession. All attempts to construe, all artificial heaping up of paragraph upon paragraph of a code, can deceive only a biassed mind as to the truth that a decision according to a legal proposition is possible only where there is a legal proposition already in existence.

It is true, according to juristic terminology the question to be determined in a case of this kind is one of fact and not of law. But the judicial decision was rendered not only on the basis of the facts ascertained but also on the basis of a norm for decision which the judge had drawn from the facts. This norm for decision, indeed, is not as yet a legal proposition. It lacks the formulation in words, the claim to universal validity, the authoritative publication,

决;但现在,这种萌芽深埋在法官的潜意识中。如果我们想当然地认为,在原始时代法官保护占有或者契约,仅仅是因为他设想存在着一个法律命题,按照该命题占有或契约应当被法律保护,则我们是在把我们的观念强加于他。他仅仅考虑具体的事情,而不考虑抽象的事情。那些设法从这些判决中搜集以往法律的法律史学家,最多可以发现其中那些普遍存在的法律、普遍存在的习惯,不过却不是普遍有效的法律。然而,尽管缺少法律命题,但裁判规范并非纯粹是一种反复无常的东西。法官总是从法律事实——即从习惯、支配和占有关系、意思表示,以及主要从契约——中获得法律命题,这些法律命题或者建立在法官自身知识基础上,或者建立在证据的基础上。一旦给定这些事实,规范也随之确定;事实问题和法律问题是不可能分开的。

今天,当需要裁决的案件没有对应的法律命题存在时,我们遇到同样的情形。法官只能查明诉讼中涉及的习惯、支配关系、法律关系、契约关系、联合体章程和遗嘱处分的存在,并在此基础上独立发现法律规范。在有关占有命题的诉讼中,作为小前提的既不是事实的确定,也不是规范的自由发现。所有解释的尝试、法典条款的人为堆积,只能蒙蔽那些对——依法律命题裁决只可能在法律命题先已存在的情形下才有可能——这一真理有偏见的人。

诚然,依照法律术语学,在此类情形下要决断的问题是事实问题而不是法律问题。但是,司法裁判的作出不仅要以确证的事实为基础,而且也要以法官从事实中得出的裁判规范为基础。这种裁判规范当然不仅仅是到那时为止的法律命题。这种裁判规范缺乏明确的语言表达、普遍有效的宣称、权威性的公布,但是它

but it is a part of the valid law, for if this were not true the judge would have no authority to decide the litigation according to it. Even in this case therefore the question of fact cannot be separated from the question of law.

But even where a legal proposition has been found which covers the instant case, the legal proposition does not yield the decision without more ado. The legal proposition is always couched in general terms; it can never be as concrete as the case itself. It may define the term "accessories" (*Zubehör*) never so minutely, the question still remains whether the subject of the litigation falls within this definition or not. Here too the judge must ascertain the facts; here too he must decide independently whether the ascertained facts correspond to the definition of "accessories" contained in the legal proposition. Whether the judge answers this question in the affirmative or in the negative, the judgment is always rendered on the basis of a norm for decision which he has found independently, and which decides the question whether or not the subject matter of the litigation is part of the "accessories." Even where this norm for decision merely individualizes the content of the legal proposition in concrete form, it is nevertheless not identical with the norm found in the legal proposition; for the question what constitutes "accessories" is something different from tile question whether a certain object is a part of the "accessories." In such a case, the prevailing tendency in juristic science invariably assumes that we have a decision as to a question of law; one speaks of a question of fact only where the subsumption under the legal proposition is not controverted or is incontrovertible. But it is clear that in this case, as in the earlier cases, the question of fact, the ascertained facts, cannot be dissociated from the question of law, the norm for decision which the judge has found at this very moment. This concrete norm for decision, which the judge has deduced from the facts, is introduced between the legal proposition which contains the general norm for decision and the ascertainment of the facts by the judge.

Whether the judge, therefore arrives at his decision independently of a legal proposition or on the basis of a legal proposition, he must find a norm for decision; only, in the latter case, the judicial norm for decision is determined by the norm contained in the legal proposition, whereas in the former case it will be found quite

是有效法律的一部分,因为如果不是这样,那么法官将没有权力据此裁决讼案。因此,即使在这一情形下,事实问题也不能和法律问题分开。

但是,即使发现法律命题涵盖一个即时的案件,也不能干脆直接地基于该法律命题作出判决。法律命题总是用一般的术语表达;它从来不可能如案件本身那样具体。法律术语从来不可能如此详细地定义“从物”(*Zubehör*),诉讼主题是否在这一定义的范围内仍然是一个未决的问题。在这里,法官也必须确定法律事实;他还必须独立判定已确证的法律事实是否符合包含在法律命题中“从物”的定义。不管法官是以肯定的方式,还是以否定的方式回答这一问题,判决总是以法官独立发现的裁判规范为基础的,该诉讼裁判决定诉讼标的是否属“从物”的一部分。甚至在裁判规范仅仅是通过具体的方式把法律命题内容个别化的地方,它仍然不同于法律命题中发现的法律规范;因为哪些事物构成了“从物”这个问题,不同于某特定客体是否为“从物”的一部分这个问题。在那种情况下,主流法学的倾向总是假定:我们有一个关于法律问题的裁断;一个人只会在法律命题下的小前提未遭到反驳或无可辩驳的情形下才会提及事实问题。但是非常明显,这种情形下和先前的情形下一样,事实问题,确证事实,不能够与法律问题——法官在这一刻发现的裁判规范——分开。此具体的裁判规范——法官从事实中推导出的裁判规范——是作为介于包含一般裁判规范的法律命题与法官确证的法律事实之间的事物而被引入的。

因此,不管法官是独立于法律命题作出裁决,或者是以法律命题为基础作出裁决,他必须找到裁判规范。仅仅在后一种情形中,裁判规范才由包含在法律命题中的规范决定;反之,在前一种

independently. The more concrete the legal proposition, the more precisely the judicial norm of decision will be determined by the norm of the legal proposition; the more general the legal proposition, the more independently and the more freely the judicial norm will be found. But there are legal propositions which grant an unlimited discretion to the judge. Examples of this kind in private law are the legal propositions on abuse of a legal right, on *grobes und leichtes Verschulden*, on good faith, on unjust enrichment. In criminal law and in administrative law they also play an important part. In these cases, the legal proposition does indeed appear to contain a norm for decision; actually, however, it is merely a direction to the judge to find a norm for decision independently. It is as if the legal norm left the decision to the free discretion of the judge. These cases seem to belong to the second group. This however is a matter of appearance only; in reality they belong to the former, where the judge finds the decision freely. The upshot of all of this is that the difference between a decision according to a legal proposition and one not according to a legal proposition is a difference of degree merely. The judge is never delivered up to the legal proposition, bound hand and foot, without any will of his own, and the more general the legal proposition, the greater the freedom of the judge.

Every norm for decision contains the germ of a legal proposition. Reduced to that part of its content that is basic principle, couched in words, proclaimed authoritatively with a claim to universal validity, the norm for decision becomes a legal proposition. This is true even where it is merely a concrete individualization of the concept contained in the legal proposition. Let us say, for example, that the norm has declared that a certain object is subsumed under the legal concept of "accessories"; there lies in this declaration the germ of the legal proposition that objects of this kind are always "accessories." Considering the matter historically, we may say that most legal propositions arose out of norms for decision. As to the greater part of our codes we call show positively how the legal propositions were extracted from the decisions contained in the *corpus iuris*; and where the *corpus iuris* does not state decisions, but legal propositions, these, with rare

情形下,裁判规范要由法官完全独立地发现。法律命题越具体,裁判规范就越精确地由法律命题的规范决定;法律命题越概括,裁判规范的发现就越独立、越自由。不过,授予法官不受限制之裁量权的法律命题也是存在的。在私法中,此类例子有涉及权利滥用、重大过失或轻微过失、诚信、不当得利等法律命题。在刑法和行政法中,此类命题也起到了非常重要的作用。在这些情形中,看上去法律命题的确包含了裁判规范,然而,实际上它仅仅是指导法官独立发现裁判规范。这些法律规范好像是留给了法官自由裁量的空间。这些情形似乎属于第二种类型。然而这仅仅是表面现象,实际上它们属于法官可以自由作出裁决的第一类情形。这全部的结论就是:在法官依据法律命题作出裁决和法官没有依据法律命题作出裁决之间的区别仅仅是程度上的差异。法官从未把权力完全交给法律命题,从未被法律命题束缚住手脚,从未没有任何自己的意志,并且法律命题越概括,法官就有越大的自由空间。

每一个裁判规范中都包含着法律命题的萌芽。约简为基本原则的那部分自身内容,用文句表达出来,以权威的形式宣称具有普遍效力,这样,裁判规范就变成了一个法律命题。甚至当裁判规范仅仅是包含在法律命题中之概念的具体个别化时,情形也是如此。例如,一个规范宣布特定的物包含在"从物"的法律概念中;此处存在一个法律命题萌芽的宣告:这种类型的物总是"从物"。历史地考察这件事情,我们可以说大部分的法律命题都产生自裁判规范。至于我们的法典中的更多内容,我们可以肯定地证明,这些法律命题是如何从《国法大全》所包含的裁决中抽取出来的。在《国法大全》并没有介绍裁决的地方,则很少有例外,

exceptions, undoubtedly have had their origin in norms for decision which were first enunciated by a jurist when a dispute was submitted to him for decision.

It is possible that now and then legal propositions were thought out by jurists without reference to a definite decision. The rule of the Prussian law about the "*Erbschatz*" perhaps arose in this way; for, according to credible reports, an "*Erbschatz*" has never been met with, either before or after; the same may be said of the so-called *Schulfälle* (moot cases). Of course these can be only very insignificant legal propositions. We can also say that a legal proposition is prior in time to the norms for decision where a statute regulates an institution in order to introduce it, particularly where the latter is imported from a foreign country, as, for instance, the statute concerning companies with limited liability or the statute containing the *Höferecht* of the Austrian peasants. But apart from these exceptions the concrete, as is usual, is prior to the abstract; the norm for decision, to the legal proposition.

The creation of a legal proposition out of the norms for decision requires that further intellectual effort be applied to the latter; for we must extract from them that which is universally valid and state it in a proper manner. This intellectual labor, whosoever it may be that is able to do it, is called juristic science. The Historical School of jurisprudence has taken infinite pains to show how "customary law," or, to put it more accurately, legal propositions of "customary law," arise immediately in the popular consciousness. It is a vain endeavor. Lambert has shown conclusively that with the exception perhaps of legal maxims, legal propositions do not arise in the popular consciousness itself. Legal propositions are created by jurists, preponderantly

这些法律命题毫无疑问地起源于法学家——对提交给他予以裁断的争议——首次阐明的裁判规范。

法学家偶尔也会想出一个与具体裁决无关的法律命题，这种情况也是有可能的。普鲁士民法中关于"*Erbschatz*"[1]的规则可能就是通过这种方式产生的；因为依据可信的报告，"*Erbschatz*"在此前和此后均从未有过。所谓的 *Schulfälle*（模拟法庭所审理的案件）也属这类情形。当然这些都是一些非常无关紧要的法律命题。在制定法为了引进一个裁判规范而调整相关制度时，我们也可以说一个法律命题在时间上先于裁判规范，特别是当裁判规范是从外国引进时，例如，关于有限责任公司的制定法，或者包含奥地利农民的有关农场继承法的制定法。但是除了这些例外，通常情况下，具体先于抽象；裁判规范先于法律命题。

从裁判规范中创设法律命题，需要对裁判规范付出进一步的智力劳动；因为我们必须从裁判规范中抽象出普遍有效的命题并通过适当的方式表达。无论是什么智力劳动，只要能完成这一任务，都可以被称为法学。历史法学派的法学家付出不懈的努力来揭示什么是"习惯法"，或者更确切地说，"习惯法"的法律命题是如何直接从民众意识中产生的。这是一种徒然的努力（Lambert）。兰伯特确凿无疑地证明，或许除了一些法律格言外，法律命题不可能从民众意识自身中产生。法律命题是由法学家主要

〔1〕 按照普鲁士法典中的规定，*Erbschatz* 是一种夫妻共同生活期间共同使用的部分财产。这种财产是丈夫和妻子的一部分财产，在丈夫和妻子共同生活期间，由丈夫和妻子共同使用。最后，这些财产归依旧生存者所有，然后毫无阻碍地变为子女的婚姻财产。

on the basis of norms for decision found in the judgments of courts. The judge therefore who, when he gives the reasons for his decision, states the norm for decision in the form in which it is to be binding in future cases, may be said to be engaged in juristic labor. Judge-made law is always merely a subdivision of juristic law. Juristic science is created by the writer or teacher, an Eyke yon Repgow or a Bratton, who endeavors to extract the law of his day from the judicial decisions; and he does this even where, as editor of a collection of decisions, he states the legal propositions that are derived from the decision in the form of a head note, or where, as editor of a statute, he adds them to the various sections in the form of annotations. And *a fortiori* we may speak of juristic science when a juristic writer or teacher, in his writings or in his teaching, states the legal propositions which in his opinion are applicable to the cases he is discussing. And lastly the legislator who puts the norms for decision into statutory form is also engaged in scientific juristic labor, provided they contain more than mere state law. And every such legal proposition, wheresoever it may have had its origin, lays claim to universal validity. This is self-evident; for it would be a senseless procedure to write down, teach, or publish as a statute a legal proposition without the intent that it should be valid in all cases to which it is applicable. To be sure, as a rule, only the legislator has the power to make his will prevail. In the case of a judge or a writer the value of the performance is decisive of the success of his intellectual labor. If the legal proposition is good and practical, its chances of gaining recognition are as fair as the chances of a good and practical idea in any other sphere, perhaps as fair as the chances of a good and practical invention. The few words of Pomponius on the *disputatio fori* illustrate a process which may be considered fairly typical. The legal proposition is accepted

基于从法院的裁决中发现的裁判规范而创设的。当法官给出裁决理由时,他就通过拘束未来案例的形式表达了裁判规范,因此可以说,法官从事着法学劳动。法官法始终仅仅是法学家法的一个分支。法学由法学著作家或者法学教师创设,如艾克·冯·雷普戈或布拉顿这样的人,他努力从司法裁决中抽取他那个时代的法律;甚至当他如判例的编者那样以批注的形式阐述法律命题时,或者当他如制定法的编者那样以注解的形式把它们添加至各组成部分时,他也会这样做。而且当法学著作家或教师在其作品或教学中,阐述依他之意可适用于正在讨论之案件的法律命题时,我们更有理由可以提到法学。最后,倘若制定法中不仅仅包含着国家法,则把裁判规范转化为制定法形式的立法者也在从事着科学性的法学劳动。并且每一个这样的法律命题,不管它们源自何处,都宣称具有普遍的效力。这是不证自明的;因为若没有这种法律意图——法律命题在其可适用的所有案件中普遍有效,则记录、教授和出版作为制定法的法律命题,将是一个毫无意义的过程。的确,通常只有立法者才有力量推行自己的意志。在法官或著作家的情形,其工作表现的价值对其智力劳动成果的成功具有决定性的意义。如果法律命题是良善的和实用的,则它获得承认的机会,就如同在任何其他领域中的良善的和实用的想法获得承认的机会一样公平,或许如同良善的和实用的发明获得承认的机会一样。彭波尼[1]关于法庭上的辩论寥寥数语的论述阐明了一个可能被认为非常典型的过程。法律命题的

---

〔1〕 彭波尼斯·米拉,古罗马重要的地理学家。

not *ratione imperii but imperio rationis*.

After all, as daily experience shows, the success of a thought in every field of human activity does not depend exclusively upon its inner value but also upon certain outward circumstances, particularly upon the weight generally attached to the words of the person who has given utterance to the thought. This weight very often increases with the power of the author of the legal proposition in the state, his position, and his personal reputation. In several countries a definite usage has developed as to this matter. Occasionally this usage is well settled; usually it is rather uncertain. This side of the question was discussed exhaustively by Lambert with an admirable knowledge of the literature on the question in his work *La fonction du droit civil comparé*; I have done this as to the Romans in my *Beiträge zur Theorie der Rechtsquellen*. Under different names and under very different attendant circumstances, four kinds of persons have attained to prominent positions in history. They are: the judge, the juristic writer and teacher, the legislator, and the official who has been entrusted with this matter by the state. In order that the norm may become a legal proposition, it must pass through the alembic of juristic science, judicial, literary, legislative, or magisterial.

The prevailing Continental doctrine, at the present time at least, denies, it is true, that the judge has the right to call new legal propositions into being. It contends that new law can originate only in the popular consciousness in the form of customary law and in legislation; that the function of the judge is merely to apply the statute; that judicial decisions are merely juristic literature, interpretations of existing law, to be rejected wherever they purport to do more than this. Indeed the Continental commonlaw juristic science of the Historical School has quite consistently dealt with judicial decision in this way. Its older representatives, Savigny, Puchta, Vangerow, and Brinz, paid no attention to it at

接受并不是由权力说了算，而是由合理性来决定。

毕竟，如日常经验所示，人类活动每一个领域思想的成功并不完全依靠它内在的价值，而且也取决于特定的外在环境，特别是取决于一般归因于表达该思想之人言辞的重要性。这种重要性通常随着法律命题的创造者在国家中的权力、地位及其个人声誉的增长而增长。在一些国家，一个涉及该问题的明确惯例会发展起来。有时候这一惯例是非常固定的，通常情况下它却是不确定的。兰伯特在其著作《比较民法的功能》中，以其对该问题令人惊叹的文献知识，对该问题的这一方面进行了详尽的讨论。关于罗马法方面，我在《法源理论的贡献》中也进行了相应的讨论。在不同的名义和在非常不同的伴生环境下，四种不同类型的人在历史上获得了显著的地位。他们是：法官、法学著作家和法学教师、立法者以及被国家授予这方面权力的官员。一个规范要想变为法律命题，必须通过法学、司法、法学文献、立法或者地方执法官的提炼转化。

诚然，欧洲大陆的主流学说至少在目前是否认法官有权创设新法律命题的。它主张新的法律只能产生于以习惯法的形式存在的民众意识，只能产生于立法；法官的职能仅仅是适用制定法；已有的司法裁决仅仅是司法文献，是对现行法的解释，任何场合下它们想要逾越分际，都会被拒绝。的确，历史法学派的欧陆共同法学始终如一地如此处理司法裁决。历史法学派早期的代表人物萨维尼、普赫塔、凡格罗和布林兹根本就没有注意到这一问题；历史法学派后来的人，特别是温德沙伊德

all; the later ones, particularly Windscheid, as a rule merely inquired whether the decisions are in accord with the *corpus iuris*, and which of the points of view represented in juristic literature they follow. Over and above this, they regarded them merely as evidence of the customary law. Even Seuffert's *Archiv* in its first volumes reprints chiefly the literary discussions contained in the decisions. But all of this was mere theory; in actual fact one always felt that judicial decisions are something more than, and different from, juristic literature. Demand was always being made that the administration of law should be stable, a demand which is quite incomprehensible from the point of view of the prevailing trend in jurisprudence. If the judge is to follow the statutes and the customary law exclusively, he cannot, at the same time, follow principles which have not been laid down by statute or by customary law, but by another judge. If we demand that the judge should not depart from previous decisions, in order that the administration of justice may be stable, the decisions are more than literature, more than non-obligatory literary views on the interpretation of a statute or the construction of a case at law; they are judge-made law.

The case of scientific law is different. It is a matter of elementary truth that science can only know that which is, and cannot command what should be, that science therefore creates no norms, but merely investigates, presents, and teaches. The question as to creative juristic science must therefore be formulated in a way quite different from that in which this is usually done. The question is not whether new law arises from the knowledge of law, but whether the jurist, as a person versed in the law, claims the right to create new law. It is self-evident that this question can be answered historically only, and the answer will be in the affirmative wherever juristic science is not content to be limited to making a most faithful and unprejudiced presentation of that which is law, but strives, over and above this, to create norms independently which shall be binding upon the judges for all cases for which none can be found in the other sources of law. Among the Romans, juristic science was a science of this kind,

照例仅仅考察了司法裁决是否与《国法大全》相符,以及它们遵循了法律文献中表述的哪一种观点。除此之外,他们仅仅将司法裁决看做是习惯法的证据。甚至是绍依菲尔特的《档案》,也是在他的第一卷中主要再版了包含在司法裁决中的文献讨论。但是,这全部仅仅是理论;实际上,一个人经常感觉到司法裁决不仅仅是法律文献,它们不同于后者。法律实施应当保持稳定,这样的要求总是会产生,这种要求从法学的主流倾向的视角来看,是完全不可理解的。如果法官要完全遵循制定法和习惯法,那他就不可能同时遵循制定法或者习惯法或习惯法尚未规定,而是由另外一位法官确立的原则。如果我们要求法官不能偏离先前的判决,以使司法保持稳定,则司法裁决就不仅仅是文献,不仅仅是对制定法解释或对法律案例诠释的、不具法律约束力的学术观点;它们是法官法。

法学家法的情形有所不同。科学仅仅能够知道实然并且不能够把握应然,因此科学不创造任何规范,而仅仅研究、表述和教授规范,这大概是一个基本真理。因此,关于创造性法学的问题必须以一种完全不同于法学惯常之表述方式的另外一种方式清楚地表述。这个问题并不是新法是否产生于法律知识的问题,而是法学家作为一个谙熟法律的人是否主张创造新法权利的问题。不言而喻,这一问题只能从历史角度来回答,而且,在任何地方,只要法学不满于仅仅对"什么是法"这个问题做一个非常可靠且公正的表述,而是除此之外还要努力独立地创造——拘束法官并对所有案例适用的规范,因为没有人能从其他法源中发现它,则对这一问题的回答就是肯定的。在罗马人中,法学正是这种类

i. e. a science which is always creative, even when it is not conscious of it. It came into vogue in all common law countries when the Roman law was received. As late as its last classical period, which indeed was limited to Germany, the juristic science of the common law produced an abundance of new legal material, of which the German Civil Code affords an approximate idea. It is strange that hitherto no one has undertaken the grateful task of sifting the content of the Code historically and of showing the contribution that was made by the juristic science of the Continental common law. The juristic science of the Orientals (Islamic, Hindu) and at least the older science of the Scandinavians (the *Rechtsprecher*) may perhaps be of this kind, as Lambert has shown. On the whole it is very rarely limited altogether to receiving and stating law. In the main it is such only among the present-day English; less so, it seems, among the Americans.

Great differences, indeed, appear in details. It is self-evident that the importance of science is in an inverse ratio to that of the statute and that of the judge; the higher the position of the judge the greater the jealousy with which he guards his independence; the more omnipotent and comprehensive legislation, the more limited the sphere it is willing to concede to the jurist. For this reason juristic science declines whenever a codification has been made and does not awaken to a new life until the people become aware of defects and gaps in the latter. The jurist tries to influence the judge through his opinions, his teaching, and his writings, and through his criticism of judicial decisions; he either finds norms for the decision of the individual case or seeks to set up general principles, in the manner of the traditional juristic technique, which may serve as guides for the judge in the decision of individual cases. All these forms occur in the course of history. In Rome the influence of the jurists was based at first solely perhaps on their activity as *prudentes*, giving *responsa* as to individual cases; thereafter also on their activity as teachers of law; in later Imperial times, preponderantly on their literary works. The importance of the Continental common law juristic science consisted chiefly in the literary process of extracting general principles which were to guide the judge in the decision of indi-

型的科学,即科学总是一种创造性的科学,即使当它没有意识到这点时也是如此。当罗马法被继受时,在所有的共同法国家,这也成为了一种时尚。迟至最后的古典时期,事实上仅限于德国,共同法学产生了大量的法律新素材,《德国民法典》提供了近似的观念。非常奇怪,迄今为止,没有人承担这项令人愉快的任务——从历史角度筛分《德国民法典》的内容,并揭示出欧陆共同法学所作的贡献。如兰伯特所示,东方法学(伊斯兰法学、印度法学),以及至少斯堪的纳维亚更古老的科学(法律的公布)或许就属于这一类型。总的来说,它很少被完全限于接纳和表述法律。大体上,仅仅在如今的英国人中还是如此;似乎在美国人中,那种自由度还稍稍差些。

的确,在细节上还存在很大差别。不言而喻,科学的重要性与制定法及法官的重要性成反比。法官的地位越高,他就越珍视维护自己的独立性;立法越是无所不能和包罗万象,它乐于放弃给法学家的领域就越有限。因为这个原因,无论何时,法典编纂后,直到人们意识到其中的缺陷和漏洞才唤起新生活,法学在此期间会处于衰落的状态。法学家尝试着通过他的主张、他的教学和他的著作,并通过他对司法裁决的批评来影响法官。法学家或者为个案发现裁判规范,或者以传统法学技巧的方式建立作为法官裁断个案时之指导的一般原则。所有的这些形式在历史的进程中都发生了。在罗马,法学家的影响或许首先纯粹基于他们作为法学家对独立案件给出释疑解答的活动;从那时以后,这种影响也基于他们作为法学教师的活动;在后来的帝国时期,这种影响则主要基于他们的文献著作。欧陆共同法学的重要性主要在于提炼指导法官个案裁决的一般原则的著述过程。最近,法学

vidual cases. In most recent times, jurists have regained an established position as critics through the annotations which they have appended to the judicial decisions in the great collections of reported cases. These critics, the *arrêtistes*, have made the study of French judicial decision their life's work; in their annotations they are attempting to give, in addition to a detailed scientific critique, a history of the course of decision on the question as to which the judicial decision has been rendered. The originator of this tendency is Labbe, one-time professor of Roman Law at the University of Paris. A most attractive history of the *arrêtistes* is given by Meynial in the *Livre de Centenaire du Code Civil*.

It is self-evident that where scientific or judge-made law prevails there must be valid traditional or established criteria governing the evaluation of judicial or juristic decisions. Of course it could never have been the understanding that in general every judicial decision and every opinion of a jurist should be binding as such. In the case of judge-made law perhaps the official position of the judge is decisive, as a rule; in the case of juristic law there is very often no external criterion; the question is decided by the value of the work, or—a circumstance that often has no bearing on the value—the reputation of the author. The statements of Pomponius in the *Enchiridion* afford an insight into the manner in which a jurist of the Republican era achieved the reputation which a *conditor iuris* was required to have until the matter was finally settled in the days of the emperors. In England there is a definitely fixed regulation as to the binding quality of judicial decisions. In general the decision of a higher court prevails over that of a lower court, but the "great judges" whose names have become historical are being cited with an incomparably greater measure of reverence than the great multitude of the others.

A limitation exists, however, beyond which the judge and the legal writer must not go. Their decisions must be in harmony with

家通过对重要的被报告案例集中的案例附加评注的方式重新获得了作为批评家的显赫地位。这些批评家,即判例评注汇编者,把研究法国的司法裁决作为了他们日常的工作。在他们的评注中,除了给予一种详尽而科学的批评外,他们还尝试给出裁决所涉问题的裁断过程。该倾向的创始人是拉贝,他曾经是巴黎大学的罗马法教授。梅尼亚在《民法典百年文集》一书中给出了一段关于判例评注汇编者最吸引人的历史。

不言而喻,在法学家法或法官法盛行的地方,那里必定存在有效的传统标准或既定标准,用以规范对司法裁决或者法学家裁决的评价。当然,从来都不可能这样理解:通常,每一个司法判决和法学家每一主张都应当同样具有拘束力。在法官法的情形下,一般说来,法官的官职具有决定性作用;在法学家法的情形下,经常没有外部标准;这一问题由著作的价值决定,或者由——经常和著作的价值毫无关系的情形——作者的声望来决定。彭波尼在《指南》中的介绍深刻洞察到,在罗马帝国时期法学家的声誉这一问题获得最终解决之前,罗马共和国时期的法学家获取声誉所采用的方式,这种声誉是法的创建者必须具有的。在英国,关于司法裁决的拘束力,也存在一个明确而固定的规定。通常情况下,上级法院的判决优于下级法院的判决,不过,那些名字获得了历史性意义的"伟大法官"的判决也被人引用,相比其他大多数法官,他们获得了无与伦比的尊崇。

然而,也存在法官和法学著作家无法逾越的限制。他们的裁

the principles of the existing valid law and of juristic science. Its function is therefore often, though not always, conceived to be this: It is not to create new law, but to discover the principles and rules of justice already existing in the law. Flexible and elastic though this limitation may appear, it must not be overlooked; for it, as well as the limitation of the statute, is an expression of the strong conviction that the judge and the jurist are qualified to build on the foundation of the existing legal order, but not to shake it or substitute another for it. The remark is often found in French juristic literature that the famous article 1382 of the French Civil Code would suffice for the solution of the social question. Now the enormous power which this article entrusted to the French judge was used by him to create a judge-made law of damages which, in its basic outlines, is perfectly clear and consistent, and which is essentially new, although formally at least it is based on the existing law. But no attempt was ever made to utilize it for the solution of the social problem or for the introduction of any revolutionary innovation into the legal system. And one may safely set one's mind at rest, for such an attempt will never be made. It will not be made for the same reason that an attempt of this kind has never been made under normal circumstances. The introduction of the English common law into Ireland through a judicial decision (case Gavelkind) is even today regarded as a daring Cossack *coup de main*; and in that case a people which had been crushed by defeat was involved; furthermore it was done at the command of the victor, who has often enough had occasion to regret it. A similar attempt in Bengal failed; the judge and the sovereign power of the state had to yield in the face of a general uprising. The power of the judge is not sufficient to overcome the enormous powers of resistance inherent in society which would rise up in opposition to an attempt to place society on a new foundation by means of a judicial pronouncement;

断必须与现行有效的法律原则和法学原则相一致。因此,其功能常常——虽然并非总是——表达如下:它不是要创造新法,而是要发现法律中已有的原则和规则。虽然这一限制似乎具有灵活性和变通性,但却不容忽视;因为它与制定法的限制一样,也表达了一种强烈的信念:法官和法学家有资格去创立现存法律之制度的基础,但不是动摇它或以他物来取代它。在法国的司法文献中经常可以发现这种评论:《法国民法典》著名的第1382条足以解决社会生活中的问题。现在这一条授予法官的巨大权力正被法国法官用来创设有关赔偿金的法官法,该法在基本原则方面非常清楚和连贯一致,并且尽管它至少在形式上是以现行法为基础,但其在本质上是全新的。不过,从来没有人尝试利用这一条文来解决社会问题或者往法律制度中引入任何革命性的新方法。人们大可放心,因为那样的尝试永远没有人会去做。之所以没有人做正是基于同样的原因——在正常的情况下这种尝试从来没有过。通过一个司法判决(case Gavelkind),[1]把英国的普通法引入爱尔兰,即使在今天,这也会被认为是一个大胆的哥萨克式的突然袭击。那种情形下涉及到一个被失败完全压垮的民族;而且,这一过程是在胜利者的命令下完成的,而这个胜利者有足够多的机会可对此表达悔意。同样的尝试在孟加拉以失败告终。法官和国家主权面对普遍的抗争不得不屈服。法官的力量不足以克服社会中固有的抵抗力,后者反对尝试通过司法宣告的方式将社会置于一个新的基础之上;并且,法官需要足以

〔1〕 肯特郡土地保有习惯案例:一种英国的土地保有制度,始于盎格鲁——撒克逊时期,废于1926年,即把其土地平均分配给有资格的继承人。

and a judge requires knowledge of the world sufficient to be able correctly to estimate these powers of resistance as well as his own power. The judge has often, it is true, disregarded the law in the service of an unscrupulous sovereign power; occasionally, supported by the law, he has been able to offer successful resistance to a strong sovereign power; but he has never risked a conbat with the state, society, and traditional law. Much less has juristic science, with its limited powers, ever done this.

Both judicial and scientific law are always subject to the critical inquiry whether they have remained within the limitations with which they are hedged about—a criticism which has given the quietus to many an attempted innovation. Great though the power of the Roman jurists may have been, it would never have sufficed to abolish the Praetorian law of succession or the *fideicommissa*, perhaps not even the *actio de effusis et deiectis*; and Pollock says of the English judge: "Failing a specific rule already ascertained and fitting the case in hand, the

正确评估抵抗力及其自身力量的世界知识。的确,法官经常在效力于臭名昭著的最高权力时漠视法律;偶尔,在法律的支持下,他能够成功地抵抗强大的最高权力。但是他从来都不冒险与国家、社会及传统的法律斗争。更不用说拥有有限权力的法学家曾经这样做。

法官法和法学家法总是遭到批评性的质问:它们是否仍然留在为它们划定的界限范围内——这种批评使许多的革新尝试归于死寂。尽管罗马法学家的权力可能非常强大,但这种权力从来就没有强大到足以废止对裁判官法的继承或者遗产信托,〔1〕或许甚至也无法废止坠落物或投掷物致害之诉。〔2〕 波洛克在提及英国的法官时说:"如果没有已确定的、适合于手头上案件的特定规

---

〔1〕 (拉)*fideicommissa*(遗产信托),遗产信托是一种死因财产处置行为,表现为遗产处置人委托其继承人、受遗赠人实施某种使第三人受益的行为。例如要求受托人将遗产的全部或者部分转移给第三人,要求受托人解放某个奴隶等;第一种信托属于真正的遗产信托,第二种信托有时候也被称为解放信托。遗产信托具有比较灵活的特点,可以弥补罗马遗产继承制度的某些欠缺,例如:可以使处置人在未立遗嘱的情况下处置自己的遗产,可以使不具有遗嘱继承能力的人继承遗产。在罗马法中遗产信托不要求有严格的形式,它对受托人只产生一种道义上的义务,最初并不具有法律上的约束力;奥古斯都首先在一些特殊的情况中从法律上认可了这一制度,允许对不履行义务的受托人进行非常审判,后来甚至出现了两名专门负责审理遗产信托案件的裁判官。

〔2〕 (拉)*actio de effusis et deiectis*(坠落物或投掷物致害之诉),如果从建筑物中落下或者投出任何物品在公共场所造成损害,无论该建筑物的住户是否具有过错,均可对其提起此诉讼,以此要求给予双倍的损害赔偿。在优士丁尼法中,对住户上述责任的追究则以具备过错为条件。如果上述行为造成某一自由人死亡,则任何市民都有权提起民众诉讼,要求对责任人给以50金币的处罚。

king's judges must find and apply the most reasonable rule they can, so that it be not inconsistent with any established principle." The freedom of the Continental administration and science of law, at this moment, is still more narrowly limited. So juristic and judge-made law are always exposed to the danger of being crushed by the mass of the traditional element. The thought of a remedy through legislation does not suggest itself nearly so readily to man on a lower stage of development as it does today. The legislative machinery operates slowly and haltingly as yet, and the thought that it might alter the customary law has not yet occurred to anyone. One need but read Gaius and note how circumspectly he discusses the *senatusconsulta* and the *leges* of the Empire which were in conflict with the ancient *ins civile*.

These might be the historical presuppositions for magisterial law. Like judge-made law, the latter is posited by persons to whom certain functions have been assigned in the administration of justice in the course of the performance of these functions. It is not being posited however on the basis of the usual judicial authority and powers, but on the basis of authority and powers granted by the state that far transcend these. It has happened twice in the history of law that a state official acted when it became necessary to end the sway of norms for decision that had become rigid and antiquated. The Roman praetor and the English chancellor fulfilled their historic mission by opposing an altogether new legal system to the traditional system. Since the Middle Ages, magisterial law has no longer been able to gain a footing on the Continent. The royal courts of the Frankish and of the German kingdom failed to achieve a stable administration of justice; the capitularies of the Frankish kings were not magisterial law, but an echo of the legislative power of the Roman Caesars. In Rome as well as in England, the magisterial law became a fixed, fully developed system of legal rules, which confers upon the person entrusted with its application no greater freedom than do the other parts of the law.

则,国王的法官必须发现和适用他们能够发现和适用的、最为合理的规则,所以它将不会与任何已确立的原则相矛盾。”而这时候,欧洲大陆的司法自由和法学还在受着严密的限制。因而,法学家法和法官法总是承受着被大量的传统因素压垮的危险。与在发展的低级阶段相比,人们从来没有像在今天这样如此轻易地产生通过立法进行救济的思想。立法机器至今仍缓慢地、步履蹒跚地运行着,任何人都未曾想过它可以修改习惯法。人们只需要读读盖尤斯的东西,并注意他在讨论与古代市民法相冲突的元老院决议及帝国的法律时,有多么的谨慎。

这些可能是对地方执法官法的历史预设。如法官法一样,地方执法官法是由赋予其在司法中特定职能的人在履行职能过程中提出来的。然而,这些法律的提出并不以通常的司法权威或者司法权力为基础,而是以远远超越这些的、国家授予的权威和权力为基础。当有必要结束已变得僵化、过时的裁判规范的支配时,国家官员发挥了作用,这种情形在法律史上发生过两次。罗马的裁判官和英国的御前大臣通过使一种全新的法律制度与传统的法律制度相对照的方式完成了他们的历史使命。中世纪以来,地方执法官法无法再在欧洲大陆上获得立足点。法兰克王国和德意志王国的皇室法院未能实现司法的稳定性。法兰克国王的法令集不是地方执法官法,而是罗马恺撒之立法权的一个仿效。在罗马和英格兰,地方执法官法成了一个固定和充分发展了的法律规则体系,不过它授予其适用者的自由与其他部分的法律授予的自由一样大。

Norms for decision found in statutes are juristic law if they are the product of the same kind of intellectual labor as the norms for decision of the judge-made and of the literary juristic law. As to the nature of a legal proposition, it is manifestly quite immaterial whether it is found in the reasons given for a judgment, in the discussions of a writer, or in the paragraphs of a code, though this may be quite important where its effectiveness is in question. As it is, a large part of the juristic law contained in statutes has been taken from the juristic law existing at the time. But if the legislator has not prescribed a new norm for decision but has merely stated it, it is none the less juristic law, in spite of the fact that that which might have been said in a judicial opinion or in a treatise has been said in a statute. This statutory juristic law is just as susceptible of expansion and development as law that has been created in any other way. On this principle, the adoption of foreign statutes is based. State law, too, can surely be adopted from foreign countries, but only by the will of the state, i. e. by a statute, an ordinance, or any other enactment of the sovereign power of the state. It is manifest that universal compulsory military service, income tax, or regulation of self-defense could not by any manner of means be adopted from foreign law in any other way than by an act of the sovereign power of the state. But juristic law, even in the form of a statute, may migrate from one country into another like a scientific doctrine or like a practical invention. It makes its way into the literature, and thereby, or perhaps independently, into the judicial decisions. Even apart from the reception of Roman law, there are numerous examples of this phenomenon. The Austrian Civil Code at the present time actually is valid law in Hungary; indeed it is being taught by the law faculties, although it may not be cited in judicial decisions. The French Civil Code has gained recognition in Russia, the German Commercial Code in Switzerland and in the Scandinavian countries; and at the present time the German Civil Code is gaining a footing in the Scandinavian countries.

如果制定法中的裁判规范如法官法的裁判规范以及文献中法学家法的裁判规范一样是同一种智力劳动的成果，则制定法中发现的裁判规范也是法学家法。关于法律命题的性质，不管法律命题是存在于判决给出的理由中，还是存在于著作者的讨论中，或是存在于法典的条文中，这明显是无关紧要的。尽管这可能在正在讨论该裁判规范效力的地方相当重要。实际上，制定法中所包含的大部分法学家法都取自于当时存在的法学家法。然而如果立法者没有规定一个新的裁判规范，而是仅仅陈述它，则这个规范依然是法学家法，而不管在司法意见或在论文中可能表述的东西在一个制定法中是否已经得以表述。这种制定法中的法学家法与通过任何其他方式创设的法律一样，非常容易扩充和发展。对外国法的继受都是以该原则为基础。当然也可以从外国继受国家法，但必须通过国家的意志方可，即，通过制定法、行政法规或者国家主权进行的任何其他形式的立法。很明显，具有普遍强制性的军事服役法、税法或者自卫法，只能采用国家主权法令的方式，不能以任何其他方式从外国法律借用过来。但是法学家法，即使是通过制定法的形式表现出来的法学家法，也可以如科学原则或实践发明一样从一个国家移植到另外一个国家。法学家法不断发展，成为文献，或许藉此独立地成为裁判规范。除了罗马法的继受外，有关此种现象还有许多例子。《奥地利民法典》目前在匈牙利实际上是有效的法律；确实，法律教员们也正在教授《奥地利民法典》，尽管在司法判决中，《奥地利民法典》并未被引用。《法国民法典》在俄国获得了承认，《德国商法典》在瑞士和斯堪的纳维亚国家获得了承认。现在，《德国民法典》也正在斯堪的纳维亚国家取得立足点。

Norms for decision in statutory form, whether taken from juristic law or created by the legislator, are a precarious matter. It is much more difficult for the legislator to formulate a correct general rule than for the judge to decide an individual case; and it is a much more hazardous thing for him to posit an absolutely binding dogma for all time to come than it is for a jurist, who is proceeding scientifically, to enunciate propositions which are continually being examined and re-examined. The norm for decision becomes an entirely different thing when published in a statute from what it was before. Hitherto merely a presentation of what appears to be the proper rule, it now becomes a precept as to what ought to be the rule. It loses the pliability which had enabled it to adapt itself to every better insight and to every development. How often has a juristic doctrine been thrown overboard, and another substituted for it, although behind the pretense of a better insight there lay hidden the need of taking a new development into account. A method of procedure that is permissible where a legal doctrine is involved might not be permissible at all, or at least only with greater difficulty, when one is dealing with a statute. The legislator therefore ought to attempt to mould life according to his own ideas only where this is absolutely necessary; and where he can let life take care of itself, let him refrain from unnecessary interference. This doubtless was the leading, though unexpressed, thought in the fight which Savigny, for a time, waged against legislation, not merely against codification as is often mistakenly asserted today. Every superfluous statute is a bad statute.

Nevertheless it would be childish to give up altogether the thought of expressing juristic law in statutory form. Scientific and judge-made law everywhere surpasses statute law in wealth of material, adaptability, and mobility; but in more advanced stages of development mankind is brought face to face with a number of problems of legal life that can be satisfactorily dealt with only by the state.

The experience of thousands of years has shown that only moderate local needs can be satisfied when the creation of law is split up locally; legal development can take place on a grand scale only when it takes place in a vast area and originates in a single

以制定法形式存在的裁判规范,不管是源于法学家法还是由立法者创制,都是不确定的。立法者清楚阐明一个确切的一般性原则要比法官裁判一个个案更加困难。对于立法者来说,设定一个对未来所有时候均有绝对拘束力的法则要比正从事科学研究的法学家阐释一个不断受到检讨和再检讨的法律命题更加棘手。当裁判规范在制定法中公布时,它就完全不同于以前的规范。迄今仅仅是“恰当的规则似乎是什么”的表述,现在却变成了一个关于“该规则应当是什么”的规定。它丧失了使它自己适应每一次更深的洞察与每一次发展的可塑性。一个法学学说被推翻并弃置在一边,再被另外一个学说取代,这是多么常见的事情,虽然在更深洞察的主张后面隐藏着考虑新发展的需要。在涉及法律学说的场合,一个可行的诉讼方法,若涉及制定法,可能根本不被允许,或者至少会带来更多困难。因此,立法者只在那些有绝对必要之处,才应该尝试按照他自己的想法去塑造生活;在那些生活本身可以运转良好的地方,还是让立法者避免不必要的干涉为好。这无疑是萨维尼一度反对立法——不仅仅是反对我们今天经常误称的法典化——的主要想法,尽管该想法没有明确表达过。每一项多余的制定法都是糟糕的制定法。

尽管如此,不过完全放弃以制定法形式表达法学家法的想法却是幼稚的。法学法和法官法在素材的丰富、适应性和灵活性方面都胜过制定法。但是在更发达的发展阶段,人类必须面对大量的、只有通过国家才能圆满解决的法律生活问题。

数千年来的经验表明,只有当法律的创设是局部分离的时候,适度的局部需要才能被满足;只有当法律在一个辽阔地域产生,并从唯一的中心点形成时,法律的发展才能大规模地出现。

central point. In order to attain a rich development it requires an abundance of stimuli, which are given only by the variegated manifoldness of legal relations that may be found in a country of considerable size, and a central point where all these stimuli converge. Such a central point however can be created only by the state. This of course presupposes a thoroughgoing legislative activity. Legislation has not served this purpose in the two grandest legal systems of the world. The Roman and the English law did not arrive at the perfection which they have attained through legislation. In Rome the jurists were working at it with the immense intellectual resources of a vast empire; in England the judges, sitting in London, who for centuries had had to find the law for a great, economically developed, and politically advanced country. The common law is chiefly the product of the labors of the courts in London. Only the third world system of law, the French, owes its success to legislation. A highly developed legal system then may arise without legislation by the state, but surely not independently of the state. As a rule, however, statutes are indispensable for the purpose of getting rid of antiquated law and of quickly bringing about necessary innovations; for the rule that juristic science and administration of justice must not get into conflict with the law that has already been posited is an insuperable limitation upon their creative activity. With the exception of magisterial law, which down to the present day has had only two opportunities for free development, and which itself soon hardened into an inflexible rigidity, it may be said that it has always been the statutory law that was able to come to the assistance of the process of legal development when the latter had arrived at a dead center. This is the reason why one can say that the state, which in times of economic or political disturbance always is both an effect and a cause, may be called the most important lever of social progress. This is the reason why revolutionary parties which are violently attacking the state, from which legislative action proceeds, have often demanded legislative intervention, while conservative groups, which support the state, are filled with silent mistrust of its labors. But also in times when the course of events was undisturbed, legislation has proved an indispensable instrument for the removal of antiquated institutions and the advancement of legitimate interests which are struggling for recognition.

为了获得丰硕的发展,法律需要大量的刺激——只有斑驳多样丰富多彩的法律关系才能给予这样的刺激,而那些法律关系可能存在于相当大的国家内——还需要一个所有的刺激交汇的中心点。不过,那样的一个中心点只有国家能够创建。这当然要以彻底的立法活动为前提。立法无法在世界上两大法律体系中满足这一目的。罗马法和英国法并没有达到他们通过立法所达到的完美程度。在罗马,法学家通过辽阔帝国浩瀚的智识资源来研究这一问题;在英国,生活在伦敦的英国法官几个世纪以来不得不为这个经济发达、政治繁荣的伟大国家寻找法律。普通法主要是伦敦的法院的劳动成果。只有第三个世界性的法律制度——法国法,其成功可归功于立法。因而,一个高度发达的法律制度可以不通过国家的立法而出现,不过它确实不能离开国家。然而,通常制定法对于革除过时的法律和迅速促成必要的变革这一目的而言是必不可少的;因为法学和司法不得与已设定的法律相冲突这一规则是针对它们的创造性活动而设置的不可逾越的界限。除了地方执法官法——此种法律迄今只有两次自由发展的机会,其本身很快就凝固成了僵硬的刻板之物——外,可以说,能够在法律发展到达僵固点时有助于法律发展进程的始终是制定法。这就是为什么一个人可以说以下这些话的理由:国家——在经济或政治动荡的时期它总既是结果又是原因——可以说是社会进步最重要的手段。这也是为什么激烈攻击国家并发起立法行动的改革派政党经常要求立法干预,与此同时那些支持国家的保守团体对国家的工作满腹猜疑的原因。但是,同样在安定有序的社会中,立法也被证明是革除过时制度和提升正奋力争取承认之正当利益的不可或缺的工具。

In addition to the norms for decision of the juristic law, modern codes contain *Kautelarjurisprudenz* in the form of the so-called *Reglementierungsbedingungen*; occasionally, at least according to the intent of the legislator, in the form of *nachgiebiges* (noncompulsive), contract law or of precepts concerning testamentary dispositions. The legislator by means of subsidiary law requires the inclusion of those provisions that, in his opinion, the prudent draftsman ought to include in the document. These statutes likewise are, essentially, juristic law. Moreover, they also contain state law, e. g. the provisions concerning entry in a book of record and concerning the supervision to be exercised in the matter.

At the present time the magisterial law has become silent in England also. Since equity has been elaborated into a fixed system of law, its decisions contain judge-made law, not magisterial law. When the Continental common law withdrew into the background in Germany, the literary juristic law went with it; the teacher of law confines himself to the teaching of existing law, and the discussions in the works of juristic literature are no longer treated as legal propositions but merely as suggestions for judicial decision and legislation. At the present time juristic law flourishes only in the form of judge-made and statute law.

A glance at a modern edition of a code "with annotations taken from the judicial decisions" shows the relation between judgemade law and the law contained in statutes. To the various provisions the editor has appended legal propositions drawn from judicial decisions. These purport merely to individualize concretely that which is laid down in the statute; actually however they are of equal value with the juristic law of the statute, both as to content and as to purpose. And as a matter of fact the element of concreteness lies in the cases on which

除了法学中的裁判规范外,现代法典中包含以所谓的官方监督、管理的条款形式存在的 *Kautelarjurisprudenz*;[1] 有时候,至少按照立法者的意图,制定法包含以 *nachgiebiges*(非强行性)[2] 的形式存在的契约法或有关遗嘱处分的规定。立法者通过附属法要求包含一个谨慎的起草者应当在文件中包含的所有的那些条款。这些制定法本质上同样是法学家法。而且,法典中也包含了国家法,例如:涉及到登记簿的登入以及涉及到这方面监管的条款。

现在,地方执法官法在英格兰也已经变得沉寂了。自从衡平法被详尽阐述,成为一个固定的法律体系之后,其裁决中就包含了法官法,而不是地方执法官法。当欧陆共同法在德国退居幕后,文献法学也跟随之。法学教师仅限于教授现行法,法学著作中的讨论不再被视为法学命题,而仅仅被视为一种对司法裁判和立法的建议。目前,法学家法只是在法官法和制定法方面呈现繁荣。

对带有"来自司法裁判之注解"的现代版法典粗略打量,便可明白在法官法和制定法中所含法律二者之间的关系。对于各种不同的法律规定,修订者都附加了来自司法裁判的法律命题。这些活动声称仅仅是为了使制定法中的规定具体性地个别化;然而,实际上,就内容和目的而言,它们与制定法中的法学家法具有同等的价值。而且事实上,具体化的要素存在于作为它们之基础

---

〔1〕 (拉)*Kautelarjurisprudenz*,一些法学家使用这一废弃不用的术语来指那些涉及预防性规定的那些法学活动(*Reglementierungsbedingungen*),当正在进行法律交易或者正在起草法律文件的时候,这些规则必须被遵守。它完全包括起草法律文件的整个的技艺和学问。

〔2〕 (拉)*nachgiebiges*,调整除非双方当事人另外通过协议作出规定的情形的法律。

they are based. When the statute is restated, as was done, for example, in the case of the German Commercial Code, these annotations are received into the statute. Occasionally the decisions are in conflict with one another. This however proves only that the juristic law is still uncertain. If they are in agreement it is as difficult to prevail against them as against the actual words of the statute.

It would seem to follow from this discussion that there is no occasion for decisions that are found freely. But a more careful examination of the annotations shows that their connection with the provisions of the statute is quite external; that actually they are quite independent of them. The French editions of the Civil Code append the decisions on unjust enrichment to the provisions as to management of another's affairs without authority. The French jurists do not doubt that they have nothing to do with this subject-matter. In this case, therefore, we may say that the decisions have created the juristic law as to unjust enrichment quite independently.

The situation is the same where the statutory provision is so general as to amount to no more than a direction to the judge to find the norm for decision himself. In such case, the legal propositions extracted from these norms for decision do not elaborate the statute, they add new law to it. What is meant in German law by abusive exercise of a legal right, when the performance of an obligation is a violation of good faith, when a contract is immoral (*den guten Sitten widerspricht*), we do not know as yet, for the German Civil Code contains no provisions on these subjects, and we probably shall not know from judicial decisions until a century has elapsed. And these decisions will be so far from being based on the Civil Code that a judge in any other jurisdiction may adopt the norms contained therein, without any hesitation, e. g. for the concept of an immoral contract, or of abusive exercise of a right, unless the statutes of his jurisdiction contain divergent provisions.

In my book on the declaration of the will by silence, I have shown that among the Romans this term meant only a declaration made in a manner other than by means of words and the meaning of the declaration as discovered by means of an interpretation based on the experience of the ordinary intercourse of life. The decisions of the German, Austrian, and French courts take it to include, in addition, the follow-

的案件中。当制定法重述时,例如在《德国商法典》中所做的那样,这些注释被吸收进了制定法中。偶尔,裁决相互冲突。然而这仅仅证明了法学家法具有不确定性。如果它们达成一致,则压倒它们与战胜制定法中的实际措辞一样困难。

似乎可以从这一讨论得出结论:裁决是没有机会自由发现的。但是对注释的详细的审视表明,它们与制定法条款间的联系是相当表面的;实际上它们完全独立于他们。《法国民法典》把不当得利的裁决引向有关无因管理的条款上。法国法学家并不怀疑他们并未涉入此主题。因此,我们可以说司法判决创造了关于不当得利的法学家法。

在那些制定法条款是如此的概括以至于对法官而言不过是等同于要其自己发现裁判规范的地方,情形也是如此。那种情形下,从裁判规范中提取出来的法律条款并没有详细地阐述制定法,它们毋宁是加入了新的法律。当债务的履行违反了诚信原则时,当一个契约是不道德的时候(*den guten Sitten widerspricht*),我们到目前为止还不知道,在德国法中,法定权利滥用条款要达到的意图是什么,因为《德国民法典》并没有包含针对这些问题的条款,而且直到一个世纪已经过去之后,我们才可能通过司法判决得知其意图。这些判决远远不是以民法典为基础,以至于任何拥有其他司法权限的法官也可以毫不犹豫地采纳包含在其中的规范,例如不道德契约的观念或者权利滥用的观念,除非规定法官司法权限的制定法另有规定。

在我论及默示之意思表示的书中,我已经说明,在罗马人中该术语仅仅指以言辞和表示意思之外的方式所做的表示,如同基于生活中日常交往的经验而进行的解释所能发现的意思一样。德国、奥地利与法国三国法院的裁决认为这一术语除上述含义外

ing: the acceptance of an offer by performance or by acts of appropriation; the binding force of a declaration which imposes an obligation on one of the parties only, e. g. of *Verbürgung* (becoming surety) or of *Verpfändung* (giving a pledge), or of *Verzicht* (disclaimer) without any acceptance by the other party ("*stillschweigende Annahme*") (acceptance by silence); the extinguishment of an obligation by long continued failure to exercise one's rights ("*stillschweigender Verzicht*," properly speaking, a hidden prescription) (disclaimer by silence); expiration of the right to make a transaction effectual after a lapse of time by approval or confirmation ("*stillschweigender Verzicht*," properly, a hidden limitation as to time) (relinquishment by silence); the power of the contents of an invoice to bind the person receiving the same where the latter had not provided against this ("*stillschweigende Annahme*") (acceptance by silence). DeLivery by silence ("*stillschweigende Übergabe*") in the case of the *societas omnium bonorum* and of the fruits to the usufructuary lessee means that, by way of exception, ownership is transferred without transfer of possession, i. e. solely on the basis of the agreement. It is impossible to regard all of these merely as concrete individualizations; all of these, undoubtedly, are special, independent legal propositions of juristic law, connected in a purely external way with the Roman norm for decision concerning declaration of the will by silence.

The borderline between state law and juristic law is not easily determinable. In the first place juristic law consists of the norms for decision which the jurist has created by universalization.

还包括如下内容:通过履行行为或者付款行为对要约的接受;仅仅强加给一方当事人义务之表示的约束力,例如 *Verbürgung*(作保证人)或 *Verpfändung*(提供质保),或者在没有另外一方当事人任何承诺(“*stillschweigende Annahme*”)(默示承诺)的情况下 *Verzicht*(弃权)等的效力;某人权利长期不行使导致债务消灭(“*stillschweigender Verzicht*”,恰切地说,隐含的诉讼时效)(默示弃权);在同意或确认的期间届满后缔结有效交易之权利的失效(“*stillschweigender Verzicht*”,恰切地说,默视放弃,暗含的期间限制)(默示弃权);在收受发票的一方当事人并没有预先反对发票的内容时,发票的内容对他的拘束力(“*stillschweigende Annahme*”)(默示接受)。在共同合伙[1]情形下与有用益权之承租人的孳息情形下的默示交付,意味着通过一种例外的方式在不转移占有的情形下所有权发生转让,即,所有权的转让仅以协议为基础。把所有的这些都视为具体的个别化,是于理不通的;毫无疑问,所有的这些都是特殊的东西,它们独立于法学家法的法律命题,通过纯粹的外在方式与有关默示意思表示的罗马裁判规范联系到一起。

国家法和法学家法之间的界线不容易确定。首先,法学家法由法学家通过一般化创造的裁判规范组成。国家法由国家向

〔1〕 (拉)*societas omnium bonorum*(共同合伙),指合伙人以自己现有的或未来的全部财产参加合伙,他们按照一定的比例分摊产生于合伙的赢利和亏损。在罗马法中,共同合伙最初表现为家子在家父死亡后联合在一起的不分遗产共同体(*Consortium ercto non cito*)。

State law consists of commands directed by the state to its tribunals. The jurists cannot issue commands, they can only find law. The state does not find law, it can only command. Norms directing administrative action therefore are always state law. But as to many a statutory norm for decision one may well be in doubt as to whether it contains a statement of grounds for decision based on juristic law or a command by the state directing the judge how to decide the litigation. The principles governing the passing of the risk in case of a sale doubtless are juristic law. The norms for decision found in the German Civil Code on the prerequisites to the acquisition of legal capacity by organizations undoubtedly are state law. But between these there are a number of borderline cases, as to which it is not clear where they are to be counted.

External criteria however are not lacking. The jurist draws his law from the social relations; juristic law therefore does not extend beyond the relations from which it was taken. All true juristic law therefore is limited to the persons and the things that are connected with the relations for which the jurist has made his law. Juristic law is dominated by the personal principle as was the whole law at the time when there was no law but juristic law. The Roman *ius civile* and the Germanic popular laws were personal and real, as is the Mohammedan law today. The state, on the contrary, enacts its statutes for a given territory, and all true state law therefore is territorial law. The Roman *leges*, therefore, with the exception of the *leges de iure civili* and the Frankish capitularies, were territorial law. In the modern law this criterion has disappeared outwardly; but if one examines the principles of private international law, which somehow or other have come into vogue between the time of the theory of the "statutaries" and Zitelmann, one will find that, nevertheless, it makes its way everywhere. That part of modern law which is juristic law is effective as personal or as real law beyond the territory of the state; but state law is effective only within the territory of the state. The most precise

其裁判机构发布的命令组成。法学家不能发布命令，他们只能发现法律。国家不能发现法律，它只能发布命令。因此，指导行政行为的法律总是国家法。然而，对于许多制定法上的裁判规范，人们有充分理由怀疑，它是否包含基于法学家法或国家指示法官如何裁断诉讼之命令的裁判理由说明。规制买卖中风险转移的原则无疑是法学家法。《德国民法典》中存在的涉及通过组织取得法律权利之必要条件的裁判规范无疑是国家法。但是，其中存在着大量的介于两者之间的情形，至于这些情形，它们到底是属于国家法还是法学家法并不清楚。

然而，外部的标准并不缺乏。法学家从社会关系中提炼出法律；因此法学家法不能超越作为法学家法来源的社会关系。因此，所有真正的法学家法限于那些与作为法学家创造法律之服务对象的关系相联系的人和物。法学家法受到个人原则的支配，如同在没有法律只有法学家法的时代，全部的法律都受到个人原则的支配一样。罗马的市民法和日耳曼的民间法是动产法和不动产法，如同今天的伊斯兰法律。相反的，国家在一个特定地域颁布了它的制定法，因此，真正的国家法都是地域法。因此，罗马法除了有关市民法的法律和法兰克人的法令汇编外，都是地域法。在现代法律中，这一标准已经在表面上消失；但是，如果人们审视一下国际私法——因这样或那样的原因在“制定法”理论的时代与齐特曼的时代间变得流行起来——的原则，就会发现这一标准无论在什么地方都在继续发展着。现代法律中那部分属于法学家法的、涉及动产法或不动产法的法律，其效力超越了国家的版图。但是国家法仅仅在国家的地域范围内有效。已经被

formulation of this principle is found in the national theory of private international law which has been received into the Italian Civil Code, and according to which the law of a citizen of a state follows him everywhere, with the exception of the *lois d'ordre public*, whose validity is always territorial.

The two kinds of legal propositions also differ in force and effecttiveness. This is not a question of the distinction between compulsive (*zwingendes Recht*) and non-compulsive law, which, as I have shown in my book on the compulsive law, is of significance only in so far as it refers to the legal consequences of transactions which in part can be excluded by the will of the parties, and in part take effect unconditionally. In this sense, there is also a compulsive juristic law; and state law occasionally, though not often, is non-compulsive. But certain kinds of legal propositions are always juristic law—rules of interpretation, subsidiary law—whereas only state law can confer advantages, which the person advantaged cannot relinquish, and can impose disadvantages as to which there is no dispensation. On the other hand, state law, as the *corpus iuris* shows, has much less power of resistance to the changes of time than juristic law; almost all of the juristic law, but very little of the state law, contained in the *corpus iuris* has been received into the Continental common law.

The legal propositions which are contained in the legal commands of the state directed to courts and administrative tribunals are based on the will of the person who has power and control over the courts and the administrative tribunals; but their content does not always proceed from the state. The distinction between *Gesetzesbefehl* (command contained in a statute) and *Gesetzesin*halt (content of a statute) which prevails today is based on sound sociological discernment. But the answer to the question by whom the command must be issued is a matter which in no wise depends upon the constitution of the state but upon the questions: in whose hands do the military and the police powers of the state lie, is the person in whose hands these powers lie thereby enabled to exercise control over courts and administrative tribunals, will he be able to induce judges and administrative officials to do his bidding? If he has the seat of the administration of justice and

《意大利民法典》吸收的国际私法之国家理论中存在着对该原则最精确的阐述,按照该法典,除了效力总是地域性的治安法外,国家公民的法律将跟随他到所有地方。

这两种类型的法律命题在影响力和效力方面也有所不同。这并不是强行法和非强行法的区分的问题。如同我在论强行性法的书中表明的那样,这种区分只有在涉及交易的法律后果时才有意义,此种法律后果部分可被当事人的意思排除,部分可无条件地生效。在这种意义上,也存在强行性的法学家法;国家法偶尔——虽然不是经常——也是非强行性的。但是,特定类型的法律命题总是法学家法,如解释规则、辅助性法律等,然而,只有国家法可以授予某人不可放弃的利益,强加给某人的不可免除的不利益。另一方面,正如《国法大全》所示,国家法比法学家法在抵制时代的更替方面力量更弱;《国法大全》中包含的几乎所有的法学家法——但只有很少的国家法——被欧陆共同法继承下来了。

国家指示法院和行政裁决机构的命令中包含的法律命题乃是基于对法院及其他裁决机构拥有权威和掌控力之人的意志;但它们的内容并不总是源于国家。如今盛行的、在 *Gesetzesbefehl*(制定法中包含的命令)与 *Gesetzesinhalt*(制定法的内容)之间的区分是以可靠的、社会学的辨别力为基础的。但是,对于谁可以发布命令这一问题的答案绝不依赖于国家的宪法,而是取决于如下这些问题:国家的军队和警察力量掌控在哪些人手里,拥有这些力量的人能够借此支配法院和行政裁决机构吗,他能够促使法官和行政官员服从他的命令吗?如果他在能力所及范围内在司

of the civil administration in his power, even the content of a statute that has been enacted in a constitutional manner is powerless against him, and he can give effect to state law even though it be unconstitutional. It is well known that the legislation of the Roman emperors down to the days of Diocletian was based on the possession of power of the kind described, and each of a number of rival Caesars had the power to legislate within his particular sphere of power. Accordingly the Prussian government was in position to impose the constitution which it granted; the Russian, to change the election laws; the Danish, to carry out a reform of the military system by royal decree. The constitutionality of the Austrian so-called paragraph 14 decrees, as is well known, is being disputed by many; but their validity, in view of the character of the Austrian officials and judges, is being denied by no one. The force of these facts is so overwhelming that even a government which denies the legality of a preceding one will, as a rule, acknowledge the validity of legislation that was enacted meanwhile. Accordingly the Stuarts recognized the legeslation enacted during the Usurpation; the Bourbons, the legislation of the French Revolution and of the Empire.

法和民政管理方面拥有影响力,则即使是通过合乎宪法的方式颁布的制定法,其内容对他来说也是没有任何权威的。他可以赋予国家法效力,即使该法是违宪的。众所周知,下至戴克利先时期的罗马皇帝的立法都是基于上述这种权力的享有,大量的具备同等实力的统治者,他们每一个都有权在其特定权力范围内立法。因而,普鲁士政府有能力强制实行它所批准的宪法;俄国人修改了选举法;丹麦人通过皇室的命令实施了军事体制的改革。众所周知,奥地利所谓的第十四条法令的合宪性受到许多人的质疑;但是,在奥地利的政府官员和法官的显要人物眼中,没有人否认它们的效力。这些事实的力量是如此的具有压倒性,以至于即使一个否认前任政府合法性的新政府通常也会承认其间所颁布立法的效力。因此,斯图亚特王朝承认僭主政治期间颁布的立法;波旁王朝承认法国大革命和拿破仑帝国时期的立法。

# IX

# The Structure Of The Legal Proposition

The immediate basis of the legal order of human society is the facts of the law: usage, relations of domination, relations of possession, declarations of will, particularly in their most important forms, to wit: articles of association, contract, and testamentary disposition. From these facts the rules of conduct which determine the conduct of man in society derive. These facts alone, therefore, and not the legal propositions, according to which the courts render decisions, and according to which the administrative tribunals of the state proceed, are of authoritative significance for the legal order in human society. Nevertheless the legal propositions gain significance for the latter inasmuch as the decisions of the courts and the measures taken by the administrative agencies affect the facts of the law and thus bring about changes in the existing usages, relations of domination, relations of possession, articles of association, contracts, and testamentary dispositions, i. e. on this presupposition the decisions of the courts and the measures taken by the administrative agencies, which are based on the legal propositions, in turn produce norms which regulate the social conduct of human beings. New facts of the law therefore can be established not only, as in past centuries, by the application of force, or, as is usual in our days, by the silent, unobserved sway of social forces, i. e. particularly by new kinds of associations, new kinds of agreements, and testamentary dispositions, but also, at least indirectly, by means of legal propositions. For this purpose however it is not sufficient that the legal proposition should have formal validity, or that it should be applied in isolated cases; for an isolated fact is not a social fact. It is necessary for this purpose that men regulate their conduct according

# 第九章　法律命题的结构

人类社会法律秩序的直接基础是法律事实：习惯、支配关系、财产关系以及意思表示，特别是其中最重要的表现形式，即联合体的章程、契约和遗嘱处分。决定社会中人们行为的行为规则正是产生于这些事实。因此，对于人类社会法律秩序具有权威性意义的不是法院据以裁判、国家行政裁决机构据以处断的法律命题，而仅仅是上述这些法律事实。但是，法律命题为法律事实增添了重要性，因为法院的裁决和行政机构所采取的措施会影响到法律事实，进而改变现存的习惯、支配关系、占有关系、联合体的章程、契约和遗嘱处分，即：在这种假设下，建立在法律命题基础之上的法院裁决和行政机构的措施，反过来也产生调整人类之社会行为的规范。因此，新法律事实的建立不仅可以像过去的几个世纪那样靠施加武力，或者，像现今通常的那样，借助于无声的、不被察觉的社会力量的影响，即，特别是通过新型联合体、新型协议和遗嘱处分的方式，而且也可以——至少是非直接地——依靠法律命题。然而，法律命题具有形式上的有效性，或在孤立的案件中获得应用——因为孤立的事实不是社会事实——并不足以满足此目的。为了这一目的，人们有必要依据法律命题来调整他们的行为。一

to the legal proposition. A legal proposition which dictates to the courts and administrative tribunals the course of action which they are to follow contains what amounts to a legal norm for the courts and administrative tribunals as soon as these bodies actually carry it out; it becomes a rule of conduct only when the social relations are actually being ordered thereby.

The legal norms which are deriving from the legal propositions, therefore, always have reference to social relations, but the nature of this reference varies. The sum total of the legal norms which have validity for courts and other tribunals has never been identical with the sum total of social law; there have always been a number of social legal relations which have been free from all intrusion from this quarter. This appears more clearly in Roman law than in any other legal system, for no jurists ever had a clearer conception of the extent of their legal propositions than did the Roman jurists as to their *ius civile* and *ius honorarium*. There is a kind of official Roman family law; but side by side with it there were family relationships which were recognized socially only and which were regulated by no norms for decision, or almost none. These are concubinage and the matrimonial relation of a Roman with a person who did not have *connubium*—a relation which has been called by modern writers *matrimonium iuris gentium*—and the issue of these relationships which in their nature are very like marriage. The Romans have, at all times, exercised a peculiar kind of control over their freedmen concerning which a few precepts arose at a very late date in the Praetorian law. Up

旦法院和行政裁决机构实际执行了要它们遵守的法律命题,则这些命题实际上等于是包含了为法院和行政裁决机构设定的法律规范;只有当社会关系实际上因此被规整时,法律命题才能变为行为规则。

因此,源于法律命题的法律规范总是与法律关系有关,但是这种关联的性质各不相同。所有对法院和其他裁决机构均有效的法律规范的总和从没有跟社会法的总和相一致过;总是有很多的社会关系不受来自这方面的侵扰。在罗马法中要比在任何其他法律制度中表现得更清楚,因为没有法学家对他们的法律命题比罗马法学家对他们的市民法和荣誉法〔1〕有更清晰的概念。有一种官方的罗马家庭法;但与之并存的是指只被社会认可的、不受,或几乎不受裁判规范调整的家庭关系。后者就是罗马人跟没有通婚权〔2〕的人之间的非法同居关系和婚姻关系以及这些关系所产生的问题,现代著作家称此此种关系为万民法婚姻的一种关系,其性质很像婚姻。罗马人一直对自由民实施一种特殊的支配,关于这些特殊的支配,有一些规则到很后期的裁判官法中才出现。一直到那时,这种规则的实施主要靠社会手段。

---

〔1〕（拉）*ius honorarium*(法官法,荣誉法,裁判官法),指由执法官在司法审判过程中创立的法律规范总和。由于在罗马社会执法官是一种荣誉职位,因而此类法律规范常常被称为“荣誉法”。创立法官法的执法官主要为享有司法权的裁判官,因而,法官法有时也被称为“裁判官法”。

〔2〕（拉）*connubium*(通婚权),具体指罗马公民间的通婚权利以及伴随合法婚姻所形成的各项特殊权利,如父亲所拥有的家长权。

to that time it was enforced preponderantly by social means. The *precarium* is a typical instance of a possessory relation which was protected only by social law. The praetor began to extend a certain measure of protection to it, at least against third parties, by means of the *interdictum de precario*, but this was not done until the last days of the republic. For the longest time, the relations of possession of the *ager publicus* were of the same nature. The contradistinction between the *pacta*, which have only social validity, and the *contractus*, which are enforceable in the courts, is found throughout the whole course of Roman legal history. Express statements have been handed down to the effect that all testamentary declarations of the will, the *donatio mortis causa*, the *testamentum per aes et libram*, the *fideicommissum*, originally were transactions about which the state and the courts did not concern themselves. It is self-evident that this enumeration by no means

临时让与[1]是一个只被社会法律保护的占有关系的典型例子。裁判官开始通过针对临时让与的令状[2]提供对临时占有的特定范围的保护，至少是针对第三人的保护，但是这些直到共和国后期才完成。在最长的一段时间里，公田的占有关系也一直是这种性质。罗马法律史的整个进程中都可以发现在只有社会效力的简约和在法庭上可强制执行的契约之间一种对比的区别。对于所有遗嘱中之意思表示的效力，流传下来的表述是：根据遗嘱声明，死因赠与、[3]称铜式遗嘱[4]遗产信托，最初都是国家和法院并不关注的交易。不言而喻，这种列举决不能

〔1〕（拉）*Precarium*（临时让与），无名契约中的一种，表现为一方当事人允许另一方当事人取得对前一方物品的占有。受让人的这种占有是有条件的，即：有义务在出让人提出要求的情况下立即向该人实行返还，因此，有时候它可以被认为是受令状保护占有，但不能构成时效取得占有。

〔2〕（拉）*interdictum de precario*（针对临时让与的令状），当某人对某物虽不享有市民法所有权，但属于善意拥有者时，如果他人拒不向其返还被临时让与的该物，前者可以向执法官申请此令状以要求后者实行返还。

〔3〕（拉）*donatio mortis causa*（死因赠与），一种特殊的赠与，它的最终效力以赠与人先于受赠人死亡为条件，赠与人在死亡前有权随时撤销该赠与。受赠人不对赠与人的债务以及在占有问题上的恶意负责。在优士丁尼法中，死因赠与被遗赠所彻底取代。

〔4〕（拉）*testamentum per aes et libram*（称铜式遗嘱）。一种出现在公元前2世纪的遗嘱形式，具有一定的信托特点，表现为遗嘱人采用家产要式买卖的方式将遗产转让给自己的一位朋友，即家产买受人，委托其依照遗嘱人的意愿加以处置。此种遗嘱也称为民法遗嘱。

purports to be exhaustive. A reference may suffice to the *statu liberi*, to the position occupied by those freedmen who had not been formally manumitted before the praetor began to protect them in the enjoyment of their freedom, to the *fiducia*, to the oldest form of *locatio conductio*, to the *clientela*, which, even at the latest times, existed solely as a social institution.

We meet this relation between the norm for decision and the social law elsewhere. In the thirteenth century, Bracton, employing the phrases of Institutes 1, 3, 18, says concerning the English law of contracts: *Conventionalis (stipulatio) quae ex conventione utriusque partis concipitur, nec iussu iudicis vel praetoris; et quarum totidem sunt genera quot paene rerum contrahendarum, de quibus omnibus omnino se curia regis non immiscet, nisi aliquando de gratia.*

By way of illustration from modern law we may be permitted to mention the important role played by the religious marriage in many parts of Italy where a civil marriage is required by law; the various free associations which are not covered by the law of associations and on which, until a very recent date, the system of associations in France was based; the family community (Sadruga), which is still in existence among the southern Slavs of Austria but unknown to the positive law of Austria; the agreements found everywhere which are unenforceable legally and enjoy social recognition only; the testamentary gifts given in trust, by means of which religious associations which, until the

说是毫无遗漏的。不过提及一下半自由人、[1]那些在裁判官开始保护他们享有自由前还没有正式解放的自由民所居地位、信托、租赁最古老的形式以及受保护的地位,[2]就已经足够了,所有这些,即使是在现代,也只是单纯作为一种社会制度存在着。

我们在其他地方也遇见过裁判规范和社会法之间的这种关系。在13世纪,布莱克顿用了一些《法学阶梯》(Institutes,3,8)中的措辞,提到有关英国契约法:协议是根据双方的约定而产生的,它不是基于承审员的命令,也不是基于裁判官的命令。契约的标的有多少种,契约的种类就有多少种。

以现代法为例,请允许我们提及,在民法上的婚姻需要法律确认的意大利,宗教婚姻所发挥的重要作用;未被联合体法律涵盖的,乃至于直到最近法国联合体制度仍基于其上的,各种各样的自由联合体所发挥的重要作用;仍然存在于奥地利南部斯拉夫民族的,但却为奥地利实证法所不知的家长制家庭公社(Sadruga)所发挥的重要作用;在法律上不可强制执行、只能获得社会认可的、随处可见的协议所发挥的重要作用;通过信托方式的遗嘱赠

[1] (拉)*statu liberi*,半自由人;自由权附条件的人。指依照遗嘱在一定条件下获得自由的人,或在一定的时间或一定的条件下将获得自由的人。

[2] (拉)*clientela*,受保护的身份;受保护的地位。

most recent legislation on the subject, had not been recognized in France had accumulated property worth untold millions.

In my book, *Das zwingende und nichtzwingende Recht im burgerlichen Gesetzbuch für des Deutsche Reich* I have discussed the nature of the legal proposition and its relation to the situations of fact which it regulates. Referring the reader to this book, I shall introduce here only so much as is indispensable for the present discussion. Every legal proposition that contains a norm attaches a command or a prohibition to a given state of facts as the legal consequence of the latter. The state of facts which conditions the norm, the command, or the prohibition, is a fact of the law, i. e. a usage, a relation of domination or of possession, or a declaration of the will. In the case of a legal proposition which functions as a norm, we are always concerned, therefore, with the relation of the command or the prohibition which has been converted into a norm to one of the above named facts of the law. We must accordingly distinguish three classes of legal propositions.

In the first place there are legal propositions that accord the protection of the courts and other tribunals to the facts of the law as they exist in society. They do this either unconditionally or under certain-conditions by recognizing the usages of the associations as being legally effective, protecting relations of domination and of possession, enforcing contracts and testamentary directions. In all these instances the norms of the legal proposition conform as a matter of logical necessity to the norms which derive directly from the facts of the law, i. e. from usage, domination, possession, declaration of the will. These are the norms that result "from the concept," "from the nature of the thing." This is the proper place in law for the logical element, and logical necessity is raised to a sort of mathematical precision in so far as the concept of value enters in; for value, in fact, partakes of the nature of the mathematical: it is an equation. This juristic mathematics, "an arithmetic of concepts," therefore is found in the law of claims for damages and unjust enrichment; in the law of claims arising from contracts in which value is given for value, from contracts of barter, and from contracts for furnishing things for use (*Gebrauchsbeschaffungsverträge*). Distinguished from legal

与——通过该制度(直到最近,相关立法在法国才获得认可)宗教联合体积累了数不清的财富——所发挥的重要作用。

在我的《德意志帝国民法典中的强行法和非强行法》一书中,我已经讨论了法律命题的性质及其与所规制之情势的关系。建议读者参看这本书,我在此仅仅介绍对于目前讨论必不可少的部分。每一个包含规范的法律命题,对于一个给定事态,都会规定一个命令或禁令,以作为该情势的法律后果。这种以规范、命令或禁令为条件的事态就是法律事实,即习惯、支配关系或占有关系、或意思表示。因此,在法律命题作为一种规范来实施的情况下,我们一直关注已经转变为针对上述法律事实之一的规范的命令或禁令关系。因此,我们必须区分法律命题的三种类型。

首先,存在着与法院和其他裁决机构对社会中现存法律事实的保护相一致的法律命题。他们或者无条件履行职能,或者在特定条件下,通过认可联合体的习惯在法律上具有实际效力、保护支配关系和占有关系、执行契约和遗嘱指示而完成此项职能。在所有这些例子中,基于逻辑的必要性,这些法律命题的规范符合直接来自法律事实(即习惯、支配、占有、意思表示)的规范。这些规范从“观念”、“事物的本质”中产生出来。这是法律中逻辑要素的正确位置,就价值观念的注入而言,逻辑的必要性上升为一种数学的精密性;因为,事实上,价值具有数学的性质:它是一个方程式。因此,这些法律数学,“一种数学观念”,可以在要求赔偿金和不当得利法律中发现;可以在有关等价有偿的契约、易物契约和物之使用契约(*Gebrauchsbeschaffungsverträge*)所产生之请求

propositions of this kind are those that negate existing facts of the law or that self-actively create facts of the law. On the basis of legal propositions courts and other state tribunals artificially create or dissolve associations, establish or abolish relations of domination, give, take away, or transfer possession, rescind articles of association, contracts, testamentary declarations of the will, or occasionally create them by compulsion. Under this head are found chiefly the legal propositions that decree expropriation or forfeiture of things; that declare certain relations invalid, null, voidable, or punishable. Modern statutes undertake to coerce parties into performance of legal acts employing chiefly for this purpose a device called "*Reglementieren*," i. e. they prescribe a definite content for articles of associations and contracts, and supervise the observance of these regulations through state officials (registers).

It is self-evident that a social relation that is void, invalid, or punishable is something quite different from a relation that the courts and other state tribunals regard as lying outside of the legal sphere; a void marriage is something different from a relation that is no marriage at all; a society, membership in which subjects a man to punishment, is something different from a free association which lies outside of the scope of the law of societies; a prohibited contract is something different from a contract on which neither a complaint nor a defense can be based. They are denied the protection of the courts and other state tribunals, not on the ground that the law does not make provision for them but on the ground that they are to be banished from society. Of course, if courts and other tribunals tolerate them, or permit them to continue, in spite of the prohibition, then, from the point of view of the sociology of law, they do not constitute relations which are excluded from society by the legal propositions, but merely relations to which legal protection is denied; for the sociology of law is concerned, not with interpretations of legal precepts, but with the attitude of society toward them. We can see every day that void, forbidden, punishable marriages, societies, relations of domination and possession, contracts, *gifts mortis causa*, are actually being

权的法律中找到。与这种法律命题不同的一种是否定现存法律事实、或是自身积极创造法律事实的法律命题。以这些法律命题为基础,法院和其他的国家裁决机构刻意创造或者解散一些联合体,建立或废除一些支配关系,赋予、取走或者转移占有物,废除联合体章程、契约、遗嘱声明,或者不时地通过强制手段创造它们。在此条目下,主要是一些有关物之征用和没收的法律命题;还包括宣布特定关系无效、未成立或可撤销、可罚的等这样一些法律命题。现代制定法强制当事人从事合法行为,为此,主要采取了一种叫做"政府监督"的策略,即它们为联合体的章程和契约规定了明确的内容,并且通过国家官员(登记官)来监督这些规定的遵守情况。

显而易见,一种未成立的、无效的或可惩罚的社会关系完全不同于法院和其他国家裁决机构认定的处于法律范围外的社会关系;一个无效的婚姻关系与一个根本不存在的婚姻关系有些不同;一个社团——其中成员关系能使个人服从惩罚的社团——与处于法律范围之外的自由联合体有些不同;一个被禁止缔结的契约与一个既不能据以起诉又不能据以抗辩的契约有些不同。法院和其他国家裁决机构拒绝保护它们,不是因为法律没有为它们作出规定,而是因为它们被社会排斥。当然了,如果法院和其他国家裁决机构能容忍它们,或者允许它们继续下去,那么,它们尽管受到禁止,但是从法律社会学的角度来看,它们并没有构成被社会通过法律命题排除在外的关系,而仅仅构成了法律拒绝保护的社会关系;因为法律社会学所关注的并不是对法律规定的解释,而是社会对它们的态度。每天我们都能看到,无效的、被禁止的、可惩罚的婚姻,社团,支配和占有关系,契约,死因赠与实际

sustained; that even slavery, thinly disguised, flourishes, in spite of abolition and amenability to punishment, in South America, in the Congo Free State, in Russia.

A third species of legal propositions attaches legal consequences to facts of the law, quite independently of the norms that result from the usages, the relations of domination and of possession, and the dispositions created by these facts. Let us bear in mind certain rights and duties connected with ownership, i. e. *Bannrechte* and trade rights, the obligation to pay taxes, the duty to insure in connection with certain contracts, the duty of the owner of poisons and explosives to give notice.

The norms prescribed by the legal proposition therefore can either secure absolute enforcement for the norms that flow from the facts of the law or they can hinder them or invalidate them; and, lastly, they can attach legal consequences to them that bear no relation whatsoever to the legal consequences that flow from the facts. Accordingly the legal order which society self-actively creates for itself in the facts of the law, in the existing usages, relations of domination; and of possession, articles of association, contracts, testamentary dispositions, is brought face to face with a legal order which is created by means of legal propositions, and enforced solely by means of the activity of the courts and the other tribunals of the state. And norms, rules of conduct, flow from this second legal order no less than from the former, to the extent that it protects, gives form and shape to, modifies, or perhaps abolishes the facts of the law. And only those norms that are contained in these two legal orders constitute the whole law of society. The important thing for the norms of the second legal order is not the distribution of interests in the individual social associations, but the distribution in society as a whole, which comprises all the associations within a certain territory. The second legal order then is an order which has been imposed by society upon the associations.

The juristic writer, the teacher of law, and the legislator, who formulate the legal proposition, always act as persons commissioned by society, whether it be in virtue of the confidence which society places in them, as in the case of the Roman and of the common law jurists up to the time of the recent codifications, or in virtue of social or official position, or, as in the case of the legislator, upon the authority of the constitution of the state. The

上一直继续存在着；还有奴隶制度，尽管已经被废除，并且违法存在将会受到惩罚，但是，在稍稍伪装后，这种制度在南美、自由刚果、俄国还很活跃。

第三种法律命题为法律事实规定了法律后果，完全独立于由习惯、支配和占有关系以及这些法律事实所创造之处分而产生的规范。让我们记住有关所有权的特定的权利和义务，即禁令权和贸易权利、纳税的义务、与特定的契约联系的保险责任、毒药和炸药的所有人给予通知的义务等。

因此，法律命题所规定的规范要么能够确保源自法律事实之规范的绝对实施，要么阻止它们或使它们无效；最后，法律命题可以给这些规范附上与后者没有任何关系的法律后果。因此，社会在法律事实、现存的习惯、支配关系、占有关系、联合体的章程、契约、遗嘱处分中自身创造的法律秩序，就与通过法律命题创造的、并仅仅通过法院和国家其他裁决机构的活动来实施法律秩序，面对面地出现了。并且，从第二种秩序中产生的规范、行为规则与由前者创造出来的规范、行为规则一样，在其所保护的范围内，赋予法律事实以形式和形态，对其进行修改，或者废除它。仅仅包含在这两种法律秩序中的规范构成社会的全部法律。对于第二种法律秩序的规范来说，重要的不是在单个的社会联合体内进行利益分配，而是在某一地域内所有联合体组成的社会整体内进行利益分配。因此，第二种法律秩序就是一种由社会强加给联合体的秩序。

系统阐述法律命题的法学著作家、法律教师和立法者，不管是出于社会对他们的信任（正如在罗马的情形或是直到最近法典编纂时的共同法法学家的情形），还是凭借他们的社会地位或官

form and the content of a legal proposition are the result of the joint labors of society and of the individual jurist, and the sociology of law will have to distinguish the contribution of the former clearly from that of the latter.

The impulses to create law which result from the distribution of power in society have their source in society. The frequently used word *Machtverhältnisse* (distribution of power) indeed is not available as a scientific term because of its indefiniteness; we are using it here as referring to the distribution of power which is based on position in the state, on economic or on social position. Furthermore the legal proposition does not owe its existence to any consideration of the interests of individual classes or ranks, but of those of all social strata; and it is immaterial whether actual general interests are involved or merely imagined ones, as in the case of the superstitious belief in the existence of witches. Under this head comes the defense against external enemies and elemental forces. In the last analysis, at least in the judgment of those that act, the interests of individual strata of the population are general interests when popular opinion does not regard the interests of the other strata as worth taking into account, e. g. the interests of the slaves in Rome; up to the nineteenth century, quite generally, the interests of the unfree peasantry; in the Polish republic, and in ancient Hungary, usually, the interests of those who were not members of the nobility; and until late in the nineteenth century, the interests of the non-propertied classes. And for most modern men and women the interest of the utterly neglected (*Verwahrlosten*) and submerged (*Verlorenen*) perhaps is but little more than something to be protected against. In their opinion, the general interest includes protection of the social order against individuals who are beyond the pale of society. This protection may be effected by means of a part of the criminal law, police law, and procedural law. In reality all of this is a matter of the distribution of power. A decision rendered for the protection of the general interest may be said to be a decision based solely upon considerations of expedience. Wherever there is no doubt as to where the power lies in a state, or where the voice of popular consciousness speaks in no uncertain tones,

职，或者如在立法者的情形下，基于国家宪法的权威，总是作为社会的受托人行事。法律命题的形式和内容是社会和法学家个人共同的劳动结果，法律社会学必须对社会和法学家个人所作出的贡献予以清晰的区分。

源于社会中权力分配的创造法律的动力有其社会根源。因为 *Machtverhältnisse*（权力分配）这个词的不确定性，被频繁使用的这个词的确很不便作为科学术语；我们在此用这个词的意义是基于在国家中的地位、经济或社会地位之上的权力分配。而且，法律命题的存在并不归因于对个别阶级和阶层的利益的任何考量，而是归结为是对社会所有阶层之利益的考量；正如在相信巫婆存在之迷信观念的情形下，是涉及实际上的一般利益还是仅仅为想象的利益，都是无关紧要的。在这些人的领导下会出现对外部敌人和自然力量的反抗。归根到底，当大众观念认为其他社会阶层的利益——例如：罗马奴隶的利益；下至 19 世纪仍很普遍的非自由农民的利益；在波兰共和国和古匈牙利，通常不属于贵族成员的那些人的利益；直至 19 世纪末，那些无产阶级的利益——不值得考虑时，至少在对那些行为的评判中，个别阶层的利益就是一般利益。并且对于大多数现代男性和女性来说，完全被忽略（*Verwahrlosten*）和埋没（*Verlorenen*）的利益或许只不过与受到保护的利益是一样的。在他们看来，一般利益包括对社会秩序的保护——免受在社会范围之外的个人的侵扰。这些保护可以借助一部分的刑法、治安法和诉讼法实现。实际上，以上所有这些都大概是权力的分配。为了保护一般利益而作的裁决可以被说成是完全基于目的性考量的裁决。毋庸置疑，无论在哪里，只要权力在国家手中，或者只要公众意识的声音是坚定一致的，那么法学家的

the task of the jurist is a merely technical one. The content of the legal proposition is given by society. His function is merely to provide the wording of it and to find the means whereby the interests which are to be secured can be secured most effectively. This technical function however must not be underrated. The clumsiness of procedure and the limited capacity for expression of the material law often cause enormous difficulty in this matter. They are the cause of all formalism in law. Formalism is not an admirable quality of law, but a technical defect which must be overcome. A glance at Roman and English legal history reveals the difficulty which in time past was caused by the clumsiness of procedure. The state of our doctrine as to statement of the cause of complaint, as to proof, and as to content of the judgment shows that it is still troubling us. The invention *of the bonae fidei iudicia* by the Romans may be counted among the greatest achievements of the human mind in the field of law. Their work was continued in a splendid manner by the French courts; and, in Germany, by the Hanseatic courts, by the Nürnberg Court of Commercial Appeals, and by the Imperial Supreme Court of Commerce. Unfortunately the achievements of the German Commercial Courts have already been forgotten in part. The investigations that have been instituted in the field of the history of legal doctrine can give us an idea, as to Roman law at least, of the labor that had to be expended before the action of theft became an action *in rem*, before the liability of the possessor for pretended possession or for possession surrendered, for the

任务仅仅是技术上的。法律命题的内容是由社会赋予的。法学家的职责仅仅是提供表达法律命题的措辞,并找到可以为需要保护之利益提供最有效保护的手段。然而,这种技术性的职能不能被低估。诉讼程序的简陋性和对实体法律表达能力的有限性经常在这个问题上造成极大的困难。它们是造成所有法律形式主义的原因,形式主义并不是法律的一个可欲的品质,而是一个必须要克服的技术上的缺陷。粗略浏览一下罗马法和英国法的历史,就会明了在过去因诉讼程序的简陋所造成的不便。我们关于起诉事由的陈述、证据、裁决内容之学说的情形表明,它还在困扰着我们。由罗马人所创造的诚信审判〔1〕可以称得上是人类思想在法律领域中最伟大的成就。法国的法院以一种让人推崇的方式仍在继续着罗马人的工作;而在德国,这一工作由商业同业公会法院、纽伦堡商事上诉法院、帝国商事最高法院继续进行着。但不幸的是,德国商事法院所取得的成就已经被部分地遗忘了。在法律学说史领域发起的调查给我们一些有关这种工作的概念,至少就罗马法而言,在盗窃诉讼变为一种对物诉讼之前,〔2〕在占有人对冒充占有或抛弃占有的责任、对物(*Sache*)的毁损责任、对

〔1〕 (拉)*bonae fidei iudicia*(诚信审判),该词同 *actio bonae fidei*(诚信诉讼)。在诚信诉讼中,由于审判标准不是严格地由法律或裁判官的告示确定的,因而审判员享有较宽的裁量权,可以根据诚信的标准决定被告是否应当承担给付义务。诚信诉讼特别适用于委托、买卖或租赁契约有关的争议。它通常也被称做诚信审判。

〔2〕 确定当事人自身对诉讼标的享有的权利和利益的诉讼。其判决不仅对诉讼当事人有效,而且对所有的任何时间对该财产主张权益的人有效。在罗马法中称 *actio in rem* 或 *actio realis*。

destruction of the thing (*Sache*), for fruits and for damage done, was established and defined. The present most unsatisfactory state of many legal institutions is attributable, in a measure, to the fact that we have not as yet been able to establish technically perfect legal propositions concerning them.

The decision as to the interests involved in a dispute is entrusted by the state to the jurist when it is dearly indicated neither by the general interest nor by the distribution of power in society as a whole. This situation may be brought about by various causes. In the first place very often the parties to the dispute are quite unaware of the great social interests involved in the decision; very often the latter are distributed among the various classes and ranks in such a manner as to place them above the struggles of class and rank; in many cases these social interests are too inconsiderable and insignificant to become involved in the dispute. Very often, too, the possessors of power, who are called upon to render the decision, are not at all involved in the conflict of interests. The most important cause however is the fact that the powers that are engaged in the struggle in behalf of the different interests counterbalance one another or that the influences that proceed from the groups that are most powerful politically, economically, or socially, are checked or thwarted by other social tendencies, which are based on religious, ethical, scientific, or other ideological convictions.

When the jurist is asked to draw the line between the conflicting interests independently, he is asked, by implication, to do it according to justice. This implies, in the first place, something negative. He is asked to arrive at a decision without any consideration of expediency and uninfluenced by the distribution of power. In recent times, it is true, it has often been said that justice, too, is a matter involving questions of power. If the writer means to say that the idea of justice, on which the decision is based, must have attained a certain power in the body social at the time when it influences the judicial finding of norms or the activity of the state, he is indeed stating a truth, but it is a self-evident truth; and a self-evident truth does not require statement. But if he means to say that, under the cloak of justice, effect is always being given to the influence of political, social, or economic position, the statement is manifestly incorrect. A legal

孳息和对已造成之损害的责任被建立和界定之前，付出上述劳动是必不可少的。目前，许多法律制度令人最不满意的状况，某种程度上可归结为如下事实：关于这些法律制度，我们至今还没有能力建立技术上完善的法律命题。

在一个纠纷所涉利益明显既非普遍利益、亦非社会中整体的权力分配时，国家会把此类纠纷的裁决委托给了法学家。导致此种情形的原因多种多样。首先，很多时候，纠纷当事人没有注意到裁决中所涉及的重大社会利益；很多时候，这些重大社会利益在各种不同的阶级和阶层中以一种使他们超脱阶级和等级斗争的方式分配；很多情况下，这些社会利益太微不足道、太无关紧要，因而在纠纷中不会被提及。很多时候，需要作出裁决的权力人根本就没有卷入利益冲突。不过，最重要的原因是：斗争中代表不同利益的各种力量彼此相互抵消；或者是因为：产生于最强大政治、经济或社会团体的影响力被基于宗教、伦理、科学或其他意识形态之确信的社会趋势阻止或者抵制。

当要法学家在冲突的利益间独立地划一条界线时，其实是含蓄地要他依据正义来完成这一任务。这首先意味着一些反面因素。要求他在作裁决时没有任何目的性考量，不受权力分配的任何影响。的确，近来有人常说，正义也涉及到权力的问题。如果言说者的意思是——作为裁判基础的正义观念，当它影响到审判上规范的发现或影响到国家活动时，它必定已经在社会团体中获得了特定的权力，那么他确实陈述了一个事实，但这是一个不证自明的事实；一个不证自明的事实不需要陈述。不过，如果他的意思是说——在正义外衣下，政治、社会或者经济地位的影响总是产生效力，则这一表述就明显不正确了。一个起源可以追溯到

norm whose origin can be traced to such influences is usually stigmatized by that very fact as something unjust. Justice has always weighted the scales solely in favor of the weak and the persecuted. A just decision is a decision based on grounds which appeal to a disinterested person ; it is a decision which is rendered by a person who is not involved in the conflict of interests, or which, even though it be rendered by a person involved in this conflict, nevertheless is such as a disinterested person would render or approve of. It is never based on taking advantage of a position of power. When a person who is in a position of power acts justly, he acts against his own interest, at any rate against his immediate interest, prompted by religious, ethical, scientific, or other ideological considerations; perhaps merely by considerations of prudent policy. The parties of political and social justice, e. g. the doctrinaire liberals, the English Fabians, the German Socialpolitical or National-Socialist parties, the French Solidarists, find their adherents chiefly among ideologists who are not personally interested in the political and social conflicts of interests. In this fact lies their strength and also their weakness.

But all of these are negative characteristics. Which are the positive characteristics of justice? The catch phrase about balancing of interests which is so successful at the present time is not an answer to this question; for the very question is: What is it that gives weight to the interests that are to be balanced? Manifestly it is not the balancing jurist, writer or teacher, judge or legislator, but society itself. The function of the jurist is merely to balance them. There are trends caused by the interests that flourish in society which ultimately influence even persons that are not involved in these conflicting interests. The judge who decides according to justice follows the tendency that he himself is dominated by. Justice therefore does not proceed from the individual, but arises in society.

The role of the person rendering the decision is of importance only inasmuch as, within certain limitations, he can select the solution which corresponds most nearly to his personal feelings. But in doing

那种影响的法律规范通常会被那样的事实上打上不公正的烙印。正义总是使得裁断标准有利于弱者和受迫害者。一个公正裁决的基础是由公正无私的人来审判;那是一个与纠纷无利害关系的人所作出的裁决,或者即使他卷入到冲突中,不过他正如一个公正无私者那样来裁断该纠纷,或他就该纠纷所作的裁断会让一个公正无私者感到满意。这一裁决永远都不能以利用权力地位为基础。当一个当权者公正行事时,他其实是基于宗教、伦理、科学或者其他的意识形态的考量,而违背了自身的利益,至少是违背了其直接的利益;或许,他仅仅是出于谨慎策略的考虑。政治正义和社会正义的政党,例如:教条的自由主义者、英国的费边主义者、德国的社会政治党或者民族社会主义政党、法国的社会连带主义者,他们发现其追随者主要在那些自身对政治和社会利益冲突不感兴趣的思想家中。他们的力量在于此,弱点也在此。

但是所有的这些都是反面特征。什么是正义的正面特征?目前如此成功的、有关利益平衡的随兴而发的措辞并不是该问题的答案;因为真正的问题是:是什么给那些有待平衡的利益加重了分量?显然并不是那些在权衡的法学家、著作家或教师、法官或立法者,而是社会自身。法学家职责仅仅是平衡他们。社会中普遍存在的利益会导致某些倾向,这些倾向最终会影响到那些甚至没有卷入这些冲突利益之中的人。依据正义裁判的法官遵循着支配他自己的倾向。因此,正义并不是源自个人,而是产生于社会。

裁决者的作用之所以如此重要,仅仅是因为在特定的界限内,他可以选择最符合他个人情感的解决方案。但是这样做时,

this, he cannot disregard the social basis of the decision. If a Spartacus, favored by fortune, had abolished slavery in antiquity, or if the socialists should abolish private property, let us say in a beleaguered city, as was done in Paris during the days of the Commune, these facts would have nothing to do with justice. And a judge who, in a decision which he renders, recognizes private property in means of production in spite of the fact that he is a socialist, or who admits the defense that the debt sued upon in a stock-exchange transaction is a gaming debt although in his opinion the setting-up of this plea is a breach of good faith, does not thereby contradict himself. In doing these things he is merely being guided by social tendencies against his own individual feeling in the matter. A rebellious slave, the government of a beleaguered city, like that of Paris during the Commune, can indeed proceed according to their individual feelings, but they can do so only because they have been removed from social influences by the force of circumstances. Justice is a power wielded over the minds of men by society.

It is the function of juristic science, in the first place, to record the trends of justice that are found in society, and to ascertain what they are, whence they come, and whither they lead; but it cannot possibly determine which of these is the only just one. In the forum of science, they are all equally valid. What men consider just depends upon the ideas they have concerning the end of human endeavor in this world of ours, but it is not the function of science to dictate the final ends of human endeavor on earth. That is the function of the founder of a religion, of the preacher, of the prophet, of the preacher of ethics, of the practical jurist, of the judge, of the politician. Science can be concerned only with those things that are susceptible of scientific demonstration. That a certain thing is just is no more scientifically demonstrable than is the beauty of a Gothic cathedral or of a Beethoven symphony to a person who is insensible to it. All of these are questions of the emotional life. Science can ascertain the effects of a legal proposition, but it cannot make these effects appear either desirable or loathsome to man. Justice is a social force, and it is always a question whether it is potent enough to influence the disinterested

他也不能忽视裁决的社会基础。如果一个受命运青睐的斯巴达克斯党人在古代废除了奴隶制度，或者社会主义者——比方说在一个被包围着的城市里，如巴黎公社时期的巴黎——废除了私有财产，则这些事实与正义没有什么关系。一位法官尽管事实上是一个社会主义者，但在其作出的裁决中承认生产资料中的私人财产，或者一位法官认可了被告的抗辩——在证券交易中产生的债务是赌债的辩护，尽管该法官认为这种辩解有违诚信原则，这两种情形下，法官并未自相矛盾。这样做时，他仅仅是受到社会倾向的指引，而不受此事上个人感情的主导。一个反叛的奴隶、被包围之城市政府(如巴黎公社时期的巴黎)，确实能够按照他们个人的情感而继续存在下去，但是他们可以这样做，仅仅是因为已经除去了环境力量的社会影响。正义是社会对于人之心智所施加的力量。

法学的功能首先是记录社会中存在的正义倾向，并且确定它们是什么、来自何处和将导向何方；但是法学不可能确定哪一种倾向是唯一的正义。在科学的论坛里，它们都是同等有效的。人们所考虑的不过是取决于那些理念——在我们这个世界上人类努力的日标，但是表明人类最终的目标并非科学的功能。这是宗教的创始人、传教士、先知、道德规范的布道者、实用法学家、法官和政客们的功能。科学只能关注那些容易被科学证实的事情。某个事情是否正义，就像哥德式人教堂的壮丽或贝多分交响乐的华美对于一个对此毫无感觉的人一样，无法在科学上被证实。所有的这些都是情感生活的问题。科学可以确定法律命题的效果，但它却不能使这些效果看上去可欲或可恶。正义是一种社会力量，它是否有能力足以影响那些无利害关系的人——他们的职能

persons whose function it is to create juristic and statute law.

But although science can teach us nothing concerning the ends, once the end is determined, it can enlighten us as to the means to that end. The practical technical rules that perform this function are based on the results of pure science. There is no science that teaches men that they ought to be healthy, but practical medical science teaches men who desire to be healthy what they can do, according to the present state of the natural sciences, to bring about that result. Practical juristic science is concerned with the manner in which the ends may be attained that men are endeavoring to attain through law, but it must utilize the results of the sociology of law for this purpose. The legal proposition is not only the result, it is also a lever, of social development; it is an instrumentality in the hands of society whereby society shapes things within its sphere of influence according to its will. Through the legal proposition man acquires a power, limited though it be, over the facts of the law; in the legal proposition a willed legal order is brought face to face with the legal order which has arisen self-actively in society.

The idea that society must be governed by laws (legal propositions) is found among the ancient Greeks. It plays an important role among the Romans, appears again in the sixteenth century, and since that time has been the basic idea in all the great political and social trends in Europe down to the beginning of the twentieth century, especially in the absolute *Wohlfahrtsstaat* (state promoting the public welfare), in the mercantilistic, natural-law, and social-political movements. For the modern development of law it has attained an enormous, a fateful significance.

What can the sociology of law offer to juristic science in this sphere? The ultimate ends of our pilgrimage on this earth doubtless shall ever remain hidden from our eyes, but we can, at any rate, overlook a small part of the way. The highest aim of all science is to vouchsafe to us a glimpse of the future; the investigator gradually becomes a seer. As the physicist endeavors to determine the course of a cannonball in advance, so the disciples of the social sciences endeavor to calculate in advance the unifying regularities in the course of the future

是创造法学家法和制定法,这永远是一个问题。

虽然科学不能告诉我们关于目标的任何东西,但是目标一旦确定,它可以给我们有关到达目标之途径的启发。那些履行此功能的实践性技术规则,是以纯科学的成果为基础的。没有哪种科学告诉人们,人们应当保持健康,但是实践医学告诉那些渴望获得健康的人,按照现在的自然科学状态,人们能够做什么就会获得健康。实践性法学关注人们正努力通过法律达致其目标的方式,但是它为此必须利用法律社会学的成果。法律命题不仅仅是社会发展的结果,也是社会发展的手段;它是社会手中握有的工具,由此社会可以依其意志在其影响范围内塑造事物。通过法律命题,人类可以获得一种对法律事实的控制力,尽管这种力量是有限的;在法律命题中,一种具有某种意志的法律秩序与社会中自发产生的法律秩序面对面地产生了。

古希腊人中就存在社会必须受法律(法律命题)统治的观念。这一观念在罗马人中发挥了重要的作用,并在 16 世纪重新出现,从那时起,一直到 20 世纪初,这一观念成了欧洲所有重大的政治和社会运动的基本观念,尤其是成了在绝对的 *Wohlfahrtsstaat*(福利国家)、重商主义、自然法和社会政治运动中的基本观念。由于现代法律的发展,这一原则获得了重大的至关重要的意义。

在这一范围内,法律社会学给法学提供了什么?我们在这地球上的朝圣之旅的终极目标无疑将会隐藏在我们视线背后,但是至少我们可以眺望到旅程的一小部分。所有科学的最高目标是赐予我们对未来的一种瞰览;研究者逐渐变成一个预言家。如同物理学家努力地提前确定古炮炮弹的轨迹,社会学的信徒们也努力提前计算出社会事件未来发展进程的统一规律性。他们可以举出

development of social happenings. They can point to many great successes, particularly in the general sphere of economics, and every advance in sociological study will bring new successes.

Sociology teaches us the laws governing the development of human society and the effects of the legal propositions. It teaches juristic science how the legal propositions may be adapted to the laws of social development in accordance with their effects. Sociology indeed is just as far from teaching us that we must regulate our lives according to these scientific laws in the matter of our legal propositions and our conduct generally as the natural sciences are from telling us that we must be healthy. But men usually wish to do that which is expedient, just as, with very rare exceptions, they desire to be well. Accordingly on the basis of the results of the steady progress of the science of sociology, juristic science will be in a correspondingly better position to tell the judge and the legislator when they are performing useful labors, and when, inasmuch as they are resisting the laws of development and failing to understand the effects of the legal propositions, they are bootlessly frittering social forces away. If there is such a thing as *richtiges Recht* or to be more exact *richtige Rechtssätze*, they are those that advance the human race in the direction of its future development. It is true that inexpedient conduct can never be prevented altogether, for doubtless it has its function somewhere in the universal scheme of things, but solely in the nature of a hindrance, of a resistance of the means employed.

The sociologist, therefore, who on the basis of his scientific knowledge is endeavoring to draw a picture of the social order as it will exist in the future, and of a legal system that, even in the present, shall be adapted to the future, is by no means engaged in an unscientific undertaking. Marx's attempt to show the necessity of socialism by showing that social development must needs lead to socialism is not unscientific, at least no more so than the weather predictions of the meteorologist for the guidance of tillers of the soil, or the writings of geologists on the future of gold for the benefit of those engaged in directing monetary policy. It is true, unfortunately, that in investigations of this kind very much that is untenable sails under the

大量的成就,尤其是在通常的经济学领域内,社会学研究的每一个进步都会带来新的成就。

社会学教给我们支配人类社会发展和法律命题效力的规律。它告诉法学,法律命题可以怎样依其效果来适应社会发展。社会学的确绝不是教导我们,就我们的法律命题和我们的行为而言,我们必须依据这些科学规律来调整我们的生活,正如自然科学绝不会告诉我们必须保持健康一样。但是,人们通常总希望做合算的事情,正如人们渴望健康而很少有例外一样。因此,以社会学稳步前进的成果为基础,法学相应地也能够更好地告诉法官和立法者,他们什么时候正在做有用的工作,什么时候由于违背了发展规律、未能了解法律命题的效果而正在徒劳地消耗社会的力量。如果存在正义的法律——或更确切地说存在正义的法律命题——这样的东西,那么,它们就是能够推动人类奔向未来发展的力量。的确,不适宜的行为永远无法完全避免,因为无疑该行为会在事物的全部发展进程中的某处发挥自己的作用,不过却仅仅具有一种所采用手段之阻碍、抵抗的性质。

因此,社会学家正根据自身的科学知识,努力勾画未来的社会秩序和法律制度——即便在目前,它们也应当适应未来——的图景;他们绝不是在从事一项非科学的事业。马克思通过揭示社会发展必然会导致社会主义,试图证明社会主义的必要性,这种尝试不是非科学的,它至少和气象学者为了指导农夫耕种土地所做的天气预测一样,或者如同地质学者为了那些从事指导货币政策的人所撰写的有关黄金前景的论著一样。不幸的是,的确,在这种类型的研究中,许多站不住脚的东西在科学的旗帜下大行其

flag of science, but the blame for this must not be attributed to the subject but to the newness and incompleteness of this whole field of knowledge. And the query why every sociologist presents that which seems to him to be the end of the development as the end of all development beyond which mankind will never be able to go is, possibly, based on a misapprehension. The astronomer who is examining the uttermost nebulae that his telescope can reach, the microscopist who shows us the smallest particles that his instrument can lay hold on, do not deny that behind these worlds there are other worlds; behind these minute particles there lie things that are still more minute. So every sociologist knows that behind the horizon which limits his vision at the time there lie other horizons, which are withdrawn from his view, but he is content with that which is attainable. All these matters that have been presented up to this point, the relation of the legal proposition to society and its being conditioned by the social development, were clearly discerned by the founders of the Historical School; for what they call the legal consciousness of the people is but the trends of justice in society. It is true they were in error as to the scope of their doctrine, for the latter did not give an explanation of the law but only of the legal proposition; and not of every legal proposition, but only of the proposition that is based on justice; but even admitting this limitation we must say that their work of more than a century ago was a mighty deed. To what heights they towered above their successors appears from the fact that there has not been found among the latter a man able to continue building on the foundation which they had laid.

Perhaps the task which science must perform with reference to justice can best be shown by discussing a question which at the present time is violently agitating the colonial politicians of France. The nomadic tribe of Arabs on the rim of the desert in Algiers and in Tunis, who are owners of immense herds of sheep, camels, and horses, require not only extensive pastures for their herds but also long stretches of roadway in order to be able to

道,但是,对此不应当归咎于该学科,而应归咎于整个相关领域知识的崭新性和不完备性。而且,为什么每个社会学家将他认为是发展目标的东西当做是全部发展的目标——人类从来不能超越此目标——而提出来,这样的质疑很可能是基于一种误解。分析其望远镜所能看到的最远星云的天文学家,为我们展示其工具所能捕捉到的最小微粒的、使用显微镜的技术人员,他们并没有否认在这些世界后面还有其他的世界;在这些微小的粒子后面还存在着更为微小的粒子。所以每一个社会学家都知道,在限制其视野的地平线后面,还存在着他视线所不能及的其他地平线,但社会学家已经对他所达到的范围感到满足了。到此刻为止所阐述的全部内容、法律命题与社会的关系以及法律命题受制于社会发展,这些都被历史法学派清晰地辨别出来;因为他们所说的民众法律意识不过是社会正义的倾向。至于他们的学说范围,他们的确是弄错了,因为他们的学说并没有给出对法律的解释,而仅仅给出了对法律命题的解释;而且并不是所有的法律命题,而仅仅是那些基于正义的法律命题。不过,尽管承认此种局限性,我们还是必须说,他们在一个世纪前所做的工作是伟大的功绩。在何等高度上他们的成就超越了他们的继任者,可以从以下事实中看出:在他们的继任者中,没有发现一个人能够在他们建立的基础上继续构建。

或许科学必须完成的涉及正义的任务,可以通过讨论目前让法国殖民地的政客们极端激动的一个问题而得到最好的揭示。在阿尔及尔和突尼斯沙漠边缘上的阿拉伯游牧部落,他们拥有大量的绵羊、骆驼和马匹牧群,不仅仅为了他们的牧群需要广阔的牧场,而且为了能够在季节变化时,把他们的牲畜从一个牧场

drive their cattle from one place of pasture to another at the time of the changes of the seasons. Doing this, they cannot avoid entering upon land that is being tilled. Thereby agriculture on a large scale becomes impossible. Now is agriculture to continue in this wretched state in order that a few hundred Arabs may be able to find food for their herds? By way of reply one may put the counter question: Should several hundred thousand sheep as well as a great number of horses and camels be sacrificed for the benefit of agriculture on the rim of the desert, extremely precarious as it is in view of the "desperate uncertainty of rain," and incapable of development, since only ten thousand hectares are involved at most? A similar battle was raging in Switzerland about the middle of the nineteenth century between the tillers of the soil and the breeders of cattle (*Grossvieh*) on one side and the breeders of small cattle (*Kleinvieh*) on the other. The agriculturalists were on the side of the breeders of cattle because agriculture could expand only at the expense of the pasture for small cattle not of that for large cattle. It is said that there is a similar conflict of interests awaiting adjustment at the present time in Norway and Sweden between the Lapps, who are breeding reindeer, and the farmers, who are crowding them out of their pastures. Everyone who has concerned himself with Spanish national economics knows of the vast importance of the role played in Spain today by the pastures for Merino sheep, which make agriculture impossible in many parts of the country.

Questions of this nature and scope confront the jurist every day. Whether it be a question of defining the limit up to which a person engaged in an industrial enterprise may inconvenience a neighbor by noises and odors; of determining the extent to which the life, the health, the mental and the physical development of the workman must be considered in the case of a labor contract; of determining the standard according to which the usufructuary, after the usufruct has terminated, must make compensation for deterioration or may demand reimbursement for expenses incurred; of laying down a rule fixing the

赶到另一牧场,还需要长长的一条路线。这样做时,他们难免要进入正在耕种的土地。因此,大规模的农业生产就变得不可能。那么,为了让数以百计的阿拉伯人能够为他们的牧群找到食物,在这个不幸的国家有必要继续农业生产吗?人们可以提出相反的问题作为回答:鉴于此处沙漠地区那种“令人绝望的雨水之不确定性”和农业的无从发展性,难道仅仅因为这至多涉及到的10万公顷土地,几十万只绵羊和大量的马匹以及骆驼就应当为在沙漠边缘极不稳定的农业生产利益作出牺牲吗?大约在19世纪中期,相似的斗争也在瑞士激烈地进行着,那场斗争是土地的耕种者和牲畜的饲养者(*Grossvieh*)组成的一方和作为另一方的小牲畜的饲养者(*Kleinvieh*)之间展开的。农业学家站在了牲畜的饲养者一方,因为农业生产只有以牺牲放养小牲畜之牧场的利益,而不是以损害放养大牲畜之牧场的利益为代价的情况下,才能够发展。据说,目前在挪威和瑞典的卢普兰人,驯鹿饲养者与将前者挤出他们牧场的农民之间有一个类似的利益冲突等待裁决。任何一个关注西班牙国民经济的人都知道,饲养美利奴细毛羊的牧场今天在西班牙国民经济中所起的巨大作用,这些牧场使得这个国家许多地方的农业生产无以为继。

法学家每天都面临这种性质和这一范围内的问题。例如:确定一个从事工业企业生产的人因为噪音和气味而可能给邻人造成不便的限度的问题;确定在劳动契约中工人的生命、健康、身心发展必须被考虑到的程度的问题;确定标准在用益权终止以后,用益权人必须依据该标准,对损坏进行赔偿或者可以对发生的费用要求补偿的问题;制定一条规定竞

extent to which the clause concerning competition may limit an employee in the free exercise of his power to work; or of drawing up in statutory form the regulations according to which society should guarantee to the non-propertied classes a certain standard of living by means of a minimum wage, provision for illness, old age, unemployment, for widows and orphans: the just decision should always protect the higher interest where the interests are in conflict. But which is the higher interest?

If a decision were rendered, or a statute enacted, according to the wishes of the breeders of cattle or of the agriculturalists, of the persons engaged in industrial undertakings or of their neighbors, of the owners of land or of the usufructuaries, of the employers or of the employees, of the propertied or of the non-propertied classes, the decision would not be according to justice but according to power. If justice is to govern, the decisive factor must not be the wishes of one party or the other, but the question which of the conflicting interests are of greater importance to society, i. e. the interests of cattle-raising or of agriculture; of industry or of the sanitary condition of the neighborhood; of the owner of land or of the usufructuary; of the employer or of the employee; of commerce or of free exercise of one's powers; of increase of wealth in the hands of the propertied classes or of the welfare of the non-propertied classes. And he who is called upon to render a decision must take into account not only the present moment, but also the coming generations; not only the economic needs, but also the political, ethical, and cultural significance of cattle-raising and of agriculture, of industry and of public hygiene, of great landed estates and of rights of usufruct, of employer and of employee, of commerce and of free activity, of property and of the welfare of the non-propertied classes.

To render a decision of this kind is one of the greatest and most difficult tasks, and one most heavily freighted with responsibility. To answer questions of this kind means to be able to read the signs of the development of the future in the society of today, to sense its needs in advance, and to determine its order in advance.

争条款可能限制一个雇员自由运用其劳力范围之规则的问题;或者以制定法的形式作出那些规定依据该规定社会应当通过最低工资以及为疾病、老年、失业、寡妇与孤儿而采取的相应措施,从而保证无产阶级一定的生活水平的问题;在利益冲突时,公正的裁决应当总是保护更高的利益。但是,哪一个才是更高的利益呢?

倘若一个裁决的作出或一项制定法的颁布,是依据了牲畜饲养者的愿望或者农业学家的愿望,依据了工业企业的愿望或其邻居的愿望,依据了土地所有者的愿望或用益权人的愿望,依据了雇主的愿望或雇员的愿望,依据了有产阶级或无产阶级的愿望,则这一裁决就不是依据正义作出的,而是依据权力作出的。如果让正义去支配,则决定性因素不是一方或者另一方当事人的愿望,而是哪一种冲突的利益对社会更重要,即牲畜的饲养者的利益或农业的利益;工业的利益或邻近地区卫生条件的利益;土地所有者的利益或用益权人的利益;雇主的利益或雇员的利益;商业的利益或一个人自由行使权利的利益;有产阶级手中财富增加的利益或者无产阶级的福利利益。需要作出裁决的人不但要考虑当前的情形,还要考虑未来的几代人;不仅要考虑经济需要,而且也要考虑牲畜饲养、农业、工业和公共卫生、大宗土地产权和用益权利、雇主和雇员、商业和自由活动、有产阶级和无产阶级的福利在政治上、伦理上和文化上的重要性。

作出此种裁决是最伟大而艰巨的任务之一,裁决者承担着最沉重的责任。回答这种问题意味着能够理解当今社会中未来发展的迹象,能够预先感知社会的需要,并且能够预先确定社会的

If we shall ever be able to attempt this on the basis of scientific knowledge—and in a most modest measure it is being done to day—it will be found that only an intellect equipped with the full armament of science can be called upon to perform this task. Meanwhile our sense of justice is merely one of those great indefinite divinings of hidden interrelations in the vast scheme of things, which, like religion, ethics, and perhaps art, lead mankind to distant unknown goals. In these paths the genius is the born leader of mankind. Even in the most primitive days, the legislator and the judge stand in the thoughts of men by the side of the founder of a religion, the prophet, the poet. The genius is the more highly developed man in the midst of a human race that has remained far behind him; the man of the future, born, by a mysterious coincidence, into the present, who today thinks and feels as some day the whole race will think and feel. Therein lies his tragic fate, for he is lonely; and his sole compensation lies in this, that he shows the way to others. The divinings which conjure up the picture before the mental eye of the genius bestow upon him such a masterful insight into hidden interrelations as ordinarily might be expected only as a result of the most perfect knowledge. In his speech in the English House of Lords for the protection of laborers who were working at machines, Byron developed ideas of justice which did not penetrate into the consciousness of men who were trying to bring about social justice for at least fifty years; in his speech on the Irish question, he gave expression to a concept of justice that was first embodied in a bill by Gladstone; at the beginning of the nineteenth century he assisted in the renascence of Greece, which we all are marveling at today. For though justice is based on social trends, it requires the personal activity of an individual to make it effective. In this it is most like art. The artist, too, as we know today, does not produce his work of art from his inner self; he can but give shape to that which society

秩序。如果我们曾经能够以科学的知识为基础尝试这样做——今天正在一个最适度的规模上如此做——则可以发现,只有用全部科学装备武装起来的知识分子才会被要求去完成这一任务。与此同时,我们的正义感也仅仅是隐含于事物在宏大系统内相互关系中的那些巨大而不确定之预言的一部分,这种正义感也像宗教、伦理,或许也像艺术一样,引导人类通向遥远的未知目标。在这些道路上,天才是人类天生的领袖。即使在最原始的时代,立法者和法官也和宗教的创始人、先知和诗人一样,并立于人们心中。天才是人类中智力高度发达的人,其他人远远落后于他;天才是未来时代的人因为神秘的巧合而降生在今天的人,他今天的思考和感觉,正如将来某一天整个人类的思考和感觉一样。这也正是他悲惨的命运所在,因为他是一个孤独者;他所获得的唯一的补偿在于:他向其余的人指明了道路。用魔法描绘出的图景呈现于天才之慧眼前的这种先知,赐予他那样一种通透隐藏之相互关系的高超洞察力,这种洞察力通常只能认为是拥有最完美知识的结果。拜伦在英国上院发表的为保护在机器旁边工作的人的讲演中,他发展了一种正义观念,这种正义观念至少在五十年内,并没有渗入试图带来社会正义之人的意识中;在他关于爱尔兰问题的讲演中,他表达了一种首先体现在格莱斯顿法案中的正义观;在 19 世纪初,他协助希腊复兴运动,我们所有人现在对此极为惊讶。因为虽然正义以社会的倾向为基础,但是它需要个人的独立活动来使它产生效力。在这一点上,它与艺术最为相似。如我们今天所知,艺术家也不能通过内在自身创造出艺术作品。他只能塑造出社会提供给他的东西。但是,正如艺术作品需要艺术家为其覆盖上可见的形式一样,正义——尽管它

furnishes him with. But just as the work of art, although it is a result of social forces, requires an artist to clothe it in a visible form, so justice requires a prophet to proclaim it. And again like a work of art, which, though shaped out of social materials, nevertheless receives from the artist the stamp of his whole individual personality, justice owes to society only its rough content, but owes its individual form to the artist in justice who has created it. There is no such thing as one justice only, as there is no such thing as one beauty only, but in every work of justice there is justice, just as beauty speaks to mankind in every true work of art. Justice, as it has been given individual form in statutes, judicial decisions, works of literature, is, in its highest manifestations, the resultant of an inspired synthesis of opposites like every other grand creation of the human mind.

The mind of man is so manifold, the stratification of society is so variegated, that it is impossible to state the concept of justice in a single formula. Perhaps none has met with so much success as the formula which Bentham borrowed from Beccaria, to wit the greatest happiness of the greatest number. But it has never been "demonstrated," and it cannot be numbered among those truths that are evident without demonstration.

In the first place Bentham's formula will by no means convince everyone. Not the religious ascetic to whom earthly happiness in general appears as of no value whatever; not the member of the aristocracy according to whose ideas the "greatest number" has not been created for happiness but for labor and obedience; not the aesthete, to whom a Michelangelo or a Napoleon outweighs millions of the all-too-many; not the patriot, who is much more concerned with the power and greatness of his country than with the happiness of the individuals that constitute its citizens; not the energist, to whom striving and making his efforts effective is of much greater importance than happiness. This formula will gain adherents only among those who are convinced of it from the outset—those who consciously are democrats. It is a

是社会力量的结果——需要一个预言者来宣告它。其次,正义与艺术品第二个相似的地方在于,虽然艺术品从社会的素材中成形,不过它从艺术家那里获得了自己的全部个性标记,而正义源自社会的只是其大致内容,但正义的个别形式却归功于创造正义的艺术家。就像没有唯一的美一样,也没有唯一的正义,但是在每一本正义的著作中都存在正义,正如同美对于人类来说,存在于每一件真正的艺术作品中。如同制定法、司法裁决和文献著作中赋予正义的个别形式一样,正义,在其最高表现形式,是对立面在神灵的启示下综合的结果,如同人类思想每一个其他的伟大创造一样。

人类的思想是如此纷繁复杂,社会的层次是如此丰富多样,所以无法用单一的公式来表达正义的观念。或许,从来没有哪个人像边沁从贝卡里亚借用的公式那样取得那么多的成功,这个公式即最大多数人的最大幸福。但是,它从来没有被"证实"过,并且,它也不属于那些不证自明的真理。

首先,边沁的公式决不会让每一个人都服膺。"最大多数人"不是宗教禁欲者,世俗的欢乐对他来说通常没有任何的价值;不是贵族成员,依据他们的观念,"最大多数人"生来就不是享福的,而是劳动和服从的;不是审美学家,对他来说,米开朗基罗或拿破仑要比太多太多的普通人重要得多;不是爱国者,他们关心国家的强盛和伟大要比关心构成国家公民的个体快乐为甚;不是干劲十足的人,于他而言,努力奋斗并使之产生效果,要比幸福更重要。这个公式只能在一开始就深信它的人中获得拥护者——那些自觉要成为民主主义者的人。它是一个民主主义者的口号,这样说我们其实是

democratic catchword, and saying this we have said by implication that it expresses the thoughts and feelings of a small minority only. For democracy is an aristocratic thought. There are no true democrats other than those who are aristocrats in their intellectual natures; among those who are aristocrats by birth only those are democrats who have inherited this distinctive feature with their rank. The plebeian is never a democrat. He demands equality only with those who are above him, never with those that are below him. There is something of the highest quality of nobility, a consciousness of enormous power, an unconquered defiance, in not only refraining from demanding privileges but also rejecting them when they are offered.

And what did all these democrats among aristocrats and aristocrats among democrats take the words "greatest number" to mean? To the Gracchi they were several hundred thousand proletarians among the Roman commonalty; to Ulrich von Hutten, the German order of knights, which certainly was not more numerous; to Bentham himself, the middle classes of the urban bourgeoisie; to Marx, the millions of the laboring classes. If one had demanded of the Gracchi that they should grant to the non-Italic peregrine equal rights with the citizens, or of Hutten that he should grant to the peasants equal rights with the knights of the Empire, they

在暗示,它仅仅表达了一小部分人的思想和情感。因为民主政治是一种贵族式的思想。除了那些在智识天性上的贵族外,没有真正的民主党人。在那些因为出生而成为贵族的人当中,只有那些继承了该等级独特特征的人才是真正的贵族。贫民从来都不是贵族。他要求的平等,仅仅是和那些地位高于他们的人平等,而不是与那些地位低于他们的人之间的平等。贵族的最高品性,一种对巨大权力的警觉,一种未曾被征服过的反抗,不仅仅在于克制而不要求特权,而且也在于拒绝不请自来的特权。

所有这些贵族中的民主主义者和民主主义者中的贵族,使用“最大多数人”这样的措辞意指什么呢?对于格拉古兄弟[1]来说,他们是罗马平民中好几十万的无产者;对于乌尔里希·冯·胡腾来说,他们指的是德国的骑士阶层,当然后者的数量并不更多;对于边沁本人来说,他们指的是城市中的中产阶级;对于马克思来说,他们指的是有数百万人的工人阶级。倘若某人向格拉古兄弟要求他们应当授予非意大利的外来民族以平等的市民权,或者向胡腾要求他应当授予农民与帝国的骑士平等的市民权,

〔1〕 古罗马的 Gracchi 兄弟,哥哥叫 Tiberus,于公元前 133 当选为保民官,提出土地改革,规定公民每户公有地不能超过 1000 尤格,超出的土地由国家买入收归国有。由一个三人委员会负责分配土地并划分每块 30 尤格给贫农。法案通过的来年他却被利益冲突的元老院贵族挑起的械斗杀害。弟弟 Caïus 于公元前 123、122 任保民官,他重申哥哥 Tiberus 的土地法案,还提出了实行赈济城市贫民的粮食法、授予骑士司法权的审判法、国家向平民廉价供应粮食、在亚细亚行省由包税人负责征收什一税、改组审理行省中官员违法案件的法庭、在迦太基遗址设殖民地、授予意大利人罗马公民权等。弟弟也被反对改革的元老院贵族杀害,但是他通过的法案大多保留下来,促进了罗马社会改革。

would have considered such a proposal most unjust. Bentham contented himself with the cold comfort that it is possible even for the lowest working-man to rise into the middle classes—perhaps for one among ten thousand. Is that the "greatest number"? The idea of offering some sort of assistance to factory workers by means of a very moderate social policy first occurred to Bentham's greatest disciple, John Stuart Mill. From the standpoint of pure arithmetic, Marx surely was right. But in his whole book there is not a single line on the question how the socialization of the means of production can be made to benefit those who are beyond the pale of society. And if one considers the population of the whole world, the latter surely are the "greatest number." And in a socialistic Utopia published, prefaced, and recommended by Kautsky, one of his most faithful disciples, we find the doctrine that the socialistic society will secure tropical fruits and other products through enforced negro labor, for "the negro will not work voluntarily."

And finally, what is the meaning of the "greatest happiness"? To Bentham and his disciples these words meant, in a general way, the economic well-being of the middle classes and the greatest possible scope for the free exercise of the powers of the individual. But is it not true that they who have the deepest insight into human nature have pointed out that the "greatest number" are happiest when they are led by strong men who forge their fates for them? When their individuality is merged in a community, or even when they serve a master who provides for the day, and in the evening protects them from privation and misery? Is it not true that a perhaps equally "great number" experience the greatest happiness when they live in contemplative laziness, at the expense of someone else, albeit suffering great privations withal? Bentham's conception of the greatest happiness is that of a certain class, in a certain country, at a certain time, to wit the middle classes in England at the beginning of the last century.

则他们会认为这样一个建议是极不公正的。边沁自己满足于冷漠的安慰:即便是生活水平最低的工人,他们也有上升为中产阶级的可能——或许只有万分之一的人有此幸运。这就是那个"最大多数人"? 边沁最伟大的弟子——约翰·斯图亚特·密尔首先想到,通过非常温和的社会政策,为工厂工人提供某种帮助。从纯粹的算术的立场来看,马克思当然是正确的。但是,在他的整部书里,关于——生产资料的社会化如何能够造福于那些游离于社会范围之外的人——这个问题,他没有提供任何的解决途径。并且,如果有人考虑到整个世界的人口,那么后者确实是"最大多数人"。在由他的一位最忠实的信徒考茨基出版、作序和推荐的一本社会主义的《乌托邦》中,我们发现了以下学说:社会主义社会将通过强制黑人劳动来获得热带水果和其他产品,因为"黑人是不会自愿劳动的"。

最后,"最大幸福"是什么意思呢? 对于边沁及其门徒而言,这几个词一般说来意指,中产阶级在经济上富裕,并且个人在最大可能范围内自由行使权力。但那些对人性有最深刻洞察力的人指出:当"最大多数人"被那些塑造他们命运的强人所带领时,是最幸福的,难道这不是真的吗? 当他们的个体性融入一个团体时,或甚至当他们服务于一个主人——白天供给他们食物,晚上使他们免于贫穷和凄惨——时,他们不是最幸福的吗? 当或许同样"多数"的人以其他人——虽然后者同时遭受了巨大的困苦——为代价而生活在沉思冥想的懒散中,他们难道不的确是在体验着最大的幸福吗? 边沁的最大幸福的概念指的仅仅是特定时代、特定国家之特定阶级的最大幸福,即19世纪初英格兰的中

Carlyle submitted a concept which was diametrically opposed to this, and which was equally good for a different social stratum of the same country at the same time. Happiness is a meaningless word in general, which does not correspond to any actuality. It would be hard to find a man to whom it means anything definite; perhaps no two men to whom it means the same thing. And in general happiness has nothing to do with legislation and the administration of justice. Nevertheless Bentham was right and carried his point; for he put into the form of a clear juristic demand that which in his day had been the vague ideal of a powerful trend of justice. But his doctrine is of no significance beyond the class, the time, and the place.

There is no formula in which the idea of justice is summed up and fully expressed; it is a term that expresses a way and a goal—a goal which lies in the sunlit distance, which the human mind can divine, but not know, and a way which man must tread with faltering and uncertain steps. He who shall be able to speak the last word on the subject of justice will thereby have found the law of the development of the human race, perhaps of the universe. Meanwhile science must rest content to contemplate the line of development which has been graven into the past and to divine that which the near future will trace out for it.

It is a long way that leads from the inner order of the associations to the legal propositions of our codes and juristic handbooks. In primitive times only the legal propositions governing procedure and the regulations concerning penalties are being created; and they are being created solely according to considerations of expediency. The norms that are contained in these propositions belong to those that constitute the second order of society, for they do not order and regulate the associations directly but are designed merely to ward off dangers. The norms of the first order, which are required by the exigencies of litigation, do not as yet exist in the form of legal propositions; they derive from the inner order of the associations through univer-

产阶级的最大幸福。卡莱尔提出一个与此截然相反的观念，该观念对某个时代某个国家的所有不同社会阶层均有利。总的来说，幸福就是一个没有任何意义的词语，幸福不对应于任何现状。要找出幸福对一个人的确定含义，是非常困难的；或许它对任何两个人来说，含义都是不同的。所以，通常情况下，幸福与立法及司法无任何关系。然而，边沁也是对的，并且也达到了他的目的；因为他植入了一个清晰的正义要求的模式，那种正义要求在他那个年代还只是有关正义强大趋向的模糊理想。但是他的学说一旦超越特定的阶级、时间和地点外，就变得没有任何意义。

不存在任何一个公式，能够总结正义的理念并将之充分表达；正义是表达一条道路与一个目标的术语；那个目标就躺在阳光照射的远方，人类思想能够察觉，却不能认知，那条道路是人们必须用蹒跚而不确定的步伐行走于其上的道路。任何一位能够对正义这个话题作总结陈词的人，将会由此而找到人类发展的规律，或许能找到宇宙发展的规律。同时，科学必须乐于思索铭刻于过往的正义发展路径，并预言不远的将来正义会被描绘成什么样子。

从联合体的内在秩序到我们法典和司法手册中的法律命题，其间有长长的一段路。在远古时代，只创立了管控法律诉讼和有关刑罚规定的法律命题；创立这些法律命题也纯粹是基于目的性考量。包括在这些法律命题中的规范属于构成社会次级秩序的规范，因为它们不直接规整和管控联合体，它们的设计目的仅仅为了避免危险。诉讼所迫切需求的一级秩序规范，还没有以法律命题形式出现过；这些规范通过一般化和化而

salization and reduction to unity, or they are being obtained by a process of free finding, and are not being developed into universally valid legal propositions until a later time. At the same time the legal propositions of the second order grow in number and power, an ever richer procedural law develops, the regulations as to penalties are being converted, in part, into a law of damages, and, in part, into a law of crimes. Finally state law arises as the norm for the decisions of the courts, and as the basis for action by the state.

At each of these stages, society is as active as the jurist. Every legal proposition is shaped out of materials furnished by society, but the shaping is done by the jurist. It is indeed the norms that are already prevailing in society that, universalized and reduced to unity, become legal propositions; but in the last analysis the jurist decides what is to be universalized and reduced to unity, which of the various orders of the family that come within his sphere he is to treat as the model order according to which he decides the controversies that arise in the others, which of the various contents of contracts that occur furnishes the standard for the decision of controversies arising from all like contracts. The purpose of the free finding of norms is merely to eke out and to take the place of the inner order of the associations where the latter fails in the adjudication of litigation; and the whole "second order" is destined, from the very beginning, to surround the inner order of the associations, as it is being created anew every moment by usage, relations of domination and of possession, with a wall of defense against attack and danger. The law governing interference by society and the state with the inner order of the associations also proceeds at all times from a larger social or state association, which is endeavoring to exert influence over the smaller associations of which it is composed. However great the extent to which these norms arise from the relations already existing in society, the jurist who transforms them into legal propositions must supply not only the wording but also a great deal of the content. But the jurist who in this manner places the stamp of his personality upon the legal proposition in turn is subjected to the influence of society. Its distribution of power, its ideas of the general interest, its trends of justice dictate to him what he is to

为一的方式，从联合体的内在秩序中产生，或者它们在自由发现的过程中产生，并且，直到后来，它们才发展成为普遍有效的法律命题。与此同时，次级秩序的法律命题在数量和权威上有所增长，一个内容不断丰富的诉讼法发展起来，关于刑事赔偿金的规定部分地转变为损害赔偿法，部分地转变为刑法。最终，国家法作为法院的裁判规范和国家行动的基础而发展起来。

在每一个发展阶段中，社会和法学家一样积极。每一个法律命题都是源于对社会所提供之素材的塑造，但这种塑造却是由法学家完成的。经一般化与化而为一之后成为法律命题的，的确是已盛行于社会的规范；但归根到底，要由法学家来决定对哪些予以一般化和化而为一；在他的领域内，纷繁多样的家庭秩序中，他要将哪一种作为模范秩序，在其他类型家庭秩序中产生的争议均按照此标准来裁断；各种各样的契约内容，哪一种将作为标准，用以裁断所有类似的契约。规范之自由发现的目的不过是在联合体内部秩序不能解决诉讼的裁断时补充并取代它。从最开始时，整个"次级秩序"就注定要围绕在联合体内在秩序周围，就像它由惯例、支配和占有关系每时每刻重新创制出来，保护联合体免受攻击和危险的防护之墙。调整社会和国家对联合体内部秩序干涉的法律，也始终产生于一个更大的社会联合体或国家联合体，后者会努力地对构成它的较小联合体施加影响。然而，这些规范无论多大程度上源于已存社会关系，把它们转化为法律命题的法学家不仅要为它们提供措辞，而且也要为它们提供大量的内容。但是，这些通过这种方式在法律命题上烙下自己个性的法学家，反过来也要受到社会的影响。权力的分配、普遍利益的观念以及正义的倾向，都指令他要对哪些内容予以一般化和化而为一，

universalize and reduce to unity, what norms he is to find for the relation that is in dispute, what is to be protected against attack and danger, what is to be surrendered to the latter, where the selfcreated order of the associations is to be modified or abolished. Only a small part of the legal proposition therefore is the expression of the personality of its author to such an extent that one might assume that it would not have been worded as it is had it been created by a different person. And even at this point we must not fail to observe to what extent every man, even the most individual genius, is a resultant of the influences of his environment, that every man can be born and work only in a given society, that everywhere else he would be impossible and would make shipwreck.

The prevailing school of jurisprudence, which sees in every legal proposition only the expression of the "will of the lawgiver," altogether fails to recognize the important part of society in its creation. The teachers of the Natural Law School, in their day, had a much deeper insight into the matter inasmuch as they endeavored to base the law upon the sense of justice, i. e. upon the social trends of justice; Savigny and Puchta with their doctrine of the popular consciousness of right and law as the basis of legal development merely restated thoughts of the natural law in terms of a social point of view. Bentham, by his principle of utility, with which Jhering's *Zweck im Rechte* coincides in the main, for the first time, in a comprehensive manner, directed attention to the general interest, which, it is true, he often enough confused with the interest of a single class, the bourgeois middle class. The materialistic interpretation of history went much further than the natural law doctrine, than the Historical School, than Bentham and Jhering. It pointed out to what extent the law, and therefore also the legal propositions, are a superstructure erected on the foundation of the economic order, and also to what extent the legal propositions are being fashioned and created under the pressure of the distribution of power in society. But in doing this it became biassed, for it intentionally excluded from its consideration the element of human personality, the trends of justice as well as all non-economic influences which it always, and occasion-

要为处于争议关系发现什么样的裁判规范,哪些(关系)应当受到保护以免受到攻击和危险,哪些要向后者屈服,在哪些地方联合体自己创立的秩序要被修改或废除。因此,只有一小部分的法律命题是其作者的个性表达,在那样的范围内,人们可以设想,当法律命题由不同的人创立时,其措辞是不一样的。而且,甚至在这一点上,我们也不能不注意到,在何等程度上,每个人——即使最有个性的天才——也都是其周遭环境影响的结果,每个人都只可能在一既定社会中出生和工作,在其余任何地方,他都将不可能存在,必会走向毁灭。

把每一个法律命题仅仅视为“立法者的意志”的主流法学流派,完全没有认识到社会在法律命题创设中的重要作用。自然法学派的教师们在他们生活的年代对这一情况有深刻的洞察,因为他们努力把法律建立在正义感之上,即建立在社会的正义倾向之上;萨维尼与普赫塔把民众的权利和法律意识作为法律发展基础的学说,仅仅是用社会视角的术语重述了自然法学的思想。边沁藉着他的效用原则——耶林在其《法律的目的》中大致表达了相同的理念——首次以一种全面的方式,把人们的注意力集中到普遍利益之上,当然,他经常将这个普遍利益与单一阶级,即资产阶级的中产阶级的利益混为一谈。历史唯物主义的解释远远超越了自然法学说,超越了历史法学派,超越了边沁和耶林。历史唯物主义指出,在何种程度上,法律——因此亦即法律命题——是建立在经济秩序基础上的上层建筑,并且在何种程度上,法律命题在社会权力分配的压力下被塑造和创立。但是,这样做时,历史唯物主义开始变得有了偏见,因为它故意排除了对人类个性因素、社会正义倾向和非经济因素影响的考量,

ally in an extremely arbitrary manner, traced back to economic ones, and usually, though quite unintentionally, all consideration of the general interest. The sociology of law must not overlook any of these things; it must consider everything that takes part in the creation of the legal proposition.

它总是——偶尔以一种极端恣意的方式——将这些追溯到经济因素,并且通常——尽管是完全无意识地——追溯到对普遍利益的所有考量。法律社会学不能忽略这些事物中的任何一个;它必须考虑到法律命题创设中起作用的全部因素。

# X

# The Varying Content Of The Concept Of Justice

The creation of the legal proposition takes place everywhere under the influence of the concept of justice. On the basis of this concept, the judge finds the norms for his decision when there is no legal proposition to guide him. A statute, a judicial decision, an administrative action by the state, is judged according to its inherent justice. Every political party has chosen justice, at least according to its alleged conviction, as its goal. In all these cases, what is the concrete content of the concept of justice? And since, in the case of the norm for decision, of the legal proposition, of criticism, of political parties, in general in the case of all law, we are dealing with interests which are to be protected, or to be given effect to by law, we must put the question thus: Which are the interests that are considered just? Hedemann has investigated this question in a wider connection, limiting his investigation however to the private law legislation of Germany, Austria, and Switzerland in the nineteenth century, and has solved it in a manner that meets the most rigorous demands of science. Here however we must disregard the usual classification of law. We are not concerned with the influence of justice upon private law, criminal law, administrative law, procedural law, but with interests which are to be protected by private law, criminal law, administrative law, and procedural law, according to justice.

The legal history of the primitive period of the nations of Europe presents a picture of an administration of justice by the state which is limited altogether to things that immediately concern the state: attempts on the life of the king, trading with the enemy, violation of military discipline. Apart from these things, legal protection is a matter for the primitive or genetic associations, the

# 第十章　正义观念多变的内容

在正义观念的影响下，法律命题的创设无处不在。以此观念为基础，法官在没有可资指导的法律命题时，会自己去发现裁判规范。评价一部制定法、一项司法裁决与一个国家行政行为，依据的都是其内在的正义。每一个政党，至少按照它自称的信念，都选择正义作为自己的目标。在所有这些情形中，正义观念的具体内容是什么？既然在裁判规范、法律命题、批判、政党等情形下，通常在所有的法律情形下，我们处理的是要受到法律保护或由法律赋予效力的利益，那么，我们必须提出这一问题：什么样的利益被认为是公正的？黑德曼虽然把自己的研究限制在19世纪德国、奥地利和瑞士的私法立法，但是，他在更广阔的背景下研究了该问题，并以一种符合最严格的科学要求的方式将其解决。然而，在这里，我们必须不理会法律的通常分类。我们不关注正义观念对私法、刑法、行政法、诉讼法的影响，而关注依正义观念，私法、刑法、行政法和诉讼法要保护的那些利益。

欧洲民族原始时期的法律史呈现了一幅国家司法的图景，那时，国家司法完全限于跟国家直接相关的事情：企图杀害国王、通敌和违反军纪等。除了这些以外，法律保护是原始或原生性联合

clan, the family, the household, which are being held together by the strong conviction of each individual member that he can maintain his existence in this world, filled with violence and outrage as it is, only by the closest possible union with his own. These genetic associations create the courts, regulate procedure, create the first legal propositions. We are fairly well informed on these matters through a series of statements of law which date from the earliest times. As to the law of Europe, it is chiefly the Twelve Tables of the Romans, the Germanic popular laws, which came into existence at about the same stage of development, the Scandinavian sagas, and a few Slavic sources of law that are to be considered. From these we gather that in the society in which this law was in force thc most vital concern was to repel violence directed against the state, the person, life, and possession. These ancient regulations refer almost exclusively to murder, homicide, wounding, robbery, theft, and despoiling of inheritances. The legal precepts contained therein are engrossed with concern for the state, for the life of the people, for the peace of the domestic hearth, of possession, and of the workshop. These are the only interests that are considered worth protecting, and legal protection is extended by means of self-help, vengeance of blood, outlawry, and finally by means of a money penalty. These legal propositions, which according to the modern conception should be included in criminal law, are the prototype of all those upon which, down to the present day, the legal security of the state, of the person, and of possession are based.

It is a remarkable fact that everywhere, after the first codifycations, tradition is silent for a long time. Among the Romans as well as among the Germans the dark centuries begin. Very little information has been handed down to us concerning the creation of law during this time. As soon as the sources begin to flow more plentifully, we see a picture that is quite different. This took place in Rome about the end of the Republic; among the Germanic peoples about the thirteenth century; in England the darkness was dissolved at a somewhat earlier date; among the Scandinavians, in the fifteenth century.

体、氏族、家族、家庭的事，这些联合体因每个成员的此等强烈信念——要是想在这样一个充满暴力和暴行的世界中维持自己的存在，就只能与其所属联合体保持可能的最亲密的契合——而结合在一起。这些原生性联合体建立了法院，规范了诉讼程序，创设了第一批法律命题。通过源自最早年代的一系列法律陈述，我们熟悉了这些事情。至于欧洲的法律，要考虑的主要是罗马人的《十二铜表法》、大约在同一发展阶段形成的日耳曼民间法、斯堪的纳维亚的中世纪传奇和一些斯拉夫人的法律渊源。从这些资料中，我们可以得知，社会中生效的法律最主要关注的是抵御对国家、人身、生命和占有的暴力侵害。这些古代规定几乎全部指向谋杀、杀人、伤害、抢劫、偷窃和掠夺遗产。那时这些法律规定的全部关怀落实于国家、人民的生命、国内家庭的和睦、占有和工场。所有的这些被认为是唯一值得法律保护的利益，并且法律通过自救、血亲复仇和放逐、并最终通过赎罪金的方式对它们提供保护。这些法律命题——按照现代法律观念应当包含在刑法中——直到今天仍是对国家、人身和占有进行法律保护所立基的原型。

一个显著的事实是：第一次法典编纂以后，在所有地方，传统都沉寂了很长一段时间。在罗马人和德国人当中，黑暗的世纪来临了。在这段时期内关于法律的创设方面，几乎没有什么信息传继下来。原始文献之水流一旦增大奔涌而来，我们就立刻看到了一幅完全不同的画面。在罗马这大约发生在共和国末期；在日耳曼民族这大约发生在 13 世纪；在英国，黑暗则在更早一些的时候就被驱散了；在斯堪的纳维亚人中，这大约发生在 15 世纪。

The interests that are considered worth protecting are the same as in earlier days, i. e. the state, the human body and human life, possession ; but the means are considerably more ample and diversifted. First of all the state acts much more frequently, exercising its power to punish not only when the state itself is concerned but also, and with increasing frequency, when the security of the bodies, of the lives, and of the possessions of the people is concerned. Furthermore the state has secured control of the social courts to a great extent, and through these affords a much more effective protection than society was able to afford at an earlier time. At the same time that the state administration of justice undertook the protection, by means of deterrence, against violence, crafty and thievish interference, the conversion of the penalty into payment of damages for damage done made it possible to grant satisfaction for the wrong done not only in case of violent, crafty, thievish interference, but also in case of interference of other kinds. And lastly we find the action for the vindication of a right in the narrowest sense of the term, the object of which is to secure for the person entitled the very subject matter of his right, i. e. the thing of which he claims ownership or possession, or which the defendant owes.

The prevailing school of jurisprudence has precluded itself from an understanding of this development by assuming a basic difference between a claim for damages and a claim which asserts a right. It deals with the claim for damages in the law of obligations; the claims in the nature of a vindication of a right it deals with in connection with the various rights to which they refer, e. g. in the case of a property claim, in connection with the doctrine of ownership. But Mauczka has correctly pointed out that the rights of personality, the rights in one's life, body, honor, good name, cannot be protected, even against violation without culpability, except through a claim for damages. These claims therefore are not a part, analytically, of the law of obligations,

被认为值得保护的利益还和早期一样,即国家、人身和生命、占有;但是保护的方式却相对地更加丰富和多样化。首先,国家更频繁地行动起来,国家不仅仅在涉及到国家自身时行使其惩罚权,而且当涉及到人身、生命和财产占有的安全时,国家行使惩罚权的频率也在不断增加。此外,国家在很大程度上获得了对社会法院的控制,通过这些,国家提供了一个比早期的社会所能提供的保护更有效的保护。与此同时,国家司法开始通过对暴力、欺诈和隐秘妨害的威慑来提供保护,对已造成的侵害由刑罚改为支付赔偿金,这种转变使得不仅在暴力、欺诈和隐秘妨害等不正当行为的情形下,而且也在其他类型侵扰的不正当行为情形下,提供赔偿。最后,我们发现了最狭义术语上的权利主张诉讼,[1]这种主张活动的目的是确保该人对其权利的特定标的享有权利,即保护他主张拥有所有权或者占有之物,或者被告所欠之物。

当前法理学的主流学派由于认定损害赔偿请求权和主张权利的请求权之间存在区别,因而不可能理解这种发展。它处理债法中的损害赔偿请求权;它处理的是与各种各样权利相关的、权利主张性质的请求权,例如,在涉及财产请求权时,相关的是所有权学说。但是毛次卡正确地指出,除了通过损害赔偿请求权外,人格权、生命权、身体权、荣誉权和名誉权无法获得保护,甚至在无过失侵害的情况下也是如此。因此,通过分析,这些请求权并不是债法的一部分,而是人法的一部分。其他主张权利的请求

[1] 在罗马法中,指物的返还之诉(*rei vindicatio*),即所有权人藉以取回财产的一种诉讼形式。

but of the law of persons. The same is true of the other claims that assert rights. The action *in rem* based on loss of possession—incidentally the action brought for protection against interference with a relation of domination has the same origin—arose from the action for deprivation of possession either by thieves or robbers. It is therefore intimately related to the action for damages because of robbery and theft. The claim for damages therefore, even today, takes the place of an action *in rem*, whenever the recovery of possession is impossible, occasionally even when it is not desirable. In modern English law and to a certain extent in classical Roman law the claim to a thing (*dinglicher Anspruch*) can be effectively asserted only in the form of a claim for damages. The claim for damages in these cases therefore is, in part, the necessary, and in part the historically given, form of the action for deprivation of ownership and possession, a certain form of the action based on ownership and possession. Likewise the action for damages because of damage done to a thing of which the plaintiff was owner or which he had in his possession always remains an action based on ownership and possession. As in the case of the action brought because of deprivation, so in the case of this action for damages, ownership or possession is the basis of the action, in fact, since the *actio negatoria* is today no longer conceived of, as was the case among the Romans, as an action involving a question of servitude but as an action based on ownership inasmuch as, though the object of the action is the protection of one's property against an asserted servitude, its basis is

权也是如此。基于占有的丧失——顺便提一下,保护支配关系免受干涉的诉讼也基于此——的对物之诉,产生于针对小偷或者强盗剥夺占有的诉讼。因此,对物之诉与因抢劫和偷窃而引发的损害赔偿之诉密切相关。因此,即便是在今天,每当回复物的占有不可能时,损害赔偿请求权就会取代对物之诉,甚至当回复占有并不合算时,偶尔损害赔偿请求权也会取代对物之诉。在现代英国法和一定范围内的古典时期罗马法中,物权请求权(*dinglicher Anspruch*)只有通过损害赔偿请求权的形式才能有效主张。因此,在这些情形下,损害赔偿请求权成为所有权和占有被剥夺之诉讼——这是一种基于所有权和占有的特定诉讼形式——的必要形式,某种程度上是必然的,某种程度上则是历史赋予的。同样,因原告所有之物或占有之物遭受损害而引发的损害赔偿之诉,始终是一种基于所有权和占有的诉讼。如同在因剥夺致诉时一样,在损害赔偿之诉中,所有权或占有都是这些诉讼的基础。事实上,既然排除妨害之诉[1]如今已不再被想象为涉及地役权问题的诉讼(罗马人则是如此想的),而是被设想为一种基于所有权的诉讼——因为尽管该诉讼的目标是为了通过挫败他人声称的地役权以保护某人的财产,但其基础是所有权——

〔1〕 (拉)*actio negatoria*(排除妨害之诉),所有人针对侵害其权力的轻微行为提起的诉讼,这种行为主要表现为行为人非法行使他物权,例如:非法对所有人的物行使用益权或者役权等。在此种诉讼中,原告应当证明自己对有关物享有所有权并证明被告所造成的侵扰,但不必证明被告不拥有他物权,因为关于这一点的举证责任应当由被告承担。通过这种诉讼,所有人获得对侵扰的排除或者对不造成侵害的保证。

ownership, we shall have to consider the *actio legis Aquiliae*, not according to its object but according to its basis, as an action based on ownership.

The actions which are based on unjust enrichment are also actions based on ownership or on possession. They are actions by the owner or by the possessor for compensation, up to the amount of enrichment of the other party, for the loss which he has suffered by being deprived of his ownership or his possession for the benefit of another. When a creditor sues to have a transfer of the debtor's property set aside, the basis of the action is the loss of his security. It is therefore in reality an action based on the law of obligations. In the Roman law the claim for the return of unjust enrichment has attained a rich development: *condictiones sine causa*, *actio negotiorum gestorum*, *actio de in rem verso*, *actio Pauliana* as the

那么，我们就不能依据其目标，而应依据其基础，将阿奎利亚诉讼[1]看做是一种基于所有权的诉讼。

基于不当得利提起的诉讼也是基于所有权或占有的诉讼。它们是所有者或占有者为了获得价值相当于另一方当事人所获利益的补偿而提起的诉讼，以弥补其因所有权或占有被剥夺而遭受的损失，他人同时因此而获益。当一个债权人起诉要求撤销债务人转移财产的行为时，该诉讼的基础是他的债之保全利益的损失。因此，实际上，这是基于债法的诉讼。在罗马法中，返还不当得利的请求权获得了充分的发展：无债因请求返还之诉、[2]无因管理之诉、[3]

---

〔1〕（拉）*actio legis Aquiliae*（阿奎利亚诉讼），由《阿奎利亚法》*lex Aquiliae* 创设的诉讼，可由受害人向侵害人提起；为了能够提起诉讼，损害必须具有实在性，它应当是由物体造成的，即直接由行为人的身体活动造成的，并且应当对某一物造成损害。此诉讼属于罚金之诉和损害赔偿之诉。最初的阿奎利亚法诉讼只能由所有人提起，在后来的司法实践中，人们也允许善意占有人、用益权受益人、使用权受益人或者质押债权人等人员采用扩用的方式提起仿效诉讼。

〔2〕（拉）*condictiones sine causa*（无债因请求返还之诉），解决不当得利问题的诉讼手段。当某人根据不存在的债因实行了给付（即非债清偿）时，可以采用此诉讼要求返还已给付的钱财。

〔3〕（拉）*actio negotiorum gestorum*（无因管理之诉），在罗马法中无因管理之诉可区分为直接诉讼和反诉讼两种。无因管理直接诉讼是所有人针对经管人提起的诉讼，在此诉讼中，前者否认后者的诉讼具有无因管理的性质，从而要求其承担相应的赔偿责任。无因管理反诉讼是由经管人针对所有人提起的诉讼，在此诉讼中，原告要求被告向自己支付产生于无因管理的费用并且使自己摆脱因经营管理行为而承担的债务。保佐人也可以通过无因管理反诉要求被保佐人对于产生于保佐行为的费用给予补偿。无因管理之诉的一种特殊形式是丧葬之诉。

action of the creditor to set aside the transaction. It was elaborated to a much greater degree of refinement by the Continental common law, especially under the influence of Windscheid. Since the French Civil Code contains provisions only for the repayment of money paid that was not owed, the development of the claim based on unjust enrichment in French law took place almost exclusively through legal decisions which, in point of form, as a rule were based on the *actio in rem verso*. Planiol contented himself with basing it on the principle *neminem cum alterius detrimento et iniuria fieri locupletiorem*: "C'est une des rares règles de droit naturel, qui dominent toutes les lois, alors même que le legislateur n'a pas pris specialement le soin de les

转化物之诉、[1]作为债权人申请撤销(债务人不当)交易之诉的保利安之诉。[2] 欧陆共同法,尤其是在温德沙伊德的影响下,对不当得利制度的系统阐述,在很大程度上更加精致化了。由于《法国民法典》仅仅包含了有关返还非债清偿之价金的条款,因而在法国,不当得利请求权的发展,几乎完全是通过法律裁决——就形式而言,通常是基于转化物之诉的裁决——而出现的。普兰尼奥尔满足于把不当得利请求权建立在"这是一个自然法规则,适用于一切法律,因此立法者并没有特意作出专门规定"这一原则的基础上。"目前在德国法和法国法的观念中,所有并非基于当事人意思、且没有给与支出费用一方当事人补偿的获益,都可以作为这种不当得利之诉的根据。"在英国法中,

---

〔1〕 (拉)*actio de in rem verso*(转化物之诉),属于主人或者家父责任之诉的一种,当奴隶或者家子把与他人交易所取得的收入转化到主人或者家父的财产中时,人们可以针对奴隶或者家子实施的交易活动提起此诉讼,要求主人或家父在其获利的范围内对产生于上述交易活动的债务承担责任。

〔2〕 (拉)*actio Pauliana*(保利安之诉),如果资不抵债的债务人为对债权人实行欺诈而将自己的财产转让给第三人,从而使债权人得不到清偿,即可对该债务人提起此诉讼,要求执法官撤销债务人实施的转让行为。提起此诉讼所需要具备的三项条件是:(1)债务人有意采用减少自己的财产的手段致使债权人得不到清偿,即具有欺诈意图;(2)对债权人造成损害结果;(3)接受转让的第三人对上述欺诈行为知情。保利安诉讼是由优士丁尼法创设的,在此之前,它表现为两种不同的诉讼手段,一种叫欺诈给付令状,它要求欺诈知情的第三人必须返还所获得的物;另一种叫做恢复原状。

formuler." At the present time in the view of the German as well as of the French law, all gain which is not based on the will of the parties, and for which compensation is not given to him at whose expense it was made, will serve as the basis for an action based on this unjust enrichment. In English law the relation between the claim for unjust enrichment and the claim of ownership or possession, is marked much more clearly because the usual actions for the enforcement of both claims (*trover and indebitatus assumpsit*) originally were actions for interference with possession (trespass). Trover, which originally was an action for things found, now covers all cases in which the defendant has converted to his own use things that belonged to the plaintiff or of which the plaintiff had possession, or has unjustly deprived the latter of their possession and use. *Indebitatus assumpsit* usually covers cases of the same kind as trover where money is involved.

The actions that assert rights, or demand damages, or ask for restitution of unjust enrichment, together with the criminal law that is applicable, are merely various forms of protection of the person, of the relation of domination, of possession. Justice demands that the person, the relations of domination, and possession be protected. Justice also demands that the protection be extended and improved; but in every case the technical question remains to be solved: In what manner shall the requirements of justice be met? Justice must be patient so long as norms for decision and legal remedies sufficient to carry out its demands have not yet been found. The development of the law of damages offers a good illustration of this. The owner of a thing that was stolen or lost can demand its surrender even from an innocent purchaser, but he can demand damages from a person who injures the thing only in case he is able to show that the latter is culpable. This more lenient manner of dealing with the person who injures the thing is not a requirement of justice. The reason for it is historical to begin with. The action for the vindication of a right against a third person in possession of the article that had been stolen or acquired in some other wrongful manner had grown out of the action of theft at quite an early date. But the original action for damage done, which was looking toward the payment

不当得利请求与基于所有权或占有的请求权,此二者间的关系划分得更加清楚,因为,实现这两种请求权追索侵占物和损害赔偿之诉的常见的诉讼,最初都是针对侵害占有(trespass)的诉讼。追索侵占物诉讼,最初是有关发现物的诉讼,现在包含了所有下列情形:被告把属于原告的物转归自己使用,或被告把属于原告占有的物转归自己使用,或被告不正当地剥夺了原告占有和使用之物。损害赔偿之诉通常包括与涉及金钱时追索侵占物之诉相同的情形。

主张权利的诉讼或要求损害赔偿的诉讼,或是要求归还不当得利的诉讼,连同可适用的刑法,这些仅仅是保护人身、支配关系和占有关系的各种形式。正义要求人身、支配关系和占有应受到保护。正义也要求这种保护能不断地扩展和改善;但是,在每一种情形下,技术性问题还有待解决:以何种方式正义要求会得到满足呢?只要足以实现正义要求的裁判规范和法律救济措施尚未被发现,正义就必须耐心一些。损害赔偿法的发展为此提供了一个适当的例子。被窃物或者遗失物的所有权人甚至可以要求一个不知情的购买者交还原物,但是该所有人仅仅在能证明损坏物的人可归责时,才能向其要求损害赔偿。这种对损坏物的人更为宽大的处理方式并不是正义的要求。这种现象的发生首先有其历史原因。针对通过偷窃或者其他某种不正当手段占有物品之第三人的那种主张权利的诉讼,在很早的时候就从盗窃之诉中发展起来了。但是,最初的损害赔偿之诉——原先是带有惩罚性

of a penalty, which is in the nature of a punishment, has, in every system of law that has reached a more advanced stage of development, presupposed culpability in the person doing the damage. Because of this historical connection with the ancient action for a penalty, the action for damage done had to be based on culpability even at a time when the penalty had become compensation for damage done. In order to subject it to a development parallel to that which led from the action of theft to an action based on ownership, one would have to find a legal proposition that can make a clear-cut distinction between damage caused without fault and damage that is the result of pure accident. Neither the Romans nor the modern jurists down to the present day have been able to do this, and because of this technical difficulty we still cling, as a matter of principle, to the legal propositions, which, in very many cases, are felt to be unjust, to wit *casum sentit dominus*, loss from accident must lie where it falls. Roman law and our older law knew a few exceptions to this. In the nineteenth century at least a few undertakings that can be prosecuted only with great danger to others have, by statute, been made liable for the damage caused by them, but hitherto only the French judicial decisions have given wider application to the principle of liability for damage caused without fault. But it has been possible only in part to deduce clear legal propositions from their norms for decision.

The oldest contract involves transfer of possession. In the contract of barter possession of goods is being transferred; when a person voluntarily surrenders himself into bondage for a debt, i. e.

的赎罪金的支付——在每一个发展到较高阶段的法律制度中,都要求以造成损害之人可归责为先决条件。因为和古代赎罪金诉讼的这种历史联系,所以,即便在赎罪金变成了对已造成损害的补偿时,损害赔偿之诉也不得不建立在可归责性的基础之上。为了能使损害赔偿之诉经历一个与导致盗窃之诉转向基于所有权之诉讼的发展类似的发展,人们必须找到能够在无过错所致损害与纯粹意外事件所致损害之间作一个清晰区分的法律命题。不管是罗马的法学家还是现代的法学家,直到今天都没有能力做到,并且,由于该技术难题,我们原则上仍然僵守着在很多情形下我们都感到不公正的如下法律命题——意外事件让债务人倒霉,〔1〕即由意外事件导致的损失必须由意外降临处之人承担。罗马法和我们古老的法律中在这方面有一些例外。在19世纪,至少有一些企业——只有在对其他人造成重大危险时方能被起诉——按照制定法,对于它们造成的损害承担责任,〔2〕但是迄今为止,只有法国的司法判例对无过错致损的责任原则给予了更宽泛的适用范围。不过,只在某种程度上从他们的裁判规范中推演出清楚的法律命题,还是可能的。

最古老的契约涉及到占有的转移。在易物契约中,物品的占有发生转移;当某人自愿受债务拘束时,即在所有令某人有义务

〔1〕(拉)*casum sentit dominus*(意外事件让债务人倒霉),这句格言是有关契约责任的一项基本原则,根据此原则,在双务契约中,如果某一意外事件致使契约一方无法履行自己的契约义务,作为债权人的契约另一方当事人则应当免除相应的给付义务,例如:在房屋租赁中,如果已出租的房子因地震而倒塌,承租人可以免除交纳房租的义务,由此产生的损失由出租人承担。

〔2〕即不考虑过错的无过错责任。

in the case of all contracts that obligate a person to render services and performances (in the contracts of subjection), possession of one's own person is being transferred. In the beginning the contract is ineffectual without such transfer of possession; and we may say accordingly that the courts do not protect the contract itself but merely protect the possession which has been transferred to the recipient against deprivation through robbery, theft, or deceit. The situation is not changed when a pledge is substituted for the subject matter of the contract, or when a third person is substituted, as a hostage, for self-delivery into bondage. The creditor can now rely on the possession of the pledge or the hostage, and is protected in this possession in the same way in which he is ordinarily protected in the possession of a thing; he has no other rights as yet that he can enforce at law against the other party.

A true law of contracts does not come into existence until the *Haftung* (liability) arising from the debtor's word is greater than the liability arising from that which he has transferred to his creditor. For a long time stress was laid upon the relation in thought between the symbols which were delivered to the creditor, i. e. the *arrha*, or earnest-money, the part performance, and the giving of security by means of delivery of the subject matter of the contract or of the debtor into the possession of the creditor; but this relation evaporates more and more, until finally the promise as such, in an ever increasing measure, creates the *Haftung* (liability).

Originally legal protection of the contract always meant only the legal protection of the disposition that was made in connection with the contract either of a thing or a person, either one's own or another's, at any rate the legal protection of the disposition of one's own person for the purpose of rendering services or of furnishing goods. If the disposition is not carried out at once, it creates at first merely an obligation (*Schuld*) owed by the person making the disposition; to this obligation is added the *Haftung* (liability) arising from the word of the party making the disposition as soon as the courts compel him actually to carry out the disposition. The law has taken these steps hesitatingly and in a certain sense reluctantly—always as a concession to the

提供劳务或履行的契约(在隶属契约)中,对自己人身的占有也被移转了。起初,这种契约在占有未转移时是没有效力的;因此,我们可以说,法院并不保护契约本身,而仅仅保护已经转移给受让人的占有,使其免受以抢劫、盗窃或诈骗方式实施的剥夺。当担保物代替契约的标的物时,或者当作为人质的第三人代替契约的标的物时,这种情况也没有改变。债权人现在可以依赖对担保物的占有或对人质的占有,并且可以凭借这种占有而受到保护,这与他通常因占有某物而受到保护的方式完全一样;目前为止他还没有其他可以强制实施法律来反对另一方当事人的权利。

直到因债务人的承诺而产生的 *Haftung*(责任)远远大于因他转让给债权人之物而产生的责任时,真正的契约法才开始产生。在很长的一段时间里,重点都放在了思考这些交付给债权人的标志,即 *arrha*[1] 或定金,部分履行与借助于契约标的物的交付或债务人将占有移交给债权人而给后者的保证之间的关系上;但是,这种关系在不断消失,直到最终,承诺就这样在越来越大的程度上创设了 *Haftung*(责任)。

起初,契约的法律保护总是仅仅意味着对与物或人自己或他人的契约有关之处分的法律保护,至少是为了提供劳务或提供商品而对某人人身的保护。如果这种处分没有立即履行,它首先仅仅产生一种处分人所欠之债(*Schuld*);当法院强迫他实际履行其债时,因当事人的承诺而产生的 *Haftung*(责任)就附加到这种债务之上。法律犹豫不决地、并在某种程度上不情愿地采取了这些

---

〔1〕 (拉)*arrha*(定金),债的担保形式之一,根据具体功能的不同,可区分为确认定金(*arrha confimatoria*)和反悔定金(*arrha poenitialis*)。

most urgent and imperative demands of life. *Haftung* (liability) makes its earliest appearance in the case of the compromise as to the payment of a penalty and in the case of the contract to extend credit in connection with the symbolic self-sale of the debtor; the *Haftung* (liability), which, in the case of a sale, is based on the warranty (that the thing has not been stolen), arises at a later time. True *Erfüllungshaftung* (liability for the performance) of the promise connected with the contract of barter presupposes a great amount of commercial intercourse and of division of labor in society. Roman law has not yet reached the stage at which the seller is compelled to perform his promise. It merely compels him to transfer possession and to assume the *Haftung* (liability) for the promise that the buyer shall be permitted to keep the thing. The *locatio conductio* and the other contracts of exchange, the so-called innominate contracts, have not reached even this stage. They give rise, essentially, to an obligation, not to a *Haftung* (liability). The modern *Übereignungsvertrag* (contract to convey title) was the first to create the duty to transfer the property. But it is only the French consensual contract and the English deed that produce the effect of the disposition, i. e. the complete transfer of ownership at the very moment the contract is entered into. It may be said therefore that the development of the idea of justice everywhere strives to make the word (promise of the parties) the all-efficient source, in the contract, of legal effects enforceable at law. But primarily the contract appears as nothing more than the exercise of the right of disposition over one's person or one's possessions. Manifestly the basic thought is merely this: Just as the owner may burn the thing he owns, or cast it into the sea, so he can also transfer it to someone else. Just as the will of the owner is authoritative in general as to anything that is subject to it, so it is also in case the will is declared in a contractual disposition. The contract, from this angle, is a means of utilizing one's property.

Herein lies the germ of another thought sequence. Since the power of disposition over one's property by means of a contract is a means of utilizing the property, that which is to be effected by utilizing the property is part of the content of the contract. In the contracts which are of the greatest importance for commerce the

措施——始终是作为一种对最紧急、最迫切的生活需要的让步。*Haftung*(责任)首先出现在支付赎罪金的和解契约情形下,以及与债务人象征性自售有关的信贷契约情形下;在买卖的情形下,基于保证(标的物未曾失窃)的责任后来才产生。与易货契约相关的允诺所产生的真正 *Erfüllungshaftung*(履行责任)是以社会中大量存在的商业交往和劳动分工为前提的。罗马法还没有达到强制一个人履行其允诺的阶段。罗马法仅仅强迫债务人转移占有,并承担其允诺的责任,根据其允诺,买者可拥有契约标的物。租赁契约与其他的交易契约,所谓的无名契约甚至还没有到达这一阶段。实质上,它们引发了一项债务而不是责任。现代的 *Übereignungsvertrag*(所有权转让契约)首次创设了转移财产的义务。不过,只有法国的诺成契约和英国的契据才能产生处分效力,即,在契约订立的那一刻完成所有权的完全转让。因此,可以说,正义观念在各处的发展均是努力要使言辞(当事人的允诺)成为所有效力的源泉,在契约法中是作为法律上可强制执行的法律效力的源泉。但是,契约似乎主要是对个人人身或其所有物处分权的行使。显然,最基本的思想就是这样的:正如所有者可以烧掉他所拥有的物,或把它扔到海里,他也同样可以把它转让给其他任何人。正如一般言之,所有人的意思对于任何隶属于他的东西都具有权威性一样,同样,契约上的处分所含的意思表示也是如此。从这个角度来讲,契约是个人利用财产的一种手段。

这儿存在另外一个思维次序模式的萌芽。既然借助契约对个人财产的处分权是利用财产的手段,那么,通过利用财产将会实现什么目的,这个问题就成为契约法内容的一部分。在那些对于商业而言具有最重大意义的契约中,其目标是,以让与一当事

object is to acquire, in exchange for the disposition of one's property, a counter-performance from the other party, which in turn consists in a disposition of property. At a very early date therefore, at first in contracts of exchange, later, to an ever increasing extent, in other bilateral contracts also, performance by one side became the basis of a judicially recognized claim to counterperformance by the other side. But tile contract comprises two dispositions which not only condition each other, but which are in an intimate relation with each other and which are intertwined with each other, and a legal system which concerns itself exclusively with the two dispositions contained in the contract without considering their mutual relations, gives expression only to a part of the content of the contract, not to the whole content.

The book of Zitelmann, *Rechtsgeschäft und Irrtum* (Legal Transaction and Error), contains a model analysis of the psychological processes that go on when a disposition is made. Since every contract contains dispositions, both the point of departure and the result of Zitelmann's book are absolutely correct. But Zitelmann stops with the disposition, lie divides the contract into two independent dispositions. To him a contract still is two dispositions, not the intertwining of two dispositions. Inasmuch as this intertwining is a part of the psychological process in the making of the contract, it is not appreciated at its full value by him. The abundant modern literature of the Continental common law and of the law of the German Civil Code first paid attention to this point. Incomparably more profound studies of it are contained in the doctrine of value in economics. As is well known, the adherents of the English classical school have written on this subject, as well as the economists of the school which is usually called the Austrian school because its chief exponents were Austrians, although among its founders must be numbered, in addition to the Austrian Karl Menger, the Englishman Jevons, and the Frenchman Walrus, and although it has many adherents and outstanding exponents not only in Austria but also in France and England, and especially in Italy and America. Apparently

人的财产为代价,换取另一方当事人的对待给付行为,后者反过来也构成了财产的转让。因此,在很早的时期,首先在交换契约中——稍后,随着范围不断扩大,也在其他的双方契约中——一方当事人的给付行为成了司法认可的,要求另一方当事人对待给付的基础。但是,这个契约中包含了两个不仅互为条件,而且彼此关系密切,相互交织缠绕在一起的处分,仅仅关注包含在契约中的两个处分,而不考虑两种处分之间相互关系的法律制度,仅仅表达了契约的部分内容,而非全部内容。

在齐特曼的著作《法律行为和错误》中,包含了对一个处分作出时整个心理过程的典型分析。既然每一个契约中都包含着处分,那么齐特曼之著作的出发点和结论都是完全正确的。但是齐特曼在处分方面戛然而止了。他把契约分成两个独立的处分。对于他来说,契约仍然是两个独立的,而不是两个交织缠绕在一起的处分。因为这种交织缠绕也是契约缔结之心理进程的一部分,因而他并没有对它的全部价值作出评估。欧陆共同法和《德国民法典》中的大量现代法律文献首先注意到了这一点。经济学中的价值学说包含了关于这一问题的无与伦比的深刻研究。众所周知,英国古典学派的信徒曾经论述过这一主题,通常被称作奥地利学派的那一派经济学家们也论述过这一主题,之所以被称作奥地利学派,是因为尽管这一学派的创始人除了奥地利人卡尔·门格外,还必须列举出英国人杰文斯和法国人瓦勒赫斯的名字,尽管这一学派不仅在奥地利,而且在法国和英国,特别是在意大利和美国也有很多追随者和杰出的倡导者,但是这一学派的主要代表人物都是奥地利人。显然,古典学派和奥地利

the classical school and the Austrian school have reached highly divergent results; actually, however, it seems, they have thrown light upon the identical problem, albeit from different angles. The concept of value of the classical is as truly justified as is that of the Austrian school. But for the question we are now discussing, the concept of value of the Austrian school alone is important.

We are concerned with the contract that has been entered into according to economic principles. "In every concrete economic unit, innumerable tendencies are conceivable in the conduct of the economically active subjects; it is true however that, disregarding economically irrelevant diveigencies, but one way of conducting economic undertakings can be the expedient, the economic one; or, in other words, there are innumerable uneconomical ways of conducting every economic undertaking, but, disregarding economically irrelevant divergencies, in every case only one, a strictly determined, strictly circumscribed, way of conducting it along economic lines is conceivable." (Karl Menger.) The economic contract is a contract in which equal values are exchanged.

The investigations of the Austrian school were confined chiefly to sale and barter; and in these spheres, to the subject matter of the mutual performances, especially to the price. In most recent times, Kleinwächter has included the urban contract of lease (*Bodenrente*). It is self-evident that investigations of this kind might be instituted with reference to contracts of all kinds, even those that are altogether unilateral, and that do not involve any exchange at all, also to contracts that have no economic content, especially contracts of family or of public law. In every case the contract is based on a psychological process which can be analyzed just like the process which underlies the contract of exchange. In this respect the English doctrine of consideration yields valuable results, as Pollock has shown in his work on contracts. An investigation cannot be said to be complete or exhaustive which does not take into account every single understanding arrived at in the contract as well as all *Haftungen* (liabilities), conditions, periods of time, limitations of time; for the eco-

学派两派得出的结论有严重分歧;然而,实际上它们似乎在揭示同一个问题,只不过切入的角度不同而已。古典学派的价值观念如同奥地利学派的价值观念一样,被证明是完全正确的。但是对于我们正在讨论的问题而言,只有奥地利学派的价值观念是重要的。

我们关注按照经济原则订立的契约。"在每一个具体的经济单位中,在经济上活跃的主体之行为中,可以想见,有无数种意向;然而,忽略掉经济上不相关的差异,的确只有一种管理经济企业的方式是合宜的,即是经济的方式;或者,换句话说,事实上存在着无数种管理每个经济企业的不经济的方式,但是,忽略掉经济上不相关的差异,在每一种情形下,只有一种依循经济的路线精心确定并严格限制的管理经济的方式是可想象的。"(卡尔·门格)经济的契约是一份交换同等价值的契约。

奥地利学派的研究主要限于买卖和易货交易方面;在这些范围内,又主要限于标的物的相互给付,尤其是价金的相互给付。最近,克莱因瓦赫特把城市租赁契约(*Bodenrente*)也囊括了进去。不言而喻,开始这种类型的研究可能会牵涉到所有类型的契约,甚至会涉及到那些完全是单边的契约以及那些根本不涉及任何交换的契约,也涉及到那些没有任何经济内容的契约,尤其是家庭契约或公法契约。在每一种情形下,契约都是基于一个可以分析的心理过程,正如作为交换契约基础的过程一样。在这方面,如同波洛克已经在其论契约的著作中所示,英国的对价学说产生了有价值的结论。一项没有考虑到契约中的每一个默示条款、所有的 *Haftungen*(责任)、条件、期间、期限的研究不能说是完整或详尽的;因为经

nomic situation is determined not only by the subject matter and the price, but by the whole content. Until now however Böhm-Bawerk has considered only the influence of time, i. e. the periods of time, in his work on *Kapitalzins* (simple interest).

The ideal of a perfectly just contract is one that is based throughout on the principles of sound economics. If the norms for decision were to follow this ideal, they would necessarily be altogether inapplicable to an uneconomic contract or they could give effect to it only as it ought to have been made according to the principles of economics. This ideal however cannot be attained by practical juristic science. In the first place the principle that a contract must be based on the principles of economics perhaps cannot be expressed in a general juristic formula, much less in a legal proposition; furthermore the jurist lacks the requisite procedural devices, especially in the matter of proof. Juristic science therefore must set itself a much more modest task. On the one hand it must reject the most glaring instances of uneconomic action; on the other hand it must, in proper cases, correct details of the content of the contract according to sound economic principle. Legal history shows that the norms for decision in the law of contracts are in fact developing in this direction under the influence of the idea of justice.

The causes that bring about uneconomic contracts are carelessness, error, necessitous situation, duress. The legal propositions that make against taking advantage of these things in entering into contracts are among the oldest everywhere on the whole earth; in particular, the oldest statutes are directed against it. These are the statutes against usury and fraud. Statutes against usury and fraud are found in Greece, in Rome, in the Middle Ages in Europe; they are the expression of the earliest development of penal law beyond its primitive stage, and they are gaining ground more and more even today.

Beyond this point the law of contracts moves very slowly. In the view of all the older legal systems, of the Roman, of the mediaeval,

济形势不仅仅由标的物和价格决定，而且也由整个内容决定。然而，直到现在，博姆·巴维克在他论《资本利息》的书中，还仅仅考虑到了时间因素，即期间的影响。

一个完全公正的契约之理想始终建立在合理的经济学原则之上。如果裁判规范遵循这种理想，它们肯定全部不适用于不经济性契约，或者只有当它应当依据经济原则创立时，它们才被赋予效力。然而，实践性法学是无法达到这一理想的。首先，契约必须以经济原则为基础这一原则可能无法用一个普遍的法学公式来表达，更不用说用一个法律命题来表达了；而且，法学家缺少必要的程序设计，尤其是在证据方面。因此，法学必须为自己设定一个更为适度的任务。一方面，法学必须否定那些不经济活动的最明显情形；另一方面，在适当的情况下，法学必须按照合理的经济原则修正契约的细部内容。法律史表明，在契约法方面的裁判规范在正义理念的影响下，事实上正向着这个方向发展。

引起不经济契约的原因是疏忽、错误、紧迫之形势和胁迫。针对契约订立时从这些因素中获利的法律条款在世界上的任何地方都是最古老的；尤其，最古老的制定法都针对了这些情形。这些就是反对高利贷和欺诈的制定法。在希腊、罗马与中世纪的欧洲，都可以发现针对高利贷和欺诈的制定法；它们是刑事法律超越原始阶段之最早发展的表达，甚至在今天，它们也正在获得越来越广泛的认同。

除了这一点之外，契约法发展得非常缓慢。在所有的古老法律制度的观念中，在罗马人的观念中，在中世纪的观念中，甚至在

and even in the more recent Roman law in the view of the legal propositions as to *stipulatio* and the other contracts which give rise to *actiones stricti juris*, in the view of the older Continental common law, and in many respects even of the modern English law, the contract, is, essentially, nothing but a disposition. This point of view appears to have been overcome, to a limited extent, only in the later Roman law, in the later Continental common law, and in the latest Continental law.

But neither the Roman nor the modern law has arrived at a final conclusion. The root of the difficulty is the law of error in the making of the contract, and the law governing the interpretation of contracts. To direct the judge to decide according to business usage and *bona fides*, according to good faith and *boni mores*, as was done by the Romans and much more frequently by moderns, is by no means a solution of the difficulty. This is not a legal proposition that contains norms for decision but a direction to the judge to find norms for decision according to justice, i. e. according to the principles of sound economics—norms which will give the fullest possible effect to all those considerations on which each party based its calculation of value, and, on the other hand, will deny legal protection to the incurably uneconomic, especially to the incurably immoral, contract. These judge-

新近的罗马法的观念中,有关要式口约[1]和其他导致严法诉讼[2]的契约的观念中,在古老的欧陆共同法的观念中,甚至在现代英国法的许多方面,契约在本质上仅仅是一种处分。这种观念似乎于有限的程度上在后期罗马法、后期欧陆共同法和最近的大陆法中被克服了。

但是,不管是罗马法还是现代法律都没有得出最后结论。困难的根源在于有关缔约中错误的法律和规范契约解释的法律。如同罗马人和现代人更为经常做的那样,指示法官按照商业惯例和善意、诚实信用和善良风俗进行裁判绝不是解决这一困难的办法。这并不是一个包含裁判规范的法律命题,而是一种对法官依据正义原则寻找裁判规范的指导,也就是说,依据合理的经济学原则,将会最大可能实现所有考量的规范,基于那些考量,每一方当事人作出价值评估,并且,另一方面,对于那些无可补救的不经济契约——特别是那些无可补救的不道德契约——拒绝提供法

---

[1] (拉)*stipulatio*(要式口约),罗马法中的口头契约之一,表现为作为要约人一方当事人向作为承诺人的另一方当事人进行提问,后者对该提问所涉及的义务作出承诺或保证。要式口约的特点在于:第一,采取固定的套语,套语使用错误将导致缔约行为无效。第二,完全以口头的形式进行,有关当事人面对面地完成缔约行为。第三,一般不问缔约的具体原因,只注重形式上的合法。第四,有关的提问和回答必须是连续的(一次性完成)和相互对应的。随着书面契约形式的发展,要式口约后来也采用有关的文书加以证明,出现了要式口约约据。

[2] (拉)*actiones stricti juris*(严法诉讼),这是罗马法上的一种对人之诉,法官审理时受限于法律的字面意义,而没有进行衡平考虑的自由裁量权。严法诉讼的程式中如果没有列入被告的抗辩,则虽然法官明知被告是受原告的欺诈和胁迫,也不得免除被告的责任。与诚信诉讼相对。

made norms for decision however are susceptible of universalization, and can, therefore, at a subsequent time, be converted into legal propositions. A large part of the Roman law of contracts is based on universalization of decisions rendered on the basis of *bona fides*, and the moderns have developed additional legal propositions from the decisions reported in the Roman sources. In my book *Die stillschweigende Willenserklärung* I believe I have given an intimation of the wealth of legal propositions on the law of contracts that is found in modern judicial decisions. It is self-evident that legal propositions of this kind should not be included in a code; they are juristic science in the narrowest sense of the term.

Among the legal propositions that have been derived from the principle of good faith (*Treu und Glauben*) in this manner, there is one that merits a more careful consideration. It is the proposition that each party is held responsible for the truth of the statements he makes when the contract is entered into. If the other party has made his calculations of value in reliance upon these statements, the norms for decision give effect to the contract in accordance with this calculation. The so-called declaration theory has understood this correctly. This legal proposition can be applied to a third party. Whenever a third party by his conduct has induced this calculation of value, he is bound by the contract as it was made in consequence of his conduct. This is the principle of "reliance on collateral facts" (*Vertrauen auf äussere Tatbestände*), as Welspacher has named it. An application of it is the legal proposition "*Hand muss Hand wahren.*" It means that a contract which was made in good faith with a possessor is valid against the owner who had entrusted the thing to the possessor and in this way had created the collateral state of facts, in reliance upon which the good-faith purchaser made his calculation. Another application of the principle is found in the case of public records. The records supply the parties with official information on which the latter can base their calculations. A person who by his conduct has caused the register to be false or incomplete cannot prosecute his right against

律保护。然而,这些法官制定的裁判规范容易走向一般化,并因而在随后能够转化为法律命题。大部分的罗马契约法都是基于善意所作出之裁判的一般化之上,并且,现代法从罗马的原始文献中记录的裁决中,发展了另外的法律命题。在我的《默示的意思表示》一书中,我相信,我在有关现代司法裁决中存在的契约法法律命题的丰富性方面已经给出了暗示,不证自明的是,这种类型的法律命题不应被包含到一部法典中去;它们是最狭义的法学。

在以这种方式从诚实信用(*Treu und Glauben*)原则衍生出来的法律命题中,有一个法律命题值得更细致的考量。该命题就是:当契约订立时,每一方当事人都必须对自己陈述的真实性负责。如果另一方当事人在信赖这些陈述的基础上作了价值计算,则裁判规范依照这种计算赋予契约的效力。所谓的公示理论正确地理解了这点。该法律命题也适用于第三人。只要第三人通过其行为导致了这种价值计算,他就会受到契约的拘束,因为契约是由于他的行为而产生的。正如韦尔斯普拉赫命名的,这就是“表见事实信赖”(*Vertrauen auf äussere Tatbestände*)原则。此原则的应用就是“以手护手”的法律命题。它意味着:(第三人)善意地与占有人缔结的契约对于所有人——该所有人把一个物委托交付给占有人保管,这样就创造了间接事实状态,善意购买人据此做出计算与规划——来说,也是有效的。此原则的另外一个应用存在于官方记录的情形下。这些记录为当事人提供官方信息,当事人据此可以做出相应的计算。一个因为自己行为而导致登记错误或者登记缺漏的人,不能针对信赖此种不确登记而计算之人起诉以寻

a person who made this false or incomplete record the basis of his calculation; at best he can proceed against the person who has profited thereby. A few legal propositions carry the principle of reliance upon collateral states of fact considerably further than this limit; these however are not based on good faith but on practical considerations, security of business transactions and of credit, the social importance of the public record.

It is interesting to note that the English law of contracts in its norms for decision adheres to the older conception of the contract as a disposition to a much greater extent than the Continental law. Until recently it knew of no public land records. They were introduced tentatively only a few years ago. Until recently, with the exception of a few instances, e. g. the doctrine of market overt, it did not know the prindple "*Hand muss Hand wahren*," which was first laid down in a series of statutes of the years 1823 to 1877, in the so-called Factors' Acts, and then only for commercial purposes, and it holds the parties bound by their declarations to a much greater extent irrespective of whether they correspond to the presuppositions of upright business dealings.

It is impossible to extend these investigations to contracts other than those of the law of property, especially to the contracts of family law and public law. Although the canon law as to the grounds of invalidity of marriage, which is a result of the experience of a thousand years and of deep insight into human nature, is out of date, self-evidently, in a few particulars today, it may serve as a sample of what the human mind can accomplish in a field of such difficulty. This achievement has not been equaled in any other legal system, not even in the modern law of marriage, nor in the modern law of the contract concerning property.

求保护自己的权利；最多，他只能起诉因此而受益的人。一些法律命题贯彻间接事态信赖原则的程度远远超过了该限制；然而，这些都不是以善意原则为基础，而是基于实践考量、商业交易与信用安全以及官方纪录的社会重要性等。

注意一下这种情形是很有趣的：英国契约法在裁判规范方面固守作为一种处分的古老的契约观念，其程度远甚于欧陆法。直到最近，英国才知道有公共土地登记制度。该制度只是在几年前才被尝试引入英国。除了少数几个例子——例如公开市场原则——之外，直到最近，英国才了解“以手护手”原则，该原则首先在1823年到1877年期间的一系列制定法中被规定下来，在所谓的《代销商法》[1]中规定下来，那时它仅仅是为了商业目的，并且，该原则使当事人受他们自身宣示之约束的背景是，在相当大程度上不考虑它们是否符合诚信的商业交易所要求的先决条件。

把这些研究延伸到财产法以外的契约，尤其是延伸到家庭法和公法中的契约是不可能的。尽管不言而喻，有关无效婚姻基础的教会法——它是几千年人类经验和对人类本性深刻洞察的结果——如今在一些细节方面已经过时，但是，它可以作为在如此困难的领域人类思想所能实现之成就的榜样。在任何其他法律制度中，还未取得过同样的成就，甚至在现代婚姻法和有关财产的现代契约法中也是如此。

---

〔1〕 英美两国规范代销业的立法。根据这些立法，代销商有权占有并出售委托人的货物，并有权以委托人的全部或部分货物设定抵押，从而保护善意第三人的权利。

We have shown what role justice plays in the law of contracts. It progresses, one may say, along the path of penal law protection of faithful performance of contractual duty by means of penalties for usury and fraud from Zitelmann's conception of the contract to the conception of the Austrian school of economists, from the contract conceived of as a mere disposition to the contract which serves the purpose of acquiring a counter-performance by means of this disposition. In the early law, the contract is merely a means of utilizing one's possessions. The more the law develops, the more it sees in the contract an instrumentality of honest commercial intercourse. It is self-evident that, at every stage, the contract was not only the former but also the latter, i. e. both a means of utilizing one's possessions and, at the same time, an instrumentality of honest commercial intercourse. But the question is not what the nature of the contract is, but how the norms for decision give effect to it. For the purpose of giving effect to the contract as an instrumentality of upright commercial intercourse, even irrespective of questions of the material law, a refinement of procedure was required such as the Romans did not have before the praetorian procedure with its *exceptiones* and *bonae fidei iudicia* came into use. The mere *denegatio actionis*, even though it did actually serve this purpose, surely was not sufficient to accomplish it. And even today the goal has scarcely been approximated.

Because of the great influence of purely military considerations upon the development of the law of inheritance, it is not easy to recognize the part played by the idea of social justice in the devel-

我们已经揭示了正义原则在契约法中所起的作用。有人可能会说,契约法循着借助于针对高利贷和欺诈的刑罚从而对契约义务诚实履行的刑法保护这样的路径,从齐特曼的契约观念一直发展到奥地利经济学派的观念,从仅仅被想象为一种处分的契约一直发展到服务于借由这种处分获得对待给付目的的契约。在早期的法律中,契约仅仅是利用一个人财产的手段。法律越发展,契约越像是一种诚实商业交往的媒介。不言自明的是,在每一个发展阶段,契约都既是前者也是后者,也就是说,契约既是利用个人财产的手段,同时也是一种诚实交往的媒介。但是,问题不是契约的性质是什么,而是裁判规范如何赋予它效力。为了赋予作为诚实商业交往媒介的契约以效力,甚至不理会实体法上的问题,需要一个精致的诉讼程序;就像罗马法在存在抗辩的裁判官程序和诚信审判[1]产生以前就缺乏这种程序。单单诉权——[2]尽管它实际上也服务于这一目的——还不足以实现此目标。甚至在今天,也极少能够接近此目标。

因为纯粹军事的考量对继承法的发展产生了巨大的影响,所以要认识在继承的发展中,社会正义观念发挥了什么作用并不容

---

〔1〕(拉)*bonae fidei iudicia*(诚信审判),又称做"诚信诉讼",在此类诉讼中,由于审判标准不是严格的由法律或裁判官的告示确定的,因而审判员享有较宽的裁量权,可以根据诚信的标准决定被告是否应当承担给付义务。诚信诉讼特别适用于与委托、买卖或租赁契约有关的争议。

〔2〕(拉)*denegatio actionis*(诉权),在程式诉讼的法律审阶段,如果执法官对有关诉讼要求进行审查后认为该诉讼请求缺乏根据或者缺乏形式上的合法性,可以对原告的诉权予以否定,阻止诉讼继续进行,从而使有关诉讼在进入裁判审阶段之前终结。

opment of the latter. The law and right of inheritance began everywhere contemporaneously with the house community. The part of the property of the deceased that was not given to him to take with him on his last journey remained to the members of the household. The further development is based in the first place upon a fiction of membership in the household, except in so far as military considerations were given weight. If there are no members of the household, the inheritance, which would have been without an heir, is offered to those who had been members of the household of the deceased, or would have been had there not been a division of goods. This is the basic idea of the agnatic law of inheritance. An agnate is an actual or a fictitious member of the household, a person who would be a member if he or his ancestor had not withdrawn from it. When the Romans say that an agnate is anyone who is under the same *patria potestas* as the deceased, or would be if the ancestor were still alive, this is merely another mode of expressing the same thought, for the *patria potestas* is the power of the head of the household over the members.

The agnatic law and right of inheritance, therefore, is not a law and right of inheritance by relatives. It must be immediately apparent to everyone that its basis is the house community as long as the greater part of the people live in house communities, and inheritances actually go to present or former members of the household. But it becomes increasingly less apparent the more the rule becomes the exception, the rarer house communities, excepting those of parents and offspring, become. Finally, the whole relation between agnatic law and right of inheritance and house community is forgotten, so that the agnatic law and right of inheritance appears as a species of capricious and irrational law and right of inheritance in the relatives limited to the male line. This was the conception of the Romans as early as the days of the Republic, and it is the conception of the modern English. Now justice demands that these utterly incomprehensible caprices and accidental features of the law of inheritance should be abolished, and that simply the nearest relatives, i. e. those that are not excluded for some particular reason, should be entitled to the inheritance. In this way the agnatic law and right of inheritance becomes a law and right of inheritance in the family. The justice of the family right of inheritance is obvious especially at

易。继承权在所有地方都是与家庭共同体同时产生的。亡者没有带去天国的那部分财产仍然属于家庭成员所有。继承法的进一步发展首先基于一种家庭成员资格的拟制，涉及军事方面考量的范围除外。如果没有家庭成员，则没有继承人的遗产归那些曾经属于亡者家庭成员的人所共有，倘若不涉及到财产分割，则此遗产归原本属于亡者家庭成员的那个人所有。这就是男性亲属继承法的基本观念。一个同族父系亲属是一个真实的或者拟制的家庭成员，倘若他或其被继承人没有离开这个家庭，则他也将是该家庭的一员。当罗马人说，父系亲属是像亡者一样处于同一父权之下的任何人，或者是，倘若其祖先还活着，那么他就是处于同一父权之下的任何人，这仅仅是同一思想的另外一种表达方式，因为父权是家庭的首领对家庭成员的权利。

因此，父系亲属继承权并不是按照亲属关系确定的权利。对每个人来说，显而易见的是，只要大部分人都住在家庭共同体中，并且遗产实际上留给现在或以前的家庭成员，则继承权的基础就是家庭共同体。但是，该基础变得日益模糊，变成例外的规则越多，家族共同体就越来越稀少，那些父母和儿女共同生活的家庭共同体除外。最后，父系亲属继承权和家族共同体之间的整个关系被遗忘，[所以，父系亲属继承权看上去像是一种多变的和非理性的亲属继承权，其仅限于男性血统。]这是罗马早在共和国时期的观念，它也是现代英国人的观念。现在，正义要求废除这些继承法中完全不可理解的怪念和非本质特征，它要求只有最近的亲属才能被赋予继承权，即，那些因为特殊原因没有被排除在外的成员应当被赋予继承权。这样，父系亲属继承权变成了家庭内的继承权。家庭继承权的正义是显而易见的，尤其是当死者遗留

a time when the deceased himself has, in most cases, inherited the property which he leaves, i. e. has acquired it from the family. A special development of this right has found expression in the maxim *paterna paternis*, *materna maternis*. All inherited property, according to this maxim, should revert to the side from which it came.

Ficker's investigations have shown that the fictitious house community and the family community are of no significance for the original law of inheritance of the Germanicpeoples. In so far as the free man was not prevented by actual members of the household, he could dispose of his property *inter vivos* as he saw fit; after his death it was without an heir unless it escheated to the state or to the commune. The same situation obtains among the Romans and the Slavs. The right of the agnates or of the relatives (*Beispruchsrecht*), that their consent must be obtained before land can be sold, belongs to a later order everywhere. And the fact that there are no legally effective testamentary dispositions in primitive times is attributable to the lack of legal remedies to enforce them; but the *Treuhandgeschäft* (trust transaction), the contractual gift *inter vivos* coupled with a postponement of legal effect until after death, is not made impossible thereby. The great importance of the trust transaction was set forth in the excellent book of Robert Caillemer on the basis of a great wealth of material. The *Treuhandgeschäft* (trust transaction) is a contract, and the element of justice in this transaction is identical with the element of justice in the contract: the power of disposition of the owner over his property. And this remains the basic idea of the law and right of inheritance by testamentary disposition even after the *Treuhandgeschäft* has become a unilateral testamentary declaration. The will of the owner, as in the case of contract, controls the disposition of his property, in this case, even beyond the grave. The more the agnatically fashioned *rechte Erbrecht* (true law of inheritance)—to rehabilitate this fine term which Puchta had suggested as a substitute for *gesetzliches Erbrecht* (statutory law of inheritance), which is very likely to be

下的财产多半是自己先前从家庭中继承所得的时候。继承权的特殊发展,可以在格言由父系后裔继承父系财产,由母系后裔继承母系财产发现其表达。按照该格言,所有通过继承获得的财产都应当归属给遗产来源方。

非克尔的研究表明,拟制的家庭共同体和家族共同体对于日耳曼民族的最初继承法来说是没有任何意义的。只要自由人并没有受到实际家庭成员的阻碍,而且他认为合适,他就可以在生前处分他的财产;在他死后,其财产将没有继承人,除非其财产被收归国家或公社。在罗马人和斯拉夫人中也存在着同样的情形。父系亲属或亲戚的同意权(*Beispruchsrecht*)——即,出卖土地前必须征得他们的同意——在各地都属于后来形成的秩序。原始时期不存在具有法律效力的遗嘱处分,此等情形可归因于缺乏执行它们的法律救济;但是,*Treuhandgeschäft*(信托行为)、即附期限的生前契约性赠与(死因赠与),却并非不可能存在。罗伯特·凯勒默以非常丰富的材料为基础,在其杰作中阐述了信托行为的极大重要性。*Treuhandgeschäft*(信托行为)是一种契约,这种交易中的正义要素与契约中的正义要素一致:所有者对自己财产的处分权。甚至在 *Treuhandgeschäft*(信托行为)变为一种单方遗嘱宣告后,这还是凭借遗嘱处分所享有的继承权的基本理念。如在契约中的情形一样,所有人的意志支配着对其财产的处分,这样的话,则所有人的意志甚至延伸至其死后。男性亲属继承模式的 *rechte Erbrecht*(真正的继承法)——为了复兴这一精致的术语,普赫塔曾建议以它来代替 *gesetzliches Erbrecht*(制定法上的继承法),不过后者可能更容易被

misunderstood—appears to be out of harmony with the family order which prevails in society today, the more the disposition by last will and testament grows in importance. Before long it has come to be considered a misfortune to die intestate. This was the case in Rome and in the early Middle Ages. Since the middle of the twelfth century, actuated by self-interest, the church has prepared the way for the last will and testament. Thereafter the endeavor to provide for one's family, for pious and public uses, for the economic undertaking that one has been engaged in, looms large in the minds of men.

These clear trends of justice in the law of inheritance are being crossed by a series of thoughts that belong to entirely different orders. In the ancient city states, the parcels of ground owned by countrymen and by city dwellers are at the same time warriors' portions. These were not to be diminished in number by the death of the possessors, and, on the other hand, they were not to be weakened by the division of inheritances to such an extent as to make it impossible for the possessor to gain his livelihood from them. The right of inheritance of the freeman among the Germanic peoples seems to have been influenced by the same considerations. This accounts for the limitations on the right of women to take by inheritance. These military points of view are most strongly expressed in the law relating to the right of the *Erbtochter* to take. The purpose of the whole feudal law was to provide an expensively equipped horseman for the army of the feudal lord, and the feudal law of inheritance is designed to effectuate this purpose. As to the right of inheritance of the villeins the constitution of the manor and the will of the lord are decisive. The latter's concern is undiminished revenues and services; his endeavor is to establish a law and right of inheritance according to which every parcel of ground will have an owner able to render the required services. Again there is the desire to assign the various parts of the inheritance to those to whom they would be of benefit: the arms to the men; the *Gerade* (i. e. the paraphernа-

误解——越是显得与当今社会中盛行的家庭秩序不相容,遗嘱处分就会变得越重要。不久以后,未立遗嘱即死亡者开始被认为是一种不幸。这是罗马和中世纪早期的情形。自 12 世纪中期以后,受自身利益的驱使,教会已经为遗嘱的设立制定出方式。此后,在人们的脑海里,为供养自己的家庭而努力、为宗教事业和公共事业而奋斗以及为所从事的经济事业而打拼,这些念头大量隐现。

继承法中这些清晰的正义倾向与属于完全不同体制的一系列思想相交错。在古代的城邦,农民和城市居民所拥有的一块块土地同时也是战士所分得的一份。这些土地不会随着占有者的死亡而在数量上减少,另一方面,它们也不会因为遗产分割而稀薄到占有人无法从这些土地中谋得生计的程度。在日耳曼民族中,自由人的继承权似乎受到相同考量的影响。这解释了对妇女靠继承取得财产之权利的限制。这些基于军事角度的见解在涉及取得 *Erbtochter*[1] 之权利的法律中得到了最强烈的表达。整个封建法的目的是为了为领主的军队提供配备昂贵装备的骑兵,封建继承法也是为实现这个目标而设计的。关于农奴的继承权,庄园的章程和领主的意志具有决定性的意义。领主关心的是收入和役务不能减少;领主的努力目标是:建立一部继承法,据此,每一块土地都会有能够提供所需役务的保有者。同时,还有这样的愿望,即把遗产的各部分分给那些可从中受益的人:把武器分给男人,把 *Gerade*(即已婚妇女特有的动产)分给女人。

---

〔1〕 与 *Stammgut* 最后的所有人关系最近的女性家系有权取得。*Stammgut* 是一块地产,其移交由特别的继承法规范。

lia), to the women. Again in the higher ranks of the nobility there is the rooted idea to establish the law and right of inheritance in the interest of the glory of the family. Among the free peasants the principle of the house community survives here and there; to wit one of the sons takes possession of the farm, the other heirs are provided for as servants. Elsewhere the elder sons are portioned off, and the youngest son, who has remained with the father, gets the farm (ultimogeniture, borough-English).

The English law of inheritance has, preponderantly, been under the sway of such trends ever since the influence of the London courts in the fifteenth century caused the feudal law of succession, which had been confined to the holders of knight's fees, to be extended to all classes. The immovable property descends to the first-born son according to feudal law; in default of a first-born son, to the first-born male child among the children of the nearest relative (with a rather complicated computation of the degrees of relationship); while as to movables, the right of succession of relatives together with the right of the surviving spouse has been making its way for two centuries. In the seventeenth century an unlimited freedom of testamentary disposition prevails, which is not even limited by a law providing for a *Pflichtteil* (duty part, or compulsory portion). The attachment of the English to their law of inheritance is not easily understood by a Continental. They have made only minor changes during the course of the nineteenth century.

In the most recent development of the law of inheritance, only a few leading thoughts are discernible. In the law of testamentary disposition, the tendency is toward untrammeled power of disposition, limited only by the law creating a duty part, or compulsory portion, in favor of the descendants and the ancestors of the testator, occasionally also in favor of the surviving spouse. The duty part, or compulsory portion, is thought of as making provision for those persons for whom the testator is under a duty to provide. The *rechte Erbrecht* (*supra*) is characterized by a state of extreme perplexity. It almost seems as if the idea were this: Someone must take the property after the death of the owner; who takes, and what the taker does with it after he has it, is a matter of indifference to the law provided only that it remain in the family. In Germany and Austria a contrary tendency has set

此外,在等级较高的贵族中,有一种根深蒂固的观念,为了家族的荣耀而构建继承法。在自由农民中,家庭共同体的原则到处还存留着;即,其中一个儿子继承了农场,另外的继承人就要作为仆人。在别处,年长的儿子从家庭中分离出去,而仍与父亲一起生活的幼子继承农场(幼子继承制)。

自从15世纪伦敦法院的影响导致了封建继承法——原先仅适用于骑士封地的拥有者——扩展适用于所有的社会阶层之后,英国的继承法就主要受到那些倾向的影响。依据封建法,不动产要由长子继承;在没有长子的情况下,不动产要由所有近亲中第一个出生的男孩继承(存在相当复杂的计算亲等的方法);不过对于动产,亲属继承权和健在配偶的继承权在两个世纪中齐头并进。在17世纪,盛行不受限制的遗嘱处分自由,这种自由甚至不受规定*Pflichtteil*(特留份)之法律的限制。欧洲大陆的学者不容易理解英国人对其继承法的那份执迷。在整个19世纪,英国继承法只作了很小的修改。

在继承法最近的发展中,只有一些最主要的思想可以辨明。在遗嘱处分法中,其趋势是朝着不受约束的处分权方向发展,它仅仅受到规定特留份之法律的限制,这种特留份是为了立遗嘱人的子孙与长辈,偶尔也是为了依然健在的配偶。特留份被认为是为立遗嘱人有义务供养的那些人准备的。*rechte Erbrecht*(真正的继承权)具有表述极其混乱的特征。它近乎是这样的观念:一个人必须在所有人死亡之后取得财产;只要这些财产仍然保留在家庭内,则谁继承财产以及继承者在继承后如何利用这些财产,法律并不关心。在德国和奥地利,一个相反的趋势正

in, but only in the peasants' law of inheritance, i. e. the tendency to preserve the farm in such condition and extent as will insure adequate husbandry. The Swiss Civil Code contains an interesting attempt to arrive at a profounder understanding of the problems of the law of inheritance.

In spite of all this, the leading ideas of justice in the historical development of the law of inheritance can easily be traced. Remaining in possession of the goods that were left, by a process of extension, became a right of inheritance in the fictitious members of the household, the agnates, and this is transformed into a right of inheritance in the members of the family. To this is added the trust (*Treuhandgeschäft*) in the form of a contract *mortis causa*, and out of this grows the testamentary disposition as soon as the necessary juristic technique has been developed. The law and right of inheritance by last will and testament is limited—in part—only by the right of the members of the household and of the nearest relatives to take by inheritance, and in England not even by that. Secondary trends lead to a law and right of inheritance in the interest of the preservation of the glory of the family, of husbandry, of economic undertakings, to gifts to the church and other public institutions, especially in testamentary dispositions. In the beginning the criminal law affords no protection, even against theft and robbery; for the inheritance is considered ownerless in case there are no members of the household. Later however state regulations appear for the safeguarding of the rights of the heirs (sealing of the inheritance, permission to take possession of the goods of a deceased person granted only after a court proceeding).

An idea of justice that has become widespread is that labor should be placed on a par with property as wealth that is entitled to protection. It has been recognized in the word of Scripture, "The laborer is worthy of his hire"; and in the socialist assertion of a claim to the fruits of one's labor it has been given a clearly defined expression, which, of course, as long as the present social order continues, does not demand that it be realized by means of legal propositions. But the norms for decision do not even make provision for it to the extent to which it could easily be received into the framework of the present-day social order; and, to a great extent at least, the cause of this is the difficulty of adequately

在形成，但仅存在于农民的继承法中，即该趋势就是在确保足够的农业耕作的条件下和范围内保护农田。《瑞士民法典》则包含了一个有趣的尝试，企图获得对继承法问题的更深刻理解。

尽管存在这一切，但是，在继承法历史发展中，正义的主导观念仍然可以轻易地跟踪到。继续占有遗留下来的财产，经过一个扩展的过程，变成了家庭中拟制成员（父系亲属）的继承权，接着，这种权利又转变成为了家族成员的继承权利。除此之外，还有以死因契约存在的信托行为（*Treuhandgeschäft*），当必要的法律技术获得发展，从信托行为中就立刻衍生出遗嘱处分。依据遗嘱而享有的继承权受到限制（部分的限制），只有家庭成员和最近的亲属才有权获得遗产，在英格兰，甚至不存在这些限制。第二个趋势引致了一种为了维系家庭荣耀、农业生产、经济事业，而把财产捐赠给教会和其他公共机构的继承权，尤其是在遗嘱处分中此种继承权更为常见。起初，刑法不提供任何保护，甚至对偷窃和抢劫遗产也置之不理；因为在家庭没有成员的情况下，遗产被认为是无主财产。不过，后来国家法令开始保护继承人的继承权（封存遗产，只有在经过司法程序后获得授权，才允许占有亡者的遗产）。

一个广泛流传的正义理念是：劳动应当和作为财富的财产同等地受到保护。该理念在《圣经》的经文中获得认可，“劳动者应当获得酬金”；在社会主义者对自己劳动成果的权利主张中，这一观念被清晰、明确地表达出来。当然，只要现在的社会秩序继续下去，这一理念就不要求借助法律命题的方式来实现。但是，裁判规范甚至没有在非常容易被今天的社会秩序框架接受的范围内，预先做好准备；至少在很大程度上，导致这一问题的原因是充

formulating the legal proposition. Accordingly a cause of action which is similar to the cause of action for unjust enrichment through the property of another lies only in the rarest of cases against the person who has unjustly enriched himself through the labor of others. It is only in one field, the field of creative intellectual labor, that the difficulties, which in this sphere were enormous, have been overcome by the combined labors of the jurists of almost all civilized peoples, and a considerable part of the problem has been adequately solved. To it we owe our law protecting literary and artistic creation and the criminal law protection of intellectual property. It is true, much remains yet to be done. So in France the idea is being agitated to secure for the artist whose works have been sold at a ridiculously low figure a share of the increase in value of these works after he has become famous. The justice of this idea is not being disputed, but it is impossible to find the technical solution of the problem. The means proposed, to wit to assure to the artist and to the members of his family after him as a matter of law two percent of the price obtained at a public auction as an inalienable right, clearly is utterly ineffectual. The correct thing would be to grant him a right of preemption in respect of his work, but even here the closer one approaches the problem, the more the difficulties accumulate.

The ideas of justice therefore give rise to legal propositions that supply society with increasingly rich and varied means of defense against attacks upon its order. In all these cases, it is always a question of developing materials rather than of transforming those already existing. Personality, domination, possession are protected by the inner order of society. They are protected in the first place by means of a threat of punishment, by giving causes of action for damages, and lastly, especially in the case of possession, by giving causes of action for the assertion of rights and for unjust enrichment. The causes of action arising from contract are realizing, more and more perfectly, the original peculiar purpose of the contract, i. e. to utilize the power of disposition over one's possessions in order to acquire a counterperformance, and, in the case of the *Kreditaustausch* (exchange of credit) and of the contract for furnishing things for use, to obtain equal value. Judicial and state protection of the right of inheritance likewise, in so far as it is based on justice, carries out a

分而明确表达该法律命题的困难。因此,一种类似于不当得利诉因的另外一种诉因,只存在于针对那些通过他人劳动使自己不当获益的极为罕见的情形中。仅仅在一个领域中,即创造性的智力劳动领域中,这方面的巨大难题被几乎所有文明国家的法学家的共同劳动所攻克,并且很大一部分问题已经被充分解决了。我们应该把保护文学和艺术创造的法律和保护知识产权的刑法归功于该正义理念。的确,还有许多事情有待去做。因此,在法国,为了确保艺术家——其作品曾经以一个离谱的低价出售过——获得在其成名后这些作品不断增加之价值的部分份额,这一理念正在被激烈地辩论着。该理念的正义性并没有引起争论,不过,却无法找到解决这一问题的技术方案。提议的措施——即,确保艺术家及其逝世后的家庭成员一项不可剥夺的权利:依据法律获得公开拍卖会上所拍得价款的百分之二——很明显是完全行不通的。正确的方法是赋予他在涉及其作品时的优先购买权,但即使这样,人们越研究这一问题,堆积的难题也就越多。

因此,正义的观念促生了——为社会提供日益丰富多样的防御手段从而使其秩序免受攻击的——法律命题。在所有的这些情况下,它总是一个开发素材而不是改造那些已有素材的问题。人格、支配和占有受到社会内部秩序的保护。它们首先凭借一种刑罚威胁的方式、通过规定损害赔偿诉因的方式而受到保护,最后,尤其在占有的情形下,通过规定权利主张的诉因与不当得利的诉因而受到保护。产生自契约的诉讼事由正越来越完美地实现契约最初的特殊目的,即:利用对自己财产的处分权来获取对待给付,在 *Kreditaustausch*(信用交易)和借用契约中,则是获取对等的价值。继承权的司法保护和国家保护,就其基于正义而言,同

series of thoughts which are already in existence in life. They are the following. The inheritance, to begin with, is the store from which the members of the household and the nearest relatives of the deceased derive the means of sustenance. Over and above this, it belongs to the family of the deceased; the dispositions made by the deceased are effective beyond the grave. The fact that the protection of intellectual labor by means of legal propositions and legal remedies was effected only in the last centuries must be attributed to the fact that intellectual labor did not come into its own before that time. Thus far then the whole law, which is based on justice, is nothing more than an expression of the existing facts of the law, an expression of social statics. In contrast to, and distinct from, this justice there is another justice, which is an expression of social dynamics. In the latter the idea prevails not only that the legal proposition is able to preserve the *status quo*, but that it is a means whereby society can order the relations within the various associations in its interest. The powerful impelling forces of this dynamics are individualism and collectivism. It is believed that, through judicial decisions and administrative action, the existing facts of the law can be modified or abolished and that by this means the progress of society can be guided into certain channels.

The significance of individualism and of collectivism for the development of the law I have discussed with so much detail in my book on legal capacity (*Rechtsfähigkeit*) that I may be permitted to limit my present discussion of this point to a reference to this book. In the present connection, the important thing is their effect upon the norms for decision. The culmination of individualism is the principle that every man is an end unto himself and is not subject to any power that would use him for its own ends: neither to a domination that would subject him to the individual will of another nor to a domination that would subject him to the will of an association in which he does not serve himself but only the whole. The ideal of justice of individualism is the individual and his property, the individual who has an untrammeled power of disposition over his property, who recognizes no superior but the state, and is not bound by anything but the contracts he has freely entered into. Individualism therefore dissolves all relations of dependence established by custom, i. e.

样贯彻了生活中早已存在的一系列的思想。这些思想如下:首先,遗产是源自亡者的积蓄,是其家庭成员和近亲属得以维生的手段;除此之外,遗产属于亡者的家庭;亡者生前所作的处分在其亡故后仍然有效。借由法律命题和法律救济保护智力劳动只是在19世纪才实行的,原因在于,智力劳动在此之前尚未获得应得的认可。到那时为止,整个基于正义的法律不过是对已存法律事实的表达,仅仅是社会静态学的表达。除了这种正义,还存在另外一种与之相反、截然不同的正义,即一种表达社会动力学的正义。在后者中,盛行这样的理念:法律命题不仅能够维持现状,而且也是社会能够为其利益而规整社会联合体内各种关系的手段。这种社会动力学强大的强制性力量是个人主义和集体主义。据信,通过司法判决和行政行为,现存的法律事实能够被修改或废止,并且通过这种方式,社会进步可以被导向特定的路径。

个人主义和集体主义对于法律发展的重要性,我已经在我的著作《权利能力》(*Rechtsfähigkeit*)中作了详细的探讨,因此,请允许我将对此探讨限于参考这本书。在当下的背景中,重要的是它们对裁判规范的影响。个人主义的顶点是这样的原则:每一个人对于自己来说都是目的,他不屈服于任何力量而为他所用;具体包括:不受使自己受控于他人意志的支配,也不受使自己受控于一个联合体——其中他不为自己工作,只为联合体效劳——之意志的支配。个人主义的正义理想就是个人及其财产,个人对其财产享有不受妨碍的处分权,他不承认除了国家之外的任何其他的上级,并且,除了他自己自由缔结的契约外,他不受任何其他约束。因此,个人主义废除了所有通过习惯建立起来的依赖关系,

slavery, domination, and subjection, and abolishes, or at least weakens, the family law powers. The power of the husband falls into disuse under its influence; marriage itself is loosened to a considerable extent by more easily obtainable divorce; the paternal power, guardianship, and curatorship gradually cease to be selfserving rights of a master, and become an office, the duties of which are being performed for the benefit of the person subjected to it. This development, which reached its culmination in the Austrian Code at the beginning, in the Swiss Code at the end, of the nineteenth century, is destined to reach its culmination in France in the revision of the Civil Code. Only a modest beginning is to be found in the German Civil Code. After the associations, into which the individuals appear to have been placed as members by society, have been dissolved and destroyed, the only connecting links that remain between the individual and society are ownership, contract, and the state, to which even individualism concedes the unlimited right to use the individual as a means to an end. Between the state and the individual are only those associations which the state creates as its institutions or endeavors to treat as such (commune, country, church), and those that the individual enters voluntarily either by joining or through contract (clubs, societies). All the rights that the individual is entitled to are transmuted by norms for decision into individual rights, real rights or obligatory rights. This may be said even of the time-honored community of ownership in the family: the right to maintenance becomes a claim for maintenance. The German Civil Code puts the matter in a form that indicates the true situation: maintenance shall regularly be paid in the form of a money annuity. This precept, as such, which has been derided a great deal, is quite proper in the system of the Code; for whenever maintenance is to be awarded in a judicial proceeding—and this is preponderantly the case in the individualistic private law —it will regularly be done in the form of a money annuity. In general duties are imposed upon an individual by norms for decision only in a case where the individual has undertaken a duty contractually or has brought it upon himself through fault (*Schuld*).

即奴隶制度、支配关系、服从关系，并且，废除或至少削弱了家庭法中的权力。丈夫的权力在它的影响下，开始被废止；在很大程度上婚姻关系自身由于越来越容易实现的离婚而变得更为松散；父亲的权力、监护权和保佐权逐渐不再是主人为自己利益服务的权利，而是成为一种公职，是为了承受对象的利益而履行的一种职责。这种发展——19 世纪初曾在《奥地利民法典》中达到顶点，19 世纪末曾在《瑞士民法典》中达到顶点——注定在《法国民法典》修订时在法国达到顶点。在《德国民法典》中仅存在它的一个谨慎的开始。在——个人似乎被社会作为成员置入其中的——联合体遭到解散和摧毁之后，个人和社会之间所保留的唯一连接就是所有权、契约和国家，对于这些，甚至个人主义也承认利用个人作为达到目的之手段的无限权利。在国家与个人之间，只存在国家作为自己机构创立的或者国家努力按自己机构对待的(社区、乡村、教会)那些联合体，以及由个人或通过加入或通过契约自愿建立的那些联合体(俱乐部、社团)。个人被授予的一切权利，被裁判规范转化成了人身权、物权或债权。甚至对于历史悠久的家庭财产所有权共有也可以这么说：要求抚养的权利变成了抚养费请求权。《德国民法典》以一种能表明真实情形的方式对此作了规定：抚养费将定期通过年金的形式支付。像这样受到大量嘲笑的规定在法典体系中是相当合适的；因为每逢在司法诉讼中抚养费被判决给予时——这主要是在个人主义的私法中的情形——抚养费将定期通过年金的形式支付。一般而言，由裁判规范强加给个人的义务仅发生在如下情形：该人以契约方式承担了一项义务，或者这个人因为过错而自己招致了一项义务(*Schuld*)。

The individualistic law of things is striving for a liberty of property which shall set the latter free from all relations with, and considerations for, the community. The individualistic law of contracts demands liberty of contract, with the limitation indeed that the individual shall not have power of disposition over his own person inasmuch as the individualist has always considered the person inviolable. The individualistic law of inheritance culminates in the endeavor to accord the fullest practicable equality of treatment to the heirs that are entitled to take, and to provide society with the greatest possible number of individuals that are endowed with property and freedom of contract. The individualistic law of the state places the individual in a direct relation to the state: its ultimate mode of expression is the right of suffrage. Every form of limited suffrage hitherto has always been found to be a veiled right of suffrage in the householder or in the head of the family. This disappears where the right of suffrage is universal; the state appears as consisting of individual human beings. Woman's suffrage, it would seem, presents the public law dissolution of the household and of the family into individuals as its component parts as well-nigh completed. Thus, severed from all relations, judged, essentially, according to identical norms for decision, human beings are equal before the law.

The world-historical significance of individualism lies in this, that it has done more than merely to create legal propositions, that it has, through the legal propositions, directly affected the facts of the law. It has done away with the usages in the associations by abolishing the associations; it has changed them by changing the structure of the associations, especially by loosening the structure of the family and by bringing the state into an entirely new relation to the individual; and, in particular, it has given a deathblow to the power of domination in the family and in the ruling associations among civilized peoples. Through the establishment of liberty of property and the liberation of land from all burdens and charges, which followed in the train of liberty of property, it has utterly changed the relations of possession; through liberty of contract it has freed trade and commerce from untold fetters; and through liberty of industrial activity it has shifted the center of gravity in the acquisition of wealth to movable property. But the very greatness of the revolution most effectively bears witness to the fact that the legal propositions

个人主义的物权法正在为——使得财产从所有团体关系与团体考量中解放出来的——财产自由而努力奋斗。个人主义的契约法要求契约自由,真正的限制是个人无权处分自己的人身,因为个人主义者总是认为人身是神圣不可侵犯的。个人主义继承法的最终目标是,努力将最充分可行的平等待遇给予有权取得财产的继承人,并为社会提供最大可能多数的、拥有财产和契约自由的个人。国家的个人主义法使个人与国家直接发生联系:其最终表达方式就是选举权。迄今为止,每一种受限制的选举形式总是被认定是一种被遮掩在户主或家长阴影下的选举权。在选举权普遍的地方,这种现象消失了;国家以独立个人组成的形式出现。妇女的选举权似乎在公法上把家庭或者家族分解为个体,以作为其几乎完整意义上的组成部分。这样,人类跟所有的关系断绝了,本质上,仅依据同样的裁判规范来接受裁判,从而人类在法律面前获得平等。

个人主义世界史的重要意义在于:它不仅仅创设了法律命题,而且通过法律命题,它直接影响了法律事实。它通过废除联合体方式取消了联合体内的惯例;它通过改变联合体的结构而改变它们,特别是通过疏松家庭结构和通过在国家和个人之间建立全新的关系来改变它们;而且,尤其是,在文明民族中,它给予家庭中和统治阶级中的支配权致命的打击。在财产解放之后,通过财产自由的建立和土地从所有负担费税中的解放,个人主义彻底改变了占有关系;通过契约自由,个人主义使贸易和商业从数不清的桎梏中解放出来;并且通过工业活动的自由,它使财富取得的重心转向了动产。但是,此革命的伟大之处是最有效地证明了这一事实:那些法律命题主要通过这些基本的社会力量产生了这

have brought about these effects solely through the elemental social forces, to which they in turn owed their very existence.

In the nineteenth century collectivism appeared as a reaction from individualism. Inasmuch as it found expression in socialism or communism it has no place in this discussion; for in this form it has had no influence upon the present-day development of law. Other, more moderate, forms of the idea, however, particularly in the last decades, have come to be of great significance in all departments of the law.

Collectivism expresses the opposite of the idea of isolation (*Einzelgedanke*) of which individualism is the protagonist. According to the individualistic idea of isolation, it is the duty of each individual to look out for himself, utilizing his property and his work as advantageously as he can. But individualism, even in the days of its greatest power and influence, was not able to prevent communities from coming into existence, and continuing to exist, in which at least certain claims of the members were satisfied by the whole body according to quite different principles. In the house community of the family, in the corporations, in the societies for the promotion of the public welfare, in the state in so far as it is a military community or a community of officials, or a welfare community, there are no performances and counterperformances nicely calculated according to property and contract. The individuals render services according to their powers and abilities, and receive according to their needs. Although collectivism, unlike socialism and communism in this, does not endeavor to erect the whole social structure on the basis of principles of this nature, it does attempt to introduce into society some of the principles which appear fully realized in the existing communities. For the free utilization of property through contract there is to be substituted an order under which the individual, at least in emergencies, would render services to the whole according to his powers and abilities, and the whole would provide for the needs of the individual—at least in emergencies.

The point of departure is the great inner contradiction with which

些效果,反过来,这些社会力量的存在本身又归功于那些法律命题。

19世纪,集体主义作为对个人主义的回应而出现。由于在社会主义或共产主义中存在它的表述,因此,此处讨论中不会涉及它;因为在这种形式下,集体主义对今天的法律发展不会产生任何影响。然而,更为温和的集体主义观念形式,特别是在最后的十年中,却在所有的法律部门中都具有了重大的意义。

集体主义表达的是个人主义所倡导的个体思维(*Einzelgedanke*)的反面。按照个人主义的个体思维的观点,照料自己是每个人的责任,每个人要尽可能以最有利的方式利用自己的财产和工作。但是个人主义,即使在它最强大、最有影响的时候,也不能阻止社会团体的形成和继续存在,其中,成员的特定权利要求至少有一些,整个团体依据完全不同的原则满足了它们。在家族里的家庭共同体中,在公司里,在为促进公共福利的社团里,在还只是一个军事共同体、官员共同体或福利团体的国家里,根本没有依据财产和契约精确计算过的给付和对待给付。每个人根据他们的力量和能力提供服务,并且根据他们的需要获得物品。虽然,在这方面不同于社会主义和共产主义,集体主义并不努力以此种性质的原则为基础建立整个社会结构,集体主义确实尝试着向社会中引进了一些似乎在现有社区中可以完全实现的原则。对于通过契约自由利用财产将被一种秩序所替换,在这种秩序下,至少在紧急事态时,个人要根据自己的力量和能力为整个社区提供服务,同时整个社区至少在紧急事态时也要向他提供需要的物品。

个人主义的出发点就是一种巨大的内在矛盾体,个人主义因

individualism is afflicted. In spite of the endeavor to treat all men alike, it permits some of the greatest inequalities to remain, especially the inequality in wealth, which the equality before the law merely serves to accentuate. The more the rich and the poor are dealt with according to the same legal propositions, the more the advantage of the rich is increased. In contrast to socialism, the social movement that is based upon collectivism does not attempt to abolish the inequalities, but merely to mitigate them. Its aim is to counterbalance the advantage in fact which the rich enjoy by means of social institutions and legal propositions which impose limitations upon the rich and prevent them from availing themselves of these advantages in too great a measure.

In spite of the apparent conflict between them, both individualism and collectivism are after all nothing but the expression of a tendency running counter to the legal order which is founded on ownership of property. The latter gives to the possessor the exclusive power of control over the economically profitable forces of nature, and this is the sense not only of the law and right of ownership but also of almost all the other legal institutions. According to its inner nature, every contract, even the contract of labor, is a utilization of one's property by the exercise of the power of disposition over it; and although the workman is not exercising this power of disposition over his property in the narrower sense of the term, but over his physical and mental powers, he does it for the sole purpose of enabling the owner of the means of production to acquire the working power of the workman, and thereby make his property productive. Whether the family serves the purpose both of production and of consumption of goods, as it did in the past, and as the family of the peasant still does even today, or whether it serves only the purpose of consumption as is the case preponderantly today, it is being kept together by the owner of property and receives its content from the ownership of property. The state and the public corporations are the organs of a society which is based on property; other associations exist for the administration and utilization of property which is held in common for common purposes. These purposes, of course, may possibly be ideal purposes. In the days

此承受着巨大痛苦。尽管个人主义努力以同样的方式对待所有人,但它允许巨大的不平等存在,尤其是允许财富的不平等存在,法律面前的平等也仅仅是为了加剧这种不平等。越是依据同样的法律命题处理富人和穷人,就越增加富人的优势。与社会主义相比,以集体主义为基础的社会运动并不试图废除这种不平等,而是仅仅试图减轻这种不平等。它的目的是,通过给富人强加限制的社会制度和法律命题来抵消富人事实上所享有的优势,并防止富人过度地利用这些优势。

尽管个人主义和集体主义存在明显的冲突,但是它们都不过是一种与基于财产所有权的法律秩序相反倾向的表达。后者赋予了占有者控制经济上可获利之自然力的绝对权利,并且,这不仅是所有权的意旨,而且是几乎所有其他法律制度的意旨。按照其内在性质,每一个契约,即使是劳动契约,也是通过实施对财产的处分权来利用其财产;虽然工人并非是在对其财产行使狭义上的处分权,而是行使处分其体力和脑力的权力,但是工人这么做的唯一目的是,使得生产资料所有人获得工人的劳动力,并使其财产增值。不管家庭是同时具有生产和消费职能——如同过去的家庭一样,甚至如今的农民家庭仍是如此——还是仅具有消费的职能(如今主要就是这种情形),它都是由财产的所有人撮合筹建起来的,并从财产所有权中获取内容。国家和公法人都是以财产为基础的社会机构;其他联合体存在的目的是为了管理和利用为共同目的而共有的财产。当然,这些目的很可能是观

when society consisted of slaveholders, in the feudal society in Europe down to the days of its last offshoots in the nineteenth century, and in the family down to the nineteenth century, property was invested with certain rights of domination which were exercised by the owner either directly or through the state and through the public corporations, and by the owner of means of production through the guilds. It was at this point that individualism made its attack. When it demanded liberty of property and contract, it meant merely that no rights of domination should be connected with property. Since vestiges of these can be found today only in the state and in the family, the historic mission of individualism has well-nigh been fulfilled. Collectivism goes deeper than this. It is not directed against the direct right of domination but against the indirect right and power of domination in the owner, particularly against the personal subjection which appears as the consequence of exclusive right and power of disposition over the resources of nature. Collectivism seeks to counteract this right and power of domination by endeavoring to bring about the creation by the state or by society of new communities or the development by the state or by society of those that are already in existence. This, it is hoped, will aid and support the individual in his struggle for existence (right of combination, trade-unionism, organizations for the common welfare). On the other hand, it is urged that this be done by direct action of the state, this greatest, this all-inclusive association, which, it is urged, should interfere more vigorously than it has done hitherto through legislation and through its agencies in the interest of those who are laboring under a handicap because of the property system. The state limits the rights of the owner in so far as they might become dangerous to the person or the property of another (extension of liability for damage done, usually up to but not including damage done by *vis major*), and imposes special duties toward the workmen and other employees (legislation for the protection of workmen in the narrower sense). Just as the old usury legislation tried to prevent the owner of money and consumable goods from availing himself of his ownership for the purpose of exploitation in the contract for the extension of credit, so the state today forbids the owner of the means of production (*Arbeitsmittel*) to resort to certain kinds of exploitation in the contract of labor (limitation of the labor of women and children, of the working day, Sunday rest, prohibition of payment in kind (*Trucksystem*)).

念中的目的。在社会由奴隶主组成的年代，在欧洲封建社会下直到 19 世纪其最后分支的年代，在下至 19 世纪的家庭中，财产被赋予了特定的支配权，该支配权要么由财产的所有者直接行使，要么由他通过国家和公法人来行使，还可以由生产资料的所有者通过同业公会来行使。正是在这一点上，个人主义发起了进攻。当它要求财产自由和契约自由时，它仅仅意味着财产不应该与任何支配权相连。既然今天只有在国家和家庭中才可以发现这种残余，则个人主义的历史使命几乎完全实现了。集体主义走得更远。它不是反对直接的支配权利，而是反对所有者间接的支配权利和权力，尤其是反对作为对自然资源独享处分权的结果而出现的人身从属。集体主义寻求抵消这种支配的权利和权力，其方式是通过努力使国家或社会创设新的团体，或者通过国家或社会来发展社会已经存在的团体。集体主义希望这能帮助和支持个人为生存而进行的斗争（联合的权利、工会主义、公共福利组织）。另一方面，集体主义督促国家通过直接的行为来实现这些，集体主义督促最伟大的、无所不包的联合体应当为了那些因为财产制度而处于不利地位的劳动者的利益，而通过立法和国家机构比迄今为止更为积极有效地干预。国家就它们可能对其他人的人身和财产产生危险的情况，限制了所有者的权利（对已造成损害责任的扩展，但不包括不可抗力造成的损害），并且强加给他们对工人和其他雇员的特殊责任（对狭义上工人的保护立法）。正如旧的高利贷立法试图防止金钱和消费品的所有者为了在信贷契约中的剥削目的而利用自己的所有权，今天的国家也禁止生产资料（*Arbeitsmittel*）所有者在劳动契约中采取特定的剥削方式［限制妇女和童工的劳动、工作日、星期日休息、禁止以实物付款（*Trucksystem*）］。

It compels the owner of the means of production (*Arbeitsmittel*) to permit the workman to receive a greater share of the fruits of his labor (wage policy, minimum wage in England, Australia, and New Zealand). It expends a part of the produce of the national economy for the benefit of the non-propertied classes (old age pensions, social insurance, state institutions for the public welfare, the public welfare law of inheritance of the project for the Swiss code, state housing policy). The state takes over a part of the production of goods in order that the fruits and profits arising from it may accrue to all strata of the population (movement toward state ownership and control). Similar action by the communes is of similar significance (municipal socialism). In the case of collectivism, too, it appears that the world is not ruled by legal propositions. It produces its effects only by creating associations, imposing charges on property, limiting the liberty of contract, i. e. by creating facts of the law.

The social idea of justice therefore has not destroyed the individualistic idea of justice; it has fulfilled it. However much the idea of individualism and that of collectivism may clash, in the course of histoy the spheres within which each of them is justified are gradually being delimited. Individualism, too, must concede to the state whatsoever it requires for the purpose of doing justice to each individual, and collectivism, too, must be in position to justify its existence by promising to the individual a better present, or at least a better future, than he could obtain as an individual.

Individualism and collectivism are not confined to the legal sphere. They have made their influence felt in art and literature; in philosophy and ethics; perhaps in every sphere of human activity. And in the legal sphere, they undoubtedly have been active at all times. The "individualism" of the Roman law and the "social trends" of the mediaeval German law but recently were fashionable terms, although surely there was no dearth of social trends in Roman law and none of individualistic trends in German law, and although the outward impression that one receives is determined by the stage of development that the person who is forming a judgment on these two systems of law has in

它强迫生产资料的所有者(*Arbeitsmittel*)允许工人取得自己劳动成果的更大份额(工资政策,在英国、澳大利亚和新西兰的最低工资制)。它将国民经济生产总值的一部分花费在非有产阶级身上(养老金、社会保险、国家的公共福利机构、《瑞士民法典》设计之公共福利性的继承法、国家的居住政策)。为了让源于商品生产所得的成果和利润能够增加所有阶层的福利,国家接管了一部分的商品生产(以国家所有权和国家控制为目标的运动)。公社的类似行为具有类似的意义(市政社会主义)。在集体主义的情形下,似乎世界也不是由法律命题统治的。集体主义只有通过创设联合体、强制征收费税、限制契约自由——即通过创设法律事实——才能产生自己的效果。

因此,社会的正义理念并没有摧毁个人主义的正义理念,而是实现了它。无论个人主义的理念与集体主义的理念可能发生多大的冲突,在历史的进程中,各自的领域——其中它们各显正当——都正在逐渐被界定。为公平对待每个人,无论国家要求什么,个人主义都必须向国家让步,与此同时,集体主义也必须通过承诺给个人一个比他作为个人所能取得的结果更好的现在,或至少承诺一个更好的未来——而更有资格正当化其存在。

个人主义和集体主义并不限于法律领域。在艺术和文学中也可以感受到它们的影响;在哲学和伦理学中也是如此;或许在每一个人类活动的领域都是这样。在法律领域,它们无疑一直都是活跃的。但是,罗马法的“个人主义”和中世纪德国法的“社会性倾向”是最近时髦的术语,尽管罗马法中的确并不缺乏社会性倾向,而德国法律中并不缺乏个人主义倾向,尽管人们接受的外在表达取决于对这两种法律制度形成判断之人考

mind. Every article on the *artele* bears witness to the influence of collectivism in Russian law. Whenever several Russians embark on a common undertaking, even though it be merely a hunting expedition, they form an *artel*, an association. But for two centuries, at first individualism, then collectivism, have consciously been the motive power in the creation of law. They have not only brought about legal propositions, but have powerfully influenced human conduct, and have given rise to much new law. There is much in the work of individualism that has called forth just criticism, nor have all the results of collectivism stood the test. It seems that we are again facing an individualistic tendency, which undoubtedly will be followed by a tendency of the opposite kind. Like the thread of a screw, these two ideas of justice alternately have been drawing the human race upward.

Among all of the ideas of justice that have been described until now there is not one that has failed to encounter an antagonist in the course of historical development who, in the deepest chest-tones of genuine conviction, would proclaim the opposite as that which alone is just. This affords a deep insight into the nature of justice. It would be difficult to find a principle that is so widely recognized as being just as the "sacredness" of property. One need not point to the jibe of the socialists at the sacredness of property, "of which they prate most to whom nothing else is sacred." It may suffice to call attention to the fact that expropriation for the benefit of the public is held to be fully as just as property itself. This of course, by itself, would not be convincing. But a more searching investigation of the modern development of law reveals the fact that the expropriations by the state which are generally being demanded and which are actually taking place either quite openly or most thinly veiled, have become so numerous and so extensive that the principle seems to have been converted into its opposite, and that every instance of interference with property by the state is felt to be just, provided only that it seem somehow covered by a reference to the public interest. This is by no means a new phenomenon; for even a man with the highly developed sense of justice of an Adam Smith has justified the incredible confiscations perpetrated

虑到的发展阶段。每一篇关于合作社的论文证实了集体主义在俄国法中的影响。每当几个俄国人着手一项共同的事业,即使它仅仅是一项狩猎旅行,他们也都会织一个合作社、一个社会联合体。但是在两个世纪里,先是个人主义,然后是集体主义,自觉地成为了法律创设的动力。他们不仅促生了法律命题,而且还强有力地影响了人类行为,并且导致大量的新法律产生。在个人主义作品中,存在很多招致公正批评的东西,集体主义的全部成果也都无法经得住此种标准的检验。似乎,我们又一次面对一个个人主义倾向,毫无疑问,在这之后将是一个相反类型的倾向。像螺丝上的线一样,这两种正义的观念交替引领人类上升。

在迄今描述过的所有正义理念中,还没有哪一个在历史发展进程中没有遭遇过反对者,这个反对者出于最真诚的确信宣称,只有相反的正义理念才是唯一正确的。这提供了对正义性质的深刻洞察。难以找到一个原则能恰如财产权"神圣"原则一样被广泛接受。人们不必指出社会主义者对财产神圣原则的嘲笑,"他们对那些人——对他们来说没有什么是神圣的——空谈了许多"。以下事实足够引人注意:为公共利益对财产的征收被认为与财产权本身一样是完全正当的。当然这本身并不那么令人信服。不过,对现代法律发展的一份更为详细的研究报告却揭示了如下事实:通常所要求的、实际上总是或公开或稍稍有些隐蔽的国家征收变得如此频繁、如此广泛,以至于这一原则似乎转至其反面,以至于只要披上公共利益的外衣,则国家干涉财产权的每个例子,人们都觉得是正义的。这绝非是一种新的现象;因为即使是一个具有亚当·斯密那种高度正义感的人也

under the Navigation Acts on the ground that they were being perpetrated in the interest of British naval power. This applies also to the contract. It is just that every man should be bound by the contract as he has made it, but demands are continually being made in the name of justice for new limitations of the liberty of contract in the interest of public morals, of personal liberty, of social policy, of honesty in daily life. Anton Menger says of the reliance upon collateral states of fact in matters covered by the maxim "*Hand muss Hand wahren*" that, in the interest of the security of commercial transactions, the whole national wealth is thereby subjected to an expropriation, which indeed is limited, but which is operating without interruption. Anton Menger also combats individualism in the law of the family. He says that in modern society the family is practically the only place where love and devotion are being cultivated, and that it is to the interest of the non-propertied classes that it be maintained and strengthened. Nothing seems to most people to be more just than that all the children of the deceased should inherit equally, and the legislation of the French Revolution seems to have been altogether unable to persuade itself that it had sufficiently given effect to this idea. Nevertheless I am convinced that the German peasantry of Austria regard the law and right of the single heir (*Anerbe*) which prevails among them as just. According to this law all the children, with the exception of the single heir (*Anerbe*), are limited to a very niggardly duty part, or compulsory portion (*Pflichtteil*). Not even those children that are being disadvantaged make any complaint about it. In this whole matter it is by no means a question of subjecting a universally valid principle to salutary limitations in one detail or another. The point is that often enough, at the same time, opposing principles are conceived to be just, sometimes in different strata of society, in circles that are remote from each other, but just as frequently by people who are in a very close relationship to each other. Both the two parties to a law-suit are usually convinced of the justice of their cause, and perhaps they may

已经为依据《航海法案》所进行的邪恶的、令人难以置信的征收而辩护,理由是:此乃为了英国海军的利益。这也应用到了契约领域。每一个人都受到他所订立之契约的拘束,这是符合正义的。但是对契约自由的新的限制要求正在不断以正义的名义提出,即为了公共道德利益、为了个人的自由以及为了社会政策和日常生活中的诚实。安东·门格尔提到了在"以手护手"原则所涵盖事项中对间接事态的信赖,即,为了商业交易安全的利益,整个的国民财富都因此受到征收的影响,此种征收虽然的确受到限制,但在运作中却没有任何阻断。安东·门格尔也和家庭法的个人主义作了斗争。他说在现代社会中,家庭实际上是唯一可以培育爱和献身精神的地方,并且,维护和强化它正是为了那些无产者阶层的利益。对于大多数人来说,没有比亡者的子女平等继承遗产更公正的了,法国大革命时期的立法似乎根本不能说服自己,立法本身已经充分赋予过这种观念以效力。尽管如此,我还是确信,奥地利的德国农民认为在他们当中盛行的单一继承人(*Anerbe*)的继承法是合乎正义的。依该法,除了单一的继承人(*Anerbe*)外,其他所有子女的权利都仅限于一个极少的特留份(*Pflichtteil*)范围内。即使是那些处于不利地位的子女对此也没有任何抱怨。在这整个事情上,绝对不是使一个普遍有效的原则受制于在这个或那个细节上所作出的有益限制的问题。关键在于,太多时候,同时存在的相互对立的原则都被认为是正义的,这种情形有时候发生在社会的不同的阶层中,发生在彼此相隔遥远的圈子中,但发生在彼此关系非常亲密的人中间的频率也一样多。一个法律诉讼中的双方当事人经常都确信他们的诉因是正义的,并且他们也许有充足的理由认为如此;因

well be; for each is appealing to a different idea of justice.

But a searching consideration of the facts of legal history permits us to pick out a clear line of development everywhere in the variegated diversity of the phenomena. Among the conflicting ideas of justice there always has been one that gained the victory at the time, and the victories were gained not because of historical accident but in accordance with an inner unifying regularity. As everywhere else in the universe, so also in society, the yesterday is contained in the today, and the today in the tomorrow. In the sphere of law, justice is the idea of today which has grown out of the idea of yesterday and the idea of tomorrow which is growing out of the idea of today. In order to become a legal proposition, the legal today and the legal tomorrow, born in society, must be given form and shape by a personality who thinks and senses what the future will bring. This is the basis of all practical juristic science, of all legislative policy, of all the systems of legal philosophy that have hitherto come into existence. It is true, we are in no better case than the herbalists of past centuries, to whom thousands of years of experience of the human race had given a vague idea of the virtues that are inherent in the various plants. The jurist and the legislator will gradually become more and more like the modern scientifically trained physician in proportion as sociology is able to trace and present the laws of the development of human society. At the present time there are a few modest beginnings in, and only in, the science of economics.

为每一方都诉诸于一个不同的正义理念。

但是，对法律事实的历史的透彻考量使得我们可以在各处纷纭复杂的现象中勾画出一条清晰的发展脉络。在相互冲突的正义理念中，在那个时期总是有一种正义理念会获得胜利。这些胜利的获得并不是因为历史偶然，而是因为它符合内在的、一致的规律性。在社会中与在宇宙中其他地方一样，昨天包含于今天当中，今天也包含于明天当中。在法律领域，今天的正义理念产生自昨天的正义理念，明天的正义理念产生自今天的正义理念。为了成为一项法律命题，孕育于社会的今天的法律和明天的法律都必定由思考、感觉着未来所能带来之一切的人来形塑。这是所有实用法学的基础、所有立法政策的基础和迄今为止形成的所有法律哲学体系的基础。的确，我们并未处于比过去几个世纪中的草药医生更好的一个状态，人类数千年来的经验赐予后者一个模糊的概念：各种各样的植物各自具有哪些内在价值和功效。依社会学所能追踪和展示人类社会发展规律的程度而定，法学家和立法者会逐渐地越来越像现代的受过专门训练的医师。当前，这种趋势在经济学中，也仅仅在经济学中，有一些不大起眼的苗头出现。

# XI

# Juristic Science In Rome

Everyone who has compared a statute with a book that has been written about it has observed that the bulk of the book is many times greater than that of the statute, occasionally as much as several hundred times greater. The idea suggests itself to inquire into the cause of this phenomenon. How did it come about that so large a volume was written about so brief a statute? To this question the jurists have a very plausible answer at hand. Every statute, be it never so clear and detailed, leaves room for all manner of doubt. To resolve these doubts is the function of juristic literature. Now the doubts must be rather great if they can be resolved only in books that are of so much greater size than the statutes themselves. Under these circumstances, I take it, the further question is justified: Why are the statutes not couched in terms that leave no room for doubt? For nothing is gained under our present-day method if, in order to arrive at a clear understanding of what the statute ordains, one must refer to a book that has been written about it. The statutes therefore ought to be more detailed or juristic literature is superfluous.

Time was when the jurists themselves entertained this idea. They endeavored to draft the statutes in such minute detail as to make doubt as to their meaning altogether impossible. The immediate result was that the statutes became bulkier, but the bulk of the juristic volumes was not decreased thereby. In the course of time jurists began to awaken to the fact that each word that is added to a statute gives rise to

# 第十一章　罗马法学

但凡把某一制定法与论述它的法学著作相比较的人，就会发现：后者的篇幅是前者的许多倍，偶尔可能达到几百倍。这种发现让人想要探究此种现象之成因。那样简短的制定法怎么会有如此浩大卷帙的相关著作呢？对于该问题，法学家手头上有一个似是而非的答案。即每一部制定法，即便是空前的清晰和详尽，它总会留下疑问的空间。解决这些疑惑就是法学文献的功能。如果这些疑惑只能在规模要比制定法自身大得多的书籍中解决，那么疑惑必然是相当多。在这些情形下，我认为，有充足的理由继续追问：为什么制定法不使用不会留下疑问空间的术语来表达？因为，如果为了达到对制定法规定的清晰理解，任何人都必须参考一本论述制定法的著作，那么在我们如今的方法之下，任何东西都不能获得。所以，制定法应当更加详备，或者说法学文献是多余的。

有一段时间，法学家他们自己接受了这一观点。他们努力更加详尽地起草制定法——在每一细节上都如此详备以至于其条款的意思完全不可能产生歧义。直接的结果是制定法变得篇幅巨大，但是法律论著的篇幅并没有因此而减少。经过一定的时间，法学家开始醒悟：每一个增加到制定法的词语都会引发更多

further doubt. Today almost all jurists of true insight incline toward the opinion that the briefer, the more chary of words, the statute is, the better it is. The current answer, therefore, to the question why that which is written in the books is not contained in the statute cannot possibly be satisfactory.

Further inquiry will convince one that the difference between a statute and a book that discusses the statute is not quantitative but qualitative. The juristic books do not offer something additional but something different. For they contain the juristic technique, practical juristic science. Technique is out of place in a statute. If it is put into the statute, as has been attempted by those that demand that everything be found in the statute, it at once loses its characteristic nature and becomes a hybrid, which not only does not aid the development of the technique, but disfigures the statute, and not infrequently interferes with its operation.

Practical juristic science, which is to be the sole subject matter of our discussion at this point, is the art of making law subserve the legal needs of daily life. It is therefore something quite different from the science of law. Although there might be as many kinds of practical juristic science as there are kinds of legal needs in daily life, only two branches of this technique have become important. These are, first, judicial technique, which arises from the need of adjudication of legal controversies, secondly *Kautelarjurisprudenz*, the art of drawing up legal documents. A clean-cut line of demarcation between the two cannot be drawn; for in drawing up legal documents one must consider the question how a legal dispute arising from the document would have to be adjudicated, and on the other hand judicial juristic technique must continually consider the question how legal disputes which involve documents must be dealt with. Judicial juristic technique always was the leading one and is often considered the only one. It is indeed the older of the two; for the art of drawing up legal documents does not come into being until a relatively more advanced stage of development has been reached. Judicial juristic technique therefore must needs be the point of departure for a scientific presentation of practical juristic science.

的疑惑。今天几乎全部有真知灼见的法学家都倾向于认为:制定法越简洁,措辞越简练,制定法就越好。所以,对于——为什么著作中撰写的内容没有包含在制定法中——这一问题当前的回答很可能无法令人满意。

进一步的研究将使人确信:制定法和探讨制定法的著作之间的差异不是量上的,而是质上的。法学著作并没有提供一些附加的东西,而是提供一些不同的东西。因为法学著作中包含法学技术——实用法学。在制定法中存在技术是不合适的。如果把技术置入制定法中,正如那些要求制定法中什么都有的人曾试图做的那样,那么制定法马上就会丧失它的独特性质,而变为一个混生物,这不但无助于法律技术的发展,而且会毁损制定法,并经常会妨碍制定法的施行。

实用法学——我们此刻讨论的唯一主题——是使法律促进日常生活之法律需要的艺术。因此,实用法学完全不同于法律科学。尽管可能存在如同日常生活法律需要之类型那么多的实用法学,但是,此技术只有两个分支很重要。它们是:首先,司法技术,它产生自裁断法律争议的需要;其次,*Kautelarjurisprudenz*,即草拟法律文件的艺术。在这两者之间无法划出一条轮廓清晰的界线。因为在草拟法律文件中,必须考虑产生于法律文件的纠纷将如何被裁决的问题,另一方面,司法技术必须连续不断地思考,涉及法律文件的法律纠纷必须如何处理。司法技术总是主导性的分支并经常被认为是唯一的分支。司法技术确实是两者中较古老的一个,因为直到人类达到了相对更发达的发展阶段,草拟法律文件的艺术才形成。所以,司法技术务必要成为对实用法学予以科学揭示的一个出发点。

Practical juristic science did not arise from the need of applying existing law according to rules of art, but from the need of fashioning a legal system so that it might be practically applicable. The law as a rule of conduct, the law in the sense of a social order, is as old, indeed, as society itself; but the law never arises spontaneously in such a form as to be immediately available for use as a norm for decision, and does not suffice for the decision of all causes that may arise. The earliest function of the jurist, then, is to fashion the social law into norms for decision, and, furthermore, to find the norms required for the adjudication of the legal controversy. Legislation, or creation of law by the state, is not found at this stage, and for a long time to come will not be found to an extent worth considering. The jurist is not yet an organ of the state, but of society. He fulfils his task as law-finder not in virtue of a commission from the state but in virtue of the reputation and the confidence he enjoys in society, just like the soothsayer and the medicine man. The fact that as a rule (it seems, not always) he is a priest does not argue a close relation between law and religion; for the other arts and sciences, too, were fostered chiefly by the priesthood, e. g. the arts of healing, music, and poetry. In a stage of development in which society is as yet altogether unorganized, the priesthood is the bearer of all intellectual life.

A practical juristic science of this kind must needs exist in every society that has attained even the lowest degree of civilization. On a soil that is especially adapted—such as never existed in Greece, but did exist in Rome and in Iceland in the greatest conceivable measure—it can develop most luxuriantly. In the more advanced stages of legal and social development, a few additional functions are being added to the earlier ones of juristic science: a knowledge of the existing law; a deeper insight into human nature, which is developing more and more, and into human relations, which are continually becoming more and more complicated; the ability to formulate the existing law in a legal proposition that will meet the present need; the ability to find the proper solution in case a practical need arises, and to make use of legal knowledge for the solution of practical problems. In the course of historical development, one or the other of these quailties comes to the fore. But let it be said most emphatically that

实用法学并非源自依技术法则适用现行法的需要，而是源自塑造一个法律制度从而使其变得实际可行的需要。作为行为规则的法律与社会秩序意义上的法律，确实像社会自身一样古老，但是，法律从未以那种可立即作为裁判规范适用的方式自然地产生，法律也不能满足可能发生的所有诉讼的裁断需要。于是，法学家最早的功能就是将社会法塑造为裁判规范，此外，就是发现裁断法律争议所必需的规范。在此阶段，尚不存在国家的立法或法律创设，接下来很长的一段的时间里，国家的立法或法律创设也没有达到值得考虑的程度。法学家到那时为止还不是国家的元件，而是社会的元件。他作为法律发现者完成任务并不是因为来自国家的委托，而是由于他在社会上所享有的声誉和信任，正如占卜者和巫师一样。通常，法学家（似乎，但并非始终）是一个牧师的事实并没有证明法律和宗教之间存在紧密的关系；因为其他的艺术和科学，也主要是由神职人员来培养，例如医术、音乐和诗歌。在那时社会是完全缺乏组织性的发展阶段，神职人员是所有智力生命的承载者。

此种类型的实用法学必然存在于每一个社会中，甚至存在于仅有最低程度文明的社会。在那些特别适宜的土壤上——譬如说，它在希腊从未存在过，但在罗马、冰岛，它在可想见的最大范围内存在过——它可以生长得最茂盛。在法律和社会更发达的发展阶段，法学又增添了若干新的功能：对现行法的认识；对日益发展的人性和对越来越复杂的人类关系更深刻的洞察；以满足目前需要的法律命题阐述现行法的能力；在实践需要时找出恰当解决办法、并利用法律知识解决实践问题的能力。在历史发展过程中，法学的这些功能之一就会适时涌现出来。但是，应强调的是，

it is the Continental idea of the last two or three centuries only that would limit practical juristic science to a knowledge of the existing law, and to the solution of practical problems. The wise men in the court scene on the shield of Achilles are not expected to proceed according to established rules, but, on the basis of their deeper insight into human nature, to find a judgment which will compose the quarrel about the penalty which is to be paid for the man that was slain. The ten men who composed the Twelve Tables, or those other four men who proclaimed the *lex Salica per tres malleos*, had been asked to make a comprehensive statement of that part of the law which had already penetrated into the consciousness of men in the form of clear legal propositions, and where such propositions were lacking, to eke out the law suitably and in conformity with the rules of juristic technique. This was also the function of the Scandinavian *Rechtsprecher* (declarer of the law) and of every other codifier of the law in time past. In those days the scientific training was lacking which is necessary in order to enable one sharply and clearly to draw the line of demarcation between codification of laws and the creation of law, and which is presupposed today in, and only in, the juristic faculties of universities. Accordingly, juristic science, historically speaking, comprises all of the following: knowledge of the law, application of the law, and creation of law; and, essentially, this has remained true to the present day.

The position of practical juristic science in the development of law in its great historical continuity has never been made the subject of investigation. Only the work of Lambert, which has repeatedly been mentioned, *La fonction de droit civil comparé*, contains an attempt of this sort. The object of this book however is the clarification of a different problem. Hitherto practical juristic science has always developed only in connection with a certain legal system; and, as a matter of fact, there are as many practical juristic techniques as there are legal systems. An understanding of the significance of practical juristic science for mankind could be gained only from a comparative history of the juristic science of the civilized peoples at least. Self-evidently however the solution of a problem of this kind is not to be thought of at this point. Nevertheless there is a practical juristic science which has become of world-historical significance, i. e. the legal science of the Romans, and that of the Continental common law, which

将实用法学局限于对现行法的认识以及对实践问题的解决仅仅是最近两三个世纪欧洲大陆的观念。人们并未期待法庭上佩有在阿基里斯之盾的贤明人,会按照已确立的规则进行诉讼,而是期盼他会基于对人性更深刻的洞察来作出一个调解争议(关于应当付给被杀害的人的赔偿金的争议)的判决。制定《十二铜表法》的十个人或者颁布《萨利克法典》的四个人被要求对已经以清晰的法律命题形式嵌入人们的法律意识中那部分法律作出全面陈述,在缺乏法律命题的地方,则被要求适当地补充法律的不足,并且使其符合法律技术的规则。这也是过去斯堪的纳维亚的法律的宣布者和法律的每一个其他编撰者的职责。那时候缺乏那种——为了使人们能敏锐、清晰地在法律编纂和法律创设之间划出界线所必要的,并且在当今法学院(也仅仅在法学院)作为先决要件的——科学训练。因此,从历史角度来说,法学包含所有的下列部分:法律的知识、法律的适用和法律的创制,并且本质上,这对于今天而言也是正确的。

实用法学在具有伟大历史延续性的法律发展中的地位从未被当作过研究课题。只有早已反复提及的兰伯特的著作《民法比较法的功能》,包含了此种努力。然而,这本书的目的是澄清另外一个不同的问题。迄今,实用法学的发展毫无例外地与特定的法律制度相联系;事实上,存在着与法律制度同样多的实用法律技术。实用法学对人类的意义,无论如何只能从文明民族的比较法学史中得到理解。不过,不言而喻,目前尚未想到对此类问题的解决。尽管如此,还是存在具有世界历史意义的实用法学,即罗马人的法学和由罗马人的法学发展而来的欧陆共同法学。下面,我

has grown out of it. We shall deal chiefly with these hereafter. Anglo-American juristic science will be presented but very briefly, and that of the Scandinavian legal system will be merely touched upon. Since that of the Continental common law has in many ways served as a model for the other important juristic sciences, except the Mohammedan, a more detailed presentation of its nature will be conducive to an understanding of the others.

Before we shall enter upon a discussion of the practical juristic science of the Roman law and that of the Continental common law, let us but glance at the statements of German law and at the German law-books; for they belong to a much more primitive stage of legal development than our tradition of the Roman law. It is true, the German popular laws are not an original source of law. Drawn up in territory that at one time had been Roman and had enjoyed a high degree of legal development, influenced by the latter, and also by the church, they contain much that is not native to the soil, particularly much state law, and much that surely never had been law, and that never did become law at a later time. If we eliminate these borrowings, which belong, in the main, to the field of public law, there are left, as the content of these laws, chiefly precepts as to legal procedure, criminal law, law of damages, and as to the law and right of inheritance of collateral relations, and a few private law regulations, the majority of which had manifestly got in quite accidentally and had been received merely because they had been applied shortly before in the adjudication of litigation. But it is not only the narrowness of the legal material that is striking, but also the dearth of legal propositions. A few centuries later, in the Middle Ages, the number of legal propositions has indeed increased considerably, in several regions at least; particularly the laws of the cities contain an incomparably greater number of them than the leges *barbarorum*. But the number of divisions of

们将主要处理这些问题。英美法学将会被介绍但仅是简要地介绍,斯堪的纳维亚的法律制度法学仅仅会被简单提及。既然欧陆共同法法学在很多方面都是除伊斯兰法学以外的其他重要法学的典型,那么详细地介绍欧陆共同法法学的性质将会对理解其他法学大有裨益。

在我们开始讨论罗马法和欧陆共同法的实用法学以前,让我们浏览一下德国法的陈述和德国法律书籍;因为它们属于一个比我们所讨论的罗马法传统更原始的发展阶段。的确,德国民间法并不是最初的法源。德国民间法制定于一度属于罗马的、并享有过法律高度发展的区域,它受到罗马的影响,也受到教会的影响,包含了很多不是本国的东西,特别是许多国家法,还有很多确实先前从来不是法律、后来也从未变成过法律的东西。如果我们排除这些大体上属于公法领域的法律借鉴,那么剩下的就内容而言,主要是一些关于法律诉讼、刑法、损害赔偿法、涉及旁系亲属继承权的规定,以及一些私法方面的规定,这些私法规定的大多数得来明显纯系偶然,并且它们之所以被接受,也仅仅是因为它们在诉讼判决前不久才刚刚被适用。但是,令人惊异的不仅是法律素材的狭隘,而且还包括法律命题的匮乏。几个世纪以后,在中世纪,至少在几个领域中,法律命题的数量确实获得相当的增加;尤其是城市法中包含了蛮族法[1]无可比拟的大量法律命题。但是它们所提及的法律部门的数量要比法

---

〔1〕 中世纪日耳曼各族法典的统称。指从公元5世纪起入侵罗马帝国的日耳曼主要民族的法律。虽然被称为法典或法典汇编,实际上只是当时部落习惯法的汇编并非制定法。这些法律大约在5世纪到9世纪完成,除盎格鲁-萨克逊法是用本族语言外,其余均以拉丁文编写。

the law to which they refer is not greater than it was in Frankish times, to wit procedure, criminal law, criminal procedure, law of damages, and law of inheritance; we might add a part of the law of suretyship, pledge, warranty in sales. Perhaps in addition to the rules that may be found in the collections a few other rules were in use here and there about the form of certain classes of contracts. At any rate there were not many of them.

We can positively assume, then, that practically the whole store of rules of law that the contemporaries knew of at the time the popular laws or the city laws were collected has been handed down to us. But they could not possibly have contained a sufficient legal order; not even from the point of view of the requirements of the administration of justice. Where then did the judges and the *Schoeffen* get the norms for decision which they required? To answer this question by referring to their sense of fairness and justice would be inexact. For tradition shows that, in the majority of the cases, the inner order of the individual legal relation which was the subject matter of the particular controversy served as the source of the norms for decision. Long before norms for decision couched in general terms were in existence in sufficient numbers, such norms were taken from the content of the subjective rights as they severally appeared. In mediaeval German law every tract of land may properly be said to be an individual. It has its own law which arises from custom or from the document of grant or from the contracts that were entered into concerning it or from its location in the mark. All this, and nothing but this, is conclusive as to the extent of the rights of the landowner, the rights of property and the rights to emoluments, the relations between neighbors, ground rents and other returns, and the permanent charges on land. Likewise there is no general law of corporations. The corporations make their own law or they receive it from the king or from some landowner. Every man belongs to some one or more legal group or groups; and the

兰克时代要少,即诉讼法、刑法、刑事诉讼法、损害赔偿法和继承法;我们可能还要增加部分保证法、担保法、瑕疵担保法。或许,除了存在于汇编中的规则外,偶尔还有关于特定类型契约形式的其他一些法律规则在各处盛行。无论如何,它们的数量并不多。

因而,我们可以肯定地认为,当时那代人知道的、收集民间法或城市法的法律规则全部的库藏,都传给了我们。但是,它们不太可能包含一个满足需要的法律秩序,甚至从司法需要的角度来看也是如此。那么,法官和陪审法官从哪里获得他们需要的裁判规范?以什么公平正义感来回答此问题并不严谨。因为传统证明:在大部分案件中,作为特定争议标的之个别法律关系的内在秩序充当了裁判规范的来源。用一般术语表达的裁判规范大量存在的很久之前,那些规范从那些各别出现的主观权利的内容中抽象而来。在中世纪的德国法中,每一块土地都完全可以说是一个个体。每一块土地都有自己的法律,这些法律产生自习惯,或者产生自授权文书,或者产生自订立的涉及这块土地的契约,或者产生自它在马尔克公社土地[1]中的位置。所有的这些并且只有这些,对于土地所有人权利的范围、财产权、报酬请求权、相邻关系、地租及其他利润以及固定的土地负担具有决定性的意义。同样,也不存在任何的社团一般法。社团创造他们自己的法律或者从国王或者土地所有者那里获得法律。每一个人都属于特定的一个或多个法律群体,法律群体大

〔1〕 在早期条顿法律和英国法律中的一种村落共同体,是当时最基层的政治组织;也指这种村落共同体所共同所有的土地;这些共同体相互联合可以组成更高一级的组织,即百户区。

legal group, in the main, determines the legal status of its members independently. Moreover most of the free families, especially the noble families, have created their own law through ordinance, agreement, or tradition. This law governs the rights of personality, family, and inheritance of its members. The most subjective law however is the material law of contract, which is based almost exclusively upon the content of the various contracts. The declarations of law and the judgments that have been handed down to us show that the basis for the adjudication of a legal controversy was the law, as ascertained in each case, of the parcel of ground, of the corporation, of the family, of the noble house, or the content of a contract, i. e. the inner order of the relations, which clearly appeared from tradition, the documents submitted, or commercial custom.

All of this, as is well known, did not prevent the mediaeval writer from writing the *Sachsenspiegel*, in which, no doubt, he stated a much greater number of legal propositions than he found in existence at the time. It is known today, to a certain extent, how he came to do this. In the public law parts he worked with an ideal conception of the ancient glory of the Empire. This we shall not discuss here. But if we examine the private law, the part we are most concerned with here, we shall see that he is vigorously and consciously universalizing the form of the subjecttive legal relations within the borders of his narrower homeland, with which he had had opportunity to familiarize himself while acting as *Schoeffe* (lay member of a court), and that, most likely, he has invented more or less of it. In spite of the great diversity in the orderings of the family, the relations of possession, the contents of contracts, and the relations of the various ranks and classes, there have developed in certain districts under the influence of economic uniformity, of the system of legal documents, and also through direct imitation and borrowing, certain common features in the law of real property, of rank, of the family, and of contract. They attracted the attention of Eike von Repgow, doubtless a man of vide experience and keen powers of observation, who made a systematic presentation of these features in his book. Since he was not writing a code but a book of law, he was chiefly concerned with preserving that which was common to legal relations of the same kind, without expressing

体上独立决定其成员的法律地位。此外，大部分的自由家庭，尤其是贵族家庭通过风俗习惯、协议或传统创设他们自己的法律。这一法律调控着人格权、家庭以及成员的继承权。然而，最私人的法律是实体契约法，契约法几乎完全建立在各式各样的契约的基础上。传下来的法律和判决公告表明：法律争议的裁判基础是在涉及每一宗土地、每一个社团、家庭、贵族家族或者契约内容的情形下所查明的法律，即从传统、提交的法律文件或商业惯例中清晰显现的各种关系的内在秩序。

众所周知，这一切都没有阻止那位中世纪的作者撰写《萨克森法典》，无疑，该作者在《萨克森法典》中陈述了比他发现的当时存在的法律命题数量更多的法律命题。今天，人们某种程度上已经知道他是如何完成这项工作的。在公法领域中，他带着帝国古老荣耀的理想观念工作。这里，我们将不讨论这些。但是，如果我们研究一下私法——此处我们最关心的部分——我们将会发现：作者有力、自觉地对在他狭小的祖国疆域内的私人法律关系形式予以一般化，在作者担任陪审法官时，他有机会熟悉了这些法律关系，最可能的是，他曾经或多或少创造过这些法律关系。尽管对家庭、占有关系、契约内容和各种阶层和阶级关系的法律规整存在巨大的多样性，但在受经济统一性和法律文件制度影响的特定地区，通过直接的摹仿和借鉴，在不动产法、专门职业法、家庭法和契约法中共同的特征发展起来。他们吸引了艾克·冯·凡格罗的注意力，无疑，他是一个有丰富经验和观察力敏锐的人，他在他的书中系统地介绍了这些特征。由于他不是在起草一部法典而是在撰写一本法律书，所以他主要关心对同类法律关系的共性予以支持，而对

disapproval of that which was divergent or peculiar. The latter was not to be done away with; for it was just as much entitled to continue as that which is general. But the effect was a different one; for posterity did not treat the *Sachsenspiegel* as a book of law, but as a code. The divergent and peculiar was greatly disadvantaged by these universalizations, which he had laid down and, in part, had laid down quite arbitrarily; for in every instance it had the burden of proving that it was permissible. Success in this matter was a matter of comparatively rare occurrence, much rarer than it had been before the general had been laid down. We must assume that it was successful only when the parties concerned had already become aware of it, especially when it had been recorded in writing either in a collection of laws or in a document containing a grant. Accordingly the mere fact of universalization in the *Sachsenspiegel* became a self-active, law-creating force; the general became a rule; the divergent and peculiar, an exception. In this way, the *Sachsenspiegel* has become a universal norm for decision even beyond the boundaries of the German Empire; of course not in the form of a universalization but as a precept, as a norm in the sense that now the decision based on the universalization of the *Sachsenspiegel* has been substituted for the decision based on the subjective nature of the individual legal relation, at least in all cases where the divergence and peculiarity was not clearly and unmistakably manifest. It is weil known that this development has often gained legal force for the doctrines of the *Spiegler*, even when the latter did not contain universalizations but free inventions. This highly remarkable peculiarity of juristic science, the conversion of its forms of thought, of its legal theorems, into norms, this great antinomy of juristic science, is the basis upon which its worldhistorical position rests.

The *Schwabenspiegel* and the smaller *Kaiserrecht* arose in the same

殊的内容没有表达否定。不过,后者并没有被清除;因为它们正如一般的东西一样,有权继续存在下去。但是,效果却有所不同;因为后人并没有将《萨克森法典》当作一本法律典籍来对待,而是当作了一部法典来对待。分歧的或特殊的内容被作者规定的——相当程度上是相当武断的——这些一般化置于一种极为不利的位置。因为在每一种情况下,后者都有责任证明它是被允许的。在这件事情上,成功是相当罕见的,比一般化内容制定之前成功的几率更为罕见。我们必须承认,只有当相关当事人早已意识到它、尤其是在法律汇编或包含有授权的文件中书面记录了它的时候,它才是成功的。因此,《萨克森法典》中一般化的单纯事实变成了一种自动的法律创制力量;一般化的东西变成一个规则,分歧的或特殊的东西成为了例外。通过这种方式,《萨克森法典》变成了一种一般性的裁判规范,这种裁判规范甚至超越了德意志帝国的国界;当然它不是以一般化的形式,而是作为如下意义上的一种规定、一种规范的形式:现在以《萨克森法典》一般化为基础的裁决代替了那些基于个别法律关系的主观性质的裁决——至少在分歧和特殊性并不是非常清晰和明显的时候都是如此。众所周知,这种发展经常为施皮格勒[1]的学说赢得法律效力,即使在后者包含的不是一般化而是自由创设时,也是如此。该法学显著的特殊性、其思想形式、法律规则的形式向规范的转变、以及该法学巨大的自相矛盾是该法学在世界历史上的位置得以奠立的基础。

《施瓦本法典》和一本短小的《帝国法律其中分歧的或特》

〔1〕 即《萨克森法典》的作者。

way and have attained a similar importance. In France the same thing occurred in the case of several books of law, especially the *Grand Coutumier de Normandie*, the *Etablissements de Saint Louis*, the *Somme rural*, and, although not until long after the death of the author, the *Beaumanoir*; in England, in the case of Bracton, much more so, in the case of Littleton and Coke. We may pass by the Swedish, Norwegian, and Icelandic books of law, since they are closely connected with the peculiar *Gesetzsprecheramt* (office of declarer of law); the Danish law-books however do not differ much from the works named above. The same may be said of the records of the feudal law, the Assizes of Jerusalem, the *Libri feudorum*, the feudal law of the *Sachsenspiegel*. In this way the great work of Hugo Grotius

都是通过这种方式产生，并且具有同样的重要性。在法国，同样的事发生在几本法律著作中——尤其是《诺曼底大习惯法》、[1]《圣路易汇编》、[2]《乡村合集》，[3]还有直到作者去世很久以后才成名的《博马努瓦尔》；[4]在英格兰，就布莱克顿而言，情形也是如此，关于利特尔顿和柯克更是如此。我们可以省略瑞典、挪威和冰岛的法律典籍，因为，它们和奇特的 *Gesetzsprecheramt*（宣布法律的官员）密切关联；不过，丹麦的法律书籍和上面提到的著作没有多大的差别。这话也同样适用于封建法的历史记载、《耶路撒冷法律和法律论文集》、[5]《封土之律》、[6]《萨克森法典》中的封建法。通过这种方式，胡果·格劳秀斯的伟大

---

〔1〕 法学家莫赛于1270～1275年编纂的著名习惯法汇编。

〔2〕 1269路易9世颁布的法律法规汇编。

〔3〕 法国自15世纪以后出现的习惯法汇编。

〔4〕 即《博瓦西斯习惯法》，作者是菲利普·德·博玛努瓦尔（Phillipe de Beaumanoir），13世纪的法国行政官兼法学家。《博瓦西斯习惯法》是论述古法国传统习惯法的最重要的著作之一。在这本书中，博玛努瓦尔详细记述了博瓦西斯的法律，同时也提出了某些私法原则。这些私法原则对于近现代私法的发展，起到重要的影响作用。

〔5〕 法律和法律评论的汇编。1009年，克罗塞蒂斯征服巴勒斯坦后，布由林的戈弗雷根据传统的习惯规则，为东方拉丁王国政府制定的。它主要基于学者归纳的一些本国习惯法，实质上反映了整个欧洲法律的共同性。旧版丢失后，新版的内容基础主要是13世纪的情形。它们强调了贵族高级法院的法权和特权，并描绘了一个理想的封建制度。

〔6〕 该律乃12世纪编定的伦巴第地方（意大利北部）的习惯法，记载着关于封臣以服军役为条件领有封土及其相关权利义务等。

has created the modern law of nations.

The significance of the books of law lies not only in the fact that they universalize but in the fact that this process of universalization leads to reduction to unity. He who universalizes merely states that which is universally valid; but reduction to unity always imports a precept to the effect that the particular should conform to the universal. Universalization in itself is merely a logical process without which scientific and practical thinking is impossible. But in juristic science it is norms that are being subjected to this process, not the unifying regularity of phenomena, as in the other practical sciences and in the true sciences. And in consequence it is not more nearly universal unifying regularities that result from the logical process, as is usual in cases of universalization, but universal norms. The great antinomy of juristic science which, I presume, the latter has in common with all other practical sciences that deal with norms, but not with the other practical sciences and with the true sciences, lies in this, that its modes of thought and its doctrines are being converted into norms.

To begin with, it would be most amateurish forthwith to draw inferences as to Roman legal development from mediaeval, especially Germanic, legal development. In the days of the Republic, the Roman law was valid, in the main, only in a very small area, and a legal system of this kind is something quite different from a legal system that is valid in a vast area like the German. On the other hand one cannot compare it with the Italian or the German city laws; for in the latter the city population, which is engaged in commercial and industrial pursuits, was the important consideration, while the Roman law of the more ancient times dealt preponderantly with the nobility and the peasantry of the adjacent open country. In the days of the Empire it was being transformed, rapidly and positively, into a system of law adapted to the needs of an empire. The development was supervised and in part directed from a single center, and in this respect can be compared only with the English law, as to which the London courts have been fulfilling a similar function from the days of Henry II. But the Roman Empire was much larger than England, so far as the London courts are concerned, ever has been, and the provinces enjoyed a much greater measure of independence in the matter of law than the

著作建立了现代国际(公)法。

法学著作的重要性不仅在于它们一般化的事实,而且在于这种一般化的过程导致了化而为一。那些进行一般化的人仅仅表述那些一般有效的东西;但是化而为一总是意味着一个效力准则:具体应符合一般。一般化自身仅仅是一个逻辑过程,没有它,科学和实践的思考都不可能。但是,在法学中,经历此过程的是规范,并不是现象统一的规律性,如同在其他实践科学和纯科学中一样。结果,从该逻辑过程中产生的并不是更接近一般的、统一的规律性,而是一般性的规范。我相信,法学的巨大矛盾——法学与处理规范的所有其他实用学科(而非与其他实用科学和纯科学)共同均存在的巨大矛盾——在于,法学的思考模式和学说模式正在被转变为规范。

首先,毫不犹豫地从中世纪、尤其是日耳曼的法律发展中获得有关罗马法的推论将是最业余的。在共和国时期,罗马法大体上只在非常狭小的范围内有效,此种法律制度非常不同于像在德国这样广阔的地区有效的法律制度。另一方面,任何人都不能把罗马法和意大利或者德国的城邦法相比较;因为在城邦法中,从事着商业或工业经营的城市人口是一个重要的考虑因素,然而更古老时代的罗马法主要处理邻近的空旷乡村里的贵族和农民。在帝国时期,罗马法迅速、彻底地转变为适合于帝国需要的法律制度。罗马法的发展受到单一中心的监督和部分指导;在这方面,它只能和英格兰的法律相比较,伦敦法院在亨利二世时代就在履行类似的功能。但是罗马帝国要比英格兰广阔得多,就伦敦的法院而言,罗马帝国各行省在法律事务方面享有的独立性比英格兰各地区所享有的大得多,或许要比今

various parts of England; perhaps more than is generally believed today. A comparison with France, at least up to the time of the Revolution, would be much more fitting were it not for the fact that the French provinces, in spite of their subjection to the Parliaments, were so much more independent in their creation of law than the Roman, at least so far as the law pertaining to Roman citizens is concerned. Moreover, we must take into account the condition of the Roman tradition. As to the time of the Republic it is extremely fragmentary, and as to the days of the Empire it presents only that in which the jurists of the capital were interested, and it presents this with a marked metropolitan coloring that dominates the whole presentation. In addition to the discussion of the law concerning the peasantry and the rural nobility, which undoubtedly constitutes a heritage from the days of the Republic, there is a presentation only of the law concerning the magistrates of the capital and the official class; commerce and industry receive scant attention.

If one bears in mind these extraordinarily important differences, one has eliminated the most important sources of error in the comparison of the development of the mediaeval law with that of the Roman law. In the first place this comparison shows the historical position of the law of the Twelve Tables. We must concede to Pais and Lambert that throughout historical times there has been no authentic tradition of its text. This is proved by the comparatively modern language, by the fact that its text varies in different quotations, by the many interpolations that date from a later time, e. g. the statement as to the division of the *nomina* and the *aes alienum* among the heirs, or the proposition that the title to the thing sold does not pass to the buyer until the price has been paid. But I think that there is abundant testimony that the Romans had a codification, perhaps an official one, albeit one poorly transmitted, of the old customary law, which goes back in substance to the fifth or fourth century before our era. So far as one can judge from the content that has been handed down, it parallels the Germanic folk laws throughout. In the main, it contained precepts as to procedure, penal law, law of damages, right of collateral relations to inherit, rights of neighbors, *ius sacrum*. Over and above this there are a few propositions about forms of contracts and testaments. The former perhaps are interpolations; the latter, perhaps, originally had a

天通常所相信的还要大。倘若不是因为这一事实:尽管服从于议会,但法国各省在创制法律方面要比罗马更独立,至少就适用于罗马公民的法律而言,那么,拿罗马和法国比较,至少和直到法国大革命前的法国比较,会更加恰当。另外,我们必须考虑到罗马传统的状况。在共和国时期,罗马的传统是不连续的;在帝国时期,罗马的传统仅展现了首都的法学家感兴趣的部分,并且这种展现始终贯穿着一种支配性的、明显的大都市的色彩。除了对涉及到农民和乡村贵族的讨论外,这种讨论毫无疑问地构成了来自共和国时期的遗产,那里仅有涉及到首都地方行政官和官员阶层的法律介绍;商业和工业极少受到重视。

如果一个人牢记这些格外重要的区别,那么他就消除了在对中世纪法律的发展和罗马法的发展比较中最重要的错误根源。首先,这一比较揭示了《十二铜表法》的历史地位。我们必须向帕艾斯和兰伯特让步:整个历史时期中并不存在那种文本所说的正式传统。这一点被比较现代的文本用语、被其文本在不同的引用中的变化、被来自稍后时代的许多添写所证明,例如继承人中关于任命和信托让与区分的介绍,或者是出售之物所有权在价款被付清以前所有权并不转移给买方的命题。但是,我认为大量的证据证明罗马人有一部法律汇编,或许是一个官方文本(尽管传播的情况糟糕),基本是关于可以追溯到我们时代以前四五个世纪的旧习惯法。单就其流传下来的内容来判断,它完全和日耳曼民间法相似。大体上,它包含了关于诉讼法、刑法、损害赔偿法、旁系亲属继承权、相邻权和奉祀礼仪法的规则。除这些之外,还包含了一些关于契约和遗嘱形式的法律命题。前者或许是一些添写;后者或许

meaning quite different from that which was attributed to them at a later time.

If this is correct, it follows that, at the time the Twelve Tables originated, the store of legal propositions was in a general way comparable to that which existed among the Germanic peoples in the sixth or in the eighth century. The chief significance of this fact is that by that time the Roman of those days had become aware of only a very small part of the law of society. As in mediaeval German law, the majority of the norms for derision had to be derived, in each individual case, from the subjective nature of the various legal relations. The fact that we find no trace of the great diversity which we meet with in the history of the German Empire and of German law can be explained by the fact that the territory in which the Roman law of the Twelve Tables, as well as that of the period immediately following, was valid was a very minute one in comparison with that in which the German law prevailed; but, in proportion to the extent of territory, the Roman legal institutions of the time of the Twelve Tables surely were not more unitary than those of the kingdom of the Franks or of mediaeval Germany. The idea that there ever was a unitary law of the Roman *gentes* is out of the question. Each *gens* had its own law, which was based on tradition, perhaps upon precept, surely not, upon legislation. An abundance of vestiges of this law of the individual *gentes* may be found in historical times. Surely there were common features which permitted of a comprehensive presentation such as was perhaps contained in the lost pages of Gaius. Nor must it be thought that the law of the Roman household, as we know it, was quite generally the inner order of the Roman house. In my book on Legal Capacity, I have shown that the family law that has been handed down by tradition referred only to the relations of the family to the outer world. The inner order of the family must have been subject to very great variations according to rank, calling, wealth, place, descent, *gens*, and also as to time, from century to century. It is quite unthinkable that the Roman artisan or the small merchant or even the proletarian ever was a member of the larger family as we know it, or that the foreigner who had acquired

最初完全不同于在后来所加给它的意义。

如果这是正确的，那么可以得出结论：一般而言，在《十二铜表法》产生的时代，大量的法律命题与在6世纪或8世纪日耳曼民族中存在的法律命题相似。这一事实的主要意义是：在那以前的时代，罗马人仅仅注意到社会法律中的很小一部分。如同在中世纪的德国法中，每一个案中的大多数裁判规范都不得不从各种法律关系的主观性质中推得。我们在别处根本不会发现如同在德意志帝国和德国法历史中所遇到的那种巨大多样性，这一点可以被如下事实所解释：《十二铜表法》及紧接着那段时期中的法律，仅仅在一个与德国法盛行的地域相比而非常狭小的地域范围内有效；但是，依照其地域范围的比例而言，《十二铜表法》时代的罗马法律制度，确实不比法兰克王国或中世纪的德国法律制度更统一。那种认为曾经存在过统一的罗马宗族法的观点是不可能成立的。每一个宗族都有自己的法律，宗族的法律是以传统，或许是以训诫为基础，但确实不是以立法为基础。这种个别宗族法的大量残余可以在若干历史时代中看到。确实，存在着容许全面陈述的共同特征，譬如在盖尤斯的丢失的书页中可能包含的共同特征。同时不能认为：如我们所知，罗马家庭法通常完全是罗马家庭的内部秩序。在我的著作《权利能力》中，我已经证明，通过传统传给我们的家庭法仅仅涉及家庭和外部世界的关系。家庭的内在秩序依据等级、职业、财富、地位、血统、宗族会有极大的变化，同时在从一个世纪到另一个世纪的斗转星移中，它也必定经历巨大的变迁。无法想象：罗马的工匠或小商人、或者甚至无产者是我们所知道的一个庞大家庭的成员；也无法想象，一个获得罗马市民身

Roman citizenship at once began to regulate his life and that of his family according to the precepts of the Roman jurists. The sources are silent on this subject because that which goes on in the bosom of the family is no concern of theirs. What does concern them is the fact that the *pater familias*, and he only, represents the household in court, and that he alone has the power of disposition over its wealth. But before this outer order had been established, the Roman family, just like the Roman *gens* down to Imperial times, had no law other than its inner order, which, just like the *gens*, it had, in the main, established itself. That the divergencies in the order of clans and families influenced the law of inheritance in the far distant past is, to say the least, very probable, in spite of the fact that the law of inheritance was the first to be regulated by general propositions. Even in Cic ero' s day inheritance among the patrician *Claudii* was regulated differently from inheritance among the plebeian *Claudii*. As to Roman land law, there is today a growing recognition of the fact that we know it only in the form into which it was put when the original constitution was abolished. That this was brought about by the Twelve Tables is the more improbable the earlier the time into which one places them. In the fifth century, the *fundus* was not yet *res mancipi*. Accordingly the *mancipatio* of the law of the Twelve Tables, if it dates from that time, could not possibly have been applicable to the *fundus*. Moreover, before the village organization and the dis-

份的外国人马上开始按照罗马法学家的规则来调节他的生活和他的家庭。原始文献在这个问题上保持了沉默，因为在家庭内部发生的事情并非法学家的关注点。他们关注的是如下事实：家父是唯一可以在法庭上代表家庭的人，他有权单独处分家庭的财产。但是，在这种外部秩序建立以前，罗马人的家庭，正如帝国时期以前罗马的宗族一样，除了它的内部秩序外没有法律，这种内部秩序，正如宗族一样，大体上也由家庭自己建立。退一步说，氏族和家庭内部秩序的差异影响了遥远过去的继承法是很可能的，尽管继承法是第一个受到法律命题调整的法律部门。即使在西塞罗的时代，对贵族克劳狄〔1〕间的继承的调整不同于对平民克劳狄间继承的调整。关于罗马的土地法，今天，人们日益认同如下事实：当最初的宪法被废除时，我们仅仅通过土地法所采取的形式而知道了它。人们认为这由《十二铜表法》在更早的时期所带来——这更是不可能。在5世纪，土地还不是要式物〔2〕。因此，如果追溯到那时，那么《十二铜表法》中的要式买卖〔3〕不可能适用于土地。而且，在村庄组

〔1〕 一个氏族名称。

〔2〕 （拉）*res mancipi*（要式物），这类物对于早期的罗马社会和经济曾经具有至关紧要的意义，因而对它们的转让必须通过要式买卖或者拟诉弃权的方式进行，例如：土地、房屋、奴隶、用于运输的牲畜、乡村地役权，等等。

〔3〕 （拉）*mancipatio*（要式买卖），市民法上最古老的一种所有权转让方式。要式买卖必须遵守一定的仪式和程序，如买卖双方当事人必须亲自到场，有五个证人和一个司秤参加，使用一套规定的术语和动作即“铜块和秤”的方式等。最初要式买卖中的仪式是实质的，以铜块击秤来检验其成色，但后来是一种象征性仪式，要式买卖也随之从财物买卖扩大适用于立遗嘱、收养子女、解放子女和奴隶等假设买卖。要式买卖在尤士丁尼时废除。

trict organization were abolished every parcel of Roman land was an individual in the same sense as the German parcel of the Middle Ages. The law that governed it was not determined by legal propositions; the latter had to be ascertained in each individual case on the basis of tradition, contracts, document of grant, location in the village mark, relations between neighbors. The Roman law of agreements, even in historical times, was by no means laced so tightly within formulae as modern presentations would lead us to believe. Of course one would have to give up at the outset the preconceived notion that the classes and the contents of agreements that the Romans were familiar with can, in some way or other, be gathered from the classes and contents of their *contractus*. So far as we can decipher the Roman law of agreements, we conclude that an agreement had to be of considerable importance in daily life before a contract action could be brought on it. The prior in time was the agreement, not the action. This was the situation in primitive times, and it was the situation in Imperial times also; there always were more agreements than *contractus*. And if one had to, or wanted to, enter into an agreement on which an action could not be brought, one would rely on *iuramentum*, *satisdatio*, *pignus*. The Catonian formulae, even though one should refer them exclusively to legally enforceable agreements (and this can hardly be correct), constitute the best evidence that assurance that the agreement would be performed was not sought for in the right to sue but in the security that was given. The sources show that in other relations, too, the Romans did not set great store by the right to sue. The great significance of *fides* appears from the rôle that was played as late

织和地区组织被废除前，罗马的每一宗土地都是一个个体，它与中世纪德国的一宗土地意义相同。调整土地的法律并不是由法律命题决定；后者不得不在每个案件中以传统、契约、转让文件、村庄马克尔土地中的位置、相邻关系为基础确定。罗马的协议法即使在历史上，也决不像现代的表述让我们相信的那样编织得如此紧密。当然，人们将不得不放弃起初预想的观念：罗马人熟悉的协议的类型和内容可以通过这种或者那种方式从他们的契约类型和内容中推测出来。在我们可以解释罗马契约法的范围内，我们断定：在可以提起契约诉讼以前，协议无疑在日常生活中相当重要。时间上在前的是协议，而不是契约诉讼。这是在原始时期的情形，也是在帝国时期的情形；协议总是比契约要多。如果一个人必须或者打算缔结一个不能据以提起诉讼的协议，那么他将依靠宣誓、担保、质押。即使一个人完全将它们称作法律上可强制执行的协议（这几乎不可能是正确的），Catonian 的公式（程式）也构成了最好的证据：协议会被履行的担保并不能诉诸于法庭，而只能在提供的担保本身中寻求。原始资料表明，在其他的关系中罗马人也没有设定大量的诉讼权利。信任的重要意义源于信托[1]在帝国后期所

〔1〕（拉）*fiducia*（信托），当事人一方（受信人）根据协议从另一方当事人（信托人）那里以要式买卖或者拟诉弃权的方式接受某物，承担义务为一定目的使用该物并且在实现此目的之后予以返还。在古典法中，信托关系一般采用信托简约的形式缔结，并且主要被用来实现担保、寄托、使用接待以及解放奴隶的目的。受信托人对信托物区的形式上的所有权，但实际上他按照简约的条款占有、使用或处置信托物。对于违反信托义务的受信托人，信托人可以提起信托之诉。

as the days of the Empire by the *fiducia*, on which an action could not be based until a very late period. The same phenomena may be observed in the case of the *fideicommissa*. The *iuramentum liberti*, too, was in vogue for a long time before an action could be brought on it. For a few contractual claims for *cerra pecunia* or *certa res*, it is true, an action lay, the *condictio*, which did not go out of use until a later period; it is possible, as many believe today, that after the adoption of the formulary procedure an *actio in factum* was given in these cases. The further we penetrate into the past, the more of contract law is found to be outside of the *ius civile*, and there were relatively fewer universally valid rules governing them.

This, it is true, is flatly contradictory to the prevailing view that the rigidity and the strict adherence to forms which characterized the older law was not relaxed until a comparatively late date, and then only gradually. The latter view, however, is based, perhaps, on several misunderstandings. It is not true that life and intercourse among men were bound by rigid forms; but appeal to the courts

起到的重要作用，不过，直到帝国后期才能以信托为基础提起诉讼。在遗产信托[1]的情形下，可以观察到同样的现象。宣誓解放自由人也是在可诉诸法庭前流行了很长一段时间。确实，对于一些关于确定金钱或者某物的契约请求权而言，诉讼以请求给付之诉的形式被提起，这种请求给付之诉直到后来才被废止；情况可能是这样：如同今天很多人相信的那样，在采用了程式诉讼后，事实之诉[2]就被限制在上述这些情形下。我们越是深入地探究过去，我们就会发现更多的契约存在于市民法外，调整它们的一般有效的规则相当稀少。

的确，这与主流观点截然对立，主流观点认为作为旧法特征的僵化和严格遵循形式直到相对后来的时期才有所松动，而且当时仅仅是逐渐地松动。然而，后一种观点或许建立在几个误解之上。人们之间的生活与交往受到严格形式拘束——这并不真实；

---

〔1〕 (拉)*fideicommiss*(遗产信托)，是一种死因财产处置行为，表现为遗产处置人委托其继承人、受遗赠人实施某种使第三人受益的行为。例如：要求受托人将遗产全部或者部分转移给第三人，要求受托人解放某个奴隶。在罗马社会中，遗产信托不要求严格的法律形式，它对受托人只产生一种道义上的义务，最初并不具有法律约束力；奥古斯都首先在一些特殊情况中从法律上认可了这一制度，允许对不履行义务的受托人进行非常审判，后来甚至出现了两名专门负责审理遗产信托案件的裁判官。

〔2〕 (拉)*action in factum*(事实诉讼)，当某一新的关系不涉及由市民法所调整的权利，并且关系人不能借助法定诉讼程序解决该关系产生的争议时，裁判官允许当事人针对创造上述关系的事实提起诉讼；在此种诉讼中，裁判官所维护的不是法律明确承认的权利，而是事实上存在的、新的公平关系。从一定意义上讲，所有的裁判官诉讼在最初的时候均表现为事实诉讼，随着它们的逐渐发展与成熟，其中一部分上升为权利诉讼。

was permitted only under very strict conditions. In general, one must get rid of the idea that the courts were open to everyone in primitive times, as they are today, just because one's right had been violated. In order to appeal to the courts, one had to be a man of power, and such a person engaged in litigation only with his equals. The appeal to law took the place of the feud. Even in historical times, instances can be found on every page of legal history that show the importance of having a powerful patron in litigation. In the typical action against a poor man, the *legis actio per manus iniectionem*, the decisive question was whether the defendant could find a man of rank and wealth, an *assiduus*, to take his part. The rigid, staccato forms of the court procedure correspond to the relation between two mortal enemies as they stand before the judge; they are of the same coinage as the rules of single combat.

But the prerequisites to resort to law have nothing to do with the forms and formalities of legal life. Originally the basis for a cause of action could consist only in an accusation that the accused had perpetrated a misdeed. The *malo ordine tenes* of Frankish times was, as is now admitted, the basis of the *rei vindicatio* also. As to this basis of a cause of action the formalities of commercial intercourse are altogether immaterial. The claim arising from contract, the only one as to which rigid forms could be decisive, is one of those that did not become justiciable until a very late period of time. Since the oldest form of legal protection provided for the contract consists merely in the protection of the possession which was transferred by means of the contract, it is self-evident that the contract is enjoying legal protection only in-

不过,诉诸于法庭只在非常严格的条件下才被许可。总的来说,人们必须摆脱这样的观念:法庭在原始时代正如今天这样,它们向每一个(仅仅)权利受到侵犯的人敞开着大门。为了诉诸于法庭,一个人必须有权利,而且这样的一个人也只能与跟其地位对等的人进行诉讼。诉诸于法律代替了世仇。甚至在历史上,在法律史的每一页上都能发现那样的例子,证明有一个强大的保护人的重要性。在典型的针对一个穷人的诉讼——拘禁之诉中,决定性的问题是被告能否找到一个拥有地位和财富的人、一个有固定住所者参加到他这一方。僵化的、不连贯的法庭诉讼程序与站在法官前之死敌的关系相符合;他们同属作为"单挑对决"规则的那枚硬币。

但是,付诸法律的先决条件与法律生活的形式和手续没有关系。最初,诉因的基础仅在于对被指控者犯有罪行的控告。如同现在所承认的,法兰克时期的违法占取也是返还所有物之诉[1]的基础。关于这种诉因的基础,商业交往的手续是完全无关紧要的。产生自契约请求权——关于严格的形式具有决定性意义的唯一的请求权——是直至很靠后的时期才成为可诉的那些请求权的一种。既然提供给契约的最古老的法律保护形式仅仅在于对依契约所转移之占有物的保护,那么不言而喻,契约享有法律保护仅仅是

---

〔1〕(拉)*rei vindicatio*(返还所有物之诉),典型的要求维护市民法所有权的诉讼,表现为物品的所有主针对非法占据其物品的人提出归还该物品的要求。在这种诉讼中首先需要认定的是物品的归属,它最初采取的是对物的誓金法律诉讼形式,即双方当事人当着法官的面各自提出所有权主张并进行赌誓,宣称有关物品归自己所有。

as much as it is accompanied by transfer of possession. But the fact that the contract was protected only where it was accompanied by transfer of possession does not make transfer of possession a formality of the contract. In the gradual severance of the obligation of the contract from the transaction of transfer of possession, the gradual strengthening of the idea of the independent contract may be seen. Not until then did symbols of possession become a matter of form. The calling of witnesses to assure the buyer that the thing sold had not been stolen, or of relatives whose consent was necessary to make the alienation binding—these things are not formalities. And it is just as improper to conceive of the crudeness and the clumsiness of the oldest form of procedure, which made a straightforward presentation of the state of facts, a more careful elaboration of the claim, and the effective assertion of defenses, impossible, as strictness of form. These things were merely defects of technique, not formalism. Primitive times know of awkward and naive, but not of rigid, forms. Wherever the latter arise, in religion, in art, and in law, the order of development, as history teaches us wherever we can trace it far enough, is a hardening of forms that originally had been soft and flexible, not the reverse. It is true, a time comes when they become an unendurable fetter, which occasionally is thrown off all of a sudden, but we must not on that account believe that the fetter lies at the beginning of all development. Wherever we are enabled to survey a longer period of time, as in Germany, France, and England, we become convinced that the law has always developed from freedom to rigidity. At any rate we may be permitted to quote the words of Maitland concerning English law, which ever since the fifteenth century had been stifling more and more in a veritable bog of formalism until it regained a fair measure of freedom through the influence of Bentham in the nineteenth century. Says Maitland: "It is a mistake to suppose that our common law starts with rigid, narrow rules—knows only a few precisely defined forms of gift, and rejects everything that deviates by a hair's-breadth from the established models. On the contrary, in the thirteenth century it is elastic and liberal, loose and vague." Accordingly Roman juristic science found itself, at the beginning of its career, probably in the fourth century B. C.,

因为契约中伴随着占有的转移。但是,契约仅仅在伴随着占有转移的地方才受到保护并没有使占有转移成为契约的形式。在契约债务逐渐从占有转移交易中分离的过程中,可以看到独立的契约观念不断强化。直到那时,占有的象征才变为了一个形式问题。邀请证人使买方确信出卖物并不是偷来的,或者寻求亲戚的同意从而使转让具有拘束力——所有的这些都不是手续。想想最古老诉讼程序形式的生硬和笨拙,它使得对事态的直接陈述、对请求权更细节的表达、对抗辩的有效主张变得不可能,这正如形式的严格一样不妥当。这些情形仅仅是技术的瑕疵,而不是形式主义。原始时代知道有笨拙的和幼稚的形式,却不知道有僵化的形式。无论后者在什么地方——在宗教、艺术或是在法律中——产生,发展的次序如历史告诉我们的那样(只要我们追溯得足够久远)——都是由最初曾经柔和、灵活的形式逐渐走向僵化的过程,而不是相反。的确,当形式变成不能忍受的桎梏,一个时代到来了,这种桎梏偶尔会突然被尽数除去,但是,我们不能据此就相信,桎梏存在于所有发展的开始阶段。在我们能够考察更长时间的任何地方,如在德国、法国和英格兰,我们会确信,法律总是从自由向僵化发展。至少,请允许我们引用梅特兰关于英格兰法的陈述,从那时到 15 世纪,英格兰法越来越窒息在名副其实的形式主义沼泽中,直到 19 世纪在边沁的影响下,英格兰法才重新获得了合理程度上的自由。梅特兰说:“那种以为我们的普通法始于僵硬、刻板的规则——仅仅知道一些精确界定的赠与形式,拒绝对已建立模式的任何微小偏离——的观点是错误的。相反,在 13 世纪,普通法是富有弹性的、自由的、宽松的和不清晰的。”因此,罗马法学大概在公元前 4 世纪其事业刚起

face to face with the same task that confronted the writer of the *Sachsenspiegel* when he began writing his book. There were only a few universal legal propositions in a comparatively small number of branches of private law. In other cases, the norms had to be found by observing life; one had to ascertain what custom was in vogue in the *gens* or in the family on the point in question, what agreement the parties had reached and entered into, what was commercial or trade usage in a given region or class. If we take a look at the fragments of the juristic science of the Republic, or at Labeo, or at Sabinus, we shall discover that the Roman law has traveled a long way in the course of fewer centuries by far than separate the *lex Salica* from the *Sachsenspiegel*. In this extremely fragmentary tradition we find a wealth of legal propositions, which, in part, have been elaborated to a marvelous degree of refinement. In spite of the great amount of labor that has been bestowed upon the study of the history of Roman law, no satisfactory answer has been found to the question whence the Romans got their legal material. In time past the belief was universal that they had obtained it by a process of interpretation from the statutes and from the edict.① But this answer would merely shift the question somewhat, for we should then be constrained to ask whence the statutes and the edict got their legal materials. But we may now regard this doctrine as generally abandoned. At the present time, we have sufficient knowledge of the Twelve Tables, of the later private law statutes, and of the edict to know that this great wealth could not possibly have been obtained there. At most, they have made contributions of consequence

① This clearly is the view of Mommsen, *Staatsrecht*, III, p. 604, n. 2.—*Author's note*.

步时，发现自己面临着与《萨克森法典》的著者开始写这本著作时所面临的相同的任务。只有很少普遍有效的法律命题在相当少的私法部门中存在。在其他的情形下，规范必须通过观察生活获得。在有疑问时，人们必须探明：什么样的习惯在宗族或者家庭中流行，当事人达成和缔结了什么协议，在一特定地区或阶级中有什么样的商业或贸易惯例。如果我们看一下共和国时期或拉贝尔时期或萨宾时期的法学文字片段，那么我们将会发现：迄今罗马法在比《萨利克法典》[1]与《萨克森法典》分离过程更短的几个世纪内，走过了长长的一段路。在这极不完整的传统中，我们发现了丰富的法律命题，这些法律命题部分地被详细阐述到一种不可思议的程度。尽管对罗马法历史的研究投入了大量的劳动，但是对罗马人从何处获得法律素材这一问题仍没有得出满意的回答。过去，人们普遍相信：罗马法学家是从对制定法和告示[2]解释的过程中获得法律素材的。① 但是，这一回答仅仅是稍稍转换了问题，因为我们将会接着被迫追问：制定法和告示从哪里获得它们的法律素材。但是，现在我们可以认为这一学说已被广泛摒弃。目前，我们已经有了关于《十二铜表法》、后来的私法制定法以及告示的充足知识，知道大量的法律命题是不可能从那里获得的。至多，

---

① 这明显是 Mommsen 的观点，《国家法》，III，p. 604，n. 2。

〔1〕（拉），*lex Salica*，《萨利克法典》。这是现存最古老的日耳曼法典，是关于萨利安法兰克人的法律和后经修订、增补，形成文字的古代习俗的汇编。它编纂于公元 5 世纪，在法兰克各民族中有极高的权威并产生了重大的影响，成为了同时期其他法典的重要渊源。

〔2〕（罗马法）告示：罗马地方长官，如裁判官、监察官等在各自辖区内以公告发布的命令。

only to the law of unlawful acts and of intestate succession. Perhaps I may claim for myself the credit of having shown in my *Beiträge zur Theorie der Rechtsquellen* that Roman juristic science has created its material independently of any other source of law. The main root of the Roman law is the *proprium ius civile*, i. e. the juristic law which the jurists themselves have created. According to the words of Pomponius, it is the *ius quod sine scripto venit compositum a prudentibus*, *ius quod sola prudentium interpretatione consistit*, or according to Boethius, *probatae civium iudiciis creditaeque sentenciae*. Although in form an interpretation of the Twelve Tables, this *ius civile* was an absolutely independent creation of the Roman jurists. For a further discussion I must refer the reader to the book mentioned above, the conclusions of which have quite generally been accepted.

Even though it has been established that juristic science in Rome has itself furnished its material, the question where the jurists got it remains unanswered. On this point, the writings of the Roman jurists contain a great amount of information which has not yet been made accessible, and which I may possibly turn to account at some future time in a second volume of *Beiträge zur Theorie der Rechtsquellen*. Moreover there are some scattered references on this point in the literature of recent date. The *veteres*, including Labeo and Sabinus, employed the same methods that were employed by the author of the *Sachsenspiegel* (the later writers, to a great extent, merely continue working on the basis of the tradition), i. e. they have consciously, forcefully, and intelligently universalized that which they had observed within a narrow sphere, the inner order of the relations, of which they had a lively understanding from actual observation. They did not, however, select a certain place or a single class, rank, or profession as their point of departure—a proceeding which would be most unlikely at all events. Their point of view was changing continually according to the legal institution they were dealing

它们对违法行为法和无遗嘱继承法作了重要贡献。或许,我可以把我在《法源理论的贡献》中已经证明的结论归功于己:罗马法学独立于其他任何法源创造了自己的法律素材。罗马法的主要根源是自有的法学家法,即法学家自己创设的法学家法。按彭波尼的话来说,它是没有书写成文,而是通过法学家的解释来建构的法,或者按波伊丢斯的话,它是为城邦的法官所批准以及判决所赞同的。虽然是以一种对《十二铜表法》解释的形式,但法学家法完全是罗马法学家独立的创造。对于进一步的讨论,我必须让读者参阅上面提到的书,这本书的观点已经获得非常普遍的接受。

尽管已确证罗马法学为自己提供了素材,但是,法学家们从哪里获悉它这一问题却仍然没有回答。在此问题上,罗马法学家们的著作中含有大量目前尚不可理解的信息,并且我有可能在将来某个时间,在第二版《法源理论的贡献》中利用这些信息。另外,关于这个问题,在一些近期的文献中也有一些零散的参考资料。早期那些人,包括拉贝尔和萨宾,他们都用《萨克森法典》一书作者曾使用过的方法(很大程度上,稍后的著者们都仅仅以传统为基础继续工作),即:他们一直自觉地、有力地、聪明地将那些他们已在小范围内观察到的那些关系的内部秩序一般化,他们基于实际观察对这种关系的内部秩序有真切的了解。不过,他们并没有筛选一特定地域或者一单独的阶级、阶层或职业作为他们的出发点——无论如何这是最不可能的做法。他们的观点一直随他们所应对的法律制度而改变,之所以这样,

with, partly because, at the time when juristic science began to consider the question, the views of a certain class, profession, rank, or perhaps of a certain locality were dominant; partly because certain legal institutions appeared chiefly in certain social strata. But a point of view once adopted is usually maintained quite consistently throughout. The basis of the Roman family law is the constitution of the family of the Roman peasantproprietor; and this state of affairs continued after the latter had disappeared from Roman society. The enormous revaluation of all human life at the end of the Republic and in Imperial times had surely revolutionized the inner order of the family, but this fact found incredibly little of corresponding expression in the norms concerning the capacity to appear in court, the inheritance and the contract of the *filii familias*—the *senatus consultum Macedonianum*, a little mitigation of the old precepts as to the incapacity of the *filii familias* to appear in court and to acquire property or rights, a few slight changes in the law of inheritance, and nothing more. Only the law and right of *dos* in the free marriage and perhaps the free marriage itself as we find it at a later time arose among the nobility and the well-to-do middle classes. The Roman testament, too, seems to have arisen among, and to have been concerned primarily with the interests of, the peasantry. The Roman law of sales is concerned chiefly with parcels of ground, slaves, cattle—in brief, with the individual transactions of the dealings of peasants and small men; a few principles of the law of the market were universalized at a later time so as to cover other sales also. Scarcely a trace can be found of consideration of wholesale trade and industry. The *mandatum* manifestly

部分是因为，当法学开始思考此问题时，一特定的阶级、职业、阶层或者可能一特定地域的意见会主导这种思考过程；部分是因为，一些法律制度主要出现在特定的社会阶层。但是先前一度被采纳的观点却在各处完全一致。罗马家庭法的基础是罗马自耕农家庭的构造；当自耕农从罗马社会消失后，这种情势还继续着。在罗马共和国末期和帝国时期，对所有人类生活的广泛再评价无疑从根本上改变了家庭的内部秩序，但是令人难以置信的是，该事实却几乎没有引起有关出庭资格、继承和家子所缔结之契约——马切多尼安元老院决议——这些规范表达的变化，也几乎没有改善有关家子没有资格出庭、没有资格获得财产或权力的旧规定，除了在继承法中有一些轻微的改动外，没有其它任何更多的变化。如我们在后来发现的，只有在贵族和富裕的中产阶级中才能产生自由婚姻中的嫁资[1]权，或自由婚姻本身。同样，罗马的遗嘱看起来是从农民阶级中产生的，并且最主要关心的是农民阶级的利益。罗马的买卖法主要关注一块块的土地、奴隶、家畜，简而言之，关注的是农民们和小人物们的个人交易；为了涵盖其他的买卖，后来市场上的少数法律规则也被一般化了。几乎不存在考虑批发贸易和工业的痕迹。很明显，委任[2]源于贵族；它产生

〔1〕（拉）*dos*（嫁资），是妻子、她的家父或者第三人为维持婚姻生活的目的而向丈夫转让的财产；嫁资与婚姻有着必然的联系，如果婚姻无效，嫁资也就无效。在婚姻关系存续期间，嫁资归丈夫掌管，可用来补贴婚姻生活的花费。当婚姻关系解除时，丈夫应当将稼资退还妻子或其亲属；妻子或其继承人可以通过妻物之诉或者嫁资诉讼要求返还。

〔2〕（拉）*mandatum*（委任），罗马法中的合意契约之一，表现为受委托人根据委托人的指示经营一项获数项事务，后者有义务承担因上述经营行为发生的费用或损失。罗马法的委托是无偿的。

is of aristocratic origin; it arose from the relations between the great lord and his *clientes* and stewards. The roots of the law of partnership have been traced; they lie in the household of the peasant family, later in occasional associations for purposes of gain or speculation, and lastly in permanent associations for the purpose of conducting joint enterprises. *Sachmiete* (letting and hiring of a thing) involves almost exclusively law pertaining to great landed estates and tenement houses. Studies of this kind yield some information as to the time at which the law governing these institutions arose.

What the mutual relations between the two parts of the Roman law, the *ius civile* and the *ius gentium*, were while these developments were taking place is of little importance for the question we are discussing here. It is possible that the Romans in their universalizations also took the general commercial law of the nations of the Mediterranean littoral into account, but, according to what has just been stated, this does not seem probable; at any rate, they did this only to a limited extent. Moreover, transactions that manifestly were parts of the *ius gentium*, like sale, ordinary and usufructuary lease, were a basis for juristic law only in the form in which they were in use among Roman citizens. This self-evidently applies, even to a greater extent, to the *mandatum* and to the *societas*. This is the only way one can account for the fact that the law of sales remained the law chiefly of the traffic in land, slaves, and cattle and that so little is said of the subject matter and the forms of wholesale trade and other commerce, in which foreigners took part also. We must not forget that the *ius gentium* applied to Roman citizens only so far as it had become juristic law, and that to this extent, as I have shown in my book,

封建领主及其门客[1]还有管家的关系中。合伙契约法律的根源也已经被探寻到了，它们存在于农民家庭户中，后来存在于以盈利或投机买卖为目的的临时联合体中，最后存在于以管理合办企业为目的的常设联合体中。*Sachmiete*（物之租赁）几乎完全涉及适用于大宗不动产和租住房的法律。对这一问题的研究产生了一些关于这个时期的信息，在这个时代，统治这些制度的法律产生了。

罗马法的法学家法和万民法这两部分的相互关系是什么呢？难道这些正在发生的进步对我们目前正在讨论的问题不重要吗？很有可能，罗马人在法律一般化的过程中，也把地中海沿海国家的普通商法考虑在内了，但是，依据刚才所言，这个似乎不可能；无论如何，他们仅仅在有限的程度上这么做。此外，交易很明显如买卖、普通租赁和附用益权租约一样，只是万民法的一部分，仅在它们为罗马公民所运用的形式上，它们是法学家法的一个基础。不言自明，甚至在更大程度上，这也适用于委任和合伙[2]。这是唯一能解释一下事实的方法：买卖法仍然主要是土地、奴隶和家禽方面的法律，同时外国人也参与的批发贸易和其他商业的主题和形式所言极少。我们不能忘记，只有在万民法成为法学家法的时候，它才适用于罗马市民；也不能忘记，在此范围内，

---

〔1〕（拉）*clientes*（门客），依附于庇主并且处于其保护之下的从属者。门客对庇主负有遵命、服务、忠诚和提供劳务的特殊义务，他们通常从庇主那里获得一份被临时让与的土地，并且依靠庇主的帮助和保护；他们也是氏族战争和家庭圣事的参与者。

〔2〕（拉）*societas*（合伙），合伙属于合意契约之债的一种。

the Romans, when they spoke of the *ius civile*, included the *ius gentium*.

The juristic universalizations, as I have said a propos of the *Sachsenspiegel*, are one thing as to their purpose, another as to their effect. They purport to be statements of that only which is universally valid, and their effect is that everything that has been stated becomes a norm according to which everything is judged that has not been able to maintain itself as something of a distinct and particular nature. Here the great antinomy appears again to which, in every instance, juristic science owes its position in the history of the world. Universalization in its nature is a logical process through which the human mind extracts the universal from the diversity of things which would otherwise be beyond comprehension. But in juristic science the universal becomes a norm, a precept; the particular, an exception, which must justify its existence in each and every case. What the relation was between the universalizations of the Roman jurists and life cannot readily be shown in detail; but this much is certain: the latter did not follow the former in everything. It has already been pointed out that the inner order of the family of the later times did not correspond to that which the jurists had borrowed from the family of the peasant-proprietor. Another example of this is the sale, which became a contract of transfer not because of the juristic law but in spite of it. But the universalizations demonstrated their enormous power in their function as norms for decision for the courts. They were unreservedly recognized as such in Rome; and in the last analysis, even today, controversies that are covered by the law of family, of the matrimonial régime, of things, of obligations, of inheritance, and, occasionally, even of corporations are being decided according to universalizations at which the Roman jurists arrived through observation and study of indigenous relations, and which have passed over into modern law.

It is with these universalizations that have become norms for decision that is connected the boundless wealth of norms for decision which the Romans found solely for the purpose of satisfying the requirements of litigation because they believed them to be app-

如我在书中所揭示的那样，当罗马人提到法学家法时，其实是包括万民法的。

如同我已经说过的《萨克森法典》的有关情形一样，法律的一般化，其目的是一回事，其效果则是另外一回事。它们声称只陈述那些普遍有效的东西，其效果就是，所有被陈述的东西都变成了一个规范，任何不能主张自己拥有独特性和特殊性的东西都必须根据此规范来接受裁断。这里，再一次出现了巨大的悖论，在所有情况下，法学在世界历史中的位置都归因于这种悖论。一般化在本质上是一个逻辑过程，通过此过程，人类智力从事物的多样性——这种多样性以别的方法无法为人所理解——中提取一般性。但是，在法学中，这种一般性成为一个规范、一个规定；作为一种例外的特殊性，它们必须在每一种情况下证明其存在的正当性。罗马法学家一般化与生活之间到底是什么关系——这并不能轻易地详尽揭示，但可以肯定的是：生活并非在所有事情上都遵循法学家的一般化。前面已经指出，稍后时期的家庭内部秩序并不符合法学家从自耕农家庭借鉴来的内部秩序。这方面的另一个例子是销售，它变成一种转让契约不是因为法学家法，而是因为并没有理会法学家法。但是，一般化显示了它们作为裁判规范的功能对于法院的巨大作用。它们在罗马被毫无保留地承认；归根到底，甚至在今天，家庭法、婚姻制度法，物法、债法、继承法、偶尔还包括法人社团法所涵盖的法律争议，都根据罗马法学家通过对本土关系的观察和研究而获得的，并已转化为现代法的一般化来裁判。

与这无尽丰富的裁判规范相联系的正是这些已变成裁判规范的一般化，而罗马人发现这些一般化仅仅是为了满足诉讼要

ropriate means to the ends sought and to be meeting the demands of justice. They include first of all the highly ramified subsidiary and non-compulsory law of contracts, in addition, the rules relating to liability for *dolus*, *culpa*, and *mora*, to bearing the risk, to the legal consequences of mistake, to the point of time at which a legal right is acquired or lost, to claims for compensation for unjust enrichment, to the extent and the content of the procedural claim, to *Rechtskraft* (force of law), to conflict of claims. Of all of this nothing, or very little, is to be found both in the *Sachsenspiegel* and in other law-books so far as they are independent of Roman law. Even the modern English law, which in many respects is more richly elaborated than any other legal system in the world, has remained far behind the Roman law in the matter of legal propositions of this kind. For various reasons, but especially because they can most easily be transplanted to foreign soil, I am inclined to believe that it was the great store of norms for decision, clear, well thought out, and well adapted to the purpose intended, that qualified the Roman law to become a world system of law.

In spite of their fragmentary condition, the sources make a deep insight into the workshop of Roman law possible. The system of

求，因为他们相信它们是达至目标的恰当手段，且能符合正义的要求。它们首先包括分支众多的补充性和非强行性的契约法，另外还包括：与故意[1]、过失[2]和迟延责任有关的规则；有关风险承担的规则；与错误的法律后果有关的规则；有关权利取得或丧失之时点的规则；有关不当得利补偿的规则；有关程序性权利的范围和内容的规则；有关 Rechtskraft（裁决既判力）的规则；有关请求权冲突的规则等。在所有这些中，只要它们还独立于罗马法，则它们的内容不会——或只有很少的内容——能同时在《萨克森法典》和其他法律书籍中找到。即使对于在许多方面比世界上其他法律体系都要阐述得更丰富详尽的现代英国法而言，它在此类法律命题方面也要远远落后于罗马法。原因是多方面的，但特别是因为它们可以非常轻易地被移植到外国土壤中，我倾向于相信，正是这些清晰的、深思熟虑和具有良好的目的适应性的大量裁判规范，使得罗马法有资格成为一个世界性的法律制度。

尽管原始文献不太完整，不过还是让我们可能对罗马法的“制造车间”有一个深刻的洞察。在对法律发展最重要的时刻，罗

---

〔1〕（拉）*dolus*（故意，欺诈，恶意），此术语在罗马法中不仅表示一种有着明确意识和意愿的心理状态，而且可以被用来表示欺骗行为，即：一方为蒙蔽、欺骗、欺诈他人而采用的计谋、骗局和手段。

〔2〕（拉）*culpa*（过错，过失）。有两层含义，一层含义是指非法行为本身，相对应的中文术语是“过错”；另一层含义是指判定某人（特别是债务人）承担责任的主观标准，相对应的中文术语是“过失”。从前一种含义上讲“*culpa*（过错）”也包含故意而实施的非法行为；从后一种含义上讲，“*culpa*（过失）”是一种不同于故意的规则标准，主要表现为不同程度的疏忽，即：勤谨注意的缺失。

actions which prevailed in Roman law at the time that is of the greatest importance for legal development indicates that there is a distinct procedure for each claim. The parties must express their desires and requests in clear and definite terms, and at the same time perform certain acts, and all of this is definitely prescribed in the forms for each *actio*. The system of actions grew out of the procedure of primitive times. Originally an appeal to the court lay only in case of certain misdeeds, and in making his appeal the plaintiff had to state in advance not only the misdeed but also the sum which he demanded by way of penalty. Out of the complaints, which varied according to the misdeed, there arose, at a later time, actions which varied according as the claims varied. In the Roman *rei vindicatio* the connection with the old action for theft still appears quite clearly. Since it manifestly was a matter of extreme difficulty to obtain a new *actio* for a claim, the existing forms had to be worked over continually in order that the system of actions might meet the needs of life. This required great legal knowledge and technical ability. The forms had to be drawn up so that they might readily conform to the claims, and also that the very greatest possible number of claims might be asserted by means of each form. The drafts man required a keen eye for the various relations of life out of which the claims arose, and for that which was common to the great number of claims for which he was drawing up a new *actid*. All of this was of decisive importance for the art of drawing up legal documents. Because of the comparatively great rigidity and inflexibility of the *actiones* it was important to draw up a document so that an existing *actio* would fit it, or to protect the parties so fully by means of securities that they could dispense with the *actio*.

Under this system the process of universalization in a certain sense took place mechanically. Every lawyer would, as far as possible, squeeze the legal relation for which he was about to draw up a document into one of the existing documentary forms, and the claim which he was about to assert, into one of the existing litigious forms; and for each claim the *actio* yielded not only the

马法中流行的诉讼制度表明,每一种请求权都有一个独特的诉讼程序。当事人必须用清晰明确的术语来表达他们的愿望和请求,同时要履行一定的行为,所有这些都在针对每个诉讼的形式中有明确规定。诉讼制度由原始时期的诉讼程序发展而来。最初,仅仅在特定的犯罪行为下,才能诉诸于法庭,并且在控诉时,原告不但必须提前陈述犯罪行为,而且也要表明请求获得赎罪金的数额。除了因犯罪行为的不同而有所不同的原告起诉状外,随后又出现了随请求权的变化而变化的诉讼。在罗马,返还所有物之诉和针对偷窃行为的旧诉讼的关系到现在仍然很清楚。很显然,由于为一个请求权获得一个新的诉讼极为困难,所以现有的诉讼形式不得不被持续研究,以便可以使之符合生活需要。这要求有渊博的法律知识和过硬的专业技能。这些诉讼形式必须被草拟出来,以便让它们很容易符合那些请求权,同时也为了使最大可能数量的请求权能够以这些诉讼形式中的每一种来主张。起草人需要对产生那些请求权的各种各样的生活关系有敏锐的观察力,并且要对那些——他正起草的新诉讼所服务的——很多请求权共有的东西保持敏锐观察力。这一切对法律文献起草艺术而言都是至关重要的。由于诉讼相当地僵化和不灵活,所以重要的是:起草一个文件以便使现存的诉讼能适合它,或者通过担保充分保护当事人,这样他们无需诉讼也行。

在这种制度下,一般化的过程在某种意义上机械地发生了。只要可能,每位律师都会尽可能地把他将要起草文件的法律关系纳入到一个现有的文件形式中;把他即将要主张的请求权纳入一个现有的诉讼形式中;对于每一个请求权,产生的不仅是诉讼程

procedure but also, in connection with the appropriate document, a large part of the material law. The claims based on the same documentary forms and drafted according to the same litigious forms, therefore, had a series of rules of law in common. Once the document and the *actio* for a contract of *dos* have been established, a universal law of dos has been established, for everyone would draw up the contract according to the existing document in order to be enabled to avail himself of the recognized *actio*. The endeavor to economize in the use of forms led to combining quite heterogeneous relations into a common *actio*, e. g. to subsuming the contract of labor under the category of the contract of letting and hiring; or the claim of the guardian or of the curator under the category of *negotiorum gestio*. It often therefore led to very unnatural juristic constructions and to a very unsatisfactory distortion of the material law. The Romans called the art of drawing up documents *cavere*, the drawing up of the forms for litigation, *agere*; in addition there is the *respondere*, the giving of juristic opinions, which self-evidently also became a lever for universalization. There is a good deal of Roman law that we shall never understand until at least a small portion of the industry that has been expended upon the reconstruction of the praetorian edict is devoted to the practice of the lawyers who drew up legal documents. Difficult though it is to find traces of the Roman forms for contracts in our tradition, in many ways much more could be done than has been done until now. Further study will make many things clear that until now have been incomprehensible to us. By the time the freer procedure according to written formulae replaced the older spoken formulae, the technique of the jurist had become fixed to such a degree that this innovation remained without any influence whatever on it.

In my book on the theory of the sources of the law (*Theorie der Rechtsquellen*), I have dealt with the question how the opinions of the jurists became a part of the law that was binding in the law courts, i. e. of the *ius civile*. From the fragment of the Enchiridion

序，而且还包括与适当文献相联系的很大的一块实体法。因此，以相同文件形式为基础的、根据相同诉讼形式设计的请求权有一系列共有的法律规则。一旦适于嫁资契约的文件和诉讼建立起来，则有关嫁资的普遍法就建立起来了，因为每个人都会根据现有的文件起草契约，以便能利用已承认的诉讼。竭力有效利用现有诉讼形式导致把完全异质的关系融合到一个共同的诉讼中，比如：把劳动契约归入到租赁契约这一种类中，或者把监护人或保佐人请求权归入到无因管理中。因此，这经常导致法律的解释非常勉强，并且导致非常令人不满意的对实体法的曲解。罗马人把起草文件称作提供、把规划诉讼形式称作协助，另外还有解答，是给出法律意见的，不言而喻，它也成为一般化的手段。有大量的罗马法，直到耗费在裁判官告示重建上的辛勤劳动——其中至少一小部分被用于研究起草法律文件之律师的实践后，我们才终于理解。尽管从我们的传统中找出罗马契约形式的痕迹很困难，但是，我们原本可以在很多方面比迄今所做的做得更多。进一步的研究，将会使迄今我们无法理解的东西变得非常清晰明白。随着代替古老的口头程式的书面程式而变得更自由的诉讼程序出现的那个时候为止，法学家的技巧已经变得那么固定，以至于这种革新仍旧不会对该技术产生任何的影响。

在我的有关法源理论的书中，我已经处理了这个问题：法学家的见解如何成为了在法庭上有约束力的法律的一部分，即成为市民法的一部分。通过彭波尼《指南》的片断（不幸的是

of Pomponius, which unfortunately is very incomplete, we can gather only that in the days of the Republic the only requisite was that they should emerge victoriously from the *disputatio fori*. According to a remark of Suetonius, Caesar was anxious to regulate the matter (*ius civile ad certum modum redigere*); perhaps Augustus merely carried out this intention when he regulated the *ius respondendi*. But the jurists were not creating law solely by giving opinions; their influence as teachers and writers must have been much more effective. A glance at the juristic literature that has come down to us will show what method they pursued. The jurist usually introduces his opinion with extreme modesty, e. g. *et puto*, *magis arbitror*, *sed magis sentio*, *aequius est*, *magis est*; but occasionally a more forcible expression like *existimo constituendum* is found. At this point the *disputatio* begins, no longer in the forum but in the literature, employing phrases like the following: *et magis placuit*, *sed magis visum est*, *et magis putat Pomponius*, *el ego puto*, *secundum Scaevolae sententiam quam puto veram*, *et magis admittit* (*Marcellus*) *tenere eum*, *el est aequissimum*, or a phrase of rejection: *quae sententia vera non est et a multis*

《指南》非常不完整),我们只能了解到,在共和国时期,唯一的要件是它们能从法庭辩论中成功地脱颖而出。根据苏维托尼乌斯[1]的评论,凯撒急于规范这件事(即以某种方式编辑市民法);或许奥古斯都[2]仅仅是在它规范解答权时实现了这个意图。但是法学家们不完全是通过给予见解来创造法律的;他们作为教师和作者的影响力肯定是更有效的。稍稍浏览一下流传下来的法学文献就能看出他们运用的哪种方法。法学家经常用极端谦虚地姿态提出他们的观点,比如:我觉得,最好是这样说,如果就更好的而言,公正地来说;偶尔也会用比较强硬的表达:我的判断是。在这一点上,辩论不再在法庭上而是在文献中开始,并使用如下的短语,较好的决定,从较好的观点看,彭波尼认为最好是,我认为,根据谢沃拉的观点,(马切勒)认为最好采纳这样的观点,根据被认为是正确的观点来判断,或者关于反对的短语:正确的判断

〔1〕 公元二世纪的罗马史学家,著有《罗马十二帝王传》(又译《诸凯萨生平》)。

〔2〕 即屋大维(Gaius Julius Caesar Octavianus),又名奥古斯都。屋大维是凯撒大帝的甥孙和养子,亦被正式指定为凯撒的继承人,罗马帝国开国皇帝。

*notata est*, *nec utimur Servii sententia*; until finally the rule is established: *maiores constituerunt*, *Cassii sententia utimur*, *Labeo scribit eoque iure*, *el hoc et Julianus admittit eoque iure utimur*, *haec Quintus Mucius referter vera sunt*, *abolita est enim quorundam veterum sententia*. Until one could say of a rule which had been stated by a jurist, *eoque iure utimur*, it had not finallv won its way to victory.

It seems that the praetorian law did not begin its powerful and independent development until the formulary procedure had been introduced. Doubtless the creative activity of the praetor has been overestimated for a long time. Lenel' s reconstruction of the edict shows sufficiently how small the contribution of the praetor to the whole proud structure of the Roman law was. The edict contains legal propositions of very diverse kinds: procedural law, penal law, police regulation. So far as it contains civil law, it is, for the greater part, juristic law, and, what is more, judgemade juristic law. It was found by the praetor in the course of his judicial activity. His norms closely follow the norms of juristic law, the procedural forms of which the praetor availed himself, often with very insignificant changes, for his purposes; and there can scarcely be any doubt that the same jurists who were perfecting the *ius civile* inspired the thoughts which the praetor embodied in his edict. And so his finding of norms, just like that of juristic law, is based upon universalization of the concrete nature of the various relations of life, and in part upon the same principles of justice and fairness that the jurists follow. It is true, the praetor was limited by the *leges* and the *ius civile*, and perhaps had to render obedience to the commands of the senate; in any case, however, relying on his *imperium* he could proceed

不是这样的,正如许多人知道的,塞尔维的观点不正确;直到最终建立起如下规则:多数人认为,卡西最后认为,拉贝奥认为法应该是这样,尤里安最后认为法的规则应该是,昆图斯.穆齐认为正确的应该是,在这一问题上,先前的观点被否认。直到任何人都能提到一个被法学家表述过的规则,最后所认可的法,该规则才最终赢得了胜利。

似乎直到程式诉讼被采用之后,裁判官法才开始获得有力而独立的发展。毫无疑问,很长时间以来,裁判官的创造活动被高估了。莱内尔对告示的重新完整揭示充分证明,裁判官对整个辉煌的罗马法大厦的贡献是多么小。告示中包含了多种多样的法律命题:诉讼法、刑法、治安条例。就它所包含的民法而言,大部分都是法学家法,而且是法官创设的法学家法。裁判官在其司法活动中发现了它。裁判官规范紧紧遵随法学家法的规范,他在利用该规范的诉讼形式时,经常会基于特定目的而做一些无关紧要的变化;几乎毫无疑问,完善法学家法的法学家同时也是启迪裁判官的人,在裁判官告示中体现前者思想。正如法学家法一样,裁判官发现规范也是基于对多种生活关系之具体性质的一般化,部分则是基于法学家遵循的正义和公平的原则。诚然,裁判官受到法律和市民法的限制,或许裁判官还不得不服从元老院的命令;然而,无论

much more boldly and with much more determination than the jurists. It is difficult to determine at the present time where the line was drawn for him; perhaps it varied with the time and the personality of the praetor.

But the purely practical activity of the jurist does not explain everything. A legal system that is the outcome of a purely practical legal activity leads only to a series of legal propositions loosely strung together, like the mediaeval German law and, in many respects, the modern English law. The fact that the Roman law, as early as the days of the jurists of the later Republic, seems to be a well ordered and perfect structure, containing a great number of universal legal propositions, must be attributed to the fact that the Roman jurists were not only practicing lawyers, but also writers and teachers. Of course, had they been writers and teachers only, their word would have had no greater weight than that which is given to it by their reasoning; they must needs, like the English writers of text-books, have been confining their activities to collecting the results of the judicial decisions, occasionally embroidering them with a modest criticism, and here and there timidly drawing an inference which no one as yet had dared to draw. Before long, however, it became the customary practice to concede the same importance to the literary utterances of the jurists that the utterances indisputably had which they made in the exercise of their practical calling. And so they dared to undertake, even in their capacity as writers, not only to tell him who sought advice in their books what had been customary in the past, but also, anticipating possibilities that had been overlooked until that time, to make additional universalizations and to create new norms for decision. Of still greater consequence is the fact that they were teachers. It is a characteristic peculiar to the teacher to exhaust the content of a legal proposition altogether, to reveal everything that it contains. A teacher, it is

如何，裁判官依赖其治权[1]，他能够比法学家更大胆、更果断地开展工作。目前，尚难以划定裁判官活动的界限；或许它随着时代和裁判官个性的变化而变化。

但是，法学家纯粹的实践活动并不能解释所有的事情。作为纯粹实践性法律活动之结果的法律制度仅仅会导致一系列松散排列在一起的法律命题，如同中世纪的德国法一样，在许多方面也像现代的英国法。早在共和国后期法学家时代的罗马法，似乎就是一个有序排列的、完善的结构，同时还包含了数量众多的一般性法律命题——这肯定要归功于罗马法学家既是实践律师又是著作家和教师的这一事实。当然，倘若他们仅仅是著作家和教师，那么他们的话就不会比仅仅由理性赋予他们的更有分量，他们必定像英国教科书的作者一样，把他们的活动限制在收集司法裁决的成果，偶尔用适度的批评加以修饰润色，偶尔提心吊胆地得出一个迄今没有人敢提出的推论。然而，不久以后，承认法学家的书本意见具有同样的重要性成为了一种习惯性做法，这些意见是法学家在他们的实践职业操练中给出的，因而是不容置疑的。所以，甚至在他们作为著作者时，他们也敢于：不仅仅告诉从他们的书中寻求指点的人过去的习惯是什么，而且在预料到那时为止被忽略的可能性时进行另外的一般化，创造出新的裁判规范。更重要的是，他们还是教师。详尽无遗地阐述法律命题的内容并揭示法律命题包含的全部意义是专属于教师的一个特征。的确，教

---

〔1〕 (拉)*imperium*(治权，统辖权)，在古罗马意味着最高指挥权、司法权和强制权，一般只有君主、执政官、独裁官和裁判官才拥有；享有此权利的人可以决定召集民众，行使刑事和民事司法权，建议修改或制定法律。

true, does not desire to create law, but he desires to develop it. When a practicing lawyer is dealing with a breach of contract he will confine himself to the points upon which the decision must hinge. When a writer deals with it he will chiefly consider the contingencies that might give rise to a legal controversy. But the teacher will be anxious to say everything, that is: who has the right; against whom it can be asserted; when and where the correlative duty must be fulfilled; what its content is and what content it can possibly have; what are the consequences of delay, and of non-fulfilment. The Roman law owes its great systematic completeness and perfection of form to the teaching activity of the jurists.

If one would, to some extent, justly appreciate the work which juristic science has done in Rome in this manner; if one would be convinced that Roman law has become what it is through the labors of the jurists and not because of any inexplicable innate juristic gift of the Romans, one should compare the *ius civile* with any one of the departments of their law that customarily was not influenced by their juristic science—among others, the legal relations concerning the *ager publicus*, public law, and a large part of administrative law, criminal law, which did not become the subject matter of juristic activity until a late period, and then only in a limited measure and only inasmuch as it was regulated by the *leges iudiciorum*. Here one finds nothing of that which appears so admirable elsewhere in Roman law. As to the *ager publicus* there were scarcely any universal principles; every single usufructuary lease was a distinct legal relation, and the Roman magistrate, like the German *Sckoeffe*, had to derive his decision from the particular form of the legal relation. In criminal law, a universal theory is sought for in vain ; on all questions of principle there is an embarrassed stammering; norms for

师并不渴望创设法律,但是他渴望发展法律。当一个职业律师处理违约时,他会将自己限于裁判必须依赖的关键点上。当一个著作者处理违约时,他会主要考虑可能引发法律争议的可能性。但是,一个教师会渴望论述每一个问题:谁拥有权利;可以向谁主张权利;何时何地相关义务必须被履行;它的内容是什么,它很可能会有什么样的内容;迟延履行和不完全履行的后果是什么;罗马法伟大的体系完备性和形式的完善性归功于法学家的教育活动。

如果任何人想在某种程度上公正地评价法学以这种方式在罗马所完成的工作;如果任何人想要确信:罗马法变成现在这个样子,是由于法学家的努力而不是因为罗马人任何神秘而固有的法学天赋,那么他应该把市民法和通常未受到法学影响的任何一个罗马法律部门比较——在其他的法律部门中,涉及公田[1]、公法、大部分的行政法以及刑法的法律关系,直到后来才成为法学活动关注的对象,而且也仅仅在一个有限的范围内,仅仅因为它受到所公布之法律的调整。那些在罗马法其他领域令人如此钦佩的东西在此处一无所见。关于公田,几乎没有任何一般的原则;每一单个的用益租约都是一个独特的法律关系,罗马的地方执法官,如德国的陪审法官一样,必须从法律关系的具体形式中推得裁决。在刑法中,人们徒劳地探寻一个一般的理论;在所有的原则问题上,有的只是一种令人尴尬地结结巴巴,裁判规范

〔1〕(拉)*ager publicus*(公田),最初指位于罗马城以外的、用于放牧或耕作的土地,后来也包括被罗马人征服的民族的土地;这些土地归罗马国家所有,但国家允许市民临时占据和使用。

decision are found exclusively by means of interpretation of the statutes. This surely is not inherent in the material, but is caused by the lack of a great juristic tradition; for *iniuria* is not treated in a less intelligent manner than any other subject matter of private law. Whether the juristic science of Roman public and administrative law ever amounted to more than an orderly collection of statutes and ordinances and of the results of the course of the judicial decisions cannot be determined from the tradition with any degree of certainty.

Still the very history of juristic science in Rome discloses that essentially, like juristic science everywhere, it was a preserving rather than a propelling force. Hesitatingly, unwillingly, and dispiritedly, it yields to the imperative exigencies of life, and never goes further than is absolutely necessary. And even that which is absolutely necessary it prefers to do unobservedly, disguising the new as something old, doing this by means of impossible interpretations, fictions, and constructions. Innovations that are very useful but somewhat daring are rejected even by the classical jurists. It is certain that the jurists were bound by that which was existing valid law. Over and above this, the limit of their power was a sense of that which might be permissible rather than a clearly defined line. Had their power to find law been quite unlimited, there would have been no need either of private law legislation (*leges de iure civili*) or of a praetorian edict; juristic science would have been able to satisfy every need of new law. The way in which Roman juristic science in its endeavor (which moreover it has in common with the juristic science of every other system of law) to make that which it has at hand suffice, sought to go not one step beyond that which is necessary—the economy of the law, as Von Jhering has called it—has in many ways served as a model for the juristic science of the Continental common law.

完全依靠解释制定法而获得。这确实不是法律素材的固有性质，而是由于缺乏伟大的法学传统所导致的；因为侵辱[1]并没有以一种比处理私法的任何其他对象更缺乏睿智的方式来处理。罗马公法法学和行政法法学是否曾经达到过那种超越对制定法、条令汇编、对司法裁决成果汇编的程度，无法从任何确定程度的传统中推得结论。

尽管如此，罗马法学的历史揭示，本质上，罗马法学如同任何其他地方的法学一样，是一种维护力量，而不是一种推动力量。法学犹豫地、不情愿地、意志消沉地屈服于生活的迫切需求，并且从来没有超越绝对必要的程度。甚至对于绝对必要的东西，法学也喜欢不被察觉地行动，将新的伪装为旧的，依靠于理不通的解释、拟制和推定来达到目的。非常有用但稍稍大胆的创新甚至被正统的法学家拒绝。法学家受现行法的约束，理所当然。不过除此以外，他们权力的界线是一种或可被许可的感觉，而不是清晰明确的界线。倘若他们发现法律的权力完全没有限制，那么就不必有私法立法（*leges de iure civili*）或裁判官告示了；法学将会能够满足新法的每一个需要。罗马法学通过自己的那种努力，即使当下的需要获得满足，且设法不越“必要之举”一步（而且，这是它与每一个其他法律制度的法学共有的特征）——耶林称之为“法律的节约”——在很多方面，充当了欧陆共同法学的楷模。

---

〔1〕（拉）*iniuria*（侵辱），罗马法中私犯的主要形式之一，表现为通过行为或者语言在身体上或精神上对人造成侵害。

# XII
# Juristic Science In England

In The last analysis it is an extraordinary piece of good luck for the sociology of law that from the early Middle Ages the English jurists ( more Roman than the Romanists, says Maitland) steadfastly closed their minds to the Roman law. To this fact must be attributed the other fact that among the nations of European civilization, in addition to the Roman or Continental common law, another legal system, the Anglo-American, has attained a high and altogether independent development. If it is the function of all scientific study to demonstrate the unifying regularity of the phenomena, sociology could never fulfil this task if no other legal system besides that of the Roman law and that of its offspring, the Continental common law, had attained to a more advanced stage of development. For the other legal systems of the globe, which have remained uninfluenced by Roman law, have continued in so undeveloped a condition that they cannot be adduced for purposes of comparison except with earlier stages of our law. A comparison of the whole course of development of Roman and English law is outside of the scope of the present inquiry, which is limited to a study of legal science in England with continual reference to that of Rome and of the Continent. It is impossible to appraise legal science in England justly without a fleeting glance at the development of English procedure.

The oldest English procedure does not differ from the original procedure of the other Germanic peoples. We may assume there-

# 第十二章　英格兰法学

归根到底，从中世纪早期开始，英国法学家（按梅特兰的话说，他们比罗马派法学家更“罗马”）就决意抵制罗马法，对于法律社会学而言，这是一段特别的好运。此等事实必须归功于另外一个事实：在欧洲文明国度里，除了罗马法或欧陆共同法之外，另外一种法律体系——英美法系——也获得了一个高度且完全独立的发展。如果说证明此等现象具有统一的规律性是所有科学研究的功能，那么若不是罗马法及其后世各类衍生形态、欧陆共同法之外的法律体系曾达到过一个更先进的发展阶段，则社会学永远不可能完成此项任务。因为世界上其他未受罗马法影响的法律体系，仍旧停留在一个欠发达的状态之下，以至于它们除了和我们更早期的法律比较之外，我们不可能基于比较的目的将其作为例证拿出来。罗马法和英国法整个演进过程的比较不在我们此处探究的范围之内，此处仅限于对与罗马法学及欧陆共同法学有持续关联的英格兰法学的研究。要是没有对英国诉讼程序发展的简要回顾，就不可能对英格兰法学有一个公正的评价。

最古老的英国诉讼程序与其他日耳曼民族所拥有的原始诉讼程序没什么两样。因此我们可以认为，在本质特征上，英国

fore that it coincides in its essential features with the prehistoric procedure of Roman law. This view, which perhaps appears strange to many, is based on the fact that all those things in Roman procedure in historical times that appear to be striking peculiarities, the two stages, a preliminary proceeding followed by the *Beweisverfahren* (the proceeding in which proof is made) and the division effected by the litis *contestatio*, manifestly are survivals from an earlier stage of the development of procedure, and, unless indications are deceiving, are found in essentials among all Germanic peoples. The formula of the later Roman procedure is none other in form and content than the *conditional Beweisurteil*, which is followed among the Romans as well as among the Germans by the *Beweisverfahren*. Since there is absolutely reliable evidence that the two-fold division of the trial existed in the procedure by *legis actio* also, inasmuch as the *litis contestatio* in this form of procedure effects a division just as it does in the formulary procedure, there is no doubt that in the *litis contestatio* of the *legis actio* procedure an alternative *Beweisurteil* was rendered which, though perhaps it was not drawn up in writing, was very similar to the formula both in form and in content.

The actual development of English law and English procedure begins with Henry II, in the twelfth century. This king was perhaps one of the greatest juristic geniuses that ever sat on a throne,

法最初诉讼程序与罗马法有文字记载之前的诉讼程序是相同的。这种或许看起来对许多人而言比较奇怪的观点,却是基于以下事实:在罗马法被认为具有鲜明特色的历史时代,罗马法程序中所有的那些事项,两个阶段的诉讼程序——即审前预备程序和 *Beweisverfahren*(证据程序)——以及这种受到争讼程序[1]影响的划分,显然都是诉讼程序更早发展阶段的残余,并且除非相关迹象是误导的,否则在所有属于日耳曼民族中,那些特征的主要方面皆有显露。后期罗马法诉讼程序模式在形式和内容上与传统的根据证据裁判完全一致,后者既被罗马人遵从,也被有着证据程序的日耳曼人遵从。既然有绝对可靠的证据证明审判程序的这种二分法也存在于基于法定诉讼[2]的程序中,既然这种诉讼形式中的争讼程序也影响到诉讼阶段的划分——正如它在程式诉讼中所发挥的相同作用,那么就不应怀疑,在争讼程序中,提供了一个可供选择的根据证据裁判的程序,尽管它或许并未被书面记载下来,但是它肯定在形式和内容上与程式诉讼是相同的。

英国法和英国诉讼程序的实际发展始于亨利二世时代,即12世纪。这位国王或许是曾经登上王位的最伟大的法学天才之一,

〔1〕 (拉)*litis contestatio*(争讼程序),它是古罗马法诉讼程序中的一个承上启下的程序,旨在确定诉讼标的,并将争议提交审判员。

〔2〕 (拉)*legis actio*(法定诉讼),古罗马法上的法定诉讼,指罗马司法官使用的两种诉讼程序制度中较古老的一种,不同于审讯诉讼程序。该程序严肃、刻板并且注重形式。该诉讼制度被公元前约150年颁布的《爱布蒂亚法》(*Lex Aebutia*)所引进的程式诉讼制度取代。

and although, as Maitland puts it, he sold his labor, inasmuch as he demanded heavy payments therefor from the parties, he has achieved better results than any other vendor of justice ever has. First of all we wish to present, at this place, a brief sketch of his legal reform. But we wish to preface this with the statement that he converted his *curia regis* into a permanent court of justice, over which he, a jurist in heart and soul, used to preside.

Perhaps the most important of his procedural innovations is the *assisa novae disseisinae*, which seems to have been invented under the influence of the canon law *actio spolii*, and which granted to everyone who had been disseised the right to obtain a writ which directed the sheriff to form an *assisa* consisting of twelve men of the neighborhood (*duodecim liberos et legales homines de visneto*) who, as soon as the royal justices should arrive in the vicinage, should make answer to the justice whether or not a disseisin had taken place. This *assisa novae disseisinae* was followed at a later time by other assizes, the basic features of which were: summons by royal writ to appear before the justice and judgment based on a verdict of men of the neighborhood. In addition the king had granted to everyone who desired to assert a claim to land the privilege of taking the matter out of the local communal court by means of a royal writ and of bringing it before

并且尽管如梅特兰所言，由于他需要从政党那里获得大量的款项，他曾经出卖过他的职业，但是他还是比任何其他的正义卖主获得了更好的结果。首先，我们希望在此介绍其法律改革的简要框架。但我们希望借以下陈述作为序言：他将御前会议[1]转变为一个常设法院，作为一个全心全意的法律人，亨利二世曾经主持过那样的法院。

关于他的诉讼程序改革，或许最重要的是新型侵占土地之诉，那似乎是在教会法侵夺之诉影响之下发明的，该程序授权给任何不动产遭到侵占之人以获得令状的权利，依据该令状，地方行政司法长官将任命一个由事发地附近地区的12个人（*duodecim liberos et legales homines de visneto*）——一旦王室法官到达附近地区，则这些人应该回复法官此地是否发生了侵占不动产的事件——组成的状召咨审团[2]。这个新型侵占土地之诉被后来其他的咨审团所遵随；该程序的基本特征是：在法官基于邻近之人的事实认定而作出裁决之前，首先有一个皇家令状所作的传唤。此外，国王以颁发皇家令状的形式授予所有渴望对土地主张权利的人以特权，将所涉争议的裁决权从地方社区法院那里移走，并将其转给御前会议。这些革新为当

---

〔1〕（拉）（英格兰古法）*Curia regis*（御前会议）。作为封建法庭，它对国王的直属封臣之间或其他显贵之间的纠纷有一审裁判权，并享有过去贤人会议所享有的上诉管辖权。普通民众缴纳一笔费用后，可以将在郡或百户区法庭审理的案件移至这里。

〔2〕（拉）（英格兰、苏格兰古法）*assisa*（状召咨审团），咨审团的最早形态。

the *curia regis*. These innovations offered many advantages to the parties, especially since the *curia regis* enjoyed a much greater measure of confidence than the local courts, employed a procedure that was much more expeditious and technically on a much higher plane than the clumsy ancient Germanic procedure, and had substituted for traditional, highly imperfect means of proof, such as trial by combat and oath with oath-helpers, the testimony of the men of the neighborhood.

We are dealing here with the first germs of the English jury. As Brunner has shown—and the results of his investigations have been generally accepted in England—this procedure originated in Normandy. Henry II, who at the same time was the Duke of Normandy, most probably had become familiar with it in his native country. But it was adapted to new needs in a manner so magnificent that his innovation may be called one of the greatest legislative acts of all time. The assize, it is true, is not yet the English jury. The latter grew out of the assize at a much later time. In the case of the assize the *homines liberi et legales* are called together by the summons, but the *jurata* presupposes a submission to the verdict of the neighborhood by mutual consent. The *jurata* arose later, when the parties, in order to avoid the unwelcome methods of proof, the trial by combat, and the oath with oath-helpers, agreed, without demanding an assize, to submit their controversy to the verdict of the men of the neighborhood. But even when there was an assize, the parties often agreed to ask men of the neighborhood to render a verdict on matters not mentioned in the writ. The mediaeval English jurists say: *assisa vertitur in iuratam*.

Because of the technical superiority of the procedure of the king's courts, because of the greater assurance of a just judgment, and because of their impartiality, the ancient Germanic mode of

事人提供了很多便利,特别是因为御前会议比地方法院拥有大得多的信心度,采用一种迅捷得多的诉讼程序,并且在技术上与笨拙的古代日耳曼诉讼程序相比,它有着更高的水准,因此替代了传统的、有极大缺陷的证明程序——诸如通过决斗并在助誓人见证之下的宣誓来裁判以及通过邻人的宣誓证言等方式进行的裁判。

我们在此首先探讨英国陪审团制度的最初萌芽。如布伦纳曾揭示的那样——他的研究成果已经在英格兰获得普遍接受——这种诉讼程序最初起源于诺曼底。亨利二世(当时也是诺曼底公爵)对于在他家乡本土的这种程序最有可能早就熟悉。但它在被改变后以一种如此宏大的形式来适应新的需要,以至于他的革新可以被称作所有时期最伟大的立法行为之一。的确,这种咨审团还不是英国的陪审团。后者在一个相当迟的后期才由前者发展而来。在巡回审判的情形下,状召咨审团的成员全部由传票召集,但是当事人合意咨审制基于合意预先假定(双方)提请由邻人作出裁决。当事人合意咨审制在后来产生,当时当事人为了避免不受欢迎的证明手段(决斗裁判、通过在助誓人见证之下宣誓的方式裁判),一致同意不要咨审团来审理他们的争议,而是把它们提交给相关的邻人作出裁决。但是即使在咨审团存在的时候,当事人经常也会一致同意:请求邻人对于令状中未提及的事项作出裁决。中世纪的英国法学家说:状召咨审团存在于宣誓之中。

由于王室法院诉讼程序在技术上具有优越性,由于对正义的审判有了更大的保障,由于它们本身的公正性,古代日耳曼人审

trial gradually disappears altogether, and is replaced by divers new modes of trial patterned after the *assisa novae disseisinae*. The complainant applies to the king' s chancellor, and, upon payment of a fee, obtains a writ which summons his opponent to appear in the king' s court. Each kind of claim has an appropriate writ, stating the claim and prescribing the procedure. Some of these writs are writs of course, but for a claim not falling within one of these writs, a new writ, more expensive and presupposing some influence with the king' s courts, must be drawn up. In the later actions the jury displaces the assize altogether. The difference between the two is this: The jury is no longer summoned by the writ but at the request of the parties, and the question as to which the jury are to give their verdict is no longer stated in the writ but is to appear from the proceeding.

Every Romanist who reads this description is at once reminded of the Roman formulary procedure and of the praetorian *album*, on which all the formulae that were in current use were recorded. From these the plaintiff had to select the one that was appropriate, while if there was no appropriate formula the plaintiff had to have one made especially for his purpose or secure one from the praetor. In fact English legal historians very often compare the procedure which prevailed in England down to the Judicature Acts of the nineteenth century to the Roman formulary procedure. The comparison however is based upon a very superficial study of the situation. The common element is this, that the writ and the formula (the latter, at least according to the prevailing view) were written documents, and that each contained the plaintiff' s claim. But the formula concludes the proceeding before the court; the writs open it. The formula is a *Beweisurteil*; the writ,

判模式逐渐完全消失，取而代之的是在新型侵占土地之诉之后出现的若干新的审判模式。原告求助于王室大法官，在支付一定的费用后，获得一个令状，该令状会将被告传唤至王室法庭。每一种诉讼请求都会有适当的令状来标明该种请求并指示相应的诉讼程序。有些令状属于常规令状，如果一个诉讼请求不能归入这些令状中的任何一种，则必须创设一种更昂贵且必定对王室法院产生更大影响的新的令状。在后来的诉讼中，陪审团完全取代了咨审团。二者的区别是：陪审团不再由令状召集组建，而是基于当事人的申请而组建，并且陪审团待决事项不再由令状载明，而是源于诉讼的需要。

每个罗马派法学家看到以上说明，定会立刻想起罗马法上的程式诉讼以及（古罗马）裁判官的布告栏，当时可用的所有程式均载于布告栏中。原告必须从这些程式中挑选一个合适的，同时如果没有合适的程式，原告则必须请人特别制作一个程式来满足其需求，或者直接从裁判官那里获得一个新的程式。事实上，英国法律史学家经常将英格兰盛行（一直到 19 世纪的《司法组织法》[1]颁布实施为止）的这种诉讼程序比作是罗马法上的程式诉讼程序。然而，这种比拟却是基于对此种情形极为肤浅的研究而作出的。二者共同的要素是：令状和程式（后者，至少按通说）都是书面公文，并且每一种都包含原告的诉讼请求。然而，程式终结法庭上的诉讼程序；令状则是启动诉讼程序。程式是一个根据证据裁判的程序，令状则是一个传票。进一步审视

〔1〕 英国 1873～1875 年间对高等法院的组织和审判程序进行改革的法律。

a summons. Upon a closer investigation, one will not compare the older English procedure with the formulary procedure but with the Roman procedure by *legis actio*. The fact that the latter was begun by a private summons, the *in ius vocatio*, the English proceeding, by an official summons, may be considered an immaterial difference. But as in Rome, so in England, both the plaintiff and the defendant were required to state their proposals in definitely fixed terms, following the statements of the royal writ and in accordance with the legal basis of the action. As in Rome, so in England, the formal law and right was also the material law and right. Each kind of claim had its appropriate procedure, and the law of procedure determined the material legal bases of the claim. As in Rome, so in England, the material law was chiefly the law of the several actions (*actiones*). Each action has its own precedents, and English jurists write their text-books on the several actions. "To a considerable degree the substantive law administered in a given form of action has grown up independently of the law administered in other forms." (Maitland.) The oldest English law, then, like the Roman law, was a law of actions. In comparison with this great number of analogies, I presume, the differences become insignificant, but we shall not pass over them altogether in silence. The English judge directs the whole proceeding in the presence of the jury; in the more developed procedure he no longer pronounces a conditional judgment like the Roman judge, but permits the parties to formulate the question of fact—frame the issue—upon the determination of which they are willing to let the outcome depend, submits this question to the jury, and pronounces his final judgment according to the

之后，任何人都不会把古代英国的诉讼程序与古罗马人诉讼程序的程式诉讼相提并论，而是会把它与古罗马人的法定诉讼程序作比较。后者由一个私人传票[1]启动，而和在罗马一样，英国诉讼程序由一个官方传票启动——这个事实可能被认为是一个无关紧要的区别。不过，在英格兰，在皇家令状声明之后，原告和被告都被要求在一固定期限内陈述他们的主张，并且各自主张均须符合诉讼的法定事由。在英格兰和在罗马一样，形式上的法律和权利也是实体上的法律和权利。每一种请求权都有其合适的诉讼程序，程序法决定了该种请求权的实体法律基础。在英格兰和在罗马一样，实体法主要是几个诉讼（*actiones*）之法。每一个诉讼都有其自身的先例，英国法学家为这几种诉讼撰写了教科书。"以某种给定诉讼形式实施的实体法发展到一个相当高的程度，并独立于其他形式实施的法律。"（梅特兰）最古老的英国法，和罗马法一样，是一个诉讼法。与二者之间这么多的共同点比较起来，我以为那些差异变得无关紧要，不过，我们不能一言不发整个儿忽略了它们。英国法官在存在陪审团的场合下指挥着整个诉讼程序；在更先进的程序里法官不再像罗马法官一样宣布一个有条件的判决，而是允许当事人自己整理事实问题——拟出争点——他们乐意让最后裁决结果以前述争点为基础和范围，法官将该争点提交给陪审团，并基于陪审团的裁决而作出最后的判决。陪审团

〔1〕（拉）*in ius vocatio*（传唤受审），原告向被告发出口头通知，要求其与自己一起至执法官处出庭，以便进行对抗式诉讼。在被告拒绝出庭的情况下，原告有权在见证人的协助下采用武力强制被告出庭。

verdict of the jury. The jury has nothing to do with the question of law. The latter is a matter for the judge.

The English system of *legis actiones* was not replaced by a system essentially similar to that of the Roman formulary procedure until the Judicature Acts were passed, which abolished the old formulae, and permitted the parties to submit their written proposals to the court in a manner that seemed good to themselves. This proceeding, too, is divided into two parts just like that of the Roman formulary procedure (in chambers and in court), with this difference: The proceeding before the judge, i. e. the proceeding *in iure*, follows the preliminary procedure; furthermore the proceeding before the judge includes the proof.

The personal interest which the judges had in the law-suits that came before them, because of the large fees they received, constitutes an extraordinarily important element in the development of English procedure. It explains their persistent endeavor to enlarge their jurisdiction and to adapt the forms of action most practically to the needs of the parties in order that their activity might increase. Strangely enough they have shown no interest in a more expeditious and more simple procedure. Perhaps they feared that they might reduce their perquisites.

In order to justify these extensions of jurisdiction, the English jurists resorted to the use of fictions. There were three king's courts of major importance, all of them sitting in London: Common Pleas, King's Bench, and Exchequer. The true civil court was the court of Common Pleas. The jurisdiction of the court of

与法律问题无关。后者是法官的事情。

英国的法定诉讼制度并未被一个与罗马法程式诉讼相似的制度所取代，这种状况一直持续到《司法组织法》通过为止，它废除了古老的程式，并允许当事人将他们的书面申请以一种看似对他们有利的方式提交给法庭。这种诉讼程序也恰如罗马法的程式诉讼一样可分为两个部分（在法官办公室[1]和在法庭上），二者的区别是：这种在法官面前的程序（即 *in iure* 程序）[2]紧随审前准备程序之后；而且在法官面前的程序包括证明（阶段）。

法官在其审理之诉讼中的个人利益——由于他们从中接受了高额费用——构成了英国诉讼程序发展中的一个额外重要的因素。它可以解释，英国法官为什么极力扩大他们的管辖权，并将诉讼形式改造得能够最切实地满足当事人的需要。令人极感奇怪的是，他们对于一种更快捷、更简单的诉讼程序并未显示出丝毫兴趣。或许他们担心他们的津贴会因此而减少吧。

为了使管辖权的这些扩张合法化，英国法学家诉诸法律拟制的运用。三个最重要的国王法庭均位于伦敦：英格兰皇家民事法庭、王座法庭以及财税法庭。真正的民事法庭就是

---

〔1〕 在英国，法官包括主事法官和地区法官，他们在法官办公室处理不需在公开法庭上处理的法律事务，如听审申请、签署文件等。

〔2〕 罗马法程式诉讼两个阶段之一，*in iure* 即法律审，与事实审（*in judicio*）相对，在裁判官面前进行，包括介绍部分及对法律问题的解决。

King's Bench, which would ordinarily be of rare occurrence in an action between private persons, was based on a fiction that the defendant was *in custodia Mareschalli*, held in confinement for the king, and therefore subject to the jurisdiction of the court of the King's Bench. The court of Exchequer, which in fact was a fiscal board, based its jurisdiction upon the fiction that the plaintiff was in arrears in the payment of his taxes to the king, and was unable to pay them because he could not collect his money from the defendant.

The functioning of the court is conditioned upon the plaintiff's securing a proper writ for the cause of action. If he does not secure the proper writ, he loses the law-suit. In the early Middle Ages, it is true, writs were readily issued for any claim that appeared justified, and so Bracton could write: *Tot erunt formulae brevium quot sunt genera actionum*. But in the course of time this matter becomes more difficult. Only writs of course (*de cursu*) are being issued without more ado. The barons, assembled at Oxford (1258), pass a resolution: *Ke il ne enselera nul bref fors bref de curs sanz le commendement le rei e de sun conseil ke serra present* (*ut praetores ex edictis suis perpetuis ius dicerent*). But the statute of Westminster (1258) permitted the *clerici de cancellaria*, when they were unanimous, to issue a writ *ne contingat de cetero quod curia diu deficiat querentibus in iustitia perquirenda*. If the *clerici* cannot agree, let them report to Parliament. Nevertheless since the beginning of the fourteenth century it becomes increasingly difficult to obtain a new writ, especially since the judges became jealous of the chancellor and began to quash new writs. Bracton's proposition was converted into its converse: *Tot erunt actiones quot sunt formulae brevium*.

Only one writ constitutes an exception: the writ of trespass.

英格兰皇家民事法庭。王座法庭的管辖权——在私人之间发生的诉讼极少由它审理——乃基于这样一种假定:被告是在最高指挥官保护之下,仅限于由国王来审判,因此属于王座法庭管辖的范围。财税法庭,事实上是一个财税委员会,作为其管辖权基础的假定是:原告对国王欠税并无力清偿,原因是他无法从被告那儿收取债权。

法庭的功能取决于原告为诉因求得一个恰当的令状。如果他不能获得一个恰当的令状,他将会败诉。在中世纪早期,令状的确可以因任何看似正当的诉求而签发,所以布莱克顿写道:有多少简要程式就有多少种诉讼。但是随着时间的推移,这种事情变得越来越困难。只有常规的令状(*de cursu*)才会无须多费周折就能申请到。1258 年,贵族在牛津集会,并通过一项决议:*Ke il ne enselera nul bref fors bref de curs sanz le commendement le rei e de sun conseil ke serra present*(*ut praetores ex edictis suis perpetuis ius dicerent*)。但是《威斯特敏斯特制定法》(1258 年)允许御前会议事务官在全体无异议的情形下,签发一个——*ne contingat de cetero quod curia diu deficiat querentibus in iustitia perquirenda*——令状。如果事务官不同意,则将之呈报议会。尽管如此,自 14 世纪初开始,获得一个新型令状还是变得日益困难,尤其是在普通法官变得对御前大臣有了嫉妒之心并开始宣布新的令状一律无效之后。布莱克顿的主张事实上正好被颠倒过来:所有的诉讼都要有一个简要程式。

唯一构成了例外的令状是侵害之诉的令状。最初它是作为一

Originally a criminal action for breach of the King's Peace *vi et armis*, trespass became a civil action about the sixteenth century, and all the actions that were in use in the eighteenth and nineteenth centuries were derived from it. Its three oldest forms are: assault and battery (bodily injury), *de bonis asportatis* (depriving one of the possession of chattels), and *quare clausum fregit* (interference with one's possession or depriving one of possession of immovables).

Trespass became very popular, and exhibits a series of new forms, which during the course of the seventeenth and eighteenth centuries practically superseded all the older forms of action. As early as the beginning of the sixteenth century, it came into close contact with ejectment, which thereafter took the place of the real action for immovables. On the basis of the provision of the Statute of the second Parliament of Westminster in *consimili casu*, case branched off from trespass. From case, the chief difference between which and trespass is that the plaintiff did not have to allege *vi et armis*, several important actions developed in turn. Chief of these is assumpsit, which branched off at the beginning of the sixteenth century. The defendant has undertaken by contract to deal with the plaintiff's goods in a certain way, e. g. to perform some labor in relation to them, and in doing so has caused damage to the plaintiff. This action of assumpsit subsequently becomes an action on the promise, a contractual action which takes the place of the old action of debt. In Slade's case (1602) it was held that "Every contract executory imports in itself an assumpsit, for when one agrees to pay money or to

种针对破坏国王和平之行为的刑事诉讼,后来在 16 世纪左右变成了一个民事诉讼,并且在 18 世纪和 19 世纪适用的所有种类的诉讼都源于它。它的三种最古老的形式是:恐吓和殴打(身体伤害)、*de bonis asportatis*(剥夺他人对动产的占有)以及 *quare clausum fregit*(妨碍或剥夺他人对不动产的占有)。

侵害之诉变得非常普遍,并发展出一系列新的形式,在 17 世纪和 18 世纪它实际上取代了所有更古老的诉讼形式。早在 16 世纪初,它便与逐出租地之诉紧密相连,后者在那以后代替了不动产返还之诉[1]。根据威斯特敏斯特第二议会关于 *in consimili casu* 制定法的规定,间接侵害之诉[2]自侵害之诉发展而来。间接侵害之诉与侵害之诉的主要区别是,原告不必主张被告使用了暴力,从间接侵害诉讼开始,几种重要的诉讼类型相继发展确立。其中首要类型是违反简式合约索赔之诉,于 16 世纪初建立。被告根据契约以某种特定方式承诺处理原告的货物,即履行有关于这些货物的劳务,在此过程中造成了对原告的损害。这种损害赔偿诉讼后来变成了基于允诺的诉讼,这是一种取代旧式债务诉讼的契约诉讼。在斯莱德的案子中,法院认定,"每一个有效契约本身都意味着一个有效力的承诺:当某人同意付款或交付任何东西

〔1〕"逐出租地之诉"是一种古老的侵害之诉类型,原先仅可请求损害赔偿,15 世纪开始这一救济扩大到可以是承租人收回被占租地。后来这一诉讼程式又被用于可继承完全保有地产的占有权争议的诉讼中,从而绕过了不动产诉讼的繁琐程序。

〔2〕Trespass on the case 的简称。

deliver anything, thereby he assumes or promises to pay or deliver it." This is indebitatus assumpsit, which later became in part an action for unjust enrichment, "in which the element of contract is purely fictitious." About the middle of the sixteenth century trover begins to germinate within the sphere of trespass on the case. The accused has found a chattel which the plaintiff had lost, and though demand has been made, refuses to return it; he has converted it to his own use (conversion). Subsequently trover lies against a third person; loss and finding is feigned; the only essential thing is the detention and the conversion to the defendant's own use. Trover becomes a general action *in rem* for movables and, at the same time, a very convenient action for unjust enrichment (conversion of another's goods to one's own use). According as these actions are used to demand either the thing itself or compensation, or both, they are real actions, personal actions, or mixed. Ejectment is a real action; assumpsit and trover are personal actions, for in the case of movables and of contractual relations the plaintiff in an action at law can recover only damages (it is otherwise in equity). For this reason the English call movables and obligations personal property.

时,他将因而承担付款或交付该物的义务,或对此种义务给予保证。"这是普通简约之诉[1],后来部分地演变为一个对不当得利的诉讼,"其中,契约的要素纯粹是拟制性的"。大约在16世纪中期,动产侵占之诉[2]开始在间接侵害之诉的范围内萌芽。被告发现一个原告丢失的动产,尽管原告提出返还请求,但仍拒绝返还;被告将该动产视为已物而加以利用(此种情形构成,即侵占)。随后,动产侵占之诉延伸至针对第三人;丢失和发现由法律拟制;唯一的要素是被告扣留该物,并视作已物加以利用。动产侵占之诉成为一种笼统的、有关动产的对物诉讼,同时,它也是一种针对不当得利(将他人之物作已用)的很方便的诉讼。这些诉讼可分别被用来寻求索回原物、损害赔偿或同时诉求此二者,基于诉讼请求的不同,这些诉讼分别对应为不动产返还之诉、损害赔偿诉讼或者同时包含二者的混合诉讼。逐出租地之诉属于土地返还之诉;违反简式合约索赔之诉与动产侵占之诉均属于损害赔偿诉讼,这两种情形下,原告只能依据契约关系(向违约人)请求损害赔偿或就被侵占的动产(向侵占人)请求损害赔偿(否则就是衡平法上的权利请求)。基于前述理由,英国人称动产和债务为个人财产。

---

〔1〕 即"普通简约之诉",与特殊简约之诉相对应。前者基于默示合约,而后者则基丁明示的承诺;前者多发生于出卖、运输货物、完成劳务所引起的价金给付,后者则常见于不履行协议所造成损失,偶尔也见于合同条款需要解释的情况。

〔2〕 即对非法占有或使用动产者的损失赔偿诉讼。

Trespass owes its enormous success to various causes. In the first place it was a proceeding that was more vigorous and more expeditious than the older forms. Its origin as a penal action for breach of the King's Peace accounts for the practice of beginning the action with provisional arrest of the defendant. The matter of proof, too, was regulated much better. In the case of the old actions *in rem* (writ of right, detinue) and of contractual actions (debt), oath with oath-helpers (wager of law) was still available. In the assizes the sworn triers had to be called at the time the original writ was issued, and were permitted to make answer only to the question that was put in the writ itself. In trespass there was a jury; it was summoned during the course of the proceeding, and was required to answer the questions that arose from the pleadings of the parties. The influence of the attorneys was of importance also. Trespass was reserved to the King's Bench. In the court of Common Pleas a certain class of attorneys, the sergeants-at-law, who were appointed by royal writ, were enjoying a monopoly. All other attorneys therefore had an interest in getting suits into the court of King's Bench, in which they themselves could appear as attorneys, and therefore also in increasing the number of causes over which this court had jurisdiction.

The extension of the various actions to new situations was brought about in part by the judges holding that a certain action lay in a given case. Thereafter there was no more difficulty. In this way Slade's case made assumpsit a general contractual action. Still more important is the system of fictions. The most famous is the fiction in the action of ejectment, the *actio in rem* for the determination of ownership in later English law. Ejectment originally was an action of trespass by the lessee against any third party who deprived him of possession. At the beginning the owner, John Rogers, availed himself of this action in the following manner: Basing his claim on title, which he asserted to be in

侵害之诉巨大的成功乃归功于各种各样的诉由。首先它是一个比其他更古老的诉讼形式更有力、更迅捷的诉讼程序。它最初是作为对破坏国王和平行为的一种刑罚,这也解释了该诉讼起初的实践包括对被告人的临时拘押。证明问题也得到了更好的规范。在古老的对物诉讼(权利令状,收回被占财产之命令)以及契约(债务)诉讼情形下,在助誓人见证之下的宣誓(即宣誓断讼)仍然可用。在启用咨审团的情形下,宣誓过的咨审员必须在令状签发之时召集,并被允许仅仅对令状本身提出的问题作答。在侵害之诉情形下,则存在一个陪审团;它在诉讼过程中被传唤,并被要求回答源自当事人诉状中的问题。其中,律师的影响也很重要。侵害之诉保留给王座法庭管辖。在英格兰皇家民事法庭,一个特定的由皇家令状任命的律师阶层享受着垄断利益。所以让诉讼进入到王座法庭审理,这对所有其他律师而言利益攸关,此种努力若能成功,则他们在王座法庭可以作为辩护律师出现,并因此也能增加这种法庭拥有管辖权之诉由的数量。

因应新情况的各种诉讼类型的扩张部分归由于法官的这种认定:某特定诉讼属于既有诉讼类型的范围。如此认定之后,类似诉讼的归属就没有更多的困难。通过这种方法,斯莱德的案子让违反简约索赔之诉成为了一种普通的契约诉讼。尽管如此,更重要的还是拟制制度。最著名的是关于逐出租地之诉中的拟制,即后期英国法中有关所有权确权的对物诉讼。逐出租地之诉最初是由承租人针对任何剥夺其租地占有的第三方提起的侵害之诉。起初,所有人约翰·罗杰斯以下列方式应用该诉讼:基于其本人所享有产权之上的请求权,他(为占有)实际进入该土地,

himself, he made actual entry, and then made a lease to Richard Smith, who was thereafter ejected by William Stiles and brought suit against the latter. William Stiles, the casual ejector, thereafter gave notice of the suit to the present tenant, George Saunders.

In the suit against the present tenant the lessee at first had to prove the following: 1. That the demandant was entitled to lease the land to him, i. e. that the demandant was the owner; 2. That the latter had actually leased it to him;3. That he, the lessee, had actually taken possession of the land; 4. That he had been ejected by the casual ejector. This procedure however was simplified considerably by means of a number of fictions which were invented by Chief Justice Rolle during the Commonwealth. The lease, the entry, and the ejection by William Stiles now are purely fictitious. The latter, the fictitious casual ejector, simply gives notice of the pendency of the action to the tenant, George Saunders. If the tenant George Saunders remains silent, the land is awarded to the lessee (in behalf of the actual plaintiff); for the casual ejector has no intention to defend his right. If the tenant chooses to defend, he is permitted to do so only upon condition that he admit the lease of the land by John Rogers to Richard Smith, the entry by the latter and his ejection by Stiles. Thereafter the suit is confined to the question of the right of John Rogers to lease the land to Richard Smith, in other words, to the question whether John Rogers has title.

The question obtrudes itself why this roundabout way was selected for the purpose of giving to the owner the remedy of the lessee instead of creating a direct remedy for him. Maitland thinks it was impossible to do this inasmuch as the owner had the

然后他与理查德·史密斯签订了一份土地租契,但威廉·斯蒂尔斯后来将史密斯逐出了这块土地,于是史密斯起诉斯蒂尔斯。威廉·斯蒂尔斯,这个意外驱逐者之后将该诉讼通知给了当前的土地保有人乔治·桑德斯。

在针对当前土地保有人的诉讼中,土地承租人首先必须证明如下事项:1. 原告[1]有权将土地租给他,即原告是所有人;2. 原告实际上曾经将土地租给了他;3. 承租人实际上曾经占有过这块土地。4. 他被意外驱逐人逐离了这块土地,然而这个程序通过大量的拟制而被极大的统一化了,这些拟制是首席大法官罗尔在英联邦时期所创造的。(土地)租契、(为占有而对土地的)进入以及斯帝尔斯的驱逐现在都是纯粹的拟制。后者,拟制的意外驱逐者,只是将未决之诉讼通知给当前的土地保有人桑德斯。如果桑德斯保持沉默,该土地将被判给承租人(代表实际的原告);因为意外驱逐者斯帝尔斯无意为其权利辩护。如果当前的土地保有人选择答辩,则他只有在——承认罗杰斯与史密斯之间的租契、承认后者曾进入该土地并遭到斯帝尔斯的驱逐——这样的条件下才能获得允许。接下来,诉讼将限于罗杰斯将土地出租给史密斯的权利问题,换言之,即罗杰斯是否对该土地享有产权的问题。

问题是为什么偏偏要采用这种拐弯抹角的方式来为所有人提供这种承租人的救济,而不是为其创设一种直接的救济方法。梅特兰认为,由于所有人有返还土地之诉、权利令状以及回复占

---

〔1〕 demandant,指的是"实际的原告",在该案中,即土地产权人罗杰斯。下同。

real action, the writ of right, and the possessory action (the assizes); that it was impossible to leap over this obstruction. And since trespass with its fictions, after all, served the purpose best, there was no need of a change. Since there was no disadvantage involved, the law contented itself with discussing the legal relation between the actual plaintiff and the actual defendant in a suit in which the formal issue was an interference with the possession of a fictitious lessee by a fictitious ejector who gave notice to the defendant. By a series of Judicature Acts in the nineteenth century this system of *legis actiones* was abolished and replaced by a free formulary procedure, which will be discussed later.

In the twelfth and thirteenth centuries the English law as it was applied in the royal courts was extraordinarily fluid and flexible. But in the fourteenth and fifteenth centuries it became rigid and formal, chiefly because of the great difficulty experienced in obtaining new writs. This state of affairs prompted the chancellor to take a considerable part of the development of the law into his own hands. From ancient times the parties had been accustomed to apply to the king for relief from a wrong they had suffered. This is a part of the ancient jurisdiction of the king, upon which, in the last analysis, the whole jurisdiction of the king's courts, which are gradually replacing the older courts, is based. Especially after the chancellor refuses to issue new writs as a matter of course, the number of such appeals to the king is increasing at an extraordinarily rapid rate. These appeals are petitions praying for relief either in a case where relief cannot be had at the hands of the courts because of the lack of a suitable writ or in a case where relief is sought from an unjust judgment rendered by the courts. The king refers the parties to the chancellor, who investigates the matter, and, if he has satisfied himself that an injustice has been done to one of the parties, interferes, and sees to it that the latter obtains justice. This procedure

有之诉,因而创新之举概无可能;他认为跨越这些障碍是不可能的。而且,既然侵害之诉有了拟制——已经尽可能地方便了原告,因而就无需再创新改变了。既然没有什么相关的不利情形,法律便满足于讨论一件讼案中实际的原告与实际的被告之间的法律关系,其中,正式的问题是拟制承租人的占有受到一个拟制驱逐者(他通知被告应诉)的妨碍。随着19世纪《司法组织法》一系列规则的确立,这种法定诉讼被废止,取而代之的是一种自由的程式诉讼程序,下文将要谈到这种新型诉讼程序。

在12世纪和13世纪,皇家法院适用的英国法特别易变与灵活。但是在14世纪和15世纪,它变得僵硬与刻板,主要原因是在获得新的令状时遭遇到巨大困难。这种状况促使御前大臣将英格兰法发展的相当大的部分纳入自己的掌控之下。从古代起,当事人就习惯对于他们遭受的不公正向国王申请救济。这是国王的古代司法管辖权——归根到底,也是国王法院(正逐渐取代旧式法院)的整个司法管辖权——赖以存在的基础。特别是自御前大臣势所必然地拒绝签发新的令状之后,向国王发出那种诉求的数量以一种惊人的速度增长。这些诉求是一些在下列场合下请求获得救济的诉状:由于缺乏合适的令状而不能通过法院[1]获得救济;或是法院作出了一个不公正判决。国王将当事人委托给御前大臣,由后者调查案情,如果他自认为其中一名当事人受有冤屈,则予以干预,并负责让受冤者获得公道。这种程序大体上是

[1] 此处的法院指的是普通法法院。此章中的法院未作特别说明的,皆为普通法法院。

is in a general way modeled upon the procedure of the ecclesiastical courts. It is a very natural thing for the chancellor to take his procedure from the ecclesiastical courts; for, as a rule, he is a cleric. It is self-evident that this does not make an end of the activity of the courts or render it superfluous. The chancellor is not permitted to interfere directly with the administration of justice. But, in his capacity as a royal official, he has at his disposal remedies by means of which he exercises his power, which in turn he derives from the fullness of the king's power. In virtue of this delegated royal power he has the power, in the first place, to enjoin the parties in a given case both from appealing to the courts and from availing themselves of a judgment already obtained in a court; and finally he has the power to enforce his decree through his own officials.

Accordingly, the chancellor actually has the power, on petition by one of the parties, to withdraw any litigation, whether it has already been adjudicated or not, from the jurisdiction of the courts and to take it into his own hands. The commands and prohibitions directed to the parties are called injunctions. They can be enforced by the chancellor by means either of imprisonment or of fines. They are being issued *sub poena*. They can of course refer not only to a matter submitted to the courts by one of the parties to a controversy but also to the greatest possible variety of other matters.

The courts did not submit to these interferences by the chancellor without some show of resistance, especially since, although only in rare cases, the injunctions applied even to the courts as such. Resistance to the chancellor began in the reign of Edward IV, and, in the reign of James I, led to a conflict between Justice Coke and the chancellor, Lord Ellesmere. The chancellor contended that his decrees were not addressed to the courts but to

对教会法庭之诉讼程序的模仿。对于御前大臣而言,这种效法是很自然的一件事;因为通常来说,他是一个神职人员。这(御前大臣对司法的介入)并未终结法院的活动或者使它显得多余,此点不言而喻。御前大臣并不能直接干涉司法的施行。不过在他作为一名皇家官员的职权范围内,他负责通过行使权力(其权力则来源于国王的完整权力)的方式来给予法律救济。依据这种被授予的皇家权力,他享有如下权力:首先,在一特定案件中禁止当事人向法院提出诉求并且也禁止他们利用自法院已获得的判决;其次他还有权执行由其所属官员作出的裁决。[1]

因此,御前大臣实际上有权根据当事人的申请将任何诉讼——无论该诉讼是否已经有了判决结果——从法院的管辖范围内取回,并将其纳入自己的掌控之下。(御前大臣主持的)大法官法庭对当事人(积极性)命令和(消极性)禁令被统称为禁制令。御前大臣执行禁制令的方式可以是将当事人监禁,也可以是对其课以罚金。在需要辅助性惩罚的时候,就会签发禁制令。它们当然不仅指向当事人一方提交给法院的事项,而且也指向具有最大可能多样性的其他事项。

法院不可能在毫无反抗的情形下就屈服于御前大臣的这些干涉,特别是因为禁制令甚至同样约束法院本身(尽管此等情形极为罕见)。对御前大臣的抵制始于爱德华四世以及詹姆斯一世,这种抵制引发了一场英格兰皇家民事法庭法官柯克和御前大臣埃尔斯米尔之间的冲突。御前大臣强调说,他的裁决不是针

〔1〕 decree 一般指的是衡平法院和御前大臣法庭所作的裁决。

the parties; that "Injunctions did not interfere with the common law. The judgment stood. All that the chancellor was concerned with, was the conduct of the parties to the case in which the judgment had been given." On this basis James I, following an opinion of Bacon, at that time attorney-general, decided the quarrel in favor of the chancellor. Thanks to the recognition of the validity of the injunctions, the chancellor definitively prevailed. During the seventeenth and eighteenth centuries the courts made repeated attempts to put the matter to the test again, but without success. Thereby the chancellor, entrusted with a jurisdiction of his own, was enabled to create a legal system which, in many respects, is a perfect analogy to the praetorian law of Rome.

It would of course be a very superficial procedure, if, relying upon a few similarities in external matters, one should permit oneself to be misled into placing the chancellor and the praetor side by side. Not external details, but the whole inner structure of the legal systems created by them, justifies one in seeing the same historical phenomenon in the two officials. This view, it is true, does not appear to any appreciable extent in English books, for the English take little interest in a conceptual understanding of their law. But a reading of the presentation of the matter by Professor Langdell, an American scholar, resolves all doubts. From Langdell's book, entitled "Survey of Equity Jurisdiction" (Cambridge in the United States 1905), I quote the following:

"As legal rights have in them no element of equity, so equitable rights have in them no element of law... As law is a creature of the State, so equity was originally a creature of the supreme executive of the State, i. e. the king. What then was the power of the king which enabled him to create equity? It may be answered that he had in him the sole judicial authority as well as the sole executive power, but none of the legislative power, i. e. he could not alone exercise any portion of the latter. By virtue of his judicial power he had entire control over procedure, so long as the legislature did not interfere; and this it was that enabled him to create equity. As he had no legislative

对法院,而是针对当事人,并且"禁制令不会干涉普通法。审判停滞了。御前大臣所关心的是当事人对这个已决案件的行为"。在此基础上,詹姆斯一世听取了当时是总检察长培根的意见,作出了有利于御前大臣的裁决。由于禁制令的有效性获得确认,御前大臣在这场冲突中确定无疑地占了上风。在17世纪和18世纪,法院一再试图将此事重新提请决断,但没有成功。因此,由于其自身被赋予了一种(特定的)司法管辖权,御前大臣能够创设一种法律制度,这种法律制度在很多方面与古罗马帝国的裁判官法完全相似。

这当然是一个很表面化的程序,如果基于外部事项的一些相似性,人们或会产生一种错误印象而把御前大臣和裁判官相提并论了。不是外部细节,而是他们所创设的法律制度的内部结构才是人们在了解这两种官员身上发生的相同历史现象时获得正确认识的依据。确实,在英国的书籍中这种观点并未达到任何值得重视的程度,因为英国人对于他们法律的概念性理解兴趣甚微。但是美国学者兰德尔的一本阐述此事的读物解决了所有的疑问。从兰德尔名为《衡平法院司法管辖权概观》美国剑桥出版社,1905年版的书中,我摘引了如下部分:

"正如普通法上的权利本身不包含衡平法上的元素,衡平法上的权利本身也不包含普通法上的元素……正如法律是国家的创造物,衡平法最初也是国家最高执行者,如:国王的创造物。那么让国王得以创设衡平法的权力是什么呢?回答可能是:国王本身拥有独一无二的司法权威,同时也拥有独一无二的执行权力,但是他没有丝毫的立法权,亦即,他不能单独行使任何立法权。依据他的司法权,他完全支配诉讼程序,只要议会并未干涉;而且这种权力能够让他创设衡平法。由于他没有立法权,所以他不能给

power, he could not impart to his decisions in equity any legal effect or operation, but when he had by the exercise of his judicial authority rendered a decision in equity in favor of a plaintiff, he could enforce it by exerting his executive power against the person of the defendant, i. e. he could compel him to do or to refrain from doing whatever he had by his decision directed him to do or to refrain from doing..."

A Romanist need not be told that only a slight change in the wording of this statement will make it equally applicable to the praetor.

Moreover the inner similarity between the praetorian law and equity appears also in a series of details, first of all in the fact that the latter is directly connected with the *ius civile*, the common law. It is not an independent system, but can be understood only as an appendix to the common law. Without equity the latter would indeed be a hard, rigid system of law, ill adapted to the requirements of life, but after all it would be a system of law. Equity without the common law simply could not exist. Just as the work of the praetor constituted an appendix to the *ius civile* in content as well as in form, just as he created praetorian institutions on the model of those of the civil law, created remedies by means of *actiones fictitiae* and *utiles*, which were analogous to those of the civil law, and created a praetorian law of inheritance to follow and supplement the civil law of inheritance, so the chancellor imitates the common law. A principle of equity is: *aequitas sequitur legem*. For almost every common law rule which

予他的衡平法上的裁决以任何普通法上的效果和效力，但是当他通过实施其司法权力而给予原告一个衡平法上的有利判决时，他可以通过运用针对被告人人身的执行权来执行它，亦即，他可以强迫被告做或不做任何事情——只要此事是他依其裁决命令他做或不做的……”

一个罗马派法学家无需别人告诉他，以上表述的措辞稍微变动一点点即可同样适用于罗马裁判官。

此外，罗马裁判官法与英国衡平法之间的内部相似性还体现在一系列的细节上，首先是后者与市民法、普通法有直接联系。衡平法不是一个独立的法律体系，而是可以被来理解为普通法的一个补充。如果没有衡平法，普通法将是一个刻板而僵硬的法律体系，无法适应现实生活的需要，但毕竟普通法还是一个法律体系。要是没有普通法，衡平法根本就无法存在。正如裁判官的工作在内容和形式上均构成市民法的补充一样，尽管他以市民法的制度为模型也创立了裁判官制度，通过拟制诉讼[1]和扩用诉讼——与市民法的相应制度类似——创设了救济制度，并创造了裁判官继承法来仿效和补充市民法继承法一样，御前大臣（的司法程序）也效仿普通法。衡平法的一个原则是法律第一，公平第二[2]。对于几乎每一个非程序性规则的普通法规则而言，

---

〔1〕（拉）*actiones fictitiae*（拟制诉讼），是扩用诉讼（*actio utilis*）的一种，在此种诉讼中，执法者假设在实际关系中尚缺乏的条件具备，并把这一虚拟条件作为扩展适用某一法定诉讼程序的依据。罗马法中最典型的拟制诉讼是善意占有之诉（*acito Publiciana*）。

〔2〕直译为：衡平法次于普通法。

is not simply a procedural rule there is a corresponding rule of equity. And the praetor's success in creating legal institutions quite independently, e. g. the praetorian property law or the praetorian law of inheritance, is paralleled, and perhaps surpassed, by the success of English equity in the same sphere of endeavor.

Nevertheless the basic differences between the praetorian law and equity must not be overlooked. The Roman *iudex* was subordinate to the praetor, who could therefore issue directions which the former had to obey. The English judge is quite independent of the chancellor. All the latter can do is to enjoin the parties not to appeal to the courts or not to avail themselves of a judgment rendered by the law court. He can summon the parties to appear before him, and can issue a decree which he can enforce by means of his own. In consequence, equity is much more independent of the common law than is the praetorian taw of the *ius civile*. Equity is not, like the praetorian law, a component part of the whole legal system, but is a separate legal system side by side with the other. And in the course of time equity becomes just as fixed and inflexible as the common law. The chancellor no longer creates new legal remedies, but develops those that are already in existence, just as the judges develop the institutions of the common law. The chancellor enunciates no new legal principles, but develops his precedents in precisely the same manner as the judges develop theirs. Equity has become the legal system according to which the chancellor proceeds, just as law is the legal system according to which the courts render their decisions. There are differences in procedure; chiefly this, that there is no jury in the court of chancery. There is a difference too in the legal consequences (*Rechtsfolgen*). But in the last analysis the chancellor is a judge just like the others. Whether equity or the common law shall apply ultimately depends upon whether the parties appeal to the chancellor or to the courts, and whether the chancellor or the courts to which the party applies is the tribunal competent to render judgment in the matter. If a person asks for an intervention of a nature for which equity has made

并不存在一个相应的衡平法规则。而且裁判官在创立法律制度方面的成功十分独立,例如,英国衡平法的成功在相同的努力范围内与罗马裁判官财产法或裁判官继承法相比毫不逊色,或许还有所超越。

尽管如此,裁判官法和衡平法之间的差别仍不容忽视。罗马法中的审判员从属于裁判官,因此后者签发命令,前者必须遵守。英国法官则相当独立于御前大臣。后者可以做的一切不过是禁止当事人向普通法院起诉或者禁止当事人利用普通法院下达的裁决。御前大臣可以传唤当事人前来,并可以发布一个其自身可以执行的裁决。因此,与裁判官法和市民法之间的相对紧密的关系相比,之于普通法,衡平法要独立得多。衡平法并非像裁判官法那样是整个法律体系的一个组成部分,相反它是一个与普通法并立的法律体系。并且随着时间的推移,衡平法变得和普通法一样的固定和僵硬。御前大臣不再创设新的法律救济,而是不断完善现有的救济手段,正如普通法法官不断完善普通法制度一样。御前大臣也不再阐明任何新的法律原则,而是不断完善既有的法律原则,这与普通法官对待普通法法律原则的态度如出一辙。衡平法变成了御前大臣据以行事的那种法律制度,正如普通法是普通法法院据以作出判决的法律制度一样。它们在诉讼程序上存在区别;主要是,在衡平法院的法庭上不存在陪审团。在法律后果上也存在一个区别。但是归根到底,御前大臣与其他法官一样也是一名法官。究竟是适用衡平法还是普通法最终取决于当事人是向御前大臣提起诉讼还是向普通法法院提起诉讼,以及究竟是御前大臣还是普通法法院对争讼事项享有司法裁决权。如果一名当事人请求御前大臣对一个衡平法未加规定的事

no provision, the chancellor refers him to the courts.

Since the Judicature Acts, equity has become a division of the Supreme Court of Judicature. It is a court in name also. In case of a conflict between equity and law, the principles of equity prevail. Certain legal remedies, it is true, can be applied only in chancery; others, in the other divisions of the Supreme Court. But once the jurisdiction of the division has been determined, chancery as well as the courts, wherever the case may be pending, can apply either law or equity. Only the procedure still varies. Although every English barrister may practice both in chancery and in the courts, it is customary for those barristers that have their offices in Lincoln's Inn to practice in chancery. Equity comprises, in the main, the law of trusts, a considerable portion of the law of pledge, a few legal remedies of the law of inheritance, specific performance (the right in case of contractual obligation to demand performance of the promise, not merely damages), finally the injunctions, i. e. the preliminary prohibitions directed to one party where the party applying for the injunction anticipates irreparable damage. Equity therefore covers only a small number of legal institutions and remedies. But among them is one which in itself constitutes a distinct legal system—the trust.

Trusts can be traced back to the fourteenth century. The original term was use (from *ad opus*). The trust is a transaction, which was well known on the Continent in the Middle Ages, and which was named the *Treuhändergeschäft* (fiduciary transaction). The fiduciary is called the trustee; the person for whose benefit the transaction is entered into, the *cestui que* trust. In Germany and France, as well as in England, in the later Middle Ages, the fiduciary transaction was a substitute for the last will and testament. Whenever anyone wished to leave a thing to the church or to someone else, he delivered it to the trustee

项提供干预，则御前大臣将会让他寻求普通法院的帮助。

自《司法组织法》颁布实施以后，衡平法院已变成英国最高法院的一个分庭。名义上它也是一个法院。在普通法和衡平法冲突时，衡平法原则优先。当然某些特定的法律救济只有衡平法庭可以决定适用；其他的法律救济则在最高法院的其他分庭中亦可适用。但是一旦该法庭的司法管辖权被确立以后，则衡平法院和普通法院可以适用普通法或者适用衡平法——无论该案件已经被审理到什么阶段。只是二者的诉讼程序仍有不同。尽管每一个英国巴律师既可在衡平法院又可在普通法院执业，但是对于那些将办公室设在林肯律师学院的巴律师而言，在衡平法院执业是一个惯例。衡平法大体上包括信托法、相当大比例的担保法、继承法上的一些法律救济、特定履行（在合同之债中要求履行承诺、而非仅要求损害赔偿的权利）以及禁制令——亦即在当事人预期到有无法弥补的损害时向衡平法院申请的，约束另一方当事人行止的预先命令。因此衡平法只包括少量的法律规范和救济。但是其中，有一个部分本身即构成了一个独特的法律制度，即信托。

信托可以追溯到 14 世纪。最初的术语叫做用益（源自 *ad opus*）〔1〕。信托是一个交易，它在中世纪的欧陆为人所熟知，被称作 *Treuhändergeschaft*（信托交易）。受信托的人被称作受托人；因加入该交易并从中获益的人被称作信托受益人。中世纪后期，在德国、法国和英国，信托交易是遗嘱的替代物。无论何时，某人想要给教会或其他人留下某物，他就将该物交给受托人，并附有如何处理该物的指示。御前大臣对此

〔1〕（拉）*ad opus* 为了工作，为了需要。

with directions how to deal with it. The chancellor assumed jurisdiction over this matter and compelled the trustee by the application of the means of power (*Machtmittel*) at his disposal, just as the Roman emperor compelled the fiduciary, to perform the last will of the deceased. Before long transactions of this kind were entered into *inter vivos*, and a thing that had been delivered to the trustee was treated as belonging in equity to the beneficiary from the moment of delivery. The great extent of these transactions was brought about chiefly by the feudal system with its numerous limitations on freedom of action and the ever present danger of escheat to the feudal lord, which made circumventions of this sort necessary. The great feudal lords were vitally interested in the use. It is true the vassal was thereby enabled to prevent many an estate from escheating to the lords, to the great detriment of the latter, by enfeoffing a feoffee to uses who was to hold for the vassal himself; for a person who enfeoffed a feoffee could impose a condition that the trustee should hold for the feoffor. But the great feudal lords themselves were feudatories, the greatest among them holding directly from the king, and they in turn derived advantages from the trust over against their own feudal lord, the king. Their influence for a long time was sufficiently great to cause the chancellor to extend vigorous protection to trusts. But Henry VIII, who had everything to lose and nothing to gain by the use, wrung from an unwilling Parliament a law according to which every use gave to the beneficiary a legal estate, i. e. the corresponding common law right. The statute had scarcely been enacted, when it was interpreted away by an interpretation which limited its application in a manner that took away all its practical significance. It has not hindered the development of the trust.

The law of trusts is not an isolated trust relation but a whole legal system. It comprises first of all the law of corporations. A considerable portion of the ecclesiastical law of the numerous English religious denominations and of the Catholic church, the whole English law of societies,

享有司法管辖权,并通过运用自身权力迫使受托人受其支配,正如罗马皇帝强制受信托人履行亡者的遗嘱一样。不久以后,签订的这种交易当事人活着时亦有效,并且交付给受托人的物品在交付的那一刻起在衡平上被视为属于受益人所有。大部分的这些交易主要由封建制度所引发,因为后者对行为自由有大量的限制,而且对于封建领主而言还存在土地因无继承人而被迫充公这样永恒且现实的危险,这使得此种规避行为有了必要性。大领主对用益极为感兴趣。事实上,通过授予封地受领人以用益权(由该受领人为附庸本人而占有土地)的方式,附庸也因此能够避免让许多土地因无继承人而被迫归还给领主,这对后者非常不利;因为授予封地的人可能强加一个条件,即受托人应该为封地授予人而占有土地。但是大领主自己也是封臣,他们中最大的封地直接来源于国王,他们反过来通过信托又可从他们自己的领主即国王处获得利益。他们长期的影响如此之大,足以促使御前大臣为信托提供强有力的保护。但是亨利八世——这个通过用益丢了所有却什么也得不到的人——逼迫并不情愿的议会制定一部法律,根据该法律,每份用益都将给受益人一个普通法上的地产权,亦即,相应的普通法上的权利。该立法刚一颁布,就有一个解释对其适用作出阐释说明:即该法仅限于以一种实际上剥夺了其所有现实重要性的方式被适用。因此,它并未阻挡信托的发展。

信托法并非是一个孤立的信托关系,而是一个完整的法律制度。它首先包括所有的法人社团法。英国许多教派的教会法和天主教的教会法以及英国的社团法,它们中相当大的比例均基于以下这种主张:受托人为信徒以及为社团成员占有

is based upon this proposition: The trustees hold the property in trust for the believers, for the members of the societies. A special law of things has arisen within the law of trusts. As soon as the subject matter has been transferred to the trustee, the beneficiary at once acquires all rights of use, consumption, and disposition which were intended for him and which he can transfer except in so far as he is limited by the trust. The trustee indeed retains the legal title, but solely as a *nudum ius*. Only a purchaser who has bought the legal estate *bona fide* for value and without notice can deprive the beneficiary of his interest. Since the courts, at least where land is involved, treat the least negligence in the investigation of title as constructive notice, this case could arise only where the documents had been forged very skillfully. The law of the assignment of obligatory rights, as a whole, is a part of the law of trusts. Not until a most recent date was it régulated, in part, by statute.

The English law of family property also developed within the law of trusts. The family settlements provided that the family property was to be held by the trustee for the benefit of the wife, the children born or not yet born. In this way the wife, at a time when the matrimonial community of goods prevailed at common law, was placed in a position of complete independence of her husband in the matter of property law and right, because that which had been given to her in equity was not touched by the community of goods. At the present time this equitable right has been established by statute as the general matrimonial régime. In part, the English law of the declaration of the will by last will and testament is also based on the law of trusts. Historically speaking it was here that the law of trusts had its beginning.

Of no less importance was the influence of the chancellor on the English law of pledge. The pledge law of the common law, the mortgage, corresponds to the oldest form of the Roman *fiducia*. The pledgee obtains full legal ownership of the thing pledged as soon as the debt is due and unpaid. But the chancellor compels him to return the thing pledged to the debtor in case the debt is paid at a later time, and thus enables the pledgor who, indeed, has

被托管的财产。在信托法中产生了一种特别的物法。标的物一旦转移给受托人,受益人立刻就获得所有的用益、消费以及处置的权利,并且除了信托有限制外,他还可将这些权利进行转让。受托人当然保有普通法上的所有权,但后者仅仅是一个裸权。只有支付对价且预先未获通知的善意购买该法定地产权的人才能剥夺受益人于该物中的利益。既然法院——至少涉案土地所在的法院——将(买受人)调查土地权利过程中最小的疏忽视为一种推定通知,那么这种情形仅仅在书面文件先前已经被非常巧妙地伪造时才会发生。债权转让法,总体说来,是信托法的一部分。直到最近,债权转让才部分地由制定法来规范。

英国家庭财产法也是在信托法的范围内发展起来的。家庭财产协议规定家庭财产由受托人为妻子、孩子或尚未出生的孩子的利益而占有。这样,当夫妻财产共有在普通法盛行之时,妻子同时还被置于一个在财产法和权利事务上完全独立于其丈夫的地位,因为在衡平法上给予她的这种利益并不受财产共有的影响。如今,这种衡平法上的权利作为一般的婚姻制度已经由制定法加以规定。在某种程度上,由遗嘱进行意思表示的相关英国法也是以信托法为基础的。从历史角度言之,此处正是信托法发展的始点。

御前大臣对英国担保法的影响绝非较不太重要。普通法上的担保法,按揭,对应于罗马法上最古老的形式信托。一旦债务到期且未偿付,质权人就获得担保物完整的法定所有权。但只要该债务在后来某个时间获得清偿,御前大臣就强制担保权人返还该物给债务人,这样就使得担保人——他的确已经让渡了该物的

already aliened the property, to create additional pledge rights in the thing, which of course could only be equitable rights.

Here the Romanist self-evidently is reminded of the two-fold ownership in Roman law. Indeed even the external similarity is extremely striking. Just as the praetor had developed the transfer of possession into a real contract, so the chancellor utilized a contract for the benefit of a third party—and that is what the trust is in the last analysis—in the same way. And even though Maitland in his work on equity most emphatically denies that the trust is a right *in rem*, this applies only to the juristic construction of the whole legal relation. The extent to which the whole inner structure of the equitable right and the praetorian rights correspond is pointed out by Langdell's presentation:

"As equity wields only physical power, it seems to be impossible that it should actually create anything. It seems moreover to be impossible that there should be any other actual rights than those that are created by the State, i. e. legal rights. So, too, if equity could create actual rights, the existence of rights so created would have to be recognised by every court of justice within the State; and yet no other court than a court of equity will admit the existence of any rights created by equity. It seems therefore that equitable rights exist only in contemplation of equity, i. e. that they are a fiction invented by equity for the promotion of justice. Still as in contemplation of equity such rights do exist, equity must reason upon them and deal with them as if they had an actual existence."

And at another place Langdell, again speaking of the chancellor, says:

"Through his physical power he could imprison men's bodies and control the possession of their property, but neither his orders and decrees nor any acts as such done in pursuance of them had any legal effect or operation; and hence he could not affect the title of property except through the acts of its owners. Even when

所有权——能够在该物上创设附加的担保权利，这种权利当然只可能是衡平法上的权利。

不言而喻，罗马派法学家此处会想到罗马法上的双重所有权。的确，就是这种外部的相似性也是令人极为惊奇的。正如裁判官曾经将占有的转让发展为一种不动产契约，御前大臣也为了第三方的利益同样地利用了一种契约——归根到底那正是信托法的本质。尽管梅特兰在他关于衡平法的作品中最大程度地极力否认信托是一种对物权，但这只适用于整个法律关系的法学建构。关于衡平法上的权利与裁判官法上的权利二者整个内部结构相对应的程度，兰德尔指出：

"由于衡平法仅行使人身强制力，所以它实际上能够产生任何结果似乎都不太可能。另外看来同样不可能的是，除了由国家创设的权利即法定权利外，还存在任何其他实际的权利。因而，如果衡平法能够创设实际权利，那么这些新创权利的存在也必须获得全国每一个法院的认可；然而，正是衡平法院才会承认由衡平法创设的任何权利。因此，衡平法上的权利似乎仅存在于衡平法的思维中，亦即，它们是衡平法为了促进正义而创设的拟制物。尽管如此，由于在衡平法的思维中那样的权利的确存在，因而衡平法必须在它们的基础上推理，并设法处理它们——就好像它们是一种真实存在。"

在另外一个地方，兰德尔又一次谈到了御前大臣，他说：

"通过他享有的人身强制权力，他可以将人投进监狱，并占有他们的财产。但无论是他的命令、裁决还是在劝诫当事人过程中的任何行为都不具有任何法律效果或效力；因此除了通过财产所有人自己的行为之外，他无法影响到财产的权利。即使当他为改

he made a decree for changing the possession of property, it took the shape of a command to the defendant in possession to convey to the plaintiff, and it was only as a last resort that the chancellor issued a writ to his executive officer, commanding him to dispossess the defendant and put the plaintiff in possession."

This presentation shows that the norms for decision in English as well as in Roman law are preponderantly juristic law. The statutes, it is true, seem to be of greater significance than in Rome; but this may be attributed to the fact that we have altogether too low an opinion of the productivity of the Roman legislative machine in the days of the Republic. The original body of English norms for decision however does not derive its origin from statutes. We may consider the assizes of Henry II as a part of the law created by the state, although they do contain much that is juristic law; but the later *formulae*, to which, as all English jurists admit, a considerable part of the English substantive law, the material law, owes its existence, doubtless belong to the category of juristic law. We know the authors of a few of these *formulae*. The writ *quare ejecit infra terminum* was an invention of Bratton's teacher William Raleigh; Lord Chief Justice Rolle refined and improved the writ of ejectment. The situation is not altered by the existence of the fictions, which are in no wise different from the fictions of the praetor and of the juristic science of the Continental common law. On the whole it is admittedly an error, based on the mistaken idea that all creation of law is within the sphere and province of the legislator, to believe that fictions must not be originated by jurists. It is true, the Roman jurists did not employ them, but the older juristic science of the Continental common law and of the French law made

变财产占有而发布裁决，那也不过是采取了命令的形式，从而要求占有财产的被告将该财产转让给原告，而且御前大臣签发令状给他的执行官，命令他剥夺被告的占有并让原告成为占有人仅仅是最后的救济手段。”

这段陈述表明，英国法和罗马法上的裁判规范主要都是法学家法，（英国的）制定法的确似乎比古罗马的制定法具有更大的重要性；但这可能归因于这样的事实：我们全都对罗马共和国时期立法机器的立法能力评价过低。然而，英国裁判规范的最初内容并非来源于制定法。我们可能把亨利二世的法令视为国家所制定法律的一部分，尽管它们确实包括很多法学家之法；但是，后来的诉讼程式——所有的英国法学家都承认，相当大的一部分英国实体法之存在端赖于该诉讼程式——毫无疑问属于法学家法的范畴。我们知道这些诉讼程式中其中一些的作者。期前被逐出租地[1]令状是由布拉顿的老师威廉·罗利发明的；皇家首席大法官罗尔对逐出租地之诉进行了提炼和改善。这种情形并未因法律拟制的存在而有所改变，在裁判官的拟制和欧陆共同法的拟制之间没有任何差异。总的看来，基于错误的想法——所有的法律创制都属于立法者的权力和职权范围——而认为法律拟制不得由法学家创造，这显然是一个谬见。的确，罗马法学家不曾使用它们，但欧陆共同法与法国法的古老法学都曾广泛使用过它们。

---

〔1〕“期前被逐出租地”是一种令状名称。土地承租人在租期届满前就被驱逐出土地租地的情形下，可向封地受领人或出租人提起的诉讼。后来，该令状被租地逐出之诉取代。

extensive use of them. It would be a difficult matter to state wherein the constructions of the Roman and of the Continental common law differ from fictions—as a rule only in the mode of expression.

Now where did the English judges get the norms according to which they decided the law-suits that were brought before them? How did the English common law develop from them in the course of the centuries? Undoubtedly it developed in the same way as the Roman *ius civile*. The basis of the decisions here also is the inner nature of the legal relation, agreement, articles of association, last will, custom, commercial usage, which, universalized, yield a unitary norm for decision in other situations. Since the history of the older English law is better known than the history of Roman and of German law we are in a better position to trace the process of reduction to unity and of universalization. We see how the courts evolve the law of things by universalizing feudal law; how the husband' s sole ownership of the property which the wife brought into the marriage relation is gradually being adopted by the courts; how they gradually substitute the right of the first-born to inherit for the right of all children to take equally, which had been the law until that time. Everywhere the endeavor appears to be to make the law unitary by extending the legal principles that prevail among the upper classes to the whole people. In a similar way the law of commerce is created as late as the eighteenth century by a process of universalization and reduction to unity. Furthermore, from the very beginning the English judge thought himself empowered to find norms for decision according to justice and fairness.

It is self-evident that the development of equity in a still greater measure takes place in the light of history. Sir George Jessel, Master of the Rolls, one of the greatest of equity judges, says on this point:

"It must not be forgotten that the rules of equity are not, like the rules of the common law, supposed to have been established from time immemorial. It is perfectly well known that they have been established from time to time, altered, improved, and refined from time to time. In many cases we know the name of the

要说出罗马法、欧陆共同法的推定与法律拟制的区别在哪里，这是一件困难的事情——通常它们只是在表达的方式上有所不同。

如今英国法官从何处获得他们据以断讼的规范？在几个世纪里，英国普通法是怎样从这些裁判规范中发展出来的？无疑，它与罗马市民法的发展道路一样。裁决的基础也是法律关系、协议、社团章程、遗嘱、习惯、商业惯例等一系列事物的内部性质，这些基础在一般化之后，产生了一个可适用于其他场合的一元化的裁判规范。既然古代英国法的历史比罗马法、德国法的历史更为人所知，我们就更容易探寻这种统一化和一般化的演进过程。我们了解法院如何通过使封建法一般化而发展物法的；丈夫对妻子结婚时带入夫家之财产的独占所有权如何逐渐为法院所承认；它们又是怎样为了所有孩子的平等权而逐渐代替了长子继承权的，在这种代替发生之前，长子继承制一直为有效的法律规定。无论何处，这种将仅盛行于上层社会的法律原则扩大适用于全体人民的努力似乎都是为了让法律一元化。同理，商业法在18世纪因一般化和统一化的过程而得以创立。而且，从一开始，英国法官就认定其自身被授予权力以发现符合正义和公平的裁判规范。

历史清楚地表明，衡平法的发展程度甚至更为深远。掌卷法官乔治·杰塞尔爵士，这位最伟大的衡平法官之一就此说道：

“不能忘记，与普通法的规则不同，衡平法的规则不能被认定是远古以来就已建立，大家都很清楚，衡平法的规则不时有所建立、改变、完善与精炼。许多情况下，我们知道创造它们的御前大

Chancellor who invented them. Take such things as these: the separate use of the married woman, the restraint on alienation, the modern rule against perpetuities, and the rules of equitable waste. We can name the Chancellors who first invented them, and state the date when they were first introduced into equity jurisprudence, and therefore in cases of this kind the older precedents are of little value. The doctrines are progressive, refined and improved, and if we want to know what the rules of equity are, we must look, of course, rather to the more modern than the more ancient cases." (Quoted by Holdsworth, History of English Law, from an opinion.)

Equity has been created in the same way in which all other juristic law has been created. The law of trusts and family settlements and of the equitable mortgage is based chiefly upon universalization of the traditional content of agreements. The remainder of the law of equity, as Sir George Jessel has put it, consists essentially of norms for decision, freely found by the chancellors, in finding which they consider themselves far less bound by previous decisions than do the common law judges.

The thing that may seem most striking to the Continental jurist in English judge-made law is the importance attached to the personality of the individual judge. A lawyer citing a case refers to the judge by name. If the decision is rendered by the whole bench, each judge states the reason for his decision separately, and thereafter these norms are cited under his name. It is true, each one of the high courts as such has weight and influence, but what that weight and influence is depends not upon the court but upon the judge. There are judges who were epoch-making in the history of English law and whose names are spoken of with reverence centuries after their death; the rank and file have long since passed into the great silence. Each one of the great judges has a pronounced personality, which is described in the history of law very much in the manner in which that of

臣的名字。那些可指出其创设人的规则有如下这些:已婚妇女(对特有财产)的单独使用、对(财产自愿)转让的限制、现代的禁止永久权规则以及衡平法上之损耗的规则。我们可以说出首次创设出上述衡平法规则的御前大臣的名字以及它们首次被引入衡平法的日期,因此在这些规则适用的场合,古老的先例价值极小。这些理论是先进的、精制的、完善的,而且假使我们想知道衡平法的规则是什么,那么我们当然必须看更现代的案例,而不是去看更古老的案例。”(霍兹沃思在《英国法律史》引用的一种观点)

与所有其他法学家之法的创建方式相同,衡平法也创建起来了。信托与家庭财产协议法、衡平法上的抵押法主要都是以协议之传统内容的一般化为基础。衡平法上的剩余地产权,如乔治·杰塞尔所言,本质上包含裁判规范——这种情形由御前大臣们主动发现,在此过程中,御前大臣认为他们自己断讼时受到先例拘束的程度远较普通法官小。

在英国法官法中,似乎最令欧陆法学家吃惊的事情就是法官个性的重要性。律师在引证某个案例时会提到审理该案法官的名字。如果裁决是由全体法官作出的,那么每一名法官都要单独陈述其裁决的理由,此后这些规范被引用时都置于某法官名下。的确,每一个高等法院因其地位,都具有重要性和影响力,但是那种重要和影响并非依赖于法院,而是取决于法官。有些法官在英国法律史上具有划时代的意义,在他们死后数世纪,人们谈及他们的名字仍然会有崇敬之情;尽管他们的职位和卷宗都早已作古。这些伟大的法官,每一个都有很鲜明的个性,法律史中对这些个性着墨甚多,至于描述方法,则与文学史和艺术史中对伟

the great poets and artists is described in the history of literature and of art. The following are mentioned as the most famous: Coke, Hardwick, Mansfield, Stowall, Grant, Willes, Jessel, Cairns, Bowen, Parke; and among American judges perhaps: Marshal, Kent, Story, Shaw, O. W. Holmes, Jr. In a book of Maitland's, I find the following significant words: "I have mentioned this case, because we may say that when the court of Appeal overruled Jessel, M. R., the case was very near the border line."

Juristic science in England also comprises the business of drawing up documents, and in this respect, too, it has become a perfect art, chiefly in the matter of documents concerning land and marriage contracts (family settlements). Its basis is the established custom of the attorneys, which however closely follows legislation and decided cases. The judicial decisions that deal with documents are being carefully recorded and taken into account. Frequently the judges say that they cannot depart from the decided cases although they consider them wrongly decided, on the ground that the conveyancers may possibly have been following them in the preparation of legal documents.

The nature of English juristic law was stated by Sir James Parke, later Lord Wensleydale, in a case that was argued before the House of Lords in the following words:

"Our common law system consists in applying to new combinations of circumstances those rules of law which we derive from legal principles and judicial precedents; and for the sake of attaining uniformity, consistency and certainty, we must apply those rules, where they are not plainly unreasonable and inconvenient, to all cases which arise; and we are not at liberty to reject them, and to abandon all analogy to them, in those to which they have not yet been judicially applied, because we think that the rules

大诗人和伟大艺术家的描述方法并无二致。以下法官被认为是最著名的:柯克、哈德威克、曼斯菲尔德、斯托瓦尔、、格兰特、、威尔斯、杰塞尔、凯恩斯、鲍恩、帕克;在美国法官中,最著名的或许是以下这些:马歇尔、肯特、斯托里、肖、霍姆斯。在梅特兰的一本著作里,我发现下列重要的一句话:“我已经提到过这种情况,因为我们可以说,当上诉法庭推翻 M·R·杰塞尔的判决时,这个案子已经非常靠近界线。”

英格兰法学也包含制定书面文件的事务,并且在这方面,它也成了一件完美的艺术,主要是有关土地和婚姻契约(婚姻财产协议)文件的事务。它的基础是已确立的律师习惯,不过这种习惯紧跟立法和已决案例。处理文件的司法裁决均被认真记录,供人参考。法官经常会说,尽管他们认为先前案件判决有误,但他们仍不能背离这些已决案例,因为不动产转让律师很可能在准备这些法律文件时就已经打算遵循它们了。

关于英国法学家法的性质,詹姆斯·帕克爵士,亦即后来的温斯利戴尔勋爵,在一个由上议院审理的案件中说过如下的话:

“我们的普通法制度在应用于复杂的新情况时所包含一些法律规则,是我们从法律原则和司法先例中推导出来的;为了保持法律的一致性、连贯性和确定性,除非显然不合理或不合适,否则我们必须在所有的案例中都适用那些规则;并且我们不得随意拒绝运用它们,不得随意废弃对它们的所有类推,在那些案例中,后者尚未获得司法适用,因为我们认为,那些规则并不像我们自己

are not as convenient and reasonable as we ourselves could have devised."

On this occasion I may be permitted to correct an erroneous opinion that is very widespread on the Continent, i. e. the opinion that the free finding of law in England in some way is in a causal connection with the fact that the law of England has not been codified. For the free finding of law is a valid method even when applied to statutes. Here too the judge, by a free finding of law, determines the meaning where there is an ambiguity, and supplies the omitted words where there is a gap; and these decisions are as binding upon the court for the future as those that deal with the common law. Only where the meaning is plain, the court is not bound by previous decisions. On the other hand, where an erroneous interpretation is very old the courts may not lightly disregard it (Hardcastle, The Construction and Effect of Statute Law, Third Edition, p. 93 et seq.). Consequently the glorious freedom of action which the English judge enjoys would be preserved even if the English law were codified. In an article in the Law Quarterly Review (Vol. 19, p. 15) on the Codification of Mercantile Law, Chalmers quotes the following words from a report of the Royal Commissioners on the Criminal Code Bill, which had been prepared by the judges Lord Blackburn, Lord Justice Lush, Sir James Stephen, and Mr. Justice Barry:

"The great richness of the law of England in principles and rules embodied in judicial decisions, no doubt, involves the consequence that a code adequately representing it must be elaborate and detailed, but such a code would not, except in a few cases in which the law at present is obscure, limit any discretion now possessed by the judges. It would simply change the form of the rules by which they are bound."

English and British juristic literature, on the other hand, has created law only in a very limited measure. Holdsworth in his History of English Law mentions only five juristic writers who have become figures of outstanding importance in the history of English law.

原本能够设计得那样适宜与合理。”

在这里，请允许我纠正一个错误的、但在欧陆非常普遍的观点，即：在英格兰，在某些方面对法的自由发现与英格兰法律尚未法典化这个事实之间存在因果联系。因为即使在应用于制定法时，法的自由发现也是一个行之有效的方法。这种情况下，法官在遇到法律有歧义时，同样通过法的自由发现确定其含义，并且在遇到法律有漏洞时填补了被忽略的内容；这些裁决在后来对法院断案也有约束力，这与适用普通法断案的先例裁决效力一样。只有在（法律规则的）含义非常简单清楚时，法院才可不受先例裁决的拘束。另一方面，当一个错误的解释非常古旧时，法院也不能轻易地忽视它。（哈德卡斯尔，《制定法的解释与效力》，第 3 版，第 93 页及以下）因此，即使英国法进行了法典化，英国法官也会享有显赫的行动自由。《法律季评》（第十九卷，第 15 页）中有一篇文章专门讨论商法的法典化，在文中，查默斯从皇家委员会关于《刑法典议案》的报告中引用了下面一段话：

“英格兰法原则和规则的极大丰富体现在司法裁决中，无疑，这种丰富必然会带来如下结果：充分表现这种丰富的法典必定是精心创制、详尽无遗的，但这样的法典除了在某些情况下——现行法含糊不清——之外，将不会限制法官现在享有的任何自由裁量权。法典将仅仅改变他们受拘束之规则的形式。”

另一方面，英国和不列颠法学文献仅在非常有限的程度上创建了法律。在英国法律史上，具有杰出重要性的法学文献作者，霍兹沃思在其《英国法律史》中只提到了五位。他们是：格兰维尔

They are: Glanvill, Bracton, Littleton, Coke, and Blackstone. But it is impossible to show that the Tractatus de legibus, which is usually attributed to Glanvill, the chief justiciar of Henry II (died about 1190), and the work of Henry de Bratton (usually called Bracton) exerted any influence upon the development of English law. Blackstone's book is a presentation of the existing law, not a work of practical juristic science in the sense of a literary development of law, and but few of his doctrines have gained general recognition. Only Littleton (? -1481) and Coke (1552-1628) remain. Pollock mentions Sir Michael Forster's Treatise on Crown Law, the first edition of which was published in 1762, as "the latest book to which authority in the exact sense can be ascribed."

Moreover the juristic writers of England make no attempt to find norms independently in the manner of the Continental writers. They content themselves with collecting the decisions. Furthermore there is an utter absence of commentaries on the statutes in the Continental sense, for a statute can be interpreted only by judicial decisions. "English text-books are almost entirely a collection of cases with comments interspersed. Sometimes a general rule is stated which may go a trifle further than the cases do; sometimes an opinion is thrown out on a point not covered by authority. Still the cases are the gist of the book," says Bryce. It is only in recent times that books that contain independent inquiries and attempt deeper study, like the works of Sir Frederic Pollock or of the American writers Langdell and O. W. Holmes, Jr., are beginning to appear.

The English common law is the law not only of England, Ireland, and Wales, but to a great extent of Scotland, also of the United States, of almost all the English colonies except perhaps where aborigines are concerned, and even in dealings with them

布莱克顿、利特尔顿、柯克和布莱克斯通。但是,要指出《英格兰的法律与习惯论》——该书作者通常被认为是亨利二世时的最高司法官格兰维尔(约卒于1190年)——这部作品、以及亨利·布拉德(通常被称作布莱克顿)的作品对于英国法的发展发挥过什么影响,是不可能的。布莱克斯通的著作是对现行法的阐述,而不是在法律文献的发展意义上的实用法学的作品。但是他的有些学说已获得普通承认。这样,只剩下利特尔顿(?—1481)和柯克(1552—1628)可以归入到有重大影响的法律文献作者。波洛克提到了迈克尔·福斯特爵士《论刑法》的专著,该书第一版出版于1762年,“精确地说,这本最新著作称得上是此领域的权威论著”。

此外,英格兰的法学作者从未打算像欧陆法学作者那样独立地发现规范。他们满足于收集判例。而且在英格兰,对制定法还完全缺乏欧陆意义上的释评,因为这种对制定法的解释只能在司法裁判中由法官进行。布赖斯曾说,“英国教科书几乎完全是带有评论的案例集。有时候,一个一般规则可能被阐释得极其琐碎,远超过案例的篇幅;有时候,一个(法官)意见会被弃置一边,不为权威著作所容。尽管如此,案例仍然是教科书的精华。”直到最近,一些包含独立的探究并尝试进行更深研究的作品——比如弗里德里希·波洛克的著作或是美国作者兰德尔以及O·W·霍姆斯的著作——才开始出现。

英国普通法不仅是英格兰、爱尔兰和威尔士的法律,而且在苏格兰法中也占有极大的比重,它还是美国法以及几乎所有的英属殖民地(除了涉及当地土著居民,不过即使涉及他们,普通法通

it is usually applied as subsidiary law. The Indian codifications as a rule preserve the common law unchanged. One may well say that it is valid law in states and nations that are counted among the wealthiest and most advanced of the whole world. And since it does not presuppose particular laws which it must supplement, its influence is much more direct and effective than that of the Continental common law. Moreover it comprises not only private law, but also criminal law, mercantile law, and—purely historically—procedural law. It is true, it has never attained the finish, the perfection, and the fine elaboration in detail which is characteristic of the Continental common law, but it surpasses the latter by far in wealth of legal propositions, in variety of legal institutions. The juristic science of a legal system such as this must not be ignored in the development of legal science. It can be traced back in its beginnings to the time of Henry II, i. e. to the middle of the twelfth century. One of its first achievements, the assize of novel disseisin, dates from the year 1166. In point of venerable age indeed it is surpassed by the Continental common law juristic science, but this is counterbalanced to a great degree not only by the enormous extent of the territory in which it is valid and in consequence by the great diversity of situations with which the English jurists are called upon to deal, but also by the early and great development of commerce and industry as well as of the social and political relations of the peoples concerned. All of this has provided an invaluable amount of stimulation.

Since the movement toward free finding of law has directed the attention of Continental jurists to English juristic science and the English method of finding law, the statement is often made on the Continent that the English are satisfied neither with the results of their juristic science nor with their method of finding the law. May I therefore in conclusion be permitted to quote the words of two eminent English jurists, who moreover are considered experts in Continental affairs. Both of them, it is true, are not speaking directly of the free finding of law but of case law, the legal system based upon it; but inasmuch as this presupposes free finding of law, their opinion must be referable to both. One of these is the aged author of the American Commonwealth,

常还是作为辅助性法律而获得适用法律中最重要的组成部分，括号部分。印度法典化总体上让普通法保存完好。人们可以理直气壮地说，普通法是世界上最富裕、最发达的国家和民族中行之有效的法律。而且，既然它不以其必须辅助的其他特定法为前提，那它的影响就比欧陆共同法来得更直接、更有效。此外，它不仅包含私法，还包括刑法、商法以及——纯粹就历史角度而言诉讼法。诚然，它从未达致完整、完善以及细节上的精雕细琢——这是欧陆共同法的特征，但它在法律见解的丰富性上、在法律制度的多样性上远胜于后者。因此，英国普通法的法学在法学发展上不容忽视。普通法可以被追溯到亨利二世时它的发展源头，亦即12世纪中叶。它的首要成就之一就是创立了新型侵占土地之诉，这种诉讼形式源自1166年。就古老程度而言，英国普通法的法学的确不如欧陆共同法的法学，但这一弱项很大程度上不仅被它所适用领土的广袤范围以及由此带来的英国法学家需要加以应对的多样性局面所抵消，而且还因其统治下之民族的商业、工业以及社会和政治关系的提早的巨大发展而获得弥补。这一切提供了一个极其珍贵的激励。

由于有关法的自由发现运动将欧陆法学家的注意力集中到英国法学和英国有关发现法律的方法之上，所以欧陆经常有这样的论调：英国人既对法学的成果不满，又对发现法律的方式不满。因此最后请允许我引用两位杰出的英国法学家，他们也被认为是欧陆事务方面的专家的话。的确，他们二人并没有直接说到法律的自由发现，而是谈论判例法——英国普通法制度赖以存在的基础，但由于这是法律自由发现的先决条件，所以他们的意见可以看成是同时论及此二者的。其中一位是

James Bryce, who in his youth sat at the feet of Vangerow in Heidelberg and dedicated his first work to the Holy Roman Empire of the German Nation. What he says about case law sounds almost like a *hymnus*, which he prefaces with the following words: "It is an abiding honor to our lawyers and judges, to have worked it out with a completeness and success unknown to any other country." (Studies in History and Jurisprudence, Vol. II, p. 289 et seq.)

Let him who would be informed as to what so distinguished an English jurist thinks of the grandeur of the English legal system, as compared with the Continental system, read the three pages following the words quoted from the work cited above. They seem so much more persuasive since Bryce, as is well known, is an unbiassed observer of foreign institutions and is by no means blind to the disadvantages of the English method.

Perhaps the following remark of Pollock's, quoted from the book already referred to, will be found more persuasive than all of this. Says Pollock: "Where the two systems have come into competition as they have done in the Province of Quebec, the Cape Colony, and other British possessions originally settled under Continental systems of law, the method ascribing exclusive authority to judicial decisions has invariably, so far as I know, been accepted." In other words, wherever the English case law system, which is founded upon the free finding of law, comes into contact with the Continental methods of applying law, the latter are inevitably thrust aside. Anyone who knows the conservative turn of mind of the jurist can judge from this how obvious the superiority of the English method of finding law must be. In this connection one must not fail to note that both in Canada and in South Africa many a feature of the English organization of the administration of justice which is usually

《美利坚共和国》[1]年长的作者詹姆斯·布赖斯,他年轻时在海德堡曾在凡格罗手下任职,将他的第一部作品《神圣罗马帝国》献给了日耳曼民族。他关于判例法的言谈听起来像一个圣歌,他是这样开始谈起的:"设计出判例法且获得不为任何其他国家所知的完备性和成功,这对于我们的律师和法官而言,是一个恒久的荣耀。"(《历史和法学研究》,第Ⅱ卷,第289页及以后)

那样一个杰出的英国法学家想到了与欧陆法律制度相比,英国法律制度的伟大之所在,对此熟悉的人不妨读一下上面所引著作中紧接着的三页话语。众所周知,由于布赖斯是一个对于外国法律制度的评论不怀偏见的评论者,而且对英国模式的缺陷绝非熟视无睹,因此,它们似乎更容易让人信服。

或许波洛克下面的评语(同样引自该著作)将比所有的这一切更具有说服力。波洛克说:"就我所知,在这两种法律制度竞争的地方,比如在魁北克省、开普殖民地、以及其他原处于大陆法律体系统治下的不列颠殖民地,将排他性的权威归于司法裁决的方法一直获得认可。"换句话说,无论在哪里,只要建立在法的自由发现基础上的判例法制度与欧陆的法律适用方式方法碰到一起,后者都不可避免地遭到弃绝。任何了解法学家之保守性情的人都能从中判断出英国的法律发现方法具有多么大的优势。关于这一点,人们不能不注意到,在加拿大和南非,经常被指出的英国司法施行机构的许多特征并不存在,例如法院高度的集中化、法官

〔1〕 美利坚共和国,指宾夕法尼亚州、肯塔基州、弗吉尼亚州和麻萨诸塞州等四州最初组成的政治实体。

pointed out is absent, e. g. the extraordinary centralization of the courts and the high position of the judge, although even as it is, the position of the judge in these countries might be higher than it is in central Europe.

In conclusion I would quote the words of Holmes, an American jurist. He says of the common law that it is "a far more developed, more rational and mightier body of law than the Roman."

The complaints that are being heard in England about case law refer exclusively to its terrible lack of systematic arrangement. In fact, scattered throughout thousands of volumes, it is like a tropical primeval forest, where the wanderer who has lost his way is threatened with new surprises and dangers at every tree that he sees. But this fault does not lie at the door of the free finding of law, but at that of the absolute binding force of all judicial decisions, which continues at least until such time as they are reversed by a higher tribunal. But even though the free finding of law gives rise to the idea that the law that has been found should not readily be given up, the evils that have arisen from it in England as consequences of the historical development do not, by any means, have to be taken into the bargain. They can easily be avoided.

Juristic science in England differs from juristic science in Rome chiefly in this, that it is not preponderantly literary as was the latter, at least in the days of the Empire, but almost exclusively judicial. In spite of this, as our inquiries have shown, the two systems have developed on parallel lines throughout. Procedure passes through the same stages as in ancient Rome, the judges create the common law by employing the same methods of universalization and of finding norms that the *prudentes* employed in creating the *ius civile*, and the English magisterial law presents the same essential characteristics as the Roman, not in a few externals merely, but in its whole inner structure. Is there need of further proof to show that we are face to face with a natural unifying regularity of events?

的崇高地位等，即便如此，在这些国家中法官的地位可能比中欧国家的法官地位还要高。

最后，我想引用美国法学家霍姆斯的话。在提到普通法时，他说，普通法是"一个远比罗马法发展程度更高、更理性、更强大的法律体"。

在英格兰，关于判例法常听到的抱怨是它缺乏体系化的安排。事实上，由于散落并遍及于数千卷中，因而它就像一个热带原始森林，迷路的漫游者在他看到的每一个大树下都会遭逢到新的意外和危险。但是这个缺陷并不应归咎于法的自由发现，而应归因于所有的司法裁决所具有的绝对拘束力——这种拘束力至少能维持到该裁决被更高层级的法院推翻时为止。不过尽管法的自由发现会带来这样的观念：已经被发现的法律不应该轻易放弃，但在英格兰，作为历史发展的结果，因该观念而产生的弊端无论如何也不必带到交易中。它们可以很容易被避免。

英格兰法学不同于罗马法学之处主要在于，它并非像后者一样主要是以书面著作形式呈现的（后者至少在罗马帝国时期是如此），相反，它几乎全部是以司法裁决为载体。尽管这样，正如我们的研究所表明，两种法学体系自始至终都在两条平行线上发展。（英格兰的）诉讼程序经历的各种阶段与古罗马帝国的情形完全相同，英格兰的法官通过运用了与罗马法学家创造法学家法所使用的同样的法律一般化与规范发现的方法创造了普通法，而且，英国的治安官法展现了与罗马执法官法本质上相同的特点，它们并非仅仅在一些外部特征相同，而是在整个内部结构上一致。还需要更进一步的证据来证明，我们直接面对了自然趋同的事物规律性吗？

# XIII

# The Juristic Science Of The Older Continental Common Law

The reception of Roman law in the Middle Ages and in modern times may properly be considered here, for it undoubtedly created a new and unique phase of juristic science. It is clear in the first place that the kind of juristic activity which occupies the foreground in every indigenous legal development, i. e. the creation of norms for decision through universalization and free finding of law, thereafter necessarily had to be thrust into the background by the wealth of norms for decision which the Roman law books offered ready for use. This appeared so much more clearly inasmuch as the Roman universalizations in part lost the characteristic quality of universalizations when Roman law was received. On the soil on which it had its origin, a universalization must be felt as what it actually is, i. e. as a universalization. Transplanted to a soil on which the phenomena that have been universalized do not occur, it ceases to be a universalization, it becomes a rule, occasionally appearing to be quite arbitrary, which knows neither universal nor particular, and according to which legal disputes are being decided. The whole Roman law, which had been given the force of law in this way, became a collection of juristic norms for decision. Whereas in Rome it had grown directly out of life, it now faced life as a fixed, immovable standard. Legal life no longer was the subject matter of juristic science, as it is to a certain degree in an indigenous legal development, but its object. And

# 第十三章　古老的欧陆共同法学

在这里，我们将适当讨论中世纪和近现代罗马法继受的情况。因为罗马法的继受毋庸置疑地创造了法学发展的一个崭新和独特的阶段。首先，继受罗马法的法律活动——通过罗马法的一般化和自由发现法律创造裁判规则的活动，明显地占据了所有国家法律本土化发展过程中的显著位置。此后，这一研究活动必然由研究罗马法著作提供的大量裁判规范推进到了研究罗马法演变、适用的特定背景上。就罗马法的普遍性而言，当罗马法被各国接受时罗马法也部分地丧失其独特的普遍性品质。在罗马法的发源地，一般化肯定是一种被真切感觉到的一般化。当罗马法被移植到另外的一些国家时，罗马法的一般化现象没有发生，它不再是一种一般化，而是变成了一个用以裁断法律纠纷的规则，此种裁判规则偶尔显得相当恣意。它既未经历过一般化也未经历过个别化。通过这种方式获得法律效力的全部罗马法，变成了裁判规范的集合。尽管在罗马，罗马法直接来源于生活，不过现在它却开始用一种固定不变的标准面对生活。在法律本土化的发展过程中，法律生活不再是法学的主题，如同在法律本土化发展过程中某种程度上所表现的那样，而是成为了法学的客体。

thereby juristic science became something quite different from what it had been before that time. It now faced life as something approaching from without. It undertook to force rules upon society which it had not invented itself but which it had taken over from elsewhere, without any thought of whether society desired them or not, without any concern as to how society fared under them, simply because they were in existence. And in a great measure it has been successful. The great antinomy of juristic science, in the hands of which all modes of thought become forces that have the power to create norms, has again demonstrated its historic significance.

Although the reception of Roman law relieved the jurist of the burden of dealing with life by continally creating the law which the latter requires, it brought him face to face with another, perhaps a greater, difficulty, i. e. the difficulty of adapting the new law to legal relations that were altogether foreign to it. How could the jurists, in the years immediately following the reception, get the idea into their heads that the Roman sources were dealing with the same institutions that they themselves had to deal with? Was it so obvious that the peculiar mediaeval rights in land or the contracts, which in part were of a totally different nature, must be adjudged according to Roman law? The mere fact of the reception is sufficient to establish the basic presupposition of the sociological science of law that there are legal institutions that exist independently of the positive law; at any rate it proves that among all the peoples by whom the Roman law was received there were legal institutions which they had in common with the Romans, at least to such an extent that the application of the Roman law did not appear to be altogether impossible.

This must be attributed in part to the state of the Roman law into which Roman juristic science had put it. With inimitable mastery the latter had selected those elements that are universally human, and that must exist in every society. The concepts of corporation, family law powers, ownership and real rights, the various agreements, inheritance,—all of

因此,法学完全不同它先前的样子了。现在,法学把生活看成了一种从外部接近的事物。法学开始把并非法学自己创立而是从别处得来的规则强加给社会,而不考虑社会是否想要它们,也不关注社会在那些规则之下如何发展,它将那些强加于社会,仅仅是因为它们实际存在着。在很大程度上,法学曾经是成功的。法学的巨大悖论——在这种悖论的控制下,所有的思想方法都变成有权创造规范的力量——又一次证明了法学的历史重要性。

虽然罗马法的继受减轻了法学家必须不断创造出生活所需法律来应对生活的负担,但是它也提出了另外一个或许是更大的必须面对的困难,即全然异质的法律体系接纳新法律的困难。在紧接着罗马法继受的年月里,法学家怎样才能把握罗马法原始文献中曾经处理过而他们现时又必须进行处理的同样的法律制度?中世纪的土地权利或契约权利在某种程度上与古罗马土地权利或契约权利具有完全不同的性质,(可现在)它们必须依据罗马法来审判——这样做很容易理解吗?单单罗马法继受的事实就足以建立法律社会学的基本假设,即法律制度是独立存在于实在法之外的。至少它证明了在所有继受罗马法的民族中存在着与罗马人相同的制度,至少在——罗马法的适用并非显得完全不可能——这一范围内是如此。

这必须部分归功于罗马法学使罗马法所达到的那种状态。凭借对法律无与伦比地精通,法学家们选择出那些具有普遍人性和必然存在于每一个社会中的要素。法人社团、家庭法权力、所有权和物权、各种各样的协议和继承等概念——所有的这些概念

these and many other basic concepts of juristic science in general, not only of juristic science as it exists among a certain people, it had developed and set forth, and had found the proper norms for the decision of the most important questions that might arise in a legal controversy. But mediaeval society was so totally different from Roman society because it was in a stage of development so far removed from that of Roman society that, at the time of the reception, the number of legal institutions as to which one could be certain at the outset that they were identical with those of Roman law must have been exceedingly small. It was the case perhaps only as to this or that family relation, a small number of agreements, let us say, as to sales and loans. Apart from these, though there were many external similarities, the differences must have preponderated.

The situation that the jurists of the time of the reception found themselves in can perhaps be illustrated best by means of a comparison. Let us suppose that by a miracle, the law of England should, at this very moment, become the valid law of some part or other of the European continent. Let us suppose further that the Continental jurist consults the Stephen-Jenks commentaries on the Laws of England (incidentally the only work on English law that can be compared with the comprehensive presentations that are in vogue on the Continent). He would be surprised to find that the basic concept of his whole legal thinking up to the present time — the concept of ownership — is not being discussed at all. To begin with there is no concept of ownership which comprises the law both as to movables and immovables. A concept that corresponds to ownership of immovables is there called a freehold, and is defined as "an estate, either of inheritance or for life held by free tenure." Here almost every word is unintelligible to a Continental jurist, and the concept itself is still more so. For "freehold" refers, in the first place, to immovables only. It is a sort of real right which includes usufruct, heritable lease, and heritable building right, and which excludes the free ownership of land of the Continental law inasmuch as it presupposes tenure. He would find it necessary in the first place to resolve all doubts

和其他法学中通常所含有的基本概念不仅仅存在于一个特定民族的法学之中。它在不断地发展和表达,并且为法律争议中出现的最重要问题找出恰当的裁判规范。但是因为中世纪在发展阶段中与罗马社会相距甚远,所以中世纪的社会完全不同于罗马社会。在这一个时期的罗马法继受中,可以确信刚开始时曾与罗马法保持一致的法律制度数量肯定已经极少了。这种一致性可能仅仅存在于家庭关系的某些方面,少量的协议(比如买卖与借贷)。除此之外,其余的制度可能表面存在许多相似性,但差异已明显是主要的了。

当时继受罗马法的法学家发现他们自己所处的境况或许可以通过比较得到最好的说明。让我们假设在那个特殊的时期,英国法奇迹般地成为当时欧陆某些地域有效的法律。让我们进一步假设,大陆法学家参考了斯蒂芬·甄克的英国法的评述(碰巧是关于英国法的唯一能与当时盛行于欧陆全面著述相比拟的作品)。他肯定会惊讶地发现:直至当时其法律制度的基本概念——所有权的概念——根本无人讨论。首先,包含动产和不动产法的所有权概念根本不存在。与不动产所有权概念相对应的是自由保有地产权,其定义是“一种继承的或终身自由保有的地产权”。这个定义不仅让大陆系的法学家们一头雾水,而且定义本身也含混不清。首先,“自由保有地产权”这一术语仅指不动产。它包括用益权、可继承租赁权和可继承建筑权等物权;大陆法中无任何限制的土地所有权因为不能预先设定使用期限而被排除在外。他发现有必要首先要澄清由以下问题而产生的种种疑虑:既然在大陆法系,无

as to the question whether the free ownership of the Continental law, since it is not a feudal fee, is covered by this concept. This question the Continental jurist, whether he likes it or not, will find himself constrained to answer in the affirmative, for the reason that tenure in modern English law is a pure fiction, and for the further reason that, if this were not so, there would be no legal regulation at all, not only of ownership but also of usufruct, of heritable lease, and of heritable building right, all of which are conditioned upon acquisition from an owner. And apart from this, the difficulty of working with a concept of property which comprises also usufruct, heritable lease, and heritable building right, and among the sub-divisions of which are found the base fee (property to which most strange resolutory conditions are attached) and the fee tail (inalienable property which passes to certain definite heirs, our Continental *fideicommissum*, and, after all, not a *fideicommissum* at all). What does all of this refer to?

The famous decretal of Pope Alexander III, which regulated the passing of the advowson to the *firmarius*, proves that this imagined and impossible illustration quite faithfully reflects all the

任何限制的不动产所有权不是一种封建世袭地产，因而该所有权是否包含在“自由保有”这一法律概念之下。对于这个问题，欧陆法法学家不管喜欢与否，都将被迫作出肯定的回答。因为在现代英国法中，土地使用期限根本就是一种纯粹的拟制。更深层的原因是倘若不是这样，那根本就不存在任何法律规则。不光没有所有权，也没有用益权、可继承租赁权和可继承性建筑权，所有后面这些权利都是以从所有者那里获得为条件的。除此之外，困难还在于如何界定不动产权利这一概念，财产权包括用益权、可继承租赁权和可继承性建筑权，对上述权利再往下细分，还可以派生出：附条件自由继承地产权〔1〕（这一不动产权利上附着一些最奇特的解除条件）；限嗣继承地产权〔2〕（不能转让的只能指传给特定继承人的财产权，类似于我们大陆法系的*fideicommissum*，〔3〕但毕竟根本不是*fideicommissum*）。所有的这些指的是什么？

教皇亚历山大三世——规范如何将圣职推荐权〔4〕传给适格继承人——著名的教令证明，所有这些臆想的、于理不通的解释都忠实地反映了中世纪在继受罗马法时所必然遇到的困难。

---

〔1〕 base fee，在这里指的是附（解除）条件地产权，其成就和存在以其他条件的存在为前提，并且是在该条件终结时终结的地产权或权利。

〔2〕 fee tail（限嗣继承地产权），这种地产的继承只限于特定的继承人，通常是土地所有者的直系卑亲属（issue）。另外，这类限定可以只限定于一类人。一旦持有这种地产，除持有者本人享用终身外，还可以沿特定方向往下传承，直至不再有符合条件的继承人时，该地产终止。

〔3〕 （德）特定世袭财产。

〔4〕 （英）（教会法）圣职推荐权，本质上兼具世俗财产和宗教责任的特征。作为世俗财产，它可以被继承、买卖，甚至出租或无偿让渡；作为一种责任，圣职推荐权人有义务保护特定的圣职的特权。持续的圣职推荐权是不动产，而一次性的圣职推荐权是动产。

difficulties that necessarily had to arise from the reception of Roman law in the Middle Ages. A vast literature rich in disputes and teeming with false conclusions and misunderstandings concerned itself for centuries with the question to whom, as persons having a *real* right, the advowson passes, since it was impossible to decide which kind of Continental *real* rights corresponds to the English *firma*. In a thorough historical and doctrinal inquiry, Wach has indeed presented an exhaustive discussion of the nature of the *firma*; but he has not solved the practical question, i. e. which Continental institution must be regarded as a *firma*, for the simple reason that it cannot be solved. There is nothing on the Continent that could be said to be a *firma*. The question cannot be answered; it would have to be decided.

At the time of the reception, irresoluble questions of this kind cried out to the Continental jurists from every line of the *corpus iuris*. Had they been men of scientific training, let us say of the Historical School of Savigny or of the modern sociological school, they surely would never have undertaken this task, which cannot be performed scientifically. They would have said to themselves at the outset: The kind of ownership that the sources speak of does not exist among us (in the Middle Ages, not even the name; much less the concept); the unfree person that we are dealing with is not

由于无法断定哪种欧陆物权与英国适格继承人制度相对应，充满争论并充斥着错误结论与误解的大量文献几个世纪都关注这个问题——圣职推荐权会传给谁（作为物权享有者）。在彻底的历史和学说探究中，瓦赫对适格继承人的性质予以详细的论述。但是他仍然没有解决这一实践性问题，即到底大陆法中的哪一制度应该被当作适格继承人制度。其实原因很简单——那本就是一个无法解决问题。欧陆没有哪一制度可以被称为适格继承人制度。这个问题无法回答；它必须被裁断。

在继受罗马法的这段时间中，存在于《国法大全》字里行间的这类无法解决的问题摆到了欧陆法学家的面前。如果他们都是接受过科学训练的人——让我们设想是萨维尼的历史法学派或者是现代社会法学派——他们确实无法承担起这项任务，因为那是用科学方法难以完成的。法学家们在开始时就自言自语：原始文献中提到的所有权在我们的生活中并不存在（在中世纪的时候连所有权的名称都没有，更不用说概念了）；我们所涉及的这种非自由人不是罗马法上的奴隶。就像现在不存在先取遗赠[1]或

[1] （拉）*legatum per praeceptionem*（先取遗赠），罗马法中遗赠的主要方式之一。类似于直接赠与，表现为向数名继承人中的一人转移对某一单项财物的所有权，使该物不参与遗产分割，也就是说，它是对某一遗产物的预先提取。先取遗赠的典型表现形式："你将先取"。普罗库勒学派认为对于非继承人也可以实行先取遗赠，而萨宾学派则认为它只是适用于数名继承人之间。

the Roman slave. Institutions like the *stipulatio*, the *cautio indiscreta*, the *mandatum*, or the *locatio conductio operis* or *operarum* do not exist today, just as there is no *legatum per praeceptionem or peculium profectitium*. Doubtless there are phenomena of legal

者父予特有产[1]一样,现在也不存在如要式口约[2]不可分割的保证、委托[3]和承揽租赁或雇佣租赁[4]这样的罗马法制

---

〔1〕 (拉)*peculium profectitium*(父予特有产),指由家父给予家子个人支配和经管的钱财。对于此种特有产,家子按照家父的要求进行管理,并且向家父汇报有关的经营情况;家父只有在该特有产的范围内对有关的债务承担责任。在优士丁尼法中,家父为该特有产的形式所有主,不再享有处分权。

〔2〕 (拉)*stipulation*(要式口约),罗马法中的口头契约之一,表现为作为要约人的一方向作为承诺人的另一方进行提问,后者就该提问所涉及的义务作出承诺或保证。要式口约的特点在于:第一,采用固定的套语,套语使用错误将导致缔约行为无效。第二,完全以口头的形式进行,有关当事人面对面地完成缔约行为。第三,一般不问缔约的具体原因,只注重形式上的合法。第四,有关的提问和回答必须是连续的(一次性完成)和相互对应的。随着书面契约形式的发展,要式口约后来也采用有关的文书加以证明,出现要式口约约据。

〔3〕 (拉)*mandatum*(委托)。罗马法中的合意契约之一,表现为受托人根据委托人的指示经营一项或数项事务,后者有义务承担因上述经营行为而发生的费用或损失。罗马法的委托是无偿的。一些罗马法学家认为:如果受托人向委托人收取报酬,他们之间的关系就变成了承揽租赁(*location conducio peris*)。受托人有义务根据受托人的指示或者事务的性质经管受托事务,汇报账目,返还为用完的钱物以及在办理事务期间收取的钱款;他可以通过其他人执行有关的受托事务。委托人不仅应当承担受托事务的费用和损失,而且还应承担受托人因执行委托事务而对外缔结的债务。根据受益人的不同,委托可以分为为己利益之委托(*mandatum mea gratia*)、为他人利益之委托(*mandatum aliena gratia*)、为彼利益之委托(*mandatum tua gratia*)和共同利益之委托(*mandatum mea et tua gratia*)。

〔4〕 (拉)*location conducio operis*(承揽租赁),*location conducio operarum*(雇佣租赁)。*location conducio operis*(承揽租赁),租赁契约的主要形式之一,表现为一方向另一方提供需要加工的原材料或者某一需要通过工作加以完成的项目,后一方则向前一方提供特定的加工或者工作成果,并且有权利为上述加工或成果的实现而从前一方那里获得相应的报酬。与雇佣租赁

life which present a certain similarity to the above-named Roman institutions, but the divergencies are so great at every point that it would be a highly unscientific procedure to deal with them according to identical principles. What prevented the juristic science of the Romanist jurists from bleeding to death was the fact that it never undertook the scientific task which Savigny in his day suggested to it. The jurists of the time of the reception had law cases in hand and they searched the *corpus iuris* for decisions that might fit them. And the decisions did fit whenever there was a certain amount of similarity between them and the cases. Scientific exactitude was not sought after. The function which their juristic activity subserved was not a scientific one but the eternal, practical one of all juristic science, to wit to make the law subserve the requirements of life.

This practical labor however was made considerably easier for all the generations of jurists since the Middle Ages by the fact that it had already been done, in part at least, by the glossators under most extraordinarily favorable conditions. For in the tenth and eleventh centuries, when the glossators began their work, the relations with Roman antiquity were extremely close, at least in the parts of Italy where the glossators lived and in southern France. Many Roman legal institutions, though distorted during the course of the centuries, may still have been in existence at the time, at least to an extent sufficient to establish the connection in a certain measure. A still more important

度。毫无疑问,呈现与上面所称的罗马法律制度的某些相似性的法律生活现象是存在的,但是它们在各方面差异又是如此巨大以至于按照同样的原则去处理它们将是极不科学的处置方法。使罗马法学派法学家的法学幸免于难的是,这一法学没有承担起萨维尼在世时所倡导的科学研究的任务。罗马法继受时期的法学家接到案件以后,就寻找《国法大全》中适合于案件的判决。当案件事实和《国法大全》中的判决有一定的相似之处时,就会适用这一判决。在这里,科学的严格性无人探求。法律活动所具备的功能不是科学性功能,而是所有法学永恒的实用功能,即,使法律服务于生活需要。

不过,对于中世纪之后的每一代法学家而言,此种实践活动变得更容易,因为注释法学家在非常有利条件下至少已部分地完成了它。在10世纪和11世纪,当注释法学家开始他们的工作时,至少是在注释法学家所生活的意大利部分地区和法国南部地区,他们与罗马古代人的关系极为接近。许多罗马的法律制度尽管在几个世纪的时间里被曲解了,但是在那时可能仍然存在,至少足以在一定范围内与古罗马法律制度建立联系。一个更重要

---

不同的事,在承揽租赁中,提供劳务的是承租人,而且这种劳务是特定的。此外,在雇佣租赁中承租人应当亲自提供劳作,而在承揽租赁中承租人则可以通过第三人提供劳作。*location conducio operarum*(雇佣租赁),租赁契约的主要形式之一,表现为一方向另一方提供自己的劳作,后一方则向前一方支付相应的报酬。罗马法的雇佣租赁不以某些自由职业者的智力劳动为对象;对于这些智力劳动的报酬只是到了帝国时期才通过非常审判给予法律保护。作为提供劳作的出租人只对自己的故意和过失行为承担责任;作为雇佣方的承租人应当按照契约取得的时间段向出租人支付报酬,即使该出租人在此期间由于不可归责于他的原因而没有提供劳作,雇佣租赁因约定的期限届满或者出租人死亡而消灭。

factor was the part played by the language alone. At that time, Latin still was a spoken language, and in its own way interpreted the Roman world to the person who used it, without however laying any claim to historical accuracy. The Roman *miles* surely was something quite different from the mediaeval knight; but since the knight was called a *miles*, the doctrine of the *peculium castrense* was applied without more ado to the knightly *filius familias*.

In spite of all this there were many difficulties that stood in the way of applying Roman law to the existing legal relations. And these difficulties were the cradle of the jurisprudence of conceptions. Everywhere, even in an indigenous legal system, there must be some sort of relation between the legal norm and the legal relations, but in by far the greatest number of cases actual observation of life is sufficient for this purpose. The great objection that one could make to the definition of a railroad given by the Supreme Court of the Empire is the fact that it is so altogether superfluous. Do we not know without this definition what a railroad is? At any rate we shall find that, after innumerable readings of the definition given by the Supreme Court, we have not added to our knowledge. A few borderline cases may indeed be doubtful, but what are they among the vast number of cases that are being decided quite clearly and unmistakably by actual observation for everyone that has ever seen a railroad—and who is there today that has not seen a railroad? And actual observation taught the Roman, with the same certainty, what *a delegatio* and a *mandatum in rem suam* was; and the Salic Franks what a *chrenechruda* was. But in the Middle Ages

的因素是单单语言本身在这一过程中所发挥了独特作用。在那时,拉丁语仍然是重要的会话语言。它以自己的方式向使用它的人解释着罗马世界,但从未自以为具有历史传承上的精确性。罗马的兵士肯定与中世纪的骑士相当不同,但是既然骑士也曾经被那么叫过,那么就可以干脆痛快地将军营特有产[1]的相关原则适用到骑士的家子身上。

尽管如此,将罗马法适用到现有法律关系中还是存在着许多困难。这些困难就是概念法学产生的根源所在。在每个地方,即使在本土法律制度中,法律规范和法律关系之间也必然存在某种联系。但到目前为止,在绝大多数的情形下,对生活的观察就足以解决这个问题。人们可以对帝国最高法院所作出的“铁路”定义提出众多异议,这说明该定义完全是多余的。难道没有这个定义我们就不知道什么是铁路了吗?无论如何我们会发现,在读过最高院给出的“铁路”定义无数遍之后,我们没有增加任何知识。在一些界限模糊的情形下,也许值得怀疑,但是,在绝大多数的情形下,对于见过铁路的所有人来说,通过他们的实际观察是可以作出准确无误的判断的。现在谁还没有见过铁路呢?实际观察以同样的确切度告诉罗马人什么是为自己利益的委托;告诉法兰克族的萨利人什么是 chrenechruda。但是在中世纪,很多时候,缺

---

〔1〕(拉)*peculium castrens*(军营特有产),一种由家子直接占有和经营的特有产,主要来自该家子在服役期间取得的钱财、战利品、战友的赠品。家子可以通过遗嘱处置此特有产。只有在家子未立遗嘱而死亡的情况下,它才成为家父的财产。

often enough there was no actual observation to aid the jurist in his attempts to gain an understanding of the Roman law, and this lack the jurisprudence of conceptions was designed to make up for.

For practical juristic science the important problem was how to apply Roman law. It does not loom very large in the work of the glossators, for with them the scientific interest outweighed the practical. They are occupied more with ascertaining the content of the *corpus iuris* than with the manner of its application. The *corpus iuris* was a new code to them, and their attitude toward it was very much like that of jurists toward any new code, even that of the present-day German jurists toward the German Civil Code. Their first concern was to find out what it contained. Accordingly the glossators were chiefly engaged in interpreting the *corpus iuris*, not in developing a practical juristic science. But they could not escape the questions of practical application altogether, for although they were not practical jurists, they wanted to become teachers of practical jurists. And therefore they found it necessary, in all cases in which actual observation or the language failed to give them information, true or false, to study the sources themselves for the purpose of getting a clear knowledge of what their precepts actually referred to. Accordingly we find that even the glossators engaged in investigations of concepts, for instance, of the concept *res publica*, in order to determine whether in legal contemplation, in addition to the Roman Empire, there was another community in the

乏帮助法学家试图理解罗马法的任何实际观察,概念法学正是为了弥补这一缺陷应运而生。

对于实用法学来说,重要的问题是如何适用罗马法。对于注释法学家来说,这一问题并不非常迫切,因为对于他们,科学的重要性胜过实际应用。他们更多地致力于探寻《国法大全》的内容而非其适用方式。《国法大全》对他们来说是一部新法典,并且他们看待《民法大全》的态度也正如法学家们看待任何新法典一样,甚至于有点像当今德国法学家看待《德国民法典》的态度。他们关注的首要问题是如何揭示《民法大全》的内涵。因此,注释法学家主要致力于诠释《国法大全》的内容而不是发展一种实用法学。不过,他们不能彻底地回避法律适用的问题,因为虽然他们不是实用法学家,但他们想成为实用法学家的老师。因此,在实际观察或语言都不能给他们信息(无论正确与否)的所有情形下,他们发现有必要亲自研究原始文献,以便对它们的规定实际所指获得清晰的了解。因此我们发现,甚至连注释法学家也会从事概念探究,例如,为了确定在法律思维中除了罗马帝国外是否还有其他具有国家性质的"共同体",他们会对公有物[1]的概念以及集合体、替代[2]、

---

〔1〕 (拉)*res publicae*(公有物),最初是指归罗马共同体所有的物品,后来也指供公众使用的非交易物,例如:河流、道路、桥梁、广场、戏院,等等。

〔2〕 (拉)*delegatio*(替代),债的更新形式之一,表现为单方面指定或者准可某人接替原债关系中的债权人或债务人的地位或者代替债务人或债权人实行清偿或接受清偿;在此情况下,债权人与债务人之间原有的债的关系因更新而消灭,并且被原债务人与新债权人之间的债的关系或者原债权人与新债务人之间的债关系所取代。罗马通过此种替代清偿实现债权或债务的转移。

nature of a state, of the concepts *universitas*, *delegatio*, *possessio civilis*, and *naturalis*.

This purely practical side of the work in turn involved great practical difficulties. The pure concepts of the sources of the Roman law, the universalizations of the facts of Roman legal life as such, which the Roman jurists had but rarely formulated in words, and even more rarely had formulated correctly (*omnis definitio periculosa*), would be just as unavailable to the jurists of the Middle Ages as the concepts of freehold or of *firma* of the English law would be to the Continental jurist. In order that the Roman concepts might be available, they had to be extended so as to include the phenomena not only of the Roman law but also those of the mediaeval law. For this purpose everything had to be eliminated from the concept that did not fit into the present, that is, everything that was given by the particular social and economic relation out of which the concept had arisen in Rome. The more empirical content is taken out of a concept, the more abstract it becomes; and so the Roman universalizations became abstractions in the Middle Ages. The mediaeval and modern abstractions are Roman universalizations which to a considerable extent have been emptied of their content.

It would be unfair to take this to mean that in their abstractions the jurists had given up all connection with economic and social life. A juristic concept without any relation to life, and therefore without empirical content, is simply unthinkable. But here the situation was the following. The practical purpose which the legal relation subserved in Rome did not exist in modern society. At the same time

市民法占有[1]和自然等概念进行研究。

这种工作纯粹实用性的一面反过来也必然遭逢到巨大的实际困难。罗马法原始文献里的纯粹概念以及诸如那些罗马法学家极少明确阐述、或几乎没有正确阐述(*omnis definitio periculosa*)过的那些罗马法律生活事实的一般化,对于中世纪的法学家来说,就像大陆法系的法学家难以接受英国法里的自由保有地产权和适格继承人制度的概念一样,是难以接受的。为了让罗马法的概念可用,法学家必须把这些概念扩展,使其不但包含罗马法的现象而且还包含中世纪的法律现象。为此,与现在不相符的所有东西都应该从该概念中清除出去,也就是说,由特定的社会和经济关系所给予的全部东西,都出自罗马概念。概念里经验的东西抽掉得越多,概念就会变得越抽象;所以罗马法的一般化在中世纪变成了抽象化的过程。中世纪和现代的抽象化是在很大的程度上被抽空了概念内容的罗马法一般化。

如果认为这意味着,在抽象化的过程中,罗马法家不考虑概念与经济和社会生活的任何联系,那是不公平的。一个法学概念和社会生活没有联系,并因而没有经验的内容,简直是不可想象的。但是,这里出现了如下的情况。罗马法律关系所促进的实践目的在现代社会不存在。同时,在现代社会也存在着一个不同的

〔1〕(拉)*possessio civilis*(市民法占有),指以正当原因为基础,真正受到诉权保护的占有。例如:时效取得占有,通过先占而获得的占有。实际上,这种占有已经变为受市民法保护的法定权利,因而可以将其理解为依据是民法所有权的占有。

there was a different practical purpose in modern society for which, at any rate, the Roman precepts could be utilized. The thing to do therefore was to receive only so much empirical content into the concept as was necessary in order not to interfere with the utilization of it in mediaeval society. The correality of the sources of Roman law, like every joint liability, has arisen out of relations of community between the co-obligors, especially out of family communities, partnership relations, and relations of suretyship. Undoubtedly the nature of these community relations has had a bearing upon the nature of the joint obligation. The correality of husband and wife, of brothers holding goods in joint ownership, was something different, even in Rome, from the correality of persons engaged in a joint adventure. The Roman jurists did not fail to take account of these differences; although this fact does not appear very clearly since with them it was always a freely chosen correality. The community relations however out of which joint obligation arose in the Middle Ages and in modern times were so totally different from the Roman relations that the Roman law of joint obligation would have been unavailable for the modern relations if in defining joint obligation the Roman community relations which constituted its basis had been taken into account, and the classes of joint obligation had been dealt with separately according to the differences in the character of these community relations. Therefore an abstract concept of joint obligation was formed. Its whole economic content is limited to the fact that the creditor can demand the whole performance from each joint debtor. The relation of the joint debtors to the creditor and to each other, which would vary according to the kind of community relation that subsisted between the joint debtors, is left out of account in this abstract joint obligation. And so Roman law remains applicable although it manifestly presupposes community relations of a kind quite different from those that were in existence in the Middle Ages. It was intended at the outset that this abstraction should be utilized only for the purposes of litigation. In actual life there are no abstract joint debtors. Each class of joint obligations has an economic basis of some sort, and according to the various kinds of economic bases there are different classes of joint obligations. The brothers who are holding their goods in common the joint adventurers, the

实践目的，不管怎样，为该目的，罗马的规定还是可以一用。因此，要做的就是必要时在那些旧规定中注入如此多的经验内容，从而使那些旧规定在中世纪社会的应用能够顺畅无碍。罗马法原始文献的“连带责任”，如同每一类共同责任一样，源于共同债务人之间的共同体关系，特别是家庭统一体、合伙关系和保证关系。无疑，这些共同体关系的性质对于共同债务的性质产生了影响。夫妻之间、共有财产的兄弟之间的“连带责任”，即使在罗马，也不同于从事联合经营者之间的连带责任。罗马法学家不可能没有考虑到这种差别；虽然，由于对于他们来说它总是一个可自由选择的“连带责任”，所以这种事实看上去并不清晰。然而，这些产生自中世纪和现代的连带债务的共同关系完全不同于罗马的那些关系，以至于如果在对连带债务进行定义时，考虑到构成其基础的罗马的共同体关系并依据这些关系性质上的差异分别处置它们，就会使罗马的连带债务法无法适用于现代的这些关系。因此，连带债务的抽象概念就形成了。它的整个经济内容仅限于：债权人能够要求每一个连带债务人完全履行。每个连带债务人分别与债权人的关系以及连带债务人彼此之间的内部关系——它们会依据存在于连带债务人之间的共同体关系的种类而有所变化——在这种抽象的连带债务中未予考虑。所以，虽然罗马法预设的共同体关系与中世纪存在的共同体关系完全不同，但罗马法仍是可适用的。从一开始时，这种抽象的应用就只是为诉讼的目的。在现实中，没有抽象的连带债务人。每一种类型的连带债务都有一定种类的经济基础，依据各种不同的经济基础，就会产生不同种类的连带债务。共有财产的兄弟、联合经营人、以主债务人面目出

sureties who assume this relation as principal debtors, become abstract joint debtors, and so it became possible to utilize the rules which had arisen in Rome for the regulation of these relations indiscriminately for the modern abstract joint debtor whether he be a joint debtor because of a matrimonial community of goods, a joint making of a bill of exchange, suretyship, mercantile association, joint adventure, or civil law partnership. The well known difficulties which have sicklied o' er the Romanist doctrine of correality and solidarity have their origin in the concept of abstract joint obligation.

The adaptation of Roman law to the needs of a society that was altogether foreign to it was facilitated by the form which the basic concept of every legal system, the concept of ownership, had received as early as the days of the Republic. It certainly is not true that ownership in Roman law was an abstract ownership. At Roman law, ownership was just as truly an economic matter as ownership necessarily must be anywhere else. But this Roman economic ownership of the Italic *fundus*, of which alone the jurists are speaking, was of such a nature, because of the Italic system of ownership of land, that at the time of the reception it inevitably led to an abstract concept of ownership.

Had the Roman jurists been dealing with land in its original village community, with all its relations to neighbors and the relations of subjection to the lord of the manor, which inevitably result from situations of this kind, it would scarcely have been possible to adapt such a law of real property to the needs of mediaeval society; the reception of Roman law would have been as impracticable perhaps as the reception of the English law of real property would be on the Continent today. But since the Romans, as is well known, had abolished their original village community at a time prior to that of the historical tradition, Roman law knows nothing of the village, but knows only the individual farm (*Hof*). Confronted with the task of creating a new land law for the *fundus*, which had been severed from all its former

现[1]的保证人,都变成了抽象的连带债务人,所以,就有可能利用罗马的旧规则来一视同仁地调整现代的这些抽象的连带债务人,而不管这些连带债务人的存在是因为婚姻共同财产、汇票共同出票、保证关系、商事合伙、联合经营还是民事合伙。给罗马法研究者的连带责任学说带来巨大困扰的、众所周知的难题源自抽象连带债务的概念。

改变罗马法使其适应完全相异的社会的需要,这一过程受到了每一个法律制度的基本观念形式的推动。所有权的观念早在共和国时期就已被接受。可以肯定,以下看法是错误的:罗马法的所有权是一个抽象的所有权。在罗马法中,所有权就像在其他任何地方必然存在的所有权一样仅仅是一个经济性的事物。但是,罗马法学家所提起的意大利土地的罗马经济性所有权,由于意大利的土地所有权制度,因而具有那样的一种性质,以至于在罗马法继受时,它不可避免地演变成了一种抽象的所有权观念。

倘若罗马法学家正在处理原始村落共同体内的土地,由于此种情形必然导致的相邻关系以及与庄园主之间的服从关系,那就几乎不可能使这样一种不动产法律适应中世纪社会的需要;今天在欧陆对罗马法的继受就可能会像对英国不动产法的继受一样不切实际。但是,众所周知,因为罗马人在村落共同体的历史传统形成之前就已经废除了村落共同体,所以罗马法对村落一无所知,而仅仅知道个人农场(*Hof*)。面对要为已经切断与先前所有关系的土地创设一种新的土地法律的任务,罗马法学家

〔1〕 即放弃了先诉抗辩权的连带保证人。

relations, the Roman jurists created it in the likeness of the ownership of movables. They simply dealt with the owner of land according to the same rules according to which they dealt with the owner of a movable thing. That is to say: The *fundus* is a *res mancipi* like the slave, like the head of cattle. Were it not for the fact that a few remnants of the older order had been retained, such as the servitudes, especially the *servitutes praediorum rusticorum*, the *actio damni infecti*, the *operis novi nuntiatio*, the *actio aquae pluviae arcendae*, there would be practically no peculiarities in the classical Roman law, at least as to the *ager privatus*. Indeed it is very doubtful whether this was the

就像创设动产所有权一样创设了土地所有权。他们仅仅依据他们对待动产所有人的同样规则来对待土地所有人。也就是说,土地就像奴隶和牛一样是要式物[1]。倘若不是因为以下这个事实:更古老秩序的一些残余仍然存在,如役权[2]、尤其是城市地役权[3]、损害赔偿之讼[4]、新施工告令[5]、排放雨水之诉[6],则古典时期的罗马法实际上不具有任何特色,至少对于私有土地来说是这样。当然,这是不是罗马的全部的土地法,再有,除了这

---

〔1〕 (拉)*res mancipi*(要式物),这类物对于早期的罗马社会和经济曾经具有至关紧要的意义,因而对它们的转让必须通过要式买卖或者拟诉弃权方式进行,例如:土地、房屋、奴隶、用于运输的牲畜、乡村地役权等等。

〔2〕 (拉)*servitudes*(役权),指对归他人所属的物享有的有限权利,可分为地役权(*sevitutes praediorum*)和人役权(*servitutes personum*)。

〔3〕 (拉)*servitutes praediorum rusticorum*(城市地役权),地役权的类型之一,以维护需役地所有人或其建筑物所有人的一般生活需求为特点,例如:伸出役权、加高役权。

〔4〕 (拉)*actio damni infecti*(损害赔偿之讼),要求损害赔偿的一系列诉讼的总称,包括因非法或者过失行为所致损害引起的各种诉讼。它相当于"action for damage"。

〔5〕 (拉)*operis novi nuntiatio*(新施工告令),当所有人在自己的土地上开始的建设或拆除作业有可能改变该地的原貌时,相邻土地的所有人如认为此作业会对自己造成潜在的损害,可以发出此告令,要求作业人提供潜在损害保证。这种保证采用口头形式在作业现场向有关的责任人发出。被告者必须中止施工或者提供潜在损害保证;告令人也应当立即为证明自己的权利受到妨害而提起诉讼,否则,裁判官可以根据被告者的申请决定撤销新施工告令。当公共利益可能遭受正在开始的施工的侵害时,人们也可以要求发布新施工告令。

〔6〕 (拉)*action aquae pluviae arcendae*(排放雨水之诉),在相邻关系中,土地的所有人因邻居改变雨水的自然流道而提起的诉讼。

whole of Roman land law, whether there was not, in addition to this, much local and economic law, which varied according to the use to which the land was being put and of which we no longer have any knowledge; at least some law regulating the right to build and some mining law can be found even in the sources of the classical period. But all of this seems to have been outside of the sphere of interest of the jurists. We must point out most emphatically however that even this juristic law of ownership and possession was the law of a certain economic order of possession, thc economic order of the possession of the *ager privatus* in Italy, and that it did not extend beyond this order. It applied neither to the *ager publicus* in Italy nor to the *solum provinciale*. But of all of these divergent orders of possession only a few scanty provisions about the *ager vectigalis* and the *emphyteusis* found their way into the sources. In the Middle Ages only the church was able to utilize these.

If we treat land like a movable thing, the relation of the ownership of land to society is eliminated from the concept of ownership, and there remains only one question that has any bearing on the right of ownership and the right of possession connected therewith, to wit the question of the actions claiming ownership or pos-

些，是否就没有依据土地用途的不同而内容有所不同的，并且我们尚不了解的许多地方性的、经济性法律，这些问题都是很有疑问的；至少有些调整建筑权和采矿权的法律甚至在古典时期的原始文献中也能找到。但是，这一切似乎超出了法学家感兴趣的范围。不过，我们必须着重指出：甚至这种有关所有权和占有的法学，也是有关占有——意大利的私有土地的占有——的特定经济秩序的法律，它没有超出这种秩序。在意大利它既不能适用于公有土地也不能适用于外省土地[1]。但是在这些形态各异的占有秩序中，只有关于赋税田[2]和永佃权少数几个单薄的条款在原始文献中有所规定。在中世纪只有教会能够利用这些条款。

如果我们把土地视为动产，那么土地所有权与社会之间的关系将会从所有权概念中消失。这样，就剩下唯一能对所有权和占有权产生影响的问题，即，主张所有权与占有之诉讼的问题。在

---

〔1〕（拉）*solum provinciale*（外省土地），指罗马帝国在所征服的国家设置的行省的土地。这种土地的最终的所有权属于国家或皇帝，占有土地的人只享有占有权而无权以法律（市民法）规定的方式转移土地的所有权。与之对应的是意大利的土地（lolum italiacum），到优士丁尼时取消了此二者之间的区别。

〔2〕（拉）*ager vectigalis*（赋税田），指既未被加以分配或出卖，也未由私人占据的，而是被以一百年期限或永久出租的公田，这些田地在法律上归自治市或僧侣团体所有，但承租者只要正常纳税，即可平安享用土地，并且可以获得关于占有令状的保护，也可提起一种对物之诉——赋税田之诉。赋税田的拉丁名称来自于承租者交纳的税赋的名称“*vectigal*”。如果承租者不交纳上述税赋，其享有权将可能被撤销。这种对赋税田的长期享用权可以说是永佃权的前身。

session. The Roman jurists who, in the case of land, can disregard its economic relations and the economic constitution of Italy are concerned chiefly with the actions claiming ownership or possession. Practically everything therefore that the Roman jurists have to say about ownership of land clusters around the various forms of the actions claiming ownership or possession. The acquisition and the loss of ownership and of possession, considered chiefly as the presuppositions for the actions, the parties to an action for the protection of ownership and to the interdicts, the problem of proof: this is practically all that we can learn from the Roman jurists.

The law of ownership and of possession of the Roman jurists then was a legal order based on the Italic system of landholding, and the fact that it contained chiefly regulations concerning actions claiming ownership or possession must be attributed to the fact that because of the peculiar nature of the Italic system of landholding, it was only these actions that required regulation. But even in the code of Justinian it had taken on an altogether different significance. And this was due not only to the fact that the Italic system of landholding meanwhile had undergone a complete change but also to the fact that the Roman land law meanwhile had become the law of the Empire, and was to be the law of the provinces also, the system of landholding in which was altogether different from the Italic system. This new land law was stated, albeit in a very incomplete and imperfect form, in the Imperial constitutions, which are found in the Code and in the Novels. Perhaps for the greater part there were no regulations at all, and the civil service as well as the administration of justice had to make shift as well as it could. At the same time the law of property and of possession of the classical jurists was received into the Institutes and into the Digest, and was thereby engrafted upon the new system of landholding. In this connection however it no longer was the law for a certain system of landholding but a law which contained a few precepts, chiefly concerning actions claiming ownership or possession by way of supplement to a regulation of the system of landholding which was laid down in the Code and in the Novels. In this form it was admirably fitted for

土地的情形下,能忽略其经济关系和意大利经济体制的罗马法学家,主要关注主张所有权和占有的诉讼。因此,实际上,罗马法学家对于土地所有权要说的所有东西都集中围绕着主张所有权或占有之讼诉的各种形式。被认为主要是这些诉讼先决条件的所有权和占有的取得与丧失、保护所有权之诉讼和申请禁令之诉讼的当事人以及证明问题:这就是实际上我们可以从罗马法学家那里学习到的一切。

因而,罗马法学家的所有权与占有方面的法律就是以意大利的土地所有制度为基础的法律秩序。这种法律中主要包含了有关主张所有权或占有之诉的规定,这主要是因为如下事实:由于意大利土地所有制度的独特性质,因而需要规定的只有这些诉讼行为。但是即使在东罗马帝国皇帝尤士丁尼的法典里,它也呈现出了一种完全不同的重要性。这不仅是因为意大利的土地制度在其间经历了一种彻底的变化,而且也是因为其间罗马的土地法律变成了帝国的法律,也变成了在土地所有制度方面完全不同于意大利的各行省的法律。这种土地法在收于《法典》和《新律》的皇帝谕令中有所表述,尽管采用的是一种不完整和不完善的表述。也许对于更大的一部分土地,根本就没有什么规章制度,文职部门和司法也必须尽可能地转变。与此同时,古典法学家的所有权和占有的法律被吸收到《法学阶梯》和《学说汇纂》中,从而建立起新的土地所有制度。不过,在这种背景下,它不再是关于特定土地所有制的法律,而是一个为补充《法典》和《新律》原有相关规定而包含一些主要涉及主张所有权或占有之诉规定的法律。在这种形式下,它是最适于继受的。继受国的法学家当然没

the reception. The jurists of the countries which received it of course did not, and self-evidently could not, entertain the idea of receiving the Roman system of landholding when they received the Roman law. Neither the ancient Italic system of landholding, which the classical jurists presupposed, nor the later system of the Imperial *constitutiones* became valid law in the Middle Ages, which had developed a possessory order based on the feudal system. They conceived of the Roman law of property and possession as a legal order which, disregarding all actual systems of landholding, regulated merely actions claiming ownership or possession. As a law which regulated merely actions claiming ownership or possession it was not incompatible with any system of landholding, not even with the mediaeval system. The abstract Roman concept of ownership is therefore, properly speaking, not an achievement of the Roman law but of the reception. It is a law of ownership, whose whole economic content is the action claiming ownership, which does not regulate the economic possessory order but presupposes it.

Accordingly the creation of abstract concepts was merely an altogether indispensable juristic device for the adaptation of the Roman norms to the requirements of a different society. The result on the whole was the same in every case as in the case of joint obligation and ownership. The indigenous social order remained in existence as one freely chosen, based on customary law, on particular law; to it, usually in a quite arbitrary manner and only for the purposes of procedure, the Roman norms were added so far as it was possible to comprehend them in a legal concept which had been emptied of its peculiarly Roman content. But this process was permissible only to the extent to which the concepts which had been created in this manner could be applied to mediaeval and modern situations. A limitation therefore was imposed upon the jurisprudence of conceptions at the point at which it became impossible, even though the greatest possible measure of abstraction be employed, to subsume legal relations which belonged exclusively to mediaeval or modern law under the Roman legal concepts. The jurists of the early days of the reception both in Italy and in Germany avoid these difficulties with a marvelous lack of embarrassment. The glossators pay very little attention to this matter. It is their business to interpret the Roman

有——不言而喻也不可能——在继受罗马法时抱有继受罗马土地所有制的想法。不管是古典法学家所预设的古老的意大利土地所有制,还是后来的皇帝谕令中的土地所有制,都没有在中世纪成为有效的制度。中世纪发展出了一种以封建制度为基础的占有秩序。他们认为,罗马的所有权和占有法是一种不考虑所有的实际的土地所有制,而只是规范主张所有权和占有之诉的法律秩序。作为一种只是规范主张所有和占有之诉的法律,罗马法是与任何土地所有制不相容的,更不用说与中世纪的土地所有制相容。因此,恰当地说,抽象的罗马法所有权观念不是罗马法的成就而是罗马法继受的结果。这是一种所有权的法律,它的整个经济内容就是主张所有权之诉,这种法律并没有规制经济性的占有秩序,而是以其为前提条件。

因此,抽象法律概念的创制不过是使罗马法规范适应一个不同社会之需要的,完全不可或缺的法律方法。大体上,这种结果在每一种情形下与连带债务和所有权的情形下一样。基于习惯法和特别法的固有的社会秩序依然存在,如同自由选择的那样;通常,只要能以一个被抽去了罗马社会独特内容的法律概念涵括这些固有社会秩序,罗马规范就会以一种相当恣意的方式,并且只是为了诉讼程序的目的,而被加诸于这些秩序之上。只有这样创造出来的法律概念能在中世纪和现代情形中应用时,这种过程才是允许的。因此,要将完全属于中世纪法或现代法的法律关系包摄于罗马法律概念之下,哪怕运用最大可能的抽象化方法,也是不可能的;在这一点上,概念法学受到了限制。在德国和意大利,罗马法继受早期的法学家避免这些困难的过程有着令人惊奇的顺畅。注释法学者几乎没有注意到这一点。他们的工作就是

law, not to apply it. To which of the relations of their day that are foreign to the Romans the Roman law should not be applied is discussed by them, on principle, only once as far as I know, i. e. in the gloss to 1.32. D. leg. 1, 3: *de quibus scriptis legibus non utimur*: *in feudis*. Nowhere in the gloss is there a hint as to how, for example, the mediaeval community relations, bearer papers, which are met with in Italy as early as the eleventh century, and the *commenda*, which can be traced into antiquity, are to be dealt with juristically, although the glossators must have been familiar with all of these things. From their whole attitude one can infer that they believed Roman law to be applicable only to those relations which were regulated therein. Whatsoever had been ordained by other statutes, ordinances, customs, was outside of the sphere of Roman law; they therefore without more ado recognized the ordinances of the Italian cities as valid side by side with the Roman law. Perhaps the gloss to 1.7 C de agr. 11, 47 is a typical case; there decisions based on the passage from the Code appear side by side with decisions based on *communis consuetudo*. There is a close connection between this attitude of the gloss and the fact that it reflects the state of affairs in the early years of the reception of the Roman law. Roman law is being applied only where its application is, in a sense, a matter of course. It is a significant fact that Zasius, who in point of time occupies the same relative position to the reception in Germany as the later glossators to the reception in Italy, preserved the independence of the institutions based on German law with the same lack of embarrassment.

But when in the days of the postglossators as well as in Germany in the seventeenth century, the Romanist jurists obtained control over the practical application of law as well, the principle came into vogue that every case must be adjudged according to Roman law unless a different norm has been established for its decision. Thereafter the jurisprudence

解释罗马法,而不是应用它。据我所知,依据原则,他们只就——因关系性质不同,因而他们所在时代的哪些关系不应当适用罗马法——这个问题讨论过一次,即在对"1.32. D. leg. 1,3:成文的法律没有什么帮助,最终要靠盟友关系"的注释中有过一次讨论。尽管注释法学家必定对所有的这些事情都很熟悉,但是对于如何在法学上处理这些事情,例如如何处理中世纪团体关系、早在11世纪的意大利就已出现的无记名票据以及可以追溯到古代的康孟达组织,在注释中没有任何提示,从他们的总体态度中,我们可以推出:他们认为罗马法只适用于那些在那里已经受到规范的关系。由其他制定法、法令、习惯作出的任何规定,都已经超出了罗马法的范围。因此他们干脆痛快地承认,意大利城邦的法令与罗马法都是同样有效的法律。或许,对1.7 C de agr. 11,47的注释就是一个典型情形;在那里,依据法典作出的判决和依据共同的习惯法作出的判决同时出现。该注释的这种态度和它反映罗马法继受的早期情势这一事实之间有一种密切联系。罗马法只在那些应用乃理所当然的地方才被适用。一个重要的事实就是:正如后注释法学家在意大利的罗马法继受中占据的位置一样,扎休斯在同一时间也占据了德国罗马法继受的相应位置。扎休斯在同样遇到极少阻碍的情况下保持了基于德国法之制度的独立性。

但是,到了后注释法学派时期和17世纪的德国,罗马法研究学者获得了对法律实际应用的控制,而且,每个案件除非一个不同的裁判规范已经确立,否则所有案件都要依据罗马法判决的原则就变为了时尚。自那以后,概念法学不再有用;因为罗马法的概念,至少流传下来的各种原始文献中的概

of conceptions could no longer avail; for the Roman concepts, at least the concepts of the sources that have been transmitted to us, were not adequate to the requirements of the much richer and much more complex modern life. Apart from this, it was inevitable that most unsatisfactory results should be brought about when the institutions of two such *toto caelo* dissimilar societies as the Roman on one hand and the mediaeval and modern on the other were to be jumbled together and to be judged by the same norms for decision, regardless of the gulf that was fixed between them in point of time as well as of economic and of social development. There were several ways of escaping from these difficulties. One could distort the Roman concept in such a manner as to adapt it to the foreign institutions; one could combine the heterogeneous institutions of Roman law in such a manner that the norms for decision that resulted from this combination would meet the requirements of the case in hand; one could falsify the Roman norms for decision so thoroughly that they yielded the desired result. In fact, all of these methods were employed at different times according to the requirements of the individual case. We have now reached the jurisprudence of constructions.

The exigencies of the system of actions caused the Romans themselves to resort to a jurisprudence of constructions whenever it became necessary to meet new requirements of life with such legal means as were at hand. It is true, the praetor and the jurist could find new legal propositions for new legal institutions; but this power doubtless was hedged in by traditional limitations, of which we have no detailed knowledge. On the other hand, proceeding by means of constructions offered the advantage that one could, to a certain degree, work with the law that had already been established, and could thus avoid the many dangers involved in a new finding of law. This method does not include the use of fictions; for only the legislator and the praetor could avail themselves of the latter as finders of law, and not, as in England, the jurists. True juristic constructions are the following: the construction of suretyship as *mandatum pecuniae credendae*, of assign-

念,已经不能满足更丰富、更复杂的现代生活的需要。除此之外,当两种那样有天壤之别的不同的社会制度——即罗马社会制度与中世纪和现代社会制度——搅和在一起,不考虑它们在时间上、经济上和社会发展中形成的巨大鸿沟,坚持适用同样的裁判规范时,出现令人最不满意的结果就是不可避免的了。有几种方法可以避免这些难题。人们可以极力扭曲罗马法概念,以便使罗马法适应外国制度;人们可以将完全不同的罗马法制度强行结合起来,使源于这种结合的裁判规范可以适用于手头的案例;人们可以彻底伪造罗马法从而获得他渴望的结果。实际上,在不同时期根据不同案件的需要,这些方法都曾被采用过。我们现在已经达到了一种"建构法学"的层次。

诉讼制度的迫切需要,促使罗马人在有必要使手头的法律工具适应生活的新需要的任何时候,自身诉诸建构法学。诚然,裁判官和法学家能够为新的法律制度寻找到新的法律命题。但是,无疑这个权力要受到我们尚未详细了解之传统的限制。另一方面,通过解释方式行事有这样的好处:人们可以在某种程度上与已经创建起来的法律合作,从而避免在发现新法律的过程中牵扯到的许多危险。这种方法并不包括采用拟制的方式,因为只有立法者和裁判官作为法律的发现者才能利用这种方式,法学家(如在英国一样)不可以这样做。真正的法学解释是这样的:将保证解释为委托借贷;[1]

---

〔1〕 (拉)*mandatum pecuniae credendae*(放债委托,委托借贷),也被称为特定委托,表现为委托他人向第三人借贷钱款或者一定数量的可替代物。作为一种为彼利益之委托,它的效力得到了罗马法的承认。在第三人不能够向受托人履行还款义务的情况下委托人将承担担保责任,因此,此种委托实质上是一种人的担保。

ment as a *mandatum in rem suam*, of the payment of a debt by the surety as a purchase of the obligation, of the dormant commercial partnership as a *depositum irregulare*. These Roman constructions however did not yield binding rules of law; to the Romans they were merely technical remedies. The Roman jurists did not hesitate to reject such inferences from their constructions as did not suit their purposes; and so the surety who had paid was not entitled, like the purchaser of an obligation, to demand a warranty from the creditor, or to demand more from the debtor than he had paid to the creditor.

The glossators likewise resort to construction and they by no means do this in a very modest measure. The proposition of Roman law, *alteri stipulari nemo potest*, they limit by holding that though a third party does not, indeed, get the right to bring the *actio directa*, he may be permitted to sue directly by means of the *actio utilis* without obtaining an assignment, which the sources

将转让解释为为自己利益的委托;将保证人的债务清偿解释为一种债务购买;将隐名的商业合伙解释为非常寄托[1],然而这些罗马人的解释并没有产生拘束性的法律规则;对于罗马人来说这些仅仅是技术上的补救。当这些解释不符合罗马法学家的目的时,罗马法学家就会毫不犹豫地拒绝从解释中得出的推论。因此,清偿债务的保证人与真正的债务购买人不同,他无权要求债权人提供保证,或者从债务人那里取得比他支付给债权人更多的东西。

同样,注释法学家也会诉诸法律解释,并且,他们决不会在一种很有节制的程度上来做这件事。对罗马法的法律命题"任何人不得为他人缔约",他们也作了限制,他们所采取的方式是认定:虽然第三人的确无权提起直接诉讼[2],但他可以借助扩用诉讼[3]的方式,

---

〔1〕(拉)*depositum irregulare*(非常寄托),以可替代物作为对象,例如寄存钱款,因此,与普通寄托不同,非常寄托中的受托人只负有归还同等数量的同质物的义务,这意味着受托人可以使用被寄存的可替代物,从而使得这种寄托具有消费借贷的作用。对于非常寄托,人们可以附加利息简约,要求受寄托人为物的使用支付一定的利息。

〔2〕(拉)*actio directa*(直接诉讼),即指市民法诉讼,它的适用范围和对象是由法律专门规定的。法学家们一般使用"直接诉讼"一词表示市民法诉讼与裁判官法诉讼的区别,后者是裁判官根据司法实践的发展对直接诉讼的扩展适用。

〔3〕(拉)*actio ulilis*(扩用诉讼),将适用于特定情况或关系的法定诉讼形式扩展应用于某些相似的情况或关系的诉讼;这种相似的情况或关系反映着受法定诉权保护的情况或关系的发展和衍生,由于法律不及为其规定专门的司法救济手段,只好由执法官在司法实践中以变通的做法参照现有的法定诉讼模式提供司法保护。扩用的方式可以表现如下:假设法定诉讼模式要求的身份或条件存在,即实行拟制诉讼;更换诉讼主体,以法定诉讼所要求的主体身份起诉,以另一种身份承受判决结果,比如鲁第里诉讼;或者模仿现有的诉讼创造一种相似的诉讼,比如仿效诉讼。

presuppose. They construe the *constitutum possessorium* as abstractly as possible in order to weaken the requirement of delivery in a case of transfer of ownership. They distort the Roman *dominium*, perhaps unconsciously, by making a distinction between *dominium directum* and *dominium utile*, and thereby obtain appropriate norms for decision applicable to the mediaeval rights to take fruits and profits (*Nutzungsrechte*). In order to give to corporations the power to adopt resolutions of the whole body, they misinterpret the Roman proposition1, §2, D. 42, 2 *municipes per se nihil possidere possunt, quia universi consentire non possunt*, by adding an arbitrary gloss: Gloss V° *non possunt: subaudi hic facile vel commode.* They distort the concept, consciously I am sure, of the *servus publicus* by calling the notary of

在未获得原始文献所规定的先决条件(即转让)时亦可直接起诉。他们将占有转移协议[1]解释得尽可能抽象,以便弱化转移所有权情形中的交付要件。他们通过对直接所有权和扩用所有权的区分,从而获得可适用于中世纪的孳息和利润取得情形下的恰当的裁判规范,这样做时,他们(或许无意之中)曲解了罗马人的所有权概念。为了使自治城镇[2]有权采纳整个团体的决议,他们通过增加一个专断的注释——Gloss V°*non possunt*: *subaudi hic facile vel commode*,[3]错误地解释了罗马法的法律命题 1, §2, D. 42,2 *muni-cipes per se nihil possidere possunt, quia universi consentire nonpossunt*。[4] 我确信,为了使文书记述人[5]能够像代理人一样能够代表他的指示人[6]订立契约,他们把当时的公证人——文书记述人称作公奴

---

[1] (拉)*constitutum possessorium*(占有转移协议),拟制让渡的形式之一,表现为物的所有人通过改变对有关的权利的心理态度实现对该物的所有权转让,例如:某甲自己的房子卖给了某乙,但希望以承租人的名义继续使用该房子,它可以与某乙达成占有转移协议,改变自己权利的性质,从作为所有人的占有变为作为承租人的使用。

[2] 原先指的是享有地方自治权和某些罗马公民权的意大利城镇,后来地域范围扩大至任何地方。

[3] (拉)不可能,这里的是言外之意是不容易或不方便的意思。

[4] (拉)自治市本身不能占有,因为所有的市民不可能都同意。

[5] (拉)*tabellio*(文书记述人),在后古典法时期出现的、根据当事人的要求起草私人文书的人,他也发挥着文书证明人的作用。

[6] (法)*mandants*(指示人),等于 *mandan*(拉),即(寄托契约的)的寄托人、授权人、指示人。

their day, the *tabellio*, a *servus publicus* in order that he might be able to enter into contracts in behalf of his mandants as their representative. *Quia publice servit*, *non quia servus est*, says Accursius.

Bartolus and his pupils however gave an incomparably greater impetus to juristic construction. They gave direction to the Continental common law technique for many centuries. The most famous of these constructions are the following: (1) The whole theory of the territorial validity of statutes, almost without any basis in the *corpus iuris*, the only point of contact, and a purely external one at that, *being l.* 1. C. *de summa Trin.* 1, 1. (2). The *aequitas Bartolina*, the obligation, established by Bartolus, of the *ecclesia* as owner of a parcel of ground held under a perpetual lease (*emphyteusis*), to let the land, after the direct line of descent of the *emphyteuta* has become extinct, to the collateral relatives of the latter by heritable usufructury lease. This is based on 1. 1, § 43 D. *de aqua quot et aest* 43, 20. All that Ulpian says in this passage is that the purchaser of a parcel of ground has a legal right to have the right to draw water from a public aqueduct restored to him if he can show that the right had been granted to the land and not only to the person of his predecessor—a case that is in no wise connected with the grant of an *emphyteusis* to the collateral relatives of the *emphyteuta*. (3) The doctrine that a servitude can be established by the mere appointment of the *pater*

隶[1]，从而有意地曲解了公奴隶这一概念。阿库修斯说，“那些为公共服务的人不是奴隶。”

然而，巴托鲁斯[2]和他的学生给予法学解释以无与伦比的巨大动力。在几个世纪里他们引导了欧陆共同法的法律技术。最著名的这些解释如下：(1)制定法的整个地域效力理论，几乎没有《国法大全》的任何基础，唯一的并且纯粹表面上的联结点在于。(2)巴托里纳衡平规则，即巴托鲁斯创设的教会义务，其内容是：设有永佃权之一宗土地的所有人，有义务在永佃权人的直系血统的后人断绝后，根据可继承的附用益权租约把土地租给永佃权人的旁系亲属。这是以1. 1，§43 D. de aqua quot et aest 43，20 的规定为基础的。乌尔比安在这一节里说：一块土地的购买者如果能够证明：从归还给他的公共沟渠中取水的权利不仅授予给他的前手所有人，而且也授予给这块土地，那么他就享有一个法定的取水权。显然，原始文献中的这种情形与“把永佃权授予给永佃权人的旁系亲属”之间压根没有任何联系。(3)地役权可由家父单纯的指定而设定的学说，该学说也源于巴托鲁斯，巴托鲁斯

---

〔1〕（拉）*servus publicus*（公奴隶），指在国家开办的厂矿工作的、丧失自由人身份的人。实际上，此种奴隶享有一定的程度的权能，例如，通过遗嘱处置其特有产的一半。

〔2〕巴托鲁斯（1313～1357），评论法学派（亦称后注释法学派）的代表人物。

*familias*, which also owes its origin to Bartolus, who based it on a very unsatisfactory interpretation of the sources. (4) The denial, by Cinnus and Baldus on the basis of C 4, 28, 5, of the *exceptio* of the *senatusconsultum Macedonianum* against the *filius familias* in mercantile matters. (5) The construction, by Baldus, of the bill of exchange as a purchase in order to circumvent the law prohibiting usury. (6) The construction, by later commentators, of the power of a general partner of an unlimited mercantile partnership to enter into a contract with a third person in behalf of the partnership as a mutual *praepositio institoria*; of the assets of the unlimited mercantile partnership as a *corpus mysticum expluribus nominibus conflatum*; of insurance against risk as *emptio venditio periculi*.

将该学说建立在对原始文献的一种非常令人不满的解释之上。(4)辛努斯和巴尔杜斯[1]基于C 4, 28, 5马切多尼安元老院决议[2]中的抗辩[3]而就家子从事商业事务这一问题所给出的否定意见。(5)为了规避禁止高利贷的法律,由巴尔杜斯所作的把汇票看作是一种买卖的解释。(6)由后期的评注法学者所作的关于无限商业合伙的普通合伙人代表合伙与第三人缔结契约的权利是一种相互设置经管人[4]的解释;无限商业合伙的财产是一种一个显名合伙人加多个隐名合伙人组成的团体的解释;风险保险是一种风险买卖的解释。

---

〔1〕 巴尔杜斯(1327~1406),意大利法学家,巴托鲁斯的学生,著名的注释法学家。

〔2〕 (拉)*senatuconsultum Macedonianum*(罗马法马其顿决议),又称"*Macedonian decree*"。是罗马元老院针对高利贷者马其顿通过的法律。主要内容包括为保护未成年人及其家庭免受高利贷的盘剥,规定对高利贷给未成年人的钱款,不能提起偿还之诉。

〔3〕 (拉)*exceptio*(抗辩)。法律尤其是裁判官法赋予被告的、据以对抗原告诉权的权利。最初它曾是介于原告诉讼请求和判决程式之间的一项诉讼程式,是被告有可能证明存在某种情形,足以让原告的请求丧失合法性或有效性;一旦被告在抗辩中提出的某种情形被得到证实,原告的主张将被驳回。因此,抗辩是被告的辩护手段;在诉讼中这种手段可以多次使用,被告针对原告的答辩可以提出再抗辩,并且以此类推。抗辩的类型主要是由裁判官通过自己的告示引进的,在个别情况下是由法律引进的。抗辩可以区分为无限期抗辩和有限期抗辩。

〔4〕 (拉)*praepositio institoria*(设置经管人),一种单方的法律行为,表现为某人授权他人经营自己的商贸事务,该授权人对经营人在履行义务期间的负债承担责任,对之可以提起经管人之诉。最初,这种设置经管人的行为不被视为委托,在优士丁尼法中被纳入委托的范畴,并且可对之适用无因管理的规则。

Outwardly the jurisprudence of conceptions and the jurisprudence of constructions manifestly are the very antithesis of the method of the Roman jurists. The latter sought to investigate the various legal relations, as they occurred in daily life, by a searching study of life. They universalized the results of these investigations, and thereby either found, through immediate observation, the norms for decision which naturally flow from the economic and social connections of the legal relation, or invented norms that were adapted to the nature of the legal relation. Both the jurisprudence of conceptions and the jurisprudence of constructions however do not seek to get first-hand knowledge of the affairs and happenings of daily life. They purport to establish the concept of the legal relation just as the Roman jurists had it, for the sole purpose of subsuming all the legal relations of their own time with which they had to deal under the Roman concepts and of then applying the Roman norms for decision to them. For the greater part, however, this is seeming only and not reality. The jurisprudence of conceptions and of constructions would amount to pure logical operations, to an arithmetic of conceptions if, and only if, it had brought about the application of the Roman norms for decision to modern situations without any consideration of the question whether the result is appropriate to them or not. But it is easy to demonstrate that this was not the case. Without a certain first-hand observation of the legal relations of life there can be no juristic science. The Romanist jurists must understand the relations of the life of their own time in order to be able to subsume them under the Roman concepts. Like the jurists of all times they therefore sought to understand the legal relation that was submitted to them for decision. Accordingly, proceeding on the basis of the records, the documents, the testimony of witnesses, on the basis of what they knew from other sources as to custom and business usage, they ascertained in every single case the rights of the parcel of land, of the family, of the human beings, of the content of the agreement in question. This knowledge of life furnished the basis for the formation of concepts and for the constructions which we find in the writings of the glossators and of the postglossators. It was life, and life only, that could teach the glossators what is the content of the real rights to take fruits and profits which they construe as *dominium utile*; life only could tell the commentators something about

从表面上看来，概念法学与建构法学明显是罗马法学家方法上的直接对立。罗马法学家试图通过透彻的生活研究，来探究各种法律关系在日常生活中实际发生的状态。他们把这些研究的结果一般化，从而通过直接观察发现自然产生于法律关系之经济和社会联系的裁判规范或者创造适于此种法律关系性质的裁判规范。然而，不管是概念法学还是建构法学都没有试图探求日常生活事务和事件的第一手的知识。他们旨在建立了法律关系的概念，正如罗马法学家曾经做过的那样，其唯一目的就是使他们那个时代必须应对的所有法律关系都包摄在罗马法的概念之下，从而可以适用罗马法的裁判规范来解决这些问题。然而，在很大程度上，这只是表面上的，并不实际。如果只要法学和建构法学把罗马法裁判规范应用于现代情势，而丝毫不考虑其结果是否妥当，那么这样的法学就会等同于纯粹的逻辑运作和一种概念算术。不过很容易证明，实际情形不是这样。没有对生活中法律关系的直接观察，就不可能有任何法学。为了使罗马法研究学者所处时代的生活关系被包摄在罗马法的概念之下，他们必须很好地理解他们那个时代的生活关系。就像所有时代的法学家一样，他们必须努力理解交由他们裁断的法律关系。因此，他们依据记录、文件、证人证言，或者依据从其他来源获悉的有关习惯和商业惯例的内容，在每一个个案中确定关于土地、家庭、人类以及正在讨论的协议内容的权利。这些生活的知识为我们在注释法学家和后注释法学家的作品中所见到的概念和解释的形成奠定了基础，生活，只有生活可以告诉注释法学家，收取孳息和利润之物权——被他们解释成为了所有权收益——的内容究竟是什么；只有生活才能告诉评论家风险保险的一些东西，而他们试图通过风

insurance against risk, which they tried to reach by means of the concept *emptio venditio periculi*. The concepts of the modern legal relations which the Italians developed in this manner they do not naively subsume under the Roman concepts, but they take the results of this operation into account in advance. They did not utilize the Roman concepts for the purposes of juristic science in the form in which they found them in the sources, but first of all refashioned them according to the rules of the craft by means of abstraction and construction so as to produce a result that was suitable for the new universalization, or at least not altogether too objectionable. If the Roman norms for decision were absolutely inapplicable, they made no use of them. Accordingly they never attempted to apply the Roman law of slavery to the serfs of the Middle Ages, except in a case where temporarily, as was the case for instance in Prussia in the seventeenth and eighteenth centuries, the serf lived in a state of oppression so great that the existing modern relations suggested the application of the Roman norms. This characteristic of juristic science appears much more clearly in the case of construction than in the case of mere creation of concepts. In this case the jurist has not only acquired a first-hand knowledge of the legal relation but has also found the norms which he intends to apply by means of universalization and free finding of law. All that he is now looking for is texts in the sources that will provide him with the norms he desires. Since he proceeds with the greatest conceivable measure of arbitrariness, rejects everything that stands in his way, does not stick at falsifications and distortions, there can be no doubt about his success. There can be nothing that more exactly describes the nature of the juristic construction than the well known story that Bartolus would first find the solution of a legal problem that was submitted to him, and would then direct his pupils to gather texts from the sources to support his solution. Bartolus surely was not the only one who had the solution before he had the texts.

Lastly the jurisprudence of conceptions and the jurisprudence of constructions caused the juristic concepts of the sources, which, in a great measure, had lost their original content, to be filled with an

险买卖的概念来解释它。意大利人通过这种方法发明了现代法律关系的概念,但他们并没有天真地把他们都包摄在罗马法概念之下。他们已经预先考虑到了这样做的结果。他们并没有为法学的目的,以他们在原始文献里看到的形式利用罗马法的概念,而是首先依据专业规则,通过抽象和解释的方法重新塑造它们,从而产生一个适于新的一般化的结果,或者至少不会产生一个完全要不得的结果。如果罗马法裁判规范绝对不可用,那么他们就根本不会用它。因此,他们从来不会把罗马法上的奴隶制度适用于中世纪的农奴,除非在一种情况下临时适用,就像17、18世纪的普鲁士,农奴生活在一种高度受压迫的状态,现实存在的现代关系要求适用罗马法规范。法学的这种特征在解释中要比在纯粹的法律概念创造中表现得要清晰。这样,法学家不但得到了法律关系第一手的资料,而且还发现了他打算借助一般化和法之自由发现的方式而适用的规范。他现在所要找的就是那些能够给他提供其所欲求之规范的原始文献的原文。由于他的方法最大的可以想见的恣意程度,拒斥所有妨碍他的东西,不坚持篡改和歪曲,所以他的成功是毫无疑问的。没有任何东西比——巴托鲁斯对交给他的法律问题,首先得出解答,然后令其学生在原始文献中搜集支持其观点的原文——这个众所周知的故事,更准确描述法学解释的本质。当然,巴托鲁斯并不是唯一一个在找到原始文献原文之前就有解答的人。

最后,概念法学和建构法学令法学概念——在很大程度上已失去最初内容——被填入了全新的内容。如基尔克所展示,在讨

entirely new content. The gloss, in the discussion of the *universitas personarum*, could not avoid, as Gierke's presentation has shown, expressing an opinion about the phenomena of the life of its time which, in its view, were *universitates*, i. e. about the empire, about cities, villages, guilds, about churches in charge of a *collegium* of clerics and convents, about churches at which only one cleric was employed; it began to distinguish between different kinds of property of the *universitas*, between the *res in patrimonio universitatis* and the *res universitatis*, and, in the arrangement of the inner affairs of the latter, to keep separate and distinct the various amounts of goods belonging to each—each of which was governed by legal principles peculiar to itself. The *miles* of the sources, who has capacity for the acquisition of a *peculium castrense*, becomes the mediaeval knight in the writings of the glossators, as Fitting shows; it was required that he should not be a trader; that he have passed the squire's examination, that he have taken the oath of knighthood; that he have been girt with a

人的集合体[1]时,注释不可避免地要表达有关他们那个时代生活现象的观点,在他看来,那些生活现象都是集合体,即有关帝国、城市、乡村、行会以及由教士和修女社团[2]管理的教堂,有关只雇用一个教士的教堂;他开始区分不同财产集合体,区分财产集合体中的物与团体物[3],在后者内部事务的安排中,使得分立的、不同种类的、各种数额的财产归属于每个人,而它们每一个都有专适用于他的法律原则来规范。正如菲廷所示,原始文献中有资格获得军营特有产[4]的士兵,变成了注释法学家著作中的中世纪骑士;这就要求他不是一个商人。他必须通过侍从[5]考试,必须宣誓(进入骑士阶层的仪式),他还须佩戴一把剑,并

---

〔1〕 (拉)*universitas personarum*(人的集合体),特指为一定目的而组织在一起的人群,也可称为社团或团体。

〔2〕 (拉)*collegia*(社团),由至少3人为一定目的而组成的私人团体。根据结社的不同目的,社团可以分为宗教社团、行业社团和政治社团。罗马社会自古就承认结社自由,这种自由的限制是不得有损公共秩序。到了帝国时期,由于政治社团的大量涌现,奥古斯都于公元前7年颁布了《关于团体的尤利法》,规定:组织社团必须获得国家的批准。社团可以拥有自己的财产,但在古典法中,社团尚不具备完全的法律人格;只是到了帝国时代,这种法律人格才逐渐完善起来;社团获得了解放奴隶的权利、接受遗赠的权利、充任继承人的权利等其他民事权利。

〔3〕 (拉)*res universitati*(团体物),指属于自治市、殖民区或其他共同体的物品,它们专门为公众所使用,属于非交易物和人法物。

〔4〕 (拉)*peclium castrense*(军营特有产),一种由家子直接占有和经营的特有产,主要来自于该家子在服役期间取得的钱财、战利品、战友的赠品。家子可以通过遗嘱处置此特有产。只有在家子未立遗嘱而死亡的情况下,它才成为家父的财产。

〔5〕 侍从:护卫骑士且在封建等级制度中地位比骑士低的年轻贵族。

sword; that he have received the *nota publica*, which the gloss does not refer to the accolade, but to the knot, which the knight wore on his sleeve until some prince or some lady of high noble rank took it off; and that his name have been entered in the list. On an equal footing with this *militia armata*, with reference to the *peculium quasi castrense*, was the *militia inermis*, which was sub-divided into a *caelestis* for the clerics and a *litterata* for the jurists. In a similar fashion the postglossators utilized the concepts of Roman law for the purpose of construing the absolutely modern concepts of the bill of exchange, of the mercantile partnership with unlimited liability, of the assets of a corporation, and of insurance.

Accordingly the new juristic science is based, to precisely the same extent as was juristic science among the Romans and in the *Sachsenspiegel*, on the individual legal relation, out of which the norms for the decision of the individual legal controversies arise. As at all times, so also in the days of the glossators and the postglossators, the great mass of decisions was rendered on the basis of the nature of the individual relations, knowledge of which had been gained in the manner indicated, on the basis of actual observation, on the basis of what is found in the records, on the basis of the documents and of the testimony of witnesses. To state this in modern parlance, in most legal controversies the question of fact, not the question of law, was being adjudged. Whenever the question of fact was of general significance, or admitted of, and actually occasioned, a universalization, it became a legal proposition. These new legal propositions served the purpose of pouring a new content, adapted to the needs of the time, into the concepts of the *corpus iuris*. This was done in the guise of formation of concepts and of constructions. The juristic science of this period therefore is only to a limited extent that which it purports

得到公开的标记——此处注释指的不是爵士授予仪式,而是指徽章,爵士必须一直把它戴在套袖上,直到王子或者高等贵族的女子帮他取下;他的名字已经列入名单。同样配备这个作战武器,涉及到准军营特有产[1]的是无防御的军队,后者又被细分为教士中的卓绝者和法学家中的博学者。多少有一点相似,后注释法学家利用罗马法的概念来解释完全属于现代的概念——汇祟、无限责任的商事合伙、法人资产以及保险等。

因此,新的法学,如罗马人中的法学和《萨克森法典》中的法学一样,同等程度地基于个别法律关系之上,从这些法律关系中,个案裁判得以产生。一直以来,自然也包括注释法学和后注释法学时代,大部分的裁决都是基于个别法律关系——它们的相关知识是通过上述方法获得的——的性质、基于实际观察、基于记录中所载内容、基于文件和证人证言中而作出的。用现在流行的用语来说就是,在大多数的法律争议中,接受裁断的是事实问题而不是法律问题。每当事实问题很重要,或者容许有——实际上引发——一种一般化时,它就会成为一个法律问题。这些新的命题会服务于这样的目的:将适应时代需要的新的内容注入到《国法大全》中的概念中去。这些都是在概念法学和建构法学的伪装下进行的。因此,这个时代的法学仅仅在有限的程度上才是

〔1〕 (拉)*peclium quasi castrense*(准军营特有产),一种由家子在担任公职、教职或者从事自由职业期间取得的特有产。在君士坦丁时期,它被等同于军营特有产。

to be, i. e. a presentation and explanation of the content of the sources. To a much greater extent, it is a new juristic science, which, in the new period, is fulfilling the eternal task of all juristic science, i. e. the task of making the law subserve the needs of life.

Creation of concepts and construction have remained the tried household remedies of Romanistic juristic science wherever the latter has made its way, especially of its, historically and scientifically, most important branch, German juristic science, from the sixteenth century onward. The attempt of Zasius to place the German villein on a level not with the Roman slave but with the Roman freedman is first of all an attempt—abortive, it is true—to create an abstract concept of freedman. If Zasius had been at all willing to consider the economic and social relations of the two statuses, he would, self-evidently, have realized that Germanic villeinage is much more like Roman slavery than like the condition of the freedman; for in both villeinage and slavery, we are dealing with a status acquired at birth. The villein becomes a freedman, as Zasius himself observes, through manumission. But Zasius altogether disregards the economic and social relation, considers only the provisions of the Roman law about freedmen which seem to correspond, to a certain extent, to the condition of the Germanic villein, and utilizes it for the creation of the concept, according to which he judges Germanic villeinage. In order to be able to do this, it was necessary to have a clear understanding of the concept of villeinage, and this he owes to a searching and deep study of life.

There is nothing that can give us a better idea of the way the Continental common law originated than this attempt of Zasius. Had Zasius been successful, his attempt would have brought into existence a general concept of "villein" on the basis of the Roman concept of freedman. The norms of the Roman law concerning freedmen that are applicable to the ordinary villein would have become a part of the Continental common law; the others would have been rejected. Over and above this, self-evidently, everyhring would have remained in force, as a matter of local law, that had been established concerning them according to custom, customary law, regulation, contracts, statutes. The

它所声称的那种样子,即是对原始文献内容的表述和解释。在更大的程度上,它是新时代的新法学,承载着法学的永久的任务,即,使法律服务于生活需要。

概念的创造和解释仍然是罗马派法学可靠的、家喻户晓的纠正方法,不论哪里,后者都一路高歌,特别是自16世纪以来,历史上和科学上它的最重要的分支——德国法学更是迅猛发展。扎休斯试图使德国的农奴不同于罗马的奴隶,而是和罗马的自由民一样,这种尝试首先是一种创造抽象的自由民之概念的尝试,的确,该尝试失败了。倘若扎休斯曾经愿意考虑一点儿这两种法律的经济和社会关系,则不言自明,他就会意识到德国的农奴与罗马法的奴隶而不是自由民更相像。因为,不管是农奴还是奴隶,我们都是以出身来判断的。如扎休斯自己所观察的那样,农奴是通过农奴解放变为自由人的。但是,扎休斯完全忽略了经济和社会关系,只考虑到了罗马法上有关自由人的条款——这些条款在一定程度上似乎与德国的农奴状况相符——并利用它来创造概念,他根据这个概念,来判断德国的农奴。为了能够做好这件事,有必要对农奴的概念有清楚的理解;而要想获得这种理解,他认为需要对生活进行透彻、深入的研究。

没有什么事情比扎休斯的尝试能更好地为我们揭示欧陆共同法学的起源方式。如果扎休斯成功了,他的尝试将会带来基于罗马法之自由人概念的一个一般性的"农奴"概念。罗马法上与自由人有关的、可适用于普通农奴的法律规范也将变为欧陆共同法学的一部分;其他的将会被舍弃。除此之外,不言自明的是,作为依据习惯、习惯法、条例、契约、制定法已建立起的相关地方法而存在的所有东西,仍然继续有效。有关所有权、担保、债、继承

Continental common law of ownership, of pledge, of obligations and of inheritance have all been created and elaborated in this fashion. But Zasius's attempt to create this concept failed. It seemed altogether too much like a *tour-de-force*. And as a result of this failure, the legal situation of the villein was determined exclusively by contracts, local regulations, custom, customary law, and statute. One hundred years after Zasius, Mevius admitted this unreservedly in his book entitled *Von dem Zustande der A-bforderung und der verwiederten A-bfolge der Bauers-Leute*, which contains the words, quoted by Stintzing: "*Worinn aber ihre Dienstbarkeit und Freiheit soviel sie beyder theilhaft sein, bestehe, lässet sich in universum nicht wol beschreiben. Angesehen ein jedwedes Land und Territorium seine eigne Weisen, Gewohnheiten und Gebräuche hat. . . Darumb dieselbe wol erforschen und beleuchten muss wer von der Bauern Zustand, Gebühr und Recht urtheilen wil.*"

The first achievement of German juristic science, the creation of the concept of Gattung (*genus*) and of fungible goods by Zasius, was also brought about in this manner, i. e. by first-hand observation of the contract for supplying goods (*Lieferungsvertrag*), which became a thing of practical importance in the sixteenth century, but was unknown to the Roman jurists. In this way, the things that had been done by the glossators and the postglossators were being repeated everywhere. The concepts that were taken over from the Romans were being filled with a new content. The individual legal relation as it is reflected in the documents, in the testimony of witnesses, in records, in custom and business usage, provides the material, which is being universalized, and then judged according to the statements of the sources. But in many cases this has been preceded by a working over of the matter by local law. It is well

的欧陆共同法都是通过这种方法而创立的。但是,扎休斯创造此概念的尝试失败了。这似乎太需要花费力气。由于它的失败,农奴的法律状况完全由契约、地方条例、习惯和习惯法、制定法来决定。在扎休斯的一百年以后,梅维斯在他名为《Von dem Zustande der Abforderung und der verwiederten Abfolge der Bauers-Leute》的书里率直地承认了这一点。该书有施廷兹(Stintzing)引用的句子:“那里不论有怎样的服从和自主,单就二者皆有的情形而言,那种共存并立不可能被描述得很完整。鉴于每个国家和地区都有自身的风俗、习惯和惯例……因此评价农民状况、义务和权利的人必须很好地调查和研究它们。”

德国法学的第一个成就,即扎休斯创立的 Gattung(种类物)和可代替物概念,也是以这种方法获得的,即通过对代物清偿契约的直接观察,这在 16 世纪成为一种具有实际重要性的东西,而罗马法学家是不知道的。这样,注释法学家和后注释法学家做过的事情在所有地方都一再被重复着。从罗马人那里取来的概念被注入新的内容。如同在文件、证人证词、习惯,记录、商业惯例里所反映的那些个别法律关系提供了正在被一般化的素材,然后根据原始文献的说明来判断。但是,在许多情况下,对地方法问题的研究更领先一步。众所周知,17、18 世纪

known to what extent the famous German Romanists of the seventeenth and eighteenth centuries were endeavoring to present, not Roman law, but the law of their native country in Roman garb. Each one of them is being referred to as of the part of the country to which his life's work belongs. So Carpzov and Struve are being referred to as of Saxony; Mevius, as of North Germany; Lauterbach, as of Württemberg; Stryck, as of the Mark. For the investigation of the legal relations of their native country they made use of judgments, opinions of faculties, records of trials, as well as of the positive law of the territory in which they were working and for which they were writing. Here too then the first-hand observation of the individual legal relation constitutes the beginning.

By the reception of the Roman law therefore the jurists were not spared the necessity of observing life, or of universalizing its facts. But the center of gravity has been shifted somewhat. So far as the Roman norms were simply taken over, the jurists could limit themselves to a mere presentation and explanation of Roman law. Apart from this, the original free procedure, as it was customary among the Romans and among the German *Schoeffen*, was

著名的罗马派法学家在何种程度上竭力介绍在罗马法外表下的本国法,而不是罗马法。这些法学家每一个人都作为其毕生工作所属国的一分子而被提及。因此,卡普佐夫和斯特鲁维就作为萨克森[1]的一分子而被提到;梅维斯,属德国北部;劳特巴赫,属符腾堡[2];施特吕克,属马克·勃兰登堡[3]。为了研究他们本国的法律关系,他们利用了判决、庭审记录以及他们在其中工作的、并为其写作之地域的实证法。这里同样以对个别法律关系的直接观察作为开始。

并非通过罗马法继受,法学家们就可以不必观察生活,或者可以不必进行一般化的工作。只是,重心有所转移。就罗马法的简单继受而言,罗马法学家可以限于只是介绍并解释罗马法。除此之外,原始的自由诉讼程序——如同在罗马人和德国陪审法官中是习惯做法一样——则被一些由概念和解释所创立的高度

---

〔1〕 萨克森,位于德国北部,原来是萨克森人的家园,8 世纪被查理曼征服,并在他死后成为一公国。由于分裂和重新划分,这一地区的边界最终向东南方向拓展,1356 年萨克森大公成为神圣罗马帝国的诸侯,1860 年萨克森大公加冕称帝,但是将他的一半领地给予普鲁士(1815 年),后来的萨克森王国成为德意志帝国(1871 ~ 1918 年)的一部分。

〔2〕 符腾堡,是一个历史地名,位于德国西南部的施瓦本,今天巴登—符腾堡州的一部分。东边与巴伐利亚接壤,南边与奥地利,瑞士共享博登湖,西部与巴登、霍亨索伦,北边又与普法尔茨,黑森为邻。历史上很长一段时间,符腾堡首都在斯图加特,其他时间,君主们则选择路德维希堡或乌拉赫为首都。符腾堡得名于斯图加特一座叫 Wirtemberg 的山。

〔3〕 即 Mark Brandenburg,勃兰登堡是德意志联邦共和国的一个州,位于德国东部。其北部是梅克伦堡—前波美拉尼亚州,东临波兰,南滨萨克森州,西南部临萨克森—安哈尔特州,西部是下萨克森州。它环绕柏林州。

replaced by the highly artificial but essentially similar procedure by creation of concepts and construction. The use of such unscientific means as the distortion of concepts and falsification of norms—a thing that was done consciously to a very great extent —would have been reprehensible only if they had been under an obligation to work scientifically. But they had no scientific aims; but only the eternal, constant aim of practical juristic science to make the law subserve the needs of life.

人工的、但本质上相似的诉讼程序所代替。只要那些法学家有义务以科学地态度和方法工作，那么那些诸如概念歪曲和规范篡改的不科学方法——很大程度上这些做法是有意为之——就理应受到谴责。然而，他们没有科学目标，只有永恒不变的实用法学的目标，即，使法律服务于生活需要。

[英 汉 对 照]

西方学术经典文库

# 法律社会学基本原理

FUNDAMENTAL PRINCIPLES OF THE SOCIOLOGY OF LAW

[奥] 尤根·埃利希 著

叶名怡 袁震 译

(三)

九 州 出 版 社
JIUZHOUPRESS

# XIV
# The Historical Trend In The Juristic Science Of The Continental Common Law

Since the middle of the sixteenth century Romanistic juristic science is under the steadily growing influence of the historical trend. The aim of all history of law is to discover the original meaning of the legal propositions and the original significance of the legal relations. These are purely scientific endeavors, which, as such, have nothing to do with practical, juristic science, and which we need not therefore discuss at this point. In so far only as the historical jurists are working in the interest of the application of law, they are concerned, not with pure science, but with practical juristic science. I have not been able to ascertain as a fact that the French and Dutch legal historians anywhere asserted in plain words that the results of their investigations should be authoritative for the practical application of law, but this may be attributable to the fact they do not recognize any science of law other than the historical science. Such an assertion could have only one meaning, to wit that the historical, theoretical science of law is also practical juristic science. At any rate the Historical School of the nineteenth century in Germany has been entertaining this thought, and has been acting according to it. This can be inferred not so much from the faltering and uncertain statements of their programs, several of which, by Savigny, indeed can scarcely be interpreted in any other way, as from their other writings. Especially Savigny's *De possessione*, which has practically become a model for the writing of monographs in the Historical School, proclaims this thought to the world with all the force at its command. Six hundred and ten of its six hundred and fifty-four pages are devoted exclusively to Roman law, without deigning the modern development worthy of as much as a

# 第十四章　欧陆共同法法学的历史倾向

自从16世纪中叶以后,罗马法学越来越为持续的历史学倾向所左右。法的一切历史的目的都是为了揭示法律命题的原初含义和法律关系的原初意义。这些是纯粹科学的努力,其本身与实用法学无关,因而我们也就不必在本书中予以探讨了。仅就历史法学家为法律之运用而开展工作来说,他们关注实用法学而非纯粹科学。在这里,我并不能够肯定地断言,法国和荷兰法律史学家在某处曾明确表示他们的研究将为法律的实际运用提供权威依据,不过这一点或许可以归因于这样一个事实:除了历史法学之外他们未认可其他任何法律科学。这种断言可能只有一种含义,即,历史的、理论性的法学同时也是一种实用性的法学。无论如何,19世纪德国的历史法学派一直以来都浸淫于这一理念之中,并且,一直依照这一理念而行动。这与其说是从他们的学术研究路径——其中萨维尼的若干研究路径几乎不能以任何其他方式来解释——迟疑而不确定的表述中推断出来,不如说是从他们其他的作品中推断出来。尤其是萨维尼的《论占有》,这一作品实际上成了历史法学派专题著作的范本,它以其掌控的所有力量向世界宣布了这一理念。《论占有》全书654页中的610页全都用来论述罗马法,却对法律现代发展中的值得探讨之处几

single word. As soon as the meaning which a statement of the sources bore in the mouth of a Roman has been ascertained, the practical question is disposed of also. There is nothing in it that might be of any further interest to Savigny. A meager section of thirty-five pages hastily disposes of the "modifications of the Roman law." He examines them to ascertain whether or not they can be harmonized in principle with that which was law among the Romans. If it can be shown that this is possible, one may accept them. If not, they are to be turned aside with a contemptuous gesture. At a later time, in his *System*, Savigny preached quite different principles of dogmatic treatment of the law, but until that time the *De possessione* alone was authoritative as to method. It would be a difficult matter to find a book of equal influence in the monographic literature not only of Germany but of the whole Continental common law. I have gained the conviction on my travels that in the literature of the world there is not another monograph the name of which and, in part, the content of which is so well known to the jurists of each and every legal system as Savigny's *De possessione*. It is the true *Programmschrift* (program book) of the Historical School for practical juristic science.

It is not therefore the guiding principle of the historical jurists that a scientific understanding of any legal system can be gained only from history. That is a scientific axiom without any practical significance. The guiding principle is, rather, that this scientific understanding must suffice for practical juristic science. And this thought received its specific coloring from the fact that in the basic conception of law of all legal historians of the Romanistic tendency since the days of Cuiaccius—a conception which they never expressed, but according to which they always acted—law does not consist of legal relations but of legal propositions, so that all that is necessary for a scientific understanding of law is to ascertain the meaning which the legal propositions bore in the mouth of those who first enunciated them. As a practical matter, therefore, the historical conception amounted

乎只字未提。出自罗马人之口有关原始文献之表述的含义一旦确定,实践性问题也随之获得解决。它们无法引起萨维尼的深入兴趣。在区区35页的最后一小节中,萨维尼只是草草地提了一下"罗马法的修正"。他探讨罗马法的修正问题是为了确定,这些修正原则上是否能够与罗马人之法律相协调。如果这种协调是可能的,我们就可以接受它;如果这种协调是不可能的,那么我们会嗤之以鼻地将其弃置一边。在之后的《当代罗马法体系》一书中,萨维尼宣扬一种完全不同的对待法律的教条主义原则,但是即使在那个时候,《论占有》一书至少在方法上仍然是不二的权威。很难找到这样的一本专题的学术著作,它不但在德国,而且在整个欧陆共同法领域都具有同等重大的影响。据我的经历,我确信,在世界法学文献中,再也找不到另外一部像萨维尼《论占有》这样的作品,它的书名,乃至其中的部分内容为每个法律体系的法学家所熟知。这本书成了历史法学派为实用法学所作的真正的*Programmschrift*(纲要书)。

不过,这本书并未因此为历史法学家提供如下指导性原则——任何法律体系都只能从历史中获得科学性的理解。那是一个不具有任何实践意义的科学公理,这个指导原则毋宁是,这种科学性的理解必须满足实用法学的需要。这一思想从以下事实获得了明晰的特色,该事实即:自从居雅士时代起,在研究古罗马法律倾向的所有法律史学家的基本法律观念——他们从未表达过此种观念,但他们总是据此行事——中,法律不是由法律关系而是由法律命题组成的,所以,为获得对法律的科学理解,所需做的一切就是确定某法律命题第一个表述者赋予它的含义。因此,实际上,历史观念等于是:在法律的实际运用时,该法律

to this, that the practical application of law must attribute only that meaning to a legal proposition which was intended by its originator. Here again the historically significant antinomy of juristic science which converts its modes of thought, even against its own will, into norms becomes operative.

Only this limitation of the "historical view of law," as Savigny has called it, to the legal propositions can explain the attitude and the conduct of the legal historians. Since the days of Jhering, the founders of the Historical School have often been called romanticists in Germany. But this is unjust; for neither the founders of the Historical School nor any of their adherents among the Romanists actually were romanticists. The yearning, which is characteristic of the romanticist, to turn life back into the past was utterly foreign to them. They surely have never evinced any desire that the *patria potestas* should be revived, or that contracts should be made in the form of the *stipulatio*. And if Savigny has spoken bitter words in a book-review of the modern system of land registration, he surely did not mean to urge the adoption of the Roman law of pledge. Since the law, in the eyes of legal historians everywhere, was not the legal relations but the legal propositions, they have not been concerning themselves about the form which the legal relations assume in actual life. They let life take its course; but they did insist that the courts should adjudge the legal relations according to the Roman legal propositions in the form in which they have been ascertained by scientific investigation. But as to this, they could not but make shipwreck. Had life, under the influence of the Historical School, again become Roman, the application of Roman law would have followed as a matter of course. But since life remained modern and necessarily had to remain modern, it was impossible to apply Roman law to legal relations that in part were unknown to the Romans and in part were totally different from those that had existed among them.

之含义的权威表述只能是该法的原创者所创立的法律命题。这里又一次出现了历史视角下法学所呈现的重大自相矛盾：它将自身的思维模式——甚至与它自身的意志相违背地——转换成了规范。

只有这种萨维尼所谓的“历史的法律观”对法律命题的限制才能解释法律史学家们的态度和行为。在德国，自耶林以降，历史法学派的创建者常被冠以浪漫主义者之名。然而如此称呼并不公允；因为，不管是这一学派的创建人，还是罗马派法学家中该学派的支持者，他们都不是浪漫主义者。富有浪漫主义气息的对旧日美好生活的向往与这些人格格不入。不管是家父权应该得到复兴，抑或是契约应该以罗马法上的要式口约的形式缔结，对于这些，他们从来就没有表现出哪怕是丝毫的渴望。即使萨维尼在他对《现代土地登记制度》的书评中言语刻薄，但是他并没有明确主张要采纳罗马担保法。既然在所有的法律史学家眼中，法律并非法律关系，而是法律命题，他们也就不关注实际生活中呈现的法律关系的形式。一方面，他们让生活顺其自然；但另一方面，他们又坚持法院必须依照罗马法的法律命题来调整法律关系，这些法律命题的形式他们都已经通过科学研究予以确定了。在这一点上，他们就无法自圆其说了。只有当我们的生活在历史法学派的影响之下回到古罗马时代时，我们适用罗马法才是顺其自然的。然而，鉴于我们现在过着现代的生活，并且将来势必继续保持这种现代性，而且由于古罗马人对部分现代法律关系一无所知，部分现代法律关系与它们在古罗马时候的状况截然不同，将那种生活中的罗马法适用于现代的法律关系，肯定是行不通的。

Accordingly the legal historians again found themselves face to face with the problem of applying Roman law. And they sinned most grievously as to this difficulty by not seeing it. They did not even investigate it, although, from their point of view, it would have been their first duty to do this rather than to throw light upon a few dark points in the history of Roman law. They never inquired how the glossators, the postglossators, and the German Romanists of the sixteenth century performed the adaptation of Roman law. Savigny's history of Roman law in the Middle Ages was a history of juristic literature. Apart from this, in the hands of the legal historians, the legal history of the time following the reception is almost exclusively a history of legal doctrine. Wherever their glance touched upon jurists of past centuries, they were interested in the way in which the latter understood Roman law, not in their attitude toward the law of their own day. To the present day, we have no presentation of the law of the gloss, of the postglossators, or of the German *usus modernus*. Indeed, even the number of treatises on the history of legal doctrine that treat of the way in which the glossators, the commentators, and the *usus modernus* dealt with individual legal institutions is extremely small.

But you cannot do away with a difficulty by ignoring it. The question of the adaptation of Roman law must be solved daily by judicial decisions. A juristic science that ignores the adaptation of law of the past to the legal relations of the present does not offer practical law but historical law. This judgment does not condemn the Historical School of the French and of the Netherlanders very severely; for, it seems, their aim was to teach law and to let the administration of law get along with it as best it could. But the German legal historians did not profess to teach Roman law but law that was applicable in Germany, and therefore it was incumbent upon them, will he nill he, to consider both the Roman law and its adaptation. Their method of procedure usually was simply to take over the results of the adaptation as

因此,法律史学家又一次发现他们在将罗马法适用于现代生活的这个难题上面面相觑。他们最严重的罪过正是在于对这一困境视而不见。尽管自他们的角度看,他们的第一要务应当是解决这一难题,然而,法律史学家甚至都不曾研究过这个难题,相反,他们将阐明故纸堆里的罗马法中的意义不明之处作为他们的首要职责。他们从不探究注释法学派、后注释法学派和16世纪德国的罗马派法学家是如何对罗马法进行修正的。萨维尼的《中世纪罗马法律史》是一部法学文献的历史。除此之外,在法律史学家的手中,自罗马法继受以降的法律史仅仅是一部法律学说史。当他们面对过往的法学家时,他们只关注这些法学家理解罗马法的方式,对这些法学家对待他们自身时代的法律的态度则显得漠不关心。时至今日,我们没有介绍过注释法学派的、后注释法学派的以及德国的学说汇纂现代应用学派的法律。实际上,即便是在论述法律学说史的文献中,探讨了注释法学派、评注法学派和法律学说汇纂现代应用派对待他们自己独特的法律制度的方式的文献也是极少的。

但我们并不能以忽略的方式来摆脱难题。罗马法的修正问题必须通过日复一日的司法裁决来加以解决。忽视将过去之法修正以适应近日之法律关系的法学无法提供实用之法,而只能提供历史之法。这一判断并不是对法国和荷兰的历史法学派的严苛指责;因为他们的目的似乎是讲授法律,并且让司法尽可能与之协调发展。但是德国的法律史学家认为他们教授的不是罗马法,而是可适用于德国的法律,因此,不管他愿意不愿意,考虑罗马法及其修正对他们来说是责无旁贷的。他们的行动方式常常只是接管他们的先辈先前完成了的修正结果。他们以与他们的

it had been performed by their predecessors. They applied the legal propositions of Roman law to the same modern relations to which they had already been applied by the glossators, the postglossators, and the teachers of the *usus modernus* in Germany. The pandects of the Historical School differ from the older works chiefly in this, that they no longer discuss the adaptation but presuppose its results. In all essential respects they present merely those results that the Continental common law jurists attained as early as the eighteenth century. But they have persistently refused to quote the writings of the latter; for in spite of the fact that they were deeply indebted to them, they despised them unspeakably with all their hearts. And, therefore, thanks to these legal historians, we have lost all knowledge of the historical connection between the adaptation of the nineteenth and that of the earlier centuries. But resort to this device failed when questions were involved that had not arisen before the nineteenth century. Inasmuch as the Historical School provided no new means of solving these problems, the old ones that had stood the test of experience had to suffice. Jurists proceeded, just as they had done before, by immediate observation and universalization, concealing their methods according to approved models under the guise of construction and creation of concepts.

As an illustration let us take the vast Continental common law literature on the making of contracts where the parties are not in the presence of each other. It discusses questions which have arisen thanks to the modern development of the postal and telegraph systems, and about which of course nothing is to be found in the Roman sources. The solution therefore had to be found quite independently. The basis was observation and the universalization of experience; subsequently however the solutions which had been arrived at in this manner were read into the sources. This happened also in the case of Jhering's doctrine of *culpa in contrahendo* and of the negative interest in a contract, More important are Einert's and Liebe's works on the bill of exchange. After the law of bills of exchange has been developed, it is being pressed into the Romanist formulae of the "literal

先辈相同的方式将罗马法的法律命题运用到现代关系之中，这些前辈包括注释法学派、后注释法学派以及德国的学说汇纂现代应用学派的教授者们。历史法学派的潘德克顿法学与之前那些古老作品的主要不同之处就在于，他们再也不谈论修正问题，他们把修正的结果作为谈论的前提。在所有基本的方面，他们仅仅介绍欧陆共同法法学家早在18世纪时就已经获得的那些结果。不过他们坚持不引用这个时期之后的作品；尽管他们从这些作品中受惠良多，但他们还是一心一意地对这些著作表现出无法形容的蔑视态度。因此，因为这些法律史学家，我们丧失了有关19世纪的修正与更早的几个世纪的修正二者之间历史联系的知识。但是当19世纪之前从未出现过的新问题出现时，他们所凭借的这个策略就会马上失败。既然历史法学派没有提供解决这些问题的新方法，过去的那些经受住了经验考验的旧方法还是必须够用才行。一如法学家们长久以来所熟识的那样，他们借住直接的观察和一般化来处理他们的问题，并且依照在解释和概念创设的幌子下所获得首肯的模式隐藏了他们的方法。

为了阐明以上观点，我们以欧陆共同法系中论及契约双方当事人不在场的缔约的浩瀚文献为例进行说明。这些文献讨论了由于现代社会邮政和电报的高速发展所带来的新问题，在罗马法的原始文献里面并没有这些问题的现成答案，所以我们必须独立地寻求问题的解答。解答的基础就是对经验的观察和一般化；然而接下去这些新问题的解答却会以解释以前的学说的方式进行。这在耶林的缔约过失学说和契约的消极利益中一样存在。另外，更为重要的是恩内特和利伯关于汇票的著作。自从汇票法得到发展以来，它就被塞进罗马法中的"书面契约"和要式

contract" and of the *stipulatio*. Bähr's work was done solely on the basis of observation; the derivation from the sources is mere external adornment.

All that we can say of the upshot of the endeavors of the legal historians for practical juristic science is that construction by means of conscious distortion and falsification has been limited to a considerable extent. They insist that the legal propositions should everywhere be employed according to their original meaning. Though this may appear to be a rather insignificant result, the effect of the historical trend in practical juristic science was an enormous one. By making the ascertainment of the meaning of the legal propositions at the time of their origin the sole function of juristic science, they intentionally shifted the center of gravity of the juristic interest into the past. They excluded the present from juristic science, and actually transmuted a creative art into a manner of science, but only into a kind of philology, which did not concern itself with the knowledge of things but with the knowledge of what has been said about things. They took no further interest in the whole development from the time when the proposition had been stated in the form in which it is binding today down to the present; they refused to go beyond Sabinus or beyond Papinian, or if Justinian had inserted an interpolation into the text, beyond that. The practical effect of thrusting creative juristic science into the background has been the doctrine that the solution of all problems must be reached by interpretation of the sources. The doctrine of the legislator who foresees everything that may arise and of the perfection of the legal system, which existed, in the germ, in the writings of the postglossators, has received its scientific consecration at the hands of the legal historians, especially of those of the German school.

But precisely for the reason that the legal historians actually rejected the thought of any and all conscious creative development of the law beyond the content of the sources, they were compelled to continue the development of juristic methods. All the arbitrary proceedings, the naïve misunderstandings and conscious falsifications, of former schools of jurists had served the purpose of adapting the law to new needs, and of enriching it by means of norms that the present time required. But

口约这两种形式里面。贝尔的作品完全以观察为基础;从原始文献中衍生仅仅是外在的装饰而已。

我们对于法律史学家为实用法学所作努力的结果能够说的一切就是:通过蓄意歪曲和篡改而进行的解释限于一种相当的程度。法律史学家坚持所有地方的法律命题必须以它原初的涵义来予以运用。尽管这看上去是个相当无关紧要的结果,然而实用法学中的这种历史倾向却是影响深远的。在使探明法律命题在其初创之时的原初涵义成为法学的唯一功能的过程中,他们对法律旨趣的重心变成了过往的历史。他们将当下从法学中拒斥出去,实际上是令作为创造性艺术的法学蜕化成一种科学,蜕化成一种只关注对事情只有言说的知识,而不关心事情本身的知识的文献学。他们对既存命题的从古至今的演变没有更多的兴趣;他们拒绝超越萨宾和帕比尼安,或是超越优士丁尼——如果他在原文中插入了某个添加。这种将创造性法学置于次要地位所产生的实际影响就是:所有问题的解决都必须通过解释原始文献来达成。预见了可能出现之一切的立法者的学说与——其萌芽存在于后注释法学家作品中的——法律体系完善的学说在法律史学家,尤其是德国学派的法律史学家手中取得了科学的神圣地位。

但是精确地说,由于法史学家事实上拒绝了所有超越原始文献内容之外的、自觉创造性的法律发展的思想,他们被迫发展了法律方法论。前述法学学派的恣意的解释、幼稚的误解和蓄意的篡改,都是为了两个目的:让法律适应新要求;以当下所需的新的规范来丰富法律的内容。但是法律史学家想要回到

the zeal of the legal historians to go back to the original content of the sources brushed aside, if not all of this most valuable legal material, certainly a considerable portion of it, and by so doing impoverished the law. The gulf that was fixed between the traditional law and the present time had continually been becoming wider and wider, and had to be bridged somehow. This was done chiefly by converting the creation of juristic concepts and juristic construction into a mathematics of concepts and into a constructive systematism (*Systematilk*).

The nature of the juristic mathematics of concepts can be shown by means of a comparison of juristic with mathematical concepts. Juristic concepts are empirical. They are a synthesis of the norms that govern an empirically given legal relation, and that are so essential to it that they distinguish the given legal relation from other similar relations. By means of formal logic therefore no other norms can be derived from a concept than those that have been utilized in creating the concept, for formal logic cannot, by any means, provide new thought material; it can only unfold such material as is already in existence and analyze it.

Mathematical concepts on the other hand are arbitrary, or as the famous French mathematician Poincaré has called them, conventional. Properties or necessary characteristics are being attributed to the concept, quite without any concern as to the question whether they are actually conceivable or not. Take for instance the imaginary number, infinity, Riemann's plane. And it is not required that the deductions that may be made from the concept should in any way harmonize with reality; all that is required is that they should not be self-contradictory. This disregard of reality by mathematics is absolutely justifiable; for the mathematician does not lay claim to any ability to exercise control over the world of reality by means of his concepts. Mathematical thinking is a source of purest delight to some natures which are especially adapted to it; to others it is, in

原始文献的最初内容上来的过度热情把——即使不是全部也至少是其中相当可观的一部分的——最有价值的法律材料给丢弃了,这样做也使得法律变得相当贫乏。传统法律和当前时代之间的鸿沟变得越来越大,必须以某种方式在它们之间架起桥梁。将法律概念的创造和法学解释转变为一种概念数学和解释体系在完成此项任务中起到了主要作用。

这种法律中的概念数学的性质可以经由法律概念和数学概念的比较得到。法律概念是经验性的。它们是调整经验上给定的法律关系的规范综合,规范的综合这一点相当关键,它使得特定的法律关系与类似的法律关系区别开来。因此,借助于形式逻辑这个工具,除了在创设概念中已运用的那些规范之外,没有任何其他规范可以从该特定概念推导出来,原因在于,不管怎样,形式逻辑无法提供新的思想材料;它只能展开那些已有材料并加以分析。

在另一方面,数学概念则是相当任意的,或者如著名的法国数学家庞加莱所说,它们是相当因循守旧的。数学概念具有某些属性或必要的特征,而不会担心这些属性或特征事实上是否可以想象得出。比如以虚数、无穷大或者黎曼平面为例。数学并不要求从概念中演绎出来的结果无论如何要与现实相符合;所有的要求只是它们不至于自相矛盾即可。数学的这种对现实世界不理会是完全有理由的;因为数学并不自以为以它的概念作为手段就有能力对现实世界施加影响。数学上的思索对某些人来说是一种纯粹的愉悦的源泉,这些人特别适合数学思维;对另一些人,数学在某种程度上是不可亲近的;对剩下的那些

part, inaccessible; upon others, among whom, unfortunately, I must be numbered, its effect is positively repellant.

But it is not impossible to treat empirical concepts as if they were mathematical concepts, to attribute properties to them arbitrarily, and to make deductions from them that are foreign to reality. Natural philosophy in past centuries has followed this path often enough. A procedure of this kind suggests itself to juristic science with an exceptional degree of force because of the fact that there actually is in its concepts something arbitrary, conventional. The legal institutions, the norms for decision, the statutory provisions, from which it draws the essential Characteristics of its concepts, the inner empirical necessity of which often is not apparent to us, are the product of the labor of the human mind, and that which is being adduced on the basis of this material often makes the impression that, at the pleasure of the originator, it might just as well have been arranged otherwise. It surely was purely a matter of convention that the Roman jurists of the Empire made the order of the family of the peasant proprietor of the days of the Punic war, which had long since disappeared, the basis for the concepts of the law of the family; that the French Civil Code made community of movables, and the German Civil Code community of administration, the statutory régime. And how many other things connected with each of these legal institutions might be regulated in a way quite different from the way it was actually done! The similarity between juristic and mathematical concepts indeed is merely an outward one; for the concept itself was not created arbitrarily, its empiric basis alone rests—and this, too, is only seemingly true — on human volition. Nevertheless this superficial similarity has been sufficient to produce a juristic method which is closely related to the mathematical method. But this alone does not suffice to explain the enormous importance of the juristic mathematics of concepts.

We must add the remarkable fact that juristic science, although it is basically different from mathematics, has at all times had a strange power to charm mathematical minds. A juristic mathematician is not endeavoring by means of juristic science to satisfy the needs for which the latter really exists, but to secure

人来说——很不幸，我也是其中一员——它的影响肯定受到排斥。

然而，将经验性概念当作数学概念也并非不可能，只需要专断地将属性加诸经验性概念之上，并且从它们那里演绎出完全不同于现实的结论即可。过去几个世纪的自然哲学家采取此种进路的时候已经足够多了。这种进路也让法学获得了很不一般的影响力，因为事实上法学中的概念也是专断而墨守成规的。法律风俗、裁判规范和制定法的规定——法学从它们之中提取了法律概念的本质特征，它们内在经验上的必然性对我们来说并非显而易见——都是人类智力劳动的产物，而且根据该材料常被引证的东西经常导致这样一种印象，即概念的创始人完全可以随心所欲地对概念作另外的处理。迦太基战争期间罗马帝国的法学家建立了——早已消失但成为之后家庭法概念的基础的——自耕农家庭的秩序，这的确纯粹是一种习俗惯例；《法国民法典》建立了动产的社会，《德国民法典》建立了行政管理和制定法体制的社会，这些也都是一种惯例。然而，有太多的、与这些法律习俗相联系的其他事项被规范的方式可能完全不同于其实际运作的方式！法学上的概念和数学上的概念只是在外表上相似；因为法学概念本身不是任意地创设出来的，法学概念的经验基础完全建立在——这同样只是似乎正确而已——人类意志之上。尽管如此，这种肤浅的相似性已经足以令他们建立一门与数学方法相似的法律方法。但是仅仅这一点并不能解释法律概念数学的重要性。

我们还必须指出这样一个显著的事实：法学尽管与数学有着根本性的不同，但法学一直都拥有吸引数学心智的奇异力量。法律数学家并不是努力要以法学来满足数学实际存在的要求，他们

the high intellectual enjoyment which analytical mathematics or the theory of numbers could afford in a much less questionable manner. Like the mathematician, he creates juristic concepts which, in part at least, he creates arbitrarily; but unlike the mathematician since the great antinomy of juristic science at once asserts itself, he demands that the conclusions, which he arrives at by unfolding the concept, be at once realized; that they be recognized as norms; that the judge render his decisions, and the legislator legislate, in accordance with them. In his judgment the solemnity and dignity of the art to which he has dedicated his life lies in this very thing, that it bestows entity upon the figments of his imagination.

The juristic mathematician may be found in all latitudes, occasionally even among the Romans, where he flourishes most luxuriantly perhaps in the doctrine of the *ius accrescendi* in case of legacies, and among the present-day French and English; but the Continental common law was an extraordinarily favorable soil. For the universalizations, the historic basis of which had long since been forgotten; the norms for decision, the social justice of which belonged to a distant past, which, in the main, we cannot understand; the statutes, the expediency of which, as in the case of the *lex Falcidia*, is a mystery to us today: all of these things could very easily—here more than elsewhere—give rise to the idea that a considerable portion, or the greater portion, of the law is arbitrary and conventional. The Historical School, which ought to have fostered an understanding of the economic and social relations out of which the legal propositions, as is well known, arose in Rome, has always been antiquarian rather than historical, and was not equal to a task of this magnitude. Inasmuch as the Historical School accentuated the practical necessity of going beyond Roman law, it is easily understood that the mathematics of concepts had never flourished so abundantly as under the domination of the historical school in Germany. Its most outstanding representatives were preponderantly mathematicians, to wit Puchta, Vangerow,

只是想要得到如分析数学和数论那样能以一种更可靠的方式提供的、高层次的智识享受。与数学家一样,法律数学家至少部分程度上有些任意地创设法律概念;但是由于法学中重大的自相矛盾会立刻表现出来,因而法律数学家与数学家不同,他会要求通过概念的展开得出的结论应当立即获得实现;要求承认该结论为规范;要求法官作出裁决、立法者进行立法,都应以该结论为依据。在法官的审判中,他为之贡献一生的这一艺术的庄严和神圣正是在于,它给予想象中的虚构之物以实体。

法律数学家无处不在,甚至在古罗马人中偶尔也有法律数学家存在,或许在遗产继承时"生存者取得权,"学说中,法律数学家最为活跃,现在的法国和英国也有这样的人;但是欧陆共同法是法律数学存活的最佳沃土。由于一般化的过程,原先的历史基础早已为人所遗忘;裁判规范和社会正义,这些都属于久远的过去,大体上,我们无法理解它们;历史上的制定法及其要实现的目的——比如《法尔奇第亚法》,对我们当代的人们来说就是一个谜:所有的这些事情可能非常容易——此处比别处更容易——引发这样的思想:相当部分的,甚至是更大比例的法律是恣意的、因循守旧的。历史法学派本该努力理解(众所周知)出现于古罗马的法律命题赖以存在的经济和社会关系,然而,法律史学家却总是食古不化,缺乏历史的眼光,他们无法胜任这一宏大的工程。由于法律史学家如此强调超越罗马法的实践必要性,因而很容易理解为何概念数学在德国历史法学派主宰下的德国会如此地繁盛。这一学派中最杰出的代表人物主要都是数学家,它们是普赫塔、凡格罗、温德沙伊德和布林兹,还有比他们更早一点

Windscheid, Brinz, and, in his earlier days, Jhering. It may suffice to point out the things that once upon a time were "conceptually" impossible, to wit assignment of an obligatory right, testamentary creation of a foundation which was to be established by the testament itself (*Staedelscher Erbfall*) ; the maxim *Kauf bricht nicht Miete*, the ser vitude of a shareholder in a parcel of land belonging to the share company. On the other hand it was "conceptually" necessary that a swindler who sold a cargo of coal which was on the high sea to several people should be permitted to recover the whole purchase price from each buyer in case it sank at a later time, because of the maxim that *the buyer bears the risk.* I wonder whether a Roman would ever have rested content with a formula of this kind, and whether he would not have freely found a suitable norm.

A typical instance of the mathematics of concepts is the concept of ownership of the Historical School. Its empirical basis comprises the following: ownership of movable things, which as a consequence of its economic purpose, as a rule, permits every possible use and consumption; the Roman ownership of the *fundus Italicus* and the modern ownership of land which have arisen out of the removal of all burdens and charges from the land, both of which, because of the Roman and of the present-day system of landholding, permit of extensive rights of taking fruits and profits; the right of the lord in land which is held in feudal tenure. Now these, I take it, are legal relations which economically are so unrelated that it is scarcely possible to create an empirical concept common to all of them, for this empirical concept must needs be expressed in economic terms. The Romans were able to get along without a concept of ownership in the *ager publicus* or in the *solum provinciale*, and the English of today can quite well dispense with a universally valid concept of ownership; the older Continental common law juristic science, too, did not have it, but made a distinction between *dominium directum and utile*. The Historical School was not willing to dispense with an omnipresent ownership. Searching for a concept which should cover the most heterogeneous relations,

的耶林。过去在概念上不可能的事情，概念数学可以办得到，这些事情包括：债权的转让、有待遗嘱本身加以证实的遗嘱基金的建立（*Staedelscher Erbfall*）以及“买卖不破租赁”的准则、股东在一块土地上的地役权归属于股份公司等。另一方面，以下情形则属“概念上”的必然：一个骗子在公海上向多个人出售一船煤炭，后来船沉没，这种情况下他向买受人提出给付价金的要求应当是允许的，因为“买受人承担风险”是法律上的一个准则。我想知道一个古罗马人是否会满足于这种表述，他是否不再自由地发现一个合适的规范。

概念数学最典型的例子就是历史法学派中的所有权概念。所有权的经验基础由以下部分组成：动产所有权，作为其经济目的的结果，通常允许每一种可能的使用和消耗；意大利土地的罗马法上的所有权和因免除土地上的负担和捐税而出现的现代土地所有权，由于古罗马和现代土地所有制，它们都允许拥有广泛地收取孳息和收益的权利；封建领主在保有地内的权利。我是这样理解的，这些属于在经济层面上不存在相互关联的法律关系，想要创设一个它们共有的经验性概念是不可能的，因为经验性概念必须可以通过经济术语来表述。古罗马人无需所有权这个概念就可以妥善处理公地或是行省土地，今天的英国不必使用所有权这个普遍有效的概念，却也运转顺利；早期的欧陆共同法学也没有这个概念，却可以很好地区分领主对领地的权利和附庸的权利。历史法学派却不想摒弃这个普适的概念。为了找到可以覆盖所有各异的经济关系的概念，他们不可避免地需要一种完全

they inevitably had to arrive at a concept that was altogether uneconomic. The most acceptable formulation, perhaps, is that of Windscheid. The latter defines it as follows: Ownership is the right which in itself makes the will of the person entitled decisive as to the thing in the totality of its relations. Manifestly, this concept is absolutely arbitrary. If one compares it with an economic juristic concept, e. g. the law and right of pledge, of usufruct, of sale, one will perceive at once that, as contrasted with these, it does not import any economic relation at all, but is merely a formula, designed to give a common name to a man's manifold economic relations. Nevertheless a number of inferences were drawn from it, to wit that there can be only one ownership of a corporeal thing; that a *real* right in a thing that one owns is impossible; that the extinction of a real right frees the thing from the limitations imposed by the *real* right; that in the *actio negatoria* the owner need prove no more than that he is the owner. Do these norms really flow from the concept of ownership as Windscheid has formulated it? The words, indeed, are so indefinite that they can mean not only this but many other things besides. But could one not speak of ownership even if these four elements were not present? It is certain that, in various legal systems, the owner may have the right to hunt, the water right, the mining right in a thing which he owns; that if another has the real right to hunt and to mine, and this right is destroyed, the right of the owner is not by this very fact at once extended so as to include these rights; that the owner remains owner even if in the *actio negatoria* the burden of proof is regulated differently. On the other hand one might say of the usufructuary that he can have no right in the thing as to which he has the right of usufruct; that the destruction of a *real* right frees his right from the limitation that had been resting upon it, and that it is sufficient if, in an *actio negatoria*, he establishes his right. After this, not much remains of the concept of

没有经济意味的概念。或许是温德沙伊德创造了最为广泛接受的所有权的定义。他将所有权定义如下:所有权是其自身能够使权利人的意志对该物之上的关系总体具有决定性影响的权利。显然,这一定义是绝对专断的。只需要比较一下经济层面上的法律概念,比如担保权、用益权、出售权等权利,我们马上可以洞察到这一点,即与以上两个概念形成对比的是,所有权的这个概念没有引入任何经济关系,它仅仅是一个惯用提法,用来为人们多样化的经济关系提供一个共同的名称。尽管如此,我们还是可以从这个概念中得到一些推论,就是:每个有体物之上只有一个所有权;在他人的所有物之上不可能再存在一个完整的物权;物权的消失使受该物权限制之物不再受其拘束;排除妨害之诉中,所有权人只需要证明他是物的所有者即可。那么这些规范实际上真的来自于温德沙伊德所构造的这个概念吗?其实,这些言辞是如此地不明确,以至于它们不仅意指如此,而且还意味着很多其他东西。当这四个要素缺场的时候,我们就没法谈论所有权了吗?在各种法律制度中,以下这些是确定不疑的,即:所有者在其所有物上可以拥有狩猎权、水权、采矿权;如果其他人享有狩猎与采矿的物权,之后这些权利遭到终结,所有者的权利并不由于这个事实而可以立即延伸以至于涵盖这些权利;即使排除妨害之诉的证明责任不是如此规定的,所有者依旧是所有者。另一方面,我们也可以说,用益物权人在该物之上除了用益物权之外不再享有其他权利;主物权的消灭使得用益物权人的权利从加诸其上的限制中解放出来,而且如果在排除妨害之诉中,他证实了自己的权利,这就足够了。在这之后,所有权这个概念已经没多少内容了。然而,被人们认为是从所有权这个概

ownership. But the norms, which are said to flow from the concept, in actual fact originated in Roman law; they are therefore empirical, and it is undoubtedly quite arbitrary to say that since they arise from the concept, they are valid even where their validity cannot be established empirically. The allocation of the burden of proof in the *actio negatoria* is a part of the latest development of juristic law, and is so far from being conceptually necessary that it has failed to gain universal recognition.

A second typical example of Savigny's mathematics of conceptions is his doctrine of essential error. According to Savigny the legal transaction is, conceptually, a declaration of the will. Consequently, there is no legal transaction where, because of essential error, the will and the declaration do not coincide, whether or not there be fault (*Verschulden*) on the part of the person in error. Since the contract is only a species of legal transaction, he says, the above statement applies also to the contract, even though the other party be not, and could not be, aware of the error. In so far as the legal transaction, empirically, is nothing more than a declaration of the will, this doctrine is correct, i. e. it is correct as to gifts, and other transactions imposing a unilateral obligation (suretyship, acknowledgment, ratification), declarations by last will and testament, agreements of family law, perhaps also most compromises. But as applied to mercantile contracts it is manifestly incorrect. It is so far from being conceptually necessary that the courts, as my investigations of the course of decisions of the last century have shown, have only rarely, and then solely on doctrinal grounds, rendered decisions according to Savigny's theory. Where an agent without fraudulent intent meant to enter into a contract in the name of the principal, and the other party had no means of knowing this, no attention has ever been paid thereto, although this is perhaps the most common instance of error *in persona*.

念推导出来的,而实际上是源于罗马法的这些规范,它们是经验性的,所以如果还是主张——由于这些规范来自于所有权这个概念,所以即使这些规范的有效性在经验层面上无法被证实,它们依然是有效的——那毫无疑问将是相当武断的。排除妨害之诉中的证明责任分配是晚近所发展出来的法学家法的一部分,并且由于它远非是概念上所必需的,所以它没有获得普遍的认同。

第二个关于萨维尼的概念数学的典型例子就是他的“重大错误”学说。依萨维尼,法律行为,在概念上,是一种意思表示。因此,不管错误一方是否有过错(Verschulden),在重大错误的情况下不存在法律行为,因为重大错误中意思和表示不一致。他说,既然契约只是法律行为的一种,则以上表述同样适用于契约,即使另一方不知或者不可能知道该重大错误的情况下亦然。如果在经验层面上法律行为仅仅是意思表示,那么这个学说是正确的,比如在涉及赠与和另外一些单方债务(保证、承认[1]和追认)、遗嘱宣告、家庭法上的安排,或许还包括大多数的和解等法律行为中。但是当把它应用到商业契约的时候,这个学说就明显不正确了。在商法中,萨维尼的这个看法绝非概念上的必然,许多本世纪的对法官判决的研究表明,法官的判决是很少仅仅建立在该学说基础之上并依照萨维尼的理论作出的。当无欺诈意图的代理人想以本人名义缔结契约,而另一方对此无从知晓,在这种情况下,尽管这或许是最常见的当事人错误,但是我们并不理会他

〔1〕 这是一个涉及许多法律行为的一般性术语,比如对债务、责任、正当性和对方主张的有效性等的承认。

These two examples afford a deep insight into the nature of the mathematics of concepts. The concept of ownership which the Historical School has created and Savigny's concept of the legal transaction have arisen from observation of actual life and are therefore empirical. We know the individual legal relations which constitute the basis of these concepts; the norms which purport to result from the concept belong, in part, to the existing law. But these concepts were not abstracted carefully from the facts of experience like those of the natural sciences, nor were they created, like the concepts of practical juristic science, with a view to the requirements of the application of law. They are universalizations of reality; they are not scientific, however, but superficial, unprofessional, containing a series of quite arbitrary admixtures, like those of the older natural philosophy or of Shelling's philosophy, by which, as is well known, Savigny and Puchta were influenced. Nor are they practical, for all consideration of expediency is foreign to them to begin with. The fact that formal logic deduces norms from them is due to the fact that these identical norms were utilized in the creation of these concepts. Formal logic, at all times, can derive those norms from a concept which it has first put into it. In so far as norms have been created empirically, they are *richtig* (correct), but if they are not based on reality, they are independent creations of juristic science. They differ from the other parts of juristic law in this, that, seemingly at least, they were created independently of social influences, distribution of power, considerations of expediency, or trends of justice. But to this very fact the success of the mathematics of concepts may, in a great measure, be attributed. The latter attained its fullest development at a time when it was believed that all creation of law should be reserved to the legislator. Whenever the administration of law found that which was offered by the Roman and also by the modern legislator insufficient for its purposes, that which men were least unwilling to place at its disposal was a juristic technique which was altogether divorced from society, and which purported to be derived exclusively from concepts. It can be shown that when Savigny and Puchta presented their doctrine of a scientific law they had this kind of creation of law in mind. Others, it is true, would have none of it. To speak of juristic

们双方的主观状态。

上文的两个例子提供了深刻审视概念数学的视角。历史学派提出的所有权的概念和萨维尼的法律行为的概念都是来自于对实际生活的观察,因而是经验性的。我们知道单个的法律关系构成了概念的基础;声称由概念而产生的规范部分地属于现行法。但是这些概念并非如同自然科学的概念一样审慎地从经验事实中抽离出来,它们也不像实用法学的概念那样着眼于法律适用的需求而被创造出来。它们是现实的一般化;相对而言,它们不是科学性的,而是肤浅的、不专业的,它们包含了一系列相当恣意的杂质,一如旧日的自然哲学或是谢林的哲学——众所周知,萨维尼和普赫塔深受它们的影响。它们也不是实用性的,因为最起码所有的合目的性考量都与它们无关。所谓形式逻辑可以推导出规范,实际上是基于这一事实,即这些规范在概念的创造中得到了利用。形式逻辑,无论何时,只有在原先就包含有这些规范的时候才可以推导出它们。当规范是基于经验而被创设的时候,它们就是 *richtig*(正确)的,但是,如果这种创设不是基于现实,那它们只不过是独立于法学的创造物罢了。它们与法官法的其他部分不同之处在于,它们至少表面上独立于社会影响、权力分配、合目的性考量和正义的趋向。在很大程度上,概念数学的成功可以归于这一事实。概念数学正是在那个坚信只有立法者创造法律的年代得到了完满的发展。每当司法发现,古罗马人和现代立法者提供的东西不足以满足其目的时,人们至少不愿意受制于一种完全与社会隔绝的,声称完全来自于概念的法律技艺。可以证明,当萨维尼和普赫塔介绍他们的科学法律的学说时,他们想到了这种法律创造。的确,其他人一点儿也没这么想过。依

science as a source of law, according to Windscheid, is to confuse the woman in childbed with the midwife.

A finding of norms which is absolutely divorced from social influences, and which consists in logical inferences from given concepts, can scarcely be called a creation of law, and a juristic science which is confined to it can scarcely be considered a source of law. The mathematics of concepts, however, as a matter of fact never attained its goal. Artificially created as they were, these concepts were always susceptible of transformation wherever the distribution of power, considerations of expediency, and trends of justice demanded it. Whether the transaction which was entered into by an agent is treated as having come into existence by the will of the agent or of the principal depends upon which construction yields the more satisfactory result. And admitting this, we have again recognized the social influences. Moreover on countless occasions the mathematics of concepts has been used as a means of warping justice.

The last building stone employed by the Continental commonlaw juristic science is its *Systematik*(systematism). The origin of the latter does not lie in the requirements of the practice of law. It is true, books that are merely practical, that are designed exclusively for the practice of law, must needs have a certain orderly arrangement; but this arrangement is designed merely to facilitate quick orientation; like the alphabetical arrangement of dictionaries, it has no effect whatever upon the content. The systematism of juristic science grew out of the necessities of teaching. It is the function of teaching to present the material to the learner in an orderly, lucidly organized arrangement. A learner will remember a few comprehensive truths more easily than a great number of unrelated details. While it is important for practical purposes to state at each point everything that refers to that point, a teacher will strive to formulate as many general principles as possible, and derive particulars from them. Hence the endeavor to group the legal phenomena as to which general statements can be made, and to discuss the legal relations to which the same rules are applicable, in the same chapter. It is true, these are external considerations, but probably the legal relations which have been grouped because the same rules, let us

温德沙伊德的说法，将法学当作法律渊源，无疑是将产妇与接生婆混为一谈。

完全与社会影响相隔离并存在于已有概念的逻辑推理中的规范的发现，很难被称为法律的创造，一种局限于此的法学也很难被看作是法律的渊源。不过，概念数学事实上从来没有达到过它的目的。这些概念在创设过程中人工的痕迹如此明显，以至于它们在权力的分配、合目的性考量和正义的趋向需要的时候总是容易变化。代理人缔结的交易是依代理人的意思还是依本人意思而成立，取决于何种构造可获得更令人满意的结果。承认这一点的话，我们就又一次认识到社会影响的有效性。此外，在无数的场合下，概念数学还被作为扭曲正义的工具。

欧陆共同法学采用的最后一种建构材料是 *Systematik*（体系理论）。体系理论的源头不在于法律实践的需要。的确，仅仅是注重实用的、专门为法律实践而撰写的书籍，（其内容）非得有某种有序的安排不可；但是如此安排只是为了便利快速的定位；就如同词典依照字母顺序排列，它并不会对内容造成影响。但是，法学中的体系论却已经超出了教学的需要。教学的功能是将材料以一种有序、明了、有条理的安排方式提供给学习者。与识记一堆杂乱无章的细节相比，学习者会更容易记住一些综合的事实。尽管，在讨论任一知识点时，将涉及到该知识点的所有东西都表述出来很重要，但教师还是会努力整理出尽可能多的一般原则，并从中推导出个别的内容。自此以后，教师努力将可给予一般性表述的多个法律现象进行分类，将可以用相同的规则处理的法律关系放在同一章进行探讨。尽管这些确实是外部考量，但是类型化的法律关系由于在不得不诉诸法律来执行它们时

say, of procedure apply in case resort is had to law to enforce them are related internally as well. The division of rights into real and obligatory rights, which is connected with the important distinction between *actiones in rem and in personam*, the orderly statement of the rules concerning *real* rights and concerning the law of inheritance on one hand and concerning contracts, damages, and other obligatory rights on the other, have originated here. Accordingly *Systematik* begins at Rome in the text-books. The system of Gaius, which surely was derived from an older source, dominates the teaching of law down to the time of Justinian and is found in the Institutes of the latter. In the Middle Ages and in modem times, the elucidation of Justinian's Institutes serves the purpose of an introduction to the study of law, and since the seventeenth century numerous books have been making their appearance in Germany which contain the whole body of legal material, arranged according to the system of the Institutes. It is followed by the French Civil Code and the Austrian Civil Code, and, with a few exceptions that touch the surface only, by the pandect system of the nineteenth century, which begins with Hugo and Heise, and by the German Civil Code.

At first jurists were not conscious, to any considerable extent, of the inner interrelationship of the legal institutions which was being expressed quite undesignedly by these systematic presentations. But in the course of time it became more conspicuous, and occupies the foreground in the systematic endeavors of the Ramists and of Donellus. Later the legal relations which were being dealt with together appeared as variations of the same legal relation. The periods of life appear as species of status; ownership and the other *real* rights, as classes of *real* rights. The more comprehensive legal relation receives a distinct name and a universal definition is being sought for it. The next step is, that all legal precepts which contain identical provisions for several related legal relations are no longer referred to these individual legal relations but to the legal concept which embraces them all; and in the end, unless there are particular reasons against doing so, everything

要适用相同的规则(如程序规则),因而它们内部也相互关联。将权利分为物权和债权与"对物诉讼"和"对人诉讼"之间的重要区别有关,这种有条不紊的涉及物权的规则表述与涉及继承、契约、损害赔偿及其他债权的规则表述两分正是来源于此。可见,体系论发端于古罗马的教科书。盖尤斯的体系也是来自于更为久远的原始文献,它支配着下至优士丁尼时代的教学方法,这一点可以在后者的巨著《法学阶梯》中发现。在中世纪和现代,对《法学阶梯》的阐明一直适于法律研究的入门需要,直到 17 世纪,德国才涌现了一大批书籍,它们拥有完整的内容,并且依照《法学阶梯》的体系来编排。这个传统的后继者包括《法国民法典》和《奥地利民法典》,它们略微动了一些皮毛,还包括 19 世纪的胡果、海瑟开创的潘德克顿体系,另外还有《德国民法典》。

起先,法学家并没有在任何可观的程度上意识到——在这些体系化的介绍十分偶然地表达出的法律制度中——内在的相互关系。然而,随着时间的流逝,这种倾向变得更为明显,拉米斯主义者和多内鲁斯的体系化方面的努力使这种倾向变得更为显著。接着,那些被放到一起讨论的不同法律关系被看作是同一种法律关系的变种。人一生中的不同时期以不同的法律地位出现;所有权和他物权都被归类为物权。更为复杂的一些法律关系获得了独特的名称,并且人们试图为其找到一般的定义。接下来的一步就是,所有包含处理若干不同法律关系的相同条款的的法律规定也不再被一一援用到这些个别的法律关系之上,而是援用到把它们全部包括进去的法律概念;除了有特别的反对理由,对这些关系之一规定的所有内容,被认为对所有的

that is predicated as to one of these relations is considered valid as to all of them. The achievement of *Systematik*, then, is the consistent continuation of the process of universalization. Accordingly we find that even the Romans had universalized a number of norms solely in the interest of systematic presentation, e. g. the norms about *actiones in rem* and *actiones in personam*, about *obligationes naturales*, about liability for fault and for delay in contractual relations. An admirable modern example of systematic universalization is Windscheid's doctrine of claims based on unjust enrichment. Systematic universalization is very closely related to juristic construction. The Romans very often employ universalization for purposes of pure construction. When they subsumed the agreements for work, labor, and services under the *locatio conductio* (contract for letting and hiring), their object was to make them actionable *contractus*. The attempt to make barter actionable in the same way has, it is true, failed.

The German Historical School, however, went one step beyond this universalization. Even the *jurisprudence of constructions* was able to utilize for its purposes the fact that identical facts and identical legal effects occur in distinct legal relations. When the Romans construed the payment of an obligation by the surety as a purchase of the obligation, they did this on the basis of the observation of the fact that both in the payment of an obligation and in the purchase there is a counting out of money. They gave the same effect to the counting out of money in a case of payment that it would have in a case of purchase. In this case the counting out of money is lifted out of its connection, and is

这些法律关系都有效。体系论的成果就是持续地将学说的一般化进行下去。与此相似，我们在古罗马人那里也发现他们仅仅出于体系化的目的而对一些规范进行了一般化，例如对物诉讼和对人诉讼、自然之债、契约关系中的过失责任和延迟责任。体系性一般化的一个极好的现代范例就是温德沙伊德的不当得利基础之上的请求权。体系性的一般化与法学的推构解释存在很密切的联系。罗马人经常将一般化用于纯粹解释的目的。当他们把工作、劳动和服务这些协议涵摄到 *locatio conductio*〔1〕（租赁契约）之下的时候，他们的目的是让这些协议成为可诉契约。不过当他们想要以同样的方式把易货交易也变成可诉契约时，他们却失败了。

然而，德国的历史学派在此种一般化上却多跨了一步。即使是建构法学也可以为了它自身的目的而利用这样的事实论据——即相同的事实与相同的法律效果可以出现在不同的法律关系中。当古罗马人将保证人对（主）债务的清偿解释为债权购买的时候，他们的分析是基于对以下事实的观察，即不管是债务清偿还是债权购买，这里都要经过一次金钱的清点。所以，他们就给予保证人清偿债务和购买债权以相同的法律效果。这样，金钱的清点从两者的关系中被提取出来，作为一种独立的

---

〔1〕（拉）*locatio conductio*（租赁），罗马法中双务合意契约之一，表现为一方向另一方允诺以接受一笔报酬为条件使后者在一定时间内享用某物，或向其提供一系列服务或特定的劳作。严格地讲，租赁不是一种单独的契约，而是一些具有相同性质但有不同表现形式的契约总和。它可以划分为三类：物的租赁、雇佣租赁、承揽租赁。

treated as an independent legal transaction, the effect of which is the right to demand the transfer of the obligation. Likewise the construction of the *offene Handelsgesellschaft* (unlimited mercantile partnership) as a partnership contract with *mutua praepositio* of the partners is based upon the separation of a legal effect of the *praepositio*, of the power of agency, from the *praepositio*, and upon a combination of it with the partnership contract, which in its nature is quite foreign to the *praepositio*. The characteristic feature of this kind of construction is that a certain fact or a certain legal effect which is found only within the sphere of a legal relation as a whole is singled out and used as a building stone in the construction of another legal relation.

According to this method the German legal historians have been building the "general part" of the whole system of private law and of the law of obligations. It is based upon the conscious endeavor to utilize constructively certain facts and legal effects which occur again and again in the most diverse legal relations. On the same basis rest the doctrines of conditions, of qualification as to time, of error, of duress, and of fraud, of representation, alternative obligations, contracts for the benefit of third parties, of plurality of creditors and debtors, of payment, and of many other things. In connection with these, another universalization was introduced. A precept as to one of these elements which was found in the sources in connection with a certain legal relation was referred to this element as such in whatever legal relation it might be found. A typical illustration is the way in which the Continental common law juristic science dealt with the retroactive force of the condition. A series of decisions recorded in the sources, which referred exclusively to certain individual legal relations in which a condition occurred, or perhaps only to one individual case of that kind, was applied quite indiscriminately to every condition, whether it was contained in a testament, a marriage contract, a gift, a purchase, or the giving and taking of a pledge. The way the doctrine of mistake in a legal transaction was dealt with is stranger still. Interesting specimens of this method are also found in the doctrines of representation and of the protection of legal rights.

法律行为予以对待，而这样做的结果就是要求债的转移的权利。同样，他们把“*Offene Handelsgesellschaft*（负无限责任的商事合伙）”解释为一种合伙人之间具有相互监督关系的合伙契约，这种解释是基于代理权之监督与监督二者的法律效果不同，另外还基于监督与合伙契约的结合，后者性质上与监督完全无关。这种推构性解释的显著特征在于，仅在某种法律关系中出现的特定的事实或特定的法律效果作为一个整体被挑选出来，并作为另外一种法律关系建构的建筑材料。

按照这种方法，德国法律史学家建立起了整个私法体系和债法中的“总论部分”。这种体系的建立是来自于刻意的努力，这种努力建设性地利用了屡次出现的、十分不同的法律关系。在这同一个基础之上，建立了条件学说、附期限学说、错误学说、胁迫学说、欺诈学说、代理学说、选择之债学说、利益第三人契约的学说、多数债权人债务人学说、清偿学说以及其他很多学说。与此相联系的另一种一般化方法也被引入了进来。与这些因素之一——它在与某种法律关系有关的原始文献中被发现——相关的法律规定也被运用到其他任何具有这种元素的法律关系中。欧陆共同法中典型的例子就是所谓的条件的追溯力。原始文献中收录的一系列裁决——它们全都涉及某条件出现于其中的个别法律关系或者个案——必须毫无差别地适用于每一个条件，而不管该条件是否包含在遗嘱、婚约、赠与、买卖、或是担保物的给予及取得之中。但是法律行为中的误解学说似乎是个例外。这种方法的例子还有很多，比如代理学说和法定权利的保护等等。

*Sysiematik* was of much greater importance for the notion of a perfect legal system than was the mathematics of conceptions. A system indeed is nothing more than an arrangement of that which is in existence, but in addition it always gives rise to a conception of the whole. Before long the legal system was treated as if it comprised not only the legal material in hand but the whole law. The concepts, whose content no longer was individual legal relations but whole classes of legal relations, became so comprehensive that they took on the appearance of logical categories, which comprised the whole world of legal phenomena. If there was something that was not subsumed under the concept of contract of a certain kind, it was a contract *simpliciter*; if it was not a contract, it was a legal transaction; and if it was not a legal transaction, it was a juristic fact, to say the least. A private right was either a right of family law, a *real* right, or an obligatory right. Much skill was employed to determine whether proscriptive rights and perpetual charges upon land belonged under the former or the latter head, or whether possibly they were to be placed under a third. Copyright and the right to one's name seemed to defy classification under any of these heads. Accordingly the right to one's name became a right of personality, the *real* rights became absolute rights, which included among other things the law of copyright. The important thing was that a place was found for everything in the legal system, and that norms for decision, too, were to be found at each of these places. As it was, the Continental common law possessed a vast wealth of norms, but this procedure of making every norm for decision which had been created for a given legal relation or for a given case applicable to all kinds of legal relations, related and unrelated, increased the number of norms a thousand-fold. The life-work of Schloss-

对于一个完善的法律体系观念而言，体系论相较于概念数学来说更为重要。一个体系事实上不过是对存在物的排列，但除此之外，它总是导致整体的观念。不久，法律体系不仅被看作是包含现有的法律材料，而且还包含法整体。法律概念——它的内容已经不仅仅是单个的法律关系，而是法律关系的整个类别——它的内容如此广泛，以至于它们以合乎逻辑之范畴的形式表现出来，这些范畴囊括了整个法律现象界。如果存在某些无法被某类契约的概念涵摄的东西，那它就是绝对契约；[1]如果它不是契约，那么就是法律行为；如果它也不是一种法律行为，那至少可以说它是一种法律事实。一种私权，要么是家庭法上的权利，要么是物权，要么是债权。为了确定排斥权和永久性土地负担究竟是属于上述哪一种类型的权利，抑或很可能需要另外创设一种新的类型权利来统领它，需要运用很多技巧。而著作权和姓名权似乎不能归入上述的任何一种。最终姓名权成为了一种人格权，而物权变成了一种包含著作权的绝对权。重要的是我们要为法律体系中的每一样东西找到它的位置，而裁判规范也要能在这样的每个位置上找到。欧陆共同法本来就已经拥有数量惊人的法律规范了，但是这种建构方法使得每个裁判规范——本为某特定法律关系或特定情形而创设——能适用于所有类型的相关或不相关的法律关系，并使得规范的数目增长了一千倍。施洛斯曼毕生的事

〔1〕 这里指不可被概念和推构解释加以定性归类的契约。*simpliciter*，胡塞尔又称之为“单纯者”，此类现象原本非为人类知性所建构或加工。例如：“树，之为单纯者属于自然的物理事物，不是作为所知觉而被知觉的树。”

mann was directed chiefly against this kind of finding of norms.

Manifestly this method of dealing with the law presented something labeled *Systematik* that no longer was *Systematik* at all. Its object was not a presentation of the material of the sources in an appropriate arrangement but instead an attempt to present an entirely new content. It surely is not one and the same thing that a norm which decides a case of mistake in a transaction of purchase be limited to a transaction of purchase and that its scope be extended to every contract, nay, what is more, to every legal transaction. Moreover these jurists were not drawing inferences from analogy. Every analogy must be justified by a similarity of legal situation. But the jurists were proceeding here as if all of these norms for decision had been laid down as principles in the *corpus iuris*, and as if the individual decisions of the sources were merely applications of a principle applicable to all of the legal situations that had been collected. This was indeed a gain in the number of norms, but to a great degree it was a questionable gain, for in the last analysis the important thing is the kind and nature of the norms. A decision that might be quite satisfactory for an individual case will often be ill adapted to the legal relation as a whole. In most cases it will be absolutely impossible to find a norm that will be equally applicable everywhere, e. g. in the law of the family, of things, of obligations, and of inheritance. In fact the doctrines of conditions, of plurality of creditors and debtors, of conflict of claims, contain more controversial questions than legal propositions. Every jurist knows how to deal with a contract of insurance or of assumption of an obligation; but what if these two contracts, which are in no wise related to each other, are submitted to him as contracts for the benefit of third persons? In consequence of all this, the Continental common law juristic science of the nineteenth century consists of two quite distinct groups of material. The law of persons, things, contracts, and the family deals with formations that are imbued with life; the general part of the system and the general part of the law of obligations is a playground for bloodless abstractions that scarcely touch the earth with their toes. In the *Systematik* of the historical

业主要就是为了反对这种发现规范的方法。

很显然,这种处理法律的方式展现了某种纯粹是徒有"体系"虚名的东西。它的目标已经不是为了通过恰当的安排来陈述文献材料,相反已经是为了努力提出新内容。很显然,这已经不是之前的那种规范了,之前决定买卖交易中错误的案件运用的规范仅仅限于买卖交易,但是现在的这种规范的适用范围扩展至全部契约,甚至全部的法律行为。此外,这些法学家也并不是在使用类推推理。任何类推必须证成法律情势的相似性。这些法学家在处置案件的时候似乎把这些用来判决的规范当作是《国法大全》里面的原则了,似乎个案判决只不过就是将能够适用于全部法律情势的原则应用于个案而已。在规范的数量上,这确实是一种收获,但是这种收获在很大程度上是值得怀疑的,因为归根到底,要紧的是规范的种类和性质。能够很好地满足某个个案的裁决在应用到作为整体的法律关系时常常会很不恰当。在大多数案件中,想要寻找到在各个地方——例如在家庭法、物权法、债法和继承法领域内——都可以适用的规范是完全不可能的。事实上,在条件学说、复数债权人债务人学说、请求权冲突学说中包含着比法律命题本身更多的争议。每个法学家都知道怎么处理保险契约或债务承担契约;但是如果这两种契约之间绝没有一点关联,我们怎么把它们都涵摄到利益第三人契约之下呢?由于这个原因,19 世纪欧陆共同法法学由两组相当不同的材料组成。人身法、物权法、契约法以及与生活的塑造息息相关的家庭法;整个体系中的(民法)总论和债法总论都是毫无生气的概念抽象的游乐场,它们的脚趾很少触及生活的地面。在历史学派的体系论中,在将思维形式转化为规范的过程中持

school, the great antinomy of juristic science, which is continually at work transmuting forms of thought into norms, is celebrating its last, its most fateful triumph.

But we must not undervalue *Systematik* on this account. It can render only those services for which it exists. *Systematik* is not juristic science, and therefore its function is not to put the law into condition to meet the requirements of the administration of justice. If it is misused for this purpose, as was done by the Continental common law juristic science, it is in fact a construction, but a construction undertaken according to points of view quite other than those of juristic science, a construction in which the economic and social relations in which the legal institutions appear are being given expression to, at most , by sheer accident only. Undoubtedly a great deal of juristic scholasticism must be attributed to the Continental common law systematic constructions.

We must not however overlook an important difference between the most important, who are also the most numerous, adherents of the Historical School, on one hand and the jurists of other schools on the other. No other jurists were as indifferent as they to the question whether or not the results of their constructions or of their systematic finding of norms were in harmony with their sense of justice. This must be attributed in part to their conception of the function of juristic science. Inasmuch as it was primarily incumbent upon them to ascertain the intention of the originator of the legal proposition, they were in a position to decline to assume personal responsibility for the decision. Again, the fact that the jurists who have attained a great reputation in the Historical School were scholars rather than men of affairs, as one might expect in view of the preponderantly scientific trend of this school, may have been of still greater importance. A professor of anatomy used to ask a student, who, while dissecting a corpse was trying to rectify a false cut by following it up with a right one, whether he would also rectify his false cuts in the case of an operation on a patient. For there is a difference between developing one's manual skill and one's acumen on a *corpus vile* and on living human flesh.

续发挥作用的法学之巨大悖论,正在庆祝它最后的、最为致命的胜利。

但是,我们也不能因此低估了体系论。它只能够为它存在的理由服务。体系论不是法学,因此它的功能不是使法律适于满足司法的要求。如果它为此目的而被误用——如同欧陆共同法法学所做的——那么它实际上就是一个构架,只是此构架是按照与法学的其他构架迥异的视角着手进行的,此构架内,显现法律制度的经济和社会关系至多是在纯粹偶然的情况下才得以表达。毫无疑问,相当多的法律经院哲学可归咎于欧陆共同法的体系构架。

另一方面,我们也不能忽略在这些最重要的——同时也是人数最多的——历史学派拥趸们与其他学派的法学家之间的重要差别。再也没有任何其他法学家对于——他们构架的结果或者他们体系化的规范发现的结果是否与他们的正义感一致——这个问题会比他们更加无动于衷。这一状况部分必须归因于他们在法学功能问题上所采取的态度。由于他们将自己的主要职责看成是确定法律命题原初创设者的意图,因而他们能够倾向于为法律裁决承担个人责任。再者,在历史学派中赢得巨大声誉的法学家是学者而非实务人士——正如考虑到该学派的主要学术倾向的人所能够预料的那样——这一事实可能还具有更大的重要性。一个解剖学教授问他的一个正在解剖尸体的解剖学学生,该生正在试图以正确的刀法来纠正刚刚的错误刀法,解剖学教授问他,要是在病人身上做手术时,他是不是也会如此纠正。因为,在尸体上培养一个人的手工技巧和敏锐与在活生生的人体上培养他的手工技巧和敏锐,二者显然有别。

This discussion has led us to a point where we can survey the work of the Continental common law juristic science in its totality. Of course, for a long time no thinking person has failed to realize the obvious truth that the Continental common law is not the law of Rome nor even that of Justinian. If one should eliminate from the *Manuel* of Girard everything that refers to the ante-Justinianian law, one would by no means have a text-book of pandect law. The text-books of Puchta or of Arndt, even though they utterly ignore post-Roman creation of law, and confine their presentations to Roman legal material, are something quite different from dogmatic presentations of Justinianian law. A further question is wherein these differences consist; as far as I can see, it is in creation of concepts, in constructions, and in *Systematik*.

There can be no doubt that the pandectists of the Historical School were honestly convinced that they were defining the legal concepts according to the law of Justinian. But in actual fact they did not do this. Every one of their concepts had to be formulated at the outset so as to include not only the Roman but also the modern phenomena. The definition of ownership indeed was suitable for the *fundus optumus maxumus*, which was being discussed by the jurists of a time as late as the days of the Republic, but it had to cover not only this but also the ownership of the feudal lord and of the holder of shares of stock. Even if the same words had been used by Labeo and Sabinus, they would have meant something different in the mouths of the latter from what they would mean in the mouths of Vangerow and Windscheid. In the case of more concrete concepts, especially those of the law of pledge or of the law of obligations (for an example, let

此种讨论已经让我们可以对欧陆共同法学作一个通盘考察。当然，任何一个理性的人都不可能长时间体认不到这样一个显而易见的事实，即欧陆共同法并非罗马法，甚至也不是优士丁尼法。如果我们将《吉拉德手稿》谈到优士丁尼之前的法律全部排除的话，那么无论如何我们都不可能有潘德克顿法的教科书了。尽管普赫塔或阿恩特的教科书完全忽略了后罗马时代的法律创造并且将他们的说明限于古罗马法律材料，但是他们所写的教科书还是与优士丁尼法的教条式说明存在很大的不同。接下来这个进一步的问题就是他们的不同之处在哪里；就我所知，概念创设、解释和体系论构成了他们的不同之处。

毋庸置疑，历史学派中的潘德克顿派真诚地相信，他们都是依照优士丁尼法来对法律概念进行定义的。然而事实上，他们并不是这么做的。在他们最初确定法律概念的过程中，不管哪个概念，都不仅仅来自于古罗马，它还来自于现代现象。事实上，所有权的定义同最优越的土地[1]是相适应的，迟至罗马共和国时期人们还在讨论它，但是这一概念除了最优越的土地之外还必须涵盖封建领主和股份持有者的所有权。即使是拉贝尔和萨宾所使用的这个词，它的涵义也不同于凡格罗和温德沙伊德口中的所有权。在另一些更为具体的概念中，尤其是在担保法和债法（例如替代[2]之中，问题马上就显得很清楚

〔1〕 即没有任何法律上负担的土地。

〔2〕 （拉）*delegatio*（替代），债的更新形式之一，表现为单方面指定或准可某人接替原债关系中的债权人或债务人地位，代替债务人进行清偿或代替债权人接受清偿；这样，原债关系被新债关系取代。罗马法通过此种替代清偿实现债权或债务的移转。

us say, *delegatio*) this fact is apparent at once. No doubt the pandectists of the Historical School endeavor to state every legal proposition in the form in which it was to be valid according to the law of Justinian. But their very statement was a construction of it. Every word they employed was not used with reference to the Roman situations but was adapted to the modern German relations. In all these respects they were children of their time, and — a fact that is still more significant — they were the heirs of the practitioners from the eleventh to the eighteenth century. The fact that their *Systematik* was not that of the Roman jurists would have made no difference. Every legal historian creates a system for his presentation which in his opinion is most appropriate to the matter he is presenting. But their system was not a system of an historical presentation of the law of Justinian, but a picture, clumsy, schematic, and imperfect though it was, of the legal organization of a modern society. At the same time, thanks to their *Systematik* they arrived at a system of doctrine that was utterly foreign to the doctrine of the Romans; and this fact is of so much greater importance in view of the fact that many, e. g. Savigny, Puchta, Unger, consider the dogmatic fruitfulness of the system the chief element of value in the science of law.

The day of the Continental common law juristic science is done. The Civil Code for the German Empire has driven it out of its last place of refuge, and no power in the world will be able to restore its glory that has passed away. Whatsoever of value its labors of more than two thousand years have produced must be preserved for the future by the sociological science of law. But the latter will not be a juristic science. The deathless function of all juristic science, however, i. e. to make the law subserve the ever changing, ever new needs of life, will remain. No code will be able to destroy it. For this task there will always have to be a juristic science, though it may be of a nature different from that of the present, though it may employ other instrumentalities, and have other aims. That it will be different from that of the present is self-evident; for every age has not only its own

了。历史法学中的潘德克顿学者确实是努力地想要严格依照优士丁尼法来表述每个法律命题。但是他们的表述只是在优士丁尼法之上所进行的解释。他们所用的每一个词语都不是用来指称罗马的情形的,而是被改变来适应现代德国的经济社会关系。不管从哪个方面来说,法律史学家都是他们那个时代的孩子,更为显著的一个事实是——他们都是从11世纪至18世纪的执业者的继承人。他们的系统与古罗马人的系统并不相同,此等事实没有什么影响。每一个法律史学家都创造出一套自己认为最切合他所述事物的叙述体系。但是他们的体系并不是优士丁尼法的历史叙述的体系,他们的体系毋宁是一幅现代社会法律体制的图景,尽管这一图景尚存在粗糙、简略、不完美这些缺陷。尽管如此,正因为他们有了(独特的)体系论,他们才获得了一个完全不同于古罗马的学说体系;鉴于诸如萨维尼、普赫塔、昂格尔等很多人认为此种体系的教条主义的成效是法学价值的主要成分,获得一个完全不同于古罗马的学说体系这一事实才会变得如此重要得多。

欧陆共同法学的时代已经终结了。《德国民法典》已经将它从最后的避难所中逐离,这个世界上的任何一种力量都无法让它恢复逝去的荣耀。它两千多年间的任何工作价值,都必须由法律社会学为未来而保存,但是后者将不再是法学。不过,所有法学永恒的功能——例如使法律服务于变动不居、永远更新的生活需要——将得到保留。没有任何法典可以毁灭它。尽管(将来的)法学可能在本质上不同于当前,可能采用其他的手段或是会拥有其他目标,但是为了实现这个功能,它将一直留存下去。但是,不言而喻,它将不同于现在的法学;因为每一个时代不止是拥有它

art, its own science, religion, and philosophy, but also its own juristic science. The Roman jurists, too, presented something different in each century. Justinian presented something different from that which the classical jurists presented; and the Romanists of the Middle Ages and of modern times do not present the Roman law of Justinian.

In the same way, the juristic science of the future, though organically connected with the traditional materials, will find that it must refashion these materials in order to satisfy the new requirements. It is true that the sociological science of law must needs furnish the scientific basis; but it can take root only in a soil which has been furrowed and plowed by the Continental common law juristic science. There will be a repetition of the process that has been going on wherever sciences have grown out of practical activities. The natural sciences have repaid all their borrowings from medicine with compound interest. The juristic science of the future, I believe, will discard for good and always all the mummery of creation of abstract concepts and of construction. But it must be admitted that these things always only served the sole purpose of concealing a necessary social process from the eyes of busybodies. Free finding of law is not, as some have thought, a finding of law that disregards the statute, but a finding of law that is untrammeled by useless and superfluous confinement in abstraction and construction.

In the years last past many a bitter word has been spoken concerning "pandectology," and although these words were not spoken by me, I will not deny that they were spoken, for I know that I bear a great deal of responsibility in the matter. In the heat of battle, this was justified, and perhaps it was necessary. I therefore feel it incumbent upon myself to point out the great achievements of "pandectology." I would remain true especially to the memory of Bernhard Windscheid. In my youth I studied his writings with great enthusiasm, and if I and those who are pressing forward with me have gone beyond him, we are indebted to his teachings for it. Time has done the rest. Before long the eyes of the last of the German jurists that have seen a living Continental common law will have been closed in death; the last voice that has taught a living Continental common law will have been silenced. Let them see to it that the valuable creations of the labors of two thousand years, separated like wheat from the chaff, are

自己独有的艺术、科学、宗教和哲学,还有它自己独有的法学。罗马法学家也是如此,他们在每个世纪呈献了不同的东西。优士丁尼展示了不同于古典法学家的东西;中世纪和现代的罗马主义者也没有(重复)展现优士丁尼的罗马法。

同样地,未来的法学,尽管与传统的素材有机相连,但还是会发现,它必须对这些传统材料进行翻新,从而满足新时代的需要。法社会学必然要提供科学的基础;但是它必须扎根于欧陆共同法学业已耕耘过的土壤之上。当科学与实践活动脱节的时候,这一过程将不断地再现和重复。自然科学已经将所借之物连本带息地偿还给了医学。未来的法学,我坚信,将会永久地抛弃所有抽象概念和建构的可笑创造。必须承认,这些东西总是服务于唯一的目的:对爱管闲事的人们隐瞒必然的社会进程。法律的自由发现并非如某些人所想的那样不重视制定法,倒不如说是不为抽象和建构中无用冗余的限制所羁绊。

在刚过去的几年中,"潘德克顿法学"遭到了严酷的批判。尽管这些批判并非出自我口,但我不会否认这些批判,因为我知道,我在此事上负有很大的责任。在白热化的论战中,这是正当的,或许还是必要的。因此,我觉得自己有责任指出"潘德克顿法学"的伟大成就。我还将一如既往特别忠实地怀念伯恩哈德·温德沙伊德。在我年轻时,我曾以极大的热情学习他的作品,假使我以及与我奋力同行的人可能超越他的话,我们都会感谢他的教导。时间已经湮灭了其余的痕迹。过不了多久,曾看到过鲜活的欧陆共同法的德国法学家将阖然长辞;最后一个教授欧陆共同法的声音也将要就此沉默。务必让他们将这两千年来劳动的珍贵创造物——如同麦子分离于糠秕那样去芜存菁——

handed down to the coming generation. What they do not save will be lost forever. But the three volumes of Windscheid's Pandects will remain as a link between a great past and an unknown future. And therefore we shall be grateful to Kipp for keeping this treasure abreast of the times with a tireless diligence that is worthy of its great creator.

传给下一代。他们没有保存下来的,将永远地遗失。但是温德沙伊德三卷本的《潘德克顿》仍将成为架起伟大的过去与未知的未来之间的桥梁。我们得感谢基普保全了这一顺应时代的宝藏,他那不倦的勤奋无愧于该宝藏的伟大创造者。

# XV

# The Function Of Juristic Science

The role of juristic science in history is quite different from everything that men have from time to time thought to be its function, just as our notions of the meaning of our activities can give us no information about their true significance. Juristic science has never been what, at the present time, it is generally thought to be, i. e. a presentation of that which has been delivered to us by tradition as law, nor has it ever been a set of rules directing us how to proceed on the basis of the rules that have been delivered to us as law. A juristic literature which has no other aims, such as the English text-books and in part our own *Lehrbücher*, is not juristic science, and no legal system could subsist on intellectual juristic labor that does not do more than that. There must always be a creative juristic science. But in order to appreciate its labors from every point of view, we must consider separately the three elements that are comprised in it, i. e. the element relating to the function of the attorney; the element relating to the legal transaction; and the element relating to the judicial function.

Let us begin with the function of the attorney. The forms of the procedure at law, in a sense, are the weapons which society, or the state in the name of society, has placed at the disposal of conflicting interests. The means that society has provided for this purpose are limited in number; for society could not possibly provide aid for all interests that are being contested or attacked. It must select those that are most important and most worthy of assistance. But no society could at the outset state once for all which interests it will protect; for in every developing, progressive society new interests are continually

# 第十五章　法学的功能

法学在历史上的作用不同于其功能，尽管两者常被人混为一谈，正如仅从行为本身，无法探知当事人的真正意图一样。法学从来不是现在通常被人们所认为的那样——亦即，法学是对传统上作为法律提供给我们的那种东西的说明；法学也从来不是指导我们按照法律规则的基本原理行事的一系列规则。一部没有任何其他意图的法学著作，比如英国的教科书以及某些我们自己的教科书，(其实)不是法学，而且没有一种法律制度会维系于仅仅那种程度的法学智力劳动之上，总是必须有一种创造性的法学才行。不过为了从每个角度都能正确评价法学劳动，我们必须将它包含的三个要素分别予以考虑，这三个要素分别是：律师功能；法律行为；司法功能。

让我们首先讨论律师的功能。在某种意义上，法律诉讼程序的构造是一种武器——社会或以社会为名义的国家在处理利益冲突时设置的武器。社会为此目的而提供的解决手段数量有限；因为社会不可能为所有相互对抗或侵害的利益都提供帮助。它必须选择那些最重要和最值得援助的利益。不过没有哪个社会能够从一开始即能立刻说出它要保护的所有利益都是哪些；因为在每一个发展、前进着的社会，新的利益日显重要，并且那些业已

gaining importance, and those that have already been recognized are continually being subjected to new attacks. Whether society will or will not protect an interest is determined by the courts. It is the function of the attorney to persuade the court that society has provided a remedy for the interest which he represents. This is the art of *Klagebegründung* (establishing the basis for an action) Secondly, he must show the court that the interest in question is worthy of protection. This is the art of *Beweisführung*(making proof). If the attorney has persuaded the court, he has secured protection for an interest to which it had been denied until then, or he has secured protection against an attack to which the interest had been exposed until then. This, doubtless, is a step forward in legal development, which he has brought about by his individuai activity.

The proceeding at law originally merely served the purpose of preventing feuds or of mitigating and regulating them. By skillfully developing the art of establishing the bases for actions, the inventive genius of the attorneys has brought it about that the legal proceeding also grants satisfaction for injury suffered, and that it finally becomes a universal remedy for the establishment of justice without a feud. The book of Declaireil, entitled *Les preuves judiciaires en droit franc*, which in general affords the most profound insight into the nature of the most ancient form of legal proceeding, has shown that the law of proof owes its origin, growth, and development to the activity of the parties; that it was not created by the judges prescribing the mode of proof to the parties, but by the parties continually seeking and finding new ways of persuading the courts of the justice of their respective causes. The forms established for the pursuit of one's right, for the making of proof, for compulsory execution, are given at all times by the traditional organization of the courts, by the content and the nature of the means at the disposal of the courts for giving effect to their powers, by the form of the proceeding at law. But it is the business of the attorney to adapt these over and over again and again to the attainment of new ends. The attorney who for the first time brought the action *de arboribus succisis* when he brought suit for cutting down vines would have obtained the same protection for the interest in vines that bad already been secured for the interest in trees if he had not made the mistake as to form that Gaius speaks of. A similar service

获得认可的利益正在持续受到新的攻击。社会是否将会或不会保护一种利益,这个问题要由法院来判断。律师的功能即是说服法院,社会已经为他所代言的那种利益提供了救济。这是诉求表达的艺术(为诉讼奠定基础)。其次,他必须向法院表明,所述利益值得保护。这是*Beweisführung*(论证)的艺术。如果该律师说服了法院,他就为在此之前一直受到否定的利益求得一条保护之道,或者说,他为那种在此之前一直受到攻击的利益寻得了保护。无疑,这是法律发展中向前迈的一步,这一步是由他的个人行为带来的。

法律诉讼程序最初仅仅是为了避免或减轻、控制长期争斗。通过富有技巧性的发展建立诉讼基础的艺术,律师的创造性天才使得法律诉讼为受到的损害提供了补偿,并且使诉讼最后变成实现不会带来世仇之正义的一般性救济。德克勒赫伊的名为《法兰克时期的司法证据》的书,大体上深刻阐释了最古老的法律诉讼形式;该书已经表明证据法的萌芽、成长以及发展均归功于当事人的相关活动;它并非是由为当事人指定好了证据模式的法官所创造,而是由当事人在不断探索并发现说服审理其案件之法庭的新方法中创造的。为了权利实现、进行证明以及强制执行而建立的诉讼程式,一直都是由法院的传统结构所孕育,由法院——为赋予其权力以法律效果——争议处理手段的内容和性质所决定,并取决于法律诉讼程序的形式。但是将这些诉讼程式一再地改变并使之适应新的目的,则是律师的事。当一个律师起诉要求砍倒葡萄藤,并选择了修剪树枝这种诉讼程式时,如果他没有弄错盖尤斯曾经说过的诉讼程式,那么与他在葡萄树中的

was rendered by the German attorney who, according to Hedemann's report, brought action in order to have the defendant enjoined from defaming a woman, and by that other attorney who brought about the well-known *Freskenurteil* of the Imperial Court(*Reichsgericht*).

The branch of juristic science that deals with the legal transaction is chiefly concerned with the legal document, although it is also concerned, of course, with the oral transaction. The legal document, like the legal transaction in general, does not exist exclusively for use in the proceeding at law. Its chief function is to provide the order of the legal relation. It is the task of the draftsman of the legal document to organize the relation that the parties are about to establish, to find the legal means whereby their objects can be realized, to state their duties and obligations in correct legal terms. This order, which is based on the document, is in itself a product of creative juristic science. That which the parties vaguely had in mind is given a fixed, definite, tangible form by the jurist, without which it could not exist. As a result each one of the parties concerned knows exactly what he is to do and not to do. It is well established that the jurists who were drawing up legal documents have created the *Kommenda*, and the economic community, i. e. the right of the single heir (*Anerbenrecht*) among the German-Austrian peasantry. But it is immaterial whether the legal relation is a new one in its entirety; the insertion of a clause into a well-known contractual form may be a creative act.

But the branch of juristic science that deals with legal transactions must not content itself with merely organizing; it must make

利益所受到的保护相同，他在葡萄藤上的利益也将获得同样的保护。根据黑德曼的报告，德国律师也提供相似的服务，比如为了阻止被告诋毁一个女人而提起诉讼，再比如众所周知的帝国法院的壁画裁决[1]中律师所提供的诉讼服务。

尽管处理法律行为的法学部门当然会涉及到口头行为，但它主要与法律书面文件相关联。法律文件，比如法律行为，通常并不单单为了在法律诉讼程序中用到而存在。它的主要功能是为了提供法律关系的秩序。构建当事人打算建立的关系，找到可以实现他们目标的法律途径，并用正确的法律术语来表述彼此的权利义务关系，这些是法律文件起草人的任务。立基于该法律文件上的这种秩序，本身就是创造性法学的一个产物。法学家将当事人头脑中不甚明朗的想法转变成了一种固定的、明确的、可感知的形式，没有法学家，后者不可能存在。由此，相关的当事人一方准确地了解他将做什么、不做什么。很容易证实，草拟法律文件的法学家已经创造出了康孟达和经济共同体，亦即在德裔奥地利农民阶层中单一继承人（*Anerbenrecht*）的权利。但法律关系是否是一个全新的东西并不重要；在一个众所周知的契约形式中插入一个条款，这可能就是一个创造性的行为。

但是处理法律行为的法学分支不可仅仅满足于法律文件的

---

〔1〕 德国帝国法院于 1912 年应一个著名画家的要求，责令柏林一个别墅的主人将修改过的一幅壁画恢复原状，因为对该壁画的修改只改变了该建筑物的外观而对该建筑物的功能毫无影响。该判决传达的信息是，在德国，建筑物的所有人不能对建筑作品随心所欲地翻修、改建和扩建，即须受著作权法的限制。

provision for the protection of the products of its labor against attack and violation. We are not concerned exclusively, nor even primarily, with the case in which recourse is had to law. The forms handed down by Cato refer both to actionable and, with a single exception, non-actionable agreements, but it is certain that *iuramentum*, *satisdatio*, *pignus* are of much greater importance than *actio* and *exceptio*. The branch of juristic science that deals with legal transactions has made extensive contributions particularly to the development, if not to the invention, of security without resort to litigation, from the Roman *fiducia* and the ordinance of German city law down to the modern *Vinkulationsgeschäft*. The more imperfect the administration of justice, the more seriously people will endeavor to put the transaction in a form that makes resort to law unnecessary. Descriptions of commerce in the Orient show to what lengths people will go in order to attain this end. Nevertheless the chief function of the branch of juristic science that deals with legal transactions is to put the relation into such form as will enable it to prevail even if resort is had to litigation, and the parties are interested not only in having a legally enforceable cause of action but chiefly in a proceeding that is free from difficulties and delays and does not involve much expense. Up to this point, then, the aims of the branch of juristic science that deals with legal transactions are not essentially different from those of the branch that deals with the function of the attorney. The object of this branch like that of the other is to utilize the means that are at hand for the best possible protection of the interests in question. Like the branch that deals with the function of the attorney, it does creative work for interests that without it would either be not protected at all or, at best, very imperfectly, that are indebted to it either for all the protection they receive or, at least, for the fact that the protection they receive is effective. And often enough it is a protection that the existing law

编制;它还必须针对该法学劳动成果可能遭受的攻击和违反制定保护条款。我们并非仅仅,甚至主要不是关心诉诸法律的事例。由加图传下来的诉讼程式既包括可诉的协议,又包括不可诉的协议(有一个例外),但宣誓、诉讼担保、质押肯定比诉权和抗辩重要得多。从罗马法上的信托、德国城市法上的条例到现代的凭单借贷协议[1],处理法律行为的法学分支特别对于不诉诸诉讼之保证的发展——如果不是说对它的创立——发挥了重大作用。司法越不完善,民众就越努力地使得交易采取一种不必诉诸法律的形式。在东方,关于贸易的描述表明人民为达此目标而付出的努力程度。尽管如此,但处理法律行为的法学分支,其主要功能还是将那种关系纳入到可以使之普及的形式——即使当事人不得不诉诸法律诉讼,并且,他不仅对拥有一个法律上可执行的诉讼根据感兴趣,而且主要对没有困难和拖延、以及无需支付很多花费的诉讼程序感兴趣。为达此要求,处理法律行为的法学分支的目标就与涉及律师功能的法学分支的目标,二者本质上并无什么不同。二者的目标都是为了利用手边的工具,为涉争利益提供最佳可能的保护。和涉及律师功能的法学分支一样,处理法律行为的法学分支为那些利益作出了创造性的工作——那些利益或是未获得任何保护或是最多受到非常微弱的保护,(而现在)那些利益或是由于受到所有的这些保护而受惠,或者至少由于受到了有效的保护而受惠。而且大多数时候,这种保护,现行法

〔1〕 一种常见的商业协议:根据可流通提货单和汇票而装货的卖方基于该票据从其借款人处获得信贷。

was inclined to deny to them. The pledge in the form of a sale with right of repurchase, the forbidden loan at interest as the *Kommenda*, unenforceable obligations made effectual by means of contractual penalties or bills of exchange, are so many triumphs of this branch of juristic science over backward or undeveloped administration of law.

The work of the attorney-at-law and of the lawyer who draws up legal documents, therefore, is a technical one. They must, in the first place, get a clear understanding, through first-hand observation and study, of the interests that are entrusted to them in order that they may be enabled to make them comprehensible to the courts, and, by making proof, induce the courts to take cognizance of them. The imperfection of human nature, limited means and limited understanding, with which the courts are afflicted like all other creations of the human mind, render a technique of this sort indispensable. It would be superfluous if the courts were omnipotent and omniscient, just as we could dispense with the telescope and the microscope if our eyes were so much more efficient. Therefore every improvement of the tools of the profession renders a considerable amount of juristic technique superfluous. Such improvements are the transition from the procedure by *legis actio* to the procedure by formula both in Rome and in England, the substitution of the direct procedure for the indirect one on the Continent, which was brought about by permitting a free evaluation of proof in the place of a restricted one.

The attorney and the lawyer who draws up legal documents attain their purpose only if they succeed in persuading the judge to adopt their views. Their labor is in vain unless the judge considers the remedy a suitable one, the proof admissible and sufficient, and—most important of all—recognizes the interest which is seeking protection as worthy of it. The judicial decision therefore is a decision of two questions. In the first place, it decides the technical question whether society is able and willing to grant protection to the interest that is being asserted, and whether the existence of the latter has been demonstrated to the satisfaction of the court; and in the second place it renders

是倾向于拒绝提供的。以含有买回权的销售形式存在的担保，作为康孟达形式存在的被禁止的附息贷款、不可强制执行的债务通过约定罚款或汇票的方式而获得实效性，相对于每况愈下或不发达的法律实施而言，上述事物的存在全都是这种法学分支的胜利。

因此，法律事务代理人的工作与起草法律文件之律师的工作具有技术性。为了让法院对于托付给他们管理的利益更容易理解，他们首先必须通过直接观察和研究对这些利益有一个清晰的认识，其次通过提出证据，劝导法院受理它们。与所有其他人类思维创造物一样，法院也会受困于人性的瑕疵、有限的方法及有限的理解力，因而需要这种不可或缺的技巧。如果法院是全知全能的，那么这种技巧则是多余的，正如倘使我们的肉眼具有无比高超的能力，我们就可以将望远镜和显微镜废弃不用。因此，该职业工具的每一次改进都会使得相当数量的法律技巧变得多余。那样的改进体现为：在英格兰和罗马，诉讼程序由法定诉讼发展为程式诉讼；在欧陆，直接诉讼程序代替间接诉讼程序，这种代替是由对证据的严格评价到允许证据的自由评价而带来的。

法律事务代理人和起草法律文件的律师只有成功说服法院接受他们的观点，才算达到他们的目的。除非法官认为救济恰当、证据可采且充分——最重要的是认识到：正寻求保护的此种利益值得保护，否则他们的工作是白费力气。因此，司法裁判是对两个问题的裁判。首先，它是对以下技术问题的判定：社会是否能够并乐意为正被主张的这种利益提供保护，以及对后者存在的证明是否已经让法院感到满意；其次，它对以下问题给予了一

an independent decision on the question whether the interest merits protection. And if it is true that the attorney and the draftsman cannot possibly limit their activity to representing interests that have already been recognized by the courts, but that they must be ready at all times to bring about the recognition of interests that are newly arising, it follows that they must again and again raise the technical question as well as the question whether the interest is worth protecting, and thereby again and again confront the judge with a new task.

The norm according to which the judge renders his decision is the outcome of a most complex proceeding. It was necessary for the attorney or the draftsman to have knowledge based on actual observation of the relation of life within which the conflict of interests had arisen, to put it into a form suitable for protection by law, and to demonstrate its existence to the judge from his own knowledge as far as possible, through the testimony of witnesses and experts, and by means of documents (in ancient days perhaps also by means of oracles, judgment of God, and the casting of lots). This is followed by a balancing of interests on the part of the judge, the determination of the question whether the interest merits protection. This in turn leads to universalization, reduction to unity, and finding of norms. Of course it is a matter of little importance whether the balancing of interests is done independently or on the basis of norms that are already in existence.

We have been considering the contributions made by the attorney, the draftsman, and the judge separately for the sake of a better understanding of the nature of the process as a whole. Ultimately, however, the contributions which the attorney, the draftsman, and the judge have made to the norm for decision must be fused into a unit in the norm itself. In fact often enough the judge, for lack of an attorney or of a draftsman, undertakes the technical problem himself. And he often enough solves it in a way quite different from the way the latter would have solved it. Just as all of these elements enter into the norm for decision, so they must also enter into the legal proposition, which contains a norm for decision; for the latter is merely a more developed form of the norm for decision. And in the legal propositions of judgemade law, which are to be found in the reasons given for the

个独立的判定:该利益是否值得保护。如果法律事务代理人和法律文件起草人的确不仅将他们的行为限于为这种已被法院所认可的利益代言,而且他们还必须时刻准备让正在新生的利益获得承认,那么由此可以断定,他们必须一再地提出技术性问题以及这些利益是否值得保护的问题,因此他们也必须带着新的任务一再出现在法官面前。

法官据以作出裁判的规范是一个非常复杂的诉讼程序的结果。法律事务代理人和法律文件起草人有必要拥有基于对生活关系——利益冲突发生于其中——实际观察之上的知识,并将该知识纳入适于法律提供保护的形式,还要尽可能从自身的知识出发,通过证人和专家的证词,以及通过书面文件(在古代或许还需要借助于神谕、神明裁判以及抽签的方式)等方式向法官证明这种知识的存在。接下来,法官通过对利益的权衡,对该利益是否值得保护这个问题作出判定。这反过来又会导致规范的一般化、统一化以及规范的发现。当然,利益权衡的工作是独立完成还是依据现有的规范而完成,这是一件无足轻重的事情。

为了更好地从整体上理解上述诉讼程序的性质,我们已经分别考察了法律事务代理人、法律文件起草人以及法官的贡献。然而,从根本上而言,法律事务代理人、法律文件起草人以及法官为裁判规范作出的贡献必须在规范本身中融为一体。事实上,由于缺乏法律事务代理人或法律文件起草人,法官经常必须自己解决上述技术性问题。而且他解决此问题的方法与后者应会采用的方法迥异。正如所有的这些元素加入到裁判规范当中一样,他们也必须加入到包含裁判规范的法律规定当中。在法官法的法律规定——我们将会在裁决理由中看到这些命题——中,我们发现所有的

decisions, we find all these elements side by side, to wit observation, putting into proper form, proof, balancing of interests by means of universalization, reduction to unity, and finding of norms. But in the legal propositions presented in juristic literature or in legislation, these elements have become intermingled and it is often difficult to separate them. The composition of the legal proposition appears historically only when the latter is traced back to its inception. I shall attempt to do this in the following discussion.

When the four men promulgated the law to the Salic Franks (*per tres malleos*), they most probably were sincerely convinced that they had not overlooked anything that was essential. Today every young jurist who is preparing himself for his examination finds out to his sorrow how greatly they were in error, how much more he must know about the law of the Salic Franks, merely in order to pass his examination, how small a portion of the whole was embodied in the *lex*.

For each homicide the *lex Salica* provided a wergild, graduated according to the rank of the person slain. These provisions are stated in a few, readily understood propositions. But in the background there is the whole of Frankish society, organized according to rank and other considerations. Who may demand the wergild? Who other than the guilty person, is obligated to pay it? What is the manner of payment? What happens if it is not paid? The number of such questions concerning the provisions about the wergild is infinite. On the basis of proof and of his own knowledge, the judge must find additional norms; and, on the basis of these norms, the judgment determines whether the plaintiffs are entitled to the wergild, whether the defendants are liable, whether or not it has been paid according to law. Of all of these questions, not a trace is to be found in the *lex Salica*; manifestly, because they had not yet been brought to the attention of the authors of the *lex*; because, unlike the very provisions about

这些元素并存,包括敏锐的观察,以恰当形式呈现的证据,通过规范的一般化、统一化以及规范的发现而进行的利益权衡。但是在法学文献或立法中提出的法律规定里,这些元素互相混杂,经常很难分离。法律规定的这种结构历史上看似乎只有当后者被追溯至它的开端时方会呈现。下面的讨论中我将努力区分这些元素。

当那四个人向萨利克—法兰克人(*per tres malleos*)宣传法律时,他们很可能真诚地相信,他们没有忽略任何必要的东西。今天,每一个正准备考试的年轻法科学生都会遗憾地发现他们的错误有多大,并且会了解,仅仅为了通过考试,他就必须知道多少有关萨利克—法兰克法的知识,还会发现,包含在 *lex*[1] 里这种法的内容占多小的比例。

对于每一个杀人者,《萨克利法》根据被杀死之人的等级,规定了凶手需要承担的不同等级的赔偿金额。这些规定以一些容易理解的法律规定的形式呈现。但是在背后,存在根据等级和其他考量组合而成的整个法兰克人社会。谁可以要求赔偿金?除了犯罪人,谁应当支付这笔赔偿金?支付方式是怎样的?如果赔偿金没有支付,又该当如何?围绕有关赔偿金之规定的类似上述的问题是无限的。基于证据和个人知识,法官必须找到额外的规范;并且基于这些规范,判决需要确定原告是否有权获得赔偿金、被告是否有责任,以及根据法律该赔偿金是否已经被支付。所有的这些问题,没有一个可以在《萨利克法》中寻得踪迹;很明显,因为这些问题还未引起《萨利克法》作者的注意;因为不像这些赔偿

〔1〕 即 *Lex Salic*,《萨利克法》。

the wergild, they had not yet been made the subject matter of the juristic science of the Salic Franks.

A legal proposition about a penalty to be paid by a thief to the person from whom the thing was stolen presupposes a rather definitely fixed right of ownership in movables. It follows therefore that there must have been rules about acquisition, loss, and forfeiture of the right of ownership, some notion as to the difference between a person who acquires property lawfully and a thief or a robber. The provisions as to a penalty to be paid by the abductor, in the case of abduction of a woman, to her father or to her relatives are manifestly based upon a certain order of the family in virtue of which the woman is under the power (*potestas*) of her male relatives, who also have the right to give her in marriage. The content of all of the norms for decision, therefore, that have been developed into legal propositions about wergild, theft, abduction of women is being eked out by norms for decision that have reference to the inner order of the clan, of ownership, of the family, and that have not yet been expressed in legal propositions.

This is the beginning of juristic science. It is concerned at the outset solely with a series of norms for decision that can be made the bases of judicial decisions. These norms indeed are connected with other norms for decision which are given by the relations of human life. But these are as yet unknown to juristic science; they lie beyond its horizon, and the judge acquires them unconsciously from observation of the relations of life. But the more the science of law develops, the greater is its sphere, the deeper it penetrates, and the greater are its efforts to prepare for immediate use in the administration of justice not only the ultimate norms for decision but also those that these latter

金规定本身，这些问题尚未成为萨利克—法兰克法学的研究主题。

一个关于窃贼向被窃失主支付赎罪金的法律规定的先决条件是：被窃失主对动产享有相当肯定明确的所有权。因此可以断定，该法典必定存在有关取得、损失以及所有权丧失的一些规则，肯定还包含关于合法取得财产的人与窃贼或强盗之间区别的一些观念。在诱拐妇女的情形下，有关诱拐者需要向被诱拐人父亲或其亲戚支付赔偿金的规定明显是建立在家庭的特定秩序之上，依据这种秩序，妇女处于其男性亲戚的支配权（*potestas*）[1]之下，这些男性亲戚也有权把她嫁出去。因此，所有的这些已在有关杀人者所付赔偿金、妇女诱拐等法律规定中出现的裁判规范的内容正在获得那些关涉到部族、所有制、家庭等内部秩序的裁判规范——这些裁判规范尚未以法律规定的形式体现——的补充。

这是法学的开始。它起初仅仅涉及到一系列裁判规范——这些裁判规范可以作为司法裁决的基础。这些规范实际上与其他因人类生活关系而产生的裁判规范彼此相关。但是后者对于法学而言，尚属未知；它们都还位于法学的视野之外，法官也只是基于对生活关系的观察无意识地获悉它们。但是法学越发展，法学的领域越大，法学的研究越深入，这些规范在司法中准备即刻派上用场的成果就越多，这不仅包括那些最终裁判规范，也包括

〔1〕（拉）*potestas*（支配权），一般是指某一主体根据法律或者习俗对其他主体行使的权力。例如家父对家子行使的父权。在公法领域，它也指执法官所享有的治权。

presuppose and those that the last named presuppose in turn. As a result, the legal propositions are becoming more numerous and detailed. All of this is done partly by means of universalization and reduction to unity of the inner order of the relations of life, partly by means of finding new norms, according to the distribution of power that obtains in society and according to the ideals of justice that rule the hearts of men. In this way Roman law and English law have developed, and in this way the Continental common law has been rejuvenated time and again, and in this way law is developing at the present time.

These norms for decision which have been transformed by the jurists into legal propositions can be distinguished, even by their outward form, from those that constitute the inner order of human relations and, in general, the rules of human conduct, and that, serf-evidently, also find their way into the works of the jurists. One can know them by their fine dialectic formulation, the formally correct delimitation of justice and injustice. There is no possibility that men could ever regulate their lives according to such juristic subtleties.

In the terminology of modern juristic usage one might say that all development of juristic science consists in the conversion of a question of fact into a question of law. The only difficulty is that today "question of fact" has two distinct meanings. On one hand it refers to the inner order of the relations of human life brought about by usage, regulation, contract, inheritance, last will. On the other hand it refers to a violation of this inner order, which leads to a law-suit or to a criminal proceeding. But "question of fact" in the first sense is a constituent part of "question of fact" in the second sense of the term. In order to know to which one of the *Claudii* the inheritance of a freedman belongs, a judge must know the order of inheritance in the *gens Claudia*; in order to determine whether or not the maternal uncle of the slain man is entitled to the wergild, he must have information about the order of the family of the slain man; in order to ascertain whether a contract has been broken, the content of the contract must be shown.

The question of fact becomes a question of law through universalization, reduction to unity, and free finding of norms. Until this has been done, there is no antithesis between "question of

这些裁判规范必然含有的那些规范，以及后者必然含有的那些规范。结果，法律规定变得数量越来越多，也越来越详细。这一切某种程度上是按照在社会中获得之权力的分配以及支配人类心灵的正义理想，通过生活关系内部秩序的一般化和统一化的方式达成的。以这种方式，罗马法和英国法获得了发展；以这种方式，欧陆共同法一次又一次地恢复活力；以这种方式，当下法律正在向前发展。

这些已由法学家改造并加入到法律规定中的裁判规范，即使根据它们的外部形式，也可以与那些构成人类关系内部秩序的规范区别开来，而且，大体上，它们与人类行为规则以及那些明显设法进入到法学家作品中的规范也可以依据外观区分开来。人类绝不可能永远按照那些法学上的微妙思想来调控他们的生活。

在现代法学习语的术语学中，有人可能会说，法学的所有发展都存在于由事实问题向法律问题的转化中。唯一的困难是，在今天，“事实问题”有两个截然不同的含义。一方面，它指由惯例、条例、契约、继承及遗嘱而缔建的人类生活关系的内部秩序。另一方面，它指对这种内部关系的违反，这将导致民事诉讼或刑事诉讼的启动。但第一种意义上的“事实问题”是第二种“事实问题”的组成部分。为了了解自由民的遗产归哪一个克劳狄所有，法官必须知道在克劳狄宗族中遗产的继承顺序；为了判断被害人的舅舅是否有权获得凶手给付的赔偿金，法官必须了解被害人家庭的情况；为了确定一个契约是否已经被违反，该契约的内容必须揭示出来。

通过一般化、统一化以及规范的自由发现，事实问题变成了法律问题。在此项工作完成之前，在“事实问题”和“法律问题”之

fact" and "question of law." The jurist of the hoary past dealt exclusively with questions of fact, for there were no juristically formulated norms for decision in existence. The law that he required for the decision of the cases that came before him was supplied by custom, witnesses, and documents. All of these were questions of fact. The principles that resulted from the decisions as to questions of fact, after they had been recognized and universalized, were the first legal propositions. Ever since that time, every day has added new ones to those that were already in existence. This is going on today. Although a paragraph of the code is cited in every judicial decision, as a matter of fact, by far the greater number of judicial decisions is rendered, not on questions of law, but on questions of fact. But in all these decisions on questions of fact, general legal principles are lying imbedded, which practical juristic science brings forth into the light of day, as a rule in the headings of the collections of decisions, and also in the annotations to the codes— unpretentious as they are. Thereafter juristic literature and doctrine take possession of them; and finally they are added to the mass of existing legal material and appear in the codes themselves.

A very graphic picture of this method of procedure employed by legal science is presented by the development of the law of the contract of current accounts (*Kontokorrentvertrag*). The first step was that the practical jurists who dealt with mercantile affairs became aware of the fact that they were dealing with a peculiar contract as to which there were no legal propositions in existence. A few judicial decisions were rendered on this contract, and the judges whose duty it was to render them found it incumbent upon themselves to make a statement as to the nature and content of the contract, which was based in part on their own knowledge and in part on opinions of merchants, on the testimony of witnesses and of experts. At that time all of this was a question of fact. The decisions were rendered on this question of fact, i. e. the nature of the relation resulting from the current accounts (*KontRorrentverhältnis*) that had been submitted to them for decision. Before very long, however, jurists began to realize that this form of contract was in great vogue in mercantile circles, and that it was as well worth considering as the contracts of sale and lease. They thereupon began to universalize the contents

间没有任何对立可言。久远年代的法学家只探究事实问题,因为那时不存在任何法律上成型的裁判规范。他为裁判案件所需的法律由习俗、证人以及书面文件提供。所有的这些都是事实问题。源于裁决的有关事实问题的原则,在获得认可和一般化之后,成为第一批法律规定。自那以后,每天都有新的法律规定加入到已经存在的法律规定中。这种情况一直持续到今天。尽管法典的一段在每一个司法裁决中都被引用,但事实上,数量更多的司法裁决并非是基于法律问题、而是基于事实问题作出的。不过在这所有基于事实问题作出的裁决中,一般性的法律原则总是内含于其中,实用法学使之清楚呈现出来,其位置通常是在裁决集的标题,同时也在法典的评注中——没有任何虚饰的存在。此后,法学著作与学说也囊括了它们;最后它们被加入到大多数现存的法律素材中,并在法典本身中出现。

法学所运用的这种程序方式由关于往来账户(*Kontokorrentuertag*)的契约法律极其清晰地展现出来。第一步是处理商务的法律执业人开始意识到这个事实:他们正在处理一个金钱契约——没有任何现行的法律规定可循。有些司法裁决是基于这种契约作出的,法官的职责让他们发现他们有义务对于契约的性质和内容作一个陈述,这种陈述部分基于他们自己的知识,部分基于商人的意见以及证人和专家的证词。那时候,所有的这些都是事实问题。那些裁决正是基于这个事实问题作出的,亦即源于往来账户(*KontRorrentverhältnis*)之关系的性质,该账户已经作为裁决的参考依据而提交给了法庭。然而,很久以前,法学家就开始意识到,这种契约形式在商人圈子中非常流行,并且人们也完全有理由将之视为销售和出租契约来思考。于是他们开始让往来账户

of the contracts of current accounts, and by this process obtained a general law of the contract of current accounts. This work of universalization was done chiefly in juristic literature, especially in the book of Grünhut and in the book of Levy; translated by Riesser. These were followed by a few treatises, text-books, and handbooks, and finally the results were embodied in the new Commercial Code. Indeed treating the contract of current accounts as a contract of mutual granting of credit or as a novation of the individual obligations was a superfluous and not very happy construction, for when applied to the contract of current accounts the legal propositions concerning granting of credit and novation underwent a radical change. The whole process however was typical, i. e. observation of the legal relation in actual life, a few decisions on the basis of this observation, universalization of the results in juristic literature, superfluous construction, and finally codification. The taw of the contract for services has been created before our very eyes by the same process. A century ago not a trace of it was in existence. The *locatio conductio* of the Roman law was absolutely inapplicable to our relations; the modern codes were silent on the subject, the French Civil Code contained two articles, one of which has been rescinded since that time. In Germany — not in France — there was a small number of legal propositions concerning a few sub-varieties, particularly concerning the contract for domestic service. Now on what basis did the judge render his decisions as to suits arising from a contract for domestic service? On the basis of the content of the given contract, i. e. on the basis of proof by testimony of witnesses and by documents, and of custom, as to which, if he did not know what it was, he heard the testimony of witnesses who did know; and all of this he would eke out according to justice and fairness. Out of these elements a fixed judicial custom arose in France, which provided a detailed regulation of the contract for services; and in Germany there grew up at least a general consciousness of right and law, which however did give rise to a series of legal propositions that are now embodied in the German Civil Code.

This appears very clearly wherever, because of procedural institutions, the question of fact and the question of law are treated

契约的内容一般化,通过这个过程,他们获得了关于往来账户的一般法。这个一般化的工作主要在法学著作中完成,特别是在格吕胡特和利维的书中,该书由里泽翻译。此后是一些专题论文、教科书以及简明手册,最后,这些成果体现在商法典当中。实际上,将往来账户契约看作是相互给予信贷的契约或个人债务的一次更新,这种做法是多余的,也不是非常理想的解释,因为当这种想法应用于往来账户契约时,有关给予信贷和债务更新的法律规定要经历剧烈的变化。不过整个过程是典型的,即,对实际生活中法律关系的观察,基于这种观察所作的一些裁决,法律著作中这种成果的一般化,多余的解释以及最后的法典化。服务契约的法律在我们的眼前已经以同样的方式被创造出来。一个世纪以前,还没有它的一丝踪迹存在。罗马法上的租赁绝对不能套用到我们的关系之上;现代的法典对该主题也未作规定,法国民法典包括两个相关条款,其中一个条款自那时起已经遭到废除。在德国——不是在法国——关于此类契约的一些亚变种,特别是关于家政服务契约,存在少量的法律规定。关于家政服务契约引起的诉讼,法官如今基于什么作出裁决呢?基于给定契约的内容,即,基于证人证言和书面文件以及习俗——如果他不知道该习俗内容是什么,那么他将听取了解它的证人证言;并且对于所有的这些,他将根据正义和公平加以补充。在所有的这些因素之外,法国出现了一个固定的司法惯例,该惯例对服务契约提供了详细的规定;在德国,至少发展出一般性的权利和法律意识,不过该意识导致了一系列法律规定,这些法律规定如今体现在德国民法典当中。

因为诉讼程序制度的缘故,事实问题以及法律问题被分别看

separately. As it is usually understood, the separation is meaningless indeed, for there is no question of fact that is not, at the same time, a question of law. The question of proof itself is a question of law. In the matter of proof, we are concerned not only with the question whether the facts are established but also, in every case, with the question whether a legal relation arises from these facts and whether this legal relation has been violated by the conduct of either party. Accordingly there lies within the sphere of the question of fact the proof, not only of the existence of a contract, of a section of the articles of association, of a last will and testament, but of the whole inner order of the relations, of all rights and duties which are actually expressed in the words of the articles of association, the contract, the last will and testament, and, where a question of unlawful conduct is involved, the proof whether an interference with a right of another has taken place. The question of law thus becomes a matter of universalization, of reduction to unity, and of finding of norms. We may disregard the doctrine, for which Wlassak has gained general recognition, that the *formula in ius concepta* arose from the formula *in factum* among the Romans, for the reason that, though it is not improbable, it is too doubtful, and that it is probable that the Roman jurists quite frequently created a formula *in ius concepta* without the intervention of

待,这一点似乎在每个地方都很清楚。如通常理解的那样,事实问题与法律问题的这种分离实际上并无意义,因为没有任何一个事实问题同时不是法律问题。证据本身的问题是一个法律问题。就证据而论,我们不仅关心该事实能否被确证,而且在所有情形下,我们还会关心某一个法律关系是否因这些事实而产生,以及该法律关系是否由于任何一方当事人的行为遭到破坏。因此,在事实问题的范畴中,不仅包括契约存在、社团章程某个条款、遗嘱等证据,而且还包括法律关系的整个内部秩序、社团章程、契约、遗嘱中以文句实际表达出来的所有权利与义务,以及在涉及违法行为的场合,该行为是否已经构成对他人权利妨碍的证据。这样,法律问题就变成了一个一般化、统一化以及规范发现的问题。我们可以不考虑如下这种学说——乌拉沙克已因该学说获得普遍认可——在罗马人中,权利诉讼程式[1]产生于事实诉讼程式[2],因为此情形尽管不是不可能,不过还是太可疑了,并且很可能,罗马法学家十分频繁地创造权利诉讼程式,而根本没有事实诉讼程式的介入,这也是可能的。但是即使我们不考虑发展演

---

〔1〕 (拉)*formula in ius concepta*(权利诉讼程式),为维护法定权利而提起的诉讼,在此种诉讼的原告请求中,应当明确列举得到法律承认的权利。该术语的拉丁文有时候被表述成"*actio in ius*"。

〔2〕 (拉)*in factum*(事实诉讼程式),当某一新的关系不涉及由市民法所调整的权利,并且关系人不能借助法定诉讼程序解决就该关系产生的争议时,裁判官允许当事人针对创造上述关系的事实提起诉讼;此种诉讼中,裁判官所维护的并不是法律明确承认的权利,而是事实上存在的、新的公平关系。从一定意义上说,所有的裁判官法诉讼在最初时都表现为事实诉讼,随着它们日益成熟,其中一部分上升为权利诉讼。

the formula *in factum*. But even if we disregard the question of the development, the distinction is quite in harmony with what is being presented here; for the *factum* comprises the whole inner order of the relation, e. g. duties arising from contract and from the *patronatus*, i. e. the relation between an owner and his manumitted slave, and the violation of these duties; the *ius* comprises the universalization, the reduction to unity, and the finding of norms. In the development of English law, of which we have a more comprehensive knowledge, all these things are obvious with an almost plastic clearness.

When the English discuss the advantages of the jury, they are in the habit of saying among other things that a jury can decide a case "without making bad law." This means: Had the judge decided the case, the decision would have given rise to a new legal proposition of judge-made law, possibly a bad one, but the verdict of the jury does not do this. This affords a deep insight into the origin of all juristic law, not only of that of English law. The jury purports to decide the question of fact; the judge, the question of law; but if the judge had rendered the decision instead of the jury, a legal proposition would have resulted. This, I take it, clearly indicates the nature of the distinction between the question of fact and the question of law. All law has arisen from the universalization of that which had originally been a question of fact in the individual case, or from the finding of norms on the basis of this universalization; and the reason why no law arises from the decision of the jury is that universalizing of this nature, if it is to contain a legal proposition which shall be binding for the future, must be done, not by the jury, but by the judge. But unless the judgment rendered by the judge on the basis of the verdict of the jury happens to be merely an application of an already existing legal proposition to the case in hand, it always creates new law

进问题,这种区分与此处所表述的情形也是相当地一致;由于事实包含此法律关系的整个内部结构,例如,契约规定的义务、因庇主权[1]而生的义务——后者指的是主人与由他解放的奴隶之间的关系——以及对这些义务的违反。该权利包含一般化、统一化以及规范的发现。在英国法的发展过程中,所有的这些事情都显而易见,有一种几乎立体感的清晰。

当英国人讨论陪审团的优点时,他们尤其习惯说,陪审团可以裁决一个案件,同时又"不会制定恶法"。意思是说,假使法官裁决该案,则该裁决将会带来法官法上的一个新的法律规定,而该新规定很可能是一个糟糕的规定,但是陪审团的裁决则不会带来这样的结果。这提供了一个针对法学家法审视的深刻视角,不限于英国法。陪审团旨在判断事实问题;法官则判断法律问题;但如果法官代替陪审团作出裁决,一个(新的)法律规定则会产生。我认为,这清楚地表明了事实问题和法律问题之间区别的性质。所有的法律都是源于最初存在于个案中一个事实问题的一般化,或是源于在这种一般化基础上的规范的发现;为什么没有一个法律源于陪审团之裁决的原因是,如果此种一般化会包含一个将约束将来的法律规定,则它只能由法官来完成,而不能由陪审团来完成。但是,除非法官基于陪审团的裁决对某个案件作出的判决碰巧仅仅是将一个现行法律规定适用于该案件,则根据英

---

〔1〕 (拉)*patronatus*(庇主权)。指解放奴隶者对于被解放的奴隶所享有的权力,依据这种权力,后者对前者负有服从义务、劳作义务和某些财产性义务(例如赡养)。此种权力可向庇主的卑亲属转移。

according to the Anglo-American view; for, except in the case of a mere application of law, the judge has always created a new norm by universalizing the facts established by the verdict of the jury, or he has found a new norm on the basis of this universalization.

The famous justice of the Supreme Court of the United States, O. W. Holmes, Jr., has stated the application of this doctrine to liability for culpability with great acumen. The jury passes on the question of fact; the court, on the question whether the facts constitute culpability, which gives rise to liability in damages. The second question involves a standard. Did the defendant exercise the measure of care which is required of a man in the conduct of the affairs of life? Who is to decide whether this measure of care has been exercised or not? Holmes thinks that this second question is a question of law. Says Holmes: "It is that the court derives the rule to be applied from daily experience, as it has been agreed that the great body of the law of tort has been derived," ① "and in this way the law is gradually enriching itself from daily life as it should." ② Whether therefore the facts established by the jury constitute culpability on the part of the defendant is a question to be decided by the judge. And out of these decisions the whole law of damages has grown. Now doubtless there are cases in which it is perfectly clear that they fall on this side of the line or on that. In such case, the judge renders the decision as to liability in damages quite independently, on the basis of the facts established by the jury. Why the judge? In these clear cases, a fixed rule of law as to the standard to be applied is already in existence. There are other cases however in which there is doubt. In those cases the jury passes not only on the facts but also on the question whether there is culpability; for in those cases the judge does not have a rule of law at

---

① Holmes, Common Law, p. 123.

② Holmes, op. cit., p. 121.

美法的观点,该判决总能创造出新的法律;因为,除了在仅仅适用法律的场合,法官总是通过对建立在陪审团裁决基础上的事实进行一般化的方式创造着新的规范,或者他基于这种一般化而发现新的规范。

美国联邦最高法院著名大法官奥利弗·温德尔·霍姆斯曾经非常敏锐地指出了将这种先例形成的原理适用于可归责责任的情形。陪审团就事实问题发表意见;法庭就该事实是否构成有责性——如果具备有责性则需承担损害赔偿责任——作出判断。第二个问题涉及一个标准。被告尽到了一个人在那种生活事务的行为中应该尽到的那种程度的注意义务了吗?谁来判断被告是否已经达到了该种注意程度?霍姆斯认为第二个问题是一个法律问题。霍姆斯说:"法官据以判断的规则来自日常生活经验,正如大家都同意,侵权法的大部分内容均来自于日常生活经验。"①"以这种方式,法律从日常生活中不断丰富其自身内容,事实上也理当如此。"②因此,陪审团所确定的事实是否构成被告的有责性是一个将由法官作出判断的问题。通过这些裁决,整个损害赔偿法成长起来。现在无疑存在许多案例,其中能很清楚地看出,它们是落在分界线的这一边还是那一边。在那种情形下,法官在陪审团所确定的事实基础上,对于损害赔偿责任相当独立地作出裁决。为什么法官会如此独立?在这些事实清楚的案件中,关于将要适用之标准的一个确定的法律规则已经存在。然而还存在其他一些案例,其中还有些疑问。在那些案例中,陪审团不仅判断事实问题,而且还判断是否存在有责性的问题;因为在那些案例

① 霍姆斯,《普通法》,第123页

② 同书,第121页

hand concerning the standard to be applied to determine the question whether there is culpability. As soon as a rule has arisen, the question as to the existence of culpability is a question for the judge. In other words, it is a question of fact whether the defendant by his conduct has violated the legal relation in a blameworthy manner; but the question whether this conduct, judged according to an already established standard, obligates him to pay damages is a question of law. The difficulty in the law of damages, says Holmes, is this, that certain cases of negligence occur too rarely "to enable any given judge to profit by long experience with juries to lay down rules, and that the elements are so complex that courts are glad to leave the whole matter in a lump for the jury's determination."

And in fact in one case it is actually possible to show historically how a whole legal system has been developed from such adjudications of individual cases by the jury, based solely upon the concrete nature of the legal relation in question as a question of fact. It is the English commercial law, the law merchant, the creator of which, in the opinion of the English, is Lord Justice Mansfield of the middle of the eighteenth century. He became the creator of this law inasmuch as he universalized the facts which were the basis of the individual decisions into legal propositions. I am quoting from the book of Carter, entitled A History of English Legal Institutions, the words of Justice Buller, taken from his opinion in a case decided in the year 1787, in which he describes the development graphically, almost as if he had been an eyewitness:

"Before that period (i. e. about 1750) we find that in courts of law all the evidence in mercantile cases was thrown together; they were left generally to a jury (i. e. the rules were treated as a matter of usage to be proved by evidence, without distinction of law and fact), and they produced no established principle. From that time we all know the great study has been to find some certain general principles which shall be known to all mankind, not only to rule the particular case then under

中,法官手头上还没有关于将要适用之标准的、确定的法律规则,从而判断是否存在有责性的问题。一旦某个规则产生,关于有责性存在的问题就会成为法官要解决的问题。换句话说,被告的行为是否以一种可责的方式破坏了法律关系,这是一个事实问题;但根据已确立的标准判断,该行为是否使他有责任支付损害赔偿是一个法律问题。霍姆斯说,损害赔偿法中的困难在于特定的过失案件发生的情形过于罕见,"以至于不能使法官在陪审团的长期经验中获益并进而制定出规则,并且构成要件如此复杂,使得法官乐于将那整个事务一次性全部交给陪审团裁断"。

事实上在一种情形下也有可能揭示,历史上一整套法律制度如何仅仅基于所涉及法律关系的具体性质,就从陪审团对个案的那种裁决发展起来。英国商法,从英国人的观点来看,是11世纪中叶由上诉法院法官曼斯菲尔德所创立。由于他将作为个案裁决基础的事实进行一般化而整合成法律规定,因而成为商法的创立者。以下是我从卡特名为《英国法律制度史》的著作中引用的布勒法官的话,这段话摘自他在1787年审理的一个案件,其中他生动地描述了这种发展过程,就好像他曾亲眼见到过一样:

"在那个时期(大约1750年)以前,我们发现在法庭上,商事案件中所有的证据都是胡乱拼凑而成;它们通常都留给陪审团(即,该规则被当成一个有待于证据证明的惯例问题,没有对法律和事实的区分),并且它们没有带来任何确定的原则。从那时起,我们知道更广泛深入的研究不是为了找出仅仅当时的特定案件需要加以考虑的规则,而是为了发现一些特定的一般性原则——这些原则将为世人所知,这些原则还要为将来的审判作指导。我

consideration, but to serve as a guide for the futurc. Most of us have heard these principles stated, reasoned upon, enlarged, and explained, till we have been lost in admiration at the strength and stretch of the human understanding." (Lickbarrow v. Mason, per Buller J., 2 T.R. 63.)

Without this constructive activity of the jurists, without their universalizing and reducing to unity, general legal propositions cannot arise from the inner order of human associations. The inner order as such remains a legal norm; to be exact, a norm for decision. An example, which extends down to our own time, is found in the private law of princes. Dungern has rendered the great service of showing that, materially, the latter consists exclusively of those rules which the individual princely houses have laid down as their inner order with reference to the questions that fall within the sphere of their autonomy. Not one of these regulations has attained the significance of a legal proposition that is binding upon anyone outside of the family that has set it up. Indeed, for centuries attempts to create a universal private law of princes have not been lacking; but the jurists that made these attempts evidently were not sufficiently influential among the higher nobility, in whose power this matter lies, to prevail.

In the numerous cases in which the jurist must draw his norms for decision from the inner order of the relations, actual experience of life must supply him with the necessary materials. How did the Roman know that in a marriage with *manus* all of the wife's property became the property of the husband, and that in case of the freer marriage she retained it? He knew it because he knew the inner order of the Roman family. How did Thöl know, when he wrote the second edition of his *Handelsrecht* (mercantile law), that each partner in a mercantile partnership with unlimited liability was entitled to the "*rechtmässige Gebrauch der Firma*" (rightful use of the firm name), so that each partner in virtue thereof could bind the remaining partners? He knew it because he knew the organization of commerce. In primitive very simple and transparent relations, an unconscious

们许多人都曾听说过这些原则(如何)被介绍、推理、详述和解释,最后总是会让我们对人类理解力的效能强度和弹性范围赞叹不已。"(Lickbarrow v. Mason, per Buller J., 2 T. R. 63.)

若没有法官的这种建设性活动,若没有他们的一般化与统一化,一般性的法律规定不可能从人类联合体的内部秩序中产生。那样的内部秩序本身依然存在于一个法律规范当中;准确地说,存在于一个裁判规范当中。一个可延伸至我们这个时代的例子可以在亲王的私法中找到。敦根已经付出很多努力来表明,实质上,后者仅仅包括那些单个亲王家族对于涉及他们自治范围内的问题已经制定的,作为他们内部秩序的规则。这些规则没有一个获得了法律规定的意义,它们不能约束制定它们家族之外的任何人。确实,几个世纪以来,试图创立一个一般性的王族法的努力从未欠缺过;但是作出这些努力的法学家显然在更高的贵族——该事务属于他们的权力范围之内——中没有足够的影响力,因而无法获得成功。

在为数众多的案件中,法官必须从生活关系的内部秩序中提炼出裁判规范,实际生活经验必须给他提供必要的素材。罗马人如何知道在一个带夫权的婚姻中,妻子的所有财产变成了丈夫的财产?罗马人又是如何知道在给予自由之身的婚姻中妻子可以保有其财产?罗马人之所以知道这些,是因为他了解罗马人家庭的内部秩序。特约尔撰写第二版的商法书时,他如何知道:因为无限责任商事合伙的每个合伙人都("rechtmässige Gebrauch der Firma")有权合理使用商号的名称,所以每个合伙人都可以约束其余的合伙人?他之所以知道这个是因为他熟悉这种商业组织。在原始的、非常简单和透明的关系中,对那个时代偶然

mental working over of the happenings of the day suffices to give to the jurist who has some sense of reality the required knowledge of the affairs of life round about him; in the manifold, highly complex, and, in part, confused situations of our day, very often long, searching investigation is required. In every case, however, it is mere knowledge, not authoritative regulation, that we are concerned with.

This presentation alone is sufficient to show that the current teaching that it is the function of juristic science to range states of fact under established legal concepts is a fatal error. The inner order of human relations which results from the traditional constitution of the family, the corporation (*Körperschaft*), the association (*Genossenschaft*), from the relation between serf and feudal lord, from the content of contracts, articles of association, and last wills and testaments, from usage—this inner order, from which the judicial decision derives the greater number of its norms for decision, which juristic science universalizes, subsumes under the juristic concepts, or construes with the help of the latter, is not a part of the world of fact, like an eclipse of the sun, or the chemical composition of water, but is in itself a part of the law. Not facts are being adjudged but legal relations. Juristic science creates legal propositions only on the basis of legal relations. Family, corporations, ownership, real rights, purchase, usufructuary lease, ordinary lease, loan, were legal relations before the Roman jurist had made his first universalization; likewise in the Middle Ages they were legal relations before they were being adjudged according to Roman law. And after the reception, in so far as the Romanistic art and science of drafting legal documents did not interfere, they remained what they had been before, even as to content. The only difference was that thereafter they were adjudged according to Roman Law. Likewise, if English law should be introduced anywhere on the continent of Europe, the family, the corporations, ownership, the real rights, and the contracts would remain what they had been until then; and even though they should be adjudged according to English law, they would not become English legal relations. Legal relations are created by society, not by legal propositions.

Now let us consider the work of juristic science since the reception of Roman law. First of all we must put aside everything that served only the purpose of setting forth most faithfully the content

发生之事的一种不经意的脑力劳动，足以给有某种程度现实感的法官带来有关他周遭生活事务的必要知识；在我们这个时代繁复、高度复杂以及有些混乱的情形下，彻底的调研绝大多数时候都是必要的。然而，任何一种情况下，我们涉及到的还仅仅是知识，不是权威的规定。

单单上述介绍就足以表明时下的教学——（认定）将事实情形排列到已建立的法律概念之下是法学的功能——是一个致命的错误。源于传统家庭情况的人类关系的内部秩序，源于农奴和封建领主之间关系、契约内容、社团章程、遗嘱以及习俗的法人（*Kǒrperschaft*）和社团（*Genossenschaft*）的内部秩序——根据这种内部秩序，司法裁判推导出数量更多的裁判规范——并非如同日食或水的化学组成一样，是事实世界的一部分，相反，其本身就是法律的一部分。判决的对象不是事实而是法律关系。法学仅仅基于法律关系创立法律规定。家庭、法人、所有权、物权、购买、有用益权的租约、普通租约、贷款，这些在罗马法学家第一次进行一般化之前，都是法律关系；同样，在中世纪，在根据罗马法对其作出裁判以前它们也是法律关系。在罗马法继受之后，在罗马法学家起草法律文件的技艺和学问没有对它们带来影响的范围内，它们还保留着先前的样子，甚至内容上也是如此。同样，如果英国法能够被介绍到欧陆的任何地方，家庭、法人、所有权、物权以及契约也将保持着（英国法引入前）原先的模样；即使根据英国法对这些进行裁判，它们也不会变成英国的法律关系。法律关系是由社会创造的，不是由法律规定创造的。

现在让我们思考一下罗马法继受之后的法学著作。首先我们必须把所有那些仅为了最忠实地阐明原始文献内容而存在的

of the sources; for this merely served to transmit that which had itself been transmitted, it did not continue the development of the art and the doctrine. The new material however that was added to that which had been transmitted was always based on what had been gained from actual observation of the legal relations and had been universalized. In this respect the method of the modern jurists does not differ from that of the Romans. There is a difference only in this, that they did not, like the Romans, derive the norms for decision directly from the universalizations or find them freely, but that they fitted the results of their labor into the Roman system of concepts, and, in appearance at least, attempted to utilize the Roman norms for decision for this purpose. But since they did not approach their task without preconceived notions, but had arrived at their decisions in advance, to which they subsequently adapted their concepts and constructions, their method, in fact, was a rather free finding of law on the basis of reasons that were adduced afterwards.

For the norms which are taken directly from the organizations, the term "*Natur der Sache*" (nature of the thing) has become current in the German juristic science of the Continental common law, particularly since the beginning of the nineteenth century. The "nature of the thing" is derivable from the forms of the associations of the state and of society and of economic associations which life has created self-actively. This is the *naturalis ratio* of the Romans; this is hidden behind so many of their *sed aequius est*, *sed melius est*, *sed humanior est eorum sententia*, and this, too, is one of the active forces of the natural law movement, down to its last offshoot, the "*Lehre von dem richtigen Recht*" (theory of the true or just law). German common law juristic science as a rule summed up in concepts that which itself or the legislator had learned from direct observation of the associations which life had created, and then deduced the norms from the nature of the thing, i. e. "from the concept." The latter was merely another technical term for the "nature of the thing." No jurist, not even a jurist of the last century, has ever been able, in spite of the positiv-

东西抛在一边;因为那仅仅为了传播已被传播的内容,所以它无助于那种艺术和学说的继续发展。然而,被传播之内容的新素材总是建立在经由法律关系的实际观察和一般化所获得的成果之上。在这方面,现代法学家的方式与罗马人的方式没有什么不同。唯一的区别仅在于,他们不像罗马人那样,直接从一般化或法的自由发现中获取裁判规范,而是将他们的劳动成果配合罗马人的概念体系,并且至少在表面上,为此而努力利用罗马人的裁判规范。但是,由于他们没有预先形成的观念就无法处理他们的任务,他们若是提前得出裁决,则他们随后就会使他们的概念和解释适合于这些观念,所以实际上,他们的方式是一种相当自由的法的发现,相关理由下文将要论述。

对于直接从组织中提取的规范,“*Natur der Sache*”(事物的本质)这个术语,特别是自19世纪初开始,在欧陆共同法的德国法学中变得流行。“事物的本质”可以从国家、社会的联合体以及经济联合体——生活会自发能动地产生出这些联合体中推导出来。这就是罗马人的自然之理;这隐藏在他们如此多的(类似)“如果这符合衡平,如果这符合善良,如果这符合人道的要求”的话语中,同时这也是自然法运动——一直到它的最后分支,即 *Lehre von dem richtigen Recht*“正法理论”——的一股积极力量。德国共同法法学一般习惯总结概念,法学本身或立法者从对于生活创造出来的联合体的直接观察中总结出概念,然后从事物的本质中,即“从概念中”推导出规范。后者仅仅是“事物的本质”的另外一个专业术语。没有一个法学家——尽管上个世纪实证法学潮流汹涌,甚至上世纪没有一个法学家——曾经能够完全抛开基于“事物的本质”

ist tendency, to dispense altogether with considerations based on "the nature of the thing," even when, like Windscheid, he apparently rejected them. They have been recognized expressly—to name only a few of the greatest names—by Savigny, Puchta, Wachter, Unger, Goldschmidt, Bähr. Adickes devoted his first book to them.

The norms "derived from the nature of the thing" or "deduced from the concept" are the rules of conduct that govern a legal relation in life; they are a product of the labor of life, not of that of a legislator or of any other power that has authority to posit norms, and they can be the subject matter of scientific knowledge, but they cannot be ordained or prescribed. Therefore, however they may have been formulated, even though it be in a statute, their scientific content can be examined into. One can always ask the question, not only whether the definition of *Erbleihe* (freehold) or of usufructuary lease, as contained in the statute, but also whether the norms which the statute merely derives from the concept, correspond to that which is considered valid in everyday life as to these legal relations. Therefore it is justly denied that definitions, and—this ought to be added—the norms that derive from them, "from the nature of the thing," should ever be put into a statute; for, if they are correct, they are superfluous when put into the statute; they would be in existence even if there were no statute; if they are incorrect, they constitute what has often been called the "*unverbindlicher Gesetzesinhalt*" (nonobligatory content of the statute), and must needs cause mischief; for men are not readily given to ignore even the non-obligatory content of a statute. The Roman maxim, *omnis definitio in iure periculosa*, indeed appears to go beyond this; for *ius civile* does not mean statute but juristic science—a fact which can be explained by the further fact that Roman juristic science could posit binding juristic law. It does however contain merely the monition that it is easier for a jurist to infer a single norm

的思考,甚至当温德沙伊德明显抵制它们的时候,也是如此。它们获得了以下法学家——仅列举一些最伟大的名字——明确的认可:萨维尼、普赫塔、瓦赫塔、昂格尔、戈尔德施密特以及拜尔。阿迪克斯把他的第一本书献给了他们。

“从事物的本质推导出来”或“从概念推导出来”的规范是支配一种世间法律关系的规则;它们是现实生活的产物,不是有权制定规范的立法者或任何其他权力机构的产物,并且它们可以是科学知识的主题,但它们不能基于命令或规定而产生。因此,不管它们可以如何被规划整理,即使它成为制定法,他们的科学内容还是可以受到检验。一个人总是可以不仅问制定法中的“自由保有(*Erbleihe*)”或“附用益权租约”的概念是什么,还可以问仅仅从此概念中推导出来的制定法的规范是否与被认为在日常生活中对这些法律关系有效的规范相一致。因此,有理由拒绝如下观点:定义与——应该加上——源于它们以及“事物的本质”的规范应该总是被植入立法中;因为,如果该观点是对的,则就此立法时,它们就成了多余的了;即使没有制定法,它们也将存在;如果它们是错误的,则它们将构成经常被称为“*unverbindlicher Gesetzesinhalt*”(制定法上无约束力的内容),并且非得引发危害不可;因为人们不大容易忽视制定法上的内容——即使是没有约束力的。罗马法上的谚语——民法中的任何一个定义都是危险的——的确超越了这个;因为民法并非意味着制定法,而是法学——这是一个可以被更深一层的事实(罗马法学可以提出有拘束力的法学家法)解释的事实。然而,它仅仅包含这样的忠告:对于一个法律人而言,从社会联合体的秩序中推导出一个单个规范要比融

from the order of the social associations than to combine all the norms that constitute the framework of a living association in a definition.

All of this self-evidently refers only to the juristic definitions of the institutions that are created by actual life itself. The *Tatbestand* (constitutive facts) to which, according to the precept contained in the statute, a statutory norm for decision or any other statutory command is to be applied is also frequently called a definition (*Begriffsbestimmung*). The empirical content which has been included in this *Tatbestand* indeed indicates the relation of life that is to be protected against interference. The existence and the qualities of the latter are independent of the legal proposition; for example bodily injury is as far from being the work of the legislator as extra-marital paternity. But the legal proposition alone determines the circumstances under which a relation of life should receive legal protection, and when the established legal consequences should ensue, e. g. what kind of bodily injury is to be punishable, when extra-marital paternity obligates a person to provide support and maintenance. The author of a legal proposition then is, if not absolutely free in determining the *Tatbestand* of social institutions, at any rate freer than in defining them. The *Tatbestand* is a part of the content of the statute and cannot be said to be either superfluous or incorrect. It may be stated too narrowly or too broadly with reference to the intent of the legislator or with reference to the purpose which the statute was designed to accomplish, and the judicial decision may disregard the wording of the statute. But in so doing it does not emend the statute; it interprets it or ekes out its meaning. The constitutional rights and duties of a citizen of a state and the rights, powers, and privileges of an owner are quite independent of the statutory definition (*Bestimmung*) of state and of ownership; nothing is to be punished as theft but what is included in the *Tatbestand* of theft; and no legal transaction can be set aside by means of the *actio Pauliana* except those which the statute gov-

合所有——构成一个定义中的现存联合体的框架——的规范更容易。

这一切显然仅仅指由现实生活本身所创立之制度的法律定义。根据立法中包含的规则，一个制定法上的裁判规范或任何其他制定法上的命令将要适用于其上的(*Tatbestand*)推定事实经常被称作定义(*Begriffsbestimmung*)。在推定事实中包含的经验内容实际表明，生活关系将会受到保护，免遭危害。后者的存在和质量与法律规定无关；例如，身体伤害远不是立法者的作品，正如婚姻外父子关系也不是其作品一样。但是只有法律命题确定了生活关系应受到法律保护的情形，以及什么时候会触发预先规定的法律后果，例如，哪一种对他人身体的伤害行为应该受到惩罚，什么时候婚外父子关系使得某人必须提供抚养费等。如果法律命题的作者不能自由决定社会习俗的推定事实，那至少也比界定它们更自由。推定事实是制定法内容的一部分，既不能说是多余的，也不能说是错误的。关于立法者的意图或者制定法企图实现的目的可能被表述得过于狭窄或过于宽泛，因而司法裁判可能不考虑制定法的措辞。但在如此做的时候，它不会修订制定法；它解释或补充制定法。国家公民的宪法权利和义务以及所有人的权利、权力和特权都独立于制定法上国家和所有权的定义(*Bestimmung*)；除了被“盗窃”的推定事实所囊括的范围之外，什么都不会作为盗窃行为受到惩罚；没有一种法律行为可以通过撤销转让行为之诉[1]的方式被撤销，除非规范法律行

〔1〕（拉）*actio Pauliana*(撤销转让行为之诉)。如果资不抵债的债务人有欺诈性转让行为，债权人可以申请撤销。该诉讼是由优士丁尼法创设的，在此之前，它表现为两种不同的诉讼手段，一种是欺诈给付令状，另一种是恢复原状。

erning avoidance has declared to be voidable (*anfechtbar*). In the case of the state and of ownership the question is one of the form of organization; in the case of theft and in the case of the *actio Pauliana* it is a question of the *Tatbestand* contained in a norm for decision. The present discussion establishes a palpably clear contradistinction between these two situations.

With rare exceptions, practical juristic science creates the legal proposition on the basis of observation of the facts of legal life, on the basis of universalization of the results of such observation. Its method presents an unmistakable similarity to the methods of the pure sciences, which also are regularly based on observation and universalization of that which has been observed. This similarity quite readily accounts for the fact that juristic science is often being conceived of not as a practical science but as a pure science, and that demand is frankly being made in its behalf for a method like that of the natural sciences. Though the method of pure science and that of juristic science appear to be very similar to each other, they are, as Rumpf has convincingly demonstrated, very dissimilar. The object of the former is knowledge; that of the latter, finding of norms. The observation and universalization of the jurist does not proceed without bias, in the spirit of pure science but, from the outset is dominated by consideration of the distribution of power, of expediency, and of ideals of justice, which give direction to the process of finding of norms. And therefore juristic observation and universalization is directed to different objects from the beginning, and attains results different from those of pure science. On the basis of scientific proceeding, the Roman jurists would never have treated the family order of the free peasant proprietor as the only order of the Roman family, the English judges would never have universalized the law of inheritance of the knights into a law for all classes, and the authors of the German Civil Code could not possibly have made community of administration the general régime. All of this becomes explicable only if we bear in mind that they were not bent upon ascertaining facts in a scientific manner but upon establishing practical precepts for the future.

The course of decisions as to rights of personality which is going

为效力的制定法已经宣告那些为可撤销的(*anfechtbar*)。在国家和所有权的情形下,该问题是一个组织形式问题;在盗窃和撤销转让行为之诉的情形下,它是一个裁判规范所包含的推定事实问题。现在的讨论证实了这两种情形之间存在的一个清晰可见的对比。

仅有极少的例外,实用法学在对法律生活事实的观察基础上,并基于对那种观察结果的一般化创立了法律命题。它的方式呈现了一种与纯科学的方式之间明确无误的相似性,后者通常也是基于观察和对观察结果的一般化。这种相似性可以十分容易地解释如下事实:法学经常不被作为实用科学来理解,而是作为纯科学来看待,并且对其方式坦率地提出的要求也类似于自然科学的要求。尽管纯科学和法学的方式二者表面上看来有很多相似的地方,但正如朗夫有力地论证过的那样,它们其实有很大的不同。前者的对象是知识;后者的对象则是规范的发现。法律人的观察和一般化不可能不带丝毫的偏见,但纯科学的灵魂,从一开始就受到对权力分配、便利以及正义理想等考量的支配,这些直接决定了法之发现过程的方向。因此法学上的观察和一般化从一开始就会指向不同的目标,并获得与纯科学不同的结果。在科学程序的基础上,罗马法学家从来不会把自耕农的家庭秩序当作是罗马人家庭的唯一秩序,英国法官也永远不会将骑士继承法一般化而扩展成所有社会阶层的法律,《德国民法典》的立法者也决不可能使(夫妻财产)共同管理成为一般性的制度。只有当我们记住它们并非系于以一种科学方法确定的事实,而是系于制定的今后的实践性方案,所有的这些都是可解释的。

一直持续到如今的有关人格权的裁决过程是一个有益的例

on at the present moment is an instructive illustration of this. Its points of departure are two statutory provisions. One is the recognition in the Austrian Civil Code of the "innate rights, whose existence is made manifest by the light of reason"; the other is the action permitted by the Swiss Civil Code for "an injunction against interference" in a case of unauthorized violation of personal relations. The fact that the juristic science of the Continent required such crutches for the development of the rights of personality is an indication of the sad plight it is in today. It is not likely that the Roman jurists would have resorted to this method in order to find the *bonae fidei contractus*. In France, too, the rights of personality were protected to a great extent without the aid of statutes. Since the course of judicial decisions, except in France, has not been playing a prominent role, the development of the doctrine is chiefly literary. The leading works are those of Specker in Switzerland and of Mauczka in Austria. It is extremely instructive to observe the manner in which these writers developed a detailed law of personality. The statute affords no help for this purpose; for legal precepts which are so utterly lacking content as those of the Austrian and Swiss codes mentioned above leave the development of the law where they found it. What Specker and Mauczka say about the rights of personality is so absolutely independent of the statute that it would be applicable without more ado within the sphere of the German Civil Code, which does not mention rights of personality at all other than the fight to a name, if only the Germans could make up their minds to recognize the creative power of juristic literature.

It is true, Specker and Mauczka include many a thing in the law of personality, which might more properly be included in a revised copyright law, or a more advanced law of possession, or of neighbors' rights (prohibition of the publication of private letters or of a photograph of a private dwelling, protection against noises or unpleasant odors). If these things are excluded, the law of personality may be defined as the social and judicial protection of the interests of the individual which arise from his position in his social association (his family, his household, his social life) or in society as a whole. The point in question, in the words of Jung, is "the fact that since we are living together in this world, each of us demands a certain amount of

证。它的出发点是两个法律条款。一个是对在奥地利民法典中“先天性权利,其存在由理性之光所证实”的承认;另外一个则是由瑞士民法典对于擅自破坏人身关系的情况下允许为“阻止妨害”而实施的行为。欧陆法学要求为人格权发展提供那些支撑——这一事实表明当下存在的一种窘境。罗马法学家不太可能为了发现善意契约而诉诸这种形式。在法国,人格权在制定法之外也受到很大程度的保护。既然除了在法国,人格权司法裁判的过程并未发挥至关重要的作用,那么该理论的发展主要就是书本上的。最主要的作品是瑞士的斯佩克和奥地利的毛茨卡的著作。观察这些著者发展出一部翔实的人格法的方法极具启发意义。制定法对此没有提供任何帮助;因为奥地利民法典和瑞士民法典中相关法律规定的内容极度匮乏,省略了该法的发展历程。斯佩克和毛茨卡就人格权所作的阐述如此绝对地独立于制定法,以至于只要德国人能下决心认可法学著作的创造性权力,那么在德国民法典范围内,它也可以无需多费周折地适用,德国民法典除了提及该权利的名称外再无相关的其他内容。

的确,斯佩克和毛茨卡所阐述的人格法中包含了很多东西,这些可能放到一个修订的版权法或是一个更先进的占有法或相邻权法(禁止出版私人信件或私人寓所的照片,保护免受噪音或不良气味的妨害)中更合适。如果把这些排除在外,人格法将被界定为对源于其所处社会联合体(他的家庭、家族以及社会生活)或整个社会中地位之个人利益的社会与司法保护。问题的关键,用容格的话说,就是“这个事实——既然我们共同生活在这个世界上,则我们每个人都需要知道一定数量的他人的想法”。考虑

consideration from the other. "The measure of consideration is always determined by the position which the usage of the association assigns to the individual. For this reason, the norms which safeguard the rights of personality are based upon usage. And in an association in which the position of an individual has been reduced to a mere nothing by the usage of the association, as was the position of the Roman slave or of the *filius familias* in the household, there is no right to life. And what is the extent, even among the civilized nations of our times, of the right to physical inviolability and liberty in women and children? But the recognition, in a general way, of the right of every human being to life, physical inviolability, and liberty merely proves that the idea of the equal value of all human beings has made its way to this extent in the usage of society. In the same sense every person nowadays is entitled to the protection of his honor, a right which formerly was conceded only to members of the privileged classes. The other rights of personality that are being recognized today, such as the right to one's picture, to privacy, to protection of one's emotional and aesthetic life, are merely extensions, granted because of the recognition of the heightened inner life of our time, of the protection which the associations in time past had granted to their members from the protection of the sensibilities of their bodies to protection of the sensibilities of their souls. No innovation in principle is involved. Of course it is apparent without argument that the right to one's name, seal, and coat-of-arms merely serves to protect the interest of the position which is indicated thereby. The social norms, moreover, that protect the interests of personality at the present time are a part of the law to a very limited extent only; they are preponderantly norms of morality, ethical custom, decorum, and tact. They are being converted into legal norms by an extremely gradual process.

At the present time, legal protection of the interests of personality is given chiefly by criminal law, and therefore only against the grossest attacks. The movement for the recognition of the rights of personality is

的程度总是由联合体的习俗给个人确定的地位决定的。因此,维护人格权的规范建立在习俗基础上。在一个联合体中——个人地位由该联合体的习俗推导出来的结果是一无所有,正如罗马人家庭中的奴隶或家子的地位——没有生存权。甚至在我们这个时代文明的国度里,妇女儿童身体不受侵犯和自由权的范围是什么?但是,以一般方式对每个人生存权、身体不受伤害权、自由权的认可,仅仅证明所有人具有平等价值的理念某种程度上在社会习俗中一直在前进。在同样的意义上,如今每个人都有权保护其名誉,此种权利在以前被认为只能由特权阶层成员享有。由于对我们这个时代被抬高的内心生活的承认,以及由于过去该联合体给予成员的保护已从对他们身体的情感保护扩展到他们精神情感的保护,因而当今被认可的其他人格权,诸如肖像权、隐私权、保护个人情感和美感生活的权利,不过是先存权利的扩张和延伸,基本上并未涉及到革新。当然无需论证的是,某人的姓名权、印章权、纹章权[1]仅仅是为了保护已经由此表明的地位利益。此外,当今保护人格利益的社会规范仅仅在非常有限的程度上是法律的一部分;它们首先主要是道德规范、伦理风俗、礼节和得体的言行。它们正通过一种极其缓慢的进程转化为法律规范。

如今,人格利益的法律保护主要由刑法来提供,因此仅仅针对最显著的攻击。对人格权承认的运动正寻求为人格利益获得

---

〔1〕 纹章是起源自西欧中世纪,即“画在盾牌上的图案”,用来标示在护具上的辨示图形。纹章图式的编成有相当严格的规则,最初是为了军事上醒目易辨,后来则成为各特定家族的“符号”。

striving to gain the much more effective protection of private law for these interests. If its objects were of a purely scientific nature, it would necessarily confine itself to the observation of the usage in the household, in the family, in business life, in social life, and gather therefrom what interests of personality are to be found there, and to what extent they are being protected by social norms. But inasmuch as it is a *Kunstlehre* (practical science) it poses its problem quite differently. It is concerned with the creation of clearly formulated legal propositions, which are to determine under what presuppositions, by means of what legal remedies and of what kinds of compulsion, the rights of personality, which arise from social usage, should be protected. But this investigation must be preceded by observation and universalization of the interests of this nature that are in existence in society, and their significance must be determined. But this process of observation and universalization not only ceases when there is nothing left of practical importance, but culminates in a most unscientific procedure, to wit in the balancing of interests as the basis of the finding of norms.

It is true, juristic science would be in a much better case if instead of instituting observations and universalizations for its purposes it could draw on an already existing store of scientific knowledge, as can be done today in the case of medicine perhaps, and in the technical practical sciences. But for the present, since there is no sociology of law which could do the preliminary work for practical juristic science in this manner, the jurist must rely on his own experience for the knowledge of the relations of actual life which he requires in order to be enabled to create norms for decision on its basis. Apart from this, the statutes and the various branches of the social sciences will serve as sources of knowledge. But however great the amount of information he may receive elsewhere, in view of the inexhaustible and enormous diversity of the affairs of life it cannot possibly suffice. It must be supplemented at all times by the fullness of his own observation and his own experience. From this discussion it is apparent that a young man is not qualified for a seat on the bench who has merely demonstrated that he is able to master the most important statutes and a number of text-books. The best that a judge can give must be drawn from his inner self; the sections of the statute book and the text-books are like an imperfect sketch for a picture; and only the observations

更多私法上的保护。如果它的目标具有纯科学的性质,则它必然专门观察家族、家庭、商业生活、社会生活中的习俗,并从中积累将被发现的人格利益,以及在何种程度上他们将受到社会规范的保护。但是由于它是一个*Kunstlehre*(实践科学),所以它相当不同地提出了它的问题。它涉及到清晰而系统的法律规定的创制,这些法律规定将要根据什么先决条件,借助于什么样的法律救济以及何种强制,这些源于社会习俗的人格权应该受到保护。但这种调查必须在存在于社会的这种性质之利益的观察和一般化之后,并且必须确定它们的重要性。但是,这种观察和一般化过程在没有任何实践重要性时不仅会停止,而且会以一个极其不科学的程序——即,将利益平衡作为规范发现的基础——而告终结。

的确,如果法学为了它能利用已有的科学知识——正如今天的医学,或许还有技术性的实用科学能够做到的那样——而非为其目的进行观察和一般化,则情况将会好得多。但是既然暂时不存在可以以这种方式为实用法学做 些初步的工作的法律社会学,那么为了创立裁判规范,法律人对于他需要了解的实际生活关系的知识,就必须依赖于自己的经验。除此之外,制定法和各类社会科学分支也可以作为知识的来源。但是不管他可以从别处获取的信息量有多大,鉴于生活事务的无穷尽和巨大多样性,那还是不可能足够的。任何时候都必须要有他自己的知识和经验来作为补充。由这个讨论可以明显看出,一个年轻人,若仅仅证明他能够掌握最重要的制定法和大量教科书的内容,那他还是没有资格在法院当法官。一个法官能够提供的最好的东西必定是来自于他的内在品质;制定法书籍和教科书的部分就像一幅图画不完美的大致轮廓;只有对生活有一个完整丰富的观察和体验才

and experiences of a full and rich life can give form and color to it.

The legally binding force of juristic law, it is true, is an enigma. The legal norm is always a command, and we ask, "How can the discussion of a jurist contain commands?" The question cannot be disposed of but can only be touched upon here. First of all we must point out that this is not an isolated occurrence. The writer on ethics formulates ethical norms, and the norms of outward decorum, of honor, of etiquette, of fashion, of games, must likewise be originated by someone. When one is in doubt, one refers to a book, e. g. to a book on decorum, a code of honor, a book of etiquette, a journal of fashions, a collection of rules for games. Whatever is printed in the books is accepted as binding, and very often there is no other reason for this than that it is assumed—and very often the assumption is not justified—that the man who wrote the book somehow was authorized to lay down such rules.

In general the psychological basis of juristic law is the same. It is true the basic function of the jurist is to give information about the norms that are already in existence; but how shall one teach what it is that has validity as a norm unless the content of that which is taught in turn becomes a norm? Whom should we ask for instruction on the question what norms are valid but him who teaches the norms? The line of demarcation between *Normenlehre* (the science of norms) and *Lehrnormen* (norms that are being taught) manifestly is so tenuous that it must needs be overlooked in actual life; and in this way the great antinomy of law arises, which continually converts doctrine into norms, but veils the process itself from the eyes of those who are taking part in the process.

But in the case of legal norms, unlike the case of a norm of decorum, etiquette, fashion, or of a game, it is not sufficient that they are being taught by someone. They must become established, they must prevail in the struggle. This often happens in society, without anyone's taking notice of the fact, when society automatically accepts that which is suitable and rejects that which

能给这幅画以形态和颜色。

的确,法学家法在法律上的拘束力是一个谜。法律规范总是一个命令,我们问,"法学家的讨论如何能够包含命令?"这个问题此处无法解决,仅能简单涉及。首先,我们必须指出这不是一个孤立的事例。探讨伦理学的作者构想伦理规范、外在礼仪的规范、荣誉规范、礼节规范、时尚规范、游戏规范,列举的这些规范也必定同样是由某个人创造的。当某人陷入怀疑时,他就会参考书本,例如,有关礼仪的书,礼法习惯的书、礼节的书、时尚期刊、游戏规则集。书里面印的不管是什么,都会作为有拘束力的规范而被接受,很多情形下,这种接受除了基于以下这种假定——写这本书人的人获得授权来制定那些规则——之外,没有其他的原因,但很多情况下,这种假定理由并不充分。

通常,法学家法心理学上的基础是同样的。法学家的基本功能的确是提供有关已经存在之规范的信息;但是如果被教授的内容没有变成规范,那么人们该如何教授此具有规范效力的东西?对于哪些规范有效这个问题,我们除了向教授该规范的人求教之外,还能向谁求教呢?在 *Normenlehre*(规范科学)和 *Lehrnormen*(正被教授的规范)之间的分界线显然如此细浅,以至于它在实际生活中必定被忽略;这样,法律上巨大的悖论产生了,一方面法律不断将学说变成规范,但同时从参与此过程的人看来,它自己又将此过程遮掩起来。

但是在法律规范,情况与礼仪规范、礼节规范、时尚规范或游戏规范不同,它们正在由某个人教授,这是不够的。它们必须被证实,它们必须在斗争中获胜。社会自动接受合适的东西并拒绝不合适的东西,这经常在社会中发生,不过任何人都不会注

is unsuitable. Perhaps no one has ever stated this better than the authority followed by Boethius. In his view juristic law ( *ius civile* ) is *probatae civium creditaeque sententiae*. Occasionally this struggle of the norms for existence takes place according to an orderly process, e. g. the *disputatio fori* of the Romans and the citation of the Continental common law writers. And in this struggle the reputation of the originator is usually decisive. Most norms draw their vitality from the reputation of the man who has enunciated them. It is only very rarely however that the intellectual greatness of the person is the sole decisive factor, as in the case of the elder jurists of the Roman Republic, of the authors of the German and French books of law in the Middle Ages, and perhaps of the Islamic jurists. Practically in every case a high official position is an additional requisite. The Roman jurists of the Empire became *iuris conditores* in virtue of the *ius respondendi*; even the Nordic declarer of the law is a public official; since the days of the glossators, the university professorship is the decisive thing among the Continental common law jurists. As late as the nineteenth century the jurists who exercised any great influence in the matter of creating law in Germany, with few exceptions (Bähr, Liebe, Einert, perhaps Salpius), were academic teachers. In England and in America high judicial office is required. But even in these countries judges are not "fungible" personalities in virtue of their office. Even though judge-made law is binding as such, it is by no means a matter of indifference by whom the proposition which one cites in court has been enunciated. Decisions of courts are, it is true, cited by attorneys in great numbers, but only a few have abiding value. The great jurists who have been actively engaged in the development of the law are always numbered among the greatest men of the human race. Their names are being mentioned and their works are being read centuries after they have departed this life.

意这个事实。或许没有人曾经比波伊丢斯信奉的观点更好地表述过这点。在他看来，法学家法(*ius civile*)[1]是为市民的合理的观点所认可的。偶尔，规范“求生”的这种斗争按照一个有序的过程发生，例如，罗马人的法庭辩论和欧陆共同法作者的引用。并且在这种斗争中，创制者的名望通常具有决定性的作用。许多规范从发表它们之人的名望中获得自身的生机。然而，该发表人智识的伟大是唯一的决定性因素，这种情形还是非常罕见的，比如在罗马共和国年长的法学家、中世纪德国和法国法律著作的作者，或许还有伊斯兰的法学家们。实际上，任何时候，一个较高的官方职位都是另外一个不可缺少的条件。罗马帝国的法学家凭借法律解答成为法的创建者；甚至该法律北欧的宣布者也是一个公共官员；自注释法学派的时代以来，大学教授职位在欧陆共同法的法学家中具有决定性的意义。迟至19世纪，在德国对立法事项能发挥任何重大影响力的法学家，除了少数例外(贝尔、利伯和恩内特，或许还有萨皮乌斯)，其余都是大学教师。在英格兰和美国，较高的司法职位同样是必要的条件。但是即使在这些国家，由于职位的缘故，法官也不是“可代替的”存在。尽管法官法本身具有拘束力，但是由法官对人们在法庭上引用的法律规定进行清楚地阐明，绝非是无关紧要的事。法院的裁决的确被律师大量地引用，但仅有一些有恒久的价值。积极从事法律发展的伟大法学家总是被列为人类最伟大的人物。在他们离开这个世界后数百年中，他们的名字还在被提起，他们的著作也还在被阅读。

---

〔1〕 此处应指习惯法。

# XVI

# The Law Created By The State

Unlike the legal norms that have arisen in society, norms that have been created by the state are rarely being enforced by purely social compulsion. The state has need of its own peculiar means of power (*Machtmittel*) for this purpose, i. e. of its courts and other tribunals. And for this reason, the most important question is whether the state has suitable agencies that can give effect to these norms. The question then whether there is state law in any given state is not only a constitutional question but also an administrative one. The significance of the statutes of a state cannot be understood until one knows the agencies whose function it is to put them into effect. Everything depends upon their educational and cultural endowment, honesty, skill, and industry. For this reason a legal proposition will be given widely divergent interpretations in various sections of human society. After large portions of English, French, and Belgian constitutional and procedural law had been transplanted into foreign soil in the nineteenth century, men became convinced that they had effects quite different from those they would have at home. Transplantation has been most successful in the sphere of commercial law; for commerce is regulated essentially alike everywhere in Europe and the agencies of the state have little to do with it.

Permit me to adduce an example. Austrian jurists who, about twenty years ago, had come to Brussels in order to take part, as invited guests, in the dedication of the palace of justice heard with great astonishment that the Emperor Josef II had introduced the oral trial procedure in Belgium. The statute that achieved this miracle was the *Allgemeine Gerichtsordnung* (General Code of Judicial Procedure), the much maligned *Josephina*, which had been in effect in Austria for

# 第十六章　国家创制之法

与源于社会的法律规范不同,国家创制的规范极少由纯粹社会强制的方式来执行。国家需要其特有的权力工具(*Machtmittel*),即,法庭和其他审判机构。因此,最重要的问题是,国家是否是可以使这些规范生效的合适的机构。在任何特定国家是否存在国家法——这个问题不仅是一个宪法性问题,而且还是一个行政性问题。人们在了解其功能为使国家制定法生效的机构之前,是不可能了解国家制定法的意义的。一切都取决于他们的教育和文化方面的天赋、诚实、技巧以及努力。因此一个法律规定在人类社会的不同领域将会获得广泛多样的解释。在 19 世纪英国、法国和比利时的宪法和诉讼法中很大一部分被移植到他国之后,人们逐渐确信它们具有十分不同于它们在本国的效力。法的移植在商法领域最为成功;因为在欧洲每个地方对商业的法律调整方式基本相同,国家机构对此可做的极少。

请允许我举一个例子。大约二十年前,奥地利法学家应邀来到布鲁塞尔参加司法大厦的落成典礼,他们吃惊地听说,约瑟夫二世皇帝已经在比利时引入了口头审判程序。完成此等奇事的制定法是《一般司法程序法》(*Allgemeine Gerichtsordnung*),遭人贬斥的约瑟菲娜,曾经在奥地利生效长达一个多世纪,从来没有

more than a century without being credited by anyone with the power to bring about an oral procedure. It is true, the Code of Procedure did provide that, in the country (i. e. everywhere outside of the provincial capitals), the proceedings should be oral. In Austria the oral procedure consisted in this, that the writings were not filed, but were drawn up in the form of protocols and were handed to the judge. Occasionally, it is true, it did happen that the statements of the parties were reduced to writing on the day in court (*Tagfahrt*). The law-suit however was decided in every case solely on the basis of the protocols, and as a rule by a judge who had not participated in the preliminary proceedings. In the Netherlands, which at that time belonged to Austria, the oral procedure was taken seriously. The proceedings in court were conducted orally; at the end, the discussion was embodied in a protocol; and the judge who had conducted the proceedings at the day in court decided the case, with the aid of the protocol, it is true, but chiefly on the basis of the impression received at the oral proceedings. So the identical statute brought about a written, indirect procedure in Austria, and an oral, direct one in the Netherlands.

But even the best state agencies are neither omnipotent nor omnipresent. If a statute is being obeyed only where the agencies of the state compel the people to do so, not much more has been achieved than the noisy creaking of the official mill. The art of regulating rivers does not consist in digging a new bed for the river all the way down to its mouth, but in directing the current so that it self-actively creates a new bed for itself. Likewise statutes fulfil their functions only where the great majority of the people obey them in obedience to the promptings of an inner impulse.

There are two ways in which a state can act through its law. One is through the norms for decision. The state issues directions to its courts and other tribunals as to the manner in which they should decide the cases that are being submitted to them by the parties. The majority of norms for decision, it is true, have been taken from juristic law; they are state law only when they have arisen independently of juristic law and are designed to subserve the purposes of the state.

任何人相信它有力量创设一个口头诉讼程序。的确,该诉讼法典规定,在乡村地区(即该省省会以外的其余地方),诉讼程序应以口头方式进行。在奥地利,口头诉讼程序存在于这种情况:文书(对应于英国法的诉答程序)并未提交,但是已根据备忘录的形式写好,并交给法官。当然,偶尔当事人的陈述也会碰巧在开庭(*Tagfahrt*)日用书面表达出来。然而,法律诉讼任何时候都会仅仅基于该备忘录而作出判决,并且该裁决通常由未参加此案审前预备程序的法官作出。在荷兰——当它还属于奥地利的时候——口头诉讼程序就受到重视。法庭上的诉讼程序都是以口头形式进行;最后,讨论将体现在一份会议纪要中;曾经在开庭日主导该诉讼程序的法官在该会议纪要的帮助下——但主要基于在口头诉讼程序中获得印象——裁决该案。所以同样的制定法在奥地利带来的是书面的、间接的诉讼程序,在荷兰带来的却是口头的、直接的诉讼程序。

但是,即使是最称职的国家机构也不是无所不能、无处不在的。如果一项制定法仅仅在国家机构强迫人民遵守的时候才得以遵守,那么,其收效不过是国家研磨机发出来的嘈杂的咯吱声。治理江河的艺术不在于为江河挖一条新的由远至近的河床,而在于引导水流,以便让其为自身自动开辟一条新的河床。同样,只有当多数民众出于内心驱使而遵守制定法时,制定法才会实现其功能。

国家能够推行其法律的方式有两种。一种是通过裁判规范,国家向其法院和其他裁断机构发布指令,指明后者裁判当事人提交给他们处理之案件的方式。大多数裁判规范的确来自法学家法;只有当它们不依赖于法学家法而产生,并被设计用来促进国

The other form of state law are *Eingriffsnormen*( norms directing state agencies to proceed). They direct the authorities to act irrespectively of whether they have been appealed to or not. Although the state norms for decision and the norms directing state agencies to act are not, indeed, in all instances, based upon statutes, we are concerned chiefly with instances where this is the case. Whether a legal proposition brings about direct action or whether it is but a norm for decision does not depend exclusively upon the intent of the legislator or the wording of the statute, but is determined by actual usage. In civil affairs they are preponderantly norms for decision. Exceptions are: matters relating to matrimony, to guardianship, to corporations, to records (land register, commercial register, register for matters of the matrimonial régime), and the state proceeding in the matter of the estate of a deceased person where such proceeding is required. In these cases, in part at least, direct action actually takes place. Originally criminal law consisted exclusively of norms for decision. The injured party himself had to bring the matter before the court. And even today criminal law consists in part of norms that are mere norms for decision even where the action is to be brought by officials of the state, for it is the custom of the authorities to wait for a notice or some other move by the parties. In case of an offense against the state, however, of murder, arson, and other crimes that are considered dangerous to the common welfare or to the state, the state calls upon its agencies to hale the guilty person into court. The same relation between direct action and decision is found in administrative law.

The effect of state norms for decision is usually very much overestimated. The whole matter hinges upon action by the parties, who very often faiI to act altogether. Often the statute remains unknown to a considerable part of the population; again the parties for whose benefit it was enacted often lack the material means to enforce their claim, or, because of the actual distribution of power, they lack self-confidence or confidence in the authorities. For this reason legislation for the protection of working-men, so far as it contains only norms for decision, as a rule remains ineffectual. A few years ago I instituted an inquiry which dealt with the question to what extent the Austrian

家的目标时，它们才是国家法。国家法的另外一种形式是*Eingriffsnormen*（指令国家机构行事的规范）。不论此类规范是否被援用，它们均指示这些权力机构按此类规范的规定行事。尽管国家裁判规范和指令国家机构行事的规范实际上并非在所有情形下都建立在制定法的基础上，但我们此处主要探讨的就是这种情形。一个法律规定是否引发直接行动或者它仅仅是一个裁判规范，并不单单取决于立法者的意图或者制定法的措辞，而是由实际的惯例来决定。在民事案件中，它们主要是裁判规范。例外的情况有：有关婚姻、监护、法人、记录（土地登记、商事登记及婚姻领域事项的登记）的事务，以及国家在死者财产的事务上所必需的程序等。在这些情况下（至少部分如此），实际会带来直接的行动。最初，刑法仅仅包括裁判规范。受害方自己必须将相关问题提交到法院。甚至在今天，即使在诉讼由国家工作人员提起的情形下，刑法部分地仍由仅仅是裁判规范的规范构成，因为等待当事人的通知或提议是权力机构的习惯。不过，在发生攻击国家、谋杀、纵火以及其他犯罪行为的场合下，国家会命令其相应机构强制犯罪人入庭受审。直接行动和裁判之间的关系，在行政法中也可以同样看到。

国家裁判规范的效能通常被高估了。整个事情关键在于当事人的诉讼，而当事人经常压根就没有诉讼行为。相当一部分民众经常不了解制定法；另外，利益受到立法保护的当事人往往又缺乏行使他们请求权的物质手段，或者，由于权力的实际分配，他们缺乏自信或不信任权力机构。因此，有关劳动者保护的立法，就其仅包含的裁判规范而言，通常是没有实效的。一些年以前，我着手进行了一项调查，内容涉及在何种范围内，奥地利民法

Civil Code, which by this time has been in force for a century, had actually become part and parcel of everyday life. It produced remarkable results. Of the law of warranty, a part of the law which apparently is of extremely great practical importance, only a few regulations concerning defects in cattle are actually effective today—and these, perhaps because they had made their way into the statute from daily life. In case of immovables, warranty is usually excluded by contract; in case of movables, rules obtain which have no connection whatsoever with the Civil Code. But even apart from this, one would not believe to what extent the ineffectual law overbalances the effectual law. A conjecture to the effect that the number of sections of the Austrian Civil Code that have had no influence whatever upon life amounts to about one-third is not too high an estimate. Among them there are some that contain provisions of very wide scope, provisions that might become applicable at any moment but that have not been cited once in the more than 20,000 decisions reported in the Glaser-Unger collection of the decisions of the Supreme Court. It is self-evident that the situation is not altered by the fact that a given legal proposition has been applied here and there. That is far from proving that it has actually become part and parcel of, and regulates, daily life.

Perhaps I may be permitted to illustrate this statement by an example which I have adduced in another connection. The family law of the Austrian Civil Code, as is well known, is extremely individualistic, perhaps the most individualistic in present-day Europe. The relation of the wife to the husband and of the children to the parents, in general, is one of complete independence, almost as if they were strangers to one another. A child may have property of his or her own, and his or her power of disposition over it is as free and untrammeled as that of the parents over their property. Whatsoever the child acquires, accrues to the benefit of the child not of the parents. The child has full power of self-determination and can utilize his or her earning power freely for his or her own purposes. Only so long as the child is a minor is it under the power of his or her father; but the father, the bearer of this power, is not much more than a guardian. His

典——此前已生效了一个世纪——实际上已成为日常生活中不可缺少的一部分。如今,在明显具有极大现实重要性的那部分瑕疵担保法中,只有一些涉及牲畜缺陷的规定是实际有效的——这些,或许因为它们是从日常生活转入立法中的。在不动产场合下,瑕疵担保通常被合同所排除;在动产场合下,通行的规则与民法典都没有任何关系。但即使除此之外,人们也不会相信,在何种程度上没有实效性的法律的价值超过具有实效性的法律。奥地利民法典中对生活没有发生任何影响的条款数量占到总条款数的三分之一——这样一个推测并非是一个极端的估计。其中存在一些包含十分宽泛范围的条款,还有一些可能在任何时候都是可适用的但在最高法院格拉泽-盎格判例集中超过20000个的裁决并未曾引用过的条款。显然这种情况并未因以下这种事实而改变:一个特定的法律规定到处被适用。那远不能证明,该规定已经实际上成为日常生活中必不可少的一部分,从而对日常生活起着支配调整作用。

或许我可以引用在别处的一个例子来证明我的陈述。众所周知,奥地利民法典中的家庭法特别的"个人主义"——或许是当今欧洲最个人主义的一个法律部门。妻子和丈夫的关系以及孩子和父母的关系是完全独立的,几乎好像他们彼此之间都是陌生人。一个孩子可以拥有他或她自己的财产,他或她处置其财产的权利与其父母处置自有财产的权利一样自由和没有限制。孩子无论获得什么,都归于其自身利益,而非其父母的利益。孩子享有充分的自我决定权,能够自由利用他或她的收益能力追求其自身的目的。孩子作为未成年人在其父亲支配下的时间并不长;但是父亲作为这种权力的承有者,只不过是一个监护人。他的主要

chief function is to see to it that the child suffers no injury in consequence of inexperience, lack of discretion, or weakness. Only in this sense does the father have the right of disposition over the property, the earning power, and the destiny of the child. And even in this, he is under the supervision of the Supreme Court of Guardians, which will adjudge a complaint of a child against a father.

In Bukowina, however, although it is a part of Austria, and although the Civil Code is in force there as well as in the other parts of Austria, the power of the father is an extremely serious matter. The Roumanian peasant, perhaps the only true Roman of our day, exercises a *patria potestas*, which seems strikingly familiar to the student of Roman law. There the children actually belong to the father, although not all their lives, nevertheless until they attain their majority at the age of twenty-four; and though this ownership is not as absolute as it was in Rome, it is an ownership of body, property, and earning power, not only so long as they live in their father's house, but even while they are among strangers. If such a *filius* or *filia familias* is in service, the father or the mother appears punctually every month at the employer's residence or place of business and, quite as a matter of course, carries the wages home. And the parents dispose just as freely of the property and the income from the property of the child. And if one asks why the children submit so docilely, the answer is that resistance is something unheard of.

Ever since I directed attention to this phenomenon in an article in Harden's *Zukunft*, I have again and again received the reply that those things that are in conflict with the Civil Code are ethical custom, not law. This reply is based on the same old idea, to wit that we are here dealing with a question of terminology, i. e. with the question just what is to be called law. But we are here dealing with something quite different from this, i. e. with the fact that the Austrian Civil Code has not been able to root out this custom, which is in such decided conflict with the Code-irrespective of whether we call it law or

作用是照看孩子,不要让他由于无经验、缺乏判断力或虚弱而遭受伤害。只有在此意义上,父亲才有权处置孩子的财产、收益能力以及决定孩子的前途方向。并且即使在这种情况下,父亲也会受到最高监护法庭的监督,该法庭会对孩子针对其父亲提起的诉讼作出判决。

然而,在布科维纳,尽管它是奥地利的一部分,并且奥地利民法典在该地同样有效,但该区域内,父亲的权力是一个极为严肃的事情。罗马尼亚农民,或许是我们这个时代唯一真实的罗马人,他们行使着父权,研习罗马法的学生似乎对此极为熟悉。在那里,孩子属于父亲,尽管不是他们所有的生命,这种状况一直持续到他们24岁成人的时候;尽管这种所有关系并非像在罗马帝国时那样绝对,但那仍然是包含身体、财产以及收益能力等诸方面,不仅他们住在其父亲的家里时如此,而且即使当他们独立在外居住时也是如此。如果那样一个子或家子在作帮工,那么父亲或母亲每个月会按时出现在雇主的住处或营业地,不用说,他们是来领取工资的。父亲可以自由地处置由孩子的财产而衍生的财产和收入。如果有人问,为什么孩子如此温顺地驯服,答案就是"反抗"闻所未闻。

自从我在《哈登的未来》上的一篇文章中指出这种现象后,我一再收到回复,说与民法典相冲突的那些事情是伦理习俗,不是法律。这种回复是基于同样陈旧的观念,即,我们此处正在探讨一个术语学问题,亦即什么将会被称为法律。不过我们此处探讨的东西非常不同于这个问题,即,我们探讨的是奥地利民法典并不能扎根于这种习俗之外的事实,这种习俗与民法典处于那样一种明显的冲突中——不管我们是把它叫做法律还是伦理

ethical custom. It is true that since I first mentioned this custom about ten years ago I have noticed that it has markedly been beginning to fall into disuse; but this must be attributed to the breaking up of the old family order which is being brought about by modern social relations and by modern modes of thought, and which is very clearly perceptible in this country in other ways also, rather than to the influence of the Civil Code, which, we must admit, did not become effective until now, i. e. after the lapse of a whole century. If the jurists were more in the habit of observing life at first hand, they would discover a great number of instances of this kind. The famous investigation of the South Slavic customary law, which Bogišič had instituted, revealed that among all the southern Slavs within the territory in which the Austrian Civil Code is in effect, the well known South Slavic family community, the *Sadruga*, is in existence; this is altogether unknown to the Civil Code and absolutely irreconcilable with its principles. Moreover on almost every page of the book in which he summed up the results of his investigation we find the remark, with reference to the most diverse subjects, particularly with reference to the law of inheritance and of the family, that the people know that the precepts of the statute have a content quite different from their customary usage, but that they do not follow the statute. In his book, *Das Gewohnheitsrecht und die sozialen Verbände*, Dniestrzanski tells of a sort of primitive mercantile partnership which complies neither with the provisions of the Austrian Commercial Code nor with those of the Civil Code. I myself am continually meeting with phenomena of this nature and hope to be able to discuss them in a detailed juristic exposition. All of this shows to what extent the effectiveness of state law is being interfered with by other social forces.

Direct action by the state is much more effective than a norm for decision. This is convincingly demonstrated by the history of legislation for the protection of working-men. These statutes were originally enacted in order that they might serve as norms for the decision of disputes arising from contracts for wages and from bodily injuries. This applies also to the French statute relating to the twelve-hour day and to the German statute relating to liability in case of accident. These

习俗。的确，自从我十年前首先提到这种习俗，我已经指出，它显然已经逐渐遭到弃用；但这必须要归因于古老家庭秩序因现代社会关系和现代思维方式而逐渐瓦解，这在该国的其他方面也是清晰可见的，相反，它不能归因于民法典的影响，我们必须承认，经过了整整一百多年后，民法典迄今尚未"生效"，如果法学家更习惯于直接观察生活，那么他们将会发现大量的这种例子。由鲍季斯克曾经进行的关于南部斯拉夫习惯法的著名调查表明，在所有的南部斯拉夫人中，在奥地利民法典生效的区域内，众所周知的南部斯拉夫家族共同体"家长制家庭公社"依然存在；民法典对此一无所知，它也绝对与民法典的原则不相容。而且在总结其调查结果的该书的几乎每一页，我们都会发现涉及最多样主题的说明——特别是有关继承法和家庭法方面的问题——即人们知道制定法的规定非常不同于他们通行的习惯法，但他们仍然不遵循制定法。在《习惯法与社会联合体》一书中，作者丹尼斯特扎斯基介绍了一种原始的商事合伙，该合伙既非以奥地利商法典的规定组建，亦非按照奥地利民法典的规定组建。我自己也碰到这种性质的现象，希望能够在更详细的法律阐释中讨论它们。所有的这些都表明，国家法的效能在多大程度上正在受到其他社会力量的干扰。

由国家发动的直接行动比裁判规范有效得多。保护劳动者之立法的历史有力地证明了此点。这些规定最初制定是为了它们能够作为裁判规范，用于裁决因工资契约和身体伤害引起的争议。这同样适用于有关一天12小时（工作时间）的法国制定法和有关意外事故责任的德国制定法。这些制定法全都不具有实效

statutes were altogether ineffectual. The office of industrial inspector, as a state agency for the enforcement of the legislation for the protection of workingmen, first breathed some life into them by means of direct official action.

It is self-evident of course that a direct command of the statute directing the authorities of the state to proceed in a certain manner is not always sufficient to bring about such action. The French statute of the year 1806 relating to the cessation of labor on Sunday was never enforced. "Il ne se trouvait presque jamais un commissaire de police ou un garde champêtre qui osât dresser un procès-verbal contre les coupables," de Rousiers says on this subject.

So even state law often fails completely. Often the measures taken by the state for supervision and enforcement are unequal to the task of converting the rule laid down by the state into a rule of conduct. Often it fails because of the unwillingness, the weakness, or the incapacity of the authorities; the indictment which should be brought as a matter of official duty often waits notice from the parties involved. The law of the State regulating corporations and societies is evaded by means of free associations, e. g. in France and, in part, in Austria; partnerships and agreements are withdrawn from state supervision through failure to have them registered; contracts which are prohibited by the state are being entered into and voluntarily performed by the parties; invalid testaments are not being submitted to the obligatory proceedings for the distribution of the estates of deceased persons and the inheritances are being distributed by free partitioning. In such cases the other social associations have proved more powerful than the great social association, which has created the state as the instrument for carrying out its will. But as soon as the measures taken by the state for the purpose of supervision and enforcement fail in case of a statute that is to be enforced by direct action of the agencies of the state, the statute is reduced to the status of a norm for decision, which is able to manifest a trace of life only in case the whole apparatus is set in motion by the parties concerned.

The effectiveness of the law of the state is in direct ratio to the force which the state provides for its enforcement, and in inverse ratio to the resistance which the state must overcome. The fact that a

性。工业巡查处,作为实施保护劳动者立法的国家机构,通过直接的官方行动首次为这些立法规定注入生机。

当然很明显的是,指令国家职权机构以某特定方式行事的一个制定法的直接命令并不总是足以使那种行为发生。法国1806年关于周日停止工作的制定法从未实施过。胡适耶就此发表评论说:"敢于对违法者提起口头程序的专职人员几乎从未存在过。"

所以,甚至是国家法也经常完全不能发挥作用。国家为监督和实施而采取的措施经常不等于将国家制定的规则转变为行为规则的任务。这些措施经常由于机构的不情愿、虚弱或无能为力导致无效;应作为一个官方职责而产生的控诉经常需要等待有关当事人的通知。规范法人和社团的国家法由于自由结社方式而正受到规避,例如在法国以及某种程度上在奥地利;合伙和协议由于不登记而脱离国家的监督;(法律上)无效的遗嘱不会屈从于为分配死者财产而存在的强制性程序,遗产被自由瓜分。在这样一些场合下,其他社会联合体要比创立国家作为执行其意志工具的巨大联合体更为有力。但是,对于将要被国家机构通过直接行动执行的制定法,一旦由国家为监督和执行目的而采取的措施无法奏效时,该制定法将弱化至裁判规范的地位,它只有当整个机构由相关当事人激活而处于运转当中时,才会显示出"生命的迹象"。

国家法的效能与国家为执行该法投入的力量成正比,与国家必须克服的阻力成反比。社会行动相当大的部分焦点集中在立

considerable part of social activity has found its focus in legislation, administration of justice, and civil administration has not done away with the forces which are operative in society apart from these things. The church, economic life, art, science, public opinion, the family and personal associations, after all, have maintained their independence over against the state either altogether or to a great degree. They are, indeed, *foci* of development of purely social forces with which legislation, administration of justice, and civil administration by the state must cope at every moment. It is an error to think, as often happens, that all the modern state need do is simply to employ the means of power at its disposal in order to overcome everything that comes in its way. It is true that no one can offer legally justifiable resistance to the modern state as one could to the feudal state, to which the great feudal lord was bound solely by agreement. But the forces which the state has at its absolute disposal, the army, the police, and, supported by these, the civil officials, in the nature of things, are equipped for conflict with society only inasmuch as they are called upon to overcome a forcible insurrection, to attain a success which can be gained by a single effort. In the course of time they finally grow weary and their energies flag, and they themselves are too much exposed to social influences to follow the power of the state wherever it would lead them. History shows that the military and semi-military organization of the state, in spite of the great impetus which it can develop, and which can, at a given moment, overcome all resistance, is not a match for the uninterrupted sway of elemental forces which have their life and being in the social associations. They operate with less force at the beginning perhaps, but they operate steadily, decisively, and without faltering. Sufficiently developed, the religious, economic, political, and ethical trends created by them sooner or later gain influence, and, under favorable circumstances, gain control over the legislative and magisterial machinery of the state. The French express the thought that the state cannot permanently base its right upon might in the very expressive words: *On peut tout faire avec les baionettes*,

法上、司法上以及民政管理上，这一事实并未消除社会中在除了这些事项之外的领域起作用的力量。毕竟，教堂、经济生活、艺术、科学、公众观点、家庭和个人联合体，相对于国家，这些还保留着它们的独立性，要么是完全独立，要么是相当大程度上的独立。实际上，它们是纯粹社会力量发展的中心点，由政府进行的立法、司法和民政管理必须时刻应付它们。经常有一种观点，认为所有的现代国家为了克服阻碍之物需要做的仅仅是自由地使用权力工具，这种观点是错误的。的确，没有人能够提供在法律上正当的理由来反抗现代国家，这与人们有理由反对封建国家不同，对于封建国家，大封建领主仅仅受协议约束。但是由于国家享有的绝对自由的支配力量——军队、警察以及以它们做后盾的民事官员——被要求镇压强有力的暴动，并获得一蹴而就的成功，所以它们理所当然被装备起来以应付与社会的斗争。随着时间的流逝，它们最后变得疲倦，它们的能量开始衰弱，并且它们自己也受到太多社会的影响，而不能追随处处领导它们的国家的力量。历史表明，国家的军事和半军事组织——尽管可以显示出很强大的推动力，甚至在特定时刻，可以克服所有阻力——仍然比不上那种在社会联合体内部拥有其自身生命和存在之“自然力”不间断的支配。或许后者在一开始起作用的力量较弱，但它们稳定地、决然地并且没有任何犹豫地发挥着作用。充分发展之后，由它们创造的宗教的、经济的、政治的以及伦理的趋向或早或迟取得影响力，并且，在合适条件下，还会获得对国家立法和权威机器的控制。那个法国人用极具表现力的话表达了这种思想——国家不可能永久地将其权利建立在强权之上：我们可以用刺刀做一切事

*exceptés' y asseoir*. Even state law must, therefore, continually take the social forces into account.

And to begin with, the state cannot destroy the economic presuppositions of its own existence. The state is conditioned upon the production of economic goods within society in sufficient quantities to supply it with nourishment. It can, of course, find the means for the erection of its own structure by committing depredations upon the national economic system, and it is doing this even today to a terrific extent; for the ruin which will come after the lapse of decades or centuries need not worry the persons that are in power at the present time. But it cannot destroy the national economic system, for it must derive its sustenance from the surpluses of the latter.

Stammler says a fully developed despotism is a legal order which consists of but one paragraph, to wit: The legal relations among those that are subject to the law shall be adjudged and given effect solely according to the concrete decision of the ruler in the individual case. If the ruler had a band of foreign mercenaries at his beck and call, such a legal order would not, in itself, be inconceivable. But how long could it endure? If no one were secure in the possession of his property because a concrete decision of the ruler could deprive him of it at any time, if no one could act in reliance upon a contract because a similar decision might rescind the contract, agriculture, trade, and commerce would be in such a state of disintegration that before long the ruler would have no one left to rule. The many despots of whom history tells, therefore, were very careful not to supply us with warning examples of an essentially unsound legal order (*unrichtiges Recht*). They did not hesitate in individual cases to plunder, rob, and pillage as much as they thought feasible, and occasionally permitted their creatures to do this, but in general they permitted people to attend to their affairs, and unless they were particularly interested in warping justice they suffered legal disputes to be decided according to law and custom. Their own interest, clearly seen, quite readily taught

情,但我们不能坐在刺刀上面。因此,即使是国家法也必须连续不断地考虑社会力量。

起初,国家不能破坏其自身存在的经济方面的先决条件。国家以社会中足够数量的经济产品的生产为条件,以此来使国家保持繁荣。当然它能通过从事掠夺国民经济体系的方式找到建立起自身结构的方法,甚至在如今,国家从事这种恶行也达到了一个惊人的程度。数十年或数百年之后方才到来的经济崩溃不会让现时掌权者担心。但是它不能破坏国民经济体系,因为它必须从后者的盈余中获得自身的维系。

施塔姆勒说,一个充分发达的专制统治是一个仅由一个条款组成的法律秩序,即:在服从法律的那些人之间的法律关系将仅仅根据个案中统治者的具体决断而判决并赋予法律效力。如果统治者有一批外国的唯利是图者对其唯命是从,那样一个法律秩序本身将不会难以想像。但是它能维持多久?如果由于统治的具体裁决能随时剥夺人们的财产占有,因而没有人可以确保其财产占有,如果由于一个相似的裁决可能撤销某种契约,因而没有人可以信赖该契约而行事,那么,农业、贸易以及商业将会处于那样一种解体的状态,以至于没有多久,统治者就会发现无人再听他的统治。因此,许多专制君主的历史已经表明,他们非常注意不给我们留下有关根本不稳定的法律秩序(*unrichtiges Recht*)的前车之鉴。在认为可行的范围内,他们在个案中抢掠、抢劫、掠夺不会有丝毫犹豫,而且偶尔他们也会允许他们的奴才这样做,但是总体上,他们允许民众从事各自的事务,并且除非他们对扭曲正义特别感兴趣,否则他们还是会按照法律和习俗对相关法律争议作出裁决。他们清晰可见的自身的利益会轻易地让他们懂

them the value of a legal order.

This is the reason why it is frequently being said, albeit not by modern jurists but by economists of the classical school, that the power of the state is limited by the laws of economics. The state, which has the power to ruin very many things, which can take very much away from one person and give it to another, is nevertheless unable to make one more blade of grass grow than the economic resources of the nation permit. The significance of the knowledge of this fact as a means of preservation is enormous, for a revolutionary if he should seize control of the state would no more be able to do this than is the present state. It too could take away from one man and give to another, could ruin many things, but could not cause one more seed-corn to sprout than the economic resources of the nation permit. The best that the state as well as its adversaries can do for the future economic welfare of the nation is to treat the economic system of the present with extreme tenderness.

We shall have to get used to the thought that certain things simply cannot be done by means of a statute, that the intent of the author of a statute is a matter of absolute indifference so far as its effects are concerned. Once in force, it goes its own way. Whether the legal proposition is effective, whether it has the effect that was desired, depends exclusively upon whether it is a means adapted to this purpose. And lastly we must get used to the thought that the effect of a legal proposition is determined not so much by the interpretation which jurists place upon it as by other circumstances, which are of much greater significance in the matter, e. g. the individual peculiarity of the people, the prevailing ethical views, the means of power used to enforce it, the kind of legal procedure employed. A statute is effective not by dint of its mere existence, but by dint of its force.

The commands of the state are most effective when they are exclusively negative, when it is not a matter of compelling people to act but of constraining them to refrain from action, when they are given in order to forbid, to attack, to destroy, to extirpate. In this manner the state has been engaged in innumerable contests with religious trends,

得法律秩序的价值。

这也是为什么经常有古典学派的经济学家——尽管不是法学家所说——会说,国家的权力受限于经济学的法则。国家有本领毁灭很多事物,可以从一个人手中夺走很多,并将它给另外一个人,尽管如此,国家却无法在国家允许的经济财力之外给予某人额外的一丁点利益。了解作为一种维系方式的此等事实的意义是巨大的,因为一个革命者如果控制了国家,他能做的也不过是和现在的国家做到的一样。他也能从一个人手中夺取某物并将之交给另外一人,能够毁灭很多东西,但是仍无法让一个人在国家允许的财力之外多出一颗发芽的谷种。国家与其反对者对于未来国民经济福利能做的,充其量就是以极大的和善去对待当下的经济体系。

我们不得不习惯于这么思考:某些事情不能简单地通过制定法的方式来做,就制定法的效果而言,制定法的立法者的意图是一件绝对无关的事情。制定法一旦付诸施行,它就完全按自己的规律向前发展。该法律规定是否有效,它是否有欲求的效果,均只取决于它是否是一个适于该目的的方式。最后我们还必须习惯于这么思考:与其说法律规定的效力取决于法学家加之于上的解释,不如说取决于其他条件,在此问题上,这些其他条件具有更大的重要意义,例如,民族的独特性格、主流的伦理观点、用于执行该制定法的权力工具、所适用法律程序的种类等。一个制定法并非借助于自身存在而有效,而是借助其实施而有效。

当国家的命令全都是否定性的,且其目的不是强制人们做什么而是限制人们做什么时,当其目的是为了禁止、攻击、破坏、肃清什么而作出时,该命令最为有效。这样,国家已经与宗教倾向、

societies and other communities, to which for some reason or other it had become opposed. This is the content of the whole penal law of the state, and particularly of the only part that in fact has a certain measure of social influence. This sphere includes chiefly police legislation by the state, i. e. legislation for the public safety and the public health, and for the supervision of trades and occupations. In the economic sphere also action by the state is most effective if carried out by means of prohibitions (tariff legislation). The proscriptive rights and the monopolies of the state are mere prohibitions. The state has hindered the free activity of economic forces, and by doing so perhaps has destroyed incalculable economic values, but perhaps has made possible and fostered a given economic venture at their expense. Copyright laws have the same significance. The state issues a prohibition directed to all men, excepting only the author, forbidding them to engage in any activity of a certain kind. This is the whole content of the law in so far as it is of state origin. The only difference between this right and the proscriptive rights and the monopolies is this, that the object of the former is to stimulate or to reward the inventive genius. And so far as the law of the family and of property is not of social but of state origin, its content is almost exclusively negative, e. g. marriages, societies, contracts, last wills and testaments, that are being forbidden, dissolved, declared void, or voidable; property that is being forfeited; heirs that are being excluded.

Wherever the state wishes to constrain men to perform an affirmative act, it must proceed much more cautiously. To guide and direct great multitudes of men is a matter of enormous difficulty under all circumstances. It presupposes a great and rare gift. It is most difficult perhaps when it is to be done on the basis of universal abstract rules. Whenever men consider a task useful and profitable, they will combine on their own initiative in order to perform it; often economic and social pressure will also induce them to do so, and action by the authorities serves rather to disturb, to hinder, and confuse than to promote. For this reason it will, most likely, be impossible to impose the will of another upon a superior number of unwilling men. This is shown by the many attempts made in former days to compel striking workmen with the aid of gendarmes or policemen to return to work.

社团以及其他共同体进行了数不清的斗争,国家有这样或那样的原因反对后者。这就是国家整个刑法的内容,特别是——事实上拥有特定规模的社会影响力——仅有部分的内容。这个领域主要包括由国家进行的政策立法,即,为公共安全、公共卫生以及贸易和职业监督而进行的立法。在经济领域,国家行为如果凭借禁令(关税立法)来推行,则最为有效。国家剥夺公民权利与禁止垄断都仅仅是禁令。国家阻碍经济力量的自由行为,或许会破坏不可计量的经济价值,但是或许会以可能制造和培育一个特定的经济投机为代价。版权法具有同样的重要性。国家签发一个禁令,禁止除了作者之外的所有人从事某特定种类的任何行为。这就是国家制定的这种法律的全部内容。赋予、剥夺公民权利及禁止垄断之间的唯一区别在于,前者的目标是为了激励或奖赏这种创造性的天赋。家庭法和财产法不是社会立法而是国家立法,就此而言,它们的内容几乎全都是否定性的,例如婚姻、社团、契约、遗嘱,它们会被禁止、解散、宣告无效或可撤销;又如被征收的财产以及被排除在外的继承人等。

当国家希望强迫人们"为"某种肯定性行为时,它必须更加小心地从事。指导与指挥广大民众无论如何都是一件极其困难的事情。它需要有高超且罕见的天资。或许当基于普遍的抽象规则而做这件事情时,它是最难的。无论何时,只要人们认为,一项任务有用、有利,他们为了完成这项任务就会主动联合;经济和社会压力经常也会促使他们这样做,权力机构的行为所起的作用不是打扰、阻碍与扰乱,而是促进。因此,强行将另外一个意志加到数量更庞大的不乐意的人们身上,多半是不可能的。这可以由以下事实所证明:以前,政府付出许多努力,试图在宪兵或警察的帮

The *lex Julia et poppaea* perhaps secured many a rich inheritance for the Roman fisc; but whether even one single child owes its existence to it is a matter of much less certainty. The Austrian tax on bachelors and childless persons is striving for the same results in behalf of the fisc without the addition of flourishes about increasing the population. In the rare cases in which the state successfully compels affirmative action, especially in the administration of the army and of taxation, a specially trained and skilled technique has been developed on the basis of the experience of millennia, or at least of centuries. Face to face however with a breakdown of discipline which had been caused by special circumstances or with a well thought out refusal to pay taxes, the state, on several occasions, had to admit that it was powerless. Similar results are sometimes encountered in prisons and boarding schools, because of the great helplessness and suggestibility of the persons involved. All other cases in which the law of the state produces an affirmative effect are cases of direct dealings between the authorities and the population in which the latter realizes, at least to a certain extent, that obedience to the law of the state will redound to its advantage. The law of procedure perhaps rests chiefly on this idea. Perhaps the most successful venture of this nature that the state has undertaken in recent years is the matter of social insurance. It is a great misfortune for the state that all its institutions tend to become governmental agencies, even foundations for the advancement of education, of art, science, and the public welfare; even schools, museums, expositions, railroads, state monopoly of tobacco, and hospitals. This causes them to lose not only their adaptability to the changing needs of life but also their adherents among the people, who could make them instruments of social progress.

助下强迫罢工的工人回去工作。《关于婚姻的巴比·波培法》[1]或许可以使古罗马的皇室财库获得很多富足的遗产;但是,是否连一个孩子的存在也归于它,就远不敢确定无疑地回答了。奥地利对单身汉和无子女之人所征之税正在为国库争取同样的结果,但并没有带来人口的增加。在极少的情况下,国家成功地强制人们从事积极性的行为,特别是在军队和税收管理中,基于一千年的经验——至少是数百年的经验——经受过专门磨炼、日臻娴熟的技术已经被发展出来了。然而国家偶尔必须承认,当纪律由于特定环境而遭到破坏时,或者遇到有人想出了巧妙的避税方法拒绝纳税时,它是无能为力的。由于相关人员的极大无助和易受影响,在监狱和管理学校中,国家也会面临相似的结果。国家法律产生一个肯定性效力的所有其他情形,都是权力机构和民众之间的直接交往,这种情形下,民众意识到,至少在某种程度上,服从国家法律将会获得有利的回报。诉讼法或许主要基于这种理念。或许国家最近一些年正在从事的这种性质的商业投机中,最成功的要数社会保险事业。所有的公共机构都倾向于变成政府机构,甚至为促进教育、艺术、科学和公共福利而建立的公共机构也这样,对于国家而言,这是一个很大的不幸;甚至学校、博物馆、展览馆、铁路部门、国家烟草专营事业以及医院也都有这种趋势。这不仅让它们无法适应不断变化的生活需要,而且也让它们失去民众中的支持者——这些支持者原本能够使它们成为推动社会进步的手段。

---

〔1〕(拉)*lex Julia et poppaea*,一部罗马法规,规定限制未婚者或未生育子女的已婚者根据遗嘱而得益,以达到鼓励结婚和提高生育率的目的。

Now how did the law which had been created by the state succeed in impressing its stamp upon society and what social formations has it brought about in the course of historical development? When a state lays down for itself or for its agencies its or their position and functions, it does not thereby create state law in the proper sense of the term, but law of the state. The state thereby creates its inner order for itself and its agencies, just as every other social association must create an order for itself: the church, the commune, the family, the society. The state does no more than this when it engages in economic ventures of a private nature, railroads, banks, or mines. Its law here is the same in principle as that upon which any other economic venture of a private nature is based.

The state actually creates the people of the state (*Staatsvolk*), and it does this, in part at least, through its law. This, it is true, is something quite different from the people in the national sense, which is exclusively a product of society. Most of the latest efforts to nationalize by action of the state, and that means to unite the various peoples which are united in one state not only into one *Staatsvolk* (people of the state) but also into one people in the national sense, have failed. Hitherto it has not been the state but only society that has been able to nationalize effectually. Nevertheless the *Staatsvolk* is an entity of extremely great importance. The unity of a common constitution, a common army, a common language throughout the state; of a unitary system of civil administration, though the unity of the latter be outward and partial only; the unity of economic territory, which functions chiefly in the collections of duties, taxes, and fees, and in the establishment of means of communications; the unity of legislation and the resultant unity of juristic science and technique and of judicial decision, and finally the capital, the common center, toward which there is a constant flow of the population, and from which a great number of suggestions emanate—all of these things make the *Staatsvolk* a unique unified entity. They exercise a profound influence upon creation of law by society. To attempt to exclude the *Staatsvolk*, as has been

那么国家制定之法如何给社会留下其印记，在历史发展的过程中，它又带来了什么样的社会信息呢？当国家为自己与其所属机构规定其地位和功能时，它并未随之创立恰当意义上的国家法，而是创立了国家之法。国家因而也为自己与其所属机构创建起内部秩序，正如其他社会联合体——教会、公社、家庭、社会——必须为自身创建一个秩序一样。当国家从事私营性质的经济经营以及铁路、银行或矿山经营时，它能做到的仅仅是这个。它的法律大体上与任何其他私营性质的经济经营赖以存在的规则没什么两样。

国家实际上创造了“国民”(*Staatsvolk*)，这至少是部分地是通过法律而达成的。的确，国民与“民族意义上的人民”区别甚大，后者完全是社会的产物。最近通过国家行为而进行的大部分的国家化的努力，以及统合不同民族——不仅使不同民族统一在一国之内，而且还使它们在民族意义上“归一”——的方法，已经失败。迄今为止，能够有效实施国家化的不是国家而仅仅是社会。尽管如此，国民仍然是一个极为重要的实体。通过国家而获得的一个共同宪法的统一、一个共同军队的统一、一个共同语言的统一；一个统一的民政管理制度，尽管后者的统一是外在的，而且只是部分的；经济领域的统一，这方面的主要功能是收取关税、税收、费用以及建立通讯工具；立法的统一以及作为其结果的法律科学与技术的统一、司法裁判的统一，最后是首都的统一，大量的人口不断涌向那个共同的中心，大量的建议从那儿散播开去——所有的这些都使得“国民”成为一个独一无二的“一元化”实体。它们对于由社会所进行的法的创设产生深刻的影响。在法律发展的研究中，将国民排除在思考之外——如最近一段时期

done repeatedly in recent times, from consideration in the study of legal development is to misapprehend utterly the weight of these facts.

Furthermore the state creates the peace of the state. It constitutes agencies whose function is to preserve it, the administrative tribunals, the police; it assumes control of the criminal courts and by creating state law, supplies them with a basis for their activity. The norms of state law that we are concerned with here are parts of police law, of procedural law, and of criminal law. They are norms of secondary rank in every respect; they create neither social nor state institutions; they merely provide state protection for those that are already in existence.

In matters economic, the state wields a decisive influence through state law by establishing economic rights that are not conditioned upon the economic production or exchange of goods. At every stage the state, being a predominantly military association, is, in a certain sense, in opposition to the national economic system. It takes no active part in it; for we may disregard its inconsiderable contributions in its capacity of landowner and of industrial entrepreneur. The economic goods that it requires, it secures indirectly from the returns of other economic undertakings. Therein lies the whole economic content of the state law of finance. Through it the state, relying on its means of power, determines how much of the returns of the national economy it claims for itself. Even when the state, in a private economic contract, obligates itself to render some performance, it must draw upon other economic undertakings for this, for it is not engaged in economic activity of its own, except when it acts in the capacity of a great landed proprietor or of an industrial entrepreneur. It is self-evident that we are not denying that what the state offers to the people is, or at least can be, of the greatest possible economic significance; but it is not a result of economic activity. For this reason the state can furnish the basis for economic rights only by distributing economic values that are already in existence in a way different from the distribution that would be effected by the undisturbed operation of economic activity or by taking a value that has already been created or that is about to be created from one economic undertaking and placing it at the disposal of another. In doing these things, the state relies upon the instrumentalities of power that are at its disposal, The state law of ownership, the state law and right of inheritance of collateral relatives, the state annuities and monopolies, the effect of prohibitions by

一再做的那样——是对这些事实之重要性的极大误解。

此外,国家创立了国家的秩序。它设立了专门用于维护这种秩序的机构、行政法庭及警察局;国家掌控刑事法庭,并通过创设国家法为刑事法庭的行为提供基础。我们此处关注的国家法的规范是治安法、诉讼法、刑法的一部分。从各方面来看它们都是次级序列的规范;它们既未创立社会机构也未创立国家机构;它们仅仅是对那些已经存在的规范提供国家保护。

在经济事务方面,国家通过创设不依赖于经济生产或商品交换的经济权利。在每个阶段,作为支配性的军事联合体,国家在特定意义上与国民经济体系处于对立的地位。它并不积极参与经济生产;因为我们可能忽略了它作为一个地主和企业家的无足轻重的贡献。对于它需要的经济产品,它从其他经济企业的经营成果中间接获取。其中存在国家财政法的整个经济内容。通过财政法,国家凭借其权力工具,决定国民经济的利润中多大的份额归于它自己。即使当国家因一份非行政性的经济契约而有义务履行某种义务时,它也肯定利用其他经济企业为其服务,因为除了当它作为一个大土地所有者或企业家时,它不直接从事经济活动。很明显,我们不会否认,国家为其人民提供的——或至少能提供的——东西具有最大可能的经济重要性;但那不是经济行为的结果。因此,国家能为经济权利提供基础的方式只能是分配已经存在的经济价值,这种分配非常不同于因经济活动未受干扰的运行或从一个经济企业获取已被创造或将要被创造出来的价值,并将之交给另外一个企业自由支配而受到影响的分配。国家的所有权法、国家的旁系亲属继承法律和权利、国家的养老金和专利权、国家在共有法、财产法、契约法以及继承法中禁令的

the state in the law of joint ownership, of things, of contract, and of inheritance are based on such distribution and transfer of economic values.

The order of possession is of social, not of state, origin, and therefore is a creation of society and not of the state. The order of ownership, on the other hand, derives its origin chiefly from juristic science. It comprises the norms for decision which determine which one of the parties to the controversy about possession should win, to which one the courts of the state should grant protection. So far as this protection is granted according to the order of possession, inasmuch as the state does nothing more than to give effect to the order of possession as it has arisen in society, the legal propositions according to which this is done are not state law but social law, and, indeed, juristic law. On the other hand, the greater security which the state provides for the order of possession through criminal law, the police, and the law of procedure is an achievement of the state. Society, juristic science, and the state therefore have cooperated in the creation of the law and right of possession and of ownership. Possession is the social constitution; ownership is the sum total of the norms for decision of juristic law, according to which one's possession is protected by the courts, is restored if interfered with, and is regained if lost. This greater security is state law.

In Roman law and in the systems derived from it, this relation is obscured by the dichotomy of the protection of possession into protection of ownership and of possession in the narrower sense of the term. The idea underlying this dichotomy is the following: Unconditional protection is given only to a specifically qualified possession, to ownership; over and above this, a preliminary protection, which is preponderantly in the nature of police protection, is granted to all possession even to the altogether non-economic possession of the thief and the robber. Moreover all protection is denied to various forms of possession that rest on a sound economic basis, especially the possession of the ordinary and of the usufructuary lessee, both of whom are limited to an action on the contract. According to Roman terminology, which is followed by that of the modern Continental law, ownership is not in a general way, as it is in English and Scandinavian law, all legally protected possession, but only such possession as is protected by special remedies (*actio* and *exceptio* asserting ownership). But over and above this almost all possession enjoys some measure of protection,

实现全都是建立在那种经济价值的分配和转移之上。

占有秩序是社会的,而非国家的,因此其起源应该是社会的创造而非国家的创造。另一方面,所有权秩序,其本源主要来自法学。它包括裁判规范——决定哪一方诉讼当事人会胜出,国家的法院将会给予哪一方以保护。就这种按照占有秩序而给予的保护而言,由于国家所做的仅仅是使一个在社会中已存在的占有秩序实际生效,因此,据以实现此占有秩序的该法律规定不是国家法,而是社会之法,实际上是法学家法。另一方面,国家通过刑法、警察机构、诉讼法为占有秩序提供的更大的保障是国家的一项成就。社会、法学以及国家因此在该占有法和所有权法的创制中有所合作。占有是社会构造;所有权是法学家法的裁判规范的总和,据此,一个人的占有受到法院的保护,如果受到干涉则可回复原状,如果丢失则可取回。这种更大的保障是国家法。

在罗马法及其派生的制度中,这种关系由于将所有权保护中的占有保护与狭义上的占有保护作出区分而显得难以理解。这种二分法的理念如下:无条件的保护仅仅给予一个特定的合法占有与所有权;除此之外,所有的占有——甚至包括窃贼和强盗完全非经济性的占有——都会获得一种初步的保护,这种保护主要是治安性的保护。此外,基于一个稳定经济基础上的各种形式的占有,特别是普通承租人和享有用益权之承租人的占有都被拒绝给予全部的保护,这两类人仅能基于契约而起诉。按照现代欧陆法遵循的罗马法的术语学,所有权,一般说来,并非是所有法律上受到保护的占有——这与英国法及斯堪的纳维亚法不同——而仅仅是那些受到特定救济方法(主张所有权的诉和抗辩)保护的占有。但是除此之外的几乎所有占有都享有一定程度的保护,而

and bona fide possession can avail itself of remedies in the nature of the *actio Publiciana in rem* which are modeled upon the remedies of ownership. The private law protection of the economic constitution therefore is extraordinarily well provided with forms, and this fact makes it very difficult to see it in its social interrelations.

We have no information as to the historical reasons for the dichotomy and trichotomy of the Romans. But Jhering in his day has shown with admirable acumen that, among the Romans, possession was merely an outwork of ownership, and that protection of possession was merely an aid to better protection of ownership. If we understand possession to mean the economic constitution, and ownership to mean merely the sum total of the norms for decision through which the economic constitution is preserved and restored, the doctrine that protection of possession is merely an aid to protection of ownership manifestly means only that protection is granted to possession and to ownership for the sake of the economic constitution and that the difference between the two is merely a matter of a few presuppositions and of a few diversities in the effect of legal remedies. Jhering, I think, has found the reason why the possession of the ordinary and of the usufructuary lessee was not protected. It was the fact that these possessors, in fact, were serfs among the Romans. The protection which the non-economic possession of the thief and of the robber enjoyed even against the victim of the theft and the robbery probably never was anything more than a bit of scholastic wisdom. Definitive protection of possession in the form of protection of ownership is granted, at least in the fully developed Roman law, to all economically acquired possession, even though it has been acquired by means of a slight disturbance of the economic order (bonitary ownership); and after a short period of usucapion, even against the person whose possession has been interfered with.

Other legal systems, chiefly the Germanic system of the Middle Ages, the modern English and Scandinavian systems, do not differentiate between protection of possession and protection of ownership. Every economic possessor is granted the identical remedies. And in a case of possession of movables this is done also in modern German and

且善意占有可以获得“善意占有之诉”的救济，这种救济乃仿自所有权的救济。因此，经济制度组织的私法保护类型特别完善，并且该事实使得在社会相互关系中理解它非常困难。

罗马人这种“二分法”与“三分法”的历史缘由，我们没有任何资料。但是耶林在他那个时代已经以令人敬佩的敏锐指明，在罗马人当中，占有仅仅是所有权的“简易外围工事”，对占有的保护仅仅是为了更好保护所有权。如果我们把占有理解成经济结构，将所有权理解成只是——经济结构据以维持与回复的——裁判规范的总和。那么“占有保护仅仅是所有权保护的帮助”这种学说明显仅仅意味着，保护施与占有和所有权是为了经济结构的缘故，两者之间的区别不过是一些先决条件与法律救济效力上的少许差异性。我认为，耶林已经找到普通承租人与享有用益权之承租人的占有为什么不受保护的理由。事实就是，这些占有人实际上是罗马人中的农奴。窃贼和强盗对其非经济性占有享有的——甚至针对盗窃与抢劫受害人的——保护很可能永远只是一个学究性的知识。至少在充分发达的罗马法中已经规定，所有经济上获得的占有，这种占有即使是通过对经济秩序造成轻微扰乱的方式(无所有权而有使用权的“所有权”)而获得的占有，都将获得以所有权保护形式存在的限制性占有保护；并且在短期的取得时效后，即使针对其(原先的)占有受到妨碍之人而言，也享有所有权。

其他法律制度，主要是德国中世纪的法律制度，现代英国与斯堪的纳维亚的法律制度，并未区分占有保护和所有权保护。每一个经济上的占有者都受到同样的救济。在动产占有的情形下，

French law. This perhaps is the most convincing proof that the Roman dichotomy is based solely on a dichotomy of legal remedies, not upon a difference in the nature of the thing protected. The question has often been raised whether, in view of the expeditiousness of the modern Austrian procedure, the dichotomy is justifiable at the present time.

In addition to this social ownership, which consists solely in the protection of the economic constitution by the state, there is an ownership which is purely a matter of state law, and which arises and exists solely through the will of the state independently of the economic constitution. The state can grant the same protection that it grants to the possessor to a person who has no possession, who has never acquired possession economically, by cormmissioning its agencies independently of all economic presuppositions, in the first place to secure possession for the person favored in this manner, and thereafter to protect him in this possession and repel attacks that may be made upon it. It will also, of course, instruct its courts in case of litigation to decide in favor of the person whom it has thus made the owner. The most important instance is that of the great landowner and the disencumbrance of land of its burdens and charges.

The ownership of land by the peasants is purely economic, and arose independently of the state and outside of the state, and to a great extent prior to the state. Ownership of great proprietary estates, however, apart from the rare cases of purchase of peasant lands, which hardly ever occurred in the very distant past, owes its existence to the state. The great proprietary estate, in contrast to the economic ownership of the peasant, is a political ownership of the ruling classes, created by the power of the state. In the last analysis therefore it is merely the expression of political ascendancy. When the *populus Romanus* asserted a claim to the ownership of the *solum provinciale*, when the king of England declared himself owner of all the soil of England, they meant to say that in virtue of the right of conquest they would dispose of the land according to their arbitrary will.

现代德国法与法国法也是如此规定的。这或许是最有说服力的证据,证明罗马法上的占有保护的“二分法”仅仅是基于法律救济的“二分法”,而非基于受保护事物的性质上的差异。鉴于现代奥地利诉讼程序的快捷,这种“二分法”在当代是否仍有充分的理由——这个问题经常被提起。

除了这种社会性所有权——仅存在于国家给予的经济制度组织的保护内——之外,还有一种纯属国家法事务的所有权,它仅仅凭借与经济结构无关的国家的意志而产生和存在。国家可以将给予占有人的保护同样地给予从未曾占有过的人、从未在经济上获得过占有的人,国家通过委托独立于所有经济先决条件之外的机构,首先以这种方式使受优待之人获得占有。此后保护他维持这种占有,击退所有可能针对它的攻击。当然,若就此引发诉讼,国家也会指示其法院作出有利于被其确定为所有人的那个人的裁决。最重要的例子就是大土地主对土地的占有以及他对其土地上的负担和捐税的摆脱。

农民所享有的土地所有权纯粹是经济性的,它是不依赖于国家且在国家外而产生的,并且在很大程度上先于国家。然而,大地产的所有权,除了购买农民土地这种极少情形之外——在非常遥远的过去这种情形几乎从未曾发生过,其存在皆归因于国家。这种巨大私人财团,与农民的经济性所有权相对,是统治阶级政治性所有权,是由国家权力创造的。因此,归根到底,它仅仅是政治上支配的表达。当罗马城人对仅属外省者的所有权主张权利时,当英格兰国王宣布自己是英格兰所有土地的所有人时,他们其实是在说,凭借征服者的权利,他们可以按照自己的独断意志来处分被征服的土地。

The principle, *nulle terre sans seigneur*, merely reflects the fact that the powers that rule the state, the king, and the nobility, have succeeded in overcoming the resistance of the peasant landowners. Likewise every grant of ownerless or of occupied lands by the king to his grandees was merely an exercise of the power of the state. And it is exactly the same thing when counts and princes in the Middle Ages appropriate rights in forests, rivers, and mines, when they compel their subjects to receive their own lands in feudal tenure. Probably this device of subduing the peasants was never successfully carried out to any appreciable extent without the aid of the state. Occasionally the mere formal declaration of the sovereign power of the state that it had determined to treat a person as the owner of land was sufficient to make that person the owner. One of the most famous cases of this kind is the creation of great proprietary estates in Scotland. When the English, after the battle of Culloden, proceeded to destroy the ancient Gaelic clan organization, they accomplished their purpose by declaring that the chieftains of the clans were the proprietors of the whole clan territory, which had, until then, been held in common. The ownership of great proprietary estates in Bengal began with an error of the English, who in the eighteenth century mistook the tax on land for rent, and thought that the peasants who were obligated to pay a tax were tenants of the maharajahs.

There is no doubt that the great proprietary estates owe their existence to the power of the state. When the state created these estates it was acting as the association of powerful warlike nobles. The individual noble to whom enormous domains had been assured or given in fee found among his fellow-nobles, who, united, constituted the state, a measure of support which might, on occasion, become very useful. But he had to do the actual taking possession himself. Without personal means of power, relying merely on a document of grant, no one would have undertaken to take possession of these estates or have been able to maintain possession. The situation is the same as that which one finds in other spheres when a man secures the aid of those who are associated with him in a smaller association in order to attain his object.

“无领主则无土地”这个原则仅仅反映了这个事实:统治国家的权力、国王以及贵族在镇压农民土地所有者的反抗方面获得了成功。同样,国王每一次授予其贵族无主土地或已被人占有的土地,都不过是国家权力的行使而已。当中世纪的伯爵和王族径自取得对森林、河流、矿山的权利,当他们强迫其属民以封建土地保有的形式接受他们自己的土地时,这些行为其实都具有完全同样的性质。若没有国家权力的帮助,这种驯服农民的设计很可能永远不会成功地达到任何可观的程度。有时候,单单国家主权关于决定视某人为土地的所有人的正式宣布就足以让某个人成为所有人。这种情形最著名的例子之一是苏格兰大地产的创立。当英国在卡洛登战役后继续破坏盖尔宗族组织时,他们通过宣布该宗族的酋长是整个宗族领土的所有人(在此之前土地皆为共有)的方式达到了他们的目的。在孟加拉,大私有财团的所有权因英国人的一个错误而开始,18 世纪英国人误将土地税理解为地租,并认为有义务纳税的农民是土邦邦主的佃户。

无疑,大地产的存在归功于国家的权力。当国家创造了这些地产时,它是作为强大的军事贵族之间的联合体而发挥着作用。以世袭地产形式获得或被赐予巨大领地的单个贵族,在其伙伴贵族——他们共同联合起来建立国家——中得到了某种程度的支持,而这种支持有时候非常有用。但是,他不得不亲自进行实际占有。若没有个人权力工具,仅仅依赖于一份授权文件,没有人能够着手占有这些地产或维持这种占有。这种情况正如在其他领域,当有人为了实现目标而取得其所属的一个较小联合体内那些同伴帮助时,他所发现的那种情况。

The state-created ownership of great proprietary estates as such has no economic content. The state cannot breathe the breath of life into an economic institution by decrees based merely on the possession of power. What is the effect of a grant of land by the state? Is it anything other than the promise of the state to support the grantee in his attempt to take possession, to repel attacks upon this possession by others, and to aid him in securing income from the land? In the case of a new and feeble state this may not amount to very much; it furnishes a sufficient pretext, however, for the powerful noble to exert his own strength to convert the peasant, who until then has been an owner, into a usufructuary lessee or into a serf in order thereby to secure for himself a share of the returns of the economic activity of the latter, or, to state the matter technically, to get ground-rent (*Bodenrente*). Giving uncultivated land amounts to a warrant for the returns that may accrue to the donee from his own economic labor or from any other form of economic activity, e. g. from colonization.

Disencumbrance of the soil is the opposite of the feudal grant. It is the abolition of the right to ground-rent which had been created by the nobility and the state through the exercise of their own power. Numerous disencumbrances of this nature took place in antiquity; for example, among the Romans perhaps in the fourth century of the city, at least in the immediate vicinity of Rome. In England, an incomplete one took place in the year 1660 (12 Car. II); in France, after several earlier attempts, a complete disencumbrance in the year 1789; in the rest of Europe everywhere during the course of the nineteenth century.

When the state proceeds to emancipate the peasants and to disencumber the soil, the situation is quite different from that of the time when the land was granted to the nobles. The driving force in modern instances of disencumbrance is a powerful urban citizenry which enters into direct relations with the state. The state is no longer exclusively an organization of the landowning nobility. The urban citizenry takes a lively interest in the emancipation of the peasantry, because this emancipation makes it possible to draw them into the general commercial life, into the economic system of finance and credit, and because the domination of the nobility is held in check thereby. The king becomes independent of the nobility, inasmuch as he has already

国家像那样创立的大私有地产的所有权没有经济内容。国家无法仅凭基于强力占有的命令就把生机注入到经济结构中。国家授予土地的效果是什么？相对于国家承诺支持正设法取得占有的被授予人击退其他人对该占有的攻击，并帮助他从该土地中获得收入，那有何不同吗？在一个新生、无力的国家，这可能没有多大价值；然而，对于强大的贵族运用其强力将先前是土地所有者的农民转化为享有用益权的佃户或农奴，以便可以因此确保自己能享有后者经济行为的利润份额，或可以技术性地表述此事，或获得地租(*Bodenrente*)，那却能提供一个充分的借口。赠与未开垦土地等于是保证将因其自身经济劳动或任何其他形式经济活动，例如通过殖民地化，而可能累积的利润给予受赠人。

土地负担的消除是领主赏封土地的对立面。它是对地租权的废除，这种地租权是先前由贵族和国家通过行使自身权力而创设的。在古代，这种性质的负担消除大量发生；例如，或许在4世纪的罗马人中，至少在紧挨着罗马城附近是这样；在英格兰，1660年(查理二世在位)出现了不彻底的负担消除；在法国，经过早期的几次努力，彻底的负担消除发生于1789年；在19世纪，欧洲的其余地方到处都发生了这种负担消除。

当国家开始解放农民并消除土地负担时，情形十分不同于土地被赐予贵族时的情形。现代消除土地负担的事例中的推动力是有影响力的都市市民，他们与国家发生直接的联系。国家不再专门是拥有土地之贵族的组织。都市市民对解放农民抱有强烈兴趣，因为这种解放有可能将他们纳入到一般的商业生活、金融和信贷的经济制度中去，贵族对农民的这种支配因而被制止了。国王独立于贵族，因为他已经创建了一支常备的军队，因此不再

created a standing army and is therefore no longer limited to the military service of the nobility; he begins to administer the affairs of the state himself through officials who are dependent upon him. The king is desirous, in his own interest, of improving the economic condition of the country, and the modern science of economics, which was originated and developed by the urban citizenry, shows the way in which it may be done, i. e. by advancing industry and commerce through the liberation of economic forces from feudal fetters. The newly developed science of agriculture teaches that progress in agriculture and feudal landholding are incompatible. The nobility gradually loses interest in continuing the servile state of the peasantry, having become convinced that the returns from unfree labor are inadequate, and in view of the changed economic situation welcomes the substitution of a money payment for the feudal burdens. So the state, in emancipating the peasants, merely does that which the general economic situation seems to demand. We may therefore say that both the state-created ownership of the great landed proprietor and the disencumbrance of the soil are achieved by social forces. Apart from such disencumbrance, landholding on a smaller scale very rarely owes its existence to the state. Instances of this are the sale by the state of confiscated estates during the French Revolution, and here and there colonization by the state.

The right of collateral relations to take by succession probably owes its existence everywhere to norms for decision which the state has received into its law and developed. The whole process of development is little understood, for the reason that historical investigations in the field of law have consistently overlooked the relation between the law of inheritance and the military constitution of the state. The fact that in primitive times the estate of a deceased person who had been living alone without clan or family connection became ownerless, and therefore became the property of anyone who seized it, was a matter of little importance as long as there were few persons who lived alone, and as long as, because of the simplicity of the economic constitution, the destruction of economic values incident to ownerlessness did not import great loss. But as soon as the situation changed, it became necessary for the state to make provision for estates of persons that died without heirs. In the ancient state the citizen was also a warrior; and when a citizen died without heirs, his collateral relatives were called to the inheritance in order that the number of warriors might not be diminished. In the feudal state the vacant feud had to be

受制于贵族的军事服务;他开始通过所属官员自己管理国家事务。国王从自己的利益出发,希望改善国家的经济条件,并且由都市市民创造和发展的现代经济学表明了可能的改善方式,如,通过将经济力量从封建束缚中解放出来,以促进工业和商业的发展。新发展的农学指出,农业进步和封建土地所有二者是不相容的。贵族慢慢丧失了继续维持农民被奴役状态的兴趣,开始相信,不自由的劳动产生的利润并不充分,并且鉴于已改变的经济状况,他们乐于以金钱支付代替封地负担。所以国家在解放农民的过程中,仅仅做了一般经济状况要求做的那些事情。我们因此可以说,国家创设的大土地所有者的所有权与土地负担消除二者均由社会力量所实现。除了那种土地负担消除外,小规模土地所有的存在极少归因于国家。法国大革命期间国家将已充公的财产出售,以及国家到处进行的殖民地化,即为适例。

在各个地方,旁系亲属通过继承取得遗产的权利很可能归因于国家已接受为法律并加以发展的裁判规范。整个发展过程很难被理解,因为法律领域的历史研究一贯忽略了继承法和国家军事机构之间的关系。远古时代,原本单独生活、没有宗族或家庭联系之死者的财产变成无主财产,因而变成任何取得者的财产,这一事实其实无关紧要,只要极少有人寡居,只要经济价值因财产归于无主而导致的毁灭由于经济结构简单故而损失不会太大就好。但只要情形发生改变,国家就有必要对无继承人的死者财产作出规定。在古代国家,公民也是一个战士;当公民没有继承人而死亡时,他的旁系亲属将会被召去继承,以便使得战士的数量不会减少。在封建国家,无继承人的领地必须给某个人,因为不这样的话,封建徭役就无人承担了。如果除此之外,在封建国

given to someone, for otherwise the feudal services would not have been rendered. If in addition to this there exists in the feudal state a right of inheritance in the collateral relatives, with a preference given to the male relatives, this is a survival from the days of the universal duty of freemen to render military service, which must now seek to hold its own against the will of the king. Fixed principles determining the question to which collateral relatives the feud should be given were arrived at very slowly. The broad lines of this development in Germany, France, Engand, and Italy are well known.

Accordingly a right of inheritance in the collateral relatives, comparable to that which probably had been in existence among the Romans and the Germans in prehistoric times, arose everywhere among the Slavic peoples in the fourteenth century. But it developed chiefly at the expense of the right of escheat of the princes and the noble landowners, which had by that time been fully developed. The transition can be seen quite clearly in the code of Czar Duschan. Article 41 provides: "Whenever a noble landowner dies who has had no child or who has had a child which has died, his inherited lands shall be considered ownerless until someone is found of his house to the third child of a brother. This child shall inherit from him." We shall here merely point out the fact that the very wording of this paragraph shows that it is an innovation. Take also paragraph 48: "When a noble landowner dies, his best horse and his armor shall belong to the Czar, his great festive garment and the golden girdle shall belong to the son, and the Czar shall not take it away from him. If he has no son, it shall belong to his daughter, who shall have the disposal of it."

The payments made by the state to its creditors, the salaries of officials, the pensions of officials and of their families, are *rentes* derived from the state. In the earlier days payments by the state to especially favored persons were also of great importance. Payments out of the treasury of the state were an appropriation to a private person of a share of the returns of the national economy which the state had

家还存在旁系亲属的继承权,并且此种继承权优先给予男性亲属,那么这是自由人提供兵役之普遍义务的时代的残留物,它现在必定寻求坚持自身的立场,而与国王的意志相对立。决定领地该给予哪一个旁系亲属这个问题的固定原则确立得非常缓慢。它在德国、法国、英格兰以及意大利发展的大体线索众所周知。

因此,旁系亲属的继承权,相当于史前时期很可能存在于罗马和日耳曼人中的那种权利,在14世纪斯拉夫民族中处处都曾产生过。但它主要是以无继承人的土地归还诸侯和贵族地主为代价而发展起来的,后者在那之前一直获得了充分的发展。这种过渡在杜尚别沙皇[1]法典中可以十分清晰地看出来。该法第41条规定:"当无子女或虽有一孩子但已亡故的贵族地主死亡时,其遗留土地属于无主财产,但在其家族中有人被认定是其兄弟的第三个孩子之后,该子女将继承其财产。"这里,我们仅指出以下事实:这一段的文字表明它是一个创新。同法第48条规定:"当一个贵族地主死亡时,他最好的马匹和盔甲将属于沙皇,他最好的节日盛装和金色腰带将属于其子,沙皇不应将它拿走。如果他没有儿子,相应的物品则归于其女,后者有权处置它。"

国家对其债权人的支付款、官员的薪水、官员及其家庭的养老金,均是来自国家的岁入。在较早时期,由国家对特殊受宠之人的给付报酬也具有很大的重要性。出自国库的支付是国家已宣布归其所有的、构成国民经济利润一部分之私人的拨款。在以

〔1〕 塔吉克斯坦首都。

claimed for itself. In the days when payment was made in kind, the state directed the person entitled to collect directly from the person obligated to pay.

In time past the private monopolies granted by the state were chiefly the proscriptive rights; today they are the rights granted for the protection of literary and artistic creation, and in part the income from certain professions that are favored by the state. The state forbids the practice of a certain trade in general terms, and excepts a certain favored person from this prohibition. By doing this, it permits the privileged person to engage in an economic activity, to engage in which he normally would not require the permission of the state; but the prohibition of the state enables him to sell the products of his economic activity or his services at a higher price than their economic value warrants. This overplus is a profit, which accrues to him because of the monopoly, and which he receives at the expense of other economic undertakings. State monopolies therefore are creations of society to the same degree as of the state. Economic undertakings, inventions, do not owe their existence to the state. Only the norms of the second order, the norms of penal law, of police law, of procedure, through which the state excludes competition, proceed from the state.

And lastly the state acts through its courts and agencies by imposing limitations upon free activity. It prohibits certain communities or it dissolves them, especially certain family relations (void and punishable marriages); it takes away, and limits, rights of ownership; it denies recognition by courts and administrative tribunals to dispositions by last will and testament and, if need be, destroys them by its own action; it has, in the past at least, not only maintained existing conditions of serfdom by refusing legal protection, but has also exercised an active influence upon the content of this condition of serfdom by the extent to which it granted or refused legal protection, and in the end has abolished them altogether. In this very matter the state proceeds by means of norms of decision. And it does this in essentially the same manner as does juristic science.

Summarizing the influence of state law upon the state of the law

实物支付的时代，国家指令被授权人直接从负有支付义务之人处收取实物。

在过去，国家授予的私人垄断主要是排斥权；如今它们主要是给予文学和艺术创作保护的权利，部分是对源于受到国家优待之特定行业的收入给予保护的权利。国家概括地禁止特定行业的执业，除非某人受到特殊批准。通过这样的规定，它允许享有特权之人从事经济活动，从事那种他正常情况下不会要求国家给予许可的职业；但是国家的禁令使得他可以以比它们的经济价值更高的价格出售其产品或服务。这种溢值就是利润，是由于垄断而给他增加的利润，而且以牺牲其他企业为代价。因此，国家垄断既是国家的创造物，也是同等程度社会的创造物。经济企业、创造物之存在并不依赖于国家。只有次级规范、刑法、治安法及诉讼法规范——国家通过这些规范来排除对抗——来源于国家。

最后国家通过对其法院和其他机构的自由行为施加限制而发挥作用。国家禁止成立特定的共同体或下令解散它们，特别是针对特定种类的家庭关系（无效的与可受处罚的婚姻）；国家剥夺、限制所有权；国家通过其法院和行政法庭拒绝承认当事人遗嘱所作的财产处置，并且如果有必要，它会以其自身行动推翻它们；至少在过去，国家不仅通过拒绝给予法律保护的方式维持现存的农奴制状况，而且还通过给予或拒绝给予保护程度的大小对这种农奴制的状况发挥积极的影响，并且最后彻底废除了这种农奴制度。正是在这方面，国家借助于裁判规范而持续运作。它这样的运作方式与法学的方式本质上相同。

总结一下迄今为止历史发展进程中，国家法对此种法律所属

in the course of its historical development down to the present day, we may say the following: By creating constitutional and administrative law, the state has created its own law for its own needs. It has fused the various groups that are occupying its territory into a unified people of the state (*Staatsvolk*) and by doing so has prepared the way for a unitary development of law. Through its courts and administrative tribunals, with the aid of its secondary norms, penal law, police law, procedural law, it has brought about for the state and social institutions an increased measure of security. It has established ownership as distinguished from possession, and made possible the right of succession in the collateral relatives. It has created *rentes* and monopolies. By its prohibitions and limitations it has exerted a powerful influence upon social institutions, upon communal life, relations of domination, ownership, possession, contract, succession.

Thereafter society keeps on building on the foundation laid by the state. Communities, relations of domination and of possession, contracts, articles of association, declarations by last will and testament establish their inner order, in part at least, according to the directions of the authorities, according to the kind and measure of protection which they can expect to receive from the courts, or they make special arrangements to avoid the hindrances and traps put in their way by the latter. So in the last analysis the state of the law is a resultant of the cooperation, the interaction, and the antagonism of state and society. And in this way state law, too, can become juristic law.

As soon as state law has actually become part and parcel of everyday life, and has exerted a moulding influence upon it, jurists will no longer confine their attention to the words of the statute but will be concerned with the forms of life that have come into being under its influence. The universalizations which they arrive at in doing this, the norms which they find, will, of course, be juristic law. This happened in Rome in the case of the *Lex Falcidia* and of the *senatus-*

的国家所带来的影响，我们可以说：通过创造宪法和行政法，国家为其自身需要创造了自己的法律。它融合了各种各样的团队，这些团队在共同的土地上生活并融合成统一的“国民”（*Staatsvolk*），并且通过这样做，它也为法律的一元化发展开辟了道路。国家通过其法院和行政法庭，在次级规范、刑法、治安法、诉讼法的帮助下，为国家结构和社会机构带来了更高程度的安全程度。国家建立了区别于占有的所有权，并使得旁系亲属继承权成为可能。国家建立了定期收益与专利权。通过其禁令和限制令，国家对社会机构、公共生活、支配关系、所有权、占有、契约以及继承施加了强有力的影响。

此后，社会继续在国家建立的基础上发展。共同体、支配和占有关系、契约、社团章程、遗嘱的声明建立了它们的内在秩序，这种建立至少部分地按照权力机构的指令，按照它们可以期待从法院获得保护的种类与程度，或者它们为避免后者设置的阻碍与陷阱而作出的特别安排而进行的。所以归根到底，此种法律所属的国家是国家与社会合作、互动以及对抗综合作用的结果。同样以这种方式，国家法也能变成法学家法。

一旦国家法实际上成为日常生活不可或缺的一部分，并对日常生活产生一种“形塑”的影响，则法学家不再将其注意力局限于制定法的条文，而将关心在此种影响下所形成的生活的形态。在此过程中他们获得的一般化以及他们发现的规范当然是法学家法。在罗马时期，这种情形发生于《法尔西地亚法》[1]

---

〔1〕（罗马法）《法尔西地亚法》，颁布于公元前40年，该法规定，在任何情况下，遗产的四分之一必须保留给继承人；为此目的，必要时应当按比例缩减超过四分之三限额的遗赠。

*consultum Velleianum*, and has happened again and again since that time. English commerce is regulated by the Statute of Frauds to such an extent that the English were unwilling to change it although it is quite antiquated, but took it over in part almost verbatim into the Sales of Goods Act of the year 1893. Inasmuch as the German testament is derived from the Roman testament, the *Lex Falcidia* was received into German law together with the latter, and has become a part of the living German law no less than the testament. It is well known and generally understood that the canon law prohibition against usury is in exactly the same case. It has all the hall-marks of state-made law. The church, which promulgated it, was an association partaking of the nature of a state, and was, in this case, as the state is in other cases, an agency of society for the purpose of creating law. Through its own courts and through its influence upon the courts of the state, the church was enabled to give effect to its law as readily as a state.

Accordingly we shall have to call the part played by the state in the creation of law a very limited one. Nevertheless we are all under the influence of the notion of the omnipotence of the state; and this conception has undoubtedly given rise to a series of social thought sequences which, though they are conditioned historically, and therefore destined to perish at some time in the future which cannot be determined in advance, nevertheless dominate the thinking of the whole civilized human race at this time. Chief of these is the thought that the power to legislate is the highest power in modern society, and that resistance to it is to be condemned under all circumstances; that there cannot be any law within the territory of the state that is in conflict with statute law; and that a judge who in the administration of law disregards a statute is guilty of gross violation of duty. Since it is the

和《韦勒雅元老院决议》[1]的场合，并且在此后一再发生。英国商业由《欺诈法》来调整，英国人对该法依赖如此之深，以至于尽管该法已经相当不合时宜，但仍不愿意改变它，而是将其部分一字不差地移入1893年《货物买卖法》。由于德国的遗嘱制度源于罗马的遗嘱制度，所以原来就是继承制度的《法尔西地亚法》与后者也被德国法继受，并成为德国现行法的一部分。众所周知并了解的是，禁止高利贷的教会法也完全属于同一情况。它具有国家制定法的全部特点。宣扬教会法的教会是带有几分国家性质的联合体，并且这种情形下的教会类似于其他场合下的国家，是一个为了创设法律而存在的社会机构。教会通过自己的法院并通过对国家世俗法院的影响，使得它能够与国家一样让其法律毫无困难地生效。

因此，我们不得不说，国家在法律的创制中发挥的作用十分有限。尽管如此，我们还是全都受国家全能观念的影响；这种观念毫无疑问引发了一系列社会思潮，尽管它们都受制于历史条件，并因而注定在不可能提前确定的将来某个时间消亡，但它们仍然在当时支配了整个文明人类的思维。其中主要的是这种理念：立法权是现代社会的最高权力，对它的反抗无论如何都将被声讨；在国家的领域内不存在与国家制定法相冲突的任何法律；司法裁判中对制定法置之不理的法官，是对其职责的公然违反，应受到谴责。既然记录事实——不是评价事实——是法律社会

---

[1] （罗马法）《韦勒雅元老院决议》，一项于公元46年发布的元老院决议，该决议禁止妇女为他人实行债务承包，并且规定，由妇女提供的担保是无效的。

function of the sociological science of law, like that of every other science, to record facts, not to evaluate them, it cannot possibly, as some have believed, tend to establish, at the present stage of human development, a doctrine which might lead the judge to violate his judicial oath. And even though it cannot but state that the judge in the performance of the duties of his office is frequently quite unconsciously, albeit sometimes consciously, guided by non-legal considerations, in making this statement it is merely recording facts, not evaluating them.

But the basic social institutions, the various legal associations, especially marriage, the family, the clan, the commune, the guild, the relations of domination and of possession, inheritance, and legal transactions, have come into being either altogether or to a great extent independently of the state. The center of gravity of legal development therefore from time immemorial has not lain in the activity of the state but in society itself, and must be sought there at the present time. This may be said not only of the legal institutions but also of the norms for decision. From time immemorial the great mass of norms for decision has been abstracted from the social institutions by science and by the administration of justice, or has been freely invented by them; and legislation by the state, too, can generally find them only by following the social institutions and by imitating scientific or judicial methods.

学的功能,这与其他科学的功能一样,那么如某些人相信的那样,它不可能在人类发展的现阶段倾向于建立一个可能引导法官违反司法誓言的学说。即使它不得不说,法官在履行其官方职责时经常在十分的不经意中——虽然有时是有意识的——受到非法律考量的引导,但在作这种表述时,它也仅仅在记录事实,而非评价事实。

然而,基本的社会机构、各种各样的法律联合体,特别是婚姻、家庭、宗族、社区、行会、支配和占有关系、继承以及法律行为,它们要么是整个儿独立于国家,要么是很大程度上独立于国家。因此法律发展的重心从无法追忆的远古时代起就不是存在于国家的行为之中,而是内存于社会本身,因而现在必须在后者中探寻。这不仅可以适用于法律机构,也同样适用于裁判规范。从远古时代起,大量的裁判规范就已经通过科学和司法从社会机构中提取出来,或者由那些机构自由创造出来;国家的立法通常也只能通过追随社会机构以及模仿科学模式或司法模式的方式发现裁判规范。

# XVII

# Changes In The Law In The State And In Society

And now may we be permitted to enter upon the discussion of one of the most popular questions of juristic metaphysics, to wit the question whether at the present time the law grows through legislation only or through legislation and "customary law"; whether there is such a thing as "customary law" today; and if so, whether it can be rendered superfluous by legislation. All of these questions, rightly understood, automatically become superfluous when the origin and the growth of law are rightly understood, i. e. when they are understood to mean the origin and the transformation of social institutions. There can of course be no doubt that in this sphere as well as elsewhere the state can bring about or prevent many things by direct interference and by decisions of its tribunals. But it cannot be disputed that it is unable either to set the whole course of development in motion or to bring it to a standstill, that in a progressive society at least, new institutions are continually coming into being, and existing ones are developing irrespective of what the state may do about it.

A glance at legal history will show that even at a time when the state had already gained control over legislation, great changes were always taking place in the law that were not brought about by legislation. Slavery disappeared from Europe during the course of the Middle Ages; from the beginning of the sixteenth century the peasant in England was gradually acquiring an ever increasing measure of liberty, while in Germany his freedom was being progressively curtailed; and wherever modern large-scale industry has been introduced, it has given rise to countless new kinds of contracts, real rights, rights of neighbors, forms of succession, and has influenced even the family

# 第十七章 法律在国家与社会中的变迁

现在我们可以对最流行的属于法学形而上学的问题进行讨论,这个问题即目前法律仅仅通过立法还是通过立法与“习惯法”的方式来不断成长;今天是否还存在诸如“习惯法”这样的东西;如果它的确存在,那么由立法提供的东西是否显得多余。如果能对法律的起源和成长有一个正确的理解——即把法律理解为社会习俗制度的起源和转化——那么所有的这些问题,会自动成为多余的问题。当然,不用怀疑,在此领域和其他领域,国家可以通过直接的干涉及其法庭的裁判引发或阻止许多事情。但是无可置疑的是,国家要么无法加快整个发展进程的速度,要么无法让这种进程停止,至少在一个进步社会,不论国家可能施加何种影响,新的习俗制度总会不断产生,现有的习俗制度也不断发展。

简略回顾法律史可知,即使是在国家已经取得立法控制权的时候,在并非由立法产生的法律方面,也总是有巨大的变化发生。奴隶制在中世纪时于欧洲消失;从 16 世纪开始,英格兰的农民逐渐获得日益增多的自由,与此同时,在德国,农民的自由则逐渐被缩减;在大规模工业被引入的任何地方,它总能带来无数的新型契约、物权、相邻权、继承形式,现代大规模工业甚至影响到家庭

law. In the beautyfully developing cities of detached houses of our time a servitude requiring the building of detached houses has arisen. Electrical works have given rise to new kinds of real rights, among others the rights of transmitting currents, and new kinds of obligatory contracts, among others the contract to supply electrical current. These doubtless are changes in the law, and, in part, such changes as history tells of in tones so loud that no one can fail to hear. Perhaps recalling to memory a few pictures from the days of our own youth will enable us to answer the much mooted question whether new customary law can arise today. The family of today is not the family in which we spent our youth; the marriage of today is not the marriage that we grew enthusiastic about when we were young; commerce and life have changed; contracts of purchase and sale, of ordinary or of usufructuary lease, for services and for wages, of a nature quite different from those of the past, are being made. The relations of master and servant, of employer and employee, of producer and consumer, are quite different from those of former days. Share companies, undertakings for the transportation of persons or goods, associations, banks, stock exchanges, and dealings in futures can scarcely be recognized. But a few decades ago, where were the trusts, cartels, unions, strikes, and *Tarifverträge* (collective labor agreements)? Surely no period of time has ever made such rapid progress as has our time. Never have father and son stood so alarmingly far apart in thought, sentiment, and conduct as today. These, to be sure, are new forms of life; in part, basically changed forms of our whole social and economic life, i. e. new law.

To all of these the state is not a party. The law changes because men and things change. To use an illustration of Herbert Spencer's, one can heap up cannon balls to form a pyramid or a tetrahedron, but one cannot pile them vertically, one above the other, so that they form a wall; one can build a wall with hard, sharp-edged bricks, but one cannot heap them up like cannon balls

法。在我们这个时代有着独立式住宅、漂亮地发展着的城市，要求进行独立式住宅建设的地役权产生了。电力工厂带来了许多新型物权，其中包括输电权，也带来了许多强制性契约，其中包括供电契约。这些无疑都属于法律上的变化，并且，那些诸如历史的变化某种程度上如此明显以至于无人不知。或许，回想起从我们年轻时至今的一些图景，能让我们回答这个非常有疑点的问题——如今是否还会产生新的习惯法。今天的家庭不是我们年轻时的家庭；今天的婚姻也不是我们年轻时曾热心的那种婚姻；商业和生活都改变了；买卖契约、普通租约以及附用益权租约、劳务与工资契约，它们的性质与过去的那些契约有相当大的不同，这些新型契约正在产生。主仆关系、雇主和雇员的关系、生产者与消费者的关系都十分不同于过去。公司资本由股份组合而成的公司、旅客或货物运输的企业、社团、银行、证券交易所以及期货交易等几乎不能被认可。但是几十年前，信托、卡特尔（商业组织联合体）、工会、罢工以及 *Tarifvertrage*（集体劳动协议），这些都在哪里呢？的确，没有哪一个时段能像我们这个时代这样以飞快的速度发展着。父子之间在思维、情感以及行为上的距离从来没有像今天这样惊人地疏远过。这些的确是新的生活形态；它们在某种程度上是对我们整个社会和经济生活作了根本改变后的形式，即新的法律。

对于所有的这些变化而言，国家不是一方当事人。由于人和事的变化，法律也随之改变。借用赫伯特·斯宾塞所举的一个例子，一个人可以将炮弹堆成一个金字塔或四面体，但是他不可能将它们垂直堆立——以至于形成一堵墙；一个人可以用硬质、边角齐整的砖块砌墙，但是他不可能用砖块像用

to form a pyramid. In this sense the qualities of a composite body are always determined by the qualities of its component parts, and the qualities of a human association by the qualities of its members. No two marriages and no two families will ever be found in which the same order obtains, for the simple reason that in the whole wide world there are no two married couples that are exactly alike, nor two sets of parents and children that are exactly alike. The family law of the Romans or of the *Germans* of the Frankish period was the general order of the Roman or of the Frankish family—an order which was not a creation of Roman or Frankish law but which arose directly out of the qualities and needs of the human beings who lived in these families. Were the eyes of the jurist trained to observe his own time as those of the legal historian are trained to observe past centuries and millennia, he could not possibly fail to see that our modern family law, too, is primarily an order that is not created by the precepts of the statute-book, but one that grows out of the needs of the human beings that live in families, and that it changes and develops according to these needs. What has been said of the family may self-evidently be said of every other association, of the state, of the commune, of the associations of employers and employees in the workshop and in the factory, of national and world economics, i. e. the form of the whole is always conditioned by the nature of its component parts. When men change in the course of time, their law changes with them. The great error of the jurists, even of those of the Historical School is that they are always inquiring into the development of the legal proposition. Let them get used to observing the development of the legal relations and of the legal institutions, and they will see that the legal propositions have developed with them though not even a comma has been changed. All historical development of law is based on the fact that men and their relations to each other at any given time are of such marked individuality that they can be what they are at a given time only at that particular time, and that they therefore are subject to ceaseless change in the course of time. Within the short span of human life, the change as a rule is not sufficiently great to attract much attention, although there have always been old people who can tell how different all things were in their youth. But in the course of historical development minute changes grow into vast accumulations. The

炮弹那样堆砌成一个金字塔。从这个意义上说,一个组合体的特性总是取决于单个组成成分的特性,人类联合体的特性同样取决于其成员的特性。永远不可能发现两个婚姻、两个家庭有同样的秩序,理由很简单,因为大千世界没有哪两对配偶完全相像,也没有哪两组父母子女完全相像。罗马人的家庭法与法兰克人时期的日耳曼家庭法,分别是罗马人家庭与法兰克人家庭的一般秩序——这些秩序不是罗马法或法兰克法的创造,而是直接产生于在这些家庭中生活之人的特性和需要。倘若受过训练的法学家打算像法律史学家那样观察他自己所处的时代,他就决不会不明白,我们现代的家庭法也主要是并非由法条书的规定创造的秩序,而是源于生活在现代家庭中人们需要的秩序,并且它将按照这些需要不断变化和发展。前面阐述的关于家庭的道理很明显可以同样适用于每一个其他联合体、国家、社区、车间和工厂里的雇主和雇员联合体、国民经济和世界经济,即,整体的形式总是取决于其组成部分的性质。当人们随着时间推移而变化时,法律也随之变化。法学家——即使历史学派的法学家也是如此——的重大错误在于,他们总是探究法律命题的发展。让他们习惯于观察法律关系以及法律风俗的发展吧,他们将会明白,尽管连一个逗号都不曾改变,但法律命题是追随法律风俗的发展而发展的。法律的所有历史发展均基于如下事实:任何特定时代,人们及其相互关系具有鲜明的特性,以至于他们只是在那个特定的时代呈现当时的那种状态,他们也因此会随着时间的推移而发生永不停歇的变化。在人短暂的一生中,这种变化通常并未大到能够引起很多的注意——尽管总有老人说他们年轻时所有的事情“现在”是如何的不同。但是在历史发展的进程中,微小的变化发展为巨大的

gulf that is fixed between the legal order of the Middle Ages and that of the modern period, vast though it may seem to us, owes its existence to the accumulation of minute changes, the significance of which probably not one of their contemporaries surmised.

That which is primarily subjected to ceaseless change is the distribution of power among the associations themselves, among the individuals that are members of the same association, and among the various associations that together constitute an association of a higher order. And every change in the relation of power necessarily effects a change in the social norms that obtain in the association. For the associations unite their members for the pursuit of common aims, and the norms that arise within them are, in the first place, merely an expression of that which the community, according to the views and moods that prevail within it, quite without justification perhaps, thinks the interest of the whole justifies it in requiring at the hands of the individuals and groups that it is composed of. But the individual in an association lives his own life, having his own ends in view; and where society has reached a more advanced stage of development, he is a member of several associations which make diverse and perhaps conflicting demands upon him. The norms of the community therefore are not only the sum but also the extreme limit of that which the community may demand of the individual, they constitute a compromise between the demands which the whole makes upon the individual and those which the individual makes upon the whole. And this compromise shifts continually according as the content or the effect of the forces within the association varies.

In my book on legal capacity I have shown that the mere fact that the family household as a self-sufficing economic establishment was gradually disappearing necessarily put the whole family law upon an altogether new basis. As long as the household as an economic unit produces almost everything that the members of the household require, the members of the family remain at home; each member has a sphere of activity corresponding to his ability and his position, and is supplied with most of the things which he requires to keep body and

聚集。中世纪的法律秩序与现代的法律秩序之间的鸿沟是固定的，尽管在我们看来它是非常大，但其存在根由在于微小变化的积累，那种微小变化的意义恐怕不是它们同时代的人所能猜度的。

主要地经历永不停歇之变化的是在该联合体本身内部、在同属该联合体的各成员之间以及在构成一个更高等级联合体的各该等级联合体之间的权力分配。权力关系的每一次变化必然影响到在该联合体内流行的社会规范的改变。因为该联合体将其具有共同目标追求的成员统合到一起，并且其中产生的规范首先不过是如下理念的表达：社区按照其内部流行的观点和倾向——或许并没有多少合理性——认为，整体利益使得它有充分理由要求其所属个人成员与团体成员来贯彻实现这些整体利益。但是联合体中的个人有他自己的生活，他有自己的目标需要考虑；在社会达至一个更高级的发展阶段时，该个人成为几个联合体的一个成员，而这几个联合体对他会有不同、或许是相互冲突的要求。因而该社区规范不仅是规范总合，而且还是该社区对该个人可能要求的极限，它们在所有联合体对他的各种要求以及他对所有联合体的各种要求之间达成一个妥协。并且这种妥协随着该联合体内部力量的内容或效果的改变而不断变化。

在我那本论法律资格的书里，我已经表明，家庭户作为一个自足的经济机构逐渐消失，单单此种事实就必然使得整个家庭法置于一个完全崭新的基础之上。只要家庭户作为一个经济单位几乎能生产其成员所需要的一切东西，那么该家庭成员都会呆在家里；每一成员都会有与其能力和地位相应的活动领域，他需要保养其身心的大多数东西都会获得供应。家庭户作为一个经济

soul together. The dissolution of the household as an economic establishment compels the members to leave the household, to seek their livelihood in the world, and with the returns from their labor to buy what they need to keep body and soul together outside of the home in the open market. For goods are no longer produced in the home but in the factory, in the workshop, in a different agricultural establishment. This emancipation from economic dependence upon the household frees the members of the household from the control of the head of the family; the economic struggle which every individual must now wage outside of the house gives him the economic and the psychological self-dependence which enables him to maintain his independence against the head of the household. This appears with the greatest possible clearness in the rights of the married woman, whose sphere of activity in the organized economy of the household was one of equality with that of the husband, but which she has lost, with the exception of a few insignificant remnants, thanks to the modern division of labor, and the modern economic systems of finance and credit. She therefore seeks a sphere of activity outside of the home, and the limitations upon the legal capacity of women, which the German Civil Code has carried over to our time from a time long past, will undoubtedly be smashed by colliding with these simple facts. This was the fate of similar provisions in the French Civil Code, which, it must be admitted, was right in this, inasmuch as it came into existence at a time when the organized family household still possessed a considerable amount of vitality. As is well known, neither the French Civil Code nor the German Civil Code deny legal capacity to the married woman, but in actual fact the statutory matrimonial régime of each country practically reduces the married woman to a state of nonage. Nevertheless the married woman of France is as free and unrestrained in her movements as the married woman of any other country in the world. In his book "La femme dans le ménage" Binet says on the subject: "Les mœurs de notre pays nous offrent depuis longtemps le spectacle de l' épouse vaquant en toute libertéaux diverses opérations du ministère domestique, sans qu' il vienne a l' esprit de personne de lui demander de justification du consentement marital. Et ce n' est pas là un des moins remarquables exemples de l' antinomie apparente, si souvent signalée chez nous, entre

机构的解体迫使成员离开家庭，在世界范围内寻找他们的生计，并用他们的劳动报酬在他们家庭之外的公开市场上购买他们需要保养其身心的东西。因为物品不再在家中生产，而是在工厂、在车间、在每一个不同的农业机构生产。这种对家庭户经济依赖的解放使家庭成员免受家庭首脑的控制；每个个体必须在家庭之外为经济打拼，这给了他经济和心理上的自立，使得他可以相对于家庭首脑而保持独立。此点在已婚妇女的权利上表现最为清楚，在传统家庭户组织的经济中，妇女与其丈夫的活动领域一样，但由于现代劳动分工以及现代金融信贷体制，除了一些无关紧要的残余外，她的活动领域丧失了。因而她必须在家庭之外寻求活动领域，同时《德国民法典》之前曾众相当长时期内规定的、对妇女法律资格的限制无疑因与这些简单的事实相抵触而被革除。这也是法国民法典中类似条款的命运，必须承认，由于它是在家庭户组织的经济还拥有相当旺盛的生命力时开始出现的，因此在这一点上它当时是对的。众所周知，法国民法典和德国民法典均否认已婚妇女的法律资格，但事实上，每个国家制定法上的婚姻制度都将已婚妇女纳入未成年的状态。尽管如此，法国的已婚妇女在活动的自由和不受限制上与其他国家的已婚妇女一样。在名为《家庭中的妇女》中，彼勒说道：依据我们国家的风俗，长期以来

la loi et les mœurs, entre le droit et le fait." Binet adds the words of Tissier, which he quotes from a report on the Sociétéd'études legislatives (I[re] année) : "Celui qui, sur le rôle de la femme mariée dans la famille en France, sur ses droits et ses pouvoirs concernant les intérêts pécuniaires du ménage, ne connaît que les textes de notre loi en a une idée certainement bien fausse, et on peut affirmer que ces textes ne sont plus en harmonic avec notre manière de penser, ni avec, notre manière de vivre." Without doubt the family law of the French Civil Code has been abrogated, in part, by new customary law.

From the law of property we shall adduce only the *Lieferungs und Gattungskauf.* It was not known to the Romans in the Middle Ages it is not found in Germany, at least in ordinary business dealings. When it first appeared in commercial life cannot be readily ascertained; but in view of the peculiar nature of mediaeval commerce, at least in Germany, it is not to be assumed that it happened before the reception of the Roman law. Until that time the goods were regularly examined by the purchaser or his agent before the sale was concluded. At the beginning of the modern age it gained in importance, and Ulrich Zasius devotes one of his best known treatises to it. Since that time it has gradually become the transaction that prevails in business generally. One would look in vain for a precept that has introduced it into the legal system and has established its extremely complicated forms.

都是妇女在从事各种家务劳动,然而,这是否合乎婚姻的合意是值得置疑的。这是一个典型的法律与风俗、法律与事实相违背的例子,而这种违背,经常发生在我们身边。”彼勒还援引了迪斯耶《社会立法研究》报告的话:“我们的法律对已婚妇女在家庭中地位的规定,以及其在夫妻财产关系中的权利及权力的规定,其观念是肯定错误的。我们可以确信的是,这些规定已经不再符合我们的思想,也与我们的生活模式相违背。”毫无疑问,法国民法典中的家庭法之所以被废除,某种程度上是因为有了新的习惯法。

从财产法中我们将只列举按种类命名的货物销售契约。这是罗马人所不知道的。在中世纪的德国,至少在一般的商业交易中,也没有这种东西。当它首次在商业生活中出现时,不可能很容易就确定下来;但是考虑到中世纪商业的独特性质,至少在德国,并不认为它在罗马法继受之前就出现了。在那之前,货物通常要由买方或其代理人检验后,销售才可能完成。在现代的开始阶段,它的重要性逐渐增强,乌尔里希·扎休斯最有名的论文中有一篇就是关于它的。自那时起,它已经变成在企业中普遍流行的一种交易。若有人试图寻找一个已经将其纳入到法律制度、并建立起多层次的、极其复杂的形式的规则,则是徒劳的。这种已经

manifold and This contract, which has impressed its stamp upon our whole legal life, came into use without the aid of a single legal proposition. It owes its existence almost exclusively to the rise of large-scale industry, to the introduction of regular postal service, to improved roads, improved facilities for the transportation of freight; and lastly, it owes its perfection of form to the railroads, to navigation, to the telegraph. Is not that new "customary law"?

All legal development therefore is based upon the development of society, and the development of society consists in this, that men and their relations change in the course of time. Other men will live and have their being in other legal relations, and since legal relations are to a great extent based on legal transactions, new legal transactions will emerge in the course of time and the older ones will disappear. New associations will be formed, new kinds of contracts will be entered into, new kinds of declarations by last will and testament will be made. A11 of this must appear most palpably in the content of the legal document. The truth, well understood among legal historians, that the law of a given period must be found in the documents of the period has very rarely penetrated the consciousness of the jurist. The reason for this is the fact that he does not see the law, but only the legal proposition. The legal proposition which says that articles of association, contracts, declarations by last will and testament, are legally binding under certain circumstances has remained unchanged while the content of the contracts, testaments, articles of association, has changed. And for this reason the jurist thinks that the law has not changed. If this were true, only that could be called a change in the law which cannot be explained on the basis of the principle of liberty of contract, of testamentary disposition, and of association. But liberty of contract, of testamentary disposition, and of association are mere blank forms or set patterns. And for the very reason that they are merely blank forms or set patterns, the development of the law goes on, within their compass indeed, but not through them. When the Roman

在我们的法律生活中留下深深印记的契约，在没有一个法律规定支持的情形下开始获得应用。其出现的原因几乎只是大规模工业的兴起、常规邮政服务的引入、改善的道路、货物运载设备的改进；最后，这种契约形式的完善还有赖于铁路、航运以及电讯的发展。那不就是新的"习惯法"吗？

因此，所有法律的发展都以社会发展为基础，社会发展存在于人们以及他们的关系随着时间的推移而发生的变化。其他的人们将生活并存在于其他的法律关系中，而且既然法律关系很大程度上基于法律行为，则新的法律行为将会随着时间的推移而出现，旧的法律行为将会消失。新的联合体将会形成，新型契约将会被缔结，新型遗嘱声明将会作出。所有的这些在法律文件的内容中必定有明显体现。在法律史中，很容易理解的一个事实——特定时期的法律必定在该时期的法律文件中出现——却极少能够深入到法学家的意识中去。理由在于，他看不到法律，而仅仅看到法律条款。当契约内容、遗嘱、社团章程已经改变时，说社团章程、契约、遗嘱的声明在特定情况下具有法律约束力的法律条款尚未改变。因此，法学家认为法律尚未改变。如果这是真的，那么只有那些在法律中按照契约自由、遗嘱处分自由、结社自由等原则无法解释的东西才被称为"变化"。但是契约自由、遗嘱处分自由以及结社自由都仅仅是空白形式或模式集合。正因为它们仅仅是空白形式或模式集合，所以法律的确在它们的范围界限内——但不是通过它们——继续发展。当罗马祭司[1]

---

〔1〕 *Pontifices*，罗马社会的僧侣，其名称起源于 *pontem facere*（建桥），因为这些人往往同时也是一些重要技术、知识和传统的保存者或专家，他们曾经垄断着法律文献和有关的解释。

*pontifices* for the first time put the testament into the form of a *mancipatio*, they thought perhaps that they had merely been applying the principle of liberty of contract, did not think that they had made a change in the existing law. As a matter of fact however they introduced a most momentous innovation into the law. They put a new picture into the old frame. It is true, a single arrangement or agreement in a contract, in articles of association, or in a will is not new law; for the law deals only with that which has a great vogue and which is a matter of customary practice. But a juristic act is never an individual, an isolated, thing; together with the greater part of its content, it is a part of the prevailing social order. The needs that occasion certain legal transactions, e. g. the creation of corporations, contracts, wills, are general social needs, and the means to satisfy these needs are as general as the needs themselves. Accordingly identical articles of association, contracts, testamentary declarations of will, occur again and again at a given period ot time and in a given region—identical not only in content but also in wording. Nobody knew better than the Romans that the traditional content of the declarations of the parties are a part of the existing law. One glance will convince us that practically the whole contract law of the Digest, including the matrimonial régime and the law of pledge as well as the law of wills, is based upon the agreements and declarations that the parties are in the habit of making.

The situation is the same today. To a person who has any conception of the importance of the usufructuary lease in agriculture, a glance at the few meagre provisions of the Austrian or of the German Civil Code will suffice to convince him that they cannot possibly be sufficient to meet the needs of agriculture in Austria or Germany. It is a

第一次将遗嘱纳入到要式买卖[1]形式中，他们或许认为仅仅在运用契约自由的规则，而不会认为他们对现行法作了改变。然而，事实上，他们已经将一个十分重大的革新引入法律。他们为旧的框架植入了一幅新的图景。的确，契约、社团中的章程或遗嘱中的个别的安排或协议不是新法律；因为法律只处理广泛风行且属习惯做法的内容。但是司法行为从来不是个人性质的、孤立的事务；与其更大部分的内容一起，它是主流社会秩序的一部分。引发特定法律行为的需要，例如法人、契约、遗嘱的创设，一般都是社会需要，满足这些需要的手段与这些需要本身一样普遍。因此，在特定时期、特定地点，相同的社团章程、契约、遗嘱声明一再发生，说它相同，不仅指内容，而且也包括措辞。没有人比罗马人更懂得，当事人声明的传统内容是现行法的一部分。简单的扫视会让我们确信，实际上，《学说汇纂》中整个契约法，包括婚姻制度、担保法以及遗嘱法，都建立在当事人作出协议与声明之习惯的基础上。

今天的情形也一样。对于任何一个对农业中附用益权租约的重要性有认识的人而言，简单回顾一下奥地利民法典或德国民法典中些许单薄的相关条款，就足以让他确信，它们绝不可能满足奥地利或德国农业的需要。那是对罗马大地产的附用益权租约

---

〔1〕 *Mancipatio*，一种据以转让市民法所有权的古老方式，表现为受让人在5名见证人和1名司秤面前，手持作为价金象征的铜块，宣布买卖标的物是他的，随后以该铜块击秤并将其交付给转让人。此种转让行为只在罗马市民之间实行，不得附加任何期限或条件，并可借助合法性之诉保障被转让物所有权的合法性。随着贸易活动的发展与扩大，这种使用范围狭窄、手续繁琐的转让方式逐渐消亡。

very superficially modernized law of the usufructuary lease of the Roman latifundia. Shortly after the German Civil Code had become effective, Schumacher repeated Blomeyer's statement, made long before, that the contract of usufructuary lease ought to be drawn up in such form that no legislation would be required for the regulation of the legal relations between the lessor and the lessee. Whether there is any sense in enacting legislation of this kind, to avoid the conesquences of which the parties must call in the aid of the notary, I shall not discuss here, but I would say that the course which German agriculture was to take had been clearly marked out for it quite independently of legislation. The question as to the form and the content of the contracts of usufructuary lease has been discussed repeatedly, and a small, extremely interesting and valuable literature has grown up on the subject, which, of course, the jurists know nothing of. ① A study of this literature reveals that the agricultural contract of usufructuary lease is an institution, which was carefully elaborated according to technical rules during the course of a century of development, and which possesses a degree of elasticity that enables it to conform to the existing status of the agricultural production of goods; that there are many forms, widely used in Germany, one of which, the one employed in the administration of the royal Prussian domains, possesses a great reputation, although it must be admitted that this reputation has often been impugned.

The law of agriculture offers another illustration. At the request of the German Agricultural Association, Professor Dr. Otto Gerlach, with the cooperation of Dr. Franz Mendelssohn and *Regierungsbaumeister* (architect to the government) Alfred Blum, has studied the workers' settlements in North Germany, and has published the results of his investigations in the reports of the German Agricultural Association.

---

① Schumacher, Das landwirtschaftliche Pachtrecht, Berlin, 1901. Cf. Preset, Pacht, Pachtrecht und Pachtvertrag über grössere Landgüter in Österreich (1880); von Batocki und Bledau, Praktische Ratschläge für den Abschluss von Privatverträgen 1909. —*Author's note.*

很肤浅地现代化后的法律。在德国民法典生效后不久,舒马赫重复布洛梅尔在很久之前就作过的陈述,即,附用益权租约应该以这样的形式草拟,这样就不需要什么制定法来调整出租人与承租人之间的法律关系。仅为避免当事人必须寻求公证人的帮助所产生的后果而通过这种立法是否有任何意义,这个问题在此不予讨论,不过我会说,德国农业走过的历程已经清楚地表明它十分独立于立法。关于附用益权租约的形式与内容的问题已经一再被讨论,并且产生了一些为数不多但极为有趣而珍贵的文献,当然,法学家对此一无所知。① 文献研究表明,农业上的附用益权租约是一种习俗,它在一个世纪的发展进程中按照技术性规则获得了精心而详尽的阐述,而且它拥有一定程度的弹性,因而能够符合农业商品生产的现实状况;在德国,广泛应用的此类租约存在许多格式,其中一种是在皇家普鲁士领地的管理中得以运用,享有很高的知名度——尽管必须承认,这种声誉经常受到责难。

农业法提供了另外一个例证。应德国农业协会的请求,教授奥托·格拉赫博士,与其合作伙伴弗朗兹·门德尔松博士以及*Regierungsbaumeister*(政府的建筑师)阿弗雷德·布卢姆,一道研究德国北方工人的移民问题,并出版了研究结果,发表在德国农业协会的报告中。从研究结果中,法学家首先能够了解:农业中存在劳动力问题,并且德国乃至欧洲将来的经济和社会结构取决

① 参见舒马赫(Schumacher);《农业用益租赁权》,柏林,1901. Cf. 普雷瑟,《奥地利的用益租赁、用益租赁权与租约》(1880); 以及巴托基与布莱道,《和不契约缔结的实用建议》1909.

From it the jurist can learn first of all that there is a labor problem in agriculture, and that the future economic and social structure not only of Germany but of all Europe is conditioned upon its solution; that for more than a century, and to an ever increasing extent, with ever increasing methodicalness and clarity of purpose, attempts have been making to solve it, chiefly by inducing workers to settle in the country; that these attempts have brought about various new kinds of agreements, i. e. pure contracts of usufructuary lease, contracts of usufructuary lease in connection with contracts for work and labor, and contracts of purchase and sale with special provisions. Perhaps all of these formations are still too heterogeneous and each kind too individual in its nature; but if they are not yet fully developed law, they are law in the process of becoming. Suppose that one of the many systems suggested and tried should meet all the requirements, and come into general use in all Germany or at least in a part of Germany, can there be any doubt that this, even without any legislative interference, which, as can readily be foreseen, would be quite superfluous, would bring about an enrichment not only of economic life but also of the law?

The reason why the law is in a perpetual state of flux is that men, whose relations the law is designed to regulate, are continually posing new problems for it to solve. The family and the marriage relation are not changing at the rate of one change in a century. as the printed histories of law seem to assume; it is a daily, an hourly change, and the great changes that history records are produced by the vast accumulation of these smaller changes. The concept of ownership, too, has been developing hitherto without ceasing, and continues to develop before our very eyes. Doubtless it is not all one, either economically and socially or legally, whether the owner of large tracts of land grants them to vassals or whether he hires a manager with a staff of assistants; whether he carries on with villeins or lets the estate to lessees well supplied with working capital; whether he conducts his economic undertaking according to the three-field system or establishes

于此问题的解决;一个多世纪以来,关于解决此问题的努力,程度不断增强,目标的条理性与清晰度不断提升,主要方式是诱导工人在这个国家定居;这些努力带来了各式各样的新型协议,即,纯粹的附用益权的租约、与工作量和劳动成果联系在一起的附用益权租约以及附特别条款的购销契约。或许所有的这些契约结构具有不同性质,每一种都具有自身独特的性质;但如果它们还不是成熟的法律,那么它们也是正处于转化(为法律)进程中的法律。假设提出并经受过考验的这么多制度的其中之一能满足所有的要求,并在整个德国或至少在半个德国获得广泛运用,那么还有任何理由怀疑,即使没有任何制定法的介入——很容易可以想像,制定法在此是多余的——该制度也会给经济生活与法律带来繁荣吗?

为什么法律永远处于一种流动的状态,理由是人们——他们的法律关系受到调整——不断提出新的问题,需要用法律来解决。一个世纪之内家庭和婚姻关系变化的速度与写进书面的法律史认定的速度并不一样;它是每天、每小时的变化,历史记载的巨大变化是这些微小变化长年累月的积累。所有权的概念,迄今为止,同样经历着未曾停歇的发展,并且继续在我们的眼前发展着。无疑,它不是整个的单一所有权,相反,或是经济与社会方面的所有权,或是法律上的所有权,大片土地的所有人是将其赐予其封臣,还是雇佣一个经理人及一班助手,或者他利用农奴继续持有土地,或者将土地出租给佃户并提供流动资本;他是按照"三区轮作制"[1]经营他

[1] "三区轮作制"是中世纪欧洲采用的农业耕作体制,相对于旧的二区轮作制,它标示着农业生产的重大进步。

sugar factories. Each of these methods of operation is subject to its own law, and whenever agriculture turns from one method to another, the law regulating it changes with it. Whether a waterfall turns the wheels of a modest little water mill or supplies an electric power plant with hundreds of units of horsepower is not without a bearing upon the law and right of ownership thereof. The formal principle of liberty of contract cannot prevent the law and right of contract from changing when the contracts that have been customary until that time are being entered into with a new content which meets the new requirements. And the law of inheritance? Surely it is not immaterial whether one leaves a great proprietary estate or a factory, a mercantile establishment or millions in stocks or other securities. The enormous economic progress of our day, which has not yet run its course by any means, must exert the greatest possible influence not only upon the content of last wills and testaments and upon the division of estates in cases of intestate succession, but also upon the whole process of transfer of property *mortis causa*. The matrimonial régime of personal property under French law, the distinction made by English law between succession in case of real and of personal property, have been deprived altogether of their former significance by the fact that the importance of personal property, especially of the ownership of securities, has increased immeasurably during the course of the last century. This, too, proves that the great revolutionary changes in law do not take place in the legal propositions but in the social relations. Would anyone doubt that customary law can arise even now without the expressed permission of the legislator?

It is clear that as compared with the unceasing development of the social law, the rigid, immobile state law lags behind only too often. The law, whatever its form, is always a manner of rule of the dead over the living—to use Herbert Spencer's translation of Goethe's famous words. It is this, perhaps, that makes every collision with the state or its agencies an experience so painful to every person of refined sensibilities—the more painful, the more intimately the relation with which the state interferes is connected with his emotional life. This unpleasant situation becomes endurable only inasmuch as these collisions do

的经济事业还是建立糖厂。这些运作方式每一种都受其自身法律的约束,任何时候,当农业从一种方式转为另外一种方式,调整它的法律也会随之发生变化。瀑布是否开始为小水轮机提供动力,或是提供数百马力的电场,与其中的法律和所有权无关。在那之前一直是惯例的契约在缔结时加入了适应新要求的内容时,契约自由的形式原则不可能阻止契约法律和权利发生改变。法律的继承呢?确实,一个人是留下一大片地产,还是留下工厂、商业机构或价值数百万的股票或其他证券,这并非无关紧要。我们这个时代巨大的经济进步——无论如何仍未按常规发展——不仅对于遗嘱的内容与法定继承情况下的遗产分割带来了最大可能的影响,而且对于因死亡而生效的财产转让的整个过程也产生了最大可能的影响。在法国法制下有关动产的婚姻制度,英国法对动产继承与不动产继承的区分,由于以下事实失去了它们先前的重要意义:动产,特别是证券的所有权的重要性在最近一个世纪获得了不可估量的增强,这也证明,法律中巨大的革命性变化不是发生在法律规定中,而是发生在社会关系中。还有人怀疑:即使在如今,没有立法者的明确批准,习惯法也能够产生吗?

与社会法律的永续发展相比,显然,僵硬、固定的国家法绝大多数时候都落在后面。借用赫伯特·斯宾塞翻译的歌德著名的话即是,法律,无论其形式如何,总是一种"死"统治"活"的方式。或许正是这一点,使得每一个高度敏感的人与国家或其机构的每一次冲突的体验都是那么的痛苦——越痛苦,国家对其情感生活的相关介入关系就越密切。这种不愉快的状况之所以变得能够忍受,仅仅是因为这些冲突不会太经常地发生,而且通常给予

not occur too frequently, and can be avoided as a rule by the exercise of a certain measure of care. Fortunately the great maiority of men know the state, its courts, its agencies, and its law only from avoiding them. But there are others who see to it that the latter do not become superfluous altogether, and we must therefore discuss the question how the problem of this conflict is being solved in actual life.

To the extent that the law of society is being fitted into the frame of the traditional, especially the frame of liberty of contract, of association, of testamentary disposition, either directly or with the aid of the art and science of drawing up legal documents, it creates the norms for decision which it requires, and according to which it would be judged. The effect of contracts, of articles of association, and of testamentary dispositions is determined chiefly by their wording. In part this law goes beyond the literal meaning of the words, for, in the course of time, the course of judicial decision has learned to interpret them according to *bona fides*, *Treu und Glauben* (good faith), and according to business usage. This does not mean, as is usually believed, the unexpressed, surmised intent of the parties but the social and economic relation to which these declarations of will belong. *Bona fides*, *Treu und Glauben*, and business usage accordingly become not only sources of the living social law, but also sources of norms for decision and finally of legal propositions.

It is otherwise where the change has taken place outside of the forms of the established state law. In that case the law is not touched by the change; its norms of administrative action and for decision remain unaltered. The great never-ending task of juristic science is to resolve the conflict between the changing demands of life and the words of the established law. For this purpose it has developed its own technique in its most important branches, to wit the branch dealing with the art of drafting legal documents, that dealing with the work of the attorney, and that dealing with the work of the judge. It is by no means the same everywhere. It was one thing among the Romans; it is another at the present time on the Continent on one hand, and in the territory of the Anglo-American law on the other. It would be an error to suppose that the means adapted to the accomplishment of this purpose have been found once for all. On the Continent juristic science still operates in part with certain very flexible concepts of traditional law and in part with a still more arbitrary and whimsical construction of the whole content of the code. And the chief cause of the movement

一定程度的注意后就能避免它。幸运的是,对于国家及其法庭、管理机构、法律,绝大多数人只是从规避它们的过程中加以了解。但是还存在其他一些人,他们留意使它们不致变得纯属多余,因此我们必须讨论这个问题:在现实生活中,当这种冲突发生时,如何加以解决。

在使社会的法律适合传统框架,特别是契约自由、社团自由、遗嘱处分自由等框架的范围内,它或直接地或在草拟法律文件的技艺和学问的帮助下,创造了它所要求并据以断案的裁判规范。契约、社团章程以及遗嘱处分的效力主要取决于它们的措辞。在某种程度上,此方面法律超出措辞的字面意义之外,因为,随着时间的推移,司法裁判的过程已经学会按照善意、*Treu und Glauben*(诚信)来解释它们。这并不意味着(如人们通常认为的那样)当事人未明确表达但可检测的意图——这些意思表示将属于给定的社会经济关系。因此善意、诚信商业惯例不仅成为活的社会之法的源泉,也成为裁判规范的源泉,最后也成为法律命题的源泉。

变化有时还会在已建立的国家法规范之外发生。那种情况下,法律不为此种变化所动;它的管理性行为规范和裁判规范保持不变。法学重大而永无止境的任务就是要解决生活变动的需求与已立之法的措辞之间的冲突。为此,法学在其最重要的分支——即,涉及起草法律文件技艺的分支、涉及律师工作的分支、涉及法官工作的分支——中发展出自己的技术,它绝非处处都一样。在罗马人中间,它是一种样子;在当下的欧陆以及在当下的英美法系所辖领域,又是另外一种样子。我们不可能一劳永逸地发现用以适于达成此种目的的方式。在欧陆,法学部分地仍然运用某些非常灵活的传统法律概念,部分地还在依靠法典整个内容方面更加专断和古怪的解释。法的自由发现运动的主要缘由是

toward free finding of law is the susceptibility to attack and the insincerity of these methods, which are always seeking, by stealth, to reach a predetermined, definite, desired result, by interpreting the words of a statute the meaning of which is contrary to the result sought. Wherever state law is applied to cases which the legislator did not definitely have in mind, it must needs be subjected to a process of revaluation. It would be superfluous to enter upon a discussion of this whole problem since it has recently been made the subject of a brilliant presentation in Wurzel's book entitled "Das juristische Denken." perhaps the best book that has appeared on the Continental juristic method of the present time. Wurzel calls this process "projection," i. e. application of a juristic concept of the legal proposition as it has been formulated, without any change, to phenomena which were not within the contemplation of the proposition or, at any rate, were not demonstrably so. In public law, Jellinek has treated these phenomena as changes of the constitution.

Juristic projection in its essence is merely the immediate effect of the inner changes in the life of society upon the norms for decision. Without this process of projection, to which resort must be had by the jurist every day and every hour, administration of justice would be utterly unthinkable under state law, particularly in view of the present absolute sway of the latter. Without it, it would have been altogether impossible to retain the traditional constitutional law, the state private and administrative law of the stormy movement which is under way in society at the present time, and with which legislation is altogether unable to keep pace. To a great extent, it is true, this retention is apparent only. Large-scale industry, railroads, telegraphs, and telephones have imposed new tasks upon the administration of justice and upon civil administration. Unequal to the unaccustomed labor of free finding of law, they made shift by projecting the traditional norms of state law, as well as they could, upon the new relations. A similar thing is going on before our very eyes today. About a quarter of a century ago large-scale industry gained control over a new source of power, electricity. This, without more, imports new social law, but new state law will not fail to appear. The *arrêtisles* in France who are writing the commentaries in the great collections of judicial decisions by Dalloz

对攻击的敏感性以及这些方式的虚伪性，这些方式总是试图通过秘密行动——即，当制定法的含义与欲追求的结果相悖时，通过解释制定法的文句——获得一个预先决定好的、明确的理想结果。当制定法被应用于一个当初立法者并未明确设想过的案件情形时，该制定法必定经受一个再评价的过程。既然最近乌策尔在名为《法学思维》的著作中对该主题已经有了极为精辟的阐述，那么对整个问题进行讨论就是多余的。乌策尔把这个过程称为“投射”，即，将法律规定中的法学概念——如同它曾被系统表述过一样，不作任何改变——运用到法律规定未曾预期过，或至少能证明未曾预期过的现象中去。在公法上，耶里内克曾经将这些现象称为宪法的变化。

法学投射本质上仅仅是社会生活中的内部变化对裁判规范的即刻影响。没有法学家每时每刻必须借助的这种投射过程，则依据国家法实施司法是完全不可想像的，特别是考虑到目前后者占据绝对的统治地位。没有这种投射过程，维系传统宪法，维系当下在社会上风起云涌般运动——立法完全不可能跟得上这种运动——的国家私法和行政法，将是完全不可能的。的确，很大程度上，这种维系只是表面上的。大规模工业、铁路、电报、电话已经赋予了司法与民政管理以新的任务。不等于法的自由发现那种不同寻常的劳动，他们必须尽他们所能，通过“投射”国家法传统规范，设法应付新的关系。如今，同样的事情在我们眼前继续着。大约 25 年前，大规模工业获得对新的能源电力的控制，仅此就意味着新的社会法，但是新的国家法必定会出现。曾经在达洛兹和西

and Sirey are concerned at the present time with the development of the law contained in the judicial decisions, which is essentially a projection of the law upon new facts of life.

Projection is midway between application of law and finding of law. Now it partakes to greater extent of the nature of the former, now of the latter. Apart from the cases in which the judicial activity is something quite different from application of law, even in the cases in which it actually is application of law, it is a creative act on the part of the judge. But a creative act presupposes a creative mind. When the administratio of justice is unequal to this task, it becomes a dead weight upon legal life. When the Austrian court of cassation, without stating the legal grounds for its action, as it usually does even in its best decisions, found a man guilty of abduction who had bought a railroad ticket for a woman who was fleeing from the brutalities of her husband, it rendered a decision which is felt by every jurist like a blow in the face. Still all that is lacking in this case is a projection in time and space. In a state of slaveholders a decision of this kind would be quite in order; for everyone would be convinced that it is not permissible to help a slave make good his escape. In fact as long as slavery existed in the southern states of the United States of America, i. e. until the war of abolition, such an act was properly punishable there. The Romans, it is true, although they were a nation of slaveholders entertained milder views than the southern states and our court of cassation. A person who *misericordia ductus* freed a slave who had been chained could not be held liable in an *actio doli*, which was penal in its nature, and

雷[1]所出版的司法判例集中撰写评注的法国判例评注汇编者,现在关注司法裁判中所包含的法律的发展,那本质上是法律对新的生活事实的“投射”。

投射位于法的适用与法的发现的中点。它时而带有前者的性质,时而带有后者的性质。除了那些审判活动十分不同于法律适用的场合之外,即使在那些审判活动实际就是法律适用的场合下,它也是法官的创造性行为。但是创造性行为需要有创造性的头脑。当司法不能胜任此项任务时,它就变成了一种法律生活的沉闷的负担。当奥地利最高法院在未说明其行动理由的情况下,甚至在其最好的判决中也通常如此就裁决一个人——为一个从其残暴丈夫身边逃走的妇女买了一张火车票——犯有诱拐罪时,这样的一个裁决会让每一个法学家都感到脸上被猛击了一拳。尽管如此,这种情况下所缺的正是在时间和空间方面的投射。在一个蓄奴者的国家,这样的一个判决将会相当适宜;因为每个人都确信,帮助一个奴隶顺利逃脱是不被允许的。事实上,只要奴隶制存在于美国的南部州,即在废除黑奴战争之前,那样的“助逃”行为在那里受到惩罚是正当的。的确,尽管罗马帝国也是一个蓄奴制的国家,但还是拥有比美国南部州和奥地利最高法院更温和的观点。当一个受慈悲之心支配的人解放了一个受到囚禁的奴隶,他可能在一个期诈之诉[2]

---

〔1〕 Dalloz 与 Sirey 原为两位法国法学家,后来二人分别创立以他们姓名命名的出版社,并各自成为法国最权威的出版社之一,1953 年,达洛兹出版社买下西雷出版社。

〔2〕 (拉)*actio doli*(欺诈之诉),是指被欺诈人对因欺诈行为而获益的欺诈人及其继承人提起的诉讼。要求返还因欺诈而被剥夺之物及其所有添附;如果返还不可能,则要求给予赔偿金。

condemnation in which subjected the party to infamy, but only in an *actio in factum* for damages.

The sway of social forces brings about a continual shifting of the boundaries between the law of society and the law of the state. Interests which had been protected only by norms of social law obtain the protection of state legal norms as soon as their importance is more perfectly understood. A change of this sort can be brought about by judicial decision; the judge, acting solely in the capacity of a functionary of the state, projects a social norm as a state norm upon legal relations to which it did not originally refer. An instructive case of this kind is the defense of gaming. Originally based upon a social norm for decision, it began to take on the character of state law during the last quarter of the last century; in part this was brought about by state legislation and in part by judicial decision, since the courts avail themselves of this defense in order to curb the activities of persons not entitled to operate on the stock exchange. In my book, *Das zwingende und nicht zwingende Recht im Bürgerlichen Gesetzbuch*, I have endeavored to show how numerous regulations of the Civil Code which were intended to be social regulations must become state regulations as soon as the public becomes aware of the social interests involved.

This explains how it came about that many a rule of law was received from the law of society into the law of the state without any external change, purely as the result of moral or social changes.

中不会被认定为有责，这种诉讼性质上是刑事诉讼，在这种诉讼中被定罪，将会使当事人丧失公权，但若想诉求损害赔偿金，则只能选择事实诉讼[1]。

社会力量的影响力使得社会法与国家法之间的界限不断变化。仅由社会法规范所保护之利益的重要性一旦被更好地理解，那么它就会获得国家法规范的保护。这种变化也会因司法裁判而发生；仅仅作为国家公务员，法官将一个社会规范作为一个国家规范投射到后者当初未曾预期过的法律关系之上。这种富有启发意义的一个情形是赌博抗辩权。它最初建立在社会性裁判规范的基础之上，在最近一个世纪的最后 25 年，它开始具有国家法的特征；这种转变部分是由国家立法而促成，部分是由司法裁判而导致，因为法院为了抑制无权进行股票交易之人的活动而利用了这种抗辩权。在我的《<德国民法典>中的强行法与非强行法》中，我竭力表明，一旦公众开始意识到奥地利民法典中先前被确定为社会性的规定涉及社会利益，则数量如此庞大的那些社会性规定必定变成国家性规定。

这解释了许多法律规则在没有任何外部变化的情形下如何从社会法变为国家法，那纯粹是由于道德或社会而引发的演变。

---

[1] （拉）*actio in factum*（事实之诉），是指当某一新的关系不涉及由市民法所调整的权利，并且关系人不能借助法定诉讼程序解决就该关系产生的争议时，裁判官允许当事人针对创造上述关系的事实提起诉讼；在此种诉讼中，裁判官所维护的不是法律明确承认的权利，而是事实上存在的、新的公平关系。从一定意义上讲，所有的裁判官法诉讼在最初时均表现为事实诉讼，随着它们的逐渐发展与成熟，其中一部分上升为权利诉讼。

The family law powers which in Rome originally were a matter of private law and right similar to the law and right of ownership lose this characteristic quality, in part, as early as the days of the Empire. This is true especially of guardianship. And in modern law the *patria potestas* is gradually being converted into a public office. A large part of the law of contracts, especially the law of the contract of labor, is being converted into state law before our very eyes. The oldest Roman penal law was state law only inasmuch as it was applicable to *parricidium* and *perduelio* although the private law proceeding could often lead to a punishment as severe as that of public law. But this private penal law was displaced by public law to a great extent in the days of the Republic and to a still greater extent during the days of the Empire. The right of the husband to kill his adulterous spouse and her paramour, which has been recognized indirectly at least by the *Code pénal* (Art. 374 A1. 2, and cf. Art. 375), is the last trace, perhaps, of private penal law to be found in a modern penal code. It may possibly assert itself much more strongly in judicial decisions, especially in jury trials. A French prosecuting attorney stated only a very short time ago that a wife who had killed her husband's paramour must be found guilty because she had not selected the right victim, the husband.

The assumption of control over civil procedure by the state is of great interest inasmuch as the impulse that was causing this change was not supplied by the legal proposition but by the changing ideas of men concerning the function of the administration of justice by the state. This change is a process that extends over thousands of years. Originally legal procedure was "organized self-help," and it remained self-help in essence as long as its basic principle was the idea of a transaction between the parties. The state assumed control over penal procedure at an early date. Roman procedural law in the formulary procedure, and still more so in the *cognitiones*, contained a few isolated elements that may be said to be state law. These however disappear at a later time in the procedure of the Continental common law. This seems to indicate that in some respects human society in the last century had not advanced as far as that of the Romans. Since

在罗马,家庭法权力与所有权法和所有权一样,最初是私法和私权上的事务,早在帝国时期,就部分丧失了其这种独特性。特别是在监护制度上情况更是如此。在现代法中,父权就逐渐转变成一个公共职位。最古老的罗马刑法是国家法,仅仅由于它可适用于弑亲罪和叛国罪,尽管私法诉讼程序获得的惩罚结果经常与公法诉讼程序获得的惩罚结果一样严厉。但这种私刑法在罗马共和国时期很大程度上被公法取代了,到了罗马帝国时期,被取代的程度则更大。丈夫杀死其不贞之妻及妻之情夫的权利——至少被《刑法典》(Art. 374 A1. 2, and cf. Art. 375)间接认可——或许这是可在现代刑法典中看到的私刑法最后的痕迹。很可能在司法裁决中,特别是在陪审团审判中,它会更加强烈捍卫其自身的正当性。仅在不久以前,一名法国检察官说,一个妻子杀死其丈夫的情妇,她必定被判定有罪,因为她选错了受害人,正确的报复对象应该是其丈夫。

国家接手对民事诉讼程序的控制很有意思,因为引起该变化的冲动并非来自法律规定,而是来自人们对国家司法功能转变的理念。该变化是一个持续了数百年的过程。最初,法律诉讼是"由自力救济建立起来的",并且只要它的基本原则是当事人之间事务的理念,它的本质就仍然是自力救济性的。在早期,国家接管了刑事诉讼程序。处于程式诉讼时期的罗马诉讼法——在确定精神状况的诉讼中尤其如此——包含一些独立的,可以被说成是国家法的因素。然而,到了后来,这些在欧陆共同法的诉讼程序中全都消失了。这似乎表明,在某些方面,最近一个世纪的人类社会还不如罗马时期的人类社会那样先进。自 18 世纪时

the eighteenth century the thought is making its way more and more, in legal science at least, that procedure is a part of state law. This is the period of the *Preussische Allgemeine Gerichtsordnung*, the first departure from the principle of a transaction between tim parties, the first great attempt, even though it was undertaken with insufficient means, to convert not only the administration of law and penal procedure but also civil procedure into a matter of state law. The Austrian revision was the first attempt to establish a procedure which in most respects would be a true state law procedure, not merely in respect of administration. It sought definitively to subject the administration of law to the purposes of the state. The resistance that was encountered by the departure from the old idea of a transaction between the parties, an idea that had not a single consideration of expedience to support it, is an echo of the primeval legai ideas of the human race in the midst of the whirl of modern life.

How this inner change takes place within the legal institutions and the norms for decision is a question we can discuss only in a most general way. Doubtless a great deal of it goes on in the subconscious mind. A large part of the social norms has not been formulated in words once for all time, but must continually be abstracted anew from the regular, universally approved, actual course of human conduct. This is true without qualification in the case of the norms of morality, ethical custom, good breeding, tact. It is impossible to state any basis for them other than the fact that they have been acted upon with universal approbation. And in the case of the legal norm the situation often is the same. A number of rules of law are based upon precedents. The importance of the *Konventionalregel* in public law has heen set forth by the Jellinek school, especially by Hatschek, in a very thorough manner. It seems to me that this rule very frequently is a legal norm, but a norm which has been abstracted from actually approved conduct. Such norms, which are based on the general conception of actual conduct, are not only being confirmed by every new course of actual conduct, but are apparently being sup-

起,“诉讼是国家法的一部分”这种思维正稳步向前发展,至少在法学上如此。这是一个《普鲁士普通法院规则》时期,尽管所采取的手段尚不充分,但那是首次偏离“当事人之间事务”的原则,也是首次重大的努力,试图将法律的实施与刑事诉讼程序、乃至民事诉讼程序转变为国家法上的事项。在奥地利,类似上述的“修改”是首次试图建立一个大多数方面属于国家法上的诉讼程序,而不仅仅在法律实施方面如此。它明确寻求将法律实施置于国家的目的之下。背离“当事人之间事务”的古老理念——这并非是一个单纯权宜考量即可支撑的理念——所遇到的阻力,是人类的原始法律思想在现代生活的疾速流转中所发出的回响。

这种内部变化在法律惯例与裁判规范中如何发生,是一个我们只能以最一般方式讨论的问题。无疑,它大部分是在下意识的情形下发生的。大多数社会规范措辞上的系统表述并非一劳永逸地达成,而必定是从经常性的、获得普遍赞同的、人类行为的实际惯例中不断重新抽象而获得的,此点在道德规范、伦理习俗、良好教养以及社交中的机敏等方面更是绝对正确。对于它们,不可能说除了下列事实还有任何其他的基础:它们能发挥作用是因为它们获得普遍的嘉许。在法律规范的场合,情形经常是相同的。大量的法律规则建立在先例的基础之上。传统规则在公法上的重要性已经由耶里内克学派,特别是哈谢克以一种非常全面彻底的方式阐述。于我而言,该规则绝大多数时候是法律规范,是一个从实际获得肯定的行为中抽象出来的规范。那些基于实际行为之一般观念的规范,不仅被每一个新的实际行为惯例所肯定,而且显然正因内容上的变化而获得增补或正经历内容上的变化。

plemented or are experiencing a change of content. The insignificant divergencies involved at first remain unnoticed and the parties concerned imagine that the old rule still obtains; but in the course of time they accumulate to such an extent that the original legal institution is converted into something quite different. So it has happened more than once that, thanks to a slight shift in the norms, slavery became villeinage and villeinage became slavery. So a self-serving guardianship was converted into one requiring care and protection; the trustee transaction, into pledge-right and testament; the bilateral *real* contracts, into consensual contracts; *Vorleisitung*(prior performance), into a simulated performance(*Arrha*).

Even the wording itself is affected by the lapse of time. It often happens that norms that have been formulated in words receive not merely a new interpretation but a new wording. This too can be done quite without the knowledge of the person introducing the change; for the language of men involuntarily follows their new lines of thought. Quite properly therefore Girard has shown, by way of reply to Lambert, that from the fact that the wording of the propositions of the Twelve Tables, as transmitted to us by tradition, could not possibly have been in existence at the time of the decemvirs, it does not follow that the Twelve Tables were not in existence at all. In the course of the centuries they may have received not only a new meaning but also a new wording suited to the new meaning. And he directs attention to the fact that many of the *brocards* of Loisel have a wording which is quite difierent from that of the time of the ancient jurist, and that Lambert himself writes: "La caution n'est pas solvable," although the original wording was "La caution n'est pas bourgeoise."

The conscious act of an individual, may participate in the dewwvelopment of law, even though it is usually forgotten within a very short time. The idea of Tarde's that all human progress is based

这种重要的偏离最初未获注意，相关当事人以为，旧规则还在适用；但随着时间的推移，它们累积到一定程度，原先的法律惯例变成了迥异的东西。所以下列情形不只一次地偶然发生：由于规范中细微的变化，奴隶制变成了农奴制，农奴制变成了奴隶制。所以自利式的监护转变成一种要求有照料和保护的监护；受托人交易，转变成质权和遗嘱；双方的要物契约，转变成诺成契约；*Vorleisiung*（先予履行），转变成模拟履行（定金）。

甚至措辞本身也会受到岁月更替的影响。以文句系统表述的规范经常不仅容纳新的解释，而且还会接受新的措辞。即使完全不知道谁引入这种转变，这种转变也会发生；因为人类的语言会不知不觉地遵循他们新的思考方法。因此，吉拉德借回复兰伯特，很恰当地表明：口传至今的《十二铜表法》规定的措辞，不可能在古罗马"十大执政官"时期就已存在——这一事实不能推导出，《十二铜表法》根本就不曾存在过。在数世纪的历程中，他们可能不仅容纳了新的含义，而且还可能接受了适于表现新含义的新的措辞。而且他着力强调这一事实：洛瓦塞许多（法律谚语）的表述迥异于该谚语在古代法学家时期的表述，而且兰伯特自己也写过："保证人没有清偿能力"，尽管最初的表述是："保证人不是有产者。"[1]

个人有意识的行为，可能也会部分地参与法律的发展，尽管它在非常短的时期内通常被忘却。塔尔德的理念——所有的人

〔1〕 此两处法语皆省略了前面一句话："我不需要该保证人，因为"。

upon an invention made by an individual and upon the imitation of this invention by the great mass of the people is one of those self-evident things that, once they have been enunciated, Constitute important scientific knowledge. If the question is asked why the Romans did not permit representation in legal transactions, the reply must be that it had to be invented at some time or other, just like the locomotive. The Historical School which taught that the law was created by the people doubtless was wrong as to this point. There was always one person who did it first; the others followed. One must not, however, even in this matter of invention, over-estimate that which is individual, for it, too, is conditioned upon social presuppositions. The art of pottery, the bow and arrow, the rowboat, and the sailing-vessel, without doubt, were invented thousands of years ago quite independently in different parts of the world. For just as long a time it has been the desire of men to be able to soar in the air like birds, but this desire was not realized before the present century, and then in several places at the same time. An invention is not the deed of an individual, but a deed of society through an individual. The individual performs it as soon as society has supplied the conditions which make the deed possible. We do not owe the invention to a man sent by Providence. The inventive thought will spring up in every mind that has received sufficient training as soon as the requisite conditions exist. These conditions are, among others, a certain amount of knowledge of the laws of nature, a certain mastery of technique, a certain degree of economic development, which enables the inventor to provide himself with the necessary aids and appliances. The extended use of an invention, too, is conditioned upon certain presuppositions. The fifteenth century would have been unable to build railroads because the necessary capital was not in existence at the time, and, perhaps, also because they would have been believed to be the work of the devil. Where the social presuppositions are lacking, i. e. the economic development and the general appreciation, an invention must fail, like the invention of the steam engine by Denis Papin. The tragedy of the lot of the inventor lies in this fact, that the social presuppositions for the invention and for the appreciation of it by society very often do not coincide. For quite simple inventions like pottery, the bow and arrow, the rowboat, and the sailing-vessel, all presuppositions

类进步都立基于个人所进行的发明创造以及广大人民群众对这种发明创造的模仿——是那些不证自明的情形之一，一旦它们被清晰阐述，它们就构成重要的科学知识。如果问，为什么罗马人不允许在法律行为中进行事实陈述，那么回答必定是：它只得在未来某个时间或另外一个时间才被发明，正如机车一样。宣扬法律是由人民创造的历史学派，在此点上无疑是错了。总是有一个人首先创造了它，其他人跟随之。然而，即使就发明创造而论，人们也不得高估那个率先发明创造之人，因为，这种发明创造也是取决于社会的先决条件。陶瓷艺术、弓和箭、划艇、航船，毫无疑问都是数千年前世界上的不同地方各自独立发明出来的。因为正如人类能够像鸟儿一样翱翔在蓝天的愿望虽然早已存在，但直到本世纪，在世界的不同地方，这个愿望才同时实现。发明创造不是个人的功绩，而是社会通过个人而实现的成就。一旦社会提供条件使该成就有可能达成，个人就开始完成它。我们并不把该发明归功于神意送来的个人。一旦先决条件存在，创造性的思维会在每一个接受足够训练的头脑中萌芽生长。其中的先决条件是：一定数量的自然法知识、对技能某种程度的掌握以及能够为发明者提供必要帮助和设备的某种程度的经济发展。发明的广泛利用也取决于特定的先决条件。15 世纪时不可能修建铁路，因为那时候没有必要的资本，或许还因为它们会被认为是魔鬼的作品。社会先决条件缺失时，亦即，经济发展和一般评价尚未达到一定水平时，发明必定会失败，比如丹尼斯·帕皮对蒸汽机的发明。发明者的一切不幸均在于这个事实：关于此发明的社会先决条件与社会对此发明的一般评价经常并不一致。对于十分简单的发明如陶瓷、弓箭、划艇以及航船而言，数千年前所有的先决条

were in existence thousands of years ago. For the flying-machine, they were first supplied by our century.

The greater number of juristic inventions probably are found among those the presuppositions for which were in existence at an early time and in many places. They are to be found therefore in all parts of the world, like pottery, the rowboat, and the sailing-vessel. But there are some legal transactions, norms for decision, and procedural forms that require a great measure of independent conscious labor such as can be performed only by specially trained minds. They are the creations of jurists of a scientific bent, of judges, attorneys, and practitioners of the art of drafting legal documents. *Multis vigiliis excogitata et inventa*, Bracton says of the *Assisa movae disseisinae*, the pioneering feat of Henry II. From this point of view, we may say, it is not an error whe the various peoples attribute their laws to a personal lawgiver. They are merely symbolizing the many long-forgotten workmen who took part in their creation. And this fact makes the reception of a foreign legal system possible. A reception actually transfers into foreign countries only norms for decision, model forms for contracts and for articles of association, procedural precepts, which have been invented elsewhere. This is done by means of judicial decision, drafting of legal documents, juristic literature, and, occasionally, legislation. It is a characteristic feature of our time however that a great deal of that which, in the past, was done by the jurist of a scientific bent, by the attorney, by the draftsman of legal documents, is, at the present time, generally assigned to the legislator. It is considered the function of the legislator to create noms for decision, model forms for contracts, for articles of association, for societies and corporations. Indeed all modern procedure is created by legislation. It is difficult to determine what may be the causal relation; at any rate it is by no means a gratifying phenomenon. It brings about a onesidedness and a retardation of legal development, and, to a quite unnecessary degree, delivers the state into the hands of those who at a given time are in power.

件即已存在。对于飞行器,相应的先决条件是到我们这个世纪才具备的。

更多的法学创造,很可能存在于那些先决条件在早期不同地方存在的事物之中。它们因此也将和陶瓷、划艇、航船一样,在世界的所有地方都会被发现。但是还存在一些法律行为、裁判规范以及程序规范,它们要求较高程度的独立性、有意识的劳动,这些是只有经过特别训练的头脑才可能完成的劳动。它们是具有科学爱好的法学家的创造物,是法官、律师以及起草法律文件艺术之实践者的创造物。很多的认识和创造性的深思熟虑,布拉克顿说新型侵占之诉,是亨利二世开创性的功绩。从这个角度,我们可以说,当各式各样的人把他们的法律归功于一个私人立法者,并非是一个错误。他们不过是将许多曾参与创造过程,但长期被遗忘的工作者用特定符号表示而已,而且这也使得对外国法律制度的继受成为可能。法律继受实际上仅仅将外国已经创设出来的裁判规范、契约典型形式以及社团章程、程序规定引入己国。继受的方式可以是司法裁判、法律文件的起草、法学文献等,有时也可以通过立法的方式来继受。不过,在过去,大量的继受是由具有科学爱好的法学家、律师、法律文件起草者来完成的,而现在,此项任务通常由立法者来完成,这是我们这个时代鲜明的特征。创设裁判规范、契约的典型形式、社团章程、团体和法人规范被认为是立法者的功能。事实上,所有的现代诉讼程序都是由立法创造的。很难确定其中的原因与结果关系可能是什么;无论如何,它绝非是一种令人满意的现象。它带来了法律发展的片面和迟滞,并十分不必要地将国家交付给了在某特定时间掌权的人。

It seems however that a change is imminent, that today much less is expected of legislation by the state than a decade ago, tnat there is much more insistence upon limiting its power and a much greater demand that the state stop and reflect upon itself, its functions, and its duties. This must be attributed to a growing understanding of what can be effected and promoted by the means which the state has at its disposal. But the question as to the present-day extent of the sphere of authority of the state and, incidentally, of the statute, is a quite different one. The presentday conception of the state is that of an omnipotence which is contemplated with a certain religious awe, and against which resistance is as impossible as it is impermissible. It is easily demonstrable that this omnipotence is historically conditioned throughout and is based chiefly on the military powers which the state possesses at the present time. Whenever there is a possibility of the state being confronted by another military power within its own territory, as was the case during the days of feudalism, the state is not conceived of as omnipotent. But even today its irresistible power is limited to such things as can be accomplished by means of military power. As a purely social organization the state is but one of many, and, apart from the military power, has only social powers at its disposal, which are by no means superior at all times to those of the other social associations.

The classical school of economists, basing its teachings upon the doctrines of the physiocrats, has subjected the question of the limitations upon the power of the state and of the consequences of state activity, especially of legislation, to a thorough and exhaustive examination. This examination showed that the laws of economics, which, in the view of this school, to a great extent comprise many social processes of a non-economic nature, impose limitations upon the activity of the state beyond which the state may not go, and, beyond which, to a certain extent, it cannot go. It cannot go beyond them without obtaining results that are contrary to its intention; it cannot go beyond them without beating the air. They have also successfully demonstrated that he who can issue a command that a certain measure be taken does not thereby have the power to control its effects. These investigations laid a solid foundation for modern social science.

然而,似乎某个变化近在眼前,如今对国家立法的期待要比10年前少得多,对于限制国家权力则有更多的坚持,并对国家停下来去反省其自身、其功能及其职责有更强烈的要求。这必定归功于人们对——由国家支配的手段能够影响和促进什么——这一问题的理解不断成熟。但是如今关于国家的,顺带也是制定法的权威领域的限度,则是另外一个十分不同的问题。今天的国家观念是把国家设想成带有宗教敬畏色彩的全能概念,对于国家的反抗既不被允许,亦不可能。很容易证明,这种全能在历史上完全取决于国家当时拥有的军事力量,并主要建立在这种军事力量的基础之上。每逢国家在其领土内面临另外一个军事力量时,正如在封建时代的情形一样,国家就不会被认为是全能的了。但是即使是在今天,国家不可抗拒的力量也仅限于那些可以通过军事力量达成的事情。作为一个纯粹的社会组织,国家只是许多社会组织中的一个,并且除了其军事力量之外,也仅有社会力量可以支配,而国家拥有的社会力量也绝非任何时候都强于其他社会联合体所拥有的社会力量。

古典经济学学派——其教义是建立在重农主义学说之上——已经对限制国家权力的问题和国家行为,特别是立法之后果的问题作了一次彻底、详尽的考察。考察的结果表明,在该学派看来,经济学法则很大程度上包含许多非经济性质的社会进程,并对国家的活动施加了限制,国家的活动不得逾越此限,而且一定程度上,它也不可能逾越此限。若结果与其意图一致,则它不可能逾越此限;否则,便是白费力气。他们也成功地证明,能够签发一个采取某种措施之命令的人,并不因而就有力量控制该命令的结果。这些调查研究为现代社会科学奠定了坚实的基础。

For the latter comes into being as soon as that which goes on in society is referred not to the will of the human being who is acting but to the forces which are acting independently of him in society, just as the beginning of the natural sciences is the knowledge that the processes of nature must be explained not as being caused by the will of the gods but by the forces of nature. If these suggestions had been followed, they would have led to an art of legislation resting on a scientific foundation. As it is, the results of these investigations have long since been forgotten. As a result, legislation is characterized by a most naïve dilettantism, which is satisfied in its own mind that all that is necessary in order to abolish an existing evil is to forbid it.

因为一旦在社会上发生的事情并不归因于正在采取行动之人的意志,而是归因于社会上与他无关的那些力量,社会科学就产生了,正如自然科学的出发点是这样一种认识:自然进程不得被解释为神的意志,而只能解释为自然的力量。如果这些建议获得采纳,它们将会使立法技术建立在科学基础之上。事实上,这些调查成果很长时期以来被遗忘了。结果,(对相关技艺)相当幼稚的浅薄涉猎成了立法的特色,它内心确信:为了结束目前的这种"不幸",需要做的就是禁止它。

# XVIII

# The Codification Of Juristic Law

The *Corpus iuris civilis* contains a text-book (the *Institutes*), excerpts from juristic writings (the Digests), and constitutions (the Code), i. e. it contains in the first place juristic literature both in the form of a text-book and in the form of excerpts from works on the existing law, and a collection of statutes. But only a very small part of the excerpts from the writings of the Roman jurists purports to limit itself to a presentation of the law contained in the *praetorian* edict, the *leges*, and the *constitutiones*. The greater part establishes legal norms independently. Their content therefore is juristic law, which, in part, has been presented in literary form, and, in part, appears in the form of responses and decisions. The older imperial constitutions are chiefly

# 第十八章　法学家法的法典化

《民法大全》包含一部教科书(《法学阶梯》)、源自法学著作(《学说汇纂》)的摘录以及法规(《法典》),也就是说,它首先包含以教科书形式和源自关于现行法之著作的摘录形式存在的法律文献,还有一些法令集。但是,在源自罗马法学家作品的摘录中,仅有很少的一部分旨在将其自身局限于对裁判官法、法律[1]以及谕令[2]中所包含法律的阐述。更多的则是独立地创立法律规范。因此,它们的内容就是法学家法,它们一部分是以文学形式呈现,一部分是以答复和裁决的形式来阐明。更古老的皇帝谕令主要

---

〔1〕 (拉)*leges*(法律),在后古典时期,人们对君主谕令(*constitutiones principum*)的笼统称呼,可区分为一般法律(*leges generales*)和特别法律(*leges speciales*),与另一种规范渊源——法(iura)——相对应。

〔2〕 (拉)*constitutiones*(谕令),罗马君主各种指令的总称,构成罗马法的重要渊源之一。它的表现形式有:①诏谕(*edicta*);②训示(*mandata*);③裁决(*decreta*),君主在正式或非正式的审判中宣告的判决;④批复(*rescripta*),君主应私人或执法官的请求,针对某一具体的法律问题作出的答复;最初时,这种答复的约束力一般仅以具体案件为限,后来对类似案件也同样具有指导作用;⑤诏书(*epistulae*),君主撰写的书面答复,其意义与批复相同。

decisions of law cases, and therefore they also are juristic law; some, the *mandata*, are commands addressed to imperial officials, and therefore are administrative regulations. The later ones however are statutes in the narrower sense of the term, i. e. "state law," which provide what is to be law in the future. In addition there are *leges*, *senatusconsulta*, *constitutiones*, i. e. statutes, which contain state law. They are being cited in all parts of the *corpus iuris*. The praetorian edict, which also constitutes a large part, is either juristic law or state law, the latter containing chiefly police regulations. The work of Justinian therefore comprises juristic literature (text-book and literary presentation), juristic law (in the form of literary presentation, responses of jurists, and judgments of the praetor and of the Emperor), and state law (*leges*, *senatus consulta*, *edict*, *constitutiones*).

According to the prevailing view, all of this has been fused into a unit by the will of Justinian, and has become a code. But the various parts of the *corpus iuris* have met widely different fates in the course of time. The parts which at the outset did not contain legal propositions but legal science, i. e. discussions of the nature of law, sources, divisions, system, definitions, content of rights, have remained what they were from the beginning, i. e. a science of law. In so far as it has proved itself to be scientific doctrine, it has gained recognition even in countries in which it has never been

是法律诉讼的裁决；因此它们也是法学家法；一些如训示，[1]主要是向皇帝官员发布的命令，因此它们属于行政法规。不过，后来的皇帝谕令则属狭义上的制定法，即"国家法"——规定了那些在将来成为法律的东西。此外，还存在法律、元老院决议、[2]谕令，即制定法，其内容包含国家法。在《国法大全》的所有地方，它们均被引证。裁判官法令也构成很大的一块，其性质要么是法学家法，要么是国家法，后者主要包含治安法规。因此，优士丁尼的作品包含法学文献（教科书和著作阐述）、法学家法（以著作阐述的形式呈现的法学家的回复、裁判官与皇帝的裁判）以及国家法（leges、senatus consulta、edict、[3] constitutiones）。

按照主流观点，所有的这些都因优士丁尼的意志而合为一体，成为一部法典。但是《国法大全》的不同部分随着岁月的推移各自有着完全不同的命运。一开始未包括法律规定而是包括法律科学——即研究法的性质、来源、部门、体系、概念以及权利内容——的部分，还保持着最初的状况，即还是法律科学。在它证明自己是科学学说的范围内，即使在从未将它作为该国法律接受

---

[1] （拉）*mandata*（训示），罗马帝国时期皇帝向帝国官员特别是行省总督和官员发布的指示，它的内容是各种各样的，可以包含一些新的规范（比如关于军人遗嘱制度的新规范）。

[2] （拉）*senatusconsulta*（元老院决议），罗马法的重要渊源之一，表现为以书面形式向最高执法官提供的咨询意见。由于元老院成员所享有的威望和权力，这类咨询意见在事实上具有法律（*lex*）的效力。

[3] （拉）*edict*（诏谕），君主向全体或者部分臣民发布的通告；最初其效力有限，在发布诏谕的君主去世后，该诏谕即丧失其效力；后来这种限制逐渐消失。

received as the law of the land; it dominates the general theory of law even among the English, the Americans, and the Scandinavians. And the juristic law has become, and has remained, the basis of the common law of most of the civilized nations of the Continent of Europe to the present day. On the other hand that part of it which is state law has, in the main, gradually been eliminated. This applies to those parts of the edict that chiefly contained police regulations and to those imperial constitutions that do not, like many a novel of Justinian, simply modify and replace juristic law.

But though Justinian collected propositions of such diverse descent into a code, he was not thereby enabled to fuse them into a unitary mass. Even within the code they retained the stamp of their origin. Manifestly this fact was of very great influence upon their history. Moreover, a more detailed examination would show how widely they differ in structure and effect.

To form a correct estimate of a modern code, particularly of one of the private law codes of the territory in which the Continental common law used to be in force, the Prussian Code, the French Civil Code, the Austrian Civil Code, and, lastly, the German Civil Code, one must subject it to the kind of examination that the *corpus iuris* by its very outward form challenges one to subject it to. One must separate its three parts from one another, i. e. science of law, juristic law, and state law. In doing this one must of course not fail to observe that juristic law does not cease to be juristic law, does not become state law, simply because it was modified, made milder, adapted to the existing situations, or even found anew, when it was received into the code; for in doing this, the jurist is not working as a legislator but as a jurist. There is a very palpable difference between the provisions of the German Civil Code on the liability of innkeepers, which have been made more rigorous, and the regulation of associations that do not have legal capacity; between the provisions of the French Civil Code that title shall pass at the time the contract is made (*contra* to the rule of the Continental common law), and the precepts as to civil marriage or civil death (*la mort civile*).

的国家,它也获得了认可;即使在英国人、美洲人、斯堪的纳维亚人中间,它也支配着法的一般理论。这种法学家法已经成为大多数欧陆文明国家共同法的基础,并一直维持着这种地位,直到今天。另一方面,包含国家法的那一部分,大体上已经慢慢消亡了。那些主要包含治安法规的诏谕部分,以及那些——并非像优士丁尼新律一样仅仅修正和取代法学家法的——皇帝谕令,都是这种命运。

但是尽管优士丁尼将那些不同"渊源"的规定汇编成一部法典,但是他并未因此使它们成为一元的整体。甚至在法典内部,它们还保留着它们各自最初的印记。显然,该事实对它们的历史具有很重要的影响。此外,一个更详细的调查将会表明,它们在结构和效力上的差异是多么的巨大。

为了对现代法典——特别是对欧陆共同法一直有效适用的地区所存在的某一私法典,如普鲁士法典、法国民法典、奥地利民法典,或德国民法典——形成一个正确的评价,必须让该法典经受某种检验,即以《国法大全》的外在结构作标尺的那种检验。人们必须将它其中三个部分与另外一个部分分开,即法律科学、法学家法以及国家法。当然在这样做时,不能不看到,法学家法一直未曾改变性质,没有变成国家法,原因仅仅是它被修正,变得更和缓,能够适应当前的形势,或者当它被加入法典时,它甚至重新被发现;因为在这样做的时候,法学家不是作为立法者而是作为法学家工作的。在德国民法典关于旅馆主人责任的规定——该规定非常严厉——和关于不具有法人资格之联合体的规定之间,存在十分明显的差异;法国民法典有关"所有权在契约缔结时转移"的规定(与欧陆共同法的规则相对)与有关世俗婚姻、剥夺公权终

Moreover juristic science in Germany has, to a certain extent at least, prepared the way for a critical analysis of the content of the codes such as is suggested here. The doctrine of the non-obligatory content of a statute applies particularly to the purely scientific elements in a statute, and it has succeeded in causing them to disappear almost altogether from the German Civil Code. This cannot be said of juristic law and of state law, although Savigny has brought out the distinction most clearly. In his *Beruf* he most emphatically directs attention to the "two-fold element in the law," the "political" and the "technical." As an example of the former, he cites the *lex Julia et Papia Poppaea*; the latter is the "whole legal store, or capital," that which is law without having been enacted. The further elaboration of this distinction by Savigny shows that it coincides with the distinction between state law and juristic law.

The sifting of state law from juristic law in the modern codes would be a task not only of great scientific but also of great practical importance. It would not be difficult today; for by this time we have pretty accurate knowledge of the sources trom which the codes have drawn their materials. They are the content of the Continental common law as it existed at the time and in the country in which the code originated, the indigenous law of the time and country, and the law of nature.

身[1]的规则之间也存在十分明显的差异。此外,德国法学至少在一定程度上为对民法典的内容进行诸如此处提到的这种批判分析开辟了道路。制定法的非强制性内容的学说特别适用于制定法中纯粹的科学性要素,并且成功地使它们几乎完全从德国民法典中消失。这不可能适用于法学家法和国家法,尽管萨维尼曾经对该区别作了非常清晰的阐述。在他的《论当代立法和法学的使命》[2]中,他着力强调法律中的"两重要素",即"政治的"和"技术的"。关于前者的例子,他提到了《巴比·波培法》[3];关于后者的例子,他提到了"整个法律库藏或资产",它们是未曾正式立法的法律。[4] 关于这种区分,萨维尼更进一步的详细阐释表明,它与国家法和法学家法的区分相一致。

现代法典中,从法学家法到国家法的转变不仅是重大的科学任务,而且还是具有重大实践意义的任务。在今天,这种转变并不困难;因为迄今为止,对于法典据以从中提取出素材的那些来源,我们已经有了非常精确的了解。它们是那个时代、法典诞生地的那个国家欧陆共同法的内容,是彼时彼国的本土法,也是自然法。

---

〔1〕(法)剥夺公权。

〔2〕Savieny,《论当代立法和法学的使命》(Von Beruf unserer Zeit fiir Gesetzgebung und Rechtswissenschaft),Heidelberg,1840.

〔3〕(拉)*lex Julia et Papia Poppaea*(《巴比·波培法》),一部罗马法规,规定限制未婚者或未生育子女的已婚者根据遗嘱而得益,以达到鼓励结婚和提高生育率的目的。

〔4〕原文是"Ohnehin bestehende Recht",照字面意义就是"无论如何都构成法律",即,虽未经立法通过也有效力的法律。

The chief constituent part of the codes everywhere is the Continental common law. For the most part, the common law, which had been received on the Continent of Europe during the Middle Ages and in the modern period, had remained a mere norm for decision for the courts. But one must not limit the importance of the Continental common law to this. Modern investigations have shown that the legal document, especially the notarial document, which, self-evidently, was based on the Italian formbooks, had adapted itself very readily to the common law in every country. Thereby a great deal of the Continental cornnon law became part and parcel of everyday life, became the living law in the territory in which it was valid. The nations of the Continent of Europe are indebted to the Continental common law for the last will and testament, and it can be shown that it was the lawyers who drew up the legal documents that transmitted it to them in the Roman form. It is true the last will and testament would have come into vogue even if conveyancers had not introduced it, albeit in a somewhat different form. But this cannot be said of the Roman law of contracts. In virtue of the fact, and only in virtue of the fact, that the Roman law of contracts as developed in the Continental common law has been made the basis of the legal document, the Continental common law system of contracts, the fundamental principles of which are Roman, has attained such a preeminent position in the modern legal consciousness that we are inclined today to look upon the Roman contracts as understood by the Continental common law as something that is, in a certain sense, self-evident. Nevertheless a glance at the mediaeval German legal sources, especially at the documents dating from the time before the reception, shows that, in Germany and France at least, the law of contracts would have developed along entirely different lines had there been no reception—probably along lines similar to those of the development in England. And lastly, as a consequence of the reception, the fixed and clear juristic terminology and the whole juristic technique of the Continental common law juristic science has become part and parcel of the Continental common law everywhere. All of this has exerted a profound influence upon the codes.

The second constituent part of the codes are the legal propositions taken from the codifications of the indigenous law. The various *Landrechte* ( laws of the various states ) and the revisions in the sixteenth century in Germany as well as the official statements of the *coutumes* in France at the end of the fifteenth century have been of great importance for later legislation. They are not merely,

在所有地方,法典的主要组成部分都是欧陆共同法。一般说来,在中世纪和现代,欧陆所接受的共同法还仅保留着供法院适用的裁判规范。但是不得将欧陆共同法的重要性仅限于此。现代的调查表明,法律文件,特别是公证文件——显然以意大利的格式书为基础——在每个国家都被调整得非常容易适合该国共同法。因而,大量的欧陆共同法变成了日常生活不可或缺的一部分,变成了在它所适用的疆域内的活法。欧陆国家在遗嘱制度方面受惠于欧陆共同法,可以证明,是将该制度以罗马法上的形式传至这些国家的律师起草了那些法律文件。的确,即使传播者没有引进遗嘱制度,该制度还是会流行开来,虽然是采取另外不同的形式。但这并不适用于罗马契约法。罗马契约法,如同在欧陆共同法中的发展一样,已经被当作法律文件的基础——根据并仅根据这个事实,欧陆共同法契约制度(其基本原则源自罗马法),已经在现代法律意识中获得那样一个突出的位置,以至于我们今天倾向于把根据欧陆共同法来理解的罗马契约视为在某种意义上不证自明的东西。尽管如此,但若对中世纪德国法律渊源,特别是对早在罗马法继受之前的法律文件浏览一番,就会看出,至少在德国和法国,倘若没有发生罗马法继受,契约法将按照不同的轨迹向前发展——很可能类似于英国的发展路径。最后,作为继受的结果,固定而清晰的法学术语与欧陆共同法学的全部法学技术在欧陆的所有地方都成为欧陆共同法必不可少的一部分。所有这些都对那些法典产生了深远的影响。

法典的第二个组成部分取自本土法汇编中的法律命题。各种各样的 *Landrechte*(国家法)以及 16 世纪德国的修正本、15 世纪末法国习惯法官方陈述对于后来的立法具有重大意义。它们不

official statements in writing of the indigenous law of France and of Germany that had been in use until that time. The revisions, it is true, were drawn up, in part at least, by jurists who had a knowledge of the indigenous law; and the laws of the various states and the *coutûmes* were based on information given to the authors by experts in the indigenous law; the official drafting of the French *coutûmes*, in particular, was done with extreme care. But only a very small part of this information stated legal propositions that had previously been formulated, and that the persons who gave the information knew in that form. For the most part they were formulated by these persons on the basis of individual impressions at the moment they gave the information. They are therefore universalizations of actual observation of indigenous legal relations, made by the persons who gave the information at the very moment of giving it. We know furthermore that the persons who drew up the statements, in many instances, modified the law intentionally, mitigated its rigors, supplemented it, and, in particular, attempted to assimilate it to Roman law. Apart from this, many rules were taken directly from Roman law and from other statements of law. The *Constitutiones Saxonicae* professedly purported, not to codify existing law, but to harmonize it with the common law of the Continent. One cannot therefore unqualifiedly say that the codifications of the fifteenth, sixteenth, and seventeenth centuries were codifications of the then valid German law. If by law we do not mean the legal relations but the legal propositions, it would be more nearly correct to say that practically all the law contained in these works came into existence through the codification. Thereby it became juristic law as to form and content. The revisions in the cities, the laws of the states (*Landrechte*), and the *coutûmes* owe their existence in part to universalization, and in part to juristic finding of norms such as undoubtedly can be found elsewhere both in the juristic writings of the Romans and in those of mediaeval German writers.

The third kind of material that entered into the modern codes is the law of nature. It is customary to consider the law of nature as a defense set up by the German legal consciousness against the invading Roman law. This view contains a great deal of truth, but

仅仅记录直到那时仍在使用中的法国和德国本土法的官方陈述。的确,修正本至少部分是由对本土法有所了解的法学家草拟的;各种各样的国家法和习惯法都是建立在本土法专家给那些立法者提供的信息基础之上;起草法国习惯法的官员是带着极度的细心完成工作的。但是仅有少量的这种信息说明那些先前已经被系统表述过的法律命题,同时说明提供此等信息的人了解该法律规定先前的表述方式。在极大程度上,这些人阐明这些法律规定主要是以他们在提供此等消息时的个人表达为基础。因此,这些法律命题是对本土法律关系实际观察的一般化,实施一般化的主体则是,在提供信息的那一时刻的信息提供者。而且我们还知道,很多情况下,起草陈述的人,有意识的修正法律,减轻其严酷性,增补它,并特别试图将它吸收到罗马法中。除此之外,许多规则直接取自罗马法与其他法律陈述。萨克森法规集自称不仅旨在编纂现行法,而且努力将现行法与欧陆共同法调和。因此人们不能斩钉截铁地说,15 世纪、16 世纪以及 17 世纪的法典化就是对当时有效的日耳曼法的法典化。如果说法律时我们不是意指法律关系,而是法律命题,那么以下说法将会更接近正确:实际上,这些作品中包含的所有法律都是通过法典化而产生的。因此,它们在形式和内容上都变成了法学家法。在城市中的修订本、国家法、习惯法,这些的存在部分都归因于法的一般化,部分归因于法学上规范的发现——诸如毫无疑问的可以在罗马人的法学作品中和中世纪德国作者的法学作品中到处可见的那些规范。

进入现代法典中的第三个素材是自然法。习惯上认为,自然法是德国法律意识反对入侵的罗马法而建立的。这种观点包含

it is not the whole truth. For the teachers of natural law, beginning with Pufendorf at least, were practical and theoretical economists, not jurists, and represented, at first unconsciously perhaps, later consciously, the claims and demands of the urban middle classes. The final expression of the natural law movement is by no means to be found in the writings of the juristic ideologists of Germany and France, but in the writings of the French physiocrats whose demands and doctrines, were, in many instances, anticipated in Germany by Pufendorf and Wolf. The urban middle class is the class which was engaged in the trades and in commerce in the seventeenth and eighteenth centuries, and which was just beginning to turn to industrialism. It was already making political demands albeit they were rather modest in Germany. They demanded a powerful state, participation in the power of the state, and a weakening of the power of the feudal nobility.

These demands explain the absolutist trend of the older, especially of the German, teachers of natural law; but the call for an absolute form of government was merely an outward disguise for a developing tendency of much wider scope. The monarch alone was able at this time to create a powerful state; he alone was able to break the power of the nobility. The middle classes of the population could enter into a direct relation with the state, whose embodiment to them at the time was the monarch, only through absolutism. The absolutist welfare state, of the German natural law teachers in particular, is the state which aids commerce, trade, and industry, increases the population, and by so doing provides workmen for commerce, trade, and industry, forcibly curbs enemies of the latter at home, provides legal security and protection against foreign enemies. As is well known, the later teachers of natural law gave up these ideas and demanded constitutionalism in the English sense, and finally, popular sovereignty. In so far at least as all of this was the case, the teachers of natural law surely were not combating the Roman law but feudalism. In doing this they were not espousing the cause of German law but were striving for a political and legal order different from that which was in effect at the time.

很大的真实性，但并非完全正确。因为自然法的教授者，至少从普芬道夫开始，都是应用和理论经济学家，而不是法学家，并且在一开始就下意识地，或许后来是有意地代表都市中产阶级的主张和要求。自然法运动的最终表述绝不是在德国和法国法学理论家的作品中看到的那样，而是在法国重农主义者的作品中看到的那样，后者的要求和学说很多情况下德国的普芬道夫和沃尔夫都已论及。都市里的中产阶级是17世纪、18世纪从事贸易和商业的这一阶层，他们正开始转向工业主义。虽然他们在德国还很低调，但是他们已经开始有政治上的要求。他们要求建立一个强大的国家，并分享这个国家的权力，同时削弱封建贵族的权力。

这些要求说明了自然法较古老的教授者们、特别是德国的教授者们的专制主义倾向；但是有关绝对形式之政府的要求对于一个更广泛范围内的发展趋势而言仅仅是一个外部的掩饰。当时君主一个人就能建立起强大的国家；单单君主自己也可以拿掉贵族的权力。中产阶级的居民可以与国家发生直接的关系，对于他们而言，国家的化身就是君主，发生联系的方式则仅仅是专制主义。专制主义的福利国家——特别是德国自然法教授者心目中的福利国家——是扶助商业、贸易、工业的国家，增加人口，并且通过这样做来为商业、贸易、工业提供劳动力，并约束后者在国内的敌对势力，为抵抗外国敌对势力提供法律安全和保护。众所周知，自然法后来的教授者放弃了这些思想，并要求英国意义上的立宪主义，最后，主张的是人民主权论。至少就所说的这种情况下，自然法的教授者们确实没有同罗马法进行斗争，而是同封建主义进行斗争。这样做时，他们并不是在拥护日耳曼法的事业，而是在为一个不同于当时有效的政治和法律秩序

But for legislation the economic demands of the urban middle classes are much more important than the political ones. It was these that were chiefly making for a reorganization of the private law by means of the codes. The endeavors of the teachers of natural law, along this line also, were directed chiefly against feudalism, which interfered with and hindered trade and commerce in the country, and, to a certain extent, in the city also, by means of proscriptive rights and of restrictions of trade, withdrew the peasant from the sphere of the interests of the middle classes, restricted his working power in the interest of the landowner, and made it impossible to utilize it for the purposes of industry. Over and above this, however, they were bent upon the establishment of a legal order, based on liberty of contract and freedom of commerce, which should overthrow the restrictions placed on free activity, and abolish inequalities before the law between classes and localities.

The efforts of the urban middle classes suggested a legislative policy to the teachers of natural law, as their spokesmen, which indeed was in conflict with the existing order inasmuch as the latter restricted the free activity of the individual. Individualism became the ideal of the teachers of natural law, i. e. a system under which the individual, unhampered by class distinctions (equality before the law), can do with his own as he will, and is bound only by contracts voluntarily entered into. That this ideal entailed new and very great obligations, they did not see as yet, and in fact could not see at that time. But they imagined that this very ideal had been realized in Roman law. In so far as Roman law recognizes oppressive class distinctions—binds and fetters the individual by means of public law, penal criminal law, and family law—it usually was not received. All that remained of Roman law was abstract ownership, a soil free from burdens and divisible, liberty of contract, and an essentially equal right of inheritance. These were also the principles of the natural law legislative policy, which from the very beginning had put on the garb of an individualistic legal philosophy. Within the framework of free ownership

而奋斗。

但是对于立法来说,都市中产阶级的经济要求比政治要求重要得多。通过法典形式促进对私法的整编,主要力量就是他们的经济要求。同样沿此路线前进的自然法的教授者们,他们的努力主要是反对封建主义,后者干涉和阻碍了一国的贸易和商业,并在某种程度上,也干涉和阻碍了一个城市的贸易和商业,凭借排斥权以及对贸易的限制,使农民从中产阶级的利益范围内撤出,将他的劳动力限于为地主的利益服务,使得其劳动力不可能被用来为工业的目的服务。然而,除此之外,他们基于契约自由和商业自由,致力于一种法律秩序的建构,这种法律秩序将会推翻加于自由行动之上的限制,并废除不同阶级之间和不同地区之间法律上的不平等。

都市中产阶级的努力要求自然法的教授者——作为他们的代言人——有某种立法政策,这种新的立法政策与现行秩序相冲突,因为后者限制了个人的自由行动。个人主义成了自然法教授者的理想,即,在这种个人主义制度下,个人不会受到阶级划分的阻碍(法律面前平等),能够按自己意志做自己的事情,并仅仅受自愿签订的契约的约束。这种理想必然伴有新的更大的义务,只不过他们当时尚未看到,事实上,他们当时也不可能看到。但是他们认为,这个新的理想在罗马法中已经获得实现。就罗马法承认压迫性的阶级划分——通过公法、刑法以及家庭法制约和束缚个人——来看,该理想并未被接受。罗马法中所存留的是抽象的所有权,没有负担、无须分割的土地,契约自由,本质上平等的继承权。这些也都是自然法立法政策的原则,从一开始,它们就披上了个人主义法律哲学的外衣。在自由所有权和契约自由的框

and liberty of contract, the urban middle classes were able to create most of the legal institutions which they required for their future development. Wherever therefore the teachers of natural law—by way of exception—make a more detailed statement of their law, they create it by means of abstraction from the existing institutions of the urban middle classes in the manner in which Wolf created his law of bills of exchange, or they formulate it according to the wishes of the urban middle classes. They transform the wishes of the middle classes into legal propositions, somewhat in the manner in which the lawyer who draws up a legal document expresses the wishes of his client in the conditions of the contract.

The law of nature went one step beyond this, for it was actually bent upon creating its own particular legal system, in particular its own private law, based upon an individualist idea of justice. The principles of individualist liberty of ownership and liberty of contract, as expressed in the abstract concept of ownership and in the system of contract of the Continental common law in the service of the as yet very limited traffic in goods of the seventeenth and eighteenth centuries; in addition thereto, the traditional morality of middle-class family life; the idea of the right of the owner to dispose of his property beyond the grave carried out to its logical conclusion by means of last will and testament; and the idea of a right of inheritance, intended for the time being for the nearest relatives, and equal among equally close relatives—these indeed are a basis sufficiently broad for them to develop a system of private law upon, in broad outlines at least, and often with an almost mathematical precision. The attempt of the law of nature school to do this manifestly amounted to a finding of norms, i. e. juristic science. It is true, it was a juristic science which was based, in the main, on the living law, and whose relation to the existing law was one of comparative freedom, but, by no means, of absolute independence; for it presupposed the existing social and economic order which, for the most part, has arisen and taken shape under the influence of the existing law.

Accordingly Roman law was more in harmony with the teachings of the Natural Law School than any other system of law, especially ancient German law, could be. With few exceptions, there-

架内,都市中产阶级能够创造出他们未来发展所需要的大多数法律惯例。因此,无论在哪里,作为例外,自然法的教授者们会对他们的法律进行更详尽的表述,他们要么通过对都市中产阶级的现行惯例予以提炼、抽象的方式——那正是沃尔夫创造汇票法的方式——创造了它,要么按照都市中产阶级的愿望对它进行了简洁的表述。他们将中产阶级的愿望转化成法律规定,转化的方式有些类似于起草法律文件的律师以契约的条件明确表达出其代理人愿望的方式。

自然法超越了这一阶段,因为它实际上是致力于以个人主义者的正义理念创立自身独特的法律制度,特别是创建自身的私法制度。个人主义者的所有权自由原则、契约自由原则,如同在所有权的抽象概念中以及欧陆共同法的契约制度——运用于截至17、18世纪时非常有限的货物运输——中表达的那样;除此之外,还有中产阶级家庭生活的传统道德;所有人通过遗嘱使其处置财产的权利在其死后仍可得以实现的理念;暂时仅适用于最近的亲属、并在其近亲属中同等对待的继承权的理念——这些实际上足以构成一个广阔的基础——至少是一个主要的轮廓,从而在其上发展出一套私法制度来,并且经常带有几乎数学上的精确性。自然法学派如此做的努力显然实际上就是规范的发现,即法学。的确,它是一种科学,其基础主要是活法,它与现行法的关系相当自由,但又绝非完全独立;因为它以现存的社会和经济秩序为前提,而这种秩序极大程度上又是在现行法的影响下产生和成形的。

因此,罗马法律制度比其他任何法律制度——特别是古代德国法——都更能与自然法学派的教义相和谐。因此,仅有极少的

fore, among these perhaps Thomasius, they did not by any means oppose Roman law; on the contrary, they generally were adherents of it. They never tired of emphasizing that Roman law, in its essence, is natural law, or that it differs from the latter only in unimportant details. It must be admitted however that in spite of this the content of Roman law did not fully satisfy the needs of society in the seventeenth and eighteenth centuries and that a few changes would have been very welcome indeed. But it is not so much the principles of German law that bring the teachers of natural law into occasional conflict with Roman law as the demands of a new era. Offense was not taken at the content, but at the form, of Roman law. What the teachers of natural law were impugning and desired to modify was this cumbersome, voluminous code in a foreign language, utterly lacking clearness of arrangement, weighted down by a mass of material long since antiquated, trailed by a vast juristic literature and interminable controversial questions, among which no jurist, much less a layman, could find his way. Hotomanus, the actual originator of the idea of codification, in his day demanded a brief code, which meets the requirements of the administration of justice, is drawn up in language that is within the grasp of an ordinary intellect, does away, once for all, with the controversial questions, and offers a clear and fair solution of every case that may arise.

Still the teachers of natural law have been successful in advancing juristic technique by one important step. It was impossible indeed to derive legal propositions of any appreciable utility from the principles of natural law, which were merely the principles of an individualistic property and contract law; but the tendency to derive law from principles made it easier for them to discern what is basic, in the

例外——其中或许有托马西乌斯,[1]他们无论如何不会反对罗马法;相反,他们通常是罗马法的追随者。他们从来都是不厌其烦地强调,罗马法本质上是自然法,或者强调罗马法不同于自然法之处仅仅在于无关紧要的细节上。不过,必须承认,尽管在 17 世纪和 18 世纪,罗马法的内容并没有充分满足社会的需要,但实际上还是发生了一些可喜的变化。但是,与其是说德国法的原则使得自然法的教授者们与罗马法偶尔发生冲突,不如说新时代的要求使然。违背之处不在罗马法内容,而在其形式。自然法的教授者所攻击并渴望修改的是:用外语表述的笨重的长篇法典,特别缺乏安排的清晰性,大量过时的材料使之沉重不堪,浩瀚的法学文献和冗长的争议问题牵扯于后,任何一个深陷其中的法学家——更不用说门外汉——都会迷失方向。霍托马努斯,法典思想的实际创始人,在他的那个时代要求创立一部简要的法典来满足司法的要求,该法典以平常智力的人即能掌握的语言写出,一劳永逸地解决争议问题,为每一种可能发生的案件提供了一个清晰而公平的解决办法。

尽管如此,自然法的教授者们还是成功地将法学技术推进了重要的一步。实际上从自然法的原则中推导出任何获得可观效用的法律规定是不可能的,后者仅仅是个人主义财产法和契约法的原则;但是从原则中推导出法律的偏好至少使得在现行法中区分什么是基本的东西更加容易。自然法的教授者们起初认识到

---

〔1〕 托马西乌斯,德国法学家,他在莱比锡大学和哈利大学任教授,他坚持讲授德国法,并主张在实践中确立德国法以取代罗马法。他在促进德国法的发展中曾有极大的影响。他视法律为自然法,认为法律是建立在神明裁判基础上,由上帝对人们心灵所讲的话。

existing law at least. The teachers of natural law perceived an important truth at the outset which the Continental common law had failed to observe until then, to wit that a considerable part of the sources of Roman law merely contains particular applications of legal norms of a much more general tenor, and that a code could be made much briefer, much more easily comprehensible, by including only the general legal propositions and omitting the particular applications. They took it to be their chief function therefore to find these general legal propositions, which, they believed, the Romans had simply derived from the law of nature; and their theory permitted them simply to exclude from the system of natural law any decision which did not suit them, on the ground that it was a deviation from the law of nature. Their method of proceeding was based indeed on a considerable lack of understanding of the heterogeneous tendencies that necessarily run counter to each other within a legal system and of that which is positive and historically given therein, but it was also based upon the valid, good, and new thought, as its true content, that there are general principles in law upon which the individual decisions are based and that exceptional features are not to be accepted without more ado, but are to be examined as to their bases. This is a reliable criterion according to which they were able to eliminate those elements from the positive law that were merely arbitrary exceptions or survivals which can only be explained historically.

The doctrine of the natural law school therefore is, primarily, a criticism of the form and, secondarily, a criticism of the content of Roman law. The latter is leveled generally and essentially at matters of secondary importance. It became authoritative for the later form of the tiny code, which is divided into brief chapters and lays down general principles only. It did not contain very much positive material, and this was taken, in part, from the German legal consciousness, in part from the institutions of commerce, trade, and large-scale industry, which was coming into existence at that time. In other words it arose from the institutions of the urban middle classes in all these fields.

Lastly the teachers of the law of nature taught out-and-out individualistic juristic law. Not being practical jurists, they did not enter upon a discussion of details. They had a general picture in their minds of what they were demanding, but they were unable

一个重要但欧陆共同法直到那时尚未发现的事实，即，罗马法相当大的一部分来源仅仅包含更有一般生活倾向之法律规范的个别应用，并且通过仅包含一般的法律规定，同时省略个别应用的方式，法典原本可以更简洁、更容易理解。因此他们将发现这些一般性的法律规定作为他们的主要职责，他们认为，这些一般性法律命题是罗马人直接从自然法中推导出的；他们的理论允许他们直接将他们不满意的任何裁决排除在自然法体系之外，因为那是对自然法的背离。他们的诉讼方式的确是基于对相异的倾向——在一个法律体系中它们必然相互冲突——相当缺乏了解之上，也是基于对实证的、历史上的东西缺乏了解之上；但是它也建立在正当的、良善的以及新式的思想基础之上，并作为其真实的内容，这种新思想就是在法律中存在个别裁判必须遵循的一般性原则，例外性特征不是很干脆地予以接受，而是就其基础接受审查。这是一个可靠的标准，据此，他们能够消除仅仅是恣意的例外或只能在历史上予以解释的那些源于实证法的因素。

因此，自然法学派的学说首要是对罗马法形式的评判，其次是对罗马法内容的评判。后者一般实质上被置于次要位置。对于微型法典后来的形式，它变得具有权威性，后来的法典通常被分为简要的章节，并且只规定主要的原则。它并不包含很多实证的材料，此种设计部分来自德国法律意识，部分来自当时出现的商业、贸易以及大规模工业的惯例。换言之，它源于都市中产阶级在这所有领域内的惯例。

最后，自然法的教授者们不折不扣地教授个人主义法学家法。由于不是从事实践的法律人，他们没有参与细节的讨论。他们的脑海中有一幅关于“他们正在要求的”图景，但是他们不能提

to propose a practically applicable system of juristic law as a substitute for the Continental common law. Law of this kind does not spring from discussions of legislative policy, but only from the administration of justice, from the decision of individual practical law cases. Even Wolf, who more than any other teacher of the law of nature concerned himself with detailed problems, does not state true legal propositions, but sets up demands as to economic policy, legislative policy, and social policy, according to the idea of the *Wohlfahrtsstaat* (state promoting the public welfare), which, together with those things that he simply borrowed from the existing law and a critique of Roman law, constitute the principal content of his prolix book.

The building stones, then, which were used in the construction of the codes of the end of the eighteenth and the beginning of the nineteenth century were: *first*, the Continental common law juristic science; *secondly*, the legal propositions of indigenous law which were contained in the law of each of the various states (*Landrechte*), the revisions, and the *coutûmes*, and *lastly*, the demands of the teachers of the law of nature. The first two are chiefly juristic law. The law of nature, being juristic law also and, in addition, a critique, from the point of view of legislative policy of the existing feudal law and of juristic law, contained no legal material of its own. It did however exert a decisive influence upon the external form of the codes.

In these three codes these constituent elements are mixed in varying proportions. The Prussian Code, private law only being considered, contains more Roman law than the others; the French Civil Code, the greatest number of provisions taken from indigenous law (the *coutûmes*); the Austrian Civil Code is dominated chiefly by the law of nature. There is very little of actual state law to be found in any of them. The codes, then, in the main, contain juristic law put into statutory form; they are statutory juristic law. This shows wherein lay their chief significance for the development of law. The men who drew them up knew quite well, and Savigny knew, that their function was not to create new law but to organize the existing law and put it into suitable form, to eliminate that which had become antiquated, and here and there to adapt the part that was valid to new needs. In

出一套实际可行的法学家法的制度,来作为欧陆共同法的代替。这种法律并非来自立法政策的讨论,而仅仅来自司法,来自实际法律诉讼的个案裁决。甚至比任何其他人更关注细节问题的沃尔夫也没有表述真实的法律规定,而只是按照 *Wohlfahrtsstaat*(促进公共福利之国家)的理念,提出有关经济政策、立法政策以及社会政策的要求,那种福利国的理念加上他直接从现行法中借得的东西以及对罗马法的评论,共同构成了他那本冗长著作的主要内容。

这样,用于18世纪末、19世纪初的法典建构的"建筑石料"包括:首先是欧陆共同法法学;其次是在每个国家法(*Landrechte*)中包含的本土法的法律命题、修正本、习惯法;最后是自然法教授者们的要求。前两个主要是法学家法。自然法,也是法学家法,此外,从现行封建法的立法政策和法学家法的角度来看,评论本身并不包含法律素材,然而它对法典的外部形式产生了决定性的影响。

在这三个法典中,上述这些构成要素混合的比例各不相同。普鲁士法典,仅考虑了私法,它包含的罗马法因素最多;法国民法典,最多数量的条款取自本土法(习惯法);奥地利民法典则主要受到自然法的支配。三者之中,极少发现有现实的国家法。这样,这些法典大体上包含的法学家法取得了制定法的形式;它们是制定法形式的法学家法。这表明,其中法学家法对于法律的发展发挥了首要的意义。起草这些法典的人十分了解——萨维尼也了解——他们的功能不是创造新法典,而是将现行法整合起来,并将其置入一个合适的形式,并消除已经陈旧过时的东西,同时到处改变仍有效的部分,使之适应新的需求。用萨维尼的话说

the words of Savigny "the existing law is to be recorded, with such modifications and emendations as may be necessary for political reasons."

Although the German Civil Code was composed a century later, it bears the same stamp as the eighteenth-century codes. The juristic science on which it is based is indeed younger by a century than that of the other codes, but after all it is merely the science of the Continental common law—younger by a century. Apart from this, thanks chiefly to Gierke's influence, it contains much German private law; this, too, in the form of juristic law, as it was fashioned by the Germanists of the last century in their text-books and handbooks of German private law. For this reason it is much more important to emphasize its relation to the law of nature. In form and content it realizes the demands of the teachers of the law of nature much more completely than any previous code, and the reason why this fact has been overlooked so often is that the demands of the teachers of natural law, meanwhile, have become self-evident commonplaces. Accordingly in the sphere of intellectual endeavor the greatest success comes when the truth becomes a commonplace.

A characteristic of the Roman juristic law which has been handed down in the *corpus iuris* is the fact that it is judicial juristic law exclusively. The Roman art and science of drawing up legal documents seems to have had no influence whatever upon the sources of Justinian, which do indeed concern themselves with the content of documents, not, however, with the question how they are to be drawn up, but how the controversies that arise from them are to be decided. The juristic science of the Continental common law, however, was, in a great measure, a science of legal documents. The latter plays a particularly important rôle in the writings of the commentators, who are continually putting the question how the document must be drawn up in order to avoid this or that undesirable legal consequence. In the writings of the German and the French jurists of the seventeenth and eighteenth centuries, however, this point of view is being emphatically relegated into the background; they concern themselves, just like the teachers of natural law, chiefly with judicial law. Nevertheless even in the French Civil Code and in the Austrian Civil Code, the idea of a model contract is faintly discernible—in the French Civil Code, chiefly in the provisions regulating the matrimonial régime; in the

就是，“现行法将要被记录下来，并作出可能基于政治理由是必要的那些修改和修正”。

尽管德国民法典的编纂要晚一个世纪，但它与18世纪的法典具有相同的特征。它所基于的法学实际上比其他法典要年轻一个世纪，但毕竟是年轻了一个世纪的欧陆共同法法学。除此之外，主要鉴于基尔克的影响，德国民法典中包含很多德国私法；这也采取了法学家法的形式，如同最近一个世纪德意志学者在他们有关私法的教科书和手册中所塑造的形式。因此，强调它与自然法的关系重要得多。在形式和内容上，它实现自然法教授者之要求的程度要比先前任何其他的法典彻底得多。为什么此事实如此经常地被人忽略，原因在于自然法教授者们的要求已经变成了不证自明的老生常谈。因此，在知识分子奋力进取的范围内，当真理变成一种常识，最伟大的成功降临了。

在《国法大全》中传下来的罗马法学家法的特征在于：它完全是司法性的法学家法。罗马人起草法律文件的技艺和学问似乎对于优士丁尼的原始文献没有任何影响，后者实际上只关注文件的内容，即关注的不是如何起草它们的问题，而是源于它们的争议如何被裁决的问题。不过，欧陆共同法的法学在很大程度上是起草法律文件的科学。后者在评注法学家的著作中发挥了特殊的作用，评注法学家不断地提出这样的问题：法律文件必须怎样起草才能避免这样或那样的不良法律后果？但是，在17世纪、18世纪德国和法国法学家的著作中，这种观点被着力置于次要地位；他们就像自然法的教授者们一样，主要关注司法之法。尽管如此，甚至在法国民法典和奥地利民法典中，典型契约的观念也是依稀可辨的。在法国民法典中，主要体现在调整婚姻制度的条

Austrian Civil Code, in the chapter on loans and usufructuary leases. Such legal conesquences are to be provided for as the parties themselves would have provided for, had they drawn up a detailed document. Since it is almost exclusively subsidiary law, it does not require the parties to adopt a definitely prescribed content of the contract, but it does compel them at least to bear in mind the contractual content for which regulations have been provided by the statute if they are desirous of bringing about other legal consequences than those provided for by the statute. Nevertheless even here the consideration of a possible legal controversy seems to have most weight.

It was not before the nineteenth century that statutes were enacted which, following French and English example, purported, in part at least, to state the content of a legal document. Their object was to introduce certain institutions which until then had been unknown at home; which, perhaps according to the then state of the law had been forbidden, or whose permissibility had been in doubt. The plan was to permit the parties, according to foreign models, to establish these institutions by agreement between themselves either by contract or by articles of association. This implies a determination of the content of the declaration of will—for the most part, by non-obligatory law, to a great extent, however, by obligatory law. The object of these statutes manifestly is to prepare the ground for the legal document which the parties necessarily must draw up with reference to the transaction in such a way as to protect them against being overreached (*Reglementierung*). Institutions of this kind are the legal order of societies, of stock companies, of the Schulze-Delitzsch associations, of partnerships with limited liability, of the heritable building right. Very often the state supervises the making of these contracts in order to ascertain whether they are drawn up in such a way as to meet the statutory requirements. This supervision may be exercised, e. g. by state action

款中;在奥地利民法典中,主要体现在贷款和附用益权租约的章节中。那样的法律效果将会产生,因为倘若当事人起草了一份详细的文件,那么当事人自己就会规定那样的法律效果。既然它总是毫无例外地属于辅助法,那么它不会要求当事人采用明确指定的契约内容,但是如果当事人希望产生不同于调整该契约的制定法所规定的其他法律后果,它至少会强迫他们记住契约内容。尽管如此,甚至此处对可能产生的法律争议的考量似乎也是沉重的负担。

直到19世纪,追随法国和英国的榜样,至少部分地旨在表述法律文件内容的制定法才得以颁布。他们的目标就是将直到那时国内尚未知的特定制度引进来;这种惯例按照当时的国家法来看,或许是被禁止的,或者其是否被许可尚有疑问。按照外国的模范,该计划打算允许当事人通过他们之间的协议而建立这些机构——协议形式或是契约或是社团章程。这也意味着遗嘱内容的确定一般依据非强制法,不过很大程度上也依据强行法。这些制定法的目标显然是以那样一种方式为当事人提供他们在交易中必然要制订的法律文件,从而保护他们免受欺诈之害(*Reglementierung*)[1]。这种制度是社团、股份公司、舒尔策·德里施合作社[2]、有限责任合伙、可继承建筑权的法律秩序。国家经常会监督这些契约的制定,以便确定它们的起草方式是否满足制定法

---

〔1〕 (德)Reglementierung 严格控制、集中统一管理。

〔2〕 1846年时,德国作物欠收和饥荒,舒尔策(Herman Schulze-Delitzsch)组织了一个合作经营的磨坊和面包店,以特别优惠的价格向成员卖面包。1850他又以这种精神组织了第一个信用合作社。

when the agreement is presented for recording or for approval. All of this however must not obscure the fact that what we are dealing with is essentially the art and science of drawing up legal documents, i. e. with juristic law, which is being found by the legislator. In antiquity, in the Middle Ages, even in modern times, it was the art and science of drawing up legal documents that invented both the new institutions and the necessary forms which economic life required. When it became necessary to make provision for the protection of third parties, the courts provided norms for decision which science and judicial decision created out of their own materials. Even today our legal life for the most part is based upon these achievements of the past. It may be admitted that these statutes are more closely related to state law than any other part of private law legislation. In this form the art and science of drafting legal documents got into the German Civil Code (law of societies, matrimonial régime, law of partnership), and, to a still greater extent, into the Commercial Code.

All in all it was the task of the codes to sum up the development of juristic law which had taken place until that time, and in so doing to make the necessary changes which legal technique, being bound in a great measure by tradition, lacked the power to make. For the second task, legislative intervention was actually indispensable. On the other hand a code is far from being the only means whereby the greatest of inconveniences connected with juristic law can be remedied, i. e. its enormous extent, its lack of systematic arrangement, its interminable controversies. This has been accomplished more than once by other means. It was accomplished in part by so mechanical a device as the law of citations of Valentinianus III. At the present time, the English, who have to deal with more than twenty thousand volumes of juristic law, contained in their collections of decisions, make shift by considering it highly improper for a barrister to cite opinions to the court that are more than one hundred to one hundred and fifty years old. This surely is a drastic remedy for this, the greatest of inconveniences connected with juristic law, but it is inescapable. Very often the works of private individuals undertake this task. This is the significance of the

的要求。例如,当协议为登记或批准而提交时,国家行为就可能对该协议实施这种监督。然而,所有的这些不得模糊一个事实:我们正在讨论的东西实质上是制订法律文件的技艺和学问,即讨论由立法者正在发现的法学。在远古时代,在中世纪,甚至在现代,正是制订法律文件的技艺和学问创造了新机构和经济生活所要求的必然体制。当有必要为第三人保护预先采取措施时,法院提供了裁判规范,其学问和司法裁判均源自它们自身的素材。即使在今天,我们的法律生活极大程度上也是建立在过去的这些成就之上。可能会承认,这些制定法,想必任何其他私法制定法的部分,跟国家法的关系更近。以这种形式,起草法律文件的技艺和学问进入了德国民法典(社团法、婚姻制度、合伙法),并且,还在更大程度上进入了德国商法典。

总而言之,那些法典的任务就是总结截止到当时的法学家法的发展,这样做可以进行必要的变革——这是很大程度上受传统所限的法律技术无力推行的变革。对于法典的第二重任务来说,立法干预实际上是不可或缺的。另一方面,法典远远不是改善有关法学家法最大不便——即它庞大的内容、缺之体系化的安排以及无休止的争议——的唯一手段。运用其他手段也曾不止一次地解决过此种不便。运用诸如瓦伦提尼安Ⅲ的“援引例证”这样的技术设计就曾部分地解决过该问题。当时,不得不应付在他们裁决集中超过 20000 卷的法学家法的英国人,认为对于一个巴律师而言,引用超过 100 年到 150 年前法院的意见是极不合适的,由此,他们做了变革。对此种有关法学家法的最大不便,这确实是一个巨大的改善,但它并非是必然发生的。私人作品也很经常地从事此项任务。这就是

*Decretum Gratiani* and of the gloss of Accursius. The Continental common law at all times had some book or other which was looked upon as the summing up of all juristic science. In the last period of its validity it had Windscheid, and after him, Demburg. The code therefore is merely one of the many possible means of giving to juristic law a suitable form for the administration of justice.

The immediate effect of the reduction of juristic law to statute law in the codes is merely this, that the juristic law which has been in existence until now reappears as statute law. This change of form is not without effect upon the state of the law. For until that time juristic science drew its content from society, it created legal propositions on the basis of the social facts under the influence of social trends. Henceforth this is to be changed. Among the various thought sequences that result from the introduction of the codes, perhaps one of the most important and widespread is that juristic science henceforth may work only on the basis of the code. The social material that has passed from the earlier stage of juristic science into the code is to be developed by juristic science in its present stage, which is based on the code; but science is not permitted to fashion new materials independently. Here as elsewhere the intentions and the effects of legislation are at variance with each other.

Since the codes are primarily juristic law, they, like all juristic law, contain a social morphology. They describe the social relations of a legal nature to the extent to which the legislator has

《格拉提安教令集》[1]与阿克索斯[2]评注的意义所在。任何时候,欧陆共同法都有一些或另外一些被看作是对所有法学进行总结的著作。在其有效的最后时期,它有温德沙伊德,在他之后,有德恩伯格[3]。因此,法典仅仅是赐予法学家法一个适于司法之形式的许多种可能手段之一。

法学家法被纳入法典、成为国家法,所产生的即刻影响仅仅是迄今一直存在的法学家法作为制定法重新出现。这种形式上的变化对该法的状况决非没有影响。因为直到那时,法学的内容来源于社会,它在社会事实的基础上、在社会潮流的影响下创设了法律命题。自此之后,这将要被改变。在法典引入所带来的各种各样的思潮中,或许最重要、流传最广泛的是法学自此可能只基于法典而运转;但是科学不能独立地创造出新素材。此处与别处一样,立法的意图和效果彼此间并不一致。

由于法典首要就是法学家法,所以它们像所有的法学家法一样,也包含一个社会形态。法典描述这样一种法律性质的社会关

〔1〕 1140年的《格拉提安教令集》概括了大部分教会习惯,成为标准的教科书。它标志着早期编纂教令汇编时代的结束,同时,也为进一步教会法典创造了条件。

〔2〕 阿克索斯(约1182~约1260),意大利法学家,阿佐的学生,后成为博洛尼亚大学的教授。他是法学研究复兴运动的领袖人物。他把大量有关查士丁尼《法学阶梯》、《学说汇纂》和《查士丁尼法典》的注释及评论整理成册,这些典籍经他编纂后比以往更加条理化,因此取代了以前所有的注释和概要,成为著名的《注释大全》

〔3〕 德恩伯格·海因里希(1829~1907),德国法学家,是《学说汇纂》的权威学者。著作有:《论盖尤斯的〈法学阶梯〉》、《普鲁士私法教科书》及《论〈学说汇纂〉》等。

become conscious of them and has thought it necessary to regulate them or at least to mention them. This morphological content of the code, of course, cannot become state law; for state law is not a morphology. The state gives form only to itself, to its own institutions, its army, its tribunals. It does not give form to society. It can only issue commands or prohibitions to the latter. But the question can be raised whether or not, according to the intention of the legislator, the morphology of the code is to be an exhaustive one, whether it is not accompanied by a command issued by the state that no institutions should be established except those that are permitted and regulated by the state; whether therefore social associations, family relations, forms of undertakings, contracts, dispositions by last will and testament of a kind not described in the code are permitted.

The state can of course issue a command forbidding certain institutions by omitting any mention of them in the code. This has the same effect as any other prohibition by state legislation. By failing to mention juristic persons, the French Civil Code undoubtedly meant to check, perhaps to prevent, the development of corporations, and it has actually affected French corporations very adversely thereby. Likewise the German Civil Code intended to make the creation of *real* rights other than those regulated by the code impossible, and when new contracts are being entered into the question will often arise whether or not they should be recognized under the code. The Austrian Civil Code has abolished ownership of a story of a building by failing to mention it. The only question is whether the state is able to enforce the prohibition. This is of course extremely doubtful where the latter is enforceable only by resort to private law, and where the prohibition of the new institution merely takes away the protection which lies in the right to sue and defend. Prohibited contracts, societies, testamentary gifts (for example, gifts in mortmain) have been able to hold their own even against the codes.

It is true a jurist of the traditional school is inclined to believe that every legal relation that is not mentioned in the code is forbidden. Even the innocent *fidei commissum eius quod supererit*, according to a remark of Pfaff and Hofmann's, is believed by many to be forbidden, although the only reason why it is not

系——立法者已经认识到它们,并认为有必要规范它们或至少提到它们。当然,法典的这种形态内容不可能变成国家法,因为国家法不是一个形态。国家仅给予其本身、自己的机构、军队、法庭以形式。它并不给予社会以形式。它只能对后者提出命令或禁令。但是,以下问题可能会被提出:按照立法者的意图,法典的形态是否详尽无遗漏,是否并没有附加一个国家签发的命令——除了那些国家允许或规范的机构之外,任何机构不得建立;是否因此这些未在法典中描述的社会联合体、家庭关系、企业形式、契约、遗嘱的财产处分都是被允许的。

国家当然可以通过在法典中不作任何提及的方式签发一个命令,禁止特定的机构建立。这与国家通过立法所作的任何其他禁止效果相同。通过不规定法人制度,法国民法典毫无疑问想要控制——或许是阻止——法人的发展,这实际上对法国的法人造成了非常负面的影响。同样,德国民法典打算创设物权,而不是那些法典不可能加以规范的权利,当新契约缔结时,经常会出现这样的问题:它们是否被法典认可。奥地利民法典通过对建筑物楼层所有权只字不提,从而废除了该制度。在后者仅诉诸私法才可强制执行时,当对新制度的禁止仅仅是去除了存在于诉权和抗辩之中的保护时,这种做法当然极为可疑。被禁止的契约、社团、遗赠(例如,“死手保有权”中的赠与)已经甚至能够对抗法典。

的确,传统学派的法学家倾向于认为,在法典中未提及的每一个法律关系都是被禁止的。甚至在清白的那些超过一定限度的信托,按照普法夫和霍夫曼的评论,也被许多人认为是被禁止

mentioned in the Austrian Civil Code is that it was thought unnecessary to state a legal precept for this case. As a rule, however, the juristic morphology, of social phenomena does not import such a prohibition by the state. The four kinds of contracts of the Roman jurists did not abolish agreements of other kinds, and the Roman testament did not make gifts *mortis causa*, which were not testaments, impossible. Likewise the reception of various legal relations into the code and the description of them therein does not have the effect of excluding from the law everything that does not fit into these relations.

So long as the legal relations as to which no provision has been made in the code do not come into contact with the agencies of the state, the practical jurist has no occasion to concern himself about them. From his point of view they are outside of the legal sphere. The modern development of trusts and cartels and of collective labor agreements, demonstrates to what an enormous extent the social development of law can go on independently of and in conflict with positive law. But the situation changes when a legally recognized basis is to be created for these new legal relations by means of legal documents, when litigation arises, or when, for some other reason, perhaps in the course of supervision by the state, interference by an administrative body becomes unavoidable. Then, and not until then, the question confronts the jurist whether he can find suitable forms and norms for decision in the code, or, as the German common law juristic science used to express it, whether he can construe the relation juristically. This is a question of juristic technique, and must be variously answered according to the stage of development which the technique has attained. The answer must be a different one under the Roman system of legal actions from what it would be in the juristic science of the Continental common law or in that of Anglo-American law. And under a system of free finding of law it would present an entirely different appearance from that which it presents at the present time.

In every legal system there has been an abundance of cases in which juristic construction seemed impossible. One of the most famous examples of the most recent time is the obligation of the

的,尽管它未被奥地利民法典提及的唯一理由不过是:这种情况下,没有必要作一个法律规定。然而,通常,社会现象的法律形态并不含有国家那样一种禁止的意思。罗马法学家的四种契约并未废止其他种类的契约,罗马法遗嘱制度也并未使死因赠与——死因赠与不属于遗嘱——成为不可能。同样,对进入法典的各种各样法律关系的接纳,以及在其中对它们的描述并没有将未曾提及的任何其他事项排除出法律的效力。

只要法典未曾提及的法律关系不与国家机构发生联系,实用法学家就没有必要关注此类法律关系。从他的角度看,它们处于法律领域之外。信托和卡特尔(即企业联合)、集体劳动契约的现代发展,已经在极大的程度上证明,法律的社会发展能够独立于实证法继续前行,并能在与后者的冲突中向前发展。但是,当为了这些新的法律关系而借助于法律文件创设一个获得法律认可的根据时,当诉讼发生时,或者当行政机关的干预由于某些原因,或许在国家监督的过程中变得不可避免时,情况就改变了。那时,直到那时,该法学家就会面临这样的问题:他是否能够在法典中发现合适的类型与裁判规范,或者,如同德国共同法法学过去曾表述的那样,它是否能够在法学上解释该法律关系。这是一个法律技术的问题,按照该技术达到的不同发展阶段,回答必定有所不同。在罗马法律诉讼制度下的回答与在欧陆共同法法学之下的回答,或与英美法法学之下的回答,肯定各有差异。并且在法的自由发现制度下,它将展现一个与目前展现的外观相比完全不同的景象。

在每一个法律制度中,都存在丰富的案例,其中,法学建构似乎是不可能的。最近最著名的一个例子是,糖厂的股东供应甜菜

shareholders in a sugar factory to furnish sugar beets. The consequence of this impossibility is that the given relation, since it lacks protection by the courts and administrative tribunals, must rely exclusively upon social forces for recognition, protection, and enforcement, or perish. This is indeed a sad result, especially where there is a great social and economic need for this relation, where neither prohibition by the state nor public interest stands in the way. And it must be stated emphatically that the trouble lies not with the relation but with juristic science, whose technical resources are insufficient for the satisfactory performance of its never-ending task, to wit to make the law subserve the needs of life. The codes inevitably increase the difficulties which new phenomena of legal life cause to legal science. For contemporaneously with the codes the idea arises almost automatically that an authoritative command of the legislator has made an end of the activity of juristic science not only as to the past but also as to the future; that thereafter a jurist must seek the solution of every problem that confronts him exclusively within the code. The precepts of the code as to filling up the gaps are a matter of indifference in view of the fact that the code confronts the legal profession as the embodiment of perfection of the legal system. Henceforth juristic science, judicial as well as literary, has only one task to fulfil, i. e. to judge the phenomena of life according to the code. Its starting point must be the code in every case. If the code were able to prevent economic development from going beyond the code, it would also be able to compel juristic science to stand still; for it would thereby deprive the latter of all new subject matter that it might possibly find new norms for. But it has been shown that the code neither produces nor strives to produce this effect. For the new needs of society there must always be new juristic law. The popular reference to remedy by legislation indicates a failure to understand the nature of the function both of juristic science and of legislation. Difficulties of construction like the difficulty involved in the obligation to supply sugar beets to the sugar factories arise at every moment. They constitute the daily bread of the practical jurist. The legislator who would keep pace with all of them would indeed be a busy man. Moreover, in that case, who would be able to find his way through the labyrinth of statutes? And lastly it is by no means the intention of the private law codes to bind the

的义务。这种不可能性的后果是，该给定法律关系，由于缺乏法庭和行政裁决机关的保护，不得不完全依赖于社会力量寻求认可、保护及执行，或消灭。这实际上是一个令人悲哀的结果，特别是在对这种关系存在很大的社会和经济需要的场合，以及国家的禁令或公众利益都未妨碍该法律关系的场合。并且必须着重指出，麻烦并不在于该法律关系，而在于法学，后者的技术手段并不足以为其永不完结的任务给出令人满意的表现，即，使得法律能够有益于生活的需要。法典不可避免地增大了法律生活的新现象给法学带来的困难。因为伴随着法典，几乎会同时自动产生一种观念：立法者的权威命令已经为法学活动画下句点，不仅针对过去，而且也包括未来；此后法学家必须为他面临的每一个问题完全在法典框架下寻找解决办法。考虑到这个事实——法典视法律职业为法律制度完善之体现，法典中填补该鸿沟的规则，则是不重要的事情。此后，法学，无论是司法方面的还是著作方面的，都只有一个要实现的任务，即，按照法典裁判生活现象。在每一种情况下，它的出发点必定是法典。如果法典能够不让经济发展超出法典的范围之外，那么它也能够迫使法学静立不动；因为它可以因此使后者丧失所有可能发现新规范的新的论题。但是已经证明，法典既未展现也未努力展现这种效果。因为社会的新需要必定总是新的法学家法。通过立法提供救济的流行提法表明没有理解法学功能与立法功能的性质。解释的困难，如同糖厂供应甜菜义务所遭逢的困难，在每时每刻都会发生。它们构成实务法律人的必不可少的生计。试图即时回应这些难题的立法者肯定将是一个忙碌的人。此外，那种情况下，谁能够找到通往穿越制定法迷宫的道路？最后，约束一国的社会与经济力量，直至

social and economic forces of the nation until such time as the legislature acts again or perhaps to destroy them.

Human society, particularly human economic life, imperatively demands new legal forms for new forms of life. In actual fact the three older codifications, the Prussian *Landrecht*, the Austrian Civil Code, and the French Civil Code, have not been able to prevent social and economic development from outstripping them. New, and theretofore unknown, associations, new kinds of contracts, new forms of undertakings, new kinds of declarations of will in case of death have come into use, and juristic science has found appropriate norms for decision and appropriate remedies both within the framework of the code and without. The new situation under the new German Civil Code, as is clearly discernible even now, will not be different.

The "*Geschlossenheit des Rechtssystems*" never was anything but purely theoretical pedantry. Juristic science has never been able to offer prolonged resistance to great and justifiable social or economic needs, and jurists have always believed that its most important function is to find forms for new social and economic developments that fit into the frame of the code (the art and science of drawing up legal documents) and to establish norms for decision adapted to these new developments without directly doing violence to the code. Anyone who has observed the development of juristic science must admit that the task which daily and hourly confronts the jurist not only can be performed by the jurist but is actually being performed daily and hourly. To cite an important and famous example, permit me to mention the matter of life insurance. It is passed over in silence both by the French Civil Code and by the Austrian Civil Code, not by chance, but with the intent to forbid it. That this is true is shown as to the former by a remark of Portalis, one of its authors, and by a remark of Merlin, a contemporary, in his Repertoire; as to the latter, it was proved by v. Herzfeld by quotations from the source material. Speculation as to the length of human life

立法再一次发挥作用或者可能破坏它们时为止,这绝不是私法典的意图。

人类社会,特别是人类经济生活,不可避免地要求有适于新的生活形式的法律形式。实际上,这三个较老一些的法典——《普鲁士邦法》、《奥地利民法典》以及《法国民法典》——都未能阻止社会与经济的发展超越其调整范围。新的、在那以前尚属未知的联合体、新型契约、新的企业形式、在死亡场合下新型的意思表示,都获得了运用,并且法学在法典框架范围内和范围外也都发现了合适的裁判规范与合适的救济办法。新的《德国民法典》之下的新形势,如同即使到现在也清晰可辨的那样,没有什么不同。

“法律制度的完善”从来只是纯粹理论上的学究式思维。法学从来不能对巨大而正当的社会或经济需求提供长时期的抵抗,法学家也总是相信,法学最重要的功能是为新的社会和经济发展发现适于法典框架(制订法律文件的技艺和学问)的新的规范,并在无需直接违反法典的情况下建立适于这些新发展的裁判规范。任何观察过法学发展的人都必须承认,法学家不仅能够履行他们时刻面临的任务,而且事实上他们也正在每时每刻履行这样的任务。举一个重要且有名的例子,请允许我提及人寿保险事务,法国民法典和奥地利民法典对此都未予规定,这种“沉默”不是一种偶然,而是有意要禁止它。关于前者,那的确已经被包塔利斯——他是立法者之一——的评论证明,也被与包塔利斯同时代的人梅林在其文集中的评论所证明;关于后者,它为赫兹菲尔德引用的原始文献所证明。推测人的寿命被认为是不道德的,

was considered immoral, and fears were entertained that it might stimulate crime. If a contract ought to be held bad in any case on the ground of the silence of the statute in regard to it, this is such a case. What would this world look like if in this case juristic science had not been mindful of its unending task?

The new law which is imperatively demanded by new relations is drawn by the jurists who are working under a code, as was done by the jurists of all times, from the concrete structure of the legal relations themselves, chiefly from declarations of the will, documents, and business custom; it is enriched by means of universalization and finding of norms, and gauged by the content of the codes. This is the way in which the law of insurance arose from the contracts of insurance during the course of the nineteenth century. The codes facilitate the execution of the juristic tasks, both of the judges and of the lawyers who draw up legal documents, in part unconsciously perhaps, nevertheless very effectively, through the extraordinary flexibility of their provisions. Liberty of association, liberty of contract, liberty of testamentary disposition form an enormously wide frame within which most of the things that life requires can be provided for. Moreover the codes invariably contain a series of concepts which make it possible, for judicial decision at least, to create legal norms that are adapted to the new institutions. These are the concepts of declaration of will by silence, business usage, the principle of *gute Treue* (good faith, *bonne foi*), the principle of *Treu und Glauben* (good faith); in addition there are the old tried and proved home remedies of practical juristic science which have been in use since the days of the glossators, to wit the creation of concepts and construction. Accordingly judicial decision in Austria, in France, and in a modest measure also in the territory of the Prussian Code has in fact succeeded in pouring a new content into the law of the codes just as the juristic science of the Continental common law has ever been able to adapt the law of the *corpus iuris* to the needs of life at the proper time and place. At the present time the French Civil Code and the Austrian Civil Code, the two of the older codes that are still in force, are covered with a crust of new juristic law so thick that the original content can scarcely be discerned, and this in a few places only. One can readily understand that in both countries the call for a re-

同时还考虑到可能刺激犯罪。倘若一个契约仅因法典没有规定它,而无论如何应被认定无效,那么这就属于此种情形。如果此种情形下,法学已然忘却了其永恒的使命,则这个世界看起来像什么样子?

新关系必然需要的新法律由那些法典下工作的法学家——正如所有时代法学家做的那样——从法律关系本身的具体结构中提取,主要从意思表示、(法律)文件以及商业惯例中提取;新法律通过一般化与规范的发现不断获得丰富,并经受法典内容的测评。就是采取这种办法,19 世纪时,保险法产生于保险契约。法典凭借其条款特别的灵活性,促进了起草法律文件之法官和律师的法律任务的执行,这种促进尽管非常有效,但或许还是无意识的。结社自由、契约自由、遗嘱处分自由,这些构成了一个广阔的框架,大多数生活所需的东西在其中都能有所规定。此外,法典总是包含一系列规定,使得至少对司法裁判而言,有可能创设适于新形势的法律规范。这些包括默示意思表示、商业惯例、*gute Treue* 原则(善意原则、*bonne foi*),*Treu und Glauben* 原则(诚信原则)等观念;此外,自从评注法学家时代开始,还存在古老的、可靠的并经过证明的实用法学上的有效救济,即,概念创设和解释。因此,在奥地利、法国——较低程度上也包括普鲁士法典的范围内,司法裁判事实上在为法典之法注入新内容方面获得了成功,正如欧陆共同法曾经能够成功地使得《国法大全》中的法律在合适的时间和地点满足生活的需要。目前,《法国民法典》和《奥地利民法典》,这两个较老一些但仍有效的法典,蒙上了如此厚实的法学家法的外壳,以至于其原初的内容极少能被分辨出来,仅在某些地方可以。人们能很轻易地理解,在这两个国家,修正民法

vision of the civil law has been heard, the task of which will be identical with that which was performed one hundred years ago, i. e. to receive into the code the substance of the law that has been created meanwhile, and at the same time to take account of many new claims and interests which the existing law has not recognized. The new law must needs be a new morphology of society, must give occasion for the creation of new norms, which self-evidently will be as far from being final as any legislator has ever been from speaking the last word on social development.

One must never overlook the fact that even in a code juristic law is not state law. Even in this form, it cannot, because of its very nature, be a command issued to persons subjected to its power, as is state law, but can only be, as it is everywhere else, a direction and an instruction. Surely no one would attribute the same force and power to the rule about the sale on approval as to the provisions of the German Civil Code about *Sachwucher* (a form of usury). Juristic law is not being imposed upon the relations; it was abstracted from the content of these relations in the past, and it is to conform to this content in the future. Compare the breadth and flexibility of the precepts of the German Civil Code concerning the legal transaction which violates good morals (*contra bonos mores*) with the rule of state law prohibiting usurious transactions, which is contained in the same section. The presuppositions and the effects of the latter must be found exclusively in the code. But as to the question when a legal transaction is *contra bonos mores*, and what its consequences are, information must be gathered from the whole body of antecedent literature and the antecedent course of judicial decision as well as from the whole body of subsequent literature.

The provisions of Roman law as to liability for *culpa lata* and *culpa levis* are typical universalizations of juristic law. In these provisions the Romans by no means intended to lay down in advance exactly what measure of fault the jurist should assume in each individual legal relation. These provisions of the Roman jurists were merely a description of the practice actually followed in the administration of justice. It was not a "should be" for the future, but merely an "is" as to the

的呼声一直有所耳闻，民法的任务与一百年前要完成的任务是同样的，即，将其间已经被创造出来的法的要旨加入到法典中，并且同时考虑现行法尚未认可的许多新的请求权和利益。新法律务必要成为一个新的社会形态，必须为新规范的创造提供根据，不言而喻，新规范远非是终局性的，正如任何立法者都决不会对社会发展说出定论。

人们永远不得忽略这个事实：即使在法典中，法学家法也不是国家法。即使在法典这种形式中，由于它自身的性质，它也不可能像国家法那样成为一个针对服从其权力之人的命令，而只能像在别的任何地方表现的那样，成为一个指示与指导。确实，没有谁能够将同样的效力和权力归于《德国民法典》有关 *Sachwucher*（高利贷形式）条款中的试销规则。法学家法并未被强加于此种关系；过去它从这些关系的内容中提取出来，在将来它要符合该内容。比较一下《德国民法典》有关违反善良道德（*contra bonos mores*）之法律行为规则的广度和灵活性与同一部分内禁止高利贷交易之国家法的规则。后者的先决条件和效果必定全部在法典中出现。但是，至于法律行为何时违反善良道德、其后果是什么的问题，相关资料就必须从早先全部的文献、司法裁决以及后来的文献中去收集。

罗马法有关重过失责任与轻过失责任的条款是典型的法学家法的一般化。在这些条款中，罗马人决不打算预先准确地规定法学家在每单个法律关系中应当采取的过错标准是什么。罗马法学家的这些条款仅仅是对在司法中事实上获得遵循之实践的描述。它不是对未来设定的“当为”，而仅仅是对现在描述的“是

present. The principles according to which the judges in Rome actually adjudged fault hardened into the doctrine of the Roman jurists about the care required in everyday life.

Received into the modern codes, these Roman universalizations were, in form, converted into legal propositions which were to bind the judge in the future. There is no doubt however that they actually do not do this. The Austrian Civil Code indeed does provide for liability in all contracts even for slight fault; only the measure of damages depends upon the degree of fault. And now let us compare the case of a man about to undertake a journey who deposits his valuables with a friend, who, as a matter of friendship, undertakes to keep them safe, with the case where he delivers them to a professional depositary for hire. That which is considered fault in the case of a professional depositary will of course not be considered fault in the case of a friend who is merely doing a favor. The course of judicial decision in Austria apparently makes the same distinction that the Romans made, i. e. in the former case there is liability for slight fault, or negligence, in the latter only for gross negligence. The only effect of the precepts of the Civil Code was that the judges made no distinction between gross and slight negligence but simply denied that there was fault in a case in which they did not think it proper to hold the party liable. The attempts, therefore, of the Austrian Civil Code to convert a doctrine of juristic law, an essential characteristic of which is adaptability, into a rigid, inflexible norm has failed. And I presume that the same result has been reached wherever the codes have recognized the degrees of *culpa levis* and *culpa lata*.

The codes therefore have had the effect neither of bringing the course of development of law to a complete standstill nor of limiting it exclusively to legislation. The development of the living social law as well as of the art and science of drawing up legal documents and of judicial decision continues the even tenor of its way. The authors of the codes did indeed believe that they would be able to exclude juristic science altogether. It was not only Justinian that entertained this idea but also the Emperor Joseph II, Frederick II, and Napoleon I. It is

(这样)”。罗马法官实际上据以判断过错的这些原则强化了罗马法学家关于日常生活所要求之注意的学说。

这些罗马法上的一般化被吸收进现代法典,在形式上转化为在将来约束法官的法律规定。然而,毫无疑问,它们实际上并未如此做。《奥地利民法典》实际上在所有的契约中甚至为“轻微过失”也规定了责任;只是损害赔偿金的范围取决于过错程度。现在让我们来比较两个案例:第一个案例是,一个要去旅行的人将其贵重物品寄托于其友处,后者出于友情而帮其照看该物品;第二个案例是该旅行者将其贵重物品交付给一个职业保管人处出租。在后一案例中被认定的过错当然在前一案例中不会同样被认定为过错,前一案例中,友人仅仅是在提供帮忙。奥地利司法裁决的行动方针显然作了与罗马人曾作过的同样的区分,亦即,在后一案例中,存在轻过错或过失责任,在前一案例中,仅存在重大过失责任。民法典规定的唯一效果在于法官对重大过失与轻过失不作区分,而仅仅是拒绝承认在他们认为让当事人承担责任并不恰当的情形下存在任何过错。因此,《奥地利民法典》将本质上具有灵活性的法学家法的学说转化为僵硬、固定之规范的努力宣告失败。并且我认为,无论何处,只要法典承认轻过失、重过失等级,就同样会失败。

因此,这些法典既不会使法律发展的进程停滞,也不会使法律的发展完全限于立法。活的社会之法、起草法律文件的技艺和学问以及司法裁决,它们的发展在其平坦的进程中持续向前。这些法典的作者实际上认为,他们能够完全把法学排除在外。拥有此种想法的不仅有优士丁尼,还有约瑟夫二世、弗里德里克二世以及拿破仑一世。据说,当拿破仑一世看到最初的评注时,

said that when the last named saw the first commentary, he exclaimed: "*Mon code est perdu.*" The reason for this is that, like all men of action, they lived only for the moment, and were bent upon doing away with a future that was independent of their wills.

During the time immediately following the appearance of a code, it is true that, to a certain limited extent, there is no need of juristic labor. Since the code has received all the juristic law that was in existence at the time, questions of greater importance at least have been settled for the moment, and when juristic science insists upon participating in the work, the authors of the code are justified in rejecting its overtures as those of an officious and superfluous intermeddler. But before very long, time will bring questions for which no answer, or no satisfactory answer at least, can be found in the code. And at this very moment, juristic science is again brought face to face with its never-ending task of making the law subserve the needs of life; and it fulfils this task by employing the same means that it has used from time immemorial. As soon as life has caught up with the code, juristic science begins to function with renewed vigor. The older a code, the more clearly its work of modifying and eking out becomes apparent. Practically not a single proposition of the *Danske Lov* of the year 1683 is valid today in its original sense. And time has had a powerful effect also upon the French codes of the beginning of the nineteenth century. He who knows only the French Civil Code has only a very imperfect conception of the civil law that is in force in the French courts. One must not seek the law that is actually valid in France in the codes, but in Dalloz and Sirey. And recent though the German Civil Code is, German judicial decision has resorted to legal material not embodied in the code in an untold number of instances, as Hedemann, Jung, and other adherents of the free-finding-of-law movement delight in pointing out.

他宣称："我的法典对此无能为力。"理由是，像历史进程中所有人一样，他们仅仅在当下生存，并致力于消除不受他们意志支配的未来之事。

在法典出现后紧接着的时期内，在某种有限的程度上，法学工作的确没有必要存在。既然法典已经将当时存在的所有法学家法全部纳入，较为重要的问题至少暂时已经解决，并且，当法学坚持参与该工作时，法典的作者完全有理由反驳说：法学提供的建议纯粹是乱出主意的多余干涉。但是，用不了多久，时间将会带来法典没有回答或至少没有满意回答的问题。至少在这个时候，法学又一次面对其永无止境的任务——使法律为生活需要服务；法学实现该任务的方式是它自远古时期就一直运用的同样的方式。一旦生活跟上法典，法学就开始带着新生的活力再次发挥作用。法典越古老，它的修改和增补工作就越清晰可见。实际上，1683 年的《丹麦法典》[1]没有一个条文在其最初的意义上说今天仍然有效。时间也给 19 世纪初的《法国民法典》带来了强有力的影响。仅知道《法国民法典》的人，对于在法国法院实际发挥效用的民法只有一个非常不完全的了解。不得在民法典中寻找在法国实际生效的法律，而应该在达洛兹和西雷(的出版物)中寻找。正如海德曼、容格以及其他一些"法之自由发现"运动的支持者所乐于指出的那样，尽管《德国民法典》颁布较晚，但在无数个例子中，德国司法裁决求助于并未体现在法典中的法律素材。

---

〔1〕 丹麦 1683 年在对各省现有法律整理之后所编纂的第一部法典，它的内容多半被 1687 的 Norske Lov (Norwegian Code)所继承。

This then is what has happened in the case of the three older codes. The French Civil Code has produced a result in this connection that is extraordinarily instructive. While juristic science in France was temporarily at a standstill, there appeared in Germany, immediately after the promulgation of the French Civil Code, the famous handbook by Zachariae, which amounts to a professed juristic development of the law of the French Civil Code, and which has been recognized as such by the French. Why did this book appear in Germany and not in France? Because to the French the code was but an orderly statement of the results of their juristic science up to that time, to which, they thought, they had nothing to add, for the moment at least. But to the German it was an altogether different thing from the very outset. It was not the results of the juristic science of his own law that had been expressed in the code, but the results of a juristic science that was based on a totally different social morphology and that created different norms. Zachariae's work was practically of the same nature as that done by any other jurist in case life has outstripped and grown away from the code. He worked into the juristic law of the code the law created by judicial decisions that had been rendered in the society of which he was a part, and which, in part, was very different from French society. In this way his handbook became a model for the later French juristic science, which found it incumbent upon itself to work into the code the law created by the judicial decisions rendered in French society, which, however, had undergone a considerable development meanwhile. The French consider his work a classic, just as they do its French continuations by Aubry and Rau.

这就是在三个较老一点的法典中发生的情况。《法国民法典》已经在这方面产生了一个特别具有启发性的结果。尽管法国的法学暂时处于静止状态,但在德国,紧跟着《法国民法典》颁布后不久,出现了扎哈里埃[1]著名的手册,这实际上公开宣称是《法国民法典》中法律的法学发展,并且本身已被法国所认可。为什么这本书出现在德国,而不是法国?因为对于法国人来说,该法典只是他们的法学截止到当时的一个有条理的表述,他们认为,他们至少暂时没有东西可加入进去。但是对于德国人来说,从一开始,《法国民法典》就是一个完全不同的事物。它不是德国人自己法律之法学在法典中被明确表达出来的结果,而是基于完全不同社会形态之上的、并创造出不同规范之法学的结果。扎哈里埃的工作实际上与任何其他法学家在生活已经超越并抛离法典的情形下所作的工作性质相同。他把在(德国)社会——他自己作为其中一部分,并且在某种程度上非常不同于法国社会——中作出的司法裁决所创造出来的法律加入到法典中的法学家法中。就这样,他的书成了后来法国法学的典范,后者认为自身有责任把由法国社会中作出的司法裁决所创造的法律加入到法典中去,不过,法国法学其间也经历了重要的发展。法国人认为他的著作是一个经典,正如他们认为由奥布里(Aubry)和劳(Rau)二位继续进行的工作也是经典一样。

[1] 扎哈里埃(1769~1843),德国法学家,著述甚多,最重要的是1868年的《法国民法手册》,这是德国人论法国法最系统的著作。

# XIX
# The Theory Of Customary Law

Mommsen has pointed out quite emphatically that among the Romans "usually and especially in the language of the law books," i. e. one may say technically, the phrase *ius publicum* did not mean law that concerns the people, but law that is posited by the commune; that *ius publicum* in this sense is that which the older legal language called *lex publica*; that *ius publicum* therefore is not *Staatsrecht*, but law posited by the state. This remark of Mommsen's is borne out by the sources. In my *Beiträge zur Theorie der Rechtsquellen*, I have shown that *ius publicum* is very seldom used in the sense of *Staatsrecht* and never, as is usually believed, in the sense of compulsory law, but regularly in the sense of law that is posited by the state. In the writings of Cicero and of the jurists of the age of the Republic, *ius publicum* is the *leges* and the *plebiscita*; in the writings of the jurists

# 第十九章　习惯法理论

蒙森曾强调指出，在罗马人中，从技术意义上说，“通常且尤其”“在法律书用语中的 *ius publicum*（公法）”，[1]不是指关涉到人民的法律，而是指由公社提出来的法律；这种意义上的 *ius publicum*（公法），在更古老的语言中被称之为 *lex publica*；因此，*ius publicum*（公法）不是 *Staatsrecht*[2]（狭义上的公法），而是由国家设定的法。莫姆森的这个见解由原始文献所证实。在我的《法源理论的贡献》（*Beitrage zur Theorie der Rechtsquellen*）中，我已经指出，*ius publicum* 很少在 *Staatsrecht* 的意义上使用，并且如同通常认为的那样，从来不在强行法意义上使用，而一般在国家设定之法的意义上使用。在西塞罗和（罗马）共和国时期的法学家的著作中，指的是 *leges*（法律）[3]

---

〔1〕（拉）*ius publicum*，公法，指调整国家或共同体的政治关系、维护其基本秩序和稳定的法律规范的总和。它具有较为强烈的强制性。

〔2〕（德）狭义上的公法，不包括国际法，而只包括宪法和行政法。

〔3〕（拉）*leges*（法律），在后古典时期，人们对君主谕令（constitutiones principum）的笼统称呼，可区分为一般法律（leges generales）和特别法律（leges speciales），与另一种规范渊源——法（iura）——相对应。

of the Empire, it comprises in addition the *senatusconsulta*, the praetorian edict, and the law of the imperial constitutions. Wherever a given precept is referred to by the jurists as belonging to *ius publicum*, it is based, as can be shown, upon a *lex*, a *plebiscitum*, a *senatusconsultum*, on a provision contained in the edict or in a constitution.

The concept of *ius privatum* is given by the contrast to this sense of *ius publicum*, i. e. it is the law that is based on the other, the non-state, sources of law; it is the Roman customary law, especially the Roman juristic law. The words of Ulpian on this point must be taken literally: *Tripertitum est: collectum etenim est ex naturalibus praeceptis aut gentium aut civilibus*. These three kinds of *praecepta*, the *praecepta naturalia*, as well as those *iuris gentium* and the *praecepta civilia*, are parts of non-state law.

和 *plebiscita*（平民会决议）；[1] 在（罗马）帝国时期法学家的著作中，它还包括 *senatusconsulta*（元老院决议）、[2] 裁判官的告示以及帝国制度组织的法律。任何一个地方，一个特定规则若作为 *ius publicum*（公法）被法学家被提及，则可以证明，它是立基于一个 *lex*（君主谕令）、*plebiscitum*（平民会决议）、*senatusconsultum*（元老院决议）之上。

*ius privatun*（私法）[3] 的概念与这种意义上的 *ius publicum*（公法）相对，即，它是建立在另外一种非国家性的法源之上的法律。它是罗马习惯法，特别是罗马法学家法。乌尔比安 Ulpian 对此发表过的言辞必须认真解读：*Tripertitum est：collectum etenim est ex naturalibus raeceptis aut gentium aut civilibus*. 它分为三个部分：要么由自然法的戒条、要么由万民法的戒条、要么由市民法的戒条组成。这三种 *praecepta*（戒条）、*praecepta naturalia*（自然戒条），以及那些 *iuris gentium*（万民法上的戒条）与 *praecepta civilia*（市民法上的戒条）均属非国家法的部分。

---

〔1〕（拉）*plebiscita*（平民会决议），罗马法渊源之一，指由平民会议（*concilia plebis*）表决通过的法律。最初只对平民具有约束力，随着《关于平民会决议的霍尔滕西法》（*lex Hortensia de plebiscitis*）的颁布，取得了约束所有罗马市民的法律效力。

〔2〕（拉）*senatusconsulta*（元老院决议），罗马法的重要渊源之一，表现为以书面形式向最高执法官提供的咨询意见。由于元老院成员所享有的威望和权力，这类咨询意见在事实上具有法律（*lex*）的效力。

〔3〕（拉）*ius privatum*（私法），指调整私人之间关系的法律规范的总和。对于罗马法来说，它最初以市民法（*ius civile*）为核心。

*Ius privatum* is a later, purely academic concept, occasioned chiefly by the notion that logic somehow required the subsumption of all classes of legal propositions that were not *ius publicum* under one head. The original legal language did not employ the term *ius privatum* but *ius civile*. The oldest meaning of the term *ius civile*, which is found wherever the term is used absolutely without an opposite, like *ius gentium*, for example, from the *auctor ad Herennium* down to the classical jurists, is the juristic law which is applicable in a proceeding in a Roman law court. In Cicero's day the opposite to *ius civile* still was *leges*. *Legibus et iure civili* is one of his standing phrases. The *leges* which govern court procedure also, chiefly the *leges testamentariae*, he *calls leges de iure civili*. The praetorian edict occupies a subordinate position in Cicero's day, and the later sources of the law, *senatusconsulta* and *constitutiones*, are not yet in existence.

Accordingly the Romans in the days of the Republic distinguish but two sources of law, *ius civile*, or, as it is still called by

*ius privatum*(私法)纯粹是后来学理上的概念,主要由如下观念引发:逻辑性以某种方式要求所有类别的非属于 *ius publicum*(公法)的法律规定包摄于一个条目之下。最初的法律语言并未使用 *ius privatum*(私法),而是用了 *ius civile*(法学家法)[1]这个术语。*ius civile*(法学家法)这个术语无论在哪里出现——例如,从 *auctor ad Herennium*(赫勒纽指南)至古典法学家——它都像 *iuris gentium*(万民法)一样,均没有相对者,其最古老的含义是在罗马法庭上的诉讼程序中适用的。在西塞罗时代,*ius civile*(法学家法)的相对者还是 *leges*(法律)。*Legibus et lure civili*(条款和市民法)是他常说的话。同样支配诉讼程序的 *leges*(法律)主要是 *leges testamentariae*(遗嘱的条款),他称之为 *leges de lure civili*(市民法上的条款)。裁判官告示在西塞罗时代占据了次要的位置,后者的法源 *senatusconsulta*(元老院决议)与 *constitutiones*(谕令)[2]尚不存在。

因此,罗马人在共和国时期仅区分两种法源,*ius civile*(习惯法),

---

〔1〕(拉)*ius civile*,一般被后人理解为"市民法",但作者认为,该术语有多重含义;在本书中,尤其是在本章中,多指"习惯法"。对此,作者作了大量的解释论证。

〔2〕(拉)*constitutiones*(谕令),罗马君主各种指令的总称,构成罗马法的重要渊源之一。它的表现形式有:①诏谕(*edicta*),君主向全体或部分臣民发布的通告,起初效力在君主去世后丧失,后来此种限制逐渐丧失;②训示(*mandata*),君主向各省总督发出的指示,具有行政命令的特点;在发布命令的君主当政期间,该训令具有法律的效力;③裁决(*decreta*),君主在正式或非正式的审判中宣告的判决;④批复(*rescripta*),君主应私人或执法官的请求,针对某一具体的法律问题作出的答复;最初时,这种答复的约束力一般仅以具体案件为限,后来对类似案件也同样具有指导作用;⑤诏书(*epistulae*),君主撰写的书面答复,其意义与批复相同。

Pomponius, *proprium ius civile*, and *leges*. The former is juristic law, which is traced back to juristic interpretation of the Twelve Tables somewhat in the manner in which the Mohammedan jurists trace their vast body of norms to a few hundred passages of the Qoran, of which only a very small number contains as much as a single legal proposition. It is self-evident that by this time no one takes this derivation of *ius civile* from the Twelve Tables seriously, as is shown by the presentation of Pomponius. At a later time the praetorian edict is added to the *leges* and the *ius civile*. It cannot be shown that it was, in theory, considered a source of law as early as the days of the Republic; but practically it was a source, as appears from Cicero's writings. The great mass of private law, without doubt, derived from the *ius civile*. The edict and the *leges* dealt with special subjects only, whenever the necessity for new regulation appeared. The two sources that were added in the days of the Empire, the *senatus-consulta* and the imperial constitutions, were not universally recognized until after the Byzantine Empire had been established.

Since I first published this view of the sources of Roman law, it has quite generally been accepted by unbiassed scholars. I should like to add here that since that time I have gathered some material which confirms my opinion. The doubts which critics have expressed

或者如旁波尼所称的 *proprium ius civile*（自有的法学家）与 *leges*（法律）。前者是法学家法，可以追溯到《十二铜表法》的法学解释，伊斯兰教的法学家也曾运用同样的方式将他们的大量规范追溯到数百页的《古兰经》经文中，只有很少的规范仅包含单个的法律命题。不言而喻，在此之前，没有人认真地从《十二铜表法》中得出——如同旁波尼的阐述所揭示的——*ius civile*（法学家法）的这种语源。后来，裁判官告示被加入到 *leges*（法律）和 *ius civile*（法学家法）中。在理论上，不可能证明裁判官告示早在共和国时期就被认为是一种法源；但实际上，如同在西塞罗的著作中所出现的那样，它是一种法源。毫无疑问，大量的私法源自（习惯法）*ius civile*。告示和 *leges*（法律）仅处理特别的事项，每当新型管控的需要出现时，二者即派上用场。*senatus consulta*（元老院决议际）和君主谕令，这两种法源在帝国时期被加入，但直到拜占庭帝国建立之后才获得普遍承认。

自从我首先提出了有关罗马法法源的这种观点后，它就十分普遍地被不含偏见的学者所接受。在此，我想补充的是，自那时起，我收集了一些巩固我的观点的材料。批评者所表达的怀疑涉及到 *ius civile*（法学家法）与 *ius honorariun*（法官法）[1] 之间的对立。

---

〔1〕 （拉）（法官法、执法官法、荣誉法），指由执法官在司法审判过程中创立的法律规范的总和。由于在罗马社会执法官是一种荣誉职位，因而此类法律规范常常被称为“荣誉法”。创立法官法的执法官主要为享有司法权的裁判官，因而，法官法有时也被称为“裁判官法（*ius praetorium*）”。法官法是罗马法的重要渊源之一，它不仅使市民法（*ius civile*）规范的运用更加适合现实的社会需要，而且还弥补了制定法留下的大量空白，大大丰富了罗马法的内容。

refer to the antithesis between *ius civile* and *ius honorarium.* In the book referred to, I made the assertion that, among the Romans, *ius civile* is contradistinguished from praetorian law down to the days of the later Empire in precisely the same manner in which it is contradistinguished from *ius legitimum*, the *senatusconsulta*, and the law of the constitutions. And there is much evidence in favor of this view. It is, I admit, in conflict with the well-known fragment of Papinian in the Digest, which divides the whole law into *ius civile* and ius *honorarium*, and which enumerates under the former head, in addition to *auctoritas prudentium*, *leges*, *plebiscita*, *senatusconsulta*, and *decreta principum.* We do not know what the passage meant in its original context, but the doctrine which it teaches has not been handed down elsewhere. There is not another passage in which the law is divided into *ius civile* and *ius honorarium* in the sense in which this is done in the passage referred to. In every other text of the sources in which we find a similar division, the latter refers exclusively to the *actiones* and to the law of inheritance. There are *actiones* that are part of the *ius civile* and there are *actiones* that are part of the *ius honorarium*; there is a *ius civile* law of inheritance and a *ius honorarium* law of inheritance. Beyond this there is no mention of *ius civile* and *ius honorarium.* But before the times of the Severi, even the division of the law of the *actiones* and of inheritance into civil and honorary is never mentioned. In particular, we find no trace of it in Gaius. I have therefore expressed the opinion that the text of Papinian in its original context referred solely to the law of inheritance, and that the doctrine of civil and honorary actions, of civil and honorary law of inheritance, which moreover is based solely on practical considerations and not upon any considerations of the theory of the sources, was invented by the jurists of the time of the Severi. But the basic idea of my book would not be shaken in the least if it could be shown, as is contended chiefly by Girard, that the doctrine of Papinian and of the jurists of the time of the Severi arose at a somewhat earlier period.

在相关的书中，我断定，直到后期帝国时代在罗马人中，*ius civile*与裁判官法一直截然有别，其对立的方式与 *ius civile*（法学家法）跟 *ius legitimum*（制定法）、元老院决议以及君主谕令区别的方式如出一辙。有很多的证据支持这种观点。我承认，它与帕比尼安在《学说汇纂》中众所周知的那个段落相矛盾，后者将整个法律划分为市民法和法官法，此外，在市民法的条项之下，还列举了 *auctoritas prudentium*（法学家的观点）、*leges*（法律）、平民院决议、元老院决议以及 *decreta principum*（皇帝敕令）。我们不知道该段最初的语境是什么，但是它教导的学说并未在任何别处传继下去。并没有任何别的段落表明，法律在此段所提及的意义上被分为市民法和法官法。在原始文献的每一个其他文本中，我们都可以发现相似的划分，后者全部指向 *actiones*（诉讼）和继承法。诉讼部分是 *ius civile*（习惯法）方面的，部分是 *ius honorarium*（法官法）方面的；既存在有关继承的市民法，也存在关于继承的法官法。除此之外，关于法学家法和法官法再无提及。但是在塞维里时代之前，甚至连诉讼法和继承法被分为 *ius civile*（法学家法）和 *ius honorarium*（法官法）的说法，也无人提及。特别是，我们在盖儿斯那里找不到它的任何蛛丝马迹。因此，我提出这样的观点：帕比尼安的原文在最初语境上仅仅指继承法，市民法诉讼和法官法诉讼相区分、有关继承的市民法与有关继承的法官法相区分——而且主要是基于实践考量、而非任何原始文献的理论考量——的学说，由塞维里时代的法学家所创立。但即使能够证明——尤其像古拉德所坚决主张的那样——帕比尼安的学说与塞维里时期法学家的学说出现于一个更早的时期，我著作中的基本思想也不会受到丝毫撼动。

This basic idea is the following: the Roman law that was applied by the courts is in its essence and as to its original component parts *ius civile*, juristic law, and remained such until the latest Imperial times. To this original part were added at a later time the *leges*, the *edictum*, the *senatusconsulta*, the *constitutiones*. It is self-evident that I do not mean to say that the words *ius civile* never had any other meaning than juristic law. There is not a single expression of human speech that for centuries had the same meaning at all times. To what degree even the technical terms of the Roman jurists were susceptible of many different interpretations and have changed their meanings in the course of centuries is shown by a glance at the *Vocabularium iurisprudentiae Romanae*. As is well known to every student of language, the meaning of words varies in accordance with the meaning of the words as the opposites of which they are being used. If the term *ius civile* is used as the opposite to *ius gentium*, or *ius militare*, or *ius criminale*, it does not mean juristic law, but the opposite to *ius gentium*, or *ius militare*, or *ius criminale*. This I have expounded in my book. And this is the reason why Gaius Inst. I, I, I does not refute my theory, as Mitteis thinks. I have by no means overlooked this passage but have discussed it at length. It is only in those passages in which *ius civile* is used absolutely, without an opposite, that it invariably, from Cicero to the *auctor of Boëthius*, means, as far as I can see, juristic science, juristic law. And I do not believe that I have overlooked a single passage. When Paulus says (Sent. IV, 8, 20): "*Idque iure civili Voconiana ratione videtur effectum*," *iure civili* can only mean "juristic law."

Unless one bears this in mind, one cannot understand the development of Roman law. And this is doubly important since we are not discussing a peculiarity of Roman law. The same phenomena

这个基本思想是：法院适用的罗马法，其本质以及最初的组成部分就是法学家法，并且这种状况一直保持到最后的帝国时期。*Leges*（法律）、*edictum*（告示）、元老院决议以及 *constitutiliones*（谕令）在较后的时期才被加入。不言而喻，我的意思不是说，*ius civile* 除了法学家法的含义外，从来没有其他的含义。人类语言的表达中，没有一例在数个世纪中含义一直保持不变。甚至罗马法学家的技术性术语，也经常被怀疑有许多不同的解释，并在数个世纪的变迁中改变了它们的含义，只要稍微回顾一下 *Vocabularium iurisprudentiae Romanae*《罗马法学词汇》，即可明白此种差异和变迁的程度有多大。每一个学习语言的学生都清楚地知道，单词的含义会随着作为正在使用的、其对立面的单词的含义不同而有所变化。如果 *ius civile* 经常作为 *iuris gentium*（万民法）、或 *ius militare*（军事法）或 *ius criminale*（刑法）的对称而使用，则该术语并非指法学家法，而是作为上述三种法律的相对物。这在我的书中已经作过阐述。而且这也是为什么盖尤斯《法学阶梯》，并不像米特艾斯认为的那样驳倒了我的理论的原因。我决未忽略这一段落，而是详细地讨论了它。仅仅在那些中，*ius civile* 被独立地使用，没有相对物，从西塞罗到波伊丢斯的 *auctor*（著述者），就我所能看到的，它总是意指法学、法学家法。并且，我认为，我并没有忽略任何一段。当保罗说："*Idque lure civili Voconiana ratione videtur effeetum* 这被认为是在市民法中的沃科尼亚法中的规则所确立的"，*ius civile* 只可能意指"法学家法"。

除非人们记住此点，否则就无法理解罗马法的发展。由于我们现在不是在讨论罗马法的特性，这就变得加倍的重要。相同的

appear in the development of the only other system that has attained to an advanced stage of development—has attained to it without a reception and without marked foreign influences. In English law we find the distinction between common law and statute law, which exactly corresponds to the distinction between *ius civile* and *ius legitimum*. The common law is exclusively juristic law; it is the custom of the realm, established by the judges. And the statute law is merely *ius legitimum*, created by the state. Here also a third component part is added at a later time, magisterial law, equity. One can justly say therefore that we are not dealing with an accidental peculiarity of the development of Roman law but with the law of all legal development, which takes place independently of the power of the state, from within, and independently of any outside influences.

The Roman jurists at the same time speak also of *mores* and of *consuetudo*. These however are not customary law such as courts would have to consider. The norms that arise in Roman society become customary law only by passing through the alembic of juristic law, by becoming *ius civile*. This is seen most clearly in the case of the rule making gifts between husband and wife invalid—a rule which is referred to, in ten different texts at least, *as ius civile*. The discussions of Pernice (*Zeitschrift der Savigny Stiftung* R. A. XX Bd. S. 127) and of Brie (*Die Lehre vom Gervohnheitsrecht*) show that *mores* or *consuetudo* cannot become customary law directly without the intervention of the labors of juristic science. These discussions appear the more convincing to me because the point of view of their authors is diametrically opposed to mine.

Customary law other than *ius civile* had not been heard of in Rome down to the end of the classical period. Among the texts of the title of the Digest, *de legibus senatusque consultis et longa consuetudine*, and of the title of the Code, *Quae sit longa consuetudo*, which were taken from writers of the classical period, there is but one that

现象出现在仅有的另外一个法律制度的发展中，后者曾经达到过一个较发达的阶段，并且没有发生过法律继受、未受到过外国影响。在英国，我们发现普通法与制定法之间的区分，它准确对应于 *ius civile* 与 *ius legitimun* 的区分。普通法完全是法学家法；它是由法官建立的王国领域内的习惯。制定法仅仅是由国家创立的 *ius legitimun*。在英国，后来也由第三种组成部分加入其间，那就是衡平法。因此人们可以公允地说，我们论及的不是罗马法发展的随机的特性，而是所有法律发展的规律，它的出现与国家的权力无关，也与任何外界的影响无关。

罗马法学家同时也提到了 *mores*（习俗）和 *consuetudo*（习惯）。然而，这些不是习惯法，譬如说，法庭并非必须要考虑它们。产生于罗马社会的规范只有通过法学家法的提炼，只有通过变为 *ius civile*，才能成为习惯法。这一点在使丈夫与妻子之间的赠与无效的规则上表现得最为清晰，该规则至少在 10 个不同的文本中被认为是 *ius civile*。珀尼斯在《萨维尼基金会期刊》的讨论，以及布里在《习惯法理论》的讨论均表明，*mores*（习俗）和 *consuetudo*（习惯）若没有法学劳动成果的介入，不可能直接变为习惯法。这些讨论对我而言似乎更具有说服力，虽然这些讨论的作者的观点与我的观点全然相反。

*ius civile* 之外的习惯法直到古典时期末也尚未听闻过。在《学说汇纂》该标题的原文中，*de legibus senatusque consultis et longa consuetudine*（关于法律和元老院决议以及长期的习惯），以及在《法典》中的该标题中，*Ouae sit longa con-suetudo*（那些属于长期习惯的东西），这些都取自古典时期的著者，只有一个论及

dealt with Roman customary law, i. e. fr. I, 3, 36. In this text gifts between husband and wife are being discussed. But this text contains only an academic laudation of this precept. The whole content of these two titles originally did not deal with questions of Roman customary law. The famous passage from Julian (fr. 2 h. t.), in its original context was a discussion of the *lex Papia et Poppaea*, probably of the provisions of this statute concerning burdensome communal offices and services. In this connection reference was not made to customary law but to the usage that obtained in the *municipia*. The fact that the two passages from Ulpian, fr. 33 and 34 h. t., as well as the constitution of the Emperor Alexander (C. I. 8, 52), were taken from Ulpian's book *De officio proconsulis* indicates that they were not discussing customary law but provincial usage. The texts taken from the *Quaestiones* of Paulus and the *Quaestiones* of Callistratus (fr. 36, 27 h. t.) refer exclusively to the traditional interpretation of statutes. The passage from Paulus, fr. 37 h. t., is taken from the disquisition *Ad legem municipalem*. That it deals only with municipal custom is shown by its very wording: *qua iure civitas retro in eius modi casibus usa fuisset*. To sum up: when the classical Roman jurists speak of *ius civile* they mean Roman customary law; but when they quite generally speak of *mores* or *consuetudo*, they do not.

I have taken the preceding paragraph verbatim from my *Rektoratsrede*, entitled The Fact of Customary Law. When I had this address printed, I did not know that Puchta had said exactly the

罗马习惯法,即 fr. I,3,36。在此节正文中,讨论了在丈夫与妻子之间的赠与。但是此节正文仅包含对该规则的一个学理上的褒扬。这两个标题下的全部内容并未涉及罗马习惯法的问题。来自尤里安(fr. 2 h. t.)著名的一段,在其最初的语境下,讨论的是 *lex Papia et Poppaea*《巴比·波培法》,那很可能是——有关繁重的社区服务和役务的——该制定法的条款。在这方面,参照的不是习惯法,而是在 *municipia*(自治市)[1]中通行的惯例。来自乌尔比安的两段(fr. 33 与 34 h. t.),以及亚历山大大帝(C. I. 8,52)的法令均来自乌尔比安的书《论行省总督的职责 *De officio proconsulis*》——这一事实表明,他们不是在讨论习惯法,而是在讨论地方惯例。摘自保罗的 *Quaestiones*(论辩集)以及卡里斯特拉图斯的 *Quaestiones*(论辩集)(fr. 36, 27 h. t.)的文章,论及的全都是制定法的传统解释。保罗的段落(fr. 37 h. t)取自《*Ad legem municipalem* 论自治市法》的专题论文。他论及的是地方惯例,这可以从他下面的这句话得到证明:*qua Iure civitas retro in eius modi casibus usa fuisset*(在同样的情况下城邦先前适用的法律)。总结一下就是:当古典时期的罗马法学家提及 *ius civile* 时,他们意指罗马习惯法;但是当他们十分普遍地提到 *mores*(习俗)或 *consuetudo*(习惯),则指的不是罗马习惯法。

前面的段落,一字不差地取自我的题为《习惯法的真相》的 *Rektoratsrede*(就职演讲)。当我将该演讲付印时,我并不知道普赫

---

[1] (拉)*municipia*(自治市),指独立享有某些民事权利的城市或居民共同体。不同于享有主权的国家,它在私法领域拥有一定的权利能力,可以在与居民个人的关系中成为原告或被告,可以成为遗赠(*legatum*)或遗产信托(*fideicommissum*)的受益人,甚至在后来还拥有接受遗产的权能。

same thing, perhaps in a better way, at any rate in a more complete statement, in his book on customary law. I have repeatedly studied this book very carefully, but have always skipped the discussion of Roman customary law because we have made such glorious progress since that time. Then I decided to read it after all, and now I am far from certain that we have advanced very far beyond Puchta. I believe that after all we could still learn something from his work. Puchta's view has met with Savigny's approval.

*Consuetudo* was first treated as a source of law by the post-classical jurist Hermogenianus and the later imperial constitutions. At that time the situation was quite different from that of the age of the classical jurists. From the days of the *Constitutio Antonina*, the Roman law was law for nations of the most varied character, civilization, and descent, whose members had indeed become Roman citizens but had not adopted Roman law and Roman custom even outwardly. They continued to live, as they had done before, according to their ancient law and customs. It was not advisable simply to ignore this fact. Though the emperors were strongly inclined simply to abolish these *consuetudines*, they had to concern themselves with them. Accordingly a post-classical text of the Digest, which was taken from Hermogenianus, expressly states that *quae longa consuetudine comprobata sunt* are binding. The Code contains three imperial constitutions that deal with this question. Justinian, who realized that he could not simply ignore these local laws and customs, took the statements of classical jurists which I have referred to above out of their context, greatly distorting their meaning in the process, construed them to suit his purpose, and added such texts as he could find on the subject in post-classical literature.

The glossators, the postglossators, the canonists, and the common law practitioners of the Continent had a task to perform that was similar to that of the post-classical Roman jurists and legislators. They too were to apply Roman law to peoples of varied

塔已经在他论述习惯法的著作中准确地说出同样的东西,而且或许采用了一种更好的言说方式,至少,那是一个更完整的表述。我非常认真地反复研读此书,但总是略过罗马习惯法的讨论,因为我们自那时起已经取得了巨大的进步。于是,我终究决定还是读它,现在我已经完全不敢肯定,我们已经远远超越了普赫塔。我相信,归根到底,我们还是能从他的作品中学到一些东西。普赫塔的观点获得了萨维尼的肯定。

最早将 *Consuetudo*(习惯)视为法源的是后古典时期法学家赫尔摩格尼亚努斯以及后期的君主谕令。那时,情形非常不同于古典法学家的时期。从 *Constitutio Antonina*(安东尼敕令)时代开始,罗马法成为最多样性格的民族之法,这些民族的成员实际上已经变成了罗马公民,但是,甚至在表面上,他们也未采用罗马法和罗马习惯。他们继续按照他们的古代法和习惯生活,像以前一样,简单地无视该事实是不明智的。尽管皇帝们强烈地倾向于直接废除这些习惯,但他们不得不关注它们。因此,来自赫尔摩格尼亚努斯的《学说汇纂》后古典时期的文本明确说道:*quae longa consuetudine comprobata sunt*(那些为长期的习惯所支持的规则具有拘束力)。《法典》包括三个涉及此问题的君主谕令。优士丁尼意识到他不可能简单地忽视这些地方法和习俗,就使我上面提到的古典法学家的叙述脱离其(原初)语境,在此过程中大大歪曲了它们的含义,使之符合他自己的目的,并加上那些他能找到的后古典时期文献中有关此主题的文句。

注释法学家、后注释法学家、教会法学家以及欧陆共同法的实践者有一项任务需要完成,该任务类似于后古典时期罗马法学家和立法者要完成的任务。他们也要将罗马法适用于各具性格、

character, descent, and civilization, to whom Roman customs and Roman law were foreign, and who had their own law and their own customs. The texts of the Justinianian sources were designed, as it were, to meet this very situation, and could be applied directly. The only question was how much of the customary particular law was to be considered valid, and how to draw the line of demarcation between it and the Continental common law. It is clear that a standard derived from the Continental common law was very welcome; it is equally clear that the jurists who were trained in the Continental common law preferred a narrower policy to a more liberal one. At any rate these texts were anything but a theory of the sources of law in the opinion of those who from the beginning of Romanist juristic science down to the days of the activity of the Historical School were relying upon them. To them they were a statutory provision concerning the validity of particular law and local customs. This situation remained unchanged until it was remedied by the Historical School of jurisprudence, which created a doctrine of such grandeur that it must stir us to unqualified admiration even today, for it has never been surpassed.

In this connection, of course, we are referring exclusively to Savigny and Puchta. Between the basic doctrine of these two pioneers of the historical interpretation of law, especially in the sphere of customary law, and their successors a gulf is fixed that cannot be bridged. Savigny and Puchta may be treated as a unit. And if, occasionally, the doctrine of one differs from that of the other in detail, it does not appear that they were desiring to give expression to a difference of opinion thereby. It is analogous to a variation between the statements of the same writer at an earlier and at a later date. It is true, the views of both have undergone modifications. Savigny's view in the Beruf is different from that in the *System*; Puchta's view in the *Gewohnheitsrecht* is different from that of the *Institutionen*; and in the notices and reviews which both have written, one occasionally perceives a modification of view. As to Puchta, we must treat the statement in the second volume of his *Gewohnheitsrecht* and in the review of Georg Beseler's *Volksrecht und Juristenrecht* as final; as to Sav-

血统和文明的民族,适用于那些视罗马习惯和罗马法为外国东西的人,适用于拥有他们自己法律和习惯的人。优士丁尼原始文献的原文似乎就是为了适应此等非常形势而设计的,并且它们可以直接适用。唯一的问题是习俗性的特殊法有多少将被认定为有效,以及如何在它与欧陆共同法之间作出划分。清楚的是,源自欧陆共同法的一个标准非常受欢迎;同样清楚的是,在欧陆共同法中受训的法学家喜欢一个更严格的政策,而不是一个更自由的政策。无论如何,在上起罗马派法学的开端下至历史学派活跃的时代一直依赖于这些法源的人看来,这些文句仅仅是一种法源理论。对他们来说,它们是有关特殊法与地方习惯有效性的制定法规定。这种情况一直到历史法学派法学对其加以改善才得以改变,历史法学派法学创造了一个那样伟大的学说,以至于甚至在今天,它也必定激发起我们称绝赞叹,因为它从来未被超越过。

当然,在这方面,我们提及的全都限于萨维尼和普赫塔。这两位是法——特别是习惯法领域——的历史解释的先行者,他们的基本学说与他们继任者的学说之间存在确定的、无法逾越的鸿沟。萨维尼和普赫塔可以被看作是一个个体。如果偶尔其中一位的学说在细节上不同于另外一个,那么看起来也不是说他们想要表达出不同的观点。这类似于同一位作者早期的表述与后来的表述之间的差别。的确,二人的观点都经历过修正。萨维尼在《论当代立法和法学的使命》中的观点与他在《当代罗马法体系》中的观点不同;普赫塔在《*Gewohnheitsrecht*(习惯法)》中的观点与他在《*Institutionen*(法理学教程)》的观点不同;并且在二者都写过的介绍和评论中,人们偶尔会觉察到观点的修正。至于普赫塔,我们必须把他在《习惯法》第二卷中的陈述与在对

igny, the *System*. We must not, of course, ignore the other works of Savigny and Puchta, especially their critical works, when these supplement or explain those mentioned above.

In forming an estimate of the doctrines of Savigny and Puchta, one must bear in mind that it was they who first introduced the idea of development into the theory of the sources of law and clearly saw the relation between the development of law and the history of a people as a whole. "This organic relation between law and the nature and character of a people is maintained throughout the passing of time, and as to this point also is to be compared with language. For both there is no moment of standing absolutely still; both are subject to the same progress and development as every other activity of the people; and the development of both law and language are subject to the same law of inner necessity. The law grows with the people, develops with it, and finally dies when the people loses its individuaity." (*Beruf.*) This view gave rise to an absolutely new conception of the sources of law: their function no longer is to determine arbitrarily and casually what should be law; they are an expression of a process of becoming and happening which takes place from an inner necessity within the popular consciousness (*Volksbewusstsein*).

And now we see the deeper root of the whole doctrine. Savigny and Puchta's chief endeavor was to establish most emphatically that the development of law goes on immediately within the legal consciousness. Usage is merely the shoot which reaches the surface. "Custom does not create law, it merely makes it possible to gain a knowledge of law," said Puchta in a reply to Beseler. But that is by no means a peculiarity of customary law; it must needs be true of every other source of law. If it is really to create law, it must be an expression of the general legal conviction of the people. For this reason a statute must be treated exactly like usage. "The common power is the *Geist des Volkes* (spirit of the people), from which legislation,

格奥尔格·贝塞勒《民间法与法学家法(*Volksrecht und Juristenrecht*)》这本书的书评中的陈述当作他的最终观点;至于萨维尼,则应将他在《当代罗马法体系》中的表述当作他的最终观点。我们当然不得忽视萨维尼和普赫塔的其他著作,特别是他们的批评性作品,当这些是对上述那些的补充和解释时,尤其不能忽视。

在对萨维尼和普赫塔的学说进行评估时,人们必须记住,正是他们首先将发展的理念引入到法源理论中,并清楚地看到在法律发展和一个民族的历史之间总体上的关系。"这种法律与民族的天性与特征之间的有机联系贯穿于时间的流逝中,关于此点,也可以与语言相比较。因为二者都没有一刻曾停滞过;它们如同人类的所有其他活动一样,都经历了同样的进步和发展;法律与语言二者的发展都受到同样的内在必要性规律的支配。法律随民族而成长,随民族而进步,最后当该民族丧失个性时,法律也随之消亡。"(《论当代立法和法学的使命》)这种观点促生了一个绝对崭新的法源观念:它们的功能不再是恣意而随便地判断什么应该是法律;它们是一种有关——因民众意识(*Volksbewusstsein*)中的内在必要性而发生的——"生成"和"出现"进程的表达。

现在我们明白了整个学说更深的根基。萨维尼与普赫塔的主要努力就是为了最有力地证明,法律直接在法律意识内持续向前发展。习惯仅仅是到达(社会生活)表面的芽。"习惯并不创造法,它仅仅使获取法律的知识成为可能",普赫塔在回应贝塞勒时如此说。但那绝不是习惯法的特性;(这一点)它对所有其他法源来说必然也是成立的。如果它实际上创造法,那它必定是对该民族一般法律确信的表达。因此,对待制定法必定要完全像对待习惯那样。"共同力量是 *Geist des Volkes*(民族精神),从中立法机

too, derives the content of its pronouncements." It is well known that there is a close harmony between this statement and the doctrines of Savigny from the beginning of his career. In his *Beruf*, he says that the sole function of a code is to state the whole existing law. In the *System*, he makes the same statement, not only, however, as is generally believed, with reference to the codes, but with reference to all statutes. He says that the already existing popular law (*Volksrecht*) "is the content of the statutes, or, to express the same thought in other words, the statute is the instrumentality of the popular law." A statute, according to Savigny, merely serves the purpose of making the popular law more definite, or perhaps, in the case of progressive development of law, "of shortening the interim of uncertainty in the law." Similarly Puchta says that the activity of legislation is a formal rather than a material one, inasmuch as the legislator is not the possessor of a peculiar legal consciousness, but receives his material directly from the *Volksgeist* (spirit of the people) and from the jurists. Frequently it exercises an exclusively formal influence upon the law, inasmuch as it states the already existing law, i. e. puts it into statutory form.

The third source of law is juristic science. Savigny in his *Beruf* has called attention to juristic science as a source of law. Puchta devoted a brief section to it in the first volume of his *Gewohnheitsrecht* but made substantial changes in the second volume. Savigny, in his *System*, follows Puchta, but there is some doubt about this, for the doctrine of neither is quite clear. According to Puchta, juristic science creates law only in case it is not a pure science but a popular one. "In addition to the usage" which is based on a legal proposition scientifically deduced, there is a usage "which expresses the popular consciousness of experts in the law and therefore contains customary law." How these words are to be understood can best be seen from Puchta's statements in his review of Beseler's book: "When we are discussing the common conviction as to the law of bills of exchange, we shall not expect to find this conviction among the peasants; again, when

关也可以推导出它宣示的内容。”众所周知，在该表述和萨维尼事业初期所持学说之间存在紧密的协调。在其《论当代立法和法学的使命》中，萨维尼说，法典的唯一功能在于陈述全部的现行法。在《当代罗马法体系》中，萨维尼作了同样的表述，不过，此处的表述不仅如一般人认为的那样针对的是法典，而且也针对所有的制定法。他说，已经存在的民间法（*Volksrecht*）“是制定法的内容，或者换句话表达同样的思想就是，制定法是民间法的媒介”。按照萨维尼的观点，制定法仅仅是为了使民间法更明确，或者在法律的渐进发展的情形下，或许是为了“缩短法律中不确定的过渡时期”。同样，普赫塔说，立法活动是形式上的，而非实质上的，因为立法者不是一个独特法律意识的拥有者，而是直接从 *Volksgeist*（民族精神）中，从法学家那里获取自己的素材。经常，他对法律会产生的影响完全是形式上的，因为他陈述了已经存在的法律，即，使之套上了制定法的形式。

第三种法源是法学。萨维尼在其《论当代立法和法学的使命》一书中，促请人们注意，法学也是一种法源。普赫塔在其《习惯法》第一卷中用了主要的篇幅来强调这一点，不过在该书第二卷作了实质性改变。萨维尼在其《当代罗马法体系》一书中追随普赫塔，不过对此存在一些疑问，因为他们俩的学说都不是十分清晰。按照普赫塔的观点，法学只有在其不是一门纯粹的科学而是一门大众的科学时，才可能创造法。“除了按科学方法可以推导出法律规定的习惯外”，还存在“表达法律专家的大众意识，因此包含了习惯法”的惯例。这些话如何理解，最好参看普赫塔对贝塞勒的著作所发表的书评：“当我们讨论有关汇票法的共同确信时，我们不会期望在农民中发现这种确信；同样，

we are discussing the law as to marking off boundaries and as to the servitude of pasture, we shall not consult a banker. But among those in whom we take an actual conviction on the legal proposition in question for granted, we shall assign a prominent place to those whose affairs bring them into more frequent contact with legal questions in general or with a certain kind of legal question. We shall not, for instance, take for granted that all persons of equal mental powers who have the legal capacity to draw bills of exchange have the same strength and extent of this consciousness. When dealing with the question of a common popular conviction, we shall select those whose experience in affairs of this kind is most varied as the representatives of the whole class. Imagine a court consisting of persons who have not made the judicial office their profession; will not the opinion of these men, provided they have been called upon repeatedly to serve in this capacity, e. g. of merchants, who have acted as lay judges in commercial courts, *ceteris paribus* be given especial weight among us on a legal question of this kind, even though we are merely seeking to ascertain the popular conviction? Now let us, in our imaginations, substitute for these judges men who do not combine any other profession with their judicial office; let us imagine further that they have received a legal training as a preparation for this office. Do they thereby lose their capacity to represent the popular conviction?"

In this sense therefore customary law and statute and juristic law are shoots from the same slip, i. e. the popular consciousness. Puchta says that ethical custom is the original body of customary law in the same sense in which the organized system is the peculiar instrumentality of juristic law, and in which the word is the peculiar instrumentality of statute law. The reciprocal relation of these three kinds of law can be most graphically presented by an extract from a notebook of Savigny's of the year 1819, which a kind stroke of fate has permitted me to read. I am quoting this passage verbatim, since it not only is of the greatest interest intrinsically but also seems to show that Savigny is the true originator of the doctrine of customary law formulated by

当我们讨论有关划分边界的法律以及牧场地役权的法律时，我们不会去咨询银行家。但是，在那些我们认为对于所谈论的法律命题他们会抱有真实的确信乃理所当然的人之中，我们划出了一块醒目的位置给那些——所从事工作通常使得他们与法律问题、或特定种类的法律问题联系得更紧密的——人。例如，我们不会想当然地以为，所有具有——签发汇票之法律资格的——同等心智的人，都拥有相同的强度和范围的此种意识。当讨论一个共同的民众确信的问题时，我们将会选择那些各自在此种事务领域内的经验最不相同的人，作为整个阶层的代表。设想一下，法庭由那些从未将审判职位作为他们职业的人组成；倘若他们被一再地要求担任此职，例如，他们是曾经在商事法庭担任陪审法官的商人，对于此类法律问题，即使我们只是试图确定该共同确信，*ceteris paribus*（在其他条件相同的情况下），在我们当中，难道这些人的观点不会被给予特别的重视吗？现在让我们在想像中代替这些未曾同时从事过任何其他职业的法官；让我们进一步设想，他们都接受过法律训练，从而为担任法官这个职位作过准备。他们因此就丧失了代表此种共同确信的资格吗？"

因此，在这个意义上，习惯法、制定法、法学家法都是源自同一幼枝——即"民众意识"——上的芽苗。普赫塔说，伦理习惯是习惯法的最初内容，在同样的意义上，其中，有组织的体系是法学家法的独特手段，命令是制定法的独特手段。这三种法律之间的相互关系可以以萨维尼 1819 年的笔记本中的一句话——偶然的幸运让我读到它——最为生动地表达。由于它不仅仅本质上是最有趣的，而且似乎也表明了萨维尼是由普赫塔系统阐述的习惯法学说真正的创始人，所以，下面我就直接引用这一段。"因此，

Puchta. "Accordingly the law can be formulated in a scientific manner, first by seientifically trained jurists, secondly through legislation. To fix the essential, invisible, law of the spirit of the people in this manner must therefore be the sole purpose of legislation. Unfortunately, in many instances, legislation has not been carried out in this spirit, and, as a result, the law has suffered grave injury. Let us adopt the view which is the only correct one, and which has stood the test of history, and let us ask how can the law, which, in accord with its true inward nature, has arisen invariably within the consciousness of the people, emerge into an outward visible existence? Our answer is: The language of the law can be provided scientifically (e. g. through books, instruction, etc.); it can also be provided by legislation. In the latter case, the written sources are not originating causes but merely marks and necessary characteristics from which we can draw inferences as to the existing law. Accordingly all statutes serve but this one purpose, i. e. to tell us what the existing law is at the present time, and to preserve it. This is borne out by experience, for most of the existing statutes are the expression of a custom which has been in existence among the people for a long time."

In this way, Savigny and Puchta are endeavoring to place the center of gravity of the development of all law—not only of customary law—into the legal consciousness, "the natural harmony of the conviction of a people, which is a popular universal conception" and to treat its emergence in usage as not essential to the origin of law. People generally, however, fail to realize the profoundness and comprehensiveness of the conception upon which this "spiritualistic" view of these two writers is based. It is presented most clearly perhaps in the following words, quoted from Puchta's review of Beseler's book: "The epoch of German juristic science which subsequently has been called the Historical School found a theory of law in existence, in which the state had been severed from its natural, basis, the nation, and had been converted into a purely arbitrary mechanical structure. All law was said to owe its existence to the legislative power, and whatever else insisted that it was a law-creating power—and

法律可以以一种科学的方式来系统表达，首先由接受科学训练的法学家，其次通过立法来表达。因此，以这种方式来明确民族精神中根本性的、看不见的法律，必定成为立法唯一的任务。不幸的是，许多情况下，立法没有贯彻这种精神，结果是，法律遭受到严重损害。让我们采纳那种唯一正确并经得起历史考验的观点，让我们问问，依其真实的内在性质总是产生于民族意识内部的法律，如何显现为外在可见的存在？我们的回答是：法律的语言可以按科学方法规定（例如，通过书本、讲授等等）；它也可以通过立法来规定。在后者，书面文献并非是创设的动因，而仅仅是标志和必然的特征——从中我们可以获得有关现行法的论断。因此，所有的制定法仅服务于这唯一的目的，即，告诉我们目前的现行法是什么，然后保存它。这由经验所证实，因为大多数现行制定法是在该民族中已经存在较长时间的习惯的表达。”

这样，萨维尼与普赫塔都致力于将所有法律——不仅仅是习惯法的发展重心置于法律意识之中，这种“一个民族确信的自然一致”，是一种大众的普遍观念，并且将其在习惯中的出现当作法律起源非本质的东西。然而，人们通常没有意识到这种观念的深刻性和广泛性，萨维尼与普赫塔他们两位作者的这种“唯心论”的观点正是建立在此种观念之上。从普赫塔对贝塞勒的著作所发表的书评中引用的下面一段话，或许最能清楚地表达这种情况：“后来被称作历史法学派的德国法学时代发现了一种现行法理论，在该理论中，国家从其自然基础的民族、上脱离，并转化成一个纯粹恣意的机械结构。所有法律的存在都被说成立法权力的结果，被认为是创造法律之权力的任何别的东西——为了不要看

it would have been necessary forcibly to close one's eyes in order to fail to see that there were legal propositions everywhere that were valid though they had never been promulgated—was somehow brought into connection with legislation, was conceived of as a direct product of the latter, and in this way the absolute supremacy of statute law was maintained—at all events this was accomplished with the aid of the division into written and unwritten law. The Historical School has taken a different path. It based its doctrine on the concept 'national,' having found in it the natural basis of law and of the state."

It would be difficult to over-estimate the importance of these discussions, particularly in view of the doctrine of evolution, which is their basis throughout. The doctrine of evolution is not merely this or that scientific truth; it is the basis of all modern thinking, one might say a "*Weltanschauung*" (philosophy). At a time when it was dimly discerned only by a few of the most select minds in the natural sciences, Savigny and Puchta successfully introduced it into the science of law, i. e. into the social sciences. They were successful because they gave an altogether new content to the theory of the sources. Their predecessors were not very much interested in this theory. There was no doubt in their minds that the question what is to be considered law is decided exclusively by the legislator, and they stated the few rules laid down by the Roman legislator on the question under what conditions customary law should be recognized. At this point Savigny and Puchta are proclaiming their views as to the origin of law. The view is here being proclaimed for the first time that the nation is an organic whole, that it is in a continuous process of development, and that all changes in the law are merely a result of the development of the whole people.

The Historical School, therefore, unlike its predecessors, is no longer interested in laying down rules for the judge as to the application of customary law, but in discovering the law-creating forces in society. The object of the jurists of the Historical School was not to teach how law should be applied, but how it originates; not to give practical directions, but to present a theory of the sources of law which discloses the nature of customary law, explains it, and justifies it. An explanation and justification of this sort they found in the concept "national," and Puchta says expressly:

到到处都是有效的法律规定,(尽管它们从未被颁布过),闭上眼睛是必要的——都会以某种方式与立法发生联系,并被想像成后者的一个直接产物,这样,制定法的绝对最高权威获得了维持——无论如何,这一点是在划分成文法与非成文法的帮助下实现的。历史法学派走的是一条不同的道路。它在'民族'的概念中发现了法律与国家的自然基础后,将其学说立基于'民族'观念之上。"

很难高估这些讨论的重要性,特别是考虑到始终作为其学说基础的进化论。进化论不仅仅是这个或那个科学真理;它是所有现代思维——也可以说是一个"*Weltanschauung*"(世界观)——的基础。当它仅仅被自然科学中一些第一流的心智所朦胧地理解时,萨维尼与普赫塔成功地将它引入到法律科学中,即,引入到社会科学中。他们成功是因为他们提供了一套具有全新内容的法源理论。他们的前辈对此理论不是很感兴趣。毫无疑问,在他们的思想中,什么将被认定为法律的问题,将完全由立法者来决定,而且他们叙述了一些由罗马立法者对此问题制定的规则,此问题即什么条件下,习惯法应该予以认可。此点上,萨维尼与普赫塔都宣示了他们关于法源的观点。下述见解乃首次于此公布:民族是一个有机整体,且处于一个持续发展的进程中,法律中的所有变化不过是整个民族发展的一个结果。

因此,历史法学派与先前的学派不同,不再对为法官制定关于习惯法适用的规则感兴趣,而是对在社会中发现创造法律的力量感兴趣。历史法学派法学家的目标不是教授应如何适用法律,而是教授它如何发源的;其目标不是给予实践指导,而是提出揭示习惯法性质的法源理论,解释它,证成它。他们在"民族"观念中找到了这种解释与正当理由,并且普赫塔明确说:"如果习惯法

"If customary law is so intimately and necessarily related to the natural concept 'nation,' and if it is the result of the direct activity of the nation with reference to law, the question whether customary law is valid and on what ground it is valid cannot, in fact, arise; for the only answer that can be given is the following: Customary law exists and is valid for the same reason that a popular conviction exists; in the last analysis for the same reason that peoples exist."

Since customary law is based exclusively on the concept "national," there are no other prerequisites to its origination than a common popular conviction. Not even ethical custom can be considered a prerequisite; for the latter is the expression of something that has already come into being, not a prerequisite to its coming into existence. But there are prerequisites to the applicability of customary law by the judge. "But if we take prerequisite to mean something else, e. g. if we take it in the sense of a prerequisite to the application by the judge, to his acceptance of customary law, then that whereof we are speaking no longer is a prerequisite to customary law itself. In this case the question to be answered is: What must the judge take into account when a party litigant appeals to customary law or when for any other reason he is called upon to consult this source of law? What are the presuppositions under which customary law can actually be assumed to exist?" (Puchta). And at another place, "According to the results of the investigations of the nature of customary law, the doctrine of the prerequisites to customary law can mean only this, that it should be ascertained under what presuppositions the fact that a proposition is customarily followed can be a means of cognition of that law for the judge. By no means must one think, in this case, of the prerequisites to the arising of customary law."

This is the sharp distinction which Puchta makes between the question as to the origin of customary law and as to its applicability by the court, which latter of course depends upon the cognoscibility of customary law. It follows therefore that there may be customary law which indeed exists in the conviction of the people, but is not applied by the courts because the prerequisites to its applicability by the court are lacking. Savigny and Puchta make this inference, at least as to

与自然观念'民族'之间存在如此亲近和必然的联系,如果这是民族关于法律的直接活动的结果,那么习惯法是否有效以及它依据什么有效的问题实际上不可能产生;因为唯一可以给出的回答就是:习惯法存在及有效的原因,与民众确信存在的原因相同;归根到底也与众多民族存在的原因相同。"

既然习惯法完全基于"民族"的观念,那么关于其起源,除了一个共同的民众确信外,不存在任何其他的先决条件。甚至没有任何一个伦理习惯能被认为是先决条件;因为后者是某些已经存在之事项的表达,而不是其开始存在的先决条件。但是对于法官适用习惯法还存在一些先决条件。"但是如果我们将先决条件理解为其他一些东西,例如,我们在法官适用其所接受的习惯法的先决条件这种意义上来理解它,那么,我们在此所谈论的已经不再是习惯法本身的先决条件了。这种情况下,有待回答的问题是:当一方诉讼当事人求诸习惯法或当他无论出于什么原因被要求查考这种法源时,法官必须考虑什么?依据哪些先决条件才能认定习惯法实际存在呢?"(引自普赫塔)。在另外一处,他又说道:"按照习惯法性质的调研结果,习惯法先决条件的学说仅能意味着:应当查明,在哪些先决条件下,一个法律命题习惯上被遵循的事实,能够成为法官对那种法律的一个认知手段?假如这样的话,人们决不必考虑习惯法产生的先决条件。"

这就是普赫塔在习惯法起源的问题与习惯法对于法院的可适用性问题之间所作的鲜明区分,后者当然取决于习惯法的可认知性。因此可以得出结论:可能有实际上存在于该民族确信中的习惯法,但该习惯法不被法院适用,因为对于法院而言,其适用性的先决条件欠缺。萨维尼与普赫塔至少对于国家禁止习惯法的

the case where the state prohibits customary law. This prohibition, they say, can prevent its recognition by the court but cannot prevent it from arising.

In this discussion, however, a basic difference between customary law and the other sources of law, i. e. statute law and juristic law, has not been sufficiently emphasized. In customary law, as Savigny and Puchta assume, that which has arisen in the legal consciousness of the people is directly converted into ethical custom; the people are not merely conscious of their law, but they live their law, they act and conduct themselves according to it, and this living according to law is not a mere form of manifestation but also a means of cognition of customary law. Customary law therefore is both a rule of conduct and a norm for decision; nay, rather, it always is a rule of conduct in the first place and thereby becomes a norm for decision. This cannot be said of the other sources, and especially of statute law. Both Savigny and Puchta say that it is highly desirable that the statute should also arise in the legal consciousness of the people, but they admit that it is not always the case. Savigny, for instance, in the passage quoted above from his notebook, emphasizes the fact that much legislation has not been enacted in this spirit, and in many ways has done grave injury to the law; and in the *Beruf*, he speaks of the "new" statutes, which "can easily become a fruitless corruption of the law"; and Puchta, too, must admit, after all, that it is not necessary that the "content of a statute should at the time of its enactment have been in existence as law, either in the form of customary law or of usage, inasmuch as a view of the people or of the jurists can be sanctioned that has not yet developed into a firm conviction, into law, or but for the aid of the legislator would never have developed. And therefore legislation is, potentially at least, a true source of law."

The situation is dearer still in the case of juristic taw. Let Savigny insist as much as he will that, at a more advanced stage of legal development, the law-creating activity was exercised by the juristic profession as "representatives of the whole"; and Puchta that, by a natural process, the jurists "become the instrumentality through which the

场合作此推论。他们说，这种禁止能够阻止它被法院认可，但不能阻止它产生。

然而，在该讨论中，习惯法与其他法源，即制定法与法学家法之间的基本差别未获足够重视。在习惯法，如萨维尼与普赫塔认定的那样，产生于民族的法律意识当中的东西直接转化成伦理习惯；该民族不仅仅意识到他们的法律，而且还实行他们的法律，依据它来行事，并且这种依据法律所过的生活不仅仅是表现的形式，而且还是习惯法的认知手段。习惯法因此既是行为规则又是裁判规范；不仅如此，更准确地说，它首先是行为规则，并因而成为裁判规范。其他法源，特别是制定法则不能这么说。萨维尼与普赫塔都说，制定法也产生于民族意识当中是极其理想的，不过他们承认，情况并不总是如此。比如，萨维尼在其笔记本中有一段话强调，许多立法并未按这种精神来制定，这在许多方面给法律带来了严重损害；在《论当代立法和法学的使命》中，他提到了那种“很容易就成为法律无用的讹误”的“新”制定法；普赫塔终究也必会承认，“制定法的内容在其制定时就已经作为法律存在，或以习惯法的形式或以习惯的形式而存在”并非必要的，“因为民族或法学家的某种观点——它尚未发展为一个稳固的确信、未发展成为法律，或者若没有立法者的帮助它就永远不可能获得发展——也能获得（官方）认可。因此，立法者至少潜在地是一种真实的法源。”

在法学家法的场合下，情况更加明朗。让萨维尼差不多如他所愿地坚持主张，在法律发展更高级的阶段，造法活动由法学家们作为“全体的代表”来进行；普赫塔认为，通过一个自然的过程，法学家“变成了民族有关法律的共同确信得以表达出来的媒介，

common conviction of the people as to law is being expressed and through which the common conviction of the juristic profession is substituted for the conviction of the members of the nation generally." But in the case of customary law, the common conviction of the members of the nation was manifested in this, that the latter as members of the nation acted according to their legal conviction; in the case of juristic law it is manifested, according to Puchta, only by the fact that "it actually was able to assert itself, in part in the conviction of the jurists, in part in the application by the courts." And this, one must admit, is something quite different. Let the jurists have what legal conviction they will, they do not live according to it, as jurists at least; as jurists, they merely apply it. All juristic law therefore appears to be solely a norm for decision, not a rule of conduct. For this reason, the idea expressed by Puchta that in other cases also the legal consciousness usually arises only in a few individual members of the nation is not a very good one; for the bankers actually live the law of bills of exchange, the peasants live the law of bills of exchange, but the jurists merely render decisions according to these laws.

Savigny and Puchta therefore have one thing in mind as the efficient force when they speak of customary law, and another when they speak of statute and juristic law. Customary law arises directly in the legal consciousness of the whole people or of various classes as a rule of conduct; the whole people or the various individual classes regulate their conduct according to it, and in this way customary law becomes ethical custom; in this form it has become cognoscible to the jurist, especially to the judge, and thereafter the jurist, especially the judge, derives the norm for decision from it. Often statutes have come into being in the same way, and this is the only form of legislation that the founders of the Historical School unqualifiedly approve of, to wit declaration of what the law is. But they do not close their eyes to

变成了法学家们之共同确信得以总体上替代该民族成员之确信的媒介。”但是,在习惯法的场合下,该民族成员的共同确信体现在,法学家作为该民族成员会按照他们的法律确信行事;在法学家法的场合下,按照普赫塔的观点,民族成员的共同确信仅仅由以下事实才得以揭示:“它实际上能够显示自己的权威,部分在于法学家的确信,部分在于法院对它的适用。”必须承认,这是完全不同的事情。让法学家拥有他们希望的法律确信,作为法学家,他们至少不会按照它来生活;作为法学家,他们仅仅适用它。因此,所有的法学家法似乎仅仅是裁判规范,不是行为规则。因此,普赫塔表达的思想——在其他场合下,法律意识通常也仅仅在民族的一些个体成员之间产生——并不十分令人满意;因为银行家实际上依汇票法行事,农民依划分地界法或牧场地役权法行事,[1]但法学家仅仅按照这些法律作出裁判。

因此,当他们时而说起习惯法时,时而又说起制定法与法学家法时,萨维尼与普赫塔将心中一样事情当作最有效的力量。习惯法作为行为规则,直接产生于整个民族或各种阶层的法律意识当中;整个民族或不同的单个阶层按照习惯法来调整他们的行为,这样,习惯法成了伦理习惯;以这种形式,它可被法学家所认知,特别被法官所认知,此后,法学家,特别是法官从中推导出裁判规范。制定法经常也以同样的方式产生,并且这是——历史法学派无条件赞成的——立法的唯一形式,即,“法律是什么”的宣告。但是他们并未无视这种事实:制定法也可以以其他方式产

〔1〕 英译本此处显然有误。对应前文,此处不应该是“农民依据汇票法(bills of exchange)行事”,而是依据“划分地界法或牧场地役权法行事”。

the fact that statutes can arise in other ways. This too Puchta was the first to state. He said it in plain words in his review of Beseler's book. Said Puchta: "A statute is valid because it has been promulgated by the legislator; it is expected to correspond to the actual national will, but its validity is not conditioned upon an investigation of this presupposition; therefore legislation is a formally distinct source of law."

In the light of what has been said this can have only one meaning, to wit: The content of a statute corresponds to the popular consciousness if and only if, it has been drawn from the prevailing rules of conduct; if not, it is foreign to the popular consciousness and does not meet Puchta's requirements; it is binding on the courts, it is true, but only as a norm for decision. It is strange that both Savigny and Puchta fail to observe that the same argument must apply to juristic law, and in a much greater measure than to statute law. For juristic law has never been drawn from the rules of popular conduct; if it were, it would not be juristic law, but customary law. It has not been drawn from the rules of juristic conduct, for the jurists do not, as such, take part in the affairs of everyday life. As Puchta has correctly perceived, it is, to begin with, only the "conviction of the jurists," and is therefore utterly ineffectual as a rule of conduct; or it appears "in the application in the judicial decision" and is a mere norm for decision.

The theory of the sources of law which the founders of the Historical School taught is explicable only on the basis of the strongly felt but not clearly comprehended distinction between rules of conduct and norms for decision in law. On this is based their well known doctrine of the antithesis between the customary law of the beginnings of legal development and the juristic law of a later time. When they assume that in the earlier times law arises immediately in the popular consciousness, their meaning is that at that time law still consists exclusively of the rules of conduct of the entire nation, which therefore constitute the sole basis for the adjudication of legal controversies. And if they contend that at a later time the law-creating activity of the people is confined, for the most part, to the legal profession, they

生。这也是普赫塔第一个指出来的。他在针对贝塞勒著作所发表的书评中用平实的语言谈及此点。普赫塔说,“制定法有效,是因为它由立法者颁布;人们预期它与现实的民族意志一致,但其有效性并不取决于有关此种预设的审查;因此,立法是一种形式上独特的法源。”

依照普赫塔的阐述,这仅可能有一种含义,即,如果且只有当制定法取自于通行的行为规则时,制定法的内容才与民众意识相符合;如果不是,则它与民众意识无关,并且不符合普赫塔的要件;的确,这种与民众意识不相符的制定法也会对法庭产生拘束力,但它仅仅是一种裁判规范。奇怪的是,萨维尼与普赫塔都没有注意到,同样的论点必须适用于法学家法,而且适用于法学家法比适用于制定法的程度高得多。因为法学家法从来不是从民众的行为规则中提取的;如果是,则它不是法学家法,而是习惯法。它并非从司法行为规则中提取,因为法学家本身并不以那个资格参与日常生活的事务。如普赫塔正确理解的那样,一开始,它就只是“法学家的确信”,因此,它作为行为规则是极度缺乏效率的;或者它出现于“司法裁决的适用中”,仅仅充当裁判规范。

历史法学派创始人所教导的法源理论,只有根据强烈的感觉方可解释,其解释的依据不可能是对法律中的行为规则与裁判规范的清晰区分。他们关于在法律发展开端的习惯法与后期的法学家法之间相对的、众所周知的学说正是建立在此点的基础之上。当他们认定在早期,法律直接产生于民众意识时,他们的意思是说,那时候法律还完全由整个民族的行为规则组成,因此,行为规则构成了法律争议裁决的唯一基础。如果他们主张,在后期,民族的造法活动极大程度上限于法学家们,那么他们的意思

merely mean to say that "for the most part" law no longer arises, as a rule of conduct among the people, but as a norm for decision among the jurists. This idea can be dimly perceived in the writings of Savigny, when he says that "moreover the occasion for juristic activity may be either the communication, by teaching or writing, of the result obtained, or the need of adjudication of a legal controversy"; likewise in the writings of Puchta, when he says: "Thus there appears by the side of customary law, which is based on the common conviction of all the people, law of a different kind which is based on the usage of the experts in the law, the jurists, as the representatives of the people." By the usage of the jurists he can in this connection mean only, as does Savigny, either the theory of decision of legal controversies or the decision itself.

But in order to do some measure of justice to the doctrines of Savigny and Puchta, we must determine what concrete cases of customary law they had in mind when they developed their doctrines? For a single glance at their work will suffice to convince one that it is not a matter of mere abstract philosophizing or of mere deduction from preconceived opinions, or of theories arbitrarily constructed, but of careful induction based upon their own observation. Nevertheless it is not an easy thing to answer this question. Though there can be no doubt that the classical writers on the science of law always had concrete cases of customary law in mind, what they write is so abstract, couched in such general terms, that not much can be inferred from it. Their endeavor is to formulate their doctrines so as to make them applicable to all customary law everywhere; we look in vain for distinctions, for a discussion of details, for an investigation of specific cases. Nevertheless they cannot altogether escape the necessity of giving an indication at least of the actual presuppositions of their doctrines and of illustrating them by a few examples. For this reason it is possible here and there to examine the factual bases of their doctrines.

From the examples adduced by Savigny and Puchta we can

是说,“极大程度上”,法律不再作为民族中的行为规则而产生,而是作为法律人中的裁判规范而产生。在萨维尼的作品中可以模糊地觉察到这种思想,他说,“而且,法律活动的诱因可能是对获得的结果通过教授或写作进行的交流,或是法律争议裁决的需要”;同样,在普赫塔的作品中也能模糊觉察到这种思想,他说,“因而,似乎和——建立在整个民族共同确信基础之上的——习惯法一起出现了一种不同种类的法律,后者建立在作为该民族代表的法律专家、法学家的习惯的基础之上。”就“法学家的习惯”来说,在此,与萨维尼一样,普赫塔仅指法律争议的裁决理论或是裁决本身。

但为了某种程度上公平对待萨维尼与普赫塔的学说,我们必须确定,当他们发展他们的学说时,他们心中考虑到的习惯法的具体情形有哪些?因为对他们的成果简单扫视一番就足以让人相信,那不仅仅是一个抽象哲学化的事情,或者仅仅是从预先形成的见解中得出的推论,或者是恣意建构的理论,而是基于他们自身的观察所进行的仔细的归纳。尽管如此,回答这个问题仍不是一件简单的事情。虽然,法学经典作家总是心存习惯法的具体情形——此点可能没有疑问,但他们写作的东西如此抽象,用极其概括的术语来表达,以至于从中无法推导出很多东西。他们的努力是系统阐述他们的学说,以便使它们适用于各个地方的所有习惯法;我们徒劳地寻找差别,寻找细节的讨论,寻找特定案例的调查。尽管如此,他们不可能完全免除至少对他们学说的现实预设给予说明,并用一些例子来证明它们的必要性。因此,各处检验他们学说的事实基础是有可能的。

从萨维尼与普赫塔所列举的例子中,我们至少可以了解,他

gather at least that they consistently conceived of customary law not as a mere norm for decision but as a rule of conduct. Puchta mentions, as modern customary law that was created by legal science, the doctrine that the ancestor of an insane person has the right of substitution to an extent equal to that of pupillary substitution; that the Roman *signatio* of a testament was replaced by the seal of attestation, which was unknown to the Romans; and finally the proposition: *dies interpellat pro homine*. As further examples he mentions the bankers' law of bills of exchange, the peasants' law of demarcation of boundaries and of the servitude of pasturage. In several instances he mentions examples of customary law which he has invented himself: "If a man adds his seal to his signature in... case of a lease of a house, a certain fixed time for the notice to quit is a *naturale negotii*." "The question is whether there is a customary law in a city according to which the lessee of a dwelling newly conditioned is under a duty to return it not in the condition into which it would be put by ordinary use but in the condition in which he has received it, or a customary law according to which the power of the lessor to terminate the lease without the consent of the lessee on the ground that he requires the house for his own purposes has been defined by the recognition of the validity of certain reasons, e. g. the marriage of a son, and has, perhaps, been extended beyond the intent of the Continental common law."

In general however there can be no doubt that they did not ar-

们一致把法律设想成并非纯粹是裁判规范，而且还是行为规则。普赫塔谈到像法律科学创造的现代习惯法一样的学说：一个精神病患者（作为被继承人）享有与为成年人指定补充继承人之权利同等程度的指定补充继承人的权利；罗马人在遗嘱上 *signatio*（签字）被见证印章所取代，后者对于罗马人而言尚属未知；最后谈到这样的命题：*dies interpellat pro homine*（期限代人催告）。[1] 作为进一步的例子，他还提到银行家的汇票法、农民的地界划分法律以及牧场地役权法。在若干场合下，他还提到他自己构想的习惯法的例子："如果某个人在房屋租约中将自己的印章加到其签名上，那么退租通知的某固定时间是一个 *naturale negotii*（自然之事）。""问题是，在城市中是否存在这种习惯法——新近整修之住宅的承租人返还租屋时，对房屋状态的要求，不是以通常使用即会产生（自然耗损后）的那种状态为标准，而是必须以他接手该房屋时的状态为准，或者是否存在这种习惯法——按照该法，出租人享有无需承租人同意即可终止租约的权力，因为他要求，对特定原因——例如儿子的婚姻——有效性的承认已经对房屋作了服务于出租人目的的限定，或许这个问题已经超出了欧陆共同法的内容。"

然而，通常没有疑问的是，他们并非通过观察此类不管怎样

〔1〕（拉）*dies interpellat pro homine*（期限代人催告），罗马法上的迟延履行制度，即，定有债务履行固定期限的情形下，若债务人届期未为履行，则债权人无需催告，债务人即构成履行迟延。无固定履行期限的债务的情形下，债务人构成履行迟延一般须有债权人催告的要件。

rive at their theory of the sources of law through observation of occurrences of this, at all events unimportant, sort, but through historical study. To them, the standard of primitive law was the law of the Roman regal period and of the early republic, as they conceived of it. In his *Institutionen*, Puchta gives a graphic description of it, and in his *Gewohnheitsrecht* he gives another description—a description which is essentially in agreement with the former. In addition, it can be shown, they had the German law of the Middle Ages in mind. Both among the Romans and among the ancient Germans, the law still consists chiefly of the prevailing rules of conduct; the people participate in the administration of justice and their legal consciousness is authoritative for the adjudication of the legal controversy. The jurists as yet have no special legal consciousness of their own; they draw the rules of law from the consciousness of their fellow citizens. Puchta refers expressly to Eyke von Repgow. As to the later period, the founders of the Historical School base their doctrine on the legal situation of the Roman Empire in which the Roman jurists are creating law directly, and their own legal consciousness supplies the basis for the creative activity. This is the empirical basis of their doctrine of juristic law. But a law which arises in this manner is not a rule of conduct but, in its very nature, a mere norm for decision.

Above all things they must come to terms with "the greatest and most remarkable act of universal customary law," i. e. the reception of Roman law in the Middle Ages. Their whole theory is designed to justify the latter. How can one harmonize their theory that the law arises in the legal consciousness of the people with the fact that in the Middle Ages a system of law which was foreign to the legal consciousness of the people became the valid law of Germany? This purpose of theirs is subserved by the theory that the people no longer participate in the creation of law after they have reached a more advanced stage of legal development, that they are being "represented" in this matter by the jurists. Roman law was received in the Middle Ages solely and alone by the jurists, but they acted as the representatives of the people.

This is, in its essence, Savigny and Puchta's theory of the sources of law, stated, as far as possible, in their own words. I have availed myself of the statements of Savigny and Puchta quite

都不重要的事件得出其法源理论，而是通过历史研究获得其理论的。对他们来说，原始法的标准是罗马君主时期以及早期共和时期的法律，如他们想像的那样。在《法理学教程》中，普赫塔对此给予了一个形象的描述，在其《习惯法》中，他给出了另外一番描述——与前者本质上相同。此外，可以证明，他们心中想的是中世纪德国法。罗马人和古代德国人中，法律还是主要由通行的行为规则组成；人民参与司法，他们的法律意识对于法律争议的裁决具有权威性。法学家还没有形成他们自身独特的法律意识；他们从他们的市民同胞的法律意识中抽象出法律规则。普赫塔明确提到艾克·冯·雷普戈。至于后期，历史法学派的创建人将他们的学说建立在罗马帝国的法律状况之上，在罗马帝国，罗马法学家直接创造法律，他们自己的法律意识为造法活动提供了基础。这是他们法学家法学说的经验基础。但是以这样方式产生的法不是行为规则，就其性质而言，它仅仅是裁判规范。

最重要的是，他们必定达成一致，认同“一般习惯法最伟大、最非凡的举动”，即，中世纪的罗马法继受。他们整个的理论就是为了用来正当化后者。如何将“法律产生于民族的法律意识中”这种理论与“中世纪时，对于德意志民族法律意识而言属于外来者的法律制度变成了德国有效的法律”这个事实调和起来？在法律意识达到一个更高的法律发展阶段后，民族不再参与法律创造，在这方面，他们由法学家“代表”——这种理论促进了他们的目标。在中世纪，罗马法仅由法学家所接纳，但是他们充当了民族的代表。

本质上，这就是他们的——尽可能按照萨维尼与普赫塔自己的话表述的——法源理论。我已经不加区别地利用了萨维尼与

indiscriminately for, I am sure, there is no doubt that, in spite of a few minute differences in details, the doctrine as a whole is a unit, a product of their joint labors. And this product of their joint labors is an achievement of the highest rank, which was not understood by the great majority of their contemporaries, and which has not been surpassed in our day. Moreover they have produced the whole doctrine by their unaided, absolutely independent labors even though certain traces of the influence of Schetling's philosophy or of Burke's *Reflections on the Revolution in France* may perhaps be found.

Their gravest error has been pointed out repeatedly in this book. It lies in this, that they manifestly conceive of the whole law as consisting exclusively of legal propositions. Legal propositions however do not, at any stage of legal development, arise, fully formed and developed, from the legal consciousness. They are always a product of the labors of the jurists. A few legal relations arise among the people, e. g. corporations and other communities, family relations, ownership and other property rights, contracts, and rights of heirs. This may be the "essential, invisible, spiritual law of the people" that Savigny is speaking of. It is only on the basis of these relations that juristic science and legislation create legal propositions. In order to attain clarity, every theory of the sources of law must carefully distinguish between the question as to the origin of legal institutions, and the question as to the creation of legal propositions.

This first error is the cause of the second, which consists in this, that the jurists of the Historical School make a distinction in principle between the earlier and the later legal development. At a lower stage of development the idea of the development of law immediately within the consciousness of the people presented little difficulty to them, for they took for granted that the whole people was called upon to take part in the administration of justice, and that the legal propositions that it applied resulted directly from the legal consciousness of the whole people. But the history upon which their doctrine was built up was not true. Even when "all the people" judge in the assemblies, it is always parts only of the people that are entitled to take part in the

普赫塔的理论,因为我相信,毫无疑问,尽管他们二人的学说在细节上存在一些微小的差异,但该学说总的来说是一个整体,是他们共同劳动的产物。并且,该产物是最高等级的成就,它并未被他们同时代的大多数人所理解,而且在我们这个时代也尚未被超越。此外,尽管或许能够发现他们受到谢林哲学或伯克《对法国革命的反思》(*Reflections on the Revolution*)影响的蛛丝马迹,但他们是在没有外界帮助、完全靠自身独立劳动的基础上创造了整个学说的。

在本书中,他们最严重的错误被一再地指出。该错误在于,他们显然认为整个的法律都是全部由法律命题组成的。然而,法律命题不是在法律发展的任何阶段都会从法律意识中产生、充分形成和发展。他们总是法学家的劳动产物。一些法律关系产生于民族之中,例如法人与其他社团、家庭关系、所有权及其他财产权、契约、继承权等。这可能是萨维尼说的“民族中本质的、看不见的精神之法”。只是在这些关系的基础之上,法学与立法才创造出法律命题。为了获得清晰的思路,每一种法源理论都必须仔细区分法律制度的起源问题与法律命题的创造问题。

这第一个错误导致了第二个错误的产生,萨维尼与普赫塔的第二个错误在于,历史法学派法学家在早期法律发展与后期法律发展之间作了大体上的区分。在法律发展的低级阶段,“法律发展直接从民族意识中产生”这种理念几乎没有给他们带来什么难题,因为他们想当然地认为,整个民族都被要求参与司法,所适用的法律命题直接源于整个民族的法律意识。但他们的学说据以建立的历史基础并不真实。甚至当“该民族全体人民”在集会上共同审判时,那也总是该民族部分民众才有权参与此审判活

assemblies, and the legal propositions are formulated and proposed by a few, i. e. by those that are "experts in the law, such as a nation possesses long before it has developed a science of law" (Puchta). It is not these legal propositions that live and have their being within the consciousness of the people, but the legal institutions and the norms of the law of corporations and other communities, of property, and of contract, upon which the institutions are based, and from which the legal propositions are deduced. On the other hand at a higher stage, at which the jurist has already appeared on the scene, legal institutions and norms appertaining to them continue to arise among the people themselves, e. g. (using Puchta's illustrations) the bill of exchange among the bankers, the demarcation of boundaries, and the servitude of pasture among the peasants; only the legal propositions are being formlulated by the jurists in their teachings and writings and in statutes. Had Savigny and Puchta distinguished between legal institutions and legal propositions, they would have realized at once that both are being created in an identical manner at a higher as well as a lower stage of development.

Immediately linked with this second defect in principle appears a third defect in the teachings of the jurists of the Historical School, an error more remarkable indeed inasmuch as it prevented them from drawing the obvious inference from their greatest achievement, which was opening up new channels for the science of law, to grasp the full significance of which was reserved for a future generation. I mean the introduction of the idea of evolution into legal history. It is positively amusing to ask Savigny and Puchta what their conception is of the way in which, at least at a more advanced stage of civilization, the consciousness of the people arrives at the legal proposition, and thereby makes its way into the law which is being recognized and applied by the courts, and which according to their conception is the valid law. In this case, they always insist, the immediate influence of the popular consciousness is "negligible." But legislation, too, as they both teach, is of minor significance. Only "in case the development of law must take account of changed customs and views, in case quite new legal institutions become necessary," they say, legislative action may become salutary, aye, indispensable, in order to make an end of the interim of uncertainty, in order to give

动,而且法律命题也仅由一些人来阐述和主张,这些人是"法律专家,譬如说在发展出法学很久之前就作为民族财产存在的法律专家"(普赫塔)。产生并存在于民族意识当中的不是这些法律命题,而是那些法律习俗,建立在那些法律习俗之上并可推导出这些法律命题的法人与其他社团法的规范、财产法规范、契约法规范。另一方面,在法学家已经登场的更高发展阶段,法律习俗以及与其有关的规范继续在该民族内产生,例如(援引普赫塔的例子)汇票在银行家里产生,地界的划分与牧场的地役权在农民中产生;只有法律命题由法学家在他们的教义和著作中、在制定法中系统阐述。要是萨维尼与普赫塔在法律习俗与法律命题之间作出区分,他们就会立刻意识到此二者在法律发展的高级阶段与低级阶段均以完全相同的方式被创造出来。

与上述第二个错误直接相连、表现在历史法学派法学家的教义中的第三个错误,似乎更加醒目,因为该错误阻止了他们从他们最伟大的成就中获得明显的推论——他们最伟大的成就是为法学开辟了新的道路,完全掌握其重要意义的工作要留待后人完成。我指的是将进化思想引入法律史当中。问问萨维尼与普赫塔,他们的观念是什么样的路径——在该路径上,至少在更发达的文明阶段,民族意识已经获得了法律命题,并因此成为被法院认可与适用的法律,而且按照他们的观念还是有效的法律——肯定很有趣。这种情况下,他们坚持,民众意识的直接影响是"微不足道的"。但是,如他们所教导的那样,立法的重要性更低。他们说,只有"在法律发展必须考虑变动的习惯和见解,且全新的法律习俗成为必要的情况下",为了终结不确定性的过渡期,为了使新法对其他相关法律命题产生均衡的影响,立法活动才可能是

effect to the equalizing influence of the new law upon other, related legal propositions. Finally, the legislator must act, perhaps, when "stages of development and situations" arise, like those under Constantinus in Rome, which are no longer favorable to the creation of law by the common conviction of the whole people (Savigny). And beyond this legislative action becomes unprofitable.

Legislation therefore is just as negligible as the activity of the totality of the people. All that remains is juristic law. But how do jurists bring about harmony between the progress of their own legal consciousness and the law? It is important to hear Savigny and Puchta themselves on this point. In the first volume of his work on customary law, Puchta says: Scientific law is not customary law; scientific activity is not popular activity; scientific convictions are not those that a man arrives at as one of the people, but such as he arrives at as an individual, therefore the *Volksgeist* (spirit of the people) is not the factor which is directly creative. But the science of law has a subject matter which is national in scope, and the science of law is a true science only if it treats its subject matter as national in scope, i. e. treats it according to its true nature. The jurists therefore must needs act as the representatives of the people if they would exercise the influence on law that has been referred to above. And the people is the original source of this kind of law also, even though it is not created immediately by the people, like customary law, but mediately, through these representatives. A juristic view is law and right whenever there is a scientific basis for it, i. e. whenever it is true. In order to be true, it must be based on the inner nature of things, and it must be in accord with the *Volksgeist*. That it is in accord with the *Volksgeist* will appear from the fact that it has made its influence felt in part in the conviction of the jurists, and in part in the application by the court. This is the significance of the authority of the jurists and of the *res iudicatae*, which therefore are not sources of law but merely sources—of course, not absolutely infallible ones—of the knowledge of such law as has already come into existence.

有益的、值得赞成的、不可或缺的。最后，当类似于罗马康士坦丁统治下的“发展阶段与局势”出现时——此时由整个民族的共同确信来创制法律不再是理想的时候——立法者或许必须行动（萨维尼）。除此之外，立法活动都是无益的。

因此，立法正如民族的整体活动一样是可忽略不计的。所有保留下来的是法学家法。但法学家如何在他们个人法律意识的进步与法律之间保持一致呢？听听萨维尼与普赫塔他们自己对此问题的看法比较重要。在其关于习惯法的著作第一卷当中，普赫塔说，科学法不是习惯法；科学活动不是大众活动；科学确信不是某人作为民族一分子、而是作为个人获得的确信，因此，*Volksgeist*（民族精神）不是直接创造性的因素。但是，法律科学包含一个题材，其范围是民族性的，并且法律科学是真正的科学，只要它将其题材限定在民族范围内，即按照其真实的性质来对待它。因此，如果法学家想要对上面提及的法律产生影响，则他们非要充当民族的代表不可。并且，尽管这种法律并非如习惯法一样由该民族直接创造，而是由其通过这些代表间接创造，但该民族还是这种法律最初的起源，任何时候法学家的观点就是法律和权利，只要这种观点具有科学基础，即，它是真实的。为了保证真实，它必须基于事物的内部性质，它必须与民族精神一致。它与民族精神一致，可通过如下事实显现出来——它已经让它的影响部分地在法学家的确信中被感知，并部分地在法院适用中被感知。这就是法学家与 *res iudicatae*（已决案）[1] 权威的重要意义，因此它不是那种已有法律知识的法源而仅仅是其来源——当然，不是绝对可靠的来源。

---

〔1〕（拉）*res iudicatae*（已决案），指已经由司法裁决加以判定的事项。

In the second volume of his book on customary law, however, Puchta says that under certain circumstances juristic law can be customary law. As the law develops, the mass of legal material increases to such an extent, and the science of law becomes so refined that a comprehensive knowledge and a scientific mastery of the law can be found only among the jurists. Therefore the conviction of all the members of the people is replaced by the conviction of the jurists. "In this connection, it might be a good thing to consider that the jurists do not possess this qualification of natural representation in virtue of their scientific activity, which as such is not a popular one, but in virtue of their preeminent legal knowledge which they have in common with the men learned in the law, who are met with among a people long before the latter has a science of law." Accordingly by the side of customary law which is based upon the common conviction of the people there is another kind of customary law, which is based upon the usage of those learned in the law, of the jurists, as the representatives of the people, provided no proposition is involved for which a scientific basis must be sought, and which is valid only because it is inherently true; and in addition to the customary practice "which is based upon a legal proposition scientifically deduced" there is another customary practice which expresses "the popular legal consciousness of those learned in the law," and which therefore contains "customary law."

Savigny, in his *System*, amplifies Puchta's remarks. Discussing the general nature of the sources of law, he says that one must distinguish between a material and a formal, purely scientific activity of the legal profession. As to the former, he says that the law-creating activity of the people is being withdrawn into the legal profession, and is being practiced by the latter as representatives of the whole people. Later, in the section on the sources of Roman law, he contrasts the theoretical and the practical activity of the jurists. The theoretical activity, according to Savigny, consists in purely scientific investigation, i. e. in establishing and interpreting the text of the sources, working up the results into a legal system, and perfecting the inner organization of the legal system. This activity, he says, does not produce new law; it merely makes possible a purer knowledge of the ex-

然而,在论习惯法著作的第二卷中,普赫塔说,在特定情况下,法学家法也可能是习惯法。随着法律的发展,法律素材的总体增加到那样一种程度,法律科学变得如此精致,以至于法律的广泛知识和科学把握只有法学家才具备。因此,民族所有成员的确信被法学家的确信取代。“在这方面,认为法学家具有自然代表的资格,不是由于他们那种本身并非大众化的科学活动,而是由于他们拥有深厚的法律知识,他们与在法律方面博学的人一样,后者在一个民族拥有法律科学很久之前在该民族中就会出现。”因此,倘若不牵涉到任何相关的命题——必须为其寻求一个科学基础,并且它之所以有效是因为它本来就是真实的——那么除了基于民族共同确信的习惯法外,还存在另外一种习惯法,它基于那些作为该民族代表的、在法律方面博学之人、法学家的习惯;除了“法律命题按照科学方法据以推导出来的”通行惯例外,还存在另外一种通行惯例——它表达出“那些在法律方面博学之人的流行的法律意识”,因此,它也包括“习惯法”。

萨维尼在其《当代罗马法体系》一书中,对普赫塔的阐述作了展开。在讨论法源的一般性质时,他说,人们必须区分从事实质性、具体实践活动的法学家与从事形式上的、纯科学活动的法学家。关于前者他说,民族的造法活动退而由法律职业阶层进行,并由后者作为整个民族的代表来实施。后来,在论及罗马法源的一节中,他比较了法学家的理论性与实践性活动。按照萨维尼的观点,理论性的活动纯粹由科学研究构成,其内容即:确证和解释原始文献的原文,然后将结果整理、加入到法律体系中,并完善法律体系的内部结构。他说,这种活动并不产生新法;它仅仅使现

isting law. By practical activity he means all investigation which has in view the relation between the content of the sources and "the condition of the living law upon which they are to act, i. e. the condition and the requirements of modern times." This activity may be occasioned by the communication, through teaching or writing, of the results obtained, or by the necessity of deciding a law-suit. In either case, the investigation is an instrumentality of customary law and, at the same time, a part of scientific law.

In the Romanistic practical legal science, Savigny would differentiate between two totally dissimilar component parts. "One part is of a healthy nature, and is based upon the modern requirements that have arisen as a natural result from the completely changed conditions, *inter alia*, from the great modifications in judicial procedure, and in part from the great transformation of the whole ethical view of life that has been brought about by the Christian religion. According to the views just stated, we must attribute to this part the power and reality of customary law which has been recognized in a scientific manner. In this connection, it is immaterial that earlier teachers of law made a misguided attempt to derive these propositions from Roman law. These jurists were sincere in their endeavors, and we must, in such cases, consider the investigation of the true Roman law an essential part of our task; not for the purpose of keeping it in force as valid law, but in order to ascertain the true extent of the innovation. The other part has arisen solely from the misguided confusion mentioned above, i. e. from a defective scientific method. It is our task to expose and to dislodge this error, without permitting long undisturbed possession of the field to protect it; especially since, to a great degree, it will be possible to prove that there is imbedded in it an inner contradiction, a basic error in logic." As an illustration he adduces the *Summarissimum* of modern usage.

In concluding this discussion, Savigny adds these words: "The part of the practical law which I have referred to as the sound part is of an importance altogether different from that which I have attributed to the theoretical labor. It is not only effective as an authority which commands respect, but in fact comprises newly

行法的知识有可能更完美。关于实践性活动,他指的是所有着眼于原始文献的内容与“现行法得以发挥作用的条件——即最新时代的状况和要求”二者之间关系的研究。该活动可能因通过教授或写作所获得之结果的交流而产生,或者因法律诉讼之裁决的必要性而引发。无论哪一种,此种研究都是习惯法的手段,同时,也是科学法的一部分。

在罗马派法学家的实用法学中,萨维尼区分了两个完全不同的组成部分。“第一个部分是良性的,并且建立在作为某种自然结果而产生的现代要求之上,该结果源于完全变化了的形势——特别是审判程序的重大修改,*inter alia*(尤其)源于因基督教带来的整个生活伦理观的重大转变。按照刚刚提到的这种观点,我们必须将这部分归于以一种科学方式获得认可的习惯法的力量和现实。在这方面,法律的早期教授者曾误入歧途地尝试从罗马法中推导出这些法律命题,这无关紧要。这些法学家在作这种努力时出于真心实意,那种情况下,我们必须将对真正罗马法的研究作为我们任务的核心部分;不是为了使它保持如同生效法一样的效力,而是为了确定革新的真实内容。另外一部分仅仅因上述误入歧途的混乱而产生,即源于一种有缺陷的科学方法。揭示并清除该错误,不允许该领域长期被错误把持、拒绝改正,这是我们的任务;特别是因为在很大程度上有可能证明,其中蕴含着一种内在的冲突、一个逻辑上的基本错误。”作为例证,他列举了 *Summarissimum* 的现代用法。

在总结此次讨论时,萨维尼又说道:“我所提到的,作为完好部分的实践法部分具有完全不同于我认定的理论性工作所具有的重要性。它不仅是一个要求被尊重的有效权威,而且事实上也

created law. Nevertheless we cannot concede even to it a conclusively perfected, immutable existence. It is true, such a proposition of the practical law cannot be deprived of its validity by a purely theoretical examination, by demonstrating its divergence from the law of the sources, for, being true customary law, it has acquired an independent existence. But there can be no doubt that it can lose its validity in the same way in which it got it."

To these words we must add the following remarks of Puchta in his review of Beseler's book: "I find that even though those powers (the powers to interpret the existing law) have been most fully developed, the judicial office requires additional powers without which it would, in very many cases, have no norm for decision at its disposal. In such cases the judge derives the legal proposition which is to be applied from the principles of the existing law. Inasmuch as the law is inherently reasonable, that which follows as a matter of inner necessity from the existing law, must also be valid law."

This can scarcely be called a scientific exposition; it is an embarrassed stammering. The question is, whether the jurists who are working according to a scientific method are authorized to introduce new principles into the law. If they are, let it be stated clearly and unmistakably, and let the methods be stated according to which they can and must do it. It cannot be done by merely developing the principles of the existing law, for they are comprised in the existing law. Puchta is right in insisting in his argument against Beseler that this scientific labor, too, is productive; but its productivity consists in discovering the content of existing law, not in creating new law. And if Savigny alludes to the misguided attempt of earlier teachers of law to derive such propositions from the Roman law, I would say that this method becomes the more hopeless the more our understanding of Roman law, and of existing valid law generally, increases. At all events it would have been the most important task of these great defenders of the creative power of the science of law carefully to develop the methods of original creation of law. But no trace of

包含了新创设的法律。尽管如此,我们也不能承认它就会最终完美、永久不变地存在。的确,那样一个实践法的命题不可能由于一个纯粹理论性的检验——通过证明它偏离了原始文献法——就被剥夺了有效性,因为,作为真实的习惯法,它已经获得了一个独立的存在。但是,毫无疑问的是,它以何种方式获得其有效性,它也可能以相同的方式失去该有效性。"

除了这些,我们还要提到普赫塔在其评论贝塞勒著作的书评中的下列评论:"我发现,即使那些权力(解释现行法的权力)已经获得最充分的发展,审判职位还是要求额外的权力,没有后者,在许多情况下,它将没有可用的裁判规范。那种情况下,法官从现行法的原则中推导出将要被适用的法律命题。由于该法律具有内在的合理性,作为一种内在必然性,从现行法推导出来的东西必定也是有效的法律。"

这几乎不能被称作是科学的阐释;它是一种困窘的口吃。问题是,按照科学方法工作的法学家是否有权将新原则引入到法律中。如果他们有权,那就清楚地、不会让人误解地说出来,说出他们能够以及必须据以履行此项工作的那些方法。不可能仅仅通过发展现行法的原则就可以达成此目标,因为它们都包含在现行法当中。在反驳贝塞勒时,普赫塔认为这种科学劳动也是建设性的,这是对的;但是其建设性在于发现现行法的内容,而不在创造新法方面。如果萨维尼指的是法律的早期教授者们从罗马法中推导出那些法律命题的误入歧途的尝试,我会说,我们对罗马法以及现行法了解越深,这种方法就会越显无用。无论如何,谨慎地发展原创性的造法方法将是这些法学创造性权力的伟大捍卫者们最重要的任务。但在他们的作品中找不到任何这方面的蛛

this can be found in their writings. All that they have to say of the science of law refers exclusively to the means of deriving norms for decision from traditional law, not to a method of find ing or inventing new law. And the juristic method which they have in fact developed most successfully, i. e. the historical and systematic method, most flatly contradicts their teachings. A school of jurisprudence whose chief concern is to establish the meaning of legal propositions at the time when they were created is manifestly little qualified for the creation of new law whenever the present time requires it.

In his book, entitled *Volksrecht und Juristenrecht* (1843), Beseler attacked the doctrine of Savigny and Puchta at two points. First of all he denies that direct participation of the people ceases at the more advanced stages of development. He adduces numerous examples from all departments of law—he devotes a whole chapter to *Genossensehaftsrecht* and another to *Standesrecht*—in order to show that the popular law is still alive in the great masses of the people. It is true, he says, the jurists know little of it and the courts pay no attention to it, but the Historical School of jurisprudence teaches that actual usage is not a necessary element of the concept of customary law, but is merely an external characteristic, that all that is of the essence of customary law is that it has arisen directly from the consciousness of the people. Therefore, he insists, it is absolutely immaterial whether this law, which is based directly upon the popular consciousness, is, or is not, known to the jurists, whether it is, or is not, applied by the courts.

Thereupon Beseler attacks the idea that, without more ado, the jurists are to be looked upon as the representatives of the people in the matter of creating law. He expresses the opinion that law might arise, "as to which it is at least a merely accidental matter whether and to what extent it retains its character as popular law." This is the case, above all, when bad laws are enacted in the state, but also "when external influence becomes so powerful from long continuance of its operation upon the state of the law that at last true norms for decision develop therefrom which everyone considers, and must consider, binding." The ultimate basis of the validity of law in this case is custom, "which therefore is no longer a mere external characteristic

丝马迹。他们必须要谈论到的法律科学的一切毫无例外全部涉及到从传统法律中推导出裁判规范的方法,而不是发现或创造新法律的方法。他们事实上发展得最为成功的法学方法——即历史的和体系化的方法——大部分与他们的教义直接相矛盾。主要的关节在于当法律命题被创立时,确立它们含义的法学流派显然不能胜任在当下有需要时创造新法的工作。

在《民间法与法学家法(*Volksrecht und Juristenrecht*)》(1843)中,贝塞勒在两点上攻击萨维尼和普赫塔。首先,他否认在法律发展更高级的阶段民族的直接参与会终止。他从所有的法律部门中引用了大量的例子——他运用了一整章的篇幅来论述 *Genossensehaftsrecht*(社团法),另外一整章来论述 *Standesrecht*(专门职业法),以此来表明,民间法在该民族广大民众当中仍然是活法。他说,的确,法学家对其知之甚少,法院也没注意到它,但是法学的历史学派教导说,实际使用不是习惯法概念的必要要素,而仅仅是一个外部特征,习惯法的所有本质内涵是它从民族意识中直接产生。因此,他坚持认为,这种直接建立在民众意识之上的法律是否为法学家所知,是否为法院所适用,绝对是无关紧要的。

于是,贝塞勒攻击这种观念:在造法方面,无需多费周折,直接将法学家视为民族的代表。他表达了这样的观点:法律可能产生,"关于它,是否以及在什么程度上它还保留了民间法的特点,无论如何仅仅是一个次要的问题。"特别是,当国家颁布劣法时,以及"当它由于长期的持续实行从而对国家产生的外部影响变得如此强大,以至于最后真正的裁判规范从中发展出来,每个人都认为且必定认为受其拘束时",就是这种情形。如果这样,法的有效性的最重要基础是习惯,"因此它不再仅仅是法律的一个外部

(*Kennzeichen*) of law but actually participates in its creation, and very often in opposition to the (spirit of the people) and to the reason of things (*Vernunft der Dinge*)." Customary law therefore, as such, is a thing foreign to the popular consciousness. Its relation to *Volksrecht*, whose origin lies immediately in the popular consciousness, is now one of hostility, now of indifference. It is incorrect therefore, he insists, to say that juristic law necessarily is a continuation of popular law; it may be merely customary law.

It is apparent that Beseler here carried Savigny and Puchta's very own thoughts to their logical conclusion. When they made difficulties about admitting that in their own day the development of law was being continued by the whole people, and were bent upon looking upon the jurists as representatives of the people, they did this solely in order to justify the reception of Roman law, which had been carried out by the jurists and had remained foreign to the popular consciousness. Beseler, who, being a Germanist, was under no obligation to defend the reception, availed himself of this freedom. But inwardly Savigny and Puchta were very close to Beseler—much closer perhaps than they themselves believed.

Beseler devoted a whole section of his book to the question how popular law must be ascertained and recognized. The people in its totality, or in narrower circles, within whose consciousness popular law lives and has its being, he says, has an immediate intuition of it, "which grasps the essential elements of everyday life contained in the circumstances and relations of everyday life, and, at the same time, knows the norms that regulate them and applies them. This may also be said of every individual, within whose consciousness, because of his position and his experience in business and life, the common knowledge of the law is being reflected.... But if anyone who is a stranger to the life of the people and the views of the people wishes to obtain a knowledge of the law contained therein, he must proceed like a natural scientist; he must acquire a knowledge of things as they are by means of actual observation." In this case, the sources of knowle-

特征(*Kennzeichen*),而是实际参与了法律创制的过程,并十分经常地与*Volksgeist*(民族精神)相对,与事物的理性相对。”因此,习惯法本身对于民众意识而言是一个外在的东西。它与*Volksrecht*(民间法)——其起源直接存在于民众意识中——的关系时而是充满敌意,时而是漠不关心。因此他坚持认为,说法学家法必然是民间法的延续是不正确的;法学家法可能仅仅是习惯法。

显然,贝塞勒在这里将萨维尼与普赫塔他们自己的思想推演出它们逻辑上的结论。当他们承认在他们当时那个年代,法律的发展由整个民族继续推动有困难,于是致力于将法学家作为民族的代表时,他们这样做仅仅是为了证明,由法学家实施的、对于民族意识尚属陌生的罗马法之继受诚属正当。贝塞勒,作为一名德意志主义者,并没有义务为罗马法继受辩护,他利用了这种自由。但是,在内心,萨维尼、普赫塔跟贝塞勒十分接近——或许比他们自己认为的那样更为接近。

贝塞勒在他的著作中,用了一整节来讨论民间法如何必定被确定和认可的问题。他说,民族整体上,或在更小的范围内——在该民族的意识中,民间法产生并存在——有一种直接有关该问题的直觉,“该直觉抓住了包含在日常生活环境和关系中的日常生活的本质要素,同时,知道调整他们和适用于他们的规范。这也适用于个人,在个人意识中,由于他在商业与生活中的地位和经验,法律的共同知识得到反思……但是,如果对于该民族的生活和观点感到陌生的任何人希望获得该民族中所包含的法律知识,他必须像一个自然科学家那样行事;借助于实际观察,他必定会获得事物的实际知识。”这种情况下,知识的来源是:在对相

dge are: inquiry among people that are interested in the matter in hand, mercantile *Pareres* (an institution that might be applied to other relations as well), legal literature, autonomous relations, through which popular law in former days so often expressed itself; in statutes, too, we often find a pure and clear expression of the popular idea of right and law.

If we examine the presuppositions of this presentation, which, as usual, are not expressed, we find that, unlike Savigny and Puchta, when this writer speaks of law he does not mean legal propositions but legal institutions. This is obscured by the fact that, apparently, the basis of the doctrine of both Beseler and the founders of the Historical School is the legal consciousness. But the latter, as to the present time at least, have in mind the legal consciousness of the jurists, who have gained control over the teaching and the administration of law; Beseler has in mind the legal consciousness of the people among whom the legal institutions develop today, just as they did many centuries ago. Savigny and Puchta themselves have put the center of gravity in the legal consciousness, and have treated customary practice as a mere "external characteristic (*Kennzeichen*)." From this Beseler draws the inference that popular law can dispense with the requirement of customary practice altogether in the practical application of law. When Puchta, quite inconsistently with his own point of view, objected to this on the score of the uncertainty of law of this kind, i. e. law without usage as an external characteristic (*Kennzeichen*), Beseler replied that in the very fact that he had declared that direct observation of the relations of life is of such paramount importance if one would know the popular law, there lay "a direct reference to the habitual customary observance of the norm (usage), which is revealed in the relations of life inasmuch as it controls them." Here the opposing views clash. On one side there is the view that the important thing is the law that is applied by the courts; on the other, the knowledge of the fact that law regulates the relations of life even without the intervention of the courts. The fact that Savigny and Puchta com-

关事项——商业方面的*Pareres*（专家意见）（可能也适用于其他关系的习俗制度）、法律文献、自治关系等——感兴趣的人之间的调查，早先时候民间法如此经常地通过它们来表达自身；在制定法中，我们也经常发现一些有关权利和法律的民间思想纯粹而清晰的表达。

如果我们对该表述的先决条件——通常它们没有表达出来——进行检验，则我们会发现，与萨维尼和普赫塔不同，当这位作者说到法律时，他指的不是法律命题而是法律习俗。此点因下列事实而模糊：贝塞勒与历史法学派建立者的学说基础显然是法律意识。但是后者，至少在当时，已经考虑到了支配法律教育和法律实施之法学家的法律意识；贝塞勒想到的是民族的法律意识，在这样一个民族中，法律习俗今天的发展正如他们数个世纪之前的发展一样。萨维尼与普赫塔他们自己把重心放在法律意识当中，把习惯性实践仅仅作为一个"外部特征（*Kennzeichen*）"。贝塞勒从中推出结论：在法律的实际应用中，民间法可以完全抛开习惯性实践的要件。当普赫塔因为这种法律的不确定性——即没有"使用"作为外部特征的法律——而与他自己的观点十分不一致地反对此点时，贝塞勒回应道，在他已经宣布的事实中——如果一个人知道民间法，则生活关系的直接观察具有那样无以伦比的重要性，存在"对规范（习俗）习惯性的遵守，由于它支配着生活关系，所以它在生活关系中能够显现。"此处存在对立观点的冲突。一方面，一种观点认为，重要的事情是法院所适用的法律；另一方面，对立的观点认为，重要的事情是了解这个事实：即使没有法院的介入，法律也调整生活关系。尽管萨维尼与普赫塔并未把习用（*usage*）作为习惯法产生的先决条件，但他们二人反

bated the latter view, although they did not consider usage a prerequisite to the arising of customary law, is further evidence of the lack of consistency that characterizes their whole controversy with Beseler. But Beseler has gone much further than Savigny and Puchta inasmuch as he is not content with stating propositions about popular law and juristic law, but is seeking methods for the direct acquisition of knowledge "in the manner of the natural scientist... by means of observation." The fact that this powerfully stimulating suggestion by the great Germanist remained unheeded is merely another proof that in science, too, it is the distribution of power (*Machstverhältnisse*) rather than the spirit that turns the scale.

The idea of Beseler was realized far from the land of its origin by a pupil of Savigny's, the Croat Bogišič, and by another student of the writings of Savigny, the Spaniard Costa. Both are endeavoring to create a science of popular law, not by establishing legal propositions but by studying legal relations and legal institutions. Bogišič drew up an extensive questionnaire containing more than eight hundred questions, and made the answers which he received from the regions inhabited by southern Slavs the basis of his work (*Zbornik sadašnih pravnih obizč aja južnih Slovena*), and Costa created the foundation of his two-volume work *Derecho consuetudinario y economia popular en España* by direct personal observation and study of the legal relations and institutions he is describing. The second volume, incidentally, also contains works of other writers. The work of Bobčev on Bulgarian customary law, *Sbornik na blgarski juriditski obitschai*, employs the method of Bogišič.

I hope to be able to make a report on all of these books at another place. Several years ago, in an article which appeared in Schmoller's Jahrbuch, I emphatically directed attention to the books of Bogišič which are written in Croatian and which, for that reason, are little known, and I am therefore in every way well armed

对后一种观点的事实是他们缺乏前后一致性的进一步证据，这种一致性的缺乏构成了他们与贝塞勒整个论争的特征。但是，贝塞勒走得比他俩更远，因为他不满足于表述民间法与法学家法的命题，而是要探求“以自然科学家为榜样……凭借观察”直接获取知识的方法。这个伟大的德意志主义者提出的具有强烈鼓动性的建议遭到了忽略，这个事实不过是又一次证明了，在科学中，改变力量对比的同样是权力的分配（*Machstverhältnisse*），而不是精神。

贝塞勒的理念由萨维尼的一个学生科洛特·波吉斯克与萨维尼著作的另外一个“学生”斯帕尼亚德·科斯塔在远离其发源地的地方实现了。他们二人都致力于创造民间法法学，并且不是通过建立法律命题，而是通过研究法律关系和法律习俗的方法来实现这个目的。波吉斯克制定了一份包含超过 800 个问题的内容广泛的调查问卷，并将他从定居在南部斯拉夫地区获得的回答作为他《*Zbornik sadasnih pravnih obizaja juznih Slovena*》这部作品的基础，科斯塔则凭借直接的个人观察和对他所描述的法律关系和习俗的研究，为他的两卷本著作《*Derecho consuetudinario y economia popular en Espana*》建立了基础。其中第二卷也附带包含了其他作者的作品。Bobčev 论保加利亚习惯法的作品《*Sbornik na blgarski juriditski obitschai*》，就是运用了波吉斯克的方法。

我希望能在别处对所有的这些著作制作一份报告。几年前，在一篇收录于《施姆勒年鉴（*Schmoller's Jahrbuch*）》的文章中，我着力向人们推荐了波吉斯克用克罗地亚语——因此也极少为人所知——写就的作品，因此，对于防御那种在维也纳时就瞄准

against the charge that has been leveled at me in Vienna that I have been trying to ignore them by not mentioning them. But I cannot admit, on the other hand, that I owe the basic thoughts of my sociological works to Bogišič. Since the works of Bogišič are for the most part inaccessible to West European readers because of the language in which they have been written, everyone cannot convince himself, by a personal examination, of the recklessness with which I have been accused of borrowing. Bogišič was a veritable genius of the concrete, and his questionnaire is a masterpiece of insight into the legal conceptions of a backward society and the order based upon them. But it would be a vain endeavor to look for general thoughts in his works. The passage from his *Sbornik* which I published in a German translation in the article referred to above is practically all that I have been able to find in his works in the nature of a discussion of principles. He has supplied us with invaluable material but has utterly failed to work out a classification and an organization of this material that I could have availed myself of. Moreover his horizon is extremely narrow; he confines himself to the institutions peculiar to a primitive society, and is not at all interested in the relations existing in a more advanced form of civilization, in a richer life, or in modern business. From this the reader may judge how far I have advanced beyond Bogišič.

I do however feel constrained to refer to the small volume of Dniestrzanski, entitled *Das Gewohnheitsrecht und die sozialen Verbände* (1905), in which may be found the germs perhaps of a number of thoughts that are somewhat like those that I am presenting in the present volume. I first became acquainted with his work while I was writing this book. There can be no thought of a borrowing; for I have expressed these thoughts as early as the year 1903, in an address entitled *Freie Rechtsfindung und freie Rechtswissenschaft*. At the same time it is apparent that the article by Dniestrzanski is absolutely independent of my address.

Moreover it is the extraordinary merit of Bogišič to have written a code which fully meets Savigny's requirements. It is a codification of the property law of Montenegro. It is based upon a very careful and

我的指控——说我通过对他们只字不提来尽力忽略他们，我在各方面都武装得很好。但是另一方面，我不可能承认，我把我的社会学作品的基本思想归功于波吉斯克。由于作品所用语言的原因，波吉斯克的作品对于西欧读者来说多半难以理解，所以，每个人不可能通过个人检验的方式就充分弄清楚有关我剽窃之指控的鲁莽。波吉斯克是具体事务的真正天才，他的问卷是对落后社会法律观念及基于其上之秩序怀有洞见的杰作。上面提及的、从他的《*Sbornik*》中抽取的那个段落——我曾在一篇文章中将它翻译成德文出版过——实际上是我在他带有原理讨论之性质的作品中所能发现的全部。他为我们提供了珍贵的材料，不过他完全没有对我可以利用的材料进行分类和组织；他将自己限于关注原始社会的独特习俗，对以更高级文明形式存在的关系、对更富裕的生活或对现代贸易一点都不感兴趣。由此，读者可以判断出，我超越波吉斯克的距离有多远。

我不得不提到的丹尼斯特扎斯基名为《习惯法与社会联合体(*Das Gewohnheitsrecht und die sozialen Verbande*)》(1995)中篇幅较短的一卷，其中或许能发现有些类似那些我在这一卷中提及的大量思想的萌芽。当我写这本书时首次熟悉了他的作品。这儿没有任何剽窃；因为我早在 1993 年的一篇名为“*Freie Rechtsfindung und freie Rechtswissenschaf*(法的自由发现和自由法学)”演讲中，就表达过这些思想。不过，显然丹尼斯特扎斯基的这篇文章也完全独立于我的那篇演讲。

此外，创立了一部完全满足萨维尼要求的法典是波吉斯克的非凡的价值所在。那是黑山(*Montenegro*)财产法的法典化。它是建立在非常仔细地、有条不紊地对南部斯拉夫法律习惯进行调查

methodical investigation of South Slavic legal custom, not merely of the legal propositions, which are very few in number, but chiefly of the concrete legal relations and legal institutions. These books, the object of which was not historical understanding, which the legislator can quite readily dispense with, but the understanding of that which is in existence, today, have enabled Bogišič to produce a recognized masterpiece.

The barrenness of all theories of customary law that have been advanced hitherto is caused by the fact that their aims are not clearly defined. While the oldest type of juristic science merely sought, under this head, to give directions to the judge in which cases he should recognize local or particular customs in preference to the Continental common law, the Historical School attempts to present the doctrine of the origin of law. But the Historical School never fully realized that the origin of legal institutions and the origin of legal propositions are two quite distinct things; that the former takes place in society, or, according to their terminology, in the popular consciousness, and becomes manifest in the rules of conduct, or in their terminology, in usage, whereas the legal propositions are being created by the jurists. Instead of dealing with these two phenomena separately side by side, they discuss one after the other; and being unaware of the fact that they are dealing with two distinct things, they propound a doctrine which, on the whole, applies only to juristic law, and then apply it to the development of law in society as well. And when Beseler points out that popular law exists even at the present time, that there are legal institutions which arise immediately in society, they do not know what to say in reply to these inferences from their own principles. In a general way, it may be admitted that the doctrines of Savigny and Puchta are correct if limited to juristic law; their continual vacillation and uncertainty is caused by the fact that they have never become aware of the existence of this limitation.

But there is another ambiguity involved. Juristic law, too, has a double function. In the first place its function is to formulate the norms for decision required for the regulation of the legal institutions which have arisen in society by universalizing the social rules

的基础上,不仅仅针对数量极其有限的法律命题,而且主要是对具体的法律关系和法律习俗进行调查。这些卷册的目标不是有关历史方面的理解——立法者可以很轻易地抛开这些——而是有关现有东西的理解,如今,这些卷册被公认为是波吉斯克的杰作。

迄今为止提出的所有习惯法理论的贫瘠源于这样的事实:它们的目标从来没有被清晰界定过。最古老的法学在此标题之下,仅仅试图为法官提供指导——在这些场合下,他应该优先承认地方习惯或特殊习惯,而不是欧陆共同法;然而,历史法学派却努力提出法源学说。不过历史学派从来没有充分意识到,法律习俗的起源与法律命题的起源是两个十分不同的东西;前者在社会中发生,或者按照他们的术语说是在民众意识,并在行为规则中变得显明或者按照他们的术语说是在习用;而法律命题是由法学家创造的。他们并没有分开论及此二者,相反,他们相继讨论了它们;在没有意识到这个事实——他们正在讨论两个性质不同的事情——的情况下,他们提出了一个学说——该学说大体上只能适用于法学家法;然后,又将它适用于社会中法律的发展。当贝塞勒指出民间法甚至存在于当下,存在直接产生于社会中的法律习俗时,他们不知道该说什么来回应这些从他们自己的原则中推导出来的结论。一般说来,人们可能会承认,如果该学说仅局限于法学家法,萨维尼与普赫塔的学说是正确的;他们持续的摇摆与不确定的根源在于:他们从来没有意识到这种局限性的存在。

但是,还存在另外一种相关的歧义。法学家法同样有双重功能。首先,它的功能是系统阐述调整法律习俗所需要的裁判规范——这些裁判规范是通过对社会行为规则的一般化以及使它

of conduct and making them unitary, but over and above this to find norms for decision independently according to the trends of justice that prevail in society. At this point, too, the founders of the Historical School failed to make the necessary distinction. This error however is less palpably felt, for the reason that, to a certain extent, the same rules apply to both kinds of juristic law. Nevertheless let me emphasize the fact that their discussions are applicable chiefly to the second kind of juristic law, albeit, as their doctrine of analogy and of the "nature of the thing" shows, they occasionally have the former in mind also.

At any rate Savigny and Puchta could not fail to realize that it was necessary not only to advance a theory of the sources of law, a science of the origin and development of law, but also to issue directions to the judge concerning the method of testing the binding force of customary law. For this reason they took over from the older juristic science in vogue among the jurists of the Continental common law the doctrine of the prerequisites of customary law, which, however, quite imperceptibly, become means of gaining knowledge of customary law such as is already in existence in the consciousness of the people or of the legal profession. From this point of view, they discuss the method, the uniformity, the long continued repetition of the acts, the recognition implied in the judgment, the *opinio necessitatis*, the reasonableness, the publicity, and the effect of error. It is apparent that these wretched *Kautelen* (prerequisites) are not necessary for testing either the legal validity of the institutions that have arisen in society or the binding force of juristic law; but they can serve the purpose for which they were found, for which the practical science of the older jurists of the Continental common law utilized them, i. e. for the ascertainment of the binding force of local and special legal customs in preference to the common law. This was recognized by Savigny, especially when he taught that this narrow point of view "that custom, as the source (*Enstehungsgrund*) of a rule of law must always be resoluble into definite, individual, demonstrable acts" is applicable at most to special (*partikuläre*) customs, of which alone one is in the habit

们归于一元的方式而在社会中产生的,但除此之外,它的功能还在于按照社会中占据主流的法学倾向独立地发现裁判规范。对于此点,历史法学的创始人同样没有给予必要的区分。然而,这个错误不太容易被觉察到,因为,在某种程度上,同样的规则适用于这两种法学家法。尽管如此,还是让我强调一下这个事实:他们的讨论主要适用于第二种法学家法,虽然,如他们类似的学说以及"事物的本质"等学说所表明的那样,他们偶尔也考虑到第一种法学家法。

无论如何,萨维尼与普赫塔不可能没有意识到,不仅有必要提出一种法源理论、一种法律起源和发展的学问,而且有必要为法官提供有关测试习惯法拘束力之方法的指导。因此,他们接手了在欧陆共同法学者中流行的古老法学,并且发展出习惯法的先决条件学说,然而,该学说几乎不知不觉地变成了获取诸如已经存在于民族意识或法学家群体意识中的习惯法知识的途径。从这个角度看,他们讨论了其途径、统一性、行为长期持续的重复、在判决中暗示的认可、*opinio necessitatis*(民族内心有关特定规则必须被遵守的确信)、合理性、公之于众的状况以及错误的后果。显然,这些让人不舒服的 *Kautelen*(先决条件)对于测试那些已在社会中产生的法律习俗的有效性或法学家法的拘束力而言均非必要;但是它们易于被发现,而且欧陆共同法年长法学家的实践科学运用了它们,即,用于查明并确定效力优先于欧陆共同法的地方性习惯与特殊习惯的拘束力。萨维尼认识到了此点,特别是当他教说如下见解时更是如此,"习惯,如同法律规则的来源(*Enstehungsgrund*)一样,必定总是可以分解为明确的、个别的、显而易见的行为"——这种狭隘的观点至多可适用于特殊(*partikulare*)习惯,人们有思考这种特殊习

of thinking. "It is not applicable at all to the great and difficult cases of modern customary law, in which the latter is identical with scientific law. The conditions that are usually assumed as conditions precedent to the genesis of customary law, refer throughout to the nature of those acts from which, as we say, it uniformly arises. For this reason they have a merely one-sided applicability to the special (*partikuläre*) customary law, and even as to the latter the various acts must not be looked upon as the sources but rather as the phenomena or characteristics of an existing common legal conviction. As thus modified, the predicate 'truth' may be applied to these conditions, and therefore they must be examined and ascertained separately." He then discusses the conditions in the form in which the Continental common law theory has handed them down. That this is a matter solely of particular customs is confirmed by the English law. The common law, which in its essence is juristic law, throughout follows the rules that Savigny and Puchta have developed for their customary law, which, they say, is chiefly juristic law. In addition, it is true, we find rules like the following: "A custom, in order to be legal and binding must have been used so long that the memory of man runneth not to the contrary; it must be reasonable, it must be continued, not interrupted and peaceably enjoyed; must be reasonable; must be certain; must be compulsory; customs must be consistent with each other; as to the allowance of special customs no custom can, of course, prevail against the express provision of an act of Parliament." The Continental common law jurist must be strongly reminded of home when he reads these words. But all of these things do not refer to customary law but to local and special customs.

The modern Continental common law and the modern German school of legal science mark a step backward from Savigny and Puchta. They are based exclusively on law that is created by the state, and therefore they can have no theory of the non-state, the social, development of law, nor of juristic law. For them the very question becomes all-important that engrossed the attention of

惯的习惯。“这种观点一点也不适用于现代习惯法的重大而困难的情形，其中，后者等同于法学家法。通常被认定为习惯法起源先决条件的条件，全都涉及那些行为的性质，如我们所言，它一律从这些行为中产生。因此，它们仅有一个方面的可适用性，即适用于特殊的（*partikuläre*）习惯法，甚至对于后者，各种各样的行为也不得被看成是来源，而应该被看成是先有共同法律确信的现象或特征。这样一修改，这些条件都可以用谓词“真”来定性，因此它们必须分开接受检验，并加以确定。”然后他讨论了以某种形式呈现的条件，正是以那种形式，欧陆共同法理论将其传递下来。这仅仅是特殊习惯的事情，此点也被英国法所确认。英国普通法——其本质上是法学家法——完全遵守了萨维尼与普赫塔为他们的习惯法所发展出来的规则，他们说，后者主要也是法学家法。此外，我们确实发现了如下一些规则：“为了成为法律并具有拘束力，习惯应用的时间必须很长，以至于人们的记忆不会转向反面；它必须是合理的，它必须是连续的、不曾中断且和平地为人所享有；它必须是合理的；它必须是确定的；它必须是强制的；许多习惯必须彼此相容；至于对特殊习惯的承认，当然没有哪个习惯能够胜过议会的制定法明确的条款。”当欧陆共同法学者读到这段话时，他们必定产生强烈的思乡情绪。但所有的这些事情并不涉及习惯法，而是涉及到地方性的特殊习惯。

现代欧陆共同法学与现代法律科学德国学派均从萨维尼与普赫塔立场倒退了一步。他们完全以国家的立法为基础，因此，他们不可能拥有“非国家的理论”、社会理论、法律发展理论，也没有法学家法理论。对于他们而言，恰恰在罗马帝国时期和欧陆共同法时期吸引法学注意的那个问题——即，一个法律制度是否以

juristic science in the days of the Roman Empire and in the days of the Continental common law, i. e. whether and how a system of law can become valid so as to displace the common law of the state. As a practical matter, this question resolves itself into a question as to the validity of special and local customs. For this reason, the doctrine of Savigny and Puchta was thrust aside and the old doctrine of the prerequisites of customary law was taken up again. Inasmuch as law, in principle, is taken to proceed from the state, permission, approval, or recognition by the sovereign power of the state is demanded in some form or other, either by express words or by silence, and thereby a thought of Justinian's and of the older trend of juristic theory of the Continental common law is being revived. But if, following Savigny and Puchta, modern writers base customary law upon a universal legal conviction as to its binding force, this, in view of the theory that all law proceeds from the state, can mean only that a special prerequisite is being added. The meaning of this doctrine is the following: All law proceeds from the state; under certain conditions, the state permits non-state law; these conditions include among others the universal conviction that the rule in question is law (*Rechtsüberzeugung*). Zitelmann, however, has conclusively demonstrated that these doctrines are untenable. He himself simply derives the validity of customary law from its validity. It is valid because it is valid. But in this tautology a deeper understanding of the non-state character of customary law, at least, lies hidden. Law can come into existence independently of the state whenever it secures validity in society. Zitelmann did not elaborate his thought. Geny, a Frenchman, however, building on the foundation laid by Savigny and Puchta, and elaborating some ideas of Jhering's, has restored the *libre récherche scientifique*, the juristic law of the founders of the Historical School, to its former position of honor. This view is diametrically opposed to the theory, which is also the prevailing theory in France, that the state is the sole source of law.

It is self-evident that the Sociological School of jurisprudence cannot make use of a concept which is composed of such heterogeneous elements as is the traditional concept of customary law. It will analyze it and resolve it into its component parts, and discuss these separately in their proper place and order. These parts

及如何变得有效,以便能够取代这个国家的共同法——变得最重要。实际上,这个问题本身可以归结为特殊的地方习惯的有效性问题。因此,萨维尼与普赫塔的学说被弃置一边,有关习惯法先决条件的古老的学说再一次受到钟爱。由于法律原则上来自国家,因而要求由国家主权所给予的批准、赞成或认可必须以某种形式存在,可以是明确的言语,也可以是默示,因此,优士丁尼的思想以及欧陆共同法古老潮流的法学理论的思想正在复活。但是,如果现代作者追随萨维尼与普赫塔,将习惯法的拘束力建立在一个普遍的法律确信之上,那么考虑到所有的法律均来自于国家,这仅能意味着,一个特殊的先决条件正在被添入。该学说的含义如下:所有的法律来自于国家;在特定条件下,国家允许非国家法的存在;其中,这些条件包括“所涉及的规则是法律”这样一种普遍确信(*Rechtsüberzeugung*)。然而,齐特曼已经确凿无疑地证明了,这些学说是站不住脚的。他自己直接从习惯法的有效性推导出习惯法的有效性。因为它是有效的,所以它是有效的。但是在这种同义反复中,至少隐藏了一种对习惯法非国家性特征的更深理解。齐特曼没有详细阐述他的思想。然而,法国人惹尼——在萨维尼与普赫塔所铺就的基础之上建立并详述了耶林的一些思想——将 *libre récherche scientifique*(“自由的科学探索”学派)、历史法学派创立者的法学家法恢复到该学说先前曾有过的荣耀地位。这种观点全然与法国的主流理论——国家是唯一的法源——相对立。

不言而喻,法理学的社会学派不可能使用一个由那些诸如习惯法的传统概念的异源因素组成的概念。它将分析习惯法,并将它分解为其各组成部分,然后在适当的位置、以恰当的顺序分别

are: the origin of legal institutions in society independently of the state, the creation of legal propositions by the jurists, as writers, teachers, judges; and the question to what extent courts and other agencies of the state are bound by non-state law. These are totally distinct fields of knowledge, and fusing them into one can cause nothing but confusion.

But confined to a limited sphere, the concept of customary law is indispensable to the Sociological School of legal science. Where the creation of juristic law is not regulated by fixed precepts, as it is in England, it is necessarily unsettled and uncertain during the time immediately following its creation. A considerable period of time must elapse before a rule of juristic law gains such general recognition that a judge will no longer consider himself authorized to disregard it even though it conflicts with his own conviction. Thereafter it is something more than juristic law, and it would be quite in keeping with modern theory to call it customary law. Whenever there is a long-continued course of decisions contrary to a statute under circumstances where there can be no error of law, it ought to be made the subject of a special study. The occurrence of such courses of decision is beyond doubt. It has been observed repeatedly in France; and it occasionally blossoms forth even in Austria, a country which in other respects is the paradise of the narrowest sort of worship of the letter. It is often being denied that customary law can arise from such usage. But this only means that the courts, in such cases, can always revert to the statute, and that a judge cannot be accused of defeating the ends of the law who decides against the existing judicial usage according to the statute, provided that in doing so he follows his conviction. This phenomenon at all events deserves a more detailed study. As compared with the theory that customary law arises simply from juristic law, it presents numerous peculiarities.

来讨论它们。这些组成部分是:社会中不依赖于国家的法律习俗的起源,法学家作为作者、教师、法官对法律命题的创造;在何种程度上法庭和其他国家机构应当受到非国家法拘束。这些完全属于不同的知识领域,把它们混在一起,除了能带来混乱,别的一无所获。

但是局限于一个有限的领域,习惯法的概念对于法理学社会学派而言是不可或缺的。在法学家法的创造不受固定规则调整的地方,比如在英格兰,在紧随其创造之后的时期内,它必然是不稳固、不确定的。在法学家法的规则获得普遍认可、以至于法官不再认为他自己有权忽略它——即使它与该法官自己的确信相冲突——之前,必定要经历相当长的一段时间。此后,它就不仅仅是法学家法了,它将与称其为习惯法的现代理论相当一致。任何时候,在制定法不可能有任何错误的场合下,只要存在与制定法相对立的持续很长的裁判过程,它就应当被当作特殊研究的主题。那样的裁判过程毫无疑问会发生。这种情形在法国可以一再看到;它偶尔甚至在奥地利——那是在别的方面对于字面意义抱有最刻板的崇拜的天堂——这样的国家也会一再出现。经常遭到否认的是,习惯法能够从那些习惯中产生。但是这仅意味着,在那种情形下,法庭总是能够回返到制定法上,并且,决心依据制定法反对现有司法习惯的法官,如果这样做他遵循了自己的确信,那么他不可能因为阻挠此种法律的目的而遭到指责。无论如何,应对此种现象进行更详细的研究。与习惯法仅仅源于法学家法的理论相比,它提供了大量的奇异的东西。

# XX

# The Methods Of The Sociology Of Law

## I. Legal History And Juristic Science

There is no antithesis between science and art. Every true work of science is a work of art, and the man who is not an artist is a poor man of science. Production of a work of science requires the same qualifications as production of a work of art; both require a certain receptivity of mind, imagination, and power to give shape to one's material. For this reason every independent investigator must create his own method, just as every creative artist must create his own technique. He who employs another's method, just like the person who employs another's technique, may possibly be a great disciple, but never more than a disciple, who continues the work of the master but does not undertake new work. It is possible therefore to teach one's own or another's method or technique, but not to teach scientific method or artistic technique. For the mind which thinks and works independently will ever be seeking new methods and new techniques which correspond to his individuality.

But whatever method or technique it may be, its starting point will always be that which the external world presents to the human mind. For the latter can work only on those impressions that it receives from without. Every deduction is preceded by an induction; all idealizing, by a reception of the outward impression of that which has been idealized. The induction and the reception

# 第二十章　法律社会学的方法

## 1. 法律史与法学

科学与艺术之间不存在对立。每一个真正的科学作品都是艺术作品，不是艺术家的人其科学也必定浅薄。科学作品的创作需要与艺术作品的创作同样的技能；此二者都需要大脑的感受性、想象力以及表达素材的能力。因此，每个独立的研究者都必须创造他自己的方法，正如每一个创造性的艺术家都必须创造出他自己的技巧一样。使用别人方法的人，就像使用别人技巧的人，很可能是一个伟大的门徒，但永远不会超越门徒本身，门徒继续做主人的工作，但不会从事新的工作。因此，可能教授自己的或他人的方法或技巧，但不可能教授科学的方法或艺术的技巧。因为独立思考和工作的人永远会寻求与其个性特征相应的新方法和新技巧。

但是无论是什么方法或技巧，它的起点总是外部世界给人类智力提供的东西。因为后者只能基于它从外部接受的那些印象之上工作。每一个演绎之前都有归纳；所有的理想化之前都有对已被理想化的外部印象的接受。然而，归纳和理想化极其频繁地

however very frequently take place with lightning-like rapidity, unconsciously, without any conscious intention, and only the subsequent process of deduction or of idealizing enters into the consciousness of the scientist or of the artist. This creates the appearance of an inductive science or of an idealistic art.

The social sciences have hitherto been working, and are still doing their work, by means of such unconscious inductions. But when Montesquieu apparently derives a considerable part of his theory of the state by a purely deductive method from his classification of the forms of government; when he bases the despotic form of government upon fear, the monarchical upon honor, the republican upon virtue, the inductions, most superficial and unmethodical as they are, which have preceded the deductions can easily be perceived by anyone. The theory as to despotism is based on the accounts of the Greek city tyrants or the Roman emperors; as to the republic, on the accounts of the small ancient free state and of the Swiss cantons. The wealth of unconscious experience that has been compressed into the theory of value of Ricardo or of Marx, a veritable model of deduction, must be sensed by everyone who has read their presentations understandingly. And in the preface to his work on *Kapitalzins* (interest) Boehm-Bawerk, one of the chief exponents of the Austrian school of economists, which allegedly is purely deductive, says that the facts on which the book is based have been learned by means of simple, informal observation directly from common everyday life as it presents itself to every one of us.

And sociology also, including the sociology of law, must be a science of observation. The man who, a century and a half ago, wrote the three words *Esprit des Lois* as the title of his book surely was seeking a sociology of law within his own soul even at that early date. And Montesquieu even then was busy for twenty years, indefatigably gathering facts on long journeys, and as an untiring reader. Although his book is not the work of a scholar, but the dilettantish, poorly arranged, desultory work of a grand seigneur, and is planned on a scale

以类似光的速度无意识地发生着，没有任何自觉的意图，只有随后的演绎过程或理想化过程加入了科学家或艺术家的意识。这造就了演绎性科学或理想化艺术的外观。

迄今为止，社会科学一直在发挥效用，并且仍然在通过无意识的归纳做着它们的工作。但是，当孟德斯鸠通过对政府形式的分类运用纯粹演绎的方式推导出其国家理论重要一部分时；当他把专制形式的政府建立在恐惧之上，把君主形式建立在荣耀之上，把共和形式建立在美德之上时，这些位于演绎之前的归纳虽然最肤浅且最没有条理，却能够很轻易地被所有人理解。有关专制的理论是基于对希腊城邦暴君或罗马皇帝的说明；至于共和理论，则是基于对小面积的古代自由国家和瑞士州的说明；被浓缩成李嘉图或马克思之价值理论——这是一个真正的演绎典型——的无意识体验的财富，任何对他们的说明给予理解性阅读的人都必定能够明白。贝姆-巴威克、这位奥地利经济学派主要的阐释者之一在其名为《利息(*Kapitalzin*)》的作品——据称该作品是纯演绎性的——中说，该书所依据的事实全部是根据对展现在我们每个人面前的、普通日常生活进行简单的、非正式的观察获得的。

社会学——包括法律社会学——也必须是一门观察的科学。一个半世纪之前写过三个单词“法律的精神”作为其书书名的人甚至早在那个时代就在其自己的精神中探寻法律的社会学。那时孟德斯鸠甚至为此忙碌二十载，孜孜不倦地在其旅行途中收集事实，并且同时也是一名不知疲倦的读者。他的书不是一个学者的作品，而是一个贵族浅显、安排欠佳、条理不够明晰的作品，而且就其规模而言整部作品被设计得过于宏大，但尽管如此，它还

altogether too magnificent, it is nevertheless an inexhaustible source of stimulation and instruction, and it would be well worth the effort to avail oneself of the resources of modern science for the purpose of investigating the innumerable problems which he touched upon and disposed of but practically never answered.

We are dealing here not with history of literature nor with methodology but with a method of the sociology of law. The most important question which our time must solve is, what phenomena should the sociologist concern himself with, and how should he gather the facts which he needs in order to understand and explain them? The social phenomena in the legal sphere, which are of importance for a scientific understanding of law, are first of all the facts of the law themselves, i. e. usage, which assigns to each member of the human associations his position and his tasks, the relations of domination and of possession, agreements, articles of association, dispositions by last will and by other means, and succession. To these must be added the legal proposition, considered only as a fact, i. e. with reference to its origin and effect, not with reference to its practical application and interpretation, finally, all social forces, which lead to the creation of law. These are the phenomena that the sociologist must keep in mind, and he must collect the facts that give rise to these phenomena, and explain them.

In the past legal science has dealt with only one of these phenomena in an exhaustive manner, i. e. with the legal proposition. The others it has merely touched upon. And the facts which it adduced for the purpose of getting an understanding of, and explaining, the legal propositions were taken exclusively from history and ethnology. What we have of true, theoretical science of law is either historical or ethnological. Basically however even ethnological science is historical, for it is based on the proposition that the law of all nations has passed through approximately the same stages of development, and that therefore the law of peoples of a lower stage of development, with which the ethnological study of law concerns itself, corresponds, in its main outlines at least, to the past of the law of all other peoples.

Undoubtedly the chief function of the history of law is to supply the subject matter for the sociology of law. But this is not, pri-

是一个取之不尽的激励与指导之源，它很值得人们去努力利用这个现代科学资源，以便研究他们遇到的、处理的但实际上从未能回答的无数问题。

我们此处讨论的既不是文献史，也不是方法论，而是法律社会学的一种方法。我们这个时代必须要解决的最重要的问题在于：什么现象是社会学家应该关注的？为了理解和解释此类现象他该如何收集他需要的事实？对于科学理解法律具有重要意义的法律领域内的社会现象，首先是法律本身的事实，即习用，它为人类联合体每个成员分配位置和任务，然后还包括支配关系和占有关系、协议、联合体章程、遗嘱以及其他方式的财产处分、继承等。除此之外，还必须加上法律命题——法律命题必须仅仅被视为一个事实，即，关于其起源和效果，不是关于其实际应用和解释，最终指向的是，导致法律创造的所有社会力量。这些是社会学家必须谨记的现象，他还必须收集引发这些现象的事实，并解释它们。

过去，法学以一种详尽的方式仅讨论这些现象中的一个，即法律命题。其余的现象，法学仅仅触及而已。为了理解和解释这些法律命题而引据的事实毫无例外地取自历史和文化人类学。我们拥有的真实的、理论性的法律科学或是历史的或是文化人类学的。然而，甚至文化人类学基本上也是历史的，因为它基于这样的命题：所有民族的法律都经历了近乎同样的法律阶段，因此，处于低级发展阶段的民族的法律——法律的文化人类学研究会关注它——至少就其主要梗概而言，与所有其他民族法律的过去相对应。

毫无疑问，法律史的主要功能是为法律社会学提供题材。但

marily, a question of the history of the legal proposition, of the history of the sources, or of the history of legal doctrine, but of the history of legal institutions. No serious legal historian believes today that he can present the whole law of a period of time that is past on the basis of the legal propositions that have been handed down, e. g. that he can present the state of the law of Rome at the time of the Twelve Tables on the basis of these Twelve Tables even if they had been preserved in their entirety, or the whole law of the Salic Franks on the basis of the *Lex Salica*, or the law of the Saxon countries on the basis of the *Sachsenspiegel*. He is bent upon gaining a first-hand knowledge of the legal institutions on the basis of a study of the legal document. Yet even the legal document will not enable one to get a perfect picture of the law of the past. It speaks only of contracts, legal relations, and decisions that have been embodied in legal documents; it is silent as to the parol legal transaction and as to the great majority of legal relations, which have been the occasion neither of a document nor of a law-suit. About the legal form of the family, of the system of landholding, of the affairs of everyday life, which would be of vast importance for the understanding of the spirit and of the order of the whole life of the past, we shall not be able to learn much from the legal document. Very often the ability to interpret a picture on an ancient vase would be of much greater value to the legal historian. It is true, in modern times the ability to read between the lines of the traditional material, to spell out of a given word everything that it presupposes, has increased in a most fearsome fashion, but it cannot compensate for the absence of a tradition. The information which could have been obtained only by direct observation is lost to posterity — perhaps forever.

Great though these difficulties may be, the chief function of the history of law, as the founders of the Historical School have pointed out in their day, must be to show that the legal propositions and the legal institutions are growing out of the life of the people, out of the social and economic constitution as a whole. For the sociology of law it is of value only in so far as it is successful in doing this. The various legal

是,这主要不是法律命题史的问题,不是渊源史的问题,或是法律学说史的问题,而是法律制度史的问题。今天,没有任何一位严肃的法律史学家认为,他可以基于已经流传下来的法律命题介绍出过去一段时期内的所有法律,例如,他无法基于《十二铜表法》——即使它们保存完好——介绍出《十二铜表法》时期罗马法的状态,无法基于《萨利克法典》介绍出萨利克·法兰克人的所有法律,无法基于《萨克森法典》介绍出萨克森国家的法律。他基于对法律文件的研究致力于获得法律制度的第一手资料。然而法律文件并不能让一个人获得对过去法律的完美图景,它仅提及契约、法律关系、已经体现在法律文件中的裁决;对于口头交易、既未体现在书面文件又未衍生出法律诉讼的大部分的法律关系则不会谈到。关于家庭的法律形式、土地所有制度的法律形式、日常生活事务的法律形式——这些对于研究过去整个生活的风气和秩序具有非常重要的意义,我们不能从法律文件中获悉更多的东西。一般说来,解释一幅关于古代花瓶画的能力比法律史学家具有更大的价值。的确,在现代,解释传统材料的言外之意的能力,清楚解释某给定单词所应予阐明之一切的能力,已经以一种非常可怕的方式增长,但是它仍不能补偿传统的缺失。只能通过直接观察获得的信息,对于后世而言是失传了——或许是永远失传。

尽管这些困难可能比较巨大,但是法律史的主要功能,如同历史法学派的创始人在他们那个时代曾经指出过的那样,必定表明,法律命题和法律制度正从民族的生活中成长起来,从作为一个整体的社会和经济构造中成长起来。对于法律社会学而言,仅仅因为它在这方面做得成功,所以它才有价值。各种各样的法律

propositions as such, the legal institutions divorced from their presuppositions, have no information to convey. If there is a unifying regularity in the phenomena of legal life, to discover and make a presentation of which is the function of sociology, it can be found only in the fact that legal life is conditioned upon the social and economic constitution; if there is a legal development which takes place according to certain laws, it can be recognized and presented only in connection with the whole social and economic development. The sociology of law therefore will not draw its materials from legal antiquities but from social and economic history.

The results of practical juristic science are equally important for the sociology of law. Every technique is, at the same time, the beginning of a true science; and this applies to practical juristic science also. In order to acquire dominion over nature, man strives to understand the laws of nature; and in order to gain mastery, over life as a jurist, he must know life. The practical jurist of course deals primarily with the norms for decision. But since the latter arise directly from the social formations, or must be referred to the social formations, they cannot enter into his consciousness in any other way, and cannot be presented by him in any other way, than in connection with these formations. It is impossible to teach the law of the family without describing the family; to explain the law of things (*Sachenrecht*) without stating what kinds of rights in things are found in life; to state the law of contracts without stating the content of the contracts that are being entered into. And together with the norms which it state practical juristic science must present a picture of the society in which these norms are to have validity, and this picture is being drawn by men who have devoted their lives to the juristic study of society, and who ought to possess that fine sense of the reality of things which we admire in the ancient Roman jurists, in Bartolus, in many a jurist of the most recent years. In this sense a famous Roman has called jurisprudence *divinarum atque humanarum retum notitia*. It is the function of law teaching to provide for the *cupida legum inventus*, who do not yet

命题本身、从其先决条件中分离出来的法律习俗都没有任何要传达的信息。如果在法律生活的现象中存在一个统一的规律性来解释和介绍社会学功能之所在,那么它只能在如下事实中出现:法律生活取决于社会和经济体制;如果有按照特定规律呈现的法律发展,那么它只可能在整个社会和经济发展方面被认识和提出。因此,法律社会学不是从古代的风俗习惯中提取素材,而是从社会和经济的历史中提取素材。

实用法学的成果对于法律社会学而言同样重要。每一个技巧同时都是一门真正学问的开始;这也适用于实用法学。为了获得对自然的支配,人类努力理解自然规律;为了获得像法学家那样对生活的掌握,他必须了解生活。实用法学家首要处理的当然是裁判规范。但是既然后者直接从社会构造中产生,或者必定涉及到社会构造,则除了与这些构造相关的方式外,它们不可能以任何其他方式考虑他自己的意识,也不可能由他以任何其他方式提出。教授家庭法却不描述家庭,这是不可能的;解释物权法(*Sachenrecht*)却不说明生活中可以见到哪些种物权,也是不可能的;介绍契约法却不说明正在缔结的契约的内容,同样是不可能的。另外,实用法学与其表述的规范一道,必定呈现一幅社会图景,其中,这些规范将会生效,并且,这幅图景正在由那些将其毕生奉献于社会法律研究的人以及那些应当对于事物的现实性拥有敏锐感觉的人绘制——那些人都是在古罗马时期、巴特鲁斯时期以及最近一些年我们所敬仰的法学家。在此意义上,一个著名的罗马人把法学称作是关于神之事物与人之事物的知识。为渴望法学创造但还不了解生活的人提供要成为法学家必定要从

know life, a substitute for the study of life at first hand which one must engage in in order to become a jurist, and also to provide them with the results of such observations as they never would institute themselves—observations that will widen their horizon and refine their sensibilities.

Direct actual observation of human relations of a legal nature, universalization of the results of this observation and the appertaining norms for decision— these are the scientific elements in juristic science. To this extent, juristic science actually is a morphology of the legal formations of social life. It presents the state in all the ramifications of its activity, the forms of the family, ownership and *real* rights, the contracts and the other forms of the economic distribution of goods, the organization of commerce, of industry, of the trades, of agriculture, of the mining industry, the fate of property after the death of the owner. The systematism (*Systematik*) of juristic science organizes all of this material, classifies and arranges it, separating the related from the unrelated The content of the much maligned " general part," too, is scientific in its nature; for by analyzing the composite complicated legal institutions into its constituent parts it reveals their inner structure and creates an accurate and at the same time flexible scientific terminology. The jurists, being under the limitation of practical interests, are concerned with social morphology and with *Systematik* from a point of view altogether different from that of the scientific investigator. The latter however is nevertheless relieved of a great deal of hard work by the fact that all he need do is to arrange the results of the observations of others for his own purposes.

It is true, practical juristic science, in the first place, deals only with legal propositions that belong to a certain system of positive law. And for this very reason, after it has completed the discussion of the legal propositions and has begun the discussion of the relations of life upon which the latter are based, it contents itself with a presentation of the morphology of a society which is governed by a certain system of positive law. But the human relations, upon which a presentation of the law must be based, are independent of the legal propositions. The state and its instrumentalities, persons, ownership, *real* rights, contracts, succession, are found everywhere; and among peoples of an approximately identical civilization and of an approximately identical stage of economic development, they are found in a form which, in addition to some diversities, exhibits a series of common traits. It is

事的第一手生活研究的替代物,同时也为他们提供那些他们从未进行过的观察——这种观察将会拓宽他们的视野、改善他们的感受力——的结果,这是法律教学的功能。

对一种法律性质的人类关系进行的直接的实际观察,这种观察结果的一般化以及附属的裁判规范——这些都是法学中的科学元素。在此程度上,法学实际上是社会生活的法律信息的形态学。它对其活动的所有衍生的结果、家庭形式、所有权和物权、契约和商品经济流通的其他形式、商业组织形式、工业组织、贸易组织、农业组织、矿业组织、所有权人死后其财产的命运给出了说明。法学的体系化(*Systematik*)将其所有的材料组织起来,并将其分类管理,同时将它与无关的事物分离开来。遭人诟病的”总论部分”的内容就其性质而言具有科学性;因为通过把综合复杂的法律制度分解成其构成部分,法学将会展现其内部结构,并创造出准确的但同时又是灵活的科学形态学。法学家,受实际利益所限,总是从一个完全不同于科学研究者所持的角度关心社会形态学和体系化。然而,后者还是能够从大量的艰苦工作中有所解脱,因为,他需要做的一切只是为其自身目的整理其他人的观察结果。

的确,实用法学首先只处理属于特定实证法律制度的法律命题。正因为这个原因,在它完成对法律命题的讨论,并开始讨论法律命题所基于的生活关系时,它满足于对受到特定实证法律制度支配的社会形态学的描述。但是法律的描述必须基于其上的人类关系,独立于法律命题。国家及其执行部门、人、所有权、物权、契约、继承无处不在,在近似同一文明以及近似同一经济发展阶段的民族中,它们呈现为一种形式——除了一些多样性外,该形式展现了一系列的共同特征。因此,描述所有的这些法律关系

quite in order therefore to describe all these legal relations without reference to any system of positive law, as has been done for some time in economics in the case of economic legal relations. For this reason, I think, it is possible to evolve a general legal science, which is based, just like economics, not on a society governed by a certain positive legal system, but on human society as such. The first and foremost function of the sociological science of law is to present an exposition of the common elements in the legal relations without reference to the positive law that governs them, and to study the elements peculiar to each relation with reference to their causes and effects. In the field of public law, of *Staatsrecht* (public law in the narrow sense), of criminal and of procedural law, much work of this kind has already been done. In the field of private law, little or nothing has been done.

Nevertheless it is particularly in the field of private law that the juristic labors of the jurists of the Continental common law have prepared the way for the sociological study of law. And they have done this in a way that can be fittingly described only by the epithet "magnificent." The juristic science of the Continental common law was itself the heir of a never interrupted, international intellectual activity extending over a period of two thousand years or more. Its basis was the *corpus iuris civilis*, which, in spite of all its defects, was a great achievement. Its roots are to be found in the juristic science of the Roman *pontifices* in prehistoric times. Since that time untold generations of jurists have been bestowing creative labor upon it, the pupil becoming the successor of his teacher both in developing the law and in teaching it, each generation receiving the benefit of the work of its predecessor and continuing to build on the foundation laid by the latter. Accordingly an unbroken chain of oral tradition unites the professors of Constantinople with those of Berytus, the compilers of Justinian's code with each one of the *prudentes* of the days of primitive Rome. It is being understood more and more clearly from day to day that this juristic science of the Roman jurist was, at all times, connected by an unbroken continuity with everything that had been accomplished in this sphere in antiquity, was always ready to appropriate the institutions of other peoples, and in its palmy days, which extend into the third century of our era, was able to weld these elements

而不提及任何实证法律制度是相当可行的，正如就经济法律关系而言，一段时期以来经济学中所发生的情形那样。因此，我认为，使一般法学——正如经济学一样不是基于由特定实证法律制度支配下的社会，而是基于人类社会本身——向前发展，是可能的。法律社会学的首要功能是在不涉及到支配它们的实证法的情形下，对法律关系中的共同要素给予解释，并研究每一种关系关于其原因和结果的独特要素。在公法领域、*Staatsrecht*（狭义的公法）领域、刑法、诉讼法领域，许多此类的工作已经被做过了。在私法领域，此类工作完成得极少或根本没有。

尽管如此，特别是在私法领域，欧陆共同法法学家的法学工作已经为法律社会学研究开辟了道路。并且用来描述他们所采取的方式的恰当形容词只能是“宏大的”。欧陆共同法的法学本身就是长达2000年或更长时期从未中断的、国际智力活动的继承者。它的基础是《民法大全》，后者尽管有这样那样的缺点，但仍然是一个伟大的成就。欧陆共同法法学的根可以在史前时期罗马的祭司法学中发现。从那时起，数不清的一代代法学家为它贡献了创造性劳动，在发展法律和教授法律方面，学生变成了其老师的继承者，每一代都继受先辈劳动的优秀成果，并在其先辈奠立的基础上继续建设。因此，一个不曾中断的耳口相传的链条将君士坦丁堡与柏利图斯两地的教授联合起来，将优士丁尼法典的编纂者与原始罗马时期的法学家联合起来。罗马法学家的法学一直以来都是通过一个未曾中断的连续性与古代在此领域所完成的一切相连，并总是愿意学用其他民族的制度，在其法学直至公元3世纪全盛时代的，它能使这些元素融入其制度体系当

into its system as an organic whole. Only that which was received during the decline of the Empire could no longer be assimilated. So in the *corpus iuris civilis*, all the results of a thousand years of ancient legal development, gathered, as it were, in a focus, were transmitted to the Middle Ages. This was followed by the work of the glossators and the postglossators, who in turn were followed by the great French jurists of the sixteenth and seventeenth centuries, by the learned and astute Dutch legal scholars, by the juristic science of the German jurists from the days of Ulrich Zasius. Thus almost all civilized peoples of Europe took part in its creation, and a structure arose which is unique in the history of law and without a peer in other spheres of intellectual life. International participation did not cease until the nineteenth century, when the national codifications brought about a practical juristic science whose sole concern was national law. In Germany, however, the Historical School of jurisprudence is still making the best possible use of the talent entrusted to it, and so the international science of law is enjoying a new, late classical period.

But if the teaching of Bartolus and Baldus was quite different from that of the glossators, that of Stryck and Lauterbach quite different from that of Ulrich Zasius, that of Windscheid and Dernburg quite different from that of Vangerow, the reason for these differences lies in the fact that different times made different demands. The differences are so great that one can almost say that each period was dealing with an entirely different subjectmatter. But if one looks at the connecting links that connect the successive schools, one marvels at the gradual, methodical transition, at the way in which each generation based its teaching directly upon that of the preceding one. It was not theories that suggested the trends and methods to the jurists; the needs created the trend, the method, and the appertaining theory. The necessity of adjusting itself again and again to the changing times gave to the juristic science of the jurists of the Continental common law its extraordinary wealth of ideas, and the fact that it was the law of a considerable part of the civilized world, where its function was to serve the most manifold needs, gave it a remarkable flexibility and expressiveness.

中，并成为一个有机的整体。只有那些在帝国衰落时期接受的东西可能不再被吸收消化。所以，在《民法大全》中，一千年古代法律发展的所有成果——宛如被收集在一个中心范围内——流传到中世纪。接下来是注释法学派以及后注释法学派的作品，他们反过来又被16世纪和17世纪伟大的法学家、被博学而敏锐的荷兰法律学者、被从乌尔里希·扎休斯时代开始的德国法学家的法学所承继。这样，几乎所有欧洲的文明民族都参与了法学的创造，并且一个在法律史上独一无二的、在智力活动的其他领域没有类似物的结构产生了。国际参与一直到19世纪才停止，当时民族法典化运动带来了实用法学，后者仅关心民族法。然而，在德国，法学的历史学派还在尽其所能地利用其天赋，因此国际法学正在享受一个新的、晚近的古典时期。

但是，如果巴特鲁斯和巴尔杜斯的学说十分不同于注释法学派的学说，施特吕克和劳特巴赫的学说十分不同于乌尔里希·扎休斯的学说，温德沙伊德和德恩伯格的学说十分不同于凡格罗的学说，则这些不同的理由在于这样的事实：不同时代有不同的要求。这些不同如此巨大以至于有人几乎会说，每一个时期处理一个完全不同的主题。但是如果他看看联结后继学派的联系纽带，他就会惊奇于渐进的、有条不紊的传继，惊奇于每一代直接将其学说建立在其前代学说之基础上的方式。表明法学家的倾向与方法的不是理论；需要创造倾向、方法以及从属的理论。一再调整自身以适应时代更迭的必要性为欧陆共同法的法学家法学带来了惊人的思想财富，它是相当一部分文明世界的法律——在这些地方，法学的功能是为最多重层次的需要服务——这一事实给予它一种非凡的适应性和表达力。

For this reason the juristic science of the Romanist jurists of western and of central Europe never was merely the science of a system of national law, much less of Roman law, but to a certain degree a science of law, a general science of law. It has created the most important presuppositions for a sociology of law which is not bound by the limitations of a given system of law, or of a given people, or by the requirements of customary observance, or usage. It has in the first place created a fixed juristic terminology and, over and above that, a juristic language which is readily understood by every jurist, for the jurists of all civilized peoples learn Roman law from text-books written by the jurists of the Continental common law school. In Germany the Germanists, particularly those of Beseler' s school, have contributed much to the development of juristic science. At the same time they have made German law a part of the juristic science of the Romanist school. They have employed its systematism, its technique, its terminology, and thereby they have actually demonstrated that it can subserve not only a Romanist science of law but any science of law. And if one removes from the German common law monographs or from the general works on the pandect law everything that might look like an interpretation of a text of the sources, there still would remain a scientific achievement which can be made the basis of the study of any system of law, not only of the Continental common law.

The sociology of law therefore must continue its work on the basis of the juristic science of the Continental common law. It must by no means be confused with "*allgemeine Rechtslehre*," or with *Rechtsenzyklopädie*, as it is called. It does not present formalistic abstractions from the juristic science of systems of national law, but its living content. Nor does it include true interpretation the legal basis of juristic science, however, must be shown as well as the form which the institutions have assumed in the course of the administration of justice and of life.

May I be permitted to illustrate by an example the fitness of the juristic science of the Continental common law to constitute the basis for a general science of law? The English doctrine that informal contracts are binding only when supported by consideration is one of the peculiarities of English law that a Continental jurist does not readily understand. Only recently a German work on legal history compared

因此,中、西欧罗马派法学家的法学从来不仅仅是一个民族法律制度的科学,更不是罗马法制度的科学,而是某种程度上的法律科学、一般性的法律科学。它已经为法律社会学创造了最重要的先决条件,此种先决条件不受特定法律制度、特定民族、惯例或习惯要件之限制的约束。它首先创立了确定的法律术语学,除此之外,还创造了易于被每个法学家理解的法律语言,因为所有文明民族的法学家都从欧陆共同法学派所写的教科书中学习罗马法。在德国,德意志主义者,特别是那些贝塞勒学派的人,已经为法学的发展贡献良多。同时,他们已经让德国法成为罗马派法学的一部分。他们运用了自身的体系化方法、自身的法律技术、自身的术语学,因此他们实际上已经证明,它不仅可以服务于罗马派法律科学,也可以服务于任何法律科学。如果有人去除掉德国共同法的专论或研究潘德克顿法中任何看似对原始文献的原文进行解释的一般作品,则还会余留下可作为任何法律制度——不仅仅是欧陆共同法制度——研究基础的科学成就。

法律社会学因此必须继续根据欧陆共同法法学来继续其工作。它决不会因所谓的"法的一般理论"或所称的法学概论而迷惑。它不是从民族法律制度的法学中,而是从民族法律制度活的内容中提出形式主义的抽象概念;它也不包括真实的解释;然而,法学的法律基础以及在司法与生活过程中习俗制度所采取的形式必定会得以揭示。

请允许我举一个例子来证明欧陆共同法的法学构成一般法律科学之基础的适切性。非要式契约仅在提供对价时才有拘束力的学说是英国法的独特特征之一,这是欧陆法学家不容易理解的。只是最近,一部研究法律史的德国人的作品才把罗马人的无

the Roman innominate contracts to the English contracts for good consideration. This, of course, is altogether beside the mark. Consideration and *res* in the sense of Roman law are things of a totally different nature, and the informal contracts of English law are not "*real*" contracts but "consensual" contracts. But an informal contract creates a legal obligation according to English law only when each party has purchased the obligation of the other party by incurring a detriment. If the debtor who owes one hundred pounds pays ten shillings one day before the debt is due at a place other than that provided for in the contract, an informal agreement by the creditor to remit the remainder is binding; for payment before the due day or at another place may be a detriment to him. But if he pays ninety-nine pounds at the time and place provided for, a formal release in writing and under seal is required, for in that case there is no consideration. The situation is different in the case of a loan for use (*commodatum*) or of a bailment (*depositum*), and also in case of a commission (*mandatum*), where the mandatary receives a res from the *mandator* for the purpose of executing the commission (e. g. to carry it to some other place). All of these are instances of gratuitous bailment and there is no consideration. The recipient is liable for failure to return in an action for damages (*assumpsit*). But is he liable also for a blameworthy defective performance of his promise or for lack of the care provided for in the contract? In this case the English say that the consideration lies in the detriment which the person who delivers the thing suffers, in asmuch as, by giving possession of the *res* to the recipient at the latter's request, he surrenders direct control over it. But this amounts merely to saying that the *res* takes the place of consideration. The loan for use, the bailment, and the commission (*mandatum*) connected with delivery of possession of a *res* are "*real*" contracts in English law, for the obligation is based on delivering and receiving a *res*. And Pollock in fact admits that where the request is not made by the person receiving the *res* but by the person delivering it, i. e. in the case of the *depositum* and the *mandatum*, an element of the contract, the request, is

名契约比作是有合适对价的英国契约。当然，这完全没有说到点子上。对价和罗马法意义上的物二者是具有完全不同性质的东西，英国法上的非要式契约不是“要物”契约，而是“诺成”契约。但是按照英国法，只有当每一方当事人通过承受不利而换得另一方的义务时，非要式契约才创设了一个法律义务。如果欠 100 英镑的债务人在债务到期之前的某天在合同约定之外的某地支付了 10 先令，则债权人免除剩余债务的非要式协议是有拘束力的；因为在到期日之前或在非约定地的支付对他来说可能是不利的。但是如果他在合同约定的时间和地点支付了 99 先令，正式免除债务就需要采取书面形式并盖章，因为那种情况下，不存在对价。在使用借贷（*commodatum*）或寄托（*depositum*），以及在委托（*mandatum*）——受托人（*mandator*）从委托人处接受某物以便执行某项任务（比如将该物送至他处）——的情形下，情况有所不同。所有的这些都是无偿寄托的例子，并且也不存在对价。接受人在损害赔偿之诉（*assumpsit*）中对于未能返还原物负有责任。但是，对于一个可责的、有缺陷的允诺履行或未能尽到契约约定的注意义务，他同样负有责任吗？这种情况下，英国人说，对价存在于交付标的物之人所遭受的不利中，因为他应接受人的要求把物的占有转移给后者，他让与了对物的直接支配。但是这不过是等于说，物取代了对价。使用借贷、寄托、委托（*mandatum*）都与物的占有交付相关，这些在英国法中都是“要物”契约，因为契约义务基于交付和接收一个物。事实上，波洛克承认，在要求并非由接受物之人而是由交付之人作出——即，在寄托和委托——的情形下，作为契约的要素，此种要求是拟制的，以便让法院找到对价。

supplied by a fiction in order to enable the court to find consideration. No greater difficulty than this is involved in stating this refined and difficult doctrine in the language and concepts of the juristic science of the Continental common law.

Where the scientific treatment of law is freed from national limitations, the mere restoration of international activity in the field of law bids fair to yield abundant returns. No science has ever grown great in national seclusion; it requires not only the preparatory work of all preceding generations, but also the cooperation of the whole contemporary generation. One nation, even the greatest and most gifted, is too small to be able to produce a science single-handed and relying solely on its own inner resources, much less a science of law. Consider how the French, the English, and the Italians were lost in the bog of a wretched system of casuistry and exegesis when they limited themselves to their own national law, and on principle rejected all suggestions from without, in spite of the fact that they have thousands of times demonstrated their high and great endowment for scientific activity, particularly in the field of law, and are demonstrating it today by the great progress they have been making in the science of law in recent years, ever since they gave over their national provincialism. Does not the history of juristic science in the countries whose law has been codified preach this doctrine most impressively? Nowhere else is the connection between rise and decline on the one hand, and opening and closing of the border to foreign suggestion on the other, more strikingly apparent.

It is true, the codes brought about the displacement of the international scientific activity of the Continental common law and the rise of a national practical and a national theoretical science of law. This however is a transient phase of development, which is largely being superseded today. In spite of dissimilarities in legislation, the institutions of civilized nations are so closely related as to permit of a common practical and scientific morphology and creation of norms. And for these, too, the scientific work of the Continental common law constitutes an excellent basis. For the law of the Austrian and Prussian codes a new era began when it came into contact with the scientific work of the Continental common law through the work of Wächter on the private law of Württemberg. Wächter was the first to demon-

在用欧陆共同法的法学语言和概念表述这种精致的、难解的学说时,再没有比这个更大的困难了。

在对法律的科学分析不受民族限制约束的地方,法律领域内单单国际活动的恢复就有希望产出丰厚的回报。没有一种科学曾经在民族隔离中长大;它不仅要求所有先辈的准备性工作,还要求所有当代人的行动。一个民族,即使是最伟大、最有天赋的民族,也太小了,无法仅依靠自身内部资源,独自创造出一门科学,更别提单独创造出法学。尽管法国人、英国人、意大利人曾经数千次证明他们在科学活动方面——特别是在法学方面——非凡而伟大的天赋,并且自从他们放弃民族性的地方观念后,今天还在通过他们最近一些年在法学方面取得的伟大进步继续证明这种天赋,但还是想想当他们把自己限制在他们本民族的法律中,并且原则上反对所有来自外部的建议的时候,他们如何在诡辩与注释之糟糕体系的沼泽中迷失。在那些已经法典化的国家中,法学历史的宣讲不是使这种学说令人印象最为深刻吗?一方面,没有任何一个别的地方存在兴起和衰落间的这种联系,另一方面,外来建议之边界的开合也变得更加惊人地显而易见。

的确,法典使得欧陆共同法的国际科学活动被民族实用法学和理论法学的兴起所置换。然而,这是一个过渡性的发展阶段,它在今天很大程度上已经被取代了。尽管立法相异,但文明民族的习俗制度还是如此紧密相关,以至于允许有一个共同的实践性、科学性的形态学和规范的创造。而且,欧陆共同法的学术著作也为它们建立了一个极好的基础。对于奥地利法典和普鲁士法典的法律而言,当它通过韦希特研究符腾堡私法的作品而接触到欧陆共同法的学术著作时,一个新时代开始了。韦希特第一个证明,

strate that a local or particular system of law does not necessarily preclude general legal science; for legal science is not primarily concerned with legal propositions but with the formations of life, of which one indeed takes the measure by means of legal propositions, but which one does not arrive at by interpretation of statutes. Unger and Koch have successfully applied this principle to the law of their respective codes, while the work of Zachariae has long ago done the preparatory work for its application to the law of the French code. The scientific labor of jurists in connection with the German Civil Code moves along the same lines. It would be absolutely erroneous to attempt to justify this procedure by saying that these codes are based on Roman law. Not Roman law, but the *usus modernus*, constitutes the basis of the Prussian Landrecht, the French Civil Code, and the Austrian Civil Code. The German Civil Code is based chiefly on the pandects of the nineteenth century. The true reason is the fact that for the presentation of the law of the codes a considerable part of the Continental common law morphology and creation of norms could be utilized without more ado; this was not the morphology and creation of norms of a certain legal system but the morphology and creation of norms of the society of the civilized nations of Europe.

When Count Thun undertook to improve the pedantic and antiquated teaching of law in Austria, he devoted one half of the time given to the study of law, the first two years of the whole *quatriennium* to the study of Roman law, of German law, and of ecclesiastical law. The result was an immediate undreamt of advancement of legal science in Austria. It is true, he did not, by his action, cause the historical basis of the Austrian law to be taught, but he opened the door to an invasion by German science. The results of the juristic thinking of the last three centuries in Germany were given academic form and literary expression in the science of the history of Roman and of German law, of the Continental common law, and of German private law; and this German science, which had been driven out of Austria as a

一个地方性或特殊[1]法律制度并不必然排斥一般法学；因为法律科学主要不是关注法律命题，而是关注生活的塑造，那是人们可以通过法律命题对其加以估量的，却不是通过制定法的解释而得到的。昂格尔和科赫曾成功地将此原则适用于他们各自的法典法当中，而扎哈里埃很久之前就为将它适用于《法国民法典》之法做过预备性的工作。与《德国民法典》相关的法学家的科学研究按照相同的路径进行着。试图通过辩称这些法典都是基于罗马法而为此等过程的辩护绝对是错误的。不是罗马法而是学说汇纂现代应用学派构成了《普鲁士邦法》、《法国民法典》以及《奥地利民法典》的基础。《德国民法典》主要基于 19 世纪的潘德克顿法。真正的理由是如下事实：对于法典法的表达而言，相当一部分欧陆共同法形态和规范创造，可以直接干脆地被采用；这不是某法律制度的形态和规范的创造，而是欧洲文明民族之社会的形态和规范的创造。

当图恩伯爵在奥地利着手改进迂腐、过时的法律教学时，他花了一半时间用在法律研究上，整个的四年规划头两年是对罗马法、德国法以及教会法研究。结果超乎想象，奥地利法学立即获得了发展。的确，他没有通过其行为讲授奥地利法律的历史基础，但他开启了一扇德国科学得以闯入的门。在德国，最近三个世纪法学思维的结果在罗马历史学和德国法学、欧陆共同法科学、德国私法科学方面被赋予了学术形式和文学表达；这种德国科学——在 19 世纪初由于奥地利私法的法典化而曾遭到驱逐

〔1〕 在这里，指的是区别于欧洲大陆上一般性的欧陆共同法。

result of the codification of the Austrian private law at the beginning of the nineteenth century, victoriously returned to Austria at the time of the reform of legal studies. The lectures on legal historical subjects, on the pandects, and on German private law made up for the lack of lectures on legal science for the simple reason that they contained all the science of law that existed in Germany. If Austria was anxious to give to its young jurists something better than the paltry instruction in statute law and in interpretation which before that time had flourished at Austrian universities, if Austria actually desired to give him instruction in legal science, the best it could do was to offer legal history, pandect law, and German private law.

As early as the last century Austin conceived the idea of a general legal science— I would say incidentally that the whole modern theory of norms is contained in his works— and he carried it out, only in part however, in his two works (*The Province of Jurisprudence Determined* and *Lectures on Jurisprudence*). His followers, chiefly Thomas Erskine Holland, Amos, and Salmond, attempted complete expositions of legal science which were to be independent of any definite system of law—Holland, in his *Elements of Jurisprudence*; Salmond, in the *Science of Law*. It is significant that both Austin and Amos perceived that the juristic science of the Romanist jurist affords a much more advantageous basis than that of the English jurists; for both made the former their point of departure. John Stuart Mill presents Austin's basic idea in an essay on the latter, and he does it much better than Austin ever did. I quote from his essay:

"The details of different legal systems are different, but there is no reason why the main classifications and heads of arrangement should not be the same. The facts of which law takes cognizance, though far from identical in all civilized societies, are sufficiently analogous to enable them to be arranged in the same cadres. The more general of the terms employed for legal purposes might stand for the same ideas, and be expounded by the same definitions, in systems otherwise different. The same terminology, nomenclature, and principle of

——在法律研究的改革时期胜利回归到奥地利。论及法律史主题、潘德克顿法以及德国私法的论文弥补了法学论文的缺失,原因很简单,它们包含了存在于德国的所有法学。如果奥地利急切地想给其年轻的科学家一些比制定法中以及在那之前曾在奥地利大学中盛行过的解释中微不足道的指导更好的东西,如果奥地利实际上渴望给他法学上的指导,那么它能做的最好的就是提供法律史、潘德克顿法以及德国私法典。

早在上个世纪,奥斯丁就意识到一般法学的思想——我想附带说一下,整个现代规范理论都被囊括在他的作品里,然而,他在他的两部作品(《法理学的范围》与《法理学讲演录》)里仅仅部分完成了它。他的追随者,主要是托马斯·厄斯金·霍兰德、阿莫斯、萨尔蒙德,他们试图完整阐释独立于任何明确法律制度的法学,霍兰德是在其《法理学的要素》、萨尔蒙德是在其《法律科学》中作此努力的。重要的是奥斯丁和阿莫斯都意识到,罗马派法学家的法学提供的基础比英国法学家的法学提供的基础有益得多。约翰·斯图亚特·密尔在一篇论及奥斯丁的论文中提及后者的基本思想,他做得比奥斯丁更好。下面一段话引自他的该篇论文:

“不同法律制度的细节是不同的,但是主要分类和排列的标题不相同就没有理由了。法律注意到的事实,尽管在所有文明社会中远非相同,但还是足够类似,以至于可以将它们以相同的基础结构来排列。在不同的法律制度中,基于法律目的而使用的更一般的术语可能代表同样的思想,可以被同样的定义来解释。使

arrangement, which would render one system of law definite and (in Bentham's language) cognoscible, would serve, with additions and variations in minor details, to render the same office for another."

This, it is true, is not the whole of sociological legal science. Austin and his followers ale formalists. In all their writings they do not concern themselves with living creations. They purpose to present only a general part in the sense of the German pandectists. And they are interested only in the forms of the legal relations, not in their content, not in the germinative powers of the development of law, nor in its unifying regularity. But it contains a part, at least, of the material which the practical science of law will be able to pass on to the sociological science of law.

得一种法律制度明确且(用边沁的话说)可知的同样的术语、专门用语、排列原则,作一些添加和细节上的变化,也可以为另外一种法律制度提供相同的功能。”

的确,这不是全部的社会学法学。奥斯丁及其追随者都是形式主义者。在他们所有的作品中,他们全都不关心有生命的创造。他们仅仅旨在提出德国潘德克顿主义者意义上的总论部分。而且,他们仅仅对法律关系的形式感兴趣,而不是对法律关系的内容、法律发展的原动力及其统一的规律性感兴趣,但是它至少包含一部分素材,那是法律的实践科学能够留给法律社会学的素材。

# XXI

# The Methods Of The Sociology Of Law

## II. The Study Of The Living Law

The reason why the dominant school of legal science so greatly prefers the legal proposition to all other legal phenomena as an object of investigation is that it tacitly assumes that the whole law is to be found in the legal propositions. It is assumed furthermore that since, at the present time, all legal propositions are to be found in the statutes, where they are readily accessible to anyone, all that is necessary in order to get a knowledge of the law of the present time is to gather the material from the statutes, to ascertain the content of this material by one's own individual interpretation, and to utilize this interpretation for the purposes of juristic literature and judicial decision. Occasionally one meets with the further idea that legal propositions may arise independently of statute. In Germany the usual belief is that they can be found in juristic literature; in France, in judicial decisions. "Customary law," on the other hand, in the prevailing view, is so unimportant that no effort is being put forth to ascertain its content by scientific methods, much less to create methods for its investigation. Only the teachers of, and writers on, commercial law still concern themselves with usage, in this case, with business custom. This explains why the efforts of those who are carrying on research in law at the present time are bent upon ascertaining the legal propositions of the past, which are not so

# 第二十一章 法律社会学的方法

## 2. 活法之研究

为什么最有影响力的法学流派如此偏爱将法律命题而不是任何其他法律现象作为研究对象,原因在于它心照不宣地认定,在法律命题中将会发现全部法律。而且还认定,既然当前在制定法中将会发现所有法律命题,这些法律命题容易为任何人所获得,那么,为了获得对当前法律的认识,所需要做的一切就是从制定法中收集素材,并根据个人自身的独特解释,确定这个材料的内容,然后为了法学文献和司法裁判的目的利用该解释。偶尔,人们会碰到另外的见解:法律命题也可能独立于制定法而产生。在德国,通常的意见是,在法学文献中能够发现法律命题;在法国,通常的意见是,在司法裁判中能够发现法律命题。另一方面,按照主流观点,"习惯法"如此不重要,以至于人们并未试图借助科学方法探求它的内容,更不要说为其研究创造方法了。只有商法的教师与作者还在关注惯例——此种语境下,指的是商业习惯。这解释了为什么研究当下法律的那些人,其成就都是致力于探知过去的法律命题——这些对于我们而言不如现代制定法所

readily accessible to us as those that are contained in modern statutes. It is believed that the scientific result of the labor expended upon the study of the law of the past consists not only in a knowledge of the development of law, which of course means only the development of legal propositions, but also in an historical understanding of the law of the present; for the law, i. e. according to the tacit assumption the legal propositions of the present time, is rooted in the past. These, I take it, are the lines of thought on which the method of research in the field of law has hitherto been based.

But the statement that the whole law is not contained in the legal propositions applies to a much greater degree to the law that is in force today than to the law of the past. For the men who composed the Twelve Tables, the *Lex Salica*, and the *Sachsenspiegel* actually had a direct personal knowledge of the law of their own time, and their endeavor was to gather up this law with which they dealt, and to formulate it in legal propositions. This however does not apply, even approximately, to the most important part of the legal material with which the jurists of the present day are concerned, i. e. the codes. For in contrast to what once upon a time the jurists had in mind under all circumstances, vaguely at least, the compilers of the modern codes very often did not have the slightest intention whatever of stating the law of their own time and of their own community. They draw their legal material, first, from the compilation of Justinian, from which, self-evidently, they are likely to obtain reliable information on almost any other subject than the law of their own time, i. e. of the eighteenth or of the nineteenth century; secondly, from older statements of law, which, even if they met the requirements of their own time, do not meet those of the time of the legislator; thirdly, from juristic literature, which was chiefly concerned with the interpretation of older laws and of older codes, and, in any case, did not belong to the time of the code in question. The truth of this statement appears most clearly in the case of the German Civil Code, the sources of which have been almost exclusively text-books of pandect law, earlier German statutes and compilations of law, and foreign codifications. Accordingly our codes are uniformly adapted to a time much earlier than their own, and all the juristic technique in the world would be unable to extract the actual law of the present from it, for the simple

包含的法律命题那么容易理解。人们相信,花费在对过去法律进行研究上之劳动的科学成果不仅在于对法律发展——当然仅指法律命题的发展——有了认识,而且还在于对于过去法律有了历史方面的理解;因为法律——即,按照对过去法律命题心照不宣的认定——扎根于过去。在我理解,这些是迄今为止,法律领域内的研究方法据以作为基础的思维路径。

但是,并非所有的法律均包含在法律命题中,这种表述适用于当下现行法的程度要比适用于过去法的程度大得多。因为编撰《十二铜表法》、《萨克森法典》的人实际上对他们当时的法律都有直接的个人认识,他们谋求的就是总括这种他们要处理的法律,并用法律命题的形式予以系统阐述。然而,这并不——哪怕是近似——适用于当今法学家关注的法律材料最重要的部分,即法典。因为与从前法学家无论如何都会考虑到——至少是模模糊糊地想到——的东西大不相同的是,现代法典的编纂者经常没有对有关表述他们自身所处时代、所处社会之法律的任何东西给予丝毫的关注。他们首先从优士丁尼的法律汇编中提取法律素材;其次,他们从法律的古老表述——此种表述即使符合它最初被作出之时的要求,也不符合立法者所处那个时代(即 18 世纪、19 世纪)的要求——中提取法律素材;最后,他们从法学文献——主要关注古老法律、古老法典的解释,并且无论如何都不属于正在谈论的法典的时代——中提取素材。该表述的正确性似乎在《德国民法典》中体现得最为清楚,《德国民法典》的资料来源几乎完全是潘德克顿法的教科书,后者要早于德国制定法和法律的汇编以及外国的法典化。因此,我们的法典一律适应于比他们自己的法典早得多的时代,并且世界上所有的法律技术将无法从当今

reason that it is not contained therein. But the territory within which our codes are valid is so vast, the legal relations with which they deal are so incomparably richer, more varied, more subject to changes than they have ever been, that the mere idea of making a complete presentation in a code would be monstrous. To attempt to imprison the law of a time or of a people within the sections of a code is about as reasonable as to attempt to confine a stream wthin a pond. The water that is put in the pond is no longer a living stream but a stagnant pool, and but little water can be put in the pond. Moreover, if one considers that the living law had already overtaken and grown away from each one of these codes at the very moment the latter were enacted, and is growing away from them more and more every day, one cannot but realize the enormous extent of this as yet unplowed and unfurrowed field of activity which is being pointed out to the modern legal investigator.

It could not be otherwise. The legal propositions are not intended to present a complete picture of the state of the law. The jurist draws them up with a view to existing practical needs, and with a view to what he is interested in for practical reasons. He will not put forth the effort to formulate legal propositions with reference to matters that lie outside of his sphere of interest, perhaps for the sole reason that they are not within the jurisdiction of the courts before which he practices, or because they do not concern his clients. Since commercial law lay outside of the usual sphere of interest of the Roman jurist, we find that the commercial law of the Roman sources is utterly inadequate; and for the very same reason the Romans and, until quite recently, the modern jurists have very little to say about labor law. Even Eyke von Repgow did not deal with the law of cities and with the customs of manors because it lay outside of his immediate sphere of interest.

的现行法中提炼出来，仅仅因为其中并不包含法律技术。但是，我们的法典行之有效的领域如此广大，与曾经的法律关系相比，我们的法典要处理的法律关系更加无与伦比地丰富、更具多样性、更能适应变化，以至于在一个法典中做一个完整的表述，单单这种想法就显得比较怪异。努力将一个时代或一个民族的法律装进法典，成为后者的一部分，大概与将一股水流限制在一个池塘一样合理。[1] 被放入池塘的水不再是活的水流，而是死水一潭，而且只有极少的水能够放入池塘。而且，如果有人认为，在法典通过的那一刻，活法已经超越了这些法典中的每一个，并且终止了同它们的亲密关系，那么他必然意识到，到那时为止，活法的庞大内容还是尚未开垦过的活动领域，此点正被现代法律研究者所指出。

它不可能是别的样子。法律命题并未被用来呈现出法律状态的完整图景。法律人从满足现存的实践需求、从基于他所感兴趣的实践理由出发，来描绘它。他将不会努力对与其兴趣范围之外事项有关的法律命题进行系统阐述，或许仅仅是因为它们不在他所执业之法院的司法管辖范围内，或许是因为它们并不关涉到他的诉讼委托人。由于商法位于罗马法学家通常的兴趣范围之外，所以我们发现，罗马原始文献中的商法极度缺乏；正因为同样的原因，罗马人以及直到相当晚近时期的法学家对劳动法所言极少。甚至艾克·冯·雷普戈也没有论及城市法和领地习惯，因为这些在他的直接兴趣范围之外。

---

〔1〕 英译文是 reasonable（合理），中译者怀疑是 unreasonable（不合理）。

On the other hand, the attempt to arrive at an understanding of the present through the study of history or of prehistoric times, i. e. of ethnology, is an error in principle. To explain something, according to a saying of Mach's, is to replace a mystery that one is not accustomed to by a mystery that one is accustomed to. Now the present contains fewer mysteries that we are not accustomed to than does the past. The paleontologist will understand the nature and the functions of the organs of a fossil animal only if he understands the nature and the functions of the organs of living animals. But the zoölogist cannot learn the physiology of the animals which he is studying from the paleontologist; he will have recourse to paleontology only for the purpose of getting a picture of the development of the present-day animal kingdom. We arrive at an understanding of the past through the present, and not vice versa. Accordingly the history of law and ethnological legal science will not be of value for the understanding of the existing law but only for the study of the development of law.

As a result of the methods employed by modern legal science, the present state of our law is, in a great measure, actually unknown to us. We often know nothing, not only of things that are remote but also of things that happen before our very eyes. Almost every day brings some juristic surprise which we owe to a lucky accident, to a peculiar law-suit, or to an article in the daily papers. This surprise may concern the peasant tenants in Schwarzenberg, or puzzling heritable building rights in the heart of the city of Vienna, in the Brigittenau, or peculiar relations involving heritable leases in Berhomet, in Bukowina. But he who observes life with careful attentiveness knows that these are not isolated occurrences. We are groping in the dark everywhere. And we cannot plead the excuse that the legal historian can avail himself of, i. e. that a bit of the past has been irrecoverably lost. We need but open our eyes and ears in order to learn everything that is of significance for the law of our time.

In the part of the Austrian code that deals with matrimonial agreements there are four meagre sections, which, according to

另一方面,通过对历史研究或史前时期(即对文化人类学)的研究努力对当前获得理解,通常是一个错误。按照马赫的话说,解释一些东西就是用一个习惯了的神秘取代一个人们不习惯的神秘,现如今比过去包含了更少的、我们不习惯的神秘。只要古生物学家了解活动物之器官的性质与功能,他就能理解化石状动物之器官的性质与功能。但是动物学家不可能从古生物学家那里了解到他所研究之动物的生理机能;他仅仅在为了获得对当今动物界的发展图景时才会求助于古生物学家。我们通过现在对过去获得了解,而不是相反。因此,法律史和文化人类学法律科学对于理解现行法没有价值,而仅仅对研究法律发展有价值。

由于现代法学所使用的方法,我们的法律现在的状况,很大程度上对于我们来说是陌生的。我们不仅经常对遥远的事情一无所知,而且对发生于我们眼前的事情也一无所知。几乎每天都带给法学家的惊奇,对此现象,我们认为那是归因于一次侥幸的偶发事件、一个特殊的诉讼或是日报上的一篇文章。这种惊奇或许涉及到黑山的佃农,或许涉及在维也纳的中心地带、在布里吉特劳令人费解的可继承的建筑权,或许涉及在贝尔霍梅特、布科维纳有关可继承租约的特殊关系。但是非常留心观察生活的人知道,这些不是孤立的事件。我们正在黑暗中到处摸索。而且我们不能以法律史学家利用过的托辞——即,过去的点滴已经无可挽回地丧失了——来为自己辩护。我们仅需要睁开眼睛,竖起耳朵,以便了解到对于我们这个时代的法律而言所有重要的东西。

在《奥地利法典》涉及婚姻协议的部分,存在四个单薄的条

the marginal heading, deal with the matrimonial régime of community of goods. Anyone who has had opportunity of coming into contact with the German peasantry of Austria knows that they live, almost exclusively, under a matrimonial régime of community of goods. But this matrimonial community of goods, which is tile prevailing, freely chosen property régime of the German peasantry in Austria, has nothing in common with the community of goods provided for in the Austrian Civil Code, and the provisions of the Civil Code are never being applied since they are always excluded by a marriage contract formally entered into. What would be the value of a science of law which failed to recognize that the community of goods that the Austrian Civil Code speaks of exists only on paper? What would be the value of a science of law which thinks it is fulfilling its whole task when it ascertains the intent of the lawgiver, which has been expressed in the above four sections, but does not concern itself with the community of goods, which is based on readily accessible legal documents, and according to which practically the entire German peasantry of Austria lives?①

Again there is the agricultural usufructuary lease. The few provisions contained in the modern codes on the subject, especially in the Austrian and German codes, were for the most part taken from Roman law, and had arisen on the exhausted soil of Italy in the days of the Roman Empire with its system of extensive *latifundia* and an oppressed peasant class. They would be altogether insufficient today. A glance at life will convince us that they are almost never being applied. Their operation is almost always being excluded and they are being replaced by the provisions of contracts of usufructuary lease such as are suitable to modern social and economic conditions, and are being entered into between the lessor and the lessee in almost every instance. Though they vary according to the region, the nature of

---

① This presentation has been taken verbatim from my essay in volume XXXV of Schmoller's Jahrbuch. Since the date of its publication, an excellent essay by Reich, the notary, on the matrimonial régime in the German parts of Steiermark, Kärnten, and Krain has appeared in the Festschrift zur Jahrhundertfeier des (österr.) A. B. G. B. (General civil code of Austria). —*Author's note*.

款，按照旁注的标题，它们涉及的是婚姻财产共有制度。任何有机会接触到在奥地利的德国农民的人都会知道，他们几乎完全生活在一个婚姻财产共有制度下。但是这种婚姻财产共有——在奥地利的德国农民中通行的、可以自由选择的财产制度——与《奥地利民法典》中规定的财产共有制度没有丝毫相同之处，后者的规定从未得到过适用，因为它们总是被正式缔结的婚约排除。未能认识到《奥地利民法典》中的财产共有制度仅仅停留在纸面的法律科学有什么价值呢？当某种法律科学探求已经表达在上述四个条款中的立法者的意图，却不关心基于能够轻易获得的法律文件之上的财产共有时——所有在奥地利的德国农民正是按照这种共有制度实际生活着，它认为正在履行它的全部任务，这种法学的价值又何在呢？①

同样的还有农业上附用益权租约。现代法典包含与此主题相关的一些条款，特别是在《奥地利法典》与《德国民法典》中，这些规定大部分取自罗马法，是在罗马帝国时期有着大地产制度的意大利枯竭的土地和受压迫的农民阶级基础上产生的。在今天，它们全都是不充分的。简单扫视一下生活，我们就会相信，它们几乎从未被适用过。它们的实施总是遭到排除，它们正被那些诸如能够适应现代社会和经济条件的附用益权租约条款所取代，同时，几乎每一种情形下都是在出租人与承租人之间签订。尽管它们因地域、被出租地产的性质、当事人的地位等之别而形态多样，

---

① 该表达直接取自于收于《Schmoller' s Jahrbuch》第 35 卷的我的论文。自从它出版后，公证人一篇极好的论文，研究 Steiermark, Kärnten, and Krain 德国部分的婚姻制度，出现在 the Festschrift zur Jahrhundertfeier des (österr.) A. B. G. B.（奥地利一般民法典）——作者注。

the estate which is being let, and the position of the parties, they have, in spite of this limitation, an ever recurring, typical content. It is apparent, I dare say, in view of this discussion, that a presentation of the law of usufructuary lease of the civil codes, be it never so careful, cannot reflect the actual state of the German or Austrian law of usufructuary lease. To do this, it would be necessary to set forth the typical content of the leases, and for this purpose it would be necessary to search the archives of the offices of notaries and lawyers, and to make inquiries at the time and place.

Or what information can be gathered from juristic literature as to the system of agriculture in Germany or in Austria? Not even the various methods of cultivation of the soil have been formulated from a juristic point of view, and that would be but a small part of the task that has to be fulfilled. All economic cultivation of the soil is linked with other relations which are of the greatest importance to the jurist. In the first place, the neighborly relations between owners of farms operated for economic purposes and of landed estates. They are being regulated in part by custom; in part, by statute. Yet the entire juristic literature has not a single word to say about any of these, except perhaps about the statute. Moreover agriculture, in so far as it is carried on on a scale larger than the very smallest and most insignificant, presupposes a certain organization of labor, which, in the case of great landed estates, becomes a most artistically interlocking and extraordinarily complicated mechanism. To everyone that takes part in it, there is assigned, partly by custom, partly by contract or statute (regulations for servants), the measure of his powers, rights of supervision, privileges and duties, without a knowledge of which this difficult piece of machinery could be understood neither from the economic, or technical, nor from the juristic point of view. In case of similar undertakings all these legal relations occur again and again in their typical form throughout the whole region and often throughout the whole realm; and for this reason it is not a difficult task to study them and set them forth.

Note also the law of the family. The first thing that attracts the attention of the observer is the contrast between the actual order of the family and that which the codes decree. I doubt whether there is a country in Europe in which the relation between husband and wife, parents and children, between the family and the

尽管有这些限制，但它们含有始终一再出现的、典型的内容。我敢说，考虑到此种讨论，很明显，民法典中附用益权租约的法律表述，不管它是怎样的详备，都不可能反映德国或奥地利附用益权租约法律的实际状况。若想完善，则有必要表达出这种契约的典型内容，为此还必须在公证部门和律师事务所的档案中搜寻，并在彼时彼地进行调查。

关于德国或奥地利的农业制度，从法学文献中能收集到什么信息呢？从法学角度看，甚至各种各样的土壤耕作方法也没有清楚阐明过，并且那仅仅是它必须完成的任务中的一小部分。所有的土壤经济性耕作都与对法学家而言最重要的其他关系相连。首先，农场主之间的相邻关系因经济目的和地产而发挥作用。它们部分由习惯调整，部分由制定法调整。然而，全部的法学文献对这些中任何一个——或许除了制定法——只字未提。而且，就农业在极小、极不重要的规模上经营来说，它预设了一个特定的劳动组织，后者在大地产的情形下变成了技术上紧密相连、特别复杂的机构。对于任何参与其中的人而言，他的权力范围、监督权利、特权和职责，部分根据习惯、部分根据契约或制定法（有关雇工的规范）而设定，不了解此点，则这种组织机构令人困惑的部分既不能从经济或技术的角度来理解，也无法从法学的角度弄明白。在类似的情形下，所有的这些法律关系以它们的典型形式在整个地区，并经常在整个国土内一再发生；因此，研究并表达它们不是一件困难的事。

同时也请注意家庭法。吸引观察者注意的第一点是家庭的实际秩序与法典确立的秩序二者之间的对立。我怀疑，在欧洲是否有一个国家，其中丈夫和妻子的关系、父母和孩子的关系、家庭

outside world, as it actually takes form in life, corresponds to the norms of the positive law; or in which the members of the family, in which there is a semblance of proper family life, would as much as think of attempting to enforce the rights against one another that the letter of the law grants to them. It is evident therefore that in this case, too, the positive law is far from giving a picture of that which actually takes place in life. So much the less must legal science and doctrine confine itself to giving an exposition of the content of the statutes; it must seek to ascertain the actual forms that the family relations assume, which are essentially uniform and typical although they differ in the various classes of society and in the various parts of the country. We shall not discuss in this connection whether the statute has lost its mastery over life or whether it never had it; whether life, in the process of growth, has developed beyond the statute and grown away from it or whether it never corresponded to it. In this connection, too, science fulfils its function as the theory of law and right very poorly if it merely presents that which is prescribed by the statute and fails to tell what actually takes place.

The peasant law of inheritance of Germany (*Sering*) and of the German parts of Austria has been investigated more thoroughly and has been juristically evaluated more nearly at its true value than any of the subjects mentioned above. For the other classes, as well as for the non-German peoples and countries of the Austrian monarchy, the work has not yet been done. Juristic literature is content with setting forth the well-nigh unrestricted liberty of testamentary disposition provided for by the civil codes. Ought it not also ask what use is being made of it in the various countries and in the various classes?

The only branch of law the juristic science of which is based not merely incidentally, but throughout, on actual usage is commercial law. The latter has been officially received into juristic science in the form of business custom and "usance." The organization of the great landed estate and of the factory, even of the bank, has, to the present day, remained to the jurist a book sealed with seven seals, but the organization of the commercial house he knows, in its main outlines at least, from the Commercial Code. He knows the position of the principal

与外部世界的关系——如它实际在生活中成形的那样——与实证法规范相符,或者在这个国家里,外部看上去过着正常家庭生活的家庭成员,试图互相针对对方行使法律文义赋予他们的权利。因此,显然在这种情况下,实证法远远没有给出生活中实际发生情形的图景。法律科学与学说必须将自身限于对制定法的内容作出阐释,那就更加不妙;它必须试图探求家庭关系所呈现的实际形式,这种形式尽管因不同社会阶层、不同地理位置而有所差异,但本质上是一致的、典型的。我们将不讨论以下内容:制定法是否已经丧失了生活的控制或它从未取得过控制;生活在其演进过程中是否已经发展得超出了制定法并疏离了它或者生活从未与它相符过。就此而论,如果法学仅仅提出制定法规定了什么,而没有指出实际上发生了什么,则科学实现其作为法律与权利理论之功能的状况也是十分糟糕的。

德国农民继承法(*Sering*)以及奥地利之德国人聚居区的农民继承法已经被调查得更为彻底,而且法学上对其的评价比起上述任何主题都更接近其真实价值。对于其他阶层、奥地利君主国内的非德意志民族和国民而言,此项工作尚未完成。法学文献满足于表达民法典规定的几乎无限制的遗嘱处分自由。难道它不应该也问问,在不同国民和阶层中,此等规定作了哪些用途?

不仅偶然、而且始终基于实际惯例的法学所对应的唯一法律部门是商法。商法正式接受以商业习惯和“惯例”的形式出现的法学。大地产的组织和工厂组织,甚至银行组织直到今天还为法学家保留着七个印章标记的一本书。但他知道的商号组织,至少其主要梗概是从商法典中了解到的。他了解负责人与拥有一

and of the holder of a general power of procuration; of the holder of a mercantile power of agency and of the mercantile employee, of the mercantile agent, of the commercial traveler; he knows the significance of the mercantile trade name (*Handelsfirma*), of the books of account, and of business correspondence. He has a conception of the significance of all of these things not only from the economic but also from the legal point of view. And the contract law of modern commercial law has not been taken over from the *corpus iuris*; nor is it a product of the diligent reflection of its authors. What the commercial statutes and the commercial codes have to say about buying and selling, about commissions, about forwarding of goods, about the insurance, the freight, and the banking business, is actually being practiced somewhere even though, possibly, not always to the extent set forth therein. Likewise many commercial institutions, particularly the Exchange, have been properly furrowed and plowed by the jurists. The fact that much hard work remains to be done in every nook and corner is caused less in this sphere than in others by the lack of understanding and appreciation of the actual realities and more by the difficulties inherent in the subject matter and by its extremely rapid development. The gigantic organization of the production of goods which is taking place before our very eyes in trusts and cartels, all the modern achievements of commerce, the numerous new inventions, lead to new formations at every moment, and open new fields of labor for the jurist.

This then is the *living* law in contradistinction to that which is being enforced in the courts and other tribunals. The living law is the law which dominates life itself even though it has not been posited in legal propositions. The source of our knowledge of this law is, first, the modern legal document; secondly, direct observation of life, of commerce, of customs and usages, and of all associations, not only of those that the law has recognized but also of

般代理权[1]之人的地位；他了解拥有商事代理权[2]之人与商业雇员、商事代理机构、商业推销员的地位；他了解商号（*Handelsfirma*）、账簿、商业信函的重要性。他不仅从经济角度，而且从法律角度了解到所有这些事项的重要性。现代商法中的契约法并未突破《民法大全》的规定；它也不是其作者努力思考的成果。商事制定法和商法典必须要涉及的买卖、委任、货物运输、保险、运费以及银行业务，实际上正在某个地方实践着，即使可能并非总是达到彼处所提及的程度。同样，许多商业机构，特别是证券交易所，也由法学家恰当地创立出来。在每一个角落里都有许多艰苦的工作有待去做，此事实在这个领域由于缺乏对现实状况的理解和正确评价，因而比其他领域更少出现，与此同时，由于该主题上的内在困难及其极为快速的发展，它在此领域又比在其他领域更多发生。就发生在我们眼前的商品生产的巨大组织托拉斯和卡特尔、所有的现代商业成就、大量的新发明，每一刻都引发新的组织形态，并为法学家开辟新的工作领域。

这就是与在法庭及其他裁判机构所执行的法律形成了对比的活法。即使活法未以法律命题的形式被提出，但它是支配生活本身的法律。我们有关这种法律的知识首先来源于现代法律文件，其次来源于对生活、商业、习惯、管理、所有联合体的直接观察，这种直接观察不仅是对那些法律已经认可的事项，而且也是

---

〔1〕 一般代理权（Prokura），加雷斯曾作过界定，即，它必须登记；它只能由制定法给予限制；它对于第三人的效力不得被当事人协议限制；它由限于这种特殊情形的正式任命而指定。

〔2〕 参见《奥地利商法典》§ 54。

those that it has overlooked and passed by, indeed even of those that it has disapproved.

In our day, doubtless, the most important source of knowledge of the living law is the modern legal document. Even today one of these documents is being studied very extensively, to wit the judicial decision, but not in the sense we have in mind here. It is not being treated as evidence of the living law, but as a work of juristic literature which is to be examined not as to the truth of the legal relations described therein and as to the living law that is to be extracted therefrom, but as to the correctness of the statutory interpretations and of the juristic constructions contained therein. Even the conception of the French *arrêtistes*, of the jurists who have made it their business to add the explanatory notes on the decisions published in the great collections of Dalloz, Sirey, and in the *Journal du Palais*, is based on a much deeper understanding than this. To them the judicial decision is an expression of the law not as the legislator has pictured it to himself, but as it has developed in the consciousness of the French judges in the course of the century during which the French codes have been in force. In the words of Meynial, who has discussed the work of the *arrêtistes* in a brilliant fashion in the memorial volume published in commemoration of the one hundredth anniversary of the introduction of the *code civil*, they see in it " *la notion du changement du droit, grâce aux inflexions que la jurisprudence fait subiràla loi; celle du consentement général facite qui fait de la jurisprudence non seulement la servante mais l' émule et comme le suppléante de la loi.* "

I myself entertained this idea when about a quarter of a century ago I began to work at my book on the declaration of the will by silence. My intention was to study more than six hundred volumes

对那些被法律忽略和遗漏的事项,甚至对那些实际上遭到法律反对的事项进行观察。

无疑,在我们这个时代,有关活法的最重要的知识来源是现代法律文件。即使在今天,这些文件中有一种——即司法裁决——还在被非常详尽地研究着,但不是在我们此处想到的意义上的研究。它并未被当作活法的证明,而是作为一种法律文献——有待检验的不是其中所描述的法律关系的真实性,或是从中抽象出的活法,而是其中制定法文义解释与法学家解释的正确性。甚至法国的判例评注汇编者——他们是把为达洛兹、西雷以及法院杂志已出版的大型判例集中的司法裁决添加注释视为己任的法学家——的观念,也是基于比这个深得多的理解。对于他们来说,司法裁决是法律的表达,这种表达不是如同立法者已经为其勾画出的外观,而是如同它在长年累月的时间里——其间法国法典已经颁布实施——在法国法官的意识中发展出来的模样。用梅尼亚——曾经在纪念《民法典》颁布百年活动中出版的纪念卷里讨论过"判例评注汇编者"的工作——的话说就是,从中他们明白了"归功于判例对制定法的发展,'法'这一概念发生了改变:判例不再是制定法的仆人,而成为了制定法有力的竞争者和替代者"。

大约 25 年前当我开始致力于我那本关于默示意思表示的著作时,我自己就抱有这个想法。我的意图是研究超过 600 卷的德

of decisions of German, Austrian, and French courts, and on the basis of these decisions to present a picture of what judicial decisions had made of the declaration of the will by silence. Before long however my attention was arrested by, and occupied with, what actually took place rather than by the judicial decision. As a result my book contains, to a great extent at least, a statement of the facts on which the judicial decisions had been rendered, as they actually happened in life, and a statement of the significance of the silent declaration of the will in legal life. In this book, I actually, though unconsciously, applied the sociological method of legal science, for which I subsequently sought to establish a theoretical basis.

At a later time, however, I realized that this method is not quite sufficient. Even the judicial decisions do not give a perfect picture of legal life. Only a tiny bit of real life is brought before the courts and other tribunals; and much is excluded from litigation either on principle or as a matter of fact. Moreover the legal relation which is being litigated shows distorted features which are quite different from, and foreign to, the same relation when it is in repose. Who would judge our family life or the life of our societies by the law-suits that arise in the families or in the societies? The sociological method therefore demands absolutely that the results which are obtained from the judicial decisions be supplemented by direct observation of life.

And for this very purpose the modern business document offers a basis which can become at least as fruitful as the method of past millennia and centuries. A glance at modern legal life shows that it is predominantly controlled not by statute law but by the business document. Non-compulsory law is set aside by the content of the business document. The living law must be sought in marriage contracts, in contracts of purchase, of usufructuary lease, in contracts for building loans, for loans secured by hypothecs, in testaments, and in contracts of inheritance, in articles of association of societies and of business partnerships, and not in the sections of the codes. In all of these contracts, there is, in addition to the individual content which applies only to the particular transaction, a typical, ever recurring content. This typical content is basically the most important thing in the document. If our literary jurists were well advised, they would concern

国、奥地利以及法国法院的裁决,并且试图基于这些裁决,呈现出司法判决先前为意思表示勾绘出的图景。然而,不久我的注意力就被实际发生的事情而不是司法裁决俘虏和占据了。因而,至少很大程度上,我的书里包含了对司法裁决据以作出之事实的描述——如同它们在生活中实际发生的那样——以及对法律生活中默示意思表示之意义的介绍。这本书里,尽管是无意识的,但我实际上运用了法律科学的社会学方法,随后我试图为其建立一个理论基础。

不过后来我意识到,该方法还十分不够。甚至连司法裁决也没有给出法律生活一个完整的图景。在法庭上以及其他裁判机构里只能得到一丁点真实的生活;很多(真实生活)原则上或事实上被排除在诉讼之外。而且,涉讼的法律关系体现了一种相对扭曲的特征,十分不同于同一法律关系处于正常时候的状态。谁会通过在家庭或联合体中产生的法律诉讼来裁断我们的家庭生活或我们的联合体的生活?因此,社会学的方法绝对必需,从司法裁决中获得的结果应由对生活的直接观察来补充。

正是为此目的,现代商业文件提供了一个能够变得至少与过去千百年的方法一样富有成效的基础。对现代法律生活的一瞥将会表明,它主要不是被制定法而是被事务文件所支配。非强行法被事务文件的内容挤到一边。活法必须在婚姻契约、购销契约、附用益权租约、建筑贷款契约、抵押担保贷款契约、遗嘱、遗赠契约、社会联合体章程以及商号章程中寻求,而不是在法典的条款中寻求。在所有的这些契约中,除了仅适用于特别交易的个别内容外,还存在典型的、反复出现的内容。该典型内容基本上是文件中最重要的东西。如果经常与文字打交道的法学家非常细

themselves primarily with it, as did the Romans, who, in their commentaries on the edict and in their *libri iuris civilis*, wrote long disquisitions on the ever recurring *duplae stipulatio* and the *institutio ex re certa*. In that case we probably should have more monographs on the beer-seller of the breweries, or on the contracts for the processing of sugar beets by the sugar factories, or on the sale of a physician's practice, than on the concept of the juristic person or the construction of a pledge right in one's own *res* (*Sache*). Of course it is a new task for the jurist to make use of a modern document for the purposes of theoretical and of practical legal science. But the historian, particularly the legal historian, is quite familiar with the study of documents, and the latter might, at the beginning at least, render valuable services both to the theoretical and to the practical jurist. The science of historical documents has developed a technique that is one of the most delicate and difficult things in scientific work, and the industry and labor of a

心,他们将会首先关注它,如同罗马人那样,他们在对法令以及《罗马法汇编》[1]的评论中写了长篇的专题论文,内容涉及始终反复出现的双倍之价赔偿的要式口约[2]和特定物继承人的设立[3]。那样的话,相比于涉及有关法人的观念或在某人的物上担保权之解释的论文,我们很可能拥有更多涉及酿酒厂的啤酒销售商、糖厂加工甜菜的契约或医师执业服务的专论。当然,对于法学家而言,为了理论性法律科学和实用性法律科学而利用现代文件是一项新的任务。但是历史学家,特别是法律史学家,十分熟悉文件的研究,后者可能至少在一开始就为理论法学和实用法学提供了有价值的服务。历史文献科学已经发展出一种在科学工作中属于最精致、最难解事项之一的技术,并且,终生的勤奋

---

〔1〕 (拉)*libri iuris civilis*,即 *libri Basilicorum*,《(罗马法)汇编》,根据东罗马帝国皇帝 Leone 四世的命令编纂的希腊文罗马法文献汇总。总计 60 编,编下分章,从各种希腊文版本中摘录了优士丁尼《民法大全》的文献,并作出评论和归纳。此《汇编》在东罗马帝国逐渐取代《民法大全》。

〔2〕 (拉)*stipulatio*(要式口约),罗马法中的口头契约之一,表现为作为要约人的一方向作为承诺人的另一方进行提问,后者就该提问所涉及的义务作出承诺或保证。要式口约的特点在于:其一,采用固定套语,套语使用错误将导致缔约行为无效;其二,完全以口头形式进行;其三,一般不问缔约具体内容,只注重形式上的合法;其四,有关提问和回答必须是连续和相互对应的。*duplae stipulatio*(两倍之价赔偿的要式口约),则是指一种在出卖人与买受人之间缔结的要式口约,前者以此向后者保证:在被卖物出现瑕疵以致影响后者正常享用的情况下,前者将向其给付相当于或双倍于被卖物价值的赔偿钱款。

〔3〕 (拉)*institutio ex re certa*(特定物继承人的设立),罗马法中,继承人的设立可以针对被继承人的全部财产设立,或者针对某一财产份额,或者针对某一特定物,或者针对除某一特定物以外的财产而设立。

lifetime will scarcely suffice for the mastery of all its refinements. But in the case of the modern document tasks must be fulfilled which in part are quite different from those involved in the case of the historical document and which are by no means lighter.

Above all, we must endeavor to treat the document as a part of the living law, and to derive the living law from it as the Romans did in their law of contracts and of testaments. The titles of the Digest *de contrahenda emptione*, *de actionibus emti venditi*, *de evictionibus et duplae stipulatione*, *pro socio*, *de stipulatione servorum*, and those that deal with the law of testaments and legacies, can still serve as models everywhere. It is a matter of the utmost importance that present-day theoretical and practical science should at last concern itself not with Roman, but with present-day contracts and documents. It would be the first task of modern legal science to examine the documents as to the part of their content that is of general importance, typical, and ever recurring, to treat juristically and to evaluate them from every angle according to their importance from the point of view of society, economics, and legislative policy.

In this way we could at last get a picture of what is taking place among us in the sphere of the document. Although in general the documents are alike, they differ very much in details according to localities, classes, ranks, races, and creeds. It seems likely that we must perform the function of legal statistics by means of the devices of the science of documents. It will not be possible to do this without new methods, and it surely will not be an easy task to devise such methods. But what splendid results are beckoning to the jurist in this connection, especially if he succeeds in laying bare the historical, economic, or social presuppositions of these diversities.

Still the value of the document would be greatly over-estimated if one should think that one could, without more ado, read the living law from it. It is not at all conclusively established that

与劳作极少能够足以掌握它所有的精妙。但是在现代文件的情形下,部分不同于那些在历史文献情形下的相关任务必须被完成,该任务也绝不比后者轻松。

综上所述,我们必须尽量将文件作为活法的一部分,并从中推导出活法,如同罗马人在他们的契约法和遗嘱法中做的那样。名为《学说汇纂》、买卖契约、关于买卖之诉、关于追夺担保和双倍要式口约、关于合伙、关于奴隶的要式口约以及那些涉及遗嘱和遗产之法的东西,在各个地方还能作为榜样。当今理论法学和实用法学最终不是关注罗马法而是关注当下的契约和文件,这是最重要的事情。调查这些文件中具有普遍重要性的、典型的、始终反复出现的内容,在法学层面描述它们,并依据它们的重要性从社会、经济、立法政策等角度全方位地评价它们,这是现代法学首要的任务。

这样,我们在文件范围内最终能够获得"在我们中间什么正在发生"的图景。尽管总体上这些文件是相似的,但它们在细节上,由于地域、阶级、阶层、种族以及信仰之别而相差甚远。看起来似乎我们必须借助文献科学的手段来履行法律统计学的功能。没有新的方法,完成该任务是不可能的,并且设计那样的方法确实不是一件容易的事。但就此而论,多么辉煌的成果正在召唤法学家,特别是如果他成功地揭示这些多样性的历史、经济或社会方面的先决条件的话,成果无疑更为卓著。

尽管如此,如果某人认为他能从文件中直截了当地读到活法,那他还是可能极大地高估了文件的价值。文件作为一个整体

the document as a whole contains and bears witness to the living law. The living law is not the part of the content of the document that the courts recognize as binding when they decide a legal controversy, but only that part which the parties actually observe in life. The effects of the transactions that are evidenced by documents cannot be learned without more ado from their enforceable legal consequences. Could anyone infer from the articles of association of a society or of a share company that the seemingly plenipotent meetings of the shareholders usually turn out to be utterly insignificant gatherings of yes-men? But the legally operative content of the document gives no reliable information as to the effects not intended by the parties nor yet as to those intended. There is much in the document that is simply traditional; this part is copied from a form book by the person who drafts the document, but it never reaches the consciousness of the parties. They will therefore neither demand nor grant the things provided for therein, and will be very much surprised to hear of them when, in the event of litigation, the document gets into the hands of a lawyer who insists upon them in court. There are other provisions which the parties will permit to be embodied in the document only in order to be prepared for the worst. It is self-evident that they are not to be mentioned as long as there is no controversy. The other party understands this very well. He accepts the most extreme rigors of a contract of this sort calmly, but haggles most obstinately over all provisions that are intended to be taken seriously. If one reads a contract of usufructuary lease prepared by the administrator of the Prussian crown-lands or of the Greek-Oriental religious foundation of Bukowina, one marvels how it is possible for the lessee to move at all within this barbed-wire fence of paragraphs. Nevertheless the lessee gets on very well. No use is ever being made of all of these contractual penalties, of the clauses appointing stated times, of the short-term notices to quit, of the forfeitures of security, of the right to compensation for damage done, as long as it is possible to get on with the lessee at all. One who is engaged in the practical affairs of life is anxious to deal peaceably with people. He is not interested in carrying on litigation even if he is bound to win.

The standard therefore according to which the Sociological School of jurisprudence must test, not only the legal propositions,

包含并见证了活法，这点根本没有获得确凿的证明。活法不是法院裁决案件时会认为此部分具有拘束力的文件的内容，而仅仅是当事人在生活中实际遵守的部分。由文件证明的交易的效力不可能直接从可执行的法律后果中了解。有谁能从社会联合体或股份公司的章程中推导出，表面上拥有公司完全“主权”的股东会通常会变成由一群只会说“是”的人组成的一个极端无足轻重的集会？但文件在法律上有效的内容对于当事人未想要的效力以及想要的效力没有提供任何可靠的信息。在文件中有很多不过是传统的东西；这部分由起草文件的人从介绍格式的书中拷贝，但是它从未影响到当事人的意识。因此，他们既未要求也未承认那儿规定的东西，并且当诉讼发生、文件传到法庭上强调这些东西的某律师手中时，他们听到这些内容会感到非常惊奇。文件中还存在当事人允许体现在文件中的其他规定，仅仅是为了预备最坏的情况。毫无疑问，只要没有争议发生，人们就不会提及它们。其他当事人能很好地理解此点。他平静接受了这种契约最极端的严苛，但是最倔强地对所有打算认真对待的条款争论不休。如果某人读到一个由普鲁士王地管理者或布科维纳东正教宗教基金会的管理者起草的附用益权租约，则他会对承租人在条款编制的铁丝网中如何能安然行动大为惊叹。尽管如此，承租人仍然过得很好。只要（出租人）有可能与承租人相处得好，所有的这些契约规定的违约金、契约制定的期间、退出的短期通知、担保的丧失、对已造成损害的索赔权这些统统都不会派上用场。从事此方面生活实践事务的人总是渴望和平地与人们打交道。即使他打官司肯定会赢，他对提起诉讼也没有兴趣。

因此，法理学的社会学学派用来检测法律命题和法律文件的

but also the legal document, is actual life. Here too it must observe the distinction between the law that is enforced by the courts and the living law. The entire valid content of the document is law that is enforced by the courts (i. e. norm for decision), for, in case the parties resort to litigation, the decision will hinge upon it; but it is living law only in so far as the parties habitually insist upon it even if they do not wish to risk litigation. Failure to observe this heterogeneousness of the component parts of the document embodying the contract results in an erroneous and distorted picture of life itself. But the contrast is of the utmost importance for the administration of justice and for legislation as well. It is questionable whether the latter should lend themselves to permitting those things to be taken seriously which were never intended to be taken seriously.

Of course we can learn only so much of the living law from the document as has been embodied therein. How shall we quarry that part of the living law that has not been embodied in a legal document but which nevertheless is a large and important part thereof? There is no other means but this, to open one's eyes, to inform oneself by observing life attentively, to ask people, and note down their replies. To be sure, to ask a jurist to learn from actual observation and not from sections of a code or from bundles of legal papers is to make an exacting demand upon him; but it is unavoidable, and marvelous results can be achieved in this manner.

From the great number of things that deserve being studied in this manner, I would select only a few. First of all the old law that still survives. The old law, which is popular law and not merely juristic law, lives on under a thin surface of modern statute law, and dominates the conduct and the legal consciousness of the people. The legal historian can not only find many things here as to which his sources are silent, but he can actually observe many things which are generally believed to belong to a time that is long since past. In doing this he can disregard the legal document; for it is well known how often it is but a poor compromise between that which is traditional and the demands of modern law, e. g. in the law of inheritance among the peasants, and in the matrimonial régime. But it is necessary to focus

标准是现实生活。它也必须观察法院执行之法与活法之间的差异。文件全部有效的内容是法院执行的法律(即,裁判规范),因为,在当事人诉诸民事诉讼的场合,裁决关键取决于它;但是仅就当事人习惯坚持的部分而言,那是活法,即使当事人并不愿意冒诉讼的危险。未能观察到包含契约之文件的不同组成部分之间的这种差异,将会导致对生活本身错误扭曲的描述。但对于司法和立法而言,这种对立是最重要的。有疑问的是,立法是否会轻易允许对那些从未打算认真对待的事情给予认真对待。

当然,我们从文件中获悉的活法内容只能达到它体现在其中的程度。我们要如何搜集那些并未体现在法律文件之中,但大量存在且十分重要的活法呢?除了睁开眼睛,通过细心观察生活、访寻民众并记录下他们的回答之外,别无他途。确实,让一名法学家通过实际观察、而不是通过法典的条款或浩繁的法律文书了解活法,其实是给他提出了一条严苛的要求;但那不可避免,以这种方法获得的结果将是最佳的。

从大量的应以此种方法研究的事项中,我只选择了一些。首先,古老的法律仍然继续存在。属于民间法而非仅仅是法学家法的古老法律,在薄薄的一层现代制定法的表层下继续存在着,并支配着民众的行为和法律意识。在此,法律史学家不仅能发现许多其来源并无记载的东西,而且他实际上能够发现许多通常被认为属于很久之前的过去的东西。这样做时,他能够忽略法律文件;因为众所周知,那么多次的情形下,它仅仅是传统的东西与现代法律的要求之间可怜的妥协,例如在农民的继承法以及在婚姻制度方面。但是,相比于迄今为止对那些虽然没有体现在文件

attention to a much greater extent than has been done hitherto upon those parts of the old law that still exist among the people though they are not embodied in legal documents, expecially since it is doubtful whether it can hold its own much longer against the impact of modern commercial life. Bogišič has discovered the ancient Sadruga, one of the most primitive of human organizations of mankind, within the very territory within which the Austrian Civil Code is in force. In another remote corner of Austria, in eastern Galicia, Dnicstrzanski (Customary Law and the Social Associations, Czernowitz, 1905) has found a mercantile partnership comprising the entire Ruthenian tribe of the *Bojken*, and having a remarkable form of organization, which of course is quite foreign to the Austrian statutes. I myself have been able to establish the fact that only about one half of a century ago there were isolated peasant family-communities in existence among the Ruthenians of eastern Galicia and of Bukowina. Today, I suppose, they have disappeared altogether. Mauczka (*Altes Recht im Volksbewusstsein—Ancient* Law in the Popular Consciousness—Wien, 1907—also in *Gerichtszeitung* Nos. 10 and 11, l007) has recently shown that there are some survivals of this institution among the German population of Austria as well. And at my suggestion, a Viennese writer, Dr. Kobler, has recorded some observations for my seminar for the study of the living law.

The germs of new law that are viable are probably of greater importance to the jurist than such dying survivals. And here we are confronted by a peculiar fact. It is generally believed that the knowledge that law is in never-ending process of development is an enduring achievement of the historical school, and one would think that this is accepted as true not only as to times long since past but also as to the last century. But science and theory are making a peculiar use of this bit of academic wisdom. So far as the ancient Romans or the Germans down to the fourteenth and fifteenth centuries are concerned, jurists are wide awake to the development of legal institutions, e. g. of the

中，但仍然在民众中存在的古老法律已经给予的关注而言，有必要给予更大程度的注意，特别是考虑到，它能否在现代商业生活的影响下坚持得更久仍有疑问，就更应对其给予关注。波吉斯克曾发现了古老的家长制家庭公社，这个最原始的人类组织就存在于《奥地利民法典》施行的疆域内。在奥地利另一个遥远的角落，在加利西亚地区，*Dniestrzanski*(《习惯法与社会联合体》，Czernowitz，1905)曾发现了一种商事合伙，它由波基垦整个罗塞尼亚人部落组成，并有一个值得注意的组织形式，该形式当然与制定法的规定十分不同。我自己也能证明以下事实：大约一个半世纪以前，在东部加利西亚地区和布科维纳地区的罗塞尼亚人中间，存在着一种独立的农民家庭共同体。如今，我认为，他们全都消失了。毛茨卡最近在《民众意识中的古代法》(*Altes Recht im Volksbewusstsein*，*Wien*，1907)以及《法院报》(*Gerichtszeitung*，第10期、第11期，1907)中也揭示，在奥地利的德国人中同样存在这种风俗制度的一些残余。并且，在我的建议下，越南的一位作者已经开始为我(主持的)研究活法的研究班记录一些观察。

对于法学家而言，有生命力的新法律的萌芽很可能比那些垂死的法律残余更重要。并且此处我们遇到了一个特殊的事实。通常认为，法律是永无止境的发展过程，这一认识是历史法学派的不朽成就，而且此点不仅为很久之前那些时代的人们所认可，而且也被上世纪的人们所认可。但是科学和理论正在对此点学术智慧进行一种特殊利用。就古代罗马人或下至14世纪和15世纪的德国人而言，法学家充分觉察到法律习俗制度的发展，例如

family, of the relations of personal subjection, of ownership of land, of contracts. Statutes, which are of no significance in those days, are scarcely being mentioned. But for the later period, this kind of legal history breaks down altogether, and for the last century, the science of the Historical School resolves itself altogether into a history of legislation. Jurists seem to assume that in this period legal institutions develop only through changes in the paragraphs of the codes. What is the meaning of this? Has the non-statutory development of legal institutions ceased altogether in the nineteenth century? But today, just as in antiquity and in the Middle Ages, legal history is based not so much upon the emergence and the disappearance of legal propositions that have been formulated in words as upon the emergence of new legal institutions and the gradual assumption of a new content by those that are already in existence. No legal historian will admit that the basic legal relations in Germany, let us say, of the sixteenth century, coincide with those of the fifteenth, or that the changes, some of which were very sweeping ones, took place solely as a result of legislation, which was enacted very rarely and was not very sweeping. Does this not hold true for the nineteenth century as well, a period which was so highly agitated socially, economically, and politically that one may say that until that time mankind had never experienced its like? It is a question of what one means by development. The family law has undergone development. This means exactly what it meant in the Middle Ages, i. e. that the relations of husband and wife, of parents and children, now bear a different stamp. Ownership of land has undergone development even apart from the fact that the soil was freed by statute and by administrative action from the burdens and charges resting upon it; this means that there is a different system of landholding in vogue because different kinds of real and obligatory rights have been established with reference to the soil, and also because the economy of the peasant and of the great landowner has undergone a change. The law of contract has undergone development; this development is based on the fact that new kinds of contracts have come into use and that the contracts of the traditional kind now have a different content. The law of inheritance has undergone development; this means, chiefly, that division of inheritance, testaments, and other dispositions *mortis causa* now have a content quite different from

家庭、人身依附关系、土地所有权、契约等法律习俗的发展。在那些时候并不重要的制定法极少被提及。但是后来,这种法律史完全中断了,到了最近一个世纪,历史法学派的科学将其完全归结为立法律史。法学家似乎认定,在这一时期,法律习俗只通过法典条款的变化来发展。这意味着什么?在19世纪,非制定法性质的法律习俗制度发展完全停止了吗?但是今天,正如在古代和中世纪一样,法律史与其说是基于以文句系统表述的法律命题的出现和消亡之上,不如说是基于新习俗的出现以及那些现有习俗的新内容的逐渐呈现之上。没有一个法律史学家会承认,比如说16世纪在德国的基本法律关系与15世纪的基本法律关系一致,法律史学家也不会承认,变化——有些是很彻底的变化——仅仅是作为极少颁布且并非很彻底的立法的结果而发生的。这难道不也适用于19世纪那样一个社会、经济、政治领域如此躁动不安以至于可以称得上是史无前例的时期吗?它是一个人们以发展来确定所指内容的问题。家庭法已经历经了发展。这确切地意味着它在中世纪的意蕴——即,丈夫和妻子的关系、父母和孩子的关系——现在有了不同的印记。甚至抛开这个事实——土地已经因制定法和行政行为从加在其上的负担和捐税中解放了出来——不谈,土地所有权亦已经历了发展;这意味着存在不同的正流行的土地所有制度,因为有关土地的不同的物权和债权已经被确立,也因为农民和大地主的经济已经经历了一个变化。契约法也经历了一个发展;该发展基于以下事实:新型契约开始投入使用,并且传统类型的契约现在有了不同的内容。继承法也经历了一个发展;这主要意味着,遗产的划分、遗嘱以及其他死因财产

that which they had a century ago. Compared with these revolutionary changes, the changes brought about by legislation are negligible.

The sociology of law then must begin with the ascertainment of the living law. Its attention will be directed primarily to the concrete, not the abstract. It is only the concrete that can be observed. What the anatomist places under the microscope is not human tissue in the abstract but a specific tissue of a specific human being; the physiologist likewise does not study the functions of the liver of mammals in the abstract, but those of a specific liver of a specific mammal. Only when he has completed the observation of the concrete does he ask whether it is universally valid, and this fact, too, he endeavors to establish by means of a series of concrete observations, for which he has to find specific methods. The same may be said of the investigator of law. He must first concern himself with concrete usages, relations of domination, legal relations, contracts, articles of association, dispositions by last will and testament. It is not true, therefore, that the investigation of the living law is concerned only with "customary law" or with "business usage." If one does any thinking at all when one uses these words—which is not always the case—one will realize that they do not refer to the concrete, but to that which has been universalized. But only the concrete usages, the relations of domination, the legal relations, the contracts, the articles of association, the dispositions by last will and testament, yield the rules according to which men regulate their conduct. And it is only on the basis of these rules that the norms for decision that the courts apply and the statutory provisions that alone have hitherto occupied the attention of jurists arise. The great majority of judicial decisions are based on the concrete usages, relations of possession, contracts, articles of association, and dispositions by last will and testament, that the courts have found to exist. If we would comprehend the universalizations, the reductions to unity, and the other methods of finding norms that the judge and the lawgiver employ, we must first of all know the basis upon which they were carried out. The more we know of the Roman banking system, the better shall we understand *receptum* and *litteris contrahere*. Does this not hold true for the law of our day? To this extent Savigny was right when he said that the law—and by law he means above all the legal proposition—can be understood only from its historical

处分现在有了十分不同于它在一个世纪之前的内容。相比于这些革命性的变化,由立法而产生的变化微不足道。

这样,法律社会学必须从探明活法开始。它的注意力将主要指向具体的、而非抽象的东西。我们能够观察到的只会是具体的东西。解剖学家放到显微镜下的不是抽象的人体器官,而是特定人的特定器官;同样,生理学家研究的不是抽象的哺乳动物的肝脏,而是特定哺乳动物的特定肝脏。只有当他完成了具体物的观察之后,他才会问它是否普遍有效,并且努力通过一系列具体观察竭力确证这个实情,为此,他不得不寻找独特的方法。这同样适用于法律的调查者。他必须首先关注具体惯例、支配关系、法律关系、契约、联合体章程以及遗嘱的财产处分。因此,活法的调查者并非仅仅关注"习惯法"或"商业惯例"。如果某人在使用这些词语时作了任何思考,他就会意识到——并非总是如此——他们指的不是具体的事物,而是普遍化之后的东西。但是只有具体的惯例、支配关系、法律关系、契约、联合体章程、遗嘱的财产处分才会产生人们据以调整他们行为的规则。并且只有在这些规则的基础上,法院适用的裁判规范与迄今唯一吸引法学家注意的制定法条款才会产生。绝大多数司法裁决基于法院认定存在的具体惯例、占有关系、契约、联合体章程以及遗嘱的处分。如果我们要充分理解这种一般化、化而为一以及法官和律师所使用的其他发现规范的方法,那么我们必须首先知道它们据以运作的基础。我们越了解罗马人的金融制度,我们就越能理解承保和通过文书订立契约。这难道不同样适用于我们今天的法律吗?在此范围内,当萨维尼说法律——他说的法律首要是指所有的法律命题——仅能从其历史背景方面来理解时,他是对的;但是历史

connection; but the historical connection does not lie in the hoary past, but in the present, out of which the legal proposition grows.

But the scientific significance of the living law is not confined to its influence upon the norms for decision which the courts apply or upon the content of statutes. The knowledge of the living law has an independent value, and this consists in the fact that it constitutes the foundation of the legal order of human society. In order to acquire a knowledge of this order we must know the usages, relations of domination, legal relations, contracts, articles of association, declarations by last will and testament, quite independently of the question whether they have already found expression in a judicial decision or in a statute or whether they will ever find it. The provisions contained in the new German Commercial Code regulating stock exchanges, banks, publishing houses, and other supplementary provisions were full of gaps when they were enacted and, for the most part, have become antiquated today. Modern commerce, especially the export trade, has meanwhile created an enormous number of new forms, which ought to be the subject matter of scientific study as well as those that have been enumerated in the statute. Very much that is of genuine value can be found on this point in the literature on the science of commerce that is blossoming forth so abundantly. A part of the order in the sphere of mining and navigation has been made accessible to legal science through mining law, maritime law, and the law of inland navigation, but for the most part this has long since become antiquated. The factory, the bank, the railroad, the great landed estate, the labor union, the association of employers, and a thousand other forms of life—each of these likewise has an order, and this order has a legal side as well as that of the mercantile establishment, which is being regulated in detail only by the Commercial Code. In addition there are countless forms in which the activity of these associations manifests itself outwardly, above all the contracts. In studying the manufacturing establishment, the legal investigator must pursue the countless, highly intricate paths that lead from the acceptance of the order to the delivery of the finished products to the customer, to wit the position of the representative and of the commercial traveler, the three departments that are to be found in every manufacturing establishment (the sales department, the technical department, and the manufacturing department), the arrival of the orders, the preparation

背景不在久远的过去，而在当下，法律命题在当下产生。

但是，活法的科学意义并不限于对法院所适用的裁判规范的影响或对制定法内容的影响。活法的知识有独立的价值，此点存在于如下事实：它构成了人类社会法律秩序的基础。为了获得对这种秩序的认识，我们必须了解惯例、支配关系、法律关系、契约、联合体章程、遗嘱的声明，这些完全独立于以下问题：它们是否已经在司法裁决或制定法中表现出来或者说他们是否总是会在司法裁决或制定法中表现出来。在新的《德国商法典》中调整股票交易、银行、出版社的条款以及其他补充条款，在它们颁布时就充满了缺漏，并且在今天这些条款已经几乎完全过时了。现代商业，特别是出口贸易已经同时创造了大量的新形式，它们应当是科学研究的主题，与那些已经在制定法中得以列举的形式一样。很多具有真正价值的东西可以在有关商业科学的文献中找到，后者现在发展得如此兴旺繁荣。在矿业和航海领域的一部分秩序，通过矿业法、海事法以及内河航运法，法学已经可以较为容易地对其施加影响，但大体上，此种秩序早已变得过时。工厂、银行、铁路、大地产产业、工会、雇工联合会以及以前多种其他的生活构造——每一种都有自身的秩序，此等秩序有其法律的一面，亦有商业的一面，在细节方面，它只受商法典的调整。此外，还存在无数的构造，其中，这些联合体的活动向外显露自身，首要依靠契约。在研究制造业公司时，法律研究者必须沿着从接受订单到向顾客交付最终产品过程中无数的、高度复杂的路径前进，即：代表人和推销员的地位、每一个制造企业都要建立的三个部门（销售部、技术部、制造部）、订单的到达、图纸的制备与保存、此笔交易

and the preservation of drawings, the computation of the cost of the undertaking, the sale price, the calculation for the purpose of checking up, the execution of the order on the basis of the drawings, the functions of the manufacturing department, of the master workman, the management of the warehouse, the computation of wages by the piece and by time, the distribution of wages among the individual workmen, the importance of the certificate showing that material has been handed over, the price list, the supervision at the gates by porters. Of equal importance for the legal side of the order of the undertaking is the keeping of books, the taking of inventories, the supervision over the warehouse, the preservation of drawings and models, the employment of workmen and of apprentices, the working regulations, and the committees, of the workmen.

Economists, it is true, have often been engaged in investigations of the kind demanded here. But this has by no means rendered the work of the jurist superfluous. The jurist and the economist are dealing everywhere with the same social phenomena. Property, money, bills of exchange, share companies, credit, law and right of inheritance — it would be difficult to find a single object that the science of law is not concerned with as much as economics. But the jurist and the economist are dealing with different aspects of the same social phenomena. One concerns himself with their economic significance and scope; the other, with their legal regulation and their legal consequences. Though the jurist can be taught much by the economist, and the economist by the jurist, the questions which the identical objects of investigation pose to their respective sciences are absolutely distinct; and for this very reason no part of the labor which is necessary for both may be thrust upon one of them alone.

The investigation of the living law will of course render neither the historical nor the ethnological method superfluous; for we can learn the laws governing the development of society only by studying the historic and the prehistoric (ethnological) facts. But the historical and ethnological methods are indispensable, too, for the understanding of the state of the law of the present time. It is true we shall never understand the past but through the present; but the path to the understanding of the innermost nature of the present lies through the understanding of the past. Within every part of the present lies its entire past, which can be clearly discerned by the eye that is able to look into these depths. This truth was not hidden from the eyes of the great founders of the Historical School, and for this reason their object was

的成本计算、销售价格、为核对而进行的计算、根据图纸对订单的执行、制造部的职责、熟练工的作用、仓库的管理、计件工资和计时工资的计算、工资在单个工人之间的分配、表明原料已经移交的单据的重要性、价格表以及门卫在大门处的监督。对于企业秩序的法律方面而言,同等重要的是账簿的保存、财产目录的编制、仓库的监管、图纸和模型的保管、工人和学徒工的雇佣、工作规程以及工人委员会等。

的确,经济学家曾经从事过此处所需的这种调查。但是这绝没有使法学家的工作变得多余。法学家和经济学家处处都应对同样的社会现象。财产、金钱、汇票、股份公司、信用、继承法律和权利——很难找到一个对象,法学对其关注得不如经济学关注得多。但是法学家和经济学家处理同一社会现象的不同方面。一个关注社会现象的经济意义和范围;另外一个关注社会现象的法律调整和法律后果。尽管经济学家可以教给法学家很多东西,法学家也可以教给经济学家很多东西,但是同一调查对象给他们各自的科学提出的问题绝对是不同的;正因为如此,对于二者均属必要的工作,没有任何部分可以单独强加于其中之一之上。

对活法的调查当然并没有使历史方法和文化人类学的方法变得多余;因为我们只能通过研究历史的和史前(文化人类学)的事实来了解支配社会发展的规律。但是,对于理解当下的法律状况而言,历史和文化人类学的方法同样是不可或缺的。诚然,我们从未仅仅通过现在来理解过去,但是对当下最核心性质的理解之道在于通过对过去的理解。在当下的每一部分中都存在其完整的过去,后者可以通过我们的慧眼清晰地分辨出来。此种真相并未逃过历史法学派伟大创始人的眼睛,因此,他们的目标绝不

by no means, as is generally believed today, to create a legal science which in its essence is a history of law, but a historical science of law. It is true, in the main they were occupied not even with legal history but with legal antiquities, and substituted dialectic speculations for historical legal science or—and this is not much better—Schelling's philosophy. They, too, were children of their time. But they wrote a legend in large letters above the gate of entrance to their school which stated what their goal was. No one however was able to read and interpret the inscription. And this fact is just as characteristic as is the other fact that at a later time the *Zeitschrift für geschichtliche Rechtswissenschaft* became a *Zeitschrift für Rechtsgeschichte*.

In order to understand the actual state of the law we must institute an investigation as to the contribution that is being made by society itself as well as by state law, and also as to the actual influence of the state upon social law. We must know what kinds of marriages and families exist in a country, what kinds of contracts are being entered into, what their content is as a general rule, what kinds of declarations by last will and testament are being drawn up, how all of these things ought to be adjudged according to the law that is in force in the courts and other tribunals, how they are actually being adjudged, and to what extent these judgments and other decisions are actually effective. An investigation of this sort will reveal that although the legislation of two different countries may be identical, e. g. of France and Roumania, the law of one country may differ from that of the other; that in spite of the fact that the courts and other tribunals of Bohemia, Dalmatia, and Galicia apply the same code, the law of these countries is by no means the same; and that because of the differences in the actual state of the law, there is no uniform law even in the various parts of Germany in spite of the Civil Code, quite apart from the particular divergencies of legislation.

Of course our knowledge in this sphere will always remain full of gaps, and unsatisfactory, and doubtless it is much easier and much more pleasant to study a few codes together with illustrative

是——如今天通常认为的那样——创建一个本质为法律史学的法律科学,而是要创建一个有关历史的法律科学。的确,他们主要不是关注法律史,而是关注法律的古老习俗,以辩证思维代替历史上的法学或并非好得多的谢林哲学。他们还是他们那个时代的产物。但是,他们在通往他们那个学派的入门处——那儿叙述了他们的目标——的上方用大大的文字书写了传奇。然而,没有人能够读懂并解释那个题字。该事实与另外一个事实恰好具有相同的特征,即:后来,《历史法学期刊》变成了《法律史期刊》。

为了理解法律的实际状况,我们必须开始一项有关社会本身与国家法所做贡献以及国家对社会法实际影响的调查。我们必须知道:在一个国家内,存在何种婚姻和家庭,缔结的是何种契约以及通常其内容是什么,起草的是何种遗嘱,这些事项按照法院和其他裁决机构所适用的法律该如何裁判,它们实际上又是如何裁判的,在什么样的范围内,这些裁判和其他裁决实际上是有效的。这样的调查将会揭示,尽管两个不同的国家的立法可能是一样的,比如法国和罗马利亚,但其中一个国家的法律可能不同于另外一个国家的;尽管波希米亚、达尔马提亚、加利西亚法院和其他裁决机构都适用同样的法典,但这些国家的法律绝不相同;由于法律的实际状况的差别,因而尽管存在《德国民法典》,但甚至在德国的不同地区,除了个别的立法差异之外,也没有统一的法律。

当然,我们此领域的知识总是充满了缺漏,总是令人不满的,并且毫无疑问,研究一些法典以及说明性的材料和注释比探明法

material and explanatory notes than to ascertain the actual state of the law. But it certainly is not the function of science to seek easy and pleasant tasks but great and productive ones. We know in part, and the science of law is no exception to this; the more truly scientific it will become, the more perfect it will be.

This exposition would altogether fail of its purpose if it were understood to convey the idea that I mean to say that the methods which I have indicated in any way exhaust the methodology of the sociology of law. New scientific aims will always make new scientific methods necessary. For this reason, in order to prove that the possibilities are unlimited, I wish to point out a few things. Political geography as created by Ratzel and as it is understood today by Brunhes in France is in fact sociology with a geographic method. As early as the fifties of the last century Le Play, a Frenchman, in his *science social* based his investigations at all points on the local conditions of social life, and the school which he founded is zealously continuing the work he began. In his book on irrigation in Spain, Egypt, and Algiers, which is at least as interesting, even to the jurist, as any work on the history of law or on ethnology, Brunhes points out that there is a great number of legal formations which are associated everywhere with the kind and nature of the irrigation plants and the amount of their output. The reason why the Arabs of the desert do not recognize property rights in the sandy plain of the desert but only in the trees of the oases cannot be given by ethnology and legal history but only by the peculiar economic institutions of the desert.

Many decades ago Ofner of Vienna pointed out the possibility of instituting a direct investigation of the sense of law and right (*Rechtsgefühl*) by means of juristic experiment. A year ago Kobler discussed the idea in detail in the Vienna *Juristische Blätter*, and actually instituted experiments in the *Freie juristische Vereinigung*, which he himself had founded. Actual or fictitious law cases, even entire court proceedings, are being submitted to the persons who

律的实际状况要容易得多、有趣得多。不过,寻求容易而有趣的任务当然不是科学的功能,科学的功能是寻求重大而具有建设性的任务。我们部分地知道此点,并且法律科学也绝非例外;法律科学越有科学性,它就会越完美。

如果这种解释被理解为传达了这样的思想,我的意思是说,我以任何方式暗示过的方法详尽论述了法律社会学的方法论,那么该解释的目的就完全没有达到。新的科学目标总是需要新的科学方法。因此,为了证明此种可能性是无限的,我希望指出一些事情。拉第尔创建的以及今天在法国被布吕纳理解的政治地理学,事实上是采用地理方法的社会学。早在上世纪50年代,勒普来,一个法国人,在其《社会科学》中将其调查完全建立在社会生活的地方条件之上,他所建立的学派热心于继续他开创的事业。布吕纳在他关于西班牙、埃及以及阿尔及利亚灌溉的书中,如同任何有关法律史或文化人类学的作品一样,他指出,存在大量的法律形态,其中每一处都与灌溉植物的种类与性质以及它们的产量相关。为什么沙漠地区的阿拉伯人没有承认沙漠的沙地平原的财产权,而只承认绿洲树上的财产权利,其原因不可能借助于文化人类学与法律史学而获得,而只能通过独特的沙漠地区的经济结构来给出答案。

许多年代以前,维也纳的欧弗纳指出,一个有关正义感(*Rechtsgefühl*)的直接调查可以通过法律试验来进行。一年前,克布勒在维也纳详细讨论了《法学通报》中的思想,并且实际上在他自己创建的《自由法律协会》进行了试验。实际或虚拟的法律案例,甚至完整的法庭诉讼程序,都取决于用于试验的人——他

are being used for the experiment, who must not be jurists, and who are requested to express an opinion on them. They can do this only by relying on their sense of law and right. Is not everyone reminded of the psychometry of the school of Fechner and Wundt? These tests are open to the same objections that have been urged against psychometry. The person who permits himself to be used for the experiment is not in his usual frame of mind, and he knows, too, that his judgment does not decide the case; the fictitious case arouses no passions, does not agitate the emotions, but addresses itself to the intellect alone. These are sources of error which a correct method must compute and take into account. In spite of this however the attempt will produce valuable results, provided one does not forget about the sources of error.

Method is as infinite as science itself .

不得是法学家，并被要求对这些事项发表意见。他们只能凭借他们的正义感来完成任务。难道每个人都没有想到费希纳与冯特学派的心理测验？这些测试面向同一组已被要求反对心理测验的对象。愿意参与此项试验的人并不在状态，他也知道，他的判决不是在裁断案件；虚拟的案件引发不起任何激情，没有刺激情感，只会让他单纯地运用智力。这些是错误的根源——正确的方法必须计算和考虑它们。尽管如此，不过这种努力仍然会产生有价值的结果，只要他没有忘记错误的根源。

科学本身是无限的，方法也是如此。

# 译者后记

埃利希(Eugen Ehrlich 1862～1922),奥地利法学家,社会学法学派在欧洲的首创人之一。他出生于律师家庭。曾在维也纳大学学法律。1899年起在切尔诺夫策大学任罗马法教授。主要著作有《法的自由发现和自由法学》(1903)、《法律社会学基本原理》(1913)、《法学逻辑》(1918)等。

埃利希在历史法学的基础之上建立了社会学法学,他以罗马法、英国普通法、欧陆普通法等不同类型法律的历史发展为纵线,以法律的结构与功能为横线,集中阐述了"联合体内在秩序(the inner order)"这个关键性概念,并就此提出"活法"的思想,埃利希宣称他的学说的中心思想是:法的发展的重心不在立法、法学或判决,而在社会本身。他认为法比国家出现得更早,国家制定和执行的法仅是法中很小的一部分。即使在现代,国家对法所起的作用也是有限的,而大量存在的是"活法"(living law)。《法律社会学基本原理》既是埃利希最重要、最负盛名的代表作,同时也是欧洲大陆上第一部自成体系的法律社会学专著。该书第一次真正自觉地把法律学与社会学(sociology)相结合,使法律社会学的研究作为独立学科而体系化。

这部著作,此前并没有完整意义上的中译本。这样一部法理学的经典,由从事民法学专业学习的我们来翻译完成,其难度可想而知。

此书翻译的完成得益于许多人的帮助。首先要真诚感谢北京大学的薛军教授,书中几乎全部的拉丁语句子、许多拉丁语短语都得益于他的不吝赐教。因此在这里,要郑重向他表达深深的谢意!其次要感谢译者的师姐,博士生罗瑶,她为全书法语词句的翻译提供了无私的帮助!再次,吉林大学理论法研究中心的博士生王勇同学,慷慨赠与译者原著的一个中文节译本,素昧平生即慷慨相助,令人感动!50年前台湾学者杨树人先生曾经出版过此书的节译本,尽管只有薄薄的几十页,尽管在专业术语的用词上当时与如今差别并不小,但它还是为译者理解原书提供了重要的帮助。最后,译者的同门,博士生舒玲敏、浙江大学法学硕士生凌皞、西北大学英语语言学硕士生李利敏对本书的部分文字进行了校对,对他们的辛勤付出也表示诚挚的感谢!

全书共二十一章,初译的分工如下:第一章至第十一章、第十三章由袁震翻译;第十二章、第十四章至第二十一章由叶名怡翻译。全书由叶名怡审校、统稿。

译事无止境。再多的时间和精力投入其中,都不会是一种多余。此书的翻译虽已“完成”,但绝非“完结”。囿于译者的学力,谬误定然存在。另外,还有个别小语种的文句因为能力所限,故保留了原貌。企求学界各位前辈、专家、学长多加指教,以利日后改正完善。

叶名怡　袁　震

2006年9月

# 《西方学术经典文库》(第一辑)

| | |
|---|---|
| 功利主义 | [英]约翰·斯图亚特·穆勒 |
| 诗学·诗艺 | [古希腊]亚里士多德<br>[古罗马]贺拉斯 |
| 经济发展理论 | [美]约瑟夫·阿洛伊斯·熊彼特 |
| 经济学原理 | [英]阿尔弗雷德·马歇尔 |
| 国民财富的性质与原理 | [英]亚当·斯密 |
| 联邦党人文集 | [美]亚历山大·汉密尔顿 |
| 就业、利息和货币通论 | [英]约翰·梅纳德·凯恩斯 |
| 尼各马可伦理学 | [古希腊]亚里士多德 |
| 道德情操论 | [英]亚当·斯密 |
| 君主论 | [意]尼科洛·马基雅弗利 |
| 新教伦理与资本主义精神 | [德]马克斯·韦伯 |
| 古代法 | [英]亨利·萨姆奈·梅因 |
| 第一哲学沉思集 | [法]勒内·笛卡儿 |
| 查拉图斯特拉如是说 | [德]弗里德里希·威廉·尼采 |
| 哲学研究 | [英]路德维希·维特根斯坦 |
| 实践理性批判 | [德]伊曼努尔·康德 |
| 社会契约论 | [法]让·雅克·卢梭 |
| 理想国 | [古希腊]柏拉图 |
| 心理学原理 | [美]威廉·詹姆斯 |
| 精神现象学 | [德]威廉·弗里德里希·黑格尔 |
| 神圣者的观念 | [德]鲁道夫·奥托 |
| 小逻辑 | [德]威廉·弗里德里希·黑格尔 |

| | |
|---|---|
| **论人类不平等的起源** | [法]让·雅克·卢梭 |
| **道德形而上学基础** | [德]伊曼努尔·康德 |
| **人性论** | [英]戴维·休谟 |
| **政府论** | [英]约翰·洛克 |
| **论法的精神** | [法]查尔斯·路易斯·孟德斯鸠 |
| **代议制政府** | [英]约翰·斯图亚特·穆勒 |
| **英国法与文艺复兴** | [英]弗雷德里克·威廉·梅特兰 |
| **法律社会学基本原理** | [奥]尤根·埃利希 |
| **论美国民主** | [法]夏尔·阿列克西·德·托克维尔 |
| **原始社会结构与功能** | [英]A. R. 拉德克利夫-布朗 |
| **政治学** | [古希腊]亚里士多德 |
| **罗马帝国编年史** | [古罗马]科尔涅里乌斯·塔西佗 |
| **普通语言学教程** | [瑞士]费尔迪南·德·索绪尔 |
| **货币哲学** | [德]格奥尔格·西梅尔 |
| **法理学讲演录** | [英]约翰·奥斯丁 |
| **思想录** | [法]布莱兹·帕斯卡 |
| **利维坦** | [英]托马斯·霍布斯 |
| **意识形态与乌托邦** | [德]卡尔·曼海姆 |
| **忏悔录** | [古罗马]圣·奥古斯丁 |
| **西太平洋上的航海者** | [英]布罗尼斯拉夫·马林诺夫斯基 |
| **历史学:理论和实际** | [意]贝内德托·克罗齐 |
| **逻辑哲学论** | [英]路得维希·维特根斯坦 |